THE ROUGH GUIDE TO
IRELAND

This fourteenth edition updated by
Norm Longley and Kate Drynan

ROUGH
GUIDES

Contents

KNIGHT'S TOWN ON VALENTIA ISLAND

Introduction to
Ireland

Ireland continues to transform itself with quiet determination. Gone is the image of a conservative, introspective, rural nation, while the infamous unrest and violence of the Troubles has, mercifully, faded away. An outward-looking Ireland has stepped forward, energized by its constantly rejuvenated cities that somehow still beat to their own drum, with age-old customs and traditions intermingled with the fresh ideas of a changing population. Of course, it's not called the Emerald Isle for nothing, and Ireland's physical beauty is, naturally, one of its greatest assets. The landscape is much more than a nondescript blanket of green – indeed, forty shades are said to be seen, even on the rainiest of days. And beyond this already pleasing palette, the country's smouldering good looks can send a tingle down your spine with the Burren's moonscape grey vistas, the dark brooding peat bogs of the Midlands and Connemara's gold- and purple-tinted mountains. And when the sun is high and a cloudless sky sparkles the brightest bold blue, it really is like nowhere else on earth – or so the Irish would have you believe.

While Dublin, Belfast and the other cities are cranking up the cosmopolitan – from hipster coffee shops to edgy, internationally relevant arts scenes – their on-message worldliness is not the be all and end all: **traditional culture** is cherished by even the most city-slicking of the Irish. Moreover, as Northern Irish historian J. C. Beckett (1912–96) noted, his homeland "has no natural focal point, no great crossing-place of routes, no centre from which influence spreads naturally." The lay of the land and the **road network** lend themselves to a democratic exploration, with each part of the country fair game, and you're unlikely to feel swallowed up by the cities' gravitational pull. In **rural areas**, switch modes to walking boots or two wheels

THE ROCKY SHORE AT DUNAFF IN COUNTY DONEGAL

(motorized or otherwise) and you'll be in no great hurry to return to the urban sprawl, however vibrant.

In some areas **public transport** coverage fades to black, and you have no choice but to feel your way – the perfect opportunity to get to grips with Ireland's rich textures. The **west coast** is famous for its long beaches and windswept cliffs with views of the western islands; the drama of the landscape here is awe-inspiring, not least to the surfers who flock to Donegal and Galway. In the **east**, outside Dublin, the crumpled granite of the Wicklow Hills sits in stark contrast to the lush central plain just a few kilometres away. Cross the border into **Northern Ireland** and it is a short journey through rolling hills – known locally as drumlins – to the spectacular coast road that leads to the geological wonder of the **Giant's Causeway**.

Scattered across these landscapes is an abundance of **historic sites**. The very earliest of these include enigmatic prehistoric tombs, stone circles and hill forts. It is possible to trace the history of successive waves of immigration, whether Christian pilgrims, Viking raiders or Norman settlers, through the stone churches, distinctive **round towers** and high crosses strewn across the landscape. Ireland's **monasteries** were important centres of Christian learning during the Middle Ages, and the monks' elaborate craftsmanship is preserved in surviving illuminated manuscripts, such as the *Book of Kells*, held at Dublin's Trinity College. Doughty **castles** and tower houses record the twelfth-century Anglo-Norman invasion, while numerous

FACT FILE

- Ireland is the third-largest island in Europe. The **landmass** has a total area of 84,412 square kilometres, with its **coastline** stretching for 3152km.
- Its longest **river** is the Shannon (358km), largest **lake** Lough Neagh (387 square kilometres), **highest point** Carrauntoohil in Kerry (1038m) and its deepest **cave** is Reyfad Pot in Fermanagh (193m).
- The Newgrange Passage Tomb in County Meath dates back to **3200 BC**, making it around a thousand years older than Stonehenge.
- The island is made up of the Republic of Ireland, consisting of 26 **counties**, and Northern Ireland, subject to devolved British rule, which comprises six counties.
- The Republic's **population** is roughly 4.4 million, with 1.7 million residing in the Greater Dublin area. Northern Ireland's population is approximately 1.8 million, with some 650,000 occupying the Greater Belfast area.
- Irish is the **national language** of the Republic, according to the constitution, with English recognized as a second official language. However, only around fifteen percent of the population has a good competence in Irish.
- Ireland is the only country in the world with a musical instrument, the Irish harp, as its **national emblem**.

stately homes from the eighteenth and nineteenth centuries attest to the wealth and political power of the Protestant Ascendancy both north and south. A remarkable aspect of Ireland's landscape is the tendency for physical features to have **sacred associations** – few counties do not shelter a pile of stones called "Diarmuid and Gráinne's Bed", where the star-crossed lovers are said to have slept together on their flight from the great warrior Fionn Mac Cumhaill.

Inseparable from Ireland's history is its cultural heritage, a happy coming together of millennia and myriad influences from home and abroad. Here you have the richest store of **mythological traditions** in northern Europe, folkloric associations at every turn and world-famous literature and poetry. But there are a couple of elements you'll likely encounter in vivid form on a daily basis – particularly if you're a pub-goer. First you have **traditional music**, with its ballads and *sean-nós* ("old-style" Irish-language singing) recounting tales of love, history and humour. Then there's the *craic*, the talking therapy of Ireland's pubs, a combination of unlikely yarns, surreal comedy and plain old chatter and gossip. **Dublin**, which has long enjoyed a reputation as a culturally rich city, remains the epicentre of artistic activity. The Republic's capital is justifiably proud of its literary tradition, which takes in (among countless other luminaries) Oscar Wilde, Flann O'Brien and James Joyce, whose famously complex and experimental *Finnegans Wake* is – besides its many other triumphs – a worthy encapsulation of the sheer weightiness of Irish culture.

Ireland is rightly renowned for the **welcome** extended to visitors, and the tourist sector is, unsurprisingly, at the centre of its plans for lasting economic recovery. Northern Ireland and Belfast, in particular, have taken full advantage of the sudden influx of visitors previously deterred by the Troubles. What they will encounter is an Ireland where, finally, the past is significant for its **cultural riches** rather than the shadow it casts – and where the future is all about that big blue sky.

Where to go

Dublin is the Republic's main entry-point, a confident capital whose raw, modern energy is complemented by rich cultural traditions, and which boasts outstanding **medieval monuments** and the richly varied exhibits of the **National Gallery** and **National Museum**. South of the city, the desolate **Wicklow Mountains** offer a breathtaking contrast to city life while just over an hour or two away, many of the islands inland gems such as Cavan, Kildare, Kilkenny and Westmeath have plenty to offer.

If you arrive on the **west coast** at Shannon Airport in County Clare, Ireland's most spectacular landscapes are within easy reach. From here the **Wild Atlantic Way** is in easy reach in either direction. This coastal driving route will take you through some of the most stunning scenery on the island, with great seaside towns dotted along the route to set up base for a night or two. **Clare**'s coastline rises to a head at the vertiginous **Cliffs of Moher**, while inland lies **the Burren**, a barren limestone plateau at odds with the lush greenery characteristic of much of Ireland.

County Kerry, meanwhile, is breathtakingly beautiful, an intoxicating brew of seascapes, looming mountains and sparkling lakes. Though the craggy coastline traversed by the **Ring of Kerry** is a major tourist attraction, it's still relatively easy to find seclusion. In County Galway, to Clare's north, lies enthralling **Connemara**, untamed bogland set between sprawling beaches and a muddle of quartz-gleaming mountains;

THE BEST PUBS FOR TRADITIONAL MUSIC

If the Irish didn't invent the **pub**, they've certainly espoused its cause with great vigour. Indeed, alongside the local church and the betting shop (for men), the pub retains a pivotal place in Irish society. It's the place where stories are narrated, deals and pacts are made, jokes are told and traditional music is heard. During the 1990s, the "Irish pub" concept (albeit with "authentic" period decor manufactured in Dublin) spread to far-flung points of the globe. Yet experiencing the real thing on its home turf to a live soundtrack of **traditional music** is still an unbeatable experience. With a pint of the black stuff in hand, here are some of the best, entirely authentic pubs to get you started on a lifelong love affair with *bodhráns*, tin whistles, pipes and fiddles:

- **Buckley's** Killarney (see page 275)
- **De Barra's** Clonakilty (see page 250)
- **The Five Points Whiskey & Alehouse** Belfast (see page 468)
- **O'Donoghue's** Dublin (see page 106)
- **Reel Inn** Donegal Town (see page 417)
- **Seán Og's** Tralee (see page 296)
- **Tigh Coili** Galway City (see page 341)

in contrast, university cities such as **Galway** and **Limerick** to the south of Clare provide year-round festivals and buzzing nightlife. Further north, **Donegal** offers a dramatic mix of rugged peninsulas and mountains, glistening beaches and magical lakes.

Dotted around the west coast are numerous **islands**, providing a glimpse of the harsh way of life endured by remote Irish-speaking communities. The **Arans** are the most famous – windswept expanses of limestone supporting extraordinary prehistoric sites – but the savagely beautiful landscape of the **Blasket Islands**, off Kerry's coast, is equally worthy of exploration. **Achill Island**, the largest and accessible by bridge, is home to five spectacular blue flag beaches.

On Ireland's southern coast, **Cork**'s shoreline is punctuated by secluded estuaries, rolling headlands and historic harbours, while **Cork city** itself is the region's hub, with a vibrant cultural scene and nightlife. Nearby, the pretty seaside town of **Cobh** (previously called Queenstown) is renowned as the departure point for over 2.5 million Irish immigrants bound for North America after the Great Famine, and as a port of call for the ill-fated RMS *Titanic* in 1912. To Cork's east, **Waterford city** houses the wondrous Viking and medieval collections of Waterford Treasures, while, in Ireland's southeastern corner, **Wexford**'s seashore features broad estuaries teeming with bird life and expansive dune-backed beaches.

Inland, the Republic's scenery is less enchanting, its **Midland** counties characterized by fertile if somewhat drab agricultural land, as well as broad expanses of **peat bog**, home to endangered species of rare plants. However, there is gentle appeal in Ireland's great watercourse, the **Shannon**, with its succession of vast loughs, and the quaint river valleys of the southeast.

Numerous **historic** and **archeological sites** provide fine alternative attractions. The prehistoric tomb at Meath's **Newgrange** and the fortress of **Dun Aengus** on Inishmore are utterly mesmerizing; County Cork features many **stone circles**; and there's a multitude of **tombs** and **ring forts** across the west coast counties. Stunning early **Christian monuments** abound, too, including those located on **Skellig Michael** and the **Rock of Cashel** and atmospheric sites at **Clonmacnois**, **Glendalough** and **Monasterboice**. Of more recent origin, the Anglo-Irish nobility's planned **estates**, developed during the eighteenth and nineteenth centuries around impressive Neoclassical mansions, are visible across Ireland.

Much of **Northern Ireland's** countryside is intensely beautiful and unspoiled. To the north are the green **Glens of Antrim** and a coastline as scenic as anywhere in Ireland, with, as its centrepiece, the bizarre basalt geometry of the **Giant's Causeway**. The **Antrim Coast Road**, meanwhile, is one of Ireland's most scenic drives. In the southeast, **Down** offers the contrasting beauties of serene **Strangford Lough** and the brooding presence of the **Mourne Mountains**, while, to the west, **Fermanagh** has the peerless lake scenery of **Lough Erne**, a fabulous place for watersports, fishing and exploring island monastic remains. Evidence of the Plantation is also provided by planned towns and various grand **mansions**, often set in sprawling, landscaped grounds.

To get to grips with the North's history, a visit to its **cities** is essential, not least for their tremendous museums: **Belfast**, with its ship-building past and grand public buildings, built on the profits of industry; **Derry**, which grew around the well-preserved walls of its medieval antecedent; and the cathedral town of **Armagh** where St Patrick established Christianity in Ireland.

When to go

Whenever you visit Ireland it's wise to come prepared for wet and/or windy conditions, especially along the west coast, which faces the Atlantic, the source of much of Ireland and Britain's weather. On average (see page 46), it **rains** around 150 days a year along the east and southeast coasts, and up to as many as 225 days a year in parts of the west and southwest. April is the driest time across most of the island, while December and January are the wettest. Whatever the case, the weather is very changeable and you'll often find a soggy morning rapidly replaced by brilliant sunshine minutes later. Most years also see a few weeks of gorgeous weather, though predicting this occurrence is well-nigh impossible. Generally, the **sunniest months** (see page 46) are May and September, while June, July and August are the warmest with temperatures sometimes reaching as high as 25°C (just don't expect them to come with sunshine to match). Overall, the southeast tends to get the best of the sunshine.

Author picks

Our authors scoured every inch of the Emerald Isle to bring you these hand-picked gems, from the best of Dublin's pubs to the glories of taking to two wheels in Co. Mayo.

Ticking off Dublin's pubs In Joyce's *Ulysses*, Leopold Bloom queried whether it would be possible to cross Dublin without passing a pub – and with more than seven hundred dotted around the city, it would be a mean feat indeed. A cliché it may be, but there's something very special about a perfect pint of Guinness in a Dublin pub – *The Palace Bar* (see page 105) and *The Stag's Head* (see page 105) are both good options.

Twitching on Rathlin Island Hop on board the Rathlin ferry from Ballycastle (see page 485) for the short crossing to Northern Ireland's only inhabited island. It's home to a colony of seals and an RSPB nature reserve attracting guillemots, puffins, razorbills and the red-billed chough.

Get poetic in Yeats Country Sligo captured the heart of William Butler Yeats (see page 392) and it's not hard to see why. Follow the famous poet's trail around Drumcliffe or enjoy hikes with dramatic views in the nearby Dartry Mountains or to the Devil's Chimney.

Drink like a Victorian in Belfast Step back in time in the fabulously intact Victorian 'gin palace' that is the *Crown Liquor Saloon*. Inside it features exquisite wood panelling and cosy nooks, alongside stained glass, beautiful tilework and age-old oak casks, all smack bang in Belfast city centre (see page 468).

Cycle the Waterford Greenway This glorious 46km route (see page 213), along a disused railway track in County Waterford, is one of the country's best off-road walking and cycling trails in Ireland. Broken down into six sections, it's a favourite with families: highlights along the route include Ballyvoyle Tunnel the section around Kilmacthomas with its viaduct and the coastal views as you approach Dungarvan – a bustling seaside town.

Our author recommendations don't end here. We've flagged up our favourite places – a perfectly sited hotel, an atmospheric café, a special restaurant – throughout the Guide, highlighted with the ★ symbol.

RATHLIN ISLAND

CYCLING THE GREAT WESTERN GREENWAY

25

things not to miss

It's not possible to see everything that Ireland has to offer in one trip – and we don't suggest you try. What follows, in no particular order, is a selective and subjective taste of the country's highlights: from geological wonders and ancient ruins to activities and experiences both on land and at sea. All highlights are colour-coded by chapter and have a page reference to take you straight into the Guide, where you can find out more.

1 WILD ATLANTIC WAY
See page 26
This coastal drive covers 2500km from Donegal to Cork and takes in some of the most rugged and awe-inspiring scenery in Europe.

2 TRINITY COLLEGE, DUBLIN
See page 64
Wonder at the ninth-century *Book of Kells*, housed in the Old Library, before wandering through the city-centre campus, taking in the best of Dublin's architecture.

3 TITANIC BELFAST
See page 453
Taking pride of place in the heart of Belfast's Titanic Quarter, this interactive museum takes visitors on a fascinating journey through the city's maritime heritage and the story of the ill-fated RMS *Titanic*.

4 TRADITIONAL MUSIC
See page 579
Often loud, often raucous and always fun, traditional Irish music can be heard in many pubs and at dedicated festivals such as the Willie Clancy Festival in Miltown Malbay every July.

5 SURFING AT TULLAN STRAND AND ROSSNOWLAGH BEACH
See page 412
Thunderous waves roll in at Ireland's surfing capital, attracting fans from around the globe.

6 BRÚ NA BÓINNE
See page 141
This extraordinary ritual landscape is simply one of the world's most important prehistoric sites.

7 MEDIEVAL MILE
See page 186
Kilkenny is one of the best medieval cities in Ireland – follow an easy walking tour and take in the museum, castle and sixteenth-century merchant's house.

8 MAYO DARK SKY PARK
See page 366
For fabulous stargazing this is the place to go. Don't miss the festival held each November.

9 SKELLIG MICHAEL
See page 281
A remarkable and inspiring early Christian hermitage clinging to a mountain summit on a wild, bleak island.

10 THE ROCK OF CASHEL
See page 222
Rising high above the Golden Vale, the Rock features an entrancing group of early ecclesiastical remains.

11 KILMAINHAM GAOL
See page 89

A grim encounter with the Spartan conditions experienced by those deemed enemies of the state, with superb displays on Irish political history and the gaol's restoration.

12 THE BURREN
See page 323

A barren expanse of cracked limestone terraces stretching towards the Atlantic, peppered with a multitude of fascinating megalithic remains.

13 GLENDALOUGH
See page 123

Often referred to as "the valley of the two lakes", this wonderfully remote and beautiful mountain valley also shelters an atmospheric monastery.

14 KINSALE
See page 245

Imposing forts and some of Ireland's finest cuisine – particularly during October's annual Gourmet Festival – in a glorious bayside setting.

15 CRAGGAUNOWEN
See page 313

A recreation Bronze Age Irish ring fort hides behind a sixteenth-century castle. A great family day out with costumed re-enactors bringing the experience to life.

11

12

16

17

16 KILLARNEY NATIONAL PARK
See page 269
The grandeur of the lakes and mountains has been drawing visitors to Killarney for over three centuries.

17 MALIN HEAD
See page 442
Beautiful beaches, mighty dunes and gusty clifftop walks with the most spectacular views await in Ireland's northernmost outpost.

18 THE GOBBINS
See page 480
One of the most hair-raising walks in Europe, this guided 2.5 hour walk crosses spectacular bridges, climbs jagged rock staircases, and follows a narrow path along a breathtaking cliff-face.

19 THE GIANT'S CAUSEWAY
See page 487
Marvel at the eerie but entirely natural basalt formation of the Causeway and discover the myths and legends that surround it in the award-winning visitor centre.

20 DERRY'S CITY WALLS
See page 496
A visit to Derry is incomplete without a stroll around the ramparts of the only completely walled city in Ireland.

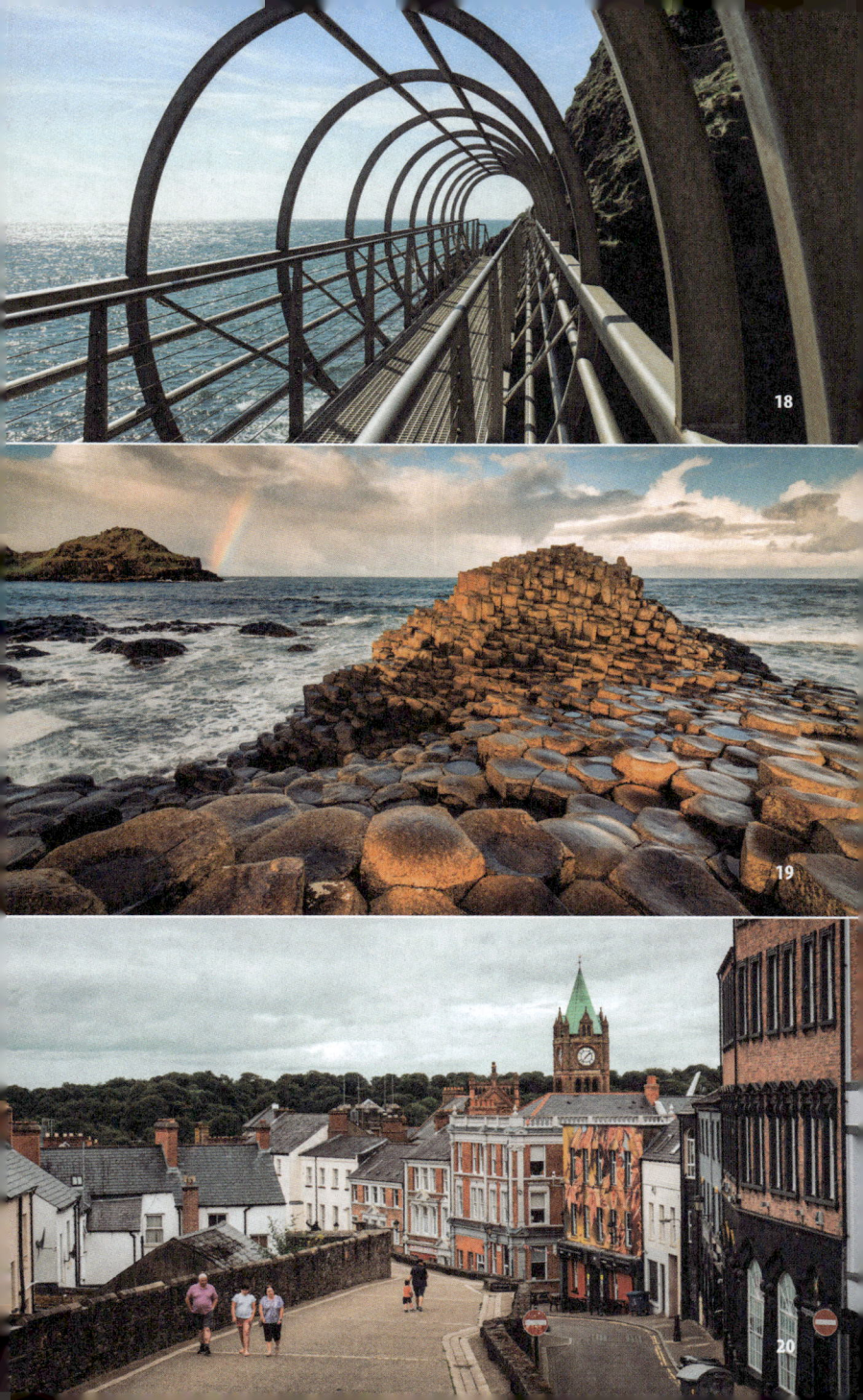

21

22

23

www.galwayoysterfest.com

21 **KYLEMORE ABBEY, CONNEMARA**
See page 364
One of Connemara's most historic sites, the spectacular Kylemore Abbey comes with a beautifully restored walled garden and Neogothic church.

22 **INIS MÓR**
See page 349
The largest of the Aran Islands, it's rugged, remote and utterly otherworldly and full of ancient forts, churches and excellent pubs.

23 **GALWAY BAY OYSTERS**
See page 334
Galway lays claim to Ireland's finest oysters – try your hand at a shucking competition during the Galway International Oyster and Seafood Festival every September.

24 **DUBLIN PUBS**
See page 104
Feel the heartbeat of the city's social life, with over seven hundred venues to choose from, fuelled by perfect pints of Guinness and healthy doses of *craic*.

25 **CROAGH PATRICK**
See page 370
It's a steep two-hour climb, but the fine views across Clew Bay, and the mountain's religious and historical resonance, make it all worthwhile.

Itineraries

Ireland is compact but it packs an awful lot in. Five days on the Wild Atlantic Way guarantees a host of unforgettable vistas, while a few days in the southwest will introduce foodies to a feast of local delicacies. The coastline around the Giant's Causeway in the North is simply one of the world's great road trips – at 120 miles (190km) it can easily be driven in a day, though you're bound to want to slow down and savour the ride.

A SOUTHWEST FOODIE TRIP

Allow three to four days to cover these 140km, sampling some of the finest produce the island has to offer, from seafood to superb cheeses.

❶ Kinsale The southwest's culinary honeypot boasts a beautiful harbour setting. For seafood lovers, the pick of the crop is the *Fishy Fishy Café and Restaurant*, serving up the freshest catch from the morning's haul. See page 245

❷ Clonakilty Heading west, you'll come to the source of the famous Clonakilty Black Pudding, sold at traditional butcher's Twomey's. Enjoy fine local produce for dinner at the *Inchydoney Island Lodge and Spa*, which overlooks the beach just outside of town. See page 248

❸ Baltimore Further southwest lies the small harbour village of Baltimore where the award-winning *Rolf's* makes a perfect leisurely lunch stop – it serves delicious local and organic lunches during the summer months. See page 253

❹ Schull Continue onto Schull where the Ferguson family produce their excellent Gubbeen cheese and meats. They sell at various local markets, including the Sunday morning Schull Market (Easter to Sept). See page 255

❺ Durrus The beautiful village of Durrus has an excellent option for dinner. In the evening head to the fabulous *Blairscove House & Restaurant*, with its impressive choice of Irish meats cooked over a roaring fire. See page 257

❻ Bantry Finish off your gastronomic gallivanting with a trip to Bantry Market, one of West Cork's largest. Located in the main square, it runs every Friday morning from 9.30am–1pm. See page 258

CAUSEWAY COASTAL ROUTE

The distances are short but the views are immense on this spectacular road trip.

❶ Carrickfergus From Belfast, head north on the M2 to Carrickfergus, home to a twelfth-

---

Create your own itinerary with Rough Guides. Whether you're after adventure or a family-friendly holiday, we have a trip for you, with all the activities you enjoy doing and the sights you want to see. All our trips are devised by local experts who get the most out of the destination. Visit **www.roughguides.com/trips** to chat with one of our travel agents.

century Anglo-Norman castle, complete with cannons, portcullis and ramparts. See page 476

❷ The Glens of Antrim A drive through the Glens of Antrim guarantees waterfalls, forests, glacier-gouged valleys and the pretty villages of Carnlough, Cushendall and Cushendun – *Game of Thrones* fans might recognize some of the location backdrops en route. See page 480

❸ Rathlin Island Explore the market town of Ballycastle before hopping on the ferry to craggy Rathlin Island, which offers fantastic birdwatching and nature walks. Get some rest at the *Manor House*, a charming, National Trust-owned B&B. See page 485

❹ The Giant's Causeway Channel your inner Indiana Jones at Carrick-a-rede rope bridge before continuing on to the Causeway, with its world-famous rock formations. See page 487

❺ Bushmills Continue along the coastline to Bushmills for a tour (and a dram) at its famed whiskey distillery before booking in to the cosy *Bushmills Inn*. See page 488

❻ Portstewart Explore ruined Dunluce Castle (believed to have been the inspiration for Cair Paravel in C. S. Lewis' *The Chronicles of Narnia*)

then continue, via the classic seaside town of Portrush, to picturesque Portstewart, with its 3km stretch of golden sand, *Harry's Shack* on the beach is the perfect place to dine before or after a stroll on the beach. See page 491

❼ Roe Valley Country Park Sample Roe Valley Country Park's riverside walks, ending your trip at the Green Lane Museum. See page 493

IRELAND'S ANCIENT EAST

Become immersed in Ireland's fascinating history, from ancient burial sites to Norman castles and Viking towns. Allow at least a day and overnight stop in each county.

❶ Greystones Forty minutes south of Dublin, this picturesque seaside village in County Wicklow is full of great places to eat and boutique shops. See page 117

❷ Powerscourt Estate Explore the most fabulous garden in Ireland on the grounds of a lavish eighteenth-century mansion. See page 120

❸ St Kevin's Way still in county Wicklow, follow the path of medieval pilgrims on this 29km trail that ends in the stunning monastic settlement

of Glendalough with its beautiful lakes. See page 123

❹ **St Canice's Cathedral** Just over an hour south of Wicklow, Kilkenny city is a rambler's dream, full of winding medieval streets and historical distractions. At its heart is its grand castle and pleasant grounds, from where you can walk along the High Street, stop in at the Medieval Mile Museum and along to Rothe House before finishing off at the magnificent St Canice's cathedral and round tower offering superb views of the city. See page 186

❺ **Dunbrody Famine Ship** On the way to Waterford it's worth the detour to visit this incredible reproduction of an 1840s emigrant vessel. With a guided tour, costumed performers, and fine exhibitions, it provides a unique insight into the lives of the many Irish forced to leave the country during the Famine. See page 202

❻ **Viking Waterford** Ireland's oldest city, Waterford is over 1100 year's old. Take a walk through the old city ("the Viking Triangle") and soak up the history, stopping in to see Reginald's Tower, the Medieval Museum and the Bishop's Palace. See page 206

THE WILD ATLANTIC WAY

At over 2500km, the Wild Atlantic Way is the world's longest defined coastal touring route. Stretching the length of the rugged Atlantic coast, from the Southern Peninsulas to the Northern Headlands, it's an unforgettable way to explore the west of Ireland. Although it's possible to travel the route by bus (and even bike), it's more relaxing to rent a car and enjoy it at your own pace. With so many tempting detours and unmissable sights, it can be a daunting task even choosing where to begin. These itineraries pick out some of the highlights on the route, starting in Cork and winding all the way up to Malin Head – the country's most northerly point. For more routes, interactive maps and a host of other resources visit http://wildatlanticway.com.

THE HAVEN COAST

Day one

Starting in the handsome heritage town of Kinsale (see page 245), head south to the Old Head of Kinsale – a remarkable little peninsula with great views looking back on the town and the surrounding countryside. Continue

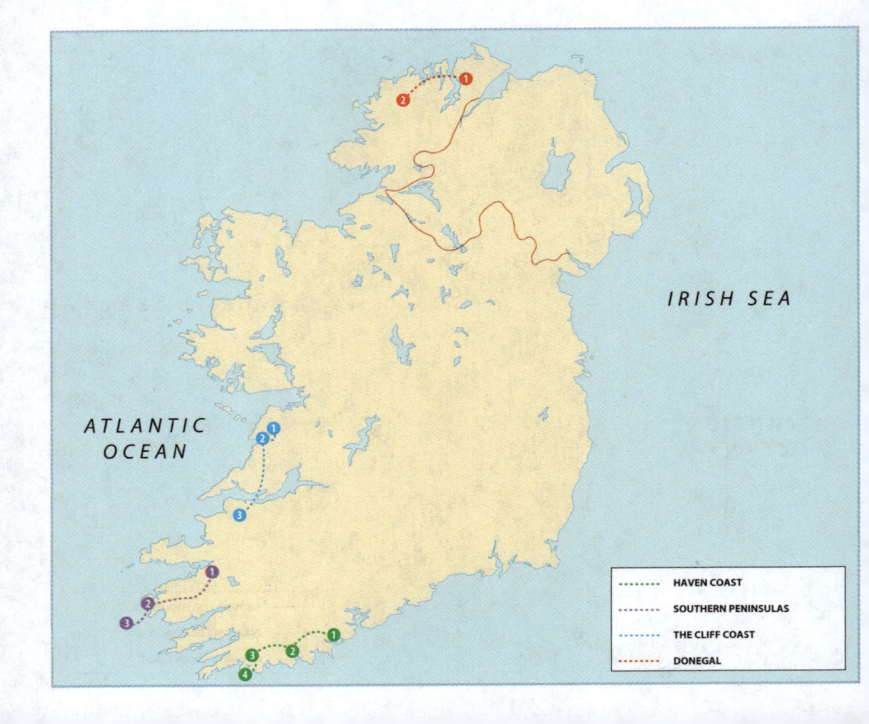

west along the R600 to the pleasant town of Clonakilty (see page 248) to spend the night.

Day two

After sampling some of the famous Clonakilty black pudding, pay a visit to Inchydoney Beach (see page 248). Just south of the town, it was recently voted best beach in Ireland – quite an achievement considering the competition. Get back on the winding road and enjoy the beautiful scenery of the Haven Coast, stopping for lunch in Rosscarbery. From there it's a short trip to the Drombeg Stone Circle (see page 249), an ancient circle of seventeen large standing stones, believed to be over 2000 years old. Continue on to Skibbereen (see page 250), home to a fantastic heritage centre with a Great Famine commemoration exhibition.

Day three

From Skibbereen it's a twenty-minute drive to Baltimore (see page 253), an idyllic village and the perfect place to do a spot of whale-watching. Humpback whales, basking sharks, and Risso's dolphins can all be seen here. Finish the day with a fantastic meal in *Rolf's* restaurant and a few pints with the locals.

SOUTHERN PENINSULAS

Day one

Starting in Killorglin (home of the Puck Festival; see page 275), it should take just under an hour to reach Cahersiveen (see page 277), a small town overlooking Valentia Harbour. From the town it's worth the fairly steep walk to the summit of Beentee Mountain to enjoy the panoramic views. Next visit Valencia Island (see page 279), a place of enduring traditional Irish culture. End the day in Portmagee (see page 278), a town of great pubs and even better seafood.

Day two

A visit to Skellig Michael (see page 281) is a must (although increased popularity due to the *Star Wars* film means advance booking is essential). A UNESCO World Heritage site, the island is home to a 1300-year-old monastic site, reached by a precarious ascent up an ancient stone stairway.

THE CLIFF COAST

Day one

Spend the morning exploring the utterly unique and otherworldly landscape of the Burren (see page 323), calling into the Burren Nature Sanctuary in Kinvara. From there it's an hour's drive to the charming little village of Doolin (see page 322). Either head to the impressive Doolin Cave or catch one of the many trad sessions in the local pubs.

Day two

Next it's a short drive to one of the highlights of the whole Wild Atlantic Way – the Cliffs of Moher (see page 322). Whether experienced on a clear day or in blustery rain, these magnificent cliffs are truly a sight to behold. It's then a fifteen-minute drive on to Lahinch (see page 321), a lively town full of surfers and great places to eat the freshest seafood and great pubs in which to enjoy a drink.

Day three

Leaving Lahinch, head for the Loop Head peninsula (see page 320), just over an hour away. The drive itself is stunning but be sure to climb the famous Loop Head lighthouse and take in the magnificent views that stretch from Kerry back up to the Cliffs of Moher. Finish the day in John. B Keane's in Listowel (see page 297), where you can learn the fine art of pulling the perfect pint of Guinness.

DONEGAL

Day one

From Buncrana (see page 440) it's a 25-minute drive to the ancient site of Grianán Ailigh (see page 438). This stone fort sits majestically on the Inishowen Peninsula, and the panoramic views are breathtaking. Afterwards continue up to Malin Head (see page 442), the most northerly point in Ireland. Enjoy a blustery walk around Banba's Crown before heading back to Buncrana for the night.

Day two

Everything that makes the Wild Atlantic Way so special is distilled in this drive around Donegal's Northern Headlands – stunning vistas, great food and drink, and a palpable connection to the past. Starting again in Buncrana, this time head for the village of Rathmullan (see page 433), from where the Flight of the Earls took place in 1607. Push onward to Fanad Head (see page 434), stopping along the way to enjoy some incredible beaches and coastal viewpoints. Pop into *The Singing Pub* (see page 433) for lunch before heading to the gorgeously picturesque Glenveagh National Park & Castle (see page 429). Here, a great hike is up to the Poisoned Glen.

Sustainable travel

Low-impact travel that gives back to the local community is a key focus on many a traveller's mind in a rapidly changing world. Here are a few easy ways in which you can make your trip to Ireland both enjoyable and sustainable.

In a land that is green and meandering, it's not hard to get off the beaten track, and be well rewarded for it. Ireland relishes slow travel and friendly locals love to stop and chat, especially in the smaller towns and villages and giving back to the local community is a sure way to win over the hearts of the Irish people.

GETTING THERE AND AROUND

Ireland is working to decrease public transport fares and improve transport links with more services running for longer. There are also a growing number of bicycle lanes in the major cities to encourage more sustainable modes of transport. With multiple ferry ports north and south, it's also easy to take the slower more sustainable route to Ireland by boat, the island has major ferry ports in Dublin, Wexford, Cork, Belfast and Larne with direct sailings to the UK, France and Spain.

EAT LIKE A LOCAL

Farming is at the root of the nation and as such, great Irish produce can be found everywhere. Even global supermarket chains stock some of the freshest Irish-farmed produce you can find, alongside home-baked treats, jams and other Irish-made sauces and condiments such as those from the famous Cork-based Ballymaloe cookery school. Come summer, don't hesitate to stop at the roadside stalls (have cash at the ready) selling Wexford new potatoes and strawberries – you'll not find tastier or better. And meat lovers should seek out the local butcher for great traditional black and white pudding, sausages and Irish farmed lamb and beef.

SUPPORT IRISH CRAFTSPEOPLE

Ireland excels at crafts, and this will soon become obvious, even in the tourist hotspots. Irish-made pottery, blankets, linen, toys, woodwork, candles and silverware are of the best quality. Art is huge also and exhibitions and festivals focusing on art and crafts run throughout the year. Kilkenny Arts Festival held annually in August has art by local artists on display and for sale in dedicated exhibition spaces, shops, cafés and pubs.

RECYCLE, RECYCLE, RECYCLE

Ireland loves recycling, at the expense it seems of finding a normal rubbish bin at the best of times. The new Deposit Return Scheme has introduced can and plastic bottle recycling banks which can be found in service stations and most supermarket chains, with refund values starting at 15c a unit. The money-back receipt can then be used in the store against any further purchases. Of course, this is not free money but rather a government-backed scheme to encourage recycling or forfeit the tax that has already been added onto any product with the return logo on it.

FERRIES RUN REGULAR ROUTES TO THE UK, FRANCE AND SPAIN

YOUGHAL

TAKE THE SLOW ROAD

Ireland's motorways may be the fastest route but getting off them can reveal wonderful surprises. Many small towns have been bypassed and as a result have witnessed an unprecedented decline in passing trade. Many of these small towns have great little shops and tearooms and traditional pubs who will be delighted to welcome travellers.

CLEAN UP

Dublin City Council (dublincity.ie) organises regular clean-up initiatives, such as the Autumn Leaf Collection, while nationwide, the National Spring Clean (https://nationalspringclean.org) throughout the month of April and the Clean Coasts (https://cleancoasts.org) programme in September are just some initiatives you can register to get involved in. While the idea of 'cleaning' isn't everyone's definition of a holiday, participating in such schemes allows visitors to help maintain the island's beauty and, better yet, cultivate long-lasting friendships with the warm and gregarious locals.

DUBLIN'S MODERN TAKE ON THE TRADITIONAL GEORGIAN DOOR

Basics

Getting there

Dublin is the Republic of Ireland's main point of arrival, Belfast that of the North, while Shannon, near Limerick city in County Clare, is the major airport giving direct access to the west coast. There's an ever-changing route map of flights between Britain and Ireland – book early to get the best price. Train–ferry and bus–ferry combinations are kinder to the environment and generally cheaper, though of course they take longer. For those bringing their own car, there's a wide range of ferry routes from southwest Scotland to Northern Ireland, and routes from Wales, France and Spain to Dublin and Wexford. North American visitors can fly direct to Shannon, Dublin or Belfast, but those from South Africa, Australia and New Zealand have to travel via Britain, Europe or the Gulf. If you're thinking of booking an organized tour, there are plenty of Irish companies offering interesting trips – check online for options departing from near you.

Flights from Britain

It's never been easier or cheaper to fly from Britain to Ireland. Dozens of **routes** are available, with new destinations regularly appearing and unsuccessful routes phased out. To this end, there are **flights to Dublin**, Cork, Knock, Kerry and Shannon airports from many English, Scottish and Welsh airports; airlines include the national carrier Aer Lingus (http://aerlingus.com), British Airways (http://britishairways.com), and Ryanair (http://ryanair.com). The cheapest, most convenient, options **flying to Belfast** and Derry include easyJet (http://easyjet.com), Emerald Airlines (http://emeraldairlines.com) and Ryanair. With so much competition, **prices** can be ridiculously cheap, but as always, the secret is to book as early as possible: fares can be obtained for as little as £40–50 return if booked well in advance, but these can rise to over £150 one-way if left till the last minute. Flight time between London, for example, and any airport in Ireland is between one hour and one hour thirty minutes.

Flights from the US and Canada

From the US and Canada, Aer Lingus offers the widest choice of routes, including nonstop flights from Boston, Chicago, New York, Orlando, San Francisco, Toronto and Washington to Dublin, and from Boston and New York to Shannon. If booked well in advance, their low-season fares can be excellent value and Aer Lingus do regular great deals with many direct routes. Flying time to Dublin, is around six hours thirty minutes from New York and Toronto and ten hours fifteen minutes from San Francisco. Ireland operates a US preclearance programme (USCBP) meaning that US immigration and customs procedures can be carried out before departure, eliminating wait times on arrival at the other end.

Flights from Australia, New Zealand and South Africa

Travel from Australia, New Zealand and South Africa is generally via London, or one of the other European or Gulf cities such as Frankfurt or Abu Dhabi. **From Australia or New Zealand**, flights via Southeast Asia or the Middle East are generally the cheapest options, with the likes of Etihad (http://etihad.com) and Emirates (http://emirates.com) and Air New Zealand (http://airnewzealand.com). There are direct flights from Johannesburg (11hr) in **South Africa** to London Heathrow with South African Airways (http://flysaa.com), British Airways (http://britishairways.com) and Virgin Atlantic (http://virginatlantic.com).

Ferries

Ferry **routes** to Ireland are detailed below, along with the length of each voyage; http://aferry.com will give you an overview of what's currently available and allow you to compare prices. High-speed catamarans

---

A BETTER KIND OF TRAVEL

At Rough Guides we are passionately committed to travel. We believe it helps us understand the world we live in and the people we share it with – and of course tourism is vital to many developing economies. But the scale of modern tourism has also damaged some places irreparably, and climate change is accelerated by most forms of transport, especially flying. We encourage all our authors to consider the carbon footprint of the journeys they make in the course of researching our guides.

(which also take cars) operate on the Dublin route only (see page 32), though they don't run in the winter and in bad weather they're more likely to be cancelled than regular ferries.

Prices vary hugely according to the time of year, and even the day and hour you travel. Most ferry companies have peak seasons of July and August and may charge higher fares around public holidays; generally, it's cheaper to travel midweek. Foot passengers can travel cheaply and will pay around £35, plus £10 per bicycle.

FERRY CONTACTS

Irish Ferries http://irishferries.com. Holyhead to Dublin Port (3hr 25min, catamaran 1hr 50min); and Pembroke to Rosslare (4hr).
P&O http://poferries.com. Cairnryan to Larne (2hr)
Stena Line http://stenaline.co.uk. Fishguard to Rosslare (3hr 30min); Liverpool to Belfast (8hr); Holyhead to Dublin Port (3hr 15min); and Cairnryan to Belfast (2hr 15min).

Trains

Combined train and boat journeys from Britain generally use one of three **routes** across the Irish Sea: Cairnryan to Belfast, Holyhead to Dublin or Fishguard to Rosslare. Journey times are generally quicker than by coach: London to Dublin, for example, takes around eight hours, Glasgow to Belfast as little as four hours fifty minutes.

Ticket prices are **calculated** partly on a zonal basis, but also depend on which boat you take and whether you book in advance. Online, you can **book** train–boat tickets through Raileasy or Irish Ferries. Otherwise, you can book tickets in person at most railway stations in Britain, including through-tickets to other places in Ireland.

RAIL CONTACTS

The Man in Seat 61 http://seat61.com
Raileasy http://raileasy.co.uk

Buses

The main bus services to Ireland from the UK are provided by National Express (http://nationalexpress. com), crossing the Irish Sea via Cairnryan (in Scotland), and Holyhead and Pembroke (in Wales). They can be cheaper than travelling by train if booked well in advance, but take far longer. The daily through service from London to Dublin, for example, takes around twelve hours thirty minutes. Similarly, National Express operate a bus service from Glasgow to Belfast via Cairnryan, with a journey time of around just under six hours

AGENTS AND OPERATORS

Bunk Campers Northern Ireland, http://bunkcampers.com. Campervan rental in Belfast and Dublin.
El Adventures Republic of Ireland, http://eiadventures.ie. Hiking and adventure multi- and one-day tours all around Ireland; activities include kayaking, horseriding, mountain-climbing and cycling.
Go Visit Ireland Republic of Ireland, http://govisitireland. com. Small-group, customized and self-guided walking, cycling and hike-and-bike tours mostly on the west coast, as well as horseriding and kayaking.
Ireland Walk Hike Bike Republic of Ireland, http:// irelandwalkhikebike.com. Kerry based outfit offering a wide range of guided and self-guided walking holidays in the region, as well as self-guided cycling holidays.
Irish Boat Rental Association Republic of Ireland http:// boatholidaysireland.com. Umbrella association of companies who rent out cruisers for holidays on the Shannon. See http:// iwai.ie or http://waterwaysireland.org for fuller listings across the country.
Irish Cycling Safaris and Irish Ways Republic of Ireland, http://cyclingsafaris.com. Long-established and well-regarded company offering guided and self-led cycling and walking tours all over the country, with accommodation and luggage transfer covered.
Irish Horse-Drawn Caravans Federation http:// irishhorsedrawncaravans.com. Companies in Wicklow, Laois and Mayo offering horse-drawn caravan holidays, driving and sleeping in traditional, wooden covered wagons.

Getting around

It's relatively easy to travel within and between the Republic's larger towns and cities by public transport. However, it's common for small towns and villages to have just one or two bus services per week, often geared towards market days. Transport in Northern Ireland is equally sparse in rural areas, with just a few train lines across the region, though the bus network is pretty comprehensive. Renting a car is perhaps the easiest way to explore rural and remote areas across Ireland, though traffic has become increasingly heavy on major routes. Picturesque areas are particularly enjoyable on a bike, though you may need to bring your own as rental outlets have dried up in rural areas. If you want to travel quickly from Dublin or Belfast to outlying areas, it's also worth considering the internal flights available.

By rail

Train services in the **Republic** are operated by Iarnród Éireann (Irish Rail; http://irishrail.ie). Prices are usually higher than taking a coach, though journeys are often much quicker – for example, the train from Dublin to Killarney can take at least two and a half hours less than the bus. Most of the lines fan out from Dublin towards the southern and western coasts, but there are few links between them, and some counties (such as Donegal and Cavan) have no rail links at all. There is free wi-fi on all trains and charging ports and plugs for devices but note that there is no catering service and alcohol consumption is not allowed.

Tickets come in a variety of formats – single, day return, open return, family day and open returns, and student tickets. Tickets booked online in advance are generally much cheaper and you can reserve a specific seat when you book, worth doing, especially when there is a concert or event on in Dublin and the trains will be packed and you might not get a seat at all; if you miss your train and have a flexible ticket, you should be able to get on the next available service.

The only line operating **between the Republic and the North** is the Dublin–Belfast Enterprise service. The **North**'s rail service is operated by Translink (http://translink.co.uk) and restricted to just a few lines running out of Belfast. Services are generally efficient. Fares are pretty reasonable – and are often comparable with bus services.

You can also **transport bikes** on trains (see page 34).

Rail and bus passes

Although rail passes for travel within the Republic represent reasonably good value, a combined bus and rail pass, such as the Irish Explorer, is probably more useful owing to the limitations of the rail network. Passes are available at all major train and bus stations.

The Trekker ticket (€88) allows unlimited travel over the Republic's rail network for four consecutive days, while the **Irish Explorer** pass (€128) covers five days' rail travel out of fifteen consecutive days.

For travellers just visiting Dublin, it can be worthwhile investing in a Leap Visitor Card, which offers unlimited travel on bus, DART, and Luas services. A one-day pass costs €8, three days costs €16, and seven days €32. If you do not have a LEAP card, you will need to have coins to pay for the bus as there is no contactless payment on buses at present. DART tickets can be purchased from the machine at the departure station.

In the North, Translink's Rambler ticket (£10) provides unlimited travel around the bus network

after 9.15am on Sundays and during school holidays (including July and August). Families can take advantage of a variety of day passes for trains and/or buses.

If your visit to Ireland is just part of a wider European trip, it's well worth investigating the range of different passes on offer, such as InterRail (http://interrail.eu) and Eurail (http://eurail.com).

By bus

Bus Éireann (http://buseireann.ie) runs express coach and slower local services throughout the Republic. Ticket prices are generally far more reasonable than trains and you can often snap up cheap deals, especially between Dublin and Cork. Timetables and fares (including special deals) for the major routes can be found on the website. The majority of buses show destinations in both Irish and English, but some in rural areas may only display the former.

A vast number of **private bus companies** also operate in the Republic, running services on major routes, as well as areas not covered by the Bus Éireann network (especially Co. Donegal). The names, contact details and routes of these companies are listed in the Guide, where applicable. These can sometimes be cheaper and quicker than Bus Éireann, but are usually very busy at weekends, when advance booking is advisable.

In **Northern Ireland**, Metro (Belfast city buses), **Ulsterbus** (local buses) and **Goldline** (long-distance), all part of Translink (see page 33), run a pretty comprehensive network of regular and reliable services across Northern Ireland.

You can **transport bikes** on buses (see page 35).

By car and motorcycle

Travelling by **car** or **motorbike** is the ideal way to explore at your leisure, especially in remote areas. You might be tempted to take on the Wild Atlantic Way, a signposted route around the west coast all the way from west Cork to Donegal (see page 26) – and if you enjoy that, you could keep going along the Causeway Coastal Route, which runs from Derry to Belfast for over 300km, mostly along the N2. If you bring your own vehicle, it's essential to carry its registration document and certificate of **insurance** – and make sure that your existing policy covers you for driving in Ireland. Whether bringing your own vehicle or renting one on arrival, you'll need to be in possession of a valid **driving licence** (and should carry it with you – a photocopy is insufficient). A driving licence from any EU country is treated like an Irish licence, while all other visitors are allowed to drive on a valid non-EU licence for a stay of up to 12 months.

At the time of writing, in the Republic, unleaded **petrol** was around €1.77 a litre; the equivalent price in Northern Ireland was about £1.45; however, prices look set to remain quite volatile for the foreseeable future. **Diesel** is almost on a par.

Rules of the road

The fundamental rule of the road in Ireland, both North and South, is to **drive on the left**. Wearing **seat belts** is compulsory for drivers and passengers, as is the wearing of helmets for motorcyclists and their pillion riders. The Republic's **speed limits** are 50–60km/h in built-up areas (though in some parts of inner-city Dublin it's 30km/h), 80km/h on rural roads (denoted by the letter "R" on maps and signposts), 100km/h on national roads (denoted by an "N", and a green colour scheme on signposts) and 120km/h on motorways ("M" roads, with a blue colour scheme on signposts). Maximum speeds in Northern Ireland are 20–40mph in built-up areas, 70mph on motorways and 60mph on most other main roads. Minor rural roads in the Republic are generally poor in quality, often potholed and sometimes rutted – a situation notably different from the North where the overwhelming majority of roads, of all categories, are well maintained. **Signposts** in the Republic generally provide place names in both Irish and English, though in the Gaeltacht (Irish-speaking areas) you'll generally only encounter signposts in Irish. Virtually all signposts in the Republic provide distance information in kilometres (with some older signposts also giving miles); in the North distances are given in miles.

Parking

Throughout Ireland many bigger town centres require payment for on-street **parking**, either using ticket machines or a disc or card parking scheme (discs or cards can be purchased in adjacent shops) – check for signs on the street to see if parking charges are in operation. In smaller, rural towns, parking is generally free. If you don't display a ticket or disc you may end up with a parking fine or, particularly in Dublin, Cork and Galway, your car being clamped or towed away.

Car rental

Outlets of multinational **car rental companies**, such as Avis and Hertz, can be found at airports, in the cities and in some tourist towns. Rental charges are fairly high – expect to pay around €35/£30 per day plus insurance – though prices are often much cheaper in the Republic than in the North, with the best offers garnered if you book well in advance, especially via the internet. Sometimes smaller local firms can undercut the big names.

In most cases, you'll need to be 23 or over (though some companies may accept younger drivers with a price hike) and able to produce a full and valid driving licence, with no endorsements incurred during the previous two years. Considering the nature of Ireland's roads, it's always advisable to pay for extra collision damage waiver (CDW). You can pay a daily rate for this from the car-rental companies or you can buy it more cheaply in advance from specialist insurance agencies (such as http://icarhireinsurance.com), but it guarantees that you won't be liable for a hefty bill if you suffer an accident or any other damage. If you're planning to cross the border, ensure that your rental agreement provides full insurance; in some cases, you may need to pay extra.

Booking a car prior to your journey saves time when you arrive in Ireland and provides the chance to shop around on the web for the best deals. We've listed the main brokers and agencies below.

CAR-RENTAL AGENCIES

Argus http://arguscarhire.com
Auto Europe http://autoeurope.com
Avis http://avis.com
Budget http://budget.com
Car Rental Ireland http://carrentalireland.com
Dan Dooley http://dan-dooley.ie
Europcar http://europcar.com
Great Island http://greatislandcarrentals.com
GoCar www.gocar.ie
Hertz http://hertz.com
Holiday Autos http://holidayautos.co.uk
Nova http://novacarhire.com
Thrifty http://thrifty.com

By bike

Apart from some steep ascents, occasional poor road surfaces and an unpredictable climate, Ireland provides ideal territory for **cycling**, one of the most enjoyable ways to explore the stunning scenery. The tourist board's website, http://ireland.com, details waymarked **trails across the island** (see page 44), as well as specialist cycling-tour operators.

If you plan to **bring your own bike**, note that some airlines will transport bicycles for free as long as you keep within your weight allowance, but it's always worth checking with them well in advance.

Across the island, minor roads in rural areas are generally quiet, but major roads are well worth avoiding due to heavy traffic. Bikes are easy to **transport** over long distances by train, but less so by bus. In the Republic, you can take a bike on a mainline train for free, but this must be booked in advance. On DART and commuter services you can take bikes with you for free but only **at off-peak hours**. Folding bicycles can be carried for free on any service.

Bus companies will generally allow bikes to be carried for a fee, as long as there is room in the luggage compartment. In the Republic, prices vary according to the company but can come to over €10 for a long journey. Folding bicycles can be brought at no extra cost. In the **North** carrying a bike is free on Ulsterbus and Goldline services and on the trains, but is only permitted on the latter at off-peak hours.

Bike rental

Thanks to a rise in insurance premiums, far fewer places in the Republic now **rent out** bikes – though **Dublin** now has a city bike scheme (see page 96) – and there are still just a small number of outlets in the North, meaning that it's always wise to book your wheels well ahead. Rental rates are generally around €15–20 per day for a standard bike, roughly double that for an e-bike, with an extra charge for hiring panniers, though a helmet is usually included free. A deposit of anything from €100 to €200 is also required. When collecting your bike, check that its brakes and tyres are in good condition, and make sure that it comes equipped with a pump and repair kit. If you're planning on cycling in upland areas it makes sense to rent a bike with at least sixteen gears, preferably 24.

By air

The quickest way to reach outlying areas is to take a scheduled flight to one of the **regional airports** dotted around the country. Aer Lingus operates the largest network. Prices can be as little as €40 one-way, if booked online well in advance, and much time can be gained; for instance, the flight from Dublin to Donegal takes only an hour, compared with at least four hours on the bus.

Accommodation

You'll find accommodation to suit most budgets across Ireland, from swish city hotels and luxurious converted castles to historic country houses and B&Bs. There are also plenty of hostels, varying hugely in quality and atmosphere, but all providing a bed and usually a kitchen; lots offer much more. Finally, there are well-run campsites and, for the hardy, the chance to pitch a tent in a farmer's field or on common land.

You'll need to book your accommodation well in advance over **St Patrick's Day**, **Easter**, summer **public holidays** (see page 50), and during all of **July** and **August**. Accommodation is at a premium in Dublin throughout the year, especially at weekends, and may be booked out in places such as the **Aran Islands**, **Belfast**, **Cork**, **Derry**, **Dingle**, **Galway city**, **Kilkenny** and **Killarney**, and during major festivals elsewhere (see page 40). Be aware that during busy periods or popular events (concerts, rugby matches, and so on) prices can be hiked to eye-wateringly exorbitant rates. Many establishments close over the Christmas period.

ACCOMMODATION CONTACTS

Adams & Butler http://adamsandbutler.com. A selection of mostly rural and historic houses and castles across Ireland for luxury self-catering.

B&B Ireland http://bandbireland.com. The major B&B association in the Republic (plus a few members in the North), with over a thousand tourist-board-approved members and booking available on its website.

Good Food Ireland http://goodfoodireland.ie. This network of high-quality food purveyors includes a large number of good hotels where the emphasis is on cuisine.

Hidden Ireland http://hiddenireland.com. Over thirty B&Bs in private homes, mainly in the Republic, most of which are selected for their historic nature or architectural merit, as well as a similar number of self-catering properties.

Ireland's Blue Book http://irelands-blue-book.ie. Upmarket country-house hotels and B&Bs, as well as restaurants, both North and South.

Irish Farmhouse Holidays http://irishfarmholidays.com. More than three hundred farmhouse B&Bs, some in exquisite rural locations.

Irish Hotels Federation http://irelandhotels.com. Covering numerous hotels and guesthouses across Ireland, with a comprehensive listing, direct booking and special offers available on the website.

Irish Self Catering Federation http://letsgoselfcatering.ie. Tourist-board-approved site, a good starting point for finding your preferred holiday home.

Northern Ireland Hotels Federation http://nihf.co.uk. Smaller than its equivalent in the Republic, but still offering an extensive range of around a hundred hotels and guesthouses.

B&Bs and guesthouses

The overwhelming majority of **B&Bs** and **guesthouses** across Ireland are welcoming family homes and provide clean and cosy rooms, usually with en-suite facilities. Most B&Bs in the Republic, and

ACCOMMODATION PRICES

Throughout this book, for hotels, guesthouses and B&Bs, we've noted how much you can expect to pay for a **double room in high season**. Unless otherwise indicated, breakfast is included, but do check this at the time of booking. For **hostels**, we've given a per-adult price for dorms in high season and, where appropriate, a per-room price for double or twin rooms. For **campsites**, we've noted the price for two adults and a tent in high season.

Some establishments provide **single rooms**, but, in most cases, single travellers will occupy a double room. In hotels, there may be no discount on the room price at all for single occupation. You're more likely to get a good deal at traditional B&Bs, where the single rate may be around 25 percent higher than the cost of a double per person.

For Ireland:
€ = under €80
€€ = €80-140
€€€ = €140-200
€€€€ = over €200

For Northern Ireland:
£ = under £75
££ = £75-120
£££ = £120-175
££££ = over £175

virtually all in Northern Ireland, are registered with the official tourist board, but many other places open their doors during local festivals or high season. Registration is usually a guarantee of well-maintained standards and good service, though non-registered places are not necessarily of lower quality. Most B&Bs and guesthouses include breakfast – at the very least a continental breakfast but more often than not there's a cooked option (see page 38).

Hotels

Hotels come in all shapes and sizes. At the upper end of the scale, and offering most character, are Ireland's country houses, mansions and castles, many of which are beautifully located; most will also offer dinner, too, often as part of a package. **Boutique hotels** are very much in fashion, though you'll generally find these in the larger towns. Most hotels in the Republic offer reductions mid-week, but in the North, especially in Belfast or Derry, you're far more likely to get a good deal at the weekend. Budget hotels, typically run by national (and international) chains, are largely confined to Dublin, Belfast and one or two of the bigger cities in the Republic, though you may find a smattering elsewhere. Overall, hotels in Ireland are pricey.

Hostels

Well-run, good-quality **hostels** – both HI affiliated and independent – can be found across all of Ireland, often in lovely, off-the-beaten-track locations. Though most hostels are efficiently run, there's generally a relaxed atmosphere, often with no curfews. In the most popular tourist areas, however, they can be crammed to the rafters at busy times. There are still shared bathrooms and traditional single-sex bunk-bed dormitories in most, though the majority now also offer smaller rooms (often en-suite) of two to six beds for couples, families and groups. Most offer kitchens, laundry facilities and lounges, while bike rental and storage are common. In high season expect to pay €20–30 for a dorm bed in Dublin, and around €15–25 elsewhere; in Northern Ireland you'll usually pay £15–20. Booking ahead is advisable, especially in Dublin and Galway at all times, and elsewhere during high season or local festivals.

An Óige and HINI hostels

The Republic's Youth Hostel Association, **An Óige** (http://anoige.ie; annual membership €25, under-25s €15), has around twenty hostels concentrated mainly in popular tourist spots. Most offer smaller dorms or private rooms, usually with very good facilities, especially in some of the urban hostels. **Hostelling International Northern Ireland** (HINI; http://hini.org.uk; annual membership £15, under-25s £10, family £30, one-adult family £15) has just three hostels, most of which are recently built or refurbished. Membership of either organization or the umbrella **Hostelling International** (HI) is not needed to stay in an An Óige or HINI hostel, but it does give you ten percent off accommodation at most hostels, as well as providing numerous **discounts**, ranging from travel to entry to attractions. So, if you're planning to use the An Óige/HINI network a lot, it's worth joining your own country's HI-affiliated association in advance of your trip. There are a growing number of independent, non-affiliated, hostels offering similar facilities to YHAs, often with a less regimented regime and no curfews or lockouts.

Camping

The website of the **Irish Caravan and Camping Council** (http://campingireland.ie) gives details of around a hundred sites all over Ireland. The price of a night's stay at a campsite depends on the area's popularity, facilities and tent size, but expct to pay around €20/£16 for two adults to pitch a tent in high season. Some hostels also allow camping on their land for around €5–10/£4–8 per person per night, with use of a kitchen and showers.

Camping rough is possible in many parts of Ireland, though the likelihood of rain coupled with the lack of proper facilities may prove a deterrent. Some of the terrain in Ireland's windy west, often boggy or rocky, may make pitching a tent difficult too. Off the beaten track, many farmers in the Republic will allow camping in one of their fields, usually for a few euros. It's permissible to camp in some state forests in the North, but not in the Republic.

Food and drink

The quality and choice of food in Ireland is good and you can get pretty much any cuisine in the big cities, and even small towns will have a Chinese, local takeaway and maybe even an Indian restaurant. Small-scale artisan producers are on the rise, too, be they cheese-makers, organic farmers, fish-smokers or bakers, and the best Irish chefs seek out this local produce to re-create and adapt traditional dishes. It's worth looking out for Good Food Ireland signs (or checking out http://goodfoodireland.ie), a network of high-quality restaurants, cafés, hotels, producers and cookery schools, who are committed to using local, seasonal, artisan ingredients wherever possible. Moreover, there's a fantastic spread of food festivals across Ireland throughout the year.

Food

Irish meat is internationally renowned, especially Aberdeen Angus beef and lamb from the west coast, the latter appearing in **Irish stew**, a classic wintery favourite made with stock, potatoes, onions and carrots. Variants to look out for include Achill lamb, what the French call *pré-salé*: as the animals graze on seaside meadows, the meat is naturally salty and a little sweet; and air-dried Connemara lamb from Oughterard, a little like Italian Parma ham. Beef, pork

TRADITIONAL DISHES

Bacon and cabbage Shoulder of pork boiled with cabbage.
Boxty Potato pancakes.
Carrageen Edible seaweed, used to make a blancmange-like dessert.
Champ Northern Irish version of colcannon, with spring onions.
Colcannon Mashed potato mixed with cabbage and often leeks.
Crubeen Boiled pig's trotters.
Drisheen Sausage of sheep and beef blood with oatmeal and pepper.
Fadge Northern fried potato bread.
Soda bread Bread baked with bicarbonate of soda, buttermilk and flour.

and lamb of course crop up in excellent sausages, which may be accompanied for breakfast by **black pudding**, a sausage of pig's blood, and **white pudding**, made from pig's offal and cereals (butchers in Clonakilty specialize in these puddings).

Seafood

Fresh **fish** and **seafood** such as prawns, lobsters, crabs and mussels, particularly from the west coast, Dublin Bay and Carlingford Lough, Dundrum Bay and Strangford Lough in the North, are also generally excellent. Among Ireland's many seafood festivals, the most famous are at Clarinbridge and nearby Galway city celebrating Galway Bay's **oysters**. These large, silky European flat oysters are some of the best in

TOP FIVE CHEESES

Ardrahan From Kanturk, Co. Cork, with powerful, complex flavours of milk and mustard.
Desmond Piquant, long-matured, Swiss-style cheese from Co. Cork; also Gabriel, a hard, aromatic and full-bodied Gruyère-like cheese from the same makers.
Durrus Semi-soft, washed-rind, raw milk cheese from west Cork.
Kilshanny Type of Gouda, sweet, hard and milky, made in Lahinch, Co. Clare; sometimes flavoured with garlic, cumin or nettles.
Wicklow Bán Hand-crafted on a family farm in Wicklow, this is a mild and creamy Brie.

THE FULL IRISH

Big **breakfasts** are an Irish tradition and are generally available at old-style cafés, often all day long; however, visitors are most likely to come across them at their hotel or B&B, where they're invariably included in the price. The "full Irish" or "Ulster fry" typically consists of bacon, sausage, eggs, black pudding and white pudding, and tomatoes, sometimes stretching to mushrooms. Many hotels and B&Bs also offer less hearty alternatives such as smoked salmon, muesli and fruit salad.

---

the world, having matured for about three years in anticipation of a season that runs from September until April. Ireland is also home to dozens of excellent **smokehouses**, which smoke not only delicately flavoured, satiny salmon, but also mussels, eels, bacon and chicken.

Cheese

Cheese-making in Ireland entirely died out during the eighteenth century, partly because of the plantations and the rise of the international butter trade. However, legend has it that Irish monks had exported the secrets of cheese-making to Europe in the sixth century, while many kinds of Irish cheese are recorded in early texts – notably the twelfth-century *Aislinge Meic Conglinne*, a brilliantly satirical tale about a king possessed by a demon of gluttony, and an underfed monk who tries to tempt the demon out with a vision of a foodie's paradise. Since the 1970s, cheese-making has blossomed once again, especially in Munster, often handmade by farmers.

Restaurants

The widest array of **restaurants** is concentrated in the big cities – where, alongside Dublin and Belfast, Cork has a particularly vibrant scene – and in gourmet hotspots such as Kilkenny, Kinsale, Kenmare and Dingle, but good places can be found all over the country, sometimes in quite unexpected locales. Between them, the Republic and Northern Ireland now have a remarkable twenty Michelin-starred restaurants, a handful of which are in Dublin. Off the beaten track, it's usually worth phoning ahead, as opening hours can be erratic and, in winter, some establishments in tourist areas close down entirely. There's no getting away from the fact that dining out in Ireland is expensive, particularly when you factor in the high price of wine, but many fine restaurants offer cheaper, simpler menus at lunch time, and plenty also lay on good-value **early-bird menus** in the evening – two or three courses for a set price, usually available until 7 or 7.30pm, though often not at weekends. To cut down on the price of an evening out, cinema meal deals are popular and offer excellent value with a meal and cinema ticket usually in the region of €20 per person.

Found in small towns across the country, though sometimes takeaway only, the most widespread ethnic restaurants are Chinese, Indian and Italian, followed by Thai; you'll also find Eastern European delis in many large towns and restaurants. There are also an increasing number of dedicated **vegan** restaurants – which are far more preferable to the token vegan dishes offered in many pubs and restaurants.

EATING PRICE CODES

Prices are based on a two-course meal for one, including a drink.

For Ireland:
€ = under €15
€€ = €15-30
€€€ = €30-45
€€€€ = over €45

For Northern Ireland:
£ = under £15
££ = £15-25
£££ = £25-40
££££ = over £40

Drink

Dark, creamy **stout** has long been Ireland's most popular drink. It's always granted two minutes' settling time halfway through pouring and you should let it settle again once it's fully poured. Brewed in Dublin, Guinness is the market leader, and now offers a 00 version which is pretty good, but Beamish and Murphy's from Cork are also worth trying, as are microbrewery-produced stouts and beers.

The other indigenous tipple is **whiskey** (from *uisce beatha*, "water of life"). Apart from an inexplicable change in spelling, the main differences with Scotch whisky is that the Irish versions generally don't have the smoky, peaty flavour found in many Scotches, as the malt is dried in smokeless kilns rather than

CRAFT BEER IN IRELAND

Not too long ago, the letters IPA (India Pale Ale – a hoppy, cloudy beer with a more bitter taste than larger) stood for little outside of a small conclave of hipsters. Now, with in excess of one hundred micro-breweries now operating in Ireland, the nascent craft beer industry shows no signs of slowing down. With most pubs and off-licences stocking a daunting selection of these beers, it can be hard to know where to start. Here are five of the best:

Black Donkey Sheep Stealer Traditionally brewed Irish farmhouse ale with a crisp finish.
Blacks of Kinsale Black IPA A suitably Irish twist on an IPA, with a nice malty taste of stout.
Brú Dubh Irish Craft Stout A traditional dry stout brewed with chocolate malt and magnum hops.
Franciscan Well Rebel Red A medium-bodied Irish red ale.
Kinnegar Brewing Scraggy Bay An India Pale Ale with a deliciously hoppy bite.

over peat fires; they are often smoother too, being triple-distilled whereas Scotch only goes round twice. The main brands are Jameson's, Power's, Paddy's – all three of which are now distilled in Midleton, Co. Cork – and Bushmills, made in Co. Antrim and the preferred drop in the North. A notable newcomer to the scene is Teeling Whiskey, a Dublin-based independent distillery producing some superb single malts.

Gin distillerys are also popping up in recent years, with companies such as The Shed Distillery making fine gin, vodka and whiskey.

Pubs and cafés

Most **pubs** across the country will be able to rustle you up a simple lunch, typically sandwiches and salads – which regularly feature crab and other seafood in coastal areas – and hot staples such as Irish stew and soups. But while occasionally the offerings can be dull, Ireland's foodie renaissance, and a commercial need to diversify, means that many have had to up their game. An increasing number of pubs also now also serve meals in the evening. Similar fare is also available in traditional daytime **cafés**, alongside cakes and scones, which are now augmented in some towns by deli-cafés, offering a more interesting array of food.

Markets

Virtually every sizeable town now hosts a **farmers' market**, often on a Saturday. The best markets – colourful, vibrant affairs that are worth a visit in their own right – are the permanent English Market in Cork city; the Temple Bar Food Market in Dublin, the Galway city market and the Midleton market in east Cork, all on Saturdays; and St George's Market in Belfast, on Fridays and Saturdays. For a full list of farmers' markets around the country, go to the Irish Food Board's website, http://bordbia.ie/farmers-markets, and, for the north, http://discovernorthernireland.com/things-to-do/shopping/best-markets.

SPECIALITY DRINKS

Black and Tan Stout and ale.
Black velvet Stout and champagne.
Hot port Winter warmer, made with port, hot water, lemon and cloves.
Hot whiskey As above, with whiskey instead of port.
Irish coffee Invented in Foynes, Co. Limerick, in the 1940s to warm up miserable transatlantic flying-boat passengers; whiskey, coffee, sugar and cream.
Poteen (poitín, "little pot") Subject of many a song, a powerful, usually illicitly distilled whiskey that varies enormously in quality – some being fit only to strip paint.

The media

Both the Republic and the North have a wide range of daily and weekly newspapers, the latter often county-based in their coverage. The choices for Ireland-based TV are more limited both sides of the border, but there's an abundance of local radio stations, together with several national stations in the Republic.

Newspapers and magazines

The Republic's most popular middlebrow **newspapers** are the *Irish Times* and the more populist *Irish*

Independent. Though generally liberal, if sometimes tinged by old-fashioned Ascendancy attitudes, the *Times* offers comprehensive news coverage of events both at home and abroad and often excellent features (http://irishtimes.com). The *Independent* (http://independent.ie) has a more right-of-centre outlook, while the *Irish Examiner* (http://irishexaminer.com) has a Munster-based focus and generally less analytical coverage of news. British newspapers are commonly available in Dublin and other cities and some produce Irish editions.

Every county has at least one weekly newspaper, often conservative and usually crammed with local stories of little interest to outsiders. However, some, such as the *Kerryman*, the *Kilkenny People* and the *Donegal Democrat*, often provide good coverage of local events and very readable features. To delve deeper into the seamy world of Irish politics, turn to the monthly *Village* (http://villagemagazine.ie) or the satirical fortnightly **magazine** *Phoenix* (http://thephoenix.ie).

The **North**'s three morning dailies are the Nationalist *Irish News* (http://irishnews.com), the Unionist *News Letter* (http://newsletter.co.uk) and the *Belfast Telegraph* (http://belfasttelegraph.co.uk). The widest circulation belongs to the *Irish News*. All UK national papers are also available in the North.

Television and radio

In the **Republic**, the three national **TV channels** are operated by the state-sponsored Radio Telefís Éireann (RTÉ; http://rte.ie). As well as imported shows, the main news and current affairs channel, RTÉ 1, also features the popular home-grown Dublin-based soap, *Fair City*, and Friday's *Late Late Show*, a long-standing chat and entertainment institution. RTÉ 2 is a little more bubbly, with a smattering of locally produced programmes, though still swamped by imported tat and overburdened by sporting events. Some of the most innovative viewing is provided by the Irish-language channel TG4 (which provides English subtitles; http://tg4.ie), including excellent traditional-music shows and often incisive features on the culture of Irish-speaking areas. In most of the Republic, the four major British terrestrial TV channels are available on cable or satellite.

RTÉ also operates four **radio stations**, three of which are English-language: the mainstream RTÉ Radio 1 (FM 88–89), whose morning shows are largely devoted to current affairs and chat; RTÉ 2FM (FM 90–92), which is more music- and youth-oriented; and Lyric FM (FM 96–99), which mixes popular classics with jazz and occasionally inspiring world-music

shows. Raidió na Gaeltachta (FM 93) is the national Irish-language station, with broadcasts including traditional music.

Northern Ireland receives television and radio programmes from the BBC (http://bbc.co.uk) and has a limited, if often keenly followed, number of locally produced current-affairs productions. On BBC Radio Ulster (FM 92.4–95.4), *Talkback* (Mon–Fri noon–1.30pm) offers lively discussions on the North's political situation. The BBC's main commercial rival, Ulster Television (http://u.tv), relies on the standard ITV diet of soaps and drama. In most parts of the North you can also watch or listen to RTÉ programmes.

Festivals and events

Ireland has a plethora of annual festivals, ranging from small local affairs to major international occasions and significant events in the sporting calendar. For more on the big events in Belfast, Cork, Derry, Dublin, Galway and Kilkenny, see the appropriate chapter sections or boxes.

JANUARY

Temple Bar Tradfest http://tradfest.ie. Sprawling music festival focusing on traditional and folk music. Venues range from intimate pubs to Dublin Castle and St. Patrick's Cathedral.

FEBRUARY–APRIL

Tedfest http://tedfest.org. A long weekend of wackiness in the Aran Islands at the beginning of March, celebrating the characters and storylines of the hugely popular sitcom *Father Ted*.

St Patrick's Day March 17; http://stpatricksday.ie. Almost every Irish town and village commemorates the national patron saint's day, though the most significant celebration is the week-long festival held in Dublin.

Irish Grand National http://fairyhouse.ie. The biggest event of the National Hunt horseracing season takes place at Fairyhouse, Co. Meath, on Easter Monday.

MAY

North West 200 http://northwest200.org. Major international motorcycle road-racing event held in Portstewart, Co. Derry, usually in the second week of the month.

Fleadh Nua http://fleadhnua.com. One of the country's biggest traditional music festivals, held in Ennis, Co. Clare, over a week in late May.

JUNE

Writers' Week http://writersweek.ie. Ireland's biggest literary festival, five days of workshops and events in Listowel, Co. Kerry, over the bank holiday weekend at the beginning of June.

Forbidden Fruit http://forbiddenfruit.ie. One of the best music festivals of the year, set in the gorgeous grounds of Dublin's Irish Museum of Modern Art for three days at the beginning of the month.

The Cat Laughs http://thecatlaughs.com. Four-day comedy festival featuring an array of renowned and lesser-known acts, staged in Kilkenny in early June.

Bloomsday http://bloomsdayfestival.ie. A week of Dublin-based James Joyce-related events leading up to June 16, the day on which his masterwork *Ulysses* is set.

Irish Derby http://curragh.ie. The major event in the Irish flat-racing season, held at the Curragh, Co. Kildare, in late June or early July.

Dublin Pride http://dublinpride.ie. Over a week of festivities at the end of the month celebrating diversity culminate in a carnival-style parade through the city centre – one of the biggest parties of the year.

JULY

Willie Clancy Summer School http://scoilsamhraidhwillieclancy.com. Hugely popular, week-long traditional music event with a host of pub sessions and several concerts, hosted in Miltown Malbay, Co. Clare, at the beginning of July.

Orange Order Parades July 12. Unionists and Loyalists commemorate the Battle of the Boyne and close down much of Northern Ireland in the process.

Galway International Arts Festival http://giaf.ie. Massive festival of music, drama and general revelry over a fortnight from the middle of the month.

Mary from Dungloe http://maryfromdungloe.ie. Ten days of entertainment in Co. Donegal, often featuring Daniel O'Donnell and culminating in a beauty contest (where one of the prizes is sometimes a date with the man himself – yes, really); runs from late July.

Yeats International Summer School http://yeatssociety.com. Sligo-based literary festival focusing on the life of the poet, usually taking place in mid-July for around eight days.

Galway Races http://galwayraces.com. The west of Ireland's biggest horse-racing event, long celebrated in the song of the same name; held over a week at the end of the month.

AUGUST

Kilkenny Arts Festival http://kilkennyarts.ie. All manner of musical and literary events, recitals and exhibitions staged in the city over ten days in mid-August.

GAZE http://gaze.ie. LGBTQ+ film festival celebrating diversity and activism, now in its 25th year. Screenings in various Dublin locations for five days at the beginning of August.

Puck Fair http://puckfair.ie. Three days of mayhem in Killorglin, Co. Kerry, culminating in the crowning of a goat as King Puck; takes place in the middle of the month.

Electric Picnic http://electricpicnic.ie. Hugely popular rock and dance festival held at Stradbally Hall, Laois, in mid-August; big names too, like Kylie.

Rose of Tralee International Festival http://roseoftralee.ie. Tremendously popular event, focused on a beauty contest, but offering an enormous range of other entertainment; late August.

Fleadh Cheoil na hÉireann http://comhaltas.ie. Competitive traditional-music festival, drawing hundreds of participants and big crowds – different towns bid for the mid- to late-August event each year.

Ould Lammas Fair More than four hundred years old, Ballycastle's traditional market fair remains a huge draw, featuring livestock sales, and bucket-loads of music, dancing and entertainment on the last Monday and Tuesday of the month.

SEPTEMBER

All-Ireland Senior Hurling and Football Finals http://gaa.ie. The zenith of the sporting year for Gaelic games, with the hurling on the first or second Sunday and the football on the third or fourth Sunday, in Dublin's Croke Park.

Lisdoonvarna Matchmaking Festival http://matchmakerireland.com. A month-long date-athon which attracts hopeful suitors from all over the world, and there's plenty of traditional entertainment too.

Dublin Fringe Festival http://fringefest.com. Lively programme of theatre, dance, performance arts and comedy, featuring hundreds of events spread over more than a fortnight.

Dublin Theatre Festival http://dublintheatrefestival.ie. Ireland's most prestigious drama festival, commencing late in the month and running for more than a fortnight.

Culture Night http://culturenight.ie. An all-island event where arts and cultural organisations open late into the night for talks, tours, performances and other events, all for free.

Galway Oyster Festival http://galwayoysterfest.com. Boisterous four-day festival to kick off the annual oyster season.

OCTOBER

Wexford Opera Festival http://wexfordopera.com. Prestigious and massively popular international festival lasting for a fortnight commencing in mid-October.

Belfast International Arts Festival http://belfastinternationalartsfestival.com. Major arts festival, running for two weeks from the middle of the month.

Cork Jazz Festival http://guinnesscorkjazz.com. Ninety venues and four days of jazz in all its forms at the end of the month.

Metropolis http://metropolisfestival.ie. An indoor music festival in the Royal Dublin Society with a heavy emphasis on the visual, from stunning set designs to unexpected installations.

Derry Halloween Carnival http://derryhalloween.com. Street theatre, music and mayhem, especially during the fireworks display on October 31.

NOVEMBER

Cork Film Festival http://corkfilmfest.org. Established in 1956 and still going strong with a broad-ranging programme of big-budget and international cinema staged over ten days in the middle of the month.

Dublin Book Festival http://dublinbookfestival.com. A five-day celebration of Irish authors and publishers, with readings, workshops, walking tours and plenty of other literary events.

DECEMBER

Wren Boys On St Stephen's Day (December 26), it was traditional for men and children carrying the corpse of a wren to go around the neighbourhood knocking on doors, asking for money to bury the bird while singing songs and telling jokes – the money, of course, would be spent on a party. The tradition can still be found in a few places, such as Dublin's Sandymount and Dingle in Co. Kerry.

New Year's Festival Dublin http://nyfdublin.com. Three days of festivities including concerts, street parties and fireworks.

Culture and etiquette

Ireland likes to describe itself as the land of Cead Míle Fáilte ("a hundred thousand welcomes"), which you'll often see inscribed on pubs, and that's essentially true for most visitors. In terms of general etiquette, wherever you go, you'll encounter the standard Irish greeting – an enquiry about your health ("How are you?" sometimes just abbreviated to "About you?" in parts of the North) – and it's reasonable to return the compliment. Also, if someone buys you a pint in a pub, then an even-handed gesture is to pay for the next round.

Alcohol

The pub has long been at the centre of Irish society and the ready availability of alcohol has played a major part in the development of the national psyche and as a Muse to some of the country's greatest writers (O'Brien, Kavanagh, Behan) and actors (Richard Harris and Peter O'Toole).

Consumption is gradually falling but the Irish are still among Europe's heaviest drinkers, imbibing as a whole on average some twenty percent more than their continental European neighbours, and that's despite the government's heavy excise duties on drink. According to Alcohol Action Ireland, more than half of the population have harmful drinking patterns (40 percent of women and 70 percent of men) and binge-drinking, especially among the 18–25 age group, is a significant problem. By contrast, thanks to movements such as the Pioneer Total Abstinence Association, around a fifth of the Irish population are teetotal.

Children

Facilities in Ireland for those travelling with children are similar to those in the rest of Europe, and generally speaking **children** are very well received everywhere. Breast-feeding is officially permitted in all public places, including in restaurants and cafés, and **baby-changing** rooms are widely available, including in shopping centres and train stations (where you may have to pay). Baby supplies are readily available in supermarkets and pharmacies, and most B&Bs and hotels welcome children, with an increasing number now providing dedicated family rooms; cots can usually be supplied in most places with little fuss. It's usually fine to take a child into a pub during the daytime, though definitely not so legally in the Republic after 9pm. Many public museums and attractions have kids' activity packs, family events, play areas and so on, and you can generally find a playground in most neighbourhoods.

LGBTQ+ Ireland

Ireland's attitude towards the LGBTQ+ community has come a long way in a remarkably short period of time. A country traditionally seen as culturally conservative, it is now one of the most inclusive and welcoming countries to visit.

Being the first country in the world to approve same-sex marriage by popular vote in 2015 wasn't just a huge step towards equal rights, it was recognition of how Irish society has changed. And it's not just the big cities, either – a closer look at the referendum results show that rural areas voted overwhelmingly to pass the bill.

This, coupled with Ireland's first gay Taoiseach (Leo Varadkar) being appointed in June 2017 with barely an eyelid batted, points to a far wider acceptance of the LGBTQ+ community than ever before. This isn't to say, however, that homophobic attitudes don't exist. While visitors are unlikely to encounter any trouble, if support is needed, contact http://lgbt.ie.

Racism

With around twenty percent of the Irish population born abroad, and a growing number of people with dual Irish nationality, Ireland continues to grow ever more diverse. That being said, it's still possible that foreign visitors could encounter **racist attitudes** at some point in their travels.

The situation differs in Northern Ireland where, following the vote to leave the EU, incidents of racial violence have been on the rise, in common with the rest of the UK. However, these are highly localised, and tourists, of whatever culture, are very rarely the victims of assaults.

Ireland also has its own recognized ethnic minority, the **Travellers** (widely known by a range of insulting epithets), against whom discrimination remains widespread, both North and South.

Women

Irish women's economic and social status has much improved over the last couple of decades, with the Republic even outranking Germany and the Netherlands in terms of gender equality.

In terms of the travel experience, **female visitors** are unlikely to encounter problems. However, as with anywhere, if you're travelling alone or to an unfamiliar area, it's worth adopting a cautionary attitude, particularly when enjoying pubs and nightlife. In the rare case of experiencing a serious personal assault, contact either a rape crisis centre (see page 47) or the Tourist Assistance Service (see page 47), as local police forces are unlikely to be experienced in these situations.

Sports

Hurling and Gaelic football are among the fastest and most physical sports in the world, and well worth catching on your travels, whether on TV or, preferably, live. Rugby and soccer are also widely followed, while going to the races is a great day out, with less of the snobbery sometimes found in Britain. Golf is also hugely popular north and south of the border.

Hurling and Gaelic football

Both Gaelic football and hurling, Ireland's two main indigenous sports, are played at a rollicking pace on huge pitches, 140m long and 80m wide, between teams of fifteen; goalposts are H-shaped, with three points awarded for a goal, when the ball goes under the crossbar into the net, and a point when it goes over the crossbar. Over two thousand clubs in villages and parishes all over Ireland vie for the privilege of reaching the club finals, held on St Patrick's Day at 83,000-seater Croke Park in Dublin, one of the largest stadiums in Europe (see page 91), while the more popular and prestigious intercounty seasons begin with provincial games in the early summer, reaching their climax in the All-Ireland County Finals in

September, also at Croke Park. Details of all fixtures for hurling and Gaelic football can be obtained from the Gaelic Athletic Association (http://gaa.ie).

Hurling is played with a leather *slíothar*, similar in size to a hockey ball, and a hurley (or *camán*), a broad stick made of ash that is curved outwards at the end. The *slíothar* is belted prodigious distances, caught and carried on the flattened end of the player's hurley. It's a highly skilled game of constant movement and aggression that does not permit a defensive, reactive style of play. Cork, Kilkenny and Tipperary are consistently the most successful counties, though Limerick have been the pre-eminent team in the 2020s. Clare has made a comeback, being crowned champions in 2024. No county from the North has ever won an All-Ireland Final, though the sport is very popular in the Glens of Antrim and parts of the Ards Peninsula in Co. Down. **Camogie**, the women's version of hurling, is becoming increasingly popular, and is also well worth watching. Dublin has won the most camogie All-Irelands, though they haven't prevailed since 1984 and the most successful team in the modern era has been Cork.

Gaelic football has similarities with both rugby and association football, but its closest relation is Australian Rules Football; indeed every autumn, Australia play Ireland in a hurly-burly series of "international rules" matches that are known for their frequent brawling. The round Gaelic ball, which is slightly smaller than a soccer ball, can be both kicked and caught. However, running with the ball is only permitted if a player keeps control by tapping it from foot to hand or by bouncing it, and throwing is not allowed – the ball must be "hand-passed", volleyball-style. Whereas hurling's strongholds are in the southern counties of the island, footballing prowess is more widely spread – Kerry is the most successful county, though Dublin are not far behind and have been the dominant force by far in recent years.

Rugby union and soccer

Rugby union and **soccer** are very popular in Ireland and tickets for international matches, especially for rugby, can be hard to come by. The Republic's home soccer matches (http://fai.ie) and Ireland's rugby matches (http://irishrugby.ie) are played at Dublin's Aviva Stadium (formerly Lansdowne Road). Northern Ireland's soccer matches (http://irishfa. com) are played at Windsor Park, Belfast (see page 471). For the international rugby team, which is a joint Republic–Northern Ireland side, the main event of the year is the Six Nations Championship, a series of international games played in February and March against England, France, Wales, Scotland and Italy. You're more likely to get tickets, however, for matches featuring the four provinces, Munster (which includes Irish rugby's natural heartland, Limerick), Leinster, Connacht and, in Northern Ireland, Ulster, who all complete in the sixteen-team United Rugby Championship (http://unitedrugby.com) with teams from Scotland, Wales, Italy and South Africa.

Soccer is played semi-professionally in both the North and the Republic, organized into the Northern Ireland Football League Premiership and the League of Ireland Premiership respectively. Both international teams field most of their players from the English leagues; Manchester United and Liverpool are the most popular clubs among Irish fans. Glasgow Celtic are also popular both north and south, Rangers in the north, with support following Catholic and Protestant divisions, respectively.

Racing

Going to the **races** is a hugely popular and enjoyable day out in Ireland. A good place to get a sense of the Irish passion for horses is the National Stud in Kildare (see page 129), while for details of all meetings, go to Horse Racing Ireland's website http://goracing.ie. The Irish Grand National is run at Fairyhouse in Co. Meath on Easter Monday (see page 107), followed in April by the five-day Irish National Hunt Festival at Punchestown in Co. Kildare (see page 130); at the Curragh, the classic flat-racecourse in Kildare (see page 130), the Irish 1000 Guineas and 2000 Guineas are held in May, the Irish Derby in late June or early July, the Irish Oaks in July and the Irish St Leger in September. Dublin's racecourse (see page 130) plus notable local meetings, such as those at Galway, Killarney, Listowel, Sligo and Downpatrick, are described in the Guide. One local oddity worth mentioning is the meeting at Laytown in Co. Meath, the last remaining beach racing under Jockey Club rules, held once a year when the tides are at their lowest (http://laytownstrandraces.ie).

Outdoor activities

Despite the weather, Ireland is a great place for getting out and about. Cycling is one of the best ways to appreciate the quiet pleasures of the Irish countryside, while walkers can take advantage of generally free access across much of the countryside and a number of waymarked trails. With over 120 sailing and yacht clubs, plenty of lakes, rivers and sheltered coastline to explore and some great beaches for surfers, there are many opportunities for watersports enthusiasts, too.

Cycling

Signposted **cycling trails** in the Republic include the Beara Way (see page 260) and the Sheep's Head Cycling Route (see page 257) in Cork, and the Kerry Way (see page 277). On- and off-road routes are detailed on http://sportireland.ie, but trails in the North are better documented and promoted: for detailed information on the many routes here, the best places to start are http://cycleni.com and http://sustrans.org.uk. They include the Kingfisher Trail (see page 552), which also stretches into Leitrim and Cavan. Other cross-border routes include the 326km North West Trail, mainly on quiet country roads through Donegal, Tyrone, Fermanagh, Leitrim and Sligo. Getting around the country by bike is a great option (see page 34).

Fishing

There are plenty of opportunities for sea **angling** and dozens of rivers and lakes for fly- and game-fishing. For information, the best places to start are Angling Ireland's website, http://fishinginireland.info, and the tourist-board site, http://ireland.com. Great Fishing Houses of Ireland (http://irelandflyfishing.com) covers a dozen or so specialist hotels and B&Bs.

Golf

Golf, which was probably first brought to Ireland by the Ulster Scots, attracts huge numbers of visitors every year, and thanks to the likes of Rory McIlroy (from Holywood, near Belfast) and Shane Lowry (form Clara in Co. Offaly), the game has never been more popular. Golf in Ireland has also received a massive boost in recent years thanks to the staging of the Open Championship at Portrush in Northern Ireland in 2019 and again in 2025. The Golfing Union of Ireland, based in Kildare (http://golfnet.ie), provides details of over four hundred clubs, north and south, with online booking.

Horseriding

Horseriding, whether over the hills or along the beaches, is also a popular pastime, for both novices and experienced riders, who also have the option of multi-day trails rides. Stables in popular locations are

BIRDWATCHING

With a wide variety of migrating flocks, including a large number of rare species, visiting its shores, Ireland is a great place for **birdwatching**; Wexford Wildfowl Reserve (see page 196), where thousands of Greenland white-fronted geese and pale-bellied brent geese spend the winter, Cape Clear (see page 254), famous for spotting rare migratory birds in October, and the wetlands at Castle Espie (see page 518) are especially fruitful hunting grounds. The best general contacts are http://irishbirding.com, Birdwatch Ireland in the Republic (http://birdwatchireland. ie) and, in the North, the Royal Society for the Protection of Birds (http://rspb.org.uk).

listed throughout the Guide, including Killarney and Clifden. The Association of Irish Riding Establishments (http://aire.ie) maintains standards among riding centres in the Republic and the North and publishes details on its website (http://discovernorthernireland. com).

Walking and mountain climbing

There are dozens of waymarked long-distance **walking trails** in the Republic, ranging from routes through or around mountain ranges, such as the Wicklow Way (see page 121), the Táin Way (see page 153), the Slieve Bloom Way (see page 178) and the Western Way (see page 357), to walks around entire peninsulas, like the Sheep's Head Way (see page 257), the Beara Way (see page 260), the Kerry Way (see page 277) and the Dingle Way (see page 295). The Ulster Way (see page 556) in the North, the oldest and longest waymarked walking trail in Ireland, is a 625-mile circuit of the whole province, taking in the Giant's Causeway, the Sperrins and the Mournes; it's now divided into link sections, which can be skipped by taking public transport, and quality sections. For information on these trails in the Republic, go to http://sportireland.ie, which also has details of hundreds of looped day walks; in the Guide, we list the very useful websites on the Wicklow, Kerry and Dingle Ways, which include details of walker-friendly accommodation. In the North, http://walkni.com has comprehensive information on all aspects of walking.

Some councils and local tourist offices have produced helpful map guides for the main routes too, but you should always get hold of the relevant Ordnance Survey map and carry a compass.

Other **walking highlights** include the ascents of Croagh Patrick in Co. Mayo (see page 370) and of Carrauntoohil, for more experienced walkers, in Co. Kerry (see page 277), the easily accessible Bray–Greystones walks in Co. Wicklow (see page 117) and just about anywhere in Connemara (see page 357), notably the excellent Diamond Hill trail in the national park; not to mention walks in the Wicklow (see page 121) and Killarney (see page 269) national parks.

Mountaineering Ireland, an organization that covers hill-walking and rambling, as well as climbing, maintains a compendious website (http://mountaineering.ie). Particularly useful walking guidebooks are listed in Contexts, see page 602. Some guided walking tour operators are detailed on page 32, while more complete lists are available on http://ireland.com.

If you need help in a real emergency on the mountains, call 999 or 112 and ask for **mountain rescue** (http://mountainrescue.ie).

Watersports

Sailing

Ireland's many **sailing** clubs include the Royal Cork Yacht Club, established in Cobh in 1720, which is

A NOTE ON ACCESS

Unlike the North, the Republic has no public "rights of way", but there is a tradition of relatively free access to privately owned countryside. In recent years, the growing numbers and occasional carelessness of walkers, as well as insurance worries, have led some farmers to bar access to their land, and, in response, the government has begun to pay farmers who maintain popular walks across their land under the National Walks Scheme. In general, the majority of landowners do not object to walkers crossing their property. For detailed advice on **access**, including a Good Practice Guide, have a look at http://mountaineering. ie or and http://leavenotraceireland.org.

thought to be the oldest in the world. Dozens of regattas, such as Calves Week in Schull, and traditional boat festivals, such as the Wooden Boat Festival in Baltimore and Cruinniú na mBád in Kinvarra, are held every year. The most popular areas for sailing are the relatively sheltered waters of the east coast, especially in Dublin Bay; Cork Harbour and west Cork; Lough Swilly on the north coast of Donegal; Strangford Lough in Co. Down; and some of the larger lakes, such as Lough Derg in Co. Clare. Popular sailing clubs are listed in the Guide; for further information contact the Irish Sailing Association (http://sailing.ie).

Canoeing and kayaking

Inland waterways and sheltered coasts – notably in west Cork (see page 251), Dingle (see page 289) and Waterford (see page 215) – offer **canoeing and kayaking** opportunities, ranging from day-trips and touring to rough- and white-water racing. We've detailed rental and guided trip providers in the Guide; Canoeing Ireland's website covers courses and clubs in the South (http://canoe.ie), while the North has a comprehensive website, http://canoeni.com, that includes canoe trails for multi-day touring. Another useful website is http://iska.ie.

Surfing, wind-surfing and kite-surfing

There are some superb beaches for **surfing** (http://irishsurfing.ie) and its spin-offs, **wind-surfing** (http://windsurfing.ie) and **kite-surfing** (http://iksa.ie). For kite- and wind-surfing, some of the best spots are: Rosslare, Co. Wexford; Tramore, Co. Waterford; Castlegregory, Kerry; Rusheen Bay, Co. Galway; Keel Strand, Achill and Elly Bay, Belmullet, in Mayo; Lough Allen, Leitrim; and Rossnowlagh, Co. Donegal. Surfers head for: Garrettstown and Inchydoney, Co. Cork; Inch and Brandon Bay, Kerry; Lahinch, Clare; Easkey, Mullaghmore and Strandhill, Co. Sligo; Bundoran and Rossnowlagh, Co. Donegal; Portrush, Antrim; and Tramore, Co. Waterford.

Scuba diving

Right in the path of the warm North Atlantic Drift current, Ireland offers some of the best **scuba diving** in Europe, notably off the rocky west coast. We've listed dive centres throughout the Guide, and you can get further information from Diving Ireland (http://diving.ie) and http://ukdiving.co.uk.

Travel essentials

Accessible Travel

Travellers with disabilities should glean as much information as possible before travelling since facilities in Ireland are generally poor – that said, the number of accessible hotels and restaurants is growing, and reserved parking bays are available almost everywhere, from shopping centres to museums. If you have specific requirements, it's always best to talk first to your chosen hotel or tour operator. The best place to start looking for information is on the joint tourist board website, http://ireland.com/en-us/ahelp-and-advice/practical-information/accessibility. It's also

---

CLIMATE

Average maximum and minimum daily temperatures (°C/°F) and monthly rainfall (mm)

	Jan	Feb	Mar	Apr	May	Jun	July	Aug	Sept	Oct	Nov	Dec
BELFAST												
Max/min (°C)	8/2	8/2	10/3	12/4	15/6	18/9	19/11	19/11	17/9	13/6	10/4	8/2
Max/min (°F)	46/35	46/35	50/37	53/39	59/42	64/48	66/51	66/51	62/48	55/42	50/39	46/35
Rainfall (mm)	88	70	71	60	60	68	73	84	70	95	100	93
CORK												
Max/min (°C)	9/4	9/4	10/5	12/6	15/8	17/11	19/12	19/12	17/11	14/8	11/6	9/5
Max/min (°F)	48/37	48/37	50/41	53/42	59/46	62/51	66/53	66/53	62/51	57/46	51/42	48/41
Rainfall (mm)	119	79	94	57	71	57	70	71	94	99	115	122
DUBLIN												
Max/min (°C)	8/2	9/2	11/3	13/4	16/7	18/10	20/12	20/11	18/10	14/7	11/4	9/3
Max/min (°F)	46/35	48/35	51/37	55/39	60/44	64/50	68/53	64/51	64/50	57/44	51/39	48/37
Rainfall (mm)	65	55	51	50	60	63	63	72	61	78	81	76

worth consulting the Disability Federation of Ireland (http://disability-federation.ie).

All new buildings and many hotels, however, now have wheelchair access. Go to http://accessible ireland.com for island-wide listings of hotels with disabled facilities, as well as visitor attractions. The main **transport** companies (see page 32) have considerably improved their facilities for travellers with disabilities, with, for example, low-floor buses in many cities and kneeling coaches on some long-distance routes. Drivers with disabilities travelling with their cars from Britain can usually obtain reduced rates for ferry travel, depending on the time of year. Motability Ireland near Dublin (http://motability ireland.com) offer vehicle rental all over Ireland.

Costs

Ireland is by no means a cheap destination, with Dublin by far the most expensive location; indeed it often ranks within the top ten most expensive cities in Europe to visit. Though it's still possible to get a main **meal** in cafés and pubs for around €10, a three-course restaurant dinner with a glass of wine will usually cost at least €35–40/£30–35, though some offer "early bird" menus and midweek set menus at reduced rates. The price of a pint in a pub is around €4–5, significantly higher in some city-centre clubs.

As a general rule, the **minimum expenditure**, if you are travelling by public transport, self-catering and camping, would be in the region of €35–40/£30–35 per day, rising to €45–50/£40–45 per day if you're using the hostelling network and grabbing the occasional meal out. Couples staying at budget B&Bs, eating at unpretentious restaurants and visiting the odd tourist attractions are looking at €75–80/ £70–75 each per day – if you're renting a car, staying in comfortable B&Bs or hotels and eating well, reckon on at least €140–150/£130–140 a day per person.

Crime and personal safety

Crime in Ireland is largely an urban affair and generally at a low level compared with other European countries. However, thieves do target popular tourist spots, so don't leave anything of value visible in your car and take care of your bags while visiting bars and restaurants. It's sensible to seek advice from your accommodation provider about safety in the local area and take as much care as you would anywhere else.

Crimes against individuals are relatively rare, except in certain inner-city areas, and seldom involve tourists. The **Republic**'s police force is An Garda Síochána (112 or 999 for emergencies, http://garda.ie), more commonly referred to as the guards or **Gardaí**, whom you'll find generally helpful when it comes to reporting a crime. The Irish Tourist Assistance Service (01 666 9354, http://itas.ie) offers support to tourist crime victims. Rape crisis support is available from the Dublin Rape Crisis Centre (1800 778888, http:// drcc.ie), which can also direct you to similar agencies across Ireland.

Away from the sectarian hotspots, crime in **Northern Ireland** is very low. In the unlikely event that your person or property is targeted, contact the Police Service of Northern Ireland (999 for emergencies, http://psni.police.uk). The presence of the British army has diminished almost to invisibility, though it is just possible you might encounter police or army security checks on the rare occasion of a major incident.

Discount cards

For all attractions in the Guide, we've given the adult entry price. The majority of sites offer reduced rates for children (under-5s usually get in free), students (for which you'll need ID such as an International Student Identity Card, http://isic.org) and senior citizens.

An annual **Heritage Card** (€40, senior citizens €30, children/students €10, family €90; http://heritageire land.ie) is worth considering if you're planning to visit many historic sites and monuments in the Republic. It provides unlimited entry to attractions run by the Office of Public Works (sites are detailed throughout the Guide) and is mostly easily purchased at the first OPW site that you visit.

Members of **An Óige/YHA/HINI** (see page 36) also receive discounts on entry to certain sites. A number of historic buildings and sites in the North are operated by the **National Trust**. Membership (£91; under-26s £45, family £159, one-adult family £99; http://nationaltrust.org.uk) provides free and unlimited entry to these and all National Trust–run sites in Britain too. More than eighty sites across Ireland are members of the independent **Heritage Island** organization (http://heritageisland.com) whose booklet provides discounted admission prices or other special offers.

Electricity

The standard **electricity** supply is 220V AC in the Republic and 240V AC in the North. Most sockets require three-pin plugs. To operate North American appliances you'll need to bring or buy a transformer and an adapter; only the latter is needed for equipment made in Australia or New Zealand.

Entry requirements

Notwithstanding Brexit, because Ireland and the UK are members of the Common Travel Area (CTA), UK nationals do not need a passport to enter the Republic, but it's a good idea to carry one – and note that airlines will require official **photo ID** on flights between Britain and Ireland. Under current EU regulations, British passport holders are entitled to stay in the Republic for as long as they like. Moreover, the **border** between Northern Ireland and the Republic has no passport or immigration controls, and remains an open border following the UK's departure from the EU.

Travellers arriving from the United States, Canada, Australia, New Zealand and South Africa can enter the **Republic of Ireland** for up to three months with just a passport. For further information on immigration and visas, contact the Irish Immigration Service, 13–14 Burgh Quay, Dublin 2 (http://irishimmigration.ie). A full list of Irish consulates and embassies is available on the Department of Foreign Affairs website, http://dfa.ie.

US, Canadian, Australian, South African and New Zealand citizens can enter **Northern Ireland** for up to six months with just a passport. Full details of British diplomatic representatives overseas are available on the Foreign Office's website, http://gov.uk. For further information on immigration and visas, go to http://gov.uk/government/organisations/uk-visas-and-immigration.

IRISH EMBASSIES ABROAD

Australia 20 Arkana St, Yarralumla, Canberra, ACT 2600, http://ireland.ie/en/australia/canberra.
Canada 130 Albert St, Suite 1105, Ottawa, ON K1P 5G4, http://ireland.ie/en/canada/ottawa.
New Zealand Handled by the embassy in Australia.
South Africa 2nd Floor, Building A, OMK House, 238 Florence Ribeiro Avenue, Nieuw Muckleneuk, Pretoria, http://ireland.ie/en/southafrica/pretoria.

UK 17 Grosvenor Place, London SW1X 7HR, http://ireland.ie/en/greatbritain/london.
US 2234 Massachusetts Ave NW, Washington, DC 20008, http://ireland.ie/en/usa/washington.

BRITISH EMBASSIES AND HIGH COMMISSIONS ABROAD

Australia Commonwealth Ave, Yarralumla, ACT 2600, 02 6270 6666.
Canada 80 Elgin St, Ottawa, ON K1P 5K7, 613 237 1530.
New Zealand 44 Hill St, Wellington 6011, 04 924 2888.
South Africa 255 Hill Street, Arcadia 0028, Pretoria, 012 421 7500.
US 3100 Massachusetts Ave NW, Washington, DC 20008, 202 588 6500.

Emergencies

Across Ireland, in the case of an **emergency** call either 999 or 112.

Health and insurance

Visitors from the United Kingdom are entitled to **medical treatment** in the Republic of Ireland under a reciprocal agreement between the two countries. This will give access only to state-provided medical treatment in the Republic of Ireland, which covers emergency hospital treatment but it does not cover all GPs' surgeries – check that the doctor you're planning to use is registered with the local Health Board Panel before you go. Citizens of some other countries also enjoy reciprocal agreements – in Australia, for example, Medicare has such an arrangement with Ireland and Britain.

None of these arrangements covers all the medical costs you may incur or repatriation, so it's advisable for all travellers to take out some form of **travel insurance**. Most travel insurance policies exclude so-called dangerous sports unless an extra premium is paid; in Ireland this could mean, for example,

---

ROUGH GUIDES TRAVEL INSURANCE

Looking for travel insurance? Rough Guides partners with top providers worldwide to offer you the best coverage. Policies are available to residents of anywhere in the world, with a range of options whether you are looking for single-trip, multi-country or long-stay insurance. There's coverage for a wide range of adventure sports, 24-hour emergency assistance, high levels of medical and evacuation cover and a stream of travel safety information. Even better, roughguides.com users can take advantage of these policies online 24/7, from anywhere in the world – even if you're already travelling. To make the most of your travels and ensure a smoother experience, it's always good to be prepared for when things don't go according to plan. For more information go to http://roughguides.com/bookings/insurance.

horseriding, scuba diving, wind-surfing, mountaineering and kayaking.

Internet

Nearly all hotels, hostels and B&Bs, as well as many campsites, will have free **wi-fi**, though it may be fairly patchy in the more remote areas. Most restaurants, cafés and bars will also have free wi-fi, though you will of course be required to make a purchase in order to use it. An increasing number of town and city centre spaces offer free public wi-fi, too, even if it is only for an hour or two. Failing that, you could always head to the local tourist office or try a public library, most of which will have wi-fi and computers for use. Where internet cafés do exist, expect to pay around €4/£4 per hour.

Mail

In the **Republic**, post is handled by An Post (the national postal service; http://anpost.com); allow two days (or more) for a letter to reach Britain, for example. Small letters and postcards to any destination overseas cost €1.40. Main post offices are usually open Monday to Friday 9am to 5.30pm, Saturday 9am to 1pm (in cities sometimes until 5.30pm on Saturday). From **the North** with the Royal Mail (http://royalmail.com), postcards and the smallest letters cost 97p to airmail abroad. Main post offices are generally open Monday to Friday 9am–5.30pm, Saturday 9am to 12.30pm.

Maps

The **maps** in this guide will provide you with sufficient detail to navigate your way around cities, towns and counties. For more detail, there's the Ordnance Survey of Ireland's (http://osi.ie) four *Holiday* maps at 1:250,000 scale, dividing the country into quadrants, and its *Official Road Atlas of Ireland* (1:210,000), produced in conjunction with the Ordnance Survey of Northern Ireland, is extremely useful if you're driving.

The majority of tourist offices will provide free local maps, but, if you're planning on walking or exploring a locality fully, then the OSI's *Discovery* 1:50,000 scale series of maps is the best bet for the Republic of Ireland. The Ordnance Survey of Northern Ireland (http://osni.gov.uk) produces a similar *Discoverer* series.

If you're walking or cycling, the OSI/OSNI also produce special-interest 1:25,000-scale maps covering areas such as the Aran Islands, Killarney National Park, Lough Erne, Macgillycuddy's Reeks, and the Mourne and Sperrin mountain ranges. All of these maps can be purchased online at various outlets.

Money and cards

The **currency** of the Republic is the euro (€), divided into 100 cents (c). Coins come in denominations of 1, 2, 5, 10, 20 and 50 cents, and 1 and 2 euros; there are seven **notes**, in denominations of 5, 10, 20, 50, 100, 200 and 500 euros. It's not common to receive change if it's only 1 or 2c owed. Northern Ireland's currency is the pound sterling (£), though notes are printed by various local banks and are different from those found in Britain; however, standard British banknotes can still be used in Northern Ireland. Coins come in denominations of 1p, 2p, 5p, 10p, 20p, 50p, £1 and £2; notes come in denominations of £5, £10, £20 and £50.

Exchange rates fluctuate, but, at the time of writing, £1 sterling was equivalent to around €1.15 and US$1.25, €1 was worth £0.88 and US$1.10. For the latest exchange rates, check http://xe.com. The best exchange rates are provided by banks, though it's easiest to use an ATM, for which your own bank or credit card company may charge a fixed-rate or percentile fee. Unless you're absolutely stuck, avoid changing money in hotels, where the rates are often very poor. In areas around the border between the Republic and the North many businesses accept both currencies.

Credit and debit cards

The handiest means of obtaining cash is to use a **debit or credit card**. ATMs are very common throughout Ireland except in remote rural areas (where you're likeliest to find one in a supermarket), with most accepting Visa/Plus, MasterCard and Cirrus/Maestro. Major credit cards, such as Visa/Plus and MasterCard, and all cards bearing the Eurocard symbol, are widely accepted, though in rural areas you'll find that they're not accepted by some B&Bs.

Opening hours and public holidays

Shops and businesses across Ireland usually open 9am to 5.30pm, Monday to Saturday, though newsagents and petrol stations (many of which also have grocery stores) are often open earlier and later. Most large towns generally have a day when all shops open late (until 8pm or 9pm), usually Thursdays, and some also open on Sundays from around noon (1pm in Northern Ireland) until 6pm. Lunch-time closing still applies in many smaller towns, where also some businesses close for a few days midweek, increasingly

PUBLIC HOLIDAYS

Holiday	Republic	N Ireland
New Year's Day	√	√
St Brigid's Day – 1 February	√	
St Patrick's Day – March 17	√	√
Good Friday	√	√
Easter Monday	√	√
May – first Mon	√	√
May – last Mon	×	√
June – first Mon	√	×
Orange Day – July 12	×	√
Aug – first Mon	√	×
Aug – last Mon	×	√
Oct – last Mon	√	×
Christmas Day	√	√
St Stephen's Day /Boxing Day – Dec 26	√	√

Mondays. In rural areas opening times are far more variable.

Banks in the Republic are generally open from Monday to Friday between 10am and 4pm, and until 5pm one day a week, usually Wednesday or Thursday, sometimes closing for lunch in remoter areas. In the North, they open Monday to Friday 9.30am to 4.30pm, with some opening for longer hours and on Saturdays, though others may close for lunch. Post offices are also closed on Sunday (see page 49).

Throughout Ireland **cafés** tend to open in the daytime, Monday to Saturday. **Restaurants** usually open for lunch and again for dinner every day, though, away from the major towns and popular tourist areas, many may be closed at lunch times or all day on certain days of the week (especially out of season).

The law in the Republic states that **pubs are allowed to open** Monday to Thursday 10.30am–11.30pm, Friday and Saturday 10.30am–12.30am, Sunday 12.30–11pm. In the North the hours are Monday to Saturday 11.30am–11pm and Sunday 12.30–10pm. Some pubs apply for late licences, usually at weekends, while across Ireland **clubs** have variable opening days, though the majority are open from Thursday to Sunday and hours tend to be from around 10pm to 2am (or later in the major cities). Note that in the Republic all pubs and clubs are closed on Good Friday and Christmas Day.

On **public holidays**, away from the cities, most businesses will be closed, apart from pubs, newsagents, some supermarkets, grocers and petrol stations. If St Patrick's Day, Orange Day, Christmas Day or St Stephen's Day falls at the weekend, then a substitute holiday is taken at the beginning of the following week.

Phones

The international **dialling code** for the Republic is +353, and for Northern Ireland, as part of the UK, it's +44. If you're calling the North from the Republic, however, knock off the 028 area code and instead dial 048 followed by the eight-digit subscriber number.

Mobile phones

Roaming charges for mobile phones within the EU were abolished in 2017, meaning that UK travellers can use their mobiles throughout the Republic at no extra cost, a situation that looks unlikely to change despite the UK's exit from the EU – that said, check with your network provider for data allowance and charges. Travellers from other parts of the world will need to check whether their phone is multi-band GSM, and will probably also want to find out from their provider what the roaming charges are. The cheapest way to get round roaming charges is to get hold of a UK or Irish pay-as-you-go SIM card to insert in your phone, which will give you a local number and eliminate charges for receiving calls.

Smoking

Smoking is banned in all public buildings and offices, on all public transport, and in restaurants and pubs, although many pubs in cities and large towns have outdoor areas allocated for smokers, some covered and heated. In addition, the vast majority of hotels and B&Bs no longer allow it. **Vaping** – the use of e-cigarettes – is not allowed on public transport and is generally prohibited in museums and other public buildings; for restaurants and bars it depends on the individual proprietor.

Time

Ireland is on **GMT**, eight hours ahead of US Pacific Standard Time and five hours ahead of Eastern Standard Time. Clocks are advanced one hour at the end of March and back again at the end of October.

Tipping

Though discretionary, **tipping** restaurant staff or taxi drivers is the expected reward for satisfactory service; ten to fifteen percent of your tab will suffice.

Toilets

Public toilets are usually only found in the big towns in the Republic (especially in shopping malls), though in the North are much more common and generally well maintained. Toilet doors often bear the indicator *Fir* (men) and *Mná* (women).

Tourist information

The Irish tourist development agency, **Fáilte Ireland** (http://discoverireland.ie), as well as the **Northern Ireland Tourist Board** (NITB; http://discovernorthern ireland.com) both provide a wealth of area-specific information on their websites. Abroad, the two boards combine as **Tourism Ireland**, with their main point of contact for the public at http://ireland.com. There are also plenty of local and regional tourism websites, and we have listed the best of these in the relevant sections of the Guide.

Both Fáilte Ireland and the NITB provide an extensive network of **tourist offices**, covering every city, many major towns and almost all the popular tourist areas – in addition, some local councils provide their own offices. As well as offering plenty of information, some tourist offices can book accommodation. Bear in mind, though, that the opening hours are especially volatile, depending on budgets and staffing levels and varying from year to year and often from month to month.

Dublin

THE HA'PENNY BRIDGE AT NIGHT

Dublin

1

Set beside the shores of curving Dublin Bay, Ireland's capital city, Dublin, is a vibrant, dynamic place, which despite its fairly diminutive size remains utterly beguiling and an essential part of any visit to the country. Much of Dublin's centre has been redeveloped over the last few decades, so alongside the city's historic buildings – its cathedrals and churches, Georgian squares and town houses, castles, monuments and pubs – you'll discover swanky modern hotels and shopping centres, stunning street architecture and a state-of-the-art tramway system.

More than a quarter of the Republic of Ireland's population of four and a half million lives within the Greater Dublin area. Most Dubliners are intensely proud of their city, its heritage and powerful literary culture, and can at times exhibit a certain snobbishness towards those living in Ireland's rural backwaters (often termed "culchies"). Locals are noted for their often caustic brand of humour, but there is also a warmth in their welcome – it's easy to find yourself drawn into conversation or debates in bars and cafés (or, if you smoke, outside them). Dubliners are also increasingly style-conscious; where once the city looked inwards for inspiration, today it glances both east and west, to Europe and America, adopting new trends and bringing a decidedly Irish slant to them.

Most of Dublin's attractions are contained within a relatively compact area, spreading either side of the many-bridged **River Liffey**, which divides the city between its **northside** and **southside**. These have very distinct characters, defined over the city's historical development: stereotypically, the south is viewed in terms of its gentility while the north is seen as brash and working class, home of the true Dub accent. Certainly, the southside is regarded as more fashionable and fashion-conscious, thanks to its **Grafton Street** shopping area and the **Temple Bar** arts quarter, yet the north possesses Ireland's two most renowned theatres and its own increasingly lively nightlife. On either side of the river it's easy to escape the city's bustle, to relax or picnic in one of the squares or green spaces; or visitors can head to the shoreline for seaside strolls and blustery cliff-top walks.

West of the centre is the green expanse of **Phoenix Park** (home to Dublin Zoo) while across the river to the south lies the grim memorial of **Kilmainham Gaol** and, to the

---

A DECADE OF CENTENARIES

The decade between **1912 and 1922** was one of the most eventful in Irish history. The passing of Home Rule, the beginning of World War One, the growth of militant Ulster Unionism, the Easter Rising of 1916, the War of Independence and Civil War, as well as the rise of the labour and suffrage movements, were among the many momentous events which radically reshaped the political and social fabric of Ireland and its relationship with Britain during that period.

The programme **A Decade of Centenaries** (http://decadeofcentenaries.com) began in 2012 to mark the 100th anniversary of these events at a local and national level, with exhibitions, public discussions and other commemorative initiatives. The programme focuses on the everyday experience of ordinary people, as well as the leaders and key actors.

The biggest event held so far has been "Ireland 2016" (http://ireland.ie), a year-long programme remembering those who fought and died in the 1916 Rising and reflecting on the legacy of that period.

TRINITY COLLEGE

Highlights

❶ Trinity College Admire the illuminated *Book of Kells* and the magnificent Long Room library, or just enjoy the architecture. See page 64

❷ The National Museum – Archaeology Prehistoric gold and Christian treasures are the highlights of this collection. See page 67

❸ The National Gallery A graceful showcase spread out over a few wings, it's especially worthwhile for Irish art and the vibrant Yeats collection. See page 68

❹ The Chester Beatty Library An elegant, world-renowned display of manuscripts, prints and objets d'art. See page 74

❺ Dublin Spire The 121m pin-like monument is also called the Monument of Light for the way it catches the sun. See page 80

❻ Bloomsday Don a straw hat and join the festivities in celebration of Joyce's *Ulysses*. See page 84

❼ Kilmainham Gaol Tour the historic prison and its museum for fascinating insights into Republican history. See page 89

❽ Croke Park Catch a hurling or football match at this stadium. See page 91

❾ The Cobblestone Traditional music in an atmospheric pub. See page 106

HIGHLIGHTS ARE MARKED ON THE MAP ON PAGE 58

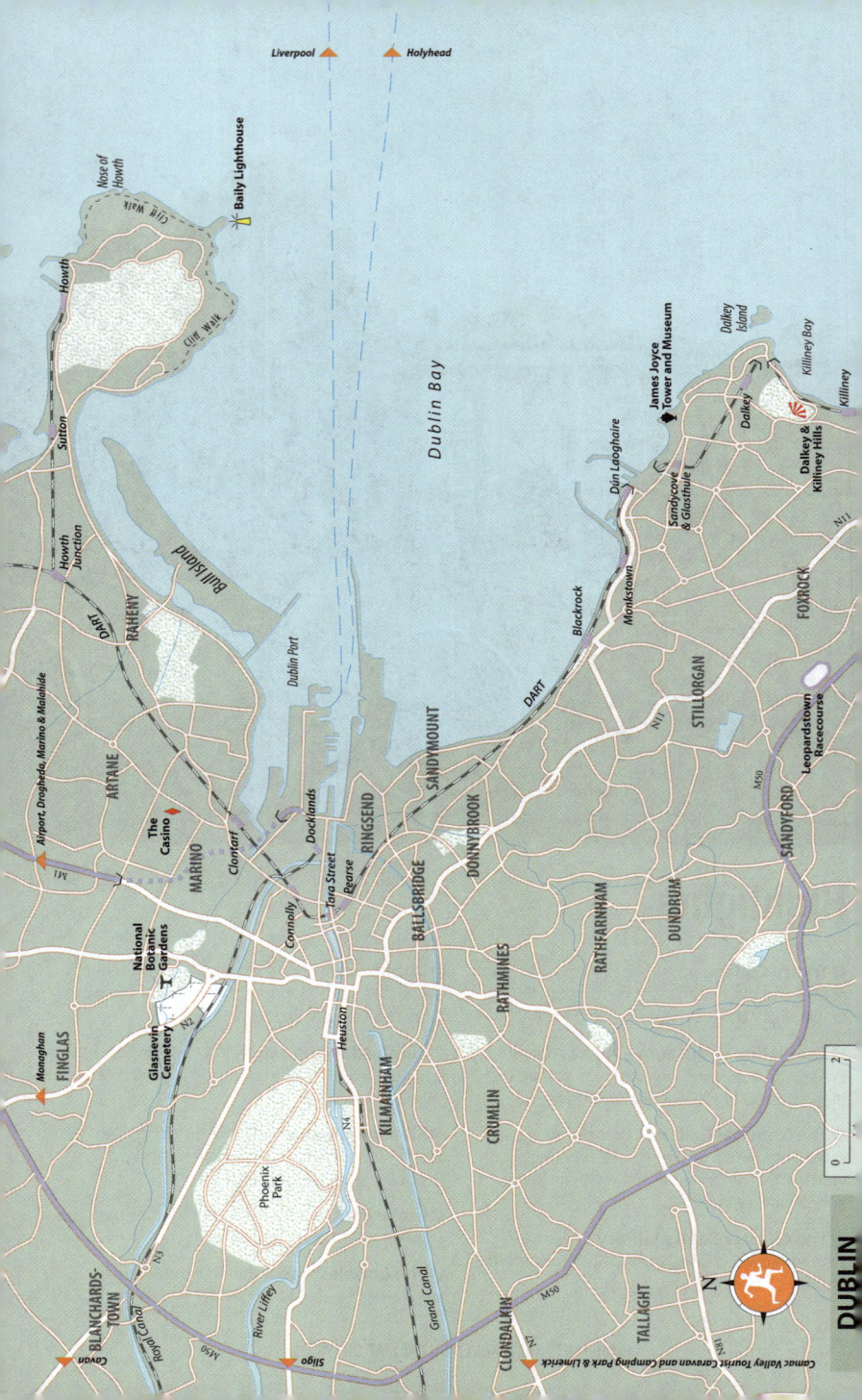

east, is the appealing **Guinness Brewery and Storehouse**. In the city's **suburbs**, the attractions of the northside have a definite edge over those to the south of the river: most compelling are the national **cemetery at Glasnevin**; the splendid stadium home of the Gaelic Athletic Association, **Croke Park**, which contains a fine museum; and the architectural wonders of the **Casino at Marino**. For a scenic breather from the city, take the southerly branch of the DART to panoramic **Dalkey and Killiney Hills**.

Brief history

Dublin's origins date back to ninth-century **Viking** times when the Norsemen saw the strategic potential of Dublin Bay and established a trading post on the Liffey's southern bank. They adopted the location's Irish name, Dubh Linn ("dark pool"), for their new home, soon amalgamating with an Irish settlement on the northern bank called Baile Atha Cliath ("place of the hurdle ford"), which remains the Irish name for the city.

The twelfth century saw Dublin conquered by the **Anglo-Normans** when Dermot MacMurrough, the deposed King of Leinster, sought help from Henry II to regain his crown. In return for Dermot's fealty, Henry sent Strongbow (see page 561) and a contingent of Welsh knights to restore MacMurrough's power. Strongbow conquered Dublin in the process and, concerned at this threat to his authority, Henry came over to Ireland to assert control, establishing Dublin as the focus for British sway over Ireland. This became the centre of the **"English Pale"** (from the Latin *palum*, meaning originally a "stake", though later a "defined territory"), ruling over the areas of Anglo-Norman settlement in Ireland; since Irish resistance to conquest was so strong in other parts of the country, the pejorative phrase "beyond the pale" evolved as a means of signifying (at least in English terms) a lack of civilized behaviour.

Only a few buildings have survived from before the seventeenth century, mainly in the area encompassing Dublin Castle and the two cathedrals, and much of the city's layout is **Georgian**. During this period, Dublin's Anglo-Irish nobility and its increasingly wealthy mercantile class used their money (often, in the aristocracy's case, derived from confiscated land granted as a reward for services to the Crown) to showcase their wealth in the form of grandiose houses, public buildings and wide thoroughfares. Wealthy members of the elite revelled in their new-found opulence, filling their houses with works by the latest artists and craftsmen, and seeking to enhance their own cachet by patronizing the arts; Handel conducted the first performance of his *Messiah* in the city, for example. Increasing political freedom resulted in demands for self-government, inspired by the American and French revolutions. The legislative independence achieved during "Grattan's Parliament" in 1782 was to be short-lived, however, and the failure of the **1798 Rebellion** (see page 564), led largely by members of the Protestant Anglo-Irish Ascendancy, inevitably led to the 1801 **Act of Union** and the removal of Dublin's independent powers.

With Ireland now governed by a British vice-regent, Dublin sank into a period of **economic decline**, brought about by its inability to compete with Britain's flourishing industries. The city remained the focus of agitation for self-rule, and by the end of the nineteenth century had also become the centre for efforts to form a sense of Irish national consciousness via the foundation of the **Gaelic League** in 1893. This sought to revive both the Irish language and traditional culture, and set the scene for the **Celtic literary revival**, led by W.B. Yeats and Lady Gregory, who established the Abbey Theatre in 1904. The political struggle for independence remained a live issue and events came to a head with the **Easter Rising** of 1916 (see page 82). The city's streets saw violence again during the **civil war**, which followed the establishment of the Irish Free State in 1921.

Austerity and much **emigration** followed Independence and it was not until the 1950s that Dublin began to emerge from its colonial past. The city's infrastructure was ravaged by ill-conceived redevelopment in the 1960s which saw the demolition of many Georgian edifices, as well as the creation of poorly planned "sink" estates to replace dilapidated tenements. A couple of decades later city planners began to address

1

the issue of inner-city depopulation, constructing apartment blocks to house Dublin's wealthy middle classes. The most obvious evidence of reinvigoration in the city centre is the Temple Bar area, though the original intention to develop a Parisian-style quarter of *ateliers* and arts centres soon fell foul of the moneygrubbers, and the area is now home to a plethora of kitsch tourist bars and fast-food chains. East of the centre, reconstruction continues in the city's docklands.

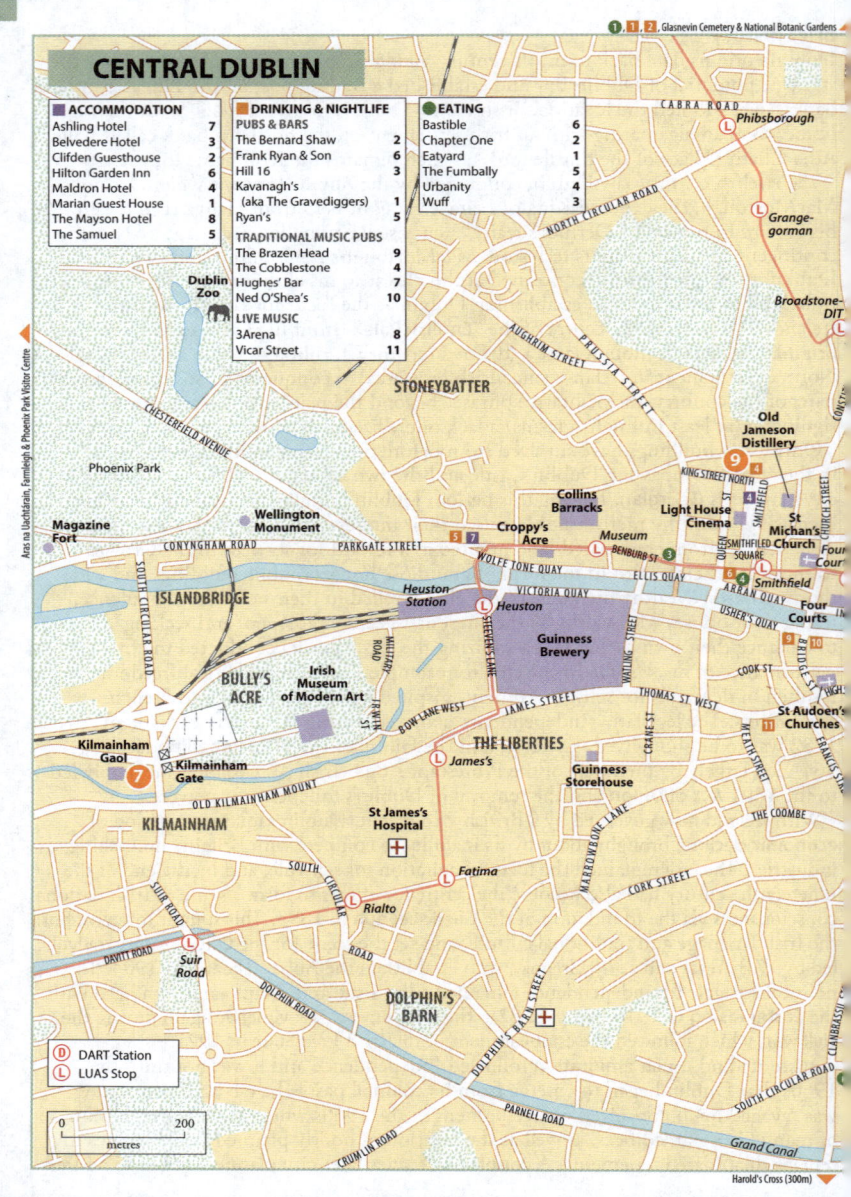

CENTRAL DUBLIN

ACCOMMODATION	
Ashling Hotel	7
Belvedere Hotel	3
Clifden Guesthouse	2
Hilton Garden Inn	6
Maldron Hotel	4
Marian Guest House	1
The Mayson Hotel	8
The Samuel	5

DRINKING & NIGHTLIFE	
PUBS & BARS	
The Bernard Shaw	2
Frank Ryan & Son	6
Hill 16	3
Kavanagh's	
(aka The Gravediggers)	1
Ryan's	5
TRADITIONAL MUSIC PUBS	
The Brazen Head	9
The Cobblestone	4
Hughes' Bar	7
Ned O'Shea's	10
LIVE MUSIC	
3Arena	8
Vicar Street	11

EATING	
Bastible	6
Chapter One	2
Eatyard	1
The Fumbally	5
Urbanity	4
Wuff	3

D	DART Station
L	LUAS Stop

0 — 200
metres

The so-called Celtic Tiger years of the late 1990s and early 2000s saw the wealth of the city grow exponentially, as a property boom drove the demolition of derelict or vacant buildings to make way for new apartments and offices.

Another legacy of the boom was the arrival of **migrants**, particularly from Africa and Eastern Europe, which, together with the city's longer-standing Chinese community, saw Dublin gradually inch towards multiculturalism.

HIGHLIGHTS

1. Trinity College
2. The National Museum-Archaeology
3. The National Gallery
4. The Chester Beatty Library
5. Dublin Spire
6. Bloomsday
7. Kilmainham Gaol
8. Croke Park
9. The Cobblestone

1

FESTIVALS AND EVENTS

JANUARY

Temple Bar Tradfest http://tradfest.com. Five days and nights of traditional music pub sessions, concerts, instrument workshops and more in the heart of the city.

FEBRUARY

Dublin International Film Festival http://diff.ie. Held at cinemas and other venues across the city centre for eleven days at the end of February/beginning of March. While screening the latest in new Irish cinema, the festival also has a decidedly international flavour and its hundred or so films include special themes and retrospectives.

MARCH

Easter Rising Commemorations take place on Easter Sunday, featuring speeches and a march from the General Post Office to Glasnevin Cemetery.

St Patrick's Festival http://stpatricksfestival.ie. Running for four days on and around St Patrick's Day (March 17), this city-wide festival includes a parade, light shows, concerts, funfair, films, exhibitions and a *céilí mór*, in which thousands of locals and visitors fill the streets in a traditional danceathon.

Mountains to Sea dlr Book Festival Celebrating the county's literary heritage, this is held over the last weekend in March at The Pavilion Theatre, Dún Laoghaire, with readings by well-known Irish and international poets, master classes, exhibitions and children's events.

MAY

International Dublin Gay Theatre Festival http://gaytheatre.ie. A fortnight of LGBTQ-focused drama, comedy, cabaret and musical theatre with international and Irish casts taking place at a variety of city-centre locations.

International Literature Festival http://ilfdublin.com. Major Irish and international writers and poets take part in ten days of readings, discussions and other events around the city centre.

JUNE

Bloomsday http://bloomsdayfestival.ie. The James Joyce Centre organizes a week of events in mid-June, culminating in Bloomsday itself (June 16), the day on which Joyce's *Ulysses* is set.

Dublin Pride http://dublinpride.ie. A week of celebration by the city's LGBTQ communities, featuring all manner of events, culminating in a vibrant and entertaining street parade.

Dalkey Book Festival http://dalkeybookfestival.org. Described by Salman Rushdie as "the best little festival in the world", this four-day literary festival attracts world-renowned writers to its picturesque south Dublin setting every year.

Forbidden Fruit http://forbiddenfruit.ie. Taking place in the grounds of the Royal Hospital.

The financial crisis of 2008 called a halt to the dizzying pace of development. Many new buildings were left half-finished, while shops and office blocks on some of the city's most prestigious streets were without tenants for years at a time. But the downturn has had an upside; cheaper rents have allowed more creative businesses to open, with new galleries, performing spaces and places to eat popping up seemingly every week. Many of the city's overpriced, overly pretentious restaurants that prevailed during the boom have withered, clearing the way for a plethora of excellent new cafés, restaurants and bars offering much more innovative dishes and better value for money. That's not to say that Dublin is a cheap destination; on the contrary, it's one of Europe's most expensive capital cities, but as long as you plan (and spend judicially) you won't have to break the bank to have a fantastic time here.

1

Kilmainham over the June bank holiday weekend, this is the city's premier annual music gathering, featuring top draw artists such as Skepta and Hot Chip.

JULY
Paddy Power Comedy Festival. A stellar line-up of mostly Irish comedians in the stunning surrounds of the Iveagh Gardens over four days.

AUGUST
Dublin Horse Show http://dublinhorseshow.com. Five-day festival of equestrian events in early August at the RDS arena in Ballsbridge, featuring major international showjumpers participating in the Nations' Cup.
*Dublin Viking Festival http://dublinia.ie. The last weekend in August sees a re-created Viking village established off Wood Quay, which features plenty of wandering inhabitants and the chance to watch re-enacted combats.

SEPTEMBER/OCTOBER
Gaze LGBTQ Film Festival http://gaze.ie. A strong bill of Irish and international LGBTQ films screened over five days towards the end of September at the Irish Film Institute (see page 74).
Culture Night http://culturenight.ie. Hundreds of arts and cultural organizations around the city open their doors until late for one Friday in mid-September, with free events, tours, talks and performances.
All-Ireland Senior Hurling and Gaelic Football finals Two of Ireland's major sporting events are staged at Croke Park (see page 91) in September: the hurling final on the first or second Sunday and the football final on the third or fourth Sunday.
Dublin Fringe Festival http://fringefest.com. Ireland's biggest performing arts festival takes place over more than two weeks from mid-September featuring music, dance, street theatre, comedy and children's events.
Dublin Theatre Festival http://dublintheatrefestival.ie. A major celebration of theatre, held during the last few days of September and the first two weeks in October, this includes performances of new and classic drama at various city-centre venues.
Dublin City Marathon http://irishlifedublinmarathon.ie. Featuring ten thousand entrants, the race takes place on the last Monday in October and involves a roughly circular course starting from Fitzwilliam Street Upper, heads north across O'Connell Bridge, and takes in Phoenix Park and some southern suburbs before the finish at Merrion Square North.

DECEMBER
NYF Dublin http://nyfdublin.com. Four days of festivities to ring in the New Year, with a "procession of light" through the city centre culminating in a big countdown concert on College Green.

As the economy continues to recover, the cranes have returned to the Dublin skyline and a fresh spate of construction is under way – only this time, its inhabitants hope that the city's planners and developers have learned from the mistakes of the past.

The Southside

The southside is home to one of Dublin's most important historic sights, **Trinity College**, whose main draw for visitors is the glorious *Book of Kells*. The area also boasts stylish Georgian streets, which lie to the east of College Green and Grafton Street, and are where you'll find the compelling displays of the **National Gallery** and the **National Museum**. On the west side of Trinity begins **Temple Bar**, which somehow manages to

INNER SOUTHSIDE

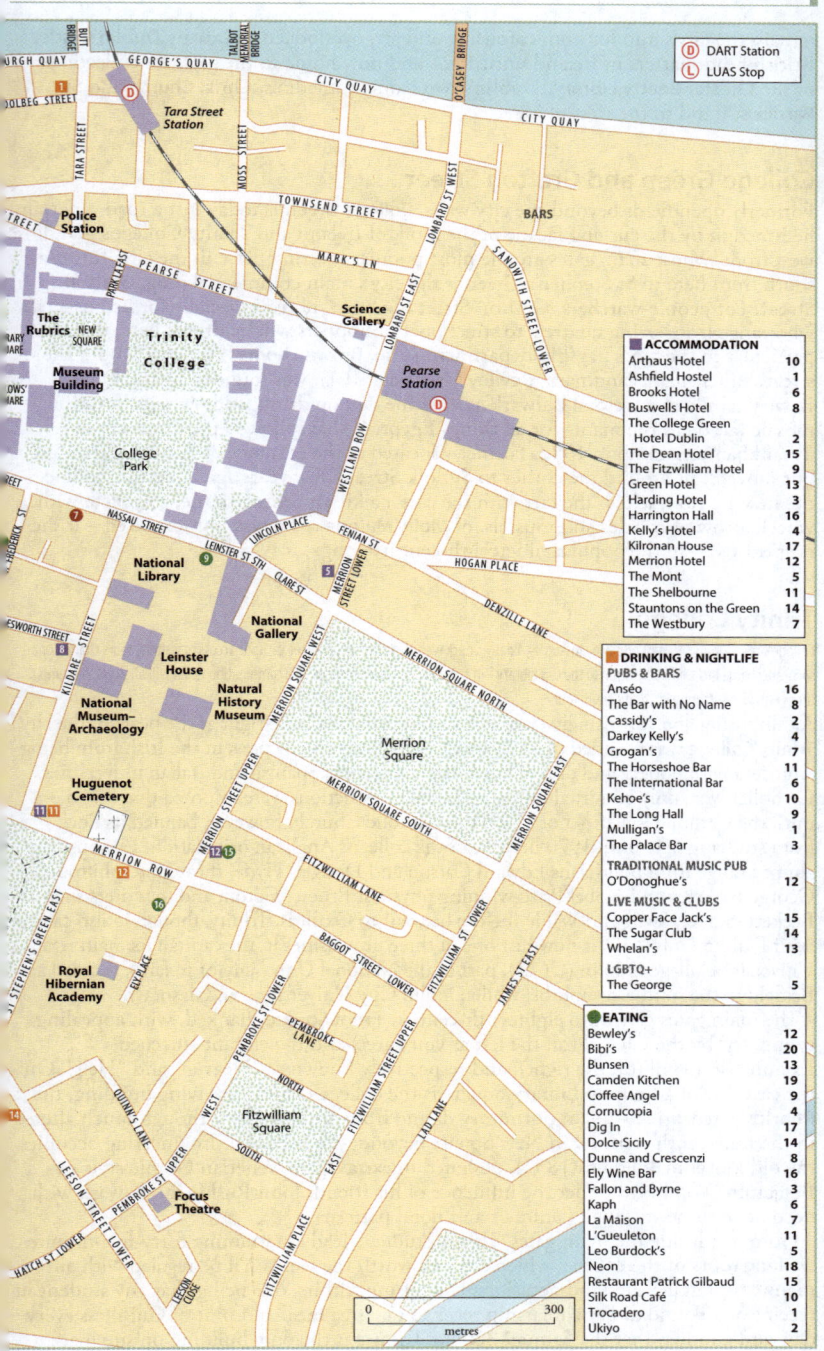

D DART Station
L LUAS Stop

■ ACCOMMODATION

Arthaus Hotel	10
Ashfield Hostel	1
Brooks Hotel	6
Buswells Hotel	8
The College Green Hotel Dublin	2
The Dean Hotel	15
The Fitzwilliam Hotel	9
Green Hotel	13
Harding Hotel	3
Harrington Hall	16
Kelly's Hotel	4
Kilronan House	17
Merrion Hotel	12
The Mont	5
The Shelbourne	11
Stauntons on the Green	14
The Westbury	7

■ DRINKING & NIGHTLIFE

PUBS & BARS

Anséo	16
The Bar with No Name	8
Cassidy's	2
Darkey Kelly's	4
Grogan's	7
The Horseshoe Bar	11
The International Bar	6
Kehoe's	10
The Long Hall	9
Mulligan's	1
The Palace Bar	3

TRADITIONAL MUSIC PUB

| O'Donoghue's | 12 |

LIVE MUSIC & CLUBS

Copper Face Jack's	15
The Sugar Club	14
Whelan's	13

LGBTQ+

| The George | 5 |

● EATING

Bewley's	12
Bibi's	20
Bunsen	13
Camden Kitchen	19
Coffee Angel	9
Cornucopia	4
Dig In	17
Dolce Sicily	14
Dunne and Crescenzi	8
Ely Wine Bar	16
Fallon and Byrne	3
Kaph	6
La Maison	7
L'Gueuleton	11
Leo Burdock's	5
Neon	18
Restaurant Patrick Gilbaud	15
Silk Road Café	10
Trocadero	1
Ukiyo	2

0   300
metres

1

remain the city's hub for both carousing and art, overlooked sternly by **Dublin Castle**, British headquarters in Ireland until 1921 and now home to the glorious collections of the **Chester Beatty Library**. Dublin's two iconic cathedrals, **Christ Church** and **St Patrick's**, stand to the west of here.

College Green and Grafton Street

Formerly open fields beyond the city walls, **College Green** is today just a road junction, hemmed in by the curving facade of the Bank of Ireland and Trinity College's grandiose west front, whose main gates are the most popular meeting place in the city. Running south from here to St Stephen's Green is the city's main commercial drag, **Grafton Street**. For people-watchers, Grafton Street is a must, noted especially for its buskers, who range from string quartets to street poets. Shoppers will be drawn here, too, in particular to the city's flagship department store, **Brown Thomas** (see page 108). The street's other major landmark, **Bewley's** (see page 101), was founded by the Quaker Bewley family as a teetotal bulwark against the demon drink, and owes its beautiful mosaic facade to the mania for all things Egyptian that followed the discovery of Tutankhamun's tomb in 1922. Formerly located at the entrance to Grafton Street but moved just around the corner to Suffolk Street a few years ago to accommodate the new LUAS track is "the tart with the cart", a kitsch bronze statue, complete with wheelbarrow of cockles and mussels, of **Molly Malone**, who was immortalized – if she ever existed – in the popular nineteenth-century song.

Trinity College

College Green • Tours (45min) mid-May to Aug 3–4 daily; check website for schedule • Free campus access to visitors; tours charge, or a separate charge including admission to the Old Library – if there are any queues there, this combination ticket will allow you to jump them • http://visittrinity.ie/trinity-trails-tour

An imposing and surprisingly extensive architectural set piece right at the heart of the city, **Trinity College** was founded in 1592 by Queen Elizabeth I to prevent the Irish from being "infected with popery and other ill qualities" at French, Spanish and Italian universities. Catholics were duly admitted until 1637, when restrictions were imposed that lasted until the Catholic Relief Act of 1793; the Catholic Church, however, banned its flock from studying here until 1970 because of the college's Anglican orientation. Famous alumni range from politicians Edward Carson and Douglas Hyde, through to philosopher George Berkeley and Nobel Prize-winning physicist Ernest Walton, and to writers such as Beckett, Stoker, Swift and Wilde (before he went to Oxford). Trinity, though it also calls itself Dublin University, is now just one of three universities in the capital: its main rival, University College Dublin (UCD), part of the National University of Ireland, is based at Belfield in the southern suburbs; while Dublin City University is in Glasnevin.

The main gates give onto eighteenth-century **Front Square**, flanked, with appealing symmetry, by the Chapel (on the left as you enter) and the elegant stuccoed Examination Hall (on the right), and respectively known as "Heaven" and "Hell". On the east side of adjoining Library Square is the college's oldest surviving building, the **Rubrics**, a red-brick student dormitory dating from around 1701, though much altered in the nineteenth century. In New Square beyond, the School of Engineering occupies the old **Museum Building** (1852), designed in extravagant Venetian Gothic style by Benjamin Woodward under the influence of his friend, John Ruskin, and awash with decorative stone-carving of animals and floral patterns.

From just inside the main gates, Trinity students lead entertaining forty-five-minute **walking tours** of the college, which are well worth the fee. You'll be regaled with all manner of fascinating (and occasionally amusing) titbits, one being that any student in receipt of a Foundation Scholarship receives one free meal and pint of Guinness every day, and another, that the Samuel Beckett Theatre is the only building on site made of wood. You'll also be shown inside the aforementioned Museum Building, which is otherwise inaccessible.

Science Gallery

Pearse St • Tues–Fri noon–8pm, Sat & Sun noon–5pm; closed for 2 weeks over Christmas and New Year • Free • http://dublin. sciencegallery.com

In the northeastern corner of the college at the Pearse Street entrance (handy for Pearse DART Station) is the excellent **Science Gallery**. Both thoughtful and thought-provoking, it hosts high-tech and interactive temporary exhibitions on all aspects of science, from how the body uses fat to the causes of extreme weather events, as well as interesting one-off lectures.

Douglas Hyde Gallery

Entrance on Nassau St • Wed, Fri & Sat noon–6pm, Thurs noon–7pm • Free • http://douglashydegallery.com

In Fellows' Square on the south side of Library Square, the modern Arts Block is home to the **Douglas Hyde Gallery**, one of Ireland's most important galleries of modern art. Temporary exhibitions focus on Irish and international artists whose work is not yet well known or has been previously overlooked. Gallery 2 regularly hosts exhibitions of ethnographic and craft artefacts.

The Old Library and the Book of Kells

Fellows' Square • Mon–Sat 8.30am–7pm, Sun 9.30am–6.30pm • charge • http://visittrinity.ie/book-of-kells-experience

Trinity's most compelling tourist attraction is the **Book of Kells**, kept in the eighteenth-century **Old Library**. Owing to years of pollution and dust accumulation, however, the library is actually due to close at the end of 2025 to undergo a major conservation project, possibly for as long as five years. On the library's ground floor, beautiful pages are displayed not just from the *Book of Kells* (around 800 AD), but from other works such as the *Book of Armagh* (early ninth century) and the *Book of Mulling* (late eighth century). The books themselves are preceded by a fascinating exhibition, **Turning Darkness into Light**, which sets Irish illuminated manuscripts in context – ranging from ogham (the earlier, Celtic writing system of lines carved on standing stones) to Ethiopian books of devotions.

Brief history

Pre-eminent for the scale, variety and colour of its decoration, the *Book of Kells* probably originated at the monastery on Iona off the west coast of Scotland, which had been founded around 561 by the great Irish scholar, bard and ruler St Colmcille (St Columba in English). After a Viking raid in 806 the Columbines moved to the monastery of Kells in County Meath, which in its turn was raided four times between 920 and 1019. Although they looted the book's *cumdach* or metal shrine cover, the pagan Norsemen did not value the book itself, however, and despite spending some time buried underground and losing thirty folios, it survived at Kells up to the seventeenth century when it was taken to Dublin for safekeeping during the Cromwellian Wars. The 340 calfskin folios of the *Book of Kells* contain the four New Testament Gospels along with preliminary texts, all in Latin. It's thought that three artists created the book's lavish decoration, which shows Pictish, Germanic and Mediterranean, as well as Celtic, influences. Not only are there full-page illustrations of Christ and the Virgin and Child, but an elaborate decorative scheme of animals and spiral, roundel and interlace patterns is employed throughout the text, on the initials at the beginning of each Gospel and on full-length "carpet pages".

The Long Room

Upstairs is the library's magnificent **Long Room**, built by Thomas Burgh between 1712 and 1732 and enlarged, with a barrel-vaulted ceiling, in 1860. As a copyright library,

1

Trinity has had the right to claim a free copy of all British and Irish publications since 1801; of its current stock of four million titles, 200,000 of the oldest are stored in the Long Room's oak bookcases, although the majority of these have already been decanted in readiness for the library's redevelopment. Besides interesting temporary exhibitions of books and prints from the library's collection, the Long Room also displays a gnarled fifteenth-century harp (the oldest to survive from Ireland), a collection of marble busts of classical and early modern luminaries (Aristotle, Newton, Swift and so on), and a rare original printing of the 1916 Proclamation of the Irish Republic, made on Easter Sunday in Dublin's Liberty Hall. Here, too, is Gaia, a huge, slowly rotating globe featuring NASA imagery of the Earth.

The Book of Kells Experience

Ahead of the library's closure, a new exhibition – the **Book of Kells Experience** – has been established in a specially constructed pavilion adjacent to the Museum Building. Cleverly conceived, the exhibition digitally transports visitors into the illuminated pages of the famous manuscript courtesy of two immersive experiences; the first charts the journey of the manuscript from Iona in Scotland to Ireland, while the second is a reimagined Long Room as seen through a series of dazzling digital projections. Here too are numerous, priceless editions, including *Frankenstein* (1818), *On the Origins of Species* (1859), and the magnificent *The Nuremberg Chronicle* (1493).

The Bank of Ireland

College Green • House of Lords: Mon, Tues & Fri 10am–3.45pm, Wed 10.30am–3.45pm, Thurs 10am–4.45pm; guided tours Tues 10.30am, 11.30am & 12.30pm • Entry and tours free • 01 677 6801

The Neoclassical granite **Bank of Ireland**, opposite Trinity on College Green, was constructed in 1729 by Sir Edward Pearce – himself an MP – as the **House of Parliament**. An Irish parliament had existed in one limited form or another since the thirteenth century, but achieved its greatest success here in 1782, when "Grattan's Parliament" (so named after the prime mover behind the constitutional reform) was granted legislative independence from the British Parliament. Catholics were still barred from sitting, but many signs of Irish sovereignty were established during this period, including the founding of the Bank of Ireland itself. Around this time, the Lords deemed it necessary to build themselves a separate entrance on Westmoreland Street, designed in 1785 by James Gandon in the Corinthian style in order to distinguish it from the Ionic colonnade of what is still the main entrance. After the Rebellion of 1798, however, the Irish House was persuaded and bribed to vote itself out of existence, and with the 1801 Act of Union Ireland became part of the United Kingdom, governed from Westminster. The Bank of Ireland bought the building for £40,000 in 1802, and the Commons chamber was demolished to remove a highly charged symbol of independence.

House of Lords

The barrel-vaulted **House of Lords** was also meant to be knocked down but survives to this day to host high-level state functions and as the main attraction for visitors, especially during its interesting, weekly guided tours. Here you'll find one or two exhibits such as the Lord Chancellor's richly embroidered purse, used to carry the Great Seal of Ireland, and tapestries showing William of Orange's victories over James II and his Catholic supporters, the *Siege of Derry* and the *Battle of the Boyne*. The richly stuccoed **Cash Hall** – an elegant spot to do any banking chores you may have – used to be the Parliament's Hall of Requests, where constituents would petition their representatives.

Powerscourt Townhouse

59 South William St • http://powerscourtcentre.ie

The **Powerscourt Townhouse**, once the eighteenth-century Palladian mansion of Lord Powerscourt (see page 120), is now home to a stylish shopping centre, harbouring some forty upscale shops and restaurants. The house's main door leads straight onto the trompe l'oeil stone floor of the entrance hall and, beyond, the central mahogany staircase, with its flighty rococo plasterwork and what are thought to be the most elaborately carved balusters in Ireland. The café-bar in the atrium is notable for its location – bathed in light on sunny days – in what was once the mansion's inner courtyard.

Leinster House (Oireachtas)

Kildare St • http://oireachtas.ie

Ireland's political and cultural establishments have their power bases in the tight confines of Kildare Street and Merrion Square. Kildare Street is dominated by the imposing **Leinster House**, the city's largest eighteenth-century mansion, designed by one of Ireland's greatest architects Richard Castle (1690–1751). Built on open fields in1745 for the Earl of Kildare James FitzGerald, the town house started a trend among the gentry and wealthy, who eschewed traditionally fashionable parts of the city to build new homes in the surrounding area. Originally called Kildare House, it was renamed when the earl became Duke of Leinster in 1766. Dublin's largest Georgian-style district grew up around Leinster House, and still survives today.

After the formation of the Irish Free State in 1922, the building was acquired by the newly formed government. It has since been home to the Irish parliament, the Oireachtas (pronounced something like "or-ruck-tas"), which is divided into Dáil Eireann (House of Representatives) and Seannad Eireann (the Senate). Portraits of two of the leading members of the first Dáil, Cathal Brugha and Michael Collins, hang opposite each other in the entrance hall, alongside paintings of past Irish presidents and an original copy of the 1916 Proclamation. It's currently no longer possible to have a guided tour of the building, but this may change in the future, so do check the website.

Natural History Museum

Merrion St • Free • http://museum.ie

The charmingly unreconstructed displays of the **Natural History Museum** have been impressing visitors since the "Dead Zoo" first opened its doors to the public in 1857. Conservation work has improved access and provided new learning opportunities – including a discovery zone where visitors can handle taxidermy and open drawers to see what is lurking inside – but overall, the exhibition style and furnishings have changed little in 150 years.

The ground floor is dedicated to native Irish species, and includes the skeleton of an 11,000-year-old deer alongside a variety of mammals, birds and fish. The upper floors feature animals from around the world, laid out in the nineteenth century by taxonomic group, which aimed to demonstrate the evolution of animal life. Note, though, that the museum is due to close its doors some time in 2024 or 2025 (for an unspecified period of time) to undergo an extensive, and much-needed refurbishment, during which time the bulk of the collection will be moved to the Collins barracks (see page 120).

The National Museum – Archaeology

Kildare St • Free • http://museum.ie

The **National Museum – Archaeology** is a must-see for visitors to Dublin. Undoubtedly the stars of the show here are a stunning hoard of prehistoric gold and a thousand years' worth of ornate ecclesiastical treasures, but the whole collection builds up a

1

fascinating and accessible story of Irish archaeology and history. The shop in the beautiful entrance rotunda sells a range of high-quality crafts inspired by works in the museum, and there's a small café.

Prehistoric gold, much of it discovered during peat-cutting, takes pride of place on the ground floor of the main hall. From the Earlier Bronze Age (c.2500–1500 BC) come *lunulae*, thin sheets of gold formed into crescent-moon collars. After around 1200 BC, when new sources of the metal were apparently found, goldsmiths could be more extravagant, fashioning chunky torcs, such as the spectacular Gleninsheen Collar and the Tumna Hoard of nine large gold balls, which are perforated, suggesting that when joined together they formed a huge necklace. Further prehistoric material is arrayed around the walls of the main hall, including the 15m-long Lurgan Logboat, dating from around 2500 BC, which was unearthed in a Galway bog in 1902.

The adjacent **Treasury** holds most of the museum's better-known ecclesiastical exhibits, notably the ornate eighth-century Ardagh Chalice, the Tara Brooch, decorated with beautiful knot designs, and the Cross of Cong, created to enshrine a fragment of the True Cross given to the King of Connacht by the Pope in 1123. Also on the ground floor is **Kingship and Sacrifice**, showcasing the leathery bodies of four Iron Age noblemen that were preserved and discovered in various bogs around Ireland.

Upstairs, **Viking-age Ireland** (c.800–1150) features models of a house and the layout of Dublin's Fishamble Street, while **Medieval Ireland** (1150–1550) moves on to cover the first English colonists, their withdrawal to the fortified area around Dublin known as "the Pale" after 1300, and the hybrid culture that developed all the while – you can listen to recordings of poetry written in Ireland in Middle Irish, Middle English and Norman French. Unmissable here is a host of strange, ornate portable **shrines**, made to hold holy relics or texts, including examples for all three of Ireland's patron saints: the Shrine of St Patrick's Tooth, the Shrine of St Brigid's Shoe (see page 128) and the Shrine of the Cathach, containing a manuscript written by St Colmcille (St Columba), legendary bard, scholar, ruler and evangelizer of Scotland.

The National Library

Kildare St • Free • http://nli.ie

The **National Library** was opened on Kildare Street in 1890, shortly after the National Museum, whose design it mirrors across the courtyard of Leinster House. Besides prestigious public talks and readings, its main draws are its long-term temporary exhibitions on subjects such as W.B. Yeats and Seamus Heaney, which are mounted in a beautiful, high-tech space on the lower ground floor. Visitors are also allowed up to the hushed domed **Reading Room** on the first floor, decorated with ornate bookcases and an incongruously playful frieze of cherubs. It is in the office here that Stephen Dedalus engages the librarians – who appear under their real names – in literary talk in the "Scylla and Charybdis" episode of *Ulysses*. In the **Genealogy Room**, library staff can give advice to anyone researching their family history on how to access the records here and elsewhere in Dublin, as well as in Belfast.

The National Gallery

Merrion Square West • guided tours Sat 12.30pm, Sun 11.30am & 1.30pm • Entry and tours free • http://nationalgallery.ie

The **National Gallery** hosts a fine collection of Western European art dating from the Middle Ages to the twentieth century, most of which is held within the gallery's two oldest, but newly modernised, buildings – namely the Milltown and Dargan wings.

A significant portion of the permanent exhibition is given over to **Irish art** from the seventeenth century onwards. The highlight is the collection of paintings by Jack B. Yeats (1871–1957), younger brother of the writer W.B. Yeats, which traces the artist's development from an unsentimental illustrator of everyday scenes to an expressive painter in abstract, unmixed colours; indeed an entire room is given over to the artist, and it is here that his long-standing affinity with all things equine is manifest in paintings like *For the Road* and the joyous *The Singing Horseman*. Other works include early twentieth-century portraits by William Orpen (1878–1931) and John Lavery (1856–1941), as well as more modern Irish landscapes by Gerard Dillon (1916–71).

Watercolours by **Turner** are exhibited every January, when the light is low enough for these delicate works. Highlights of the European collection include *Kitchen Maid with the Supper at Emmaus*, the earliest known picture by **Velázquez** (1599–1660); **Vermeer**'s *Woman Writing a Letter with her Maid*, one of only 35 accepted works by the artist, with his characteristic use of white light from the window accentuating the woman's heated emotions; and **Caravaggio**'s dynamic *The Taking of Christ*, in which the artist portrayed himself as a passive spectator on the right of the picture, holding a lamp. Moving on to European art between 1850 and 1950, big-hitters like Picasso (*Still Life with a Mandolin*), Van Gogh (*Rooftops in Paris*), and Cezanne (*La Vie des Champs*) are all represented. Also worth tracking down is the **Irish Stained Glass** room, which holds some masterful pieces by Henry Clarke, a leading exponent of the Irish Arts and Crafts movement; perhaps his most striking panel is *The Song of the Mad Prince*.

Merrion Square

Begun in 1762, **Merrion Square** represents Georgian town planning at its grandest. Its long, graceful terraces of red-brown brick sport elaborate doors, knockers and fanlights, as well as wrought-iron balconies (added in the early nineteenth century) and tall windows on the first floor, where the main reception rooms would have been; the north side of the square was built first and displays the widest variety of design.

The broad, manicured lawns of the square's gardens themselves are a joy, quieter than St Stephen's Green, and especially agreeable for picnics on fine days. Revolutionary politician Michael Collins is commemorated with a bronze bust on the gardens' south side, near a slightly hapless stone bust of Henry Grattan (see page 564), while writer, artist and mystic George Russell ("AE") stands gravely near the southwest corner and his former home at no. 74. But the square's most remarkable and controversial statue is at the northwest corner, where **Oscar Wilde** reclines on a rock facing his childhood home at no. 1 (now the American College Dublin), in a wry, languid pose. In front of him, a male torso and his wife Constance, pregnant with their second child, stand on plinths inscribed with Wildean witticisms: "This suspense is terrible. I hope it will last", "I drink to keep body and soul apart." Nearby on the railings around the square's gardens, dozens of artists hang their paintings for sale every Sunday.

The Merrion Square South terrace has the greatest concentration of famous former residents, giving a vivid sense of the history of the place: politician Daniel O'Connell bought no. 58 in 1809; the Nobel Prize-winning Austrian physicist, Erwin Schrödinger, occupied no. 65; Gothic novelist Joseph Sheridan Le Fanu died at no. 70, which is now the Arts Council; and W.B. Yeats lived at no. 82 from 1922 to 1928. At no. 39 stood the British Embassy, which was burnt down by a crowd protesting against the Bloody Sunday massacre in Derry in 1972.

The National Print Museum

Haddington Rd • Free • http://nationalprintmuseum.ie

Housed in the former chapel of Beggar's Bush barracks, the **National Print Museum** traces the history of print in Ireland, telling surprisingly affecting tales through video, rare documents, demonstrations and workshops. The ground floor is filled with original and mint-condition printing presses, still in use today, while the mezzanine level displays temporary exhibitions and a fascinating hidden library. A specialist reference library requiring an appointment to explore, it houses an extraordinary collection of

1

books, pamphlets, journals and periodicals relating to printmaking, typography, paper-making and associated crafts.

St Stephen's Green

As well as being a major landmark and transport hub for buses, taxis and the LUAS, **St Stephen's Green** is central Dublin's largest and most varied park, whose statuary provides a poignant history lesson in stone, wood and bronze. The Green preserves its distinctive Victorian character with a pair of small lakes populated by large numbers of wildfowl, bandstand, arboretum and well-tended flower displays. It was originally open common land, a notoriously dirty and dangerous spot and the site of public hangings until the eighteenth century. In 1880, however, it was turned into a public park with funding from the brewer Lord Ardilaun (Arthur Guinness), who now boasts the grandest of the Green's many statues, seated at his leisure on the far western side. Over at the northeast corner, a row of huge granite monoliths – nicknamed "Tonehenge" – has been erected in honour of eighteenth-century nationalist **Wolfe Tone**, behind which stands a moving commemoration of the **Great Famine**. Meanwhile, on the west side of the central flower display, a tiny plaque inlaid in a wooden park bench commemorates the so-called "fallen women" – mostly unmarried mothers or abused girls – who were forced to live and work in severe conditions in Ireland's **Magdalen laundries**; the last of them, in Dublin, wasn't closed down until 1996. Elsewhere, there is a statue of WB Yeats by Henry Moore, another of Constance Markiewicz by Seamus Murphy, and, inevitably, a bust of Joyce, this one located on the park's southern fringe. From the Green's northwest corner, by the top of Grafton Street, you can hire a **horse and carriage**, either as a grandiose taxi or for a tour of the sights, which will typically set you back €40–50 for thirty minutes.

The main sightseeing draws in the area date from the Georgian period: the splendid stuccowork of **Newman House** and the elegant streets and squares to the east of the Green, as well as the excellent **Little Museum of Dublin**.

Termed in the eighteenth century "Beau Walk", **St Stephen's Green North** is still the most fashionable side of the square. The **Shelbourne Hotel** here claims to have been "the best address in Dublin" since its establishment in 1824 (see page 99). Beyond the hotel at the start of Merrion Row, the tiny, tree-shaded **Huguenot Cemetery** was opened in 1693 for Protestant refugees fleeing religious persecution in France. A large plaque inside the gates gives a roll call of Huguenot Dubliners, among whom the most famous have been writers Dion Boucicault and Sheridan Le Fanu.

Museum of Literature Ireland

86 St Stephen's Green South · Charge · http://moli.ie

Newman House is home to the fabulous **Museum of Literature Ireland**, and named after John Henry Newman, the famous British convert from Anglicanism, who was invited to found the Catholic University of Ireland here in 1854 as an alternative to Anglican Trinity College and the recently established "godless" Queen's Colleges in Belfast, Cork and Galway. James Joyce and Éamon de Valera were educated at what became University College Dublin (UCD), which now occupies a large campus in the southern suburbs.

Newman House actually comprises two houses: **No. 85** is a Palladian mansion built by Richard Castle in 1738 and adorned with superb Baroque stuccowork by the Swiss Lafranchini brothers, notably in the ground-floor **Apollo Room**, where the god himself appears majestically over the fireplace, attended by the nine muses on the surrounding walls. The much larger **no. 86**, with flowing rococo plasterwork by Robert West, the notable Dublin-born imitator of the Lafranchinis, was added in 1765. Joyce studied here between 1899 and 1902 (look out for a photo of Joyce standing with his fellow students by a tree (which still stands by the way) in the back garden), while it was also the residence of English poet **Gerard Manley Hopkins** whilst he was Professor of Classics between 1894 and 1899; after five wretched years in Dublin, he died of typhoid and was buried in an unmarked grave in Glasnevin Cemetery. Inevitably it is Joyce's work that forms the centrepiece of the museum, including first editions, drafts, sketches and notebooks, and 99 different translations of his books, testament to the writer's universal popularity. But there's no doubting the star exhibit: Copy No. 1 of the first edition of *Ulysses* – as important an exhibit as any in Ireland. Other writers do get a look in, for example there's a copy of WB Yeats' *Easter, 1916* poem, one of just twenty-five copies produced. The rotating exhibitions celebrating contemporary Irish literature are first class, are there are engaging workshops for teens and children too. There's also an excellent bookshop and café here.

Little Museum of Dublin

15 St Stephen's Green North • Guided tour on the hour every hour • Charge • http://littlemuseum.ie

For a crash course in Dublin's history you could do a lot worse than pay a visit to the entertaining **Little Museum of Dublin**, crammed into two floors of a Georgian house opposite the Green. Visits are by guided tour (29-minutes long!), which are led in wonderfully entertaining (and cleverly improvised) fashion by professional actors who

---

GEORGE BERNARD SHAW

Born in Dublin in 1856, **George Bernard Shaw** grew up among a Protestant family fallen on hard times. His father was an unsuccessful grain merchant and alcoholic – prompting Shaw to become a lifelong abstainer – and there was no money to pay for his education. At 15 he started work as a junior clerk for a land agency, but five years later went to London to join his mother who had moved there to further the musical career of one of his sisters. Reliant on what little income his mother earned as a music teacher, Shaw set about educating himself by spending his afternoons in the reading room of the British Museum. He hoped to become a novelist, but following the rejection of no fewer than five novels, turned his hand to journalism instead, contributing music and drama criticism to London newspapers.

Shaw was a devout socialist, joining the Fabian Society in 1884, writing pamphlets and gaining a reputation as a natural orator. He espoused numerous causes, including electoral reform, vegetarianism and the abolition of private property. His **theatrical career** began in the 1890s when, influenced by Ibsen, he began to compose plays focusing on social and moral matters, rather than the romantic and personal subjects which then dominated British theatre.

In 1898 he married the heiress Charlotte Payne-Townshend and the same year saw the production of his first successful play, *Candida*. A stream of equally lauded comedy-dramas followed – including *The Devil's Disciple*, *Arms and the Man*, *Major Barbara* and *Pygmalion* – though he later turned to more serious drama, such as *Heartbreak House* and *Saint Joan*. Simultaneously, he maintained an active career as a **critic**, journalist and essayist, his often bitterly ironic wit ("England and America are two countries separated by a common language") becoming legendary. In 1925 he was awarded the **Nobel Prize for Literature**, but initially rejected the honour before relenting and giving his prize money to a newly established Anglo-Swedish Literary Foundation.

Shaw's attitude to Ireland was ever ambivalent – he once commented "I am a typical Irishman; my family came from Yorkshire" – and, though he remained interested in Irish affairs and became a personal friend of Michael Collins, his brand of democratic socialism would have been antipathetic to the austere Catholic and anti-British state that emerged post-independence. Shaw died in 1950 at Ayot St Lawrence, Hertfordshire.

A plaque outside 33 Synge St marks Shaw's birthplace, which, although closed to the public at the time of writing, plans to reopen as a home for writers in residence.

1

chart the history of the city over the last hundred years or so. Every square inch of every room is bursting with artefacts and curios, including newspaper clippings, old photographs, toys, ticket stubs, posters, letters and other bric-a-brac. One room is given over to rotating temporary exhibitions, which can cover anything from music to local inventions.

Fitzwilliam Square

The area to the east of St Stephen's Green is the best in the city for a Georgian architectural tour, where an aimless wander will reveal plenty of wrought-iron balconies and much-photographed doorways sporting elegant knockers and fanlights. At its centre lie the still-private lawns of the small but well-preserved **Fitzwilliam Square** (1825), where, at no. 42, W.B. Yeats lived from 1928 to 1932. His brother, the painter Jack B., had a house and studio round the corner at no. 18 Fitzwilliam Place, which together with its continuation Fitzwilliam Street forms a – now much-interrupted – kilometre-long terrace of Georgian houses, marching off towards the magnificent backdrop of the Wicklow Mountains.

Royal Hibernian Academy

15 Ely Place • Free • http://rhagallery.ie

The **Royal Hibernian Academy** is one of the country's leading contemporary art venues. Hosting major temporary shows by Irish and international artists, its well-designed viewing spaces are also home to the RHA Annual Exhibition, usually from May to July.

Temple Bar

Sandwiched between the busy thoroughfare of Dame Street and the Liffey, **Temple Bar** is marketed, with a fair dose of artistic licence, as Dublin's "Left Bank" (inconveniently, it's on the right bank as you face downstream). Its transformation into the city's main cultural and entertainment district came about after a 1960s plan for a new central bus terminal here was abandoned after much procrastination. Instead, the area's narrow cobbled streets and old warehouses, by now occupied by short-lease studios, workshops and boutiques, began to be sensitively redeveloped as an artistic quarter in the 1980s, and is now home to numerous **galleries** and **arts centres** (see page 74). It also shelters a huge number of hotels, restaurants, pubs and clubs, engendering a notoriously raucous nightlife scene that attracts more outsiders than Dubliners.

Most people enter Temple Bar from Dame Street, past the unusual and highly controversial 1970s **Central Bank**, whose floors are suspended from the roof by external cables. The main access from the north side is the cast-iron **Ha'penny Bridge**, Dublin's oldest and most renowned pedestrian river crossing, with great views of the river along the quays in both directions. It began life in 1816 as the Wellington Bridge but soon acquired its nickname thanks to a halfpenny toll, which was levied until 1919. The central **Temple Bar Square** is a popular spot for people-watching, with several open-air cafés. It hosts a small book market on Saturdays and Sundays (11am–6pm), while the nearby **Meeting House Square** has an excellent food market (see page 109) on Saturdays (10am–4.30pm). The Designer Mart on Cow's Lane every Saturday (10am–5pm) showcases Irish handmade craft and design.

At the bottom of Parliament Street are the **Sunlight Chambers**, whose curious facade merits a short detour. Built in the early twentieth century in the style of an Italian Renaissance palace by the Sunlight soap company, the Chambers' exterior sports colourful ceramic friezes on the theme of hygiene; underneath the soot you can make out farmers and builders getting their clothes dirty on the upper tier, and women washing them below.

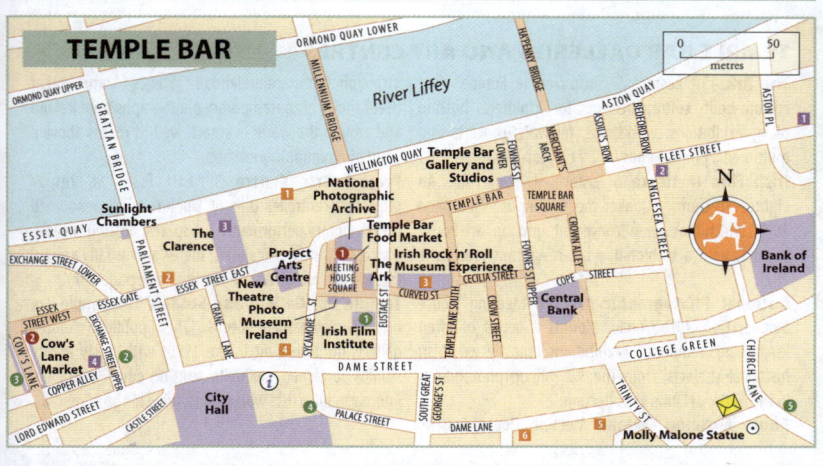

◼ ACCOMMODATION		● EATING		◼ DRINKING & NIGHTLIFE		PUBS & BARS		● SHOPPING	
The Clarence	3	Avoca Café	5	CLUBS & LIVE MUSIC		The Porterhouse	2	Cow's Lane Market	2
Hard Rock Hotel	4	Chez Max	4	Button Factory	3	The Stag's Head	6	Temple Bar Food	
Oliver St John Gogarty's	2	Irish Film Institute Café Bar	1	Four Dame Lane	5			Market	1
Temple Bar Hotel	1	Queen of Tarts	3	Olympia Theatre	4				
		Sano Pizza	2	Workman's Club	1				

The Irish Rock'n'Roll Museum Experience

Curved St, Temple Bar • Charge • http://irishrocknrollmuseum.com

Even if you're not particularly invested in Irish music, the **Irish Rock'n'Roll Experience** is an absolute blast. On hour-long guided tours, you'll get to see some priceless exhibits belonging to former and present gods of Irish rock and roll: Rory Gallagher, Sinead O'Connor, The Pogues, U2 and Fontaines D.C., among many others (indeed watching the ten-minute film montage you'll be quite surprised by the number of musicians that you never realised hailed from the Emerald Isle), at the same time as being regaled with all kinds of fascinating stories. There are plenty of other random exhibits too, such as Michael Jackson's jacket from the very last Jackson 5 tour. Thin Lizzy play a big part in proceedings here, to the extent that an entire room is given over to the band, including Phil Lynott's ripped leather pants and a Gretsch Falcon given to him by Joe Strummer. More poignantly, there is a poster advertising a gig that Nirvana's were due to play here on 8 April 1994, the day that the lead singer Kurt Cobain took his own life. It's still a working live music venue (you'll likely hear a band or two rehearsing), and you can even have a jam yourself if you feel entertaining your fellow visitors.

Dublin Castle

On a ridge above the Liffey, where previously the Vikings had established themselves, the Anglo-Norman invaders rebuilt Dublin in the thirteenth century around the doughty **Dublin Castle**. The main element of the walled city became the seat of British power in Ireland for seven hundred years, successfully withstanding all attempts to take it by force. It did, however, succumb to a major fire in 1684 and was rebuilt during the eighteenth century as a complex of residential and administrative buildings over two quadrangles, giving a sedate collegiate appearance. The outline of the medieval castle is traced by the **Upper Yard**; above its original main gate, the Cork Hill State Entrance, stands a statue of *Justice*, wearing no blindfold and turning her back on the city – a fitting symbol of British rule, locals reckon. The castle's one remaining tower (there

TEMPLE BAR GALLERIES AND ART CENTRES

The Ark 11A Eustace St, http://ark.ie Europe's first custom-built cultural centre for children, hosting plays, exhibitions, workshops, festivals, concerts and multimedia programmes for 2–12-year-olds.

Irish Film Institute 6 Eustace St, http://ifi.ie An eighteenth-century Quaker meeting house (see page 107), which has been converted into an art-house cinema, with a fashionable bar-restaurant (see page 102).

National Photographic Archive Meeting House Square, Free, http://nli.ie. Mounts a series of often fascinating temporary exhibitions, mostly on Irish historical subjects, from the 5.2 million photographs in the National Library's collection.

Photo Museum Ireland Meeting House Square, http://photomuseumireland.ie. Stages some great (free) shows of contemporary photographs from Ireland and around the world in smart, well-lit rooms above a good photographic bookshop.

Project Arts Centre 39 East Essex St, http://projectartscentre.ie. One of Dublin's most renowned contemporary performance art spaces, hosting theatre, dance, film and music shows; there's also usually a visual arts installation on at any one time (see page 107).

Temple Bar Gallery and Studios 5–9 Temple Bar, http://templebargallery.com. This publicly funded gallery, purpose-built in the 1990s with thirty artists' studios attached, exhibits cutting-edge Irish and international artists working in a wide range of media.

were four) is being converted into a museum and should be ready to view by 2026. Visitors are free to walk around the courtyards, now home to police and tax offices (Bram Stoker once worked here as a petty clerk), before taking either a self-guided or guided tour of the **State Apartments** or visiting the world-class collection of books and objets d'art from around the globe in the **Chester Beatty Library**.

The State Apartments

Daily 9.45am–5.45pm (last admission 5.15pm; sometimes closed for state occasions so check ahead); frequent guided tours (1hr 10min) • Charge; Heritage Card • http://dublincastle.ie

One of Dublin's four official government buildings, The State Apartments were built as the residence of the English viceroy and are entered from the Upper Yard. Inside the apartments, the Grand Staircase leads up to the east wing of bedrooms and drawing rooms, refurbished to their eighteenth- and nineteenth-century style after a major fire in 1941. The brass chandelier in the gaudily decorated Throne Room, with its shamrock, rose and thistle emblems, commemorates the 1801 Act of Union, while the Picture Gallery beyond is lined with viceroys, including – hiding ignominiously behind the door – the First Marquis of Cornwallis, who not only lost the American colonies, but also faced rebellions as viceroy, first of India, then of Ireland (1798). The State Drawing Room is where Margaret Thatcher, Helmut Kohl and other heads of state convened in 1990 to negotiate East Germany's entry into the European Union, while St Patrick's Hall, formerly a ballroom that hosted investitures of the Knights of St Patrick, is now used for the inaugurations and funerals of Irish presidents, photos of whom line the adjoining corridor. Its overblown, late eighteenth-century ceiling paintings show St Patrick converting the Irish, Henry II receiving the submission of the Irish chieftains, and George III's coronation.

A guided tour also includes a visit to the **Chapel Royal** in the Lower Yard, an ornate Gothic Revival gem built in 1814 but now deconsecrated, and the excavations of the **Undercroft**, which have revealed the base of the gunpowder tower of the medieval castle and steps leading down to the moat (fed by the old River Poddle on its way down to the Liffey), as well as part of the original Viking ramparts.

The Chester Beatty Library

Nov–Feb closed Mon; guided tours Wed 1pm, Sat 2pm, Sun 3pm • Entry and tours free • http://chesterbeatty.ie

To the south of the Chapel Royal lies the pretty **castle garden**; now adorned with a swirling motif taken from the passage grave at Newgrange, it marks the site of the "black pool" (*dubh linn*) from which the city derives its name. Overlooking the garden from the renovated eighteenth-century Clock Tower Building, the **Chester Beatty Library** preserves a dazzling collection of books, manuscripts, prints and objets d'art from around the world. Superlatives come thick and fast here: as well as one of the finest **Islamic collections** in existence, containing some of the earliest manuscripts from the ninth and tenth centuries, the library holds important biblical papyri, including the earliest surviving examples in any language of Mark's and Luke's Gospels, St Paul's Letters and the Book of Revelation. Elegantly displayed in high-tech galleries, the artefacts are used to tell the story of religious and artistic traditions across the world with great ingenuity. It's well worth timing your visit to coincide with lunch at the excellent *Silk Road Café* (see page 102).

The collection was painstakingly put together by the remarkable **Sir Alfred Chester Beatty**, an American mining magnate who moved himself and his works to Dublin in the early 1950s, after cutting a deal with the Irish government on import taxes and estate duties. In 1957 he was made the first honorary citizen of Ireland, and, when he died in 1968, he bequeathed his collection to the state and was given a state funeral.

It makes sense to start with the second-floor gallery, which covers "Sacred Traditions", while the first floor deals with "the Arts of the Book" (alongside a space for fascinating temporary exhibitions), with each divided into Western, Islamic and Eastern sections; exhibits range from sixteenth-century biblical engravings by Albrecht Dürer to books carved in jade for the Chinese emperors (the seventeen here are one of the largest collections in the world) and from gorgeously illustrated collections of Persian poetry to serene Burmese statues of the Buddha.

City Hall

2 Dame St • Free • http://dublincity.ie

In front of the castle stands the gleamingly restored rotunda of **City Hall**, where creamy Portland-stone columns, interspersed with statues of notables, including Daniel O'Connell (the city's first Catholic Lord Mayor), are bathed in wonderful natural light from the dome. The sumptuous Neoclassical building was constructed between 1769 and 1779 as the Royal Exchange, but fell into disuse after the Act of Union of 1801 passed governance of Ireland back to London; Dublin Corporation bought it in

---

CYCLING IN DUBLIN

Dublin is a long way behind other bike-friendly cities, but things are improving. Almost every road has a **cycle lane**, but some are so poorly designed that traffic often blocks the lane entirely. Whether in a designated lane or not, cyclists should take extreme care and remain vigilant, particularly for cars taking left-hand turns across the cycleway.

Although cycling in the city centre can be a congested and unpleasant affair, there are plenty of enjoyable routes further out. A cycle to **Howth** from the city centre takes just over an hour, and for the most part it's a beautifully scenic coastal ride. Starting at O'Connell Bridge, head east along the north side of the Liffey, through the IFSC and north through the East Wall to Clontarf. From there it's a straight and flat cycle lane for 10km into Howth.

For a shorter ride head to the **Poolbeg Lighthouse**, the perennially popular Sunday walking spot for Dubliners. A 4km-long long stone pier jutting out into the middle of Dublin Bay, it's usually a windy and cobweb-clearing walk with panoramic views of the city's coastline. The most enjoyable route is straight down the Grand Canal, through Bath Avenue, taking the first exit on the Sean Moore Road roundabout. It'll take just over half an hour, but be warned – towards the end, the route passes through a fairly unattractive industrial wasteland by the Dublin docks.

You'll find plenty more routes, maps, and safety tips on http://dublincycling.com

1

1851, and it's still the venue for city council meetings. Arts and crafts murals under the dome trace Dublin's history, while the colourful floor mosaic shows the civic coat of arms, three castles topped by flames, which apparently represent the zeal of the citizens to defend Dublin – reinforced by the city motto *Obedientia Civium Urbis Felicitas* ("Happy the City whose Citizens Obey"). The basement houses an oft-overlooked exhibition tracing Dublin's civic history from 441AD (see page 76). Closed Sundays.

Christ Church Cathedral

Christchurch Place • Charge • http://christchurchcathedral.ie

Occupying the highest point of the old city, **Christ Church Cathedral** sits above Wood Quay, the location of a Viking settlement of more than two hundred houses over which the Dublin Corporation controversially built its Civic Offices in the early 1980s.

The Gothic cathedral is now hemmed in by buildings and traffic, but inside you'll find some fascinating remnants from its long history as the seat of the (now Anglican) Archbishop of Dublin and Glendalough. From as early as the seventh century, there may have been a small Celtic church on these grounds, and in about 1030, the recently converted Viking king of Dublin, Sitric Silkenbeard, built a wooden cathedral here. This in turn was replaced by the Normans, who between 1186 and 1240 erected a magnificent stone structure to mark their accession to power. Of this, the crypt (which is Dublin's oldest functioning structure), two transepts (which retain many original Romanesque carvings) and the remarkable **leaning north wall** can still be seen. The weight of the original vaulted stone ceiling caused the roof to collapse in 1562, bringing down the south wall and pulling the north side of the nave half a metre out of the perpendicular. In the 1870s, distiller Henry Roe lavished the equivalent of €30 million on the heavy-handed restoration you can see today, and bankrupted himself.

Tomb of Strongbow

Near the main entrance at the southwest corner you'll come across the strange **tomb of Strongbow**, the Norman leader who captured Dublin in 1170 and was buried here six years later. The original, around which the landlords of Dublin had gathered to collect rents, was destroyed by the sixteenth-century roof collapse, and had to be replaced with a fourteenth-century effigy of one of the earls of Drogheda so that business could proceed as usual. The small half-figure alongside is probably a fragment of the original tomb, though legend maintains that it's an effigy of Strongbow's son, hacked in two by his own father for cowardice in battle.

The chapels

The chapels off the choir show the Anglo-Normans celebrating their dual nationality. To the left stands the **Chapel of St Edmund**, the ninth-century king of East Anglia who was martyred by the Vikings, while on the right is the **Chapel of St Laud**, the sixth-century bishop of Coutances in Normandy. The floor tiles here are original – those

---

THE STORY OF THE CAPITAL

The vaults beneath City Hall now shelter ***The Story of the Capital** (same times as City Hall; charge), a fascinating multimedia journey through Dublin's history and politics – with occasional hints of self-promotion for the exhibition's sponsors, the city council. The story is told through exhaustive display panels, slick interactive databases and a series of videos, complemented by an entertaining audio-guide narrated by Irish actress Sinead Cusack with snippets from leading historians. There are few exhibits as such, though a notable exception is the intricate city seal and its safe, which was instituted after the seal was stolen in 1305 and required the presence of all six keyholders.

1

> **DUBLIN AND THE MESSIAH**
>
> Opposite the cathedral on Fishamble Street once stood **Neal's Music Hall**, where **Handel** conducted the combined choirs of Christ Church and St Patrick's cathedrals in the first performance of his *Messiah* in 1742. As the takings were going to charity, ladies were requested not to wear hoops in their crinolines, to get more bums on seats. Jonathan Swift exclaimed, "Oh, a German, a genius, a prodigy." In a private garden on the site, the composer's reward is a statue of himself conducting in the nude, perched on a set of organ pipes. Every April 13, on the anniversary of the first performance, Our Lady's Choral Society gives a sing-along performance of excerpts from the *Messiah* here.

in the rest of the cathedral are 1870s replicas – while on the wall there's an iron cage inside which is the embalmed heart of twelfth-century St Laurence O'Toole, Dublin's only canonized archbishop. In a most bizarre incident, the heart was stolen in 2012 before being found in Phoenix Park in 2018.

The crypt

If you descend the stairs by the south transept, you'll reach the **crypt**, the least changed remnant of the twelfth-century cathedral; formerly a storehouse for the trade in alcohol and tobacco, it's one of the largest crypts in Britain and Ireland, extending under the entire cathedral for 55m. Here you'll find the **Treasures of Christ Church** exhibition, which includes an interesting twenty-minute audiovisual on the history of the cathedral, as well as a miscellany of manuscripts and church silverware, and a mummified cat and rat, which were frozen in hot pursuit in an organ pipe in the 1860s. Look out also for a ropey tabernacle and pair of candlesticks made for James II on his flight from England in 1689, when, for three months only, Latin Mass was again celebrated at Christ Church (the existing cathedral paraphernalia was hidden by quick-thinking Anglican officials under a bishop's coffin). In extravagant contrast is a chunky silver-gilt plate, around 1m wide, presented by King William III in thanksgiving for his victory at the Battle of the Boyne in 1690.

Dublinia

St Michael's Hill • charge • http://dublinia.ie

Located at the crossroads of the medieval city, and housed in the former Synod Hall of the Church of Ireland, **Dublinia** provides a lively, hands-on portrait of Viking and medieval Dublin that's especially good fun for kids. Themes such as the plague and the medieval fair are explored via walk-through tableaux of streets and houses, sound effects and lots of fun interactive displays. An archaeology room explores how the city's past has been unearthed, with a re-created excavation site and lab where visitors can examine medieval bugs under a microscope.

On the second floor, in the Great Hall, where the Anglican bishops met until 1982, the focus is on the Vikings, with all manner of objects excavated from nearby Wood Quay on display; in addition, there's a near-life-size ship, audiovisuals on the sagas and the chance to try on slave chains Before crossing the graceful, much-photographed bridge over to Christ Church Cathedral, it's worth climbing **St Michael's Tower**, a remnant of the seventeenth-century Church of St Michael and All Angels, for fine views over the city.

St Audoen's

Corn Market (near High St) • Free • http://heritageireland.ie

Just to the west of Dublinia, on the corner of Bridge Street, stand two churches dedicated to St Audoen (in French, St-Ouen, seventh-century bishop of Rouen and

1

the patron saint of Normandy). The monumental but largely uninteresting nineteenth-century Catholic version overshadows its neighbour, **Protestant St Audoen's**, which was built around 1190 and is now an intriguing tourist site. There are still services every Sunday at 10.15am – the church has been continuously used for worship for over eight centuries, longer than any other in Dublin.

The most fascinating aspect of a visit is seeing the physical evidence of how the church's fortunes waxed and waned over the centuries. As it prospered through close association with the city's guilds, St Audoen's expanded in stages around its original single-naved church, including the addition, in 1431, of **St Anne's Guild Chapel**, making a two-aisled nave. The latter is now the main exhibition area, with informative displays on the parish and the guilds.

Until the Reformation, St Audoen's was the most prestigious parish church among Dublin's leading families. Afterwards, however, many members of the all-important Guild of St Anne refused to become Protestant and the congregation declined. By the nineteenth century St Audoen's had retreated to its original single nave, by the simple expediency of removing the roofs from the other parts of the church and letting them rot. You can now poke around the open-air **chancel** and **Portlester Chapel**, where, before the building was declared a national monument, locals would hang their washing out to dry.

Behind the Protestant church, steps descend to thirteenth-century **St Audoen's Arch**, the only remaining gate in the **Norman city walls** – a dramatic, though heavily restored, remnant stretching for 200m along Cook Street, 7m high and tipped with battlements.

St Patrick's Cathedral

Patrick St • Charge • http://stpatrickscathedral.ie

The history of **St Patrick's Cathedral** is remarkably similar to that of its fellow Anglican rival Christ Church up the road. It was built between 1220 and 1270 in Gothic style, but its roof collapsed in 1544, leading to a decline that included its use as a stable by Cromwell's army in 1649. Its Victorian restoration, however, by Sir Benjamin Guinness in the 1860s, was more sensitive than at Christ Church, and it has a more appealing, lived-in feel, thanks largely to its clutter of quirky funerary monuments. Dublin has two Church of Ireland cathedrals because, in the 1190s, Archbishop John Comyn left the clergy of Christ Church and built his own palace and church here outside the city walls, and therefore beyond the jurisdiction of the city provosts.

To the right of the entrance in the harmoniously proportioned nave are diverse memorials to **Jonathan Swift**, the cathedral's dean for 32 years (see page 79), including his and his long-term partner Stella's graves, his pulpit and table, and a cast of his skull – both his and Stella's bodies were dug up by Victorian phrenologists, studying the skulls of the famous. The **Door of Reconciliation** by the north transept recalls a quarrel between the earls of Kildare and Ormond in 1492. Ormond fled and sought sanctuary in the cathedral's chapterhouse, but Kildare, eager to make peace, cut a hole in the door and stretched his arm through to shake Ormond's hand – so giving us the phrase "chancing your arm". Nearby in the north aisle of the choir, a simple black slab commemorates **Duke Frederick Schomberg**, who advised William of Orange to come to Ireland in 1686 but had the misfortune to be slain at the ensuing Battle of the Boyne. His family didn't bother to erect a memorial for him, so it was left to Dean Swift to do the honours here in 1731; in Swift's words, "The renown of his valour had greater power among strangers than had the ties of blood among his kith and kin."

In the northwest corner of the nave you'll find a slab carved with a Celtic cross that once marked the site of a well next to the cathedral, where **St Patrick** baptized converts in the fifth century. Back near the entrance, you can't miss the extravagant **Boyle monument**, which Richard Boyle, Earl of Cork, erected in 1632 in memory of his wife

JONATHAN SWIFT

"Here is laid the body of Jonathan Swift… where fierce indignation can no longer rend the heart. Go, traveller, and imitate if you can this earnest and dedicated champion of liberty."

Swift's epitaph in St Patrick's Cathedral, penned by himself and translated here from the Latin, conveys not only his appetite for political satire and campaigning, but also perhaps a certain prescience about the longevity of his fame. Born in Dublin in 1667 and educated at Trinity College, Swift went to England in 1689 to work as secretary to the retired diplomat Sir William Temple. Here he met Esther Johnson, nicknamed **Stella**, the daughter of Temple's housekeeper, who became his close companion – whether platonic or sexual, no one knows – until her death in 1728. Swift was ordained in the Church of Ireland in 1695, and wrote his first major work, **A Tale of a Tub**, anonymously in 1704, satirizing the official churches and the unscrupulous "modern" writers of his day. Sent to London to lobby the government for the relief of church taxes, from 1710 he was at the centre of England's political and literary life, a friend of Tory ministers as well as of Alexander Pope and John Gay. When the Tories fell from power, however, instead of the English bishopric he had hoped for, he was made Dean of St Patrick's, in 1713. Here he turned his caustic wit on Irish injustices, writing a series of pamphlets in the 1720s and 1730s including **A Modest Proposal**, one of the most admired works of irony in the English language, which suggests that the Irish poor sell off their children to the rich as "a most delicious, nourishing and wholesome food". At this time, too, he wrote his most famous work, the gloriously imaginative satirical novel, **Gulliver's Travels** (1726). Swift's later years were blighted by a progressive mental illness, and when he died, in 1745, he left his estate to build St Patrick's on James's Street, the first psychiatric hospital in Ireland.

Katherine who had borne him fifteen children, including the famous chemist Robert Boyle (shown in the bottom-centre niche). Viceroy Wentworth, objecting to being forced to kneel before a Corkman, had the monument moved here from beside the altar, but Boyle exacted revenge in later years by engineering Wentworth's execution.

Marsh's Library

St Patrick's Close • closed for 10 days over Christmas and New Year • Charge • http://marshlibrary.ie

Behind St Patrick's Cathedral lies the oldest public library in Ireland, **Marsh's Library**, which has remained delightfully untouched since it was built by Sir William Robinson, the architect of Kilmainham Hospital, in 1701, and still functions as a research and conservation library. Its founder, Archbishop Narcissus Marsh, was particularly interested in science, mathematics and music, and oversaw the first translation of the Old Testament into Irish. His books form one of the library's four main collections, totalling 25,000 works, relating to the sixteenth, seventeenth and early eighteenth centuries. They're housed in beautiful rows of dark-oak bookcases, each with a carved and lettered gable (for cataloguing purposes) topped by a bishop's mitre, and three screened alcoves, or "cages", where readers were locked in with rare books. The library mounts regular exhibitions from its collections on subjects such as astronomy, and displays a death mask of its former governor, Jonathan Swift, as well as a cast of his companion Stella's skull.

The Northside

Running due north from O'Connell Bridge, broader than it is long, to Parnell Square, **O'Connell Street** is the main artery of Dublin's northside. This bustling thoroughfare was originally laid out in the fashion of the grand Parisian boulevards, but poor redevelopment since the damage caused by the 1916 Rising means there are few vestiges of its former grandeur.

Nowadays, the street is lined with fast-food outlets and ugly modern shop frontages, but the historic **GPO** remains a central focal point, opposite which soars the remarkable stainless-steel **Dublin Spire**. A number of other important monuments also remain, mostly positioned in the street's broad central reservation. Just north of O'Connell Bridge, you'll encounter first the imposing figure of the politician **Daniel O'Connell**, "The Liberator", who played a major role in nineteenth-century political campaigns to secure independence. The winged figures by his side represent O'Connell's bravery, patriotism, fidelity and eloquence, while the smaller female figure nearby symbolizes Ireland unchained. At the Abbey Street junction is a statue of the trade unionist **Jim Larkin**, who led the workers of Dublin in the 1913 Lockout, caught in the act of addressing a crowd.

At the very top of O'Connell Street stands an imposing statue of **Charles Stewart Parnell**, the leading late nineteenth-century advocate of Irish Home Rule. The plinth records his famous declaration:

No man has a right to fix the boundary to the march of a nation. No man has a right to say to his country, "Thus far shalt thou go and no further."

The streets around represent a consumer's paradise and, particularly on Liffey Street Lower and in the burgeoning **Italian quarter** centred on Bloom Lane (the result of a local developer's fascination with all things Tuscan), you'll find plenty of stylish bars and cafés. Notable cultural landmarks east of O'Connell Street include the **Abbey Theatre**, centre of the twentieth-century revival in Irish theatre, and, along The Quays, the opulent eighteenth-century **Custom House**.

Parnell Square, at the top of O'Connell Street, might lack the allure of its southside Georgian equivalents, but it still has a certain grace. The Square's north side hosts one of Dublin's premier galleries, the **Hugh Lane**, while nearby **No 11 Parnell Square East** is a Georgian house currently under renovation by the Irish Heritage Trust and expected to open in summer 2025. It will be devoted to the works of the acclaimed writer **James Joyce**, Irish poetry, heritage and culture

To the west lie the **Old Jameson Distillery**, in the historic **Smithfield** area, and **Collins Barracks**, home to the National Museum's collection of decorative arts.

Dublin Spire

O'Connell St, near junction with Earl St North

The northside's most remarkable landmark marks the spot where Nelson's Pillar stood until it was blown up by Republicans in 1966. Known colloquially as "The Stiletto in the Ghetto", "The Nail in the Pale", or more simply "The Spike", the astonishing **Dublin Spire** is easily the tallest structure in the city – a 120m-high stainless-steel needle, surmounted by an illuminated beacon. Three metres wide at its base, it tapers to a mere 15cm at its summit. In the early morning or at dusk its surface takes on an ethereal blue colour, while at night it seems to loom ominously over the city. What the ghost of **James Joyce**, whose adjacent and somewhat rakish statue stands just down Earl Street North, would make of it is open to question.

The General Post Office

O'Connell St Lower • **GPO** free • **Museum** charge • http://gpowitnesshistory.ie

Just to the left of the Spire stands one of O'Connell Street's few remaining buildings of major historical importance: the **General Post Office**, whose significance lies in its role as the **rebels' headquarters** during the Easter Rising of 1916 (see page 82). The building was constructed in 1818 but only its Ionic portico survived the fighting – and

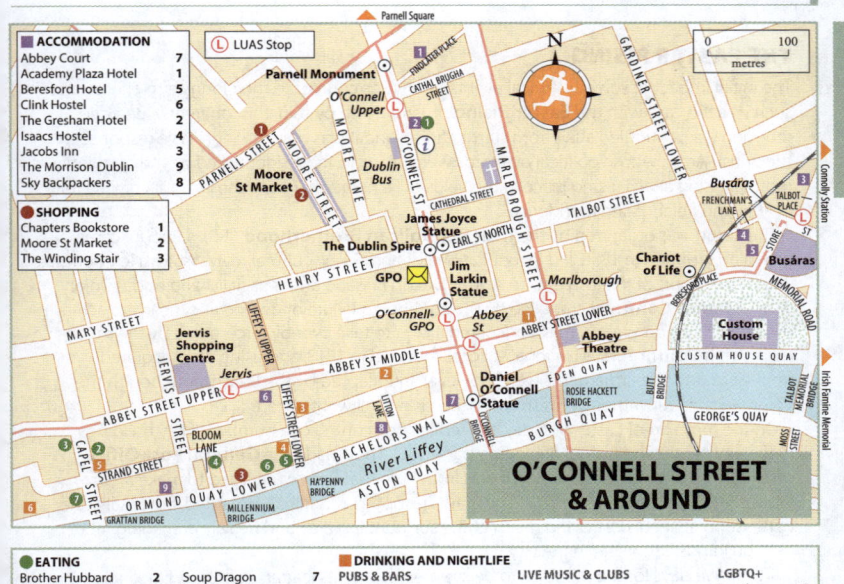

O'CONNELL STREET & AROUND

still bears the marks of gunfire. Following restoration, the GPO reopened in 1929 and inside its marble halls you'll find Oliver Sheppard's intricately wrought bronze statue *The Death of Cúchulainn*, representing a key moment in the Irish legend *Táin Bó Cúailnge* (see page 154).

The building, which still functions as Dublin's largest post office, now houses a state-of-the-art permanent exhibition called **GPO Museum**, focusing on the 1916 rising – refreshingly, it explores both sides of the conflict, as well as its causes and aftermath. Using slick touchscreens, audiovisual booths and many previously unseen artefacts it is one of the finest and most informative approaches to the subject in the city. Before examining the exhibits, it's worth making a beeline for the seventeen-minute film, *Fire & Steel*, which dramatically recreates the roles played by the leading protagonists. Among the most significant, and poignant, exhibits is a letter penned by Michael Collins and a dagger made by the republican James O'Connor whilst in prison; in a somewhat bizarre twist, the man who ordered his execution, Kevin Higgins, got married the previous year with O'Connor as his best man. The handful of civilian diaries that reflect upon the aftermath of the Rising are also worth perusing.

The Abbey Theatre

26–27 Lower Abbey St • Tours Sat 10.30am • charge • http://abbeytheatre.ie

Just east of O'Connell Street's southern end stands the **Abbey Theatre**, focal point for Ireland's twentieth-century cultural revival. It first opened its doors in December 1904 to present three plays, two by the poet and dramatist W.B. Yeats and the other by his patron Lady Gregory. The theatre's company turned professional in 1906 and Yeats and Gregory, along with J.M. Synge, became its first directors. The staging of Synge's own tragicomic *Playboy of the Western World*, with its frank language and suggestion that Irish peasants would condone a murder, provoked riots on its opening night, while later, in 1926, Seán O'Casey's *The Plough and the Stars* incited bitter outrage, the

1

THE EASTER RISING

The initial impact of some historical events often runs counter to their long-term effects, and such was the case with the **Easter Rising** of 1916. Truth be told, this inherently idealistic rebellion was a bungled affair from start to finish, and it was only the repressive response of the British Army, whose political overlords were unsurprisingly sidetracked by the seemingly more pressing affairs taking place in the fields of Flanders, that gave the event its pivotal role in attaining Ireland's independence.

The Rising was organized by the **Irish Republican Brotherhood** (IRB), a Republican grouping founded in 1858, led by educationalist and Gaelic cultural revivalist **Patrick Pearse**, with the support of the Irish Citizen Army's Dublin Brigade under socialist and trades union activist **James Connolly**. Impelled by the continuing failure of democratic means to achieve the goal of independence, they concocted a plan to take over by force, aided by the much larger **Irish Volunteers**, a Nationalist corps founded in 1913, and using arms acquired from Germany. The armaments were, however, intercepted by the British, and though the Volunteers' leader withdrew his support, the Rising still went ahead.

On the morning of Easter Monday, the rebels took control of a number of key buildings in the city centre and further afield (see page 568). They made the **General Post Office** on O'Connell Street their base, and it was from here that Pearse emerged to make his Proclamation of the Irish Republic. The British response was initially guarded, but a full-scale battle soon ensued, destroying much of the surrounding area and heavily damaging rebel-held buildings elsewhere in the city.

It took five days for the rebellion to be suppressed and its leaders captured. Dubliners decried the uprising at its outset, dismayed by the devastation ravaged upon their city by the fighting. Had the British simply imprisoned the IRB's leaders, it's extremely unlikely later political developments would have occurred as quickly as they did, but the draconian decision was made to **execute** all of them (with the exception of Éamon de Valera, who had US citizenship). In the process, the British created national martyrs, transforming the situation irrevocably and ultimately leading to a bitter war of independence.

audience regarding its view of the Easter Rising as derisive not least because the theatre had begun to receive state funding the previous year.

The original Abbey burnt to the ground in 1951 and its more modern, outwardly grim replacement opened in 1966. Informative guided tours – a must for anyone interested in the link between Ireland's culture and politics – take in both back- and front-stage areas and recount key moments in the Abbey's history. Its programme continues to include a range of drama, blending revivals of Irish classics with works by established writers such as Brian Friel and younger dramatists, while the much smaller Peacock Theatre in the basement is devoted to new experimental works. During the first years of the twenty-first century the theatre suffered disastrous financial mismanagement and was bailed out in 2006 by the largest grant ever awarded by the Arts Council of Ireland.

Seventy-five-minute-long backstage **tours** offer an insight into the history and behind-the-scenes work of the theatre; they take place while plays are running on the Abbey stage.

The Custom House

Custom House Quay, north bank of River Liffey • charge • http://heritageireland.ie

Opened in 1791, the imposing **Custom House** is one of several notable Dublin landmarks designed by the English architect James Gandon (others include the Four Courts and O'Connell Bridge). The Custom House cost the then unearthly sum of £500,000 sterling to construct, owing to its bulk and the intricacy of Gandon's architectural detail – and because it was constructed on a submerged mudflat which required covering by a layer of solid pine planks. Such cost proved even more extravagant when the Act of Union transferred customs and excise to London in 1800. The building's grandiose Neoclassical exterior, more than 100m long, features heads sculpted by Gandon's contemporary Edward Smyth, with cattle heads symbolizing Ireland's beef trade and the others representing Ireland's rivers (including the Liffey above the main entrance). Its 35m-high-dome was based upon Christopher Wren's Greenwich Hospital.

After 1801, the Custom House became the administrative centre for the city's work on public hygiene and Poor Law relief, the latter demonstrated by an enormous Famine pot. The building suffered a major fire in 1833 and was completely gutted in 1921 after being set alight by the IRA. Subsequently restored, though with significant changes to its internal structure and facade, it housed various government departments and some of its more illustrious employees, including Brian O'Nolan, better known as the comic novelist Flann O'Brien, and the songwriter Percy French. These days it's home to several governmental offices, including the Inland Revenue.

You can learn more about the building's illustrious history inside the new **visitor centre**, either on a self-guided or guided tour, the latter well worth paying the extra €2 for. Inaugurated in 2021 on the centenary of the fire, it's a beautifully executed exhibition, with interactive screens and virtual displays in each room focusing on an architectural aspect of the building or some historical element, for example the River Gods (keystones), or imports and exports. Another room is given over to documenting the fire itself, which includes some remarkable footage of the building ablaze; remarkably only nine people lost their lives, four of whom were civilians including the housekeeper. The only artefact, as such, on display is Gandon's pristine desk.

The Irish Famine Memorial

To the east of the Custom House, and set between the looming presence of the International Financial Services Centre and the Liffey, is the **Irish Famine Memorial**. These six life-sized bronze figures were designed and cast by the Dublin sculptor Rowan Gillespie to mark the 150th anniversary of the worst year of the Great Famine (see page 565). That these stark, beseeching figures are staring eastwards towards Britain is not coincidental.

The Hugh Lane Gallery

Parnell Square North • Entry and tours free, but donation suggested • http://hughlane.ie

The elegant, Georgian, stone-clad Charlemont House, with its curved outer and inner walls and Neoclassical interior, has been the home for the **The Hugh Lane Gallery** since 1933. Sir Hugh, a nephew of Lady Gregory (see page 343), wanted Dublin to house a major gallery of Irish and international art. He amassed a considerable collection by persuading native artists to contribute their work and purchasing many other paintings himself, particularly from the French Impressionist school and Italy.

The gallery holds around half of the Lane collection (the rest is in London's National Gallery) and only a fraction is on display here at any one time, though you're likely to see works by Renoir, Monet and Degas, as well as Pissarro and the Irish painters Jack B. Yeats, Roderic O'Connor and Louis le Brocquy, and there are also stained-glass pieces by Evie Hone and Harry Clarke, the latter pre-eminent in his field. The gallery usually hosts temporary exhibitions of more modern artworks.

Part of the gallery is devoted to a re-creation of Dublin-born painter **Francis Bacon's studio**, transported from its original location at Reece Mews in South Kensington, London, where the artist lived and worked for the last thirty years of his life. After his death in 1992, his studio was donated to the gallery by his heir, John Edwards, and

1

BLOOMSDAY

Perhaps no other writer has so encapsulated the life, lore and mores of his native city as **James Joyce** so successfully achieved in his remarkable novels, most notably **Ulysses** (1922). So precise are the author's descriptions of the locales visited by the book's protagonists on the date of the book's setting, June 16, that it is possible literally to follow in their footsteps. This annual pilgrimage undertaken by Joycean aficionados across the city has become known as Bloomsday. Though you can undertake to cover the **Bloomsday** route independently (a *Ulysses* map is available from the Visit Dublin Centre on Suffolk St), guided walks are organized by the James Joyce Centre (see page 84). There are plenty of other associated events, including re-creations by actors of some of the book's central passages and concerts devoted to music referenced in the novel.

Strangely, for someone who documented his native city's life with such pride, Joyce came to loathe Dublin, once describing the place in a letter as a "city of failure, of rancour and of unhappiness", and concluding "I long to be out of it." Though his early works, such as the short-story collection **Dubliners** and the semi-autobiographical novel **A Portrait of the Artist as a Young Man**, draw heavily upon his upbringing, Catholic education and Dublin experiences, by the time of the latter's publication in 1916, Joyce had long abandoned Ireland. Not long after meeting a Connemara-born chambermaid, Nora Barnacle, in June 1904, the pair eloped to Europe. Other than two brief visits to Ireland, Joyce spent the rest of his life in exile living in cities across Europe – in Pola (now Pula) in Istria, Trieste, Zurich and, notably, Paris, where *Ulysses* was published in 1922 and where he finally wed Nora in 1931. Joyce's only subsequent published work was the convoluted **Finnegans Wake** (1939). When he died in 1941, *Ulysses* was still unavailable in Ireland (though it never officially fell foul of Ireland's censorship laws, booksellers were loath to stock copies), and was not published in the country until the 1960s.

reconstructed here with astonishing precision – more than seven thousand individual items were catalogued and placed here with verisimilitude in the reconstruction. The studio can only be viewed through the window glass, but among the apparent debris are an old Bush record player, empty champagne boxes and huge tins of the type of matt vinyl favoured by Bacon, the fumes of which exacerbated his asthma. The surrounding rooms hold displays of memorabilia, such as photographs and correspondence, as well as half a dozen large canvases from the painter's last years, including an unfinished self-portrait.

The gallery runs guided **tours** of the exhibits, a programme of **lectures and films** related to its current shows (various times; €5) and very popular classical-music **concerts** (Sun noon; free).

The James Joyce Centre

35 North Great George's St · charge · http://jamesjoyce.ie

Occupying a grand eighteenth-century town house restored in the 1980s, the **James Joyce Centre** celebrates the work of perhaps Ireland's most imaginative yet most complex writer. Joyce spent part of his life living in the inner northside, and drew upon his experiences in the creation of his characters and the settings for his works. The building features decorative stucco mouldings by Michael Stapleton. The ground floor houses a small shop full of Joyceiana, such as books and prints, and an airy courtyard which includes the actual period door of 7 Eccles St, the fictional home of Leopold and Molly Bloom, two of the main protagonists in *Ulysses*, as well as a somewhat enigmatic, modernist Joyce-inspired sculpture of a cow. Here, too, are eighteen murals completed by Joyce's great grandnephew, Paul Joyce, depicting the episodes of *Ulysses*, each one in a different style.

The building's upper floors house a re-creation of the tiny room occupied by Joyce in Trieste, featuring various books, pianola music-rolls and a splendid collection of hats, as well as photographs of people and places associated with *Ulysses*, and touchscreen consoles tracing the development of the novel's plot and its variety of characters. Three short documentary films on the writer's life can also be viewed. The centre's two-hour **walking tour (charge)** which begins here, is well worth taking if you want to learn more about Joycean connections with the surrounding area.

14 Henrietta Street

14 Henrietta St • charge • http://14henriettastreet.ie

For a peek into both Georgian and tenement life on Dublin's northside, pay a visit to the wonderful **14 Henrietta St**, a neat, red-brick building nestled amongst a row of stately four-storey houses. Initially occupied by some of the wealthiest Dublin families, it was converted, in 1877, into a tenement building, at one point accommodating up to one hundred people – quite the squash. Indeed, at one point there were nineteen houses on Henrietta Street collectively housing more than 850 people. Guided tours, complemented by video footage and voiceovers, take you through a selection of rooms, most of which have been stripped back to their original 18th-century state, though what makes no.14 particularly unique is that it's installed with gas piping and two indoor flush loos. The last room has been faithfully re-created as it was when the last inhabitants moved out in 1979, with many of the family's furniture and possessions on display.

Smithfield

The area christened **Smithfield Village** by developers is more an ongoing process of urban renewal than an identifiable community, but at its centre lies the city's largest civic open space, cobbled **Smithfield**. Surrounded by rising blocks of executive flats, shops and restaurants, Smithfield still manages to host one of the city's major sights – the 300-year-old **Dublin Horse Fair**, which takes place twice a year and draws a number of traders and other horse-lovers from the city and outlying rural areas.

The National Museum – Decorative Arts and History

Benburb St • Free • http://museum.ie

The **National Museum – Decorative Arts and History** is housed in the eighteenth-century **Collins Barracks**, which surrounds Europe's largest regimental drilling square. The buildings set around this quadrangle contain a wonderful series of galleries devoted to the fine arts of Ireland and selected works from abroad. Unquestionably, the best of these is **Curator's Choice**, on the first floor of the west block, which is selected by museum curators from all over Ireland. Among its draws are a medieval oak carving of St Molaise; the extravagant cabinet presented by Oliver Cromwell to his daughter Bridget in 1652; and the remarkable fourteenth-century Chinese porcelain Fonthill Vase. The **Out of Storage** section is another highlight, bringing together everything from decorative glassware to a seventeenth-century suit of Samurai armour. There are also displays on Celtic art, coinage, silverware, period furniture, costumes and scientific instruments, and there are usually plenty of temporary exhibits. The third floor boasts a permanent exhibition on Eileen Gray, widely regarded as one of the most influential designers and architects of the twentieth century.

On the ground floor is a chain of thematically interconnected galleries, **Soldiers and Chiefs**, devoted to almost five hundred years of Irish **military history**. Apart from an array of helmets and weaponry, there's the remarkable Stokes tapestry, created by one Stephen of that ilk, a British soldier who devoted his spare time to the depiction of contemporary garrison life and was honoured to have his work shown to Queen Victoria on a royal visit to Ireland in 1849.

Croppy's Acre

Croppy's Acre, on Benburb Street, marks the location where many of those executed for their part in the 1798 Rebellion are buried ("croppy" being a derogatory term for the rebels on account of many of them sporting closely cropped hair in the style of some French revolutionaries, an act in itself considered seditious) – a Wicklow-granite monument marks the precise location of their graves. The park is also home to Éamonn O'Doherty's *Anna Livia* sculpture, a bronze embodiment of her namesake the River Liffey.

The Four Courts

Inn's Quay • http://courts.ie

The imposing riverside structure of the **Four Courts**, fronted by Corinthian columns and surmounted by an impressive dome, has seen many a legal hearing since it first opened its doors in 1802. Like the Custom House (see page 82), it was designed by James Gandon, and took some sixteen years to complete at a cost of £200,000 sterling. The Four Courts was seized by Republicans opposed to the Anglo-Irish Treaty in 1921, and heavily bombarded by Free State forces during the subsequent Civil War using, ironically, howitzers borrowed from the British. However, before the siege came to its inevitable end, the rebels accidentally set off explosives inside the building, destroying the Public Records Office and innumerable irreplaceable historic documents in the process. After rebuilding, the Four Courts reopened in 1931 and nowadays houses the **High Court of Justice** and, following the construction of the new Criminal Court of Justice on Parkgate Street, now only hears civil cases.

St Michan's Church

Church St • tours hourly • Charge • http://cathedralgroupdublin.ie

Constructed in 1095 by the Vikings in honour of a Danish bishop, **St Michan's Church** was substantially rebuilt some six hundred years later. Next to the church organ, reputedly once played by Handel, is the unusual Penitents' Pew, in which parishioners knelt facing the congregation to confess their errant ways. It is the church's **vaults**, however, that hold the most fascination. Guided **tours** descend an almost sheer staircase to view the contents of tiny crypts, which contain a dozen **bodies**, some dating back more than seven hundred years. These have been mummified by a process that involves two factors: the vaults' limestone walls, which absorb the air's natural moisture, and the methane produced by vegetation decaying below the floor. One of the mummies is believed to have been a Crusader, another a nun, and a third, which lacks a hand, may have been a repentant thief. Another crypt contains John and Henry Sheares, executed for their role in the 1798 Rebellion, as well as the death mask of one of its leaders, Wolfe Tone. Two other rebels, Oliver Bond and the Reverend William Jackson, are buried in the church's graveyard, and some reckon an unmarked grave to the rear houses the body of Robert Emmet, leader of the 1803 rising.

Jameson Distillery

Bow St • Charge • http://jamesonwhiskey.com

The buildings of the **Old Jameson Distillery**, where John Jameson set up his whiskey company, have long been turned over to a touristy but popular shrine to "the hard stuff". Forty-minute long guided **tours** whirl visitors through the process itself, from milling and mashing to the essential distillation element; while the separation of water from alcohol only occurs once in bourbon and twice in Scotch, the production of *uisce beatha* (Irish for "water of life", anglicized to "whiskey") involves a three-stage process. The tour ends with a tasting.

West of the centre

Unless you're a keen walker, you'll want to take a bus or LUAS tram to reach some of the city's western attractions. Highlights on the north side of the river include the vast grounds of **Phoenix Park**, with the dazzling interiors of **Farmleigh** mansion lying just beyond. Across the Liffey, the area west of the old city is dominated by the mammoth Guinness Brewery, whose wares are celebrated by the **Guinness Storehouse**. Further west lies the suburb of **Kilmainham**, home to the impressive **Irish Museum of Modern Art** and the forbidding **Kilmainham Gaol**, where the leaders of the 1916 Easter Rising were executed.

Phoenix Park

Main gates at Parkgate St and Castleknock Gate • Open access 24hr • http://phoenixpark.ie • Buses #25 and 26 stop near the main entrance; catch them at Merrion Square, Nassau St or Merchant's Quay

The undulating landscape of **Phoenix Park** – Europe's largest urban walled park – sprawls across some 1750 acres. Originally intended as a deer park for Charles II (a small herd still ranges across its fields), the park takes its name from Phoenix House, the original residence of the British viceroys, whose title derived from the Irish *fionn uisce* ("clear water"). These days, the park's sole residents are the Irish president and the US Ambassador. The park is bisected by Chesterfield Avenue and a few side roads open to traffic, but most of it is open space, sparsely dotted with trees, shrubs and wild flowers, with a few areas of woodland and hawthorn. It's an ideal place to escape the city's bustle, a popular venue for sports, and offers plenty of spots for a picnic.

By the park's Parkgate Street entrance lies the **People's Garden**, a pleasant area of formal flowerbeds and hedges. The nearby **Wellington Monument** took some 44 years to complete before it was finally unveiled in 1861. The obelisk – at some 60m – is the tallest of its kind in the British Isles – features bas-reliefs, using bronze from cannons captured at Waterloo, which depict scenes from the successful military campaigns of the "Iron Duke". West from here, alongside Military Road, is the derelict **Magazine Fort**, built on the site originally occupied by Phoenix House. The only way to visit the fort is on a guided tour every Sunday between April and September, with tickets (free) available on the day from the Visitor Centre (see page 88) on a first come first served basis. Otherwise, it's an easy climb up the hill to take a trip around its walls and to take in some fine views.

Dublin Zoo

Off Chesterfield Ave • Oct–Feb closes at dusk; last admission 1hr before closing • Charge • http://dublinzoo.ie

Heading northwest from the People's Garden along Chesterfield Avenue will bring you to **Dublin Zoo**, spread over sixty acres, which focuses today on raising species threatened by extinction, such as Asian elephants, Amur tigers and waldrapp ibis. The zoo is themed around different habitats, among them the African Savannah, which has giraffes, hippos and southern white rhinos, the Orangutan Forest, Wolves in the Woods, and the Gorilla Rainforest, home to a charismatic troop of western lowland gorillas. There is also a city farm for younger children.

Áras an Uachtaráin

Off Chesterfield Ave, north of the zoo • Sat 10am–3.30pm • Free guided tours; tickets from Phoenix Park Visitor Centre only on the day • http://president.ie

The impressive Palladian **Áras an Uachtaráin**, pronounced "arus an ucterawn", was the home of Britain's viceroys from the 1780s until Ireland's independence, and since 1938 it has been the official residence of the President of Ireland. Tours start from the Phoenix Park Visitor Centre (minibus transport provided) and whisk you through a section of the grandly decorated house, including the State Reception Rooms and the Presidential Office.

Phoenix Monument and Ashtown Castle

At the park's centre on Chesterfield Avenue rises the **Phoenix Monument**, dating from 1747, which more resembles an eagle or falcon than the phoenix it supposedly represents. To its southwest, by the US Ambassador's Residence, is the 30m-high stainless-steel **Papal Cross**, bearing testament to the spot where the late Pope John Paul II celebrated Mass in September 1979 before a congregation of around 1.25 million people.

Northwest of the Monument is the **Phoenix Park Visitor Centre** (daily 9.30am–6pm, Jan–April closed Mon & Tues; free), which recounts the history of the park through the ages, focusing on its flora and fauna. Adjacent is **Ashtown Castle**, an early seventeenth-century tower house whose existence was only uncovered when the former residence of the Papal Nuncio, which had been constructed around it, was demolished in 1978. Tickets for tours of the castle (Mon–Fri 5 daily; free) can be obtained from the visitor centre.

Farmleigh

White's Rd • Charge • http://farmleigh.ie • Take the #37 bus from either Suffolk St or the Quays and get off at the Castleknock Gate of Phoenix Park; upon entering the park take the path to your right, and you'll reach Farmleigh in 15min

White's Gate on the park's northwestern fringe provides access to one of the most splendid buildings in the city, **Farmleigh**. Constructed in 1752 for the Trench family, the building was later purchased by Edward Cecil Guinness, the first Earl of Iveagh, as a rustic residence offering easy access to his brewery. Extensions were made in the 1880s, and the Guinness family remained in residence until 1992. Farmleigh was then purchased by the Irish government for use as a state guesthouse (which means tours may not be available if a visiting delegation is in residence). Tours begin in the **dining room**, whose unusual decorations include statues of Bacchus either side of the fireplace and a clock inlaid in its centre. The hall features Waterford-crystal chandeliers and a pair of debtors' chairs in which the paupers' legs would be trapped until they agreed to pay their debts, while the **library** contains four thousand items on loan from the Iveagh Collection, including a first edition of *Ulysses* and books dating back to the twelfth century. The **Blue Room**, which is dedicated to Ireland's Nobel Prize winners, has another strange fireplace – this one situated below a window. However, the real treat is the **ballroom** whose Irish oak floor was constructed of wood originally intended for Guinness barrels; the doors here, fringed with delicate linen portières, lead you out to a massive, plant-stocked conservatory. Behind the house there's a tearoom in the stable block and an extremely pleasant walled garden.

Farmleigh hosts a number of free **cultural events** from July to September, ranging from ballet and brass bands in the gardens to indoor concerts in the ballroom; tickets are limited and only available via the house's website.

The Guinness Storehouse

St James's Gate • Charge • http://guinness-storehouse.com • Bus #123 (from O'Connell St or Dame St) stops outside the brewery

South of the Liffey, much of James Street, west of the old city, is centred around the colossal complex of the **Guinness Brewery**. Founded by Arthur Guinness in 1759, the Guinness Brewery initially manufactured ale, but in the 1770s started making porter, a drink so named because of its popularity with the porters of London's markets.

1

Arthur's new brew, whose distinctive black colouring derived from the addition of roasted barley to the brewing process, found such favour that by 1796 it was being exported to London, and three years later ale production ceased altogether. From that point, Guinness and his successors never looked back and, at its peak in the middle of the twentieth century, their brewery produced some 2,500,000 pints of their now eponymous product a day.

Although it is possible to experience the brewery itself on a high-end tour, most people content themselves with a visit to the seven-storey **Guinness Storehouse**, signposted from Crane Street, a high-tech temple to the black stuff. Its self-guided tour kicks off with the brewing process – a whirl of water (not from the Liffey, despite the myth) and a reek of barley, hops and malt – before progressing to the storage and transportation areas. A huge barrel dominates the section on the lost art of coopering, which faded from existence in the early 1960s when steel casks became the fashion; at the peak of barrel production, in the 1920s and 20s, over a thousand were (excuse the pun) rolled out every week. The remainder of the tour consists of an array of marketing memorabilia, including a section on the company's famous, cutting-edge adverts, perhaps the most memorable of which was the *Surfer*, which saw horses emerging from the waves to a thumping soundtrack by Leftfield. To this end there's also a gallery on John Gilroy, an esteemed painter who designed many of the company's advertisements. Right at the top of the tower is the *Gravity Bar*, where you can savour your complimentary pint of perhaps the best Guinness in Dublin while absorbing the superb panorama of the city and the countryside beyond.

The Irish Museum of Modern Art

Royal Hospital, Military Rd, Kilmainham • guided tours of the exhibitions Wed, Sat & Sun 2.30pm • Entry and tours free • http://imma.ie • Take the Luas Red Line to Heuston Station, which is a 5min walk from the museum; alternatively, the #90 bus goes frequently to Heuston Station from Connolly Station

Based on Les Invalides in Paris, the **Royal Hospital** in Kilmainham was built between 1680 and 1684 to house war pensioners. Part of the building now houses the **Irish Museum of Modern Art** (IMMA), which has a justifiable reputation for its imaginative exhibitions, covering selections from both its own permanent collection of 3500 works and loaned pieces. All shows are temporary and range from retrospectives of major international artists to new works by modern Irish painters and sculptors. Some of IMMA's most exciting exhibitions draw upon the museum's Outsider Art collection – works, largely paintings, by unschooled artists that explore the psyche – as well as the Madden Arnholz collection of Old Master prints, drawing upon the works of Goya, Rembrandt and Hogarth. The permanent "Old Man's House" exhibition recounts the history of the Royal Hospital site, from its days as an ancient burial ground and Viking settlement to the present day.

Kilmainham Gaol

Inchicore Rd, Kilmainham • guided tours (which must be pre-booked) every 45min until 1hr 15min before closing • charge; Heritage Card • http://kilmainhamgaolmuseum.ie • Buses #69 and #79 from Aston Quay, and #13 and #40 from either O'Connell St or College Green all stop at or near Kilmainham Gaol; ask the bus driver to let you off at the nearest stop

Beside **Bully's Acre**, one of the city's oldest cemeteries, lies **Kilmainham Gaol**, which holds an iconic position in the history of Ireland's struggle for independence and came to symbolize both Irish political martyrdom and British oppression. Opened in 1796, it became the place of incarceration for captured revolutionaries, including the leaders of the 1916 Easter Rising, who were also executed here. Even after the War of Independence, Republicans continued to be imprisoned here, though it closed in July 1924 after the release of its last inmate, Éamon de Valera – later to become Ireland's Taoiseach and president. Visits are by **guided tour** only and provide a chilling

1

impression of the prisoners' living conditions and spartan regime. Its single cells ensured that they were forced into solitary contemplation, and since the building was constructed on top of limestone, their health was often sorely affected by damp and severe cold in winter. Before embarking on the tour, it's well worth visiting the **exhibition galleries**. The ground-floor display includes a mock-up of a cell and an early mug-shot camera, and there's a small side gallery showing paintings by Civil War internees and a huge self-portrait of Constance Gore-Booth (see page 393), who was better known as the Countess Markiewicz, posing as the Good Shepherd. The upstairs gallery provides an enthralling account of the struggle for independence with numerous mementos, old cinematic footage of Michael Collins and the letter ordering the release of Charles Stewart Parnell.

The northern suburbs

You'll want fine weather for a trip north to the beautiful **Botanic Gardens** and the adjacent **Glasnevin Cemetery**, which has been the final resting place for major figures in Irish history since 1832. To the east lie **Croke Park**, a major sports arena and home to the innovative **GAA Museum**, the exquisite Georgian **Casino at Marino** and, at the end of the DART line, **Howth**, an attractive seaside village with a fine **cliff walk** (see page 92).

The National Botanic Gardens

Botanic Rd; entrance on Glasnevin Hill, off Botanic Rd • guided tours Sun noon & 2.30pm • Entry and tours free • http://botanicgardens.ie • From the centre, catch bus #13 from Merrion Square or O'Connell St, or #19 from South Great George's St or O'Connell St

The **National Botanic Gardens** on the south bank of the River Tolka in Glasnevin are a great place to wander on a fine day, although their magnificent Victorian wrought-iron glasshouses offer diversion and shelter whatever the weather. Laid out between 1795 and 1825 with a grant from the Irish parliament, the gardens were, in 1844, the first in the world to germinate orchids from seed successfully, and, in August of the following year, the first to notice the potato blight that brought on the Great Famine. Nowadays, a total of around twenty thousand species and cultivated varieties flourish here, including an internationally important collection of cycads, primitive fern-like trees. Highlights include the rose garden, collections of heather and rhododendrons, the Chinese shrubbery and the arboretum.

Glasnevin Cemetery

Finglas Rd (with pedestrian entrance through the original Prospect Square Gate) • guided tours (1hr 30min) daily 11.30am & 2.30pm • Charge • http://dctrust.ie • Served by buses #40 and #40A/B/C from Parnell St

Founded as a burial place for Catholics by the nationalist political leader Daniel O'Connell in 1832, **Glasnevin Cemetery** is now the national cemetery, open to all denominations and groaning with Celtic crosses, harps and other patriotic emblems marking the graves of more than 1.5 million people. You can do a self-guided tour (with audio) but it's well worth timing your visit to coincide with one of the fascinating guided **tours**, which includes access to the renovated crypt of O'Connell, who is also commemorated near the entrance by a 50m-high round **tower**; having survived a Loyalist bomb in 1971, the newly renovated tower has an exhibition recalling O'Connell's life, but in any case is well worth the 222-step climb to the top for terrific views across the cemetery grounds. In addition, a small **museum** has interactive exhibits telling the story of hundreds of the most famous people buried in the cemetery – many of them gathered around the tower.

Among them you'll find the graves of Countess Markiewicz (see page 393); Éamon de Valera, prime minister, president and architect of modern Ireland, and his old rival Michael Collins, the most charismatic leader of the successful independence struggle;

while from the arts, there's Gerard Manley Hopkins's unmarked grave in the Jesuit plot (see page 90); W.B. Yeats's muse Maud Gonne MacBride; writer, drinker and Republican Brendan Behan; and Alfred Chester Beatty (see page 75). To the right of the tower is the Republican plot, with a memorial to hunger strikers, from Thomas Ashe who died in 1917 to Bobby Sands in 1981, and in front of the tower lie the recent graves of 18-year-old Kevin Barry and eight other Volunteers who were hanged by the British during the War of Independence; originally buried in Mountjoy Prison, their bodies were moved here with the full honours of a state funeral in October 2001. For refreshment after your visit, exit via the pedestrian gate at Prospect Square beside *Kavanagh's (*aka *The Gravediggers*), a particularly atmospheric old pub (see page 105).

Croke Park and the GAA Museum

Cusack Stand, St Joseph's Avenue • **GAA Museum** charge • **Stadium tour** 3–8 daily, see website for details; note there are no tours on match days • charge includes entry to the museum • **Skyline tour** 2–6 daily, see website for details • charge includes entrance to the museum • http://crokepark.ie • Croke Park is served by numerous bus routes: from the city centre, the #1, #11, #13, #16, #33, #41 and #44 all stop within a 5min walk of the stadium; alternatively, it's a 15min walk from Connelly train station

Home of the **Gaelic Athletic Association** (GAA), **Croke Park** is a magnificent, much redeveloped and now very modern stadium whose capacity of 82,000-plus puts it among the largest in Europe. Situated under the Cusack Stand is one of Dublin's finest museums, the **GAA Museum**, whose creatively designed exhibits provide an enthralling account of not only the sports of hurling and Gaelic football, but also lesser-known games such as camogie (the women's version of hurling) and handball. Historical and political contexts are explored in a thoroughly engaging manner – since its foundation in 1884 the GAA has always been irrevocably linked with Irish Nationalism. Thus the museum does not shirk from recounting key politically sensitive events such as the first Bloody Sunday, when British troops fired on the crowd attending a match in 1920, killing twelve people in the process. On a lighter note, upstairs you can have a go at whacking a hurling ball or test your balance and reaction time via various simulations.

Taking the **stadium tour** is highly recommended, not just to view this remarkable arena first hand, but to learn more about key events in its history – including, not least, the momentous decision in 2005 to suspend the GAA's constitution to allow professional Rugby Union and Association Football international matches to take place in the stadium. Previously, only previously only games of Irish origin, played by amateurs, could be staged at what is now called the Aviva Stadium (formerly called Lansdowne Road). Visitors with no aversion to heights can take a skyline tour around a walkway 44m above the ground, for panoramic views of the city and its key landmarks.

Malahide Castle and Gardens

Back Rd, Malahide • Can be visited by guided tour only (45min) 9.30am, 12.30pm, 2.30pm & 4.30pm • Castle charge includes gardens and butterfly house; gardens and butterfly house charge • http://malahidecastleandgardens.ie • Dart trains get here in 30min from the city centre (check http://irishrail.ie for times), or take bus #32 or #42 (45min) from Connolly Station

Set in 250 acres of parkland in a pretty seaside town, **Malahide Castle** was home to the Talbot family for more than eight hundred years, until the last surviving member of the family died in 1973. The core building dates from 1185, making it one of the oldest castles in Ireland. Later additions such as the circular corner turrets, built after a fire in 1782, give it a fairy-tale appearance.

Guided **tours** take in the castle's principal rooms – the Great Hall and Oak Room are the most impressive – featuring an extensive collection of eighteenth-century furniture and Irish artworks – while an interactive exhibition in the visitor centre explores the fascinating history of the Talbot Family. The ornamental walled **gardens**, covering about 22 acres, are also worth exploring, better still on a guided tour which takes place every Thursday at 11am; they were largely created by the last Talbot to live in the

THE HOWTH CLIFF WALK

Clinging to the slopes of a rocky peninsula and overlooking an animated fishing harbour, the village of **Howth** (rhymes with "both"), at the end of the DART line, is a good place to escape the rigours of the city centre when the weather is good, with some appealing quayside restaurants and pubs. By far the best way to appreciate the location is to do the **Cliff Walk** around the peninsula, taking in great views south over the city to the Wicklow Mountains and north to the Boyne Valley. The footpath runs for some 8km clockwise from the village round to the west-facing side of the peninsula, followed by a 3km walk by the sea along Strand Road and Greenfield Road to Sutton DART station; allow at least three hours in total. (Bus #31B, serving Sutton and Eden Quay in the city centre in one direction, Howth village or The Summit in the other, runs roughly parallel but well above the path for much of the way, along Carrickbrack Road, so you can bail out of the walk if you feel like it.)

You first head east out of Howth village along Balscadden Road to the **Nose of Howth**, before the path turns south, crossing the slopes above the cliffs, which are covered in colourful gorse and bell heather in season; for refreshment on this stretch, the area known as **The Summit**, just inland of the path, has a pub and a café. The southeast point is marked by the **Baily Lighthouse**, which, until March 1997, was the last manned lighthouse on Ireland's coastline. The path along the south-facing coast of the peninsula is the most spectacular part of the walk, providing close-up views of cliffs, secluded beaches and rocky islands.

castle, Lord Milo Talbot, an enthusiastic plant collector who is also believed to have been a Soviet spy. The gardens are also home to the Republic's only **butterfly house**, where you can have fun trying to identify more than twenty colourful species.

South Dublin coast

A ride on a DART train south along the coast, as well as giving access to **Sandycove**'s James Joyce Museum, and the charming historic neighbourhood of **Dalkey**, is a scenic attraction in itself, displaying the great sweep of Dublin Bay before dramatically skirting **Dalkey and Killiney hills** and arrowing off towards Bray and Greystones (see page 117).

The James Joyce Tower and Museum

Sandycove Point • Free • http://joycetower.ie • To get here, catch the DART to Sandycove & Glasthule station, from where it's a 10min walk down Islington Ave then east along the seafront

The diverting **James Joyce Museum** in Sandycove is housed inside an impressive **Martello tower**, one of fifteen such towers erected along the coast between Dublin and Bray in 1804–06 against the threat of invasion by Napoleon. Built with 2.5m-thick granite circular walls and an armoured door 4m off the ground as the only entrance, the towers never fired a shot. Joyce stayed here for just a week, in September 1904, a month before he left the country for Italy with Nora Barnacle. At the time, his host, the writer and wit Oliver St John Gogarty, was renting the tower from the War Office for £8 a year as digs during his medical studies. Joyce immortalized the tower as the setting for the opening chapter of his masterpiece, *Ulysses* – and Gogarty as "stately, plump Buck Mulligan" – and it's now the focus for readings and celebrations every year on June 16, Bloomsday (see page 84).

Opened in 1962 by Sylvia Beach, who first published *Ulysses* in Paris in 1922, the museum displays Joyce's guitar, waistcoat and walking stick, as well as one of two official death masks (the other is in Zurich where he died in 1941). There are also copious letters, photos, and rare and first editions, notably one of *Ulysses* beautifully illustrated by Matisse. On the first floor, Gogarty's living quarters in the former guardroom have been re-created as Joyce described them, and you can climb up to the gun platform on the roof for panoramic views of Dublin Bay.

Dalkey

Around the coast from Sandycove, **Dalkey** (pronounced "Dawky") is a pretty seaside - set against the tree-clad slopes of Dalkey Hill. In medieval times, it prospered as a fortified settlement and the main port of Dublin, until the dredging of the River Liffey in the sixteenth century took away its business. Nowadays, with the building of the railway, Dalkey's characterful old houses and villas are much sought-after by well-to-do commuters, as well as celebrities seeking privacy.

Dalkey Castle and Heritage Centre

Castle St • Living History theatre tours every 30min • charge • http://dalkeycastle.com

Dalkey's main street boasts two fortified warehouses from the town's medieval heyday. Goat Castle – now known as **Dalkey Castle** – across the road from Archibold's Castle, serves as an attractive and well-designed **Heritage Centre**. The detailed exhibition, with panels written by playwright and local resident Hugh Leonard, covers the town's history, especially its transport systems and literary associations, the latter including an exhibit on Joyce, who set the second chapter of *Ulysses* in Dalkey. The castle interior is impressive in itself, and fine views are to be had from the battlements. The entry price includes Living History theatre tours in which suitably attired actors recount the lives and times of a selection of Dalkey's medieval residents.

The Heritage Centre regularly organizes interesting guided **historical walks** in the town (June–Aug Wed & Fri at noon; €7), and can also arrange guided literary tours (for groups of six or more) to settings in the work of James Joyce, George Bernard Shaw, Flann O'Brien, Hugh Leonard and Maeve Binchy. The Centre also participates in Bloomsday (see page 84), re-enacting the Dalkey schoolroom scene in *Ulysses* and staging a special Joycean evening of entertainment.

Dalkey Island

If you want to take a trip out to tiny **Dalkey Island**, some 300m offshore, then your best bet is to pay a visit to Coliemore Harbour, down Coliemore Road from the southern end of the town, and negotiate a trip with one of the local fishermen (high

---

DALKEY AND KILLINEY HILLS

A walk up adjoining **Dalkey and Killiney hills**, before descending to Killiney DART station, offers panoramic views of the city and its environs, and can all be done in an hour and a half from Dalkey DART station if you walk at a moderate pace. From Dalkey, head southeast on Sorrento Road, and then either take the easier route to the right up Knocknacree and Torca roads, or continue along cliffside Vico Road, from where steps and a path ascend steeply. On Torca Road, Shaw fans might want to track down privately owned **Torca Cottage**, where George Bernard Shaw lived for several years as a boy and where he occasionally returned to write in later years. On the way to Dalkey Hill's summit, with its crenellated former telegraph station and fine views over Dublin Bay, you'll pass Dalkey quarry, which provided the granite blocks for the massive piers of Dún Laoghaire harbour below.

From here, follow the partly wooded ridge up to Killiney Hill, where a stone obelisk, built to provide work during the severe winter of 1741, enjoys even more glorious views, north to Howth and south to Killiney Bay and the Wicklow Mountains. From the obelisk, you can quickly descend to the park gate on Killiney Hill Road; from here it's a fifteen-minute walk down Victoria Road and Vico Road through the leafy and exclusive borough of Killiney, to the DART station by the beach.

1

season only). Once a Viking base, the island features the ruins of a seventh-century church, a Martello tower and gun battery from Napoleonic times, a herd of semi-wild goats, and views of seals and a variety of seabird species.

ARRIVAL AND DEPARTURE   DUBLIN

Dublin's train and bus stations are centrally located while efficient local transport makes the city centre easily accessible from the airport and ferry terminals.

BY PLANE

DUBLIN AIRPORT
The airport (http://dublinairport.com) is 11km north of the centre and has all the facilities you'd expect of a major international airport, including a number of car rental outlets in both terminals.

GETTING TO THE CENTRE
Buses to the centre depart from outside the arrivals exit; the journey takes 30min–1hr depending upon the service and time of day.

By Express bus The most direct buses are the Dublin Express bus #782 (every 15min daily 3am–12.30am; €8 single, €12 return), which runs to Heuston railway station and Custom House Quay (for O'Connell station); and #784 (every 30min daily 5.30am–11pm; same prices), which runs to Trinity College via the 3Arena..

By city bus The slower but cheaper option (€3.30) is to take one of the regular Dublin Bus services such as the #16 to O'Connell St and College Green (every 15min Mon–Sat 6am–11.30pm, Sun 8am–10.40pm), or #41 to Abbey St Lower, just off O'Connell St (every 20–30min Mon–Sat 4am–11.50pm, every 30min Sun 4am–11.35pm).

By Aircoach Aircoach (http://aircoach.ie) operates three services: bus #700 from Dublin Airport to Stillorgan and Leopardstown via the city centre (every 30–60min daily 24hr); bus #702 to Greystones via Ballsbridge (every 2hr); and bus #703 to Dalkey via Sandymount and Dún Laoghaire (every 2hr)..

By taxi The taxi rank is outside the arrivals exit; a metered cab to the centre should cost between €25–30.

BY TRAIN
Information on train services and timetables is available on http://irishrail.ie. Services listed are for Mon–Sat; extra services may run on Mon and/or Fri, but fewer on Sun.

Dublin Connolly Services from Belfast, Sligo and Rosslare terminate at Connolly Station, a 15min walk east of O'Connell St and connected to the centre by regular buses and LUAS trams – it's also on the DART line.

Destinations Belfast (8 daily; 2hr 10min); Boyle (8 daily; 2hr 30min); Carrick-on-Shannon (8 daily; 2hr 10min); Drogheda (every 30min; 30min–1hr); Enniscorthy (5 daily; 2hr–2hr 15min); Newry (8 daily; 1hr 15min); Rosslare Harbour (Rosslare Europort; 4 daily; 3hr); Sligo (8 daily; 3hr 5min); Wexford (5 daily; 2hr 35min); Wicklow (5 daily; 1hr 10min).

Dublin Heuston Heuston Station, 3km west of the centre, serves trains from Cork, Galway, Kerry, Kilkenny, Limerick, Mayo and Waterford, and is connected to the centre by LUAS and buses #90 and #92. Luggage can be left at the nearby Tipperary House B&B (01 679 5317; €6/24hr).

Destinations Athlone (14 daily; 1hr 35min); Castlebar (5 daily; 3hr 10min–3hr 40min); Cork (hourly; 2hr 50min); Galway (10 daily; 2hr 40min); Kildare (every 40min–1hr; 40min); Kilkenny (6 daily; 1hr 45min); Killarney (7 daily, most with a change at Mallow; 3hr 30min); Limerick (hourly, most with a change at Limerick Junction; 2hr 15min–2hr 30min); Tralee (7 daily, most with a change at Mallow; 4hr); Waterford (8 daily; 2hr 25min); Westport (6 daily; 3hr 20min–4hr).

Tara Street and Pearse Two other southside stations, Tara Street and Pearse, serve DART and suburban railways. Note that some commuter trains from Co. Meath terminate at the Docklands Station, some 3km east of the centre.

BY BUS
Note that most express services to Northern Ireland and Counties Donegal and Sligo also call at Dublin Airport. Additionally, the Wexford/Rosslare Harbour service begins at the airport, picking up at Busáras en route.

Busáras Dublin's central bus station is on Store St behind the Custom House, some 10min walk east of O'Connell St. It serves Bus Éireann express coaches from all parts of Ireland (North and South) as well as the Airlink service and coaches from Britain. City buses run into the centre along Talbot St, a block to the north, while there are LUAS Red Line (see page 95) stops outside the bus station's northern exit or to the west on Abbey St Lower. Alternatively, a taxi can usually be hailed on Beresford Place just south of Busáras. There are left-luggage lockers in the station's basement (€6–10 depending on size).

Destinations Athlone (hourly; 2hr 5min); Belfast (20 daily; 2hr 30min–2hr 55min); Boyle (5–7 daily; 3hr–3hr 20min); Cahir (6 daily; 3hr 5min); Carrick-on-Shannon (5–7 daily; 2hr 45min–3hr); Carrick-on-Suir (6 daily; 3hr); Cashel (6 daily; 2hr 50min); Cavan (10–11 daily; 1hr 50min–2hr 10min); Cork (6 daily; 4hr 25min); Derry (11 daily; 4hr); Donegal town (11 daily; 3hr 45min); Drogheda (most services operate out of the Talbot St depot, but buses after 9pm leave from Búsaras; hourly; 1hr 25min); Enniscorthy (hourly; 2hr 25min); Enniskillen (11 daily; 2hr 20min); Galway (15 daily; 3hr 30min); Kildare (mostly from Connolly LUAS stop; 13–15 daily; 1hr 30min); Kilkenny (7 daily; 2hr–2hr

30min); Killarney (5 daily, change at Limerick; 6hr 10min); Limerick (hourly; 3hr 40min); Letterkenny (9–10 daily; 4hr); Monaghan (20–21 daily; 1hr 55min); Newry (hourly; 1hr 35min); Omagh (19–21 daily; 2hr 55min); Rosslare Harbour (18 daily; 3hr 20min); Sligo (7 daily; 3hr 35min–4hr); Tralee (6 daily, change at Limerick; 6hr 10min); Waterford (13 daily; 3hr–3hr 30min); Westport (4 daily; 5hr–5hr 30min); Wexford (hourly; 2hr 50min); Wicklow (from Busáras or George's Quay; every 30min–1hr; 1hr–1hr 30min).

GETTING AROUND

The best way to get to know Dublin is **on foot**; however, to visit the city's outlying attractions you'll need to make use of the efficient and comprehensive **public transport** network. The easiest (and cheapest) way to pay for journeys is with a pre-paid **Leap Card** (see page 97), which covers all types of public transport in the city.

BY BUS

Dublin Bus (http://dublinbus.ie) operates a network of more than a hundred routes covering just about everywhere in the city and extending far beyond its boundaries into Dublin County, as well as to Kildare, Meath and Wicklow. **Information** Most of its bus stops display printed timetables and a basic route map, while many now have digital displays with real-time information on when the next bus is due to arrive. See http://dublinbus.ie for more ticket and route details, or download the excellent Dublin Bus app, which allows you to plan your route and search timetables by address. All the info you need, including timetables and maps are available from the company's offices at 59 O'Connell St Upper (Mon–Fri 9am–5.30pm).
Fares All bus fares are exact-change only, therefore only coins are accepted; regular ticket prices range from €1.70 for a short ride to €2.60 for the longest journeys within the suburban area.
Timetables Most services operate around 6.30am–11.30pm on weekdays, starting later and finishing earlier on Sundays. Nitelink buses run through the small hours on thirteen routes (Sat & Sun midnight–4am; every 30min–1hr; €3); these buses run from D'Olier St and Westmoreland St, and have the suffix "N" (e.g. 46N).

BY TRAM

LUAS (http://luas.ie) – the Irish for "speed" – currently operates two overground tramway routes, which are much quicker than buses and avoid traffic congestion. Trams run every 5–15min (Mon–Fri 5.30am–12.30am, Sat 6.30am–12.30am, Sun 7am–11.30pm).
Fares Singles cost €1.70–2.60 and returns €3–4.40, though buying a Leap Card (see page 97) is a cheaper option. Tickets can be bought from machines at the tramway stops, and are not available on the trams – these should be validated on the platforms.

BY FERRY

Dublin Port All services arrive at Dublin Port, 3km east of the centre. Dublin Bus service #53 runs from Talbot St (near Busáras station) to the port (hourly; €3 single), while Nolan's Coaches (http://nolanscoaches.ie) operate a bus transfer service to the port (€3 single), departing from George's Quay..
Ferry companies Irish Ferries, http://irishferries.com; P & O, http://poferries.com; Stena Line, http://stenaline.ie.

The Green Line This north–south line commences at Broombridge, then heads through the city centre and down to the southeastern suburbs of and Brides Glen.
The Red Line This east–west line runs from The Point in Docklands, joining a small branch from Connolly Station at Busáras, before heading along Abbey St to Collins Barracks and crossing the river at Heuston Station then heading southwest to the suburbs of Tallaght and Saggart.

BY TRAIN

DART services The trains of the Dublin Area Rapid Transit system or DART (every 10min Mon–Sat 6.20am–midnight, Sun 9.20am–11.40pm; http://irishrail.ie) link Howth and Malahide to the north of the city with Bray and Greystones to the south via places such as Blackrock, Dún Laoghaire and Dalkey. It's certainly the quickest option for visiting some of the outlying attractions. Single fares cost €2.65–5, though again, buying a Leap Card (see page 97) reduces the cost.
Iarnród Éireann services The suburban train services operated by Iarnród Éireann (http://irishrail.ie) utilize the same tracks as the DART, but stop at fewer stations (Connolly, Tara St and Pearse in the centre, the new Docklands station just east of the centre, Blackrock, Dún Laoghaire and Bray to the south and Howth Junction to the north). The Northern Commuter line from Pearse Station via Tara St and Connolly is the quickest means of making day-trips to Malahide and to Drogheda for Brú na Boinne.

BY TAXI

Dublin's taxis vary in size from saloon cars to people carriers; they all have an illuminated box on the roof displaying the driver's taxi licence number. The basic rate is currently €4 for the initial charge (ie just getting into the taxi), then around €1.35/km thereafter, though rates are higher between 8pm and 8am Mon–Sat and all day Sun and public holidays. There are also extra charges for additional passengers, usually €1 each.
Taxi ranks Ranks include those at the northwest corner of St Stephen's Green, next to the Bank of Ireland on College Green, outside the *Westin Hotel* on Westmoreland St, in front of the *Gresham Hotel* on O'Connell St or on the western branch of Parnell St.
Companies and apps Smartphone users can download

1

the excellent Free Now app (free), which allows you to order an approved taxi driver to collect you from your current location within minutes. Alternatively, Lynk Taxis (01 820 2020) is a reliable option. Most companies can supply a wheelchair-accessible taxi if booked an hour or more in advance.

BY CAR

Note that during Dublin's "rush-hour" period (weekdays 7–10am and 4–7pm) traffic is very congested; some areas, such as The Quays and Dame St, are best avoided at all times.

Car rental Rental companies include Avis (airport and 39 Old Kilmainham Rd, http://avis.ie); Budget (airport and 151 Drumcondra Rd http://budget.ie); Hertz (airport and 151 South Circular Rd http://hertz.ie); Irish Car Rentals (airport and Park Lane, Spencer Dock http://irishcarrentals.com).

Parking A good southside option is the Royal College of Surgeons multi-storey off the west side of St Stephen's Green (open 24hr, €4/hr or €10 overnight). On-street spaces are hard to find, but Merrion Square and Fitzwilliam Square are often good bets.

BY BIKE

Dublinbikes (http://dublinbikes.ie) offers a single-day (€3.5) and three-day ticket (€5; credit/debit card required) and can be purchased from fourteen of the city's fifty bike stations, of which the most central are at St Stephen's Green East and West, Merrion Square West, Dame St, High St, the Custom House, Jervis St and Parnell Square North. You're provided with a personal ID number and a PIN of your own choosing and can then use your ticket to unlock a bike from the stands. Bikes are available to collect between 5am and 12.30am. The first 30min of any ride are free (as long as the bike is returned to a stand within that period); after that it's €0.50/1hr, rising to €6.50/4hr. Bikes come with automatic lights and a lock, but helmets are not provided. Note that €150 will be debited from your card if the bike is stolen or not returned within 24hr. Visitors can also rent a range of bikes, including tandems and e-bikes, from Phoenix Park Bikes, just inside the Parkgate St entrance to Phoenix Park (http://phoenixparkbikes.com; €7/1hr, €13/3hr, €20/day), which does include a helmet. Biking.ie (http://biking.ie) rents good-quality mountain bikes (Ticknock; €35/day), as well as offering mountain-biking lessons and tours of Dublin and Wicklow.

INFORMATION AND TOURIST PASSES

Tourist Information The main tourist office (Mon–Sat 9am–5pm; http://visitdublin.com) is on Barnardo Square, 3 Palace St, but, surprisingly, for such a tourist-oriented city, it's pretty useless all things told. Discover Ireland has an office at 14 O'Connell St Upper (Mon–Sat 9am–5pm).

Listings information The national daily *Irish Times* and the local daily *Evening Herald* are useful sources of information, notably for cinema and theatre listings, and the former also produces a weekly Friday listings supplement, *The Ticket*. Free listings magazines include *Totally Dublin* (http://totallydublin.ie), while listings websites http://dublintown.ie and http://entertainment. ie are also useful. The O'Connell St Lower branch of Eason's stocks just about every magazine published in Ireland, along with all Irish and UK daily and Sunday newspapers.

Dublin Pass Available at either if the tourist information centres or online at http://dublinpass.ie, the Dublin City Pass provides free entry to over thirty of Dublin's top visitor attractions, as well as a Hop on Hop off bus tour and special offers on theatre tickets, restaurants and shops. It is available for one, two, three, four or five days, costing between €74 and €149 for an adult and between €44 and €74 for a child (aged 5–15). It's well worth checking just how many attractions you'll be able to visit when judging whether this represents a good deal.

Heritage Card A Heritage Card (€40 adult, €90 family) gives free entry to attractions across the city – and the whole of the Republic (see page 47) – run by the Heritage Service (http://heritageireland.ie). Dublin attractions include: Áras an Uachtaráin, the Casino at Marino, Farmleigh, Kilmainham Gaol, Dublin Castle, National Botanic Gardens, Phoenix Park Visitor Centre, Royal Hospital Kilmainham, St Audoen's, St Stephen's Green and Croppy's Acre. Cards are available from Heritage Service sites or tourist offices, and are valid for one year.

TOURS

One of the easiest ways of seeing Dublin's attractions is a guided **city tour**, and there are plenty available – whether by open-top bus, on foot, along the river, or on a land and water tour. Adult prices are provided below, though most tour operators offer discounts for children, students and senior citizens.

OPEN-TOP BUS TOURS

If time is short a convenient way of seeing the sights is to take a ride on a hop-on-and-off open-top bus tour. Commentary is provided either by the driver (some of whom also readily break into fitting songs), an on-board guide or a pre-recorded tape. All tickets offer a range of discounts to the city's attractions. All the tours follow roughly the same route, covering Parnell Square, Trinity College, St Stephen's Green, Dublin Castle, the cathedrals, the Guinness Storehouse, Kilmainham, Phoenix Park and Collins Barracks; some tours go to Glasnevin Cemetery. The full circular tour lasts around 1hr 30min, depending on traffic congestion, and tickets are valid for 24hr from the time of first use.

TRAVEL PASSES

To save the hassle of buying individual tickets for each journey, (for which you must have the exact change) the easiest solution is a pre-paid **Leap Card** (http://leapcard.ie), available for one day (€8), three days (€16) or seven days (€32). Cards are valid for travel on all Dublin Bus services (including Airlink but excluding Nitelink), LUAS and DART services within the short-hop zone (the entire DART network and suburban rail services as far as Balbriggan to the north, Maynooth and Celbridge to the west and Kilcoole to the south), and can be purchased in most newsagents. The electronic card must be validated at the beginning and end of your journey by touching it against the machines on board the bus or at LUAS and DART stations, until you hear the tone.

A bewildering range of **travel passes** is available from the Dublin Bus office (see page 95), newsagents and other shops displaying the Dublin Bus sign, and from DART and suburban railway stations. A three-day Freedom Ticket (€49) includes travel to and from the airport on city services #16 and #41 (so is best bought at the airport's travel information desk), all Dublin bus services (except Nitelink), the company's 48hr hop-on-and-off city tour (see page 96) and all DART and LUAS services.

One-day passes for the LUAS service (see page 95) cost €5.80 (valid in all zones), and a seven-day pass costs €13.20-22 depending upon the zones. A combined one-day bus and LUAS pass is €10.

The price of most DART railway/suburban rail passes depends on the starting and finishing points of your journey. A one-day pass is €12.15 for adults or €20 for a family of two adults and two children.

Dublin Bus http://dodublin.ie. Dublin bus offer hop-on-hop-off tours which leave from outside the main Dublin Bus office at 59 O'Connell St (€32/24hr, €37/48hr daily every 20–30min 9am–7pm). Tickets can be purchased online, from the Dublin Bus office (see page 95), from the driver and from tourist information centres. The company also operates a Ghostbus Tour (daily 7pm & 9.30pm; €35; not suitable for under-14s; 2hr) visiting the city's spookier spots.

Big Bus Dublin http://bigbustours.com. This company also operates a hop-on-hop-off City Sightseeing Tour (daily every 20–30min 9am–5pm; €35/24hr, €44/48hr), departing from 13 Upper O'Connell St. Tickets can be purchased online or from any of the stops and some hotels.

RIVER CRUISES

Dublin Discovered http://dublindiscovered.ie. Forty-five-minute-long waterborne trips along the River Liffey. Sailings depart from Bachelors Walk (March–Oct 5–6 daily, Nov 4 daily Fri–Sun; €19.50).

WALKING AND CYCLING TOURS

Several general and specialist walking tours are available, covering all manner of subjects from the city's history, and its physical and social fabric, to literature and music, all led by informative and entertaining guides.

The 1916 Rebellion tour http://1916rising.com. A tour that describes the events that lead to the Easter Rising, the Rebellion itself and its aftermath. Begins inside the *International Bar*, 23 Wicklow St (March–Oct Mon–Sat 11.30am, Sun 1pm; 2hr; €19).

Dublin Literary Pub Crawl http://dublinpubcrawl.com. Starts upstairs at *The Duke* at 9 Duke St and involves actors performing extracts from major works in a number of pubs with literary connections (April–Oct daily 7.15pm; Nov–March Thurs–Sun same time; 2hr 15min; €15).

Fab Food Trails http://fabfoodtrails.ie. For those keen to enjoy the local delicacies on offer, this guided saunter around the city's range of food outlets, with a decided leaning towards the artisan, will prove agreeably satiating (10am Sat all through the year and also Fri in summer; 2hr 30min; €75); starting points vary – call for details and to book.

Hidden Dublin Tours http://hiddendublintours.com. Concentrating on the more salacious aspects of the city's history, this company offers a variety of tours (daily; 1hr 30min–2hr; €19–25), including a Haunted History tour, a "Northside Ghost Walk" and various other themed walks.

Historical Tours http://historicaltours.ie. A tour run by Trinity history graduates covering Dublin's development and major events, which starts from Trinity College's front gate (April & Oct daily 11am; May–Sept daily 11am & 3pm; Nov–March Fri–Sun 11am; 2hr; €19).

Lazy Bike Tours http://lazybiketours.com. Fun outfit offering a range of tours including a Taste of Dublin push-bike tour (2hr 30min, €35) is a whistle-stop tour of Dublin's major sights, which also takes in trendy Camden St, the fruit market, Grand Canal and the Docklands; and Dublin City e-bike tours (2hr; €45) covering all the major attractions. They also do bike hire.

1

Pat Liddy's Walking Tours http://walkingtours.ie. This renowned local historian offers a number of highly informative two-hour walking tours, including Best of Dublin, and Highlights and Hidden Corners (€25), as well as customized private tours; tours offered in French, German and Irish too.

Traditional Irish Music Pub Crawl http://music pubcrawl.com. Various musicians guide you on a tour of half a dozen pubs, performing songs and music while recounting Ireland's musical history. Tours begin upstairs at *Oliver St John Gogarty's*, Fleet St (daily 7pm; 2hr 30min; €16).

ACCOMMODATION

There's no doubt that **accommodation** in Dublin is, for the most part, very expensive, although there is better value to be found on the northside and in the suburbs. Moreover, many places do offer discounts midweek or outside high season, while B&Bs usually provide a very welcoming and comfortable alternative. If money is tight and you want to be near the action, hostels are the best option and almost all have private rooms. **Booking** in advance is always highly advisable, and is essential around major festivals such as St Patrick's Day, in July and August, and on weekends all year round, especially when major concerts or sporting events are taking place. There is one campsite on Dublin's outskirts.

HOTELS AND B&BS

Many of the city's top-range hotels are located around St Stephen's Green, though the northside also has some chic options. Temple Bar is the most central, but as the location of choice for hen and stag parties it can be very noisy at night. Dublin has a staggering number of B&Bs and you'll find economically priced options on the northside's Gardiner St or in the pleasant southside suburbs of Ballsbridge, Donnybrook and Rathmines, which are all within easy reach of the centre. All rooms listed provide en-suite bathrooms and wi-fi unless stated otherwise.

TEMPLE BAR, SEE MAPS PAGES 62 AND 73

The Clarence 6–8 Wellington Quay, http://theclarence. ie. Formerly owned by U2, this former bolthole for priests and lawyers up from the country has been transformed into an informal luxury hotel. All 58 rooms come with a state-of-the-art multimedia system, and some have balconies overlooking the Liffey. The building also contains the *Cleaver East* restaurant in the former ballroom and the swish *The Curious Mister* bar. €€€

Harding Hotel Copper Alley, Fishamble St, http://harding hotel.ie. Massively popular due to its budget-conscious high-season room rate and range of rooms (twins, doubles, triples and family accommodation), the *Harding* also includes the atmospheric *Darkey Kelly's* bar (see page xx) and *Copper Alley* bistro, venue for breakfast. €€€

★ **Hard Rock Hotel** 18 Exchange St Upper http:// hotel.hardrock.com. Rooms here at this fabulous hotel are tastefully furnished (when they might not well have been) with rock-themed artwork on the walls and some cool, or unusual, features like a coloured touch pad for lighting and the sink and mirror in the room as opposed to the bathroom.

Breakfast (cooked-to-order and continental) is taken in the *Zampas* restaurant (itself a great option for lunch, which adjoins the funky bar – the venue, unsurprisingly, for regular evenings of live bands and DJ sets. The public spaces, meanwhile, are run through with some extraordinary memorabilia, from David Bowie's orange boiler suit to Janice Joplin's harp case. €€€

Temple Bar Hotel 13–17 Fleet St, http://templebarhotel. com. From its bright and airy lobby to its attractive, modern en-suite bedrooms, the *Temple Bar* has a high reputation for service and good value, though some of its front-facing rooms can suffer from late-night street noise. The hotel's bar is a popular spot and there's reduced-rate secure car parking nearby. €€€

THE INNER SOUTHSIDE, SEE MAP PAGE 62

★ **Arthaus Hotel** Mercer St Lower, http://arthausdublin. ie. Not only is this Bauhaus-inspired hotel contender for friendliest place in town, but its plum location just of St Stephen's Green, and suite of understatedly cool rooms (Boutique, Superior and Executive), are brilliant. Size and the odd amenity aside (they all have Nespresso machines), rooms are similar, decorated in delicate shades of blue, pink or green with thick carpets and glistening bathrooms with capacious showers. €€€

Brooks Hotel Drury St, http://brookshotel.ie. Compact, four-star boutique hotel, on a quiet road that's handy for Temple Bar and Grafton St, with bright and airy bedrooms, a small gym and sauna, the well-regarded *Francesca's* restaurant and a cracking whiskey bar. €€€€

Buswells Hotel 23–27 Molesworth St, http://buswells.ie. Popular with politicians thanks to its proximity to Leinster House, *Buswells* offers pleasantly designed en-suite rooms in a converted Georgian town house. Ornate plasterwork and fireplaces testify to those origins and the hotel also has the smart *Trumans* restaurant, its own bar and secure overnight parking. €€€€

The College Green Hotel Dublin Westmoreland St, http://marriott.com. Hiding behind the facade of the old Allied Irish Bank building just north of Trinity College, the former *Westin* hotel is a marvellously luxurious establishment. Its 191 elegantly equipped bedrooms feature a blend of mahogany furniture and sensitive colour design while bathrooms are finished in gleaming Italian marble. The *Mint Bar* (live music Fri & Sat) is housed in the former bank's vaults, and the lounge has a stunning glass roof. €€€€

★ **The Dean Hotel** 33 Harcourt St, http://thedean.ie. From the eye-catching, jet-black window frames to the hipster-like reception area, the *Dean* is coolness personified. The light-filled bedrooms have a stylish industrial decor and come kitted out with record players, fully stocked smeg fridges and Nespresso machines, as well as seriously comfortable beds. Next door, the *Dean Townhouse* has a somewhat more muted atmosphere (pleasingly so) with slightly smaller but still beautifully fashioned rooms. Breakfast (a cracking affair) takes place in *Sophies*, the fantastic rooftop restaurant/bar, which is otherwise a lively nightly destination for Dublin folk. Great gym here too. €€€

The Fitzwilliam Hotel St Stephen's Green, http:// fitzwilliamhoteldublin.com. With an expansive foyer and luxurious, colourful rooms designed by Sir Terence Conran, the *Fitzwilliam* offers deluxe accommodation in a marvellous central location. Room rates vary considerably depending on size and facilities, and there's also a beauty salon, roof garden, bars, secure parking and restaurant. €€€€

Green Hotel 1–5 Harcourt St, http://thegreenhotel.ie. Swish, classy, yet thoroughly modernist, this hotel occupies a spot overlooking the southwestern corner of the Green. As well as its lively bar and economically priced bistro, fitness centre and libraries, the hotel provides 68 spacious double rooms equipped with fridges and power showers and a number of even more luxurious suites. Doubles €€€

Harrington Hall 70 Harcourt St, http://harringtonhall. com. Occupying elegant Georgian premises south of St Stephen's Green, this guesthouse has 29 thoughtfully furnished and generously sized rooms, complete with secondary glazing and ceiling fans. Substantial discounts available in low season. Free parking. €€€

★ **Kelly's Hotel** 36 Great George's St South, http://kellys dublin.com. This southside stalwart has been rejuvenated by the owners of *L'Gueuleton* (see page 103), with 16 rooms spread over three narrow floors (note that there's no lift); doubles are fashionably, but not uncomfortably, minimalist; the executive rooms offer more space, while the penthouse suite sleeps four people. The resident's only *Candle Bar* is a great spot for a nightcap. Over 18s only. €€€

Kilronan House 70 Adelaide Rd, http://kilronanhouse. com. It's hard to top the welcome at this fine Georgian town house, which features elegant decoration including Waterford crystal chandeliers, orthopedic mattresses in all its rooms and free parking. The one economy room (single) has a bathroom outside the room. €€€

★ **Merrion Hotel** Merrion St Upper, http://merrionhotel. com. The Duke of Wellington's dismissal of his Irish connections, "being born in a stable doesn't make one a horse", rings even hollower now that his birthplace at no. 24 Merrion St Upper is part of this very civilized luxury hotel. Four eighteenth-century town houses have been elegantly redecorated in Georgian style and hung with a superb collection of Irish art, overlooking a private landscaped garden. The hotel is also home to a fancy spa, the two-star Michelin restaurant *Patrick Gilbaud* (see page 103), and the infinitely less formal *Cellar Bar*. €€€€

The Mont Merrion St Lower, http://themonthotel.ie. Just off Merrion Square, this three-star hotel housed in a former bank has cool, colourfully furnished rooms all providing a high degree of comfort at excellent prices, as well as an attractive location. You can refuel well in either the *Speranza* restaurant or the funky *Sin Bin Bar*. €€€

★ **The Shelbourne** 27 St Stephen's Green, http:// theshelbourne.com. The grande dame of Dublin hotels is today looking better than ever, from the gilded lobby and grand staircase to some 265 immaculately prepared rooms. The hotel's raft of eating and drinking options include the *Horseshoe Bar* (see page 104) and the *Lord Mayor's Lounge*, where you can avail yourself of a calorific (and expensive) traditional afternoon tea, accompanied by views of the Green and the tinkling of a piano. There's a fitness room and a luxurious spa and pool. €€€€

Stauntons on the Green 83 St Stephen's Green, http:// stauntonsonthegreen.ie. Set in an unbeatable location on the south side of the Green with its own private gardens, this luxurious guesthouse has a good mix of singles, doubles (including some *very* cosy ones), triple and family rooms, which offer both comfort and style befitting this Georgian building. All the rooms overlook either the Green or Iveagh Gardens. €€€

The Westbury Harry St, off Grafton St, http://doyle collection.com. The glossy lobby of this luxurious five-star hotel is an indicator of the treats that lie in store. Its bedrooms are not so much furnished as designed to pamper, and the range of facilities on offer includes a fitness centre, a svelte bar specializing in champagne cocktails, and underground parking. €€€€

THE NORTHSIDE, SEE MAPS PAGES 58 AND 81

Academy Plaza Hotel 10–14 Findlater Place, Cathal Brugha St, http://academyplazahotel.ie. Tucked away behind O'Connell St, this busy, well-appointed hotel sports calm, colourfully furnished en-suite rooms — including triples and quads — as well as a friendly bar that rustles up decent evening meals. €€€

Ashling Hotel 10–13 Parkgate St, http://ashlinghotel.ie. Conveniently set near Heuston Station, this modern four-star hotel's luxuriously furnished rooms provide all essential amenities and plenty of space, as well as a pleasant bar and excellent breakfasts; secure parking is available. €€€

Belvedere Hotel Great Denmark St, http://belvederehotel dublin.com. The *Belvedere's* Georgian exterior encompasses a very amenable modern hotel. Rooms are attractively furnished, bright and airy, and most are wheelchair-accessible. Big discounts available during off-season. €€€

Beresford Hotel 21 Store St, http://beresfordhotelifsc. com. Though its setting opposite Busáras isn't exactly auspicious, the *Beresford's* attractive modern interior, friendly staff and over one hundred well-accoutred bedrooms more than compensate. Breakfast not included. €€€

Clifden Guesthouse 32 Gardiner Place, http://clifden house.com. One of the northside's most reliable options, this comfortable Georgian house is well maintained by very friendly hosts. Fifteen pleasant en-suite rooms include doubles as well as a triple and a family room. Off-street parking is available. €€€

The Gresham Hotel 23 O'Connell St Upper, http://riu. com. The *Gresham* isn't just a splendidly equipped four-star hotel, it is also one of Dublin's landmarks, a place where you don't have to be a guest to enjoy afternoon tea in the opulent surroundings of its lobby or sample the meals in its restaurant. Rooms are pleasantly furnished and spacious while the individually designed penthouse suites, including ones devoted to artist Marc Lamb, architect (and designer of the Spire) Ian Ritchie, and actors Liz Taylor and Richard Burton, offer differing views of the city. Rooms facing O'Connell St can be noisy. €€€

Hilton Garden Inn Custom House Quay, http://hilton. com. This sparkling hotel boasts a fabulous riverside location with staggering views of Dublin's developing docklands from rooms on the upper storeys. Immaculate rooms aside, facilities include a restaurant/bar and pantry. €€€

Maldron Hotel Smithfield Village, http://maldronhotels. com/smithfield. A great addition to the Smithfield area, this new-build hotel provides excellently equipped and furnished rooms, tastefully decorated using primary colours, and has a remarkably good-value restaurant. There's secure overnight parking nearby and it's handily placed for music sessions at *The Cobblestone* (see page 106). €€€

Marian Guest House 21 Gardiner St Upper, 01 874 4129. Immensely popular due to its budget prices and warm welcome, the *Marian* offers clean and comfortable en-suite and standard rooms, plus a filling breakfast. Most have shared bathrooms but some en suites are available. There's off-street parking, and buses #16 and #41 stop around the corner on Dorset St Upper. €€

★ **The Mayson Hotel** 82 North Wall Quay, http:// themayson.ie. From the same stable as the *Dean* (see above), this waterfront hotel has a similarly youthful, hipster-type vibe, and may also appeal if you fancy a quieter time of it, or need to be near the port or 3Arena. There's terrific coffee in the lobby bar, cocktails to enjoy in the bar, and even racks of vinyl to flick through though. Different categories of rooms run the gamut from very small doubles to suites, the latter with long velvet couches and copper baths at the end of the bed, though they all come with Marshall radios, Smeg fridges and Nespresso machines. *Ryleigh's* rooftop steakhouse is also where breakfast is served. €€€

The Morrison Dublin Ormond Quay Lower, http://hilton. com. Shiny surfaces and clean lines dominate at this swish temple of minimalism; while natural tones prevail in the lobby and ultra-cool bar, the luxurious rooms are dazzlingly white with shocks of vibrant pinks and purples. The sleek *Morrison Grill* and flashy *Quay 14* cocktail bar are the hotel's very commendable dining/drinking options. €€€€

The Samuel Spencer Place, North Wall Quay http:// thesamuelhotel.com. It could be argued that Dublin really doesn't need any more hotels, but *The Samuel* is a fine addition. The light-filled rooms' silver and mustard colour scheme may not sound particularly appealing but it works well, while the floor-to-ceiling windows offer unencumbered views of the Liffey and the Dublin skyscape. Conveniently, it's also right next to the Spencer Dock LUAS stop. €€€

HOSTELS

Dublin has numerous hostels, the majority of which offer both dormitory accommodation and private rooms, usually sleeping between two and four people. Most rooms are ensuite and the standard of private rooms is often as good as at B&Bs. Several Dublin hostels belong to the IHH, though a few are members of An Óige (see page 36) – all those listed below are affiliated to IHH unless stated otherwise. Note, though, that since the pandemic, a number of hostels (particularly some of those on or around Gardiner Place/St) have reverted to providing shelter for the homeless.

THE SOUTHSIDE, SEE MAPS PAGES 62 AND 73

Ashfield Hostel 19–20 D'Olier St, http://ashfieldhostel. com. One of the centre's most popular choices provides over 130 beds in a variety of bright and spacious rooms, all with ensuite facilities. Dorms come in a variety of sizes, from four to eighteen-bed (including female only dorms), as well as comfortable doubles. Self-catering kitchen and laundry and free daily walking tours. €-€€

Oliver St John Gogarty's 18–21 Anglesea St, http:// gogartys.ie. This well-equipped hostel above a popular tourist pub in the centre of Temple Bar has more than 130 beds in a range of accommodation, including standard and en-suite twins and four- to ten-bed dorms. Kitchen and laundry facilities are available. €

THE NORTHSIDE, SEE MAP PAGE 81

Abbey Court 29 Bachelors Walk, http://abbey-court. com. Right next to O'Connell Bridge, this upmarket, well-designed hostel provides en-suite twins/doubles and dorms ranging from four to twelve beds. Facilities are excellent for a hostel and include a self-catering kitchen (though breakfast is included), laundry, and a handful of common spaces, two of which are cinema and hammock rooms – so if you can't relax here, there's no hope. €-€€

Clink Hostel 35–36 Upper Abbey St, http://clinkhostels. com. Enormous, nine-floored hostel with neat and spotlessly clean dorms (including female only ones) and private rooms with showers. Breakfast is taken on the first floor with a ground floor bar/lounger area hosting various happenings. Breakfast costs extra. €–€€

Isaacs Hostel 2–5 Frenchman's Lane, http://isaacs. ie. Efficiently run and very welcoming, Dublin's oldest independent hostel is still one of its best and consists of four-to sixteen-bed dorms and some cosy twin-bedded private rooms. Although none is en suite, the shared bathrooms are well equipped with hairdryers and straighteners; facilities include a high-quality kitchen, a café, sauna, games room and reading room. The hostel also runs free walking tours and pizza nights. €–€€

★ **Jacobs Inn** 21–28 Talbot Place, http://jacobsinn.com. Dublin's largest hostel, which nevertheless remains one of the most convivial, with four- to twelve bed dorms plus private doubles (some ensuite) and a long, sweeping bar/lounge with pool table and large-screen TV; this is also where breakfast is taken though that does cost extra. €

Sky Backpackers 2–4 Litton Lane, http://skybackpackers. dublinhotelsweb.com. Housed in a former recording studio in a quiet side street off Bachelors Walk, this small hostel offers four- and six-bed en-suite dorms (including female only ones) as well as comfortable private rooms. There's a sizeable kitchen, and they also run free daily walking tours. €

CAMPING
Camac Valley Tourist Caravan & Camping Park Corkagh Regional Park, Naas Rd, Clondalkin, http:// camacvalley.com. The only campsite within easy reach of the city centre lies 8km southwest of Dublin. This well-equipped, family-oriented site offers excellent facilities, including kitchen, laundry and shop, as well as fine views of the surrounding countryside. Take bus #69 from Aston Quay, or it's a 5min drive from the Red Cow LUAS station. €

EATING
SEE MAPS PAGES 58, 62, 73 AND 81

It's fair to say that no one used to come to Dublin just for the cuisine, but the last decade or so has seen a complete transformation in the city's culinary fortunes. Aside from fantastic modern Irish cooking – the city now boasts six Michelin-starred restaurants, two of which have two stars – it's now possible to sample a wide variety of cuisines, from Lebanese to Nepalese. Many restaurants offer lunchtime or **early-bird** (typically before 7pm) **set menus** of two or three courses, sometimes for as little as half the cost of their regular evening meals. Some cafés and restaurants also provide good-value **weekend brunch**. In addition, plenty of pubs (see page 104) dish up decent, reasonably priced, hearty food, with more ambitious menus available at gastropubs such as *The Porterhouse* (see page 105).

CAFÉS AND QUICK MEALS
Dublin has long had a thriving café scene, and these days (like elsewhere) it's all about the artisan coffee shops which are popping up all over the city. While Irish breakfast tea is a perennial favourite, most cafés also offer a selection of herbal blends. As well as cafés, we've listed below other good spots for a quick, tasty, inexpensive meal. For a splurge with a difference, "Art Tea" at the *Merrion Hotel* (see page 99) is a lot of fun: delicious afternoon tea in the drawing rooms, with cakes that creatively reflect the surrounding paintings from the hotel's excellent collection of nineteenth- and twentieth-century, mostly Irish, art.

THE SOUTHSIDE, SEE MAPS PAGES 58, 62 AND 73

★ **Avoca Café** 11 Suffolk St, http://avoca.com. The bright, buzzy, modern Irish café on the top floor of this department store (see page 108) dishes up everything from a full Irish breakfast to organic falafel as well as an array of cakes, all beautifully presented and courteously served in a bright

dining room with vintage furniture. The food hall and deli in the basement offers salads and sandwiches to take away. €€

Bewley's 78 Grafton, http://bewleys.com. A Dublin institution, *Bewley's* serves a range of delicious breakfasts, cakes and light meals served up in a gorgeous interior spread over several floors. The window tables overlooking the street are especially sought after, and don't miss the six beautiful stained-glass windows by Harry Clarke at the back of the ground floor. €€

Bibi's Emorville Ave, http://bibis.ie. A genuinely special place to have brunch, *Bibi's* is the not-so-secret neighbourhood café that people from all over Dublin flock to on weekends. A converted house and former dress shop on a red-bricked terrace, it serves a small but perfect menu; the butternut squash eggs with chilli butter are a must. Try and get there on a weekday when it's less hectic, and enjoy the warm light and great coffee. €€

Coffee Angel 15 Leinster St, http://coffeeangel.com. There are numerous outlets of this coffee chain throughout the city, all serving superior coffee (at normal prices) and snacks.

Cornucopia 19–21 Wicklow St, http://cornucopia.ie. Friendly, vegetarian/vegan, buffet café serving an excellent range of breakfasts, salads, soups and main courses, as well as cakes, breads, juices and organic wine. €€

Dolce Sicily 20 Anne St, http://dolcesicily.ie. Arguably the most enticing looking tarts in all of Dublin, *Dolce Sicily* is the perfect place to recharge your batteries and indulge your sweet tooth. Choose from a veritable smorgasbord of treats from a famous Sicilian Cannolo to a moreish Ricotta and Nutella Tart. Unusually good vegan options too. Also serves sandwiches and wine. €

★ **The Fumbally** Fumbally Lane, http://thefumbally.ie. One of the best brunch spots in Dublin, serving excellent coffee, falafel wraps with purple slaw, and gorgeous "green

TOP 5 TAKEAWAY COFFEES

Kaph See page 102
Brother Hubbard See page 102
Urbanity See page 102
Coffee Angel See page 101
The Bernard Shaw See page 105

eggs" with avocado and fried chorizo, in a cavernous empty retail space filled with mismatched vintage furniture. €€

Irish Film Institute Café Bar 6 Eustace St, http://ifi.ie. Great for an inexpensive lunch or dinner, whether sitting in the smart bar or the echoing atrium. Simple meals range from lamb flatbreads and burgers to fish cakes and goat's cheese salad, with lots of vegetarian options.

Kaph 31 Drury St, http://kaph.ie. You'll find few folk in Dublin who don't think that this is the best coffee house in town, and it's quite simple: an ultra-cool setting, superb coffee and delicious home-made cakes – all in all, the perfect mid-morning energy boost. Great music, too.

Leo Burdock's 2 Werburgh St, http://leoburdock.com. Dublin's most famous fish-and-chipper (takeaway only, but the garden of Christ Church Cathedral is just over the road) is all gleaming surfaces and friendly service. The menu stretches to smoked cod fillet and lemon sole, but otherwise there are no surprises – it's all just very, very good. €€

Queen of Tarts Cork Hill and Cow's Lane, http://queenoftarts.ie. The former location is the cosy, original branch of this patisserie-cum-café, while the latter around the corner provides more elbow room and outdoor tables on the pedestrianized alley. Both offer veggie/vegan and meaty fry-ups and granola for breakfast; savoury tarts and other hot dishes for lunch like spicy cauliflower and caramelized onion; oh, and yummy cakes baked on the premises to keep you going between mealtimes. €€

Silk Road Café Chester Beatty Library, Dublin Castle, http://silkroadcafe.ie. Stylish and good-value museum café, spilling over into the library's sky-lit atrium. Mostly Middle Eastern food: Lebanese chicken, falafel, spinach and feta filo pie and very good salads, as well as great coffee and titbits such as Turkish delight and baklava. €€

THE NORTHSIDE, SEE MAPS PAGES 58 AND 81

Brother Hubbard 153 Capel St, http://brotherhubbard.ie. Nestled in the middle of vibrant Capel St, *Brother Hubbard* is a very busy little café serving serious food. Go for the grilled halloumi sandwich or the three salad plate, but do make sure to save room for their divine brownies. €€

Caffè Cagliostro Blooms Lane, http://wallacewinebars.ie. A tiny Italian café serving excellent espresso and pastries, with newspapers for perusal and a sunny outdoor terrace.

Eatyard Cross Guns Bridge, Glasnevin St, http://the-eatyard.com. A cool food market that attracts a lot of hungover 30-somethings on Saturday and Sunday afternoons. Plenty of stalls serving a wide selection of grub, from Taiwan street food to Venezuelan vegan wraps. Closed Mon–Wed. €

Soup Dragon 168 Capel St, http://soupdragon.com. A small and inexpensive lunchtime favourite serving the most delicious soups and stews in the city. Everything from the bread to the chowder is made on site. €

Urbanity 11 Coke Lane, http://urbanity.ie. Tucked away at the bottom of Smithfield, this trendy café has a simple philosophy: everything must be made from scratch, from the almond butter to the pickles. Even the coffee beans are roasted on site, with predictably aromatic results. Lunch ranges from mint and wild garlic grilled halloumi to a 15hr slow roast Asian-style pork belly. €€

RESTAURANTS

The majority of Dublin's restaurants are on the south side of the river in the city centre, but there are new places opening up all the time, both north and south. Eating out in Temple Bar tends to be overpriced and underwhelming, but wherever you plan to eat, it's worth booking ahead, especially in the evenings.

THE SOUTHSIDE, SEE MAPS PAGES 58, 62 AND 73

★ **Bastible** 111 South Circular Rd, http://bastible.com. A bit further south of the city centre in Portobello, this one-star Michelin restaurant is (almost) as good as anything else in Dublin. Named after a traditional Irish cooking pot, the restaurant's chef Cúan Greene conjures up magical plates like oyster tart, fermented celeriac and cucumber, and cured langoustine, sour beer and salted carrot. The decor, too, is welcomingly unpretentious. Closed Sun–Tues. €€€€

Bunsen 3 South Anne St, http://bunsen.ie. With a menu so small it fits on a business card, Bunsen does one thing, and it does it well: burgers. No fuss classic old-school burgers cooked to perfection with toppings of your choice, accompanied by a choice of different fries. Grab a soda or a shake while you're at it. €€

Camden Kitchen 3A Camden Market, http://camdenkitchen.ie. Housed in the historic Camden Market building on a residential Georgian street in Portobello, the top-class chefs combine a passion for local and wild Irish produce with inspiration from their travels abroad to create fabulous dishes such as house cured salt cod croquette and squid ink mayo, and braised ox cheek with Garryhinch oyster mushrooms. The three course early-bird menu (5–6.30pm; €39) offers the best value. Closed Sun & Mon. €€€€

Chez Max 1 Palace St, http://chezmax.ie. Archetypal French bistro at the gate of Dublin Castle, offering a wide-ranging evening menu of classic dishes, supplemented by specialities from the owner's home region in southwest France; expect the likes of beef *bourguignon* and duck *confit* alongside cold meat and cheese platters, sweet and savoury crêpes and delicious French breakfasts. €€€

★ **Dunne and Crescenzi** 14–16 South Frederick St, http://dunneandcrescenzi.com. A cosy, popular Italian café-restaurant and wine bar, with croissants and spot-on coffee, all manner of Italian sandwiches and excellent plates of antipasti, though the plates of pasta are something else, for example pasta with ragu of Irish lamb, perfumed with beer and mint. Bookings taken only for dinner. €€€

Ely Wine Bar 22 Ely Place, http://elywinebar.ie. Popular, congenial and reasonably- priced wine bar that offers snacks and main meals like pan-fried guinea fowl with barley and bacon, to accompany around eighty wines by the glass. Carefully sourced, mostly organic Irish ingredients, including fresh beef and pork from their own farm in the Burren. Closed Sun. €€€

Fallon and Byrne 11–17 Exchequer St, http://fallonandbyrne.com. Foodie heaven in a converted telephone exchange: a smart grocery store and deli (for lunch to eat in or take away) on the ground floor; a seductive, Parisian-style brasserie upstairs, offering everything from burgers to superb seared sea bream with squid terrine and smoked almond oil; and a wine bar and deli shop in the basement. €€–€€€

La Maison 15 Castlemarket, http://lamaisondublin.com. The outdoor tables at this quaint French restaurant on the pedestrianized Castlemarket are the most in demand even in winter when heaters and blankets keep diners warm while they enjoy bowls of *moules frites*. The giant 30oz *cote de boeuf* for two people is especially recommended, if your wallet will stretch to more than €90 that is. €€€

L'Gueuleton 2 Fade St, http://lgueuleton.com. Great French bistro food such as wild Wicklow venison with *pomme fondant* and cavolo nero from an open kitchen at reasonable prices, accompanied by good-value French wine. The breakfasts are ace too, for example chorizo hash with shiitake mushroom omelette. €€€

Neon 17 Camden St, http://neon17.ie. This trendy, always-buzzing Asian street-food restaurant offers an array of fiery Thai curries, Vietnamese soups and stir-fries. Enjoy over a beer or glass of wine at the rustic communal tables, before pouring your own whipped ice-cream cone for dessert. €€

Restaurant Patrick Gilbaud Merrion Hotel, Merrion St Upper, http://restaurantpatrickgilbaud.ie. The second of the city's two-Michelin starred restaurants, this is as exceptional – and as formal – as you'd expect. A la carte menus list out of this world dishes like ravioli of blue lobster with lobster coconut cream and toasted almond, and honey roast barbarie duckling, lavender and pickled daikon, all prepared with infinite class. The three-course lunch is probably better value. The prices are, of course, astronomical, but you won't forget an evening here in a hurry. Closed Sun & Mon. €€€€

★ **Sano Pizza** 1–2 Exchange Street Upper, http://sano.pizza.ie. As a sign of how expensive it can be to eat in Dublin, you'll do well to find a decent pizza anywhere for much less than €15, but Sano bucks that trend, and in some style; deliciously doughy pizzas served quickly and cheaply, and some decent vegan options too. Great stuff. €€

Trocadero 4 St Andrew's St, http://trocadero.ie. A welcoming haven, done out with plush booths, signed photos of showbiz visitors and yards of red velvet. An excellent, if heavily fish and meat skewed, menu, for example slow roasted pork belly, Vermouth jus and cauliflower puree, and glazed baked salmon with lemon dill. Closed Mon. €€€

Ukiyo 7–9 Exchequer St, http://ukiyobar.com. Chic Korean and Japanese bar-restaurant, serving bento boxes and mains like slow cooked pork with cauliflower kimchi, with a novel take on the Dublin snug. €€€

THE NORTHSIDE, SEE MAPS PAGES 58 AND 81

★ **Chapter One** 18–19 Parnell Square North, http://chapteronerestaurant.com. Housed in the cellars of the former Dublin Writers Museum, this two-starred Michelin-starred culinary gem is Dublin's big-ticket restaurant, bar none. Specializing in modern Irish food, inspired by the Irish landscape, seasons and new Irish artisan producers, the three menus (Lunch, Dinner, Tasting) might include the likes of pig's tail stuffed with Fingal Ferguson's bacon, lobster, basil puree and mustard fruits, or roast Anjou pigeon, *Céret* cherries and liver ganache. Be prepared to book weeks, if not months, in advance. Closed Sun–Tues. €€€€

Musashi 15 Capel St, http://musashidublin.com. Decent Japanese restaurants in Dublin are few and far between, but *Musashi* is up there with the best. Serving mostly sushi, the menu is just varied enough to cater for those uninterested in fish. Try the pork gyoza – as close to perfection as a dumpling can get. Vegans can satisfy themselves with a stupendous tofu steak in katsu curry. €€€

The Winding Stair 40 Ormond Quay Lower, http://winding-stair.com. Set above the bookshop of the same name (see page 108), with its views across the Liffey (ask for a seat by the window), this is one of the most enjoyable northside spots for lunch, with traditional Irish plates plates like hand smoked haddock poached in milk with onions and cheddar mash. €€€€

★ **The Woollen Mills** 42 Lower Ormond Quay, http://thewoollenmills.com. A sister restaurant to the *Winding Stair*, this "eating house" in an old haberdashery sprawls

---

TOP 5 CHEAP EATS

Bunsen See page 101
The Fumbally See page 101
Neon See page 103
Sano Pizza See page 108
Soup Dragon See page 102

over four floors, with huge windows and a roof terrace opening out over the Ha'penny Bridge. The food is fresh, local and seasonal, and caters for all types of eaters at all times of the day: grab a good takeaway coffee and a bun from their on-site bakery for breakfast, a salad box for lunch, or lounge over a supper feast of roasted Wicklow lamb with smoked violet garlic puree and a craft beer at night.

Wuff 23 Benburb St, http://wuffrestaurant.ie. A lively neighbourhood bistro in the heart of Smithfield, serving up the likes of veggie chorizo benedict breakfast, pulled jackfruit sandwiches and salads for lunch, and heartier dishes like golden beer-battered fish with twice-cooked chips for dinner. €€

THE SUBURBS

★ **Caviston's** 59 Glasthule Rd, Sandycove, http://cavistons.com. Near Sandycove and Glasthule DART station, this restaurant works to a basic but hugely successful formula – the day's freshest fish and seafood cooked simply. Booking is essential and there are a few outside tables in summer. €€€

DRINKING

Dubliners boast that their city possesses the finest **pubs** in the world. They're probably right too, but with over seven hundred watering holes to choose from, forming the backbone of the capital's social life, there's no harm in checking out their assertion. Along the way, you'll also be able to test out competing claims about the hometown drink, **Guinness**: that it tastes better here is not open to doubt, but locals argue about exactly which pub pours the best drop (is the travel-shy liquid better at *Ryan's*, just across the river from the brewery, than downstream at *Mulligan's*?). In general, the stout is best in the characterful and sociable historic pubs, many of which retain their cut-glass screens, ornate woodcarving and cosy snugs, often with a private hatch to the bar. Alongside the more traditional pubs, a plethora of cosmopolitan **bars** has sprung up, be they cavernous microbreweries serving craft beers, studenty DJ bars or chic designer cocktail lounges. Pubs operate strict trading hours, and most close at 11.30pm Sunday to Thursday and 12.30am on Friday and Saturday. Bars and nightclubs with late licences are noted in the reviews below. Traditional music pubs (see page 105) are great for a drink in their own right. Dublin also has a number of LGBTQ+ bars (see page 107) as well as some highly entertaining pub tours (see page 97).

TEMPLE BAR AND THE SOUTHSIDE, SEE MAPS PAGES 62 AND 73

Anséo 18 Camden St, 01 475 1321. Unpretentious, easy-going venue with plenty of velour banquettes to chill out on. DJs at weekends, comedy night on Wed and occasional live music.

The Bar with No Name 3 Fade St, http://noname.bar. With no formal name or a sign outside it can be easy to miss this place – it's on the first floor, entered to the left of *L'Gueuleton* (from whose kitchen weekend brunch is served). Lovely, big outdoor terrace, cool soundtrack and a loft feel, with bare floorboards, and modern art on the walls. Try one of their famous mojitos and soak up the vibes.

Cassidy's 27 Westmoreland St, 01 670 8604. With its graffitied walls, mismatched furniture and a spectacular array of craft beers on draught or by bottle, this refurbished hipster hangout also serves pizza and plays consistently great music.

★ **Darkey Kelly's** Fishamble St, http://darkeykellys.ie. Taking its name from an eighteenth-century Copper Alley (brothel-keeper), this is a highly atmospheric pub which supplies good bar food and a nightly programme of live entertainment that'll have you coming back for more.

Grogan's 15 South William St, http://groganspub.ie. Lively, eccentric traditional pub, popular with budding writers and artists. One of the most popular spots in the city on a sunny day, the outdoor seating area quickly fills, with punters taking their drinks to the street outside. On a more typically drizzly day, sit inside and order one of their delicious cheese toasties while admiring the original artwork on the walls.

The Horseshoe Bar Shelbourne Hotel, 27 St Stephen's Green, http://theshelbourne.com. In this luxury hotel, the *Horseshoe*'s deep-red leather banquettes and white marble counter maintain a cosy pub feel. The recent cleaning of the cautionary, satirical prints by Hogarth above the bar has not deterred the city's politicos and journos, who still gather here to swap tall tales and set the world to rights.

The International Bar 23 Wicklow St, http://intercomedydublin.com. Old-fashioned pub decorated with stained glass and ornate woodcarving that heaves congenially thanks to its nightly comedy shows upstairs and live music downstairs in the basement.

Kehoe's 9 South Anne St, http://kehoesdublin.ie. This meeting place used to double up as a grocery and is now a watering hole full of character, with cosy snugs and a low mahogany bar. There's barely a pub in Dublin that doesn't claim to be the best, but this place has genuine claim.

The Long Hall 51 South Great George's St, 01 475 1590. Old-time classic, sporting ornate plasterwork, antique clocks, mirrors and dark-wood panelling, a suitably long bar, friendly staff and a good pint of Guinness – and really, that's all you need.

Mulligan's 8 Poolbeg St, 01 677 5582. A little off the beaten track, this large no-nonsense pub pours an excellent pint and remains a favoured watering hole for workers at the nearby *Irish Times*.

★ **The Palace Bar** 21 Fleet St, http://thepalacebardublin. com. Relaxing, sociable, two hundred-year-old pub, former haunt of writers Behan, Kavanagh and Flann O'Brien, now famed both for the quality of its pint and for its handsome decor. The overflow bar upstairs hosts sessions of traditional music on Wed, Thurs & Sun.

The Porterhouse 16 Parliament St, http://porterhouse brewco.ie. Rambling microbrewery-bar, where you can sample a bewildering number of different stouts, lagers or ales. Live music every night, including traditional sessions on Sun, and good food.

★ **The Stag's Head** 1 Dame Court, http://stagshead.ie. Pretty Victorian bar, all dark woods and stuffed, tiled and stained-glass stags, that attracts a hugely varied crowd. Trad music Fri and Sat evenings, comedy Sun and Mon, and ukulele fun on Tues. The food's not bad either.

THE NORTHSIDE, SEE MAPS PAGES 58 AND 81

★ **The Bernard Shaw** Cross Guns Bridge, Glasnevin, http://thebernardshaw.com. Following its relocation from the southside to the northside, this long-established bar, café and creative space remains one of the city's most popular boozers, not least thanks to the colourful outdoor space with its gallery and murals; in addition there are quizzes, bingo, karaoke, and much more, as well as the neighbouring Eatyard food market with vendors from all over.

The Flowing Tide 9 Abbey St Lower, 01 874 4108. Long connected with the Abbey Theatre opposite, this pub features tasteful stained-glass windows, a mural celebrating the theatre's history and a horseshoe-shaped bar.

Frank Ryan & Son 5 Queen St, http://frankryans.com. Definitely a place for respite from the city's hurly-burly, this sociable, old-fashioned bar is cosiness incarnate. The friendly staff serve a grand pint of stout.

Hill 16 16 Gardiner St Middle, 01 874 4239. Named after Croke Park's most popular stand, the bar is a magnet for GAA devotees, particularly those who follow the fortunes of Dublin's Gaelic football team.

Kavanagh's (aka The Gravediggers) Prospect Square, Glasnevin, 01 830 7978. One of the city's finest old pubs, located just outside the old entrance to Glasnevin Cemetery, where it has consoled mourners (and changed little) since 1833. It's best reached from the present-day entrance by retracing your steps along Finglas Rd and taking the first small lane on the left along the cemetery walls.

The Lotts 9 Liffey St Lower, http://thelottscafebar.com. It's often standing-room-only at this friendly corner bar, with a snug which lays claim to being the northside's smallest. It offers a tasty selection of Mediterranean-inspired meals in its fashionable café-bar next door.

★ **Ryan's** 28 Parkgate St, http://thebuckleycollection. ie. The longtime challenger to the reputation of *Mulligan's* (see page 104) for serving the best pint of Guinness in the city, based on its proximity to the brewery just across the river, serves bar meals plus steaks and seafood in its upstairs restaurant.

Sin É 14–15 Ormond Quay Upper, http://sin.e.ie. This candlelit bar appeals to a lively cosmopolitan crowd because of its wide selection of brews and eclectic choice of nightly musical entertainment (sometimes live gigs, but mostly DJs).

LIVE MUSIC

Dublin's **music scene** is thriving but ever-changing, so it's always wise to check **listings** on http://dublintown. ie, or in *The Ticket* (see page 96), or the fortnightly rock-and-style magazine *Hot Press*. There are also a number of **open-air events** during the summer, including one-off gigs by major acts at places such as Croke Park and Marlay Park in Rathfarnham. **Traditional music** is flourishing in the city with a number of pubs offering sessions, usually commencing at around 9.30pm. Listings of these can be found at http://dublinsessions.ie.

LIVE MUSIC VENUES

3Arena Dame St, http://3arena.ie; see map page 58. Once a railway depot, the cavernous 3Arena, 1.5km east of O'Connell Bridge, is Ireland's largest dedicated music venue with a capacity of thirteen thousand. Unsurprisingly, it hosts major international names with high prices to boot. The venue is served by the LUAS red line Docklands branch.

The Academy 57 Abbey St Middle, http://theacademy dublin.com; see map page 81. The latest occupant of these premises offers a variety of largely alt/indie gigs. Fri and Sat are huge club nights in its Main Room, Green Room and Academy 2 sections.

Button Factory Curved St, http://buttonfactory.ie; see map page 73. A remarkably left-field venue with a more than eclectic booking policy covering everything from traditional music to alt/indie bands via modern jazz and tribute groups. The place transforms itself into a late club (until 3am Fri–Sun) at weekends – with a wide variety of differently themed events. Also home to the Irish Rock'n'Roll Museum Experience (see page 73).

Olympia Theatre 72 Dame St, http://3olympia.ie; see map page 73. This old, intimate and much-esteemed venue continues to stage a variety of musical events, featuring major Irish names as well as international stars.

The Sugar Club 8 Leeson St Lower, http://thesugarclub. com; see map page 62. A lush and plush southside venue, just off St Stephen's Green, *The Sugar Club* hosts a diverse and often far from mainstream variety of entertainment (bands, torch-singers, comedy, cabaret) – some divine, others dreadful, but the atmosphere is often very much on the button.

Vicar Street 58–59 Thomas St West, http://vicarstreet. com; see map page 58. Arguably the city's premier small live music venue, this three-hundred-seater has an estimable programme that includes live music, comedy and other events, and features major names.

Whelan's 25 Wexford St, http://whelanslive.com; see map page 62. *Whelan's* has remained one of the city's most successful live venues over the last two decades, thanks to an extensive programme of the old and the new – a blend of traditional music, renowned folk acts, emerging talent and occasional one-off performances by major names. As well as live music they also host some great club nights, like the ever-popular Indie and Alternative Dance Party (Thurs 10.30pm).

TRADITIONAL MUSIC PUBS

The Brazen Head 20 Bridge St Lower, http://brazenhead. com; see map page 58. Established in 1189 and laying claim to the title of Ireland's oldest pub, *The Brazen Head's* many rooms feature all manner of music-related memorabilia on the walls and ramble round a large courtyard. Traditional musicians play every night at 9pm (as well as Sun 3–6pm), though the quality of the sessions can be extremely variable.

★ **The Cobblestone** 77 King St North, http://cobble stonepub.ie; see map page 58. Arguably the best traditional-music venue in Dublin, this dark, cosy, wooden-floored bar is also a fine place to sample the hoppy products of the nearby Dublin Brewing Company. High-quality sessions take place on Mon from 7pm, Tues–Fri from 5pm, and weekends from 2pm, while the *Back Room* hosts a variety of gigs. Even during the day there's likely to be a group of musicians having a session by the front door.

Hughes' Bar 19 Chancery St, 01 872 6540; see map page 58. Tucked away behind the Four Courts, *Hughes' Bar* attracts the cream of the city's traditional musicians to its nightly sessions (10pm until closing time). Fri can draw a large crowd, so arrive early to grab a seat.

Ned O'Shea's 12 Bridge St Lower, http://nedosheas.ie; see map page 58. Opposite the more famous *Brazen Head*, *O'Shea's* nurtures the atmosphere of a homely, good-natured country pub in the centre of the city, providing sanctuary for "culchies" from any county, but especially Kerrymen. Traditional sessions are hosted every night in high season from 9 or 10pm (plus 6.30pm Sun), including set dancing on Mon, and it's a good place to watch a GAA game.

O'Donoghue's 15 Merrion Row, http://odonoghues.ie; see map page 62. The centre of the folk and traditional music revival that began in the late 1950s, forever associated with ground-breaking balladeers The Dubliners. Nightly sessions (from about 9.30pm) draw a considerable crowd of tourists, while the large heated courtyard is more of a draw for locals.

NIGHTLIFE

SEE MAPS PAGES 58, 62, 73 AND 81

It is best to check the latest listings in the *Event Guide* or *Hot Press* (see page 105), as Dublin's **club scene** is volatile. Clubs can be found in most areas of the city centre and prices vary considerably, depending on the venue, night of the week and whether a "name" DJ is spinning the turntables – the venues listed below often have free entry, but can charge up to €20 on certain nights.

Copper Face Jacks 29–30 Harcourt St, http://copperface jacks.ie; see map page 62. The most popular of several similar late-night venues along Harcourt St, and notorious for its pop tunes and groups of single lads and lasses looking for a good time..

Four Dame Lane 4 Dame Lane, http://4damelane.ie; see map page 73. Announced by burning braziers, this bar-club probably has the stylistic edge over its bare-brickwork-and-wood rivals. The tunes are good too, encompassing anything from techno to soul, with a DJ Thurs–Sun in the ground-floor bar, Fri and Sat in the upstairs Loft room.

The Grand Social 35 Lower Liffey St, http://thegrand social.ie; see map page 81. On the northside of the Ha'penny Bridge, in-house and guest DJs spin funky disco, indie, classic rock and electro at the weekends. There's a popular jazz club every Mon night, and the indoor Ha'penny Flea Market on a Sat afternoon.

Workman's Club 10 Wellington Quay, http://theworkmans club.com; see map page 73. A maze of interconnecting rooms in a red-brick building fronting the River Liffey houses dance floors, venues for live music and poetry readings, themed bars and a rooftop terrace. The bar on the ground floor serves American-style barbecues (until 9pm), accompanied by craft beers and cocktails.

ARTS AND CULTURE

Drama played a pivotal role in Ireland's twentieth-century cultural revival and Dublin's theatres continue to act as a crucible for innovation, alongside staging a range of Irish classics. Highlights include the **Dublin Theatre Festival** (late Sept to mid-Oct; http://dublintheatrefestival.ie) and the **Dublin Fringe Festival** (mid-Sept; http://fringefest. com). Ticket prices vary; as a rule, you should expect to pay €10–20 per ticket for fringe shows, €20–40 for mainstream.

If you're budget-conscious, it's worth enquiring about low-cost previews and occasional cut-price Monday and Tuesday night shows, while students (with ID) and senior citizens can sometimes find good concessionary rates. All **cinemas** operate a policy of cheap seats (around €5–7) daily before 5pm (6.30pm in some cases); standard prices are €9–12. Student discounts are often available.

The Abbey Theatre Abbey St Lower, http://abbeytheatre.

ie. The National Theatre of Ireland (see page 81) tends to show international and Irish classics plus new offerings by contemporary playwrights.

Bord Gáis Energy Theatre Grand Canal Square, http:// bordgaisenergytheatre.ie. Two-thousand-seater in the Docklands, mostly offering light entertainment and musicals.

Gaiety Theatre South King St, 0818 719388, http:// gaietytheatre.ie. Known as "The Grand Old Lady of South King Street" the Gaiety specialises in operatic and musical productions, with dramatic shows from time to time.

Gate Theatre 1 Cavendish Row, Parnell Square, http:// gatetheatre.ie. Founded in the 1920s in an eighteenth-century building leased from the Rotunda Hospital, the Gate has a reputation for staging adventurous experimental drama as well as established classics in its small, elegant auditorium, and gave an early boost to the acting careers of James Mason and Orson Welles.

Irish Film Institute 6 Eustace St, http://ifi.ie. The focus for Irish cineastes provides a broad programme of international and new Irish films in a beautifully converted Quaker meeting house. It is the hub of the International Film Festival in Feb (http://diff.ie), as well as numerous other fantastic events like Horrorthon (Oct) and the French Film Festival (Nov). They often show films using Ireland's only 70mm projector, and there's an excellent film-related bookshop beside the bar and café-restaurant (see page 102).

Light House Cinema Smithfield, http://lighthouse cinema.ie. A little away from the centre, this four-screen cinema is acclaimed for its imaginative programming and hosts the Dublin LGBTQ Film Festival (http://gaze.ie) at the end of September.

New Theatre 43 Essex St East, http://thenewtheatre.com. This theatre stages a variety of classic, rarely performed and new drama. Continually supporting new writers, it's a great place to see vibrant, emerging talent.

Project Arts Centre 39 Essex St East, http://projectart scentre.ie. Renowned for its experimental and often controversial Irish and international theatre, this flagship of the contemporary art scene also hosts dance, film, music and performance art.

SPORTS

Dublin and its surrounds offer plenty of scope to exploit the national obsessions of football (Gaelic and regular), hurling, rugby and horse and greyhound racing. If they can't attend a match or a meet, Dubliners are always keen to indulge in a second national pastime, gambling.

Soccer The Republic's national team plays most of its home games at the Aviva Stadium (http://avivastadium.ie) on Lansdowne Rd, which is situated to the southeast of the centre and is easily accessible via the adjacent DART station. The city currently has five teams playing in the professional League of Ireland: Bohemians (http://bohemianfc.com); St Patrick's Athletic (http://stpatsfc.com); Shamrock Rovers (http://shamrockrovers.ie); Shelbourne (http:// shelbournefc.ie); and UCD (http://ucdfc.ie). Standards are about the equivalent of the English Football League's Second Division. Most games take place on Fri nights and tickets generally cost around €12–15.

Gaelic football and hurling Most of the season's major games are played at Croke Park (see page 91); more info is available at http://gaa.ie. In football, the All-Ireland Final occurs on the third or fourth Sun in Sept and has been won by Dublin on 31 occasions (a record beaten only by Kerry). The Dubs have a poor record at hurling, so the crowd at the All-Ireland Final on the first or second Sun in Sept mainly consists of out-of-towners. You'll be hard pushed to get tickets for either of the finals, but you're quite likely to get in for a semi-final at "Croker" – expect to pay around €35 to stand, and sing, on the famous Hill 16, €50 to sit in the stands and less for earlier rounds.

Greyhound racing The city has one dog-racing venue: Shelbourne Park (Wed, Thurs & Sat) in Ringsend, in Docklands, east of the centre. Entry is around €10 and details of events can be found at http://grireland.ie.

Horse racing Dublin's nearest large racecourse is Leopardstown (http://leopardstown.com), in the southern suburb of Foxrock (LUAS to Sandyford station then a 15min walk). Races are held at weekends at various points of the year and on Thurs evenings during June and July, but the main events are the four-day Christmas Festival starting on St Stephen's Day (Dec 26), and the Hennessy Cognac Gold Cup in Feb. The Irish Grand National is held on Easter Mon at Fairyhouse (http://fairyhouse.ie) in Ratoath, 24km northwest of Dublin, followed in April by the Irish National Hunt Festival at Punchestown (see page 130), 40km southwest of Dublin. Flat-racing classics are held at the Curragh, nearly 50km southwest of the capital (see page 130). Bus Éireann lays on race-day transport to Fairyhouse.

Rugby Ireland's home games are played at the Aviva Stadium (http://avivastadium.ie). The provincial rugby side Leinster (http://leinsterrugby.ie) plays its own home games at the RDS in Ballsbridge, southeast of the centre. For big match days, particularly during the Six Nations in February, most pubs with a decent screen will be packed to the rafters.

LGBTQ+ DUBLIN

As attitudes to homosexuality in Dublin have become increasingly liberal over the last two decades, so the capital's **LGBTQ** community has grown in confidence, and a small but vibrant scene has established a niche in the city's social life. The latest **information** on LGBTQ events and venues in Dublin is provided by *Outhouse*, 105 Capel

St (http://outhouse.ie), a resource centre for LGBTQ people with a café (Mon–Fri 1–9.30pm, Sat 1–5.30pm) and a small library. The free magazine *GCN* (*Gay Community News* http://gcn.ie) has detailed listings of upcoming events and can be found in the LGBTQ-friendly Books Upstairs, College Green, or in clubs and bars.

The George 89 Great George's St, http://thegeorge.ie; see map page 62. Ireland's longest-established LGBTQ bar still draws huge crowds at weekends. There are two distinct sections: a lushly decorated main venue on two floors, and a quieter, more traditional pub with an older clientele to the right. Entertainment includes karaoke, game shows, DJs and Sunday-night jazz followed by bingo with drag queen Shirley Temple-Bar.

Pantibar 7–8 Capel St, 01 874 0710; see map page 81. Owned by Irish LGBTQ icon, drag queen Pandora "Panti" Bliss, this lush bar provides all manner of entertainment from Monday's "Make and Do with Panti" (an alternative take on domestic crafts and games) to various themed nights in the basement, including "Panticlub" (Thurs–Sat). Apartments are available to rent on the upper floors.

SHOPPING

The southside is the most fruitful hunting ground for shoppers, offering Irish and global designer clothes around **Grafton St**, and more alternative boutiques in the George's St **Arcade** and **Temple Bar**. Also south of the river, you'll find an attractive and eclectic range of artisan products gathered from around the country, from cheeses and whiskey to ceramics. Despite a revamp, Dublin's most extensive shopping boulevard, **O'Connell St**, is likely to hold little of interest for the visiting consumer, though the raucous Moore St market, off Henry St, is always entertaining.

ARTS, CRAFTS AND FASHIONS

Avoca 11 Suffolk St, http://avoca.com; see map page 62. Highly successful small department store, stocking its own clothing ranges for women and children, jewellery, beautiful rugs and throws woven at the original mill in Avoca, Co. Wicklow, plus deli goods.

Irish Design Shop 41 Drury St, http://irishdesignshop. com; see map page 62. Tiny shop run by two Irish jewellers, selling a range of Irish woodcraft, textiles, prints and pottery.

Kilkenny 6 Nassau St, http://kilkennydesign.com; see map page 62. A varied collection of fine Irish crafts: Newbridge silver cutlery and jewellery; Jerpoint glassware; extensive ranges of ceramics; and women's clothes and accessories by contemporary designers.

Powerscourt Townhouse Centre South 59 William St, http://powerscourtcentre.ie; see map page 62. On the second floor of the building (see page 66), the Design Centre stocks established Irish designers of women's fashion, such as Philip Treacy and John Rocha, as well as diverse international names. The Loft Market opposite is a cutting-edge showcase for young local designers of clothes and jewellery.

BOOKS AND MUSIC

Books Upstairs 17 D'Olier St, http://booksupstairs.ie; see map page 62. An excellent independent bookstore operating since 1978 with a fine selection of Irish books, as well as literary and intellectual journals.

Chapters Bookstore Ivy Exchange, Parnell St, http:// chaptersbookstore.com; see map page 81. Claiming to be Dublin's largest bookshop, its ground floor features a massive range of fiction (including lots in translation) and fact, including impressive sections on Irish literature and history. Upstairs is devoted to the secondhand section which also includes bargain-priced CDs and DVDs.

Hodges Figgis 56–58 Dawson St, http://hodgesfiggis. ie; see map page 62. A Dublin institution since the eighteenth century, behind an ornate facade, including a huge range of books on and from Ireland on the ground floor. A joy to simply browse and lose track of time.

The R.A.G.E and The Record Spot 8 Crow St, http:// therage.ie; see map page 62. This is really two shops in one: upstairs sells retro games and consoles, while the basement has a stock of over ten thousand secondhand records and various vinyl-related merchandise.

Ulysses Rare Books 10 Duke St, http://rarebooks.ie; see map page 62. A delightful little antiquarian bookshop, this is the place to come for first editions and other rare books by Irish writers, specializing in twentieth-century literature. Closed Sun.

Walton's Blanchardstown Retail Park, http://waltons. ie. Dublin's leading music shop sells traditional Irish instruments, as well as teaching aids, sheet music and recordings. The attached music school (http://newschool. ie) offers 1hr or 2hr crash courses for beginners in the tin whistle and the *bodhrán*.

The Winding Stair 40 Ormond Quay Lower, http:// winding-stair.com; see map page 81. One of the city's oldest bookshops, stocking a selection of titles you might not find in larger stores. It has a small secondhand section, which is especially good on Irish literature and biography. Upstairs is one of the northside's finest restaurants (see page 103).

DEPARTMENT STORES AND MARKETS

Brown Thomas 88–95 Grafton St, http://brownthomas. com; see map page 62. The city's flagship department store is sophisticated and pricey, featuring a long roll call of Irish and international designer labels.

Cow's Lane Market Off Essex St West; see map page 73. On a pedestrianized alley in Temple Bar, this small but lively Saturday market has stalls concentrating on contemporary women's clothes, bags and jewellery, generally sold by the designers themselves.

George's Street Arcade Between South Great George's St and Drury St, http://georgesstreetarcade.ie; see map page 62. Laidback indoor market, which claims to be Europe's oldest, offering secondhand books and records, vintage and street clothing, jewellery, cafés and speciality foods.

Moore St Market Moore St, http://moorestreetmarkets. com; see map page 81. This lively street market is a longstanding Dublin institution and much reflects the city's changing ethnicity. The traditional butchers, fishmongers and greengrocers are still present, though you're bound to see price tags in Cantonese too, and there are also a number of Afro-Caribbean stalls and shops.

FOOD AND DRINK

Celtic Whiskey Shop 27–28 Dawson St, http:// celticwhiskeyshop.com; see map page 62. Probably the best selection of Irish whiskeys anywhere, including rare examples from distilleries that have now closed down. The well-informed staff always have bottles open to taste and will ship around the world.

Sheridan's Cheesemongers 11 South Anne St, http:// sheridanscheesemongers.com; see map page 62. Fantastic, pungent array of cheeses, mostly by Irish artisan producers, plus cold meats and other deli goods, sold by knowledgeable staff.

Temple Bar Food Market Meeting House Square, http:// templebarmarkets.com; see map page 73. A magnet for Dublin's foodies, but also one of your best bets to grab Sat lunch, with stalls selling crêpes, Mexican food, olives, sushi, breads, cakes, cheeses, and a West Clare oyster bar.

DIRECTORY

Dentist For dental emergencies contact the Dublin Dental School and Hospital, Lincoln Place, 01 612 7200, http:// dentalhospital.ie.

Embassies Australia, 47–49 St Stepehen's Green, 01 664 5300; Canada, 7–8 Wilton Terrace, 01 234 4000; South Africa, Alexandra House, Earlsfort Centre, Earlsfort Terrace, 01 661 5553; UK, 29 Merrion Rd, 01 205 3700; US, 42 Elgin Rd, 01 668 8777.

Hospitals Those with accident and emergency departments include: Beaumont Hospital, Beaumont Rd, 01 809 3000; Mater Misericordiae, Eccles St, 01 803 2000; St James's, James St, 01 410 3000; and St Vincent's, Elm Park, 01 221 4000. In emergencies dial 999 or 112 for an ambulance.

Lost property Dublin Bus 01 703 1321; Bus Éireann 01 836 6111; Connolly Station 01 703 2358; Heuston Station 01 703 3299; airport 01 814 5555.

Police The main police station (Garda Síochána) is at 1–6 Pearse Street (01 666 9000). The Irish Tourist Assistance Service (01 666 9354, http://itas.ie) offers support to tourist victims of crime.

Post offices General Post Office, O'Connell St Lower (Mon–Sat 8.30am–6pm; 01 705 7600); 19 St Andrew's St (Mon–Fri 9am–6pm, Sat 9am–1pm; 01 705 8256); 31–36 Ormond Quay Upper (Mon–Fri 9am–5.30pm; 01 804 4359); 16 Merrion Row (Mon–Fri 9am–1pm & 2.15–5.30pm; 01 676 5961). Many newsagents sell postage stamps.

Around Dublin: Wicklow, Kildare and Meath

WALKERS IN WICKLOW MOUNTAINS NATIONAL PARK

Around Dublin: Wicklow, Kildare and Meath

The counties of Wicklow, Kildare and Meath equate roughly with the Pale, the fortified area around Dublin to which the English colonists retreated after 1300. The colonists coined the expression "beyond the pale" and implanted the language, customs and government of lowland England in these "obedient shires", leaving today's visitors a rich architectural legacy of castles, abbeys and, from a later period, stately homes. Wicklow, Kildare and Meath are much sought-after by modern-day settlers, too: unable to afford Dublin's property prices, thousands of the capital's workers have set up home in these commuter counties in the last twenty years.

This chapter sweeps clockwise, starting from the Wicklow coast south of Dublin and pulling up just short of Drogheda in County Louth to the north. If you have your own transport, this would make a very satisfying loop around the capital through diverse terrains, from the expansive, sandy beaches and spectacular granite mountains of County Wicklow (Cill Mhantáin; http://visitwicklow.ie), through the grassy, horse-rearing heath of the Curragh and the Bog of Allen in Kildare (Cill Dara; http://intokildare.ie), to the lush, undulating farmland of Meath (An Mhí; http://meath.ie). The **highlights** detailed opposite would form a sound basic itinerary. If you have more time to spare, in County Wicklow, add in Parnell's home, **Avondale House**, designed by James Wyatt and surrounded by forested parkland; the Neoclassical marvels of **Russborough**; the atmospheric seat of the Celtic High Kings, the **Hill of Tara**; and the impressive **Battle of the Boyne Visitor Centre** in Meath.

It wouldn't be possible to cover this same arc by **public transport**, which tends to run radially in and out of Dublin. Most of the places described in this chapter, however, are accessible on a day-trip from the capital by bus or train, with organized **tours** also

IRELAND'S ANCIENT EAST

Ireland's **Ancient East** is the east coast's answer to the Wild Atlantic Way (see page 26), although it's admittedly a more difficult sell. Whereas the Wild Atlantic Way is a clearly defined touring route, Ireland's Ancient East is a more vague proposition, geographically speaking. Stretching from the northeast to Cork Harbour, into the midlands and everywhere in between, its sheer scale can be a bit off-putting, and it's hard to know where to begin. That said, the official **website** (http://irelandsancienteast.com) is an excellent and comprehensive resource that's worth taking the time to explore. Full of **maps**, in-depth **itineraries** and featured attractions, it should be the first step in planning a road trip. Designed as a way to encourage people to explore areas outside of the capital, the focus is very much on history, from **Neolithic tombs** and **ringforts** to **Norman castles** and **famine workhouses**. Featured routes include Through the Gardens of the East (two days, 114km) from Carlow to Wicklow, Round Towers and Castles (two days, 297km) from Meath to Offaly, and Myths and Secrets of Ancient Lands (three days, 274km) from Meath to Louth via Cavan.

If driving isn't an option, Bus Éireann offer an "Open Road" tourist pass. This allows for three days of unlimited travel out of six consecutive days, with the possibility of topping up for each additional day. Further details and tailored itineraries can be found at http://buseireann.ie/openroadticket.

Highlights

❶ Walking in the Wicklow Mountains Wild and desolate terrain, traversed by the Wicklow Way, within easy reach of Dublin. See page 120

❷ Powerscourt Beautiful ornamental gardens and the highest waterfall in Ireland. See page 120

❸ Glendalough Hidden deep in this remote valley lies one of the best-preserved and most charismatic monastic sites in the country. See page 123

❹ The National Stud, Kildare town Learn all about one of Ireland's major industries at the national horse-breeding centre and enjoy the quirky gardens. See page 129

❺ Castletown Just west of Dublin, a Palladian mansion of unrestrained extravagance. See page 132

❻ Trim A historic town boasting the largest Anglo-Norman castle in Ireland and other fine medieval remains. See page 133

❼ Loughcrew Cairns These Neolithic mounds are slightly less impressive than Brú na Bóinne, but more scenic and far less touristy. See page 137

❽ Brú na Bóinne Don't miss the extraordinary prehistoric passage graves of Newgrange and Knowth. See page 141

HIGHLIGHTS ARE MARKED ON THE MAP ON PAGE 114

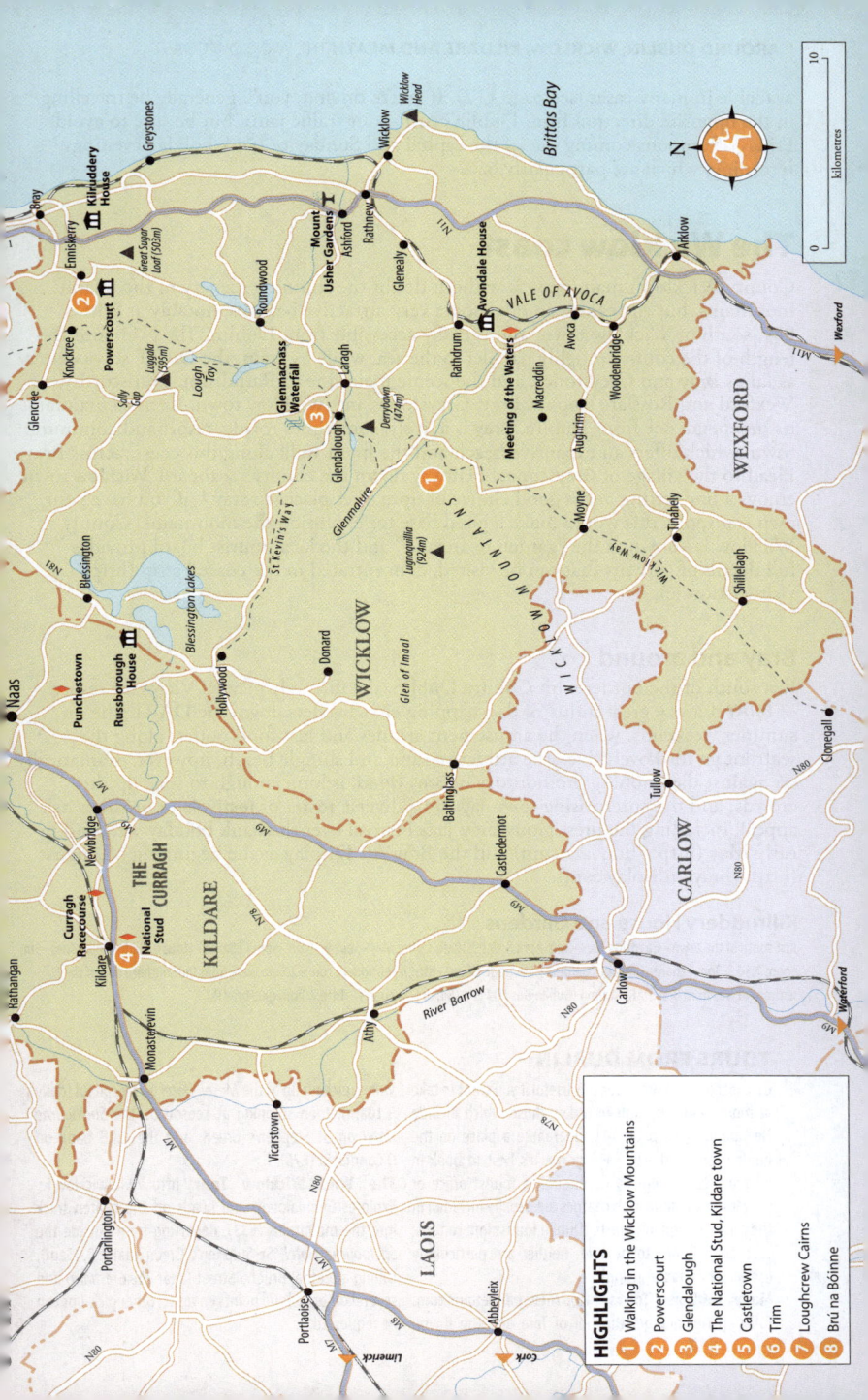

available in many cases (see page 112). If you're **driving**, you'll generally be travelling in the opposite direction from Dublin's rush-hour traffic jams, but be sure to avoid Friday afternoons coming out of the capital and Sunday or bank holiday evenings returning, which are particularly bad.

The Wicklow coast

County Wicklow's main draw is without doubt the stunning scenery of the inland mountains, but the **coast** can offer some very attractive beaches, notably at **Brittas Bay**, south of Wicklow town, and is easily accessible from Dublin. The N11 runs the length of the county roughly parallel to the sea, while by **train**, the DART service runs as far as Bray and Greystones, and the scenic main line to Rathdrum, Enniscorthy, Wexford and Rosslare stops at Bray, Greystones and Wicklow town. Keen to maintain its independence from Dublin, **Bray** is a lively, sometimes rowdy, resort and commuter town, which offers an expansive beach and the finest walk along this coast, across Bray Head to the village of **Greystones**. Halfway down the county's seaboard, **Wicklow** town enjoys a fine setting and a good choice of upmarket places to stay – if you have your own transport, this would make a good base for exploring the mountains. County Wicklow is known as the "garden of Ireland" and the local tourist board provides full details of gardens that can be visited, concentrated in the coastal strip (http://visitwicklow.ie).

Bray and around

Just south of the border with County Dublin, the formerly genteel Victorian resort of **BRAY** draws a great influx of day-tripping city-dwellers down the DART line on summer weekends, when the amusement arcades and fast-food outlets along the seafront go into overdrive. The attractive sand and shingle beach, however, dramatically set against the knobbly promontory of **Bray Head**, is long enough to soak up the crowds, and the enterprising town lays on a diverse roster of **festivals** to broaden its appeal, including the prestigious Bray Jazz Festival over the bank holiday weekend in early May (http://brayjazz.com) and the Bray Air Display at the beginning of August (http://brayairdisplay.com).

Killruddery House and Gardens

Just south of the town • **Gardens** Tues–Sun: April & Oct 9.30am–5pm; May–Sept 9.30am–6pm • charge • **House** Guided tours Tues–Sun noon, 1.30 & 3pm • charge (includes gardens); Heritage Island • http://killruddery.com • 20min walk from the southern end of the seafront or bus from Bray DART station (Dublin Bus #84 or #184, or Finnegan's – http://finnegan-bray.ie)

TOURS FROM DUBLIN

Organized **tours** are especially useful if you want to take in more than one sight in a day; those which include Newgrange (see page 141) guarantee a place on the guided tour of the passage grave. It's best to book in advance, either directly or through a tourist office or your hotel. All admission charges are usually included in the price, though not lunch. (Dublin tourist info centres: …though it has to be said, neither are particularly useful, which is surprising)

Mary Gibbons Tours http://newgrangetours.com. Takes in Newgrange, the Hill of Tara and the Boyne Valley, picking up at the *Mespil Hotel* on Mespil Rd (daily 9.10am), then stopping at Leeson St, the *Shelbourne Hotel* on St Stephen's Green, and the A.I.B bank on O'Connell St (€75).

The Wild Wicklow Tour http://wildwicklow.ie. Explores Glendalough and heads off the beaten track into the mountains (€33), departing from outside the *Shelbourne Hotel*, St Stephen's Green (daily 8.45am), calling at Cathal Brugha Street (near *The Gresham*) and several other pick-up points en route; other pick-ups can be requested.

A WALK OVER BRAY HEAD TO GREYSTONES

There's an excellent two- to three-hour **walk** from Bray seafront south across Bray Head to **Greystones**, a beautiful seaside village (see page 117) at the end of the DART line with several pubs serving food. The start of the trail is at the south end of the promenade, a five-minute walk from Bray DART station. You can follow the comparatively flat **cliff path** that runs above the rail tracks for most of the way giving close-up views of rocky coves and slate pinnacles, lashed by magnificent waves on windy days, as well as possible sightings of kestrels, peregrine falcons, dolphins, whales and basking sharks. Alternatively, if you have more time, take on the steep climb over the top of **Bray Head** for great views of Killiney Bay and the cone-shaped hills inland known as Little Sugar Loaf and Great Sugar Loaf, with a distant backdrop of the Wicklow Mountains. The latter route ascends rapidly from the end of Bray seafront through pine woods and over gorse slopes to a large cross, 200m above sea level, which was erected to mark the Holy Year of 1950; from here a track winds across the ridge below the 240m summit of Bray Head, before you turn sharp left down to join the cliff path which will bring you into Greystones.

2

Used as a film and TV location on many occasions, including for *My Left Foot* and *The Tudors*, the **Killruddery** estate is most notable for its **gardens**. Designed in the seventeenth century in early French formal style, and added to in the nineteenth, they're the oldest gardens in Ireland, featuring extensive walks flanked by hornbeam, beech and lime hedges, a café and an eighteenth-century "sylvan theatre" framed by a high bay hedge and terraced banks. The 200m-long twin ponds, once stocked with fish for the table, were designed as "water mirrors" in front of the main **house**. The latter, built in the 1820s in Tudor Revival style, is still home to the Brabazon family (the earls of Meath), and boasts some fine plasterwork ceilings. When the house is open, you can get into the **Orangery**, which was erected in the 1850s after the fashion of London's Crystal Palace, and restored in 2000 – so styling itself "Ireland's Millennium Dome". Killruddery hosts an imaginative roster of **activities**, as well as a farmers' market every Saturday (10am–4pm).

Greystones

Just south of Bray, and easily accessible on the DART line, the idyllic seaside village of **Greystones** makes a lovely day-trip from Dublin, particularly on a sunny day. Originally a small fishing hamlet, it became a popular Victorian holiday destination, and it's easy to see why. Much of it has remained the same since then – from the gently sloping main street to the leafy avenues lined with elegant houses and pretty churches. It's now a rather more upmarket settlement of boutique shops and excellent restaurants, but it still manages to retain much of its old-world charm. Watched over by the Sugarloaf Mountain, Greystones is set between the curving expanse of its **south beach** (from which the village takes its name) and the recently redeveloped **marina** and smaller north beach. Exiting the train station, the main street is to the right, while the south beach lies to the left.

ARRIVAL AND INFORMATION

By train Bray is served by frequent DART trains from Dublin (Mon–Sat roughly every 10–15min, Sun every 30min; 40min), with around every third train continuing to Greystones (Mon–Fri every 30min, Sat hourly, slightly less frequent on Sun; 50min).

BRAY AND AROUND

Tourist office Bray's tourist office is in the town council building in the Civic Centre on Main St, a 10min walk inland from the DART station (Tues–Fri 10am–1pm & 2–4.30pm; http://bray.ie).

ACCOMMODATION AND EATING

The Happy Pear Church Rd, Greystones, http:// thehappypear.ie. Starting out as a small fruit and veg shop,

The Happy Pear has now become a Greystones institution, thanks to its well-stocked shop and adjoining café serving organic vegetarian and vegan fare – much of it grown on their own farm – alongside coffee using beans from their own roastery and soda and sourdough breads. The cakes are not to be sniffed at either. €€

The Martello Hotel 47 Strand Rd, Bray, http://themartello.ie. Ideally located right on the seafront, *The Martello* provides 25 contemporaneously furnished en-suite rooms, as well as nineteen self-catering apartments sleeping up to four. There's a nightclub attached so it can get noisy on weekends. Ask for a quiet room when booking. €€

Wicklow and around

WICKLOW, 27km south of Bray, is a modest, easy-going county town, though change is under way now that it's within the ever-expanding range of Dublin commuters, as evidenced by new boutiques and galleries, and the closure of several old pubs. Transport connections are less favourable for tourists than workers, however, as there are no buses from here into the heart of the Wicklow Mountains just to the west, but if you have a car, you could base yourself at one of several fine country hotels near the town for upland jaunts.

Built around a small port that busies itself with fishing, timber and yachts, the town is enlivened by its unusual setting: the River Vartry broadens into a lough here before flowing into the Irish Sea, cutting off a narrow strip of land, **the Murrough**, that's rich in bird life, notably wintering swans and geese. On a small rise above the harbour's south pier stand the meagre ruins of twelfth-century **Black Castle**, which affords fine views of the coast, north to the Sugarloaf Mountains and south to Wicklow Head. Wicklow hosts a lively three-day arts festival in May.

Wicklow's Historic Gaol
Kilmantin Hill • charge (includes tour) • http://wicklowshistoricgaol.com

The town's major tourist attraction is **Wicklow's Historic Gaol**, dating from 1702, just up Kilmantin Hill from Market Square; after holding numerous members of Sinn Féin from 1918, the gaol finally closed for good in 1924 before it was later repurposed as a storehouse for the council. Two interactive tours are possible: a Day Tour (though it actually only lasts an hour or so) whereby you'll receive a short introductory talk before being left free to explore the facility itself; aided by videos and holograms. The tour builds up a lively and imaginative picture of life in the prison, focusing on the transportation of almost fifty thousand Irish convicts to Australia and fleshed out by sections on the 1798 Rebellion and the Great Famine. Upping the ante is the Gates of Hell Virtual Reality Tour, a fully immersive, seated experience, which transports you back to the 1700s and includes coming face-to-face with some of the gaol's most infamous inmates...

WICKLOW FILM DRIVES

From classics like *Barry Lyndon*, *My Left Foot* and *Michael Collins* to blockbusters such as *Braveheart* and *King Arthur*, Wicklow has provided the stunning backdrop to an incredibly varied selection of **films**, earning the county the soubriquet of "Hollywood of Europe". You can explore these cinematic vistas on one of the three officially designated **driving routes**. The **Braveheart Drive** (80km) starts, aptly enough, in Hollywood. A looping tour of the west Wicklow mountains, it takes in the Sally Gap, Blessington Lakes, and the spectacular Glenmacnass Waterfall. The **Excalibur Drive** (68km), starts and finishes in the village of Roundwood, and showcases some vastly contrasting scenery – bogland, mountain peaks, picturesque farms and the opulent Powerscourt Estate. Finally the **Michael Collins Drive** (72km) stretches from Wicklow town to one of the finest beaches on the east coast – Brittas Bay. For more information, see http://visitwicklow.ie.

Mount Usher Gardens

5km northwest of Wicklow, on the N11 just south of Ashford • charge • http://mountushergardens.ie • Bus #133 from Dublin

Designed by Dubliner Edward Walpole in 1868, in the Robinsonian style made famous by the eponymous gardener, **Mount Usher Gardens** shelter in excess of five thousand species, including a plethora of rare trees, shrubs and flowers, including dazzling rhododendrons, azaleas and maples, and the finest eucalyptus specimens in Europe (over fifty species), all growing in an informal style in the woodlands and meadows. Running through the gardens is the River Vartry, broken up here by a remarkable series of nineteenth-century weirs, watercourses and miniature suspension bridges.

Silver Strand and Brittas Bay

Any bus on the inland N11 to Arklow will put you off at Jack White's Crossroads, from where it's a 30min walk to Brittas Bay

Running south from Wicklow, off the R750 towards Arklow, is a series of fine, sandy beaches, beginning at **Silver Strand**, a lovely, sheltered spot just 5km from town. Backed by rolling dunes, **Brittas Bay**'s 3km strand, around 8km further on, is especially attractive and popular with weekending Dubliners, offering surfing and stand-up paddleboarding, while there's also kiteboarding on the beach; your best bet here is Brittas Bay Surf School (086 283 3075).

ARRIVAL AND INFORMATION

By train Wicklow's train station is a 15min walk northwest of the centre, off the Rathnew (Dublin) road.
Destinations Dublin Connolly (Mon–Fri 6 daily, Sat & Sun 3 daily via Greystones, Bray, Tara St and Pearse; 1hr 10min); Rosslare Europoort (3–4 daily via Rathdrum, Enniscorthy and Wexford; 1hr 45min).
By bus Buses stop either on Summer Hill, just east of Market Square, or on Marlton Rd behind the *Grand Hotel*, just west of the centre.

WICKLOW AND AROUND

Destinations Avoca (1–2 daily via Glenealy, Meeting of the Waters and Rathdrum; 35min); Dublin (airport, via several city-centre drop-off points; at least hourly; 1hr 50min); Enniscorthy (9 daily; 1hr 25min); Wexford (9 daily; 1hr 50min).
By taxi Wicklow Cabs, Main St (0404 66888).
Tourist office Rialto House, Fitzwilliam Square (Mon–Fri 9.20am–5.15pm; 0404 69117, http://visitwicklow.ie).

ACCOMMODATION

★ **Ballyknocken House** Glenealy, 8km southwest of town just off the Rathdrum road, http://ballyknocken.ie. Charming, creeper-clad 1850s farmhouse with seven rooms furnished with antiques, which serves superb breakfasts, using home-grown fruit and home-made bread and cakes. Also on offer are cookery courses with celebrity chef Catherine Fulvio and a range of walking programmes, while excellent Italian-influenced four-course set dinners are available at weekends if pre-arranged. There's also self-catering accommodation in the Milk Parlour, which has three bedrooms. €€€
★ **Hunter's Hotel** About 3km from Wicklow on the R761 north of Rathnew, http://hunters.ie. Ireland's oldest coaching inn, allegedly, dating from the early eighteenth century, is very comfortable yet unpretentious and welcoming, with an excellent restaurant; most bedrooms overlook the glorious two-acre gardens on the banks of the River Vartry, where afternoon tea is served in fine weather. Half-board packages available. €€€
Tinakilly Just over 1km out of town on the Rathnew road, http://tinakilly.ie. Grand Victorian mansion, covered in creepers and set in huge, mature landscaped gardens that run down to the sea – which is as good a reason to stay as any; some rooms have four-poster or half-tester beds. €€€

EATING AND DRINKING

Bridge Tavern Bridge St, http://bridgetavern.ie. Founded in 1759 on the site of an earlier shebeen, this venerable tavern is looking as good as ever, thanks to lots of seductive leather and dark wood filling the spacious, well-lit bars, and a flower-strewn riverside courtyard – here you can enjoy dishes like pan seared rib eye, and Thai spiced salmon with red lentil puree, coconut and broccoli. €€€
Halpin's Bridge Café Bridge St, 0404 62878. Friendly and well-kept café, where you can read their newspapers to a background of mellow jazz, while tucking into a range of toasties and wraps as well as home-made soups, gourmet sandwiches, salads, cakes and speciality teas and coffees. €
Phil Healy's Fitzwilliam Square, http://philsofwicklowtown.ie. Congenial, mid-nineteenth century wood-panelled pub with lots of craft beers in bottles and on tap, a creative food menu and traditional sessions on Wed. Closed Mon & Tues.

2

The Wicklow Mountains

If your time in Ireland is limited, it's well worth considering a stay in Dublin followed by a few days high up in the fresh air and magnificent scenery of the **Wicklow Mountains**. So close to the capital that they're often called the Dublin Mountains – by Dubliners, at any rate – they only rise to 924m at their highest point, Lugnaquillia, but form the largest area of continuous upland in Ireland. This granite mass is wild, desolate and sparsely populated at its centre, and, despite the influx of outdoorsy city-dwellers at weekends, never feels crowded. The range has been heavily glaciated to form attractive valleys, lakes and corries, while an extensive covering of peat supports purple heather and yellow gorse in abundance. To protect this huge natural playground on Dublin's doorstep, part of the massif has been designated as a national park, and walkers are signposted onto the **Wicklow Way**, a managed, long-distance trail that bisects the mountains from north to south. Wicklow Tourism's website (http://visitwicklow.ie/wicklow-walks) covers all manner of **hiking** across the county, with route maps and descriptions. One of the most popular (and satisfying) walks is to the top of the **Sugarloaf Mountain**, which, looming Vesuvius-like over the Wicklow and Dublin skyline, is the most recognisable mountain in the area. The climb is a gentle one, taking about an hour, and the views from the summit are simply stunning. To reach the starting point, take the N11 south to Kilmacanogue, go over the bridge and take the first left – the car park is the next left under the arch.

Powerscourt

1km southwest of Enniskerry • charge (includes audio-guide) • http://powerscourt.com

In the northeastern foothills of the Wicklow Mountains, just outside the village of **Enniskerry**, lies the massive **Powerscourt Estate**, where, given fine weather, you could easily pass a whole day. Although the estate is now something of an all-round destination, with two golf courses, a garden centre, craft shops, distillery and a luxury hotel, the central attraction remains the **formal gardens**, whose spectacular design matches their superb setting facing Great Sugar Loaf Mountain; indeed, so impressive are they that National Geographic voted them the third best gardens in the world.

In the late twelfth century, a castle was built on this strategic site by the Anglo-Norman le Poer (Power) family, from whom it takes its name. However, what you see today dates from the early eighteenth century, when Richard Castle designed one of the largest Palladian mansions in Ireland here, flanked by terraced gardens that were further developed in the nineteenth century. The **house** remains impressive from a distance, but most of its interior was destroyed by a fire in 1974 (on the eve of a party to celebrate major refurbishment).

The gardens

The terraced **Italian Gardens** slope gracefully down from the back of the house. The uppermost terrace, with its winged figures of Fame and Victory flanking Apollo and Diana, was designed in 1843 by the gout-ridden Daniel Robertson, who used to be wheeled about the site in a barrow, cradling a bottle of sherry – the last of the sherry apparently meant the end of the day's work. A grand staircase leads down to a spirited pair of zinc winged horses guarding the **Triton Lake**, whose central statue of the sea god (based on Bernini's fountain in the Piazza Barberini in Rome) fires a jet of water 30m skywards.

On the east side of the terraces are the curious **Pepper Pot Tower** (accurately modelled on the pepper pot from the eighth Viscount Powerscourt's dinner set), surrounded by fine North American conifers, and a colourful **Japanese Garden** of maples, azaleas and fortune palms, laid out on reclaimed bogland. To the west of the Italian Gardens lies the **walled garden**, with its rose beds, herbaceous borders and fine ceremonial

THE WICKLOW WAY

The Republic's oldest designated long-distance walk, opened in 1982, the **Wicklow Way** (http://wicklowway.com) runs the length of the Wicklow Mountains from Dublin's southern suburbs, taking in wild uplands and picturesque valleys, as well as long, boring stretches of conifer plantation. The trail cuts across the Glencree valley, passes Lough Tay and continues to Glendalough, before entering Glenmalure and skirting Lugnaquillia, the highest Wicklow peak; the walk finishes after 127km at Clonegall on the Wexford–Carlow border. The whole route is waymarked with yellow signs and can be walked in five to six days, though some people take as many as ten.

The Way begins at Marlay Park in Dublin's southern suburbs – take the #16 bus from O'Connell Street to get there. Its highlight – if you lack the time or inclination to complete the whole Way – is probably the 29km section from **Knockree to Glendalough**, which passes the Powerscourt waterfall and can be covered in one very long day – or preferably two, with a short detour to overnight at Roundwood.

Finding **accommodation** is not usually a problem, and some B&Bs will collect you from, or deliver you to, parts of the route, or ferry your bags to your next resting place, if given prior notice; there's now also a dedicated and usually cheaper luggage transfer service (http://wicklowwaybaggage.com), who also offer taxi transfers to the Way from Dublin Airport. Two An Óige hostels line the route – Glendalough (see page 125) and Glenmalure (see page 125); at the time of writing, the hostel at Knockree was hosting Ukrainian refugees and although it does have plans to reopen to the public in the future, this is likely to be some time off. Accommodation in Roundwood, Laragh/Glendalough and Glenmalure is detailed in the text. The **website** gives full details of other accommodation along the route, as well as trail descriptions, maps and other useful advice.

Ordnance Survey **maps** nos. 56 and 62 cover almost the whole route at 1:50,000, with nos. 50 and 61 picking up the extremities. EastWest Mapping (http://eastwestmapping.ie) also produce *The Wicklow Way Map Guide*, a booklet of 1:50,000 maps with accompanying text, as well as digital mapping of the region.

If you want to leave the practicalities to someone else, there are **guided walking tours** on and around the Wicklow Way by outfits such as Irish Ways (see page 32), Hilltop Treks (http://hilltoptreks.com) and Footfalls (http://walkinghikingireland.com).

entrances: the Chorus Gate, decorated with beautiful golden trumpeters, and the Bamberg Gate, which originally belonged to Bamberg cathedral in Bavaria and features remarkable perspective arches as part of its gilded ironwork design.

The waterfall

The estate's final attraction, **Powerscourt Waterfall**, is Ireland's highest at 120m. The falls leap and bound diagonally down a rock face to replenish the waters of the River Dargle in the valley below. It's 6km further down the road from the main gate, but well signposted. Note, though, that the waterfall can only be accessed by car and it's not possible to walk there.

ARRIVAL AND DEPARTURE — POWERSCOURT

By bus Enniskerry is accessible from Dublin on the #44 bus from O'Connell St, D'Olier St or Merrion Square (hourly; 1hr), or the DART train to Bray followed by the #185 bus (frequent; 30min), which sometimes continues to the main gate of Powerscourt Estate.

ACCOMMODATION AND EATING

Avoca Terrace Café Powerscourt House, 01 902 2110. Excellent, upmarket self-service café and deli, run by Avoca (see page 126), offering dishes such as lemon tart and smoked Wicklow trout salad, - though it's really renowned for its scones — and a terrace that provides sumptuous views of the garden.

2

Ferndale Enniskerry, http://ferndalehouse.com. You'll probably want to push on further into the mountains for somewhere to stay, but Enniskerry does have this good B&B on the village square, an attractive, all-en-suite place, furnished in period style, in an early Victorian house set in pretty gardens. €€

Glencree and around

To the west of Powerscourt, beyond Knockree, the village of **GLENCREE** lies at the head of its eponymous valley and on the old **military road** from Dublin south into the mountains. To flush out insurgents from the 1798 Rebellion, some of whom evaded capture in Wicklow until 1803, the authorities in Dublin were obliged to build this road right along the backbone of the range. In the village, there's a **cemetery** for German airmen who died in Ireland during the two world wars. Nearby, just south of the cemetery, is the **Glencree Centre for Peace & Reconciliation** (Mon–Fri 9.30am–5pm; http://glencree.ie), created to support people affected by the conflict in the North, fittingly occupies a former British army barracks, built to guard the military road. It houses a café with an outdoor terrace and a visitor centre that displays diverse temporary exhibitions.

South into the mountains

South of Glencree, the military road (R115) climbs past the dramatic twin tarns of Lough Bray Lower and Upper (accessible by boggy paths opposite a car park) and then through ever wilder terrain towards one of the Wicklow Mountains' two main passes, the **Sally Gap**. From here the military road continues south through superb countryside, passing the beautiful **Glenmacnass Waterfall**, down to Laragh and Glendalough. If you fancy stretching your legs along the way, pull in at the car park 2.5km south of Sally Gap, cross the road and follow the rough, boggy path for 45 minutes or so to the prominent summit of **Luggala**, or Fancy Mountain; from here, you'll be rewarded with precipitous views straight down to Lough Tay and a panorama to the south and west of Lough Dan and the major Wicklow peaks.

Lough Tay

The R759 heading southeast of Sally Gap winds its way down to Sraghmore, 3km north of Roundwood, passing impressive **Lough Tay**, where scree slopes tumble headlong into the water from the summit of Luggala. You can walk from one of the car parks above Lough Tay north up the Wicklow Way for about fifteen minutes to the memorial to J.B. Malone (one of the pioneers of Irish hill-walking and of the Way itself) for the finest view of the ensemble, and on to the top of White Hill in another twenty minutes for further scenic delights.

Roundwood

From Dublin, you can reach Glendalough on the old military road (R115), but the quicker route is along the N11 and R755 through **ROUNDWOOD**, which is accessible on the St Kevin's bus service (see page 125). This attractive village claims to be the highest in Ireland, at 220m above sea level, and enjoys a gentle setting on the eastern flank of the Wicklow range by the **Vartry Reservoir** – a good spot for an easy, flat, evening stroll. With a decent range of food and accommodation, Roundwood is a popular stop for hikers on the Wicklow Way, which is just 2.5km away. Wedged between the R759 and the R755 a little north of the village, **Ballinastoe Forest** is crisscrossed with mountain-biking trails, with bike rental, mountain-biking lessons and tours available (http://biking.ie).

ACCOMMODATION AND EATING ROUNDWOOD

Riverbank Dublin Rd, north of the village centre, 01 281 8117. Family home with a lovely garden, bright, pine-

floored and furnished en-suite bedrooms, and a drying room. Offers luggage transfer, transport to/from the trail for walkers, and packed lunches. Closed Nov–Feb. €€
Roundwood Caravan & Camping Park North end of the village, http://dublinwicklowcamping.com. Large, smart, well-equipped campsite with a shop, laundry service and campers' kitchen. Closed mid-Sept to April. €

★ **The Roundwood Inn** Main St, 01 281 8107. Roundwood's best place to drink is this cosy, seventeenth-century hunting lodge. It also serves great bar meals, ranging from local seafood to delicious Irish stew, as well as dishes such as roast leg of Wicklow lamb in its more formal, weekend restaurant. €€

Glendalough and Laragh

Visitor Centre and monastic site daily: mid-March to mid-Oct 9.30am–6pm; mid-Oct to mid-March 9.30am–5pm; last admission 45min before closing • Visitor Centre charge; monastic site free; Heritage Card • http://heritageireland.ie and http://glendalough.ie

A deep glaciated valley in the heart of the Wicklow Mountains, **GLENDALOUGH** ("valley of the two lakes") provides a delightfully atmospheric location for some of the best-preserved monastic sites in Ireland. Despite the coach parties, enough of the valley's tranquillity remains for you to understand what drew monks and pilgrims here in the first place.

The Glendalough Visitor Centre, its adjacent car park and the main monastic site are on the eastern side of the **Lower Lake**, while further west up the valley is the larger and more impressive **Upper Lake**, with its wooded cliffs and dramatic waterfall as well as more ruins, the national park information point and another car park. On the main road in, about 2km east of the visitor centre, lies the small village of **LARAGH**, which has most of the area's amenities, notably accommodation (though no ATM – the nearest is in Roundwood or Rathdrum); the Green Road from the south end of Laragh will allow you to walk along the south bank of the river to the Glendalough Visitor Centre and beyond, away from the traffic on the main road.

WALKS AND ACTIVITIES AROUND GLENDALOUGH

The **Wicklow Mountains National Park Information Office** (daily 10am–5.30pm; http://nationalparks.ie/wicklow), at the eastern end of Glendalough's Upper Lake, has details of local walking routes and conditions and sells a series of leaflets on the national park, including *The Walking Trails of Glendalough* (also available from the visitor centre), which covers waymarked routes taking anything from 45 minutes to four hours. A map of the walking trails can be downloaded from the website, while a couple of good hikes in the area are also covered by Joss Lynam's *Easy Walks near Dublin*. The visitor centre contains an exhibition on the park's **wildlife**, which includes deer, red squirrels, hen harriers, red grouse and lots of birds of prey, and runs free guided nature walks, such as bat walks in summer and rut walks to observe deer in the autumn.

St Kevin's Way follows what was the main pilgrim path to Glendalough in medieval times. Waymarked with yellow pilgrim symbols, the 29km trail runs eastwards along country tracks and quiet roads from Hollywood, near the N81 south of Blessington, climbing to the **Wicklow Gap**, before following the descent of the Glendasan River for 7km to the Glendalough Visitor Centre. *St Kevin's Way*, a booklet by Peter Harbison and Joss Lynam, covers the route with comprehensive 1:50,000 maps and text.

The easiest to follow and most satisfying short **hike** is on the south side of Glendalough valley, where it's possible to climb 474m **Derrybawn** in around an hour, for spectacular views. Follow the Wicklow Way south from the national park information point past the Poulanass Waterfall, before eventually peeling left off the waymarked forest track up a narrow path, which climbs steeply to the edge of the forest and then straight up to Derrybawn's ridge and summit cairn.

For **horseriding**, try Glendalough House, about 3km north of Laragh in Annamoe (0404 45116).

Brief history

The monastery at Glendalough was established in the sixth century by **St Kevin** (Caoimhín), who retreated to the valley to pray in solitude. His piety attracted many followers to the site, especially after his death in 618, and the monastic community here came to rival Clonmacnois (see page 174) for its learning. It was raided by the Vikings at least four times between the eighth and eleventh centuries, then by the English in the fourteenth, and was finally dissolved during the Reformation. Pilgrimages continued, however, as the pope declared that seven visits to Glendalough would earn the same indulgence as one to Rome, but the pilgrims' abstemious devotions on St Kevin's Day (June 3) were often followed by drink and debauchery, and in 1862 a local priest banned the gatherings.

The Lower Lake

The **visitor centre** features photographic displays and a film on Glendalough's place within Ireland's monastic heritage as well as a model of how the monastery is thought to have looked at the height of its activity.

Once you've entered the **monastic site**, through a double stone archway that was once surmounted by a tower, you'll come to its largest structure, the roofless but impressive **Cathedral of SS Peter and Paul**, begun in the early ninth century. Among the tombs outside stands **St Kevin's Cross**, one of the best remaining relics from the period, consisting of a granite monolith decorated with an eighth-century carving of a Celtic cross over a wheel; unusually, the quadrants of the cross have not been cut through, which suggests that it was left unfinished. Above the doorway of the nearby twelfth-century **Priests' House**, which may have been the site of Kevin's tomb-shrine, are faint carvings of figures believed to depict the saint and two (later) abbots. Downhill from here stands the two-storey, eleventh-century **St Kevin's Church**, whose steeply pitched roof and bell turret so resemble a chimney that the building is also known as "St Kevin's Kitchen", although it was almost certainly an oratory.

Glendalough's **Round Tower** rises to over 30m, its conical roof having been restored in 1876. Such tapering stone towers are found only in Ireland and probably had multiple functions, as belfries, watchtowers, treasuries and places of refuge from danger – the entrance is usually well above ground level, accessible by a ladder that could be removed if necessary.

To the south of St Kevin's Church, a footbridge crosses the river to the **Deerstone**, so called after a legend that claims that a tame doe squirted milk into the hollowed-out stone to feed the twin orphaned babies of one of Kevin's followers. In fact, it's a bullaun, one of many all over Ireland, a stone believed to have magical powers that was used for grinding medicines.

The Upper Lake

You can drive to the **Upper Lake** car park along the north side of the valley, but it's more enjoyable to walk from the Deerstone along the signposted **Green Road** (part of the Wicklow Way), a scenic track that skirts the south side of the Lower Lake. After twenty minutes or so, this will bring you to the Upper Lake and the tiny, ruined, late tenth-century, Romanesque **Reefert Church**, whose small cemetery is thought to contain the graves of local chieftains (its name means "royal burial ground" in Irish). From here a path runs up to **St Kevin's Cell**, a typically Celtic, corbel-roofed "beehive" hut on a promontory overlooking the lake. Further up the cliff, **St Kevin's Bed** is a small cave that may have been a Bronze Age tomb, into which the saint reputedly moved to avoid the allures of an admirer called Caitlín; he's supposed to have offered the final resistance to her advances by chucking the poor woman into the lake. On the opposite side of the lake, a trail runs along the north shore and on up the valley, passing nineteenth-century zinc and lead mines.

ARRIVAL AND DEPARTURE

GLENDALOUGH AND LARAGH

By bus Between March and September, St Kevin's bus service (http://glendaloughbus.com) runs daily (at 11.30am & 6pm) from Stephen's Green North in Dublin, via Bray and Roundwood, to Laragh and Glendalough Visitor Centre. Another option is to take a minibus from Rathdrum (see page 126).

ACCOMMODATION

Glendalough Hermitage Centre St Kevin's Parish Church, just west of Laragh, http://glendaloughhermitage.ie. This spiritual retreat on the north side of the road to Glendalough offers pilgrims of all faiths comfortable stone hermitages in a tranquil, gorse-strewn garden; rooms (with either single or twin beds) are simply but comfortably furnished, with a shower room and kitchenette. Restaurants and shops are a 5min walk away. Two-night minimum stay, but no limit on longer stays. €€

Glendalough Hotel Glendalough, http://glendaloughhotel.com. Bright, family-run Victorian hotel right by the visitor centre offering great views from many of the colourful, en-suite bedrooms, some of which have balconies; good-value half-board deals available. There's informal dining throughout the hotel, courtesy of *Casey's Bistro* or the *Backyard Cafe and Farm Kitchen*, the latter with a fine terrace and sweeping hillside views. €€

Glendalough International Hostel Glendalough, on the road to the Upper Lake, http://anoige.ie. Large, comfortable, all-en-suite hostel, offering breakfast and packed lunches, a well-equipped kitchen, drying room and laundry facilities. €̄

Lynham's Hotel Laragh, http://lynhamsoflaragh.ie. Airy, spacious, modern hotel overlooking the Glenmacnass River at the heart of the village, behind a popular bar with open fires in winter and outside tables by the river in summer. Bar, restaurant and lounge – all commendable – round things off nicely. €€€

Riversdale House Wicklow Gap road, just over 1km northwest of the Glendalough Visitor Centre, http://glendalough.eu.com. Hospitable, well-run B&B in a tranquil location with great views. The en-suite rooms are simply and tastefully furnished, and breakfast is taken in the picturesque sunroom overlooking the Glendasan River. Packed lunches can be arranged for walkers. Room only rates available too. €€

EATING

Glendalough Green Café Laragh, 0404 45151. Attractive, welcoming deli-café with outdoor tables on the green, dishing up tasty home-made soups, home-baked breads and cakes, salads, speciality teas and coffees.

The Wicklow Heather Glendalough road, Laragh, http://wicklowheather.ie. Just off the green in Laragh, this is a cosy restaurant with a whiskey bar and attractive patio tables. It serves everything from breakfast (excellent vegan options) and morning coffee to upmarket dinners featuring, for example, pan fried Barbary duck breast with red wine and plum sauce and garlic gratin potatoes, as well as Wicklow lamb and Irish salmon. €€€

Glenmalure

Arrowing down from the northwest around the Avonbeg River, **Glenmalure** is the next valley south of Glendalough, overshadowed to the southwest by Wicklow's highest peak, wild and lonely **Lugnaquillia** (924m). Besides the river, this peaceful, enclosed glen has room only for a thin strip of emerald fields and a narrow, gorse-flanked road between its steep slopes of scree and forestry. For drivers and cyclists, the military road offers a scenic route there, branching off the R755 just south of Laragh and continuing southwest; walkers can follow the Wicklow Way out of Glendalough, skirting Derrybawn Mountain and 657m Mullacor before descending into the valley. At the point where the military road hits the glen stands a ruined barracks, used in the suppression of the 1798 Rebellion.

ARRIVAL AND ACCOMMODATION

GLENMALURE

By bus Minibuses run to Glenmalure from Rathdrum (see page 126).

★ **Glenmalure Lodge** http://glenmalurelodge.ie. Quaint and welcoming 200-year-old coaching inn in a beautiful spot on the Wicklow Way, near the military road, offering comfortable, en-suite B&B (including a family room sleeping four), decent food and a cosy bar with a turf fire and outdoor tables; luggage transfer and packed lunches can be arranged for walkers. €€

Glenmalure Youth Hostel http://anoige.ie. Northwest of *Glenmalure Lodge*, the valley road ends at a car park and footbridge over the river, where a track runs over and up to this hostel. It's very basic (no electricity or running water) but has a gas-powered kitchen, log fire and nearby stream, and holds interest as the house formerly owned by playwright J.M. Synge and by W.B. Yeats's muse, Maud Gonne McBride. Open daily June–Aug and Saturdays Sept–May. €

Rathdrum and around

In the lush foothills at the southeastern edge of the Wicklow Mountains, the main settlement is peaceful **RATHDRUM**, its long main street and pretty village green perched high above the Avonmore River. A few kilometres downstream, the quaint village of Avoca still trades on its role as the location for the now-defunct BBC-TV series *Ballykissangel*. Venturing further afield, you might well be tempted to stay or eat at the excellent *Brook Lodge and Wells Spa* (see page 127) to the west of Avoca at **Macreddin**, a village which fell into decline in the late nineteenth century but has recently been beautifully redeveloped by the enterprising hoteliers.

Avondale House

2km south of Rathdrum village • charge; open access to grounds, though parking on-site costs €5 (coins only); Heritage Island • http://beyondthetreesavondale.com

Beautifully proportioned **Avondale House** – completed in 1779 – is the birthplace and home of **Charles Stewart Parnell**, the nineteenth-century campaigner for home rule who was dubbed "the uncrowned king of Ireland". Guided tours take in six of the ground floor rooms, which hold numerous, authentic pieces of furniture and artefacts, including an original Bossi fireplace, a walnut and mahogany dresser custom made to fit into an alcove in the dining room, and Parnell's desk and books. In the library hangs a poignant banner, representing the arms of Ireland's four provinces in pastel colours; given to Parnell in the 1880s, when home rule seemed a racing certainty, it was vainly intended for display in the future Irish House of Commons.

Recent redevelopment of the estate has incorporated Ireland's first Treetop Walk and Viewing Tower, which leads visitors on a 1.4km trail (wheelchair and buggy accessible) through the forest and above the canopy of the trees. The walk culminates in the spectacular tower, where a gentle incline leads up to a viewing platform some 38-metres above the forest floor and offering a stunning panorama of the Wicklow landscape. Learning and activity stations along the trail, and a 90-metre spiral tunnel slide, ensure maximum fun. There's also the Coillte Pavilion exhibition space, which details the history of forestry in Ireland, while numerous trails and a fine café mean that you could quite happily spend the best part of a day here.

Avoca

Set in the beautiful, thickly wooded **Vale of Avoca,** 10km south of Rathdrum on the R752, **AVOCA**'s most notable feature is its famous eighteenth-century **mill** – original home of the now-nationwide Avoca shops – where you can watch the weavers at work on a mill tour (March–Oct daily 10am–4pm; free; http://avoca.com). You can eat at the excellent **café** here and, of course, there's a shop selling the fruits of the looms as well as the other good-quality gifts the Avoca chain is known for.

ARRIVAL AND INFORMATION   RATHDRUM AND AROUND

By train Rathdrum's train station is down by the river, a 10min walk from Main St.

Destinations Dublin Connolly (Mon–Fri 6 daily, Sat & Sun 3 daily via Wicklow, Greystones and Bray; 1hr 20min); Rosslare Europort (3–4 daily via Enniscorthy and Wexford; 1hr 30min).

By bus Rathdrum (20min) and Avoca (35min) are served by one or two buses daily from Wicklow.

By minibus Roughly connecting with services to and from Dublin, there's a minibus/taxi to Glendalough and Glenmalure, via Laragh, from the train station and the market square, which would allow you, for example, to walk the Wicklow Way from Glendalough to Glenmalure (advance booking required;, http://wicklowwaybus.com).

Tourist office There's a small tourist office in Rathdrum's market square (Mon–Fri 9.30am–5pm; 0404 46262), and another in Avoca's old courthouse (Mon–Fri 9am–5pm; 0402 35022).

ACCOMMODATION AND EATING

RATHDRUM

Bates Nua 3 Market St, http://batesrestaurant.com. In a cosy, grey-stone cottage just off the market square, *Bates* is a top-quality, moderately priced restaurant with friendly service, serving dishes such as homemade pork and duck pate with sautéed cabbage, and Wicklow venison loin with butternut squash purée and thyme jus; there are some decent veggie dishes thrown into the mix too. Closed Mon & Tues. €€€

Hidden Valley Resort http://hiddenvalley.ie. Down by the river, with its own lake, this camping and caravan park has a campers' kitchen and a laundry room, as well as various self-catering lodges. Also on offer are kayak rental, swimming, aqua and splash parks, laser tag, a rock wall, cinema and lots of other activities. Closed Nov to mid-March. Camping €, lodges €€

Jacob's Well Main St, http://jacobswell.ie. Well-equipped, comfortable B&B with cheery en-suite bedrooms, great showers and a sitting room with a turf fire. It's in a separate building from the welcoming and popular pub, which offers well prepared, hearty lunch and dinner, and good Guinness. €€

MACREDDIN

★ **Brook Lodge and Macreddin Village** 12km southwest of Rathdrum, http://brooklodge.com. Located in a secluded valley, this luxurious, modern country-house-style hotel boasts impeccably appointed rooms (classic rooms and junior suites), a lovely spa, swimming pool, two excellent restaurants, pub and café, free bike hire, and a golf course designed by former European Ryder Cup captain Paul McGinley. €€€

Russborough House

3km south of Blessington village • Visit by guided tour (hourly) • charge; Heritage Island • http://russborough.ie

Standing on the western edge of the Wicklow Mountains, **Russborough House** is a lavish Palladian country house designed by Richard Castles for Joseph Leeson, later Lord Russborough and the Earl of Milltown, whose family had made their money in the brewing trade. Castle died before the project was completed, leaving Francis Bindon to oversee the fulfilment of his grand design. Completed in 1751, the Wicklow-granite building's 750m frontage, with its curving colonnaded wings, is the longest of its kind in Ireland.

Known for its outstanding **art collection** – some of which has been donated to the National Gallery for safekeeping (see page 127) – the house also boasts a sumptuous **interior**, featuring Baroque plasterwork ceilings by the Lafranchini brothers, notably in the saloon, depicting the four seasons, and in the music room, where the ingenious geometrical design seems to add height to the room. Further beautiful stuccowork, representing hunting and garlands, adorns the cantilevered main staircase, which was ornately carved out of dark Cuban mahogany by Irish craftsmen in the eighteenth century. Other highlights include the Italian-marble fireplace in the dining room depicting Bacchus and vines, and a series of French clocks dating back as far as the fifteenth century, which are still wound every Tuesday. The **grounds** contain a **maze**

PILFERED PAINTINGS AT RUSSBOROUGH

Renowned for its **art collection**, Russborough House has been **burgled** on no fewer than four occasions, though almost all of the stolen paintings have subsequently been recovered. The first burglary was in 1974, when nineteen paintings were stolen by Englishwoman Rose Dugdale in order to raise funds for the IRA – an event that featured in the 2024 film, *Baltimore*. The house was again broken into in 1986, by "The General", aka Martin Cahill, one of Dublin's most notorious criminals (this episode featured prominently in John Boorman's 1998 film *The General*). Russborough was burgled again in 2001, possibly by an associate of Cahill's, when a Gainsborough portrait was stolen for the third time, along with a work by Bellotto. Both were recovered in September 2002, only days before a fourth break-in, which netted five pictures including two by Rubens – all of which have been returned to the house, and subsequently sent to the National Gallery. Replicas of the paintings remain in the house.

and 5km of trails, which will take you past a walled garden, and it's also the location for the **National Bird of Prey Centre** (http://nationalbirdofpreycentre.ie) where you can handle several owl species and take a tour of the site (Wed–Sun 1.30pm, 2.30pm, & 3.30pm).

ARRIVAL AND DEPARTURE

By bus Blessington is about 1hr 40min from central Dublin on the #65 bus from Poolbeg St or South Great George's St (10–14 daily). Some of these services (4–6 daily) continue southwest of Blessington, towards Ballymore Eustace: ask the bus driver to let you off at the Russborough stop, which will leave you at the end of the road leading to the

RUSSBOROUGH HOUSE

house, a 15min walk away; otherwise you can walk to Russborough along the Blessington Greenway Walk, which runs through woodland along the shores of Blessington Lake from the Avon Rí Activity Centre at the south end of Blessington, which should take approximately 1hr (see http://visitwicklow.ie).

EATING

★ **Grangecon** Kilbride Rd, just off Blessington's main street, http://grangeconcafe.blogspot.com. Excellent café-restaurant in the old schoolhouse, which sources the very best, mostly organic and seasonal ingredients from the

top local suppliers and makes everything in-house, from soda bread to lemon curd for their tarts. Great sandwiches and shepherd's pie, and scrummy home-made lemonade. Closed Sun & Mon. €€

County Kildare

In contrast to the harsh landscape of the Wicklow Mountains to the east, **County Kildare** is prosperous farming country, which was gladly seized and fortified by the English as part of the medieval Pale. Rich pasture for cattle and horses in the north of the county gives way to fertile ploughland in the south, the **Bog of Allen** in the northwest providing the only unproductive blot on the landscape. The county's main attractions for visitors are neatly concentrated in two areas. Servicing the bloodstock farms on **the Curragh**'s lush heathland, **Kildare town** is generally a low-key affair, where you can explore the monastery and church founded by St Brigid in the fifth century, and see what all the equine fuss is about at the fascinating **National Stud**. To the north of town, you can trace the development of the Bog of Allen at the nature centre in **Lullymore**. Meanwhile, up on the county's northern edge lies one of Ireland's finest stately homes, **Castletown**.

Kildare town

In **KILDARE**'s quiet moments, of which there are many, you are keenly aware that the pre-eminent local business all takes place outside of town, for **the Curragh**, which stretches east from the town to the River Liffey, is Ireland's horse-racing centre. The underlying limestone of this huge plain, the largest area of semi-natural grassland in Europe, is good for a horse's bone formation, and the grass is said to be especially sweet. Consequently, the Curragh is home not only to a famous racecourse, but also to dozens of stud farms and stables, engaged in the multimillion-euro pursuit of breeding and training racehorses, one of the country's biggest sources of income – as vividly illustrated at the **National Stud**.

St Brigid's Cathedral

Market Square • tower closed in heavy rain • Cathedral suggested donation; tower charge • http://stbrigidscathedral.com

Kildare is arrayed around a triangular main square, which retains its central, nineteenth-century Market House and is overlooked by the huge Church of Ireland **Cathedral of St Brigid**. In the late fifth century, **St Brigid** is said to have founded a religious house here on a major pagan site, which became an important monastic centre of art, learning and culture – the *Book of Kildare*, for example, produced here in the seventh century but now lost, was, according to twelfth-century scholar Giraldus Cambrensis, dictated by an angel and as magnificent as the *Book of Kells*. Brigid herself, who may well have originated as the Celtic goddess Brigantia, is Ireland's second most important saint after Patrick, with many holy wells that are thought to cure sterility dedicated to her. Known also for her healing, farming and negotiating skills, Brigid has seen a recent revival of interest as an icon of feminine spirituality and an alternative to the patriarchal institutions of the Church.

The present cathedral was originally constructed in the thirteenth century, but the north transept and choir were destroyed during the 1641 Rebellion, and the building was largely reconstructed in the nineteenth century. Its twelfth-century **round tower**, the second highest in Ireland at 33m, is surmounted by mid-eighteenth-century battlements that replaced the original roof, and affords a fine panorama from the top; note, though, that it's only accessible by ladder, which may not suit all visitors. On the north side of the church is the restored **fire temple** – Brigid had cannily preserved the pagan cult of fire, and a fire is still lit here every year on **St Brigid's Day**, Feb 1 (http://solasbhride.ie/feile-bride), formerly the pagan festival of spring.

The Irish National Stud & Gardens

Tully, 2km south of central Kildare • 45min guided tours 10.30am, noon, 2pm & 4pm • charge, includes tour; Heritage Island • http://irishnationalstud.ie • Served by shuttle buses from Kildare town (see "Getting around", opposite), as well as buses from Dublin's Connolly LUAS stop

THE GRAND AND ROYAL CANALS

County Kildare is traversed by the **Royal and Grand canals**, which run from Dublin to the River Shannon. Reminders of Ireland's mercantile confidence in the eighteenth century, before the disenfranchisement of the Act of Union, they were built to service the mills, distilleries and breweries of a minor industrial revolution. Passenger boats on both canals were soon eclipsed by the railways and stopped running around 1850, but freight services continued until as late as 1960.

Completed in stages between 1779 and 1805, the **Grand Canal** heads out from south Dublin to Robertstown in County Kildare, where it splits into two branches. The 50km southern branch (aka the Barrow Line), completed in 1791, meets the River Barrow at Athy in the south of the county, allowing passage as far south as Waterford; the main waterway runs west via Tullamore in County Offaly to Shannon Harbour, a total of 114km from Dublin.

The **Royal Canal**, a rival northern route opened between 1796 and 1816, was never quite as successful, though it managed to reach a peak tonnage of 112,000 in 1847. It runs along the northern border of County Kildare, before heading northwest to Mullingar and joining the Shannon, 144km from north Dublin, at Cloondara in County Longford.

The canals are flanked by a series of pleasantly undeveloped – and easy-to-follow – **trails**, the Royal Canal Way, the Grand Canal Way and the Barrow Way; for more information and descriptions of the routes see http://sportireland.ie. Even better, rent a **barge** and hit the waterways for a few days of leisurely cruising – operating the old but ingenious locks, quietly drifting under ancient bridges and through intensely green and lush landscapes is a memorable and relaxing experience. Jennifer's Travels (http://jenniferztravels.com) has a large, beautiful four-birth barge specifically built for holiday travel, complete with kitchen, shower and peat burning stove. Pick-up is in Monasterevin, about 45 minutes from Dublin (rates are variable; call for quotes).

Another option is to go with Canalways Ireland (http://canalways.ie). They have a larger selection of barges, with a two- to four-berth costing €1295 for one week in high season. Their Grand Canal route starts in Rathangan, Co. Kildare, and ends in either Shannon Harbour, Offaly, or Lucan, Dublin. A transfer from Dublin Airport can be arranged.

The **Irish National Stud** shows the highly evolved business of horse breeding in action. Here, you can look round the stables themselves and stroll through two attractive on-site **gardens**. It's worth timing your visit to coincide with one of the entertaining **guided tours**.

The stud farm was established here, by the mineral-rich River Tully, in 1900 by Colonel William Hall Walker, of the famous Scotch whisky family. Hall Walker's methods were highly successful, though eccentric: each newborn foal's horoscope was read, and those on whom the stars didn't shine were immediately sold, regardless of their lineage or physical characteristics. In 1915, the colonel presented the farm to the British government – who promptly made him Lord Wavertree – on condition that it became the British National Stud. It was finally transferred to the Irish government in 1944 at an agreed valuation.

Within the attractive grounds, there are various yards, paddocks and stallion boxes, as well as a café. But the highlight of the tour has to be the **horses** themselves. They include retired racing stars like Hurricane Fly, Faugheen and Beef Or Salmon on the stud's 'Living Legends' team, as well as top stallions who command huge fees for what's quaintly called a live cover and who jet as far afield as Australia to mate with local mares. From February until July, you should be able to see mares and their young foals in the paddocks. Elsewhere, the **Irish Racehorse Experience** (included in the ticket) is a new state of the art experiential attraction, whereby visitors can immerse themselves in the life of a thoroughbred horse, journeying with them from birth to retirement. Here, visitors have the chance to own, train and ride their own horse, culminating in a thrilling real time race that's guaranteed to set the pulse racing.

The gardens

The grounds of the National Stud contain two beautiful gardens (included in the admission price). The beautiful and playful **Japanese Garden** was created by Colonel Hall Walker and two Japanese gardeners on a reclaimed bog between 1906 and 1910. A product of the Edwardian obsession with the Orient, it symbolizes the life of man from oblivion to eternity. Over miniature hills and waterfalls, past colourful flowers and trees, it follows from birth to death a delightful numbered trail, which yields a choice between bachelorhood and marriage, as well as a few false leads along the way.

By comparison, **St Fiachra's Garden** – named after the Irish monk who became the patron saint of gardeners – is perhaps a little less compelling. Predominantly planted with native Irish specimens, the garden comprises areas of woodland and wetland, waterfalls and streams, and a lake in which has been placed a group of 5000-year-old

---

HORSE RACING IN KILDARE

Two of Ireland's major racecourses, where you're practically guaranteed a fun, boisterous day out, are just a short trot from Kildare. The major Irish flat-racing classics are held at the **Curragh Racecourse**, about 5km east of town (http://curragh.ie): the Irish 1000 Guineas and 2000 Guineas in May, the Irish Derby in late June or early July, the Irish Oaks in July and the Irish St Leger in September. You can take special **bus** services to get to the Curragh from Dublin on race days (http://dublincoach.ie), and there are free shuttle buses to the course from Kildare town for passengers on Dublin Coach's other services (see page 131) and from Kildare **train station** (http://irishrail.ie).

About 20km east, just south of the town of Naas, **Punchestown Racecourse** (http://punchestown.com) hosts the five-day Irish National Hunt Festival in April, a more rural affair that attracts a lot of farmers. Have a look at their website for details of special buses from Dublin and Naas (which is on the train line from Connolly Station) during the festival.

bog-oak trunks, branchless and blackened, suggesting not only death but also longevity. There's plenty of native wildlife to keep an eye out for too.

ARRIVAL AND INFORMATION KILDARE TOWN

By bus As well as the Bus Éireann services to Dublin (mostly Custom House Quay, via O'Connell Bridge; Mon–Sat roughly hourly, Sun roughly every 2hr; 1hr 30min), which stop on Kildare's main square, private buses include Dublin Coach (http://dublincoach.ie) to Dublin, Dublin Airport, Limerick and Ennis.

By train The train station is a 10min walk north of the main square; there are frequent services to Dublin Heuston (20–30 daily; 40min).

Tourist office The tourist office (Mon–Sat 9.30am–1pm & 2–5pm; http://kildareheritage.com and http://intokildare. ie) and its heritage centre are in the eighteenth-century Market House in the centre of the main square.

ACCOMMODATION AND EATING

Harte's The Square, http://harteskildare.ie. A nineteenth-century pub exterior with pretty hanging baskets conceals this lively gastropub, which presents some bold and successful menu choices such as whipped brie with chorizo oil and confit fennel for starters, and braised Slane Valley lamb shank with mint and parsley chimichurri. They've also a fine selection of craft beers from their very own Dew Drop brewhouse. The three-course Sunday lunch €35 is a steal. €̄€̄€̄

★ **JJ Mahon's** Just off the square on Claregate St, 045 521316. Smartly kept, traditional pub done out in cosy dark woods and green leather. Walls cluttered with knickknacks and framed historical ephemera give it a nice old-world feel, and there's always a warm atmosphere.

Lord Edward The Square, http://silkenthomas.com. Behind – and owned by – the *Silken Thomas* pub, the *Lord Edward* offers comfortable en-suite rooms in an eighteenth-century lodge that's been smartly converted using a lot of polished wood and earth tones. Breakfast is not included in the price, but is available at the pub; half-board packages also available. €̄

Silken Thomas The Square, http://silkenthomas.com. The town's major hospitality complex, with several bars, including *Lil's* pub, the *Squires* sports bar and *Flanagan's Lounge*, which offer tempting breakfasts, lunches and dinners (most dishes €10–15), and a smart, modern and popular evening restaurant, *Chapter 16*, where main courses include items such as chicken breast with black pudding croquettes. €̄

The Bog of Allen

To the north of Kildare town lies the great **Bog of Allen**, Ireland's most famous peatland. Actually a complex of bogs that once covered two thousand square kilometres between the rivers Liffey, Barrow, Shannon and Boyne, it's now much diminished by drainage and stripping.

Bog of Allen Nature Centre

Lullymore, 16km north of Kildare town • weekend openings for special events May–Sept; closed public hols • donation requested • http://ipcc.ie

The best place to get a handle on the bog is in **Lullymore**, a tranquil parish and former monastic settlement on the road to nowhere 16km north of Kildare, which sits on an island of mineral soil, surrounded by peat. Here you'll find the **Bog of Allen Nature Centre**, run by the Irish Peatland Conservation Council, a charity whose aim is to ensure the conservation of a representative sample of Irish bogs. Informative exhibits at the centre, which is housed in the farm buildings of nineteenth-century Lullymore Lodge, trace the development of bogs, as well as their significance as habitats for rare animals and plants. The latter include species such as sundews, butterworts and pitcher plants, which have developed the capacity to eat insects, as the peat they grow on is deficient in nutrients; a greenhouse in the centre's peat free wildlife garden displays carnivorous plants from Ireland and around the world, and their various methods of drugging, gluing or otherwise catching the poor critters. Next to the centre, a 100m boardwalk has been built over Lodge Bog, a small raised bog that's home to around 150 species of plants, including carnivorous round-leaved sundews, as well as mountain hares, foxes and over seventy species of butterflies and moths.

2

BOGS

Bogs once covered around one-sixth of Ireland's surface, a higher proportion than any other European country apart from Finland. They began to form around nine thousand years ago after the last Ice Age, when retreating glaciers and ice sheets left central Ireland covered by myriad shallow lakes. Gradually the partly decomposed remnants of mosses, pondweeds, water lilies and reeds built up on many of the lake beds as layers of peat, reducing the area of open water and eventually forming **fens**.

Between 7500 and 1500 years ago, further changes occurred to most of Ireland's fens. As the fen peat became so thick that it filled up the lakes, its surface was colonized by sphagnum moss which, able to hold twenty times its own weight in water, accelerated the accumulation of peat. Thus, huge, sponge-like domes of water were formed above the level of the surrounding land, known as **raised bogs**, which have an average peat depth of 9–12m. Around 4000 years ago, a different kind of bog began to develop in areas of very high rainfall, either along the west coast or in the mountains. These **blanket bogs** carpet the land surface with a layer of black peat, 2–6m thick.

It's not surprising that, as such a prominent part of the environment, bogs occupy a significant place in Irish **folk history**, as evidenced by the many songs, poems and stories associated with the annual harvesting of the turf. They are also **habitats** of great ecological value, sheltering many rare and protected species of plant and animal. And, as well as being important to biologists and climatologists, bogs have produced some of the most spectacular finds of Irish **archaeology**. The slow rate of organic decomposition that allowed the bogs to form in the first place has also preserved thousands of remarkable artefacts from the Neolithic period to the Middle Ages. These include ornaments and weapons, some of which were deliberately left in sacred bog pools as votive offerings during the Bronze Age; surprisingly intact human bodies, a few of which are now on display at Dublin's National Museum (see page 67); elaborate wooden roads from the Bronze and Iron Ages, such as the Corlea Trackway (see page 171); and indeed, whole settlements that were engulfed by peat, as at Céide Fields (see page 378).

The bogs of Ireland, however, are under grave threat. Man has **exploited** the peatlands on a small scale for many centuries. Marl, the chalky soil found beneath the peat, is a lime-rich fertilizer; the peat itself has always been cut and dried for use as fuel; and the overlying mat of vegetation on the bog surface was once used as roof insulation. However, in the twentieth century, exploitation dramatically accelerated. Bord na Móna (the Irish Turf Board) introduced large-scale, mechanized extraction schemes, especially from raised bogs, producing fuel for power stations and domestic use, as well as horticultural peat. There have been further losses to forestry programmes and agricultural intensification, to the extent that only twenty percent or so of the original peatlands, around one-thirtieth of Ireland's landmass, remains intact.

For more information on bogs, go to the Irish Peatland Conservation Council's excellent website at http://ipcc.ie.

Castletown

Celbridge, 18km west of Dublin • 1hr guided tours daily at 11am & 3pm • €8; Heritage Card & Heritage Island • http://castletown.ie • Dublin Bus #67, mostly from Connolly LUAS stop; coming by car on the M4 take Exit 6, signposted for Castletown (access by car is through the gates off Barnhall Rd; the gates at Main St Celbridge are for pedestrians and cyclists only)

The oldest and largest Palladian country house in Ireland, **Castletown** is also one of the very finest. Its plain, grey but elegant facade, built in the style of a sixteenth-century Italian town palace, conceals a wealth of beautiful and fascinating interior detail. The nicest approach to the house is on foot through its extensive parkland, along a beautiful avenue of lime trees that begins at the northern end of Celbridge's high street.

The house was built for William Conolly, son of a Donegal publican who, as legal adviser to William III, became the wealthiest man in Ireland from dealing in forfeited estates after the Battle of the Boyne. Though construction began in 1722, under first the Italian architect Alessandro Galilei and then his acquaintance, Edward Lovett

Pearce, the interior was still unfinished at the time of Conolly's death seven years later. A second phase of work began in 1758, when great-nephew Tom Conolly married the 15-year-old Lady Louisa Lennox, who set about altering and redecorating the house to restrained, Neoclassical designs by Sir William Chambers, the architect of the Casino at Marino, Dublin.

Although you're free to explore the house and gardens at your leisure, the engaging guided tour is worth a look. It begins by the **Grand Staircase**, its cantilevered Portland-stone steps and solid brass banisters weighing at least ten tons. Rococo stuccowork by the Swiss-Italian Lafranchini brothers, depicting Tom Conolly in high relief and personifications of the four seasons, swirls extravagantly over the walls here, but in such a huge, white space manages to appear delicate and restrained. The ground-floor **Brown Study** is the only room to retain its original, rich pine panelling and narrow oak doors from the 1720s, and features a portrait of William III, donated to William Conolly by the king himself. On the same floor lies perhaps the most ostentatious display of wealth and fashion at Castletown: over six years, at huge cost and with painstaking effort, Lady Louisa had the walls of the **Print Room** papered with black-and-white prints from London and Paris, portraying everything from biblical scenes to famous actors of the day, complemented by decorative borders of swags, chains and masks; it must have looked fantastic in its original state, on a background of bright yellow paint.

The highlight upstairs is the **Long Gallery**, which was decorated by Lady Louisa with busts of Greek and Roman philosophers and murals of Classical scenes of love and tragedy, in the style of the recently rediscovered Pompeii. From the gallery's windows you can make out the **Conolly Folly**, some 3km north, an arcane, 50m-high edifice consisting of an obelisk perched shakily on top of a cascade of arches. Attributed to Richard Castle, it was built in 1740 as a monument to Speaker Conolly by his widow, and as a Famine relief scheme.

County Meath

The rich limestone lowlands of **County Meath**, bisected by the River Boyne and supporting ample cattle pasturage, have always attracted settlers and invaders. The valley's Neolithic people somehow found the resources and manpower to construct the huge, ornately decorated passage graves of **Newgrange**, **Knowth** and **Dowth**, part of the extraordinary landscape of ritual sites known as **Brú na Bóinne**, which is today one of the country's most famous and best organized visitor attractions. In contrast, the **Loughcrew Cairns**, a similarly extensive grouping of burial mounds in the far northwest corner of the county beyond the small market town of Kells, have failed to garner present-day resources for excavation and tourist development, leaving you to explore this mysterious, hilltop landscape unaided and usually in solitude. The **Hill of Tara** started out as a Stone Age cemetery, too, but evolved into one of Ireland's most important symbolic sites, the seat of the High Kings of the early Christian period. Meath also caught the eye of the Anglo-Norman invaders, who heavily fortified and held several parliaments at **Trim**, where you can visit the mighty castle and several other well-preserved medieval remnants. Meath's other noteworthy sights are on either side of Brú na Bóinne in the northeast of the county: to the west, **Slane's** historic castle and monastery, which enjoy a picturesque setting on a steep, wooded hillside above the River Boyne; and to the east, the site of one of the most significant battles in Ireland's history, the **Battle of the Boyne**, now commemorated by a high-tech visitor centre.

Trim and around

Fifty kilometres northwest of Dublin, **TRIM** is one of the most attractive towns within striking distance of the capital. Its imposing Anglo-Norman castle overlooks the curving, tree-flanked River Boyne and some picturesque ruins across on the north bank, while verdant meadows run downriver to the extensive remains of two medieval churches and a fine bridge. Trim is also the easiest jumping-off point for the Cistercian abbey of **Bective**, set in lush countryside to the northeast.

Trim Castle

Castle St · 45min guided tours of the keep every hour on the hour · charge; Heritage Card · http://heritageireland.ie

The town's outstanding centrepiece is **Trim Castle**, which is intact enough to have been used as a location for Mel Gibson's 1995 film *Braveheart*. In 1172, Henry II, fearing that the adventurer Strongbow might try to establish his own Anglo-Norman kingdom in Ireland, granted the lordship of Meath to Hugh de Lacy, who along with his son Walter gradually built the most impressive castle in Ireland, the "keystone of the Pale", at this important ford over the Boyne. It's well worth taking one of the illuminating guided **tours** of the keep, and leaving yourself enough time to poke around the enclosure's assorted towers, ruined buildings and mighty curtain wall.

The cruciform floor plan of the **keep** was a unique experiment in military architecture – the design increased possible angles of attack and thus was not emulated elsewhere. However, with walls up to 5m thick and over 20m high, which have survived to this day, the keep was obviously stout enough. The tour inside reveals a chapel, the former Great Hall, a bedroom with an early walk-in wardrobe and spectacular views of the town from the battlements.

The fording of the Boyne was defended by the castle's strongest tower, the **Magdalen Tower**, at the northern tip of the curtain wall, but during a period of greater stability and prosperity in the late thirteenth century, this was converted into private apartments, and a new **Great Hall** was built alongside. On the right-hand side of the hall, look out for a passage cut through the bedrock from the river gate, which allowed stores brought by boat from Drogheda on the coast to be delivered directly to the cellar.

Talbot's Castle

Across the river from Trim Castle · No public access

Crossing the river by the footbridge under the castle walls, you can see the only surviving remnant of the fourteenth-century outer walls, the arched **Sheep Gate**. Nearby stands the privately owned **Talbot's Castle**, a beautiful manor house built in 1415 by Sir John Talbot, the Lord Lieutenant of Ireland. In the eighteenth century, Jonathan Swift (see page 79), who was rector of nearby Laracor, bought the building and turned it into a Latin school, whose most famous alumnus was Arthur Wellesley, later the Duke of Wellington and MP for Trim. The house had been constructed on the site of an Augustinian abbey, St Mary's, which in turn had been built over one of the first monasteries in Ireland, dating from the fifth century. All that remains of St Mary's is the **Yellow Steeple**, a huge, half-ruined belfry that's so named because it glows in the evening sunlight.

Newtowntrim Cathedral

1.5km east of the town centre on Lackanash Rd, accessible off the Dublin road or by footpath along the north bank of the Boyne · Open access 24hr · http://discoverboynevalley.ie

The beautiful remains of thirteenth-century **Newtowntrim (SS Peter & Paul) Cathedral** stand in picturesque riverside meadows. The priory of Newtowntrim was founded here under the protective gaze of Trim Castle in 1202 by Simon de Rochfort, Bishop of Meath, and was soon elevated to become the seat of his diocese, with the construction of the largest and most sophisticated Gothic cathedral in Ireland. Substantial parts of the nave and chancel can still be seen, alongside a ruined refectory.

The priory and St Peter's Bridge

Just across the river from Newtowntrim Cathedral is another fine ruin, the **Priory of St John the Baptist**, also founded by Simon de Rochfort in the early thirteenth century. It was used as a hospital and guesthouse (with its own brewery) by the *Fratres Cruciferi*, the Crutched (or Cross-bearing) Friars, Augustinian monks who had attended the Crusaders. Between the cathedral and the priory, the Boyne is spanned by the wonderful Norman **St Peter's Bridge**, which is reckoned to be the second-oldest bridge in the country.

Bective Abbey

8km northeast of Trim • Open access 24hr • http://discoverboynevalley.ie • From Trim, take the Navan road, look out for a signposted right turn and then it's just over 1km on the left

In a beautiful setting by an old arched bridge on the west bank of the River Boyne, the ruins of **Bective Abbey** are a fine example of Cistercian architecture. Founded as a satellite of Mellifont (see page 152) in 1147, the abbey soon rose to prominence, its abbot holding a peer's seat in the Irish Parliament. The place was rebuilt in the thirteenth century, though only one wall of the nave remains from this phase. The majority of the extant building dates from the fifteenth century or later, remaining so remarkably intact because it was converted into a mansion house after Henry VIII's dissolution of the abbey in 1536. The sturdy and imposing fifteenth-century **tower** at the entrance is especially well preserved, and the south and west ranges of the **cloister** remain partly roofed – keep your eyes peeled for a carving of a monk near the southwest corner.

ARRIVAL AND INFORMATION

TRIM AND AROUND

By bus Buses from Drogheda (hourly via Slane; 1hr 10min) and Dublin (every 30min–1hr; 1hr) stop by the Lidl superstore, on the ring road around the east of the compact town centre, though one or two also stop near the castle.

Tourist office Next to the castle, the helpful visitor centre (Mon–Thurs 10am–5pm, Fri 10am–4.30pm; http://discoverboynevalley.ie) houses a medieval armoury exhibition. Forty-five minute medieval town tours (daily 11am; €3) also start from here.

ACCOMMODATION, EATING AND DRINKING

Franzini O'Brien's Opposite the castle, http://franzinis. com. Solid all-rounder of a restaurant with a bright, informal air, set in a peerless location right opposite the castle entrance. The global menu includes prawn tempura, chicken ruskini and beef teriyaki noodles. Early-bird three-courses deal available all day Tues–Thurs & Sun, and til 7pm Fri & Sat. €€€

James Griffin's High St, across the river from the castle, http://jamesgriffinpub.ie. *Griffin's* is a gnarly, hundred-year-old pub with bare stone walls, that offers a wide selection of Irish whiskies and craft beers, and hosts traditional music sessions on Thurs, acoustic sessions Fri & Sat. Closed Mon–Wed.

Trim Castle Hotel http://trimcastlehotel.com. Bright, spruce, four-star hotel right opposite the castle, sympathetically designed in a tasteful, contemporary style. Lots of special offers on their website, including midweek room-only and weekend breaks with dinner – indeed, there's no shortage of eating drinking options, with a multiplicity of restaurants, cafes and bars onsite. €€€

Hill of Tara

Archaeological site open access; visitor centre mid-May to mid-Sept daily 10am–6pm, last admission 5pm • charge, including a guided tour of the site; Heritage Card • http://heritageireland.ie • http://hilloftara.org

Perhaps more than anywhere else in Ireland, the **Hill of Tara** is loaded with both historical and mythical significance. It's best known as the seat of the High Kings of Ireland in the early centuries after Christ, but had been a major ritual and burial site since the late Stone Age, giving it plenty of time to accrue prehistoric legends. From 4500 to 2000 BC, it was believed to be the entrance to the otherworld. The aura of this long, grass-covered hill, covered with mostly circular mounds and ditches, is unmistakable, and the views of the surrounding countryside are magnificent.

In the **visitor centre**, an impressive twenty-minute film provides the historical and mythological background and shows some stunning views of the hill from the air. The centre occupies a nineteenth-century church, adorned with beautiful painted windows showing the Pentecost and the Apostles. Executed by Evie Hone in 1935, they commemorate the 1500th anniversary of St Patrick's mission to bring Christianity to Ireland.

The Rath of the Synods

Hard up against the wall of the church's graveyard, the first of the mounds you come to is the 83m-wide ring fort known as the **Rath of the Synods**, the reputed location of ecclesiastical synods in the sixth century. It's the untidiest of Tara's mounds: not only has it been partly destroyed by the church graveyard, but between 1899 and 1902 members of a cult, the British Israelites, dug up the rath, believing they would find the Ark of the Covenant. It's a particular shame that they kept no record of their efforts as this site went through many functions over the centuries: from early Bronze Age barrow, through palisaded ceremonial building, back to cemetery, and finally to ring fort. A Roman seal and lock have been found from this last phase, evidence of contact with the Roman world (probably Britain) in the fourth and fifth centuries AD.

The Mound of the Hostages

The next tumulus to the south is the earliest on the site, the so-called **Mound of the Hostages**. It takes its name from the primitive medieval peacekeeping practice of exchanging hostages with neighbouring kingdoms, who were supposedly imprisoned within the mound by Cormac Mac Airt. Built around 3000 BC, it's actually a Neolithic tomb with a 4m-long passage that was reputed to have given entry to the other world. Access is no longer possible, but you can admire the typical concentric

---

TARA: HISTORY AND MYTH

It's likely that people started using the **Hill of Tara** in the Neolithic period (c.3500 BC) as a place for burials and for ritual gatherings, with no resident population. Around sixty monuments, mostly barrows, have been discovered on the hill, the latest probably dating to the late Iron Age (c.400 AD). So much for the archaeology, but mythology, literature and propaganda have imbued Tara with a far greater significance, as the ritual seat of kings – who did not have to be based here, but derived their authority from association with this revered place.

The earliest Irish sagas portray the hill as the home of the master-of-all-trades **Lug**, the greatest of the Celtic gods and the divine manifestation of Tara's kingship, and the goddess **Medb** (Maeve), who could also legitimize a king, sometimes by getting him drunk and sleeping with him – if she couldn't find a suitable candidate, Medb would rule herself. Of these legendary kings, the greatest were **Cormac Mac Airt** and **Conaire Mór**, semi-divine embodiments of peace, prosperity and righteousness. On somewhat firmer ground, seventh-century historical texts tell of recent struggles between the dynasties of Leinster, Northern Ireland and the **Uí Néills** (pronounced "Ee-nails"; based in the northwest and the midlands) for the kingship of Tara. The Uí Néills came out on top, but while the title *rí Temrach* (king of Tara) would have given them special status over the other kings, territorial control over the whole island was not a possibility until the ninth century, when the island became less politically fragmented. In the eleventh century, however, geopolitical reality bit, and Tara lost out to the big city, Dublin.

Tara's significance continues into modern times: during the **1798 Rebellion** some of the United Irishmen made a dramatic last stand on the hill, while in 1843 Daniel O'Connell harnessed the symbolic pull of the site to stage his biggest "monster meeting" here, attended by up to a million people, as part of his campaign to repeal the Union with England.

circles and zigzag patterns carved on one of the portal stones. No fewer than two hundred cremated late Neolithic burials were found here, to which were added around forty from the Bronze Age, some cremated, some inhumed, the latter including a high-ranking teenage boy wearing a necklace of jet, amber, bronze and exotic faïence beads.

The Forrad, Cormac's Residence and around

A 1km-long circular bank, the **Royal Enclosure**, surrounds the Mound of the Hostages, and two larger, conjoined earthworks: the **Forrad**, a Bronze Age burial complex, and **Cormac's Residence**, an Iron Age ring fort to the east. In the centre of the Forrad is the **Stone of Destiny** (the *lia fail*), a phallic standing stone used in the coronation of the High Kings. Tradition states that the royal candidate had to drive his chariot wheel against the stone, and the gods, if they approved, would screech out his name. To the south of the Royal Enclosure lie the crescent-shaped remains of the **Enclosure of King Laoghaire** (see page 140), who is said to be buried here standing upright and dressed in his armour, facing his enemies, the Leinstermen.

The Banqueting Hall

To the north of the church, the so-called **Banqueting Hall** is actually two low banks of earth running parallel for over 200m. Though traditionally held to have been an enormous hall into which thousands of men from all over Ireland would have collected on ritual occasions, this was in fact probably Tara's ceremonial entrance avenue, aligned with the Mound of the Hostages and flanked by tombs and temples.

Gráinne's Fort

West of this avenue stands **Gráinne's Fort**, a burial mound surrounded by a circular ditch and bank. Like many ancient sites throughout Ireland, it has become associated with the tale of "The Pursuit of Diarmuid and Gráinne": the daughter of Cormac Mac Airt, Gráinne is betrothed to the king's elderly commander, Fionn Mac Cumhaill, but falls in love with one of his young warriors, Diarmuid, and elopes with him from Tara, with Fionn and his warriors in hot pursuit.

ARRIVAL AND ACCOMMODATION   **HILL OF TARA**

By bus Dublin–Navan buses from Busáras will drop you at Tara Cross, about 1km from the site (every 30min; 1hr).

Bellinter House Bellinter, 5km northwest of Hill of Tara, off the M3, http://bellinterhouse.com. This Georgian manor house set in extensive grounds overlooking the River Boyne has been converted into a stylish hotel. A bolthole for the Dublin media crowd, it offers plenty of retro chic and quirky features in its redesign, an outdoor hot tub, seaweed baths and other spa treatments, as well as wellies to borrow. In the vaulted cellar, there's an excellent restaurant, *Preston's*, that uses local, seasonal ingredients that inform exquisite plates like Listoke gin cured salmon with horseradish *mousseline* and watercress. €€€

The Loughcrew Cairns and Oldcastle

Sited on a row of four hills at the far northwestern tip of County Meath, the **Loughcrew Cairns** consist of more than thirty chambered mounds and over a hundred curiously carved stones. Local folklore has bestowed on the hills a colourful name, **Sliabh Na Caillighe** (as now marked on Ordnance Survey maps, meaning "Mountain of the Sorceress"), and foundation legend: the said witch, believing she would become mistress of all Ireland if she leapt from hill to hill carrying an apron full of rocks, performed the mighty jumps, shedding handfuls of stones on each peak, but fell at the last, breaking her neck (a cairn at the bottom of the easternmost hill is traditionally known as the witch's grave). The true story of the cairns' construction is only slightly less amazing: archaeologists believe that between approximately 3500 and 3300 BC, Neolithic people travelled considerable distances to build these communal tombs, each of which may have taken anything from four to thirty years to complete. The

2

alignment of the passage tombs and the elaborate carvings on their stone slabs display an association with sun worship, and it's obvious that this high-status ritual site was meant to be visible from afar. In reverse, the cairns afford a magnificent panorama over quiet lakes and gently undulating farmland, encompassing up to sixteen counties on a clear day.

Though on a smaller scale, the Loughcrew Cairns are contemporary with the more famous burial sites at Brú na Bóinne, but, having never been comprehensively excavated, provide quite a different experience for the modern-day visitor. If you're going to visit both complexes, it makes sense to take the guided tours of the reconstructed mounds of Newgrange and Knowth first, before letting your imagination run wild on the unspoilt ritual landscape at Loughcrew. The cairns lie around 5km southeast of **Oldcastle**, a thriving village that sports several galleries and boutiques. While you're in this area, it's also well worth visiting the attractive **Loughcrew Gardens**.

Cairn T

Carnbane East hill • Late May to early Sept daily 10am–6pm, last admission 5.15pm; outside official opening hours, you can pick up the key and a torch from the café at Loughcrew Gardens (€50 or passport as deposit) • Free • http://loughcrewmegalithiccentre.com • Coming by car, turn off the N3 at the town of Kells and follow the Oldcastle road for about 15km, before forking left towards Loughcrew Gardens; after 3km a right turn leads to the car park beneath the summit of Carnbane East after about 1km, from where it's a steep, 10min walk up to Cairn T

The majority of the Loughcrew tombs are located on top of two hills, Carnbane East and Carnbane West, though unfortunately the latter is private land and currently inaccessible to visitors; **Cairn T** is the focus of the summit of **Carnbane East**, and probably of the whole complex – most of the tombs on the other hills face towards it. The cairn's 113m circumference is reinforced by large kerbstones, behind which originally ran the thick layer of white quartz (as at Brú na Bóinne) that gave the hill its name: *carn bán* is Irish for "white cairn". On the north side is one of the largest kerbstones, known as the "Hag's Chair", where the witch of legend sat smoking her pipe (local lore adds that any wish you make while sitting here will come true). You can make out faint traces of carved Neolithic whorls on this stone, as well as a prominent cross, which strongly suggests that Masses (officially forbidden under the penal laws) were held in secret here during the eighteenth century.

The cairn's low, 5m-long **passage**, aligned with the rising sun on the equinox days in March and September (just south of east), leads into a roughly circular chamber with three side recesses. Once your eyes become accustomed to the gloom, you'll start seeing wonderful, mysterious carvings – chevrons, whorls, waves, petals – on the large stones all around you. These incisions are especially ornate in the back recess, where a prominent sun pattern may have been specifically designed to catch the first rays of the equinox sun along the passage.

Loughcrew Gardens

Loughcrew, Oldcastle • charge • http://loughcrew.com

Signposted on the southwestern side of Carnbane East, the **Loughcrew Gardens** are most famous for their impressive seventeenth-century avenue of grotesquely fluted **yew trees**. They also encompass nineteenth-century lawns, herbaceous borders, ponds and a grotto, as well as signposted woodland walks, fairy trail for kids, a café and the family church of St Oliver Plunkett (see page 149), now roofless. The oldest part of the church was formerly a tower house, the seat of the Plunketts until the 1652 Act of Settlement, when Cromwell's surveyor, Sir William Petty, installed his brother-in-law, William Naper, at Loughcrew.

INFORMATION AND ACCOMMODATION	**LOUGHCREW CAIRNS AND OLDCASTLE**
Tourist information *Kraft Kaffee*, a craft shop, café and official tourist information point on Millbrook Rd, Oldcastle	(Tues, Wed & Fri 10am–5pm, Sat 10am–4pm; 049 854 2645). **The Fincourt** Oliver Plunkett St, Oldcastle, http://fincourt.

com. This traditional inn provides a warm welcome and seven smart, comfortable and well-equipped en-suite rooms and a self-catering apartment. The pub itself has bar food, an open fire and a quiet beer garden at the back. €€

Kells

A town of unique historical and cultural significance, **KELLS** is a twenty-minute drive from the Hill of Tara on the M3. Once a major monastic site, the town is best known for **Kells Abbey**, a former monastery from which the *Book of Kells* takes its name. Although not created here, the book was safely kept in the monastery for hundreds of years, roughly from the ninth century to the sixteenth century. Today the monastic site includes a 27m **round tower**, **St Colmcilles church** and four stunning **high crosses**. Nearby on Church Lane is a tenth-century oratory known as St Colmcilles house, which is thought to have housed the saint's relics. A fifth high cross dating from the ninth century, known as the "market cross", can be found in front of the old courthouse at the east end of town. All of these sites are in the centre of Kells and a short walk from each other.

Tourist office Housed in the civic offices on Headfort Place, the welcoming tourist office has a copy of the *Book of Kells* on display (Tues–Fri 9am–5pm, Sat 9am–4pm, closed for lunch 1.30–2pm; 046 924 7508, kellscourthouse@ discoverboynevalley.ie).

The Headfort Arms Hotel Headfort Place, Kells, http:// headfortarms.ie. In business for some two hundred years, this luxury hotel is the perfect base to explore the Boyne Valley. The 45 bedrooms are a comforting mix of old and new decor and ambience, each with orthopaedic beds and excellent showers. The attached *Vanilla Pod* restaurant is the best in town, while more casual dining options are available in *Café Therese* and the *Kelltic Bar*. €€

Slane

Fifty kilometres north of Dublin, the village of **SLANE** enjoys a handsome setting on a south-facing slope above the leafy River Boyne, with the junction of the N2 and the N51 between Drogheda and Navan forming a prominent crossroads at the centre of the village.

Slane Castle

Main entrance 1km west of the village centre • Guided tours usually May to late Aug on selected dates 11am–5pm • Castle charge, distillery charge, • http://slanecastle.ie and http://slaneirishwhiskey.com

The village grew up around **Slane Castle**, whose estate extends westwards from the large Gothic gate by the bridge over the River Boyne. The main entrance for visitors, however, is now round the back of the castle, about 1km west of the village crossroads. The era's finest architects – Gandon, Wyatt and Johnston – constructed the castle, with its mock battlements and turrets, from 1785 onwards, while Capability Brown designed the grounds. A devastating fire struck in 1991, however, and it took until 2001 for the castle to open again, with its interior redesigned in largely contemporary style as a venue for conferences and society weddings. Consequently, the guided tour smacks a little of *Hello* magazine, though there are one or two points of architectural interest remaining, notably the lofty ballroom, with its ornate fan vaulting and an original carved wooden chandelier, which was built by Thomas Hopper for George IV's 1821 visit to his mistress, Lady Conyngham. The present Conyngham, Henry, Lord Mountcharles, is a friend of rock band U2, who took up residence here to record *The Unforgettable Fire* in 1984, and mounts huge concerts in the grounds each summer; REM, Bruce Springsteen and David Bowie have all performed here. Also on site is the **Slane Whiskey Distillery**, housed in the old stables building; tours take in the barley room, cooperage, production area and warehouse before concluding with a tasting.

The Hill of Slane

Around 1km north of the village centre • Open access 24hr

From the main crossroads in the village, it's a fifteen-minute walk north and west up to the **Hill of Slane**, which affords views over rolling farmland to the Irish Sea at Drogheda and the Wicklow Mountains. Here, in 433, according to tradition, **St Patrick** lit the Paschal (Easter) Fire for the first time in Ireland, signalling the arrival of Christianity. In this he challenged the pagan *Bealtaine* fire on the Hill of Tara, 15km to the south, lit by the High King, Laoghaire, to celebrate the arrival of summer. Laoghaire was soon won over, however, and although the king did not take on the new religion himself, he allowed his subjects to be converted. These included St Earc, who became Patrick's great friend and follower, and established a **monastery** here on the hill, which eventually evolved into a Franciscan house. Today you can see the extensive remains of its sixteenth-century church and fine bell tower, along with an associated college built around an open quadrangle.

Francis Ledwidge Museum

1km east of the village centre on the N51 towards Drogheda • Summer daily 10am–5pm; phone for winter hours • charge • http://francisledwidge.com

The **Francis Ledwidge Museum** is housed in a simple farm labourer's cottage which, in 1887, was the birthplace of the poet Francis Ledwidge, whose work derived inspiration from the beautiful landscape around his home here, as well as from the history and myth of County Meath. The small museum includes re-creations of the kitchen and the poet's bedroom, some fascinating display boards and a pretty, shady garden out the back. Although a member of the Irish Volunteers, Ledwidge, like 150,000 other Irishmen, joined the British Army in World War I to protect the rights of small nations, to try to secure Home Rule after the end of the war and to fight "an enemy common to our civilization", as he put it. He survived the horrors of Gallipoli in 1915 – the year in which his only volume of poems, *Songs of the Fields*, was published – but was killed by a stray shell at the Third Battle of Ypres in 1917. Inscribed on a plaque by the cottage's front door are the lines written by Ledwidge about his poet friend, Thomas MacDonagh, who was executed by the British for his part in the 1916 Easter Rising:

He shall not hear the bittern cry
In the wild sky, where he is lain,
Nor voices of the sweeter birds
Above the wailing of the rain.

ARRIVAL AND DEPARTURE   SLANE

By bus Slane is served by buses from/to Drogheda (hourly; 30min); Dublin (about 20 daily; 1hr); Monaghan (about 20 daily; 1hr); and Trim (hourly; 45min).

ACCOMMODATION AND EATING

Conyngham Arms Hotel Main St, http://conyngham arms.ie. Conveniently located just west of the main crossroads in the centre of the village, this eighteenth-century coaching inn has sixteen individually styled rooms with ornate beds, some four-poster, and nice touches such as blackout curtains, bathrobes, local handmade toiletries and Nespresso machines. Attached is a popular country kitchen restaurant serving excellent food all day. €€

George's Patisserie and Deli 51 Chapel St, 041 982 4493. Lovely little bakery-café just north of the crossroads on the N2, serving sublime strawberry tarts and chocolate Sachertorte, as well as soup and sandwiches on various home-made artisanal breads.

Slane Farm Hostel Harlinstown House, just over 2km west of the village beyond the castle, http://slanefarmhostel.ie. Comfortable, attractive, en-suite budget accommodation can be found in the converted coach house and stables of this working farm; the hostel also offers a well-equipped kitchen, laundry facilities, camping and self-catering cottages. Camping €, dorms €, doubles €€

Tankardstown Hotel Rathkenny, 5km north of Slane, http://tankardstown.ie. An elegant eighteenth-century manor house, this upmarket hotel includes an orangery, a fine restaurant, *Brabazon*, and a central courtyard of cottage suites, which include sitting rooms and kitchens and either one or two bedrooms – ideal for families. €€€

Brú na Bóinne

8km east of Slane • Knowth closed mid-Oct to Easter • charge • http://heritageireland.ie; Heritage Card • The last minibuses to Newgrange and to Knowth depart 1hr 45min before closing; for full transport details see page 142

To the east of Slane, between a U-bend in the River Boyne and the N51 to the north, **Brú na Bóinne** (the "palace of the Boyne") encompasses the spectacular 5000-year-old **passage graves** of **Newgrange**, **Knowth** and **Dowth**, high round tumuli raised over stone passages and burial chambers. Entry is funnelled through the impressive **visitor centre** on the south side of the river, which provides detailed information on the significance of the sites, their construction and artwork, and the Neolithic society that created them, as well as housing a **tourist information desk** and café. A footbridge crosses from the centre to the north side of the river, where the compulsory minibuses shuttle you to Newgrange and Knowth, which have both been comprehensively excavated and reconstructed, for **guided tours**. The passage tomb at Dowth, which has been badly damaged by roadbuilders and cack-handed nineteenth-century archaeologists, is closed to visitors.

Brú na Bóinne is one of Ireland's foremost attractions, and the **numbers** visiting each site daily are strictly limited; pre-booking your ticket is essential. Moreover, there's no point in arriving late in the day, as it takes at least three hours to see Newgrange, Knowth and the visitor centre.

Newgrange

Newgrange is unquestionably the most striking of the Brú na Bóinne mounds, not least because its facade of white quartz stones and round granite boulders has been reassembled. The quartz originally came from Wicklow, the granite from the Mourne and Carlingford areas, exemplifying the mind-boggling levels of resources and organization lavished on this project, by these farmers who used nothing but simple tools of wood and stone. It has been estimated that the tumulus, which is over 75m in diameter, weighs 200,000 tons in total and would have taken around forty years to build. It was the final resting place of a high-status family within the Neolithic community – the cremated remains and grave goods of at least five people were recovered from the burial chamber during excavation – but seems also to have had a wider purpose as a ritual site or gathering place.

The **entrance stone** is one of the finest examples of the art of the tomb-builders, who carved spectacular but enigmatic spirals, chevrons, lozenges and other geometric designs onto many of the large stones around the mound and up the 19m passage. The tomb's pivotal feature, however, is a **roof-box** above the entrance whose slit was perfectly positioned to receive the first rays of the rising sun on the day of the **winter solstice** (December 21); the light first peeps into the cruciform burial chamber itself before spreading its rays along the length of the passage. The engaging guided tour provides an electrically powered simulation in the burial chamber, while tickets for the real thing are decided by lottery each year. To prehistoric farmers, this solstice marked the start of a new year, promising rebirth for their crops and perhaps new life for the spirits of the dead.

It seems probable that by around 2000 BC, in the Late Neolithic or Early Bronze Age, the mound had collapsed and fallen into disuse, but it still provided a powerful focal point for ritual. During this era, a huge religious enclosure known as the **pit circle** was constructed here, consisting of a double circle of wooden posts, within which animals were cremated and buried in pits. To this was added a circle of around 35 **standing stones**, which may have had an astronomical function; about a dozen of them remain upright.

Knowth

It's well worth signing up for the lively guided tour of **Knowth** too, which provides some telling contrasts with the more famous Newgrange – not least in interpretation:

2

the archaeologist in charge of this site, for example, thought the white quartz stones discovered around the main passage entrance were to reflect the sun, so left them as a shimmering carpet on the ground. The Knowth mound is pierced by two passages, each around twice the length of the Newgrange tunnel, aligned roughly with sunrise and sunset on the equinox days in March and September and leading to back-to-back burial chambers. Unfortunately, it's no longer possible to follow the passages themselves, but the tour takes you inside the mound to look along the eastern tunnel, and you can also climb on top of the mound for views of the Hill of Slane and the Wicklow Mountains.

Knowth is even richer in **Neolithic art** than Newgrange, with about 250 decorated stones discovered here – over half of all known Irish passage-tomb art. The mound is surrounded by over 120 huge kerbstones, one of which supports a carved pattern of crescents and lines that may represent the equinox; elsewhere, patterns of circular and serpentine incisions have been interpreted as local maps, showing the River Boyne and the burial mounds. Hard by the main mound, you can poke around eighteen smaller or **satellite mounds**, at least two of which were built before the main tomb. The Knowth mound attracted habitation in various eras right up until the sixteenth century AD, and your guide will show you several **souterrains**, underground tunnels that were dug in the early Christian period for hiding, escape and possibly food preservation.

ARRIVAL AND DEPARTURE
BRÚ NA BÓINNE

By bus Take Bus Éireann service #100 from Dublin to Drogheda (which is also served by trains from Pearse, Tara Street or Connolly stations), and then the #163 bus to the visitor centre, which connects with the #100 twice a day (Mon–Sat).

By car If you have your own transport, follow signs, either from the south side of the bridge in Slane or from the M1 motorway to the southwest of Drogheda, to the visitor centre, which is 2km west of Donore village.

ACCOMMODATION

Rossnaree 2km west of the visitor centre on the Slane road, http://rossnaree.ie. This Italianate Victorian country house offers five luxurious, individually styled rooms, as well as art courses and fly-fishing on the estate. Sumptuous breakfasts feature eggs from their own hens, seasonal vegetables from the walled garden, freshly squeezed orange juice and home-made muesli. €€€

The Battle of the Boyne Visitor Centre

Oldbridge, 3km north of Donore Village • charge; Heritage Card • http://battleoftheboyne.ie • Bus Éireann service #100 from Dublin to Drogheda (which is also served by trains from Pearse, Tara Street or Connolly stations), and then the #163 bus to the visitor centre, which connects with the #100 twice a day (Mon–Sat); can also be reached from Brú na Bóinne by car making for Donore, then heading north for 3km to the river, or from the Drogheda–Slane road (N51) by crossing the Obelisk Bridge

On July 1, 1690 (July 11, 1690 according to our modern, Gregorian calendar, though it's celebrated by Northern Protestants on July 12, after some convoluted mathematical interpretation following the eighteenth-century change to the Gregorian calendar), William III met his father-in-law, the deposed King James II, at the **Battle of the Boyne**, the largest ever set-piece battle on Irish or British soil. At stake were the English throne, now held by the Protestant William with support from the pope and the Catholic king of Spain, and the dominance of Europe by the French, who backed the Catholic James. At the head of an army of 36,000 English, Dutch, Protestant Irish, French Huguenots and Danes, William took up position on the north side of the river just west of Drogheda, while on the opposite bank, James commanded 24,000 men, mostly Irish irregulars, but including seven thousand well-armed French soldiers. To counter William's flanking movement, upriver and around the Knowth mound, James was drawn into sending most of his force westward, which allowed the main Williamite army to cross the river to Oldbridge and put the Jacobite centre to flight. The Irish and French regrouped to carry on fighting for another year, notably at Aughrim and Limerick, but James kept running, via Dublin and Kinsale, to France, never to return.

Oldbridge House, a fine 1740s limestone mansion on the south bank of the River Boyne, houses the **visitor centre**, commemorating the battle and the 1500 men who died. It houses an impressive exhibition, delicately worded but marshalling telling quotes from participants in the battle, and an audiovisual, which puts the blame on the French. Overlooking the walled garden, there's an attractive pavilion café with outdoor tables. Admission is free to the surrounding parkland, which features display boards and five signposted battlefield walks of up to fifty minutes, and on summer Sundays and bank-holiday Mondays you can watch a musketeer and a cavalryman giving hourly "living history" displays on the front lawn.

Louth, Monaghan and Cavan

CLOUGHOUGHTER CASTLE

Louth, Monaghan and Cavan

Louth, Monaghan and Cavan all share a border with Northern Ireland and, as throughout the North, still bear many signs of the Plantation in the form of grand country estates (known simply as "big houses") and planned towns. Louth is Ireland's smallest county and the most northerly in the Leinster province, and much of its activity is focused on the historic town of Drogheda, set on the banks of the Boyne, whose fertile valley also boasts major religious sites at Monasterboice and Mellifont Abbey.

In Lough's northeast, the **Cooley Peninsula** provides somewhat dramatic relief from the county's otherwise drab coastline and played an active role in the greatest of Irish mythological epics, the *Táin Bó Cúailnge* (Cattle Raid of Cooley; see page 154).

The topography of **Monaghan** and **Cavan**, both in Ulster, is markedly different. Monaghan's landscape is characterized by eruptions of small hills, known as drumlins, and its sense of life is encapsulated in the writing of Patrick Kavanagh from **Inniskeen**. Monaghan's few towns offer little of interest, though the busy **county town** itself is attractively laid out and features a few buildings of note, plus one of the region's best festivals. To the southeast, the hilltop market town of **Clones** is a former ecclesiastical centre and also strongly associated with Irish lace-making. To Monaghan town's north lies **Glaslough**, an estate village set around the grandiose **Castle Leslie**.

In contrast, much of Cavan is defined by its waterways and small lakes, offering a multitude of choices for anglers. The **Shannon–Erne Waterway** offers the most readily navigable route through the lakes, for which **Belturbet** provides a good starting point. Away from the major roads that pierce both Monaghan and Cavan, the countryside has an unhurried charm, though it's easy to get lost when navigating its tangled grid of lanes without a map or compass. **Cavan** town itself is agreeable enough, but offers little to warrant more than a passing visit. The county's west provides some stark and rugged landscapes, ideally explored via the **Cavan Way**, which passes through **Cavan Burren**, a stunning limestone plateau scattered with prehistoric monuments.

Most of the attractions in Louth (which has rail links to Dublin and Belfast) and Monaghan are easily accessible by **public transport**, but bus services in Cavan are somewhat less frequent.

Drogheda and around

DROGHEDA (pronounced "droch – as in loch – edda") was once two separate Viking settlements, huddled together on either side of the River Boyne. These developed into twin towns during the Anglo-Norman period, whose intermittent rivalry was quashed by a royal charter uniting the pair in 1412. The town incurred the most infamous onslaught of Cromwell's Irish campaign of 1649 when its defending garrison and many inhabitants were massacred by the Lord Protector's army.

Drogheda's attractions lie both sides of the **River Boyne**. The walled town, which developed in the late medieval period, became one of Ireland's most important religious and political centres – the parliament would occasionally convene in Drogheda – and a few remnants from this time are still visible. Later constructions by the town's Protestant middle classes, such as the **Tholsel** and **courthouse**, reflect a burgeoning confidence enhanced by Drogheda's growing importance as a manufacturing town, thriving on the export of linen, shoes and alcohol. Its old **docks**, which were once the focus for the numerous trades that developed here during the eighteenth and

Highlights

❶ Monasterboice Ecclesiastical relics here include Ireland's tallest round tower and also two of the most splendid high crosses in the whole of the country. See page 152

❷ The Cooley Peninsula Closely associated with the Irish epic saga, the *Táin Bó Cúailnge*, Cooley's mountains offer tremendous views of Carlingford Lough, while Carlingford itself has some terrific restaurants. See page 153

❸ Castle Leslie Estate Glaslough's grandest residence, spend the night in a castle and enjoy fishing, falconry, carriage rides and horseriding. See page 157

❹ Inniskeen The birthplace of one of the country's greatest poets, Patrick Kavanagh, celebrates its scion through an excellent and informative resource centre. See page 158

❺ The Lakes of Cavan Known collectively as Lough Oughter and linked by an extraordinary complex of atmospheric waterways, this is the most picturesque walking territory. See page 160

❻ Cavan Burren This magnificent prehistoric landscape is replete with archaeological and geological treasures, as well as providing splendid views of the surrounding countryside. See page 161

HIGHLIGHTS ARE MARKED ON THE MAP ON PAGE 148

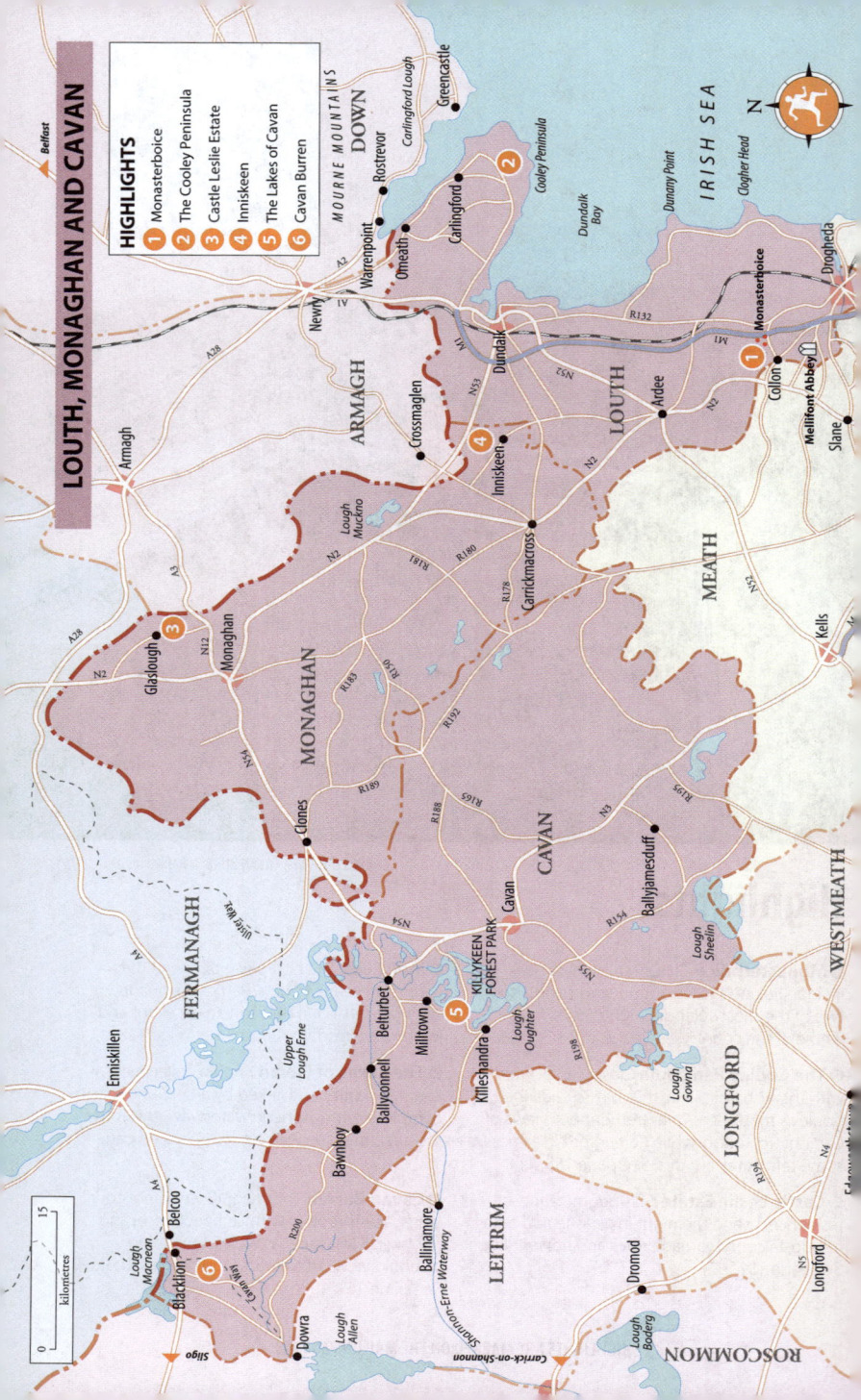

nineteenth centuries, are now being regenerated with vitality, while the town itself sports some prominent sights. The town's big annual bash is the **Drogheda Arts Festival** (www.droghedaartsfestival.ie) at the beginning of May, three fun-packed days of music, theatre, comedy and street spectacle.

To the north of Drogheda lie the remains of the monasteries of **Monasterboice** and **Mellifont**, two of Ireland's most significant ecclesiastical sites, the former including a superb high cross and the latter providing ample evidence of its erstwhile power and importance.

Tholsel, St Laurence Gate and Magdalene Tower

Positioned at the junction of West Street and Shop Street is the eighteenth-century **Tholsel**, the former town hall, a solid limestone building topped by a domed tower which features a four-faced clock; it now houses the tourist office (see page 151). A short distance east from here is **St Laurence Gate**, one of the few vestiges of the town's medieval walls. This imposing barbican, with its two tall rounded towers, once housed a portcullis protecting the tollgate just within; unfortunately, it's not open to visitors. Another dominant structure lies a little to the northwest of St Laurence Gate, in the shape of the two-storey **Magdalene Tower**, the erstwhile belfry and only remnant of a large Dominican friary founded here around 1224 by the Archbishop of Armagh, Lucas de Netterville.

The Highlanes Gallery

36 Laurence St • Tues–Sat 10.30am–5pm • Free • http://highlanes.ie

Housed in a former Franciscan church a few paces down from St Laurence Gate, the enlightening **Highlanes Gallery** features works from the municipal collection (dating from the seventeenth century) as well as a rolling programme of temporary exhibitions, taking in everything from sculpture and installations to children's art. In an unusual aside, you'll also find here the sword and mace presented to Drogheda by William of Orange shortly after the Battle of the Boyne.

St Peter's Church (Church of Ireland)

St Peter's Place, Peter St

St Peter's Church (Church of Ireland) is a graceful mid eighteenth-century edifice whose porch and spire were added by the renowned Irish architect Francis Johnston in 1793. The church replaced the original thirteenth-century structure whose stone steeple was blown down by a violent storm in 1548 and subsequently refurbished with a wooden replacement. During the massacre that followed the 1649 siege of the town, many people sought sanctuary in the steeple but perished when Cromwell's troops set it ablaze.

St Peter's Church (Roman Catholic)

West St

The town's other **St Peter's Church** (Roman Catholic) is a solidly neo-Gothic late nineteenth-century structure topped by an elegant spire and accessed via a sweeping stone stairway. Its interior is equally impressive, featuring stout granite pillars and walls of Bath stone, and just off its left-hand aisle is a small shrine devoted to **Oliver Plunkett**, Archbishop of Armagh and Primate of All Ireland from 1670. Towards the end of that decade, at a time of widespread anti-Catholic feeling in England, Titus Oates, a former Anglican clergyman and convicted perjurer who had earlier converted to Catholicism, hatched a fabricated claim (which became known as the Popish Plot) that the pope

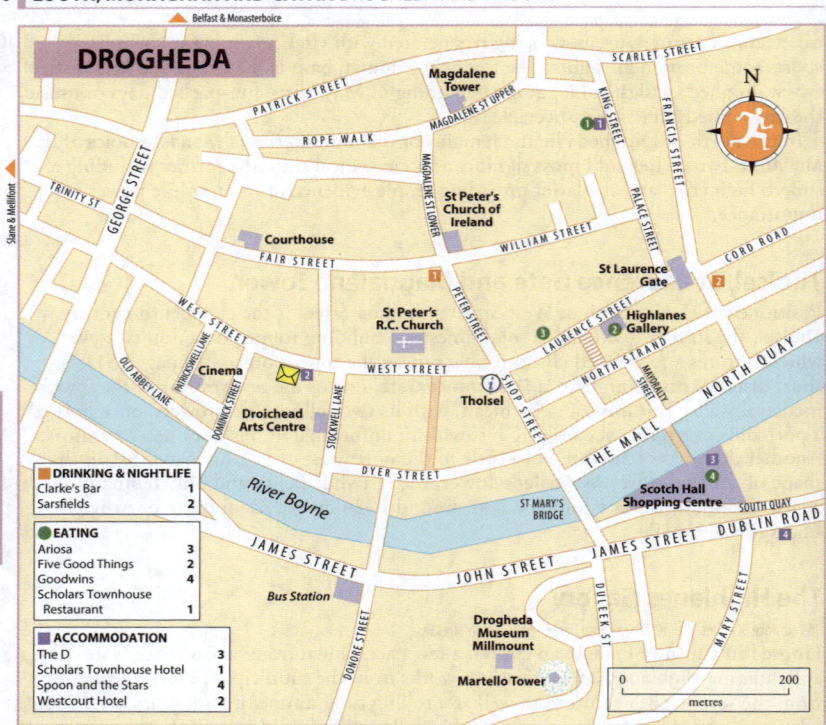

was preparing to invade the country and had installed Plunkett as one of the main organizers of the papal army. Plunkett was arrested and put on trial in Dundalk, but, when the jury failed to convict him, was moved first to Dublin and then to Newgate prison in London. Found guilty of treason on July 1, 1681, he was hanged, drawn and quartered, and his remains were thrown onto a fire, but his head and other parts of his body were rescued. The head finally arrived back in Ireland around 1722, following a circuitous route via Rome, and is now contained in a silver-ornamented box within the shrine – grisly indeed. The other parts of Plunkett's body on view (essentially a few bones) weren't returned until after his canonization in 1975 – here too is the door of his cell from Newgate prison.

Millmount Hill

Rising high above the south bank of the Boyne is **Millmount Hill**. The hill features strongly in Irish mythology, supposedly being the burial place of the Celtic poet Amergin, while its strategic value was quickly recognized by the Anglo-Normans who constructed a motte here in the late twelfth century. Subsequently, a **castle** was erected – which in later years provided the fiercest resistance to Cromwell during the 1649 siege.

Martello Tower

Mon–Sat 10am–5pm, plus summer Sun 2–5pm • charge, combined entry with Drogheda Museum • 041 983 3097

In 1808 the old fortifications were replaced by the barracks and **Martello tower** which stand here today. The tower was severely damaged by shelling during the 1922 Civil War, though it has since been restored. Inside, there's an impressive display of weaponry, including guns found hidden in the roof of the Franciscan church, but a better reason to visit is for the unhindered **views** of the town.

Drogheda Museum Millmount

Barrack St • Mon–Sat 10am–5pm, plus summer Sun 2–5pm • charge, combined entry with Martello Tower • 041 983 3097

The barracks square houses the **Drogheda Museum Millmount**, featuring a somewhat random, though occasionally stimulating, assemblage of local artefacts. The highlight is the Banners room, where you'll find a splendid collection of banners, many over two hundred years old and which represent the various crafts and trades that operated hereabouts in the late eighteenth and early nineteenth centuries; three guild banners (representing weavers, carpenters and shoemakers) stand out – these are supposedly the only remaining ones in Ireland. Elsewhere, there's a superb example of a Boyne Coracle – a circular vessel made of cowhide used by fishermen on the Boyne – while Drogheda's manufacturing history considers, among other things, the town's erstwhile role as a major producer of alcoholic beverages, when there were once no fewer than fourteen breweries and sixteen distilleries.

ARRIVAL AND DEPARTURE

DROGHEDA

By train The train station is half a mile southeast of town, just off Dublin Rd.

Destinations Belfast (7 daily; 1hr 40min); Dublin (Mon–Sat every 20–30min, Sun hourly; 30min–1hr); Newry (7 daily; 40min).

By bus The bus station is on Donore Rd, just south of the river.

Destination Matthews: Dublin (Mon–Sat hourly, Sun 10; 1hr).

Destinations Bus Éireann: Collon for Mellifont (Mon–Sat hourly, Sun 4; 15min); Donore for Newgrange (Mon–Sat 2 daily; 10min); Navan (daily hourly; 45min).

INFORMATION AND TOURS

Tourist office Inside the Tholsel on West St (Mon–Fri 9am–5pm, plus Sat April–Sept; http://drogheda.ie), the office also holds an enlightening exhibition on the town, with interactive touch screens.

Bike rental Useful for getting to either Monasterboice or Mellifont Abbey, bikes can be rented from Quay Cycles at 11a North Quay (041 983 4526; €15/day).

Walking tours Guided tours of the town are organized through the Drogheda Museum Millmount, but usually only for groups of eight or more (1hr 30min; charge; 041 983 3097).

ACCOMMODATION

SEE MAP PAGE 150

The D Scotch Hall, Marsh Rd, http://thedhotel.com. Very style-conscious riverside establishment providing swish rooms of handsome proportions – some with balcony – alongside a convivial waterside bar and restaurant (see below). Plenty of off-season and early booking bargains on offer. €€

Scholars Townhouse Hotel King St, http://scholarshotel.com. The handsome redbrick frontage of this renovated former Christian Brothers residence conceals sixteen modestly sized rooms, including a family quad; many of the original features have been retained, including the oak panelling, stained-glass windows and high-coved ceilings, lending substantial charm to the place. Faultless hospitality too. €€€

Spoon and the Stars 13 St Mary's Terrace, http://spoonandthestars.com. Cheerful and relaxed independent hostel on the main N1 road with eight- and ten-bed dorms, as well as a handful of doubles, some with bathrooms. There's also a comfy lounge, a little terrace garden, a self-catering kitchen and laundry facilities. Bus #101 from Dublin stops right outside. Breakfast included. Dorms €, doubles €€

Westcourt Hotel 29 West St, http://westcourt.ie. The most central of the town's hotels, this comfortable establishment offers variously configured rooms furnished with attractive mahogany beds with deep mattresses and tastefully upholstered chairs. €€

EATING

SEE MAP PAGE 150

★ **Ariosa** 1 Laurence St, http://ariosacoffee.com. This tiny little coffee house across from the Tholsel does the meanest caffeine shot in town; grab a newspaper and a bar stool, and savour a freshly roasted cuppa with a pastry. €

Five Good Things Highlanes Gallery, 36 Laurence St, http://fivegoodthings.ie. Refreshingly bright, conservatory-style café offering breakfasts and light bites (chorizo hash, avo toast) alongside more substantial mains such as Buffalo burger – gourmet cakes and superb coffee too. €€

Goodwins Scotch Hall, Marsh Rd, http://goodwins steakhouse.com. The D hotel's upmarket steakhouse offers more cuts than you can shake a frying pan at, as well as other meaty treats like Leinster lamb rack and roast pork tenderloin – but for a real nosh-up try the bottomless brunch. There's also the banging *Hops Bar* next door if you just fancy a pint. Closed Mon–Wed. €€€

★ **Scholars Townhouse Restaurant** King St, http://scholarshotel.com. Little has changed, ambience-wise, in this hotel's high-class restaurant over the years, as the oak-panelled walls, painted ceiling (depicting the Battle of the Boyne) and antique-filled cabinets testify. The food, however, is a thoroughly modern (and local) affair, so expect the likes of Ardsallagh goat's cheese mousse, and Skeaganhore duck breast with fondant potato and parsnip. The three-course lunch is terrific (noon–5pm; £50). €€€

DRINKING

SEE MAP PAGE 150

★ **Clarke's Bar** 19 Peter St, http://clarkesofdrogheda.com. Don't let the tatty exterior fool you: this former grocer's shop, all dark and woody with some very cosy snugs, is a fabulous boozer with bags of charm and plenty of chatter. Regular events too.

Sarsfields 128 Cord Rd, 041 983 8032. Another inviting old bar, though a bit more low-key than the others in town. Still, some terrific evenings of music await, featuring anything from modern bluegrass to singer-songwriters.

Monasterboice

6km north of Drogheda • Dawn to dusk • Free • Take the Drogheda–Dundalk bus (hourly; 20min) and ask to be set down at the Monasterboice Inn, from where it's an easy 15min signposted walk

Monasterboice has an idyllic rural setting and the remains of its monastic settlement – founded in either the eighth or ninth century – include not only one of Ireland's finest **high crosses**, dating from the tenth century, but one of the best-preserved **round towers** in the country too. The two ruined **churches** within the enclosure, which date from the thirteenth century, probably had little connection with the, by then, defunct monastery.

The crosses

The stocky **St Muiredach's Cross**, just inside the churchyard, manifests an elaborate series of carved panels depicting a variety of biblical events, loosely arranged in supposed chronological order. The base of its **east face** begins in the Garden of Eden, before moving upwards to the stories of Cain and Abel, David and Goliath, Moses bringing water to the Israelites and the Magi bearing gifts for the newborn Christ. Above these, the cross's carved wheel depicts the Last Judgement and the risen multitudes pleading for entry into Heaven. The **west face** depicts events during the later life of Christ, ranging from his arrest at Gethsemane to the Ascension, though the hub of the cross's wheel shows Moses with the Ten Commandments.

The taller **West Cross**, unfortunately chipped at its top, features another array of biblical scenes, though erosion makes most of them indecipherable. Certainly, its **east face** features David and the lion, and the **west** includes the Resurrection, but much of the remainder is difficult to discern. Adjacent to the West Cross is what's reckoned to be the tallest **round tower** in Ireland, standing at some 30m high, though it has long since lost its conical cap and cannot be entered for safety reasons.

Mellifont Abbey

R168, 10km northwest of Drogheda • May–Sept daily 10am–6pm • charge; Heritage Card • http://mellifontabbey.ie • The infrequent Drogheda–Collon bus stops at Monleek Cross, from where it's a 3km walk

Founded in 1142 by St Malachy, **Mellifont Abbey** was the first and subsequently most important Cistercian foundation in Ireland, eventually heading an affiliation of more than twenty monasteries. Set in a tranquil spot by the River Mattock, Mellifont must once have been a hugely impressive complex, though its scant ruins leave much to the imagination. After the Reformation the abbey passed into the hands of Edward Moore, who converted its buildings into a fortified residence. Here, in 1603, the great Irish chieftain **Hugh O'Neill** was besieged by Lord Mountjoy until starvation forced his surrender. During the Battle of the Boyne, William of Orange based himself at Mellifont, after which the property was abandoned and fell ultimately into dilapidation. It eventually passed into the hands of the Office of Public Works in the late twentieth century.

The site

Before touring the remains, take in the small exhibition in the **visitor centre** by the entrance, which details the foundation's history and provides a scale model of the abbey's layout. Entrance to the site is via the church's **north transept**, which features the remains of two stone *piscinae* – sinks for cleaning sacred serving vessels. As the church was built on sloping ground the broad nave has an uncommon feature, a crypt constructed to ensure it remained level. Next to the **south transept** stood the chapterhouse, whose floor features medieval glazed tiles, though some of these have been brought here from other parts of the abbey.

The tallest and finest remnant of the abbey stands in its expansive cloister garth, a remarkable, octagonal arched **lavabo**, with fountains and basins where the monks would wash. Behind the lavabo, the southern ruins included both the calefactory (or warming house), the only heated room in the entire complex, and the refectory. The remaining ruins rarely rise above knee height, and you'll need to consult the various display-boards or buy the visitors' guide to interpret them.

The Cooley Peninsula

The **Cooley Peninsula** is Louth's most hyped tourist destination, and while it's true that the mountains and surrounding rich verdure offer great walking territory and many a stunning seascape, the countryside lacks the raw, rugged and often downright exhilarating feel of the Mournes (see page 525) over the other side of **Carlingford Lough**. That said, there's still plenty here to delight, even if **Carlingford** village itself has somewhat meretriciously cashed in on its waterside location.

If you start from Dundalk, look out for signs to the *Ballymascanlon Hotel*, a kilometre or so after the R173 turn-off from the N1. A footpath from the hotel's car park runs beside the golf course to the **Proleek Dolmen**, a regular photographic feature in tourist brochures. Perched on the points of three triangular stones, its massive capstone weighs a remarkable 46 tons and, having inspected the scene, you'll probably spend the rest of the day wondering about the ingenuity of prehistoric hoisting engineers.

WALKS ON THE COOLEY PENINSULA

The varied terrain of the Cooley Peninsula offers a range of opportunities for **walking**, whether in the hills (often with sumptuous views across the lough to the Mournes), by the shore or along lush valleys. The longest waymarked walk is the 40km **Táin Way**, which takes a circular route around Slieve Foye (587m), up to the west above Carlingford village. Count on two days to complete this – you'll need proper walking equipment and clothing, adequate supplies of food and drink and the Ordnance Survey of Ireland Discovery map #36. A fabulous coastal path is the 7km-long **Carlingford–Omeath Greenway**, which tracks the old Dundalk, Newry and Greenore railway and is open to both walkers and cyclists. Otherwise, there are plenty of other walks that are easily accessible from Carlingford village; the useful **Cooley Walks pamphlet**, available from the tourist office in Carlingford (see 154) outlines ten scenic walks in the area, ranging from one to four hours in duration.

3

Carlingford

Set a short distance back from the lough's southern shore, the trim and charming former fishing village of **CARLINGFORD** is by far the best base for exploring the peninsula. Its tight and tortuous streets reflect its medieval origins and house a host of places where you can eat, drink and sleep; indeed the village has quite a reputation – surprisingly, perhaps – for being a bit of a party place at weekends, so be prepared for big crowds and no little noise. Moreover, this is not a place for the light of purse or pocket: prices here are significantly higher than elsewhere in the county or across the water in Down.

Carlingford's name is Old Norse in origin, deriving from "Kerlingfjörthr" (the fjord of the hag-shaped rock), and indicating that this was once a Viking settlement. Standing sentinel by the lough shore is the roofless ruin of **King John's Castle**, so-named after the English king who supposedly stopped in the village for two days in 1210 during the war with the Irish Knights. The village itself contains some impressive later buildings, not least the **Tholsel**, the sole surviving town gate from the fifteenth century, albeit heavily modified in the nineteenth century. Further along, and dating from the same period, stands the **Mint**, a fortified town house where coins were minted from the mid-fifteenth century onwards. Just beyond here you arrive in the market square (as central a point as any in the village) and the substantial ruins of **Taaffes Castle**, another superb medieval remnant, which was most likely a trading depot for the merchant classes.

ARRIVAL AND DEPARTURE CARLINGFORD

By bus Buses serving Dundalk (Mon–Sat 6 daily; 45min) and Newry (Mon–Sat 4 daily; 25min) stop outside the old Station House on the waterfront.

By ferry The Carlingford car ferry (http://carlingfordferry.com) makes the 15min crossing across Carlingford Lough from Greenore, 6km south of Carlingford, to Greencastle,

just outside Rostrevor in County Down, thus saving a 40min drive around the coastline; from Greenore, ferries depart on the half hour (Mon–Sat 7.30am–8.30pm, Sun 9.30am–8.30pm), and from Greencastle they depart on the hour (Mon–Sat 7am–8pm, Sun 9am–8pm).

INFORMATION AND ACTIVITIES

Tourist office The tourist office (Mon–Fri 10am–5pm, Sat & Sun 11am–4pm; http://carlingford.ie) occupies the restored railway station house on the waterfront. The office run a couple of guided tours in summer: at 3pm each day there's an hour-long Castle Tour, and on Mon, Tues & Wed at 11am there are medieval town tours.

Bike rental On Yer Bike at Carlingford Marina (http://onyerbike.ie) has a great selection of bikes (including

e-bikes) available for 2hr, half-day and full day; they also do servicing and repairs.

Activities Carlingford Adventure on Tholsel St (http://carlingfordadventure.com) offers a range of activities, including rock climbing, kayaking, paddleboarding and ziplining on the Skypark, Ireland's highest zipwire, located just outside the village.

TÁIN BÓ CÚAILNGE (THE CATTLE RAID OF COOLEY)

The location of many an Irish legend is still immediately identifiable thanks to a wealth of extant place names, and perhaps no more so than in the case of the **Táin Bó Cúailnge**. Set around 500 BC, many of the events in perhaps the greatest of the Celtic epics clearly take place in the mountains of the Cooley Peninsula. The villainess of the tale is **Medb**, the great Queen of Connacht, who so envies her husband Aillil's White Bull (Finnbenach) that she determines to capture the Brown Bull of Cooley (Donn Cúailnge). Drawing Aillil into her campaign, she begins a war against the east of Ireland, targeting Ulster in particular. All the Ulster men are rendered immobile by a curse except the tale's hero, **Cúchullain**, who is left to confront Medb's armies single-handedly. Much of the plot concerns his feats and victories, often achieved in bloodthirsty fashion, and the text is also brought to life by vivid topographical detail. The first known written version of the saga was included in the twelfth-century **Book of the Dun Cow**, and Thomas Kinsella's twentieth-century English translation encapsulates much of the vivacity of the Irish-language version (see page 599).

ACCOMMODATION

The Bay Tree 3 Newry St, http://baytree.ie. The *Bay Tree's* six rooms offer a high level of comfort, each one vaguely themed on Celtic history. The colour combinations of grey, beige and mauve are tasteful enough, while the smart furnishings include sturdy wooden bedsteads and wood-framed mirrors. €€

★ **Ghan House** Just below the Heritage Centre, http://ghanhouse.com. Sitting pretty behind a high-walled garden, *Ghan House* is a beautifully kept eighteenth-century building with eleven exquisitely furnished rooms bursting with antiques and family heirlooms — eight of these are garden rooms, all with mountain views. There is also an exceptionally good restaurant (see below). €€€

Mourneview Belmont, 2km south of Carlingford, http://mourneviewcarlingford.com. A welcome antidote to the hustle and bustle of the village itself, this charmingly run B&B sits in perfect rural isolation with delightful mountain views from its six neat rooms. €€

EATING AND DRINKING

The Bay Tree 3 Newry St, http://baytree.ie. Almost on a par with *Ghan House*, the *Bay Tree's* sparkling restaurant offers a thoughtfully crafted menu with fish to the fore — the Carlingford Oysters three ways is the perfect starter — followed, perhaps, by Char sui pork belly, soy & lime dressing, crackling, parsnip and whipped potato. Closed Mon–Wed. €€€

★ **Ghan House** Just below the Heritage Centre, http://ghanhouse.com. The undoubted culinary star in Carlingford is *Ghan House*, which serves modern Irish cuisine over a four-course dinner menu (€62.50) served at 6pm. Dishes might include treacle-cured salmon with saffron ice cream, followed by Mourne mountain lamb with artichoke and pearl barley, with ingredients from their own herb and vegetable gardens — then finish off with a Tonka bean crème brûlée. Top class. Closed Mon & Tues. €€€

PJ O'Hares Tholsel St, http://pjoharescarlingford.ie. The liveliest of the village's many pubs (and that's saying something), *PJ's* is a rambling, old-fashioned grocery-cum-pub with a warren of bars frequented by a good-natured crowd; live music or DJs at least four nights a week.

Ruby Ellens Newry St, http://rubyellens.com. An absolute gem of a tea house, from the floral-patterned cushions and fresh flowers on the tables to an outstanding range of thirst-quenching brews, served in exquisite china teacups, and assorted lip-smacking cakes. Afternoon tea is a good punt. €€

Monaghan town

All the elements of post-Plantation urban planning are well to the fore in **MONAGHAN TOWN**, which derived its prosperity from the linen industry and was long the base of a British garrison. The hub of the town plan is the **Diamond**, in whose centre stands the Rossmore monument, a flamboyant nineteenth-century drinking fountain. A short distance west is **Church Square**, dominated by an impressive obelisk commemorating a garrison member who died at the Battle of Inkerman, and is surrounded by stately, early nineteenth-century buildings, including a Neoclassical courthouse, a very fetching Regency Gothic church and an appropriately sturdy bank. Just downhill from here on Market Street is the late eighteenth-century **Market House**, a charming, arched limestone edifice whose exterior is embellished with exquisite carvings of oak apples and leaves; now home to the tourist office, it also hosts occasional arts and literary events. If you're in the region at the beginning of September, the rocking **Harvest Time Blues Festival** (http://harvestblues.ie) is well worth checking out.

Monaghan County Museum

1–2 Hill St · Mon–Fri 11am–5pm, Sat noon–5pm · Free · http://monaghan.ie/museum

To gain some understanding of the area's development, make tracks for the wonderful **Monaghan County Museum**, currently located just behind the Market House but due to move to the new Monaghan Peace Campus north of the town centre. A hugely rich and varied collection begins with some superb archaeological finds, notably the remarkably well-preserved Lisdrumturk cauldron, made from beautifully riveted bronze sheets. The most exceptional exhibit, however, is the fourteenth-century **Cross of Clogher**, a glorious, finely worked oak cross encased in bronze and adorned with bosses and panels, the uppermost of which depicts the Crucifixion. There's also comprehensive coverage of the county's various crafts and industries – many now sadly defunct – most notably **lace**, which was especially prominent in nearby Clones (see page 157).

By bus Monaghan's bus station is on North Rd, a 5min walk north of Church Square.

Destinations Bus Éireann: Cavan (Mon–Fri 7 daily, Sat & Sun 4–5 daily; 55min); Clones (Mon–Fri 4 daily, Sat 2; 30min); Letterkenny (8 daily; 1hr 50min).

Destinations Ulsterbus: Armagh (Mon–Sat 10 daily, Sun 4; 30–45min); Belfast (Mon–Sat 2 daily; 1hr 45min); Omagh (3 daily; 55min).

Tourist office The seasonal tourist office is currently located in the Market House on Market St (June–Sept Mon–Fri 10am–1pm & 2–5pm, Sat 1–5pm; http://monaghantourism.com) but like the museum, is due to relocate to the new Monaghan Peace Campus. At 11am every Saturday between April and September, there are free 1hr 30min guided walking tours of the town, departing from the *Westenra Arms Hotel* on the Diamond.

ACCOMMODATION AND EATING

Andy's 12 Market St, http://andysrestaurant.ie. If you like chicken, then this is the place to come: their garlic chicken with sweet sherry, or chicken fillet with tangy mushrooms and onion sauce – which has been on the menu for the best part of 40 years – are just two options. But if you just fancy a burger or fish and chips, then that's on the menu too. Closed Mon & Wed. €€

Coffee Break with Barbara 14 Church Square Yard, 047 72799. Secreted away in a tiny courtyard next to the courthouse, this happy little café serves the tastiest coffee in town, while carbon filament bulbs, chipboard tables and corner sofas make for a cosy ambience. Closed Sun. €

Grove Lodge Old Armagh Rd, 047 84677. Large and modern family home a 10min walk southeast of the centre, with three pleasant en-suite rooms: two doubles and one family. €€

The Hillgrove Hotel Old Armagh Rd, half a mile east of town, http://hillgrovehotel.com. Fortunately, the gaudily designed reception area doesn't extend to the rooms (including family rooms with bunks), which are far more tasteful, as well as being spacious and well furnished. There's an outstanding spa facility for guest use too. €€

County Monaghan

What few other sites Monaghan does have, besides Monaghan town, are dispersed around and about the county. In the north and west respectively, **Glaslough** and **Clones** both merit brief visits, while fans of Patrick Kavanagh can acquaint themselves with his work in **Inniskeen**, to the southeast.

Glaslough

Eleven kilometres northeast of Monaghan lies the somewhat otherworldly estate village of **GLASLOUGH**, dominated by a lengthy Famine wall (see page 565) which surrounds the estate of **Castle Leslie**. The Leslie family can reputedly trace back its origins to Attila the Hun and arrived in Ireland in 1633 in the shape of John Leslie who had been appointed Bishop of Raphoe. A colourful character, Leslie became known as the "fighting bishop", thanks to his victory as leader of an army over Cromwell at the Battle of Raphoe. When Charles II was restored to the throne, Leslie received £2000 as a reward for loyalty and used the sum to purchase Glaslough Castle and its demesne in 1665. His descendants have remained in occupation ever since and have included some equally intriguing figures. John Leslie's son Charles was charged with high treason for arguing a little too strenuously against the penal laws, but escaped and fled to France. Subsequently pardoned by George I, he returned to Glaslough where his children often entertained **Jonathan Swift**, who was not always complimentary about them in return:

Here I am In Castle Leslie
With Rows And Rows Of Books Upon The Shelves
Written By The Leslies
All About Themselves.

The current and very grand castle was built in the late nineteenth century and the family became connected by marriage to the Churchills – both Randolph and Winston stayed here. Later owners included Desmond Leslie, a former RAF pilot who authored *Flying Saucers Have Landed*, a supposedly factual account of the first alien contact with humans. His daughter now runs the castle. Even if you're not staying here, you're free to wander around the estate, which has one of the finest **equestrian centres** in the country where you can go for a 1hr hack or opt for a 45min lesson); you can also boat, fish and kayak on the lake.

ACCOMMODATION AND EATING **GLASLOUGH**

★ **Castle Leslie**, http://castleleslie.com. Often patronized by the rich and famous, *Castle Leslie* is an utterly majestic – though thoroughly unpretentious – place to stay. In the castle itself, accommodation consists of a range of sumptuously decorated and themed rooms, some defined by colour and others by historical reference (the Mediterranean room with its stone bed is brilliant), while *The Lodge*, which backs on to the stables, offers more contemporary rooms, though still imbued with spades of charm. *The Lodge* also accommodates the refined *Snaffles* restaurant, which offers an evening menu starring the likes of fillet of pork with pig cheek doughnut, sweet potato puree and cider jus (there's a dedicated vegan menu too), and the buzzy *Conor's Bar*, offering more reasonably priced two- and three-course menus. You could also stop by for afternoon tea. Lodge €€€, castle €€€€

Clones

Near the border with Fermanagh, the town of **CLONES** (pronounced "clo-nez") lies 20km southwest of Monaghan town, overlooking drumlin country from its hilltop perch. Being right on the border, Clones was hit hard during the Troubles, and today feels a little neglected, though it does merit a brief stop if passing through. It's also the location for one of the country's best small **film festivals** (http://clonesfilmfestival.com), held at the end of October. Points of interest in the town include a ninth-century **round tower** – originally five storeys high – and a richly carved **high cross**, which stands in the Diamond, somewhat overshadowed by the sombre shape of **St Tiernach's Church** (Church of Ireland). The cross's front panels depict scriptural scenes, such as the Garden of Eden, while the reverse is devoted to scenes from Christ's life.

Cassandra Hand Centre

Ball Alley Lane • Free • 047 52997

A five-minute walk south of the Diamond, the **Cassandra Hand Centre** is named after the founder of Clones Lace, whose profits went into the construction of a school here in 1859; the building functioned as such up until the beginning of World War I. Its

---

CLONES LACE

The area around Clones has a strong tradition of **lace-making**, a generally home-based industry which, at its peak in the 1850s, saw more than 1500 workers supplying markets as far afield as Paris, Rome and New York. Passed on from mother to daughter, the lace-making craft was introduced to Clones by the wife of the local Church of Ireland rector, Cassandra Hands, as a means of supplying income in the desperate post-Famine times. Rather than following the time-consuming Venetian needlework style, Clones women opted for a crochet hook as a means of expediency, and began producing work embellished by the flora of their local environs, often characterized by the multi-twirled **Clones knot**. Clones lace was embroidered into blouses and dresses, but its own elaborate style was gradually replaced by simpler designs. Nevertheless, it remains an important local tradition and, in 1989, a co-operative was established to reinvigorate the craft. There are still several lace-makers in the area and some of their work is on display at the **Ulster Canal Stores** (see page 158), where you can also purchase some of their wares.

3

main role these days is as a genealogy centre, but it's worth popping in to view the mock-up classroom and the exhibition on local folk who made good – perhaps the most notable of these is the boxer Barry McGuigan, World Featherweight champion in 1985.

Ulster Canal Stores
Cara St • Free • http://ulstercanalstoresvisitorcentre.ie

Heading further out of town on the road towards Cavan, you'll pass the **Ulster Canal Stores**, which once served as the distribution centre for wares arriving in Clones by water. Trade on the canal, which connected Belfast to Lough Erne, peaked in the 1890s, but competition from the railways led to the canal's demise, and it eventually closed in 1931. Nowadays it functions as a visitor centre with a fabulous **museum** dedicated to Clones lace alongside the history of the town; there's a welcoming little café here too.

ARRIVAL AND INFORMATION   CLONES

By bus Destinations Bus Éireann: Armagh (Mon–Sat 1 daily; 1hr); Cavan town (Mon–Sat 1 daily; 30min); Monaghan town (Mon–Sat 2 daily, Sun 1; 25min). Destination Ulsterbus: Enniskillen (Mon–Fri 6 daily, Sat 3; 50min).

Tourist information The helpful Ulster Canal Stores (see above) can furnish you with any information you might need; they also offer free guided tours of the town at 11am every Sat between May and October.

ACCOMMODATION AND EATING

Adamson's Bar Analore St, http://brianadamsons.ie. The pick of Clones' drinking dens by virtue of its traditional music sessions on Fridays and Saturdays – you can grab a stone-baked pizza to soak up the beer too. **€**
Creighton Hotel Fermanagh St, http://creightonhotel. ie. The only hotel in town is this spruce nineteenth-century building at the bottom of the street, with tip-top, though

really rather overpriced, rooms. Its restaurant and bar are easily the best places to eat in town. **€€**
Cuil Darach Fermanagh St, 047 52147. B&B above a pub/restaurant, with standard pine-furnished rooms; the restaurant itself offers a menu of attractively sauced chicken and steak dishes, though it's more fun to eat in the bar. **€€**

Inniskeen

Best accessed from Dundalk, a dozen kilometres east, the village of **INNISKEEN** was the birthplace of the influential poet and writer **Patrick Kavanagh**, born on a local farm in 1904 (see page 591). The village itself is pretty enough, with plenty of reminders of its ancient past, such as the superb tenth-century round tower and twelfth-century Norman lookout post.

Patrick Kavanagh Centre
St Mary's Church • charge • http://patrickkavanaghcentre.com

At the heart of the village stands St Mary's Church, whose annexe houses the **Patrick Kavanagh Centre**, which now looks better than ever following a major revamp. At the heart of the new visitor experience is an immersive triple-projection entitled *Pincer Jaws of Heaven*, a series of works read by Kavanagh alongside friends, associates and other poets. Elsewhere, there's stacks of memorabilia related to the poet, including photographs, manuscripts and his death mask, as well as a specially commissioned series of twelve paintings based upon his epic and extraordinarily emotive poem *The Great Hunger*. The centre hosts numerous events throughout the year and is also the venue for the annual Kavanagh Weekend in September, celebrating Kavanagh's life and work. His grave, along with that of his wife, can be found in the church cemetery. Otherwise, devotees of the poet can follow a town trail highlighting all the prominent Kavanagh landmarks, not least his home place and Billy Brennan's barn, as mentioned in *Inniskeen Road: July Evening*.

By bus Inniskeen is a 20min bus ride from Dundalk on the Dundalk–Carrickmacross service.

ACCOMMODATION AND EATING

Gleneven House 100m or so towards Dundalk from the Kavanagh Centre, http://gleneven.com. The only accommodation in the village is provided by this handsome Georgian house, which has a mix of comfy en-suite and standard rooms. Half board available and small dogs are welcome too. €€

Raglan Road Tea Room Next to St Mary's Church, 087 212 8868. If you're in need of refreshment, head to this sweet little café for a coffee with cake, a simple breakfast, or a light lunch, surrounded by books and bric-a-brac. Closed Sun. €

Cavan town and around

Nowadays a busy market town, **CAVAN** was once the seat of the O'Reilly clan who built a Franciscan abbey here in 1300, although this succumbed to a fire in 1451. Later, the town itself was razed to the ground in 1576 by a female member of the clan and subsequently rebuilt. Much of what you see today dates from the nineteenth and twentieth centuries and all that remains of the reconstructed abbey is its eighteenth-century **bell tower**, on Abbey Street, standing next to the grave of Owen Roe O'Neill. In truth there's next to nothing to see in Cavan itself, but it does possess a clutch of decent places to sleep and eat, and makes an ideal base from which to explore the county's western reaches.

3

ARRIVAL AND INFORMATION CAVAN TOWN AND AROUND

By bus The bus station is at the southern end of Farnham St. Destinations Bus Éireann: Belturbet (8 daily; 20min); Clones (Mon–Fri 3 daily, Sun 1; 30min); Donegal town (8 daily; 2hr); Dublin (hourly; 2hr); Kells (hourly; 1hr); Monaghan town (Mon–Fri hourly, Sat & Sun 3–4 daily; 55min); Navan (8 daily; 1hr 15min). Destinations Ulsterbus: Clones (Mon–Sat 2 daily; 30min);

Monaghan town (Mon–Sat 2 daily; 55min).
Tourist office and bike rental The tourist office (April–Sept Mon–Fri 9am–5pm; http://thisiscavan.ie) is 300m northeast of the bus station in the Johnston Library and Farnham Centre, itself part of the county council building. Bikes can be rented from here too.

ACCOMMODATION AND EATING

Black Horse Inn 1 Church St, 049 436 8396, http://theblack horseinn.ie. A long wooden bar with neon lighting and beer barrels for tables is the welcoming setting for this convivial boozer. The rear of the premises is occupied by a pizza outlet, *Uso*, which serves scrumptious wood-fired oven pizzas on Fridays & Saturdays – dine-in and takeaway. €

Chapter One Unit 6, Cavan Retail Park, http://chaptercavan.ie. Despite its dull and somewhat awkward location a mile or so southeast of the town centre, this is by far the most satisfying place to eat in Cavan, whether that's a breakfast of Spanish chorizo and crispy potato, a freshly made New York-style bagel, a juicy Black Jack burger, or a morsel of two from the wok. €€

Cherville B&B Drumalee, a 15min walk southeast of the town centre, http://cherville.ie. Super friendly guesthouse with four rooms decorated in deep red, vivid pink and jet black colours, alongside, for example, the occasional zebra print furnishing; a generous tray of sweet and savoury snacks and a cracking breakfast tops it off. €€

Farnham Estate Hotel 3km southeast of town on the Dublin road, http://farnhamestate.ie. Set within the grounds of a vast country estate, this super-luxurious spa hotel is as swish as you'd expect, with rooms in both the Great House itself and in a modern wing. If you fancy a bite to eat, eschew the restaurant and make a beeline for the terrific *Wine Goose Cellar Bar*. €€€

Ballyjamesduff

BALLYJAMESDUFF is a pleasant, small crossroads town, 15km southeast of Cavan town along back lanes or a little further via the N3. James Duff himself, the Earl of Fife, was an early Plantation landlord of the area, and one of his descendants, Sir James Duff, commanded English troops during the suppression of the 1798 Rebellion – making the more sombre Irish version of his name, "Black Séamus", rather appropriate to local ears.

Cavan County Museum

Virginia Rd • charge • http://cavanmuseum.ie

Housed in a former convent, the **Cavan County Museum** has an impressive collection covering all aspects of the county's history. Major items on display include the Killycluggin Stone, dating from 200 BC and decorated in classic Celtic La Tène artwork, and a replica of the Corleck Head dating from the Iron Age, as well as the impressive 1100-year-old Lough Errol **dugout boat**. Exhibitions include all aspects of the past, from pre-history to the Great Famine, folklore and archaeology. On a lighter note, also represented here is the painter, poet and songwriter Percy French who worked in the county for a spell as an inspector of drains – one of his more famous comic songs is *Come Back Paddy Reilly to Ballyjamesduff*.

Outside, there's the fun **Trench Experience**, an enormous 350m-long ditch built to the original specifications designed by Irish soldiers who fought for Britain at the Battle of the Somme during World War I. Complete with barbed wire and mock battlefield – and some clever sound and visual effects – it's impressively authentic. Some 659 men from Cavan perished in the Great War.

West Cavan

To the west of Cavan town lies the assortment of various-sized lakes that forms the system known as **Lough Oughter**, through which the River Erne contrives to manage a pathway to Upper Lough Erne (see page 555). Roads are few and landmarks limited to the occasional small hill, while the rush-fringed lakes lure many anglers. The land gradually assumes dominance over water west of the hillside town of **Belturbet**, beyond which the inhospitable and bleak strip doglegs between counties Fermanagh and Leitrim, becoming ever craggier as it rises through wild, boggy hills. At the county's northwestern tip, the **Cavan Way** terminates at the tiny border village of **Blacklion**.

Belturbet and around

One of the most pleasant bases for exploring the lough is **BELTURBET**, some 18km north of Cavan town, a hillside village rising steeply from the River Erne. Apart from the delights of lough-side walks, the major source of interest around the lakes is **Drumlane Church**, around 1.5km south of Milltown on the R201 road and which enjoys a picturesque setting between two lakes. St Mogue, a pupil of Wales's patron St David, founded a monastery here in the sixth century, while the medieval church is part of an abbey founded here by monks from Kells in County Meath. Now ruined and roofless, the church's west doorway has carved heads of possibly ecclesiastical figures or monarchs, which probably date from the fifteenth century. Nearby, an eleventh-century **round tower** features now barely distinguishable carvings of birds, thought to be a cock and a hen and believed to bear some relevance to the Resurrection.

ARRIVAL AND DEPARTURE
BELTURBET

By bus Bus Éireann services depart from outside the post office on The Diamond to Cavan town (5–6 daily; 20min) and Enniskillen (7 daily; 35min).

ACCOMMODATION AND EATING

Church View 8 Church St, http://churchviewguesthouse. com. Located just behind the library, off the main road, this friendly B&B is popular with local fishermen – there's even a tackle shed with walk-in cold room; the seven en-suite rooms are complemented by a guest lounge with complimentary refreshments. €€

The Seven Horseshoes 12 Main St, http://theseven horseshoes.com. One of the county's oldest hostelries hold a handful of functional rooms. Better is the warming, brick and wood-panelled bar, easily the most appealing spo in the village for a bite to eat (it's strong on seafood and steaks) or a pint. Closed Mon & Tues. €€

The Cavan Way and Blacklion

The county's northwestern reaches provide superb walking terrain, best accessed via the signposted 26km **Cavan Way**, which runs through jagged landscapes from Dowra in County Leitrim (see page 400) to the small border village of **Blacklion** where it joins the **Ulster Way**. The hills above Blacklion command dramatic views across Lough Macnean east to Fermanagh's lakelands and west to the mountains of Sligo and Leitrim. About halfway along the route is the **Shannon Pot**, the source of Ireland's longest river but a mere trickle here.

Cavan Burren Park

3km south of Blacklion • Dawn to dusk • Free • http://cavanburrenpark.ie

Spectacularly sited on the slopes of the Cuilcagh Mountain – and part of the Cuilcagh Lakelands Geopark – is the **Cavan Burren Park**, a remarkable limestone plateau where megalithic tombs, cist graves and ancient stone huts comprise a fantastic trove of prehistoric treasures; many examples of rock art have also been identified here. Just beyond the car park, an open-air **interpretative centre** provides information about the archaeological, geological and cultural history of Cavan Burren, and is the starting point for four short, looped **walks** through the park, ranging from 1.3km to 3km. Best of all perhaps, the park offers stunning views of Cuilcagh Mountain, west Cavan and the wider Geopark – indeed the perfect spot from which to enjoy a picnic in the designated area.

3

ARRIVAL AND INFORMATION
THE CAVAN WAY AND BLACKLION

By bus Blacklion is served by buses from/to Enniskillen (8 daily; 30min) and Sligo (8 daily; 1hr).

Tourist information Housed inside the Market House building, Blacklion's tourist office (Mon–Fri 9am–5pm, Sat 9am–4pm; http://blackliontouristoffice.com) has stacks of great info on the Cavan Way and Cavan Burren.

ACCOMMODATION AND EATING

CABÜ by the lakes Killykeen Forest Park https://holidays.cabu.co.uk. Nestled in the forest by the shores of Lough Oughter, these luxury woodland cabins offer total serenity in a fabulous, car-free setting. Take to the lakes by boat, paddleboard or kayak, or enjoy a dip in fine weather. Otherwise walk or cycle the woodland trails before reviving tired muscles in the Japanese bath, sauna and hot tub. Drinks are served and marshmallows can be toasted in the Sitooterie. Come as couples or with family and friends. Three-night min stay. Self-catering but there's a gift and grocery shop on site with ready meals and fresh pastries daily, and local takeaway fare can be ordered in. €€€€

Keepers Arms Bridge St, Bawnboy, http://keepersarms.com. Located in the village of Bawnboy, on the main road up towards Blacklion, this terrific little inn has nine tidy rooms, three of which are tucked away up on the second floor under the eaves. The downstairs bar is about as friendly as they come and the pub grub isn't half bad either. €€

★**Macnean House** Main St, Blacklion, http://nevenmaguire.com. *Macnean House* is run by one of Ireland's best-known chefs, Neven Maguire, whose modern Irish cooking is up there with the finest in the country. On the two menus (Prestige and Vegetarian) you can expect scintillating combinations like seared scallops, crab ravioli and Thai veloute, and red pepper orzo with courgette and lemongrass veloute. And if you don't fancy moving too far after an evening of gluttony, there are some beautifully appointed rooms (€€€) here too – and naturally, there's an exquisite breakfast to wake up to. Reservations essential months in advance. Closed Sun & Mon. €€€€

The Midlands: Westmeath, Longford, Offaly and Laois

CLONMACNOIS

The Midlands: Westmeath, Longford, Offaly and Laois

Obeying the siren call of the west coast, most foreign tourists, and indeed Irish holiday-makers, put their foot down to motor through the Midlands as quickly as possible. But it's the ideal area to make a stopover off the main radial routes out of Dublin and there are some compelling sights that may well surprise you.

The dairy farms of **County Westmeath** (Iarmhí) are interspersed with large, glassy lakes, including Lough Ennell to the south of **Mullingar**, the county town, on whose shores **Belvedere House** is well worth a short detour off the N4. Among the county's more northerly lakes nestle the quirky gardens of **Tullynally Castle** and the pastoral charms of the **Fore Valley**, where you can poke around medieval monastic remains and be entertained by their wondrous legends. The N4 ploughs on through **County Longford** (An Longfort), mostly rich grasslands but blending into Northern Ireland's drumlin country in its northern third. In the south of the county, the **Corlea Trackway Visitor Centre** gives a fascinating glimpse of a prestigious but ill-fated Iron Age road-building project.

The **River Shannon** and its seasonal floodplain delineates most of the Midlands' western border, running down through **Athlone**, a major junction town whose **castle** has been give an excellent, high-tech redevelopment. Just south of here, the major ecclesiastical site of **Clonmacnois** enjoys a dreamy setting above the river's meanders and meadows. Follow the river downstream and you'll come to the neat village of **Shannonbridge**, and once you cross the bridge you'll be in the neighbouring province of Connaught.

Elsewhere, **County Offaly** (Uíbh Fháilí) is known for its bogs, but the charming town of **Birr**, with its imposing castle and Georgian terraces, makes the best base in the Midlands. To its east rises the attractive bulge of **Slieve Bloom**, with a thick topping of blanket bog, beyond which **County Laois** (pronounced "leash") is mostly lush grazing and cereal land.

Brief history

These counties were mostly beyond the Pale, the enclave around Dublin that the Anglo-Normans retreated to in the fourteenth and fifteenth centuries, and indeed Offaly is named after the *Uí Failí* (O'Connor Faly), Irish chieftains who would attack the Pale and then retreat to their strongholds deep in the boglands. In the sixteenth century, however, this region was fairly comprehensively planted, when land was confiscated from native Irish owners and given to loyal English landlords. In 1541, Westmeath was split off from County Meath, and in 1556 Offaly and Laois were created as "King's County" and "Queen's County", respectively, with the latter's main town named Maryborough (now Portlaoise) after the current monarch. Bypassed by the Industrial Revolution, many of the planned estate-towns that were attached to these landholdings remain to this day, along with the vestiges of a slow, steady rural style of living.

Mullingar and around

Set in lush cattle-country, **MULLINGAR**, the county town of Westmeath, holds little of interest for visitors, except as a base for visiting **Belvedere House**, a Georgian mansion in a lovely setting on Lough Ennell, or the historically important **Hill of Usineach**.

Highlights

❶ Belvedere House A beautifully restored Georgian hunting lodge, set in attractive gardens, overlooking Lough Ennell. See page 166

❷ The Hill of Uisneach This important prehistoric site is considered by historians to be the symbolic centre of the country. See page 167

❸ The Fore Valley Explore the rich ecclesiastical history of this remote, green valley or suspend your disbelief in appreciation of its Seven Wonders. See page 168

❹ Sean's Bar Soak up the craic and great atmosphere at the oldest pub in Ireland in Athlone. See page 173

❺ Clonmacnois The Midlands' pre-eminent historical site, a prestigious complex of churches and ornate high crosses overlooking the River Shannon. See page 174

❻ Birr Castle Wander around the immense grounds and immerse yourself in the scientific exploits of the talented Parsons family at the Historic Science Centre. See page 176

HIGHLIGHTS ARE MARKED ON THE MAP ON PAGE 166

Belvedere House

5km south of Mullingar on the N52 • charge, including audio guide (see page 170); Heritage Island • http://belvedere-house.ie

Set in abundant gardens on the eastern shore of Lough Ennell, **Belvedere House** was built in the 1740s by Richard Castle as a hunting lodge for Robert Rochfort, later the first Earl of Belvedere, the so-called "Wicked Earl", whose main pastime seems to have been making life hell for his wife and brothers. In 1743 he falsely accused his wife Mary of having an affair with his brother Arthur and imprisoned her for the next 31 years at their nearby main residence, Gaulstown. It was only when the Earl died that she was released by their son, whom she no longer recognized. Meanwhile, the Earl had successfully pressed charges of adultery against Arthur, who, unable to pay the damages of £20,000, lived out his days in debtors' prison.

The **house** itself, which commands beautiful views of the lake, has been painstakingly restored and authentically refurbished by Westmeath County Council. It holds some gorgeous fireplaces of carved Irish oak with Italian marble insets, but is most notable for the exquisite craftsmanship of its **rococo ceilings**, the work of a French stuccodore,

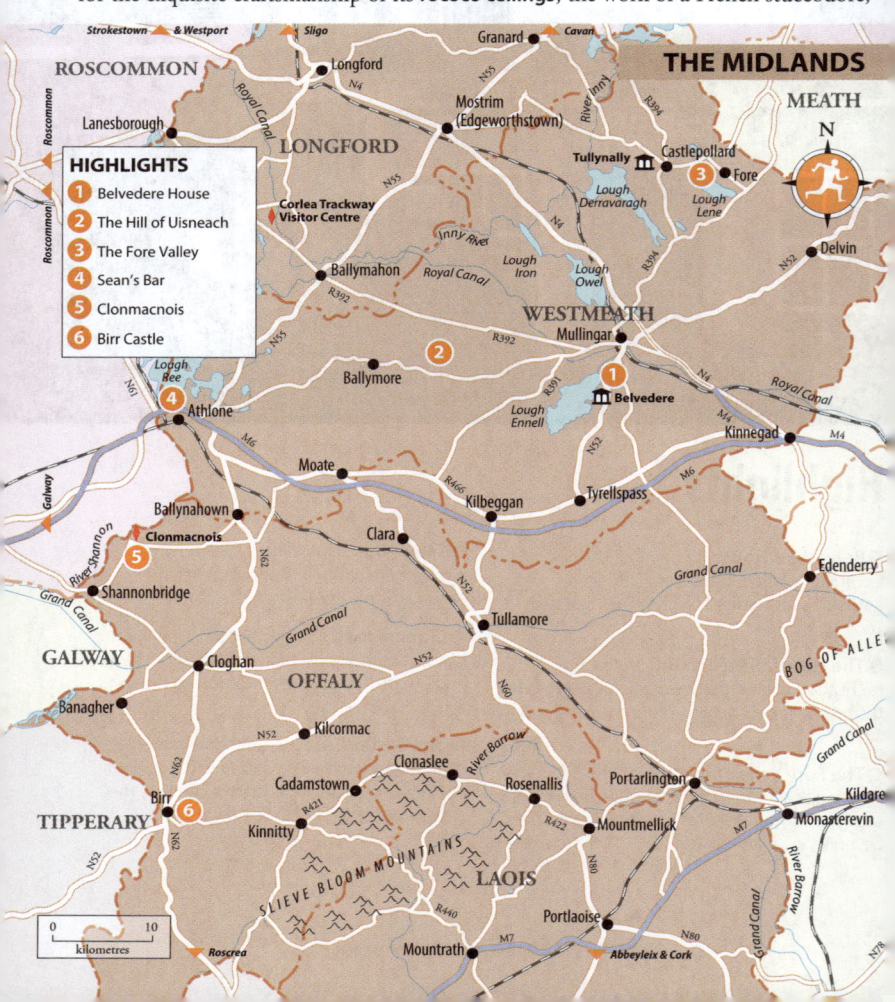

Barthelemij Cramillion. Look out especially for the vivid depictions of the Four Winds, a fire-breathing dragon and a horn of plenty in the dining room, while the library, intended for night-time use, features sleeping cherubs wrapped in a blanket of clouds, a crescent moon and stars, and on the cornice a swirl of flowers with their heads closed.

A feud between Robert Rochfort and his other brother George was behind one of the **gardens**' main sights, the **Jealous Wall**. When George commissioned Richard Castle in the 1750s to build Tudenham House, a much larger mansion than Belvedere, just 1km away, the Earl of Belvedere spent £10,000 building this huge Gothic folly, three storeys high and nearly 60m long, just to block the view. The extensive woodlands, lawns and gardens make for a pleasant stroll on the shore of the lake, past a restored ice-house and follies known as the Octagonal Gazebo and the Gothic Arch. The grounds include four children's play areas and a café.

The Hill of Uisneach

Near the village of Loughnavalley, 9km miles southwest of Mullingar • Access is by guided tour (2hr, 3km; must be booked in advance); Sat & Sun at 1pm; charge • http://uisneach.ie

The **Hill of Uisneach** is the ancient seat of the Kings of Meath and a prehistoric meeting place of renown. Its most famous feature is "**The Catstone**", a 6m-high limestone boulder that from certain angles resembles the shape of a cat about to pounce. Sitting at the centre of a low earthen ridge, the stone is known in Irish as *Ail na Mireann*, which translates as the "stone of divisions" – it marks the point where the five ancient provinces of Ireland met, and was considered the symbolic sacred centre of the country. There are now four provinces in Ireland: Ulster, Munster, Leinster and Connaught, but in ancient times there was a **fifth province**, known as **Mide** (now Co. Meath). Celtic mythology recounts that this fifth province could also refer to the magical "otherworld", and the Catstone was regarded as a gateway to it. Uisneach was said to be the home of the sovereignty goddess, Eriu, after whom Ireland is named, and according to legend she is resting beneath the catstone. For these and other reasons, the Hill of Uisneach has played a significant role in the Irish imagination; indeed, James Joyce spent time on the hill and mentioned it in *Finnegan's Wake*.

Although Uisneach is only 182m at its highest point, on a clear day, hills in twenty counties are visible from the summit, with all-encompassing views of the Irish Midlands. You're also surrounded by traces of the past, including a conjoined **ring fort** (shaped in a figure of eight), **Lough Lugh**, an ancient ritual pond named after the Sun God Lugh, and **St. Patrick's Bed**, a megalithic tomb. The hill is marked by several stretches of lazy-beds where potatoes were grown, and the ruins of small farms abandoned in the exodus from the land during the hard times of the mid-nineteenth century. The tour is an easy to moderate 3km-walk mostly over grassland, with a gentle incline to the summit. The Bealtaine Fire Festival every May celebrates the arrival of summer, with a bonfire, medieval re-enactments, art installations, music and games.

ARRIVAL AND INFORMATION

MULLINGAR AND AROUND

By train Trains on the Dublin–Sligo line stop at the station on the southwest side of the centre.
Destinations Dublin Connolly (6–9 daily; 1hr 15min); Sligo (6–7 daily; 1hr 50min).
By bus Most buses call at Castle St right in the heart of town, though some stop only at the train station.

Destinations Athlone (7–8 daily; 1hr); Dublin (hourly; 1hr 30min); Sligo (4–5 daily; 2hr 20min).
Tourist information Market House, around the corner from the Castle St bus stop, on the main Pearse St (June–Sept Tues–Sat 9am–1pm & 2–5pm; http://visitwestmeath.ie).

ACCOMMODATION

Greville Arms Pearse St, http://grevillearmshotel.ie. Bang
in the centre of town, this welcoming and refurbished old

coaching inn is mentioned in James Joyce's *Ulysses* and boasts a small first-floor museum of local life . The 38 bedrooms are either contemporary and colourful, or plush and traditional with swagged curtains, gilt mirrors and padded headboards on the beds. Naturally, there's a *Joyce* restaurant and *Ulysses* bar. €€

Lough Ennell Caravan Park 5km south of town off the N52, just beyond Belvedere House, http://caravanparksireland. com. Quiet, sheltered and well-equipped lakeside campsite. Surrounded by mature beech, birch, ash, chestnut and oak trees, it comes with a campers' kitchen, laundry, playground, minimart, restaurant and takeaway. Closed Nov–March. €

EATING AND DRINKING

Dominik's 37 Dominick St, 044 939 6696. Smart and friendly contemporary restaurant that rustles up crowd-pleasing courses such as beef carpaccio with rocket and lemon, and rack of lamb with potato. There's a two-course main menu costing €35. Closed Mon. €€€

Ilia Café 28 Oliver Plunkett St, 044 934 7354. Relaxing daytime café where the tasty menu ranges from soups, salads, omelettes, bagels and simple main courses or

curries, steaks and chicken wraps, to cakes and pastries, alongside herbal tea, filtered coffee and freshly squeezed orange juice. Closed Sun. €

Oscar's 21 Oliver Plunkett St, http://oscarsrestaurant. ie. Lively and unpretentious restaurant directly opposite *Ilia Café* that's well known locally for its reasonably priced pasta and pizza, as well as steaks and seafood. Takeaways available too. €€

Castlepollard and around

The far north of Westmeath shelters two compelling and whimsical attractions, the gardens of Tullynally Castle and the Seven Wonders of the Fore Valley, near **Castlepollard**, a pretty eighteenth- and nineteenth-century village laid out around a large triangular green.

Tullynally Castle

Just over 1km northwest of Castlepollard on the Granard road • Castle May–Sept Thurs–Sat tours at 11am, 12,30pm & 2pm; Gardens and tea rooms April–Sept Thurs–Sun 11am–5pm • charge • http://tullynallycastle.ie

Tullynally Castle has been the seat of the Anglo-Irish Pakenhams, later Earls of Longford, since the seventeenth century. Remodelled as a rambling Gothic Revival castle to the designs of Francis Johnston in the early 1800s, it remains the Pakenhams family home, open for tours from May to September and in the winter for occasional concerts. castle visits include the drawing room, dining room, library, great hall and servant's quarters. From April, the extensive **gardens**, and the Courtyard tea rooms – Patagonian cake is a speciality – are open. Terraced lawns around the castle overlook parkland, laid out by the first Earl of Longford in 1760. From here, winding paths lead through the woodland to lakes, a walled flower garden with a two-hundred-year-old yew avenue and a limestone grotto, as well as a Chinese garden with a scarlet pagoda and a Tibetan garden of waterfalls and streams. There's also a Discovery Trail for kids and a Tree Trail for committed dendrophiles, following Thomas Pakenham's remarkable collection of rare and ancient trees.

The Fore Valley

To the east of Castlepollard off the R195 Oldcastle road, the **Fore Valley** is a charming, bucolic spot, sheltered between two ranges of low, green hills and dotted with some impressive Christian ruins. Around 630, St Fechin founded a monastery here, which had grown into a community of three hundred monks by the time he died in 665. Over the centuries since, various sites in the valley have become associated with Fechin's miraculous powers, known as the **Seven Wonders of Fore**, which, while far from jaw-dropping, do add some fun and interest to an exploration of the locale. All are within walking distance of the village of **Fore** at the heart of the valley.

The Seven Wonders

To the west of the village, on the south side of the road, stands **St Fechin's Church**, now roofless, the oldest remaining building in the valley, dating probably from the tenth century. The first wonder lies over its main entrance, a massive lintel inscribed with a small cross-in-circle: the **stone raised by St Fechin's prayers**. Up the slope and across from the church, you'll find the **Anchorite's Cell**, a fifteenth-century tower to which the mausoleum chapel of the Greville-Nugent family was added in the nineteenth century (ask for the key behind the bar at the *Seven Wonders* pub in the village, which opens at around 12.30pm). Practising an extreme form of asceticism that was popular in the early and high Middle Ages, anchorites would stay in the tower, meditating and praying alone, with food brought to them by local people, until they died. Inside the chapel, an inscription commemorates the last hermit of Fore, and probably of all Ireland, Patrick Beglin, whose body is "hidden in this hollow heap of stones" – the second wonder, the **anchorite in a stone**. Like the other hermits, Beglin had vowed to remain in the cell until he died: in 1616, he fell trying to climb out, and broke his neck – thus enacting his promise.

Back down the slope and across the road you'll see the **water that will not boil**, a holy well known to cure headaches and toothaches, where in the nineteenth century rites were performed on St Fechin's Day (January 20). In the spring stands a dead ash tree, gaily festooned with sweet wrappers, stockings, knickers and coins (which caused the copper poisoning that killed the tree) – the fourth wonder, the **wood that will not burn**. Nearby, a stream that runs underground from Lough Lene to the south resurfaces at the ruined St Fechin's Mill – the **mill without a race**.

A couple of hundred metres across the marshy valley floor rise the substantial but compact remains of **Fore Priory** – the **monastery built on a bog**. It was erected in the early thirteenth century, one of very few in Ireland to follow the rule of St Benedict, the fifth-century Italian ascetic. Attached to the central cloister, of which several Gothic arches remain, you'll find the church to the north, the chapterhouse to the east, with the dormitory above, and the refectory to the south. A little away from the main buildings, up a small slope, there's a circular, thirteenth-century columbarium, where the monks kept doves, an efficient source of meat in the Middle Ages.

The seventh wonder is a little removed from the others to the south of the village – ask for directions at the coffee shop. A short woodland walk will bring you down to the attractive shore of Lough Lene, which is dotted with small, green islands. A stream flows out of the lake, apparently in the wrong direction, passing under an overgrown arched bridge, before disappearing into a sinkhole (to emerge at St Fechin's Mill) – the **water that flows uphill**.

ARRIVAL AND INFORMATION

CASTLEPOLLARD AND AROUND

By bus The daily bus service to Castlepollard from Dublin (1–2 daily; 2hr 20min) via Trim (supplemented by a weekly Mullingar–Castlepollard bus on Thurs; 30min) might work out for a visit to Tullynally, but the Fore Valley is too long a walk from Castlepollard.

By car With your own transport, Castlepollard is easily approached from Mullingar on the R394, or from the Loughcrew Cairns near Oldcastle, just across the border in County Meath (see page 133).

Tourist information The *Abbey Café* in Fore (daily 10am–6pm; http://foreabbeycoffeeshop com) hosts a 20min audiovisual on the monastery (€4), has lots of information on the area and arranges guided tours; it also sells secondhand books, local crafts, jams and other goodies. A 3km looped walk, St Fechin's Way (also known as the Nancy-Nelly Walk after two women who lived on the path) starts from the coffee shop.

ACCOMMODATION

Hounslow House Fore, about 1km from the village and well signposted, http://hounslowhouse.com. Accommodation in single, double, triple and family rooms is available at this large two hundred-year-old farmhouse set in extensive grounds with fine views of the valley. They've also got a self-catering apartment. €€

Athlone and around

Straddling the Shannon at its midpoint, **ATHLONE** is the bustling capital of the Midlands and an important road and rail junction on the Westmeath–Roscommon frontier. It probably derives its name from the *Táin Bó Cúailnge*, in which the remains of the white bull of Connacht, the Findbennach, after its defeat by Ulster's brown bull, are scattered throughout Ireland; its loins came to rest here at *Áth Luain*, the "Ford of the Loins". A bridge was first built over this ford in 1120 by Turlough O'Connor, king of Connacht, which the Anglo-Normans replaced with a stone bridge in 1210; they were also responsible for the mighty **castle**. Today, the town supports an important college, the Technological University of the Shannon (Midlands Midwest), as well as various civil-service offices and high-tech firms, but its main function for tourists is as a jumping-off point for the monastic site of **Clonmacnois** (see page 174), a 25-minute drive south of Athlone. Fewer visitors know about the **Corlea Trackway Visitor Centre**, 20km northeast, but the evocative, two-thousand-year-old wooden road preserved here is also well worth a visit if you have your own transport. Over the bank holiday weekend at the beginning of June, the **Oliver Goldsmith International Literary Festival** is held in nearby Ballymahon and Abbeyshrule (http://olivergoldsmithfestival.com). Athlone hosts a lively farmers' market every Saturday morning, held on Market Place by the castle.

Athlone Castle

Town centre, by the west side of the main bridge over the River Shannon • June–Aug Mon–Sat 9.30am–6pm; Sun 10.30am–6pm; March–May & Sept–Oct Tues–Sat 10am–5.30pm, Sun 11am–5pm; Nov–Feb Wed–Sat 10.30am–5pm, Sun 11.30am–5pm; last admission 1hr before closing • charge, combined ticket available with Belvedere House (see page 166), €6 with Viking Tours ticket (see page 173); Heritage Island • http://athlonecastle.ie

Athlone Castle still casts a formidable shadow over the town, having weathered some bloody fighting during the Cromwellian Wars and the War of the Kings of the seventeenth century. The imposing, grey, thirteenth-century fortifications have been

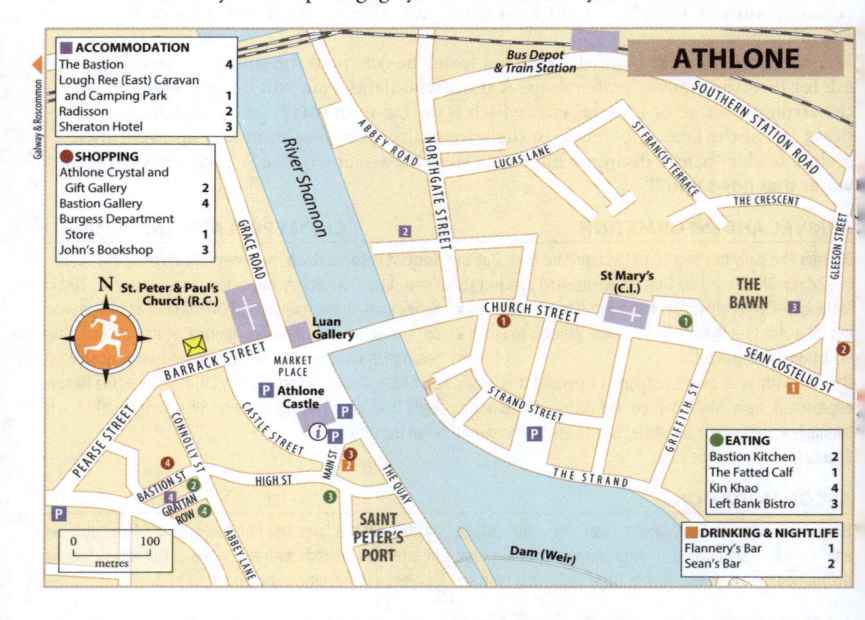

ATHLONE'S WORLD-FAMOUS OPERA SINGER

One of the best-known **tenors** of his generation, **John Count McCormack** was born in Athlone in 1884, the son of working-class parents employed at the Athlone Woollen Mills. McCormack went on to sing at the Metropolitan Opera House in New York opposite Dame Nellie Melba, and in total made more than six hundred recordings, as well as the popular Hollywood film *Song O' My Heart* (1930). His records sold in their millions, making him one of the bestselling artists Ireland has ever produced. Towards the end of his life he broadcast on the radio with Bing Crosby.

A magnificent bronze **sculpture** of McCormack now forms the centrepiece of a newly designated square beside Athlone Civic Centre. Designed by the Irish artist, Rory Breslin, the sculpture stands on a plinth and marks the starting point of a self-guided **walking trail** covering twelve stops, including the house in which McCormack was born, his old school and Athlone Castle. The castle houses a permanent exhibition displaying programmes from his time with the Dublin Amateur Operatic Society, his Papal Chain, as well as a montage of photographs and HMV recordings, including his much-loved song, *I Hear You Calling Me*.

stylishly converted to house the lively and fascinating exhibitions of the **Athlone Castle Visitor Centre**. As well as some beautiful, early Christian, carved stone slabs, the centre houses impressive audiovisuals and interactive games, focusing on the vicious Sieges of Athlone during the War of the Kings. After the Battle of the Boyne, William III's army took control of eastern and southern Ireland, while Jacobite supporters of James II attempted to defend the west along the line of the Shannon. In July 1690, Athlone Castle did its job, forcing the Williamites to retreat after a week; they returned with some serious artillery in June of 1691, however, and after crossing the river over the ancient ford and reducing much of the castle to rubble, they took it from the Jacobites, who lost over 1200 men. Within two weeks of taking Athlone, William's men won the Battle of Aughrim in County Galway, and soon after the war was ended with the Treaty of Limerick.

Aside from the noise of the sieges, warring cries and drumbeats, a different type of sensory sensation marks the end of the tour, as the lyrical voice of **John Count McCormack** serenades visitors through loudspeakers in a permanent first-floor exhibition celebrating the life of the famous Athlone-born tenor (see box).

The Luan Gallery

Opposite the castle on the west bank of the Shannon • Free • http://athloneartsandtourism.ie

It's well worth checking out the exhibitions, workshops and events at the **Luan Gallery**, a lovely contemporary art gallery. The building was constructed in 1897 as Father Mathew [sic] Hall (named after the anti-alcohol campaigner), a temperance hall for entertainments to promote sobriety among the employees of Athlone Woollen Mills. The addition of a beautiful extension has created bright, airy exhibition spaces that afford great views of the river.

Corlea Trackway Visitor Centre

2 Carton Rd, Keenagh, 20km northeast of Athlone • Free • http://heritageireland.ie

It's a little tricky to get to the fascinating **Corlea Trackway Visitor Centre**, which is actually across the county border in Longford and signposted along a minor road off the R392, 20km northeast of Athlone, but its isolation in the midst of a desolate bog only adds to the appeal of the place. In 1984, Bord na Móna (the Peat Board) discovered a buried *togher*, an early Iron Age trackway, while milling turf here in Corlea raised bog. Dated to 148 BC, the trackway was made of split oak planks up to 4m in

CYCLING AND WALKING ROUTES AROUND ATHLONE

Many regions of Ireland have repurposed old railway lines as cycling or walking routes, and the Midlands has joined the trend with the **Old Rail Trail Greenway** (http://greenwaysireland. org/old-rail-trail-westmeath**)**, which opened in 2017. Following a converted stretch of the former Midlands Great Western Railway, this 43km cycle and walking trail is a delightful rural route from Athlone to Mullingar. Generally flat and with a smooth sealed surface, it runs under historic stone arch bridges and is suitable for all ages and all types of bikes.

For those who prefer to stroll around Athlone, the **Shannon Banks Nature Trail Walk** runs along the grassy verges or the promenade of the River Shannon as part of a 5km town trail. You can start on either a green or brown route from the quay wall at the castle and follow signs pointing to tree species such as sycamore, horse chestnut and red oak. Pick up a walking leaflet at the tourist office.

length that were meant to float on the bog surface, one of the most substantial and sophisticated of many such prehistoric roads found in Europe. However, the builders knew more about woodworking than the properties of the bog, because within ten years the heavy planks had sunk into the peat – which preserved them perfectly for the next two thousand years. The road connected dry land to the east with an island in the bog to the west, but it's clear that such a prestigious construction was intended for more than just the movement of animals by farmers: it may have been part of a ceremonial highway from the Hill of Uisneach, the ritual "centre of Ireland" that marked the division of the five ancient provinces, between Mullingar and Athlone, to the royal site of Rathcroghan in Roscommon (see page 405), via the narrow crossing of the Shannon at Lanesborough.

Excellent **guided tours** begin with the 18m of trackway that's been preserved under cover in the visitor centre. Another 80m has been left outside under the turf, but the guides, as well as delving into the extraordinary ecology of the bog, will take you to the wooden walkway built over it, which gives a good idea of what the trackway would have looked like, undulating over the peaty tussocks.

ARRIVAL AND INFORMATION

ATHLONE AND AROUND

By train The train station is on the north side of the centre on Southern Station Rd.

Destinations Dublin Heuston (12–15 daily; 1hr 40min–2hr); Galway (6–10 daily; 1hr 10min); Westport (4–5 daily; 2hr).

By bus The Bus Éireann station is at the train station; Citylink's (http://citylink.ie) most convenient stop is at AIT on Dublin Rd to the east of the centre.

Destinations Bus Éireann: Birr (2–3 daily; 50min); Dublin (most via the airport; hourly; 1hr 40min–2hr 20min);

Galway (roughly hourly; 1hr 30min); Kilkenny (1–2 daily; 2hr 50min); Limerick (2–3 daily; 2hr 10min); Mullingar (up to 4 daily; 1hr); Waterford (1–2 daily; 4hr); Westport (4 daily; 2hr 45min–3hr); Ireland West Airport Knock (4 daily; 2hr 10min).

Destinations Citylink: Dublin and airport (7 daily; 2hr); Galway (7 daily; 1hr 40min).

Tourist office Inside the castle (late May to late Sept daily 9am–5pm).

ACCOMMODATION

SEE MAP PAGE 170

The Bastion 2 Bastion St, http://thebastion.net. This colourful, relaxing and funky bolthole is comfortably the pick of the town's guesthouses. The decor of polished wooden floors, white walls and crisp white linens is splashed with colour from modern artworks and Peruvian wall hangings; some bedrooms share bathrooms. Breakfast (not included) is taken in the neighbouring *Bastion Kitchen* (see below). €€
Lough Ree (East) Caravan and Camping Park 3km north of Athlone on the N55 in Ballykeeran, http:// loughreeeast.wixsite.com. Peaceful, spacious and well-

equipped lakeside campsite with a campers' kitchen, a recreation room and a 500m stretch of the Breensford trout river. Closed Oct–March. €
Radisson Northgate St, http://radissonhotels.com. This central hotel enjoys a peerless setting on the east bank of the Shannon overlooking the castle – have a sundowner at the heated riverside terrace bar to make the most of it – and offers smart, well-designed rooms with either an urban or soothing marine theme, a swimming pool and leisure club. €€€
Sheraton Hotel Gleeson St, http://marriott.com. Rooms

range from classic and deluxe to spacious suites at the top of the distinctive twelve-storey tower, where floor to ceiling windows offer spectacular views across the River Shannon. All rooms are fitted out with marble bathrooms; nice perks include late check out, complimentary parking and free newspapers. Excellent rates available for Sunday nights. €€€

EATING

SEE MAP PAGE 170

Bastion Kitchen 1 Bastion St, http://bastionkitchen. online. Small, popular and friendly health-food shop and café that serves soup with sourdough, wraps and salads, plus terrific home-baked cakes and scones, and sausage baps with tomato and onion relish for breakfast. Closed Sun. €

★ **The Fatted Calf** Church St, http://thefattedcalf.ie. With its comfortable and elegant chairs made of cowhide leather, walls spruced with Danish artwork and a first-class menu, *The Fatted Calf* has helped turn Athlone into a foodie enclave. Both the lunch and dinner menus may have suckling pork belly, farmhouse chicken or fillet of Irish sea bream among their dishes; ingredients are local and seasonally sourced, and the merits of grass-fed beef can be savoured. Artisan cheeses and home-made chutney leave a long afterglow. No children after 7pm. Closed Mon. €€€

★ **Kin Khao** 1 Abbey Lane, http://kinkhaothai.ie. Set in a cute yellow-and-red cottage, this is one of Ireland's best Thai restaurants. It specialises in spicy dishes from the Isaan region in northeast Thailand, such as Lao beef curry, and *Larb Gai*, a spicy minced chicken salad with chilli and toasted rice powder. Takeouts too. €€

Left Bank Bistro Fry Place, http://leftbankbistro. com. Stylish, laidback restaurant serving up plenty of seafood, some Asian-influenced dishes and more classic fare like rump of Roscommon lamb with garlic confit and rosemary jus. Prices for individual dishes are high, but you can ease the pain by opting for the Early Bird two-course menu (€26.95; available all evening Tues–Fri and 5–6pm Saturdays); lunch, which consists of varied sandwiches, salads and hot dishes such as spicy buffalo wings or goats cheese crostini, is cheaper again. Closed Sun & Mon. €€€

DRINKING

SEE MAP PAGE 170

Flannery's Bar 4 Sean Costello St, 086 831 3160. Monday night is blues night in this small but lively bar frequented by in-the-know Athloners. The music is top-notch and if you get talking to locals you'll hear many tall Midland tales – although don't believe all of them.

★ **Sean's Bar** 13 Main St, near the castle, http://seansbar.

ie. Another claimant to the title of Ireland's oldest pub, serving a house beer, AD 900, a pale ale brewed in Carlow. It's appealingly old-fashioned and sociable, with open fires, sawdust on the floor, live music most nights (including a traditional session Sat early evening) and a huge beer garden at the back stretching down towards the river.

SHOPPING

SEE MAP PAGE 170

Athlone Crystal and Gift Gallery St Mary's Square, 090 647 7775. Based in a restored Victorian house in the centre of town, the gallery showcases a range of Irish-designed glassware, vases and crystal bowls, plus jewellery and other gifts. Closed Sun.

Bastion Gallery 6 Bastion St, http://bastiongallery.com. The owner makes exquisite hand-crafted jewellery such as pendants and earrings based on Ogham, the first written form of Gaelic. You'll also find quilts, scarves, toys, postcards

and books, as well as unusual gifts. Closed Sun–Wed.

Burgess Department Store 1–7 Church St, http:// burgessofathlone.ie. Founded in 1839, Ireland's longest established department store occupies a substantial corner site. It stocks a large selection of fashions from well-known brand names to labels exclusive to Athlone, plus giftware, household furnishings and the like. Closed Sun.

John's Bookshop 9 Main St, http://johnsbookshop.com. A great place to while away an hour browsing secondhand

---

BOAT TRIPS TO LOUGH REE AND CLONMACNOIS

Viking Tours (http://vikingtoursireland.ie ; twenty-five percent discounts with Athlone Castle tickets) runs **boat trips on the Shannon** (March–Oct), which involve sailing in a partly open 20m wooden boat that's been made up to look like a **longboat**, with Viking helmets for all concerned (should you so wish). Every day, the boat heads north around the islands of **Lough Ree** (1hr 15min; €20), which include Hare Island, site of a Viking encampment that has yielded considerable amounts of Viking treasure. Less often, it sails south on the scenic approach to **Clonmacnois** (€30, including return by bus to Athlone; 1hr 30min), allowing you 1hr 30min to look around the site, before a bus (30min) takes you back to Athlone. Departures are from the west bank of the river below the castle, where the latest schedule of trips is always posted – or consult their website.

and antiquarian books, as well as inscribed first editions. You'll come across rare books about the Shannon, fiction and poetry by Athlone authors such as John Broderick, and new and old travel books on Ireland. Closed Sun & Mon.

Clonmacnois

6km north of Shannonbridge • Daily: Feb to mid-March 10am–5.30pm; mid-March to May, Sept & Oct 10am–6pm; June–Aug 9am–6.30pm; Nov–Jan 10am–5pm; last admission 30min before closing • charge; Heritage Card • http://heritageireland.ie

The substantial remains of **Clonmacnois**, pre-Norman Ireland's most important Christian site, enjoy an idyllic location on the grassy banks of the gently meandering Shannon, 6km upstream from Shannonbridge. Here the river descends at a shallow gradient through flat land that floods extensively in winter, but in spring the receding flow leaves beautiful, nutrient-rich water meadows, some of the last of their type in Europe. The **Shannon Callows**, as they are known, become the summer home of rare wildflowers, grazing cattle, lapwings, curlews and redshanks.

Brief history

The monastery was founded as a satellite of St Enda's house on Inishmore (see page 349) in around 548 by **St Kieran (Ciarán)**, who with the help of Diarmuid of the Uí Néills, the first Christian High King of Ireland, erected a wooden church here. Kieran brought with him a dun cow, whose hide later became Clonmacnois' major relic – anyone who died lying on it would be spared the torments of Hell – and who was commemorated in the *Lebor na hUidre* (Book of the Dun Cow), the oldest surviving manuscript written wholly in Irish. Perfectly sited at the junction of the Slí Mhor, the main road from Dublin Bay to Galway Bay, and the major north–south artery, the Shannon, the monastery grew in influence as various provincial kings endowed it with churches and high crosses. With a large lay population, Clonmacnois resembled a small town, where craftsmen and scholars produced illuminated manuscripts, croziers and other remarkable artefacts, many of which can be seen in the National Museum in Dublin. However, between the eighth and twelfth centuries the site was plundered over forty times by Vikings, Anglo-Normans and Irish enemies, and church reforms in the thirteenth century greatly reduced its influence. In 1552, Athlone's English garrison reduced it to ruins, though, as the burial place of Kieran, it has persisted to this day as a place of pilgrimage, focused on the saint's day on September 9.

The visitor centre and high crosses

Clonmacnois' three magnificent **high crosses** have been moved into the excellent **visitor centre** to prevent further damage by the weather. The finest is the **Cross of the Scriptures**, a pictorial sermon showing the Crucifixion, Christ in the Tomb and the Last Judgement. It was erected in the early tenth century by Abbot Colman and Flann, the High King of Ireland, who may be depicted together (with Flann holding a pole) in the bottom scene on the shaft's east face. Standing 4m high, the cross is carved from a single piece of sandstone and may originally have been coloured. The other two crosses are about a century older and much simpler, the **South Cross** featuring the Crucifixion surrounded by rich interlacing, spirals and bosses, while the **North Cross** is carved with abstract Celtic ornaments, humans and animals.

The site

Most of Clonmacnois' nine churches are structurally intact apart from their roofs, the largest being the **cathedral** straight in front of the visitor centre. It was built in

909 by Abbot Colman and King Flann, but its most beautiful feature now is the fifteenth-century north doorway, featuring decorative Gothic carving surmounted by Sts Dominic, Patrick and Francis. The last High King of Ireland, Rory O'Connor, was buried by the altar here in 1198. Several smaller churches encircle the cathedral, notably **Temple Ciarán**, the burial place of St Kieran, dating from the early tenth century.

In the western corner of the compound rises a fine **round tower**, erected in 1124 by Abbot O'Malone and Turlough O'Connor of Connacht, High King of Ireland and father of Rory. There's another round tower attached to the nave of **Temple Finghin**, which is Romanesque in style and thought to date from 1160–70.

In a peaceful, leafy glade about 500m away from the main site and signposted from the east side of the compound, the **Nun's Church** is the place to escape to if a fleet of tour coaches descends. Founded by Queen Devorguilla, who retired here as a penitent in 1170, it boasts a fine Romanesque doorway and chancel arch carved with geometrical patterns.

The site's tranquillity is often broken by coach tours in summer so, if you can, time your visit for late afternoon, when you might be lucky enough to catch the birds singing as the sun sets over the river.

ARRIVAL AND DEPARTURE CLONMACNOIS

By car, bike or boat There's no public transport to Clonmacnois from Athlone, 21km away, but the trip is perfectly manageable in a day by renting a bike or a car or by taking a boat tour down the Shannon (see page 173).

ACCOMMODATION AND EATING

Lukers By the bridge in Shannonbridge, http://lukersbar. com. Formerly a one-pub room dating from the 1750s, this popular establishment now also incorporates a bright stylish restaurant with a veranda looking on to the River Shannon. Steaks, burgers and fish form the basis of the lunch and evening menus and you'll also find light bites such as Galway Bay seafood and potato chowder. After your meal look into *The Old Bar* for an aperitif. Also look out for happenings in the *Boatyard*, a live entertainment venue. **€€**

4

Birr

Around 45km south of Athlone at the confluence of the Camcor and Little Brosna rivers, **BIRR** is the Midlands' most attractive town, planned around the estate of Birr Castle, the home of the Parsons family, later the Earls of Rosse. Around central Emmet Square – formerly Duke's Square, though the unpopular statue of the Duke of Cumberland, victor over the Jacobites at the Battle of Culloden in 1746, is long gone from the central pillar – you'll find several broad Georgian terraces, graced with fanlights and other fine architectural details, notably St John's Mall to the east and Oxmantown Mall to the north off Emmet Street. Running south from Emmet Square, O'Connell Street, which becomes Main Street, heads down to Market Square. Birr is not yet on the country's main tourist trail but supports some appealing places to stay and eat, making it an excellent base from which to explore the Shannon, Clonmacnois and Slieve Bloom. The town comes to life in early August during its **Vintage Week and Arts Festival** (http://birrvintageweek.com), when shop assistants, bar staff and townspeople deck themselves out in historic regalia, and there's a varied programme of street theatre, music, and art exhibitions. In October, the five-day **Offline Film Festival** (http://offlinefilmfestival.com) features screenings, workshops and a short-film competition.

Brief history

A monastery was first founded here in the sixth century, later becoming famous for the *Mac Regol Gospels* (now in the Bodleian Library, Oxford), an illuminated manuscript named after the early ninth-century abbot and bishop. Birr was settled by the Anglo-Normans, who built a castle here in 1208, later becoming the site of an O'Carroll stronghold between the fourteenth and seventeenth centuries. In the 1619 plantation of their territory (known as Ely O'Carroll), however, Sir Laurence Parsons was given Birr, which became known as Parsonstown. A descendant of his set about reconstructing the town in the 1740s in Neoclassical style, a development which continued in stages until as late as the 1830s.

Birr Castle Demesne

Town centre, to the west of Emmet Square • no under-12s, no photography • charge • http://birrcastle.com

Birr's forbidding Gothic **castle** can only be visited on a guided tour during the summer months, but otherwise there's plenty of interest in the **Historic Science Centre** in the coach houses, which also shelter a pleasant summertime café, and in the varied grounds. In the nineteenth century, the Parsons family gained an international reputation as scientists and inventors. The third Earl of Rosse, William Parsons, devoted himself to astronomy, and in 1845 built the huge **Rosse Telescope**, with a 72-inch reflector, which remained the largest in the world until 1917. It was fully reconstructed in the 1990s, along with the massive, elaborate housing of walls, tracks, pulleys and counterweights needed to manoeuvre it, and can be seen in the garden. The fourth Earl, Laurence, and his mother, Mary, a friend of Fox Talbot's, were eminent photographers, while Laurence's brother, Sir Charles Parsons, was carving himself a varied and colourful career, which included building a small flying machine and a helicopter in the 1890s and spending 25 years unsuccessfully trying to make artificial diamonds. He'll be best remembered, however, as the inventor of the steam turbine and for his exploits at the 1897 Spithead Naval Review, celebrating Queen Victoria's Diamond Jubilee when, frustrated at the Royal Navy's foot-dragging, he gatecrashed in the *Turbinia*, the first steam-turbine ship, racing through the fleet at the unheard-of speed of 34 knots. Within a few years the technology was adopted by navies and passenger liners around the world. All of this is set in historical and global context in the Science Centre, with plenty of astrolabes, cameras and other instruments, and some lively audiovisuals.

You could easily spend a couple of hours strolling around the beautiful **castle grounds**, especially if you follow the Red Tree Trail with its sixty-five most significant trees or let your kids loose on the treehouse adventure area. Beyond the wildflower meadows, which are left to grow tall until late June every year, lie

BARACK OBAMA PLAZA

He may no longer be US president, but **Barack Obama**'s name still gets top billing at a visitor centre in an unlikely setting: a motorway service station near **Moneygall** in Co. Offaly, where his ancestors came from. The village was thrust into the spotlight in 2011 when Obama paid a presidential visit to find out about his great-great-great grandfather who emigrated from the village in 1851 in search of a better life. His visit is recalled in a first-floor exhibition "From Moneygall to the White House" and in a short film at Junction 23 off the M7 Dublin–Limerick motorway. It's part of an interpretative display on Irish emigration at **Barack Obama Plaza** (0505 45810) telling the fascinating story of the Irish in America and how they prospered. In Moneygall itself (which has a population of just over 300) you can discover more about his connection to the area In Ollie Hayes' bar (0505 45230) on the main street, where Obama enjoyed a pint of Guiness. The bar features a gallery of photographs of his visit, alongside a large cardboard cut-out figure of him, and the owner will tell you about the day the president dropped in on a small Irish town. Traditional music nights, with occasional set dancing, are held on Fridays.

a nineteenth-century lake, a fernery and fountain, and the oldest wrought-iron suspension bridge in Ireland, dating from 1820. The walled gardens feature the tallest box hedges in the world, which are over three hundred years old, as well as intricate parterres and paths canopied with hornbeams in the formal, seventeenth-century-style Millennium Garden.

ARRIVAL AND DEPARTURE

BIRR

By bus Buses stop on Emmet Square.
Destinations Bus Éireann: Athlone (2–3 daily; 50min); Limerick (2–3 daily; 1hr 20min).

Destinations Kearns Transport (http://kearnstransport. com): Dublin (Mon–Fri 5 daily, Sat & Sun 2 daily; 2hr); Galway (via Portumna and Loughrea; Fri & Sat 2 daily; 2hr).

ACCOMMODATION

County Arms Hotel Roscrea Rd, http://countyarmshotel. com. Popular wedding hotel with well-appointed rooms boasting queen-size beds decorated to a high standard, and even more lavish Georgian suites with king-size beds. Facilities include two restaurants, a groovy bar, pool, Jacuzzi, sauna and steam room, or you can take a stroll around the nine acres of garden. €€€

Dooly's Hotel Emmet Square, http://doolyshotel.com. The town's social hub, a welcoming Georgian coaching inn, with a chequered history; it was here in 1809 that the Galway Hunt partied a little too hard after a day in the field and managed to burn the hotel down, thus gaining a new name, the Galway Blazers. The 17 bedrooms, some of which are on the small side, don't quite match the period elegance of the public rooms. €€€

The Stables Oxmantown Mall, http://thestablesbirr. com. Fan-lit nineteenth-century town house that's been fetchingly refurbished in a plush style, with chandeliers and gilt mirrors in the five spacious bedrooms. There's an open fire in its cosy lounge, and tea rooms in a courtyard seating. €€

Townsend House 1 Townsend St, http://townsendhouse. ie . On a busy street to the north of Emmet Square, this central, welcoming guesthouse provides en-suite rooms and wonderful breakfasts, in an airy, high-ceilinged Georgian house that's tastefully furnished with antiques. It also has a restaurant in the courtyard serving a tapas menu, with the likes of cod goujons and sticky sesame chicken. €€

EATING AND DRINKING

The Chestnut Green St, between Emmet Square and the castle, 087 220 8524. Welcoming nineteenth-century bar, stylishly outfitted with dark wood and leather seats, and backed by a large beer garden, which hosts trad music on Thursdays and acoustic on Fridays, sometimes in the garden. Closed Mon.

Craughwell's 1-3 Castle St, off the west side of Market Square, 057 912 1839. Very sociable and cosy pub, with a good pint of Guinness and traditional music on Saturday evenings.

★ **Emma's** 31 Main St, 057 912 5678. This mellow café with comfy banquettes prepares delicious panini and soup, as well as speciality teas and coffees, and a tempting array of freshly baked cakes, scones and gluten-free options.

The Emmet Dooly's Hotel, Emmet Square. The hotel's main

restaurant is a formal, luxurious affair, serving dishes such as goat's cheese bon bons, and grilled sea bass with lemon and caper cream. A more relaxing alternative is the Courtyard Bar, which, as the name suggests, is the spot for some alfresco dining in warmer weather. Closed Mon–Thurs. €€€

The Thatch Crinkill, on Military Rd, which runs east off the N62, about 2km south of Birr, http://thethatchcrinkill.com. This thatched white cottage conceals an equally appealing interior of exposed brick and stone, pine furniture, log fires and candlelight. The pub is highly regarded among locals for its food, such as rack of pork or steak and smoked hake, while early birds can sample Clew Bay crab meat with a lime olive oil and balsamic dressing for starts and mains such as lamb tomahawk with scallion mash or penne pasta with mushrooms or tomatoes. €€€

ENTERTAINMENT

Birr Theatre and Arts Centre Oxmantown Mall, http:// birrtheatre.com. Located on a fine Georgian street, the

town's main creative hub hosts a varied programme of drama, music and artistic events throughout the year.

Slieve Bloom

To the east of Birr, straddling the Offaly–Laois border, rises **Slieve Bloom**, the "mountain of Bladhma", named for an ancient Connacht warrior who sought refuge here. Although it extends only for about 20km across and down, the massif provides welcome relief from the flatness of the Midlands and a refuge for wildlife including bog plants such as the insect-eating sundew, and birds including skylarks, kestrels and the rare peregrine falcon. The waymarked 70.5km **Slieve Bloom Way** describes a heavily indented circuit of most of the range, before passing underneath the highest point – Arderin (527m), which means, rather hopefully, the "height of Ireland". But it is a sleepy landscape of bucolic laneways and gentle walking. Five short signposted loop walks created with sympathetic underfoot conditions are detailed on the useful website, http://slievebloom.ie, as are four Eco-walks. The Ordnance Survey of Ireland **map #54** covers the whole of Slieve Bloom. For something more organized, the **Slieve Bloom Walking Festival** takes place over the bank-holiday weekend in early May, with walks costing €8 per person.

The best base on the Offaly side of the mountains, within walking distance of the Slieve Bloom Way, is the charming village of **Kinnitty**, which huddles around a couple of pubs and a triangular green that's traversed by a tiny stream.

INFORMATION AND ACCOMMODATION   SLIEVE BLOOM

Tourist information See http://slievebloom.ie for information on guided walks, local accommodation and more.

Ardmore Country House Kinnitty, http://kinnitty.com. This nineteenth-century stone house with a lovely garden and a fine view of the mountain offers attractive en-suite B&B accommodation, home-baking and turf fires, and is especially accommodating to walkers, with its drying room and details on local routes. Self-catering cottage sleeping five also available. €€

Roundwood House Mountrath, about 20km southeast of Kinnitty on the R440, http://roundwoodhouse.com. On the Laois side of the range, this handsome, three-storey Palladian villa set in extensive wooded gardens offers welcoming, traditional country-house accommodation. You can stay either in the spacious main house or the earlier, more compact Yellow House whose rooms have views of the walled garden. On a wet day, any of the drawing room, study or Library of Civilisation is worth spending time in. There's first class dining here too. Self-catering cottages also available. €€€

4

Kilkenny, Carlow and Wexford

HOOK LIGHTHOUSE

5 Kilkenny, Carlow and Wexford

Ireland's southeast is largely flat and has the country's best climate. The geography helps explain why it's a hotbed of hurling, the more expansive of Ireland's traditional sports. Kilkenny's attractions centre on the city, which offers many historical sites, fine pubs and restaurants. To the south lie the evocative monasteries and trim waterside villages of the lush Nore valley, and to the east, across the River Barrow, is County Carlow and its gentle rolling landscapes and lovely formal gardens. County Wexford attracts the summer crowds with its gorgeous coastline, alongside genial Wexford town with its thriving music scene. Meanwhile, the county's southwestern corner features ruined abbeys and a sweeping arboretum, running between the bleak wonders of the Hook Peninsula and the historic river port of New Ross.

Thanks to its strategic position just across St George's Channel from south Wales, Ireland's southeast has borne the brunt of the country's colonization. The **Vikings** founded an early settlement here, which grew into Wexford town, while the **Anglo-Normans** quickly exploited the area's economic potential and greatly altered its physiognomy. They developed Kilkenny and Wexford towns and built castles across the two counties, while also transforming uncultivated areas into productive farmland. However, control was not always easily maintained. The MacMurrough-Kavanagh Irish dynasty, based in the north of County Wexford, continually frustrated English attempts to control the region, and full conquest only occurred when **Cromwell** arrived in the mid-1600s. Even after this, County Wexford witnessed some of the most bitter fighting during the 1798 Rebellion, before the insurgents were decisively defeated at Enniscorthy.

Kilkenny city and around

Unquestionably Ireland's most atmospheric medieval city, **KILKENNY** straddles the broad River Nore, doglegging past its striking **castle**. Downhill from here lies a compact grid of narrow streets, dating back to the city's origins, though little of its former gated walls remains. The main street wends its way from the castle, past **Rothe House and Gardens**, impressive evidence of the city's Tudor wealth, to Kilkenny's other main landmark, the well-preserved, medieval **St Canice's Cathedral** with its climbable round tower. North of the city the major attraction is the strange calcite formations of **Dunmore Cave**.

Brief history

The first known settlement at Kilkenny is believed to have been a sixth-century monastic community founded by St Canice (*Cill Chainnigh* means "the church of Canice"). After the arrival of the **Anglo-Normans**, Strongbow erected a motte and bailey fort overlooking the Nore in 1172, which was later replaced with a stone structure by his son-in-law, William Marshall. The latter also built a city wall and towers and forced the local population to live outside its boundaries in an area still known as "Irishtown" today. Subsequently, the city's ownership passed through various hands, before James Butler, the third Earl of Ormonde, purchased the demesne in 1391.

Following the 1641 Rebellion, Kilkenny became the focus for the **Catholic Confederation**, an unlikely alliance of royalists loyal to Charles I and Irish landowners

WOODSTOCK GARDENS

Highlights

❶ Kilkenny city Vibrant and historic, Kilkenny preserves its medieval framework, centred upon its imposing castle, and has several exciting festivals to boot. See page 182

❷ Jerpoint Abbey Atmospheric twelfth-century ruins, featuring a wonderful colonnaded cloister and fascinating carvings. See page 190

❸ Inistioge Gorgeous riverside village overlooked by the rejuvenated Woodstock Estate. See page 191

❹ Wexford Lively town that retains much of its medieval layout and is renowned for its opera festival. See page 193

❺ Curracloe Beach Seven miles of soft white sands that were the setting for the movies *Saving Private Ryan* and *Brooklyn*. See page 196

❻ National 1798 Centre Enniscorthy's enthralling multimedia account of the 1798 Rebellion. See page 198

❼ Hook Head Lighthouse The oldest operating lighthouse in the world sits at the tip of a wild strip of land. See page 200

❽ Dunbrody Famine Ship This replica "coffin ship" brings alive the hardship that emigrants to the New World had to endure. See page 202

HIGHLIGHTS ARE MARKED ON THE MAP ON PAGE 184

5

dispossessed by the Plantation. This established a parliament in Kilkenny, aimed at attaining Irish self-government and, in the process, restoring the rights of Catholics. However, its powers were short-lived, and, after Cromwell's arrival in 1650, the city's prosperity began to wane. Nonetheless, nowadays Kilkenny still possesses an undoubted grandeur, largely untarnished by modern building developments and, thanks to its castle and numerous other historic sights, as well as a lively nightlife and cultural scene, has become an integral part of the Irish tourist trail.

Kilkenny Castle

The Parade, in the heart of town • **Castle** Nov–Jan admission by guided tour only Heritage Card • http://kilkennycastle.ie

Sitting strong above the Nore, Kilkenny's stately **castle** was built in the early thirteenth century by William Marshall, Earl of Pembroke, and purchased in 1391 by James

> ## KILKENNY FESTIVALS
>
> The major event in the city's packed cultural calendar is the ten-day **Kilkenny Arts Festival** (http://kilkennyarts.ie) in August, featuring all manner of music, as well as drama, film, various exhibitions and literary goings-on. **Kilkenny Tradfest** (http://kilkennytradfest.com) brings four days of traditional music, dance and workshops around St Patrick's Day in March, while the four-day **Kilkenny Roots Festival** (http://kilkennyroots.com), over the bank holiday weekend at the start of May, spotlights American country and roots music. The bank holiday weekend in early June, meanwhile, hosts the marvellous four-day comedy festival, **The Cat Laughs** (http://thecatlaughs.com), and the bank holiday weekend in late October sees an imaginative four-day festival of food, **Savour Kilkenny** (http://savourkilkenny.com).

Butler, third Earl of Ormonde. His descendants, surviving siege by Cromwell in 1650, subsequently built the grand entrance gateway later that century and developed the broad parklands that still extend to the southeast of the castle. Further work began around 1826, enhancing the castle's medieval exterior while adapting its interior in contemporary country-house style. The Butlers remained in residence until 1935, when a decline in the family's fortunes led to their departure and the auction of the castle's contents. The building fell into disrepair, until it was acquired by the Irish state in 1969.

Inside the castle, you'll be able to see the impressive hall, whose chequered floor is tiled with black **Kilkenny marble** (actually a polished limestone, but prevalent enough in the hills around Kilkenny to have given it the nickname "Marble City"), as well as a library, drawing room and nineteenth-century-style bedrooms. En route you'll pass a portrait of the first Duke of Ormonde, which, for a period in its life, hung in the gents' toilet of a restaurant in New York – a far-flung result of the 1935 auction. The castle's crowning glory is its extraordinarily long gallery, which occupies almost the entire length of the River Wing, replete with twin fireplaces and marble carvings of key moments in the history of the Butler dynasty. Its 1825 hammer-beam roof, punctuated by curving columns bearing the heads of various mythical beasts, is decorated by whimsical Pre-Raphaelite daubs.

Beyond the castle interior, sprawling informal grounds make for a pleasant stroll around the lake and Rose Garden with its fountain, and there's a busy children's playground. Meandering paths lead down to the riverbank with further lovely walking trails under a canopy of trees.

Kilkenny Design Centre and National Design & Craft Gallery

The Parade, opposite the castle entrance • **Kilkenny Design Centre** • http://kilkennydesign.com • **National Craft Gallery** Closed Sunday and Monday • Free • http://ndcg.ie

The converted eighteenth-century coach house and stables of Kilkenny Castle house the **Kilkenny Design Centre**, which retails a broad range of premium Irish crafts, and has a recommended upstairs restaurant and a pleasant ground-floor café. Behind the shop, you'll find the attractive, airy premises of the **National Design & Craft Gallery**, which mounts a varied programme of exhibitions by Irish and international craftspeople, ranging from stained glass to quilts. Beyond the gallery, you can visit several small craft workshops in the courtyard and the beautiful walled gardens that back onto *Butler House* (see page 188).

High Street and Parliament Street

Heading down the Parade from the castle and across the junction to the High Street leads past the **Tholsel**, the city's erstwhile financial exchange and, subsequently, town hall, constructed in 1761. The High Street blends seamlessly into Parliament Street, both replete with shops and cafés, intriguing alleys and offshoots.

5

Medieval Mile Museum

2 St Mary's Lane, High St • Charge • http://medievalmilemuseum.ie

Kilkenny's magnificent thirteenth-century St Mary's Church has been brilliantly repurposed into the **Medieval Mile Museum**, with more than eight hundred years of local history at its heart. Exhibits are displayed in a modern and interactive space, with a focus on the monastic founding of Kilkenny, plus the wealthy merchants who attended St Mary's between 1200 and 1650. Treasures include replica Ossary High Crosses, the *Liber Primus* (a medieval town book) and elaborate stone tombs.

Rothe House and Garden

Parliament St • Charge • http://rothehouse.com

A complex of three dwellings linked by courtyards, **Rothe House** is the finest remnant of the city's Tudor prosperity. It was built for a wealthy Kilkenny merchant and his twelve children between 1594 and 1610, and is now, fittingly, home to the Kilkenny Archaeological Society and offers a genealogical service. Look out for two huge Kilkenny marble fireplaces on the first floor and the second floor's impressive king-post roof, made of Irish oak beams. Behind the house, two walled gardens – one for vegetables and herbs, the other a still immature orchard – have been restored to their early seventeenth-century state, stretching back to a rebuilt section of the city wall. Guided tours bookable online.

Black Abbey

Just before Parliament Street becomes Irishtown, on Abbey Street, stands the **Holy Trinity Church**, more commonly known as the **Black Abbey**, thanks to the colour of the habits of its founders, the Dominicans. Dating from 1225, the abbey was suppressed during the Reformation and fell into disrepair. Now fully restored, and again a Dominican establishment, it houses some fine carvings and a glorious fifteen-panel rosary stained-glass window.

St Canice's Cathedral & Round Tower

Coach Rd, north along Parliament St • Charge for tower • **Tower** Same hours as cathedral, access weather permitting (no under-12s) • http://stcanicescathedral.ie

Kilkenny's Church of Ireland cathedral, thirteenth-century **St Canice's**, looms above Irishtown. Though its spire collapsed in 1332, the rest of this grand Gothic structure remains true to its date of origin. The magnificently carved interior contains many splendid sixteenth- and seventeenth-century tombstones, often cut from black Kilkenny marble, including some remarkable effigies of the Butler family. In the churchyard stands a graceful ninth-century **Round Tower**, the only vestige of St Canice's monastic settlement, whose 30m summit affords a superb vista of the city spread out below.

Butler Gallery

John's Quay • Free • http://butlergallery.ie

Occupying the nineteenth-century home of Joseph Evans, the Butler Gallery's permanent collection is among the finest in Ireland. Works date from the 1830s to the present and feature the likes of Paul Henry, Louis le Brocquy and Patrick Scott, though just as important is the entire gallery devoted to local-born artist Tony O'Malley (1913–2003) and his wife Jane. Self-taught, O'Malley is best known for his abstract and colourful landscape motifs, a body of work heavily influenced by his time living in St Ives, Cornwall, between 1960 and 1990.

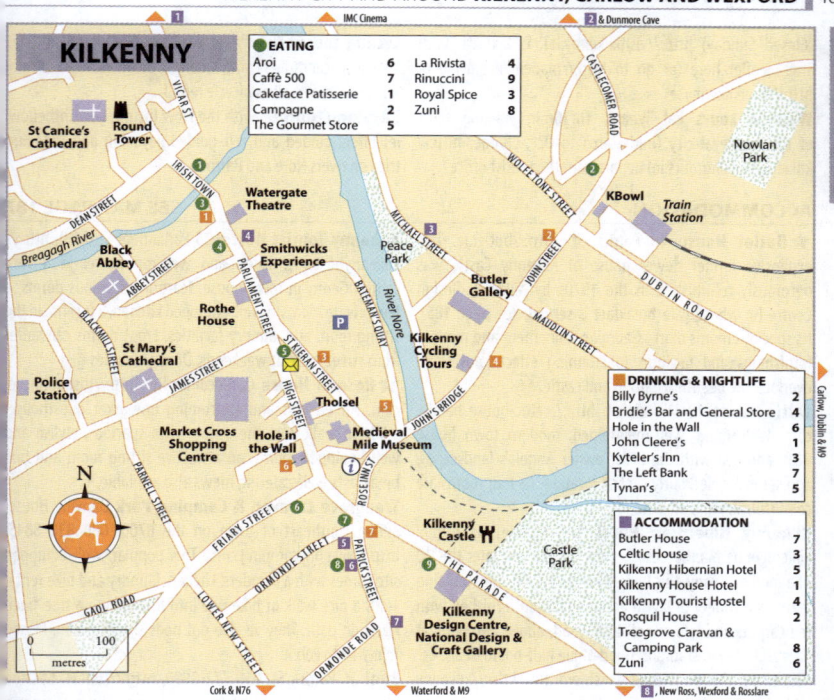

Dunmore Cave

10km north of Kilkenny, off the N78 • Charge Heritage Card • http://heritageireland.ie

Formed in a limestone outcrop of the Castlecomer plateau, **Dunmore Cave**'s series of chambers features numerous beautiful calcite creations – curtains and crystals, stalactites and stalagmites; the most remarkable of the last stands some 4.5m high. The cave is referenced in the *Annals of the Four Masters* (see page 414), which recounts that the Vikings massacred a thousand people here in 928, a tale partially substantiated in 1967 when excavations uncovered the skeletons of more than forty women and children, and a Viking coin.

ARRIVAL AND DEPARTURE KILKENNY CITY

By train The train station is off Dublin Rd, from where it's a 10min walk along John St to the city centre.

Destinations Dublin (4–6 daily; 1hr 30min); Thomastown (4–7 daily; 10min); Waterford (4–7 daily; 35min).

By bus Bus Éireann services leave from the train station and most also stop on Ormonde Rd in the centre; J.J. Kavanagh's (http://jjkavanagh.ie) stop on Ormonde Rd; Kilbride's New Ross (http://kilbridecoaches.com) buses stop on Ormonde Rd and the Parade, while their Graiguenamanagh buses stop at MacDonagh Junction, a shopping centre next to the train station, and the Parade; and Dublin Coach M9 Express (http://dublincoach.ie) stops at Ormonde Rd and

MacDonagh Junction.

Destinations Bus Éireann: Athlone (Mon–Sat 2 daily, Sun 1; 3hr); Inistioge (1 Thurs; 35min); New Ross (1 Thurs; 1hr 15min); Thomastown (Mon–Sat 2 daily, Sun 1; 30min); Waterford (Mon–Sat 2 daily, Sun 1; 1hr).

Destination J.J. Kavanagh: Dublin and airport (6 daily; 2–3hr).

Destinations Kilbride: Graiguenamanagh (Mon–Sat 2 daily; 55min); Inistioge (Mon–Sat 2 daily; 45min); New Ross (Mon–Sat 2 daily; 1hr 15min); Thomastown (Mon–Sat 2 daily; 30min).

Destination Dublin Coach: Dublin (9 daily; 1hr 45min).

INFORMATION AND TOURS

Tourist office In the Shee Alms House, one of very few Tudor almshouses remaining in Ireland, on Rose Inn St

(Closed Sunday) http://visitkilkenny.ie). Pick up a "Craft Trail" leaflet here (or go to http://madeinkilkenny.ie or http://trailkilkenny.ie).

Walking tours Pat Tynan's 1hr10min walking tours of the medieval city (mid-March to Oct; Charge; http:// kilkennywalkingtours.ie) depart from the tourist office.

Cycling tours Kilkenny Cycling Tours, 16 John St (http:// kilkennycyclingtours.com), Charge; provides tours of city and county, as well as bicycle rental.

Kayaking tours Go with the Flow (http://gowiththeflow. ie) offers guided and self-guided kayaking and canoeing trips on rivers Nore and Barrow.

ACCOMMODATION

SEE MAP PAGE 187

★ **Butler House** 16 Patrick St, http://butler.ie. This expansive former dower house of Kilkenny Castle was decorously refurbished in the 1970s by Kilkenny Design Centre (in whose café breakfast is served; see page 185). Its spacious rooms marry Georgian refinement and modern furnishings and facilities to stunning effect, and some overlook the beautiful garden and castle. €€

Celtic House 18 Michael St, http://celtic-house-bandb. com. Welcoming, well-maintained, modern town house B&B, adorned with the artist owner Angela's landscapes, and set in a quiet, fairly central location. Its four rooms are colourful, airy and en suite. €€

Kilkenny Hibernian Hotel 1 Ormonde St, http:// kilkennyhibernianhotel.com. Once a bank and later the HQ of a food company, this lovingly restored Victorian building features a variety of lavish accommodation furnished with red carpets and lots of polished wood, above two popular bars and a bar-restaurant. Good-value half-board deals. €€

Kilkenny House Hotel Freshford Rd, http://kilkenny househotel.ie. A 20min walk from the centre, this two-storey hotel features large, bright, well-appointed rooms. A real bargain from Mon to Thurs and Sun, and a likely fallback at weekends, though prices almost triple on Sat. €

Kilkenny Tourist Hostel 35 Parliament St (IHH), http:// kilkennyhostel.ie. Large and well-run hostel in a very central Georgian town house, featuring spacious dorms, a few private rooms, a well-equipped kitchen, a turf fire in the sitting room and laundry facilities. Front dorms can suffer from street noise at weekends. Dorms/doubles €

★ **Rosquil House** Castlecomer Rd, http://rosquilhouse. com. An elegant and welcoming upmarket guesthouse, a 10min walk from the centre, with spacious, stylish and well-equipped rooms, an attractive sitting room and fine breakfasts. Self-catering mews also available. €

Treegrove Caravan & Camping Park Danville House, 1.5km southeast of town on the R700, 086 830 8845, http://kilkennycamping.com. This popular, well-equipped site comes with a campers' kitchen, laundry and bike rental – it's a nice walk or bike ride into town along a tree-lined riverside path. They've also got pods sleeping two. Closed mid-Nov to Feb. €

Zuni 26 Patrick St, 056 772 3999, http://zuni.ie. Located above the restaurant of the same name in a converted century-old theatre, with thirteen luxurious contemporary bedrooms featuring a minimalist decor of creams, whites and dark wood. Half-board deals available. €€

EATING

SEE MAP PAGE 187

Aroi Friary St, http://aroi.eu. Delicious Asian food – marketed as street food, but portions are large – in a laidback but classy setting. The lunchtime special includes any main, plus gelato for dessert. Try the khao pad beef, gai pad prik or yellow prawn curry. Excellent value cinema meal deal on Tuesdays. €€€

Caffè500 1 High St Gardens. Extremely popular, buzzy, good value Italian offering a huge selection of pasta dishes alongside wood-fired pizzas, done well, and served over two floors. Favourites include the carbonara and the calzone pizza - the garlic bread and classic spaghetti bolognaise are really good too. Open for lunch and dinner. Booking at weekends is advisable. €€

Cakeface Patisserie 16 Irishtown, http://cakeface.ie. Bright, welcoming café, using local ingredients from named sources wherever possible, with a pleasant, unobtrusive retro style. There's proper coffee and hot chocolate, plus gourmet sandwiches, and of course, cakes and desserts (try the "passionate tart"). €

Campagne 5 The Arches, Gas House Lane, http:// campagne.ie. A Michelin starred restaurant since 2013, *Campagne* offers elegant and confident modern French cooking using local produce, served in olive-green booths decorated with colourful paintings of country life; expect the likes of seared scallops with braised cabbage and morteau sausage. Keep your bank manager happy by coming for the lunch and early-bird set menu with three courses. €€€€

The Gourmet Store 56 High St, http://gourmetstorekilkenny ie. Deli supplying wonderful multi-layered sandwiches, salad and cakes to take away or eat in their small café, as well as stocking a vast assortment of culinary delights. €€

La Rivista 22 Parliament St, http://larivista.ie. Hospitable Italian restaurant in a well-lit, high-ceilinged, modern space dishing up moderately priced pizzas, tasty pasta and a varie selection of main courses, all in large portions. Good-value early bird menu, offering two courses Monday to Friday. €€€

Rinuccini 1 The Parade, http://rinuccini.com. Authentic Italian-run restaurant where classily prepared traditional dishes such as *suprema di pollo ai funghi* (chicken with mushroom cream sauce) are served with some élan; early evening set menu nightly. €€€€

★ **Royal Spice** 2 Watergate, http://royalspice.ie. One of Ireland's best Indian restaurants, a stylish, modern affair that uses fresh local produce such as trout wherever possible. Less familiar dishes include a delicious lasuni prawn curry and there's a wide choice of vegetarian and vegan dishes, either as sides or mains. Three courses for early birds (5–9pm, Sat till 7pm). €€

Zuni 26 Patrick St, http://zuni.ie. Very fine and stylish modern Irish dishes with Mediterranean and Asian influences, such as sesame-seed-coated tuna with avocado and wasabi purée, served in a contemporary café-restaurant that used to be a theatre. On the pricey side but there are early bird and tapas menus every evening and a cheaper, simpler lunch menu. €€€€

DRINKING AND NIGHTLIFE   SEE MAP PAGE 187

There are loads of great bars in town, many with traditional music sessions. Weekends, however, can get a bit too rowdy for some tastes, as Kilkenny is a popular venue for Irish stag and hen parties.

Billy Byrne's 39 John St Uppr, www.billybyrnes.com. Very popular, welcoming pub close to the train station. Come in to read the paper or get breakfast, pizza or a light bite by day and enjoy some of the best live music gigs in the city by night. Great outdoor space too.

Bridie's Bar and General Store 72 John St, http://angtons.ie/bridies. Langtons owns some of the classiest bars in town, and *Bridie's*, with its traditional Irish shopfront, is a jewel in their crown. While not exactly authentic, the gleaming decor, friendly bar staff and enclosed garden will win you over.

★ **Hole in the Wall** 17 High St, http://holeinthewall. ie. Hard to categorize but impossible to ignore: Ireland's oldest-surviving town house, dating back to 1582, has been lovingly restored by a local cardiologist, who hosts regular musical evenings, including Singspiele, narrative shows on historical subjects enhanced with music, poetry and visuals. It's worth popping in to admire the architecture, even if it's just for a daytime coffee in the summer or an evening drink in the tiny tavern.

John Cleere's 28 Parliament St, http://cleeres.com. The city's longest-running traditional music session is here on Mon, as well as an open session on Wed, and other music throughout the week in the bar's theatre, which also hosts comedy and drama.

Kyteler's Inn 27 St Kieran's St, http://kytelersinn.com. This medieval inn's spooky reputation is linked to erstwhile resident Alice Kyteler who was accused of witchcraft in 1324. The bar has open fireplaces, solid oak beams and plenty of nooks and crannies, and offers traditional music at weekends in winter, nightly in summer – including free give-it-a-go *bodhrán* lessons (Mon & Tues at 6.30pm).

The Left Bank The Parade, http://leftbank.ie. This hulking, granite, Neoclassical edifice on Kilkenny's main corner, a former Bank of Ireland branch, has been reborn as a popular good-time bar, with regular live bands and DJs on Sat. The interior has been fitted out with huge carved mirrors, leather armchairs and ornate fireplaces and screens, while smokers are pampered with a covered, heated backyard with its own outdoor bar.

Tynan's 2 John's Bridge, 087 915 7121. You'll get a great pint of Guinness at this 300-year-old riverside pub, which is furnished with leather banquettes and a lovely carved-wood horseshoe-shaped bar, topped with marble.

ENTERTAINMENT AND SPORT

IMC Cinema Barrack St, www.imc.ie. Multiplex cinema with luxury reclining chairs for major new releases. Good movie plus meal deals available with a handful of local restuarants on different days mid-week.

KBowl MacDonagh Junction Shopping Centre, Hebron Rd, https://kbowlkk.ie. Busy bowling and games arcade which does what it says on the tin.

Nowlan Park O'Loughlin Rd, http://kilkennygaa.ie. The main stadium in hurling-mad Kilkenny currently holds 27,500 spectators, though there are plans to increase capacity. Match tickets cost around €15.

Watergate Theatre Parliament St, http://watergate theatre.ie. The leading venue in Kilkenny for the performing arts, the Watergate Theatre offers a varied programme of drama, classical and contemporary music, dance and comedy.

Southern Kilkenny

Some of the county's finest spots lie towards its southern extremity, countryside defined by the lush valleys of the rivers **Barrow** and **Nore**. Near the Nore are major ecclesiastical remains at **Kells** and **Jerpoint Abbey**, while above the beguiling village of **Inistioge** you can explore the extensive gardens and arboretum of the Woodstock Demesne.

Kells Priory

4km south of Kilkenny on the R697 • Open access • Enquire on-site about free tours (summer only)

5

The medieval village of **Kells** is a petite and picturesque settlement straddling a tributary of the Nore, the King's River. A short stroll east from the village centre along the Stonyford road stands one of the country's most atmospheric ruins, **Kells Priory**, set by the river. This Augustinian foundation was established in 1193 and had a turbulent history, being sacked in both 1252 and 1327, before dissolution in the 1540s. Most of its remains date from the fourteenth and fifteenth centuries, and inside the still-standing curtain wall, with its gatehouse and towers (earning it the local nickname "Seven Castles"), are a church and chapel and several domestic buildings.

Jerpoint Abbey

2.5km southwest of Thomastown on the R448 • Daily • Charge; Heritage Card • http://heritageireland.ie

The major tourist sight in the south of the county is **Jerpoint Abbey**, which lies 20km south of Kilkenny city. Originally founded as a Benedictine house in 1158, the abbey was colonized by Cistercians some twenty years later. The oldest remains are the twelfth-century Romanesque church, but the rest, set around a beautifully colonnaded fifteenth-century cloister, follows the characteristic Cistercian design. The abbey features a number of thirteenth- to sixteenth-century tomb sculptures in the transept chapels and some intriguing carvings on the cloister arcade, including the "little man of Jerpoint" whose stomach-crossed hands and open-mouthed expression suggest either mirth or dyspepsia.

ACCOMMODATION JERPOINT ABBEY

Abbey House http://abbeyhousejerpoint.com. Top-notch, all-en-suite B&B opposite the abbey, in a restored, creeper-clad eighteenth-century mill house on the River Arrigle, with freshly squeezed orange juice and local rainbow trout for breakfast. €

Thomastown

The jumping-off point for Jerpoint Abbey, **THOMASTOWN**, 2.5km to the northeast, is a pleasant riverside town on the Dublin–Waterford train line. A walled town of some note in medieval times, Thomastown now maintains scant sense of its own antiquity, other than its old **bridge** across the Nore and the thirteenth-century church of **St Mary's** at the top of the main street, which is now a private residence.

ARRIVAL AND DEPARTURE THOMASTOWN

By train Destinations Dublin (4–6 daily; 1hr 45min); Kilkenny (4–7 daily; 10min); Waterford (4–7 daily; 20min). **By bus** Destinations Bus Éireann: Athlone (1–2 daily; 3hr 20min); Dublin & Dublin Airport (7 daily; 2hr–2hr 25min); Inistioge (1 Thurs; 5min); Kilkenny (1–2 daily; 30min); New Ross (1 Thurs; 50min); Waterford (10–11 daily; 30–40min). Destinations Kilbride (http://kilbridecoaches.com) Inistioge (Mon–Sat 2 daily; 10min); Kilkenny (Mon–Sat 2 daily; 30min); New Ross (Mon–Sat 2 daily; 30min).

WALKS IN CARLOW AND SOUTHERN KILKENNY

Several worthwhile waymarked **trails** cross Carlow and southern Kilkenny. The **South Leinster Way** runs for 100km from Kildavin in County Carlow, via 800m Mount Leinster in the Blackstairs Mountains, to Carrick-on-Suir (see page 218) in Tipperary. The most attractive part is between Borris – in Carlow, where the path intersects the **Barrow Way** – and Mullinavat, especially the 16km from Graiguenamanagh to Inistioge. The southernmost section of the Barrow Way, a pretty 8km riverside path, is the most pleasant way to get from Graiguenamanagh to St Mullins (see page 193), and there are trails from **Kilkenny to Bennettsbridge** (12km) and from **Thomastown to Inistioge** (11km) along the Nore – for information on these, as well as on other walking routes, go to http://trailkilkenny.ie or http://irishtrails.ie, which feature downloadable maps.

EATING AND DRINKING

★ **Blackberry Café** Market St, http://theblackberrycafe.ie. Excellent, central, daytime café, which uses locally sourced ingredients where possible to rustle up sandwiches, soups, quiches, salads and daily specials, as well as home-baked cakes and good coffees. Closed Wednesdays.

Lekker Cafe https://www.lekkerfoodco.ie. Durban meets France at this lovely little café with great pastries. Order items like Durban Bunny Chow (curry in a bread roll), butter chicken roti, quiche or a croque monsieur for lunch or a Full Irish or French toast for breakfast. Nice selection of deli products to purchase.

Tābú Tapas Marsh's St, https://taburestaurant.ie. Arawrd-winning, upmarket, inventive tapas restaurant with a South American twist. Great outdoor space, cocktails and wine selection. The beef brisket sliders, meatballs, soft shell crab bao bun and calamari are favourites. Good value kid's menu.

Inistioge

Eight kilometres down the Nore from Thomastown is the quaint village of **INISTIOGE** (pronounced "Inisteeg"), set around a tree-lined green, an old church and a narrow-arched stone bridge over the river. Unsurprisingly, the attractive location, with its rolling hills rising above the village, has drawn film-makers, and both *Circle of Friends* and *Widows' Peak* were shot here in the 1990s.

Woodstock Gardens

1km south of Inistioge • Daily • Car park €5 • http://woodstock.ie

The steep lane rising from Inistioge's village green leads to **Woodstock Gardens**. When its owners left Ireland during the War of Independence, the estate's Georgian mansion was taken over by the Black and Tans and, like many similarly tarnished dwellings, was burnt down after independence in 1922. However, since 1999 the county council have been restoring the Victorian **gardens**, and you can enjoy walks lined by firs and monkey puzzles, an arboretum, rose gardens, rockeries and breath-taking views of the Nore valley, as well as a summertime tearoom in a cast-iron conservatory.

ARRIVAL AND DEPARTURE   INISTIOGE

By bus The first bus from Kilkenny arrives at 12.03pm, and the last bus returns at 2.25pm, so there isn't enough time to explore Woodstock in one day using public transport.

Destinations Kilbride (http://kilbridecoaches.com): Kilkenny (Mon–Sat 2 daily; 40min); New Ross (Mon–Sat 2 daily; 20min); Thomastown (Mon–Sat 2 daily; 10min).

ACCOMMODATION AND EATING

Woodstock Arms Village green, http://woodstockarms.ie. The village's main provider of hospitality is the *Woodstock Arms*, a pleasant, family-run pub with tables out on the green, offering well-appointed en-suite rooms, with good rates for singles. **€**

Carlow

The county of **Carlow** has little in the way of major sights, but **Carlow Town** warrants a visit for its contemporary arts centre, VISUAL, and its local history museum, and if you have your own transport there are a couple of worthwhile attractions nearby. Carlow is at its prettiest to the west, along the River Barrow, which for much of its length forms the boundary with Kilkenny – the village of **St Mullins** has a lovely riverside towpath that's the perfect spot for a stroll.

Carlow Town and around

For centuries, **Carlow Town**, 35 miles northeast of Wexford, was an Anglo-Norman stronghold at the edge of an otherwise fiercely Gaelic county. Today, the only thing to suggest the busy town's former frontier status is the remains of a once proud Norman **castle**, which lie beside the river at the west end of town. A far more modern attraction

5

is the €18 million development of the **VISUAL Centre for Contemporary Art**. Southeast of Carlow Town, in charming Clonegal, **Huntington Castle and Gardens** and the nearby **Altamont gardens** warrant half a day of exploration.

VISUAL Centre for Contemporary Art

Old Dublin Rd; pedestrian entrance off College St, beside the cathedral • Tues–Sun 11am–5.30pm • Free • 059 917 2400, http://visualcarlow.ie

In a vast, industrial-inspired glass and concrete space, **VISUAL** offers a varied programme of contemporary arts with a local and international focus – check online for events and workshops. Attached is the 320-seat George Bernard Shaw Theatre (named for the playwright, whose mother was from Carlow).

Carlow County Museum

College St • Jan–May & Sept–Dec Mon–Sat 10am–4.30pm; June–Aug Mon–Sat 10am–5pm • Free • 059 913 1554, http://carlowcountymuseumblog.wordpress.com

Over three floors, the county **museum** displays eclectic artefacts that relate to local historic characters and events. Highlights include a 7m hand-carved wooden pulpit from Carlow Cathedral and a pipe that belonged to Captain Myles Keogh, who was killed in the Battle of Little Big Horn in 1876.

Altamont Gardens

Between Tullow and Bunclody, 23km southeast of Carlow Town • Daily • Free; parking €2 • http://heritageireland.ie

Pathways meander the lawns, woodlands and riverbanks of pretty **Altamont Gardens**. Managed by the OPW since 1999, around 1500 different trees and shrubs are tended to, as well as 150 types of roses. The man-made lake is the romantic centrepiece, covered with waterlilies and crossed by a stone bridge. Note that some of the paths close in adverse weather as pathways are slippery.

Huntington Castle and Gardens

Clonegal, 30km southeast of Carlow • **House**: Visit by tour only, May–Sept hourly 2–5pm • Charge (includes gardens) • **Gardens**: May–Sept • Charge • http://huntingtoncastle.com

Built in 1625 on the strategically important Wexford–Dublin route, **Huntington Castle and Gardens** has been considerably altered since its early days as a granite keep. It's been a family home for generations – the first in Ireland to have electricity – and the extensive grounds include a 500-year-old Yew walk. There's also a tearoom with sporadic summer openings, toilets and children's adventure playground on-site.

INFORMATION

CARLOW TOWN AND AROUND

Tourist office College St (Jan–May & Sept–Dec Mon–Fri 9.30am–5pm, Sat 10am–4.30; June–Aug Mon–Fri 9.30am–5pm, Sat 10am–5pm & Sun 2–4.30pm; 059 913 0411; http://carlowtourism.com). Map of 1hr self-guided historic walking tour is available.

ACCOMMODATION AND EATING

CARLOW TOWN

Barrowville Town House Kilkenny Rd, http://barrowville.com. An elegant regency building a short walk from the town centre. Bedrooms have an English country cottage feel, plus there's a drawing room and garden to relax in. Breakfast is served in the conservatory and there's parking out front. €

Lennons VISUAL, Old Dublin Rd, http://lennons.ie. Stylish, award-winning bistro café on the lower ground floor of VISUAL. Produce is locally sourced and there are plenty of veggie options (warm goat's cheese and spiced pear salad they also have a coffee kiosk on Potato Market in the town centre. €

CLONEGAL

Huntington Castle http://huntingtoncastle.com Immaculately decorated period rooms in a seventeenth-century castle, with views over the formal lawns or the ruins of an early Cistercian Abbey. Full Irish breakfast is served in beautiful Victorian kitchen; there's a tearoom in a renovated

5

outbuilding, and an award-winning bistro within walking distance in the village. €€

Sha Roe https://sha-roe.ie. Gorgeous, multi award-winning, upmarket bistro in an eighteenth-century house run by a very convivial husband and wife team. The evening menu features chicken starters such as liver pâté and cauliflower soup to start while mains such as beef cheek bourguignon, pan-fried hake or the slow-roasted lamb shoulder won't disappoint. Excellent wine selection. Open for Sunday lunch. €€

St Mullins

A picturesque village on the Barrow Way walking route (see page 190), **St Mullins** is appealingly arranged at the bottom of a valley around a village green. Opposite the green is a perfectly dome-shaped castle earthwork and just behind are the remains of a monastery founded by St Moling in 696, consisting of the remnants of a medieval church and a round tower's stump. Beyond this, the road slopes down to a Barrow-side café.

EATING ST MULLINS

The Mullicháin Café The Quay, http://themullichaincafe. ie. In an eighteenth-century grain storehouse, with plenty of outdoor seating by the water. Simple menu, with soups, salads, paninis, wraps and pizzas, along with speciality tea, coffee and home-made cakes (try the lemon drizzle). €

Wexford town

WEXFORD is a happy-go-lucky kind of town with plenty of scope for enjoying music in its **pubs**, but it has its serious side too, not least in the shape of its internationally renowned **opera festival**. There are few sights to see in the town itself – more is on offer in the surrounding area (see page 196) – but the appeal of the place lies in its atmosphere and setting: its long, narrow medieval lanes huddle for shelter inland of the exposed quays, which line the southern shore of the wide Slaney estuary, with the railway line to Rosslare dividing the main road from the promenade and a busy little marina. The town's main street is lined with shops, bars and cafés, with the **Bull Ring** at its heart.

The town began life as a Viking base for incursions and trading, before becoming an early Anglo-Norman conquest in 1169. Wexford later housed an English garrison

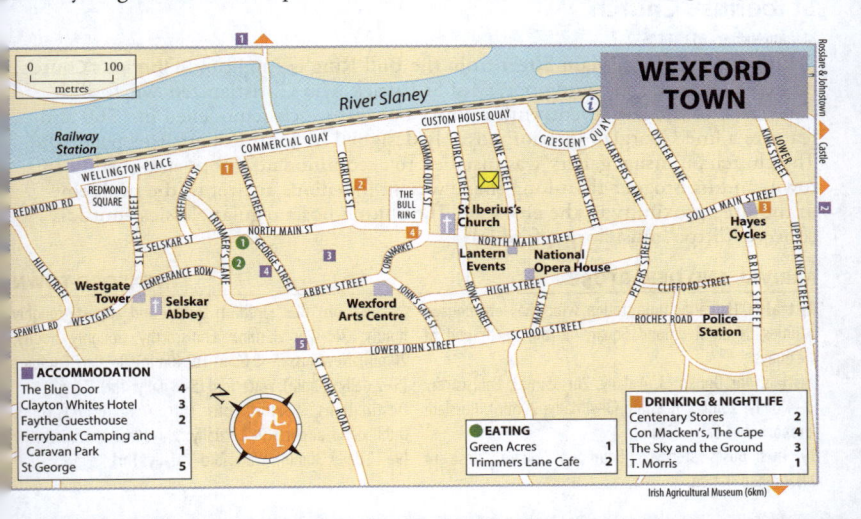

whose loyalty to the Crown resulted in vicious fighting against Cromwell's army in 1649. It also played a significant role in the 1798 Rebellion, which was finally quelled at Enniscorthy (see page 198). Wexford's lengthy quays pay testimony to its re-emergence as a prosperous trading centre in the nineteenth century, though gradual silting of the harbour's entrance and the development of Rosslare Harbour led to its demise as a competitive port.

Westgate Tower and Selskar Abbey

1 Temperance Row • Guided 45min tours (Tower and Abbey) March–Oct Mon–Sat 3pm • Charge • http://wexfordwalkingtours.net

Wexford's walls once had five gates, but the only survivor is the **Westgate Tower**, completed in 1300. The adjacent **Selskar Abbey** was founded by Alexander de la Roche who left Ireland to fight in the Crusades, but returned to discover that his fiancée, incorrectly advised of his death, had become a nun. He also took holy orders, becoming an Augustinian, and established Selskar in the early twelfth century. After the murder of Thomas Becket in 1170, Henry II came to Selskar Abbey to do penance. The abbey must have survived Dissolution since Cromwell's troops took the trouble to destroy it when they captured the town. Alongside its remains stand a fourteenth-century tower house and a nineteenth-century church, while part of the old town wall can be seen running along one side of the graveyard.

The Bull Ring

On North Main Street, the **Bull Ring** derives its name from the time when bull-baiting, a once popular form of entertainment, took place here – the bull's hide, apparently, was given to the mayor, the meat to the poor. It later became a rallying-point for politicians – Charles Parnell, James Connolly, Éamon de Valera and Michael Collins all addressed the crowd here. The bronze monument of a 1798 Pikeman that stands in the square was sculpted by Oliver Sheppard, also responsible for *The Death of Cúchulainn* housed in the GPO in Dublin. On Fridays and Saturdays, the Bull Ring hosts an interesting **market** (Fri & Sat 9am–5pm), peddling everything from artisan foods to antiques, and handmade clothes to soaps.

St Iberius's Church

31 North Main St • 053 914 0652

A little further along Main Street from the Bull Ring is Anglican **St Iberius's Church**, named after Ibar, the contemporary of St Patrick who Christianized Wexford. It dates back to the late seventeenth century but was much remodelled in 1760 and features a fine Georgian interior, possibly designed by John Roberts (see page 209). The church's unusual gallery was installed to accommodate troops stationed in the town, and its broader-than-long shape was an ingenious answer to the problem of the site's proximity to the city wall. The church hosts regular classical-music concerts (http://musicforwexford.ie).

ARRIVAL AND DEPARTURE

WEXFORD TOWN

By train O'Hanrahan train station, which has left-luggage facilities, is on Redmond Square at the north end of the quays.

Destinations Dublin (3–4 daily; 2hr 35min); Enniscorthy (3–4 daily; 20min); Rosslare (3–4 daily; 20min); Rosslare Europort (3–4 daily; 25min).

By bus Buses stop on Redmond Square, close to O'Hanrahan station.

Destinations Bus Éireann: Dublin and airport (roughly hourly; 2hr–2hr 45min); Enniscorthy (roughly hourly; 20min); New Ross (5–8 Mon–Fri; 40min); Rosslare Europort (5–7 daily; 30min); Waterford (5–8 daily; 1hr).

Destinations Wexford Bus (http://wexfordbus.com): Dublin and airport (9–12 daily; 2hr 30min); Enniscorthy (9–12 daily; 30min), Waterford (7 daily; 1hr).

INFORMATION

Tourist office Crescent Quay (http://visitwexford.ie).
Walking tours Hour-long tours of the town (March–Oct; Charge; http://wexfordwalkingtours.net) pick up from the

tourist office.
Bike rental Hayes, 108 South Main St (http://hayescycles. com) rent bikes for €20/day.

ACCOMMODATION
SEE MAP PAGE 193

Book a few months in advance for rooms during the Opera Festival (see page 195).
The Blue Door 18 Lower George St, http://bluedoor.ie. Welcoming, very central Georgian town house hung with pot plants, where the rooms are bright, attractive and comfortable and the breakfasts, served in the cheery front room, are tasty and generous. €
Clayton Whites Hotel Abbey St, http://claytonwhiteshotel.com. There's been a hotel on this site since the eighteenth century, and today's version is a lavish affair offering airy, contemporary rooms, in addition to a 20m pool, kids pool, spa with Jacuzzi and sauna, and gym. The *Terrace* restaurant, overlooking the grand courtyard, and *Library Bar*, round things off nicely. €
Faythe Guesthouse The Faythe, http://faytheguesthouse.

com. A fine Victorian house in a quiet part of town just southeast of the centre, whose pretty grounds include the remaining wall of an old castle, offering very agreeable rooms and a splendid lounge with an open fire. €
Ferrybank Camping and Caravan Park http://wexfordswimmingpool.ie. Scenic, breezy seafront camping just across the bridge from the quays, with the public swimming pool, gym, sauna and steam room on site (discounted admission for campers), as well as a campers' kitchen, laundry, recreation room and playground. Motorhome/tent pitch €
St George George St, http://stgeorgeguesthouse.com. Welcoming, remodelled Georgian townhouse set around a courtyard with bright, comfortable, en-suite rooms and plenty of local advice. Reductions without breakfast or for stays of two nights or more; very good single rates. €

EATING
SEE MAP PAGE 193

Green Acres Selskar St, http://greenacres.ie. A handsome redbrick house with a modern glass extension. Inside you'll find a well-stocked deli and wine shop, a first-floor art gallery and a bistro serving creative fare such as wild Wicklow game pie with braised kale and pickled cranberries. €

Trimmers Lane Cafe 7 Trimmer's Lane, http://trimmerslanecafe.ie. Delightful café with outdoor seating on a broad pedestrianized street. A mouth-watering array of home-made cakes and pastries, in addition to salads, sandwiches and flatbreads, and some fab pasta dishes such as watercress and almond pesto. €

DRINKING AND NIGHTLIFE
SEE MAP PAGE 193

Centenary Stores Charlotte St, http://thestores.ie. The *Stores* are most famous among Wexford's youth as a weekend nightclub, but the original pub, at the heart of this entertainment complex in two 1850s town houses, is still a very congenial spot, with its dark wood floor and panelling, and a pleasant, south-facing outdoor area. Also serves inexpensive daytime food and hosts a traditional session Sunday lunchtime.
Con Macken's, The Cape The Bull Ring. The undertaking side of the business, as claimed by the sign, has long gone,

and this popular meeting place is very much a place to catch up with local news and watch the world pass by.
The Sky and the Ground 112 South Main St, 053 912 1273. This dark and woody bar, with a large beer garden at the back, is an atmospheric place for a pint, staging regular live music, including Candlelight Sessions on Tues, which feature everything from acoustic soloists to roots/Americana bands.
T. Morris Monck St, 086 842 0498. Friendly, gnarly old bar, fitted with bare wooden floors, old grocers' drawers and

---

WEXFORD FESTIVALS

The biggest event in Wexford's cultural calendar is undoubtedly the prestigious **Wexford Opera Festival** (http://wexfordopera.com) held over two weeks in late October, which draws not only performers and companies from around the world, but international audiences too, attracted by its distinctive programme of rarely performed works – tickets (booking opens in May or June) and accommodation need to be reserved months in advance. The main performances are supplemented by a variety of concerts and talks; by a broad-based **fringe festival** (http://wexfordfringe.ie), featuring art exhibitions, drama, comedy and more music; and by an old-fashioned fairground and two **spiegeltents** on the Quays, which host cabaret, comedy and contemporary music (http://wexfordspiegeltent.com).

signs to give a relaxed, sprawling, anything-goes air. It has one of Ireland's cutest beer gardens, decorated with fairy lights, bamboo and roses, and hosts traditional music on Wednesday nights.

ENTERTAINMENT

National Opera House High St, http://nationalopera house.ie. Ireland's only acoustically purpose-built opera house is home to the acclaimed Wexford Opera Festival, as well as hosting drama, dance, comedy and music throughout the year. There's also a panoramic rooftop café.

Wexford Arts Centre Cornmarket, http://wexfordarts centre.ie. Music, theatre, dance, comedy and art exhibitions are just some of the offerings that are laid on by the Wexford Arts Centre, which is located in the eighteenth-century market house.

Around Wexford town

To Wexford's north lies Ireland's premier wildfowl sanctuary, **Wexford Wildfowl Reserve**, beyond which the coastline is punctuated by some lovely sandy beaches: 10km from town, past Curracloe, lies the powder-soft, dune-backed **Curracloe Beach**, a continuous seven-mile stretch that morphs into **Ballinesker Beach**; and further up the coast near Kilmuckridge is a broad beach popular with families, **Morriscastle**, known as "the golden mile".

To the west of Wexford is the impressive **Irish National Heritage Park**, while to the south runs rather bland countryside, though the ornate gardens of **Johnstown Castle** and the **Irish Agricultural Museum** are well worth visiting. The small seaside resort of **Rosslare** has a splendid beach, much enjoyed by families in summer, while **Rosslare Europort** is a major point of entry into Ireland. West along the south coast is the traditional fishing village of **Kilmore Quay**, with its thatched cottages, whitewashed walls, sandy beach and seasonal boat trips out to the bird sanctuary on the **Saltee Islands** (contact Declan Bates 053 912 9684). A little further out of the county town's orbit, energetic **Enniscorthy** is best known for its associations with the 1798 Rebellion, which is commemorated in an excellent museum.

Wexford Wildfowl Reserve

North side of the Slaney estuary • Daily 9am–5pm • Free • 076 100 2660, http://wexfordwildfowlreserve.ie • From Wexford, head 3km up the R741 Gorey road, then turn right for 2km

The fascinating **Wexford Wildfowl Reserve** occupies a charming patch of reclaimed land, 2m below sea level, known as the North Slobs (from Irish *slab*, meaning "mud, mire or a soft-fleshed person"), a maze of channels, reed beds, grazing lands and tillage. Between early October and mid-April, this peculiarly rich habitat is home to thousands of ducks, geese and swans, while in spring and autumn large numbers of birds on migration stop to feed here. Of particular importance in the former category are the ten thousand or so Greenland white-fronted geese, about a third of the world's population, which winter on the reserve after nesting in Greenland, as well as the two thousand pale-bellied brent geese, which arrive in mid-December after breeding in Canada. Year-round inhabitants include 42 wader species, mute swans and a healthy population of Irish hares. The reserve is home to various hides, and a well-run **visitor centre**, which houses an observation tower and an engaging little exhibition.

Curracloe Beach and Raven Nature Reserve

Accessed via Curracloe village, 9km northeast of Wexford • Free guided walks daily at noon, 2pm and 4pm, contact 053 919 6313

Curracloe Beach, which deputized for Omaha Beach as the site of the D-Day landings in Steven Spielberg's World War II epic *Saving Private Ryan*, is a wide empty bay that stretches for miles. Extending south is **Raven Nature Reserve**, an expanse of dunes and pine forest that runs down to Raven Point at the mouth of the estuary.

5

Irish National Heritage Park

4km west of Wexford off the N11 Dublin road at Ferrycarrig • Charge • http://irishheritage.ie

The carefully researched **Irish National Heritage Park** will plug the gaps in your imagination, with sixteen full-scale reconstructions of the sites and buildings that configure Ireland's known history, right through from Mesolithic times. A tour around the park, either with a costumed guide or by yourself with an audio-guide, takes you past, and sometimes into, all manner of dwellings and ritual sites, including a crannog and Viking boatyard, while the undoubted centrepiece is an impressive facsimile of a twelfth-century castle (built over the ruins of a castle of that era). The park also has a falconry centre, visitor centre, playground and restaurant.

Johnstown Castle and the Irish Agricultural Museum

6km south of Wexford • Charge • http://johnstowncastle.ie • Wexford Bus services to Kilmore Quay and to Rosslare from Redmond Square both pass within walking distance of the agricultural museum (http://wexfordbus.com)

It's well worth taking a trip from Wexford town to **Johnstown Castle**, a nineteenth-century Gothic Revival mansion. Now refurbished, it's possible to have a guided tour of the castle – the highlight of which is the remarkable 86-metre long servant's tunnel – though more appealing are the extensive grounds, featuring an abundance of trees and plants, outdoors and in hothouses, as well as ornamental lakes, rich woodland, a sunken Italian garden and a ruined medieval tower house. The estate's old farm buildings are now home to the **Irish Agricultural Museum**, which explores rural history via displays, artefacts, a wealth of furniture and machinery, and re-created workshops and kitchens. There's also a specific display on the Famine, recounting its impact, the search for a cure for potato blight, and the massive changes in rural Ireland that ensued. The grounds also incorporate a visitor centre with café, and a woodland play area.

Rosslare and Rosslare Europort

Some 11km southeast of Wexford town, with a train station on the Rosslare Europort line, is **ROSSLARE** (aka Rosslare Strand), a single-street village with a massive and popular sandy beach and a superb **place to stay**, *Kelly's* (see below). A little further southeast along the coast, **ROSSLARE EUROPORT** (http://rosslareeuroport.ie) is a major ferry terminal surrounded by hotels and B&Bs, serving arrivals from Wales, France and Spain. Should you arrive by car, there's no reason to linger, and if you come on foot there are train and bus connections to various parts of Ireland.

ARRIVAL AND DEPARTURE

ROSSLARE AND ROSSLARE EUROPORT

By ferry The terminal hosts a bureau de change, a Budget car rental outlet (053 913 3318, http://budget.ie) and offices of the ferry companies (see page 32): Irish Ferries (for Pembroke; http://irishferries.com) and Stena Line (for Fishguard; http://stenaline.ie).

By train There are stations both at the Europort and in Rosslare village.

Destinations Dublin (3–4 daily; 3hr); Enniscorthy (3–4 daily; 45min); Rosslare (3–4 daily; 5min); Wexford (3–4 daily; 25min).

By bus Buses stop at the port and the village. For Dublin, on any day except Thursday, change at Wexford.

Destinations Rosslare Europort: Dublin (Thurs; 3hr 25min); New Ross (5–6 daily; 1hr 5min); Waterford (5–6 daily; 1hr 30min); Wexford (5–7 daily; 25min).

Destinations Rosslare: New Ross (Mon–Sat 2 daily 1hr 40min); Rosslare Europort (5–6 daily; 5min); Waterford (5–6 daily; 1hr 20min); Wexford (Bus Éireann 5–6 daily, Wexford Bus 2–3 Mon–Sat; 20–40min).

ACCOMMODATION AND EATING

Ferryport Hotel St Patrick's Rd, https://ferryporthouse. com. Simple, clean rooms with no frills. At just 2km from

> ### ENNISCORTHY FESTIVALS
>
> The town's two principal festivals are the **Rockin Food Festival** (http://rockinfoodfestival. ie) over the August Bank Holiday weekend and which incorporates a huge food, drinks and craft market alongside all manner of rock'n'roll performances; and **Strawberry Weekend** (https://wexfordstrawberryweekend.ie) Festivities include loads of entertainment chef demos, and music, and punnet-loads of Wexford's famous strawberries – which you'll see for sale at roadside stalls in and around the county at this time of year.

the ferry port, it's a handy stopover before you set sail or after a long day's travelling on arrival. €
★ **Kelly's Resort** Coast Rd, 8min walk from Rosslare Strand train station, http://kellys.ie. Family-run *Kelly's* sits in lovely Mediterranean gardens right by the 8km strand and offers the highest standards of service. There's a spa with thermal, seawater and seaweed treatments, as well as a host of activities for adults and kids. Its walls – including those in its two excellent restaurants – are adorned with one of the finest private collections of modern Irish art. All manner of packages available. Closed Dec & Jan. €

Enniscorthy

Around 24km north of Wexford, the busy town of **ENNISCORTHY** straddles the River Slaney, its main streets, such as Castle Hill, rising steeply from the west bank towards Market Square.

National 1798 Centre

Parnell Rd (10min walk from Market Square, heading down Rafter St) • Charge • joint ticket with Enniscorthy Castle • http://1798centre.ie
The **National 1798 Centre** is a high-tech sound-and-vision fest, capturing the excitement of events prior to the Rebellion, the rising itself and its aftermath, all cogently set within broader intellectual and political contexts that brought about American independence and the French Revolution. An audiovisual features an enthralling debate between actors playing the roles of the Dublin-born Whig politician and philosopher Edmund Burke and Thomas Paine, the English radical and American revolutionary whose *Rights of Man* (1792) was a direct riposte to Burke's more conservative *Reflections on the Revolution in France* (1790). It was on the gorse-covered **Vinegar Hill**, opposite on the Slaney's eastern bank, that the rebels of 1798 met their bloody demise at the hands of British forces.

Enniscorthy Castle

Castle Hill • Charge, joint ticket with 1798 Centre • http://enniscorthycastle.ie
Though it's a proper castle in the heart of town, with turrets, round towers and crenellations in the traditional style of Norman stone fortresses, **Enniscorthy Castle** has spent most of its 800-year existence as a private residence. Now completely renovated, it numbers among its exhibitions a first floor that's been re-created as it might have been when it was last inhabited, in the early twentieth century. Other engaging and thoughtful displays cover 1950s Ireland and the movie *Brooklyn* (scenes were filmed in Enniscorthy), as well as pioneering modernist furniture designer, Eileen Gray, who was born at nearby Brownswood House. Staff will escort you to the crenellated roof for fantastic views of the town, the river, Vinegar Hill with its ruined windmill and, to the west, the Blackstairs Mountains.

St Aidan's Cathedral

Cathedral St • Free • http://staidanscathedral.ie
Just west of Market Square along Main Street, **St Aidan's Cathedral** is an imposing Gothic Revival edifice, designed in the mid-nineteenth century by Augustus Pugin, who is responsible for the interior of the Palace of Westminster. As well as impressively

high pointed arches, the cathedral features an oak carved pulpit and beautiful stained-glass windows depicting saints and bishops.

ARRIVAL AND INFORMATION ENNISCORTHY

By train The train station is on the east side of the river, just off Templeshannon, which leads north from Enniscorthy Bridge.

Destinations Dublin (3–4 daily; 2hr 15min); Rosslare Europort (3–4 daily; 50min); Wexford (3–4 daily; 25min).

By bus Buses set down outside the Bus Stop Shop on Templeshannon. For New Ross, Rosslare Europort and Waterford, change at Wexford.

Destinations Bus Éireann: Dublin and airport (roughly hourly; 2hr 25–3hr); Wexford (roughly hourly; 20min).

Destinations Wexford Bus (http://wexfordbus.com): Dublin and airport (roughly hourly; 2hr 25min–3hr); Wexford (roughly hourly; 30min).

Tourist office Enniscorthy Castle is the official information point (053 923 4699).

ACCOMMODATION

Monart 3km west of Enniscorthy, 053 923 8999, http://monart.ie. Lovely destination hotel-spa in a converted eighteenth-century mill with vast landscaped gardens. It's five-star and far from cheap and could do with a refresh in places but access to the thermal spa and classes is unrestricted for guests, and rates for singles are considerably reduced. Book well in advance. €€

Riverside Park The Promenade, http://riversideparkhotel.com. Top-notch hotel near the 1798 Centre, with modern, attractive rooms, many of which overlook the river, and its own indoor pool, gym and sauna. €

EATING AND DRINKING

Enniscorthy hosts a lively **farmers' market** every Sat morning on Abbey Square.

The Antique Tavern 14 Slaney St, down towards the quays from Market Square, 053 923 3428. Great spot for an atmospheric pint, a half-timbered, eighteenth-century pub with a wealth of local photos and memorabilia on its walls and a covered upstairs balcony for absorbing views of the river and Vinegar Hill.

The Bailey On the quays near Cottontree Café, http://thebailey.ie. Converted into a café-bar from a nineteenth-century malt warehouse and decorated in plush Victorian style, *The Bailey* offers good food (all-day breakfast) and regular live gigs.

Via Veneto 58 Weafer St, http://viaveneto.ie. A cosy, white-tablecloth restaurant offering authentic Italian main courses, including plenty of fresh fish, and much cheaper pizzas and pastas.

The Wilds 23 Weafer St, http://thewilds.ie. A bright, light-filled café and deli attached to a superb craft shop. Make a beeline here for breakfast (full-Irish), brunch (avocado and poached eggs on sourdough toast, roasted tomatoes and organic leaves) or lunch (selection of salads, gourmet sandwiches and burgers).

Hook Peninsula and the Barrow estuary

The sightseeing highlight of Wexford's southwestern corner is the atmospheric ruin of **Tintern Abbey**, at the neck of the blustery **Hook Peninsula**, which is punctuated with sandy beaches and a fascinating medieval lighthouse. Circumnavigating Hook Head brings you to the pleasant little beach resort of **Duncannon** and nearby **Ballyhack**, whence car ferries cross the Barrow estuary to Passage East in County Waterford. This

ACROSS THE ESTUARY TO WATERFORD: BALLYHACK

If you're heading for County Waterford, then the Passage East Car Ferry (051 382480, http://passageferry.ie) from **Ballyhack**, 1km northwest of Arthurstown, is a boon, saving time and mileage with a five-minute crossing. Ferries operate a continuous service (June–Aug Mon–Sat 7am–9pm, Sun 9.30am–9pm; Sept–May Mon–Sat 7am–8pm, Sun 9.30am–8pm; car €8 single, €12 return; cyclist €2 single, €3 return). While waiting for the ferry, you might be tempted by a visit to **Ballyhack Castle**, a fifteenth-century tower house in the village built by the Knights Hospitallers of St John (May–Aug Sat–Wed; free; http://heritageireland.ie).

5

ferry service is 20km south of the first road crossing of the Barrow, at the busy town of **New Ross**, and is certainly worth taking if you're short of time, but that way you'd miss out on a tight cluster of attractions on the east bank of the river, notably the glorious remains of **Dunbrody Abbey**, the **John F. Kennedy Arboretum**, and the charming **Ros Tapestry** and vivid **Dunbrody Famine Ship** at New Ross.

Tintern Abbey and Colclough Walled Garden

30km southwest of Wexford, off the R374 • **Abbey** Charge; Heritage Card • http://heritageireland.ie • **Walled garden** Charge • http://colcloughwalledgarden.com

On the broad neck of the Hook Peninsula lie the dramatic ruins of **Tintern Abbey**. This early thirteenth-century Cistercian foundation was constructed by William Marshall, Earl of Pembroke, to give thanks for being saved from drowning at sea, and was populated by monks from its better-known namesake in Monmouthshire, Wales. After dissolution in 1536, the abbey was granted to one of Henry VIII's officers, Anthony Colclough, who much modified the buildings, while subsequent additions, including the battlemented walls, were made by his descendants, who lived here until the 1960s. Of the original cruciform church, the tower, chancel, cloister walls and south transept chapels are extant. Beyond the abbey, verdant woodland trails lead to the restored **Colclough Walled Garden** (pronounced "coke-lee"), which is traversed by a stream crossed by five small bridges.

Hook Head

Hook Head itself is entirely exposed to the elements, serene in good weather – though very dangerous for swimming – and excitingly wild in a storm. The rocky shoreline has a wealth of fossils and it's a popular location for birdwatchers, who visit to spot migrations, as well as whale- and dolphin-watchers.

Hook Lighthouse

Accessed by guided tour (every 30min); daily: July & Aug 9.30am–7pm; Sept–June 10am–5pm • Charge • http://hookheritage.ie

The oldest operational lighthouse in the world, **Hook Lighthouse** was built by William Marshall (see above) in the early thirteenth century to guide ships safely into the Barrow estuary on their way to his thriving port of New Ross, replacing an earlier beacon. Apart from a short period during the 1600s, it has functioned ever since and became fully automated in 1996. Guided tours lead to the lighthouse's top, some 36m high, and recount its history, paying note to the monks who were the first light-keepers here; there's also a café and bakery. Check out their events roster on the website.

Duncannon and around

DUNCANNON is a small, friendly village with a lovely beach protected from the elements by a rocky coastline at its southern extremity. On the beach, you can take **kitesurfing** and **stand-up paddleboarding lessons**, and in August there's a four-day **International Sand-Sculpting Festival**, in which a host of competitors produce astonishing, but sadly temporary, artworks, followed by a two-day **kitesurfing festival**.

Duncannon Fort

Accessed by guided tour: April–Oct daily 11.30am, 12.45pm, 2.30pm & 3.45pm • Charge • http://duncannonfort.ie

Looming above the village from its lofty promontory is **Duncannon Fort**, constructed in 1586, on the site of a Celtic fort and a Norman castle, as a bulwark against Spanish invasion. Much remodelled since then, the fort was burnt down by the IRA in 1922. Informative, 45 minute tours of the fort include the ramparts, which have stunning views of the Barrow estuary and down to Hook Head.

ARRIVAL AND INFORMATION

By bus Destinations New Ross (Mon–Sat 3 daily; 35min); Waterford (Mon–Sat 3 daily; 1hr).
Tourist office By the post office (Mon–Fri 9.30am–5.30pm, plus June–Aug Sat & Sun 11am–4pm; 051

DUNCANNON AND AROUND

389530, http://hookpeninsula.com).
Hooked Kite Surfing From €50 for a 1hr 30min lesson (087 675 5567, http://hookedkitesurfing.ie).

ACCOMMODATION AND EATING

Dunbrody House Just before Arthurstown, 3km north of Duncannon, http://dunbrodyhouse.com. Sumptuous 1830s mansion set in glorious parklands. As well as a luxurious spa, the hotel houses one of Ireland's foremost cookery schools so it's unsurprising that the restaurant here is exceedingly good, if pricey; a cheaper menu is offered in the seafood bar. €€

Glendine House On the east side of Arthurstown, 3km north of Duncannon, http://glendinehouse.com. With fine views of the estuary, this welcoming late Georgian country house in expansive grounds offers luxurious, upmarket B&B. Good rates for singles; self-catering cottage also available. €

The Moorings B&B By the fort and beach in Duncannon, http://mooringsbnbwexford.com. Bright, modern, pine-floored and furnished house with comfortable, well-kept en-suite rooms and an attractive garden. Breakfast is served at a time that suits you. €

★ **Roche's** By the beach in Duncannon, http://rochesbar. ie. *Roche's* features a cosy, old-fashioned front bar – home to traditional sessions on Fri – and larger spaces beyond, including a beer garden. The food here has a definite Asian bent, with the likes of Asian prawns with basmati rice, and vegetable satay in peanut sauce, among the dishes.

Dunbrody Abbey

5km north of Arthurstown on the R733 • May to Sept • Abbey Charge; maze Charge (includes fee for pitch and putt course) • http://dunbrodyabbey.com

Overlooking the Barrow estuary are the ruins of **Dunbrody Abbey**, a Cistercian monastery founded in 1170 by Hervé de Montmorency, on the instructions of his nephew, the Anglo-Norman invader, Strongbow. Its magnificent remains centre on a 60m-long early Gothic church, whose most notable features are the elegant west doorway and east window. Following Dissolution, the abbey passed into the hands of the Etchingham family whose descendants added the tower and nearby buildings and own the land to this day. On site there's also a tearoom, pitch and putt course, and a full-sized maze, which utilizes 1500 yew trees.

John F. Kennedy Arboretum and Kennedy Homestead

8km north of Dunbrody Abbey on the R733 • **Arboretum** Last admission 45min before closing • Charge; Heritage Card • http://heritageireland.ie • **Homestead** Daily 9.30am–5.30pm • Charge • http://kennedyhomestead.ie

The horticultural connection continues at the **John F. Kennedy Arboretum**, funded by Irish-Americans in memory of the former US president, who returned to visit his ancestors' homeland in 1963. The arboretum houses an astonishing assortment of more than 4500 trees and shrubs from the world's temperate regions, as well as a summertime tearoom (May–Sept). Its grounds sweep upwards along the slopes of Slieve Coillte, whose 270m summit provides panoramic views of the surrounding countryside. JFK's great-grandfather, Patrick, was born a little to the northwest in Dunganstown, where the **Kennedy Homestead** describes his emigration to the US, fleeing the Famine in 1848, and traces the family's subsequent history.

New Ross

NEW ROSS squats beside the River Barrow, its quayside marred by poor redevelopment and heavy traffic, but there's still life in the old place, especially in the lanes behind the frontage. The river provided access to the upstream countryside of Wexford and Kilkenny, and the town's importance beyond being a local embarkation point is emphasized by the quayside presence of the **Dunbrody Famine Ship**.

5

Dunbrody Famine Ship

The Quay • Charge; Heritage Island • http://dunbrody.com

The **Dunbrody Famine Ship** tries to convey what life must have been like on a nineteenth-century "coffin ship". It's a faithful reconstruction, fully seaworthy, of the kind of three-masted barque that carried Irish emigrants to North America from ports such as New Ross, usually in appalling conditions – with death rates among the passengers commonly reaching twenty percent. Guided tours, complete with costumed actors playing passengers, take you around the ship. In the visitor centre, which houses a café, you can access a database of emigrants to the US and Canada between 1846 and 1851, the main Famine years when over a million people left Ireland.

Ros Tapestry

The Quay, opposite the Kennedy sculpture • Charge; Heritage Island • http://rostapestry.ie

It's well worth visiting the enchanting **Ros Tapestry**, a hugely ambitious and fruitful community project. Depicting scenes from the Norman history of New Ross and the locality, such as the founding of Tintern Abbey (see page 200), in 2m-wide panels, the tapestry has been hand-stitched by a hundred volunteers in various towns around Wexford and Kilkenny since 1999. There's a self-guided audio-tour to explain not only the historical detail but also the variety of pictorial styles in the vividly colourful works.

ARRIVAL AND INFORMATION NEW ROSS

By bus Buses stop on the quayside.
Destinations Bus Éireann: Dublin (4 daily; 3hr 10min); Enniscorthy (1 Weds; 1hr 30min); Kilkenny (1 Thurs; 1hr 15min); Rosslare Europort (5–6 daily; 1hr 5min); Waterford (9–10 daily; 20–40min); Wexford (5–8 daily; 40min).

Destinations Kilbride (http://kilbridecoaches.com): Kilkenny (Mon–Sat 2 daily; 1hr 15min).
Tourist office At the Dunbrody Famine Ship (051 425239; http://visitnewross.ie).

ACCOMMODATION AND EATING

Ann McDonalds Cafe 8 Mary St, http://annmcdonaldscafe. com. Popular local spot a 5min uphill stroll from the quayside. Friendly service and delicious home-cooked food, using plenty of local produce: sandwiches, soups and light bites and more substantial mains, including home-made lasagne. €̄

MacMurrough Farm Cottages 3km northeast of town, http://macmurrough.com. This welcoming working farm rents out lovely, comfortable, well-equipped self-catering cottages with central heating and stoves, one with a piano, at very good rates by the night or week. €̄

Waterford and Tipperary

CYCLISTS ON THE WATERFORD GREENWAY

Waterford and Tipperary

The attractions of County Waterford (Port Láirge, or the Déise) are gaining more attention since the designation of the Copper Coast Geopark and Waterford Greenway – alternative itineraries between Waterford City in the east and the blossoming harbour town of Dungarvan in the west. Home to almost half the county's population, including a sizeable mob of students, Waterford City supports a lively nightlife and festival scene, and three fine museums displaying the Waterford Treasures. The county's coastline takes in several sandy beaches, not least at Dunmore East and the "holy city" of Ardmore, containing enthralling relics associated with St Declan, while its northern fringe is dominated by the lonesome and boggy Comeragh and Knockmealdown mountains, the latter running down to the ancient ecclesiastical centre of Lismore, in the heart of the gorgeous Blackwater valley.

In contrast to squat, coastal Waterford, **Tipperary** (Tiobraid Árann) is the wealthiest of Ireland's inland counties, deriving its prosperity from the flat and fertile plain known as the **Golden Vale**, which provides rich pickings for dairy farmers and horse-breeders. It's also one of the largest counties, stretching over 100km from top to toe. Most of Tipp's attractions lie in its southern reaches, including the historic towns of **Carrick-on-Suir**, home to one of Ireland's most graceful mansions, and **Cahir**, with its imposing thirteenth-century castle and ornamental nineteenth-century baronial villa. But by far the county's most breathtaking lure is the **Rock of Cashel**, a magnificent isolated outcrop rising from the Golden Vale and crowned by impressive Christian buildings spanning various periods. This southern part of the county is traversed by the **Tipperary Heritage Way**, an easy 56km waymarked trail that runs down the Suir valley from Cashel to Cahir and Ardfinnan, finishing at The Vee, in the Knockmealdown Mountains near the Waterford border.

GETTING AROUND   **COUNTY WATERFORD**

If you're driving or cycling between Waterford and Wexford, note that the most southerly road crossing of the River Barrow is up at New Ross, it's worth considering the **ferry** between **Passage East**, 12km east of Waterford city, and Ballyhack (see page 199).

Waterford city

In many ways **WATERFORD** is Ireland's least discovered city, often bypassed by tourists heading from Rosslare for the more hyped destinations of Cork and Kerry further west. Even the hardiest defender of this dockland city's reputation would be hard-pressed to mount a campaign centred upon Waterford's immediate allures. Though neat, wooded hillsides figure north of Rice Bridge, the vista mainly encompasses ugly industrial development, with cranes and a refinery dominating the skyline and the unappealing quays of the River Suir offering barely a hint of the vibrant city lying behind.

But Waterford is one of those places where scraping the surface reveals numerous delights. Behind those ugly quays lies a complex of narrow lanes, first formed in medieval times, and many grand examples of Georgian town planning in the shape of sturdy town houses and elegant municipal and ecclesiastical buildings.

Highlights

❶ **Waterford Treasures** The city's history is brought evocatively to life in three museums of locally found discoveries from Viking and later times. See page 209

❷ **Waterford Greenway** A scenic 46km cycling and walking trail between Waterford and Dungarvan that follows a disused railway line. See page 213

❸ **Dungarvan** Clustered around its broad bay, this attractive town has plenty to enthral, including some great places to eat. See page 213

❹ **Ardmore** A delightful village with potent reminders of Ireland's monastic past, as well as a grand beach and exhilarating cliff-top walks. See page 215

❺ **Cahir Castle** One of the country's best-preserved Anglo-Norman strongholds. See page 219

❻ **The Glen of Aherlow** River valley in a beautiful setting, dwarfed by the adjacent Galtee Mountains. See page 221

❼ **The Rock of Cashel** Stunning medieval religious site, set high above the surrounding countryside. See page 222

HIGHLIGHTS ARE MARKED ON THE MAP ON PAGE 208

Waterford Treasures, the city corporation's historical collections dating right back to the Viking period, is split across three museums: Reginald's Tower, the Medieval Museum and the Bishop's Palace. While this does dilute their impact, each of the sites has considerable architectural interest. Along with the **Waterford Crystal** shop and factory, the three museums form the core of what's been branded, somewhat strangely, the "Viking Triangle", a wedge between The Mall and the quays that shelters some other fine buildings, including **Christ Church Cathedral**, in a complex of tiny, sometimes tortuous, lanes. To the west of here, opposite the clock tower, Barronstrand Street leads south from the quays to the main shopping streets, passing **Holy Trinity Cathedral**, and thence, via a couple of name changes, to John Street, whose bars, pubs and clubs form the nightlife focus.

Brief history

Waterford's origins are integrally linked to the River Suir. The **Vikings** built a settlement here in the early tenth century to provide shelter for their longboats and to exploit the trading opportunities offered by the river, which along with the Barrow and the Nore provided easy access to the southeast's fertile farmland. The Viking settlement prospered and controlled much of this part of Ireland, exacting a tribute from the Celts called Airgead Sróine (Nose Money) since the punishment for welshers was to have their noses cut off.

Later, the course of both local and national history was much impacted by Strongbow's assault on the city in 1170, caused by **Dermot MacMurrough**'s attempts to gain sway over Ireland (see page 561). The success of the Anglo-Norman earl's bloody offensive not only led to his marriage to MacMurrough's daughter but brought his liege lord, **Henry II**, scurrying to Ireland the following year to assume control of the country's conquest. Henry granted a charter providing royal protection to the city, and his descendant, King John, increased its size by adding new walls and towers.

Though much affected by the Black Death and frequent incursions by both Irish and Anglo-Norman neighbours, Waterford continued to flourish as a **port**, reliant on trade in wool, hides and wine. Cromwell was repelled in 1649, but a year later Ireton's troops

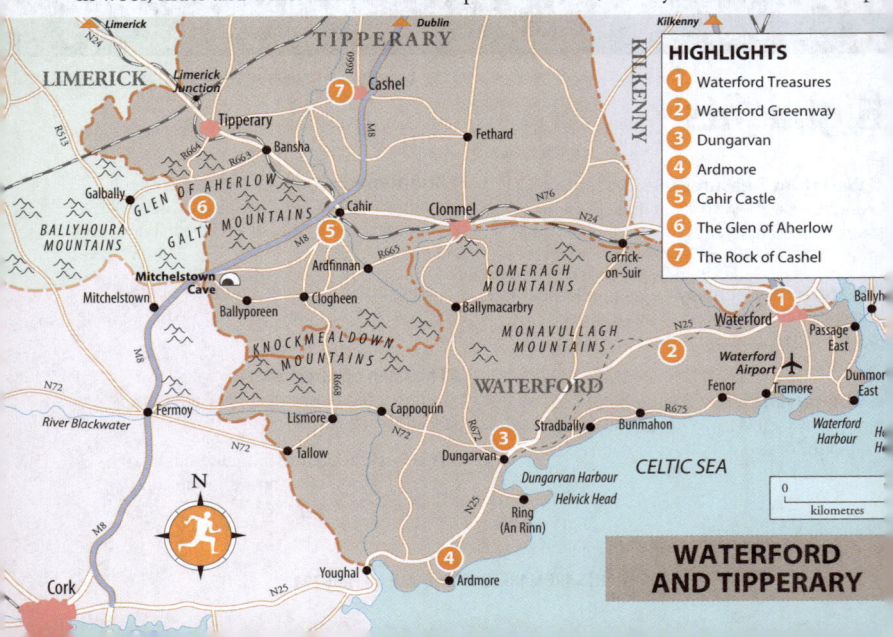

took control and expelled many of the Catholic merchants. Protestant domination of the city's trade was reinforced by William of Orange's accession. The eighteenth century witnessed major architectural developments, mostly designed by locally born John Roberts. Shipbuilding prospered during the nineteenth century, the city becoming second only to Belfast in terms of tonnage constructed, and many Waterford-built vessels transported the city's famous **crystal**, first manufactured here in 1783. However, Waterford suffered economically during the second half of the twentieth century and the beginning of this century, witnessing factory closures and the virtual end of shipbuilding here.

6

Reginald's Tower

Parade Quay • Charge; Heritage Card • http://waterfordtreasures.com

Waterford's city walls were once punctuated by seventeen towers, of which six still survive. By far the most impressive of these is **Reginald's Tower**, which stands at the corner of The Mall and the quays on the site of a Viking wooden tower and was possibly named after Ragnall, the founder of the city in 914. Dating from the late twelfth century, this circular, three-storey tower has 3m-thick walls. For a time it was a mint (the display on coinage here includes a tiny part of an Iraqi silver coin from 742 bearing a quotation from the Koran, "There is no god but Allah"), later becoming an arsenal before being used as a jail from around 1819. The tower now displays some of Waterford Treasures' Viking collection, including a meticulously carved bird-bone flute, a gaming board and a famously beautiful kite brooch.

Medieval Museum

Cathedral Square • Charge, combination ticket with the Bishop's Palace; Heritage Island • http://waterfordtreasures.com

The second of the Waterford Treasures museums is the **Medieval Museum**, whose impressive exhibits include the **Great Charter Roll** of 1373, which includes a colourful image of the walled town of Waterford, and the **Edward IV sword**, a mighty piece of silver weaponry presented to the Mayor of Waterford in 1462. Wedged between the Christ Church Cathedral and the Theatre Royal, its lovely curving facade of honey-coloured limestone is thoroughly modern, but it cleverly incorporates two medieval structures: the Choristers' Hall, the lower chamber of the cathedral deanery dating from the 1270s; and the fifteenth-century Mayor's Wine Vault, given to the cathedral by James Rice, whose graphic tomb can still be seen in the church (see page 210).

The Bishop's Palace

The Mall Charge, combination ticket with the Medieval Museum; Heritage Island • http://waterfordtreasures.com

Next door to the Medieval Museum, it's hard to miss the **Bishop's Palace**, faced with forbidding, dark-grey Leinster limestone and fronted by the outdoor tables of its popular café. It was designed in the Palladian style in 1743 by Richard Castle, but completed after his death in 1750 by "Honest" **John Roberts**, designer of many of the city's finest Georgian buildings. The ground and first floors have been refurnished in Georgian style, though the exhibits here are perhaps less compelling than in the other two Waterford Treasures museums. The highlights are three Rococo gilt mirrors carved in Dublin in the eighteenth century with lively Chinese dragons, and the oldest surviving piece of Waterford crystal, a wide-lipped 1789 decanter.

Christ Church Cathedral

Cathedral Square; services on Sun 8.30am and 10am • Donation requested • http://christchurchwaterford.com

After completing the Bishop's Palace, John Roberts designed the adjacent Church of Ireland **Christ Church Cathedral**, which took almost a quarter of a century to complete once work began in 1773. This stately Neoclassical edifice, which sometimes hosts classical music concerts, stands on the site of an eleventh-century Viking church, utilizing the base of the previous building. It features an ornate stuccowork ceiling and a fine "Arts and Crafts" window, added in the 1930s, by the stained-glass artist A.E. Child, as well as the somewhat grisly tomb of James Rice, a fifteenth-century mayor of Waterford, which graphically depicts his decaying corpse fed upon by worms and a toad. Just up from here on The Mall is another Roberts design, the squat **City Hall**.

Waterford Crystal

The Mall • Charge; Heritage Island • http://waterfordvisitorcentre.com

Waterford Crystal was founded in 1783 but moved into this gleaming new shop and factory on The Mall in 2010. Tours of the factory, which now produces 45,000 pieces a year, will show you the making of the beech and pearwood moulds that only last a week, and crystal being cut with diamond-tipped wheels. However, the highlight has to be the heat and noise of the blowing room with its 1300°c furnace, where the red-hot molten crystal is shaped with supreme skill.

Holy Trinity Cathedral

Barronstrand St • Daily Mass (see online for times) • Free • http://waterford-cathedral.com

John Roberts was the architect of the many-windowed **Chamber of Commerce** on George Street, but his prime ecclesiastical design is the Catholic **Holy Trinity Cathedral** on Barronstrand Street. This dates from 1793, but was much revised in the following century, resulting in today's flamboyant building. Its heavily ornate interior features a Baroque oak pulpit dwarfed by a soaring baldachin, all set beneath an impressively high-vaulted ceiling and ten Waterford crystal chandeliers.

ARRIVAL AND DEPARTURE
WATERFORD CITY

By train Plunkett train station is just north of the river on Dock Rd.
Destinations Dublin (4–7 daily; 1hr 50min–2hr 15min); Kilkenny (4–6 daily; 35min).

By bus Bus Éireann services use the bus station on Merchants Quay on the south bank, while J.J Kavanagh's (http://jjkavanagh.ie) terminate by the Bank of Ireland on Parnell St.
Destinations Bus Éireann: Cahir (8 daily; 1hr 15min);

Carrick-on-Suir (8 daily; 30min); Cork (hourly; 2hr 15min); Dublin and airport (hourly; 2hr 15min–3hr); Kilkenny (1–2 daily; 1hr); Killarney (hourly; 4hr 5min); Limerick (8 daily; 1hr 50min); New Ross (9–10 daily; 20–40min); Rosslare Europort (5–6 daily; 1hr 25min); Tralee (hourly; 4hr 45min); Wexford (5–8 daily; 1hr); Youghal (hourly; 1hr 25min).
Destination J.J. Kavanagh's: Dublin and airport (7 daily; 2hr 20min–3hr 30min).

INFORMATION AND TOURS

Tourist office 120 Parade Quay (Mon–Sat 9am–5pm; http://visitwaterford.com). Ask here about the city pass, which gives admission to the three Waterford Treasures museums and Waterford Crystal.

Walking tours An entertaining and informative 1hr tour of the city convenes at the tourist office (Mid-March to mid-Oct daily 11.45am & 1.45pm; Charge; http://jackswalkingtours.com).

ACCOMMODATION
SEE MAP PAGE 210

Avondale 2 Parnell St, http://avondaleguestaccommodation.com. Spruce accommodation in a sympathetically converted Georgian building, centrally located on the busy continuation of The Mall and very handy for the main sights. Breakfast not included. €

Faithlegg House Hotel Faithlegg, 10km southeast of the centre, towards the mouth of the River Suir, http://faithlegg.com. Though it extends to a large modern annexe, this hotel has at its core an attractive late eighteenth-century mansion, where its best rooms come in traditional country-house style, with lofty ceilings, four-posters and huge sash windows. There's also a good restaurant, a spa,

a large swimming pool with kids' pool, and golf course. €

The Granville Hotel Meagher Quay, http://granvillehotel.ie. This smart riverfront establishment has housed many a famous guest over the years; Daniel O'Connell and Charles Parnell both stayed here. Thoughtfully designed throughout, with large, comfortable and well-equipped rooms and good service. €

The Tower Hotel The Mall, http://towerhotelwaterford.com. Big and block-like, a prominent landmark near the river and opposite Reginald Tower, this well-equipped, 134-room hotel has generously proportioned bedrooms, a gym and a good-sized pool. €

EATING
SEE MAP PAGE 210

Bodega 54 John St, http://bodegawaterford.com. This bistro and wine bar is an attractive, informal setting for dishes such as lobster croquettes with charred lime mayo, and slow-roasted organic pork belly with black pudding crumb and celeriac remoulade. €€

Gino's 62 John St. Bright, neat branch of the long-running Cork institution, a no-frills restaurant dishing up pizzas, salads, wine, beer and ice cream. €

Granary Café O'Connell St, http://granarycafe.ie. At the back of the airy eighteenth-century granary that used

to host Waterford Treasures, this self-service café with a community feel offers a great selection of breakfasts, including espresso coffees, sandwiches, quiches, pies and a daily special main course with two salads. €

★ **L'Atmosphere** 19 Henrietta St, http://restaurant-latmosphere.com. Authentic, informal bistro with a good reputation for its unfussy, classic French dishes such as cassoulet of duck confit and Toulouse sausage. Two-course early bird menu (5–7pm). €

DRINKING AND NIGHTLIFE
SEE MAP PAGE 210

As well as some characterful pubs – some of which also serve decent food – there's a clutch of lively DJ bars and

6

WATERFORD FESTIVALS

Waterford's festivals include **Spraoi** (http://spraoi.com) during the bank holiday weekend in early August, which showcases street performances and world music. There's a **food festival** over a September weekend (http://waterfordharvestfestival.ie), while over ten days in October, **Imagine** (http://imagineartsfestival.com) encompasses music, visual arts, dance, comedy, theatre and the John Dwyer Trad Weekend.

---

clubs around the junction of Parnell and John streets, an area being developed as the Apple Market (http://facebook.com/theapplemarket.ie). Note that the city is not generally a good place to catch traditional music.

Geoff's Café Bar Apple Market, 8–9 John St., www.facebook.com/geoffscafebarwaterford/. Behind its striking facade of astroturf and electric blue window, there are lots of dark, cosy corners in this huge traditional bar, and an attractive beer garden outside. Also serves excellent food.

Kazbar Apple Market, 57 John St, http://kazbarwaterford.ie. Louche, vaguely Egyptian decor, a roof terrace and several tables outside for watching the world pass by at this busy late night watering hole, which serves good cocktails,

shows major sporting events, has live music most nights, and DJs on Friday and Saturday evenings.

Phil Grimes 61 Johnstown. Friendly, old-style bar with a small beer garden, live music in its upstairs venue and craft beers from the local Metalman and Dungarvan breweries.

★ **The Reg** 2 The Mall, http://thereg.ie. Right next to Reginald's Tower, the sprawling premises include a much-coveted, heated roof garden overlooking the tower and the river, and a whiskey bar with leather sofas. The service is very good, the excellent food comes in generous portions, accompanied by craft beers on draught, and there are traditional sessions on weeknights, plus live bands and DJs at the weekend.

ENTERTAINMENT

Garter Lane Arts Centre O'Connell St, http://garterlane.ie. Set in an eighteenth-century building, the city's most interesting arts venue hosts performances of music, dance, comedy and theatre, as well as exhibiting artworks and showing independent films.

Waterford's coast

Waterford's coastline lacks the wildness of the shoreline further east, but there are still glorious, enticing beaches – especially at **Dunmore East**, **Stradbally** and **Ardmore** – and plenty of balmy cliff-top walks, not least at Ardmore, which is also a major ecclesiastical site. Among the larger towns here, it's best to give the kiss-me-quick resort of Tramore a wide berth (though it has a vast sandy beach and is popular with surfers); more picturesque is **Dungarvan**, which enjoys a peaceful bayside setting and offers some fine places to stay, eat and listen to traditional music. Between these two, the UNESCO **Copper Coast** is an unspoilt landscape with a fascinating geological history.

Dunmore East

DUNMORE EAST, 16km southeast of Waterford, is a picturesque getaway for the city's wealthier denizens. The village is actually split in two, with the sheltered eastern part set neatly around a small, sandy beach backed by sandstone cliffs, while the much busier western half is built above and around a marina, and one of Ireland's busiest fishing harbours. There's a **food festival** over a weekend in late June, while in late August, the village comes to life for the four-day **Bluegrass Festival**. 10km inland on the Suir Estuary, **Woodstown Beach** is a popular outing – the gorgeous stretch of sand is backed by dunes and woods.

ARRIVAL AND INFORMATION   DUNMORE EAST

By bus Suirway buses (http://suirway.com) from/to Waterford (Merchants Quay; summer 8–10 daily, winter 7

Mon–Sat; 30min) stop opposite the *Bay Café*.

Tourist information See http://discoverdunmore.com.

ACCOMMODATION, EATING AND DRINKING

Bay Café Dock Rd, 087 674 3572. Inexpensive daytime café with a few outside tables above the harbour. Stuffs plenty of seafood in its sandwiches (including its famous open crab sandwich; main courses and chowder.

East Pier The Harbour, www.eastpier.ie. Seasonal, upmarket fish and chippy with outside tables only and food to go in a pretty setting with fairly lights and a small covered section by the harbour. Excellent calamari, scampi and cod straight from the sea. Toilet facilities on site.

Strand Inn 7 Wellington Terrace, http://thestrandinn. com. Life in the east village is focused around this popular eighteenth-century inn, where most bedrooms have balconies overlooking the sea, enjoying views out towards the Hook Head lighthouse; they have a fresh, modern style, with white bedding and splashes of colour, perhaps from pastel cushions or a sympathetic modern painting. Downstairs, the excellent restaurant (and the bar menu) specializes in fresh seafood, in dishes such as spicy and hot devilled crab "au gratin", alongside the usual burger, steak and pasta options, plus a kid's menu. Plentiful outdoor tables overlooking the beach. €€

Dungarvan and around

Attractive, bustling **DUNGARVAN** is splendidly situated on a large bay where the waters of the River Colligan broaden as they reach the sea, and where St Garvan founded a monastery in the seventh century. The handsome, early nineteenth-century streets of its town centre gather themselves around the main Grattan Square on the west side of the river. Unlike many of its fellow resorts, it remains largely unscathed by the blight of chain-store similitude. It plays host to the three-day **West Waterford Festival of Food** in April (http://westwaterfordfestivaloffood.com); otherwise, its fine restaurants and pubs are supplemented by a **farmers' market** of food and crafts every Thursday morning in Grattan Square.

Dungarvan Castle

Castle St • Late May to late Sept • Frequent guided tours daily • Free • http://heritageireland.ie

The town's main attraction is **Dungarvan Castle**, squatting proudly at the eastern end of Davitt's Quay, also known as King John's Castle, as the king's constable, Thomas Fitz Anthony, lived here. Built in 1185 as an Anglo-Norman command base, it consists of a shell keep with a curtain wall. Inside are eighteenth-century barracks, occupied by the IRA during the Civil War and burnt down when they abandoned the site. Subsequently, these were restored to become the local Garda station and now contain displays and an audiovisual on the castle's history.

Waterford County Museum

St Augustine St • Mon–Fri 10am–5pm, plus some Saturdays in summer • Free • 058 45960, http://waterfordmuseum.ie

Five minutes' walk west along Main Street from the castle will bring you to the spruce **Waterford County Museum** in the old town hall, which is run by enthusiastic volunteers and houses well-organized exhibits and display boards on local history. From their website, you can download a town trail app, with an audio-tour, map and lots of old photos.

THE WATERFORD GREENWAY

Fifty years after the last train rolled along the Waterford–Dungarvan line, the disused railway reopened as the **Waterford Greenway**, for **walking** and **cycling**. The 46km off-road trail meanders through countryside from Waterford's quayside along the River Suir, across historic bridges and viaducts, through the atmospheric Ballyvoyle Tunnel and eventually to the coast and Dungarvan. There are short sections that can be tackled (access with parking is available) and plenty of stops for refreshments. **Bike hire** is available in Dungarvan, Kilmacthomas and Waterford City (from €25) and comes with a free shuttle bus option. Visit http://visitwaterfordgreenway.com and http://waterfordgreenwaybikehire.com.

An Rinn (Ring Peninsula)

Nestled to the west of Dungarvan Bay is the picturesque headland of **An Rinn**, home to a vibrant Gaeltacht (Gaelic speaking) community. Explore the narrow country lanes and tiny fishing harbours, beaches and coves and enjoy spectacular views on a two hour hike out to Helvick Head from *Mooney's* pub in the village of Ring.

ARRIVAL AND INFORMATION

DUNGARVAN AND AROUND

By bus Buses stop on Davitt's Quay near the bridge at the top of the bay.

Destinations Cork (hourly; 1hr 25min); Lismore (3–7 Mon–Sat, plus 3 Sun in summer; 30min); Waterford (hourly; 50min); Youghal (hourly; 35min).

Tourist office 51 Main St (Mon–Fri 9.30am–5pm, Sat 10am–5pm; 058 41741, http://dungarvantourism.com).

EATING AND DRINKING

Gourmet House 3 Gratton Sq, http://facebook.com/www.gourmethouse.ie. Tiny coffeehouse with a fabulous selection of home-made cakes, scones and quiche, plus breakfast (scrambled eggs on sourdough toast), late night "pop-up pizza" some weekend evenings (see Facebook for dates and book ahead) and beer and wine "anytime".

The Local 10 Grattan Square, https://thelocal.ie. A cosy bar run by a famous *uilleann* piper, with traditional music sessions at weekends, plus a winter concert series that has featured big names such as Liam Clancy and Liam O'Flynn. Terrific food too.

Mooney's Tigh Tabhairne Knockanpower Lower on the R674, www.facebook.com/Mooneyspub. Friendly, traditional Irish pub in the heart of the Gaeltacht (Irish-speaking) Ring Peninsula. Come here for *ceoil* (music), drinks and merriment. Best for drinks rather than food but does seafood baskets and chicken wings for bar snacks. Has outdoor seating if you pop by on a fine day.

The Moorings Davitt's Quay, http://themoorings.ie. With waterfront tables on the quay and a large beer garden at the back, *The Moorings* is a lovely, old, nautical-themed pub serving good food. Dishes like Cajun chicken fillet burgers, and chilli beef with nachos go well with craft ales from the local Dungarvan Brewing Company. €€

Noark's Asian Cuisine Unit 25-26, Dungarvan Shopping Centre, www.facebook.com/Noarks25/. Unassuming location in the shopping centre off a carpark close to the cinema, this place does great Chinese food in a big airy space. All the usual suspects are on the menu, done well.

★ **The Tannery** 10 Quay St, near the castle, http://tannery.ie. Excellent modern Irish restaurant in a stylishly converted leather warehouse, owned by TV chef Paul Flynn, who also offers cookery courses. Local, seasonal ingredients are used wherever possible in dishes such as crab *crème brûlée*, and duck breast with potato terrine and salt baked celeriac; the three-course menu is pricey, but the early bird menu is a bargain (5.30–7.30pm, to 6.30pm Sat). Tapas and simple mains are available (Tues–Sat evenings) in the downstairs wine bar, and there are very smart and tasteful bedrooms in two nineteenth-century town houses around the corner (breakfast is served in a cosy corner of the restaurant). €€€

The Copper Coast

The R675 traverses verdant countryside along the cliff-girt littoral between Dungarvan in the west and Tramore in the east that's been christened the **Copper Coast**, after the rich deposits that were extensively mined in the nineteenth century. Because of the area's geological heritage, it's been designated a UNESCO Geopark, with a **visitor centre** at **Bunmahon**, 24km east of Dungarvan. Bunmahon's appealing **beach** supports a surf school (see page 215) and is backed by dunes, a children's playground and a caravan park. It's a good place to visit with canine companions as there's a freshwater stream to for drinking water that runs down to the sea. Scenic **Stradbally**, 8km west on a minor road off the R675, has several fabulous beaches nearby, the choicest being the sheltered, sandy **Stradbally Cove**, a little way west of the village. Seven kilometres further along the coast towards Dungarvan lies **Clonea Strand**, an expansive sandy beach, full of day-trippers in summer.

There are no buses along this stretch of coast, but the roads can be explored by **bicycle**; the first 10km from Dungarvan are off-road, along the Waterford Greenway (see page 213).

INFORMATION

THE COPPER COAST

Copper Coast Visitor Centre Knockmahon, Bunmahon (March–Oct daily 10am–5pm; Oct-Feb Thur to Sun 10am–

WATERFORD WATERSPORTS

The best way to experience Waterford's coastline is from the sea on a **kayak**, **canoe** or **SUP** (stand-up paddleboard). Guided tours take in the area's caves, islands and coves and are often blessed with sightings of **whales** and **dolphins**. Ocean swell and decent breaks attract surfers to this coastline too, particularly around Tramore and Bunmahon.

TOUR OPERATORS

Ardmore Adventures 083 374 3889, http:// ardmoreadventures.ie. Offers watersports such as kayaking, snorkelling and surfing, as well as rock-climbing and abseiling on seacliffs. From €45/half-day.

Bunmahon Surf School 087 6398 210, http:// bunmahonsurfschool.com. Small groups and beginners' boards at this friendly local surf school at the main entrance to the Bunmahon beach. All equipment is provided (including gloves and hats in winter). €35/2hr group lesson; €40 for SUP; rentals available too.

Dunmore East Adventure Centre 051 383783, http://dunmoreadventure.com. This outfit down by the harbour offers kayaking, SUP, sailing, abseiling and climbing (with indoor and outdoor climbing walls). From €40/2hr, wetsuit and equipment provided.

4pm, http://coppercoastgeopark.com). The volunteer-led visitor centre is set in a deconsecrated two hundred-year-old Monksland Church; they provide detailed information on self-guided walks of Geosites along the coast and inland, including a short boardwalk trail over Fenor Bog, 12km east of Bunmahon. See the website for their varied programme of events, including seminars and guided tours, or to download walks (some of which have accompanying podcasts).

Ardmore

The seaside village of **ARDMORE**, 20km southwest of Dungarvan, is an enchanting place, rich in religious history and relics, mainly associated with St Declan who established a monastery here some thirty years before St Patrick came to Ireland. His saint's day is still celebrated in the village with a **pattern festival** of music, theatre, walks and street entertainment in late July. There's a 1km-long sandy **beach** at the foot of the village, hemmed in by long, grassy headlands and flanked on its southern side by **St Declan's Stone**. According to legend, the saint's luggage was miraculously transported by this boulder when he travelled from Wales.

Heading up the hill towards the southern headland leads past **St Declan's Well**, where the saint apparently conducted baptisms in the early fifth century, and where he later retired to a small cell for greater seclusion; on the site of the latter, a now-ruined church was built, probably in the twelfth century. From here there's an easy 4km **cliff walk**, with stunning views, around the headland, which will bring you back to the top of Main Street.

St Declan's Cathedral

Above the town (and near the end of the cliff walk), on the site of Declan's original monastery, stands the ruins of a roofless but solid-looking twelfth-century Romanesque **cathedral** and a willowy, conically capped, 30m-tall **round tower** of the same period. The cathedral contains two carved ogham stones, one of which is the longest in Ireland, while its west outer wall features an arcade from a previous building, embellished with remarkable carvings of biblical scenes: in the lower row, you can make out Adam and Eve, the Adoration of the Magi and the Judgement of Solomon; at the right end of the upper row, look out for the scales held by the Archangel Michael, in the Last Judgement. In a corner of the graveyard is **St Declan's Oratory**, which possibly dates from the eighth century. The pit in the floor, once covered with a flagstone, is where he was supposedly buried, but pilgrims have long since scooped out the earth from the grave as it's believed to protect against disease.

ARRIVAL AND ACTIVITIES

ARDMORE

By bus As well as the direct service between Ardmore and Cork below, there are hourly buses from Waterford and Dungarvan to Youghal and Cork that pass along the N25, about 5km from Ardmore.

Destinations Cork (1–3 daily; 1hr 35min); Youghal (1–3 daily; 20min).

ACCOMMODATION

★ **Cliff House** On the southern headland, http:// cliffhousehotel.ie. Welcoming and hugely impressive hotel in an ingeniously striking but unobtrusive modern building, blending in homely touches and maritime features in a very Irish contemporary aesthetic. It makes the very most of its water's-edge location: all rooms have glorious views of the bay (many from their private balconies), as do the bar and restaurant (see Eating below), the spa, the outdoor Jacuzzi and even the 15m indoor pool. €€€€

Round Tower College Rd, http://roundtowerhotel.ie. This traditional family-run hotel offers ten restful and recently refurbished en-suite rooms, a bar and restaurant in a century-old former convent, with an attractive garden which hosts live music on Sun evenings in summer. €€

EATING

The Ardmore Gallery and Tearoom Main St, http:// ardmoregalleryandtearoom.ie. Good-value cakes, soup and sandwiches either in the bright gallery, which displays works by local artists, or out in the garden.

The House Cliff House, on the southern headland, http:// cliffhousehotel.ie. "McGrath's Black Angus Beef: Garden Spinach, Potato, Kilbeggan Whiskey, Beef Tea"... the menu entries at this superb Michelin-starred restaurant run on like a Joycean stream of consciousness. There's plenty of imagination, too, in the complex but supremely skilful combinations of unusual ingredients, and in their intricate, almost sculptural, platings. If you're not up to the Ullyssean epic of the tasting menu (wine not included), remember that the same kitchen turns out fantastic dishes such as pan-fried hake with potato gratin and salsa verde for the bar (daily from 12.30pm), which also shares the same broad deck and superb bay views.

White Horses Restaurant Main St, 024 94040. Homely café-restaurant with a back garden run by three sisters, serving everything from afternoon tea and cakes, through lunches such as deep-fried plaice with tartare sauce, to interesting evening dishes such as crispy duckling with caramelized orange and kumquat sauce.

Northern Waterford

The northern stretch of the county, along the border with Tipperary, is studded with two modest but pretty mountain ranges, the **Comeraghs** and the **Knockmealdowns**, neither of which rises higher than 800m. **Ballymacarbry**, 25km north of Dungarvan on the R671 towards Clonmel, is the best jumping-off point for the Comeraghs, while historic **Lismore**, 25km west of Dungarvan in the beautiful Blackwater valley, provides easy access to the Knockmealdowns.

The Comeragh Mountains

The best approach to the bleak moorland of the **Comeragh Mountains**, with its smattering of bogs, heather and upland lakes and its healthy ration of National Looped Walks (http://irishtrails.ie), is along the Nire valley. Now flanked by the signposted Comeragh Scenic Drive, the Nire descends westwards from beneath Knockaunapeebra (789m), the range's highest point, to waterside **Ballymacarbry**. There are three-day walking festivals in the Comeraghs in July (http://comeraghswild.com) and October (http://nirevalley.com).

ACCOMMODATION AND EATING

THE COMERAGH MOUNTAINS

Ballymacarbry Hostel Right on the R671, http:// ballymacarbry.com. Large, 25-bed en-suite dorms, as well as a gym, sauna, kitchen and dining room, are available in the villages spacious and handily located community centre. €

Glasha Farmhouse Just northwest of Ballymacarbry, signposted 1km westward off the R672, http:// glashafarmhouse.com. Bright, tasteful rooms, some with Jacuzzi baths, an attractive garden and a conservatory on a dairy farm, as well as excellent breakfasts and evening meals.

A triple and family room also available at different rates. €

★ **Hanora's Cottage** About 5km from Ballymacarbry up the Comeragh Scenic Drive, http://hanorascottage.com. This welcoming, adults-only guesthouse provides Jacuzzis in all the large, scenic rooms, a breakfast feast and splendid dinners in the restaurant; an ideal base for hiking in the mountains, *Hanora's* also offers a guided walking service, maps and packed lunches. €€

Lismore

Set amid rolling countryside on the south side of the River Blackwater lies the sleepy town of **LISMORE**, once a major religious centre. St Carthagh founded a thriving **monastery** here in 636 that became a great centre of learning and retained both religious and political importance for several centuries, despite periodic raids by the Vikings and later the Anglo-Normans. Every Sunday, Lismore hosts a farmers' and craft market in the lane leading up to the castle, plus in June there's an opera festival (http://blackwatervalleyoperafestival. com) and Immrama, a festival of travel writing (http://lismore-immrama.com).

St Carthagh's Cathedral

6 Leycester St • Free; self-guided tour booklet charge • http://cashel.anglican.org

On the site of its medieval cathedral, wrecked by Edmund Fitzgibbon around 1600, stands the Church of Ireland **St Carthagh's Cathedral**, constructed some thirty years later – to get here head east up Main Street and turn left down North Mall. Much of its appearance derives from remodelling in the early 1800s, including the addition of its tower and spire, and it remains a charming building, set in a tree-lined cobblestone courtyard. Just inside the front door is a lovely stained-glass window by the Pre-Raphaelite Edward Burne-Jones, depicting two virtues: Justice and Humility. A Romanesque arch in the nave might possibly date from the original cathedral and leads to the imposing McGrath tomb which features carvings of the twelve Apostles, the Crucifixion and the martyr St Catherine. Stones set into the back wall, including a particularly stalwart bishop, date from the ninth to eleventh centuries.

Lismore Castle Gardens and Gallery

Castle Ave • Easter to mid-Oct daily; last admission 4.30pm • Charge • **Gardens** http://lismorecastlegardens.com, **Gallery** http://lismorecastlearts.ie

Despite the cathedral's attractions it is the extravagant and graceful **Lismore Castle**, its fairy-tale turrets magnificently set above the River Blackwater, that overshadows the town. The Irish home of the Dukes of Devonshire was designed by Joseph Paxton (also responsible for the Crystal Palace for London's Great Exhibition of 1851) in the mid-nineteenth century, taking as his starting point the remains of a castle built by Prince John in 1185. Though the bulk of the castle cannot be visited, its huge **gardens**, set within the seventeenth-century outer defensive walls, present numerous exterior views from different aspects. The gardens consist of a host of magnolias, camellias and rhododendrons in season, as well as wildflower meadows and a yew-tree avenue where Edmund Spenser is believed to have written *The Faerie Queen*. Modern sculptures dot the gardens, and the formerly derelict west wing of the castle has been transformed into a **gallery** that hosts some excellent exhibitions of international contemporary visual art.

The Heritage Centre

The Old Courthouse, Main St • Charge; Heritage Island • http://discoverlismore.com

Lismore's fascinating history comes to life at the **Heritage Centre**, whose galleries recount the stories of some of the town's famous figures, including the chemist Robert Boyle who was born in the castle in 1627; and there's an entertaining 25-minute audiovisual, *The Lismore Experience*.

ARRIVAL AND INFORMATION LISMORE

By bus Change at Dungarvan Dungarvan (3–7 Mon–Sat, plus 3 Sun in summer; 30min) for a bus to Waterford.

Tourist office In the Heritage Centre (see above). Walking tours of the town depart twice daily in summer. Charge.

ACCOMMODATION

Pine Tree House Ballyanchor, pinetreehouse@eircom. net. Modern house with en-suite double, twin and triple rooms, set in a large, attractive garden on Lismore's western outskirts, well signposted from the centre. €

EATING AND DRINKING

The Classroom Bar Main St, 058 53842. Friendly, old-fashioned bar that serves a great pint of Guinness and hosts a long-running traditional music session every Thurs from about 10pm.

The Summerhouse Café Main St, 058 54148. This café is a well-established highlight on Main St, serving up tasty, simple breakfasts (full Irish with tea or coffee) and lunches (sandwiches), as well as great espresso coffees. The bakery out back is where they produce the delicious cakes and pastries.

The Knockmealdown Mountains

North from Lismore the R668 to Cahir undulates upwards through a lovely river valley, garnished with a mass of woody greenery, before heading into the mountains. To the east, after 10km, rises **Knockmealdown** itself (793m), whose name translates aptly as "bare brown mountain", while a little further up the road lies the spectacular viewpoint known as **The Vee**. At this popular beauty spot, famous for its magnificent display of **rhododendrons** in late May and early June, the valley sides offer a perfectly chevron-shaped scene of the fields of Tipperary laid out far below, a panoply of greens, browns and yellows. The **Tipperary Heritage Way** north to Cashel begins here at The Vee, while the 70km **East Munster Way** starts down at Clogheen (see page 220) and heads east from The Vee to Carrick-on-Suir, via the northern foothills of the Knockmealdowns and the Comeraghs.

The lower Suir valley

Rising in the Devilsbit Mountains in the north of Tipperary, the **River Suir**, Ireland's second-longest river after the Shannon, runs down the length of the county before abruptly turning east in the face of the Knockmealdown Mountains. Along the way it nourishes countless dairy cattle and three significant towns along the southern border with Waterford. While Clonmel holds little of interest for visitors, nearby **Cahir** is a compelling destination, with its mighty castle and the whimsical Swiss Cottage, and **Carrick-on-Suir** is the site of a rare and well-preserved Elizabethan manor house. Feeding into the Suir to the northwest of Cahir, the luscious **Glen of Aherlow** is one of the county's prettiest spots and a fine base for exploring the scenic Galtee (or Galty) Mountains. Tucked away on the south side of the range are the fantastic stalactites and stalagmites of **Mitchelstown Cave**, while the attractive villages of **Clogheen** and **Ardfinnan** lie to the east of here in the lee of the Knockmealdowns.

Carrick-on-Suir

In the far southeastern corner of County Tipperary lies the market town of **CARRICK-ON-SUIR**, famous as the birthplace of the Clancy Brothers, who are celebrated in a four-day festival over the June bank-holiday weekend that features street entertainment, art exhibitions and, of course, music (http://clancybrothersfestival.org).

Ormond Castle

Castle St • June–Oct frequent guided tours daily 10am–6pm • Charge • 051 640 787, http://heritageireland.ie

The town's main point of interest is multi-gabled **Ormond Castle**, Ireland's only surviving Elizabethan manor house, which is situated at the far eastern end of Castle Street, a continuation of Main Street. Erected in the 1560s by Thomas ("Black Tom") Butler, tenth Earl of Ormonde, for an (unrealized) visit by his cousin, Elizabeth I, the recently restored house contains numerous tributes to her, most notably in the elaborate series of panels in the long gallery. Also displayed is a fine collection of royal charters, including one of 1661 granting the title Duke of Ormonde to Tom's descendant James.

ARRIVAL AND INFORMATION
CARRICK-ON-SUIR

By train The train station is behind Greenside, the town park on the northeast side of the centre.

Destinations Cahir (Mon–Sat 2 daily; 40min); Limerick (Mon–Sat 2 daily; 1hr 15min); Waterford (Mon–Sat 2 daily; 25min).

By bus Buses stop at Greenside.

Destinations Cahir (8–10 daily; 40min); Limerick (8–10 daily; 1hr 55min); Waterford (8–10 daily; 40min).

Tourist office The tourist office and small heritage centre are in a converted church just off the north side of Main St (Mon–Fri 10am–4pm; 051 640200, http://carrickonsuir.net).

ACCOMMODATION AND EATING

The Carraig Main St, http://carraighotel.com. This smartly refurbished eighteenth-century hotel is the focal point of the town's hospitality, offering very reasonably priced rooms that have been tastefully updated in subdued colours. Downstairs, fine gastro pub fare is served in the bar (weeknight specials) and restaurant (mains such as Comeragh lamb with chive mash and shallots). Good-value half-board packages. €€

Cahir

With a name that means "fort", the dominant feature of **CAHIR** is not surprisingly its castle, one of Ireland's largest and best preserved, surrounded by the waters of the River Suir at the western entrance to the town. The castle was a power base of the influential Butlers, the Earls of Ormonde, who were known as the Fitzwalters when they first came to Ireland with Prince John in 1185 and were granted a huge swathe of land in Munster. However, Theobald Fitzwalter was soon after made Chief Butler of Ireland, entitling him to a tenth of all incoming wine cargoes, and changed his family name to "Butler".

Cahir Castle

Castle St • Daily • Charge; Heritage Card • http://heritageireland.ie

The Butlers built their stronghold in the thirteenth century, though much, including the restored outer walls, dates from more recent times. It managed to survive a siege and bombardment by the Earl of Essex in 1599, as well as the invasions of Cromwell and William of Orange. However, after Cromwell's victory in 1650, the Butlers moved out and the castle fell slowly into disrepair, until it was given new life in the mid-nineteenth century by Richard Butler, the second Earl of Glengall, who impoverished himself in the process. The castle's entrance leads to the cramped middle ward, overshadowed by the thirteenth-century keep whose chambers feature various displays, including a model of the 1599 siege. To the left of here, a gateway, surmounted by defensive viewpoints on each side, leads to the more expansive outer ward. In the inner ward, parts of the larger of the two towers derive from the thirteenth and fifteenth centuries, though the banqueting hall was redesigned by William Tinsley in 1840 for use as the Butlers' private chapel.

The Swiss Cottage

Ardfinnan Rd, 2km south off R670 • Guided 40min tours early April to late Oct daily 10am–6pm, last admission 5.15pm (maximum 12 people, so you may have a wait during the busy summer months) Charge; Heritage Card • http://heritageireland.ie

Besides its castle, Cahir's other major attraction is the **Swiss Cottage**, a thirty-minute riverside stroll through parkland south from the town. Designed by John Nash, architect of the Royal Pavilion at Brighton, this lavish, thatched *cottage orné* on the castle demesne was constructed in the early 1800s for Richard Butler, the first Earl of Glengall, though his precise reason remains unclear. A contemporary scurrilous theory held that it was to enjoy clandestine liaisons with his mistress, but there is evidence that it was used occasionally as a residence and for entertaining guests. It has now been thoroughly restored using appropriate timbers and period decor. Entertaining **guided tours** start from the basement kitchen and visit the elegant salon, whose interior is decorated with one of the first commercially manufactured Parisian wallpapers, and music room, and ascend via a spiral staircase to the grand master bedroom with its commanding views of the countryside.

ARRIVAL AND INFORMATION CAHIR

By train Cahir's train station is off Church St, a 5min walk northeast of the castle.

Destinations Carrick-on-Suir (2 Mon–Sat; 40min); Waterford (2 Mon–Sat; 1hr 5min).

By bus Buses stop opposite the castle outside the tourist office.

Destinations Carrick-on-Suir (8–10 daily; 40min); Cashel (6

daily; 20min); Cork (6 daily; 1hr 20min); Dublin and airport (6 daily; 2hr 25min–2hr 55min); Limerick (8–10 daily; 1hr 10min); Waterford (8–10 daily; 1hr 20min).

Tourist office In the castle car park (Easter to early Oct Tues–Sat 9.30am–1pm & 1.45–5.30pm; hours may be reduced from Sept; 052 744 1453, http://visitcahir.ie).

ACCOMMODATION

Apple Farm Moorstown, 6km east of Cahir on the main N24 road towards Clonmel, http://theapplefarm.com. Ecofriendly camping and caravan site on this working farm (Ireland's most famous fruit farm – you get a bottle of their apple juice on check in). The campers' kitchen and bathrooms are in a large barn. Playground, games room, tennis court and laundry facilities on-site, electric pitch €2.50 extra. Closed Oct–April. Price per person (tents free) €

Cahir House Hotel The Square, http://cahirhousehotel.ie.

Built as a townhouse for the Butlers in 1770, this Georgian mansion provides comfy, colourful rooms and a small spa, in addition to a well-regarded bistro. Good room-only and single rates. €€

Tinsley House The Square, http://tinsleyhouse.com. Just uphill from the castle on the town's main square, this B&B in a nineteenth-century town house offers en-suite bedrooms attractively furnished with antiques and decorated in bright pastel colours. €

EATING

Galileo Church St, http://galileocafe.com. Just off The Square, this café-restaurant is surrounded by crafts shops in an attractively converted granary and offers the likes of pizza, pasta and salads alongside more sophisticated mains such as smoked salmon with cherry vine tomatoes and fresh dill.

River House 1 Castle St, www.facebook.com/river house.9887. Bright, modern, self-service café opposite the tourist office, with an outdoor terrace overlooking the castle and the river. Dishes up full breakfasts, soups, all kinds of sandwiches, quiches and uncomplicated hot lunches, cakes, fresh juices and smoothies.

Ardfinnan and Clogheen

Two villages to the south of Cahir offer great places to stay and ready access to the east–west ridge of the Knockmealdown Mountains beyond (see page 218). Nine kilometres from Cahir on the banks of the Suir lies the pretty village of **ARDFINNAN**, which is traversed by the 56km Tipperary Heritage Way from Cashel, via Cahir, to the panoramic vantage point called The Vee. Nine kilometres southwest of Ardfinnan is **CLOGHEEN**, from where it's a short but steep trip up the R668 Lismore road to The Vee and into the mountains.

ARRIVAL AND INFORMATION ARDFINNAN AND CLOGHEEN

By bus The #245 runs between Clonmel and Cork and calls at both Ardfinnan and Clogheen (10min apart).

Destinations Clonmel (1–2 daily; 20–30min); Cork (1– daily; 1hr 30min–1hr 40min).

ACCOMMODATION AND EATING

ARDFINNAN

★ **Kilmaneen** 5km south of Ardfinnan on the Newcastle

road (signposted from the Hill Bar in the village centre http://kilmaneen.com. This staggeringly good B&B, set in a two hundred-year-old farmhouse and extensive gardens, not only has cosy rooms and serves delicious breakfasts, but provides the perfect starting point for walks in the surrounding countryside and offers courses in everything from cooking to beekeeping. They'll even do a packed lunch. Very good rates for singles; self-catering also available. €€

CLOGHEEN

Ballyboy House 2.5km from Clogheen along the R665 Ardfinnan Rd, 052 746 5297. Gorgeous seventeenth-century farmhouse, surrounded by lovely, diverse gardens and extensive woodland that's accessible on trails. Four-posters and other antique furniture adorn the en-suite bedrooms,

and breakfasts include home-baked bread; other meals can be provided by prior arrangement. Very good rates for singles; self-catering cottage available. €

The Old Convent On the Vee road, just south of the centre, http://theoldconvent.ie. An elegantly converted nunnery that styles itself a "gourmet hideaway", offering much-fêted, eight-course tasting menus in its restaurant (€75; non-residents welcome). Adults only. €€€

Parson's Green Off the Ardfinnan road, just north of town, http://parsonsgreen.ie. Spacious holiday park with campers' kitchens, laundry, café, playgrounds, pet farms and lots of other activities for kids. Closed Nov to mid-March. €

Mitchelstown Cave

Ballyporeen, 7km west of Clogheen • Guided tours • Charge • http://mitchelstowncave.com • From Clogheen, follow the signs up the northern route from the central crossroads; alternatively, it's easily accessed via the M8 west of Cahir

The convoluted system of grottoes at **Mitchelstown Cave** was discovered in 1833. Guided tours convey visitors through only a small section of the 3km of underground cavities, but these reveal some stunning calcite formations, such as "The Pillars of Hercules" and the frankly weird 9m-high "Tower of Babel", produced by the constant dripping of water on limestone over several eons.

The Glen of Aherlow

To Cahir's northwest lies the lush and resplendent **Glen of Aherlow**, spreading some 18km from **Bansha** in the east to **Galbally** in the west, just across the border in County Limerick. Lying beneath the northern facade of the Galtee Mountains, the glen is a marvellous place to drive or cycle around and the scenic circular route is well worth taking. The best vantage point for spectacular views is by the entrance to the Glen of Aherlow Nature Park, 1.5km north of the junction of the R663 and R664, which is the trailhead for five National Looped Walks (http://irishtrails. ie). From the wooded ridge of Slievenamuck, the glen lies spread out below, light reflecting from the river, and the mountains looming beyond. The signposted **Ballyhoura Way** runs through the Glen to Galbally, on its 80km journey from the train station at Limerick Junction via the Ballyhoura Mountains to St John's Bridge in north Cork. For information on **walking** (including leaflets with directions and maps, which are also downloadable at http://aherlow.com) and the diverse festivals in the area, contact the tourist office, while for details of local group walks throughout the year, go to http://galteewalkingclub.ie.

INFORMATION   **THE GLEN OF AHERLOW**

Tourist information At the back of the *Coach Road* pub is a small tourist office (Mon–Fri 9am–5pm, plus June–Sept

Sat 10am–4pm; http://aherlow.com).

ACCOMMODATION

All of the below establishments listed are near the R663/R664 junction.

Aherlow House Hotel http://aherlowhouse.ie. This former hunting lodge has bright, spacious rooms, a top draw restaurant and an inviting bar with log fire; traditional afternoon tea is served in the Parlour Room. Self-catering lodges also available. €€

Ballinacourty House Caravan and Camping Park http://camping.ie. Pleasant, quiet campsite in the grounds of *Ballinacourty House*, with a campers' kitchen, TV room, laundry, playground, tennis court and minigolf. Just a 15-min walk into the nearest village and loads of scenic forest walks on its doorstep. Closed Oct–March. €

6

Cashel

Though it has some other noteworthy sights, the town of **CASHEL** – the name derives from the Irish *caiseal*, meaning "stone fort" – is utterly overshadowed by the stunning **Rock of Cashel**, an outcrop that rears out of the surrounding fertile plain, the Golden Vale. Surmounted by important ecclesiastical remains, the Rock is a hotspot on the tourist trail, so is best visited in the early morning before the hordes arrive or in the late afternoon when the coaches have departed. Cashel's annual **festival** (http://cashelartsfest. com) offers a variety of cultural events over ten days at the end of September.

The Rock of Cashel

Just north of the town centre • Free 45min guided tours, call 062 61437 for times • Charge; Heritage Card • http://heritageireland.ie

Viewed from afar, the **Rock of Cashel** is a captivating sight, a freak and solitary lump of limestone, reflecting the light in diverse ways throughout the day and topped by a collection of walls, towers, turrets and crenellations of *Gormenghast* proportions. It might seem heretical to suggest so, but this vista is actually the best thing about the Rock, since, despite its staggering location and much-trumpeted billing, when you get there the site is actually far less atmospheric than other notable ecclesiastical complexes, not least Kells Priory (see page 189) and Quin Abbey (see page 314). Nonetheless, despite the swarms of coach-borne tourists, there's plenty to see and much to marvel at.

The Hall of the Vicars Choral

Once inside, the Rock's first sight is the fifteenth-century **Hall of the Vicars Choral**, which used to house the choir charged with singing at the cathedral's services. Its upper floor features a minstrels' gallery as well as a fine eighteenth-century Flemish tapestry

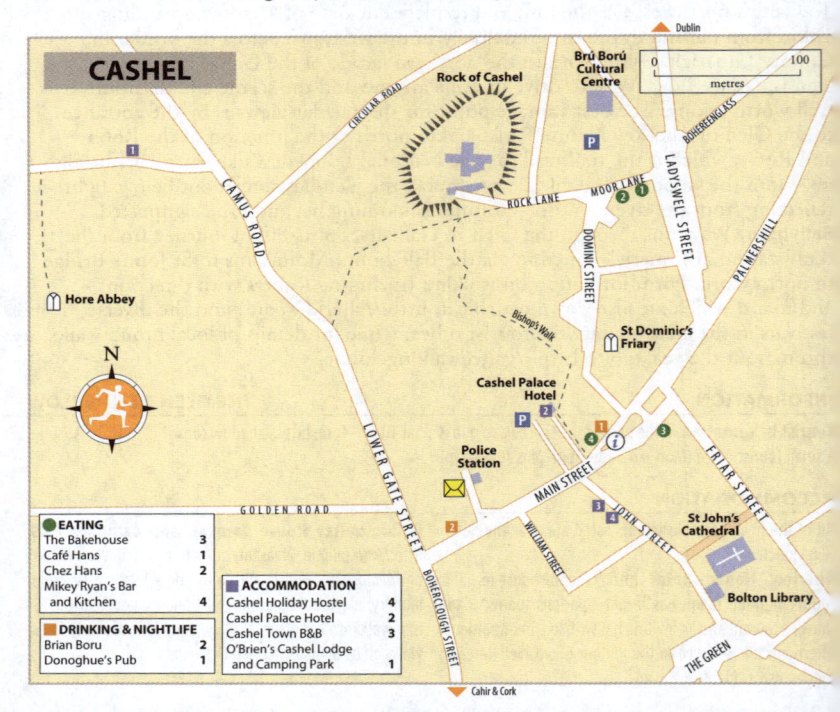

CASHEL

EATING
The Bakehouse	3
Café Hans	1
Chez Hans	2
Mikey Ryan's Bar and Kitchen	4

DRINKING & NIGHTLIFE
Brian Boru	2
Donoghue's Pub	1

ACCOMMODATION
Cashel Holiday Hostel	4
Cashel Palace Hotel	2
Cashel Town B&B	3
O'Brien's Cashel Lodge and Camping Park	1

THE RISE OF THE ROCK

According to legend, the **Rock of Cashel** first rose to political prominence in the fourth or fifth century AD, when a major fortress was established by the descendants of Eógan Mór who went on to found a dynasty of kings-cum-bishops reigning over this part of Munster. The Eóganacht were ousted from Cashel in 978 by the Dál Cais line from Killaloe in County Clare, Brian Boru becoming the overlord of Cashel, and subsequently achieving dominance over Ireland in 1002. His descendant, Murtagh, granted the Rock to the Church in 1101 and, some fifty years later, when the papacy established four archbishoprics in Ireland, one of which was at Cashel, an early medieval **cathedral** was built here. By then, however, the Eóganacht had regained control under Cormac Mac Cárthaigh, who built the adjoining **Cormac's Chapel**, finished in 1134. The whole site was sacked by Cromwell's forces in 1647, but was still used by the Church of Ireland until 1749 when cathedral status was granted to St John's Church on John Street.

6

showing Solomon receiving the Queen of Sheba, while the lower houses the original twelfth-century **St Patrick's Cross** (the one outside – on the cross's original spot – is a replica). Badly worn, it bears a carving of Christ on one side and the saint on the other, and is unusual in not having a ring around the cross head. Directly opposite the Hall of the Vicars Choral is **Cormac's Chapel**, perhaps the most atmospheric of Ireland's Romanesque churches; its appealing south facade of brown sandstone, decorated with the typical blind arcades of the period, stands in warm contrast to the grey limestone used elsewhere on the Rock and in most Irish churches.

The cathedral and round tower

Constructed on the site of the earlier establishment between 1230 and 1270, the huge Gothic **cathedral** is typically Anglo-Norman in form, with pointed arches and loftily set lancet windows. It also features some smaller quatrefoil casements, as well as a nave unusually shorter than the choir, caused by the construction of a **tower** on the west side, built for the archbishops' accommodation and refuge during the fifteenth or sixteenth century. Abutting the cathedral's north transept, the **Round Tower** is the Rock's earliest building, dating from the beginning of the twelfth century. It's nearly 30m high but cannot be climbed, so you'll have to make do with the fine views of the lush countryside around the Rock from ground level.

Brú Ború Cultural Centre

ock Lane, near the castle • Charge • http://bruboru.ie

In the eastern shadow of the Rock, beyond the car park, is the **Brú Ború Cultural Centre**, which offers a genealogical service for South Tipperary. It houses a craft shop and the entertaining **Sounds of History** multimedia exhibition, which races through the development of Irish cultural history, focusing particularly on St Patrick, Brian Ború, and traditional-music song and dance. In summer the centre's theatre hosts shows staged by the renowned Brú Ború performance group and Comhaltas Ceoltóirí Éireann, the national organization for the promotion of Irish music.

Hore Abbey and Bishop's Walk

Just downhill from the Rock's entrance, paths lead west and south. The former leads some of the way towards **Hore Abbey**, a thirteenth-century Cistercian monastery, probably built by those working on the Rock's cathedral. Set in open fields, the ruins themselves are impressive and afford an excellent unobstructed view of the Rock. The southerly **Bishop's Walk** path back to town via the grounds of Cashel Palace Hotel, which was designed in 1730 by Sir Edward Lovett Pearce, architect of Dublin's House of Parliament.

The Heritage Centre

In the market house, Main St · March · Free · http://cashel.ie

Also in the town centre, look in on the **Heritage Centre** attached to the tourist office (see below), which is home to a scale model of Cashel as it looked in 1640 (accompanied by an audio commentary on the history of the town), as well as the original charters granted to the town in the seventeenth century by Charles II and James II.

6

ARRIVAL AND INFORMATION

CASHEL

By bus Buses stop near the market house on Main St. Listed services are run by Bus Éireann.

Destinations Cahir (6 daily; 20min); Cork (6 daily; 1hr 40min); Dublin and airport (6 daily; 2hr 5min–2hr 35min).

Tourist office In the market house, Main St (March–Oct daily 9.30am–5.30pm, Nov–Feb Mon–Fri 9.30am–5.30pm; 062 61333, http://cashel.ie). A town audio-guide is downloadable from the website; enquire about borrowing a tablet.

ACCOMMODATION

SEE MAP PAGE 222

Despite the Rock's popularity you should have no problems finding **accommodation**, with plenty of B&B options in town and many more in the surrounding countryside, especially on the Dualla road.

Cashel Holiday Hostel 6 John St (IHH An Óige), http://cashelhostel.com. Appealing, central hostel in a Georgian town house, with a well-equipped kitchen and sociable dining area, a cosy sitting room, laundry facilities and a barbecue area. Dorms/twins €

Cashel Palace Hotel Main St, http://cashelpalacehotel.ie. A long-awaited renovation has seen the venerable *Palace Hotel* returned to something like it former glory. Now under the prestigious Relais and Chateaux banner, the 42 rooms are as sumptuous as you'd expect, and are complemented by a gorgeous spa complex overlooking the gardens and several first rate dining possibilities, among them the *Bishop's Buttery Restaurant* and *Guinness Bar*. €€€

Cashel Town B&B 5 John St, http://cashelbandb.com. Under the same management as *Cashel Holiday Hostel* next door, with a wide variety of cheery, colourful standard and en-suite bedrooms (extra for private bathroom), and home-made bread for breakfast, which is not included in the rates. Self-catering apartments available. €€

O'Brien's Cashel Lodge and Camping Park Dundrum Road, about 1km from the main tourist office on the northwest side of town near Hore Abbey, http://cashellodge.com. In a bucolic setting looking up towards the Rock, this well-run en-suite B&B with a self-catering kitchen is situated in an attractively renovated 200-year-old outhouse on a working farm. Camping, with shower blocks and kitchen, also available. Camping €, doubles €

EATING

SEE MAP PAGE 222

The Bakehouse 6 Main St, opposite the tourist office, 062 61680. A bakery with pavement tables and an upstairs self-service coffee shop serving cakes, pies, salads and sandwiches, such as tuna melt panini.

Café Hans Moor Lane, 062 63660. A slimmed-down, more informal and more economically priced version of its adjacent sibling, serving salads, sandwiches and dishes such as Toulouse sausage with tarragon and onion gravy, as well as great desserts. No bookings, cash only.

Chez Hans Moor Lane, http://chezhans.net. Cashel's finest restaurant, in a beautiful nineteenth-century building that was once a church lecture hall. The food is exceptional, employing locally sourced meat and wild Irish fish (crispy skinned Dingle hake with braised fennel and sauce verge).

Prices are more manageable if you come for the weekday menu. €€€€

★ **Mikey Ryan's Bar and Kitchen** 76 Main St, http://mikeyryans.ie. Outstanding gastropub with a menu that champions local artisan farmers, distillers and brewers. The two-course Sunday lunch is divine and desserts might include sticky toffee pudding or a vegan chocolate mousse. More informal lunches include schnitzel and burgers while dinner ups the ante with a selection of fish (Black sole with saffron sauce) and excellent meat and vegetarian dishes. Owned by a thoroughbred stud owner, look out for the garden horse-box bar. Lovely outdoor seating area in fine weather. €€€

DRINKING

SEE MAP PAGE 222

Brian Boru 49 Main St, 062 63381. Vast, stylish but unpretentious bar, which offers decent pub grub and hosts DJs and/or bands at weekends and a nightclub on Sat.

Donoghue's Pub 81 Main St, 086 405 5491. Tucked behind the heritage centre, this little pub has a big atmosphere. Sports on screen, a pool table, great beers and cocktails, and occasional live music.

Cork

COBH'S COLOURFUL HOUSES

Cork

Cork is far and away Ireland's largest county, though nearly all visitors simply ignore its massive hinterland of dairy farms, dotted with low mountains and evergreen plantations. The coast's the thing, and in an east–west spread of over 170km it unfurls an astonishing diversity. Based around an island near the mouth of the River Lee, Cork city the epicentre of the fondly named "rebel county", is renowned for its independent spirit, and packs a good cultural and social punch in its compact, vibrant centre. With its excellent restaurants, cafés and specialist food market, the city also sets a high culinary tone; indeed Cork is fondly known as the "foodie capital of Ireland".

7

Further reminders of a prosperous seafaring past can be seen around Cork city in the ports of **Cobh**, **Youghal** and especially **Kinsale**, each of which has reinvented itself in its own singular way as a low-key, pleasurable resort. To the west of the city as far as **Skibbereen**, the coastline, though it meanders wildly through inlets and hidden coves, remains largely gentle and green, with a good smattering of sandy beaches and a balminess that has attracted incomers and holiday-homers from the rest of Ireland and Europe. Facing each other across the shelter of Roaring Water Bay, the good-time ports of **Baltimore** and **Schull** are popular with a cosmopolitan, watersports crowd, but the offshore islands of **Sherkin** and **Clear** presage wild country ahead. **Mizen Head** is the first of Cork's and Kerry's five highly irregular, southwesterly fingers of folded rock, which afford spectacular views of each other and the Atlantic horizon. The next one along driving north up the coast, narrow **Sheep's Head**, is perhaps the most charming, where – if you get out to explore on foot – you'll feel as if you're getting to know every square kilometre of gorse, granite and pasture and just about every inhabitant. Shared between Cork and Kerry, the **Beara Peninsula** is especially dramatic, epitomized by gorgeous **Glengarriff**'s backdrop of dark, bare rock, stunning seascape and lonely mountain passes.

GETTING AROUND	**CORK**
By bus Regional services operated by Bus Éireann will get you around most of the county and you can find timetables on their website (http://buseireann.ie). Check timetables carefully (and use the journey planner), as services tend to be weekly or monthly rather than daily. **By train** The only regional train services are from Cork City,	east to Cobh and Midleton, and west to Killarney, via Mallow. **By bike/on foot** The elaborate landscape of west Cork is great country for walking or cycling, both of which pursuits are served by waymarked routes on the Sheep's Head and the Beara. Bikes can be rented in the main towns and often through rural accommodation.

Cork city

The Republic's second city, **CORK** (Corcaigh, "marshy place") is strongly characterized by its geography. The centre sits tight on a kilometre-wide island, much of which was reclaimed from marshes, in the middle of the River Lee, while the enclosing hills seem to turn this traditionally self-sufficient city in on itself. Given this layout and its history, it comes as no surprise that Corkonians have a reputation in Ireland for independence of spirit, not to say chippiness. Indeed, Cork sees itself not in second place but as a rival to Dublin. It produces its own national newspaper, *The Irish Examiner*, brews Murphy's and Beamish, its own versions of the national drink, stout (now under the aegis of the Dutch brewer, Heineken), and supports a vigorous artistic, intellectual and cultural life of its own. Even its social divisions match Dublin's: here too the south side of the river is generally more affluent, while the north side has a stronger working-class identification.

Highlights

❶ The English Market Cork styles itself as the Food Capital of Ireland, and the best producers can be found here in Cork City's bustling covered market. See page 239

❷ Kinsale A pretty harbour, impressive forts and some of the best restaurants in Ireland. See page 245

❸ Drombeg One of the country's finest Bronze Age stone circles, in a bucolic setting with views of the sea. See page 249

❹ Clear Island Hop on the ferry for varied bird-watching and pleasant walking. See page 254

❺ Mizen Head The view from Ireland's most southwesterly point – accessed by a suspension bridge across a gorge – is nothing short of stunning. See page 255

❻ The Sheep's Head Way The shortest and easiest major walking route in these parts, around a wild peninsula. See page 257

❼ Bantry House and Gardens Sumptuous art treasures in a beautiful spot overlooking Bantry Bay. See page 258

❽ Beara Peninsula and Healy Pass The loop road meanders between crashing ocean and craggy mountains; the hairpin bends of Healy Pass are unforgettable. See page 259

HIGHLIGHTS ARE MARKED ON THE MAP ON PAGE 230

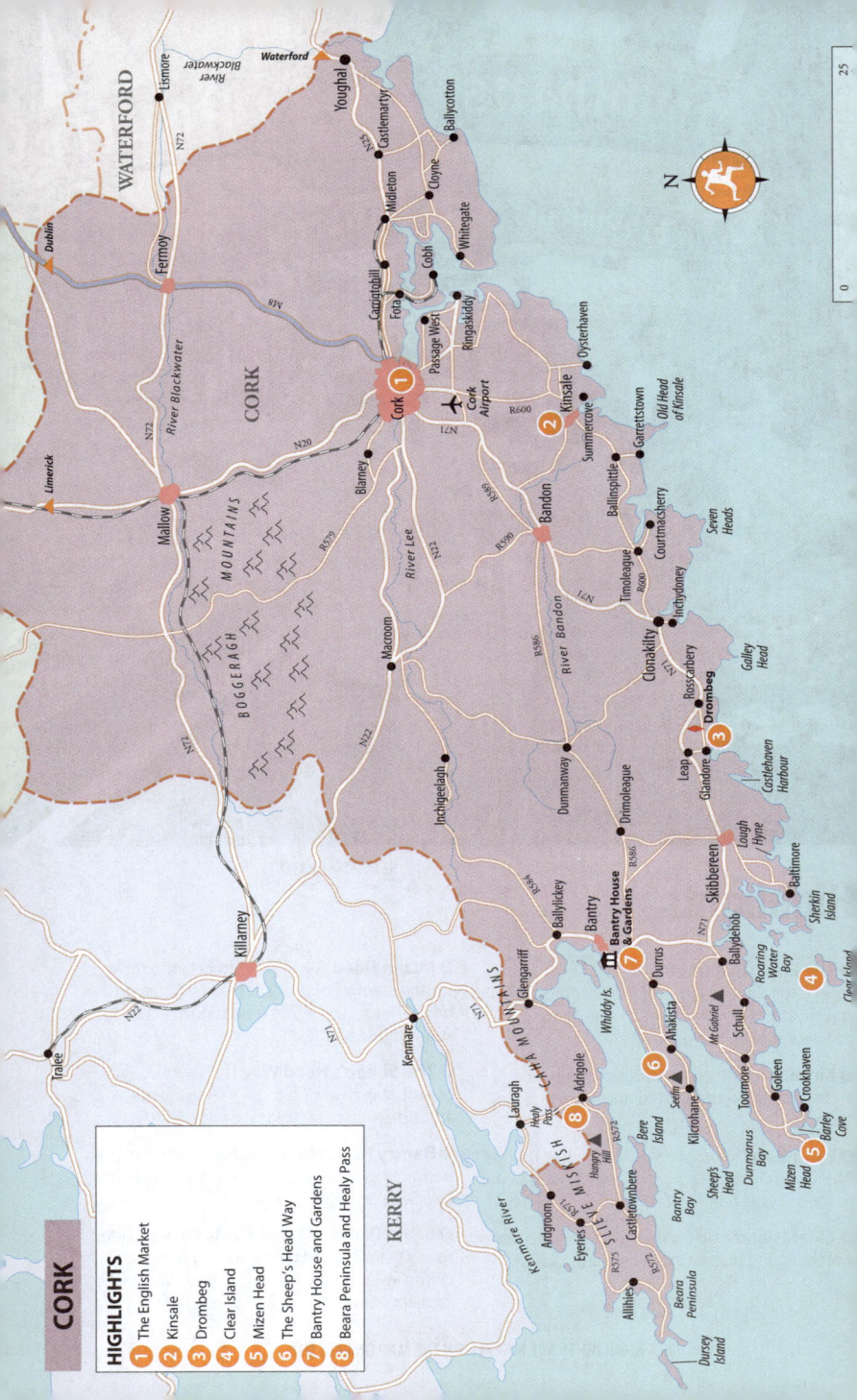

In colonial times, Cork also maintained its own strong links with London, through its role as a major **port**, proof of which can still be seen all around town. The main drag, curving St Patrick's Street, was originally a waterway lined with quays, while you can still spot eighteenth-century moorings on Grand Parade. Though contemporary Cork doesn't make the most of its long riverfront, much of which is now lined by major roads, the channels of the Lee, spanned by more than twenty bridges, break up the cityscape and pleasantly disorientate. At the start of the twenty-first century, Grand Parade and St Patrick's Street were revamped with huge criss-crossing streetlights to represent the masts of ships. The harbour area has Ireland's largest concentration of chemical factories, fortunately downstream of the centre, while the city's other main modern industry, computers, is linked to the prestigious university, to the west of the centre. All of this has spawned a widespread commuter belt, but the compact island is still the place for the many excellent restaurants, lively pubs and artistic venues.

The best of the city's sightseeing options are the **Crawford Art Gallery**, with its fine collection of eighteenth- to twentieth-century art, **Cork City Gaol**, which vividly evokes life in a nineteenth-century prison, and the hi-tech cosmological displays of **Blackrock Castle Observatory**. In truth, however, none of Cork's sights are absolute must-sees, though it's a pleasant place to stroll around on a fine day. The city centre is essentially the eastern part of the island ("the flat of the city"), with its quaysides, bridges, old warehouses and the narrow alleys of the medieval heart, plus a segment to the north of the River Lee that has MacCurtain Street as its central thoroughfare.

Brief history
In the seventh century, **St Finbarr** established a monastery at Cork, on the site of today's cathedral, to the southwest of the modern centre. Three centuries later, the Vikings created a separate settlement, an island in the River Lee's marshes, which was taken over in the twelfth century by the Anglo-Normans. They strengthened the defences of the central part of the island with the construction of vast city walls, leaving the west and east ends to the swamp and later developing suburbs on the slopes to the north and south. The fortifications were largely destroyed, however, in the successful **Williamite siege** of 1690, and became redundant when the marshes were reclaimed soon after. The

---

BLARNEY

Blarney, Blarney, what he says he does not mean. It is the usual Blarney.
So spoke Queen Elizabeth I, and a legend and its accompanying tourist phenomenon were born. Though supposedly loyal to the queen, the **Lord of Blarney**, Cormac MacCarthy, had been stalling her emissary, Sir George Carew, who had been sent to restore English control of Munster, sidetracking him with wine, women and words. MacCarthy, it was said, could talk "the noose off his head", and over the centuries blarney came to mean "flattering, untrustworthy or loquacious talk associated with…Irish people" (*The Encyclopedia of Ireland*). This story of the word's origin, however, may itself be blarney…

At some stage in the nineteenth century, with the beginnings of mass tourism to the southwest of Ireland, it became popular to kiss the **Blarney Stone**, part of the machicolations of **Blarney Castle**, a fine fifteenth-century tower house, set in attractive grounds, in the village of the same name, 8km northwest of Cork. The stone stands over a 26m drop, and planting a smacker on it is meant to grant "the gift of the gab". If you're really feeling that tongue-tied, buses run to Blarney from Parnell Place bus station (Mon–Sat every 30min, Sun hourly; 20–30min), and the castle is open year-round (daily: April & Oct 9am–5.30pm; May–Sept 9am–6pm; Nov–March 9am–5pm; last admission 1hr before closing; charge; Heritage Island; http://blarneycastle.ie). Legions of the verbally challenged queue up in summer, when it's best to turn up early in the morning or late in the afternoon.

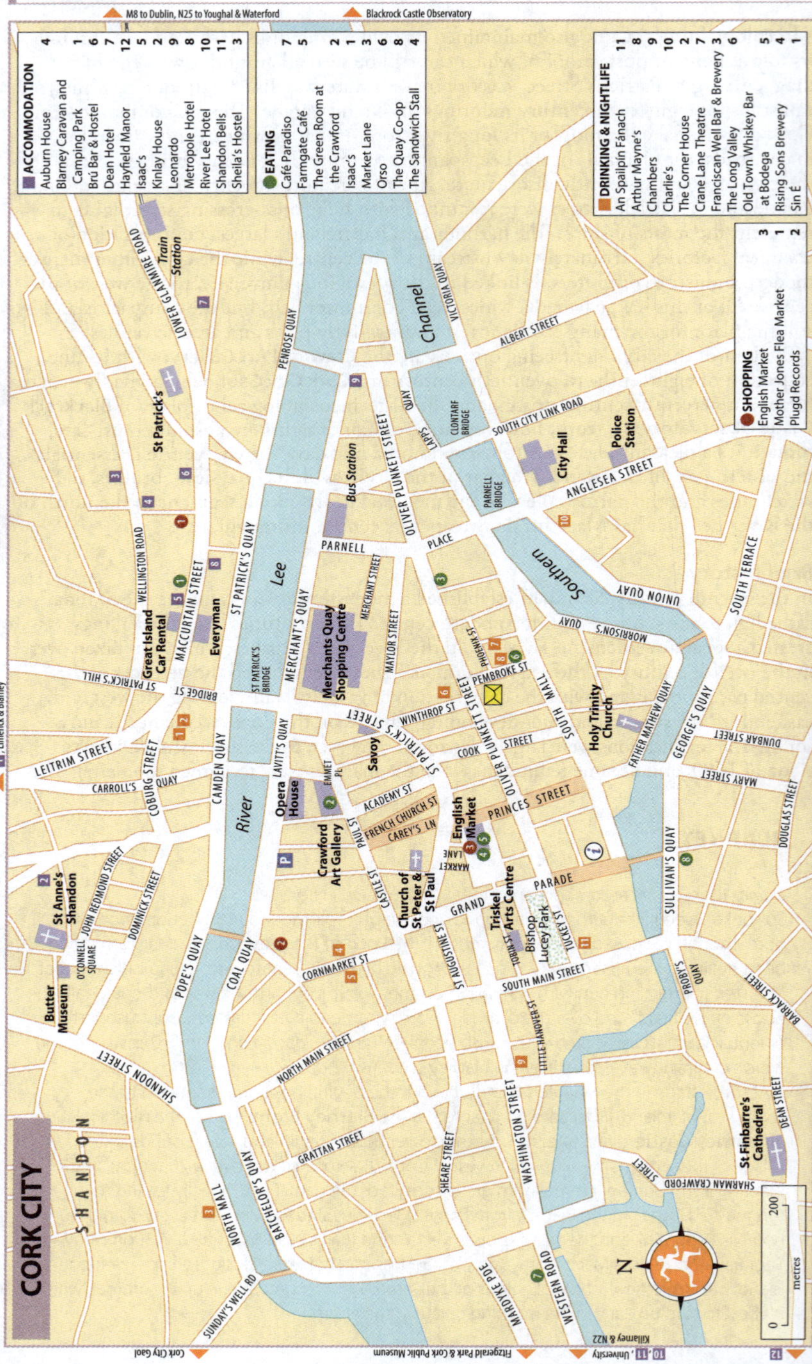

CORK CITY
M8 to Dublin, N25 to Youghal & Waterford
Blackrock Castle Observatory
ACCOMMODATION
Auburn House 4
Blarney Caravan and Camping Park 1
Brú Bar & Hostel 6
Dean Hotel 7
Hayfield Manor 12
Isaac's 5
Kinlay House 2
Leonardo 9
Metropole Hotel 8
River Lee Hotel 10
Shandon Bells 11
Sheila's Hostel 3
EATING
Café Paradiso 7
Farmgate Café 5
The Green Room at the Crawford 2
Isaac's 1
Market Lane 3
Orso 6
The Quay Co-op 8
The Sandwich Stall 4
DRINKING & NIGHTLIFE
An Spailpín Fánach 11
Arthur Mayne's 8
Chambers 9
Charlie's 10
The Corner House 2
Crane Lane Theatre 7
Franciscan Well Bar & Brewery 3
The Long Valley 6
Old Town Whiskey Bar at Bodega 5
Rising Sons Brewery 4
Sin É 1
SHOPPING
English Market 3
Mother Jones Flea Market 1
Plugd Records 2
Train Station
St Patrick's
Great Island Car Rental
Everyman
Bus Station
City Hall
Police Station
Merchants Quay Shopping Centre
Opera House
Crawford Art Gallery
Savoy
English Market
Church of St Peter & St Paul
Triskel Arts Centre
Bishop Lucey Park
Holy Trinity Church
St Anne's Shandon
Butter Museum
St Finbarre's Cathedral
SHANDON
River Lee
Channel
Southern
Lower Glanmire Road
Wellington Road
MacCurtain Street
St Patrick's Quay
St Patrick's Bridge
St Patrick's Hill
Bridge St
Penrose Quay
Victoria Quay
Albert Street
South City Link Road
Anglesea Street
Clontarf Bridge
Parnell Bridge
Parnell Place
Merchant's Quay
Merchant Street
Maylor Street
Oliver Plunkett Street
Lapps Quay
Union Quay
Morrison's Quay
South Terrace
Pembroke St
Phoenix St
Winthrop St
St Patrick's Street
Cook Street
South Mall
Father Mathew Quay
George's Quay
Dunbar Street
Mary Street
Douglas Street
Leitrim Street
Carroll's Quay
Coburg Street
Camden Quay
Lavitt's Quay
Emmet Pl
Academy St
French Church St
Carey's Ln
Paul St
Princes Street
Market Lane
Castle St
Grand Parade
Tobin St
Tuckey St
Sullivan's Quay
John Redmond Street
Dominick Street
O'Connell Square
Pope's Quay
Coal Quay
Cornmarket St
St Augustine St
South Main Street
Little Hanover St
Proby's Quay
Barrack Street
Shandon Street
North Main Street
Washington Street
Dean Street
Batchelor's Quay
Grattan Street
Sheare Street
Sharman Crawford Street
North Mall
Sunday's Well Rd
Mardyke Pde
Western Road
Limerick & Blarney
Cork City Gaol
Fitzgerald Park & Cork Public Museum
University
Killarney & N22
0
200 m
metres
N

next century witnessed great wealth, through the trade in butter and pickled meat and the development of the port for provisioning westbound sailing ships. Brewing and distilling plants were established, which persist to this day, along with glass, silver and lace industries, but the Act of Union and the introduction of steamships brought stagnation in the nineteenth century. At the start of the last century, Cork took an active part in the **War of Independence** and the **Civil War**, and suffered as a consequence. In 1920, the Royal Irish Constabulary murdered the Lord Mayor, Tomás MacCurtain, and as a reprisal for an ambush, the Black and Tans burnt much of the city centre to the ground in 1921. MacCurtain's successor as mayor, Terence MacSwiney, was incarcerated and went on hunger strike, which after 74 days led to his death on October 24, 1920.

The centre

Three roughly east–west arteries define Cork's commercial centre, bracketed to the west by the wide boulevard of **Grand Parade**: the crescent of **St Patrick's Street** (aka Patrick Street), bustling with major chainstores; **Oliver Plunkett Street**, home to more traditional shops and pubs; and the city's grand financial and legal hub, **South Mall**. On the north side of Patrick Street, restaurants line the pedestrianized alleys of the old French quarter around **Paul Street**, though the main culinary venue is undoubtedly the covered **English Market** (see page 239), a joy for the senses that's well worth wandering through. Just south of the centre, on the way to St Finbarre's Cathedral (see box 285), is the seventeenth-century **Elizabeth's Fort** on Barrack St (free; http://elizabethfort. ie). You're free to wander the star-shaped fort (there are some great city views from the walkway along the walls), or there's a daily historical tour at 1pm (€5).

The Crawford Art Gallery

Emmet Place • Free • http://crawfordartgallery.ie

The city's major set-piece sight is the **Crawford Art Gallery**, although it is due to close in 2025 for a major revamp which could take up to two years. On the Ground floor you will find two sculpture galleries painted in captivating blue; these galleries are home to a significant set of Canova Casts, a curious outcome of high stakes international politics in the Napoleonic era commissioned by Pope Pius VII as a gift to the Prince Regent in thanks for deposing Napoleon at the Battle of Waterloo. The Gallery also boasts a national collection of Irish and international art from the eighteenth century onwards that's worth a quick mosey and an excellent café, The Green Room at The Crawford (see page 237). The national collection is distributed throughout the three floors of the building. Look out for a fascinating *View of Cork*, painted in about 1740 by John Butts: you can pick out the waterway that is now Patrick Street, the 1724 Custom House (with a Union Jack in the

---

NEO-GOTHIC CORK

For those with a taste for it – and with shoe leather to spare – there's plenty of **neo-Gothic church architecture** to see in Cork, mostly along the riverbanks. The highlight is William Burges's **St Finbarre's Cathedral** on Proby's Quay (charge; http://corkcathedral.com), consecrated in 1870, whose three soaring, French Gothic spires are visible all over the city. The well-lit interior, which is elaborately decorated with red Cork marble, stained glass and Italianate mosaics, also impresses with its lofty proportions. Leading nineteenth-century practitioners Augustus Pugin and George Pain also worked in Cork. The **Church of SS Peter and Paul**, just off St Patrick's Street in the centre, was designed by Pugin and sports some fine woodcarving. Pain was the architect of **Holy Trinity Church** on Father Mathew Quay, with its handsome lantern spire, which was built in the 1830s and 1840s by booze-busting Father Theobald Mathew, who persuaded three million people to take the "total abstinence pledge", as well as of **St Patrick's Church** out to the northeast on Lower Glanmire Road.

courtyard), which is now the gallery you're visiting. There are also some fine representative works by Limerick-born Seán Keating (1889–1977), many of whose academic realist paintings have achieved iconic status. Though obviously posed in a studio, his *Men of the South* (1924) achieves the restrained grandeur of a classical frieze, depicting a grim-faced IRA column waiting to ambush British soldiers. Keep an eye out also for a piercing portrait of actor Fiona Shaw by Victoria Russell on the staircase to the first floor and – on the second floor – pencil and watercolour studies by Harry Clarke (1881–1931) for his Keats-inspired stained-glass window "The Eve of St Agnes".

West of the centre

The west end of the island narrows around a residential area, which is home to hospitals and university buildings as well as a couple of interesting small museums. North of these, to the west of Shandon in the posh suburb of Sunday's Well, is the forbidding red sandstone of **Cork City Gaol**.

Glucksman Gallery

University College Cork, 1km from Grand Parade off the south side of Western Rd • Free • http://glucksman.org

In the northeast corner of the university's main campus, it's well worth checking out the **Glucksman Gallery**. This striking building of wood, glass, limestone and steel, which was shortlisted for the 2005 RIBA prize, hosts rotating exhibitions of contemporary art, as well as free guided tours, talks, concerts and a restaurant.

Cork Public Museum

5min walk from the Glucksman Gallery off the north side of Western Rd • Free • http://corkcity.ie

Facing the leafy north channel of the River Lee, sits **Fitzgerald Park**, where you'll find the **Cork Public Museum**, a celebration of Cork and Corkonians – including sports personalities Sonia O'Sullivan and Roy Keane, both of whom have donated shirts. The museum traces the city's history through interesting documents and memorabilia, with a particular concentration on the period from the Great Famine to The Emergency, as World War II was known in Ireland. Some beautiful examples of Cork silver and glassware are on display, alongside archaeological finds from the Neolithic era onwards and engaging temporary exhibitions on subjects such as prehistoric gold.

Cork City Gaol

Convent Ave, Sunday's Well • charge • http://corkcitygaol.com • 15min walk across the river from Fitzgerald Park (signposted from the nearby footbridge)

Skilfully designed for its punishing purpose in 1818 by the Pain brothers, George and James, the **Cork City Gaol** operated until 1923 when Republican prisoners – among them Countess Markiewicz (see page 393) and short story writer Frank O'Connor – were released after the Civil War. Tours are self-guided (a guidebook is included in the entrance fee or there's an audio guide for an extra €2), but it is worth paying an additional €2 for the guided tour, which takes place at 2pm each day, but hourly in July and August.

From the late 1920s until the early 1950s, the top floor of the gaol was home to the studios of Radio Éireann (now RTÉ), which have now been replaced by the **Radio Museum**. There's lots of interesting material on the pioneers of radio here, a re-creation of the old studio, a large collection of early radios, and a "juke box" of archival recordings.

Shandon and north of the centre

To the north of the centre, **Shandon**'s narrow residential streets and alleys tumble down the slope towards the River Lee. At the centre of this area stands cobbled O'Connell Square, home to the round and tubby former **butter market**.

Butter Museum
O'Connell Square • charge • http://thebuttermuseum.com

The fascinating story of the dairy trade and its major impact on the development of the city is told in the **Butter Museum**, opposite the old butter market. The museum begins with dairy culture in early Ireland, as illustrated by a keg of bog butter: on remote grazing lands, milk was churned into butter on the spot and preserved in the bogs for later use; to this day, such kegs are often turned over by peat-cutters, who'll swear the butter is still edible. In the eighteenth century, thanks to its fertile hinterland and its site on the largest natural harbour in the northern hemisphere, Cork became the main provisioning port in the Atlantic for both the British Navy and trade convoys, with most Cork butter ending up in the West Indies. In the following century, the city managed to ride out the agricultural collapse caused by the Napoleonic Wars and the Famine, by gearing the butter trade to the English market through rigorous controls – the butter-market building you see outside was where barrels were washed and weighed, to avoid underhand practices by farmers.

St Anne's Shandon
Church St • Church free; tower and bells charge • http://shandonbells.ie

St Anne's Shandon is a graceful, early eighteenth-century Anglican church, built partly of white limestone, partly of puce sandstone – a combination that is said to have inspired the red-and-white "rebel" flag of County Cork. Its steeple, the city's most famous landmark, is flanked by four huge, notoriously unreliable clocks – earning the nickname "the four-faced liar" – and topped by a giant golden salmon as a weathervane. It's possible to climb the 132 steps of the tower for matchless views of the city and to ring the bells.

Blackrock Castle Observatory
2km east of centre on south bank of River Lee • tower and dungeon tours Mon–Fri on application, Sat & Sun 1.30pm & 3.30pm • charge • http://bco.ie • City bus #202 towards Mahon from bus station will put you off at the pier in Blackrock village, leaving an easy 10min walk to the castle

Originally built in the sixteenth century, **Blackrock Castle Observatory** is now home to two dynamic and imaginative exhibitions: **Cosmos at the Castle**, beautifully produced, large-screen audiovisuals containing up to three hours of material that you can explore interactively in as much depth as you choose, not just on cosmology, but on life, the universe and everything; and **Journeys of Exploration**, a similarly stimulating interactive experience that recalls the history of the castle and surrounding area. The visiting exhibitions are well regarded, and there's also a very good café-restaurant here.

ARRIVAL AND DEPARTURE
CORK CITY

By plane Cork Airport (http://corkairport.com) lies 7km south of the centre, off the Kinsale road. From here, Bus Éireann's #225 and 226 buses run to the bus station on Parnell Place and Kent train station (Mon–Sat every 30min, Sun hourly; 30min). If you want a quick getaway, Citylink operates through-coaches from Cork Airport to Limerick and Galway. A taxi will cost around €20.

By train Cork Kent station is 1km northeast of the city centre on the Lower Glanmire Rd.

Destinations Cobh (Mon–Sat at least hourly, 11 on Sun; 25min); Dublin Heuston (hourly; 2hr 40min); Fota (Mon–Sat at least hourly, 11 on Sun; 13min); Killarney (6–9 daily, often with a change at Mallow; 1hr 30min–2hr); Midleton (Mon–Sat at least hourly, 9 on Sun; 25min); Tralee (6–9 daily, often with a change at Mallow; 2hr–2hr 30min).

By bus The Bus Éireann station is on Parnell Place alongside Merchant's Quay. Harrington's and O'Donoghue's private buses to Castletownbere (see page 261) stop nearby on Parnell Place, while Aircoach (http://aircoach.ie) and Citylink buses (http://citylink.ie) use St Patrick's Quay on the north side of the river, the latter starting from Cork Airport 30min earlier. Most city buses stop on the central St Patrick's Street.

Destinations Bus Éireann: Adrigole (Mon, Sat & Sun; 3hr); Baltimore (1–2 daily; 2hr); Bantry (4–6 daily; 1hr 50min); Cahir (6 daily; 1hr 20min); Cashel (6 daily; 1hr 40min); Castletownbere (4 weekly; 3hr); Clonakilty (7–8 daily; 1hr 10min); Dublin and airport (6 daily; 3hr 45min–4hr

7

10min); Ennis (hourly; 3hr); Galway (hourly; 4hr 20min); Glengarriff (2–3 daily; 2hr 10min); Goleen (1–2 daily; 2hr 45min); Killarney (hourly; 1hr 30min); Kinsale (from Kent train station, via the bus station and the airport; hourly; 1hr); Limerick (hourly; 1hr 45min); Midleton (frequent; 30min); Schull (1–2 daily; 2hr 20min); Shannon Airport (hourly; 2hr 30min); Skibbereen (5–7 daily; 1hr 45min); Tralee (hourly; 2hr 15min); Waterford (hourly; 2hr 15min); Youghal (hourly; 50min).

Destination Aircoach: Dublin and airport (hourly; 3hr–3hr 20min).

Destinations Citylink: Galway (8 daily; 3hr); Limerick (8 daily; 1hr 45min).

Destinations Dublin Coach (http://dublincoach.ie): Kilkenny (8 daily; 2hr 35min).

By car If you're arriving by car, note that parking on the street requires a disc, which can be picked up from convenience stores. There's a useful multistorey car park on Coal Quay beside the Opera House.

GETTING AROUND

Bike rental Cycle Scene, 396 Blarney St (€15/day; http://cyclescene.ie), also do servicing and repairs.

Car rental Most of the big multinationals are represented at Cork Airport. There are few local outfits, but they include friendly and amenable Great Island Car Rentals,

who are centrally placed at 47 MacCurtain St (http://greatislandcarrentals.com) and can deliver to the airport.

Taxis There are ranks on Patrick St. Companies include Cork Taxi Co-op (021 427 2222, http://corktaxi.ie).

INFORMATION AND TOURS

Tourist office 125 St Patrick's St (Mon–Sat 9am–5pm; http://purecork.ie).

Walking tours Cork City Walks (http://corkcitywalks.eu) arrange a variety of tours ranging from two- to four hours and which are tailored to the needs of the individual (or group).

Bus tours Cronin's operates a hop-on, hop-off tour in an open-top double-decker (every 45min; 1hr 15min; buy tickets on board or at the tourist office; €22, valid for

24hr; http://corkcitytours.com), departing from Grand Parade outside the city library opposite the tourist office and passing the Crawford Gallery, train station, St Anne's Shandon and Cork City Gaol.

Boat tours Atlantic Sea Kayaking runs kayaking trips (April–Sept; from €60/person; http://atlanticseakayaking.com) around the city by river or out into the harbour lasting 2hr 30 minutes.

ACCOMMODATION   SEE MAP PAGE 232

Cork's **hotels** range from no-frills to luxurious, and there are scores of **B&Bs** and more upmarket **guesthouses**, which are mostly concentrated near the university along Western Road (city bus #208 from St Patrick's St or #205 from Kent train station and St Patrick's St), and at the opposite end of town on the busy Lower Glanmire Rd, near the train station. A variety of **hostels** can be found mostly on the north bank of the River Lee; for summer accommodation (June–Aug) in halls try http://studentvillage.ie or http://uccsummerbeds.com. Beds are in short supply during the city's many festivals (see page 239), when early booking is advisable.

HOTELS AND GUESTHOUSES

Auburn House 3 Garfield Terrace, Wellington Rd, http://auburnguesthouse.com. Well-maintained, en-suite B&B in a central but peaceful spot north of the river, with parking facilities. Two-night min stay and breakfast costs extra. €

★ **Dean Hotel** Horgan's Quay, Railway St, http://thedean.ie/cork. Just a hop away from the train station, the cool as a cucumber *Dean* has five categories of room, though all come with coffee machines (and good ones at that), Smeg fridges and record players, with a good choice of vinyl to boot. *Sophie's* rooftop bar and restaurant offers superlative citywide views and is a terrific spot to indulge in the

excellent breakfast, before or aftder which you can work up a head of steam in the PowerGym. €€€

Hayfield Manor Perrott Ave, College Rd, http://hayfieldmanor.ie. Giving a taste of the countryside among the terraces of the southwestern suburbs, 500m west of St Finbarr's Cathedral, this five-star 1920s manor house has been decorated in a fresh, modern, rural style and much extended. Service is attentive and congenial, while facilities include an imposing pool, an outdoor Jacuzzi in the pretty garden, a spa, a conservatory bistro and an excellent modern Irish restaurant, *Orchids*. €€€€

Isaac's 48 MacCurtain St, http://hotelisaacscork.com. Good-value, well-run hotel in a former furniture warehouse with an attractive courtyard and waterfall behind its grand, Victorian, redbrick facade, and smart, colourful, well-equipped bedrooms. Serviced apartments also available. €€€

Leonardo Anderson's Quay, http://leonardoscork.co.uk. Bright, smart accommodation in a large, efficiently run, welcoming hotel that's central but in a slightly quieter location towards the east end of the "island". Decent dining options too. €€

Metropole Hotel MacCurtain St, http://themetropolehotel.ie. A landmark building in a central location by the bus station with beautifully appointed rooms in five categories, (including cosy rooms) complemented by a welter of eating and drinking possibilities, including the glam Prosecco Lounge and the MET bar and restaurant. €€€

River Lee Hotel Western Rd, http://doylecollection.com. Pleasing modern, if very expensive, hotel decorated with pale stone and grainy wood, a 10min walk west of the centre overlooking the leafy university campus. The rooms are large and well designed with comfortable beds and their own music system. The bistro and bar feature broad terraces on the river, and there's an attached leisure club with pool, gym and spa. €€€€

Shandon Bells 44 Western Rd, http://shandonbellscork. ie. Very helpful and informative owners at this B&B 15min from the centre, overlooking the southern channel of the river near the university. Twelve bright and colourful, en-suite rooms, a varied breakfast menu and a waterside patio for fair weather. Off-street parking available. €€

HOSTELS

★ **Brú Bar & Hostel** 57 MacCurtain St (IHH & IHO), http://bruhostel.com. The city's most central hostel, a welcoming, rambling former hotel above a sociable backpackers' bar, with live music several nights a week. The clean, basic,

high-ceilinged rooms (four-bed dorms plus private rooms sleeping two or three); are complemented by a kitchen and dining and TV room. Prices include a simple breakfast. Dorms €

Kinlay House Bob and Joan's Walk, Shandon (IHH), http://kinlayhousecork.ie. Large, well-run, partly en-suite hostel, on a quiet lane next to St Anne's Church, with singles, doubles and twins alongside dorms; laundry facilities and kitchen. Price includes a light breakfast. Dorms €, doubles €€

Sheila's Hostel 4 Belgrave Place, Wellington Rd (IHH & IHO), http://sheilashostel.ie. Cork's biggest hostel, efficiently run and welcoming, with dorms sleeping up to ten and private double and twin rooms, in addition to a good kitchen, laundry facilities, a cinema room and a sauna. Dorms €, doubles €€

CAMPSITE

Blarney Caravan and Camping Park Stone-view, 3km north of Blarney, http://blarneycaravanpark.com. The nearest campsite, about 10km northwest of the city centre, with campers' kitchen, laundry, shop, play area and an 18-hole pitch'n'putt. Closed late Oct to March. €

7

EATING

SEE MAP PAGE 232

Eating out is one of the great pleasures of Cork – the city's chefs place a high premium on sourcing the best of local, artisanal ingredients, which they creatively put to good use. The best place to get a feel for Cork's culinary enthusiasm is the **English Market** (see page 239).

Café Paradiso 16 Lancaster Quay, Western Rd, http://paradiso.restaurant. Popular, unpretentious restaurant serving excellent and innovative Mediterranean-influenced vegetarian and vegan cuisine. The formula is simple: two six-course dinner menus (one of which is vegan), costing €68 and featuring the likes of parsnip gnocchi, nettle and wild garlic – and there's a terrific wine card to boot. Stylish accommodation also available for diners. Closed Sun & Mon. €€€€

★ **Farmgate Café** English Market, Princes St, http://farmgate.ie. Superb café-restaurant overlooking the market's bustling stalls. Places a strong emphasis on local ingredients and food products: daily specials depend on what's fresh from the butcher and fishmonger. Cooked breakfasts to order, great cakes and desserts and excellent lunches, which feature salads and savoury tarts, as well as many classic dishes such as tripe and onion with drisheen. Saturday brunch is also well worth considering, especially with the likes of smoky eggs and peperonata with spinach and sourdough on the menu. Closed Sun. €€–€€€

The Green Room at the Crawford Emmet Place, http://thegreenroomatthecrawford.com. Classy and affordable café-restaurant in a gorgeous ground-floor room of the gallery (see page 233) serving breakfast as well as refined lunch and dinner fare, like baked seafood crepe, and crisp

duck confit – or just pop by for coffee and cake after a short spin round the gallery. Closed Sun. €€€

★ **Isaac's** 48 MacCurtain St, http://isaacsrestaurant. ie. Popular, informal and welcoming restaurant in an eighteenth-century warehouse with bare stone walls, candles and a buzzy atmosphere. The short, global menu, supplemented by daily specials, ranges from Indian lamb curry to roast chicken with buttered leeks, while there's plenty of choice for veggies and some great comfort desserts like apple and blackberry crumble. €€€

Market Lane 5 Oliver Plunkett St, http://marketlane.ie. Crisp bistro decor featuring lots of polished wood, an open kitchen and a long bar in a bright corner location provides the setting for some outstandingly creative dishes like pan fried hake with sweet potato and coconut gratin and crispy buckwheat, and, for vegans, dal vada lentil cakes with cashew yoghurt and sweet pickled cucumber. Good value set lunch menus. €€€

Orso 8 Pembroke St, http://orso.ie. Head for this small, mellow café for great breakfasts, superb espressos and mostly Middle Eastern mains at lunch, such as flatbread with chicken shawarma and Bombay spice. Dinners are more complex and the cakes – like their popcorn, chocolate and malteser bar – serious. No bookings. Closed Sun. €€

The Quay Co-op 24 Sullivan's Quay, http://quaycoop. com. Self-service, partly organic workers' cooperative café above a health-food store, serving tasty, substantial and cheap vegetarian and vegan meals (and catering for many other dietary requirements), great salads and soups, plus a selection of desserts. Art exhibitions are a regular upstairs. Closed Sun. €

The Sandwich Stall English Market, Grand Parade, http://facebook.com/thesandwichstall. Cute corner stall in the market selling gourmet sandwiches, hot soups and channa masala. Most people grab a takeaway but you can also perch at the bar and finish off your lunch with a strong coffee. Closed Sun. €

DRINKING AND NIGHTLIFE

SEE MAP PAGE 232

The city boasts dozens of great **bars**, specializing in characterful and unreconstructed old **pubs**. These would generally be worth seeking out for their atmosphere alone, but a high proportion of them also host **music**, traditional or otherwise. For general **information** on the arts, nightlife and entertainment, consult the free monthly leaflet, *Whazon* (http://whazon.com), which can be picked up in cafés and arts venues. Plugd Records (see page 239) is a good place for info on the gig and club scenes.

An Spailpín Fánach 28 South Main St, 021 427 7949. Rambling, rustic and unpretentious, the "Migrant Worker" was established opposite the now defunct Beamish and Crawford Brewery in the eighteenth century, and hosts traditional music most nights.

Arthur Mayne's 7 Pembroke St, http://corkheritagepubs. com. Atmospheric, not to say creepy, conversion of an ancient pharmacy with dozens of old apothecary items left on the shelves, beyond which cellar-like cubicles connect with the Crane Lane Theatre bar. If you can peel your eyes away from the decor for a minute, you'll find an excellent menu of well-kept wines by the glass, as well as meat and cheese plates, sandwiches and weekend brunch.

Chambers Washington St, 021 465 8100. The city's main LGBTQ+ bar and club, with DJs every night and regular events; €5 admission Fri & Sat after 11pm.

Charlie's 2 Union Quay, http://charliesbarcork.com. Dimly lit, grungy pub with an early licence and live music three nights a week (mostly blues) plus a traditional session on Sun afternoon.

★ **The Corner House** 7 Coburg St, 021 450 0655. Welcoming pub, similar in feel to *Sin É* next door, though more spacious and airy. Great local bands from 6pm on Saturdays, Bluegrass most Sunday evenings, traditional music Mon, Wed, Thurs and every second Fri.

Crane Lane Theatre Phoenix St, http://cranelanetheatre. ie. Cosy, vibrant theatre bar, offering a wide range of craft beers, though much of the action happens under the hanging plants in the big, heated courtyard out front. Live bands – anything from folk and blues to jazz and country – and/or DJs every night.

Franciscan Well Bar & Brewery 14b North Mall, http:// franwellbar.com. On the site of a medieval monastery whose well was known for its curative properties, this microbrewery-bar knocks out great stout, lager, ale and wheat beer, which can be enjoyed out the back in the sunny/heated beer-yard. Also offers pizzas from a wood-fired oven and brewery tours (usually Thurs–Sun; charge), while diverse events include Tuesday trad sessions, jazz and indie music nights, and comedy. Upstairs at the *Monk* bar, bartenders knock up posh cocktails.

The Long Valley 10 Winthrop St, http://thelongvalleybar. ie. Fine traditional bar, sporting a large snug at the front and decorated with plants, old views of Cork and a mishmash of wooden furniture, some of it rescued from a cruise-liner. Famous for its tasty doorstep sandwiches at lunchtime. Look out for evenings of poetry readings and open-mic sessions in the upstairs *Hayloft Bar* (http://obheal.ie).

Old Town Whiskey Bar at Bodega 44–45 Cornmarket St, http://oldtownwhiskeybar.com. Barn-like all-rounder in a former covered food market on the redeveloped Cornmarket. The decor is chandeliers, arched colonnades and a lofty bar and the food's especially good here, including meat and cheese plates and brunches. Late on Fri & Sat nights, it turns into one of Cork's most popular clubs.

Rising Sons Brewery Cornmarket St, http://risingsons brewery.com. Award-winning small-batch microbrewery opposite Bodega offering tours and tastings (Tues, Thurs & Sat; charge), quality bar food and a projector showing sports events.

Sin É 8 Coburg St, http://corkheritagepubs.com. Cosy, candlelit pub – whose name means "That's It" because there used to be a funeral parlour next door – hung with all sorts of bric-a-brac and memorabilia and offering a wide range of beers. Frequent, varied live music, including traditional at 7pm every night.

ENTERTAINMENT

Cork Opera House Emmet Place, http://corkoperahouse. ie. The city's main performance venue, hosting high-quality drama, dance, opera, comedy and concerts of all hues, with more eclectic shows in the attached Half Moon Theatre.

Everyman MacCurtain St, http://everymancork.com. Cork's oldest traditional theatre, dating back to the late nineteenth century, offers a varied menu of drama, dance, opera, music and comedy.

Triskel Christchurch Tobin St, http://triskelartscentre. ie. The main contemporary arts centre is formed of two integrated buildings – Christchurch, a fine, early Georgian Protestant church, deconsecrated and beautifully renovated, where arthouse films, interesting gigs and art exhibitions are put on; and its original home on Tobin St, which includes an art gallery.

SEE MAP PAGE 232

CORK FESTIVALS

Cork city hosts plenty of lively festivals, of which the largest and most prestigious are the **midsummer festival**, a wide-ranging twelve-day celebration of the arts in mid-June (http://corkmidsummer.com), the **jazz festival** in October (http://guinnessjazzfestival.com) and the **film festival** in November, with a particular focus on short films (http://corkfilmfest.org). There's also an international **choral festival** in late April or early May (http://corkchoral.ie), the Cork **LGBTQ Pride** festival in July/August (http://corkpride.com) and **an early-music festival** in October, shared between the city and East Cork (http://eastcorkearlymusic.ie). The biggest festival in County Cork is held in September and revolves around food; **A Taste of West Cork** (http://tastecork.ie) is hosted by a number of towns, and you'll find food markets, cookery demonstrations, tastings and special events in Skibbereen, Clonakilty, Bantry and elsewhere.

SHOPPING

English Market Accessed either from Princes St or Grand Parade, http://corkcity.ie/en/englishmarket. A Victorian covered market with the city's best fishmongers, greengrocers and butchers – stocking the local delicacies of tripe and *drisheen*, a type of black pudding – and all manner of pungent specialist stalls where you could build a great picnic (perhaps for eating in the small Bishop Lucey Park, on the other side of Grand Parade): cheeses, cold meats and smoked fish, olives, salads and deli goods, bread, cakes, and even wine and chocolates. Closed Sun.

Mother Jones Flea market York St, near the corner of MacCurtain St, 085 175 1554. Fun weekend market purveying vintage clothes, antiques, books, and more.

Plugd Records 3 Cornmarket St, http://plugdrecords.com. This legendary record store not only has a prodigious stock of vinyl, but also sells publications and limited prints, and hosts in-store gigs.

DIRECTORY

Gaelic football and hurling Cork is one of the few counties that's strong on both Gaelic games, and Páirc Uí Chaoimh, 2km east of the centre off Centre Park Rd, is one of the country's major stadiums (though you might have more luck getting tickets for the smaller Pairc Ui Rinn, also 2km east, but on Boreenmanna Rd); for fixtures, consult http://gaacork.ie or *The Irish Examiner*.

Pharmacy Phelan's Late Night Pharmacy, 9 Patrick St, 021 427 2511.

Police The main police station is on Anglesea St, 021 452 2000.

East Cork

East Cork occupies a blind spot in the eyes of many visitors, their focus set on the more spectacular coastline to the west, but several interesting places are worth considering, all of them served by public transport. A suburban train service makes possible an excellent, varied day-trip across the Lee estuary to **Fota Island**, with its sensitively restored Neoclassical hunting lodge and wildlife park, and on to the attractive harbour town of **Cobh** on Great Island. Further east lies **Midleton**, the traditional home of Jameson whiskey and a culinary hub. In an expansive setting at the mouth of the River Blackwater, the historic, easy-going resort of **Youghal**, some 40km east of Cork, marks the border with County Waterford.

Fota House, Arboretum & Gardens

Carrigtwohill, Fota Island • **House** charge • **Victorian Gardens** free; guided tours (noon) €5 • **Arboretum** Free • Car parking €3 • http://fotahouse.com

If you travel from the mainland by road, you're hardly aware that **Fota** is an island in Cork Harbour. Its main attraction is **Fota House, Arboretum & Gardens**, built in the 1740s as a hunting lodge for the Barry family, whose main seat had by then moved from nearby Barryscourt Castle to Castlelyons near Fermoy. In the early nineteenth century, the house was substantially redeveloped and extended in elegant Neoclassical style, and now lies a ten-minute walk from Fota train station. Excellent guided tours reveal plenty of telling details, with the highlights being the **entrance hall**, a beautifully symmetrical space divided by striking ochre columns of *scagliola* (imitation marble), and the ceiling of the **drawing room**, with its plasterwork doves, musical instruments, hunting implements and delicately painted cherubs and floral motifs. The tour also goes below stairs to the **servants' quarters**, which include an impressive octagonal game-larder and such features as gaps at the top of the windows of the butler's servery – added so that food smells would tantalize the poor servants rather than the house guests. For visitors, there's a nice little café in the long gallery and billiard room, plus it's well worth touring the **gardens** at the rear of the house where the Victorian "Frameyard" – a complex of glasshouses – has been restored to its former glory.

Much of the estate's formal gardens and its internationally significant **arboretum**, laid out in the mid-nineteenth century, are under the care of the Office of Public Works, with free access. At its best in April and May, the arboretum hosts a wide range of exotic trees and shrubs, with many rare examples, including some magnificent Lebanese cedars, a Victorian fernery and a lush, almost tropical, lake.

Fota Wildlife Park

Carrigtwohill, Fota Island • Daily from 9.30am with seasonal variations • charge • http://fotawildlife.ie
Set within a 100-acre site on scenic Fota Island in the heart if Cork harbour, **Fota Wildlife Park** makes for the ideal family day out. The park is especially renowned for its highly successful conservation and breeding programmes, notably cheetahs, oryx, lechwe (antelope) and European bison. One of the park's most popular enclosures is the Asian sanctuary, home to Asian lions, Sumatran tigers and Indian rhinos, and elsewhere there's a tropical house, featuring snakes, lizards and turtles, while events include the daily cheetah run and other animal feeding times, as well as weekend wildlife talks.

Cobh

On the southern coast of Great Island, with extensive views of Cork Harbour, **COBH** (pronounced "cove") makes a great escape from the city on a fine day. This historic and unpretentious resort, clinging onto a steep, south-facing slope, sports a stony beach, a promenade with a bandstand and gaily painted rows of Victorian hotels and houses. Ireland's – and possibly the world's – first **yacht club** was founded in Cobh in 1720 and although the Italianate building now houses the Sirius Arts Centre (http://siriusartscentre.ie), the port's cruise-liner tradition continues. Each year, dozens of huge cruise ships dock at this fine natural harbour, said to be the second-largest in the world (by navigable area) after Sydney; Cobh was a port of call for the *Sirius*, the first steamship to cross the Atlantic, in 1838, and for the *Titanic* on her disastrous maiden voyage in 1912, while many of the victims of the sinking of the *Lusitania* in 1915 (see page 245) were buried in the Old Church Cemetery, 2km north of Cobh. The port was also a major supply depot during the American and Napoleonic wars, and became Ireland's main point of emigration after the Great Famine.

Cobh Heritage Centre: the Queenstown Story

Seafront • charge; Heritage Island • http://cobhheritage.com
Cobh's long and often tragic seafaring history is vividly detailed at the **Queenstown Story**, a multimedia heritage centre (which also offers a genealogical service) with a pleasant café in the former Victorian train station on the seafront (the town was renamed Queenstown after a visit by Queen Victoria in 1849, but its old name was restored after Independence).

The Titanic Experience

White Star Line Building, 20 Casement Square • charge • http://titanicexperiencecobh.ie

Cobh was the last port of call for the *Titanic*, with the final 123 passengers boarding here on April 11, 1912. The White Star Line ticket office where they assembled, backed by its now-ruinous wooden pier, has been turned into a visitor attraction, a short way east of the tourist office along the seafront. Amid re-creations of third- and first-class cabins, it's revealed that while first had a heated swimming pool, the seven hundred third-class passengers had to share two baths. There are some interesting audiovisuals, including footage of the wreck, discovered in 1985, passenger stories and eyewitness accounts, as well as games and interactive quizzes. An excellent audio guide helps makes sense of it all.

Spike Island

Cork Harbour, reached from Kennedy Pier • Accessible only by ferry Feb, March & Nov Sat, Sun & school hols; April–Sept daily, sailing times vary, see website • charge, includes ferry and 1hr guided tour • http://spikeislandcork.ie

At various points in history, **Spike Island** has been a monastery, a fortress, a home and the largest prison in the British Isles – earning it the rather predictable moniker "Ireland's Alcatraz". Your visit lasts around three and a half hours and includes a guided tour of the parade ground, buildings and bastions of star-shaped Fort Mitchel, prison cells (the modern-day prison only closed in 2004) and the 1950s punishment block; you are then free to wander the island, which has some well-marked out trails through open grassland and forest, not to mention some surprisingly pretty beaches. There's also a café here.

Cobh Museum

Scots Church, High Rd • charge • http://cobhmuseum.com

If your appetite for salty tales and memorabilia hasn't been sated, get along to the **Cobh Museum**, housed in a nineteenth-century Presbyterian church on the west side of the town centre, on the hillside above the railway station. The interior is crowded with engaging exhibits, much of which is focused on the sinking of Lusitania and Cobh's Naval history.

St Colman's Cathedral

5 Cathedral Terrace • Donation welcome • http://cobhcathedralparish.ie

Looming above the town is the massive neo-Gothic **St Colman's Cathedral**, which was consecrated in 1919 and has a 49-bell carillon – the largest in Europe. The views from up here are worth the steep walk and in summer (May–Sept Sun 4.30pm) you can enjoy carillon recitals (viewed from inside the cathedral on closed-circuit television – there's no public access to the bell tower).

ARRIVAL AND DEPARTURE   COBH

By train The station is towards the western end of the seafront, serving frequent trains from/to Cork (Mon–Sat at least hourly, 11 on Sun; 25min).

By ferry Cross River Ferries run between Glenbrook near Passage West, on the mainland southeast of Cork city, and Carrigaloe, a few kilometres north of Cobh on Great Island

---

COBH TOURS AND WATERSPORTS

Although the Royal Cork Yacht Club has moved across the harbour to Crosshaven, messing about in **boats** is still a strong feature of life in the town. Sail Cork, which is based 5km out at East Ferry Marina at the eastern end of Great Island (http://sailcork.com), runs **sailing and kayaking courses**, and there's a people's regatta in August. Contact Cork Harbour Boat Hire (http://corkharbourboathire.com; boat from €65/hr) if you fancy being skipper for an hour or two (though there's always a safety boat to guide you). For landlubbers, the engaging and enterprising Michael Martin (http://titanic.ie) organizes hour-long *Titanic*-themed **walking tours**, starting from the *Commodore Hotel* (daily 11am, plus 2pm in summer; charge; Oct–March pre-booking essential); the tour is also dog and wheelchair-friendly.

(daily 6.30am–9.30pm, every 10min or so; 5min; car €8 single, €10 return; pedestrian/cyclist €2 single, €3 return; http://crossriverferries.ie).

GETTING AROUND AND INFORMATION

Car rental Great Island (see page 236) has a car rental base at Rushbrooke, just north of Cobh, and meets disembarking passengers at the cruise-ship terminal.

Tourist office Market House, Casement Sq (Mon–Fri 9am–5pm, Sat 10am–4pm, Sun 10am–2pm; http://visitcobh.com).

ACCOMMODATION

Bella Vista Spy Hill, http://bellavistahotel.ie. The large en-suite rooms at this hotel have more character than the modern exterior might suggest, and the views across the cathedral and harbour are what's important here (not to mention the friendly staff); there are six categories including family rooms. Self-catering suites also available. Rooms €€, suites €€€

Waters Edge Yacht Club Quay, http://watersedgehotel.ie. Between the heritage centre and Sirius Arts Centre stands this tastefully decorated hotel, where many of the bright, spacious bedrooms – as well as the fine restaurant – have seafront verandas. The convivial *Jacob's Ladder* bar is a lovely spot for a sundowner overlooking the water. €€€

EATING AND DRINKING

Rob Roy Pearse Square, 021 481 1055. This friendly locals' pub with tables out on the square offers craft beers and a clever sampler tray of three stouts (Guinness up against the local Murphy's and Beamish). There are traditional sessions on Thurs and early evening Sun, and live music, usually traditional or blues, on Sat.

Sliced 14 Parnell Place, http://sliced.ie. Sprightly restaurant doling out cracking wood-fired, thin crust pizzas in addition to pasta, hot baps and pittas (hot cajun, Clonakilty black pudding), salads and desserts. €€

Midleton

The busy market town of **MIDLETON** is arrayed round a broad, lively main street, which is bypassed to the south by the N25, so makes a pleasant stopover, just 18km east of Cork (plenty of commuters make use of the local train line). Midleton has created a strong culinary reputation for itself and in early September hosts **fEast Cork** (http://feastcork.com), which celebrates the region's wonderfully diverse produce.

The Jameson Experience

Off the south end of Main St • charge; Heritage Island • http://jamesonwhiskey.com • Shuttle bus from St Patrick's Quay, Cork; call for details

The town's main visitor activity is **The Jameson Experience** at the **Old Distillery**. Whiskey is no longer made in this partly eighteenth-century distillery, but guided tours take you around the carefully restored machinery – including the largest pot still in the world, with a capacity of 32,000 gallons – in the atmospheric old buildings, and – on the basic 75-minute tour at least – you'll get to taste three samples of the "water of life" (*uisce beatha*).

ARRIVAL AND DEPARTURE   MIDLETON

By train Cork (Mon–Sat at least hourly, 9 on Sun; 25min).

By bus Cork (frequent; 30min), Youghal (hourly; 30min).

ACCOMMODATION

An Stór Townhouse Drury's Lane (IHH), http://anstortownhouse.com. In a converted wool store off the east side of Main St, this comfortable, welcoming town house has twin, double, triple and quad rooms, as well as a self-catering kitchen/dining room and plenty of local information at hand. Continental breakfast included. €€–€€€

★ **Ballymaloe House** Around 10km southeast of Midleton, off the R629 Cloyne–Ballycotton road, http://ballymaloe.ie. Attached to the famous restaurant (see below), accommodation in this delightful, vine-covered, originally fifteenth-century manor house and adjacent courtyard mixes country-house style with contemporary art; tea and cake upon arrival is a nice touch. Otherwise, there are numerous walks to be had around the extensive grounds, farm and the garden of Ballymaloe's nearby cookery school, while guided tours are also offered to guests, among them a biodiversity tour and a sculpture tour. Attached to the house is a seventeenth-century grain store that's been converted into a venue for music, theatre and events such as the three-day Festival of Food in mid-May. €€€€

Castlemartyr Resort 10km east of Midleton on the N25, http://castlemartyrresort.ie. Opulent hotel – think electronic curtains and traditional afternoon teas – in an eighteenth-century manor house, flanked by a striking modern extension and the ruins of the original medieval castle that was once owned by Sir Walter Raleigh. There's a luxurious spa, a staggering half a dozen dining options including the two Michelin-starred *Terre* restaurant in the Manor House and the informal *Hunted Hog* pub. Bikes are available for guests to explore the 200-acre estate, which was landscaped by Capability Brown and today encompasses an eighteen-hole golf course. €€€

EATING AND DRINKING

Midleton hosts one of the country's best **farmers' markets** (Sat 9am–1pm), offering everything from cheese, smoked fish and meats to breads, cakes and chocolate.

★**Ballymaloe House** Around 10km southeast of Midleton, off the R629 Cloyne–Ballycotton road, http://ballymaloe.ie. This stalwart on Ireland's fine dining scene offers exceptional modern dishes using local ingredients, such as housemade fettuccine with basil pesto, and Cloyne beef cheek ragout with Garryhinch mushrooms and roast parsnips, while you choose your dessert from a groaning trolley. Five-course set dinner menu €100, three-course Sunday lunch €65. Closed Jan. €€€€

Black Barrel 75 Main St, http://theblackbarrel.ie. Don't be fooled by the traditional pub frontage here – it's more restaurant than bar, decorated with colourful modern paintings, where you can choose between light dishes such as delicious chicken-liver pâté on toast and fancier meals like organic wild mushroom rigatoni. Closed Sun & Mon. €€€

★**Farmgate Restaurant & Store** Coolbawn, off the west side of Main St, http://farmgate.ie. Big sister to *Farmgate Café* (see page 237) in Cork, a bustling café-restaurant where they prepare stunningly curated dishes like braised lamb shank with spring onion champ and rosemary lamb jus. Their own bakery and deli out front sells fresh artisanal produce. €€€

JJ Coppinger 55 Main St, http://jjcoppingers.ie. Main Street's most stylish bar is all exposed brick and downlighting. They stock over a hundred whiskeys and get packed out on live music nights (Thurs, Sat & Sun).

Youghal

YOUGHAL (pronounced "yawl") enjoys a lush, picturesque setting on the west bank of the River Blackwater's estuary, the border with County Waterford. It was one of Ireland's leading ports in the medieval era, with a scattering of ancient buildings to show for it – as well as a **historical festival** in late September (http://youghalcelebrateshistory.com), when field trips, concerts and other entertainments accompany an international historical conference. It later became a centre for the carpet industry, but today is popular with holidaying Irish families, who take their leisure on the long sandy **beach** to the southwest.

Main Street

Youghal's long, gently curving **Main Street** is lined with tall, colourfully painted nineteenth-century buildings, interspersed with a few more historic structures. Bridging the south end of the street, the most obvious of these is the Georgian **clock tower**, which stands on the site of a medieval gate. It's a huge but well-proportioned sandstone affair that once served as a prison; tours (April–Oct Thurs–Sat 11am–4pm; charge; http://livingyoughal.ie) relay the building's history in entertaining fashion, but better still are the 360-degree views of Youghal Bay from the top of the tower.

Further north on Main Street, you'll find the **Red House**, a typically steep-roofed Dutch-style home built around 1710, and, opposite, a restored tower house, **Tynte's Castle**, from the fifteenth century.

Collegiate Church of St Mary's
Church St • http://youghal.cloyne.anglican.org

Turning left off Main Street, at the seventeenth-century almshouses near the Red House, will bring you to Youghal's main historic site, the Anglican **Collegiate Church of St Mary's**. On the site of the fifth-century monastic settlement of St Declan of Ardmore, it's one of the oldest functioning churches in Ireland, built in about 1250. On its north side stands an unusual, fortified bell tower, dating probably from the fifteenth century, while inside, the squat Gothic nave boasts impressive oak roof trusses.

Almost bursting out of the south transept, an extravagant, multicoloured monument commemorates Richard Boyle, the seventeenth-century Earl of Cork who did much to develop Youghal, along with his two wives and children, including the chemist Robert. Beyond the church lie the pretty gardens of The College (founded 1464) and the well-preserved thirteenth-century **landward town walls**, which provide great views of the bay.

ARRIVAL AND DEPARTURE   YOUGHAL

By bus Buses from Cork Cork (hourly; 50min) and Midleton (hourly; 25min) stop at the north end of Main St.

INFORMATION AND TOURS

Tourist information The tourist office and the attached heritage centre, which recounts the port's history since the ninth century, are on Market Square, between Main St and the harbour, near the clock tower (Mon–Fri 9am–5pm, Sat 10am–4pm, Sun 10am–2pm; heritage centre free; http://youghal.ie).

Boat tours In summer, Blackwater Cruises (http://blackwatercruises.com) runs 1hr 30min trips (€25) up the beautiful Blackwater River, lined with castles, country houses and ruined abbeys, from the jetty near the tourist office.

Walking tours Tours of the town depart from the tourist office (July & Aug Mon–Fri 11am & 3pm; at other times, book through the tourist office; 1hr 30min; €10).

ACCOMMODATION

As well as the **accommodation** below, there are also dozens of B&Bs, many of them out on the Cork road near the beach.

★ **Aherne's** 163 North Main St, http://ahernes.net. Superb small hotel in the centre of town, with spacious bedrooms around a courtyard; the rooms, with facilities for families and wheelchair users, are a little dated, but tastefully decorated with antique furniture, and breakfasts are great. €€

Avonmore House South Abbey, http://avonmorehouse.com. Bright, colourful, en-suite rooms – some with partial sea views – in an elegant, centrally located Georgian mansion, a short way south of the tourist office. Both continental and cooked breakfasts are available but do cost extra. €€

Clonvilla Clonpriest, around 7km southwest of town near the beach, on the R633 towards Ballymacoda, about 4km off the N25, http://clonvillayoughal.weebly.com. This simple but pleasant and well-kept caravan and camping park offers a campers' kitchen, laundry facilities and a playground. Closed Nov to mid-March. Camping €

Roseville New Catherine St, http://rosevilleyoughal.com. Located right in the town centre, north from the tourist office, this is an attractive, detached, period house enclosed within a large walled garden with just two rooms: the Garden Room and the balconied Garden Suite, the latter only slightly more expensive. Closed mid-Dec to mid-Jan. €€€

EATING AND DRINKING

★ **Aherne's** 163 North Main St, http://ahernes.net. The excellent restaurant here uses local, seasonal ingredients wherever possible but is known especially for its fresh seafood such as seared Kilmore scallop with beetroot and tomato salsa, and chargrilled monkfish with a smoked salmon risotto and basil pesto; three-course menu €60, and a tasting menu for €90. You can also choose from the all-day menu, including sandwiches, by the open fire in the very congenial bar. Closed Sun & Mon. €€€€

Moby Dick's Market Square, opposite the tourist office, 024 92756. One for movie buffs: for the filming of *Moby Dick* with Gregory Peck in 1954, John Huston transformed Youghal's waterfront into New Bedford, Massachusetts, and the pub where he planned each day's filming is now hung with signed photos of the shoot.

The Nook (Treacy's) 20 North Main St, by the turn-off for

St Mary's Church, http://findthenook.ie. Relaxing and cosy, traditional, hundred-year-old pub with a spruce black-and-white café at the front and a beer garden at the back, is very popular for its varied lunches (Mon–Fri). Traditional music Wed, Thurs & Fri in summer.

Priory Coffee 56 North Main St, , http://priorycoffee.com. A branch of the well regarded, Cork-based coffee chain. As well as gourmet coffee, there are pastries, nutri bites, toasties and salad boxes to choose from.

★ **Sage** North Main St, just north of the clock tower, 024 85844. Comfort food café-restaurant, where everything is home-made and locally sourced whenever possible. There are soups, salads, sandwiches and quiches, or you could round things off with a fantastic rhubarb tart, among a mouthwatering display of cakes and desserts. Closed Sun.

ENTERTAINMENT

Comhaltas Brú na Sí, Blackwater Heights, on the west side of town, http://comhaltas.ie. In summer, the local branch of this

non-profit organization for the promotion of Irish traditional music puts on a stage show of song, dance and storytelling.

Kinsale and around

KINSALE, 25km south of Cork city and the first (or last) stop on the Wild Atlantic Way (see page 26), enjoys a glorious setting at the head of a sheltered harbour around the mouth of the Bandon River. Two imposing **forts** and a fine **tower-house** remain as evidence of its former importance as a trading port, and Kinsale has built on its cosmopolitan links to become the **culinary capital** of the southwest. Add in plenty of opportunities for watersports on the fine local beaches at **Garrettstown** and **Garrylucas**, and a number of congenial pubs, and you have a very appealing, upscale resort town.

Brief history

St Multose founded a monastery at Kinsale in the sixth century, and by the tenth the Vikings had established a trading post. After the Anglo-Normans walled the town in the thirteenth century, it really began to take off, flourishing on trade, fishing and shipbuilding in its excellent deep harbour, which became an important rendezvous and provisioning point for the British Navy. The **Battle of Kinsale** in 1601 was a major turning point in Irish history, leading to the "Flight of the Earls" to the Continent six years later which saw the end of the old Gaelic aristocracy: Philip III of Spain had sent forces to Kinsale to support the Irish chieftains, but communications were poor and Chief Hugh O'Neill, more accustomed to guerrilla warfare, was defeated by Elizabeth I's army in a pitched battle.

In 1689 **James II** landed here in his attempt to claim back the throne, only to flee ignominiously from this same port a year later, after defeat at the Battle of the Boyne. His supporters fought on, however, burning the town and holing up in James Fort and Charles Fort. After a series of decisive attacks by the Duke of Marlborough, they surrendered on favourable terms and were allowed to go to Limerick for the final battle under Patrick Sarsfield (see page 303).

During World War I, in May 1915, a German submarine torpedoed the passenger liner *Lusitania* off the Old Head of Kinsale, as it was sailing from New York to England. Twelve hundred of the passengers and crew were lost, and the sinking was a major factor in the USA's eventual entry into the war.

7

KINSALE

ACCOMMODATION	
Blindgate House	6
Dempsey's Hostel	1
Garrettstown House Holiday Park	5
Old Bank House	2
Pier House	4
The White House	3

● EATING	
Bastion	3
Bulman	1
Dino's	2
Fishy Fishy	5
Max's	4

■ DRINKING AND NIGHTLIFE	
The Greyhound	3
Jim Edward's	4
The Spaniard	1
Tap Tavern	5
The White House	2

> ### KINSALE FESTIVALS
>
> Kinsale hosts a varied and prestigious weekend **arts festival** in July (http://kinsaleartsweekend. com); a weekend **gourmet festival** in mid-October (http://kinsalegoodfoodcircle.ie); and a **fringe jazz festival** to coincide with the main jazz festival in Cork over the bank holiday weekend in late October.

Kinsale Museum

Market Place • charge • 021 477 7930

The **Kinsale Museum** is immediately recognizable in the warren of lanes at the centre of town by its Dutch-style triple gables, which were added in 1706 to the market house of 1600. Upstairs, the courtroom where the inquest into the loss of the *Lusitania* took place has been left partly as it was, augmented, poignantly, by an almost pristine deckchair from the wreck, as well as a medal produced in Germany to celebrate the sinking. Otherwise, the museum is a dusty collection of tools, maps and any old rope, dotted with a few curiosities such as the shoes of the eight-foot three-inch Kinsale Giant, who made a fortune on the English stage in the eighteenth century as a novelty act.

Desmond Castle

Cork St • currently closed • charge; Heritage Card • http://heritageireland.ie

A fine example of an urban tower house, **Desmond Castle** was built around 1500 as a town residence and customs house by the Earl of Desmond, who had recently been given control of the wine trade from France, Spain and Portugal to Bristol by King Henry VII. The architectural highlight is the facade, pierced by ogival windows, including unusual corner pairs on the first floor, and stamped with the Desmond coat of arms surmounted by Henry VII's royal standard. Interesting displays inside trace the building's chequered, often grim history – including stints as a jail and workhouse – as well as local connections with the global wine trade. Many of the "Wild Geese" – Irishmen who fled the country in the sixteenth to eighteenth centuries, especially after the Battle of Kinsale and the Battle of the Boyne – went on to have successful second careers in viticulture, notably Richard Hennessy of Cork who settled in Cognac in the 1740s, and the Lynches of Galway, producers of the famous claret, Château Lynch-Bages. Note, though, that the castle is currently closed pending extensive renovation works and is not expected to reopen until 2025.

James Fort

2km southwest of Kinsale, cross the bridge over the River Bandon, turn left and continue for another 1km • Open access

On the west side of the harbour, Kinsale spreads south for a couple of kilometres to the broad mouth of the Bandon River. On a long spit of land between the river and the outer harbour, **James Fort** is a great place for a picnic, with fine views that stretch from the town around to the open sea. Built in 1602–4 on the site of a walled fortification that was easily captured by the English from the Spanish forces at the Battle of Kinsale, it's a five-sided fort whose walls are now fetchingly overgrown with ferns and brambles. The new fort, however, proved equally vulnerable when, in 1649, a well-placed gun on the higher ground to the west led to its surrender to the Cromwellians, and in the 1680s, the building of Charles Fort finally rendered James Fort obsolete. On the southeast-facing side of the narrow peninsula, there's a small and pleasant sandy **beach** (signposted).

Charles Fort

3km southeast of Kinsale, beyond the village of Summercove • closed for a week over Christmas • charge; Heritage Card • http://heritageireland.ie

Kinsale's most compelling sight, the formidable **Charles Fort**, lies on the east side of the harbour. On a fine day, the best way to get there is to **walk**, skirting round Scilly village and then following the lower, shoreline road, with refreshment available at *The Spaniard* and *The Bulman* (see page 248). It's also possible to extend the walk along the scrub-covered slopes out to the point at the end of the outer harbour (2hr return from the fort at an easy pace).

Begun in 1678, Charles Fort stands on the site of Anglo-Norman Ringcurran Castle, which had been destroyed on Cromwell's orders in 1656. **Sir William Robinson**, architect of the Royal Hospital, Kilmainham (see page 89), adapted the classic, star-shaped design of the great French military engineer Vauban, but his advice to build extra fortifications at the top of the hill was not followed – though the fort was almost impregnable from the sea, the Duke of Marlborough was easily able to unseat the Jacobites by attacking on land in 1690. Most of the buildings on the twelve-acre site were damaged during the Irish Civil War in 1922, but the eerie roofless shells are substantial enough to give a ready impression of what life in the fort must have been like for its garrison of four hundred, and you can flesh out the picture by sampling the fascinating displays and audiovisuals in the rebuilt Barracks Stores.

7

ARRIVAL AND INFORMATION

KINSALE AND AROUND

By bus Buses stop on Pier Rd, right at the heart of Kinsale; there's a direct bus hourly from Cork (50min), via Cork Airport (see page 235).

Tourist information The friendly, well-informed tourist

office, which has plenty of useful free literature on the town, is on Pier Rd (Jan–May, Nov & Dec Tues–Sat 9.15am–5pm, closing for lunch; June–Oct daily 9am–5pm; http://kinsale. ie).

TOURS AND ACTIVITIES

Bike rental Mylie Murphy, 8 Pearse St (021 477 2703, emyliemurphyshop@hotmail.com). From €15/day.

Cruises The tourist office has the times of cruises past the two forts to the outer harbour and the Bandon River on the *Spirit of Kinsale* (roughly March–Oct; €15; http:// kinsaleharbourcruises.com).

Horseriding Kinsale Equestrian Centre, 2km northwest of the centre off the Bandon road (http://kinsale-equestrian. ie), offers lessons at the centre and trekking along the Bandon River.

Walking tours From the tourist office, Dermot Ryan (daily 10.30am; 1hr; €5; http://kinsaleheritage.com) and Don and Barry (March–Oct daily 11.15am, plus 9.15am May–Sept;

1hr; €8; http://historicstrollkinsale.com) run engaging historical walking tours, while evening ghost tours meet at the *Tap Tavern* on Guardwell (April–Sept Sun–Fri 9pm; 1hr; €10; 087 948 0910).

Watersports Oysterhaven Activity Centre (http://oyster haven.com), 5km east of Kinsale on Oysterhaven Bay, has sailing, windsurfing and kayaking, while Ocean Addicts (http://oceanaddicts.ie) does diving and snorkelling. At long, sandy Garrettstown Beach, 12km southwest of town, H2O (http://h2oseakayaking.com) offers half-day and three-day sea kayaking trips, while Kinsale Surf Adventures (http:// kinsalesurfschool.com) and GTown Surf School (http:// surfgtown.com) offer surfing and stand-up paddleboarding.

ACCOMMODATION

SEE MAP PAGE 245

There are dozens of **B&Bs** and a particularly good selection of upmarket **guesthouses** in Kinsale, as well as a **hostel**. Booking is advisable in high summer and during festivals.

KINSALE

Blindgate House Blindgate, http://blindgatehouse.com. Bright, stylish and welcoming guesthouse a 5min walk west of the town centre up the hill. Decorated with natural fabrics and contemporary furniture, and offering great breakfasts and a quiet garden to relax in. Closed Dec–March. €€€

Dempsey's Hostel Eastern Rd, http://dempseyhostel.com (IHH). Basic hostel with a pleasant conservatory and garden on the main Cork road, about 1km from the centre; basic camping facilities. Dorms €, doubles €€

Old Bank House 11 Pearse St, http://oldbankhousekinsale. com. Very comfortable and luxurious Georgian town house in a central location, with seventeen handsomely furnished rooms (including triples), many of which overlook the harbour. Breakfast is a first-class affair and they've also got a terrific Indian pop-up restaurant. €€€

★ **Pier House** Pier Rd, http://pierhousekinsale.com. A charming haven in a pretty garden right in the centre of town, with a bright, contemporary-rustic look enlivened with modern art. Most of the freshly decorated rooms have sleigh beds and terraces or balconies, some with views of the harbour, and breakfast includes such delights as crêpes with fresh fruit. Closed Dec–Jan. €€€

The White House Pearse St, http://whitehouse-kinsale.ie.

Not the place if you're after peace and quiet, but if you want to be in the heart of the action above a fantastic pub, this stylish guesthouse with large en-suite rooms is great choice. €€

AROUND KINSALE
Garrettstown House Holiday Park 10km southwest of Kinsale, beyond Ballinspittle, http://garrettstownhouse. com. Campsite on the extensive grounds of the ruined eighteenth-century *Garrettstown House*, 1km from the beach, with a shop, laundry snooker lounge for adults, and lots of activities for children such as a playground and tennis. Closed mid-Sept to April. €

EATING
SEE MAP PAGE 245

There's a great **farmers' market** on Wednesday (9am–2.30pm) on Market Quay (Short Quay), with cheeses, olives, salads, breads, crafts and live acoustic music.

★ **Bastion** Cnr of Market and Main St, http://bastion kinsale.com. This outstanding Michelin-starred bistro stands apart even in foodie Kinsale. Only the best local seafood and land-based produce makes it onto the Discovery and Bastion tasting menus (€80/€150), such as cured langoustine with Pernod apple, buttermilk and horseradish, and Skeaghanore duck with plum, fennel and truffle. Closed Mon–Wed. €€€€

Bulman Summercove, 2km out towards Charles Fort on the east side of the harbour, http://thebulman.ie. This attractive restaurant, adorned with nauticalia and warmed by open fires, dishes up good food such as pan-seared monkfish, potato champ and mussel veloute, and homemade honeycomb cheesecake. Expect high quality live music on Sunday evenings. €€€

Dino's Pier Rd, 021 477 4561. Waterfront chippy of good repute, whose menu stretches to chowder, fish cakes, wine and craft beers, with plenty of comfy tables inside and a few outside if you want to sit down and eat; it's much cheaper to take away though. €

★ **Fishy Fishy** Crowleys Quay, Pier Rd, http://fishyfishy.ie. Superb seafood restaurant with very attractive tables on a quiet, leafy terrace in the summer, dishing up excellent daily specials such as scallops and Rosscarbery black pudding, as well as the trusty "Fishy Fish Pie". Reservations for dinner only. €€€

Max's 48 Main St, http://maxs.ie. Cosy, upmarket, Irish/ French spot with a small conservatory, boasting a superb seafood menu (sautéed filet of hake with creamed Jerusalem artichokes), complemented by a strong selection of meaty dishes like pan-fried lamb cutlet, black garlic jus and butternut squash. Closed Thurs & Sun. €€€€

DRINKING AND NIGHTLIFE
SEE MAP PAGE 245

The town boasts a wide array of genial **pubs**, many of which also serve good food. Pick up a copy of the free *Kinsale Advertiser* (http://kinsaleadvertiser.com) at the tourist office, or go to their website to check out what's on around town each week.

The Greyhound 6 Market Square, 021 477 2889. Popular, cosy, seventeenth-century pub with quaint wooden partitions and seats outside on the pedestrianized alley.

★ **Jim Edward's** Market Quay, http://jimedwardskinsale. com. Cosy, welcoming, central pub with an extensive choice of craft beers, wine by the glass and cocktails. There's a pleasant evening-time restaurant; the same menu of excellent, simple, fresh seafood, sourced from named local suppliers, is served in both.

The Spaniard 1km from the centre around the east side of the harbour, in the suburb of Scilly, http://thespaniard.ie. Named after the plucky leader of the Spanish at the Battle of Kinsale, a cosy flagstoned pub that offers good food, either at the bar or in the restaurant, and regular traditional music, usually Wed.

Tap Tavern Guardwell, 021 477 3231. Simple, sociable inn hung with bric-a-brac, good for a quiet pint most nights, with a nice beer garden.

The White House Pearse St, http://whitehouse-kinsale. ie. This family-friendly pub is smartly decorated and offers reasonably priced, good-quality bar food, plus frequent live music, usually traditional or ballads.

Clonakilty and around

CLONAKILTY is an appealing if undramatic service town, whose main draw is the **beach**, 4km to the south, on **Inchydoney Island**, which is now locked to the mainland by two causeway roads that enclose reclaimed pasturage. This gorgeous expanse of pristine white sand is split in two by Virgin Mary's Point, where the road ends, and flanked by headlands of rolling green fields. Clonakilty also offers plenty of traditional music in the pubs, but is most famous as the home of award-winning **black puddings** – especially from Twomey's the butcher on the main street – and as the birthplace of Republican leader **Michael Collins**. In September, the **international guitar festival** (http://clonguitarfest.com) is hosted at varied venues across town, and includes workshops and live music on the streets.

West Cork Model Railway Village

On the southeast edge of town off the Inchydoney road • **Railway Village** charge • **Road train** Usually June–Sept daily; Oct–May Sat & Sun • charge includes entry to model village • http://modelvillage.ie

Both kids and adults will enjoy the **West Cork Model Railway Village**, which replicates the 1940s West Cork Railway and the towns it served in great detail at 1:24 scale. There are also mini-diggers, remote-controlled boats which kids can manoeuvre around a miniature Kinsale harbour, and a quirky cafeteria serving tea and cakes, housed in a full-size 1940s train carriage outside. Departing from here, a "road train" makes a tour of Clonakilty several times daily.

West Cork Regional Museum

The west end of Clonakilty's main street (here Western Road) • Summer Tues–Sat 11am–4pm; staffed by volunteers, so hours liable to change • Donation requested • 023 883 3115

If poor weather rules out any outdoor exploration, you could do worse than holing up in the **West Cork Regional Museum**, which covers the area's contribution to the War of Independence and Clonakilty's once-prosperous linen industry, and displays a host of agricultural implements.

7

Michael Collins Centre

5km northeast of Clonakilty, off the R600 towards Timoleague • charge • http://michaelcollinscentre.com

The eclectic but highly recommended **Michael Collins Centre** offers engaging presentations in a theatre setting presented by Tim Crowley, a distant relative of Michael Collins. Visitors are then given a guided tour of the museum's collection, including some of Collins' personal effects and other items from the revolutionary period. Outdoor exhibits include life-size reconstructions of a firing squad execution yard and the Beál na Blá ambush site, where Collins died in 1922. If you want to explore further, you can book Tim for tours of nearby sites associated with Collins and the War of Independence, taking in the actual Beal na Bláth ambush site and Collins' birthplace, incinerated in 1921 by the Black and Tans.

Drombeg

Accessible via the R597 Rosscarbery–Glandore road, signposted after 5km • No public transport

About 17km west of Clonakilty lies one of the area's few compelling historical sites, the Bronze Age **Drombeg stone circle**. Looking out over pretty cattle pastures with the Atlantic in the distance, these seventeen well-preserved stones are associated with the winter solstice, when the sun sets on the southwest horizon at a point aligned with the lowest, axial, stone (known as the "Druid's Altar") and the two tallest portal stones. Close by in the same field sits one of the best examples of a *fulacht fiadh*, a ritual cooking site (literally "deer roast"), in Ireland. It consists of a 1.5m-long stone-lined trough for water, into which red-hot stones from the adjacent hearth would have been rolled.

Glandore

A popular yachting haven 20km west of Clonakilty, **GLANDORE** enjoys a particularly beautiful, elevated position, overlooking the turquoise waters of a deep inlet and the village of Union Hall opposite, and surrounded by lush, tree-carpeted slopes.

ARRIVAL AND INFORMATION   CLONAKILTY AND AROUND

By bus Buses stop either on Pearse St – part of the town's long, one-way (westward) high street, which to the east becomes Ashe St and then Wolfe Tone St, to the west Western Rd – or on the short bypass, just south of Wolfe Tone St.

Tourist information The helpful tourist office at 25 Ashe St (Tues–Sat 9am–5pm; http://clonakilty.ie) stocks a free

What's On guide, which includes local road-bowling fixtures (see page 535).

Surfing Inchydoney Surf School (http://inchydoney surfschool.com).

ACCOMMODATION

CLONAKILTY
An Súgán 41 Wolfe Tone St, http://ansugan.com. Lovely guesthouse in a quiet Georgian town house behind the seafood bar and restaurant (see below) with rooms (including cosy doubles) decorated in a tasteful contemporary style with comfortable beds and great breakfasts that use local produce wherever possible. €€

Bay View Old Timoleague Rd, http://bayviewclonakilty. com. Flower-bedecked, brightly decorated and welcoming en-suite B&B on the east side of town, with good breakfasts, a lovely garden and fine views of Clonakilty Bay; rooms include a garden suite with private sun lounge. €€

Desert House On a dairy farm 500m from the centre of Clonakilty, http://deserthousecamping.ie. Campsite with campers' kitchen, laundry facilities and a playground, with great views of Clonakilty Bay; head east out of town, turn right at the roundabout and follow the signs. Closed Nov–April (unless by prior arrangement). €

★ **Inchydoney Island Lodge and Spa** Mid-point of Inchydoney Beach, http://inchydoneyisland.com. Beautifully sited luxury retreat, decorated in plush but cheery contemporary style, with extravagant touches such

as espresso-makers in the rooms, which all have sea views and a balcony or terrace. Attached are a bistro-pub, a fine-dining restaurant and a well-equipped spa, offering a wide range of seawater and other treatments, as well as a large indoor heated seawater pool. €€€

O'Donovan's Hotel Pearse St, http://odonovanshotel. com. Collins, Parnell and Marconi have all stayed at this lively traditional meeting place on the main street, and it's still run by the welcoming O'Donovan family, retaining much of its period charm. €€

GLANDORE
Bay View Centre of the village, http://bayviewglandore. ie. Your best bet for B&B accommodation, a bright and comfortable, all-en-suite, waterside house in the centre of the village with great views. A terrific selection of homemade goodies await for breakfast. €€

Meadow On the R597, about 1km east of Glandore, 028 33280. Trim and peaceful campsite, with a campers' kitchen and laundry facilities. Closed mid-Sept to Easter/May (unless by prior arrangement). €

EATING

CLONAKILTY
An Súgán 41 Wolfe Tone St, http://ansugan.com. Good, fresh fish and shellfish, ranging from chowder and oysters to lobster and seafood pie, in this plush, cosy bar-restaurant with a pretty courtyard. Closed Mon & Tues. €€

GLANDORE
Hayes Bar & Kitchen Glandore, http://hayesrestaurant. ie. You can tuck into some chowder, smoked mackerel or mussels with home-made beer bread, sitting either on a sofa or armchair inside, or at one of the gorgeous tables outside, overlooking the village's beautiful community garden and harbour. €€€

DRINKING AND NIGHTLIFE

An Teach Beag O'Donovan's Hotel, Pearse St, http:// odonovanshotel.com. This storehouse, which has been reconstructed as a traditional cottage ("the little house") at the back of the hotel, hosts traditional sessions all summer (sometimes augmented by set dancing and storytelling), and there's more trad year-round on Tuesdays in the hotel itself..

★ **De Barra's** 55 Pearse St, www.debarra.ie. The pick of Clon's old-time pubs, with great live music most evenings,

including a popular traditional session on Mon and an acoustic session on Tues. Evenings of spoken word and comedy are also held here.

Shanley's Piano Bar Connolly St, running south from Pearse St, 023 883 3790. Plush, welcoming, well-tended bar with a pretty, flower-filled beer garden, hosting an acoustic session on Thurs, easy listening/jazz/American folk at weekends.

Skibbereen

SKIBBEREEN (often shortened to "Skibb"), the lively administrative centre for this part of west Cork, is a good spot to take a break and recharge your batteries, with plenty of restaurants and accommodation options and an excellent heritage centre.

To the south, it gives access to a rich coastal landscape where green pastures begin to alternate with the scrubby, rocky slopes so typical of more westerly parts. If you have your own wheels, you shouldn't miss the uniquely beautiful lagoon of **Lough Hyne**. Bypassed by the main N71 to the north, the town's **layout** is easy once you've got the hang of it, though sometimes clogged with traffic: beneath a slow bend in the Ilen River, the two narrow main streets form a V shape, North Street pointing to the northeast, and Main Street (which becomes Bridge Street) pointing northwestwards. The town's two big festivals are the **arts festival** at the end of July, featuring music, poetry, dance and drama (http://skibbereenartsfestival.com), and the ten-day **Taste of West Cork** food festival in September (http://tastecork.ie), which is actually dispersed throughout the region.

The Heritage Centre

Upper Bridge St • genealogy service by appointment • charge; Heritage Island • http://skibbheritage.com

The first-rate **heritage centre**, set in an attractively restored gasworks, first and foremost recalls the Great Irish Famine of the 1840s. Introduced by actor and local resident Jeremy Irons, *The Skibbereen Famine Story* provides a sensitive and vivid commentary on the Famine, when the Skibbereen area was especially badly hit. Nearly a third of its population of a hundred thousand lost their lives and a further eight thousand were forced to emigrate, and here you can listen to personal accounts of those who experienced those dark days – the Famine's effects on the town were widely publicized by the famous stark drawings of James Mahony for the *Illustrated London News*. You can download an app to take a virtual tour of the town's Famine sites (a leaflet is also available), including **Abbeystrewery Cemetery** on the N71 on the western edge of town, where between eight and ten thousand victims are buried. A second exhibition focuses on nearby **Lough Hyne** (see below), detailing its history and formation as well as the natural phenomena and folklore surrounding this body of water.

West Cork Arts Centre

The Uillinn, off Bridge St • Free • http://westcorkartscentre.com

The home of the lively **West Cork Arts Centre**, which hosts temporary exhibitions, especially of contemporary visual art, as well as drama, films and all sorts of other events including artist talks and discussions, is well worth a look. There are also three Artists in Residence studios, where visitors can view (and chat to) the artists as they go about their daily work; upcoming residencies are listed on the website.

WHALE WATCHING AND KAYAKING AROUND SKIBBEREEN

The seas off Skibb, rich feeding grounds for herring and sprat, are earning a reputation as one of Europe's premier **whale-watching** sites, with minke (roughly from April), fin (from June or July), more rarely, humpback (from September) and occasional killer whales, as well as scores of dolphins and porpoises, coming remarkably close to shore; September to November is the peak time. For further information, consult the website of the Irish Whale and Dolphin Group, http://iwdg.ie. Two companies run daily four-hour boat trips, costing around €60 per adult: Cork Whale Watch (http://corkwhalewatch.com) from Reen Pier, well to the southeast of Skibb on Castlehaven Harbour; and Whale Watch West Cork (http://whalewatchwestcork.com) from Baltimore. Along the coast here, there are also two and a half hour **sea-kayaking** trips (€60) run by Atlantic Sea Kayaking based in Skibbereen (http://atlanticseakayaking.com); they also offer starlight outings in Castlehaven Harbour or Lough Hyne, accompanied, at certain times of year, by an astonishing bioluminescence emitted by marine life.

Lough Hyne

If you head out of Skibb on the Baltimore road and take a left turn after about 3km, you'll come upon **Lough Hyne** (Lough Ine) after a further 3km or so. Ireland's first marine nature reserve, this tidal lake is joined to the sea only by a narrow channel, known as the rapids, but reaches depths of 45m in places. A combination of warm waters from the Gulf Stream and diverse habitats – sea caves, whirlpools, shallow and deep areas – supports an astonishingly rich variety of saltwater species here, over a thousand in less than a square kilometre. Many are rare species that are generally only found in the deep ocean or the Mediterranean, such as the triggerfish and the red-mouthed goby. Sheltered by varied slopes of gorse, woods and bare rock, the placid waters are also popular among swimmers and kayakers (see page 251).

To make the most of a visit, see the exhibit at the Skibbereen Heritage Centre first (see page 251), where you can also pick up a brochure for the **Knockomagh Wood Nature Trail**. Beginning where the road from Skibb meets Lough Hyne, at its northwestern corner, this 2km trail zigzags upwards and westwards past fine viewpoints of the lake, ancient sessile oaks and bluebell meadows, to the 197m summit of Knockomagh Hill, which affords a panorama of the coastline stretching from Galley Head in the east to Mount Gabriel above Schull.

ARRIVAL AND INFORMATION

SKIBBEREEN

By bus Buses on the Cork–Schull route drop off and pick up from *Cahalane's* bar on Bridge St.
Destinations Cork (Mon–Fri 6 daily, Sat & Sun 4–5 daily; 1hr 50min); Schull (Mon–Sat 3 daily, Sun 1 daily; 40min).
Tourist office 39 North St (April & May, Thurs, Fri & Sat 10am–3pm; June to end Sept Mon–Sat 10am–4.30, plus

Sun 11am–2pm in roughly July & Aug; http://skibbereen. ie).
Bike rental and tours Cycle West Cork, 11 Market St (€20/day; http://cyclewestcork.com), can deliver and pick up from your accommodation. They also arrange guided and self-guided tours.

ACCOMMODATION

Bridge House 46 Bridge St, http://bridgehouseskibbereen. com. Very centrally located on the busy main street, this is the standout among the town's handful of B&Bs, an eccentric, Victorian-styled place stuffed with antiques, swags and china dolls. €€
West Cork Hotel Ilen St, http://westcorkhotel.com. A

traditional hotel and hub of local social life that makes the most of its riverside setting, including spacious, colourful and well-equipped bedrooms, and tables out on the old railway bridge over the Ilen; a wide mix of accommodation includes triples and larger family rooms. Eggs Benedict and other breakfasts served until noon. €€

EATING AND DRINKING

There's a great **farmers' market** on Sat (9.30am–2pm) on Fair Field, behind Bridge St, where you'll also find crafts and antiques.
Corner Bar 37 Bridge St, 028 21522. Sessions are held at this cosy pub on Sat throughout the year and on Mon in July and Aug, with a singers' club on the first Fri of the month.
Island Cottage Heir Island, http://islandcottage.com. For a meal with a touch of adventure thrown in, make a reservation at this excellent, charming island restaurant that uses local and organic or wild ingredients whenever possible; it's lunches only though (2.15–4pm two-courses plus coffee €25), which are served between mid-June and mid-September, and even then just Fri through to Sun. To get here you'll need to drive or cycle west along the N71 towards Ballydehob for 5km, then follow the signs down the small peninsula for about another 5km to Cunnamore, from where a small boat will ferry you across to the island in

5min (€6 return, book in advance). It's also adults only. €€€
JC's Takeaway Fields car park, 028 23332. Tucked behind Main St, this family-owned business has four small tables. The open kitchen cooks up speciality burgers and freshly caught fish, with enormous portions of chips and sides of home-made coleslaw or tartare sauce. €
Kalbo's 26 North St, http://kalbos.ie. Small, justifiably popular café that uses local, seasonal produce wherever possible, in dishes such as a delicious open Castletownbere crab mayonnaise sandwich and the house chilli on rice. Closed Sun & Mon. €€
Riverside North St, http://riversideskibbereen.ie. Airy, modern café-restaurant with a pretty riverside terrace and a menu that ranges from *Huevos Rancheros* (eggs Mexican style) for brunch (all day) to home-made fish cakes and West Cork lamb koftas for lunch. Closed Sun. €€

Baltimore

Though isolated at the end of a stubby peninsula to the southwest of Skibbereen, **BALTIMORE** comes as a lively surprise, bustling with fishing and pleasure boats, and ferries to Sherkin and Clear islands. In fine weather, there are few more pleasant spots in Cork than the small, sun-trap square above the harbour, filled with café and bar tables. Basking in the shelter of large inshore islands, the port is particularly busy during the **regatta** held in early August, but there's also a fiddle **festival** in mid-May (http://fiddlefair.com) and a combined food and sailing festival during the last weekend in May (http://baltimorewoodenboatfestival.com).

Baltimore Castle

The Square • Late March to Sept daily 11am–6pm • charge • http://baltimorecastle.ie

Overlooking the square stands **Baltimore Castle** (Dún na Séad), a thirteenth-century tower house that was the chief residence of the infamous pirates, the O'Driscolls, but fell into ruins from the end of the seventeenth century until its painstaking recent restoration as a private home. It's worth a visit in summer to see the imposing great hall on the first floor and to take in the commanding views of the harbour and Roaringwater Bay from the battlements.

Sherkin Island

Ferries 5–12 daily; 10min • charge • http://sherkinferry.ie

Guarding the west side of Baltimore Harbour, **Sherkin** (Inis Arcáin, "Island of the Porpoise") is a tranquil, pretty island that shares the mixed scrub and pastoral landscape of the mainland hereabouts. On a half-day stroll around the boot-shaped island, you could take in the highest point, Slievemore, to the southwest on the toe of the boot, and the best beaches, Trá Bawn, Trá Eoghan Mhór and Silver Strand, to the north of Slievemore. **Ferries** from Baltimore land at the easterly pier, behind which stands a plain fifteenth-century Franciscan **abbey**, with its 15m tower intact; you can still see the outline of its cloister and the walls of a curious seventeenth-century fish "palace", where pilchards were salted and barrelled for export to Spain.

INFORMATION
BALTIMORE

Tourist information As well as selling some beautiful pottery and knitwear made on Sherkin and Clear islands, Island Crafts, in a hut down by the quay, provides tourist information on Baltimore and the islands in summer (Easter–Sept daily 10am–6.30pm; http://baltimore.ie).

ACCOMMODATION AND EATING

The village specializes in hospitality all-rounders, where you can **sleep**, **eat** and **drink** under the same roof. Standards are generally very high, and you'll find a surprisingly diverse range of food for somewhere so small and remote. Booking accommodation in advance is highly recommended in July and August, over bank holiday weekends and during festivals. **Bushe's Bar** On the main square, http://bushesbar.com. With the best view of the harbour from its seats outside on the

---

BALTIMORE: MESSING ABOUT IN BOATS

In summer, **boat tours** from Baltimore include trips via Cape Clear to the famous hundred-year-old lighthouse out in the open sea on **Fastnet Rock** (http://fastnettour.com), known as "Ireland's Teardrop" because it was the last part of Ireland seen by thousands of emigrants to North America. In addition, Baltimore Sea Safari offers a variety of trips in a smaller, speedier RIB (http://baltimoreseasafari.ie). You can take a **diving** course or trip at Aquaventures (http://aquaventures.ie), who also run half-day **snorkelling** trips and rent out equipment.

main square, this popular pub serves excellent cheap chowder and seafood sandwiches and platters during the day. €€

★ **Casey's of Baltimore Hotel** On the main Skibbereen road, 1km from the harbour, http://caseysofbaltimore.com. Charming, family-run hotel with large and very comfortable en-suite bedrooms, very good food in the bar and restaurant, and glorious views over the peaceful inlet to Ringarogy Island, especially from the beer garden. Also within the grounds is the Cottage, comprising five, one-bedroom apartments, and the three-room Lodge. Traditional music Sat year-round, more frequently in high summer. €€–€€€

★ **Rolf's** Left turn off the main road into the village, a 15min walk from the harbour, http://rolfscountryhouse. com. Civilized, tranquil and friendly spot in beautiful subtropical gardens with fine sea views. The ten good-value pine-furnished rooms are bright and spruce, and overlook either the courtyard or the gardens themselves, while the selection of two-bed self-catering cottages offer a touch more luxury. The relaxing restaurant uses as much home-grown, organic and local produce as possible in generously proportioned dishes such as grilled Irish salmon on spicy lentils, while the dedicated ice cream menu is fantastic. €€€

Waterfront Hotel On the main square, http://waterfront baltimore.ie. Gorgeous little family run hotel with twelve bright, pleasant, spacious, en-suite rooms, the best of which are done out in nautical blue and cream in a modern extension, and have either great views of the harbour or the patio garden. You don't have to go far to eat either, courtesy of the hotel's cool and colourful pizzeria and grill (*La Jolie Brise*) next door, which also does takeaway. €€€

Clear Island (Oileán Chléire)

Ireland's most southerly inhabited point, **Clear Island** (Oileán Chléire, also known as **Cape Clear**; http://capeclearisland.ie) is an isolated outpost of the **Gaeltacht**, which welcomes teenagers from all over the country to learn Irish during the summer, and generally reaches out to visitors, with plenty of facilities and information available. The island also holds a traditional story-telling **festival**, with concerts, workshops, walks and music, over the first weekend of September (http://capeclearstorytelling.com).

Clear describes a very rough figure-of-eight, just 6km square, with **North Harbour**, where ferries dock, and cliff-girt **South Harbour** almost meeting in the middle; the westerly part of the figure-of-eight is home to a fifteenth-century castle, **Dún an Óir** ("Fort of Gold"), a ruined O'Driscoll stronghold on an isolated rocky outcrop near North Harbour. The island's landscape of steep, rolling hills of heather and pasture is crossed by narrow, hedge-lined roads and paths, affording fine views of Roaringwater Bay and of Fastnet Rock to the west in the open sea, where whales, dolphins and sharks can sometimes be spotted. Clear Island is most famous as one of the best places to watch seabird migration in Europe, as well as supporting breeding colonies of black guillemots, choughs and rock doves; twitchers can take field courses and stay at the **bird observatory** at North Harbour (http://birdwatchireland.ie).

Up the steep bank to the east of North Harbour, visitors are welcome at **Cleire Goat Farm** (087 797 3056) which offers goat husbandry courses, starting from as little as two hours in duration, and produces ice cream, cheese and sausages. A short walk further along from the farm is the island's tiny **heritage centre** (June to early Sept daily roughly noon–4pm; charge; http://capeclearmuseum.ie) occupying an old schoolhouse building and hosting some detailed and interesting displays, especially on maritime history and archaeology. Exhibitions are rotated and often relate to anniversaries of events that took place on the island.

St Ciarán's Church

To the east of North Harbour, close to the heritage centre

The island is reputed to have been the sixth-century birthplace of **St Ciarán of Saighir** (not to be confused with Ciarán of Clonmacnois), who is (spuriously) claimed to have brought Christianity to Ireland thirty years before St Patrick. According to legend, he ended his days in Cornwall, where he was known as St Piran and credited with the discovery of tin. His twelfth-century church, graveyard and holy well lie a twenty-minute walk east from North Harbour.

ARRIVAL AND INFORMATION

CLEAR ISLAND

By ferry The *Cailín Óir* sails from Baltimore (2–4 daily; 45min; €18 return; http://capeclearferries.com), and there are summertime boats from Schull (see page 255); Baltimore–Clear return tickets are accepted on the Clear–Schull ferry. A minibus meets all ferries and charges €2/person to anywhere on the island.

Tourist information The crafts shop at North Harbour dispenses tourist information (daily: June & Sept 11am–1pm & 2.30–4.30pm; July & Aug 11am–1pm & 2–6pm; 028 39100). There's no ATM on the island – the nearest is in the supermarket in Baltimore.

ACCOMMODATION AND EATING

As the island can get busy in high summer, it's best to book **accommodation** before you come.

An Siopa Beag North Harbour, http://siopabeag.ie. The island's grocery store at North Harbour offers internet access and wi-fi, as well as a café serving sandwiches, salads, seafood and, on Fri and Sat evenings in summer, handmade pizzas. Upstairs is the island's social club, *Club Cléire*, which hosts traditional music on summer weekends.

Ard na Gaoithe Up behind the youth hostel along a steep lane above South Harbour, http://capeclearbandb.ie. This welcoming adults-only B&B, in a renovated nineteenth-century house on a working farm, has five rooms (three doubles and two twins) and good bike storage for those cycling the Wild Atlantic Way. Organic eggs and pancakes feature on a varied breakfast menu. €€

Cape Clear Hostel By the pebbly beach at South Harbour, http://capeclearhostel.ie. This basic hostel occupies the old coastguard station. As well as four- to ten-bed dorms, it offers a cosy lounge with an open fire, a large kitchen and dining room, laundry facilities and table tennis – note that there is no wifi. Minimum two-night stay in July and August and at weekends. Dorms €, four-bed room €€

Chléire Haven South Harbour, http://chleire-haven.com. The island campsite at South Harbour has expanded its horizons to offer yurts (sleeping up to six, or four adults) with wooden beds, stoves, gas cookers and cool boxes, and bell tents (also sleeping six) with self-inflating mattresses. Camping pitches must also be pre-booked. 'Cook your own' breakfast packs (€8) can be pre-ordered. Camping €, yurts €€, bell tents €€

Ciaran Danny Mike's On the road between the two harbours, 028 39153. This spacious pub with a pool table and outdoor seating is popular for lunch (until 5pm) and dinner (7–9pm) and often hosts traditional music. (It also has self-catering cottages and a guesthouse.)

The Mizen Head Peninsula

Mizen Head is a wild and beautiful peninsula, projecting southwestwards around the substantial mass of copper-rich **Mount Gabriel**. The whole of its empty northern coast presents sheer cliffs and stupendous views. The south coast is more populous, sheltering safe harbours, the large village and resort of **Schull** and the remote sandy beaches of **Barley Cove** and **Galley Cove**, while the only tourist attraction of any note is the signal station at the very tip, the **Mizen Head Visitor Centre**.

Schull

The peninsula's main settlement, **SCHULL**, is a congenial harbour town that's not only popular with yachties but also has an artistic bent, with crafts shops, galleries and a weekly country market (Sun 10am–2pm Easter–Sept; http://schullmarket.ie) in the Pier Road car park; there are some terrific food offerings here. It shelters in the lee of 407m **Mount Gabriel**, to the north, topped by an aircraft-tracking station and blessed with fine views. The walk up there (about 8km round trip) is detailed, along with four other local walks, in a very useful booklet, *Discover Schull*, that's available around the town or online at http://schull.ie; since the mountain was actively mined for centuries, take care on the way that you avoid uncovered mine shafts.

Schull also boasts a **planetarium**, developed by a local German resident in the village's community college on Colla Road, which runs south off Main Street. It's generally open only in July and August, with a programme of star shows (Mon & Fri at 5pm, Wed at 8pm; charge; http://schullplanetarium.com). Schull's annual events include a five-day **short-film festival** in late May (http://fastnetfilmfestival. com) and **Calves Week** sailing regatta in early August (http://shsc.ie).

Tourist information The community office for information and the short film festival is on Main St near the start of the pier road (summer daily roughly 10am–6pm; winter hours variable, perhaps three days/week; http:// schull.ie).

Activities Fastnet Marine and Outdoor Education Centre offers sailing courses (http://schullsailing.ie), while diving is organized by Divecology (http://divecology.com).

GETTING AROUND

By ferry Between June and August a new fast ferry runs from Schull to Clear Island (1–6 days/week; 25min; €22 return; http://capeclearferries.com); on the days when this is running, you could hook up with the Fastnet Rock tours from Baltimore (see page 253). Schull–Clear return tickets are accepted on the Clear–Baltimore ferry.

ACCOMMODATION AND EATING

★ **Hackett's** Main St, 028 28625. Great old bar with stone floors, bench seating and a vaguely alternative feel, helped along by a good soundtrack, regular live music and bottles of craft beer. Tasty bar lunches include beef in Guinness stew.

L'Escale Harbourside, 028 28599. Your best bet for dinner is this high-class chipper, which has lots of outdoor tables, some of them covered, for enjoying the harbour views. It also offers seafood platters, pancakes and wine. Note that it's only open between June and August. €

Newman's West Main St, 028 27776. Wine bar and café serving tasty breakfasts (pancakes and bagels are popular) salads and seafood (Bantry Bay mussels). Don't miss the upstairs art gallery. €

Nickie's Kitchen East End, http://nickieskitchen.com Bright, well-run country kitchen style café-deli that's popular with locals. Open sandwiches (think crab and lemon dill mayo) and homemade sausage rolls, plus tasty cakes (blueberry cheesecake) washed down with proper organic coffee. €€

Goleen, Crookhaven, Brow Head and Mizen Head

Infrequent buses run 15km southwest down the peninsula from Schull as far as the quiet village of **GOLEEN**. The southernmost tip of the Mizen Head Peninsula, **Brow Head**, which is also the southernmost point of mainland Ireland, rather surprisingly shelters a golden sandy beach in **Barley Cove**, punctured by a stream and backed by dunes, which are thought to have been thrown up by the tsunami that followed an earthquake off Portugal in 1755. A wild spit of land pushes east of here, past another beautiful sandy beach, **Galley Cove**, to the village of **CROOKHAVEN**, which would feel like the end of the world were it not for the pleasure boats anchored in the long, fjord-like inlet.

Mizen Head Signal Station

Charge; Heritage Island • http://mizenhead.ie

To the west of Barley Cove, the narrow road heads upwards and outwards to **Mizen Head**, a Signature Discovery point on the Wild Atlantic Way itself. The **visitor centre** comprises a café and gift shop alongside various maritime and environmental paraphernalia. Be sure to pay the entrance fee to walk out to the head and the hundred-year-old **signal station** (now automatic), accessed by a slender, arched bridge. Follow the narrow pathways to signposted viewpoints: with the 50m Fastnet lighthouse and the tip of the Beara Peninsula to either side and the whole of Ireland behind you, you're left to plot the folds of the jagged cliffs, the movements of the clouds and the churning contours of the ocean.

ACCOMMODATION AND EATING | GOLEEN, CROOKHAVEN AND MIZEN HEAD

The Crookhaven Inn Crookhaven, 028 35309. Cosy pub-restaurant in the village itself, with an open stove and outside tables overlooking the inlet, serving excellent food including home-cured gravlax with warm potato salad.

Galley Cove Just west of Crookhaven, http://galleycove house.com. Welcoming, if slightly old-fashioned en-suite B&B, in a spruce, modern, pine-floored bungalow with fine views of the sea and Fastnet lighthouse. €

The Sheep's Head

The **Sheep's Head**, a precarious sliver of land between Dunmanus and Bantry bays, is the quietest and smallest of the major southwestern peninsulas. Gorse and heather sprout from its long granite spine, leaving room for narrow pockets of green pasture on its north and especially its south coast. With magnificent views of the larger peninsulas on either side, it can be best appreciated by pedalling the easy-to-follow 120km **Sheep's Head Cycle Route** from Ballylickey (6km north of Bantry), or by walking the 93km **Sheep's Head Way** (http://thesheepsheadway.ie) from Bantry; the latter is relatively easy walking, avoiding the round-peninsula road for most of the way, and is covered by OS Discovery Series map number 88. It can be done in four days, with two nights in Kilcrohane after two long days' walking and a night in Durrus; the last day is missable, so you might want to catch a bus back to Bantry from Durrus.

Durrus

DURRUS is a relatively busy junction village between the Mizen Head and Sheep's Head peninsulas, supporting several local pubs and, just outside town, a fine restaurant. Sitting at the head of Dunmanus Bay, Durrus is a great place to base yourself if you're keen to go kayaking or fishing.

On a hillside just beyond the village, a farm produces the award-winning **Durrus Irish Cheese**; their shop is open Mon–Fri 10am–1pm (http://durruscheese.com), and you may also get to view the cheesemaking process whilst you are here.

ACCOMMODATION AND EATING   DURRUS

Blairscove House & Restaurant About 2km southwest down the R591 towards Crookhaven, http://blairscove. ie. In beautiful grounds overlooking Dunmanus Bay, *Blairs Cove House* combines four spacious luxury apartments mostly with open plan kitchen, living and dining areas and variously sleeping between two and four. There's also an excellent restaurant, renowned for its buffet-style starters and grilled meats and fish for mains (four-course set menu €80). Closed early Nov to mid-March. Restaurant closed Sun & Mon. €€€

Sea Lodge About 2km west of Durrus on the road to Kilcrohane, http://sea-lodge.bedsandhotels.com. On a remote country road that hugs the bay, the views from this B&B are stunning. Guest rooms and the shared lounge room are comfortable and simply furnished. Pack lunches can be arranged. Closed Oct–Easter. €€

TOURS AND ACTIVITIES

Darrens Kayaks http://darrenskayaks.com. This outfit rents kayaks (customised with motors or sails if required) and organises tuition, guided tours and fishing expeditions (rental from €25/3hr).

Kilcrohane and beyond

KILCROHANE, 15km southwest of Durrus, is a traditional sleepy village strung along the main road, with a church, a couple of decent **bars** serving food and a combined shop, petrol station and post office. The Old Creamery on the road in from Durrus shelters the Sheep's Head Producers Shop (Mon–Fri 11am–5pm, Sun 11am–4pm), where local artisans sell everything from jams to jewellery (including Sheep's Head Way maps), plus there's a café and a bike rental shop.

From Kilcrohane, a road loops along the quieter north coast of the peninsula, reaching its highest point at a spectacular pass 2km north of the village; for even better views, it's possible to walk to the top of **Seefin**, Sheep's Head's highest hill (344m), in about twenty minutes from the pass.

West of Kilcrohane, the Sheep's Head is dotted with small lakes and becomes more jagged and hummocky as it narrows to a lighthouse at the tip. The tarmac runs out at the *Sheep's Head Café*, from where it's a thirty-minute walk down to the lighthouse.

ACCOMMODATION AND EATING   **KILCROHANE AND BEYOND**

Bernie's Cúpan Tae 11km west of Kilcrohane, 086 877 8604. In a wild, end-of the-road setting, this cosy café nourishes travellers with hearty soups, sandwiches and home-made cakes and offers walking information. Closed Nov to mid-March. €

Bridge View House By the church, http://bridge viewhouse.com. This attractive house provides friendly en-suite accommodation, with six rooms in the main house and a further four in a separate private area away from the house.,There's a large garden to enjoy and a terrific

breakfast to set you up for a jaunt along the Sheep's Head Way. Self-catering available. €€

Seamount Farmhouse Glenlough, 10km from Kilcrohane towards Bantry, http://seamountfarm.com. Less than 1km off the Sheep's Head Way, this welcoming farmhouse provides rooms with magnificent views of Bantry Bay, fine home baking, walking tours and plenty of useful information about exploring the area. They can also rustle up packed lunches and can assist with luggage transfers if walking the trail. €€

Bantry

7

BANTRY enjoys a glorious location, ringed first by lush, wooded slopes and then by wild bare mountains, at the head of 35km-long **Bantry Bay**, one of the finest natural harbours in Ireland. The prime viewpoint is naturally occupied by **Bantry House**, which with its sumptuous interior and garden is one of West Cork's few unmissable historic sites. At the junction of several important roads, Bantry is also a substantial market (Fridays 9.30am–5pm) and service town, with plenty of amenities for visitors.

Wolfe Tone Square

Bantry gathers itself around the expansive, bayside **Wolfe Tone Square**, which features a statue of the eponymous United Irishman pointedly holding a telescope behind his back. In December 1796, Tone persuaded the French to send a fleet carrying some thirteen thousand seasoned soldiers to invade Ireland in support of a Republican Revolution. Contrary winds prevented them from landing in Bantry Bay – though they were "close enough to toss a biscuit on shore" according to Tone – and the fleet was forced to return to Brest. Had they landed, it's likely that they would have overwhelmed the inexperienced forces in Ireland at the time.

Bantry House

1km west of the centre of Bantry, along the bay • April to early Sept draily 10am–5pm, but often closed for weddings – check website • charge • http://bantryhouse.com

On the southern approach to town, **Bantry House** is one of Ireland's most compelling country houses, both for its lavish artworks and for its magnificent setting, among formal gardens overlooking the bay. Bought by the White family in 1739 and expanded throughout the eighteenth and nineteenth centuries, it was spared destruction during the Irish Civil War, when it acted as a hospital for the wounded of both sides. Many of its beautiful furnishings were gathered by the Second Earl of Bantry on his nineteenth-century grand tour and boast name-dropping provenances, such as the gorgeous Aubusson tapestries made for Marie Antoinette on her marriage to the future Louis

---

BANTRY FESTIVALS

Bantry hosts the prestigious ten-day **West Cork Chamber Music Festival** (http:// westcorkmusic.ie), generally at the end of June/beginning of July, followed immediately by the seven-day **West Cork Literary Festival** (http://westcorkmusic.ie /literary-festival). Mid-to-late August sees a five-day **traditional-music festival**, "Masters of Tradition" (http:// westcorkmusic.ie).

XVI. The highlight is the dining room, which resembles an extravagant stage set: rich Chartres-blue walls, a marble colonnade and vast seventeenth-century sideboards carved with cherubs and classical scenes. There's a very attractive **tearoom** located in the West Wing (formerly the nineteenth-century kitchen), which serves teas and simple lunches.

ARRIVAL AND INFORMATION   BANTRY

By bus Buses from/to Cork (Mon–Fri 5–8 daily, Sat 6, Sun 4; 2hr) and Castletownbere (Mon 2 daily, Tues, Fri & Sat 1 daily; 1hr 20min) stop on the central Wolfe Tone Square.

Tourist office At the east end of Wolfe Tone Square (April–Oct Mon–Sat 10am–6pm; Nov–March Fri 10am–2pm; http://bantry.ie). Guided historical walks (June–Aug Tues

& Thurs 11am; €2).

Bike rental O'Donovan Cycles on Market St (Tues–Fri 10.15am–4.30pm, Sat & 10am–1pm; http://odonovancycles.ie) have a selection of both touring and E-bikes (from €20/30 per day), and also do servicing and repairs.

ACCOMMODATION

There's a decent range of **accommodation** in Bantry, with dozens of B&Bs lining the Glengarriff road on the north side of town, but it's advisable to book ahead in July and Aug, especially during the town's festivals.

★ **Bantry House** On the N71 at the southern entrance to town, http://bantryhouse.com. Luxurious digs with great views in one of the country's finest mansions, which is still the home of the White family, former Earls of Bantry. The six rooms in the East Wing are sumptuous in the extreme, furnished with silk curtains and Irish woollens (bathrooms have underfloor heating), while the huge, chandeliered library, with its coffered ceiling, and the billiards room are now guest lounges. Close Nov–Easter. €€€

Eagle Point Caravan and Camping Park Ballylickey,

6km from Bantry along the Glengarriff road, http://eaglepointcamping.com. This large, well-organized campsite – with adult only pitches in the Meadow – has terraces that make the most of its Bantry Bay location; a laundry, TV rooms, tennis and basketball courts, football pitch, pebbly beaches for swimming and a slipway to launch kayaks. Closed mid-Sept to mid-April. €

The Maritime Just off Wolfe Tone Square on the main road to Skibbereen, http://themaritime.ie. This smart contemporary hotel is plush and thoughtfully equipped; all rooms can claim either a harbour or wood view, and some have balconies, with superior and penthouse rooms available for those willing to part with a bit more cash. The leisure club features a 19m pool, children's pool, gym, Jacuzzi and sauna. €€€

EATING AND DRINKING

The Anchor Tavern New St, off the southeast corner of Wolfe Tone Square, 027 50012. A popular haunt for visiting musicians, this sociable 150-year-old traditional pub is adorned with nautical memorabilia, plain stone floors and communal pews around the walls.

The Brick Oven Wolfe Tone Square, southwest corner, http://thebrickovenbantry.com. Accomplished all-rounder serving pizzas, baguettes and ribs from a wood-burning oven and tasty bistro dishes like warm smoked chicken salad with mushrooms. Closed Tues & Wed. €€

★ **Ma Murphy's** 7 New St, off the southeast corner of Wolfe Tone Square, 027 50242. Cosy bar-grocery with a cool soundtrack and a very pleasant, cobbled backyard; quirky, old fashioned and plenty of whiskeys and bottles of craft beer. Open mic Thurs, live music at weekends.

★ **O'Connor's** Wolfe Tone Square, http://oconnorseafood.

ie. Elegant, top-quality restaurant specializing in seafood (including oysters from its own seawater tank) and local lamb, pork and steaks, in ample portions. Try the Bantry Bay scallops with pea, garlic, spinach and parmesan risotto, and leave room for excellent desserts such as warm salted caramel blondie. €€€

Organico 3 Glengarriff road, 100m off Wolfe Tone Square, http://organico.ie. Popular, easy-going vegetarian and organic café, bakery and health-food store, dishing up tasty hummus salads, sandwiches and soups. Closed Sun. €

Stuffed Olive 2a Bridge St, the continuation of New St, off the square's southeast corner, http://thestuffedolive. wordpress.com. Excellent deli-café and bakery serving creative sandwiches and salads such as smoked duck, cakes, good coffees and juices. Closed Sun & Mon. €

The Beara Peninsula

The largest and most remote of Cork's peninsulas, the **Beara** (http://bearatourism.com) careers southwestwards for 50km between Bantry Bay and the Kenmare River. Patterns in the landscape are hard to distinguish here, and contrasts are frequent. Indeed, the peninsula's most popular tourist spot, **Glengarriff**, has built an industry on the stunning contrast between its lush subtropical setting and the irregular barren rocks of the Caha Mountains behind. The mountainous spine is often augmented by ribs, and particularly in the awesome Slieve Miskish Mountains at the Beara's tip, the coast road is forced to climb through whatever passes can be found. Round on the north coast, half of which belongs to County Kerry (see page 285), the only settlements occupy occasional cups of green farmland beneath the stony ridges.

The diverse scenery can be explored by car following the **Ring of Beara** (http://ringofbeara.com) around the peninsula; the 138km **Beara Way Cycle Route** mostly follows this quiet main road too. Away from the coastal route, and splicing the peninsula north–south, the outstanding **Healy Pass** is a lonely mountain road of hairpin bends and panoramic viewpoints that shouldn't be missed. For those on foot, take the **Beara Way**, a 200km waymarked walk (9–11 days) following mostly tracks and minor roads from Glengarriff west (via Adrigole, Castletownbere and a ferry to Bere Island, which can easily be missed out) to Dursey Island, then along the north coast of the peninsula (via Allihies, Eyeries, Ardgroom and Lauragh) to Kenmare and back to Glengarriff. Route guides are available locally, there's a downloadable map guide of the walking route at http://bearatourism.com, and the Ordnance Survey 1:50,000 Discovery map 84 covers nearly the whole peninsula.

Glengarriff

The founders of **GLENGARRIFF** were perhaps having an off-day when they named it *An Gleann Garbh*, the "rugged glen" – or, to be charitable, maybe the climate has changed since then. It's true that above and behind stands the magnificent backdrop of the wild, bare Caha Mountains, but the village itself sits in a sheltered oasis of balmy greenery. This picturesque juxtaposition, warmed by the Atlantic Gulf Stream, has attracted tourists since the eighteenth century, when the *Eccles Hotel* was built. The village now straggles east–west for several kilometres from the *Eccles*, with most of its amenities towards the western end around the N71–R572 junction. Glengarriff's popularity means there's a decent range of places to stay and eat, making it a good base for exploring some of Cork's most beautiful countryside or for just hopping over to see the horticultural delights of **Garinish Island**. Over a weekend in mid-June, Glengarriff hosts the vibrant **Uilleann Pipe and Trad Festival**, with concerts, workshops and sessions of traditional music (http://jimdowlingfestival.ie).

Bamboo Park

1km along the N71 Bantry Rd • charge, kids free • http://bamboo-park.com

Glengarriff's microclimate is mild enough to support the **Bamboo Park**, a beautiful thirteen-acre private garden with a tearoom towards the east end of the village, planted with thirty different species of bamboo, as well as various palms, ferns and eucalyptus. The maze of paths here are great for kids to have a very long game of hide-and-seek, while the seashore frontage, with private beach and picnic area, reveals idyllic views of tufted green islets in the bay.

Glengarriff Woods Nature Reserve and around

1km along the N71 Kenmare Rd • Free • http://glengarriffnaturereserve.ie

Glengarriff Woods Nature Reserve is a forest park of ancient sessile oaks, birch and holly, that shelters Mediterranean species such as strawberry trees. It's crossed by waymarked nature trails (about 3hr walking in total), including the short climb up to **Lady Bantry's Lookout**, which is rewarded with panoramic views of Glengarriff, Bantry Bay and the Sheep's Head; you may even see White-tailed Sea Eagles here.

Beyond the reserve you can veer west for 7km to reach **Barley Lake**, a beautiful armchair or corrie lake, or if you're keen for more rambles in nature, continue a few kilometres along the N71 to reach the **Ewe Experience** (July & Aug daily 10am–6pm 6pm; charge; http://theewe.com), a magical sculpture garden that comprises four interlinked gardens on a one-kilometre walk, which also includes elements of science and poetry; note, though, that the terrain is quite hilly so those with mobility issues or buggies may struggle.

INFORMATION
GLENGARRIFF

Tourist information There's not an official tourist office in Glengarriff, but a souvenir shop next to the Blue Pool ferry service and the bus stop has a few local brochures.

The town's website is http://visitglengarriff.ie. Note that there are no banks in Glengarriff, though there is an ATM at O'Sullivan's service station.

ACCOMMODATION AND EATING

Casey's Hotel Main St, http://caseyshotelglengarriff.ie. Friendly, family-run nineteenth-century hotel, with crisply refurbished rooms (twins, doubles and triples), a patio and garden. Very good food such as beef and Guinness pie, and plenty of seafood in the bar or smart evening restaurant. €€

Glengarriff Caravan and Camping Park (Dowling's) About 2km out on the R572 Castletownbere road, 027 63154. You can camp in some comfort at this woodland site, which has laundry facilities, a playground and traditional music in its on-site bar. Closed Nov–March. €

Glengarriff Park Hotel Main St, http://glengarriffpark. com. Tasteful, modern "classic" rooms, some with baths, plus slightly more expensive "deluxe" and "luxury" rooms

with more space, more elaborate decor and armchairs. Downstairs are a bistro and *MacCarthy's*, a pleasant, well-run bar serving tasty food. €€

Jim's Coffee House 1.5km east of Glengarriff on the N71, 027 63030. Close to the Bamboo Park, *Jim's* serves up full Irish breakfasts until midday and then light lunches and home-made cakes until close. There are a few tables outside that take in the beautiful bay view.

The Maple Leaf Main St, 027 63021. Located among a tight concentration of pubs at the main junction, this friendly spot offers live music every night in summer, at weekends in winter.

Garinish Island (Ilnacullin)

Daily: April–June & Sept 10am–5.30pm; July & Aug 9.30–5.30pm; Oct 10am–4.30pm • charge; Heritage Card • http://garinishisland. ie • Boat with Harbour Queen Ferries (every 30mins 9.45am–4.15pm, last ferry from Garinish 5.30pm; €15 return, cash only; http://harbourqueenferry.com) from opposite the *Eccles Hotel* at the east end of Glengarriff; or with Blue Pool Ferry (every 30mins 9.45am–4.30pm, last ferry from Garinish 5.15pm; €12.50 return; http://bluepoolferry.ie) in the centre of Glengarriff

In 1910, the MP Annan Bryce bought **Garinish** (aka Ilnacullin) from the British War Office and, after shipping in all the topsoil, gradually turned the rocky inshore island into an exotic garden oasis. Having passed into public ownership in 1953, the island is now a delightful and accessible escape from the mainland, especially in summer, when colourful plants from around the world set the island alight against a backdrop of the sparse, jagged mountains just across the water. The island's centrepiece is a formal **Italianate garden**, surrounded by a walled garden and wilder areas, a Grecian temple with magnificent views of the Caha Mountains, and a Martello tower. There's a coffee shop and a self-guided trail around the gardens, and serious horticulturalists should pick up the Heritage Service's guidebook, which includes detailed plant lists. The ten-minute **boat trip** (see above) to the island takes you past the lush islets of Glengarriff Harbour, where you may see basking seals.

Castletownbere and around

Over 100km west of Cork city at the end of the peninsula, the bustle of **CASTLETOWNBERE** (sometimes referred to as Castletown Berehaven or just Castletown) comes as quite a surprise. Benefiting from the country's second-largest natural harbour, it's Ireland's biggest white-fish port, and especially during strong winter gales, Atlantic trawlers of many nationalities put in here. Not surprisingly, there's a good range of amenities for visitors, with the fairly compact area around the main square offering cafés, restaurants, banks and some boisterous pubs.

Dunboy Castle

Just off the R572 Dursey road • Open access

To the west of town, there's a pleasant 3km walk through the grounds of **Puxley Mansion**, the fenced-in skeleton of a neo-Gothic pile that's been left to moulder, to the overgrown seafront ruins of **Dunboy Castle** and its dramatic views back along the Beara Peninsula. Built in the fourteenth century, the castle was besieged by the English in 1602 after the Battle of Kinsale. Facing an army of four thousand, its garrison of 143 men held out for eleven days, but in the end were all slaughtered and the castle blown up. Their chieftain, **Donal Cam O'Sullivan Bere**, then embarked on his famous long **march** up to County Leitrim (see box).

ARRIVAL AND INFORMATION
CASTLETOWNBERE

By bus Buses stop on the main square, except Harrington's, which pick up from the Supervalu supermarket just to the east.

Destinations Bus Éireann: Cork (4 weekly; 3hr); Kenmare, via Eyeries, Lauragh and the north side of the Beara (July & Aug Mon–Sat 2 daily; 1hr 20min).

Destinations Harrington's Buses (http://harringtonsbus.com): Cork (Mulligan's Bar, opposite the bus station on Parnell Place; Mon–Wed, Fri & Sat 1 daily 8am, Sun 1 at 5pm; 2hr).

Destinations Berehaven Bus Service (027 70007): Bantry (Mon 2 daily at 9.30am & 4.30pm, Tues, Fri & Sat 1 daily at 10.30am; 1hr 20min); Cork (Mulligan's Bar, opposite the bus station on Parnell Place; 1 on Thurs at 7.30am; 2hr 30min).

Tourist office Just west of the square along the main street (usually Mon–Fri 10.30am–3.30pm, but worth checking on 027 70054); they have details of short, signposted loop walks on the peninsula.

ACCOMMODATION

Berehaven Golf Club 5km east on the Glengarriff road at Filane, http://berehavengolf.com. You can camp on the shores of Bantry Bay at the golf club, shower in the clubhouse and drink in the daytime bar in the summer. Laundry room and reduced green fees for campers. Motorhomes and caravans welcome too. €

Garranes Hostel 8km west of town on the Dursey road, http://dzogchenbeara.org. Segregated dorms and a family room open to all-comers at a Tibetan Buddhist retreat centre in a traditional farmhouse cottage. It offers a fully equipped kitchen, a sitting room and plenty of tranquillity; there's a café on site too. €

EATING AND DRINKING

Breen's Lobster Bar On the main square, 027 70031. It's impossible to miss this bright pink building on the square; the interior is a little more subdued and offers a low-key menu of sandwiches, home-made burgers and seafood chowder. Closed Sun. €

Café at Dzogchen Beara 8km west of town on the Dursey road, http://dzogchenbeara.org. The small café and bookshop at this meditation retreat has unparalleled views of the Atlantic. The menu offers cakes and pastries, inexpensive vegetarian lunch specials and soups with with freshly baked soda bread; take a stroll around the meditation garden too. €

★ **MacCarthy's** On the main square, http://maccarthysbar.com. This grocery-bar-coffee shop does soups and fresh crab and smoked salmon sandwiches for lunch, and is the best place to drink, with tables on the street and regular traditional sessions.

Murphy's East of the square on the main street, 027 70244. Unprepossessing restaurant, highly regarded for its fresh simple fish and seafood (lemon sole with chips and salad).

Twomey's Ivy Bar On the main street west of the square, 027 70114. Spruce bar with a sunny yard running down to the harbour, which runs trad music on summer Fri and live music on Sat.

THE LONG MARCH OF O'SULLIVAN BERE

Beara is the ancestral lands of the O'Sullivan's, but in the seventeenth century during the Nine Years War, their leader **Donal Cam O'Sullivan Bere** (1561–1618) allied with the Spanish. After the loss of Dunboy Castle (see above) and faced with death if he was captured by the English, O'Sullivan set out to reach friends in the north. He travelled with a thousand men, women and children, and set off with only one day's worth of provisions. Harassed by the English and the Irish, and overwhelmed by harsh winter conditions, he arrived two weeks later with just 35 followers left. The march is now commemorated by the **Beara-Breifne Way** (http://bearabreifneway.ie), a 500km walking route from Dursey Island to Blacklion on the borders of Leitrim, Cavan and Fermanagh, where it links with the Ulster Way.

Garnish Bay and Dursey Island

Cable car charge (cash only) • http://durseyisland.ie

Beyond Castletownbere, you can skirt round through a few tiny, remote but dramatically set villages to the north side of the peninsula and on towards Kerry. Three kilometres before the tip of the peninsula, the R572 passes beautiful, north-facing **Garnish Bay**, which boasts one of the Beara's few sandy beaches and crystal-clear water.

The Beara lays on a bit of excitement at its very end, in the form of Ireland's only **cable car**, which teeters across the roaring sound to the bird sanctuary of **Dursey Island** and sometimes attracts long queues in summer. There are no facilities on the island (wild camping is legal), but you can walk its circular 11km stretch of the Beara Way for seemingly endless views across the Atlantic, beyond Calf, Cow and Bull islands.

Allihies

Looping round an especially harsh and rocky part of the peninsula on the R575, you'll come upon **ALLIHIES**, its brightly coloured houses dramatically huddled together against the leathery creases of Slieve Miskish's western flank and blessed with superb sunset views.

7

Allihies Copper Mine Museum

100m south of the village centre • Nov–March usually closed but may open if called in advance • charge • http://acmm.ie

In 1812, the Industrial Revolution descended on remote Allihies with a vengeance, bringing state-of-the-art engineering and Cornish mining techniques to work the copper ore in the mountains above the village. At any one time, up to 1500 people, including women and children, worked for the mines here in desperate conditions, until their closure in the 1880s, when many of the miners emigrated to the huge copper lode in Butte, Montana and Leadville, Colorado. The story is now engagingly told at the excellent **Allihies Copper Mine Museum**, set up by a group of dedicated local enthusiasts, in a renovated Methodist church that was built for the immigrant Cornish miners. Highlights of the thoughtful displays include video recollections of local men who worked in the mines when they briefly reopened in the 1950s, bits of ore that you can handle and a small-scale reconstruction of a steam pump. There's also a very attractive **café** (see below) and an upstairs exhibition area for artists. In addition, a network of **signposted loop trails** has been laid out in the surrounding countryside, allowing you to take in ruined mine buildings and spectacular views.

Ballydonegan Strand

One of the trails from the copper mine museum leads down to **Ballydonegan Strand** and its simple campsite (027 73002), 1km to the southwest. This sandy beach is actually composed of crushed quartz produced in the copper extraction process, but you'll need to beware the currents when swimming.

ACCOMMODATION AND EATING	ALLIHIES

The Copper Café Allihies Copper Mine Museum, http://acmm.ie. The café in the copper mine museum near the southern entrance to town serves good coffee, home-made cakes, chowder and lunch dishes such as West Cork mussels. €

O'Neill's Bar Main St, http://oneillsbeara.ie. Boasting an unmissable crimson facade, this pub serves inexpensive bar food such as toasties and fish and chips, and is also your best bet for traditional music (weekends year-round, more often in summer). Choose between tables out front on the street with great views, or the log fire inside, depending on the weather.

Sea View On the main street in the village centre, http://allihiesseaview.com. In a two-storey terrace house, *Sea View* offers ten comfortable en-suite bedrooms in pastel and earth tones and good breakfasts, as well as self-catering accommodation. €€

Kerry

GREAT BLASKET

Kerry

Kerry has been making visitors' romantic dreams of Ireland come true since the eighteenth century, when the grandeur of the lakes and mountains around Killarney first came to widespread attention. Encompassing the highest range in the country, Macgillycuddy's Reeks, the landscape here is, of course, still magnificent today, and the Killarney area shelters some fine, underrated architectural sights too. The town itself has plenty of amenities and entertainment, but hordes of tourists mean it can often feel a little crowded. Indeed, the launch of the Wild Atlantic Way driving route has brought a new wave of visitors to Kerry, many of them drawn to the county's three big peninsulas, seductively billed by marketing gurus as "the southern peninsulas with an edge-of-the-world feel".

Of these, the most visited is the **Iveragh peninsula**, southwest of Killarney. Measuring around sixty by thirty kilometres, it's bordered by a highly popular scenic road known as the **Ring of Kerry**, and there are plenty of tracks across its vast, rugged hinterland and coastal branch roads such as the **Ring of Skellig**, which you can explore by car, bike or on foot, and avoid the crowds. The small-scale but intriguing attractions of **Valentia Island** and **Caherdaniel**, perched on a hillside above a great beach, should be enough to tempt you off the Ring of Kerry to spend at least a night out here. Off the end of the peninsula, the island of **Skellig Michael**, one of the most remarkable hermitages in the world and now a UNESCO World Heritage Site, remains the ultimate place to get away from it all. Its profile has recently been raised since it featured in the latest *Star Wars* films, *The Force Awakens* and *The Last Jedi*, introducing the island to a new generation. At the southeastern corner of the peninsula, **Kenmare** contrasts well with Killarney, providing excellent accommodation, restaurants and nightlife in a trim setting, as well as access to further scenic delights on Kerry's part of the **Beara Peninsula**.

Kerry's other peninsula, **Dingle**, experienced its own minor visitor boom on the release of David Lean's film, *Ryan's Daughter*, in 1970, which pumped as much as £3 million into the local economy during a long and troubled location shoot here (including the near drowning of star Robert Mitchum off Dunquin and the building of an entirely new village, Kirrary, on the remote slopes above). As touristy as the Ring, it offers a jagged landscape of stark mountains and spectacular beaches, an especially rich heritage of early Christian sites, and a fine, all-round base in the (seasonally) busy main settlement, **Dingle town**.

Despite the centuries of tourist traffic, Kerry has maintained a strong sense of independence, though perhaps doesn't shout about it as much as its neighbour, Cork. It's one of the least urbanized counties in Ireland, with a sweet, country lilt to the accent. Distinctive H-shaped goalposts are everywhere, not just on village GAA fields but also on most farms, evidence of the county's obsession with **Gaelic football**. The self-styled "Brazil" of the sport, the county team has won the All-Ireland Championship far more than anyone else – 38 times and counting – and produced the finest team ever between 1975 and 1986, winning the championship eight times in those eleven years. The Dingle Peninsula, one of Ireland's strongest Gaeltacht areas, has nurtured not only great footballers, but also a fine community of musicians and the extraordinary **writers** of the wild **Blasket Islands**, who put their rich oral tradition of Irish-language storytelling to paper in the early twentieth century. The county's other most obvious concentration of literary talent has been in the flatlands of **North Kerry**, as celebrated in the genial market town of **Listowel**.

GALLARUS ORATORY

Highlights

❶ Killarney National Park Beautiful – and popular – landscape of mountains and lakes, which can be explored by boat, bike and on foot. See page 269

❷ The Puck Fair Bacchanalian festival in August, when Killorglin comes under the reign of a wild goat. See page 275

❸ The Kerry Way A 213km walking route through the wild, awe-inspiring scenery of the Iveragh Peninsula. See page 277

❹ Skywalk Rope Bridge Take a dizzying walk across Ireland's longest rope bridge for spectacular views of the Ring of Kerry. See page 278

❺ The Skelligs Spectacular, inhospitable islands; haunt of seabirds and the ghosts of early medieval hermits. See page 280

❻ Dingle town Traditional music, great pubs and seafood – what more could you want? See page 288

❼ The Blaskets Lonely islands off the scenic Dingle Peninsula, with an astonishing literary heritage that's imaginatively documented in the visitor centre. See page 292

❽ Gallarus Oratory A unique, early Christian remnant and a graceful, evocative piece of architecture. See page 293

HIGHLIGHTS ARE MARKED ON THE MAP ON PAGE 268

By bus In this deeply rural county, public buses are few and often far between. Bus Éireann is augmented by Kerry Community Transport (http://locallinkerry.ie), whose minibus network may be of use to visitors, though its complex weekly timetable is mostly designed to get people from rural areas into the big towns for the day.

Killarney and around

KILLARNEY was developed as a resort on the doorstep of Ireland's finest lakeland scenery in the eighteenth and nineteenth centuries, and has steadily grown as a tourist town since. Today it's busy, lively and easily accessible, with hundreds of places to stay across all price ranges. Backpackers are particularly well catered for, with an appealing

KERRY

HIGHLIGHTS

1 Killarney National Park
2 The Puck Fair
3 The Kerry Way
4 Skywalk Rope Bridge
5 The Skelligs
6 Dingle town
7 The Blaskets
8 Gallarus Oratory

selection of hostels and all manner of land- and water-borne tours available for those without their own transport. The town's kiss-me-quick hedonism and souvenir shops are not to everyone's taste, but its big draw is still the same as three hundred years ago: beginning in the very heart of town, **Killarney National Park** encompasses three beautiful lakes, beyond which rise the splendid **Macgillycuddy's Reeks**, the country's highest mountain range, known in Irish as Na Cruacha Dubha, the "Black Stacks". The only building of architectural interest in the town is Pugin's elegant **cathedral**, but the national park shelters three diverse and very well-preserved monuments, **Ross Castle**, **Muckross Friary** and **Muckross House**.

St Mary's Cathedral

On the west side of the town centre • Hours variable • Free

Seat of the Bishop of Kerry, **St Mary's Cathedral** is Ireland's finest neo-Gothic church, built in stages between 1842 and 1912 to a design by Augustus Pugin. Set in spacious gardens by the entrance to the national park, its exterior, with a lofty steeple over the transept, is strikingly elegant. Inside, the rough grey stonework is colourfully lit by dozens of stained-glass windows, which depict in their upper range the life of Christ, in the lower the lives of the Irish saints, notably Patrick and Brendan the Navigator, patron saint of the diocese. The redwood tree outside the west door marks a mass children's grave from the time of the Famine: work on the church was suspended in the late 1840s, when the partly roofed building was used as a hospital and shelter.

Killarney National Park

Visitor centre Killarney House & Gardens, Muckross Rd • **Information point** Muckross House, Dromyrourk, 6km south of Killarney town centre • http://nationalparks.ie/killarney

Killarney National Park now protects the glaciated limestone valleys around the three lakes, Leane (or Lower), Muckross (or Middle) and Upper. The lakeshores are covered with virgin forest that features oak, yew and such Mediterranean plants as the arbutus, or strawberry tree – so termed because of its red, but inedible, fruit. Among the park's notable mammals are Ireland's only wild herd of red deer, otter, pine marten, red squirrels and Irish hare, while its 140 bird species include the white-tailed sea eagle (reintroduced from Norway in 2007), the peregrine falcon and the hen harrier. Running roughly parallel to, but just outside, the park's western border is the dramatic glacial breach known as the Gap of Dunloe (see page 273). The **National Park Visitor Centre** at Killarney House provides information about all aspects of the park, including a twenty-minute audiovisual on the landscape, flora and fauna; a useful free **map** of the park is also available here, while the Ordnance Survey of Ireland produces a more detailed (1:25,000) map.

There's all manner of tours and transport available (many of which can be booked at the tourist office), including boats at Ross Castle and Muckross House (see page 271), and rented bikes (see page 274).

Ross Castle

Ross Island, 2km from Killarney, off the N71 Kenmare Rd • March to early Nov, last admission 5pm; maximum 15 people per tour, so you may have a wait at busy times • charge; Heritage Card • http://heritageireland.ie

The gates of Knockreer Estate opposite the cathedral and the "Golden Gates" by the National Park Information Point on Muckross Road give immediate access from the town centre to the national park. Paths through the grounds, which blaze in spring with rhododendrons, azaleas and magnolias, lead south after less than half an hour to **Ross Castle**.

The interior is only accessible on a guided **tour**, which focuses on the history, architecture and day-to-day life of the castle. It's an impressive example of a medieval tower house, probably built in the late fifteenth century by one of the O'Donoghue

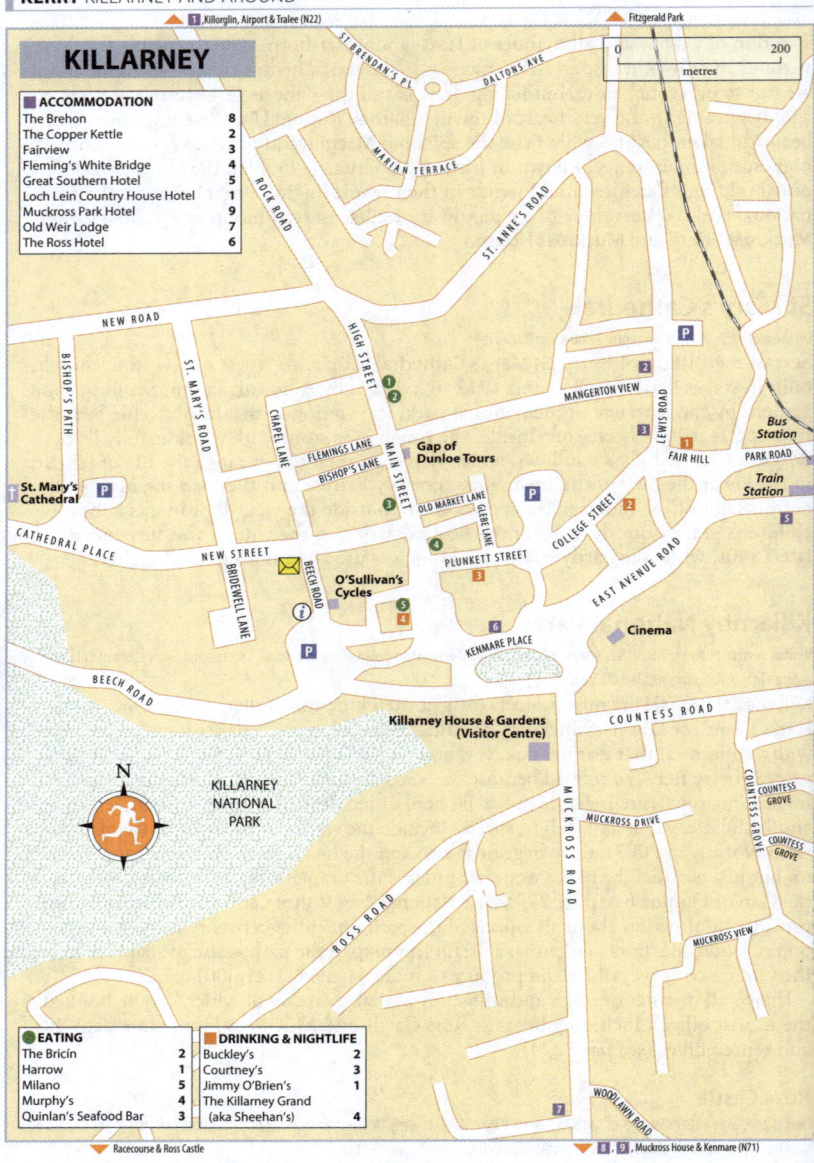

KILLARNEY

■ ACCOMMODATION
The Brehon	8
The Copper Kettle	2
Fairview	3
Fleming's White Bridge	4
Great Southern Hotel	5
Loch Lein Country House Hotel	1
Muckross Park Hotel	9
Old Weir Lodge	7
The Ross Hotel	6

● EATING
The Bricín	2
Harrow	1
Milano's	5
Murphy's	4
Quinlan's Seafood Bar	3

■ DRINKING & NIGHTLIFE
Buckley's	2
Courtney's	3
Jimmy O'Brien's	1
The Killarney Grand (aka Sheehan's)	4

Ross chieftains, who had undisputed hold over the Killarney area at the time. They clearly had something to fear, however: the austere stronghold features murder holes and stumble steps – of irregular dimensions, designed to trip unwary attackers – while the cross-planked and spiked oak doors are further protected by raised thresholds and pointed arches. The flagstoned rooms, which include a Great Hall with its own pantry and minstrels' gallery and a tiny cubbyhole for around fifteen servants to sleep in, have been decked out with authentic furniture and tapestries.

Lough Leane

Rowing boats for rent at Ross Castle (€5/hr); boat trips to Inisfallen (€10/person) are best booked through the Killarney Discover Ireland Centre (064 663 1633)

The largest of Killarney's three lakes, **Lough Leane** sits in a serene mountain-ringed valley and is dotted with uninhabited islands and a restored castle. Catch the right day and you'll be enchanted by the light – though the lake also takes on a special beauty in the drizzle. From Ross Castle you can rent a rowing boat to row out to one of the lake's wooded islands, **Inisfallen**, about 1.6km offshore, where romantic ruins date from the sixth or seventh century. It was here, between AD 950 and 1350, that the *Annals of Inisfallen* – a chronicle of world and Irish history – were written by monks; today the book survives in the Bodleian Library in Oxford. Although the original churches have disappeared, you can still see on Inisfallen the weathered ruins of a thirteenth-century **oratory** and an **Augustinian priory**.

Muckross Estate

The huge section of the national park known as **Muckross Estate** begins about 3km south of Killarney off the N71, where a gate and a gaggle of jaunting cars signal the short walk through the woods to **Muckross Friary** (free access). Founded in the fifteenth century, this strict Franciscan friary originally enshrined a miraculous statue of the Virgin Mary. It's in a remarkable state of preservation, with an intact two-storey cloister shaded by a gnarled yew tree at its centre.

Muckross House

House Guided tours daily; last tour 1hr 20mins before closing; closed one week at Christmas • charge; Heritage Card • **Farms** Mar–Oct • charge, joint ticket with the house available; Heritage Card not accepted • http://muckross-house.ie

From Muckross Friary, you can continue through the estate on foot or by bike, but car drivers will have to continue down the main road for 1km to **Muckross House**. Guided tours lead visitors around the rich Victorian interiors of this fine nineteenth-century neo-Elizabethan stately home. On the other side of the car park are the three traditional **working farms** where you can chat to actors playing out the roles of farmers and their wives. In fine weather, you can sit outside at the splendid **café-restaurant** in the crafts centre, overlooking the pretty **gardens**, which are noted for their rhododendrons and azaleas.

Muckross Lake

Boat trips can be organized at the nearby Dundag Boathouse (087 278 9335 or 087 120 0420)

KILLARNEY FESTIVALS AND EVENTS

Killarney lays on a long menu of seasonal **festivals and events**, with music and sport featuring strongly. **The Gathering** is a five-day festival of traditional music in late February (http://killarney.ie/festivals-and-events), while the **4th of July Festival** celebrates the town's strong links with the United States, with.outdoor concerts at Killarney House and a mass street parade.

In May, July and August, Killarney's **racecourse** (http://killarneyraces.ie), in a scenic spot on Ross Road, hosts boisterous, well-supported racing. The first weekend in May, when the **Rally of the Lakes** (http://rallyofthelakes.com) pulls crowds of motoring fans to the area, is not a good time to experience the serenity of the mountains.

Killarney is a good place to sample the Kerry fervour for **Gaelic football**: major matches are held at Fitzgerald Park on Lewis Road (http://kerrygaa.ie), which is named after Dick Fitzgerald, greatest player of the early twentieth century and author of the first training manual on the game, and enjoys a magnificent mountain backdrop from its north terraces. The local side, Dr Croke's, All-Ireland club champions in 1992, have their stadium across the road.

KILLARNEY NATIONAL PARK TOURS AND ACTIVITIES

GUIDED WALKS

Two-hour **guided walks** through the park set off from outside O'Shea's Funeral Home opposite St Mary's Cathedral every morning at 11am (Nov–April advance booking required; Charge; http://killarneyguidedwalks.com).

PONY TRAPS

Jaunting cars (pony traps) tout for business at several locations, including Kenmare Place in town, Muckross House and *Kate Kearney's Cottage* (see page 273) for the Gap of Dunloe. On the east side of the Kenmare Place roundabout, a sign in front of the Celtic cross war memorial and the *Killarney Avenue Hotel* gives a map of their routes and a detailed price list, though you might still have to haggle with the "jarveys" – as the drivers are known. A one-hour trip, for example, through the national park and along the lakeside to Ross Castle should cost around €18 per person. Reputable jarveys include Paul and Michael Tangney, usually to be found at Kenmare Place (http://killarneyjauntingcars.com).

HORSERIDING

Killarney Riding Stables, 1km west of town on the Killorglin road (http://killarney-riding-stables.com), offer **horseriding** in the national park on day-trips, as well as on the two- or five-day Reeks Trail.

KAYAKING

Kayaking on the lakes is offered by Outdoors Ireland (http://outdoorsireland.com); a three-hour paddle costs around €60.

ORGANIZED TOURS OF THE PARK

Several tour operators, including O'Donoghue Brothers, based at *Old Weir Lodge*, Muckross Rd (http://killarneydaytour.com), and Gap of Dunloe Tours, with a base at *O'Connors Pub*, 7 High St, in the summer (http://gapofdunloetours.com), offer full-day **combination tours**, which take you by bus to the starting point of Kate Kearney's Cottage (see page 273), from where you walk or ride a jaunting car or pony through the Gap; then after a lunch stop at Lord Brandon's Cottage you take a boat ride through the three lakes to Ross Castle, and finally a bus brings you back into town. Simpler **bike-on-boat tours** (you cycle through the Gap of Dunloe and sling your bike on a boat between Lord Brandon's Cottage and Ross Castle) can be arranged through the hostels, or O'Donoghue Brothers (as above) or Gap of Dunloe Tours. Or you can put this together yourself: from roughly early March to late October, the boats leave Ross Castle at 11am, returning from Lord Brandon's at 2pm (€15), and bikes can be rented from O'Sullivan's (see page 274).

ORGANIZED TOURS OF LOUGH LEANE

From the pier at Ross Castle, **tours of Lough Leane** are operated by two large waterbuses, which in summer each run four or five one-hour trips a day (€15): the *Lily of Killarney* (contact O'Donoghue Brothers, as above); and the *Pride of the Lakes* (http://killarneylaketours.ie), which offers a connecting shuttle bus from town.

HOP-ON HOP-OFF BUSES

Killarney currently supports two **hop-on hop-off bus** services. The Big Red Killarney Bus Tour (http://killarneytour.com), is an open-top double-decker which runs south to Ross Castle, Muckross House and Torc Waterfall half a dozen times a day and which reduces its service to once daily in winter. Killarney Shuttle Bus (087 968 7997) starts at the tourist office, offers single tickets as well as day passes, and covers three routes: west to the Gap of Dunloe (2 daily) and south to Muckross House and Torc Waterfall (5 daily), and Ladies' View (1 daily).

Starting from Muckross House (where you can pick up a walks leaflet), there's a delightful 10km **trail** around **Muckross Lake**, mostly on paved paths, but with a short section on the main Kenmare road. Passing through gnarled, mossy, ancient woods with a thick undergrowth of heather and ferns, you'll reach Brickeen Bridge where lakes Muckross and Leane meet, and shortly after the Meeting of the Waters, where the outflow from the Upper Lake runs into Muckross Lake. Just above this second meeting, towards the end of the walk, is an irresistibly photogenic, tree-shaded pool with the arches of the ruined Old Weir Bridge as a backdrop is a delightful tearoom, **Dinis Cottage**, older than Muckross House itself – you can arrive on foot, by bike or by boat as the cottage has its own pier. Originally built as a hunting lodge in the 1700s, Dinis has been used as a tearoom since the early 1800s. Some of its window etchings date from 1816. The cottage's fascinating pedigree and the area's history are displayed on walls, alongside old visitor books. Light refreshments are served all day and include sandwiches, quiches and scones. On your way back, you can take in 20m **Torc Waterfall** on a short detour, or take on the steep climb up to the summit of **Torc Mountain** (535m) for magnificent views of the lakes and the Reeks.

The Upper Lake

Further down the main N71, 16km from Killarney, is **Ladies' View**, which apparently was chosen by the ladies-in-waiting of Queen Victoria on her visit in 1861 as the finest view in the land – with some justification. From the car park here, you look directly down on the **Upper Lake**, with its many channels running down to lakes Muckross and Leane on one side, and the Carrauntoohil massif rising on the other. Just before reaching Ladies' View on the main road, there's a signposted path, part of the Kerry Way, through Derrycunihy Woods to Lord Brandon's Cottage (see below); beyond Ladies' View, spectacular vistas continue at least as far as **Moll's Gap**, where the Avoca craft shop and its good café mark the parting of the Kenmare road and the R568 to Sneem.

The Gap of Dunloe

West of Muckross Lake, the **Gap of Dunloe**, a glacial defile which cuts off Tomies and Purple mountains from Macgillycuddy Reeks, is justifiably one of the area's most popular attractions. Try, if you can, to come here late in the day, when the light is at its best and the road at its quietest.

The usual approach is from the north, where **Kate Kearney's Cottage**, a pub and restaurant 4km from Beaufort, stands at the foot of the Gap. Beyond here the narrow road is not designed to handle motor traffic at busy times, and should be left free for walkers, cyclists, pony trekkers and jaunting cars; at quiet times, you should be OK to drive it if you need to. It's a starkly beautiful 7km climb to the **Head of the Gap**, walled in by a steep patchwork of grass and bare purple rock, with tumbling waterfalls after rain, past reedy lakes and one or two sheep. Then from the Head, you can make a glorious descent into the broad **Black Valley**, hemmed in by 784m Broaghnabinnia at its western end and so named because all its inhabitants died during the Famine. It now supports a few sheep farms, a primary school and a basic An Óige hostel, on the Kerry Way 3km from the Head of the Gap. About 2km further down the road, in a delightful spot at the head of the Upper Lake, is **Lord Brandon's Cottage**, a nineteenth-century hunting lodge, now summertime café, where the boats from Ross Castle terminate (see page 269).

| **ARRIVAL AND DEPARTURE** | **KILLARNEY AND AROUND** |

By plane Kerry's airport (http://kerryairport.ie) is 15km from Killarney on the N23, 2km northeast of the village of Farranfore, which is on the Tralee–Killarney train line. Buses between Limerick and Killarney (plus a few Tralee–Killarney services) call at the airport roughly every 2hr; a taxi into town costs about €25 (a list of taxi drivers is listed on the airport website).

By train Killarney's train station is very centrally placed, off East Avenue Rd.

Destinations Cork (7–8 daily, often with a change at

Mallow; 1hr 30min–2hr); Dublin (7–8 daily, most with a change at Mallow; 3hr–3hr 30min); Farranfore (7–8 daily; 20min); Tralee (7–8 daily; 40min).

By bus The Bus Éireann station is on Park Rd, while Citylink buses (http://citylink.ie) use East Avenue Rd.

Destinations Bus Éireann: Caherdaniel (July & Aug 1 daily; 2hr 15min); Cahersiveen (July & Aug 1–3 daily, rest of year Mon–Sat 2 daily; 1hr 30min); Cork (hourly; 1hr 30min); Dingle, changing at Tralee (2–5 daily; 2–3hr); Dingle, via

Inch and Anascaul (July & Aug Mon–Sat 2 daily; 1hr 20min); Kenmare (via Kilgarvan; July & Aug 2–3 daily, rest of year Mon–Fri 2 daily; 50min); Kerry Airport (Farranfore; 6–7 daily; 20min); Killorglin (4–6 daily; 30min); Limerick (5–6 daily; 2hr); Ring of Kerry (July & Aug 1 daily; 5hr 15min, with a break in Sneem); Tralee (10–16 daily; 40min); Waterford (hourly; 4hr 10min); Waterville (July & Aug 1–2 daily, rest of year Mon–Sat 1 daily; 1hr 55min).

Destination Citylink: Galway (2 daily; 2hr 45min).

GETTING AROUND AND INFORMATION

Bike rental O'Sullivan Cycles has three outlets: Beech Rd opposite the tourist office; Muckross Road, opposite *Randles Court Hotel*; and College Street, opposite *Murphy's Bar* (all daily 9am–6pm; http://killarneyrentabike.com)); expect to pay €20 for a full day's hire.

Car rental There are half a dozen car hire companies at the

airport.

Taxis There's a taxi rank on College St or call, for example, Euro Taxis (064 663 7676).

Tourist office The tourist office is on Beech Rd (June–Sept daily 9am–5pm, Sun 9am–1pm; Oct–May Mon–Sat 9am–5pm; http://killarney.ie).

ACCOMMODATION
SEE MAP PAGE 270

It's worth booking **accommodation** in Killarney in advance, but there are scores of B&Bs, upmarket guesthouses and hotels in town – if none of the listings below can fit you in, the friendly tourist office should be able to help.

The Brehon 1km south of town on the N71 Muckross Rd, http://thebrehon.com. Imposing and stylish contemporary hotel with 125 spacious and well-equipped rooms, a fine restaurant, *Danú*, and an excellent spa. All guests have free access to the spa's vitality suite and fitness centre. €€€

The Copper Kettle 5 York Terrace, Lewis Rd, 064 663 4164. Pleasant B&B on the north side of the town centre with a variety of tasteful en-suite rooms, all with cable TV, some with Jacuzzis and king-size beds. €€

Fairview College St, http://killarneyfairview.com. Attractive and welcoming central hotel with good-sized, well-appointed rooms (some with Jacuzzi) as well as an accomplished restaurant and lounge bar. One of Killarney's more family-friendly hotels. €€

Fleming's White Bridge 1km east of town, signposted off the N22 Cork road, http://killarneycamping.com. Among several campsites around Killarney, this quiet spot on the banks of the River Flesk has a summertime shop, laundry, campers' kitchen, games room, TV lounge and bike rental. Closed Nov to mid-March. €

Great Southern Hotel East Avenue, http://greatsouthern killarney.com. This ivy-clad Victorian railway hotel comes with chandeliers and marble floors in the huge lobby, an ornate gilded ceiling in the breakfast room, and attractive guest rooms, especially in the original building. Also has extensive gardens and a sparkling spa facility with

swimming pool. €€€

Loch Lein Country House Hotel Fossa, 5km west of town off the N72, http://lochlein.com. A good-value choice if you'd prefer to stay away from the town's bustle, this peaceful, welcoming and well-run small hotel has views of Lough Leane and the mountains, spacious, tastefully decorated rooms and a restaurant that specializes in local produce. €€€

Muckross Park Hotel N71, about 5km south of town, http://muckrosspark.com. Dating from 1795, and much extended since, this opulent hotel is right opposite the entrance to Muckross Friary, giving immediate access to the national park trails (bicycles available free of charge). Some rooms have four-posters and views of the Blue Pool River, and there are eighteen two-bedroom apartments (sleeping five), available on a B&B or self-catering basis. There's a fine spa and a choice of both formal and informal dining, the latter in the convivial *Colgan's Pub*. A complimentary shuttle bus operates between the hotel and town. €€€

Old Weir Lodge Muckross Rd, a 10min walk from the centre, http://oldweirlodge.com. Thirty-room, mock-Tudor guesthouse that feels like a hotel, with spacious, well-equipped and comfortable rooms. It retains a personal touch, with a warm welcome and plenty of local information. €€€

The Ross Hotel East Avenue Rd, http://theross.ie. Luxurious boutique hotel right at the heart of the action, with bright bedrooms and excellent service. Guests are free to use the 20m indoor swimming pool, gym, sauna, Jacuzzi and outdoor hot tub at sister hotel, *The Killarney Park*, across the road. €€€

EATING
SEE MAP PAGE 270

The Bricín 26 High St, http://bricin.ie. Homely restaurant that serves traditional Irish food, notably filled boxties

(potato pancakes), as well as more eclectic dishes such as Thai red chicken curry with jasmine rice in a coconut milk

THE PUCK FAIR

For three mad days in the middle of August, the **Puck Fair** (http://puckfair.ie) draws in crowds of up to thirty thousand to the small, otherwise missable town of **Killorglin**, 19km west of Killarney. Granted its charter by James I in 1613, the fair begins when a wild goat is stalked in the mountains, then caged and crowned as king of the town, which raises the curtain on a Dionysian festival of wine and song, accompanied by a traditional horse fair. The event has pagan roots in the Celtic harvest festival of Lughnasa, though these particular ceremonies are meant to commemorate the herd of goats that ran down into Killorglin, to warn the townsfolk that Cromwell's army was on its way. For further information, contact Killorglin's Mid-Kerry Tourism office (066 976 1451, http://discoverkerry.com).

sauce; commendably, there's also a dedicated vegan menu. Excellent Early-bird menu between 6pm and 6.45pm. Closed Sun & Mon. €€€

Harrow 27 High St, http://harrowkillarney.com. Stylish brasserie – formal but far from stuffy – with a predominantly beef and seafood menu (featherblade with malt glazed carrot smoked potato purée and dried onion crumble), though there are also one or two startlingly good vegan dishes, like shallot tarte tatin with celeriac confit and walnut oil. Three-course set menu €55. Closed Mon–Wed. €€€

Milano 16 Main St, http://milano.ie. Typically fresh, contemporary setting for the Irish version of Britain's *Pizza Express*, offering a huge range of top-notch pizzas plus salads and simple pastas. €€

Murphy's 37 Main St, http://murphysicecream.ie. Branch of Dingle's excellent ice-cream shop (eat in or take away) with scrumptious flavours like Dingle sea salt, and honeycomb caramel – plus sorbets. Grab a deckchair out on the street in summer. Also serves cakes and coffees. €

Quinlan's Seafood Bar 77 High St, http://seafoodbar.ie. Branch of Tralee's superior fish'n'chip shop – take away or tuck into dishes such as lemon sole, crab, scallops or deep-water Atlantic prawns in the informal seafood restaurant. €€

DRINKING AND NIGHTLIFE

SEE MAP PAGE 270

Buckley's Arbutus Hotel, College St, http://arbutuskillarney.com. The hotel's smart, traditional bar, with long, sociable bench seats, hosts all kinds of Irish music sessions Fri & Sat, plus Sun lunch and dinner.

Courtney's 24 Plunkett St, http://courtneysbar.com. Appealingly plain, bare-wood and stone-floored pub, popular among a 20-something crowd, with a great range of whiskeys and beers. In the summer, it hosts traditional music Mon to Thurs, live bands on Fri and DJ sessions on Sat.

Jimmy O'Brien's Fair Hill, 087 961 3482. The yellow and green facade gives the game away – this traditional lounge bar is a veritable museum of Kerry Gaelic football, hung with dozens of photos (plus material on the notably lively dance music and *sean-nós* singing of Sliabh Lucra, the mountains to the east of Killarney). Decent pint of Guinness, too.

The Killarney Grand (aka Sheehan's) Main St, http://killarneygrand.com. A large but often crowded bar with nightly live entertainment courtesy of three different venues: *Paddy Sheehan's* for trad music, the *Piano Bar* for more sophisticated fare, and a straightforward nightclub for tunes every night of the week.

The Iveragh Peninsula: the Ring of Kerry

The **Ring of Kerry** is often used as a substitute name for the **Iveragh Peninsula**, but more properly it refers to the 175km road that encircles this vast, scenic leg of land. Tourists have been coming to the peninsula in ever-increasing numbers over the past century, but most of them do the Ring by bus or car in a day from Killarney. If you stay in one of the Iveragh's few small towns or venture off the main route, for example onto the **Ring of Skellig** at the very tip, you'll have to yourself this giant's landscape of mountains, lakes and long ocean views, which is at its most spectacular when illuminated by a sudden shaft of light through the clouds like a flash bulb.

GETTING AROUND

THE IVERAGH PENINSULA: THE RING OF KERRY

By bus Bus Éireann circles the whole Ring only in July and Aug (I daily; 1hr 15 min, with a break In Sneem), at other times venturing out of Killarney only as far as Waterville (1hr 55 min) via the north coast.

8

KILLARNEY NATIONAL PARK
AND THE IVERAGH PENINSULA

THE KERRY WAY AND CARRAUNTOOHIL

The 213km-long **Kerry Way** (http://kerryway.com) is a spectacular, circular, waymarked footpath that starts in Killarney, takes in the Muckross Estate, Torc Waterfall, the Upper Lake and the Black Valley before crossing to Glencar, then goes right around the Iveragh Peninsula anticlockwise, with short offshoots to Glenbeigh, Cahersiveen, Waterville and Caherdaniel, finally passing through Sneem and Kenmare. Mostly following a network of green roads, many of which are old "butter roads", the route provides magnificent views both of the Iveragh's mountains and of the neighbouring peninsulas, Dingle and Beara. OS 1:50,000 **map** numbers 78 and 83 are essential, and Cork Kerry Tourism produces a useful *Kerry Way Map Guide*. The whole thing can be done in nine or ten days, or, with careful study of bus timetables, you could do day-walks along the Way beyond Glenbeigh in summer, or on the section between Glenbeigh and Waterville in winter.

Experienced walkers may well be tempted off the Kerry Way to tackle Ireland's highest peak, **Carrauntoohil** (1038m). Two of the finest approaches are described in *Best Irish Walks* by Josh Lynam: the Coomloughra Horseshoe, a seven-hour, occasionally vertiginous circuit, starting from the bridge at Breanlee on the Beaufort–Glencar road, which also takes in the second- and third-highest peaks, Beenkeragh and Caher; and a tough, nine-hour Macgillicuddy Reeks ridge walk, beginning at *Kate Kearney's Cottage*, bagging six peaks and ending at the Breanlee bridge.

On foot You can walk around the peninsula on the Kerry Way (see page 277).

By bike Cycling, often up steep gradients and against strong winds, is a shorter option than walking (three days at the least), but perhaps just as physically demanding. The waymarked 215km Ring of Kerry Cycle Route (http://ringofkerrycycle.ie; map guide available from local tourist offices) of necessity follows the main road for around a third of its journey, but includes a long, scenic loop through Ballinskelligs, Portmagee and Valentia Island, and covers the north coast of the peninsula and the area around Killarney almost entirely on minor roads. Coach tours from Killarney, which ply the Ring of Kerry in flotillas in summer, are required to travel anticlockwise: you can weigh up the disadvantages of getting stuck in a convoy against meeting the buses on the many blind corners. We've covered the Ring anticlockwise.

8

Cahersiveen

CAHERSIVEEN (sometimes spelt Caherciveen or Cahirsiveen, but always pronounced with the stress on the last syllable) is the main service town for the west end of the peninsula. Functional rather than attractive, its one long, narrow street is at various points named East End, Church Street, Main Street and New Street. Cahersiveen holds a lively **music and arts festival** (http://celticmusicfestival.com) over the bank holiday weekend at the beginning of August. By the side of the N70 as it enters the town from the east is a striking local landmark, Éamonn O'Doherty's *To the Skelligs*. Installed in 1995, the sculpture depicts Brendan the Navigator (see page 314) and fellow monks making their way to the islands.

O'Connell Memorial Church
Main St • Hours variable • Free

The town's most famous son was Daniel O'Connell (see page 564), to whom the **O'Connell Memorial Church** on the main street was dedicated – a remarkable tribute for a politician. Built between 1888 and 1902, largely with money from the US and Australia, it's a huge, lumbering edifice made of concrete, faced with Irish granite.

The Old Barracks
Bridge St • Daily • Charge • http://theoldbarracks.net

The heritage centre in the fearsome castle-like **Barracks**, has been renovated with new exhibits on local history but still retains its external appearance of an atmospheric

SKYWALK ROPE BRIDGE

Thrill-seekers will love Ireland's longest rope bridge, the **Skywalk** (9am till dusk; Charge; http://kellsbay.ie). Known as a Burmese Rope Bridge and with a span of 34m, it is positioned 11m above the Delligeenagh River in **Kells Bay House & Gardens**, halfway between Glenbeigh and Cahersiveen on the Ring of Kerry, just south of Kells Bay beach. Spectacular views from the bridge look across to the **gardens**, which were planted more than 160 years ago and include rare flowers and ferns from the Himalayas. The admission ticket includes access to both the rope bridge and the gardens – while you're here, be sure to seek out Ireland's largest **palm tree**, found in the Succulent Garden at the front of the house: a staggering eleven-tonne specimen with a 7.5m trunk imported from Chile.

ruin. The interpretation includes the story of the Fenian Rising of 1867 and the Easter Rising of 1916. Stories about the life and times of Daniel O'Connell with touch screens are spread over two floors. There's also a café, craft shop and tourist information. The construction of these heavily fortified quarters for the Royal Irish Constabulary was prompted by the 1867 rising when local Republicans tried to cut the transatlantic cable at Valentia.

ARRIVAL AND GETTING AROUND   CAHERSIVEEN

By bus Buses from/to Killarney (2 daily; 1hr 30min) stop at the Market House petrol station/supermarket on Glenbeigh Rd.

Bike rental Casey's, New St (Mon–Sat 9am–6pm, plus July & Aug Sun 10.30am–1pm; http://bikehirekerry.com), is an excellent outfit offering touring bikes (from €20/day) as well as e-bikes (from €45/day).

ACCOMMODATION

Mannix Point Camping and Caravan Park West side of town, http://campinginkerry.com. Welcoming and very well equipped waterfront campsite with laundry, camper's kitchen and picnic garden, plus a lounge holding evenings of impromptu music sessions in July and Aug. Closed mid-Sept to Easter. €

★ **Quinlan & Cooke** 3 Main St, http://qc.ie. Beautifully designed, wood-panelled rooms in a boutique townhouse with a separate street door behind the restaurant (QC's);

large and bright with comfy beds, iPod docks, espresso machines and power showers. There's also a spacious sitting room, a sun deck and a gym. Continental breakfasts are taken in your room. €€€

Sive Townhouse 15 New Market St, http://sivebudget accommodation.com. Friendly, family-run budget hotel with simple but colourful rooms – singles, doubles, triples and family – plus a sitting room and laundry facilities. Substantial breakfast included. €€

EATING

O'Neills The Point 5km west at Reenard Point, http://oneillsthepoint.ie. Located at the terminus of the Valentia Island ferry (see page 280), this pub-restaurant is very popular for its high-quality seafood including magical dishes like casserole of monkfish on a bed of diced potato with garlic. Closed Tues & Wed. €€€

Petit Delice 11 Main St, a few doors east of QC's, 087 990 3572. Small but authentic French patisserie and café, serving quiches, filled baguettes, croissants and artisan breads, and loved by the Cahersiveen caffeine cognoscenti.

Don't leave without sampling a drool-worthy mille-feuille vanilla slice. Closed Sun. €

★ **Quinlan & Cooke** 3 Main St, http://qc.ie. One of the best places to eat on the Ring of Kerry, a nautical-themed bar-restaurant with a lovely, covered back patio. As the owners' family have their own boats and fish-processing factory, seafood is, unsurprisingly, the speciality, in dishes such as hake fillet on a broth of smoked haddock, Atlantic prawns, and sizzling Valentia crab claws; the seafood pasta of the day is always worth investigating. Dinner only. Closed Mon. €€€

Portmagee

The attractive harbour village of **PORTMAGEE** is the jumping-off point by road for Valentia, situated beside the long bridge to the island.

The Skellig Experience

Visitor centre Daily: March, Oct & Nov 10am–5pm; April–June & Sept 10am–6pm; July & Aug 10am–7pm; last admission 45min before closing • charge • **Cruises** Standard cruises 2hr (subject to demand – contact the centre in the morning); in worse weather, 45min mini-cruises around Valentia channel occasionally laid on • Standard ticket includes admission to the visitor centre; mini-cruise with admission to the visitor centre • http://skelligexperience.com

Portmagee's **Skellig Experience**, which is actually just across the bridge from the village, gives some fascinating background on seabirds and other marine life, lighthouses and early monastic life, with an impressive short film about Skellig Michael. The centre also has a café with fine views of Portmagee, and runs **cruises** around, but not on to/and on, Skellig Michael, which are useful for those who can't manage the 650 steps to the island's summit.

ACCOMMODATION AND EATING   PORTMAGEE

★ **The Moorings** 7 Harbour View, http://moorings.ie. Tastefully decorated and well-equipped accommodation is available – it's worth paying extra for a room overlooking the harbour – at this well-run, eco-conscious inn, which offers various half-board deals and activities packages. Sumptuous hot and cold seafood platters plus lots of other fishy treats are served in the restaurant, and there's traditional music most Tues, Sat & Sun nights between April and Sept in the Bridge Bar. €€€

Valentia Island

Separated from the mainland by a long, narrow channel that's now bridged, **VALENTIA** barely feels like an island. For such a small, remote spot, it boasts a surprising number of claims to fame: as well as being known from the radio shipping forecasts and for Valentia slate, which was used for the Houses of Parliament in London and the Paris Opera House, it was from here that the first transatlantic telegraph cable was laid in 1866. To add to the island's repute, the oldest fossilized footprints in the northern hemisphere, the so-called Tetrapod Trackway, were discovered here in 1992 by a Swiss geology student. Most of the island's amenities are in or around **Knightstown** at the northeastern tip, which provides dramatic views of the Iveragh Mountains, as well as a seasonal **ferry** link to the mainland.

At the western edge of the village, the **Valentia Island Heritage Centre** (April–Sept daily 10am–5pm; charge; (http://vhc.cablehistory.org) houses a display on the island's history in the old primary school.

Glanleam House

In the northern part of the island, 2km west of Knightstown • Charge • http://glanleam.com

Walking up School House Road from the heritage centre, then forking right, will bring you after about 1km to **Glanleam House**, which was formerly the seat of the Knight of Kerry. Developed in the 1850s, the beautiful subtropical **gardens** here encompass lily-of-the-valley trees, ferns and other exotic specimens from South America, Australasia and China, which thrive in this mild, sheltered location. For children, there's a pirate trail and a fairy garden.

Tetrapod Trackway

About 5km from Knightstown near the island's northernmost tip, it's possible to see for yourself the **Tetrapod Trackway**, though you might have to show some perseverance as it's not very well signposted (basically, head up School House Road from the heritage centre and take the second right). From a car park by the island's radio station, a short path leads down to a precarious shelf of black rock by the Atlantic, on which the small foot- and tail-prints of the creature – a metre-long, crocodile-like amphibian with a large, paddle-shaped tail, that lived some 385 million years ago – are quite clearly visible. What can feel like the end of the world on a stormy day is a suitably awesome location to come toe-to-toe with our first landborne ancestors.

Valentia Island Farmhouse Dairy

1km southwest of Knightstown on the main island road, the R565 • 087 349 7385

This traditional **dairy farm** makes its own delicious ice cream, which it sells at its farm and craft shop. It also offers sightseeing tours of the area around Knightstown in a horse-and-carriage (€9/person; booking recommended).

Geokaun Mountain and Bray Head

Geokaun Mountain car parking charge; pedestrians and cyclists charge • http://geokaun.com

Near the middle of the north coast, the spectacular **Fogher Cliffs** and **Geokaun Mountain**, the island's highest point, have been turned into a viewing area, with the installation of fifty information panels and a 1500m loop walk. Further exciting views are provided by the ruined lookout tower on **Bray Head**, at the southwestern end of the island.

ARRIVAL AND INFORMATION · VALENTIA ISLAND

By ferry From Reenard Point, 5km west of Cahersiveen (see page 277), a ferry operates a continuous shuttle service across to Knightstown on Valentia Island (April–Oct Mon–Sat 7.45am–9.30pm, Sun 9am–9.30pm (July & Aug last ferry 10pm); cars €10 return; cyclists €3 return; 087 241 8973).

Tourist information Inside the Valentia Island Heritage Centre on School Rd, Knightstown (April–Sept daily 10am–5pm; http://valentiaisland.ie), which also holds an illuminating exhibition on the island.

ACCOMMODATION

Atlantic Villa Behind the Y-junction at the church in Knightstown, http://atlanticvilla.ie. Overlooking the sea in the nineteenth-century former cable-master's house, this B&B offers five pleasant en-suite bedrooms, fresh produce from their organic garden for breakfast, open fires and boot and drying rooms. Two self-catering cottages also available. They can also prepare packed lunches. €€

★ **Glanleam House** About 2km west of Knightstown, http://glanleam.com. This elegant eighteenth- and nineteenth-century house set in subtropical gardens offers delightful accommodation in spacious rooms, with especially attractive bathrooms and views of Valentia Harbour. Dinner available if booked the previous day. Good rates for singles; self-catering cottages available. Closed early Nov to mid-March. €€€

EATING

Pod By the church in Knightstown, 066 947 6995. Cheery pancake café and gift shop with outdoor tables, serving imaginative savoury galettes, sweet crêpes and espresso coffees. €

The Royal Pier Knightstown, http://royalvalentia.ie. The town's landmark 200-year-old inn enjoys glorious views of the harbour and the mainland mountains from its seafront lawn, serves delectable dishes such as chowder, and Royal Smokies (smoked haddock, coley and salmon) plus fish and chips of course; takeaway also available. Also hosts traditional music on Wed and Sun nights. €€€

The Skellig Islands

An incredible, impossible, mad place…I tell you the thing does not belong to any world that you and I have lived and worked in: it is part of our dream world…

George Bernard Shaw

A voyage to the **Skelligs** (Na Scealga, "the crags"), islands of durable Old Red Sandstone that rise sharply from the sea 12km off the tip of the Iveragh Peninsula, is one of the most exciting and inspiring trips you can make in Ireland. On top of the larger of these two inhospitable, shark's-tooth islands, **Skellig Michael** (or Great Skellig), a monastery was somehow constructed in the late seventh or early eighth century, in imitation of the desert communities of the early Church fathers, and dedicated to St Michael, the patron saint of high places. The exposed, often choppy boat-ride out, followed by seabirds from Puffin Island, a nature reserve at the edge of St Finan's Bay, only adds to the sense of wild isolation. **Little Skellig** is a nature reserve too, crawling with over fifty thousand gannets;

landing is forbidden, but the boatmen will come in close so you can watch the gannets diving for fish and hear their awesome din.

The Skelligs have been thrust into the international spotlight in recent years with the filming of scenes of the Star Wars films, *The Force Awakens* (2015) and *The Last Jedi* (2017). The main island was occupied for several weeks by camera crews when Luke Skywalker took up residence. Not everyone, though, was pleased about the Irish government's decision to permit filming and allow helicopter traffic. It was criticised by heritage and ecological experts, as well as Birdwatch Ireland, who expressed concerns about the welfare of the colonies of puffin, Manx shearwaters, kittiwakes, and storm petrels that breed here.

Skellig Michael

If you come in spring or early summer, you'll have thousands of cute breeding puffins to keep you company on the 200m ascent from Skellig Michael's quay. The compact, remarkably well-preserved **monastery** in the lee of the summit is a miracle of ingenuity and devotion. It was built entirely on artificial terraces, facing south–southeast for maximum sunlight, with sturdy outer walls to deflect the winds and to protect the vegetable patch made of bird droppings; channels crisscross the settlement to funnel rainwater into cisterns. You can walk into the **dry-stone beehive huts**, **chapels** and **refectory**, which would have sheltered a total of twelve to fifteen monks at any one time and have withstood the worst the Atlantic can throw at them for 1300 years. The high cross beside the large oratory probably marks the burial of the founder, reputed to have been St Fionán, or an early saint.

At least three Viking raids in the ninth century were not enough to dislodge the monks, but during the climatic change of the twelfth and thirteenth centuries, the seas became rougher and more inhospitable. Around the same time, pressure was brought to bear on the old independent monasteries to conform, and the monks adopted the Augustinian rule and moved to Ballinskelligs on the mainland. Pilgrimages to Skellig Michael, however, continued until the eighteenth century, even after the Dissolution of the Monasteries.

A **visit to the island** is only for those with good mobility, as there's a vertical ladder up on to the quay, and then 618 steep, uneven steps with unprotected edges – slippery when wet – to the windy summit (the alternative is a cruise around the islands). Bring walking shoes, warm waterproof clothes, water and food (but take all litter away with you), as there are no facilities on Skellig Michael (toilets are on the boats).

8

ARRIVAL AND INFORMATION   **THE SKELLIG ISLANDS**

BY BOAT
Only a handful of operators are allowed to land on Skellig Michael (May–Sept, sometimes with extra departures April & Oct, dependent on the weather); landing tours are popular so book as far in advance as possible, although it's not uncommon for there to be a delay of several days before the boats will sail, due to bad weather – the captains make a decision on the weather early each morning. Boats operate mostly (but not always) from Portmagee, departing 10–11am; it takes around 45min–1hr to reach Skellig Michael and you'll typically get around 2.5hr on the island. Expect to pay in the region of €110/120 for a landing tour.

Operators John O'Shea departs from Derrynane Harbour near Caherdaniel (http://skelligtours.com), while Skellig Michael Cruises operate out of Portmagee (http://skellig michaelcruises.com). A complete list of operators is available from local tourist offices and on http://valentiaisland.ie. Most accommodation owners in the area will offer to do the booking for you, which is the easiest way to arrange your trip. **Cruises** Cruises around the islands, which typically last around 2.5hr, are a cheaper way to see them (roughly €50 per person); these are offered by the Skellig Heritage Centre (see page 279) and Skellig Michael Cruises (http:// skelligmichaelcruises.com).

The Ring of Skellig

To the south of Portmagee runs the **Ring of Skellig**, a scenic though often very steep route around the most westerly promontory of the Iveragh Peninsula, via wild and exposed **St**

Finan's Bay – which is the unlikely home of the high-quality **Skelligs Chocolate Factory** (visitors welcome to taste and buy: daily 10am–5pm; http://skelligschocolate.com) and its seasonal coffee shop (Easter to mid-Sept). From the highest point of the road between Portmagee and St Finan's Bay, you can climb the hill on the seaward side of the saddle in twenty minutes or so for magnificent views out to the Skellig Islands, across to the Dingle Peninsula and the Blaskets, and inland to the Iveragh Mountains.

Ballinskelligs (Baile an Sceilg)

On the far shore of the promontory lies the village of **BALLINSKELLIGS** (Baile an Sceilg), set behind a lovely, curving, sheltered beach with great views of Waterville and the mountains, where Skelligs Watersports (http://skelligsurf.com) offers **surfing, wind-surfing, kayaking** and **stand-up paddleboarding**. The monks of Skellig Michael retreated here in the twelfth century, constructing a new **abbey** which in turn was largely rebuilt in the fifteenth century. By walking south along the shoreline for five minutes, beyond a ruined tower house, you can still see its delicate purple-grey sandstone church and traces of its cloister. The small but sprawling village of Ballinskelligs is part of a Gaeltacht (Irish-speaking) enclave, Uíbh Ráthach, and draws hosts of teenagers to Irish college in the summer.

The striking thatched roundhouse at the north end of the village is the **Cill Rialaig Art Centre** (daily 11am–5pm; http://cillrialaigartscentre.com) and café-restaurant (Wed–Sun noon–8pm). Attached to the Cill Rialaig retreat for artists, writers and composers, it hosts art workshops for children and adults in July and August.

EATING
BALLINSKELLIGS

Caife Cois Tra 6–10 Sunny Beach Holiday Homes, 087 296 5874. In a beachside wooden chalet with plenty of outside tables on the grass, this café serves soup, sandwiches and home-baked cakes. It also houses a craft shop specializing in historical photographs. On Sun (11am–4pm) from June to Aug, there's a country market with live music.

Waterville

On the east side of Ballinskelligs Bay, **WATERVILLE** (An Coireán, "the little whirlpool") is an incongruously genteel resort in this distant wilderness. Its exposed, pebbly beach is backed by a long, grassy promenade – now sporting a statue of Charlie Chaplin, who spent several holidays here – and large, neat houses with well-tended lawns, many of them built for workers on the transatlantic telegraph cable, which was extended from Valentia to Waterville in the 1880s. August sees a five-day **festival of classic and contemporary films**, with attendant street entertainment and music (http://chaplinfilmfestival.com). There's no bank in Waterville but the post office behind the prominent *Butler Arms Hotel* on the seafront changes money.

ACCOMMODATION AND EATING
WATERVILLE

Butler Arms Hotel Seafront, http://butlerarms.com. Steeped in history, the *Butler Arms* has been welcoming guests to this part of Kerry since 1884, among them Charlie Chaplin, Walt Disney and the Queen of Tonga. There's a choice of dining, and in the sociable *Charlie's Restaurant*, overlooking Ballinskelligs Bay, you can enjoy fresh oysters, lobster and mussels, Thai-style monkfish curry, or rack of Kerry lamb. Stylishly furnished standard and executive rooms come with an Atlantic view while six on the ground floor have garden views. €€€

Old Cable House 9–10 Iveagh Terrace, http://oldcablehouse.com. Set back from the seafront in part of the nineteenth-century cable station, this attractive and congenial establishment set in a pleasant garden offers good-value, en-suite accommodation. It also houses the rather fabulous *OhMaryLoo* seafood and pasta restaurant, the latter made fresh on the premises each morning. €€

Smugglers' Inn 1km north of the centre on the beach, http://smugglersinn.ie. Comfortable upmarket rooms are provided by this well-run inn, a restored nineteenth-century farmhouse, which has the best views of Ballinskelligs Bay. Noted for its seafood such as prawn kataifi for starters and black sole for mains, it's another fantastic eating establishment in Waterville, whether in the conservatory restaurant or the *Payne Stewart Bar*, named after the late American golfer. Closed late Oct to early April. €€€

Derrynane Bay and around

Beyond Waterville, the Ring of Kerry climbs steeply to the **Coomakista Pass**, where a viewing point affords glorious views of Deenish and Scariff islands in the foreground at the mouth of the Kenmare River, and Bull, Cow and tiny Calf islands off the end of the Beara Peninsula.

Hidden away beneath, at the southernmost point of the Iveragh Peninsula about 10km south of Waterville, is **Derrynane Bay** (pronounced "Derrynaan", meaning the "oak wood of St Fionán"). From the wide, sandy beach with 3km of dunes and good swimming, you can stroll across to atmospheric Abbey Island, which shelters a graveyard and ruined abbey, founded by St Fionán in around 700. At the inlet on the western side of the island causeway, Derrynane Sea Sports (http://derrynaneseasports.com) offers canoeing, kayaking, sailing, windsurfing and other **waterborne activities** in the summer. From here you can pick your way west for over 1km along a beautiful Mass Path – which formerly led worshippers to the secret Mass Rock at Derrynane House – to Béaltrá Pier; follow the lane uphill from the pier and turn onto the Kerry Way heading east back towards Derrynane House for a satisfying circular **walk** of a couple of hours or so. Above the bay, attractively sited on its steep eastern flank, the sprawling village of **Caherdaniel** is one of the most attractive bases on the Ring of Kerry.

Derrynane House

Derrynane More, Caherdaniel • charge; Heritage Card • http://derrynanehouse.ie

On the north side of the bay, **Derrynane House** was once the home of, and is now a shrine to, **Daniel O'Connell**, the hugely popular, nonviolent campaigner who in 1829 achieved partial Catholic emancipation (see page 564). The plain, elegant house, which was largely rebuilt by the "Liberator" himself when he inherited it in 1825, contains all manner of memorabilia, as well as a tearoom and a lively, 25-minute audiovisual that's well worth catching. The most striking relic is a chariot presented by Dubliners to O'Connell on his release from prison in 1844: modelled on a Roman triumphal car, with gold and purple silk, mouldings and armchairs, it carried him at the head of a crowd of 200,000 to his home in Merrion Square, Dublin.

The pretty **gardens** are awash with plants from across the world, including South America, South Africa and Australasia, while trails give onto the beautiful Blue Flag beach in Derrynane Bay.

Staigue Fort and around

Around 7km east of Caherdaniel on the N70 a sign points left to **Staigue Fort**, near the village of Castlecove; there's a small visitor centre (charge) near the junction, attached to a café and friendly bar with outdoor tables. After 4km up a narrow road, you'll come to a sophisticated ring fort, at least two thousand years old, with 5m-high dry-stone walls surrounded by a bank and ditch; it's in an excellent state of preservation. Beyond Castlecove at Sneem, there's a fork in the main road eastward: a mountain road (the R568) heads up to **Moll's Gap** (see page 273) and from there to Killarney, while the less scenic N70 continues along the seashore to Kenmare.

ACCOMMODATION AND EATING   **DERRYNANE BAY AND AROUND**

The Blind Piper Caherdaniel, http://blindpiperpub.ie. Lovely old stone-built pub decorated with colourful flowers, with outdoor tables on a large lawn by the stream. You can eat well in either the bar or, in the summer, the restaurant, and you can often catch live music (Thurs & Sat in summer). **Derryclare** Down the lane by the Scarriff Inn, 4km west of Caherdaniel on the N70, http://iskeroon.com. Set in a peaceful location in extensive, semi-tropical gardens

running down to the sea. this delightful self-catering cottage sleeps six in two doubles and two singles. €€€ **Traveller's Rest** On the main road in the centre of Caherdaniel, 066 947 5175. Very good hostel in an attractive cottage, with small dorms (up to five beds) plus a well-equipped kitchen and a dining area with open fire. Closed Nov to mid-Feb. €

Kenmare

Sitting at the head of the Kenmare River – actually a narrow, 40km-long sea inlet – **KENMARE** is an excellent base for exploring not only the Ring of Kerry but also the **Beara Peninsula**, part of which, including the contrasting scenic beauties of **Gleninchaquin** valley and **Derreen Gardens**, lies in County Kerry. The cosmopolitan town is neat, with an array of restaurants and accommodation and a lively, sociable nightlife. Kenmare's major streets are Henry St (one-way, south–north) and Main St (one-way, north–south), which meet at Fair Green and are linked at their southern ends by Shelbourne St. Apart from its heritage centre (see below), Kenmare's only sight as such is a Bronze Age **stone circle** on the riverbank, a five-minute walk from the Green (signposted). Around 17m in diameter, it's the largest of its kind in Kerry and may be orientated on the setting sun. At its centre stands a burial dolmen, three standing stones supporting a large capstone. Otherwise, there are some nice local **walks**, including 3km of trails in lovely **Reenagross Woodland Park**, which lies between the *Park Hotel* (see page 285) and the river; you can pick up a leaflet at the tourist office.

Brief history

Kenmare was established after the 1652 Act of Settlement, which followed Cromwell's brutal campaign in Ireland and forced Irish landowners to give up their estates to English settlers. Sir William Petty, who mapped and allocated these forfeited lands, managed to get hold of a quarter of Kerry for himself, and in 1670 established **Nedeen** (or An Neidín, "the little nest") here, a colony of English and Welsh Protestants to work in his lead mines, pilchard fisheries and ironworks. His descendant, the first Marquis of Lansdowne, rebuilt the town on its current X-shape in 1775, with the pretty, tree-shaded **Fair Green** (which still belongs to the Lansdownes) at its fulcrum, and rechristened it **Kenmare** – mistranslating *Neidín* as "nest of thieves", he adapted an earlier Irish name, *Ceann Mara* ("head of the sea inlet"), with which he was also able to honour his good friend, Lord Kenmare. The town's colourful history is carefully detailed in the **heritage centre** at the back of the tourist office (same hours – see below; free).

ARRIVAL AND INFORMATION

By bus Buses stop at the top of Main St.

Destinations Castletownbere via Lauragh and Eyeries (July & Aug Mon–Sat 2 daily; 1hr 20min); Cork (via Glengarriff, Bantry, Skibbereen, Clonakilty, Kinsale and Cork Airport; July & Aug 1 daily; 4hr); Killarney (via Kilgarvan; July & Aug 2–3 daily, rest of year Mon–Fri 2 daily; 50min).

Tourist information Kenmare Heritage Centre, Henry St (Easter–June, Sept & Oct Mon–Fri 9.30am–5.15pm, July & Aug daily 9.30am–5.30pm; http://kenmare.ie).

Bike rental Finnegan's, 37 Henry St (Mon–Sat 10am–6pm, Sun 11am–6pm; http://finneganscycles.com) has touring and e-bikes for hire and also does servicing and repairs.

TOURS AND ACTIVITIES

Tours In summer Kenmare Coach & Cab (http://kenmare coachandcab.com) runs scheduled minibus tours of the Ring of Kerry (Mon, Wed & Fri), Beara Peninsula (Tues) and Glengarriff and Garinish Island (Thurs).

Cruises Seafari run seal and sea eagle cruises (roughly April–Oct; 2–3hr; €25; http://seafariireland.com) from the pier, taking in the islands of the Kenmare River, a colony of a hundred seals and prolific birdlife.

Activities Based at Dauros, 6km away on the north shore of the Beara, Star Sailing and Adventure Centre (http:// staroutdoors.ie) lays on a range of land and water-based activities including kayaking and archery, as well as boat trips on the Kenmare River (1hr; €20). Diving trips and courses are on offer from Kenmare Bay Diving (http:// kenmarebaydiving.com).

ACCOMMODATION

Fáilte Lodging Kenmare Corner of Shelbourne and Henry streets, near the post office, http://kenmarehostel.com (IHH & IHO). Spacious, well-kept hostel in the town centre, with spick-and-span dorms and en-suite and standard private

rooms, a cosy sitting room and a well-equipped kitchen though breakfast is not provided. Closed Nov–April. €

Hawthorn House Shelbourne St, http://hawthorn housekenmare.com. Highly recommended spot in the centre of town: great hospitality, attractive, well-appointed, en-suite rooms, plenty of local information and fine breakfasts, though this does cost extra. Self-catering apartments also available. €€

★ **Lagom Restaurant & Townhouse** 36 Henry St, http://lagomkenmare.com. Sleek and beautiful, this recommended spot in the centre of town: great hospitality, attractive, well-appointed, en-suite rooms, plenty of local information and fine breakfasts, though this does cost extra. Self-catering apartments also available. €€

O'Donnabhain's Henry St, http://odonnabhain-kenmare. com. The large, bright, modern rooms (including triples and family rooms), decorated in earth tones, at this friendly B&B

are spread over several floors of a long, zigzagging building, so all are well away from the pub downstairs. Self-catering also available. Closed mid-Dec to mid-Jan. €€

★ **Park Hotel** Shelbourne St, http://parkkenmare.com. Dating from the late nineteenth century, this elegant – but extortionately priced – *Relais & Chateaux* hotel stands in splendid grounds above the Kenmare River. Service is charming, and a stunning modern spa has been carefully blended into its leafy setting. There's an excellent restaurant with a tasting menu and a cheaper casual brasserie, plus elegant spa with lap pool, cinema, tennis and croquet, and golf on the adjoining course. Closed early Dec to mid-Feb. €€€€

EATING AND DRINKING

Kenmare has a good reputation for **eating out** and claims to be the only town in Ireland with more restaurants than pubs. Henry St and Main St shelter about a dozen **pubs**, so finding somewhere congenial to drink is straightforward, and many of them host traditional music once or twice a week.

Crowley's 26 Henry St, 064 664 1472. Atmospheric old-time bar with a snug and communal seating around the walls, and traditional sessions on Mon, Tues & Wed in summer, Sun in winter.

Florry Batt's Henry St, 087 961 0366. A traditional old-style Kerry bar with an open fire and regular music sessions. Worth a visit to sample a pint and soak up the local atmosphere.

McCarthy's Main St, http://pfskenmare.com. Lively, sociable spot that pulls in the 30-somethings with a popular food menu and music just about every night of the week from 8.30pm.

★ **Mulcahy's** 16 Main St, http://mulcahyskenmare.ie. Crisp, modern decor is the setting for excellent creative cuisine with global (largely French) influences, such as chicken and sneem black pudding *boudain*, and halibut grape and leek *beurre blanc*. Closed Sun & Mon. €€€

The Purple Heather Henry St, http://thepurpleheather kenmare.com. A relaxing daytime bistro-bar, serving light meals such as home-made chicken-liver pâté with Cumberland sauce. Closed Sun. €€€

8

South of Kenmare: the Beara Peninsula

To the south of Kenmare lies the **Beara Peninsula**, most of which is in County Cork (see page 259). At first the countryside here is green and thickly wooded, but head west on the R571 towards the end of the peninsula (served by buses from Kenmare in July and August), or uphill on the scenic N71 towards Glengarriff (also served by Kenmare buses in July and August), and the terrain soon becomes more windswept and lonely. The other main route across the peninsula is the R574, which heads south from Lauragh towards Adrigole, climbing to the county border at the narrow and dramatic Healy Pass and providing magnificent views.

Bonane Heritage Park

Signposted off the N71, 8km from Kenmare • Open access but there is a charge • http://bonaneheritagepark.com

Heading south from Kenmare, it's worth taking a short detour off the N71 to **Bonane Heritage Park**, where a large, grassed-over ringfort, a stone circle, and other ancient remains have been linked by a circular 2km gravel trail. There are fine views of the lush Sheen valley and the bare, wrinkly Caha Mountains behind.

Gleninchaquin

Around 13km from Kenmare along the R571, it's well worth turning onto the dramatic minor road up **Gleninchaquin**, a narrow coomb valley which bowls out at its head around the eponymous lake. After 3km, you'll come upon **Uragh Stone Circle** in a truly magical setting: hemmed in by glaciated hills, on a slender rise between lakes Inchaquin and Uragh, with views down the valley and across to the Macgillycuddy Reeks.

Gleninchaquin Park

Gleninchaquin • charge • http://gleninchaquin.com

Five kilometres further up the valley road from Uragh Stone Circle, you'll reach **Gleninchaquin Park**, where easy-to-follow **walks** have been laid out around the head of the beautiful valley. It's not the wild, man-against-nature experience of the Beara Way, but it seems to be a neat solution to the problems between walkers and farmers that have been occurring in some parts of the country – and it's hard to get lost. The main two-hour **circular trail** takes you up via a corrie lake to the top of the waterfall. If you fancy an easier outing, there's a river walk (30min) and a heritage trail (90min).

Derreen Garden

Lauragh • charge • http://derreengarden.com

On the northwest side of **Lauragh**, 25km southwest of Kenmare, the extensive, subtropical **Derreen Garden** runs down to the sea. Still owned by the descendants of Sir William Petty, it's planted with mature exotic species such as Chilean myrtles, acacias, bamboo and mighty eucalyptus trees, but the garden is known especially for it's grove of tree ferns in the King's Oozy and an extensive collection of species rhododendrons. There are plenty of marked **trails** to keep you going for anything from thirty minutes to two hours, including paths along Kilmakilloge Harbour where a belvedere affords fine views across to the Iveragh Peninsula. There is also a lovely café with homemade cake, sandwiches and tea and coffee.

The Dingle Peninsula

One wonders, in this place, why anyone is left in Dublin, or London, or Paris, when it would be better one would think, to live in a tent, or a hut, with this magnificent sea and sky, and to breathe this wonderful air, which is like wine in one's teeth.

J.M. Synge, In West Kerry

The last of southwestern Ireland's five peninsulas, **Dingle** is perhaps the most distinctive of them all. Arrowing westwards for over 50km, its heavily glaciated topography is especially irregular, with an L-shaped ridge of mountains that peaks at its north end at **Mount Brandon**, the highest summit in Ireland outside of the Macgillycuddy Reeks. Five-hundred-metre **Mount Eagle** at the very tip of the peninsula sets up a spectacular drive, cycle or walk around **Slea Head.** On the coasts, the long, exposed sandbars at **Castlegregory** and **Inch** draw surfers and wind-surfers, while the deeply recessed sandy beaches at **Ventry** and **Smerwick Harbour** encourage gentle swimming.

Dingle has an unusually rich heritage, including over five hundred Celtic *clocháns* (corbelled, dry-stone beehive huts) and the early Christian **Gallarus Oratory**, with its stunningly simple dry-stone construction. The peninsula is also one of the strongest **Irish-speaking** districts in the country, known as **Corca Dhuibhne** (meaning "the followers of Davinia", a Celtic goddess). As the main settlement at the heart of this thriving Gaeltacht (which officially begins just west of Anascaul and Castlegregory), **Dingle town** (An Daingean) feels like a capital. It supports some top-notch restaurants and places to stay, complemented by a vibrant traditional music scene, and is perfectly located for varied day-trips. One of the best of these is the boat trip to the abandoned **Blasket Islands** just off Slea Head, which were responsible for an astonishing body of Irish-language writing in the early twentieth century.

THE DINGLE PENINSULA

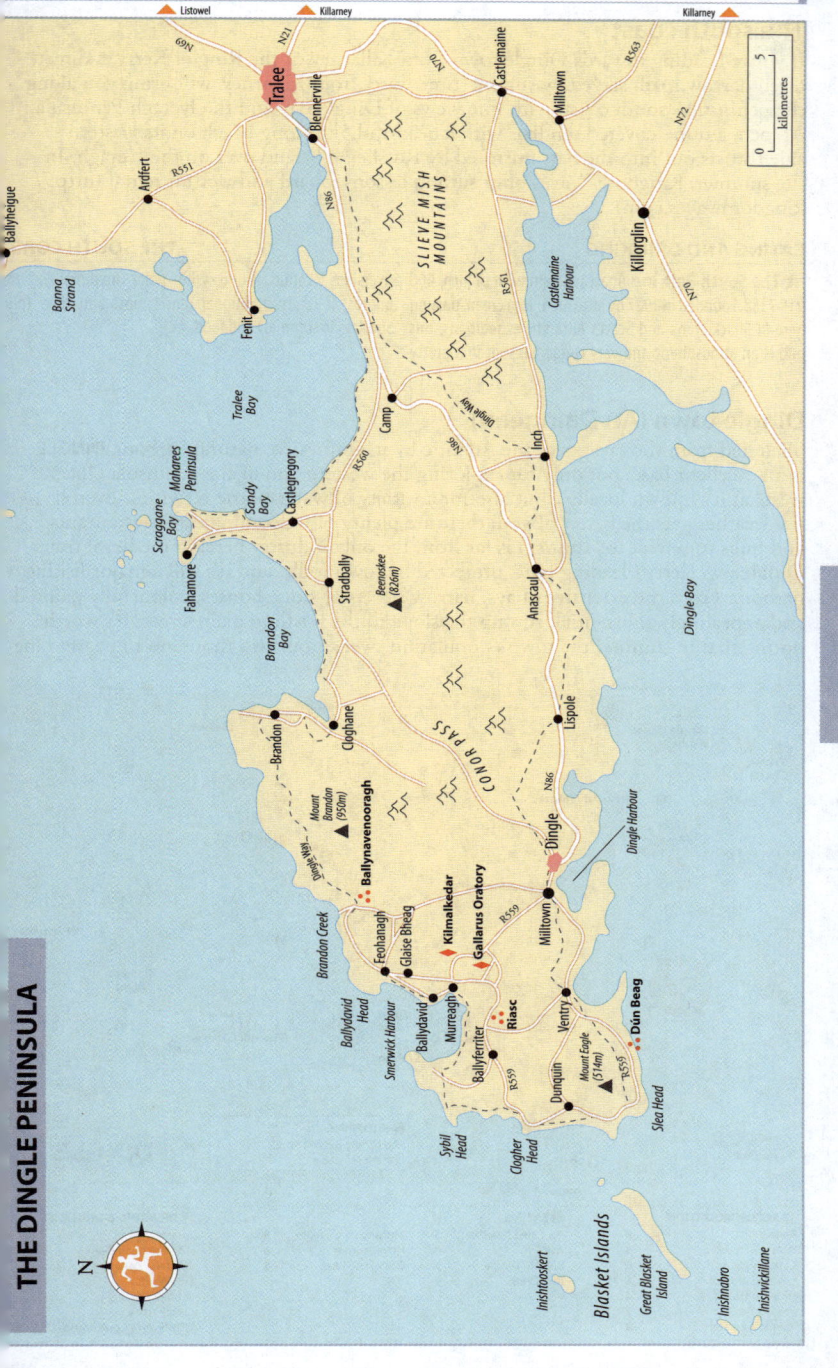

8

N

Listowel Killarney Killarney

N69
N21
Tralee
Blennerville
Castlemaine
Milltown
N70
R563
N72
Ardfert
R551
Killorglin
N70
Ballyheigue
Banna Strand
S L I E V E   M I S H
M O U N T A I N S
R561
Fenit
Castlemaine Harbour
Tralee Bay
Camp
Dingle Way
Inch
R560
N86
Castlegregory
Sandy Bay
Stradbally
Beenoskee (826m)
Anascaul
Dingle Bay
Scraggane Bay
Fahamore
Brandon Bay
Cloghane
Brandon
Lispole
C O N O R   P A S S
N86
Mount Brandon (950m)
Ballynavenooragh
Feohanagh
Kilmalkedar
Glaise Bheag
Gallarus Oratory
Dingle
Dingle Harbour
Brandon Creek
Dingle Way
Ballydavid Head
Milltown
R559
Riasc
Dún Beag
Smerwick Harbour
Ballydavid
Murreagh
Ballyferriter
Ventry
Mount Eagle (514m)
Sybil Head
Dunquin
R559
R559
Slea Head
Clogher Head
Inishtooskert
Blasket Islands
Great Blasket Island
Inishnabro
Inishvickillane

Mohorees Peninsula

The south coast

If you're heading towards Dingle town from Killarney or the Ring of Kerry, a direct, often narrow road, served by summertime buses from Killarney, will bring you along the peninsula's south coast, with fine views of Dingle Bay and the Iveragh Peninsula. At **Inch**, a dune-covered sandbar with a beautiful 5km-long beach on its western side thrusts out into the bay, mirrored by Rossbeigh Strand over on the Iveragh. In the summer, Kingdom Waves offer **surfing** lessons, board and wetsuit rental (http://kingdomwaves.com).

EATING AND DRINKING

THE SOUTH COAST

★ **The South Pole Inn** Anascaul, 7km west of Inch, 066 915 7388. Founded in 1927 by local man, Tom Crean, unsung hero of Shackleton's and Scott's Antarctic expeditions, this pub is an atmospheric and very congenial spot in a pretty riverside location. Hung with polar memorabilia and photos, it offers traditional music most Saturdays (plus Sundays in summer) and food. **€€€**

Dingle town (An Daingean)

Sheltered from the ravages of the Atlantic by its impressive natural harbour, **DINGLE** is an excellent base, not only for exploring the western end of the peninsula ("back west" as it's known locally), but also for a variety of water-borne activities. Even if the weather gets the better of you, there are plenty of welcoming cafés, restaurants and pubs to retreat to. Tourism is far from the only industry here: in medieval times, Dingle was Kerry's leading port, protected by town walls, and it's still a major fishing harbour. From the extensive quays, narrow streets of stone houses, colourfully painted and appealingly substantial, run up the slope to the bustling main street. It's worth noting that in summer the town's population swells from two thousand to nearly nine

8

■ ACCOMMODATION		● EATING				■ DRINKING & NIGHTLIFE	
Ashe's	5	An Café Liteártha	5	Murphy's Ice Cream	3	Adam's	
Benners Hotel	3	Ashe's	4	Novecento	6	An Droichead Beag	
Captain's House	6	Bean in Dingle	2	Out of the Blue	1	The Blue Zone	
Castlewood House	1	Half Door	7			Dick Mack's	
Hideout Hostel	4					John Benny's	
Pax House	7					O'Flaherty's	
Rainbow Hostel	2					O'Sullivan's Courthouse	

DINGLE FESTIVALS

The principal events on Dingle's busy calendar are a four-day **Animation Dingle Festival** in March (http://animationdingle.com); **Feile na Bealtaine** (http://feilenabealtaine.ie), a five-day multidisciplinary festival of arts and politics in late April/early May; a well-received series of **folk and traditional concerts** in summer (roughly May–Oct) at the pretty St James's Church in Main St (087 284 9656); the riotous **Dingle Races** at Ballintaggart Racecourse on the east side of town over three days in early August (http://dingleraces.ie); the **Dingle Regatta** for traditional *currachs* later in the month; a four-day **festival of traditional music** in September; a diverse **food festival** over a weekend in early October (http://dinglefood.com); and **Other Voices**, a music festival in December (http://othervoices.ie).

thousand, which means it's essential to book early for accommodation. Until 2020, most visitors to Dingle came to catch a glimpse of its most famous resident, **Fungie**, a playful 300kg bottlenose dolphin who had made the harbour his home since 1983. However, Fungie's sudden disappearance in 2020 left not only the town's residents heartbroken, but also the town without a valuable source of income.

Dingle Oceanworld

Farrannakilla, on the edge of town, on the road to Ventry · charge · http://dingle-oceanworld.ie

If nautical pursuits have whetted your curiosity, head for **Dingle Oceanworld** (Mara Beo). As well as a centre for marine conservation, Oceanworld is a richly detailed aquarium, where you can stick your hands in the touch pool, observe sharks, stingrays, piranhas, turtles and Gentoo and Humboldt penguins (feeding at 12.30pm & 3.30pm) at close quarters, and walk underneath a variety of fish from around the Irish coast in the tunnel tank.

8

Díseart

Green St · charge · http://diseart.ie

At **Díseart Institute of Irish Culture and Spirituality**, a former convent of the enclosed order of Presentation Sisters on Green Street, you can admire twelve **stained-glass windows** by Harry Clarke, one of the foremost artists in the medium in the last century; commissioned in 1922, they depict scenes from the life of Christ in opulent detail.

ARRIVAL AND INFORMATION   DINGLE TOWN

By car If you're driving, you'll need to get used to Dingle's fierce, roughly anticlockwise one-way system. Holy Ground and its continuation, Dykegate Lane, are up only (south–north), Main St is up only (east–west), while Green St, which leads back down towards the harbour, is down only. There's a useful free car park on Green St near Díseart.

By bus Buses stop in the car park behind the Supervalu store, down near the harbour.

Destinations Ballyferriter (5 daily; 20min); Dunquin (5 daily; 30min); Gallarus (2 daily; 15min); Killarney, via Inch (July & Aug Mon–Sat 2 daily; 1hr 20min); Tralee (via the N86; 3–5 daily; 1hr 20min).

Tourist office Strand St by the harbour (Mon–Sat 9am–5pm; http://dingle-peninsula.ie).

TOURS AND ACTIVITIES

Archeological tours Fascinating archeological tours of the peninsula by minibus are run in the summer by Sciúird Tours, Avondale St (daily at 10am; 3hr 30min; €50/person; http://ancientdingle.com).

Boat trips There's a choice of boat trips to Great Blasket (see page 292).

Bike rental Paddy's, Dykegate Lane (http://paddys bikeshop.com) has both touring (from €25) and e-bikes (from €45) for rent.

Kayaking Irish Adventures, off Strand St, behind *Out of the Blue* restaurant (http://irishadventures.net) offers several kayaking trips including a sunset kayak; all trips last around 3 hr.

Sailing Dingle Sailing Centre at the marina (http://dinglesailingclub.com) offers sailing courses in July and Aug.

Surfing and paddleboarding Dingle Surf, Green St (http://dinglesurf.com), for equipment rental and lessons in stand-up paddle boarding.

ACCOMMODATION
SEE MAP PAGE 288

Ashe's Main St, http://ashesrestaurant.ie. A handsome whitewashed nineteenth-century building offering three rooms above the restaurant and bar of the same name, and although breakfast is not available, each room does have a small fridge and Nespresso machine. €€

Benners Hotel 12 Main St, http://dinglebenners.com. Characterful and welcoming town house hotel and social hub that's been skilfully refurbished: bedrooms are brightly furnished with pine and floral prints, while the dark-wood lobby and bar are warm and cosy. It's not cheap mind. €€€€

Captain's House The Mall, http://captainshousedingle. com. Hospitable, central, en-suite B&B, quirkily furnished with items collected on the eponymous captain's voyages. Great breakfasts, including home-made bread, scones and jam, are served in the bedrooms. Closed Dec–March. €€€

★ **Castlewood House** 1km from the tourist office along the continuation of Strand St, http://castlewooddingle. com. Quiet, welcoming guesthouse with large and very thoughtfully and lavishly designed rooms, which stretch to DVD players and whirlpool baths; nearly all have fine views of the bay. Excellent, varied breakfasts and plenty of local information. €€€

Hideout Hostel Dykegate Lane, 066 915 0559. Friendly laidback and all en-suite hostel in a modern terrace house with a well-equipped kitchen, a sitting room with an open fire and laundry facilities; light breakfast included. Dorms €, doubles €€

Pax House Upper John St, 1km east of the town centre http://pax-house.com. Peaceful, upmarket B&B, tastefully decorated with colourful paintings in contemporary style with spectacular views of the bay from rooms and the large patio, and great breakfasts and afternoon teas. €€€

Rainbow Hostel 2km west of the centre in Milltown, http://rainbowhosteldingle.com. Sociable, family-run hostel in attractive landscaped gardens, with twin, double, triple and family rooms in addition to dorms. Amenities include large kitchen, bike rental and laundry and drying facilities. Free lift from the bus stop in town. Camping available too. €

EATING
SEE MAP PAGE 288

Although it doesn't shout about being a foodie town, Dingle has several first-rate **restaurants**. Seafood, naturally, features strongly on their menus, while homely **cafés** are great for whiling away rainy afternoons. On Fri mornings, there's a farmers' market in the car park on Holy Ground. Dingle is a hotbed of **traditional music**, with some locally based, nationally known performers turning up in the town's **pubs**. *West Kerry Live* (http://westkerrylive.ie), a free fortnightly magazine available from the tourist office, details sessions in town and across the peninsula.

An Café Liteártha Dykegate Lane, 066 915 2204. Daytime bookshop-café – with an eclectic mix of Irish language and English books, many on the local area – that offers cheap, unpretentious food, including soup, scones, cakes, sandwiches and warm brie with raspberry jam, salad and bread. Closed Sun. €

Ashe's Main St, http://ashesrestaurant.ie. Easygoing spot, more restaurant than pub, which specializes in stunningly creative seafood dishes such as crab and prawn dumplings, and roasted spiced scallops with homemade mango chutney and cumin yoghurt. The bar, too, is a terrific spot to down a cocktail. Closed Sun & Mon. €€€

Bean in Dingle Green St, http://beanindingle.com. Caffeine addicts will love the smooth and unctuous coffee full of complex flavours blended for this sleek café by the boutique roasters Badger & Dodo of Cork and served in biodegradable cups. Creamy porridge is on the morning menu and local treats such as cinnamon rolls can be enjoyed in the soothing grey and yellow decor.

★ **Half Door** 3 John St, http://halfdoor.ie. Relaxing white-tablecloth restaurant with excellent cooking, mostly seafood such as shellfish platters, mussels, crab and lobster a good wine list, desserts such as apple and pear crumble and friendly, efficient service. It's pricey, but there are various set menus on offer (including a three-course early bird menu at €45; 5–6pm). €€€€

Murphy's Ice Cream Strand St, http://murphysicecream. ie. Delicious ice cream, home-made from seawater collected to harvest the salt. Choose from a large selection of intriguing flavours, such as Irish Brown Bread and gingerbread (plus sorbets) or sample some of their desserts €

Novecento Main St, http://novecento.ie. Great pizzas either whole or by the slice, to take away in the evenings Note that it's only open Fri–Sun. €€

Out of the Blue Opposite the tourist office on Strand St http://outoftheblue.ie. Unpretentious seafood restaurant serving up the freshest and most succulent fish and shellfish, depending on what is available from the pier opposite, in excellent dishes such as Blasket Islands scallops with Calvados flambé – and don't expect chips, with anything. €€€

DRINKING
SEE MAP PAGE 288

Adam's Main St, 066 915 2133. This likeable pub offers reasonable and tasty home-made lunches – including lemon chicken and walnut salad and Irish stew – and traditional music at weekends.

★ **An Droichead Beag** At the bottom of Main St, http://androicheadbeag.com. A cosy, popular spot, "The Small Bridge" has lively sessions just about every night at 9pm occasionally followed by a DJ.

The Blue Zone Above the Dingle Record Shop on Green St, 066 915 0303. For something completely different, head for this late-night pizza and wine bar, which also offers jazz (Thurs & Fri in winter, most nights, though not Sat, in summer).

Dick Mack's Green St, http://dickmackspub.com. Crusty former cobblers' shop, with attractive tables in a quiet courtyard at the back and stars on the pavement outside to commemorate such diverse former customers as Robert Mitchum and Julia Roberts. They sell Dick Mack's IPA from a microbrewery and stock a huge variety of whiskies and Dingle gin.

John Benny's Strand St, http://johnbennyspub.com. Cosy pub popular for its microbrewed beers and reasonably priced bar food, such as Irish stew, bacon and cabbage, Glenbeigh oysters, salads and sandwiches, with vegetarian options. John and his wife are noted musicians who host traditional music every night in summer (and often enough in winter). Closed Mon. €€

O'Flaherty's Bridge St, down by the roundabout, http://oflahertysdingle.com. Spartan but sociable pub, with a flagstone floor and an old stove, its walls hung with memorabilia. Owned by a family of musicians, it hosts sessions most nights.

O'Sullivan's Courthouse The Mall, http://osullivans courthousepub.com. Another Dingle pub owned by musicians, this one by Tommy and Saundra: "no TV, no juke box, no pool table", just bare wood, white paint and an old stove – with a cute beer garden – as the setting for great nightly sessions, washed down with craft beers.

SHOPPING
SEE MAP PAGE 288

Dingle's shopping hub is **Green St**, where you'll find all manner of crafts shops, art galleries, delicatessens and bookshops. See http://originalkerry.com for information about the county's craft makers, most of whom are in Dingle.

The Dingle Record Shop Green St, http://dingle recordshop.com. This tiny shop with a big welcome has a great selection of traditional CDs, especially by local musicians, and is a good source of information about sessions, as well as selling tickets for the St James's Church concerts (see page 289). Closed Sun.

Lisbeth Mulcahy Green St, http://lisbethmulcahy.com. Gorgeous scarves, jumpers and other wool items, as well as pottery by Lisbeth's husband, Louis (see page 293). Closed Sun.

8

The Slea HeadLoop

The vast, spectacular mountain- and seascapes which stretch out to the tip of the peninsula, **Slea Head**, are the undoubted highlights here, followed by the **Blasket Islands heritage centre** at Dunquin – or even a **boat trip to the islands** themselves – and the elegant, dry-stone **Gallarus Oratory**.

Ventry (Ceann Trá)

VENTRY, the first bay to the west of Dingle, is an impressive sheltering crescent of fine, sandy, gently sloping beach and low dunes in the lee of 514m Mount Eagle. The strand here was the suitably epic location for the legendary single combat between Fionn Mac Cumhaill and Daire Donn, the King of the World, to save Ireland from invasion by Daire's armies.

Dún Beag

Slea Hed Drive, Fahan, 7km southwest of Ventry • charge • http://dunbeagfort.com

It's a fine drive or cycle out to **Slea Head** (Ceann Sléibhe), as the road narrows beyond Ventry and the slopes of Mount Eagle steepen towards the end of the peninsula. This landscape is dotted with several Iron Age dry-stone forts, known as the **Fahan Group**, of which the most interesting is the first, around 1km beyond the Celtic Museum. In a spectacular setting above the boiling sea overlooking the Iveragh Peninsula, **Dún Beag** has four lines of defensive banks and five corresponding ditches, traversed by a 16m souterrain, or underground escape route. Within the 3m-high walls stand the remains of beehive huts, or *clocháns*. Dún Beag used to be even more spectacular, but in January 2014 winter storms eroded the cliff and caused a large section of the site to fall into the Atlantic. It's worth absorbing the information (including a film) in the visitor centre before heading out to the fort itself, and once you're done exploring, make a beeline for the excellent *Stonehouse Café*.

The Blasket Islands (Na Blascaodaí) and Dunquin (Dún Chaoin)

Just off Slea Head lie the **Blaskets**, dramatic island mountains with steep, gashed sides. Despite their inhospitable appearance, the largest island, Great Blasket (An Blascaod Mór), was inhabited by up to two hundred people for at least three centuries until 1953, when, with no school, shop, priest or doctor, it was finally abandoned. Because of their isolation, however, the islanders maintained a rich oral tradition in the Irish language, which in the early twentieth century, encouraged by visiting scholars, evolved into a remarkable body of written **literature**. Works such as *An tOileánach* (*The Islandman*) by Tomás Ó Criomhthain, *Fiche Blian ag Fás* (*Twenty Years A-Growing*) by Muiris Ó Súilleabháin and *Peig* by Peig Sayers (an oral account written down by her son) give a vivid insight into the extent of the hardships of life here.

The island's story is told with great imagination at **The Blasket Centre** (mid-March to Oct daily 10am–6pm; last admission 5.15pm; charge; Heritage Card; http://blasket.ie) on the mainland opposite, at the north end of Dunquin. Excerpts from the island writers, and a moving section on Great Blasket's abandonment in 1953 and the migration of many islanders to Springfield, Massachusetts – where they still receive the *Kerryman* newspaper from Tralee every week are highlights.

If you take a boat trip (see box) to **Great Blasket**, you can wander the white-sand beach, Trá Bán, at its eastern end and the grassy footpaths that cross its 6km length, passing the ghosts of the old village. Accompanied by seals, puffins, storm petrels and shearwaters, you can contemplate the 3000km that separates you, here on Europe's most westerly islands, from North America where most of the islanders ended up, and the treacherous 2km of Blasket Sound which made living on the island untenable.

Ballyferriter (Baile an Fheirtearaigh) and around

BALLYFERRITER, 8km on from Dunquin, is a byword for remoteness in Ireland, but ticks a surprising number of boxes when it comes to amenities. There's a lovely beach, **Wine Strand**, just to the north on sheltered **Smerwick Harbour**, and pleasant walking to the northwest where the peaks of **Sybil Head** and the **Three Sisters** rise like a row of waves to meet the sea. In late February, the village hosts a five-day **traditional music school**, Scoil Cheoil an Earraigh (http://scoilcheoil.com), featuring classes, concerts and lectures.

Músaem Chorca Dhuibhne

Ballyferriter village centre • June to mid-Sept daily 10am–5pm; off-season by appointment • charge • http://westkerrymuseum.com

The old village school has been converted into the **Músaem Chorca Dhuibhne**, which houses a display on the archaeology and history of the peninsula since Mesolithic times, its geology and more recent role as a location for movies such as *Ryan's Daughter*. There's a café that does home baking at the museum, where you can find out about looped walks around the village and about the wealth of ancient ruins in the area, such as Riasc, a sixth-century monastic site, and the ring fort at Ballynavenooragh.

BOAT TRIPS TO THE BLASKETS

From **Ventry**, sea safaris operate around the Blasket Islands (3hr; €60; http://marinetours.ie), taking in the spectacular Cathedral Rocks on Inishnabro, puffins (in spring and early summer, depending on the weather) and grey seals and red deer on Inishvickillane, and possibly basking sharks, whales and dolphins; a seven-hour trip combines the guided cruise with landing on Great Blasket itself (€75). From **Dingle town,** there's the Great Blasket Island experience (http://greatblasketisland.net), with a guided cruise around the islands that include around three hours on Great Blasket, with a guided tour (6hr; €80).

Louis Mulcahy Pottery

4km west of Ballyferriter on the R559 (about 4km from Dunquin) • Daily: Summer 10am–6pm ; winter 10am–5.30pm • http://louismulcahy.com

One of Ireland's leading potters, Louis Mulcahy, has his **pottery workshop and showrooms** near the tip of the Dingle Peninsula. You may see a potter at work on the wheel, and with pre-booking, have a go yourself – and for €25 you can have your masterpiece fired and glazed, though shipping is extra. Workshop tours are also available – these too must be booked in advance.

Gallarus Oratory

5km east of Ballyferriter, off the R559 towards Ballydavid • Visitor Centre Easter–Oct 9am–5pm (site accessible year-round) • charge • http://lheritageireland.ie

(An Mhuiríoch), the beautiful **Gallarus Oratory**, is the Dingle peninsula's most compelling historic monument, dating from somewhere between the seventh and twelfth centuries. Built of dry gritstone in the shape of an upturned boat, the building – thought to be an early Christian church – sits unadorned in a field like a Platonic ideal of architectural purity.

Kilmalkedar

At the crossroads at Murreagh, the R559 turns right, passing after 2km **Kilmalkedar**, an attractive, mid-twelfth-century church in the Irish Romanesque style. Dedicated to local saint, Maolcéadair, who died in 636, it offers fine views west to the sea. Look out for a strange, carved animal head inside, above the doorway, and, in the surrounding graveyard, an early sundial, a high cross and an ogham stone, whose inscription is probably asking for a prayer for the soul of one Maile Inbir.

8

GETTING AROUND

THE SLEA HEAD LOOP

By bike/car You can make an immensely satisfying day-trip from Dingle by driving or cycling the R559 on its meandering, circular route, or by taking a tour (see page 289). Coaches are required to follow the narrow road in a clockwise direction and it's best to follow suit, rather than risk meeting them head-on.

By bus The bus schedules from Dingle (see page 289) allow you half-day trips to Dunquin or Ballyferriter on Mon or Thurs and to Gallarus on Tues or Fri.

On foot An 18km waymarked path, Cosán na Naomh (The Saint's Road), crosses this area mostly on minor roads, from Ventry Strand via Gallarus and Kilmalkedar to the foot of Mount Brandon, with an associated map-guide (http://heritagecouncil.ie).

ACCOMMODATION AND EATING

VENTRY

Páidí Ó Sé's By the church, http://paidiose.com. An old-fashioned country pub with a sense of tradition. Menu staples include bacon and cabbage, seafood chowder, chicken curry, steaks, and mixed veg and rice. At weekends musicians turn up for traditional and contemporary sessions; formerly owned by the eponymous late Kerry Gaelic star footballer and manager, it's hung with sporting memorabilia. They've also got spaces for campervans and motorhomes, which might be useful if you want to stick around for a drink or two. €€

DÚN BEAG

The Stonehouse Opposite the fort, 066 915 9970. Built in a *clochán* style with stone walls and roof, this café-restaurant menu features main courses such as enticing crab salad, Irish lamb stew, and Thai noodles, all of which you can enjoy at outdoor tables with stunning views of the Skelligs. Or simply stop by for a cup of coffee and a slice of warm apple pie after visiting the fort. €€

DUNQUIN

An Portán In the middle of the village, 066 915 6212. En-suite B&B in a one-storey quadrangle of large, bright rooms around a lawn, with a dining room for guests and a daytime café. Closed Oct–March. €€

Dún Chaoin Youth Hostel Near the heritage centre, http://anoige.ie. An Óige hostel on the Dingle Way, with great views over the Blaskets, four- to ten-bed dorms, en-suite twins, a kitchen, laundry facilities and a drying room for walkers. Note that there are no shops for 8km (Ballyferriter), but the owner can supply dry food, breakfast and packed lunches as extra. Closed Nov–Feb. €

BALLYFERRITER AND AROUND

Tig Áine Just west of Louis Mulcahy's pottery on the R559, http://tigaine.com. Boasting fine views of Sybil Head from its picture windows and outside terrace (with binoculars and telescopes for bird-spotting), *Tig Áine* encompasses an art gallery and a café-restaurant, rustling up dishes including omelettes, salads, chowder, and lamb cutlets. €€

Tigh an tSaorsaigh (Sears) On the R559 in the village, http://searspub.com. Pleasant, en-suite B&B is available at this genial 160-year-old flagstoned pub done out in striking green and red. With its piano and open stove, the bar offers simple pub grub. For €5 you can make a wish in their wishing well – alternatively put it towards hiring a bike and exploring the peninsula with the owner's brother, who runs tours. €€

The Conor Pass and the north coast of the peninsula

To the northeast of Dingle town rises an L-shaped ridge of mountains, running south from the highest, **Mount Brandon** (Cnoc Bréanainn; 950m), and across to Beenoskee (826m). The steep and narrow **Conor Pass** road, which cuts across the ridge to the peninsula's north coast, ascends to a car park at over 500m giving spectacular views of stark uplands, corrie lakes and the huge sweep of **Brandon Bay** to the north, and back over Dingle harbour to the Iveragh Peninsula and the Skelligs.

Cloghane

Signposted archaeological and walking trails, including the Dingle Way, crisscross the area around **CLOGHANE** (An Clochán), a hamlet fringed by lovely beaches on the eastern flank of Mount Brandon. Experienced walkers could take on the classic, six-hour there-and-back ascent of Mount Brandon, roughly marked by yellow painted arrows, from Faha, 2km northwest of Cloghane. Cloghane comes to life over the last weekend in July for the **Feile Lughnasa**, celebrating the Celtic harvest festival with guided walks, poetry and music.

ACCOMMODATION	CLOGHANE

Mount Brandon Hostel Village centre, http://mountbrandonhostel.com. All en-suite, eco-conscious hostel with spruce wooden floors and furniture, a well-equipped kitchen, a cosy lounge and a patio overlooking the bay. Evenings of music, poetry and storytelling are held every Monday throughout the year and in July and Aug or a Thursday. Luggage transfer can be arranged for walkers. Light breakfast included. Dorms €, doubles €€

Castlegregory and the Maharees

Separating Brandon Bay from Tralee Bay, the **Maharees** is an exposed, beach-girt spit of land to the north of **CASTLEGREGORY**. What's reckoned to be some of the best **windsurfing** in the world is possible here – it's good in all wind directions, with a variety of west-, north- and east-facing spots suitable for all levels of ability; there's a good break for **surfers**, too. If all that sounds too energetic, just flop out on the nearest beach to Castlegregory, east-facing **Sandy Bay**.

ACCOMMODATION AND EATING	CASTLEGREGORY AND THE MAHAREES

Anchor About 5km east of the village on the R560, http://anchorcaravanpark.com. This well-signposted campsite gives on to kilometres of quiet, sandy beach, and has a campers' kitchen, two play areas, TV and games room, laundry facilities and a rinsing area for wetsuits. Closed Oct–March. €

Fitzgerald's Euro-Hostel Strand St, 066 713 9951. If you're not on a package with Waterworld (see Activities below), you might want to crash at this hostel back in town, which has basic dorms, single, twin and double rooms and a large kitchen above a shop, café and bar. €

Spillane's Bar and Restaurant About halfway along the Maharees spit, http://spillanesbar.com. Your best bet for something to eat in the area, specializing in steaks and seafood, with the day's catch – maybe local mussels, crab claws and prawns – listed on a blackboard. Closed Tues & Wed. €€€

ACTIVITIES

Surfing, diving and other watersports Jamie Knox (http://jamieknox.com) offers windsurfing and surfing tuition and rental, and stand-up paddleboard rental. Diving trips, courses and accommodation packages are run by

Waterworld (http://waterworld.ie), a PADI five-star IDC   at the end of the Maharees.
Centre, from their base, Harbour House, at Scraggane Bay

North Kerry

North Kerry, flat, rich farmland that runs as far as the Shannon estuary, feels quite different from the rest of the county – and they've even been known to play hurling rather than Gaelic football up here. Instead of the remote, spectacularly set coastal villages of the peninsulas, you'll find – or avoid – the traditional kiss-me-quick resorts of Ballyheigue and Ballybunion, while the county town of **Tralee** seems quite anodyne if you've just come up from Dingle, for example. It is worth making time, however, for **Listowel**, an easy-going small town that's a hotbed of literary activity. North again from here, the useful **Shannon ferry** cuts down travelling time to County Clare from **Tarbert**.

Tralee and around

Although **TRALEE** has a long history as a market town, originally built around an Anglo-Norman castle and priory, its attractions today are modern. Among them, the County Museum, Wetlands Centre and Blennerville Windmill can be visited on a good-value combination ticket (for up to two adults and three children).

Kerry County Museum
Ashe Memorial Hall, Denny St • charge • http://kerrymuseum.ie

Chief among Tralee's sights is the **Kerry County Museum** in the centre of town, which incorporates a comprehensive run-through of the history of Ireland and Kerry since the Stone Age, with plenty of activities for kids, as well as the Medieval Experience, a series of re-created scenes of mid-fifteenth-century Tralee complete with artificial smells.

Tralee Bay Wetlands & Ecology Activity Park
Ballyard Rd, on the southwest side of the centre, just off the Dingle road • charge • http://traleebaywetlands.org

Dug out from the marshland where three rivers meet Tralee Bay, the **Tralee Bay Wetlands & Ecology Activity Park** comprises more than twenty native habitats, including coastal reedbeds, river channels, marsh, and eelgrass, all of which you can enjoy on either a guided or self-guided walk. You're likely to see herons, warblers, curlews, frogs, dragonflies and, in winter, thousands of Brent geese and the rare Whooper swans. There are also hides, a short boardwalk and a 20-metre observation tower with views of Slieve Mish on the Dingle Peninsula. In the Activity Park itself, you can let off some steam through a variety of land and water-based activities, such as climbing, rowing

---

THE DINGLE WAY

Perhaps the best way to soak up the Dingle Peninsula's dramatic, shifting landscapes is to walk all or part of the waymarked 180km **Dingle Way**, which begins in **Tralee**, heads west to Camp, then loops round the rest of the peninsula, via long, sandy beaches, the steep north face of Mount Brandon and most of Dingle's major sites and villages. The whole thing can be done in seven or eight days, catching a bus out towards Camp on the first day to avoid repeating the stretch between there and Tralee. The **website**, http://dingleway.com provides trail descriptions, maps and full details of walker-friendly accommodation, offering services such as luggage transfer, evening meals and packed lunches, along the route. On this remote peninsula, you'll need to check carefully that you'll be able to get dinner after each day's walking, especially outside of July and August. OS 1:50,000 **map** no. 70 covers most of the route, with the eastern end of the peninsula on no. 71.

and water zorbing. After all that, pay a visit to the very pleasant *Lakeside Café*, which serves snacks and hot meals throughout the day.

Blennerville Windmill

Windmill Lane, Ballyvelly, roughly 3km southwest of the centre on the Dingle road • charge • http://blennerville-windmill.ie

The largest working windmill in Ireland and Britain, the **Blennerville Windmill**, dates from 1800. It has a visitor and crafts centre where the millers will give you a 25-minute guided tour of the flour-making process; there's also an exhibition on emigration on the first floor with a short video. A word of warning: it's a steep climb of 52 steps to the top.

Ardfert Cathedral

Ardfert, 9km northwest of Tralee on the R551 • charge; Heritage Card • http://heritageireland.ie • The bus schedules between Tralee and Ardfert only allow a return trip to the cathedral July & Aug afternoons

Probably the most interesting visit you can make is to the ruined **cathedral** at **Ardfert**, on the site of a monastery established by St Brendan the Navigator in the sixth century near his birthplace. The slender tenth-to-thirteenth-century cathedral is the largest pre-Gothic church in Ireland and features fine lancet windows behind the altar. Look out for some beautiful Romanesque sandstone carving in geometric and floral designs on the west doorway and around the window of the small twelfth-century church nearby.

ARRIVAL AND INFORMATION

By train The train station, which has left-luggage facilities, is just a few mins' walk northeast of the centre of town.
Destinations Cork (7–8 daily, often with a change at Mallow; 2hr–2hr 30min); Dublin (7–8 daily, most with a change at Mallow; 4hr); Farranfore (7–8 daily; 20min); Killarney (7–8 daily; 40min).
By bus Buses stop at the train station.
Destinations Adare (7–8 daily; 1hr 40min); Ardfert (3 daily; 15min); Castlegregory (2 on Mon & Wed; 40min); Cloghane (2 on Mon & Wed; 1hr 10min); Cork (hourly; 2hr 15min);

TRALEE AND AROUND

Dingle (via the N86; 3–5 daily; 1hr 20min); Killarney (10–16 daily; 40min); Limerick (7–8 daily; 2hr 5min); Listowel (7–8 daily; 30min); Ring of Kerry (July & Aug 1 daily; 6hr 35min, with a break in Sneem).
Tourist office The friendly and helpful tourist office (Mon–Sat 9am–5pm, plus July & Aug Sun 10am–5pm; http://tralee.ie), in the Ashe Memorial Hall underneath the Kerry County Museum.
Bike rental Tralee Gas Supplies, High St, on the west side of town (066 712 2018).

ACCOMMODATION AND EATING

The Grand Denny St, http://grandhoteltralee.com. Traditional county-town hotel with lots of dark wood panelling and leather banquettes in its bar and restaurant, though its rooms, most of which are set back from the busy street, are refreshingly colourful. €€€
Quinlan's 1 The Mall, http://kerryfish.com. Your best bet for somewhere to eat is this superior chipper and

fishmonger, which serves beer-battered fish from their own boats out of Valentia, seafood chowder and deep-fried squid with home-made sweet chilli jam. Eat in or take away to the nearby town park (down Denny St by the tourist office). €€€
Seán Og's Bridge St, http://sean-ogs.com. Friendly, dimly lit, cosy pub just off The Mall, with open fires, bare stone walls and traditional music. Plus a few en-suite rooms.

ENTERTAINMENT

Siamsa Tíre (National Folk Theatre of Ireland) Next to the tourist office, http://siamsatire.com. Excellent Irish

shows in the summer, as well as a varied international programme of drama, music, dance, art and literary events.

TRALEE FESTIVALS

In mid-August, the five-day **Rose of Tralee International Festival** (http://roseoftralee.ie) takes over the town. It's a slightly questionable but generally good-natured beauty and talent contest, accompanied by much merry-making, which is open to women of Irish birth or ancestry. There's also a four-day **film festival** (http://kerryfilmfestival.com) in mid-October, held in the town and around the county, and a four-day **circus festival** at the end of October/beginning November (http://circusfestival.ie).

Listowel

Up the N69, 27km northeast of Tralee, **LISTOWEL** is a congenial market town in a leafy setting on the north bank of the River Feale. It's best known for its literary associations (see The Kerry Writer's Museum) – the town's most celebrated literary figure is probably the late **John B. Keane**, author of plays such as *The Field*, a dramatization of a shocking murder that took place in this region in the 1950s.

Seanchaí – The Kerry Writers' Museum

24 The Square • charge • http://kerrywritersmuseum.com

In a Georgian house in the imposing town square stands **Seanchaí**, the **Kerry Writers' Museum**. As well as hosting literary workshops and readings and a good café, the museum provides tourist information about the area. Its spaces are devoted to local writers such as Keane, Bryan MacMahon and Brendan Kennelly, and have been imaginatively designed, with recorded extracts, to reflect the personality of each. Audiovisuals include Kerryman Eamon Kelly, Ireland's most famous storyteller (or *seanchaí*, pronounced "shanakee"), reading stories about rural Ireland of long ago that have been handed down through the age-old oral tradition.

Listowel Castle

The Square • Guided tours late May to Sept Wed–Sun 10am–6pm; last admission 5.15pm • Free • http://heritageireland.ie

From Seanchaí's reception, informative and entertaining tours depart for formidable **Listowel Castle** next door. When the castle was built in the early or mid-fifteenth century for the Fitzmaurices, the Lords of Kerry, the adjacent River Feale would have been navigable and was probably forded at this point, but from the eighteenth century onwards, in more peaceful times, the building fell into disrepair and was quarried for stone. Nevertheless, two of the four original towers remain, rising to a height of 15m.

The Lartigue Monorail and Museum

North side of town, off John B. Keane Rd • May–Sept daily 1–4.30pm • charge • http://lartiguemonorail.com

Between 1888 and 1924 a low-cost railway system covered the 15km between Listowel and Ballybunion on the coast, attracting much interest and curiosity since it carried not only passengers but also animals and freight. A 500m section has been restored for ten-minute jaunts as part of the musuem where you can see footage of the original steam-powered monorail alongside models and memorabilia.

ACCOMMODATION AND EATING   LISTOWEL

★ **Allo's** 41 Church St, http://allosbarbistro-townhouse. com. The pick of Listowel's accommodation, off the northeast corner of the square, offering three rooms furnished with antiques, including one with a four-poster and a huge bathroom, above an appealing bar and bistro. Dine on dishes such as pork rack cutlet with sun-dried tomato tapenade, or simpler, cheaper lunches. Breakfast not served. Closed Sun–Tues. €€

★ **The John B. Keane** William St, 068 21127. At this cosy pub off the northeast corner of the town square, John B's son Billy keeps the literary flame burning, with poetry readings, history talks, music sessions and pub theatre.

Listowel Arms The Square, http://listowelarms.com. Charming traditional hotel in a creeper-covered, Georgian mansion, where some of the rooms, which are attractively furnished with antiques, have views of the river. There's very creditable food to be had in both the *Georgian* restaurant and the cool *Writer's Bar*. €€€

8

Limerick and Clare

QUIN ABBEY

9

Limerick and Clare

Although Limerick lives somewhat in the shadow of its neighbours Kerry and Clare, the county is ideal for activities such as cycling, walking and golf. Some of Ireland's most impressive archaeological sites are to be found here too, alongside cathedrals, priories and abbeys. There is a distinctly pastoral feel to much of Limerick as it sweeps from the rolling farmland of the Golden Vale over to the Shannon estuary. Limerick city, meanwhile, has gone through a sea change in recent years, reinventing itself with a vibrant cultural life.

The superb **Hunt Museum** houses the Republic's richest art and antiquities collection outside Dublin, while outside the city, the enigmatic Neolithic sites of **Lough Gur** and the historic village of **Adare** are reasons to branch out. You'll need your own transport for the former but the city is well served by trains – from Galway and points east and south via Limerick Junction – and by buses from just about anywhere.

Across the broad River Shannon, **County Clare** has a wealth of scenic attractions and is renowned worldwide for its vibrant musical traditions. Its coastline all the way from **Kilkee** to **Fanore** is dotted with golden beaches. Near the village of **Doolin**, famed for its year-long, tourist-driven diet of traditional music, stand the awesome **Cliffs of Moher**, while the county's northern interior is characterized by the craggy, mysterious landscape of **the Burren**, home to numerous prehistoric sites. Its county town, **Ennis**, is an animated place with excellent music pubs and some atmospheric religious remains, further examples of which are dotted around the countryside, such as at **Quin Abbey**, **Dysert O'Dea** and the settlement on **Scattery Island**. The castles and tower houses of Clare's erstwhile dynasties, the O'Briens and MacNamaras, inform the landscape too, notably at **Bunratty** and **Leamaneh**. At Clare's eastern extremity lies the expansive **Lough Derg**, whose waters are best explored by renting your own boat or taking a cruise. Shannon International Airport, in Clare's southeast, lies within easy reach of Ennis, which itself is the county's transport hub. Clare is reasonably well covered by buses in summertime, though the county's north is best accessed from Galway.

Limerick city and around

All manner of routes – road, rail and air – lead to **LIMERICK**, the Republic's third city and a place that has been revitalized in recent years. An imaginative urban improvement project alongside the river, the renovation of **King John's Castle** and the gloriously restored **Milk Market** in the **Market Quarter** – not to mention the newly designated **Fashion Quarter** and **Medieval Quarter** – have all contributed to a feel-good atmosphere. As well as substantial renovation of the Shannon **quays**, regeneration efforts have included the extensive campus at **Plassey**, 3km southeast, which is also the site of the **National Technological Park**. The three colleges here (the university, Institute of Technology and College of Education) certainly help to enliven the city's cultural pulse and nightlife. More than anything, though, Limerick is synonymous with sport – in particular with **rugby** – and the expansion of **Thomond Park Stadium** has helped boost the city's status.

Brief history

The **Vikings** sailed up the Shannon in about 922 and established a settlement here on a river island, formed by a narrow branch off the main flow that is today called the Abbey River. This port at the lowest fording point of the river was coveted by the

A WEEKEND NIGHT IN ENNIS

Highlights

❶ Hunt Museum This diverse, personal collection of beautiful art and antiquities is Limerick's finest attraction. See page 305

❷ Lough Gur Atmospheric rural lake surrounded by fine Neolithic remains. See page 310

❸ Quin Abbey Evocative monastic settlement in an idyllic setting. See page 314

❹ Ennis The county town offers numerous opportunities to experience Clare's lively traditional music scene. See page 314

❺ Scattery Island Deserted for more than thirty years, this tranquil island in the middle of the Shannon estuary was once a major ecclesiastical settlement. See page 319

❻ The Cliffs of Moher Massive sea-battered cliffs, providing exhilarating views of the Atlantic Ocean. See page 322

❼ The Burren A desolate rock-scape peppered with numerous Neolithic and Iron Age remains. See page 323

HIGHLIGHTS ARE MARKED ON THE MAP ON PAGE 302

9

Anglo-Normans who, in 1197, seized and set about fortifying the town. This involved building high city walls around what became Englishtown, to keep out the local Irish, who retreated to a ghetto to the southeast across the Abbey River – Irishtown.

The seventeenth century

In the late seventeenth century, the final bloody scenes of the War of the Kings were played out here. After their defeat at the Boyne in 1690, the Jacobite forces in

HIGHLIGHTS

1 Hunt Museum
2 Lough Gur
3 Quin Abbey
4 Ennis
5 Scattery Island
6 The Cliffs of Moher
7 The Burren

Limerick castle, under the Earl of Tyrconnell and local hero **Patrick Sarsfield**, refused to surrender. Though beset by a vastly superior force, Sarsfield managed to raise the siege by creeping out at night with five hundred men and destroying the Williamite supply train. When William's army came back in 1691, however, the medieval walls of the castle were unable to withstand the artillery bombardment. Tyrconnell having died of a stroke, Sarsfield surrendered on October 3, 1691, on supposedly honourable terms, according to the **Treaty of Limerick**. The Jacobites – some twelve thousand in all, later

9

known as the "Wild Geese" – were permitted to go to France, in whose cause Sarsfield fought and later died. The treaty also promised Catholics the comparative religious toleration they had enjoyed under Charles II, but the English went back on the deal, and between 1692 and 1704 the Irish Parliament passed the harshly anti-Catholic penal laws.

The eighteenth century onwards

The eighteenth century proved to be far more prosperous for Limerick, which in the 1750s received a grant of £17,000 from the Irish Parliament towards a major redevelopment.

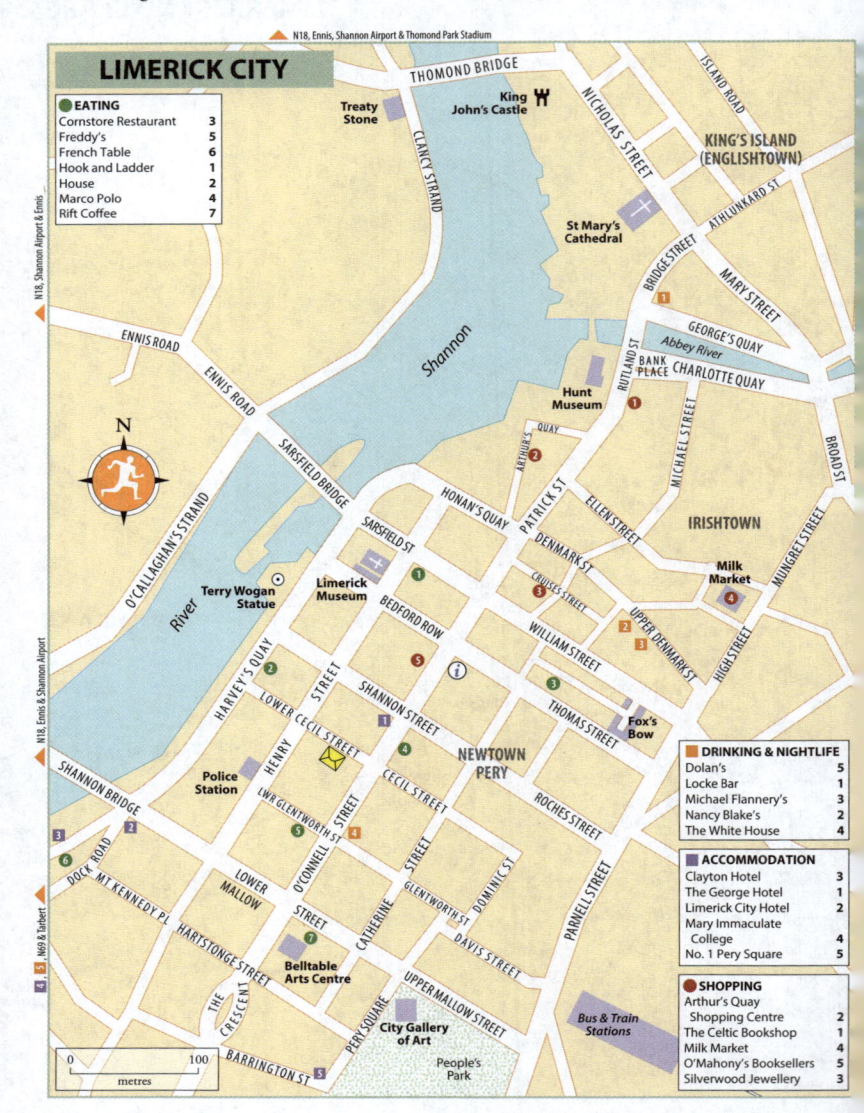

LIMERICK CITY

EATING
Cornstore Restaurant	3
Freddy's	5
French Table	6
Hook and Ladder	1
House	2
Marco Polo	4
Rift Coffee	7

DRINKING & NIGHTLIFE
Dolan's	5
Locke Bar	1
Michael Flannery's	3
Nancy Blake's	2
The White House	4

ACCOMMODATION
Clayton Hotel	3
The George Hotel	1
Limerick City Hotel	2
Mary Immaculate College	4
No. 1 Pery Square	5

SHOPPING
Arthur's Quay Shopping Centre	2
The Celtic Bookshop	1
Milk Market	4
O'Mahony's Booksellers	5
Silverwood Jewellery	3

THE LIMERICK

Limericks became common in Britain in the nineteenth century, popularized by Edward Lear, but their origin is shrouded in the mists of time. In Limerick city you'll find one on the walls of the city's oldest pub, the *White House* (see page 309):

The limerick is furtive and mean;
You must keep her in close quarantine,
Or she sneaks up to the slums
And promptly becomes
Disorderly, drunk and obscene.

Completed in 1840 and named after the local MP, **Newtown Pery** comprised a grid of broad Georgian terraced streets, built well to the south of the cramped, fetid medieval city. In the early **twentieth century**, however, Limerick suffered greatly during the Nationalist struggles, which, in 1919, gave rise to a radical movement that's unique in Irish history: in protest against British military action during the War of Independence, the local Trades Council called a general strike and proclaimed the **Limerick Soviet**. With help from the IRA, they took over the city, controlling food distribution, setting up a citizens' police force and even printing their own money. It lasted only a few weeks, however, collapsing under pressure from the Catholic bishop. In 1921 both Limerick's mayor, George Clancy, and the former mayor, Mícheál O'Callaghan, were murdered by the Royal Irish Constabulary. One of the effects of the Troubles was that the rich were persuaded to move out of the city: many of their Georgian houses in Newtown Pery became tenements and some remain dilapidated to this day. The traditional distinctions between Englishtown – focused on the castle and now signposted as King's Island – Irishtown and Newtown Pery no longer matter very much, as there's little of the medieval city left in the first two areas, while Newtown Pery's grid is scattered with modern developments.

The Hunt Museum

The Custom House, Rutland St • charge • http://huntmuseum.com

The fascinating displays in the **Hunt Museum**, dating from the Stone Age to modern times, are the best place to start a tour of the city. Over the course of the twentieth century, John and Gertrude Hunt gathered together this diverse collection of art and antiquities, especially known for its religious works, and bequeathed it to the people of Ireland. You'll get the best idea of the spirit of the place in the **Epilogue Room**, which juxtaposes pieces of wildly different origins, such as an eighteenth-century Chinese porcelain cockerel and an English stone rabbit from the fifteenth century.

There are regular guided tours every day (phone for details) and a light-filled basement café. Particular pieces to look out for include the beautiful, early ninth-century **Antrim Cross**, one of the finest examples of early Christian metalwork from Ireland. Made of bronze decorated with enamel in geometric and animal designs, it was discovered by chance in the River Bann in the nineteenth century. Keep an eye out also for the **Beverley Crozier**, a piece of walrus ivory intricately carved with miracles of healing, dating from the eleventh century. Other highlights include works by Irish artists William Orpen, Jack B. Yeats and Roderic O'Connor.

St Mary's Cathedral

Bridge St • Visits possible daily except during services • Donation • http://saintmaryscathedral.ie

Just across the river from the Hunt Museum, the Church of Ireland **St Mary's Cathedral** boasts a fine, almost homely interior of rough stone walls, brightly coloured stained glass and beautiful barrel-vaulted ceilings. It was founded on the site of the Viking *thingmote* or meeting place in 1168 – from which time dates the Romanesque west doorway, carved with monstrous heads, stylized flowers and chevrons – but has gained so many accretions over the centuries that it's now as broad as it is long, with an intriguingly confused layout.

The cathedral's highlight is its set of dark-oak **misericords** in the Jebb Chapel, the only example left in Ireland. Dating from the late fifteenth century, they're ornately carved with symbols of good and evil, including a delicate, sinuous swan, cockatrices, griffins and all sorts of other mythical monsters. Look out also for the limestone **reredos** behind the main altar, which was carved in Celtic Revival style by Michael Pearse, father of the Irish patriot, Pádraig, and the nearby tomb of the cathedral's founder, King Donal Mór O'Brien of Munster, decorated with three heraldic lions and a Celtic cross. The cathedral stages lunch-time **music recitals** every Wednesday (1.15pm) during the summer.

Limerick Museum

Old Franciscan Friary, 100 Henry St • Free • www.limerick.ie/limerick-museum

Housed within the former Franciscan friary, the **Limerick Museum** is one of the oldest and largest local authority museums in the country, housing an eclectic and varied collection dedicated to the memory of **Jim Kemmy**, a former mayor and proud Limerick man. The story of the city, and the county, is presented through a rich collection of artefacts, from Stone Age axes and medieval coins, to the civic sword of Queen Elizabeth I and a sizeable assemblage of Limerick lace and silver. More unusual items includs Ireton's Cat – a mummified cat found on St Nicholas Street in the 1890s – a 1940s diving suit, and a fragment of the largest meteorite to fall in Ireland, in 1813. If you want to see the infamous **treaty stone** on which the surrender terms of the 1691 siege were signed (see page 303), cross Thomond Bridge to the west bank, where the stone was put on a 2m-high pedestal facing the castle in 1865.

King John's Castle

King's Island • charge; Heritage Island • http://kingjohnscastle.ie

The dramatically sited Anglo-Norman **King John's Castle** is the city's most eye-catching building – especially when viewed from the banks of the Shannon. An imposing five-sided fortification inaugurated by the king himself in 1210, it had no keep and no tower at its southeast corner facing Englishtown, until a rectangular artillery bastion was added at the beginning of the troubled seventeenth century. A shiny **visitor centre** has facilitated the castle's twenty-first-century rebirth, bringing fresh life into the building with dazzling new displays. Imaginative audiovisuals cover a range of subjects, including early Gaelic society; the Normans, whose arrival in 1169 made Limerick a Royal city; the change and conflict during the sixteenth-century Reformation; the three horrendous sieges the castle suffered in 1642, 1651 and 1690–91; and the history of the castle's excavation. The sights, smells and sounds of the times are graphically captured in the galleries. Do take a walk along the battlements for fabulous views of the Shannon and the city spread out below.

Belltable Arts Centre

69 O'Connell St • Box Office Mon–Fri noon–5.30pm • http://limetreebelltable.ie

A multidisciplinary arts centre, and the oldest regional arts centre in the country, the **Belltable** is run under the auspices of the Lime Tree Theatre and houses a cinema, theatre and gallery exhibition space. Every Monday night a film is shown, while in October the **Richard Harris International Film Festival** (http://richardharrisfilmfestival.

LIMERICK FESTIVALS

The city lays on a compelling menu of **festivals** throughout the year. A key element of St Patrick's Day is the **International Band Championship**, when an array of marching bands from all over Ireland descend upon the city. At the beginning of May, it's **Riverfest** (http://riverfest.ie), one of Ireland's biggest festivals, with fireworks, fashion shows and street performances. In June and early July, **Blas** (http://blas.ie), a highly regarded two-week summer school of traditional music and dance, takes place at the Irish World of Academy of Music and Dance, Limerick University, with associated concerts and sessions around the city. A major highlight – taking place between late August and late October – is **EVA** (http://eva.ie), Ireland's pre-eminent biennial exhibition of contemporary art; works by Irish and foreign artists, as selected by a leading international curator, are installed at galleries and around the city. An international poetry festival, **Cuisle**, encompassing readings, open-mike sessions and workshops, takes place in mid-October.

com) is held here. The centre also stages a wide variety of concerts, drama, musicals and comedy shows.

Terry Wogan Statue

Harvey's Quay

Since its erection in 2017, the controversial life-size bronze **statue** of the Limerick-born BBC broadcaster, **Terry Wogan** – who died in 2016 – has attracted criticism and ridicule for its questionable resemblance to the much-loved Sir Terry (who in 2017 was named "the greatest radio presenter of the last fifty years" in a BBC poll of broadcasting experts). Sculpted by artist Rory Breslin, it depicts a seated Wogan holding a microphone in one hand and book in the other. Perhaps inevitably, given the furore surrounding it, the statue has become a popular tourist attraction.

Limerick City Gallery of Art

Carnegie Building, Pery Square• Free • http://gallery.limerick.ie

By the entrance to the People's Park stands the **Limerick City Gallery of Art**. Remodelled with renovated galleries, the building is a hybrid of the old and new. Displayed on a rotating basis, the permanent collection of eighteenth- to twenty-first-century paintings and drawings by artists such as Sean Keating, Paul Henry and Jack Butler Yeats will appeal to aficionados of Irish art, but best of all is the gallery's exciting programme of **contemporary exhibitions** by Irish and international artists. A sculpture, *The Siege of Limerick*, by the renowned New York-based artist Brian O'Doherty, was installed to mark the reopening.

Thomond Park Stadium and Museum

Old Cratloe Rd, 2km northwest of the city centre• Stadium and museum tour charge (advance booking essential; Sat or Sun tours minimum 6 people) • http://thomondpark.ie

Limerick's **Thomond Park Stadium** is home to the **Munster rugby team** – a huge presence in this part of the world – and also stages rock concerts following a redevelopment which doubled its capacity to 26,500. **Tours** offer an intimate account of the Munster players' experience on match day, taking in the dressing room, dugouts and the pitch itself. Also included is a short film recounting the team's history and a visit to the **museum**, which features club memorabilia as well as footage from the "match of all matches" when Munster beat the mighty All Blacks 12-0 in 1978.

ARRIVAL AND DEPARTURE

LIMERICK CITY

By plane Limerick is 25km from Shannon International Airport (http://shannonairport.ie), which has direct flights from North America, the UK and several other European countries, as well as Irish internal services. The airport has good bus links with Limerick and Ennis, as well as with Cork, Dublin, Galway and Killarney. The Cork to Galway bus (#51) drops off and picks up at the airport hourly en route to Limerick bus station. Shannon Airport Taxis (http://shannonairportcab.com) are the official airport service; a taxi to either Limerick or Ennis will cost around €50–60.

By train The train station is on Parnell St.

Destinations Athenry (4–5 daily; 1hr 40min); Cork (Mon–Sat hourly, Sun 7, often with a change at Limerick Junction; 1hr 40min–2hr 10min); Dublin Heuston (hourly, often with a change at Limerick Junction; 2hr–2hr 20min); Ennis (8–9 daily; 40min); Waterford (Mon–Sat 3 daily, with a change at Limerick Junction; 2hr 25min–3hr 10min).

By bus The bus station is on Parnell St, adjacent to the train station.

Destinations Adare (hourly; 20min); Athlone (2–4 daily; 2hr 10min); Birr (2–4 daily; 1hr 15min); Bunratty (hourly; 20min); Cliffs of Moher (2–3 daily; 1hr 50min); Cork (hourly; 1hr 50min); Doolin (2–3 daily; 2hr 15min); Dublin (hourly; 3hr 40min); Ennis (hourly; 1hr); Galway (hourly; 2hr 20min); Killaloe (Mon–Sat 4–5 daily; 40–55min); Killarney (6 daily; 2hr); Lisdoonvarna (2–3 daily; 2hr); Listowel (8 daily; 1hr 25min); Tralee (8 daily; 2hr); Tulla (Wed 1 at 5.30pm; 55min); Waterford (6–8 daily; 2hr 30min).

INFORMATION AND TOURS

Tourist office Inside King John's Castle (May–Sept daily Mon–Sat 9.30am–5pm; http://limerick.ie).

Bus tours A hop-on-hop-off city bus tour with nine pick-up locations is run by Red Viking Tours (April–Oct 7 daily; €12; 061 220555), operating from Arthur's Quay Park.

Rail tours Railtours (http://railtoursireland.com) takes in the Cliffs of Moher and Bunratty Castle, via Limerick on select days between April and October.

Walking tours Run by the Civic Trust, 45-minute walking tours of the city's most historic sites take place each Tues & Thurs at 11.30am and 2.30pm, costing €10 (http://limerickcivictrust.ie); must be pre-booked.

Kayaking trips Limerick City Kayaking Tours offers kayaking trips on the Shannon (€35 for 90mins; http://nevsailwatersports.ie).

ACCOMMODATION

SEE MAP PAGE 304

Clayton Hotel Steamboat Quay, http://claytonhotellimerick.com. The tallest hotel in Ireland, the building is a distinctive landmark on the cityscape, and juts out over the river with spectacular views. Fantastically plush rooms are complemented by a health and leisure club with heated indoor swimming pool overlooking the river, with dining options in the shape of the *Waterfront* and *Grain and Grill* restaurants and the excellent *Red Bean Roastery*. €€€

The George Hotel O'Connell St, http://thesavoycollection.com/the-george. Contemporary boutique hotel on the upper floors above the main street, offering well-equipped rooms in a dark wood and red or green contemporary style. The hotel also incorporates the obligatory spa, as well as the gorgeous looking *Vincenzo Grill House and Bar*. Free overnight parking. €€€

Limerick City Hotel Lower Mallow St, http://limerickcityhotel.ie. No-frills hotel with over 141 comfortable rooms. Very handy for the centre, but right on one of Limerick's busiest junctions, so unless you're eager for a view of the river, ask for a room at the back. The hotel's convivial pub, *McGettigan's*, is a good spot to catch live music at the weekends. €€

Mary Immaculate College Courtbrack, Tarbert Rd, http://mic.ul.ie. During summer (May to mid-Aug), the university's Mary Immaculate College opens its student accommodation to visitors. A light breakfast is included in the room price. €

★ No 1 Pery Square 1 Pery Square, http://oneperysquare.com. Beautifully designed boutique hotel occupying a restored Georgian town house next to People's Park. Some rooms reflect the building's period origins, featuring sash windows and individually designed beds, while others have a spruce contemporary finesse. There's a spa too and a restaurant offering everything from brunch to gourmet tasting nights. €€€

EATING

SEE MAP PAGE 304

Cornstore Restaurant Thomas St, http://cornstore.ie. Covering three floors and incorporating a wine and cocktail bar, the lively *Cornstore* specializes in seafood such as seared tuna steak with olive tapenade and garlic potato cream, and dry-aged steaks including chateaubriand to share for two. An à la carte menu is complemented by very reasonably priced set menus. €€€€

★ Freddy's Theatre Lane, http://freddysrestaurant.com. A cosy hideaway with a rustic feel, natural stone walls and a cosmopolitan menu, with dishes such as spicy Korean chicken wings in siracha sauce, and honey and soy slow cooked pork belly, plus a few vegan options. Much to their credit, there's even a dedicated coeliac menu. Closed Sun–Wed. €€€

French Table 1 Steamboat Quay, http://frenchtable.ie. Scintillating French food featuring Languedoc- and

9

Dordogne-style classics such as escargots garlic or Toulouse sausage with an imaginative Irish twist. Confit of duck leg, hake and marinated chicken are menu standards; a *Menu de Soir* costs €36 for two-courses, €45 for three. Intriguingly, they also do a lunchtime takeaway menu of salads and sandwiches. Closed Mon & Tues. **€€€**

Hook and Ladder 7 Sarsfield St, http://hookandladder. ie. This family-run establishment, housed in a former bank, is open for breakfast, lunch and early evening meals. Sandwiches, bagels and wraps as well as Mediterranean salads, chowder and chicken and bacon on a blaa (local bread) are all available. You can also indulge in home-baked cakes, pastries and breads, speciality teas, premium coffees and a wide wine selection. **€€**

House Howley's Quay, http://houselimerick.ie. Watch the swans preening in the Shannon as you dine al fresco at this elegant quayside restaurant with meat (buttermilk chicken with chipotle mayo; chargrilled steaks) and fish (Atlantic prawn Pil Pil with Gubbeen chorizo) forming the mainstay of the all-day menu, although veggies and vegans are taken care of too (vegan cauliflower wings with smoked paprika). **€€€**

Marco Polo 38 O'Connell St, http://marcopolo.ie. This buzzy restaurant offers all manner of menus including a terrific value early bird (Mon–Fri 4.30–6.30pm) at €32 for three courses, and although the dishes are not massively inventive (lemon chicken, lamb shank), the cooking is accomplished and you won't leave feeling disappointed. **€€€**

Rift Coffee 30 Mallow St, http://riftcoffee.com. A local's favourite, this is the city's top dog when it comes to coffee. Energetically run with a pleasantly pared-back interior, *Rift* also serves up soups and rolls alongside a mouthwatering selection of baked goodies – oh, and wine too, best enjoyed outside at one of the pavement tables. Closed Sun. **€**

DRINKING AND NIGHTLIFE

SEE MAP PAGE 304

Dolan's Dock Rd, http://dolans.ie. Top dog for live music, *Dolan's* features traditional tunes in the bar every night, and everything from jazz and singer-songwriters to indie and tribute bands – plus comedy nights – in its two gig venues, The Warehouse and Upstairs.

Locke Bar 3 George's Quay, http://lockebar.com. Congenial gastropub offering traditional music every night. Tables out the front overlook the River Abbey – a great spot on a sunny day; sample the Hell's Gate lager from the Treaty City Brewery or choose from the wide choice of cocktails.

Michael Flannery's 17 Upper Denmark St, http:// flannerysbar.ie. Whiskey connoisseurs love this pub with a pedigree stretching back to 1898. It has a hundred different types of Irish whiskey and once bottled its own Jameson: a "Whiskey Bible" complete with tasting notes lists them all, and you can sample three tipples in a whiskey tasting session.

Nancy Blake's 19 Upper Denmark St, 061 416443. Time-burnished watering hole with bare wooden sawdust floors, home to traditional music Mon–Wed & Sun. Through the back, a large, covered and heated courtyard and modern bar hosts a DJ on Fri.

★ **The White House** 52 O'Connell St, http://thewhite housebar.ie. Established in 1812 and furnished in dark wood, this is Limerick's oldest pub, and despite modernisation, has managed to retain some of its old essence. Tues night is the best time to pop by with trad sessions, but there's other music Wed–Sat.

ENTERTAINMENT

For details of all arts events, pick up a copy of the *Limerick Events Guide* (*LEG*), a free **monthly listings magazine** available at the tourist office and in cafés and bars. Although many poetry, music and comedy performances take place in **pubs**, Limerick has its share of quality theatre and concert venues.

Lime Tree Theatre Mary Immaculate College, Courtbrack Ave, http://limetreebelltable.ie. This 500-seater hosts drama, music and children's shows. Two excellent theatrical touring companies – the Abbey from Dublin and the Druid from Galway – stage shows here.

University Concert Hall Foundation Building, University of Limerick, Castletroy, http://uch.ie. Audiences have enjoyed large-scale operas including *Aida*, *Carmen* and *Madame Butterfly* at the UCH. Sir James Galway, Christy Moore and Billy Connolly have all performed here, and the Irish Chamber Orchestra holds an annual programme of events.

SHOPPING

SEE MAP PAGE 304

Limerick's deep-rooted connections with the past are reflected in the many **traditional shop fronts** and you will stumble across victuallers, saddlers and barbers. Don't miss **Fox's Bow**, a funky alleyway of craft, jewellery and gift shops between Thomas and William streets. For pharmacies, branches of **O'Sullivan's** are on O'Connell St (Mon–Fri 8.30am–6pm, Sat 9.30am–5pm) and round the corner on Sarsfield St (daily 10am–11pm).

Arthur's Quay Shopping Centre Patrick St, http:// arthursquay.ie. A bright mall with plenty of Irish and British chain stores and designer names.

The Celtic Bookshop 2 Rutland St, http://celticbookshop-limerick.ie. A place to lose yourself for an hour or so on a quest for rare or out-of-print Irish classics. Closed Sun.

Milk Market Cornmarket Row, http://milkmarketlimerick. ie. Saturday morning is the best time to enjoy this bustling food market, held in a stone building that was once a corn market and featuring fresh farm produce from all over Munster. Under its canopy you'll find a superb selection of stalls offering farmhouse cheeses, organic sausages, spelt breads, fruit and vegetables, chutneys, jams and artisan chocolates. You can also snack on soup, crunchy salads, inventive sandwiches, wraps and crêpes, and freshly brewed tea and coffee. Sunday is given over to monthly fairs (art, antiques, vinyl), plus there are always a few shops open and outdoor cafes doing brisk trade.

O'Mahony's Booksellers 120 O'Connell St, http://omahonys.ie. Long-established independent bookshop, particularly strong on Irish fiction and non-fiction, plus local heritage and maps.

Silverwood Jewellery 32 Cruises St, http://silverwood jewellery.com. Artfully crafted bespoke jewellery, ranging from Celtic to abstract pieces, are on sale in this eye-catching store. Brooches, necklaces, pendants and rings sit alongside gold and silver, freshwater pearls and semi-precious stones. Downstairs is an Irish graft gallery and a Goldsmiths workshop. Closed Sun.

Lough Gur

20km south of Limerick city on the R512 towards Kilmallock • Open access to site • http://loughgur.com • The only bus from Limerick to Lough Gur is the 10.30am (Mon–Sat) Kilmallock service – ask for Holycross – with returns at 12.30pm and 4.50pm; a taxi from Limerick will cost €20 each way

Set in a serenely peaceful valley 20km south of Limerick city is one of Ireland's most astonishing and atmospheric places. A cluster of grassy limestone hills springs unexpectedly from the plain, sheltering in their midst **Lough Gur**, the site of dozens of largely **prehistoric monuments**. Their importance lies in the fact that many of them are not ceremonial sites but stone dwelling places, dating from around 3000 BC onwards, which have furnished archaeologists with most of their knowledge of the way of life in Neolithic Ireland. That's not to say that this curious landscape did not have a ritual aspect, as it was also revered as the territory of the sun goddess, Áine, and accrued a powerful mythical reputation, for example as the location of some of Fionn Mac Cumhaill's adventures in the *Ulster Cycle*. Before it was partly drained in the nineteenth century, the lake (now C-shaped) formed an approximate square, with a 9km shoreline around a large triangular island, **Knockadoon**. The drainage, which left a marsh on the eastern side of the island and lowered the lake's level by 3m, revealed hoards of prehistoric items, including gold and bronze spearheads, a bronze shield, swords and stone and bronze axes.

Visitor Centre

Charge • Guided tours (2hr 30min; €50 for a minimum of two people, with admission to site included) must be booked one day in advance on 061 385386

The **Visitor Centre** features numerous exhibits and a multimedia exhibition that bring alive six thousand years of history through touch screens, listening posts and audiovisual presentations. The centre also provides a pamphlet detailing **trails** around Lough Gur (also downloadable from the website) – you can explore on your own or join a guided tour.

The stone circle

The first site you'll come to, on the R512 to the west of the lake at Holycross, is the largest and finest **stone circle** in Ireland. Now set in a grassy glade surrounded by majestic trees, it consists of 113 large stones propped upright in sockets, around an artificial floor of gravelly earth 70cm above the original ground level. Built around 2100 BC, the circle is associated with **Crom Dubh**, the harvest god. The entrance to the northeast is aligned towards sunrise around May 21 before the summer solstice and, correspondingly, around July 22 as the sun travels southwards on the horizon after the summer solstice.

Gallery grave

About 1km south of the stone circle, the access road to Lough Gur heads east off the R512 around the south shore. Just over 1km in, on the south side of the road, you'll see the so-called Giant's Grave, a wedge-shaped **gallery grave** dating from about 2600 BC, where the remains of eight adults and four children were discovered. It's yet another ancient Irish site where Diarmuid and Gráinne are meant to have lain together on their flight from Fionn Mac Cumhaill, though it has added significance as Gráinne is the alter ego of Áine, the sun goddess.

Knockadoon

Causeways lead across from near the visitor centre and the Giant's Grave to the island of **Knockadoon**, which is fun to explore though parts are covered in dense woodland. Visible from the visitor centre at the northeast corner of the island is **Bourchier's Castle**, a privately owned, fifteenth-century tower house, while the overgrown remains of the thirteenth-century **Black Castle** face the Giant's Grave from the southern shore. Working west from here, you'll see traces of huts and ring forts on the grassy slopes, and around on the northwest-facing shore of the island, a limestone seat on a small, grassy mound known as the **Housekeeper's Chair**. This was held to be the birth-chair of Áine, from which she turned green corn to gold, for Crom Dubh to carry off at harvest time. A little further on, near the northernmost point of the island, is a **cave** said to be the entrance to Tír na nÓg, the land of eternal youth.

Adare

With its broad main street lined with thatched cottages and colourful doors, **ADARE** has long been a much-admired stopping place for tourists and draws in coach parties from far afield. Its chocolate-box quaintness can be too sickly for some, however, and, sited some 15km southwest of Limerick on the N21 towards Kerry, it is also marred by its location on a major national road. As the **Heritage Centre** reveals, it was made picturesque by design: the earls of Dunraven, landlords of Adare Manor, beautified their estate village (according to the contemporary fashion for pastoral romanticism) with ornamental thatched cottages in the early nineteenth century, and with Arts and Crafts-style houses in the early twentieth century. Set beside a prim town **park** on the south bank of the River Maigue, Adare's appeal is enhanced by some impressive remnants, mostly ecclesiastical, of its medieval heyday.

Heritage Centre and castle

Main St • Free; Heritage Island • Castle tours June–Sept daily; charge • http://adareheritagecentre.ie

The best place to start is the **Heritage Centre**, centrally located opposite the park on Main Street, which houses the tourist office (see below) and sells castle admission tickets. The centre also houses a free exhibition, and there's a restaurant with outdoor terrace seating. From June to September, the restored, early thirteenth-century **Desmond Castle**, on the north side of the Maigue River bridge, can be visited on hour-long guided tours which set off by bus from the Heritage Centre (departure times vary so check with the reception desk).

The Trinitarian Abbey and Augustinian Friary

The Catholic parish church next door to the Heritage Centre, a trim, multi-aisled affair with an imposing, oak-beamed roof, was part of the **Trinitarian Abbey** until the mid-nineteenth century. Founded around 1230 with an attached hospital, it was the only house of the Order of the Holy Trinity in Ireland. Down an alley to one side is a circular stone tower with a conical roof, where the monks kept pigeons – not as a hobby, but for the refectory table. Five minutes' walk away, on the south side of the Maigue bridge, stands the **Augustinian Friary**, which is now an Anglican parish church and school. Founded in 1315, it has an attractive, fifteenth-century cloister, carefully restored by the Dunravens in the nineteenth century then spoiled by the insertion of their brutal family mausoleum.

By bus There are hourly buses from/to Limerick (20min). **Tourist office** Heritage Centre, Main St (daily 9am– 5.30pm; http://adareheritagecentre.ie).

ACCOMMODATION

Adare Camping and Caravan Park 4km south of Adare off the R519 Ballingarry road, http://adarecamping.com. This small but well-equipped site is handy for exploration of the village and countryside; facilities include laundry, camper's kitchen, a field for kickabout and a play area. Closed Oct–April. €

Adare Manor Hotel Limerick Rd, http://adaremanor.com. This Gothic pile dating from 1832 and set in 840 acres, now has 104 luxurious rooms alongside cottages and lodges, a Michelin-starred restaurant (*The Oak Room*), several bars, a swimming pool and spa, golf course, and pursuits such as falconry, archery, axe-throwing and clay pigeon shooting. It is, of course, astronomically priced. €€€€

★ **Fitzgerald's Woodlands House Hotel & Spa** 2km south of the centre, off the Limerick road, http://woodlands-hotel.ie. A gym, pool and spa are part of the deal at this welcoming family-owned hotel in a secluded setting. Many of the sizeable rooms are furnished with comfy settees, and the delightful bistro, *Timmy Macs*, features beef from the owners' very own cattle herd. Good-value midweek breaks are available. €€€

EATING AND DRINKING

1826 Adare Main St, http://1826adare.ie. The focus of this chic restaurant, set in a delightful row of thatched cottages, is on keenly priced casual dining. Their signature dish is the free-range pork tasting plate of loin belly cheek and black pudding, but you'll also find blackboard specials such as sole and braised meats. And there are worse ways to spend your Sunday afternoon than by indulging in the three-course Sunday late lunch. Closed Mon–Wed. €€€€

Aunty Lena's Main St, http://auntylenas.com. The extensive bar menu offers breakfast, sandwich and all-day menus which extend to some surprisingly sophisticated dishes like whiskey chicken and black pudding mash. Traditional music several nights a week. €€€

The Good Room Main St, 061 396218. A calming bistro café with outdoor seating, serving breakfast, brunches and lunches. Has a large selection of teas, including detox and caffeine-free varieties, plus juices, smoothies and healthy options. €

★ **The Mustard Seed** Ballingarry, 8km south of Adare on the R519, http://mustardseed.ie. Set in *Echo Lodge*, a country residence (offering stylish B&B accommodation), this is one of the country's foremost restaurants, with an inspired modern Irish menu drawing from the produce of its organic garden. The four-course "classic" dinner is served nightly and costs €72; main courses typically include rib-eye of beef, monkfish and guinea fowl. €€€€

Kilmallock

To escape the crowds and tour coaches of Adare, head south along the N20 and then east on the R515 to **KILMALLOCK**. On the face of it a workaday market town, Kilmallock's position at the centre of Ireland's political development for five centuries has made it something of a heritage hub. Wander around and you'll encounter vestiges of its medieval history, including the town walls, early church sites, a priory and castle standing foursquare, and the formidable **Blossom Gate**, the only one surviving of five sixteenth-century town gates. Kilmallock makes a superb base from which to explore the **Ballyhoura Mountains**, noted for mountain biking, cycle loops and walking trails, and you can also sample part of the **Ballyhoura Way**, a waymarked trail running through southeast Limerick and on to Tipperary.

By bus Buses run from Limerick to Kilmallock (3 daily; 40min).

Tourist office County Council Office on Millmount off Lord Edward St (daily 9am–5pm; http://visitballyhoura. com). Pick up a town map which will take you on a self-guided tour of the main historic sites. Information is also available on mountain-biking trails and looped cycle routes of the area and the Ballyhoura Way.

ACCOMMODATION AND EATING

Deebert House Hotel http://deeberthousehotel.com. This delightful family-run hotel on the site of an historic mill at the edge of town makes a good base, with twenty spacious and comfortable en-suite rooms. Its *Cloister*

Bar and Grill is open daily for lunch and dinner, offering locally sourced produce such as sausages, O'Sullivan's black pudding and cheese from Effin. There are traditional music nights on Tues in summer, and special packages for cyclists and walkers. €€

Southeast Clare

Heading north from Limerick to Galway along the busy N18, it's easy to miss some of the attractions of the county's nether region. Consisting largely of flat farmland, its lanes, ideal for cycling, lead to several sites of historic interest. The most southerly is the impressive **Bunratty Castle**, while a short hop further north lies the imaginative **Craggaunowen Project**, with its re-creations of dwellings from bygone times, and the idyllically set monastic site of **Quin Abbey**.

Bunratty Castle and folk park

Bunratty, 12km west of Limerick • castle closes 4pm • charge; Heritage Island • Banquets daily subject to demand 5.30pm & 8.45pm; charge • http://bunrattycastle.ie • Served by buses from Ennis (hourly; 35min) and Limerick (hourly; 25min)

West of Limerick, bypassed by the main N18 Ennis road, lies the village of **Bunratty** whose **castle** and **folk park** form one of Ireland's most popular attractions. A castle was first built here in 1277 during the Anglo-Normans' brief occupation of southeast Clare, though the present version dates back to the mid-fifteenth century and was constructed for the MacNamaras, a branch of the O'Brien clan. Majestically restored in the 1950s, its keep contains an impressive array of artwork and furniture, mostly dating from the fifteenth and sixteenth centuries. In the evenings, **"medieval banquets"** are staged here, as the lords and ladies of the castle welcome guests for an evening of music, mead and merriment. The expansive castle grounds host the **folk park**, a re-creation of a nineteenth-century village, replete with post office, shops, a church and a pub, all populated by actors in period dress.

ACCOMMODATION AND EATING
BUNRATTY

Bunratty Castle Hotel http://bunrattycastlehotel.com. In the village centre, this Georgian hotel has elegant accommodation in period-furnished rooms, as well as fine meals and a spa with pool. Special package rates are available for two nights' accommodation and dinner at the 'Bunratty Earl's Banquet' in the castle. €€€

Durty Nelly's Low Rd, http://durtynellys.ie. A choice of dining is available here at one of Ireland's best-known pubs. The relatively expensive *Loft* and *Oyster* restaurants offers evening menus which might include baked fillet of salmon, Nelly's surf 'n' turf or black pudding and chorizo croquettes, but there's cheaper pub grub and the bar's calendar of events includes traditional sessions Tues to Sat from March to Oct.

The Craggaunowen Project

14km north of Bunratty • April to early Sept daily 9.30am–5pm; last admission 4pm • charge; Heritage Island • http://craggaunowen.ie • By car, take the turning east off the R462 7km northeast of Bunratty, just past Sixmilebridge

The **Craggaunowen Project** features reconstructions of dwellings, hunting sites and other aspects of life during prehistoric and early Christian times. Hour-long self-guided tours begin with a sixteenth-century tower house whose displays of medieval art and artefacts include some notable European wood-carvings, before moving on to re-creations of a *crannóg*, ring fort and souterrain, as well as **The Togher**, a real Iron Age wooden roadway which was moved here from County Longford (see page 164). It's all given a dose of authenticity thanks to characters in period costume undertaking various crafts, including woodworking, blacksmithing, pottery, and dyeing and weaving of sheep's wool. Proof that replicas can sometimes match the real McCoy comes in the form of **The Brendan**, a *curragh* whose hull consists of leather hides stretched over an ash frame, in which Tim Severin and his four-man crew crossed the Atlantic in 1976.

9

A ninth-century manuscript describes how St Brendan the Navigator became the first European to reach the Americas in the sixth century in such a boat – and, though impossible to prove that Brendan did so, Severin certainly demonstrated that the technology described was sufficient for the task.

Quin Abbey

7km northwest of Craggaunowen, and 10km southeast of Ennis, on the R469 • Free

The ruined **Quin Abbey** occupies a glorious pastoral setting. Unusually, the original building incorporated parts of a castle, built by Thomas de Clare in the late thirteenth century, which was subsequently attacked by the Irish, leaving it "a hideous, blackened cave" according to one contemporary observer. In the 1430s the MacNamaras brought Franciscans to Quin to found the friary and used the ruins of the old castle as a base, constructing a remarkable edifice in the process.

Ennis and around

With a population of around 25,000, **ENNIS** is far and away Clare's largest town. It began its life in the thirteenth century as a small settlement grouped around a long-disappeared O'Brien castle. Nowadays it's a buzzing town set on both sides of the River Fergus, and still largely based around its medieval street pattern and the central, often traffic-clogged O'Connell Street. Though there's little to see here apart from the ruins of a medieval **friary**, to the north of O'Connell Street, the town has decent

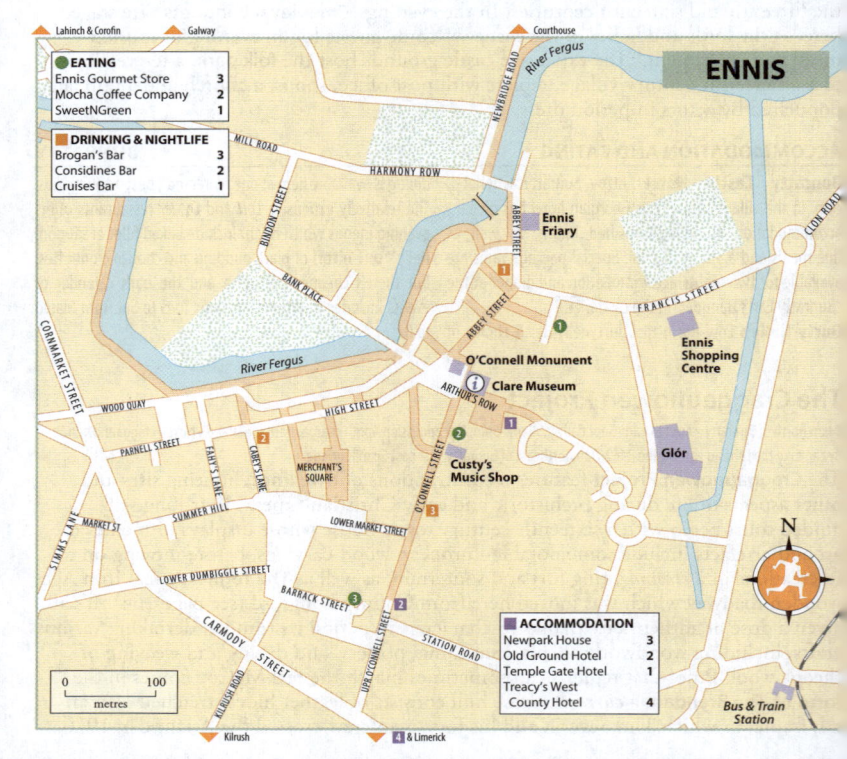

ENNIS FESTIVALS AND TRADITIONAL MUSIC

Ennis is home to two major festivals: the **Fleadh Nua** (http://fleadhnua.com), over the last week of May, and the **Ennis Traditional Music Festival** (http://ennistradfest.com), which runs for five days in early November. The best source for information about the local traditional music scene, and a good place to pick up CDs by Clare musicians, is Custy's Music Shop on Cook's Lane, off O'Connell Street (Mon–Sat 9am–6pm; http://custysmusic.com).

---

restaurants, a joyous range of bookshops and independent boutiques and, above all, a thriving **traditional music** session scene. Glór, on Causeway Link (http://glor.ie), is a purpose-built **concert hall** with traditional music concerts and festival summer schools. A **farmers' market** takes place every Friday (8am–2pm) in the car park on Upper Market Street.

The friary

Abbey St • charge; Heritage Card • http://monastic.ie/history/ennis-ofm-friary

Ennis's only real building of note is its thirteenth-century Franciscan **friary**, founded by the O'Briens, and considered, at one time, to be one of Ireland's major educational institutions. While other such establishments did not survive the Reformation, this one did thanks to Murchadh O'Brien's acknowledgement of the rule of the Tudors – he became the first Earl of Thomond in the process, though the friars were finally expelled in the 1570s. Subsequently, the buildings were used as assizes and a jail, as well as providing rooms for visiting dignitaries. In the late seventeenth century the friary became a parish church of the Church of Ireland, before finally being abandoned in 1871. In a niche on one of the fifteenth-century tower's piers is a **carved relief** of St Francis, complete with a habit whose girdle bears the three characteristic knots of the Franciscans, representing chastity, poverty and obedience. In the chancel is the **Creagh Tomb**, which dates from 1843 and incorporates sculptured panels from an earlier fifteenth-century tomb, decorated with astonishingly detailed scenes of Christ's suffering.

O'Connell Square and around

Away from the friary are several monuments devoted to Ennis's later political significance. O'Connell Square is dominated by a tall obelisk celebrating **Daniel O'Connell**, elected as Clare's MP in 1828. As a Catholic he could not take his seat, but his large majority was a factor in Westminster's subsequent implementation of the Catholic Emancipation Act and he was able to attend the Commons when re-elected in 1830. The former Taoiseach **Éamon de Valera**, who represented East Clare (including Ennis) at the Dáil for more than thirty years, is commemorated by a monument outside the Courthouse on Gort Road.

For a fuller picture of Clare's history, the **Clare Museum** (free; http://claremuseum.ie), which shares the same building as the tourist office on Arthur's Row, covers everything from local archaeological finds to the West Clare Railway (see page 321), taking in a re-creation of a Viking longboat, sport, music and dance on the way. A permanent exhibition, "The Riches of Clare", tells the story of the people, places and treasures of the county.

ARRIVAL AND DEPARTURE	**ENNIS AND AROUND**
By plane Buses and taxis run into town from Shannon Airport (see page 308).	**Destinations** Bunratty (hourly; 35min); Cliffs of Moher (5 daily; 50min); Cork (hourly; 3hr); Corofin (Mon–Sat 4 daily, Sun 2; 20min); Doolin (5 daily; 1hr 10min); Ennistymon
By bus The bus station on Station Rd is a 15min walk from the town centre.	(Mon–Sat 4 daily, Sun 2; 50min); Feakle (Thurs 1; 55min);

9

Galway (hourly; 1hr 15min); Kilkee (Mon–Sat 3 daily, Sun 2; 1hr 10min); Kilrush (Mon–Sat 6 daily, Sun 4; 55min); Lahinch (Mon–Sat 4 daily, Sun 2; 55min); Limerick (hourly; 1hr); Liscannor (5 daily; 45min); Lisdoonvarna (5 daily; 1hr 10min); Miltown Malbay (Mon–Sat 4 daily, Sun 2; 1hr 20min); Shannon Airport (hourly; 30min); Tulla (Thurs 1; 35min).

By train The train station is on Station Rd, adjacent to the bus station.
Destinations Athenry (4–5 daily; 1hr); Galway (4–5 daily; 1hr 20min); Gort (4–5 daily; 30min); Limerick (9–11 daily; 40min).

INFORMATION AND TOURS

Tourist office Inside Clare Museum, Arthur's Row (Tues–Sat 9.30am–5.30pm; http://ennis.ie).
Tours Walking tours set off May–Oct from outside the

tourist office (May–Oct Thurs & Fri 11am; 1hr 15min; €35; http://enniswalkingtours.com).

ACCOMMODATION
SEE MAP PAGE 314

Newpark House Tulla Rd, around 2km east of town off the R352 Scarriff road, http://newparkhouse.com. Occupying a lovely woodland setting, this splendid house dates from 1750 and provides stylish period rooms, some including canopy beds. Closed Nov–March. €€€
Old Ground Hotel O'Connell St, http://oldground hotelennis.com. The town's finest hotel is set in an ivy-clad, eighteenth-century building with its own relaxing gardens. The rooms are spacious, elegantly designed and furnished, and include a number of suites. There's a library too, plus a bar, bistro and restaurant. €€€
★ **Temple Gate Hotel** The Square, http://templegate

hotel.com. A soothing blend of old and new, this hotel's swish design incorporates a nineteenth-century former convent that retains its exquisite stained glass. Rooms are modishly decorated, especially the classy suites with kingsize beds and tapestry wall coverings. An on-site pub and restaurant serve a wide choice of excellent meals. €€€
Treacy's West County Hotel Limerick Rd, 1km south of town, http://treacyswestcounty.com. This modern, family-oriented hotel comes with a leisure centre featuring three swimming pools, a gym, a hot tub and sauna, and several classy dining options. Among the many varied categories of room are funky family bunk rooms sleeping five. €€€

EATING
SEE MAP PAGE 314

Ennis Gourmet Store 1 Barrack St, 065 684 3314. *The* place to pick up premium ingredients for a picnic, and also a source of terrific lunchtime sandwiches, salads, tapas and mini quiches – not to mention the town's finest coffee. Enjoy it – or perhaps a craft beer – out on the terrace or indoors. €€
Mocha Coffee Company Arthur's Row, 065 689 1326. A dazzling range of coffees and teas (everything from soya-milk lattes to wild-berry infusions) to wash down bagels, panini, Greek salads and low-carb wraps. Wine is also

available, and you can choose from indoor and outdoor seating. €
★ **SweetNGreen** Friary Car Park, http://sweetngreen. ie. Warm and appealing daytime café offering a wonderful range of tempting dishes, like halloumi chill eggs for breakfast/brunch, and baked harissa salmon with Moroccan red slaw and spiced beetroot hummus for lunch – and if you don't mind letting the calorie count slide, then tuck into one of their delicious home-baked treats. Closed Sun & Mon. €€

DRINKING AND NIGHTLIFE
SEE MAP PAGE 314

Brogan's Bar 24 O'Connell St, http://brogansbarennis. com. Local musicians feature here every night in summer with exhilarating performances and a chance to join in a sing-along.
Considines Bar 15 Parnell St, 087 908 2599. Known as *Faffa's*, this welcoming pub is highly regarded for its music and holds weekly sessions each Thurs evening, as well as

some other nights.
Cruises Bar Abbey St, http://cruiseennis.com. Dating from 1658 and named after John Cruise, an English settler and an original merchant of Ennis, this building was one of the "houses of hospitality" attached to the abbey and converted to a pub in 1993. It is still renowned for its hospitality and for links to traditional Irish music.

O'Dea Castle and Dysert O'Dea

Well signposted off the R476, 12km north of Ennis, **O'Dea Castle** (May–Aug daily 10am–5pm; charge; http://dysertcastle.ie) was the stronghold of the O'Dea branch of the O'Brien clan until 1691. Nowadays it houses an archaeological centre and is the best starting point for a history trail leading across fields to the **Dysert O'Dea** site, where St Tola founded a **monastery** in the eighth century. Several later religious remains can be found here, including a twelfth-century Romanesque **church**, extensively rebuilt in the seventeenth. This features a finely carved doorway and gargoyle-like carvings of human faces and animal heads. Nearby stands a **round tower**, badly damaged by Cromwell's guns, and the twelfth-century **White Cross of Tola**, which bears elaborate patterning and several impressive carvings.

Corofin

On the R476, **COROFIN** is a sturdy, well-defined village that makes a fine base for visiting the Burren. It is noteworthy as the birthplace of one of Ireland's foremost traditional musicians, the accordionist Sharon Shannon. The displays at the **Clare Heritage Centre** on Church Street (Mon–Fri 9am–5pm; charge; http://clareroots.com) provide a fascinating glimpse of bygone living conditions and focus on the Famine and emigration.

ARRIVAL AND DEPARTURE | COROFIN

By bus Buses drop off/pick up outside the Centra Supermarket halfway along the main street.
Destinations Ennis (Mon–Sat 4 daily, Sun 2; 20min); Ennistymon (Mon–Sat 4 daily, Sun 2; 35min); Lahinch (Mon–Sat 4 daily, Sun 2; 35min); Miltown Malbay (Mon–Sat 4 daily, Sun 2; 50min).

ACCOMMODATION

Corofin Camping & Hostel Main St, http://corofin camping.com. Comfortable budget accommodation and camping is available at this family-run hostel which has twin, double, family and dorm rooms, a sizeable kitchen for use, lounge and laundry facilities. The Burren Way walking trail starts outside its door and the owners supply maps to help you find your way. Closed Sept–March. €

Corofin Country House Station Rd, 065 683 7791. Comfortable ensuite rooms and a handy base for touring the southern Burren region and climbing Mullaghmore mountain, known as the Ayers Rock of Ireland. Closed Jan. €€

Lakefield Lodge Ennis Rd, http://lakefieldlodgebandb. com. Pleasant guesthouse on the edge of the Burren with just four rooms – a double, a twin and two triples. The owners will set up a glorious breakfast and help you plan hiking, cycling or fishing trips; they've even got boats for hire. Closed Oct–March. €€

East Clare

Less visited than other parts of the county, East Clare still has plenty of attractions, with most focused upon small towns and villages, of which **Killaloe**, sitting by the edge of **Lough Derg**, is the highlight. Offering numerous angling opportunities, the lake itself constitutes the county's eastern boundary and is popular with the more upmarket set, with its villages reminiscent of the English Cotswolds. Away from the lough, the countryside has a vastly different character from the remainder of Clare – it's a mass of hills and a warren of tiny lanes, with interest focused upon two of the county's greatest traditional music centres, **Tulla** and **Feakle**.

Killaloe

Hillside **KILLALOE** commands a strategic position above the point where the Shannon leaves Lough Derg. It was here that Brian Ború, the eleventh-century High King of Tara and founder of the O'Brien clan, built his palace, Kincora, a massive fort that was the centre of power in Ireland until Brian's death at the Battle of Clontarf in 1014 (see page 561). This stood on the summit of the hill in the spot now occupied by the Catholic church, though no trace of the building remains. About 1km to the north of the town, off the Scarriff road, is the Bronze Age ring fort **Béal Ború**, perhaps occupied by Brian Ború before Kincora's construction.

The local **festival**, Féile Brian Ború (http://feilebrianboru.com), is held over five days at the beginning of July with street entertainment.

9

MUSICAL TULLA AND FEAKLE

The villages of **Tulla** and **Feakle** are renowned for their musical pedigree. The **Tulla Céilí Band** is famed throughout the land – although you're more likely to catch them at a festival somewhere else than in Tulla. Feakle, meanwhile, 20km east of Ennis, proudly hosts the week-long **International Traditional Music Festival** (http://feaklefestival.ie) in early August, featuring major singers and musicians. You'll hear some majestic performers such as the trad superstar Martin Hayes and the celebrated accordion player Donal Murphy. If you're attending the festival, village **accommodation** consists of the lovely *Clare Ecolodge* (http://clareecolodge.ie; €€), and a friendly farmhouse B&B in *Laccaroe House* (http://laccaroehouse.com; €€). Impromptu sessions are often held in the two major **music pubs** in Feakle: *Shortt's* and *Pepper's*. Both villages have sporadic bus links with Ennis (see page 314) and each other (Thurs 1 daily; 20min), while a once-weekly bus also runs from Limerick to Tulla.

St Flannan's Cathedral

Just down Royal Parade from the bridge • http://st-flannans.weebly.com

Killaloe later became a religious centre, based around thirteenth-century **St Flannan's Cathedral**, featuring an impressive Romanesque doorway, taken from an earlier church that occupied the site, as well as a low, square bell tower. Just beside the doorway is the massive **Thorgrim Stone**, unusually bearing both runic and ogham inscription.

ARRIVAL AND INFORMATION   KILLALOE

By bus Killaloe is served by regular buses from/to Limerick (Mon–Sat 5 daily; 55min).

Tourist information There's a community-run office by the bridge (opening hours vary; http://discoverkillaloe.ie).

Boat tours Lough cruises on *The Spirit of Killaloe* (May to mid-Sept daily 1pm; €17; http://killaloerivercruises.com) leave from across the bridge in Ballina.

ACCOMMODATION AND EATING

The best options for accommodation and eating are over the bridge in **Ballina**, around 1.5km away.

Gooser's Limerick Rd, Ballina, http://goosers.com. More restaurant than pub, *Gooser's* menu features a local favourite: bacon and cabbage or a choice of steaks, mixed bean and potato curry and vegetarian specials. Their White Gypsy Ruby Ruby beer ale is noted for its caramel sweetness and toffee-roast flavour. €€€

Kincora House B&B Church St, Killaloe, http://kincorahouse.com. An attractive town house with four well-

appointed rooms that come with crisp linen, good-quality beds and modern showers – in a building whose pedigree stretches back 350 years. €€

Lakeside Hotel Ballina, http://lakesidehotel.ie. This place boasts an unbeatable waterside location with its own private jetty. Many of the 55 rooms overlook the river and there are fine views from the restaurant and bar, while the smart pool (with waterslide) will keep both adults and kids happy. €€€

Southwest Clare

It's a relatively long haul from Ennis to Clare's southwest, but well worth the effort for the attractions offered by two popular holiday spots and the chance to explore the glorious scenery of the **Loop Head peninsula**. Of the resorts, **Kilkee** is the livelier, with a sweeping beach and access to Loop Head; **Kilrush** is more stolid, but still attractive in its own way and is a base for dolphin watching and the ferry to **Scattery Island**, a major monastic site.

Kilrush

Some 40km from Ennis, **KILRUSH** is a graceful planned town whose broad main drag, Frances Street, leads down to a bustling marina where you can catch a ferry to **Scattery**

Island. At the town's core stands the **Maid of Éireann** statue, honouring the Manchester Martyrs, three Fenians who were executed in the English city in 1867 for a daring attempted rescue of some of their comrades arrested during a failed uprising.

Vandeleur Walled Garden

800m east of town by the Killimer road (N67) • charge • http://vandeleurwalledgarden.ie

In the early nineteenth century, wealthy landlord John Ormsby Vandeleur built Kilrush House, which once stood in a four-hundred-acre estate. The building was demolished in 1973, but the restored **Vandeleur Walled Garden** is an attractive spot featuring an abundance of subtropical plants. If you fancy stretching your legs a little more, directly opposite the entrance to the garden is a forest managed by Coillte, which was originally part of the estate; it's a lovely area of mixed woodland species with several easy trails.

Scattery Island

May–Sept daily 9am–6pm • €27 payable at the ticket office at Kilrush marina, includes return ferry and Island Centre admission • http://scatteryislandtours.com

In high season several daily ferries (depending on the tides) run from Kilrush's marina to **Scattery Island**, 2.5km offshore; journey time is around thirty minutes and you then have around two and a half hours on the island, which includes an hour-long guided tour (optional but well worth it). A monastery was established here by St Senan in the sixth century, and the island retained ecclesiastical importance until its exposed position attracted Viking raiders in 870, who occupied it until defeated by Brian Bórú in the late tenth century. Medieval church building is evident in the form of several ruins, and there's a reasonably well-preserved, 35m-high **round tower** which is most impressive when the sun seems to reflect off its yellowy, lichen-covered stone. Derelict since the last inhabitants left in 1978, Scattery has a timeless air. It's well worth making a trip to the island's southern point – where a **lighthouse** and gun battery remain from the time of the Napoleonic wars – for the sense of peaceful isolation and spectacular views. If you're so inclined, you are permitted to swim here too. By the pier the **Scattery Island Centre** houses an exhibition on the island's history.

ARRIVAL AND INFORMATION   KILRUSH

By bus Kilrush is served by buses from/to Ennis (Mon–Sat 5 daily, Sun 4; 55min) and Kilkee (Mon–Sat 6 daily, Sun 4; 5min).

Tourist information Ask at *Crotty's Pub* (see below) for information about the Loop Head peninsula's towns and villages.

ACCOMMODATION, EATING AND DRINKING

★ **Crotty's Pub & B&B** Market Square, http://crottyspubkilrush.com. Occupying a prime corner position with charmingly furnished rooms and good-value bar food, this is the pick of places to stay. The bar retains its original Victorian mirrors, and shelves and walls are filled with historical memorabilia. Breakfast, lunch and evening meals are available and there are traditional sessions in summer. €

The Haven Arms Henry St, 065 905 1267. Bar food is available during the day, with seafood a speciality, but you'll also find burgers and chicken curry on the menu along with other specials. €€

Katie O'Connor's Hostel 50 Frances St, http://katieshostel.com. Close to the main town square, this is a well-run place with a fully equipped kitchen. Turf fires in the living room are a big attraction. Ten-, six- and four-bed dorms are available (some ensuite), as well as private rooms. Closed Nov to mid-March. €

Kilkee and around

Thirteen kilometres northwest of Kilrush, **KILKEE** is a jaunty holiday resort, long popular with Limerick city folk, whose main attraction is a gorgeous, sandy, crescent-shaped **beach** that offers breathtaking cliff-top walks at both its ends. If the sun's hiding, alternative activities include the indoor 60m slide at **Waterworld** (June Sat & Sun 11am–5.45pm; July & Aug daily same hours; charge; http:// kilkeewaterworld.ie).

Loop Head peninsula

A tapering, elongated stretch of land, the **Loop Head peninsula** reaches southwest from Kilkee for some 25km. Though mostly low-lying, there are some staggeringly beautiful **cliff-top walks**; alternatively, it's possible to encompass virtually the whole peninsula by taking the scenic signposted drive from Kilkee or from just west of Moyasta. From the harbour at the village of **Carrigaholt**, which also houses the ruins of a fifteenth-century castle, Dolphinwatch runs excellent summer trips (2–3hr; €50; http://dolphinwatch.ie) to see and hear (through a hydrophone) the Shannon **dolphins**. The village also holds an oyster and traditional music **festival** at the end of April/beginning of May. To the north are the so-called **Bridges of Ross** at Ross Bay – natural arches formed by the ocean's erosion of the cliffs – though in fact there's now only one of the original pair.

ARRIVAL AND INFORMATION

KILKEE AND AROUND

By bus There are buses to Kilkee from Ennis (Mon–Sat 6 daily, Sun 4; 1hr 10min) and Kilrush (Mon–Sat 6 daily, Sun 4; 15min).

Tourist information In the absence of a tourist office http://kilkee.ie is a useful resource.

ACCOMMODATION

Green Acres Campsite Doonaha, http://greenacres camping.ie. A well-equipped site near the sea and handy for an exploration of Loop Head, as well as being an ideal location for a cycle tour of a section of the Wild Atlantic Way. Closed Nov–Feb. €

Kilkee Thalassotherapy Centre Grattan St, Kilkee, http:/ kilkeethalasso.com. A family-run health spa which also provides thalassotherapy in the form of seaweed baths and other related relaxations. Five en-suite rooms are available one triple, one twin, two doubles and one single. €€

EATING AND DRINKING

Kilbaha Gallery Café Henry Blake Heritage Centre, Lighthouse Rd, Kilbaha, Loop Head, http://kilbahagallery. com. Delicious home-baked snacks and lunches are one reason to visit this gallery-cum-café-cum tourist information point where they will help you navigate your way around the peninsula; you can admire local artwork and crafts as well. €

★ **The Long Dock** Main St, Carrigaholt, http://thelong dockshop.com. The best place to eat in Loop Head, with an extensive menu highlighting fruits of the sea such as fish pie, surf 'n' turf, chowder and a range of shellfish. Outdoor

tables make for a memorable dining experience. €€
Naughton's O'Curry St, Kilkee, http://naughtonsbar.com Smart, contemporary restaurant offering both land an sea based dishes, from the likes of pan-fried sea bass or colcannon mash and tarragon to Irish Angus sirloin stea with sautéed mushrooms. Closed Tues & Wed. €€€
O'Mara's O'Curry St, Kilkee, 065 906 0967. A decent old fashioned bar where the music happens spontaneousl most weekends when walk-in musicians arrive at shor notice armed with their instruments.

West Clare

More than any other area of Clare, the county's west is associated with **traditional music** – there's many a vibrant session in village pubs all along the coast and **Miltown Malbay** hosts one of Ireland's major music festivals. There are also sandy **beaches**, notably at the attractive resort of **Lahinch**, while, further north, you'll come to the towering **Cliffs of Moher**, close to the traditional music magnet of **Doolin** and, inland, the old-fashioned town of **Ennistymon**. This part of the county has also benefitted immeasurably from the **Wild Atlantic Way** driving route (see page 26), which follows the spectacular coast northwards from Spanish Point up to Ballyvaughan.

9

THE WEST CLARE RAILWAY

A few kilometres north of Kilrush at **Moyasta** is the only extant section of the **West Clare Railway** (May–Sept Mon–Sat 10am–5pm, Sun noon–5pm; charge; http://westclarerailway.ie), which opened in August 1892 and linked Ennis – via a roundabout route through Corofin – to southwest Clare until its closure in 1961. Much of the track was then sold to a Kenyan railway company, but the Moyasta station house and a 2km stretch of the line have been restored and it's possible to take a trip back and forth. The railway was immortalized by the singer **Percy French** who, in 1902, along with his troupe of music-hall entertainers, was due to play an engagement in Kilkee. Unfortunately, the train broke down in Miltown Malbay and French arrived late to discover that most of his audience had already left. He sued the railroad for damages, winning the princely sum of £10, and wrote the song *Are Ye Right There Michael?* as an account of his experiences, the Michael in question being Michael Talty, who was the guard on the train when the incident occurred.

Miltown Malbay

Though set back some distance from the sea, **MILTOWN MALBAY**, 30km northeast of Kilkee, originated as a Victorian holiday resort. Today a thriving small town with an appealing mix of modern cafés, restaurants and pubs and traditional, family-run shops, it makes an excellent base for exploring sections of the Wild Atlantic Way or to soak up some traditional music. The town hosts the week-long **Willie Clancy Summer School** (http://scoilsamhraidhwillieclancy.com), beginning on the first Saturday in July and named after the *uilleann* piper, singer and raconteur who died in 1973. More than a thousand people turn up for the music and dance classes, with seats at a premium.

ARRIVAL AND ACCOMMODATION   MILTOWN MALBAY

By bus There are bus connections with Ennis (Mon–Sat 4 daily, Sun 2; 1hr 20min), Ennistymon (Mon–Sat 4 daily, Sun 2; 25min) and Lahinch (Mon–Sat 4 daily, Sun 2; 20min).

An Gleann Ennis Rd, 1km east of town, 065 708 4281.

A friendly two-storey house with four en-suite rooms. Powerhouse breakfasts are generous, and vegetarians are catered for. €€

Lahinch

The seaside resort of **LAHINCH**, 12km north of Miltown Malbay, is renowned for its glorious sandy strand. If the Atlantic is too cold then right by the beach is **Lahinch Leisure Centre** (Mon–Fri 6.30am–9.45pm, weekends 8am–5pm; charge; http://lahinchleisurecentre.ie) with a 25m swimming pool, learner and baby pools, sauna, steam room and gym.

ARRIVAL AND DEPARTURE   LAHINCH

By bus Bus Éireann's drop off and pick up point is at the Liscannor Rd bus shelter on the edge of town.

Destinations Cliffs of Moher (4–5 daily; 10min); Corofin (Mon–Sat 4 daily, Sun 2; 25min); Doolin (4–5 daily; 45min); Ennis (Mon–Sat 4 daily, Sun 2; 55min–1hr); Ennistymon (Mon–Sat 4 daily, Sun 2; 10min); Liscannor (4–5 daily; 5min); Lisdoonvarna (4–5 daily; 25min); Miltown Malbay (Mon–Sat 4 daily, Sun 2; 20min).

ACCOMMODATION AND EATING

Atlantic Hotel Main St, http://atlantichotel.ie. Flickering log fires greet guests at this intimate, family-run hotel. Its fine selection of en-suite rooms come with crisp cotton duvets, and special offers include discounts for staying a second or third night. €€€

★ **Barrtrá Seafood Restaurant** 5km south of Lahinch on the N67, http://barrtra.com. For a sumptuous dinner, the owners of this conservatory seafood and steak restaurant rustle up some of the most praiseworthy dishes in the region. Great fun are the three "surprise" menus: seafood, meat and vegetarian (€50–60), whereby the dishes are only revealed once they arrive at the table, suffice to say that they may include the likes of baked cod with almond crust and blue cheese sauce, or pork belly tacos with apple

9

salsa. Closed Mon & Tues. €€€€
Lahinch Surf Hostel Church St, 065 708 1040. A well-appointed hostel with four- to ten-bed dorms, plus singles and doubles, which offers laundry facilities and can arrange group tours to the Cliffs of Moher and the Burren. €

Ennistymon

Straddling the River Cullenagh, the relaxed town of **ENNISTYMON**, 4km east of Lahinch, promotes itself as "the town of old shop fronts", to which its long main street bears ample testimony. The **Cascades Walk**, signposted on Main Street, leads along the riverbank past the falls, whose waters tumble over rocks by an old arched bridge. Ennistymon's most famous son was the poet **Brian Merriman**, born here in 1747, who wrote the epic and juicily salacious 1200-line poem, *The Midnight Court*. There aren't many ATMs in West Clare, but you'll find one on Parliament Street in Ennistymon.

ACCOMMODATION AND EATING

Byrne's Main St, http://byrnes-ennistymon.ie. Pleasant rooms – some looking out over the cascading Cullenagh River – in a nineteenth-century Edwardian town house. The high-ceilinged restaurant is noted for its pan-fried fresh fish. Closed Sun. €€

Falls Hotel Lahinch Rd, http://fallshotel.ie. A Georgian-style hotel set in woodlands by the water, with pleasant and spacious accommodation. It was here, in 1937, that the Welsh poet Dylan Thomas married Caitlin McNamara (when it was Ennistymon House), hence the *Dylan Thomas Bar* and its associated memorabilia. Otherwise, there's a smart restaurant (*Cascades*), while activities include an aqua and fitness centre. €€€

Doolin and around

In the 1960s the then tiny village of **DOOLIN**, 7km north of the Cliffs of Moher, developed a reputation for its **traditional music**, largely thanks to the reputation of a bachelor farmer Micho Russell, a singer, flute and whistle player who enjoyed an international touring career. Attracted by his music, a trickle of enthusiasts began to visit Doolin's pubs to hear the playing of Micho and his two brothers Packie and Gussie, all sadly departed. Today, Doolin is awash with visitors virtually throughout the year, with **pubs** such as *O'Connor's* (in Fisher Street on the way to the harbour), *Fitzpatrick's Bar* in the *Hotel Doolin* (see page 323) and *McGann's* and *McDermott's* at the northern end frequently packed with tourists. Unfortunately, most of the music churned out nightly is not the "pure drop", but either neatly adjusted to suit popular tastes or amplified garbage, and in truth there are many better places to hear Clare's often fabulous traditional music. Non-musical highlights include **Doolin Cave** (tours hourly from opening time; charge; http://doolincave.ie), where a 7m silver-gleaming stalactite hangs from the ceiling of the dome-like central cavern; and **boat-trips** from Doolin pier to the Aran Islands (see page 347) and to view the Cliffs of Moher.

The Cliffs of Moher

Visitor centre · Charge, includes car parking; Heritage Island · http://cliffsofmoher.ie · **O'Brien's Tower** Open daily but hours vary

Some 10km south of Doolin are the **Cliffs of Moher**, stretching downwards to the Atlantic for almost 200m. The cliffs take their name from an old promontory fort, Mothar, and extend some 8km from Hag's Head, west of Liscannor, to a little beyond **O'Brien's Tower**, which was constructed by a local altruist in 1835 at their highest point. Hidden within the hillside, the visitor centre is an impressive architectural feat with a first-floor **restaurant** that offers panoramic seascapes and a reasonable choice of meals. The centre houses the Atlantic Edge exhibition whose interactive touch screens, computer games and 3-D film do in part provide lucid explanations of the cliffs' evolution and wildlife, but overall form a ludicrous electronic counterpoint to the actual glories outside. The best bet is to head straight past the centre and to the steps that curve upwards towards the cliff-top. Then you can opt for turning south towards Hag's Head or in the opposite direction to O'Brien's Tower where a **viewing platform** offers the best sight of the wave-battered cliffs below, enhanced by the resonant roar of the Atlantic waves pummelling the rocks at shore level. Alternatively, you can gain a different perspective of their prodigious stature from one of the regular **boat-trips** that run from the pier at Doolin.

ARRIVAL AND TOURS

By bus All Bus Éireann services stop at the *Rainbow Hostel* on Fisher St, where you can also buy tickets for journeys. Destinations Ballyvaughan (5 daily; 50min); Cliffs of Moher (5 daily; 30min); Ennis (5 daily; 1hr 10min); Ennistymon (5 daily; 50min); Fanore (5 daily; 40min); Galway (Mon–Sat 2 daily, Sun 1; 1hr 35min–2hr 10min); Lahinch (5 daily; 45min); Limerick (2–3 daily; 2hr 15min); Lisdoonvarna (5

DOOLIN AND AROUND

daily; 15min).

By boat Doolin Ferries (http://doolinferrycom) runs services to all three Aran Islands: Inisheer (15min), Inishmaan (25min) and Inishmore (35min), between March and October (2–4 sailings daily; single €30) They also run a fifty-minute Cliffs of Moher cruise (€28).

ACCOMMODATION AND EATING

Aille River Hostel At the crossroads on the R479, 2km from Doolin Holiday Cottages (IHH), http://ailleriverhosteldoolin. ie. Centrally situated cottage-style hostel offering a variety of dorms, plus doubles, twins and family rooms, a big kitchen and wood-burning stove. Camping facilities are sheltered in a flat garden behind a stone wall; campers are free to avail themselves of the showers and kitchen. Breakfast costs extra. €

Aran View Country House Coast Rd, http://aranview. com. Dramatically sited above the village, this is a fine country house hotel offering tremendous views from its attractive rooms., which are in either the house itself or the neighbouring lodge. Two guest lounges offer good comfort after a day's sightseeing. €€

★ **Cullinan's Guesthouse** On the R479, 2km from Doolin Holiday Cottages, http://cullinansdoolin.com. Excellent B&B run by welcoming hosts, adjacent to the T-junction in the village centre. Eight well-appointed en-suite rooms, most with long views, and a warming guest lounge. Closed Dec & Jan. €€

Hotel Doolin On the R479, 2km from Doolin Holiday Cottages, http://hoteldoolin.ie. Doolin's plushest hotel also features a restaurant, pizzeria, café and *Fitz's Bar and Eatery*, where "The Trawler", a platter towering with fresh seafood, is best washed down with a glass of their own smooth red "Dooliner" ale; there's nightly music here too, while the annual Doolin craft beer festival is based here at the end of Aug. €€€

Rainbow Hostel Roadford, Doolin (IHH), http://rainbow hostel.net. Unquestionably the cosiest Doolin hostel, by *McDermott's* pub in the north of the village; single, double, triple and family rooms (all ensuite), in addition to three common areas, kitchen and dining room, and laundry. €

Sheedy's Roadford, Doolin, http://sheedysdoolin.com. Gorgeous guesthouse with five well-appointed rooms, two of which can cater for families. The owner is an accomplished chef, so you'll not have a better breakfast for miles around, whether that's stewed organic rhubarb with fresh ginger and yoghurt, or a cooked Irish complete with plump sausages and thick, cured back bacon. €€€

The Burren

The Burren's name derives from the Irish word *boireann*, meaning "stony place" – an apt description for this desolate plateau that occupies the county's northwest. Its northern and western edges hug the coast road from Doolin up to Ballyvaughan, while, to the south and east, the rocks gently slope towards lush green fields. Formed mainly of fissured limestone pavement, pitted by occasional valleys hidden beneath ominous-looking cliffs, the Burren is a thoroughly otherworldly place with barely a sign of life. The starkness of the landscape, crisp white in sunlight, deep grey-brown in rainfall, has a primeval allure and remains utterly fascinating. Few now live within its bounds, but many endured this harsh environment in the past, leaving relics of their habitation. Ancient burial practices are reflected in the abundance of **Stone Age monuments**, while later, Iron Age people built **ring**

forts and **circular stone** dwellings, many of which remain well preserved. The area's coastal outskirts include attractive resorts such as lively **Ballyvaughan** and tiny **Fanore**, while inland lie the spa town of **Lisdoonvarna**, famous for its matchmaking festival, and the renowned traditional music village **Kilfenora**; all make fine bases.

INFORMATION AND ACTIVITIES

Walking tours Themed walks and treks are organized by Shane Connolly of Burren Hill Walks at Corkscrew Hill, Ballyvaughan (http://burrenhillwalks.ie), usually all year round and often twice daily in the summer months; and Heart of Burren Walks, with the knowledgeable local author Tony Kirby (http://heartofburrenwalks.com).

Horseriding The Burren Riding Centre (087 991 9158) in Fanore offers horseriding, inclucing trails along the "green roads", trekking in the Burren and beach hacks.
Surfing The Aloha Surf School at Fanore beach (http:// surfschool.ie) offers lessons and all necessary equipment.

Lisdoonvarna

LISDOONVARNA, 8km east of Doolin, is a small town with a long street that developed in the nineteenth century around its old spa, whose sulphated waters were believed to have curative properties. Reinvigoration aside, Lisdoonvarna's calendar is focused upon its **matchmaking festival** (http://matchmakerireland.com), an annual September rally for the lovelorn, which runs for a month, believe it or not. The festival dates back to the times when dealers at street fairs acted as matchmakers, arranging marriages for bachelor farmers too land-tied to seek their own nuptial bliss.

Burren Smokehouse
Just west of the central crossroads • Free • Tours charge • http://burrensmokehouse.com

You may be tempted by the **Burren Smokehouse**, which specializes in smoked salmon and sells a tantalizing range of local artisan gourmet foods. The visitor centre includes a tour (so to speak), entitled "Taste the Atlantic – The Salmon Experience", which relates the history of Irish salmon courtesy of interactive displays followed by a sampling. You may also care to pop your head into the neighbouring **Burren Brewery** and partake in one of their tours, or just slip in for a sampling or two.

ARRIVAL AND DEPARTURE

By bus Buses drop off and pick up on the main square, beside Burke's garage.
Destinations Ballyvaughan (Mon–Sat 2 daily, Sun 1; 25–45mins); Cliffs of Moher (2–3 daily; 15–25mins); Doolin (5 daily; 10min); Ennis (4–5 daily; 1hr 10min); Ennistymon (4–5 daily; 30min); Galway (Mor–Sat 2 daily, Sun 1; 1h 20min); Lahinch (4–5 daily; 25mins); Limerick (2–3 daily 2hr).

ACCOMMODATION AND EATING

Burren Sleepzone Hostel Kincora Rd, http://sleepzone. ie. An excellently equipped An Óige-affiliated hostel set in the landscaped grounds of a former hotel; ensuite rooms (including family room) are complemented by a self-catering kitchen/dining room, TV and reading room. €
★**Rathbaun Hotel** Main St, http://rathbaunhotel. com. A well-maintained hotel with ten en-suite rooms, roughly half twins and half doubles. In the summer, music is guaranteed every night since the hotel has a pool of live-in musicians, ranging from banjo players to *uilleann* pipers who perform in the bar. Closed mid-Oct to Easter. €€
Roadside Tavern Kincora Rd, http://theroadsidetavern. ie. Just how an Irish pub should be, with mighty craic, nightly food and weekend music. Best of all though is the beer, which hails from their own microbrewery; a trio worth

sampling include the Burren Black stout, Burren Blond lager and Burren Red Ale. Closed Mon–Wed.
Royal Spa Hotel Main St, 065 707 4288, http://royalspa hotel.com. Dating from 1832, this small, family-tun hote features twelve tastefully decorated en-suite bedrooms – but ask to see a few as some are on the small side. Tasty pizzas are available in the bar all day long. €€
★**Sheedy's Hotel & Restaurant** http://sheedys. The oldest building in the village, with rooms decorated in traditional country house style, with floral patterns and mahoçany furniture, plus thoughtful touches like a jar o home-baked cookies. . In the restaurant, local produce i used for everything from bread and jam to ice cream, while the three-course menu (€58) is likely to feature ham hock duck and scallops, although the *piece de resistance* is rack

of Burren lamb served with fresh spinach and lamb gravy. Closed Sun. €€€€

Wild Honey Inn Kincora Rd, http://wildhoneyinn.com. From the stylish rooms to the Michelin-starred restaurant, this is a fantastic all-round experience. Accommodation is provided in fourteen amenable rooms, many with original features, and all ground-floor rooms have doors that open onto the garden, each with its own terrace. In the restaurant, meanwhile, chef Aidan McGrath conjures up magical dishes like *blanquette* of pork cheeks, and wild turbot with courgettes and anchovy cream. €€€

Kilfenora

Nine kilometres southeast of Lisdoonvarna, the village of **KILFENORA** is one of Clare's most celebrated **traditional music** centres. Its fame is intrinsically linked to the **Kilfenora Ceili Band**, Ireland's oldest and most illustrious, and on Wednesday nights in summer some of its members play in *Linnane's* pub. *Vaughan's* pub, meanwhile, has set dancing in its barn (Sun) as well as a session in the pub itself (Tues & Thurs in high season).

The Burren Centre
Main St • charge • http://theburrencentre.ie

The **Burren Centre** provides an entertaining account of the area's history, with its "In a Walk through Time" exhibition featuring imaginative and interactive displays and models that explain its geology and antiquities. Here too is an exhibition on traditional music (The Kilfenora Ceili Band), which traces the one-hundred-year history of Ireland's oldest and most illustrious ceili band, which sometimes performs live here.

Kilfenora Cathedral
Main St • Open access

Hard by the Burren Centre stands the ruined twelfth-century **Kilfenora Cathedral**, site of the county's largest concentration of high crosses. The twelfth-century Doorty Cross in the chancel is especially impressive; its faces depict various ecclesiasts and a scene from the Crucifixion.

ARRIVAL AND ACCOMMODATION   KILFENORA

By bus June–Aug there's a daily Bus Éireann service from Galway to Kilfenora; there is no longer a direct service to the village during the rest of the year.

Vaughan's Main St, http://vaughanspub.ie. This sparkling guesthouse offers nine lovely rooms (mostly doubles), while the neighbouring pub is forever known as the "Father

---

THE COAST TO BALLYVAUGHAN

One of the most dramatic routes around the Burren is the **R477** – now part of the **Wild Atlantic Way** driving route (see page 26) – which traces the shoreline from just northwest of Lisdoonvarna to **Ballyvaughan** (see page 326), via the tiny village of **Fanore**, (which offers a couple of peaceful accommodation options). Inland, and inaccessible by car, is a crisscross pattern of the old "**green roads**", offering upland walking and majestic panoramic views. Just 5km northwest of Lisdoonvarna, near the junction with the R479 Doolin road, you'll spot **Ballinalacken Castle**, a fifteenth-century tower house, perched high above the road. The coast road north of Ballinalacken is dramatic and sometimes shrouded in the mornings by the haze of a sea fret. The road rounds Black Head, where you can climb up to **Caheerdoonfergus** ring fort and gaze across Galway Bay before heading on to Ballyvaughan.

ACCOMMODATION

★ **Ballinalacken Castle** R477, near the ruins of Ballinalacken Castle, http://ballinalackencastle.com. Converted Victorian mansion, now a hotel, where some of the bedrooms enjoy fantastic views of the Aran Islands. Its restaurant serves sumptuous dinners (closed Tues) using local produce such as scallops and lamb, and is open to non-residents. €€€

Ted Pub", since one episode of the Channel 4 comedy series featured scenes in the bar; the folk here also have their finger on the village's musical pulse. Delicious food also available with a menu (and cooking) that's above average for a pub, for example pork belly and scallops with apple gel celeriac purée. €€

Ballyvaughan and around

Built in 1829 to assist the fishing industry, **BALLYVAUGHAN**'s harbour saw the village develop as a major trading centre and, not long afterwards, steamers began to ply between here and Galway, bringing visitors and establishing the tourist trade. It's an eye-catching village, especially when the sun gleams on its predominantly white and cream houses, and is an ideal base for exploring the Burren. Roads south from Ballyvaughan lead to a wealth of **ancient** and some **medieval sites**. The first of these, a kilometre or so down the R480 and off to the west, is **Newtown Castle** (March–Oct Mon–Fri 10am–5pm; free; http://newtowncastle.com). This restored sixteenth-century tower house with walls almost 4m thick, complete with murder holes and gun loops, is now part of the grounds of the Burren College of Art.

Aillwee Cave

Ballyallaban Rd · charge; Heritage Island · http://aillweeburrenexperience.ie

A little way south of Newtown Castle, **Aillwee Cave** is reckoned to be two million years old. Guided tours visit caverns and bridged chasms, allowing you to marvel at weird rock formations, numerous stalagmites and stalactites, and the hibernation chambers of a long-extinct species of brown bear. The ticket price also includes entry to the **Burren Bird of Prey Centre** (same hours), which stages flying displays of various avian predators and offers the opportunity to "take a hawk for a walk".

Gleninsheen Wedge Tomb and the Poulnabrone dolmen

About 3km south of Aillwee Cave, and just off the eastern side of the R480, is the **Gleninsheen Wedge Tomb**, the best preserved of its kind in the area. In 1930 a remarkable, finely worked gold collar was discovered here by a boy hunting rabbits and is now held by Dublin's National Museum. Just a kilometre south from here is the **Poulnabrone dolmen**, the best known and most photographed of the Burren's seventy or so megalithic tombs. When excavated in 1986, the remains of some thirty people were uncovered, along with tools, utensils and jewellery, providing evidence that the tomb dated from around 2500 BC.

Caherconnell Stone Fort

1km south of the Poulnabrone dolmen · charge · http://caherconnell.com

Caherconnell Stone Fort is the most substantial of the Burren's many ancient remains. Such circular homesteads, with their dry-stone walling, were built from around the fifth century onwards; this one is 40m in diameter with nearly 4m-thick walls. Displays recount how the daily life of its residents might have been spent, as well as describing the building's design and other Burren monuments. Even more fun are the sheepdog demonstrations, which take place daily at 11.15am and 2.15pm.

ARRIVAL AND DEPARTURE

BALLYVAUGHAN AND AROUND

By bus Buses stops outside the Spar Foodstore (also known as The Village Store) on Ballyvaughan's main street. Destinations Cliffs of Moher (5 daily; 55min); Doolin (5 daily; 55min); Ennis (5 daily; 2hr); Galway (Mon–Sat 2 daily Sun 1; 1hr 10min); Kinvara (5 daily; 30min); Lisdoonvarna (5 daily; 40min).

ACCOMMODATION AND EATING

An Fear Gorta Pier Rd, http://tearoomsballyvaughan. com. A daytime café with a delightful conservatory for lunches and substantial snacks, noted for its delectable cakes and lip-smacking coffee. Steven Spielberg is a fan - he has visited the café on several occasions while passing through this part of the west. €

★ **Gregans Castle Hotel** 5km south of Ballyvaughan on the N67, http://gregans.ie. A luxurious eighteenth-century building with astonishing evening dining-room views of the ever-changing colours of the limestone landscape. Some of the twenty rooms have their own private garden, while children are made to feel very welcome here. All in all, the setting and food combine to create the perfect ambience. Closed Dec to mid-Feb. €€€€

Larder Deli & Café Ballyvaughan Enterprise Centre, 086 733 3454. Local produce of Clare lamb, pork, beef and St Tola goat cheese dominates the menu along with soup and quiche for lunch. Smooth, sweet and full-bodied blends of coffee from the Anam Roastery in Kilfenora will help kick-start your limestone pavement walk. Closed Sun–Tues. €€

★ **Ó Loclainn's Bar** Pier Rd, http://oloclainnsbar.ie. As good for local lore as it is for drinks – Margaret, who runs the bar with her husband, dispenses tourist information and drams from their dazzling array of whiskies in equal measure.

The Wild Atlantic Lodge Main St, http://thewild atlanticlodge.com. Top-class accommodation in this rebranded lodge with twenty rooms (including triples and quads) that are modestly sized but pleasing on the eye, a bar and adjoining *Wildflower Restaurant* where the menu includes pork belly, cod, steak, or smoky vegetable lasagne. €€

Galway and Mayo

DIAMOND HILL

Galway and Mayo

Sweeping strokes of geology have carved up the landscape of Galway and Mayo, forming a many-pronged block between Galway and Sligo that's almost cut off from the mainland by a string of lakes. In the south, the 40km stretch of Lough Corrib neatly bisects County Galway, the second-largest county in Ireland after Cork. On one side, the flat, gentle grasslands of east Galway stretch across to the Shannon, sheltering a fascinating diversity of historic castles, cathedrals, monasteries and country estates. Between the Corrib and the sea, however, stands the violent jumble of Connemara, a much-romanticized land with glittering islands, shimmering lakes, wild mountains and bog land. Both counties are on the Wild Atlantic Way driving route, where the ocean crashes fiercely against headlands and inlets filled with deserted beaches, wide skies and seascapes. It is, in short, a place of nature on a grand scale.

If you're looking for specific tourist attractions, there's a diverting cluster around the lakeside village of **Oughterard**. Connemara's main base, however, is **Clifden**, which boasts a fine range of facilities at the heart of the mountains. On the narrow neck of land between these eastern and western halves sits **Galway city**, an animated, historical town with an enjoyable social, musical and artistic life. The city gives a whiff of the Gaelic culture that's far more noticeable out on the **Arans**, starkly beautiful islands that used to form a barrier across the entrance to Galway Bay. As well as sheltering some breathtaking prehistoric and early Christian sites, the islands are part of the country's largest Irish-speaking area, which also comprises the eastern section of Connemara.

Though ranking just behind Galway in terms of size, **County Mayo** has only half its population and is less developed for tourism. An exception is the eighteenth- century planned town of **Westport**, a comfortable, elegant base from which to tackle the pilgrims' path to the top of **Croagh Patrick**, and to visit the diverse inhabited **islands** at the mouth of Clew Bay. In the north of the county, the intriguing Neolithic agricultural remains at **Céide Fields** provide a compelling focus, surrounded by kilometre after unexplored kilometre of desolate bogland.

Galway city

Known for its festivals, music and bars, **GALWAY** (Gaillimh) is a culturally vibrant, fun-loving place and, though it has few sights to visit, many people end up staying longer than they'd intended. Conveniently, history and leisure combine here: the **pubs**, many of which retain their original, huge fireplaces and other Gothic features, are the best places to get a feel for the medieval city. As the **capital** of the Gaelic West – it's the only city in the country where you might possibly hear Irish spoken on the streets – Galway draws young people to study at the National University of Ireland, Galway and the Institute of Technology. In the summer holidays, however, its bohemian diversity becomes more overt, as hundreds of English-language students renew the city's traditional maritime links with the Continent, while dozens of buskers from all over the world sing for their supper.

This cosmopolitan atmosphere is reinforced by the setting: Galway is the only coastal city in Ireland that really seems to open up to the sea, and its **docks** sit cheek by jowl

INISHEER CEMETERY

Highlights

❶ **Galway festivals and pubs** It's hard not to have a good time in the vibrant, youthful capital of the west. See pages 334 and 340

❷ **Islands** Choose between the wild beauty of the Arans, the grandiose scenery of accessible Achill, and Inishbofin's small-scale charms. See pages 347, 362 and 374

❸ **Dun Aengus, Inishmore** The most exciting of the many ancient forts on the Aran Islands, spectacularly sited on a 90m cliff face. See page 350

❹ **Walking in Connemara** The best way to appreciate the dramatic mountains, bogs and lakes. See page 357

❺ **Croagh Patrick** A tough climb, enriched by historical and religious associations, and outstanding views. See page 370

❻ **National Museum of Country Life, Castlebar** A fascinating peek at the realities of traditional life in rural Ireland, debunking the nostalgic myths. See page 374

❼ **Céide Fields** A 5000-year-old farming community preserved under the bog. See page 378

HIGHLIGHTS ARE MARKED ON THE MAP ON PAGE 332

GALWAY & MAYO

0 — 25
kilometres

N

Map labels:

Benwee Head
Erris Head
Céide Fields 7 Ballyc
Belderrig
Pollatomish
R314
Belmullet
Carrowmore Lough
R313
Inishkea North
Bangor
Inishkea South
Aghleam
Geesala
N59
Cross
Blacksod Bay
NEPHIN BEG RANGE
Dugort
Dooagh
Keel
2
Achill Island
Achill Sound
GREAT WESTERN GREENWAY: WESTPORT–ACHILL ISLAND
N59
Newport
Newport Bay
Clare Island
Westport
Clew Bay
Murrisk
Roonagh Quay
Louisburgh
5
Croagh Patrick
MAY
Inishturk
R335
Doo Lough
SHEEFRY HILLS
PARTRY MOUNTAINS
Inishbofin
2
Mweelrea
Delphi
Inishark
Killary Harbour
Renvyle
Lough Fee
Leenane
N59
Tully Cross
Tully Hill
Cleggan
Letterfrack
Kylemore Abbey
MAAM TURKS
Omey Island
CONNEMARA NATIONAL PARK
R344
R336
Inch
Clifden
TWELVE BENS
Dan O'Hara's Farmstead
N59
Ben Lettery
Recess
Maam Cross
4
Oug
Ballyconneely
R341
BOG ROAD
Lough Inagh
N59
CONNEMARA
Gle
Errisbeg
Ballynahinch
Cashel
Screeb
R340
Roundstone
Rosmuc
R336
Carna
Costelloe
Rossaveel
Inver
Inverin Airport
Inishmore
3
2
Kilronan
Inishmaan
Aran Islands
Inisheer
Cliffs of Moher

HIGHLIGHTS

1 Galway festivals and pubs
2 Islands
3 Dun Aengus, Inishmore
4 Walking in Connemara
5 Croagh Patrick
6 National Museum of Country Life, Castlebar
7 Céide Fields

with the compact **city centre**, as you're constantly reminded by salty breezes and seagulls. Though small, the city divides into distinct areas: the **Latin Quarter**, the **West End**, **Woodquay** and the **East Village**, each with its own special ambience. The jewel in the city's crown is the long, pedestrianized main drag of **William**, **Shop**, **High** and **Quay streets**, which becomes a boisterous, Mediterranean- style promenade during summer, lined with pub and restaurant tables. At its lower, western end, the street narrows to its original medieval dimensions, then flows into Galway Bay along with the thundering **River Corrib**, providing faraway views of the Burren hills of County Clare.

10

Brief history

Strategically located in the narrow gap between Lough Corrib and the sea, Galway was little more than the site of a twelfth-century fort when it was captured from the Gaelic O'Flaherty clan in 1232 by the Anglo-Norman **Richard de Burgo**, who built a castle by the river. From the fifteenth century, the town was controlled by an oligarchy of mostly Anglo-Norman families, by the names of Athy, Blake, Bodkin, Browne, Darcy, Deane, Ffrench, Ffront, Joyce, Kirwan, Lynch, Martin, Morris and Skerrett. Cromwell later dubbed them the "**Tribes of Galway**", an epithet which they adopted as a badge of honour – to this day, Galwegians nickname themselves the Tribesmen. Under this oligarchy, Galway grew wealthy as a largely independent **city-state**, far removed from the centres of power in Dublin and London but trading extensively with Europe, especially Spain and France.

The town remained proudly loyal to the English Crown, but this only elicited harsh treatment when Cromwell's forces arrived in 1652. Thereafter, Galway went into decline, exacerbated by the **Williamite War** later in the century, and fluctuating with the development of adjacent Salthill as a seaside resort in the early nineteenth century, the arrival of the railways and the building of navigable waterways to Lough Corrib in the 1840s and 1850s, alongside the depredations of the Great Famine. Growth returned in the **late 1960s** with industrial and tourism development, and Galway is now the fourth-largest city in the Republic.

Eyre Square

The natural place to begin an exploration of the city is **Eyre Square**. This former common land, jousting ground and market square outside the city walls was until recent times a municipal wasteland, but has been pleasingly renovated. Here you'll find a splendid **fountain**, erected in 1984 to mark the city's quincentenary, which evokes a hooker (the traditional sailing boat of Galway Bay) in rusted metal and rushing water; and the **Browne doorway**, a finely carved mercantile town house entrance forlornly set in a concrete wall. The square's fourteen fluttering **flags** each represent one of the

---

GALWAY'S FESTIVALS

The city's biggest shindig is the two-week **Galway International Arts Festival** in July (http://giaf.ie), a volatile mix of drama, music, poetry, dance and the visual arts. Hard on its heels, in late July or early August, comes the even headier brew of the **Galway Races** at Ballybrit, about 5km east of town (http://galwayraces.com), when farmers and politicians rub shoulders to party and bet. The diverse festival calendar also includes part of the **Father Ted** jamboree (see page 40); **Cúirt**, an international festival of literature in late April (http://cuirt.ie); the **Galway Early Music Festival** in late May (http://galwayearlymusic.com); and a prestigious, week-long cinema festival in mid-July, the **Film Fleadh** (http://galwayfilmfleadh.com). At the end of September the riotous, four-day **Galway Oyster and Seafood Festival** (http://galwayoysterfest.com) includes the world oyster-shucking championships. Towards the end of the year, **Baboró** is an international arts festival for children in October (http://baboro.ie), while November's **TULCA** is a festival of contemporary visual art (http://tulca.ie).

GALWAY CITY

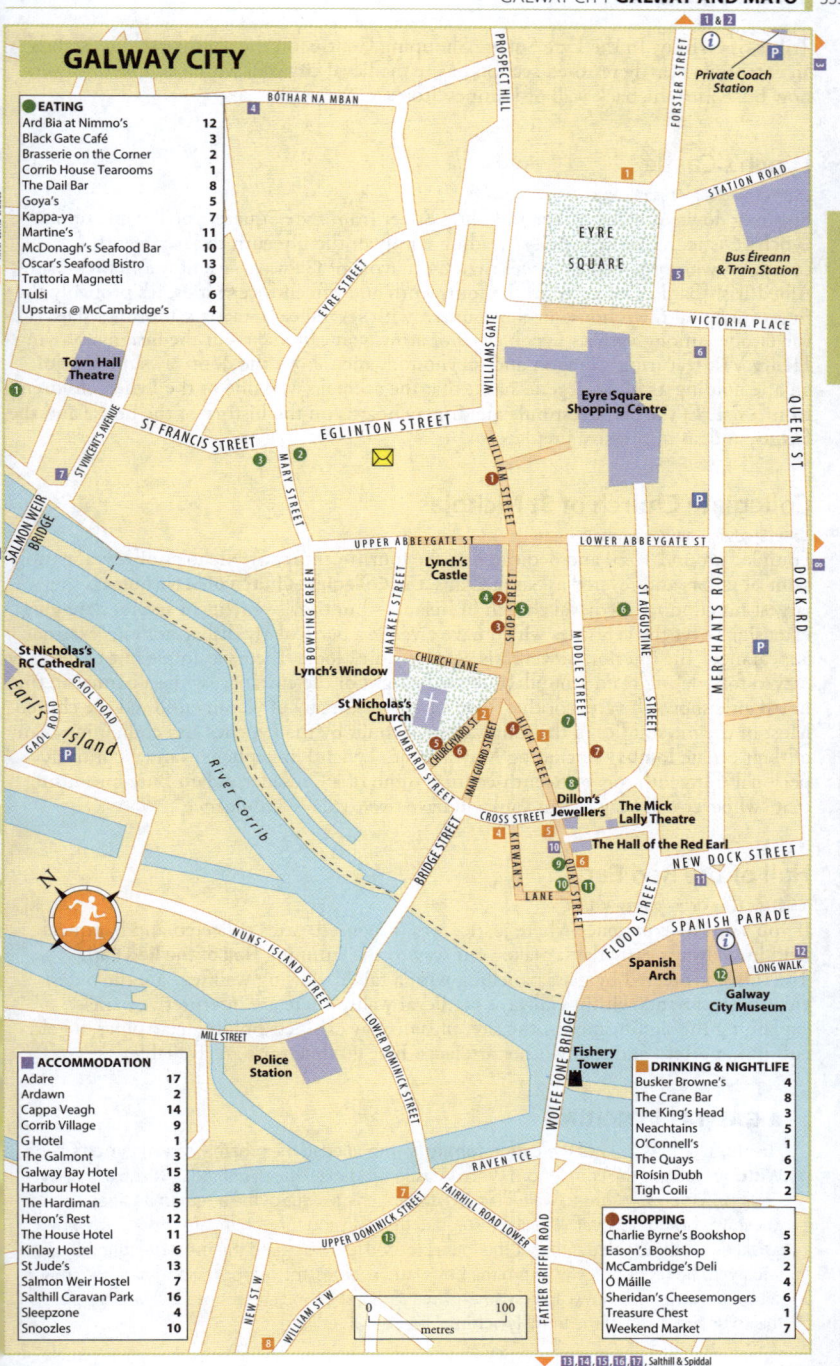

EATING

Ard Bia at Nimmo's	12
Black Gate Café	3
Brasserie on the Corner	2
Corrib House Tearooms	1
The Dail Bar	8
Goya's	5
Kappa-ya	7
Martine's	11
McDonagh's Seafood Bar	10
Oscar's Seafood Bistro	13
Trattoria Magnetti	9
Tulsi	6
Upstairs @ McCambridge's	4

ACCOMMODATION

Adare	17
Ardawn	2
Cappa Veagh	14
Corrib Village	9
G Hotel	1
The Galmont	3
Galway Bay Hotel	15
Harbour Hotel	8
The Hardiman	5
Heron's Rest	12
The House Hotel	11
Kinlay Hostel	6
St Jude's	13
Salmon Weir Hostel	7
Salthill Caravan Park	16
Sleepzone	4
Snoozles	10

DRINKING & NIGHTLIFE

Busker Browne's	4
The Crane Bar	8
The King's Head	3
Neachtains	5
O'Connell's	1
The Quays	6
Roisin Dubh	7
Tigh Coili	2

SHOPPING

Charlie Byrne's Bookshop	5
Eason's Bookshop	3
McCambridge's Deli	2
Ó Máille	4
Sheridan's Cheesemongers	6
Treasure Chest	1
Weekend Market	7

10

Tribes of Galway. In the Eyre Square Shopping Centre, on the southwest side, stands an extensive, heavily restored section of the medieval **city wall** with a couple of towers, now built into the back wall of Dunnes Stores.

Lynch's Castle

On the corner of Shop St and Abbeygate St

Strolling down William Street and Shop Street from Eyre Square, you'll come upon **Lynch's Castle**, home of the city's leading family of the fifteenth to seventeenth centuries, who provided no fewer than 84 mayors of Galway – it's now a branch of the Allied Irish Bank. Dating from the fourteenth and fifteenth centuries, it's probably the finest medieval town house in the country, with several elaborately sculptured slabs on the façade: among various Lynch coats of arms, you can make out the insignia of King Henry VII, featuring a dragon and greyhound, and, above the doorway, an image of an ape holding a child – legend has it that the animal saved one of the Lynch children from a fire. In the bank vestibule are display boards on the history of the house and the family, and an impressive fireplace.

Collegiate Church of St Nicholas

Market St • charge • http://stnicholas.ie

Founded around 1320 and dedicated to the fourth-century St Nicholas of Myra, patron saint of sailors and revered as Santa Claus, the **Collegiate Church of St Nicholas** is the largest functioning medieval church in Ireland – but only by virtue of several slate-grey extensions over the centuries which have given it a particularly disharmonious external appearance. The interior, however, is worth a quick look. There's a simple but beautifully carved font dating from around 1600 to the right of the entrance, while a banner in the north aisle shows the arms of the Tribes of Galway, many of whom endowed the church. Most of the interest lies in the south transept, built by the Lynches and containing many of their ornate **tombs** – including Mayor James Lynch Fitzstephens – and a curiously personal thirteenth- or fourteenth-century tomb of a Crusader, Adam Bure, promising that "whoever will pray for his soul will have twenty days' indulgence".

Hall of the Red Earl

Druid Lane • Free • http://galwaycivictrust.ie

If you want to experience where justice was dispensed, taxes collected and banquets held in Galway's early days, make your way to the stunning **Hall of the Red Earl**. The ruins, protected by glass panelling with a raised viewing walkway are the oldest viewable remnants within Galway's medieval walls. There are interpretive panels explaining the significance of the site, plus display cabinets holding clay pipes, a gold cuff link, pottery and many other artefacts. Free guided tours are available.

A GALWAY LYNCHING

The most famous story of the **Lynch family** is embodied in the ornately carved **Lynch's Window**, around the corner from Lynch's Castle on Market Street, behind St Nicholas's Church. In the 1490s young Walter Lynch Fitzstephens, jealous of the attentions a Spanish guest was giving his lover, Ann Blake, stabbed the man and threw him into the sea. The boy was duly sentenced to death, but the town pleaded for mercy and the usual executioner refused to do his duty. It was left to the boy's father, James, the mayor, to hang him from this jail window, which is now carved with the image of a skull and crossbones. Galwegians claim this to be the origin of the term "**lynching**".

Claddagh Museum

Quay Lane • Free • http://claddaghring.ie

A small, informal museum at the back of Dillon's Jewellers traces the engaging cultural history of the **Claddagh ring**. Designed by a late seventeenth-century Galwegian who had been captured by pirates and enslaved to a Moorish goldsmith, this style of ring has been worn by the likes of Queen Victoria and John Wayne. It features a pair of hands, symbolizing friendship, a heart, for love, and a mitred crown, traditionally for loyalty, and is often given as a love token. The museum also displays old photos of **the Claddagh** (An Cladach; "a flat, stony shore"), a former fishing village on the south bank of the river.

10

Galway City Museum

Spanish Parade • Free • http://galwaycitymuseum.ie

Down by the river, near the sixteenth-century **Spanish Arch**, stands the glass-fronted **Galway city Museum**, which hosts some temporary exhibitions. Its permanent collection has relatively few artefacts, but traces the city's history in vivid fashion, dealing with the Claddagh, the medieval town and the present day on the ground floor. On the second floor, the **Wild Atlantic Sea Science Gallery** is filled with interactive displays and a mock-up of a model submarine. Other highlights are a 9m hooker boat, suspended in all its glory in the atrium, and a statue of Galway-born **Pádraic Ó Conaire** (see page 592), the first modernist fiction writer in Irish.

Fishery Tower

Wolfe Tone Bridge • Free • http://galwaycivictrust.ie

One of Galway's most delightful landmark buildings, the unique **Fishery Tower** was built in 1852 as a draft netting station where salmon were caught. It was also used as a lookout point to monitor fish stocks coming up the Corrib River and to spot any illegal fishing.

Salthill and Silver Strand

About 1km southwest of Wolfe Tone Bridge begins the resort suburb of **Salthill**, Galway's summer playground. The long promenade is lined with high-rise apartment blocks, hotels and amusement arcades, as well as safe **beaches** with fine views across the bay to the Burren. It's a Sunday afternoon tradition to walk its length and kick the wall at the end by the diving platform (for good luck, of course) before turning back.

On the front, the National Aquarium of Ireland, **Galway Atlantaquaria** (Mon–Fri 10am–5pm, Sat & Sun 10am–6pm; Oct–Feb closed Mon and Tues; charge; http://nationalaquarium.ie), is a big hit with kids, entertainingly showcasing Ireland's sea, river and canal life. Beyond Salthill and just 5km west of the centre, **Silver Strand** is the nicest beach in the vicinity of the city, a small, sandy affair with a Blue Flag and a gentle shelf, beneath a grassy headland. It's accessible on buses towards Spiddal.

ARRIVAL AND DEPARTURE · GALWAY CITY

By train Céannt Station is on Station Rd, on the southeast side of Eyre Square.
Destinations Athenry (11–13 daily; 15min); Athlone (7–9 daily; 1hr); Dublin (6–8 daily; 2hr 30min–3hr); Ennis (4–5 daily; 1hr 20min); Gort (4–5 daily; 50min); Kildare (2–4 daily; 2hr); Limerick (4–5 daily; 2hr).
By bus The city's Bus Éireann station is beside the train station, while private companies mostly use the new coach station behind the tourist office on Forster St. Of the latter,

Citylink (http://citylink.ie) run frequent coaches between Galway city and Dublin city centre and airport, with some buses running via Loughrea and Athlone. Citylink also runs several coaches a day to Gort and Shannon Airport; to Gort, Limerick, Killarney, Cork city centre and Cork airport; and to Oughterard, Clifden, Cleggan and Letterfrack. Bus Feda (http://busfeda.ie) operates daily services between Galway city (departing from the Catholic cathedral) and Knock, Sligo, Bundoran, Donegal, Letterkenny and Gweedore.

10

Destinations Achill (Fri & Sun 1 daily; 3hr 20min–4hr); Athenry (Mon–Sat 3–4 daily; 35min); Athlone (hourly; 1hr 30min); Ballina (4–7 daily; 2hr 15min); Castlebar (5–6 daily; 1hr 45min); Clarenbridge (hourly; 20min); Clifden (summer Mon–Sat 4–5 daily, Sun 2 daily; winter Mon–Sat 3 daily, Sun 1 daily; 1hr 45min–2hr 15min); Cliffs of Moher (summer 2–4 daily; winter 1 daily; 2hr); Cong (2–3 daily; 45min–1hr); Cork (hourly; 4hr 15min); Derry (3–5 daily; 5hr 15min); Doolin (summer 2–5 daily; winter 1–2 daily; 1hr 30min); Dublin (hourly; 3hr 45min); Ennis (hourly; 1hr 15min); Gort (hourly; 45min); Ireland West Airport (5–7 daily; 2hr); Kilcolgan (hourly; 30min); Kinvarra (1–6 daily; 30min–1hr); Kylemore (summer Mon–Sat 1 daily; winter 1 weekly; 1hr 45min–3hr); Leenane (summer Mon–Sat 1 daily; winter 1 weekly; 1hr 20min–3hr); Letterfrack (winter 1 weekly, summer Mon–Sat 1 daily; 1hr 50min–3hr); Letterkenny (3–5 daily; 4hr 40min); Limerick (hourly; 2hr 15min); Loughrea (hourly; 35min); Oranmore (at least hourly; 10min); Oughterard (Mon–Sat 4–7 daily, Sun 2–3; 40min); Rosmuc (Mon & Fri 1; 1hr 15min); Roundstone (winter 3 weekly, summer 1–2 daily; 1hr 30min); Shannon Airport (hourly; 1hr 45min); Sligo (5–6 daily; 2hr 30min); Spiddal (Mon–Sat 5–9 daily, Sun 2; 40min); Westport (3–4 daily; 2hr).

GETTING AROUND

By bus Bus Éireann city and suburban services leave Eyre Square for many parts of the city including Salthill (#401; every 20min 9am–7pm; every 40min 7–11.40pm) and College Rd (#40; every 15min 9am–7pm) for B&Bs (see page 339).

By taxi Galway Taxis at 57 Lower Dominick St (091 561111, http://galwaytaxis.ie). There are taxi ranks at Eyre Square.

By car Pay and display on the street; there's a car park next to the tourist office off Forster St and multistoreys on Dock Rd and Merchants Rd.

By bike West Ireland Cycling, Unit 1, Bridgewater Ct, Fairhill Rd Lower (daily 9.30am–6pm; http://westirelandcycling.com).

INFORMATION

Tourist office Galway City Museum, Spanish Parade (daily 9am–5pm; http://galwaytourism.ie).

City listings For local listings, pick up a copy of the *Connacht Tribune* at Eason's Bookshop (see page 341).

TOURS AND ACTIVITIES

Walking tours In the summer themed walking tours of the city depart from either the tourist office (see page 337), generally lasting 1hr 30min (€20).

Bus tours Hop-on, hop-off, open-top bus tours of Galway and Salthill operate in the summer from Eyre Square North (24hr or 48hr tickets; €16/19; http://galwaycitytour.com); buses leave every 90mins and take in thirteen stops. Tours to Connemara, the Burren and the Cliffs of Moher run from the private coach station with the Galway Tour Company (http://galwaytourcompany.com).

River tours In summer, 1hr 30min *Corrib Princess* cruises (May, June & Sept 2 daily; July & Aug 3 daily; €19; http://corribprincess.ie) depart from Woodquay (beyond Salmon Weir Bridge and behind the Town Hall Theatre). Cruises head 8km up the river, passing a couple of ruined castles, before entering Lough Corrib.

Bike tours West Ireland Cycling (see above) offer bike tours of the city and longer tours around Connemara and the Wild Atlantic Way, as well as bike rental.

Watersports Windsurfing rental and tuition, plus kayaking and SUP, is available at Rusheen Bay, at the west end of Salthill (http://rusheenbay.com), while various kayaking trips are on offer with Kayakmór (http://kayakmor.ie).

ACCOMMODATION

SEE MAP PAGE 335

At festival time (see page 334), especially during the Galway Races, rooms are at a premium – often in both senses of the word. The city centre boasts a high standard of **hotels**, while the scores of **B&Bs** are nearly all on the outskirts, including large clusters on College Rd (the continuation of Forster Street) and Dublin Rd, and in Salthill (see page 339).

HOTELS

G Hotel Wellpark, Dublin Rd, 2km from the centre on the N6, http://theghotel.ie. Designed by local lad, the milliner Philip Treacy, this hotel is a bold fashion statement in an inauspicious location next to a shopping centre. The public rooms, featuring mirror-ball lamps, veer towards high camp, but the spacious bedrooms are beautifully designed and equipped, and there's an elegant, black-marble, Japanese-themed ESPA and fitness centre. €€€

The Galmont Lough Atalia Rd, http://thegalmont.com. A modern, Scandinavian-run luxury hotel overlooking Galway Bay from a fine position on the northeast side of the train station. The list of leisure facilities includes an extensive spa, swimming pool, gym, outdoor hot tub and sauna. Colour schemes in the bedrooms are dominated by purple and beige, set off with elegant furnishings and soft lighting. €€€€

★ **Galway Bay Hotel** The Promenade, Salthill, http://galwaybayhotel.net. Stylish hotel with attractive rooms and a terrace overlooking the bay. The pool and leisure centre offer added value, there are some appealing dining options, and there's a range of special offers. €€€

Harbour Hotel The Harbour, http://harbour.ie. This crisp, modern hotel offers bright, well-equipped rooms, decorated in strong colours and blonde wood, as well as a gym. €€€

★ **The Hardiman** Eyre Square, http://thehardiman.ie. This imposing Victorian railway hotel, formerly the *Great Southern*, has been superbly renovated, the bedrooms an attractive mix of traditional and modern decor, and a top-floor spa with outdoor hot tub and gym. The basement *MacNeill's* pub is a terrific place to hole up of an evening, with music Thur–Sat. €€€

The House Hotel Lower Merchants Rd, http://thehousehotel.ie. A luxurious boutique hotel converted from a warehouse, featuring well-equipped rooms with soundproofed windows and colourful, contemporary public rooms. €€€

B&BS

Adare 9 Father Griffin Place, http://adareguesthouse.ie. Just a few mins' walk from Wolfe Tone Bridge, this B&B is a convenient base, with eleven bright bedrooms. The owner likes to sing from the kitchen as she prepares the full Irish breakfast or delicious pancakes with a large choice of organic teas. Look out for the polystyrene statue of the famed Galway writer Pádraic Ó Conaire in the garden, which is in any case a lovely spot to hang out in of an evening. €€

Ardawn 31 College Rd, http://ardawnhouse.com. Welcoming, upmarket B&B a 10min walk from the centre in a redbrick, modern house. Smart, comfortable rooms – including triples and family rooms – plenty of local information and lavish breakfasts. €€€

Cappa Veagh 76 Dalysfort Rd, Salthill, http://cappaveagh.com. This comfortable and clean, modern house with three impeccably kept double rooms is close to the seafront and on the #401 bus route, with knowledgeable hosts. Minimum two-night stay. €€€

Corrib Village Newcastle Rd, 3km north of the centre, http://stay-universityofgalway.ie. In summer (June–Aug), this large complex on the campus of Galway University offers a variety of standard and en-suite B&B accommodation or apartment rentals. Sited on the banks of the River Corrib, the "village" includes a café and deli, tennis courts, laundry facilities and a complimentary shuttle bus to Eyre Square (noon–7pm). Guests also have reduced-rate access to the university's wide-ranging sports facilities. €€

★ **Heron's Rest** 16 Long Walk, http://theheronsrest.com. Hospitable B&B in a peerless location, steps from the city centre but overlooking the quiet river and Galway Bay. Two neighbouring townhouses, one with two bedrooms, the other with three, but both with self-catering facilities, plus gourmet breakfasts provided (which include a sumptuous cheeseboard and home-baked breads). €€€

St Jude's 110 Lower Salthill, http://st-judes.com. Grand, manorial 1920s family home with three elegant, en-suite bedrooms (two doubles and a twin) and good breakfasts, a 10min walk from the centre. Packed lunches can be prepared upon request. €€€

HOSTELS

Kinlay Hostel Merchants Rd (IHH), http://kinlaygalway.ie. Modern hostel that's friendly and well run, with a variety of mixed dorms sleeping six- to ten in funky pod beds with privacy curtains, plus private rooms. Facilities include laundry, kitchen and luggage storage. Prices include a simple continental breakfast. Dorms €, doubles €€

Salmon Weir Hostel St Vincent's Ave (IHO), http://salmonweirhostel.com. Simple but welcoming hostel with a wide mix of differently sized dorms (four- to twelve beds), including female only ones, plus private twins and doubles. Self-catering kitchen, laundry and bike storage. Breakfast not included. €

Sleepzone Bóthar na mBan, http://sleepzone.ie. Modern, well-maintained, 200-bed hostel affiliated to An Óige, a 5min walk north of Eyre Square. All rooms are en suite, with female only and family rooms among the many options, plus kitchen/dining area, movie and reading rooms, and laundry. Dorms €, doubles €€

Snoozles Forster St (IHH), http://snoozleshostelgalway.ie. Large and efficiently run hostel conveniently located next to the coach station, right in the hub of Galway's nightlife. All rooms are en suite, and dorms come in various sizes, from four to six beds, plus private twins and doubles. There are laundry and kitchen facilities and a light breakfast is included. Dorms €, doubles €€

CAMPING

Salthill Caravan Park Knocknacarra, http://salthillcaravanpark.com. Beside the seashore with superb views of Galway Bay and access to an excellent beach. Although it's primary focus is on caravans and campervans, there's good tent space here and good facilities including an excellent camper's kitchen. Closed Sept to mid-May. €

EATING

SEE MAP PAGE 335

★ **Ard Bia at Nimmo's** Spanish Arch Long Walk, http://ardbia.com. Set in a stone-built medieval customs house by the river, with rustic-chic decor, and modern art on the walls. The perfectly paced modern Irish food focuses on expertly prepared local, seasonal ingredients, with a few

Middle Eastern touches. Lunch includes beef and harissa *shaksuka*, with a dinner menu comprising the likes of monkfish, spiced cauliflower and chermoula. €€€

Black Gate Café 14 Francis St, http://blackgate.ie. A café-cum cultural centre set up by two young men from

10

10

Inishbofin. Lunches include charcuterie and cheese board, sandwiches and wine. With comfy chairs and a library, this is a place to linger or catch an evening of music or poetry. €€
Brasserie on the Corner 25 Eglinton St, http://brasserie galway.com. Galway is shellfish central and many come here to sample "Marty's Meaty Mussels", rope-cultivated specimens from Killary Harbour, served with zingy sauces. Delicious brown soda to mop up. Once done there it's a short hop to the adjoining *Blake's Corner Bar* for a tipple (the whiskey is especially good) and some live music. €€€
★ **Corrib House Tearooms** 3 Waterside, Woodquay, http://corribhouse.com. This delightfully situated tearoom in a Georgian-style mansion has a range of lunchtime dishes such as quiches, salads and soups plus bakes and cakes made on the premises. Grab a window seat to look out on the salmon weir and the Corrib. Closed Mon & Tues. €€
The Dail Bar 42 Middle St, http://thedailbar.com. An excellent choice for lunch or dinner, the *Dail* has raised the standard of pub grub, with its tasty light bites such as goat's cheese and sundried tomato, or southern fried chicken wings and heartier mains like bacon and cabbage, cajun chicken penne, or chilli prawn and monkfish linguine. €€€
Goya's 2–3 Kirwan's Lane, http://goyas.ie. Elegant café with tables on the alley, serving home-baked cakes and pastries that are little short of perfection. Lunchtime goodies include soups, salads, quiches and pies. Closed Sun & Mon. €
Kappa-ya 4 Middle St, http://kappayagalway.com. Small, relaxing café-restaurant serving carefully prepared and reasonably priced Celtic-Japanese food – the chicken teriyaki sushi rolls are especially good, and leave room for some wasabi and pistachio ice cream. On Sat evenings (by reservation), you can sample more elaborate dishes such as nigiri sushi. €€€

Martine's Quay St, http://martines.ie. Friendly, wood-panelled bistro with tables outside, the menu here is solidly of the steak and seafood variety, for example hake tempura in a pea and mint puree, and charcoal-flavoured rib-eye with creamed potatoes. €€€
McDonagh's Seafood Bar 22 Quay St, http://mcdonaghs. net. This Galway institution features nautical paraphernalia and a menu that casts its net wide: pan-fried mackerel, baked monkfish, lemon sole, red gurnard, grilled ray, wild Clarinbridge oysters, and scallops are all on offer, as are good old fashioned fish and chips – Galway's finest? €€€
★ **Oscar's Seafood Bistro** Lower Dominick St, 091 582180. Savvy locals like this plush bistro just a few mins' walk from the crowds of Quay St. And it's worth the short hike for some of the freshest local seafood, such as fillet of haddock, fishcakes or Galway rock oysters. Closed Sun. €€€
Trattoria Magnetti 12 Quay St, http://magnetti.ie. Cheery Italian place, dishing up some delicious pasta dishes like rigatoni with lamb and pepper ragu, alongside risottos and pizzas; there's usually a daily fish special too. €€
Tulsi Buttermilk Walk, Middle St, http://tulsi-galway. com. Galway's best Indian restaurant rustles up very good vegetarian and meaty food and even tries its hand at Indo-Galwegian fusion dishes such as tandoori mackerel for an appetizer. Takeaways too. €€€
★ **Upstairs @ McCambridge's** Shop St, 091 562259, http://mccambridges.com. A wonderful addition to the Galwegian culinary scene, above a deli that has been in business since 1925. Prepare to indulge yourself in the all-day menu featuring cold platters of cheese, meat or seafood, salads, frittatas, and hot dishes such as lamb kebabs or roasted prawns. Closed Sun. €€

DRINKING AND NIGHTLIFE

SEE MAP PAGE 335

A slow crawl through the **pubs** of Shop, High and Quay streets is a must, soaking up the atmosphere of their historic interiors in winter, and the buzzy street life at their outdoor tables in summer. You're bound to find a traditional session here, although the best pub for music is *The Crane Bar*, just over the bridge (see page 340).
Busker Browne's Cross St, http://buskerbrownes.com. This popular bar in a former Dominican convent offers medieval fireplaces, a lofty, Gothic hall, and floor upon floor of alcoves and armchairs in a complementary modern design. Food is served – try the seafood chowder – and there's live music every night, including DJs at weekends and jazz Sun lunchtimes.
★ **The Crane Bar** Sea Rd, http://thecranebar.com. Atmospheric pub with an upstairs venue, this is the top spot for traditional music with sessions every night, which can involve up to twelve musicians, plus all manner of other folk music, blues and singer-songwriters. Occasional entry charge.
The King's Head High St, http://thekingshead.ie. Busy three-storey pub in a medieval building with flagstone

floors, stone walls and an early seventeenth-century marriage stone above the 1612 fireplace. The bar's name comes from the fact that the man who requisitioned this building, Colonel Peter Stubbers, was widely rumoured to have been Charles I's executioner. Includes a popular bistro and an extensive whiskey menu, plus their own K.H. Blood Red Ale from the Galway Hooker brewery. Traditional music on Wed plus DJs on Sat.
★ **Neachtains** 17 Cross St, http://tighneachtain.com. Galway's finest traditional pub, serving a wide choice of whiskies and craft beers such as Bogmen Irish Ale or Cosmic Cow in what was once the town house of Humanity Dick (see page 360). In winter, the homely warren of small rooms, bars, bench seats and snugs draws a diverse crowd, who migrate to the plentiful tables on the busy corner of Cross and Quay streets in summer. The *Kasbah* wine bar next door (same owners) serves tapas, olives, silver darlings (aka pickled herrings) and a charcuterie board.
O'Connell's 8 Eyre Square, http://oconnellsgalway.ie. This 150-year-old pub has a traditional front bar with tiled floors

THE GALWAY WHISKEY TRAIL

In the nineteenth century whiskey distilling was Galway's largest employer – Persse Galway Whiskey was marketed internationally, and with its slogan "favourite in the House of Commons", it sold particularly well in the English colonies. A newly established **whiskey trail** around the central streets of Galway reflects this colourful pedigree in a tour of eleven bars and one off licence. Follow the trail's limestone plaques to find out about the twenty-first-century renaissance in Irish whiskey; en route, sample a dram or two and enjoy the fun of inhaling some full-bodied aromas in bars that reek of a rapturous combination of whiskey and history (http://galwaywhiskeytrail.ie).

10

and antique lighting, quirky parlour rooms behind, and a large beer garden with old shop fronts in the adjoining Gin Lane. Craft and international beers available on tap.

The Quays 11 Quay St, http://quaysgalway.ie. A regular two-storey facade conceals an eccentric, warren-like pub, decorated with mullioned and stained-glass windows, carved beams and Gothic wooden arches. Packed nightly sessions, starting at 6pm, typically feature three different artists.

Róisín Dubh 9 Upper Dominick St, http://roisindubh.net.

This pub is Galway's best general live venue, hosting gigs of every style from rock and reggae to folk and funk, with a late bar every night and a pleasant terrace overlooking the river.

★ **Tigh Coili** Mainguard St, 0http://tighcoiligalway.ie. Welcoming, central and sociable family-run pub with daily sessions in old- fashioned surroundings (Mon–Sat around 6pm & 9.30pm, Sun 2pm & 8pm). Getting a seat in here on a busy night is difficult, but on a sunny evening you can enjoy your drink outside.

ENTERTAINMENT

The Mick Lally Theatre Druid Lane, http://druid.ie/the-mick-lally-theatre. Local theatre company whose acclaimed productions have included the complete cycle of six plays by John Millington Synge.

Town Hall Theatre Courthouse Square, Woodquay, http://tht.ie. Built in the 1820s, this theatre is the city's main performance venue, staging drama, dance, music and opera by visiting companies throughout the year.

SHOPPING

SEE MAP PAGE 335

★ **Charlie Byrne's Bookshop** Cornstore Mall Middle St, http://charliebyrne.ie. A much-cherished institution with a vast selection of new, secondhand and discounted books and an extensive Irish section – the ideal place to dip into some of Tim Robinson's magisterial trilogy on the topography of Connemara or to meet writers and artists, and pick up some Galwegian gossip.

Eason's Bookshop 33 Shop St, http://easons.com. A large general bookshop that sells a wide variety of magazines and newspapers: everything from the *Connacht Tribune* (for local listings) to *Le Monde*.

McCambridge's Deli Shop St, http://mccambridges.com. A dazzling array of chutneys, preserves, olives, herbs and spices alongside Butlers Irish chocolates, Skellig truffles, hand-cut shortbread, the unique Hadji Bey's Irish Turkish delight and Murphy's ice cream. On-site café too. Closed Sun.

Ó Máille 16 High St, http://omaille.com. If you're after woollen garments such as scarves, hats, throws, rugs or Aran sweaters, this is the best place. Their proud boast is that the

shop supplied many of the tailored costumes for *The Quiet Man* (see page 366), filmed in Galway and Mayo in 1951.

★ **Sheridan's Cheesemongers** 14–16 Churchyard St, http://sheridancheesemongers.com. Outstanding Irish, Swiss and French cheeses and other speciality foods. A wine bar upstairs offers carefully sourced cheese, meat and smoked-fish plates.

Treasure Chest 31–33 William St, http://treasurechest.ie. An elegant gift, craft and fashion shop on a large corner site showcasing many of Ireland's leading brand names. You'll find Waterford and Galway crystal, Belleek china, Claddagh rings, Irish linen and knitwear.

Weekend Market Churchyard St, http://galwaymarket.com. The lively Saturday market transforms the area around St Nicholas's Church (there's a smaller version on Sunday) and hosts craftspeople, market gardeners and foodstalls. You could make up a picnic of cheese, bratwurst, home-made bread, smoked salmon, hummus, olives and doughnuts.

East Galway

East Galway (http://galwayeast.com) is a vast tract of flat, fertile land bordered by the Shannon and its tributary the River Suck, the southern half of which shelters some

10

compelling places to visit. The west's first designated "heritage town", **Athenry**, is a fascinating stop, while **Kinvarra** is a justly popular honeypot down on the shores of Galway Bay. Several historic attractions ring the town of **Gort** just inland, notably **Coole Park**, Lady Gregory's idyllic woodland estate, W.B. Yeats's tower house, Thoor Ballylee and the monastic ruins and round tower at **Kilmacduagh**. Out on a limb on the shores of Lough Derg, **Portumna** is an easy-going boating resort, with a fine castle and forest park, which gives access to **Clonfert Cathedral**, one of the country's finest Romanesque churches.

Southeast of Galway city, the N18 runs around the shores of **Galway Bay**, which are lined with native European Flat Oyster beds. The oysters are celebrated at the long-running **Clarenbridge Oyster Festival**, held over three days in early September. This kicks off the season, which lasts until April. Beyond Kilcolgan, the N18 heads inland towards Gort, Ennis and Limerick, while the N67 towards the Burren hugs the coast via the village of Kinvarra following the route of the Wild Atlantic Way (see page 26).

Kinvarra and around

Tucked away at the head of its own inlet in the southeastern corner of the bay, pretty **KINVARRA** is a popular getaway for Galwegians, with several attractive pubs and cafés. The village lays on a music **festival**, the *Fleadh na gCuach* (the Cuckoo Fleadh), over the bank holiday weekend at the start of May, and the *Cruinniú na mBád* (the Meeting of the Boats), over a weekend in August (depending on the tides). The latter features the racing of Galway Bay's traditional, wooden, red-sailed boats – known as **hookers** – which can often be seen docked in the harbour.

Dunguaire Castle
Dungory East, 2km from Kinvarra • charge • http://dunguairecastle.com

The name of **Dunguaire Castle**, an intact, four-storey tower house built in 1520, comes from Guaire – the seventh-century king of Connacht who was so renowned for his generosity that his right arm was said to have grown longer than his left – and *dún* (fort), which may refer to the ancient earthwork on the headland to the east.

Doorus Peninsula
On the west side of Kinvarra Bay, the tranquil **Doorus Peninsula**, which was an island until the eighteenth century, shelters on its north shore the Blue Flag **Traught beach** (6km from Kinvarra), and provides ample opportunity for scenic walks or cycle rides.

ARRIVAL AND INFORMATION
KINVARRA AND AROUND

By bus There's a reasonable bus service (5 daily) from Galway to Kinvarra (40min), which continues to Ballyvaughan, Doolin and the Cliffs of Moher.

Tourist information The town's website is http://kinvarra. ie.

ACCOMMODATION

Breacan Cottage Parkmore Pier, 091 638266. Out near the northeastern corner of the Doorus peninsula, this rustic, tastefully designed B&B at the water's edge is named after a holy well in a nearby field. Excellent breakfasts, including fresh fruit salad, Greek yoghurt and cold meat platter, accompany stunning views across Galway Bay. €€

Merriman Main St, Kinvarra, 091 638222. Most people visit Kinvarra for the day from Galway, but if you want to stay over the village has a good-value hotel named after the eighteenth-century satirical Irish-language poet (see page 585) from nearby Ennistymon in Clare. Boasting one of Ireland's largest thatched roofs, the hotel is tastefully decorated with well-appointed rooms. €€

EATING AND DRINKING

Connolly's The Quay, Kinvarra, http://upstairsatconnollys. ie. This flower-bedecked pub with attractive outdoor tables

has been here since 1898 and sells Kinvarra (made in Offaly) on draught. Traditional musicians flock here in the summer every night (except Thurs) and on Sun afternoon at 5pm. The restaurant (*Upstairs@Connollys*) is also well worth investigating, especially for its steak and seafood plates. €€€€
Greens Main St, Kinvarra, http://greensofkinvarra.com. Part of the fabric of Kinvarra for many generations, this is an old-fashioned spot where the shelves heave with a variety of beers and whiskies. They hold frequent impromptu sessions, so it's best to call in advance if you want to hear some trad.
Moran's Oyster Cottage The Weir, Kilcolgan, http://

moransoystercottage.com. A bar and restaurant set by the bay and famed for native oysters (from their own beds) accompanied by brown bread and a creamy pint of stout. Seafood platters, crab claws, mussels or Aran Islands prawns are all available as well as vegetarian lasagne. Closed Mon. €€€
Paddy Burke's Main St, Clarenbridge, http://paddyburkesgalway.com. A renowned pub which has fed and watered royalty and celebrities for many years. Shellfish dominates but the menu also offers cod, trout and Sun lunchtime alternatives such as duck or beef. €€€

Gort and around

About 12km southeast of Kinvarra and 19km south of Kilcolgan, **GORT** is a traffic-laden workaday town of multicoloured houses on the busy N18 Galway–Limerick road, with some relief provided by the large, triangular market square in the centre. Kinvarra and Galway make be more congenial bases for exploring the surrounding **historic sites** (for which you'll need your own transport).

Coole Park

3km north of Gort on the N18 • Free • http://coolepark.ie

Coole Park is the former estate of **Lady Augusta Gregory** (1852–1932), dramatist, folklorist and co-founder of the Abbey Theatre in Dublin (see page 81), the world's first national theatre. At the beginning of the last century, Coole was the centre of the **Irish Literary Revival**, visited by Synge, Shaw, O'Casey and, most of all, Yeats, who spent over twenty summers here or at Thoor Ballylee. After Lady Gregory's death, however, the estate passed into the hands of the Department of Agriculture and Lands, who left the house to fall into disrepair and demolished it in 1941. The demesne is now a beautiful **woodland nature reserve**, home to pine martens, red squirrels and other woodland fauna. It also encompasses **a Special Area of Conservation** (SAC) and Special Protected Area (SPA) for its unique turlough and associated habitats and wildlife. There are two signposted **nature trails** (1.75km and 4.5km), which will bring you down to the lake and its many swans and wader species. In the walled garden stands the **autograph tree**, a beautiful, swooping copper beech on which all the great writers and painters who stayed here carved their initials.

The **visitor centre** features a highly engaging exhibition based on the memoirs of Lady Gregory's granddaughter, who was born and brought up at Coole, including computer re-creations of the house, and film footage and sound recordings of Yeats. There's also a thirty-minute presentation on Lady Gregory and the Literary Revival.

Thoor Ballylee

5km west of Coole Park • Tower charge • http://yeatsthoorballylee.org

Follow signposted narrow roads from Coole to **Thoor Ballylee**, a newly renovated fourteenth-century Hiberno-Norman tower where Yeats spent summers with his family and wrote some of his best poetry. It is now a cultural and educational centre run on a voluntary basis by the Yeats Thoor Ballylee Society and stages plays, poetry readings and other literary events. The tower houses an audiovisual presentation along with two permanent exhibitions: Yeats and the West of Ireland, and Yeats and His Muses, which considers the importance of women in the poet's life. Tours are self-guided, and include tea or coffee; after exploring the tower you can wander around the grounds, bridge and riverside.

Kilmacduagh

5km southwest of Gort, off the R460 to Corofin • Open access • Free

The extensive monastic ruins of **Kilmacduagh** stand in an unspoilt setting with magnificent views of the Burren's limestone terraces to the west. The monastery was founded by Saint Colman Mac Duagh, a member of one of the local royal families, around 632, but the buildings you can see today date mostly from around five hundred years later. They're impressive by virtue of their scale and quantity – a **cathedral**, four churches, the "Glebe House" (possibly the abbot's house) and a 35m-high, leaning round tower – rather than any architectural finery, but look out for the grim-faced bishop carved over the cathedral's south doorway.

10

By bus On weekdays Bus Éireann services run hourly from Galway to Gort (Mon–Fri; 45min), dropping (and picking up) passengers outside the Allied Irish Bank in the Square.

By train Gort is a stop on the Galway–Limerick line (Mon–Sat 5 daily, Sun 4 daily; 50min to Galway, 1hr 5min to Limerick).

EATING

The Gallery Café The Square, http://thegallerycafegort. com. Formerly a spinning house, and retaining its original whitewashed stone walls, this stylish café is a popular spot. Dishes on offer include meze, pizzas and hearty salads (some with St Tola goat cheese from nearby Inagh) plus fantastic brunch dishes such as pumpkin and chorizo hash with pink onions and poached eggs. Wash it down with Con's organic cider, apple juices or lemonades. Closed Sun & Mon. €€€

Portumna and around

PORTUMNA, 47km east of Gort through the pine-clad Slieve Aughty mountains, is a compact market town surrounded by forests and open land that run down to the meeting of the River Shannon with Lough Derg.

Portumna Castle

Off Abbey St • charge; Heritage Card • http://heritageireland.ie

On the southwest side of the town centre stands the early seventeenth-century fortified mansion **Portumna Castle**, which was gutted by fire in 1826 and is currently undergoing long-term renovation. However, the ground floor is open to the public where an illuminating exhibition recalls the life of the de Burgo family who lived here, the house and its conservation. In front of the house, the elegant, geometric Renaissance **garden**, one of the first in Ireland, has been re-created, as has the walled kitchen garden to one side, and there's a coffee shop in the courtyard.

Portumna Friary and Forest Park

Off Abbey St, 400m south of Portumna Castle entrance • Open access

Beyond the castle gatehouse, about 400m down the road towards the lake, lie the extensive remains of **Portumna Friary** in a leafy setting. Originally a Cistercian chapel, it was rebuilt by the Dominicans in the early fifteenth century, with ornate traceried windows in the east wall and south transept of the church, and a small, pretty cloister, now heavily restored. Part of Portumna Castle's former estate – still home to a sizeable herd of fallow deer – constitutes the **Portumna Forest Park**, where you can stroll along marked trails through the woodland to the lakeshore.

Irish Workhouse Centre

Northern end of St Brigid's Rd • charge • http://irishworkhousecentre.ie

Buildings in the former Portumna Workhouse (a poorhouse for the destitute opened in 1852) have been converted into the **Irish Workhouse Centre**, which at one time was described as the most feared and hated institution ever established in Ireland.

Enlightening 75-minute guided tours take you through the waiting hall, boardroom, schoolroom and women's quarters, the last of which keeps an extensive collection of artefacts, including the workhouse cart, rudimentary metal cups and bowls, and tiny shoes worn by the children here.

Clonfert Cathedral

25km northeast of Portumna • Free

Infrequently used by the Church of Ireland, **Clonfert Cathedral** was founded in the sixth century by St Brendan, who was later buried here, and the present building has been in continuous service from around the tenth century. Regarded as the high point of Irish Romanesque, its rounded, golden-brown, sandstone **doorway**, topped by a triangular gable, may have been added for a synod held at Clonfert by St Laurence O'Toole, Archbishop of Dublin, in 1179. It's carved with a remarkable diversity of inventive motifs, some of which have been traced to Scandinavia and western France, including human and animal heads, interlace and other geometrical devices. Dating from around 1600, the adjacent **bishop's palace** later became home to the English fascist, Oswald Mosley, but has rapidly rotted since it was accidentally burned down in 1954.

ARRIVAL AND INFORMATION

By bus Kearns Transport (http://kearnstransport.com) runs daily services between Portumna and Dublin, via Birr, and at weekends between Birr and Galway city (Merchant's Rd) via Portumna and Loughrea.

PORTUMNA AND AROUND

Tourist office In the Irish Workhouse Centre (see page 344) on St Brigid's Rd (March–Oct daily 9.30am–5.30pm; http://visitportumna.com). Provides maps and brochures on East Galway.

ACCOMMODATION, EATING AND DRINKING

The Beehive St Patrick's St, 090 974 1830. A basic café-restaurant serving salads, sandwiches, simple pastas and other main courses and cakes, plus tasty, popular pizzas in the evenings. €€

Horan's Pub Brendan St, 090 974 1007. One of the best spots for an impromptu session on any night and a good spot to meet the locals.

Oak Lodge B&B St Brendan's Rd, http://oaklodge portumna.ie. A conveniently located guesthouse with five en-suite rooms, which are available on either a room only or B&B basis. The common room is a focal point for visitors, featuring a wood-burning stove and local interest books, while the warm welcome extends to homemade scones upon arrival. €€

Loughrea and around

LOUGHREA, 32km northwest of Portumna, is a small market town on the lake of the same name. It's unlikely that you'll want to stay here, but it's well worth detouring off the N6 bypass to visit the late nineteenth-century **St Brendan's Cathedral**.

St Brendan's Cathedral

Barrack St • Mon–Fri 10am–1pm & 2–5.30pm • http://loughreacathedral.ie • 30min audio-tour available from adjacent presbytery at weekends

St Brendan's Cathedral is a shining product of the Arts and Crafts movement – which in its Irish manifestation is often referred to as the Celtic Revival. The interior is decorated with rich marble, playfully carved Irish-oak pews and Mediterranean-style column capitals in the nave telling the story of St Brendan. Its most notable feature, however, is the stained glass, which was mostly produced by **An Túr Gloine** ("The Shining Tower"), a cooperative Arts and Crafts studio based in Dublin from 1903 to 1944. Look out especially for the 1930s works by the Dublin-born artist **Michael Healy**, who was heavily influenced by the Renaissance art he'd studied in Florence. His *St Joseph* in the right-hand aisle is sombrely emotive, but in *The Queen of Heaven*, further down the same aisle, he deals only in brilliant colours and composition, to convey Mary's regal splendour. Healy's masterpieces, however, are *The Ascension* and *The Last Judgement* in the west transept, sparkling tapestries of colour inlaid with the dramatic heads of his characters.

Clonfert Diocesan Museum

Adjoining the cathedral • Open on request Mon–Fri 10am–5.30pm • Donation requested • 091 841212

The **Clonfert Diocesan Museum** houses tapestries designed by Jack B. Yeats and made by the **Dun Emer Guild**, the weaving and printing arm of the Irish Arts and Crafts movement, founded in 1902 and named after the needleworking wife of the mythical hero, Cúchulainn. There's also a primitive, polychrome carving of the Virgin and Child dating from the late twelfth or early thirteenth century, the oldest surviving wooden statue in Ireland.

EATING	LOUGHREA

Maggie Mays Bride St, http://maggiemaysloughrea.com. A bustling bar and restaurant whose menu brims with locally sourced produce, with typical offerings including glazed pork fillet, duck, duo of salmon and lemon sole, and vegetarian dishes. The three-course set dinner menu is excellent value. €€€

Athenry

ATHENRY's name in Irish, Baile Átha an Rí, "town of the ford of the king", reveals its ancient significance as a crossing point of the River Clarin, 20km due east of Galway city on what is still the main road-and-rail route to Dublin. Many of its historic sites are well preserved, including nearly all its fourteenth-century town **walls**, plus the North Gate, five towers, and castle. In the market square stands the only **market cross** *in situ* in the country, though it's a badly damaged stump; dating from the fifteenth century, it's carved with scenes of the Crucifixion and the Virgin and Child. East from here, just across the river, the extensive remains of the thirteenth- to fifteenth-century Dominican **Priory of SS Peter and Paul** (open access) include a fine collection of carved grave slabs from medieval times onwards.

Athenry Castle

Gorteenacra, 2km off the M6 exit, on the southwest outskirts of town • charge; Heritage Card • http://heritageireland.ie

Standing at the northeast corner of the town walls, guarding the ford, the **castle** dates back to the thirteenth century. It is a forbidding, almost windowless, three-storey hall with a keep that features some fine Romano-Gothic floral carvings in the so-called School of the West Style, which is unique among Irish castles. Elsewhere, there's an empty but atmospherically cavernous basement you can wander about in, and, up on the third floor, an illuminating twenty-minute audio-visual on the castle's history.

THE FIELDS OF ATHENRY

Athenry is probably most famous for the song **The Fields of Athenry**, penned by singer-songwriter Pete St John in the 1970s as an adaptation of a poignant 1880s ballad about the abominations of the Famine. It's an emotive, catchy number, popular in pubs and at football and rugby matches, and you may well find yourself joining in, at least with the chorus:

Low lie the fields of Athenry
Where once we watched the small, free birds fly
Our love was on the wing
We had dreams and songs to sing,
It's so lonely round the fields of Athenry

Athenry Heritage Centre

Opposite the castle • Charge; 45min guided tour included in price; Medieval Experience charge • http://athenryheritagecentre.com

The lively **Athenry Heritage Centre** occupies a nineteenth-century church built within the ruins of a medieval predecessor. The big attraction for kids is the "Medieval Experience", which comes complete with stocks, a re-created dungeon, summertime archery and lots of objects to handle – and everyone, big or small, gets to wear a medieval costume.

ARRIVAL AND DEPARTURE

ATHENRY

10

By train The station is on Church St.
Destinations Athlone (10 daily; 1hr); Galway (18 daily; 45min); Limerick (5 daily; 1hr 45min).

ACCOMMODATION AND EATING

★ **Caheroyan House** Monivea Rd, 091 844858. Athenry's outstanding B&B choice is a 5min walk from the North Gate. Set in a pretty garden, this tastefully refurbished eighteenth-century manor house offers spacious bedrooms and fine breakfasts that feature home-grown grapes and home-made jam. Guests are free to explore the organic farmland and woodland. Two self-catering three-bedroom cottages also available. €€€

The Old Barracks Cross St, http://oldbarracks.ie. Set in a former RIC police barracks, this place combines pantry, bakery and a restaurant offering lunch and dinner. Mains include steak, burgers, chicken and vegetable fajitas; be sure to finish off with the delicious Linnalla artisan ice cream made in the Burren. Accommodation comes in the shape of eleven smoothly decorated rooms and suites in the neighbouring *Lodge at the Old Barracks*. €€

The Aran Islands

Once part of a land barrier across the south side of Galway Bay, the **Aran Islands** (Oileáin Árann) – **Inishmore**, **Inishmaan** and **Inisheer** – have proved alluring to travellers for centuries. Until recently, their isolation allowed the continuation of an ancient Gaelic culture, traces of which remain, while Irish is still the main language of the islands. Fishing and farming are to this day the principal activities on Inishmaan, with tourism the major earner on Inishmore and Inisheer.

As well as the islands' heritage, their dramatic landscapes, continuing the limestone pavement of the Burren in County Clare into the sea, are a major draw. This bleak geology manages to sustain over four hundred varieties of wildflower, including the rare Alpine Spring gentian, as well as a healthy population of butterflies and endangered bird species such as the chough and the little tern. Here too is one of the richest concentrations of pre-Christian and early Christian archaeological sites in Europe, including seven massive **stone forts**, some of which are survivals from the Bronze Age (1100 BC). The pick of these is **Dun Aengus**, a spectacular prehistoric ring fort on the edge of Inishmore's sea cliffs.

Brief history

From the fifth or sixth century onwards, the islands were a centre of **monastic learning**, their wildness and remoteness drawing students from far and wide. St Enda's monastery on Inishmore, the first of Ireland's dozens of island monasteries, was also one of the most influential of the age, training monks who went on to found important houses of their own, such as Brendan of Clonfert, Ciarán of Clonmacnois and Colmcille of Iona.

The monasteries of the Arans had gone into decline by the early thirteenth century, at which time Galway city began to take off as a trading port under the Anglo-Normans. For controlling piracy – and their own piratical instincts – in Galway Bay, the Gaelic lords of Aran, the **O'Briens** of County Clare, received an annual payment from the city. In the sixteenth century, however, the O'Briens fell into dispute with the O'Flahertys of west Galway over the islands – to their mutual detriment. The argument was eventually resolved by Queen Elizabeth I who, seeing the Arans as strategically important against

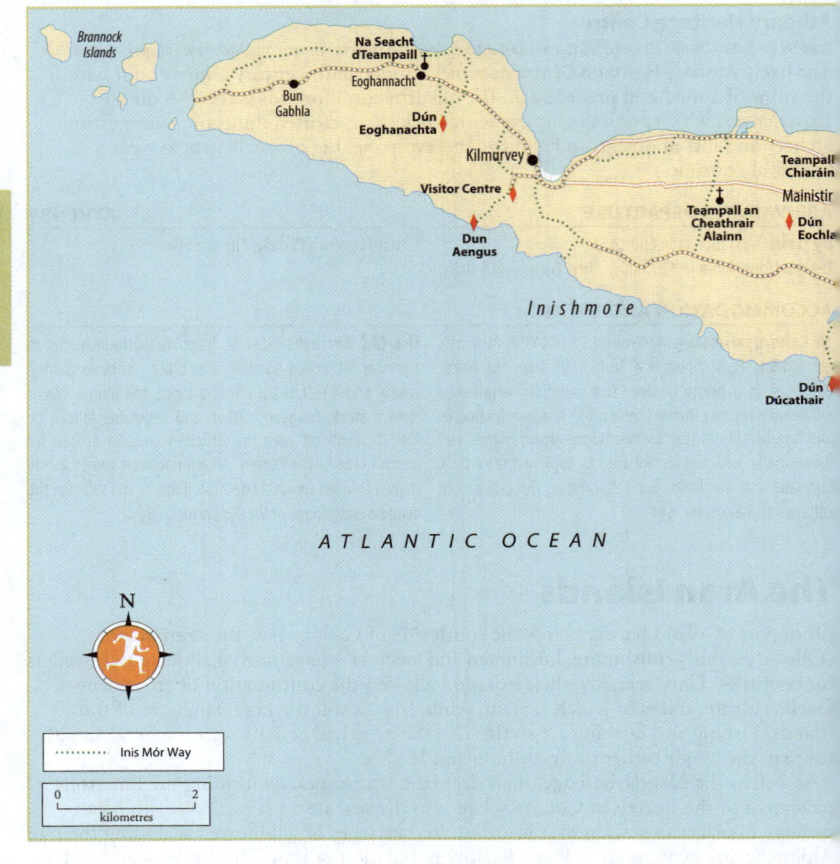

the Spanish and French, annexed the islands to the Crown. In 1588, the Arans were sold to the **Lynch** family of Galway, who were required to keep a garrison of soldiers there. The family, however, remained loyal to the king during the English Civil War of the 1640s, and the victorious Cromwell declared Sir Robert Lynch a traitor and his lands forfeit.

Thereafter, the islands passed through a succession of landowners, whose main interest was the income from ever-increasing rents. The islands escaped the worst effects of the Famine of the 1840s, as the availability of **food from the sea** and the shore helped to compensate for the failure of the potato crop. It wasn't until 1922 that the absentee landlords sold their interests and the islands' farmers finally came to own their land.

ARRIVAL AND DEPARTURE

THE ARAN ISLAND

There are coach connections from Galway to Rossaveel (25min) and Inverin airport (45min from Galway city) for most flights and boat departures.

By boat Ferries sail from Rossaveel (Rós an Mhíl) and from Doolin in County Clare (see page 322) to the Aran Islands with Aran Island Ferries which has branches on

Forster St and on Merchants Rd in Galway city (http:/ aranislandferries.com). All destinations cost €30 return o €20 single; standard bikes can be transported on the fer for a charge of €15.

Destinations Inishmore (2–3 daily with extra sailings i summer; 35min); Inisheer (2 daily; 1hr); the Inisheer boa

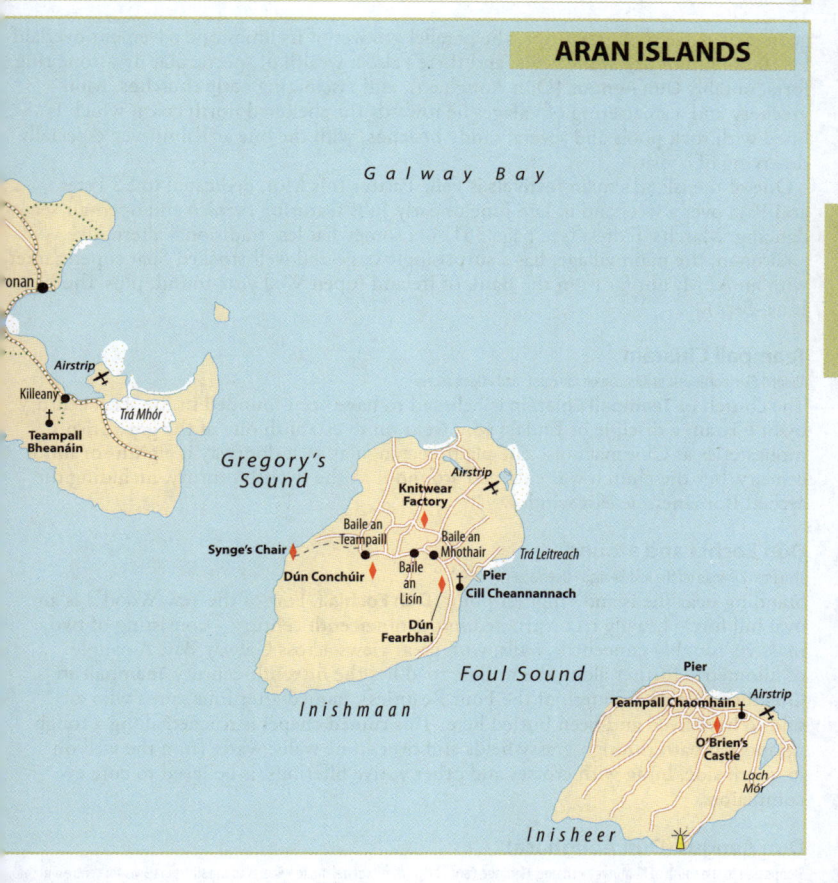

ARAN ISLANDS

alls at Inishmaan (50min from Rossaveel) on both outward
nd return journeys.

By plane Flights operate from Connemara Regional Airport

at Inverin (Indreabhán), around 30km west of Galway city,
courtesy of Aer Árann Inverin (http://aerarannislands.ie)
who fly to all three islands (up to 4 daily).

INFORMATION

Maps and guides The Ordnance Survey cover the Arans
n a single 1:25,000 map, while *The Aran Islands: A World
f Stone* is an excellent introductory book, published by
'Brien Press. Tim Robinson has produced a comprehensive
nap and guidebook of the islands, which is knowledgeable

on archaeology, local lore and the derivation of Irish place
names, while his books, *The Aran Islands: Pilgrimage* and
Labyrinth, provide even more fascinating analysis.
Website http://aranislands.ie.

nishmore

One of the great attractions of **Inishmore** (Inis Mór, "Big Island", but often referred
o simply as Árainn) is its topography, which is stark, simple and easily appreciated.
heer cliffs, lashed at their base by the relentless Atlantic, run the 14km length of its
outh coast, their tops offering an ethereal panorama, from the echoing wall of the
liffs of Moher in the southeast to the Connemara Mountains, tinged with green,
urple and gold, to the north across Galway Bay. The land declines northwards in a

10

geometric pattern of grey stone, the parallel grooves of its limestone pavement overlaid by 10,000km of **dry-stone walls**, and there's also a wealth of spectacular dry-stone ring forts, notably **Dun Aengus** (Dún Aonghasa), and fascinating **early churches**. More greenery and a smattering of villages lie towards the sheltered north coast, which is lined with rock pools and several sandy **beaches**, with the one at Kilmurvey especially deserving of a visit.

One of the island's main **festivals** is Féile Patrún Inis Mór, dedicated to SS Peter and Paul over a weekend in late June or early July, featuring *currach* and open-air set dancing. March's Tedfest (see page 351) is a somewhat less traditional alternative.

Kilronan, the main village, has a surprisingly large and well-stocked Spar supermarket, with an ATM, not far from the Bank of Ireland (open Wed year-round, plus Thurs June–Sept).

Teampall Chiaráin

About 1.5km northwest of Kilronan on the coast road • Open access

The church of **Teampall Chiaráin** is believed to have been founded in the sixth century by St Ciarán, a disciple of Enda's, who went on to establish one of the great Irish monasteries at Clonmacnois. The plain, rectangular west doorway is eighth- or ninth century, but the church was enlarged around it in the twelfth century, including the arched Romanesque east window.

Dún Eochla and around

3km from Kilronan off the middle road • Open access

Standing near the island's highest point, **Dún Eochla** ("Fort of the Yew Wood") is an oval hill fort – heavily reconstructed in the nineteenth century – consisting of two massive, roughly concentric walls, with great views across Galway Bay. A couple of kilometres further along the middle road lies the fifteenth-century **Teampall an Cheathrair Alainn** (Church of the Four Beauties), named after four saints who are said to have lived and been buried here. This ruined chapel is reached along a rough, signposted path through grassy fields and over stone walls; water from the well on its south side, hung with crosses and other votive offerings, is believed to cure eye complaints.

Dun Aengus (Dún Aonghasa)

Signposted to the south of Kilmurvey • charge; Heritage Card • http://heritageireland.ie • Access to the site is via a visitor centre and café, from where it's an uphill walk of nearly 1km to the fort

By far the Aran Islands' most compelling ancient site, **Dun Aengus** is a semicircular fort of three concentric enclosures, hard up against the edge of sheer, 90m-high cliffs. From here, on a clear day, you can see Kerry Head, northwest of Tralee, and occasionally Mount Brandon on the Dingle Peninsula – if you're truly blessed, you might spot the island of Hy Brasil to the west (see page 350). The fort is named after Aengus of the **Fir Bolg**, a legendary ancient race, said to have been of Greek

---

HY BRASIL

From Dun Aengus, you might be lucky enough to see the famous **mirage** known as **Hy Brasil** (after which the South American country was supposedly named), which appears in the sea to the west as a mountainous island. Local folklore represents this mythical land variously as the island of the blessed, the Garden of Eden, Tír na nóg (the land of eternal youth), the Isle of Truth, of Joy, of Fair Women and of Apples. In the early twentieth century, islanders believed it appeared once every seven years, but up until the mid-nineteenth century it was actually shown on some sea charts of the Atlantic. On the unforgiving, sea-battered Arans, it's easy to understand how this fantasy of a prosperous paradise grew up.

TEDFEST

During the first week of March, a friendly invasion of visitors – amounting to nearly half the island's population – arrives en masse for a madcap festival on Inishmore. Since 2006 they have been coming in their hundreds to celebrate cult classic **Father Ted**, the TV comedy whose setting, the fictitious Craggy Island, was inspired by the Arans. Based in Kilronan in *Tí Joe Watty's* bar (see page 352), the weekend is a party place for "Ted Heads". Entertainment includes comedy shows, sketches, a "lovely girls" competition and a raft of other shenanigans. Musical parameters are wide, stretching from traditional Irish, country and folk to bluegrass and rock 'n roll, featuring up to twenty bands from Ireland and the UK. Tickets are limited to around four hundred so book early and organize your accommodation well in advance. It all kicks off at noon on the Thursday, continuing unabated until the small hours of Monday morning. Go to http://tedfest.org for information and tickets.

origin and to have ruled Ireland for 37 years, before being conquered by the equally mythical Tuatha Dé Danann.

The **inner citadel** comprises a wall, 6m high and 4m wide, of massive blocks of limestone that were quarried on site and put together without mortar. In the site's heyday, the inhabitants would have lived here and in the middle enclosure, with livestock in the outermost enclosure. Some time after 500 BC, Dun Aengus contracted, and a still-imposing *cheval de frise* was constructed between the middle and outer walls, a 10m-wide field planted with razor-sharp standing stones up to 1.8m high, designed to slow down attackers.

Dún Eoghanachta

Just under 2km northwest of Kilmurvey

Look out for signposts pointing south along a dwindling trail for the twenty-minute walk up to the impressive **Dún Eoghanachta**. Probably built between 650 and 800 AD, it's the smallest of the Aran forts, a perfect circle of rectilinear, almost brick-like, light-grey, limestone blocks.

The Seven Churches

To the north of Eoghanacht village

The monastic complex of **Na Seacht dTeampaill**, or the **Seven Churches**, actually consists of the substantial ruins of two churches and five domestic buildings. It was founded by St Brecan, who arrived on the island in the fifth or early sixth century, succeeded Enda as the abbot of the main monastery at Killeany, and was famous for his piety and severity. Occupying land with some of the deepest soil on the island, the site is still used as a graveyard. The older of the churches, Teampall Bhreacáin, dates from the eighth century but was gradually enlarged with some fine arches.

Dún Dúchathair (Black Fort)

To the south of Kilronan

Enjoying a spectacular location on a promontory, **Dún Dúchathair** ("Black Fort") is guarded by cliffs on three sides, and a *cheval de frise* on the fourth. The fort consists of a single massive wall, 60m long, that slices across the neck of the headland. Once through the narrow entrance at the eastern end (the main gate here collapsed into the sea in the early nineteenth century) you'll find the remains of four oval *clocháns*.

Teampall Bheanáin

Just south of and above the village of Killeany

The eleventh-century **Teampall Bheanáin** stands in a magnificent hilltop location that's especially enchanting at sunset. Built of huge stone slabs, it's notable for its north–

south alignment, its unusually steep gables and its size – at just 5m long, some claim it to be the smallest church in Europe. It was probably part of St Enda's early monastic site (*Cill Einne*, "Church of Enda"), formed around 490, which was torn down by Cromwell's soldiers to strengthen Arkin Castle in the village in 1652.

ARRIVAL AND DEPARTURE

By boat Ferries (see page 348) dock at the main village Kilronan (Cill Rónáin) from either Rosaveel in Connemara or Doolin in Clare, usually arriving around 11am.

By plane Flights from Inverin on the nine-seat Islander

INISHMORE

planes arrive during the day into the airstrip at An Tr Mhór. A minibus will pick you up and drop you at you accommodation or chosen destination.

GETTING AROUND

By minibus Minibuses operate all over Inishmore with a basic shared journey costing €10 per person. Drivers also offer set tours that take up to 3hr, including 1hr 30min at Dun Aengus and 15min at the Seven Churches.

By bike Aran Bike Hire by the pier in Kilronan (http://aranislandsbikehire.com). It's easier if you follow a circuit going out on the coast road and coming back by the hillier middle road, with the prevailing west wind at your back; an excellent stock of bikes include mountain and e-bikes

(€20/€40/day).

On foot The most scenic way to get around is t follow looped walks of 3–5hr; route leaflets are availabl at the tourist office. Make sure you have stout walkin boots. For more information, go to http://discoverirelanc ie/walking.

By pony buggy Tours of the island with Thomas Fahert (http://aranponytrap.com) cost €40–60 for a group of up t four adults, with a choice of three set routes.

INFORMATION

Tourist office The office opposite the pier (daily: Nov–June 10am–5pm; July–Sept 10am–6pm; http://aranislands.ie) has maps and walking route leaflets for all of the islands,

information on accommodation and details of sailing an flight timings.

ACCOMMODATION

Aran Islands Hotel Lower Kilronan, http://aranislands hotel.com. Smart, modern hotel, tastefully fitted with pine floors and bare stone walls; the best rooms have kingsize beds and panoramic balconies. From the hotel's restaurant (try the seafood pasta) there are spectacular views of Kileaney Bay. €€€

Kilmurvey House Kilmurvey, http://kilmurvey-house. com. Near the Dun Aengus visitor centre, but quiet at night, this B&B occupies an impressive and welcoming eighteenth-century country house with a ruined church in its extensive garden. €€

Kilronan Hostel Kilronan (IHO), http://kilronanhostel. com. Beside *Tigh Jo Mac*'s pub, this hostel has small (four-to six-bed) en-suite dorms, with a kitchen and TV room.

Breakfast included. €

Pier House Kilronan, http://pierhousearan.com. Rich decorated guesthouse with attractive, pine-furnishe rooms, occupying a peerless spot by the jetty wit panoramic views, plus a resident's lounge and sun terra offering comfortable sanctuary in wetter weather. Sel catering apartments available. €€

Seacrest Kilronan, http://aranaccommodations.con Out of ten or so B&Bs in and around the main village, th bungalow is a good bet in the centre, with six smart, er suite rooms (singles, twins and doubles), a spacious livin room and hearty breakfasts. They also run 3hr horse-an carriage tours of the island (€25). €€

EATING AND DRINKING

The Bar Kilronan Pier, http://inismorbar.com. Convenient waterfront bar (a former priest's house) serving sandwiches, soup, fish and chips, as well as gluten-free and vegetarian meals. They also hold traditional music sessions most nights in summer and at weekends in the off season.

Man of Aran Café Main St Klronan, 085 710 5254. This is the place to come to watch the *Man of Aran* film (see page 353), which they show daily for €5. The café also sells crafts, guidebooks and maps, and offers a left luggage facility.

The Pier House Waterfront, Kilronan, 099 61811. This

is the ideal spot for food on a sunny day overlooking th waterfront. Lunches might be grilled potato fish cake smoked chicken salad or Aran seafood platter, and f dinner, expect brill, lobster or oysters. €€€

Ti Joe Watty's Cottage Rd, Kilronan, http://joewattys. A tree-shaded beer garden at a crossroads with all sorts live music (nightly in summer; weekends only from Oct). popular for varied lunches and dinners, though seafood a big deal here, such as crab claws, steamed mussels, ar fish and chips. €€

THE ARAN ISLANDS AND THE GAELIC REVIVAL

In the late nineteenth century, the Arans became a living museum for anthropologists, antiquarians and linguists, seeking out the unbroken heritage of Irish language, beliefs and customs here, which in turn provided fuel for the **Gaelic Revival** and the Nationalist movement. Written and spoken Irish was a particular focus of interest, as even by this time the islands were one of the few areas of the country where the native language was in daily use. Patrick Pearse came specifically to learn Irish on Inishmaan, which was also visited by writers Yeats, Lady Gregory and, most notably, J.M. Synge – George Russell later joked that Synge's knack was to discover that if you translated Irish literally into English, you achieved poetry.

The Arans themselves have nurtured several excellent writers, notably **Liam O'Flaherty** (see page 590) and poet **Máirtín Ó Direáin** (see page 592), both from Inishmore. In 1934 the documentary-maker **Robert Flaherty** released his classic *Man of Aran* in which he sought to record the islands' vanishing way of life – some of it had already disappeared, but he wasn't averse to re-creating scenes that were no longer witnessed. A few of the traditions captured in the film still exist – you'll still see people collecting seaweed for fertilizer, building dry-stone walls and fishing from **currachs** (traditional pointed skiffs), though these are no longer covered with animal skins. In more recent years, *The Cripple of Inishmaan*, Martin McDonagh's black comedy starring Daniel Radcliffe, has been performed to packed houses on stages in Broadway and the West End, and has captured the imagination of the critics. The storyline – about a crippled teenager who tries to get a role in the *Man of Aran* – focuses on a Hollywood director visiting the island.

10

Inishmaan

Approaching from the west or east, **Inishmaan** (Inis Meáin, "Middle Island") looks like a rising wave about to break over Galway Bay to the north. From the grey limestone pavement at its northern end, tiny pastures, separated by a maze of dry-stone walls, rise to the main east–west ridge, along which lies a ribbon of villages. The so-called "back of the island" slopes off more gradually to the south. This is the most unspoilt of the Arans, and the most thoroughly Irish-speaking (though English is understood), where people are still largely engaged in farming and fishing, with wild salmon caught from black, pointed *currachs*. The island's historic sites are on a smaller scale than Inishmore's – though the imposing ring fort of **Dún Conchúir** is worth singling out – and there are far fewer amenities, but for some people this tranquil, low-key place will be the perfect getaway.

The **Bank of Ireland** operates on the second Tuesday of every month, while Baile an Mhothair, the Inis Meáin Knitting Company (http://inismeain.ie), on the north side of the island, produces beautiful **knitwear** based on traditional Aran patterns, usually for exclusive export markets, but available here at discounted prices.

Cill Cheanannach and around

east side of the island, immediately southwest of the pier

A tiny, roofless church with steeply pitched gables, **Cill Cheanannach** was built some time before 1200. Just to the north, in the graveyard, lies a curious, roughly triangular slab of limestone: the end-stone of a tomb-shrine, it is pierced with a hole through which pilgrims could touch the bones of the saint inside (possibly the shadowy Cheanainn). On the slope above the church perches the overgrown **Dún Fearbhaí**, a small, rectilinear ring fort, probably dating from the ninth century AD or later.

Baile an Teampaill

From the pier, the island – and the main road – rises in rough steps through the adjoining hamlets of Baile an Mhothair and Baile an Lisín to **Baile an Teampaill** at its midpoint. It's well worth calling in to the village **church** here to see the gorgeous

10

INISHMAAN AND J.M. SYNGE

Inishmaan's most famous visitor was **J.M. Synge**, who, on the advice of W.B. Yeats, spent long periods of time on the island between 1898 and 1902, living on mackerel and eggs. He found artistic liberation here, as well as plenty of plot ideas in the stories told him by the islanders, writing his first play, *When the Moon has Set*, in 1901. His book *The Aran Islands* is a moving account of the way of life he encountered.

stained-glass windows executed by Harry Clarke in 1939. Made up of glass pieces of varying thicknesses, the richly coloured images swim before your eyes – look out especially for Cavan (Caomhán), the patron saint of Inisheer, with a man rowing a *currach* behind his feet.

Teach Synge

On the road a few hundred metres before Fort Dún Conchúir • June–Sept noon–2pm & 2.30–4.30pm; by appointment at other times • charge • 099 73036

Further along from the church stands **Teach Synge**, a former post office where Synge stayed, as well as Lady Gregory, W.B. Yeats and Patrick Pearse before him. It's a charming 300-year-old cottage, thatched and whitewashed, with typically small windows (rents on the islands were often calculated on the basis of the size and number of windows). A dresser, a butter churn and most of the other furniture from Synge's time are still inside, as well as fascinating photos taken by the playwright, on the first camera to be brought to the island.

Dún Conchúir

Signposted up a lane from Teach Synge

Near Inishmaan's highest point, **Dún Conchúir** is one of the Arans' most imposing forts, with fine views of Connemara and down Ireland's west coast. Its ramparted, dry-stone walls are 5m thick and 6m high, with a walled gateway defending the main entrance at the northeastern corner. According to legend, Conchúir was the younger brother of Aengus, who is commemorated with his own fort on Inishmore, backing up the theory that there was a prehistoric confederation of the islands, with its capital at Dun Aengus. The last inhabitant of the fort was a nineteenth-century Connemara man called Malley, who, having accidentally killed his father, hid out here for several months, before escaping to America – a tale used as inspiration by Synge for the plot of *Playboy of the Western World*.

Synge's Chair

About 20min walk west of Baile an Teampaill

The playwright's favourite contemplative spot, **Synge's Chair**, is a semicircle of stones he gathered himself, on the site of an old lookout facing Gregory's Sound. From here, you can take a two- to three-hour west-coast hike along towering cliffs to the blowholes at the southwest corner, before cutting up the middle of the island to the village.

ARRIVAL AND DEPARTURE
INISHMAAN

By plane Flights operate from Connemara Regional Airport at Inverin (Indreabhán). Aer Árann (http://aerarannislands. ie) flies roughly three times daily to Inishmaan and Inisheer.

By boat Ferries to Inishmaan and Inisheer sail twice daily from Rossaveel (http://aranislandferries.com) and once daily from Doolin in County Clare (http://doolinferry.com).

ACCOMMODATION AND EATING

An Dún Dún Conchúir, http://inismeainaccommodation.ie. An attractive, well-designed guesthouse with five en-suite rooms and a sauna. The restaurant menu (residents only) showcases home-grown organic vegetables, including the delectable Inishmaan floury potatoes that are fertilized in seaweed; in summer there's a daytime café. Closed Dec-

Feb. €€€
Ard Alainn 087 285 6778. A hospitable guesthouse in a lofty position between Dún Conchúir and Synge's Chair,

offering a fine panorama of Galway Bay. Modern standard and en-suite rooms and self-catering also available. Phone for free pick-up from the pier. €€

Inisheer

Lying just 10km off the Clare coast, **Inisheer** (Inis Oírr, "East Island") is the smallest and least dramatic Aran. Its historic sites aren't quite as appealing as Inishmaan's, and it's much more of a lively pleasure ground, attracting crowds of teenagers from the local Irish college and day-trippers from Doolin in summer. There's a lovely, partly sheltered, sandy **beach** east of the pier on the north coast, along which nearly all of the habitation on this 3km-wide island spreads. The 10km, waymarked **Inis Oírr Way** traces a circular route round the northern half of the island, taking in O'Brien's Castle and Teampall Chaomháin, and you could easily branch off between the latter and Loch Mór to add on a walk down the road to the **lighthouse** at the southeastern tip of the island, which affords fantastic views of the Cliffs of Moher. There are no ATMs on the island, but the Bank of Ireland visits on the fourth Tuesday of the month.

O'Brien's Castle

Above and behind the beach, **O'Brien's Castle** (Caisleán Uí Bhriain) is attractively sited above low, ivy-covered cliffs, a short, green valley and a network of dry-stone walls. It's well worth walking up to the castle for views of the harbour and the north half of the island, if nothing else.

Teampall Chaomháin

Climb the sand dune, topped with modern gravestones and wild flowers, on the southeast side of the beach and you're in for a surprise: sunk into the dune's summit lies **Teampall Chaomháin**, a roofless church dedicated to St Cavan (still a common boy's name on the island), who is thought to have been the brother of St Kevin of Glendalough. Retaining walls now help to protect the ruin from the shifting sand, but it still has to be shovelled out every year on June 14, the saint's feast day.

Áras Éanna

A 15min walk south from the West village in the north of the island • http://aras-eanna.ie

A multipurpose arts centre, **Áras Éanna** has two galleries showing temporary art exhibitions, runs demonstrations of traditional basket-making and weaving in the summer and hosts music, films and plays in its theatre.

GETTING AROUND AND INFORMATION — INISHEER

Inisheer Island Co-operative Situated beyond the east end of the beach, this business ((http://discoverinisoirr. com) can provide tourist information as well as internet access.

Bike rental Bikes can be rented from the helpful office (099 75049) in front of the pier, where you can also charter a pony and trap for a tour of the island.

ACCOMMODATION AND EATING

Island Co-operative Campsite 099 75008. The only place to camp is this site by the beach, which has toilets and

INISHEER FESTIVALS

Musicians flock here at the end of June when the island hosts a five-day **bodhrán festival** (http://craiceann.com), while mid-September sees enthusiasts of **stone walls** (and there are more than you'd think) arrive for a weekend of events and activities that include tuition on the art of stone wall building and carving.

10

hot showers. Closed Nov–April. €
South Aran House http://southaran.com. At the west end of the village, this place has bright, tasteful en-suite rooms with underfloor heating, and each room has its own private entrance. Minimum stay two nights from Oct to March.

Adults only. €€
Tigh Ned's West village, http://tighned.com. A cosy pub with a pleasant garden overlooking the harbour with lunches served in summer, locally brewed beer and traditional sessions in summer.

SHOPPING

Inisheer Heritage House This heritage house and craft shop near the main pier at the north end of the island is worth visiting to browse local sweaters, books and indigenous craftwork (099 75021).

Connemara

Comprising all of Galway to the west of the city, **Connemara** is a ravishingly diverse tract of land. Cut off from the rest of the county by the sweep of **Lough Corrib**, the lie of the land at first looks simple, with two statuesque mountain ranges, the **Maam Turks** (Mám Tuirc, the "boar pass") and the **Twelve Bens** (or sometimes Twelve Pins; Na Beanna Beola, the "Peaks of Beola", a mythical giant), bordered by the deep fjord of **Killary Harbour** to the north. The coast, however, is full of jinks and tricks, a maze of little islands, winding roads, bogs and hills, where it can be hard to tell small loughs from sea inlets. All around the littoral are quiet white-sand **beaches** that are great for swimming. It's hard to miss out **Clifden** on your travels, the likeable and lively main town, poised dramatically between steep hills and the harbour. Other likely bases are the pretty fishing village of **Roundstone**, and **Oughterard**, an angler's delight, not far out of Galway city on the lush banks of Lough Corrib. Oughterard has a good selection of visitor attractions, but the only really compelling historic sight in west Connemara is **Kylemore Abbey and Gardens**. Just off shore near here, you can sample easy-going island life on **Inishbofin**.

GETTING AROUND AND INFORMATION

By bus Bus Éireann's main services from Galway run along the coast via Spiddal to Carraroe, and along the N59 via Oughterard to Clifden, sometimes branching off to Roundstone. A few of their services to Clifden branch off at Maam Cross and detour via Leenane, Kylemore and Letterfrack, and in summer they operate a daily (Mon–Sat) bus from Clifden to Westport, via Letterfrack, Kylemore and Leenane. Citylink buses (http://citylink.ie) from Galway

serve Oughterard, Clifden, Cleggan and Letterfrack three or four times a day.
By car The major route through the area is the N59 from Galway, which cuts across to Clifden before skirting the Twelve Bens en route to Westport, but there are plenty of scenic side-roads through the mountains and around the frilly coastline.
Tourist information http://connemara.ie.

Oughterard and around

Around 28km from Galway on the N59, **OUGHTERARD** is a busy little town, at the start of the Western Way (see page 357), with plenty of varied attractions in the

CONNEMARA AND THE IRISH LANGUAGE

Connemara's harsh land has always been thinly populated and isolated, and this has ensured the persistence of rural traditions and of the **Irish language**. It contains the country's largest Gaeltacht, stretching as far west as Roundstone, with Raidió na Gaeltachta and TG4, the Irish-speaking radio and TV stations, both broadcast from here. Four-week **Irish-language courses** for adults, supplemented by cultural activities and singing and dancing classes, are held each summer by NUI Galway at Árus Mháirtín Uí Chadhain (http://nuigalway.ie) in An Cheathrú Rua (Carraroe).

WALKING IN CONNEMARA

Connemara offers a stunning variety of **walking**, including mountains over 700m – though be aware that the nearest rescue team is in Galway. A good **map** and guidebook for serious walkers is *The Mountains of Connemara*, available from local bookshops and tourist offices, with a 1:50,000-scale map derived from aerial photography and fieldwork by Tim Robinson, and an excellent guide to eighteen walks of varying length and difficulty by Joss Lynam. The Ordnance Survey has produced their own maps at 1:50,000.

A good introduction to the Maam Turks, with breathtaking views of the Twelve Bens across Lough Inagh, would be the ascent of **Cnoc na hUilleann** and **Binn Bhriocáin** from the **Inagh Valley** back road north of Recess, on a three- to four-hour circuit described in *The Mountains of Connemara*, which also covers the waymarked **Western Way**, which runs for 50km from Oughterard to Leenane. This varied, low-level trail starts as a pleasant, sometimes boggy, walk beside Lough Corrib, before crossing over from the village of Maam into the dramatic Inagh Valley, which runs between the Bens and the Turks. The walk can be done in two long days, with an overnight near Maam. You can also extend the walk into Co. Mayo. Walking trail map leaflets are available at tourist information offices.

Worthy **short walks** include the ascent of Errisbeg and other routes near Roundstone (see page 359), the sky road from Clifden (see page 360), a circuit of Inishbofin (see page 362), the excellent trails at Connemara National Park (see page 363) and the climb up Tully Hill (see page 364). **Walking tours** are organized from Clifden by Connemara Safari on the sky road (www.walkingconnemara.com), which runs five-day walking and island-hopping trips.

surrounding area to keep you occupied. Its main asset, however, is not immediately obvious from the long main street: behind the trees to the north of town lies the great expanse of **Lough Corrib**, a paradise for angling or for just messing about in boats, studded with hundreds of tree-clad islets (365 of them, one for each day of the year, if you believe the locals). May is the busiest time for fishing, when the mayflies hatch from the lake bed, while the annual agricultural and horticultural show at the end of August also attracts crowds (http://oughterardshow.ie).

Inchagoill island

If taking a boat tour (see page 358), you'll likely stop off at **Inchagoill island**. Little is known of this uninhabited island's history beyond the meaning of its name, "Isle of the Foreigners". It was, however, the site of an early monastery, featuring the Romanesque Saints' Church, which was restored by Sir Benjamin Guinness in the nineteenth century and is most notable for its attractively carved west doorway.

Aughnanure Castle

Signposted 3km from the centre of Oughterard, about 1.5km off the N59 • charge; Heritage Card • http://heritageireland.ie

Just east of Oughterard stands a particularly impressive and well-preserved early sixteenth-century tower house, **Aughnanure Castle**, which rises to six storeys and still retains its outer defensive walls; it occupies what is virtually a rocky island near the banks of Lough Corrib. The strongest bastion of the O'Flahertys, who were masters of Connemara from the thirteenth to the sixteenth century, Aughnanure boasts a frightening array of defensive features, including arrow slits aimed at the main staircase, secret prison chambers and a trap door in the hall above a subterranean river, through which were thrown guests who had outstayed their welcome.

Brigit's Garden

Pollagh, Roscahill; look for signs pointing off the N59, 4km southeast of the turn-off for Aughnanure Castle • charge • http://brigitsgarden.ie

10

The delightful **Brigit's Garden** is named after the saint (see page 128) whose feast day, February 1, and symbol, the snowdrop, mark the start of spring. This beautifully designed ten-acre garden includes an area devoted to the four Celtic seasons, featuring sculptures, standing stones, symbolic plantings and a thatched roundhouse. Beyond this, you'll find a stand of ancient woodland, a herb garden, wild-flower meadows, a small lake, a ring fort and Ireland's largest sundial, with nature discovery trails laid on for adults and kids. There's an excellent **garden café**, a gift shop and various talks and events.

Glengowla Mine
3km west of Oughterard on the N59 • charge • http://glengowlamines.ie

For a fascinating change from all the glorious scenery hereabouts, head underground into the restored **Glengowla Mine**. This silver and lead mine was worked between 1850 and 1865 and reluctantly yielded from the area's tough marble around three hundred tons of the ore galena. Entertaining guided tours (40min) bring to life the hardships of drilling by hand and blasting the rock by candlelight, often in deep pools of water.

ARRIVAL AND INFORMATION

By bus Bus Éireann services from Galway to Clifden stop in Oughterard (8 daily).
Tourist office Oughterard's tourist office is in Camp St café (daily 9am–5.30pm; 091 866066).
Boat tours On Wednesdays and Saturdays from June to

OUGHTERARD AND AROUND

August you can take a day cruise (http://corribcruises.com) across to Cong in County Mayo from the pier 2km north of the main street along Pier Rd. The tour takes in Inchagoill Island and the gardens of Ashford Castle (see page 367) and costs €28.

ACCOMMODATION AND EATING

Camillaun Eighterard, http://camillaun.com. A tastefully decorated, modern guesthouse, with a tennis court, hot tub and snooker table, set in gardens on the banks of the Owenriff River (rowing and motor boats for rent). There's a fantastic buffet or cooked breakfast to tuck into. €€
★ **Currarevagh House** Glann Rd, 6km northwest of town, http://currarevagh.com. This charming traditional country house was built in the 1840s on the lakeshore. It

has boats and ghillies, and there's walking on the wooded 100-acre estate and immaculate gardens with fine views of the lake – best enjoyed, perhaps, from the woodland sauna overlooking the lake itself. All rooms have either a lake or mountain view, while the unpretentious dinners are based on local produce and there's complimentary afternoon tea for residents. Closed mid-Nov to mid-Feb. €€€

Spiddal (An Spidéal)

The R336 coast road arrows west out of Galway through a gently sloping landscape of shrubs, ferns and boulders, offering fine views of the slate-grey Burren across the water but marred by a monotonous ribbon development of white bungalows. Relief comes after 18km with the lofty trees and church of **SPIDDAL** (An Spidéal, "the hospital"), the effective capital of the Gaeltacht, which is known for its traditional-music sessions. The daytime draw here is the **Spiddal Craft Village** (Ceardlann an Spidéil; http://spiddalcrafts.com), a group of studios – with an on-site bistro-café – making and selling pottery, weaving, jewellery, leather goods, sculpture and musical instruments. In open country 5km north of the central crossroads, **Cnoc Suain** ("restful hill"; http://cnocsuain.com) is a "cultural hill-village" of restored thatched and slate-tiled stone cottages that hosts residential programmes in Irish music, language and natural history.

ACCOMMODATION AND EATING

An Crúiscín Lán Main St, http://cruiscin.ie. An upmarket option with fourteen large, bright rooms – singles, twins, doubles and family rooms, including two with sea-view balconies – and a smart evening restaurant that serves

SPIDDAL (AN SPIDÉAL

uncomplicated but enjoyable dishes like chicken with homemade *chasseur*, and vegan cauliflower burger. Closed Jan. €€€
★ **Builín Blasta** 16 An Ceardlan, http://builinblasta

com. Tucked away at the back of the Craft Village is this top-notch café, whose name translates as "The Tasty Loaf". Lunch includes salads, soup or chowder with breads, as well as cakes, pastries and scones, all made in-house. On Fri and Sat evenings, the joint morphs into a cool little wine bar. €

Páirc Saoire an Spidéil, http://spiddalmobilehomes.ie. Campers and campervans should head for this well-equipped site, 1.5km inland from the centre of the village. Facilities include good hot showers, camper's kitchen, laundry and playground. Closed Nov–April. €

Teach an Phiarsaigh

Near Rosmuc, at the end of a small peninsula off the R340 • charge; Heritage Card • http://heritageireland.ie and http://icpconamara.ie

A thatched and whitewashed traditional cottage, **Teach an Phiarsaigh** was the summer residence of the revolutionary and writer, Patrick Pearse (see page 568). Here Pearse ran summer schools for his pupils from St Enda's in Rathfarnham, Dublin, and wrote his famous eulogy for the nationalist Jeremiah O'Donovan Rossa on his death in 1915. Inside are mementos and an exhibition on Pearse, but the cottage is more noteworthy for its atmosphere and setting, with dramatic views of Loch Oirulach and the Twelve Bens range and Maum Turk mountains. The **Connemara Cultural Centre**, with a café, exhibition space and audiovisual displays, is reached via a 400m scenic looped walk from the cottage across a newly constructed bog path with interpretation panels. The centre explains Pearse's historical and cultural legacy and looks at contemporary life in Connemara and how the Irish language is part of everyday life.

Roundstone and around

On the R341 coast road, which eventually loops round into Clifden, **ROUNDSTONE** is a delightful fishing village set amid some of Connemara's finest scenery. The stone harbour looks out on the many islands of Bertraghboy Bay and across to the peaks of the Twelve Bens and the Maam Turks, while behind looms a lone mountain, the 300m-high Errisbeg. There are some beautiful woodland **walks** along the lakeshore and riverbank in the estate of **Ballynahinch Castle** (see page 360), which are described in a leaflet available from the hotel reception. Three kilometres southwest of the village, the beautiful sandy beaches of **Gurteen Bay** and **Dog's Bay** are separated by a narrow, dune-covered isthmus.

The village is well known for its **crafts shops**, including Malachy Kearns' famous *bodhrán* workshop in a former Franciscan monastery in Killeen Park at the south end of the village (http://bodhran.com). Here you can watch the drums being made, test them out in a sound room or have one painted in the Celtic motif of your choice while you wait. Ferron's Supermarket on the main street contains a post office and ATM.

The highlight of the year for many is the Roundstone Hooker Regatta, a **boating festival** held over the third weekend of July. It includes *currach* racing, hooker sailing events, maritime heritage walks and live music gigs.

Erissbeg and the Roundstone bog

From the centre of the village, you can take a very satisfying **walk** to the summit of Errisbeg (approximately 1hr), which offers majestic views in all directions. Take the paved lane beside *O'Dowd's* bar (see page 360) and follow the rough track that it turns into; you'll have to pick your way over often boggy ground and boulders towards the top, which, despite appearances from below, turns out to be a ridge of three summits. On three sides runs a coastline of white-sand beaches, where peninsulas are barely distinguishable from islands; to the north, set against one of the finest prospects of the Bens and the Turks, lies huge, sparse **Roundstone Bog**, one of the finest blanket bogs in the country, covered with a glittering crazy-paving of tiny lakes and crossed by a single narrow road.

10

By bus Bus Éireann runs daily services to Roundstone from Clifden.

Tourist information http://roundstonevillage.ie

ACCOMMODATION AND EATING

★ **Angler's Return** Toombeola, 4km from Roundstone on the main road to Galway, http://anglersreturn.com. A no-children (under 14) policy leads to a deep sense of adult calm in this stylish 1820s sporting lodge set in semi-wild gardens, favoured not just by fisher folk but also cyclists and walkers. Home-made breads, jams and organic muesli adorn the breakfast table. Minimum stay three nights. €€€

Ballynahinch Castle http://ballynahinch-castle.com. Set on its own fishing river and lake towards the N59, this eighteenth-century castle was once the home of Richard Martin – aka Humanity Dick – the animal-rights campaigner and co-founder of the RSPCA in 1824, and later of cricketing maharaja, Ranjitsinhji. It's now a romantic luxury hotel in a gloriously peaceful setting, with an array of sumptuous (and eye-wateringly expensive) rooms, an excellent restaurant decorated with twentieth-century Irish art and a wood-panelled fishermen's bar where food is available; activities include cycling, fly-fishing tutorials, and guided walks. €€€€

Cashel House Hotel http://cashelhouse.ie. About a 20min drive east from Roundstone, this elegant country house is set in beautiful gardens. Each of the thirty rooms and suites (some garden suites) are furnished differently, and the dinner choice includes early bird, à la carte or fixed menu options. Bar meals are served during the day. Closed Jan. €€€

Gurteen Bay Caravan Site http://gurteenbay.ie. West of Roundstone, this idyllic site is right by the beach of the same name and offers self-catering apartments as well as camping pitches. Closed Oct–May. €

★ **O'Dowd's Seafood Bar & Restaurant** Main St, http://odowdsseafoodbar.com. The chowder at this sociable spot is still made daily to the same family recipe that has been in use for generations (it features stock made using brill or turbot to give it a rich kick). Daytime bar food includes a variety of shellfish as well as meat and chicken dishes. Attached to the pub is an evening restaurant, while *O'Dowd's Café* a few doors down offers coffee, salads and pizzas.

Clifden and around

CLIFDEN, the English-speaking capital of Connemara, is a popular, animated service town, enhanced by a spectacular setting: it perches on a steep, grassy hillside, where the lofty grey spires of the Catholic and Anglican churches compete for attention, while on its western side the land plunges abruptly down to the deeply indented harbour. Several stately town houses sprinkle the three major streets – **Main Street**, the continuation of the Galway road culminating in Market Square, with **Bridge Street** and **Market Street** branching off it at either end and meeting to form a rough triangle. By basing yourself here, you'll be able to explore the varied attractions of coast and mountain hereabouts, and sample the lively nightlife.

There's not much to do on a rainy day in the town itself, although you may find some diversion at the **Station House Museum** near the tourist office on the Galway road (April–Oct Mon–Sat 10am–5pm, Nov–March 11am–5pm; charge; 095 21494), which has displays on local history and on the history, breeding and racing of Connemara ponies. These rugged, passive workhorses have their day in mid-August, when they're judged at the **Connemara Pony Show** (http://cpbs.ie). The other highlight of Clifden's calendar is the prestigious and lively **arts festival** (http://clifdenartsfestival.ie) at the end of September.

The sky road and bog road

A fine diversion is to walk or cycle the spectacular **sky road**, signposted from the west side of the town, which loops scenically round the narrow peninsula on the north side of Clifden Bay (13km in total). It ends up by the long, thin inlet of Streamstown Bay, passing a quarry for the streaky, green Connemara marble, before hitting the Westport road just north of Clifden.

Alternatively, you can complete an excellent, scenic bicycle ride from Clifden by turning left off the R341, 4km north of Roundstone, on to the **bog road**, which undulates westward across the stark peatland back to town.

THE BOG ROAD TO DERRIGIMLAGH

A newly-developed 5km signposted **looped walk** across flat blanket bog at **Derrigimlagh** tells the story across seven stop points of the local area's role in two remarkable events in early twentieth-century history. Leave your car about 4km south of Clifden at the signposted parking area on the R341, where the path begins, and you'll come to the site of a telegraph station where the Irish-Italian innovator **Guglielmo Marconi** sent the **first commercial wireless transmission** across the Atlantic in 1907. A series of shelters with photoscope, panoramoscope and historioscope, as well as a parabolic mirror, create the impression of how the site might have looked in Marconi's time. The fascinating link to John Alcock and Arthur Brown, who landed here on the **first transatlantic flight** in June 1919, is also recounted. After circling Clifden twice in celebration they nosedived into the bog, wrecking their plans to continue their triumphal flight to London. Nearby, on the Errislannan peninsula, an aeroplane wing-shaped memorial, stands as a tribute to the two intrepid aviators. Depending on how long you spend at the shelters, the return walk should take approximately one and a quarter hours.

10

About 5km off the R341, southwest of Ballyconneely at Bunowen Pier, you can watch the process of preparing smoked salmon and taste some of the finished product at the **Connemara Smokehouse** (Mon–Fri 9am–1pm & 2–5pm; http://smokehouse.ie).

Dan O'Hara's Homestead and the Connemara Heritage and History Centre

Lettershea, 7km east of Clifden on the N59 • charge; Heritage Island • http://connemaraheritage.com

The area's main set-piece tourist attraction is **Dan O'Hara's Homestead and the Connemara Heritage and History Centre**, which sounds rather kitsch but is quite engaging. Fascinating displays by local archaeologist Michael Gibbons and a short video introduce you to the history of Clifden and Connemara, and to Dan O'Hara himself. A tenant farmer whose house was famous for its ceilis, O'Hara was evicted in 1845 and eventually found his way to New York, where, having little English, he sold matches and inspired the famous eponymous song. Outside, you can view reconstructions of an oratory, a dolmen tomb, a wooden ring fort and a *crannóg*, a thatched dwelling set in a small lake. You can also make your way up the hill – a pleasant fifteen-minute stroll – to Dan O'Hara's refurbished cottage for great views south over the Twelve Bens to Roundstone and Errisbeg, and for demonstrations that might include sheep-shearing, thatching and turf-cutting. There's also a craft shop and daytime tearoom for snacks such as soup and sandwiches.

ARRIVAL AND DEPARTURE   CLIFDEN AND AROUND

By bus Bus Éireann services run from Galway to Clifden, via Oughterard (2 daily; 1hr 30min), as does Citylink (8 daily) – four of these Citylink buses continue onto Letterfrack; the drop-off/pick-up point is outside the library on Market St.

INFORMATION AND GETTING AROUND

Tourist information Market St (mid-March to May & most of Sept Mon–Sat 10am–5pm; June–Aug until 5.45pm; http://connemara.net).

Bike rental Mannion's Bike Hire, Bridge St (daily 10am–6pm; http://clifdenbikes.com) has both standard and e-bikes for hire.

ACCOMMODATION

Ardagh 2km south of town on the Ballyconneely road, http://ardaghhotel.com. This former fishing lodge is a relaxing and comfortable family-run hotel with twenty beautifully-appointed rooms offering splendid views of the bay or the floral gardens, and an excellent restaurant serving four-course dinners, in addition to a lobster menu. Closed Nov–Easter. **€€€**

Ben Lettery Hostel 13km east of Clifden on the N59, http://benlettery.ie. Right at the foot of Ben Lettery, one of the Twelve Bens, with fine views, this is a cosy and welcoming forty-two bed hostel (four-, six- and eight bed dorms plus doubles), geared towards walking and cycling in the mountains; to this end it has drying rooms and bike storage, plus laundry facilities and a large kitchen. Breakfast is also included.. Closed Oct–May. **€**

10

Ben View House Bridge St, http://benviewhouse.com. Very central, flower-bedecked nineteenth-century house, offering friendly and comfortable B&B accommodation. Plenty of local information available from the owners on cultural activities in the area. €€

Buttermilk Lodge 400m out on the Westport road, http://buttermilklodge.com. A well-appointed modern guesthouse set in a large garden, offering one- and two-bed self-catering apartments sleeping two- to four people. €€

Clifden Camping and Caravan Park 2km out of town off the Westport road, http://clifdencamping.com. A quiet and efficiently run site in peaceful surroundings that's handy for the town but also a wonderful place to drink in the ever-changing light of the Twelve Bens. Amenities include games room, laundry and grocery shop. Closed Oct–April. €

★ **The Quay House** http://thequayhouse.com. Down at the harbour and set in an early nineteenth-century harbourmaster's house, which later became a convent, this is an outstanding guesthouse with a sociable, house party atmosphere. Rooms are elegantly decorated with antiques and paintings; most overlook the water, and some have working fireplaces, four-posters or balconies. The two gorgeous sitting rooms are furnished with board games and books, while breakfast is served in the large conservatory. Closed early Nov to mid-March. €€€

Sea Mist House Near Market Square, http://seamisthouse.com. Relaxing and central, this 200-year-old stone cottage in a lush garden offers four stylish en-suite rooms, great breakfasts (freshly grown garden produce and pancakes among the offerings) and plentiful local knowledge. €€

EATING AND DRINKING

Guy's Bar & Restaurant Main St, http://guysbarclifden.com. There's a tremendous range of seafood on the dinner menu here, including tempura prawns, crab salad and calamari, plus Goan chicken curry, and for lunch you can tuck into posh pizza, like the Mountain Goat (Ardsallagh cheese and marinated onions). €€€

Mannion's pub Market St, http://mannionsbarclifden.com. One of the best spots in the area for pub grub, serving big portions of Connemara lamb stew, seafood linguine, and striploin steak. Traditional music sessions take place twice daily in summer at 6.30pm and 8.30pm. €€€

Mitchell's Seafood Restaurant Market St, http://mitchellsrestaurantclifden.com. Clifden's best restaurant, providing well-judged and beautifully presented cuisine, heavily weighted towards fresh fish and seafood, like fillet of monkfish with pickled fennel and paprika mayo. Exceptional fish salad platters too. Cheaper, simpler dishes are available at lunchtime. €€€€

Walsh's Bakery & Coffee Shop Market St, http://walshsbakery.ie. Traditional daytime café serving delicious cakes, a varied menu of sandwiches and hot and cold plates at lunchtime. Closed Mon–Wed. €

Inishbofin

With just two hundred inhabitants, **INISHBOFIN** continues the diversity of the Connemara landscape into the sea, though in a gentler, miniature format. A mere 5km wide, the island – which rises to just 90m at its highest point, **Cnoc Mór** – encompasses cliffs and the rocky outcrops known as **the Stags** on its western side; tranquil, reedy **Lough Boffin**, the haunt of swans, at its centre; and several sandy beaches – the one in the southeast corner provides the best swimming, while beautiful **Trá Ghael**, beneath Cnoc Mór in the west, is also worth visiting, though its currents are too dangerous for a dip. A gift shop opens during the summer months a short way east of the pier, and over a weekend in May – or sometimes early September (check with the tourist office) – there's a lively, three-day **arts festival**. Year round you're assured plenty of traditional music, featuring the island's own renowned ceili band. Note that the only shop (and post office) near the pier is pricey, so bring as much stuff over with you as you can.

The first historical reference to Inishbofin comes from the seventh century: after the Irish and Roman Churches fell out at the Synod of Whitby in 664, St Colman

---

INISHBOFIN ACTIVITIES

Contact Deep Sea Angling (086 832 4123) to arrange **angling trips or boat hire**, while **scuba diving** is available with Islands West (087 222 7098, http://islandswest.ie). For **horseriding** get in touch with Inishbofin Equestrian Centre (daily 9am–6pm; 087 950 1545, http://inishbofinequestriancentre.com).

left Lindisfarne and journeyed here via Iona. Though the monastery he established was destroyed in 1334, you can still see the atmospheric shell of a fourteenth-century **chapel** on the site, to the east of the pier, beyond a small, lily-strewn lake. In the island cemetery surrounding the chapel, two stone crosses and a couple of **holy wells** are said to date from Colman's foundation. The island's other historic site is visible on the right as you enter the excellent natural harbour, a forbidding, mottled-black **castle**, built in the sixteenth century and strengthened by Cromwell, which is accessible at low tide.

ARRIVAL AND DEPARTURE INISHBOFIN

By bus and ferry The passenger-only Inishbofin ferry (http://inishbofinferry.ie; €25 return) crosses the 11km to Inishbofin from Cleggan, 10km northwest of Clifden, with sailings year round (40min; Easter–Aug 3 daily; 2 daily for the rest of the year). Citylink buses run from Galway, via Clifden, to Cleggan (3 daily).

INFORMATION

Tourist information You can get information and maps at the island community centre above the pier (Mon–Fri 9.30am–11pm; http://inishbofin.com.).

Bike rental If there's no sign of Paddy Joe King and his bikes, head to his house 700m east of the pier near the hostel or call 095 45833.

ACCOMMODATION AND EATING

Dolphin Hotel 700m east of the pier, http://dolphinhotel.ie. This small hotel offers eleven large, bright, well-equipped en-suite rooms (including triple and family rooms), some with outdoor terraces. Its restaurant menu includes the likes of rump of roast lamb, mackerel, pollock and shellfish. Closed Nov to mid-March. €€

Inishbofin House Hotel Just east of the pier, http://inishbofinhouse.com. The pick of the accommodation on Inishbofin, this chic, modern hotel offers rooms that mostly have balconies overlooking the harbour. There's also an evening restaurant, plus cheaper bar food. €€

★ **Inishbofin Island Hostel** 700m east of the pier (IHH & IHO), http://inishbofin-hostel.ie. Well-maintained hostel in a converted farmhouse with a conservatory and garden, laundry facilities and camping space, plus pods. Excellent facilities extend to a sitting room, kitchen/dining rooms, laundry and a bike shed; they'll also pick up your luggage at the pier. Closed Nov–March. €

Letterfrack and around

The tiny, nineteenth-century Quaker village of **LETTERFRACK**, around 15km northeast of Clifden, is the unlikely site of the Galway Mayo Institute of Technology, and plays host to two notable, longstanding festivals (http://ceecc.org), both featuring plenty of traditional music: **Bog Week**, celebrating the landscape with walking events at the end of May; and **Sea Week**, with a conference on marine heritage in late October (http://conamaraseaweek.ie). The village is also home to an official Poetry Trail, one of only two in the west of Ireland, with poems written by well-known Irish poets displayed on special plaques in various locations.

Connemara National Park and Visitor Centre

Entrance on the west side of Letterfrack • 9am–5.30pm; grounds open all year round • Free • http://nationalparks.ie/connemara

The **Connemara National Park** covers a thin slice of the northwest sector of the Twelve Bens, stretching east as far as Benbrack, Bencullagh, Muckanaght and Benbaun. It includes an excellent walkway to the top of **Diamond Hill** (445m; about 2hr 30min return), which affords fantastic views of the mountains, bays and islands all around. There are three shorter **nature trails** across the lower slopes, through some natural woodland and over bogland, with free guided walks on Wednesday and Friday mornings in July and August. The park's **visitor centre** contains a fascinating exhibition on the wildlife and geology of Connemara and a café. There's also a children's playground. A trail map is available to download from the website alongside a map of the Poetry Trail.

By bus Letterfrack is served by Bus Éireann services from   Clifden (4 daily).

ACCOMMODATION AND EATING

Cloverfox Seafood Bar By the central junction, 095 41042. This convivial restaurant pretty much does what it says on the tin, and it does it very well; all the standard fishy treats are on the menu plus a few meat options. It also offers en-suite hostel rooms. €€

Letterfrack Lodge North side of central junction (IHH), 095 41222. This partly en-suite hostel in a modern, stone-clad and pine-floored house offers local information, laundry facilities and three kitchens. Lunch and dinner are available in summer. Closed mid-Sept to late May. Dorms €, doubles €€

★ **Rosleague Manor** 1.5km west of village, http://rosleague.com. An elegant, early nineteenth-century hotel with a relaxed country-house atmosphere. Rooms and suites have either sea or woodland views, while guests are welcome to avail themselves of the charming sitting room and extensive gardens and woodlands that stretch down to the sea. The restaurant offers lamb, steak and fresh seafood. Half-board and other packages are available. Closed Nov to mid-March. €€€

Kylemore Abbey

5km east of Letterfrack on the N59 • Easter–Oct 9am–6pm; Nov–March 10am–4.30pm; 20min history talk daily at 11.30am, 1pm and 3pm; 30min garden tour Tues 2.30pm June–August; shuttle bus from the abbey to the walled garden every 15min • charge; Heritage Island • http://kylemoreabbey.com

Grey, castellated **Kylemore Abbey** sits behind a glassy lake against the rugged green backdrop of Dúchruach hill. Built with Manchester cotton money in the 1860s, it's now a small Benedictine convent, but you can still visit three of the restored reception rooms and the main hall, and learn about the place's history from the display boards, historic costumes and audiovisual presentations. There's an extensive crafts shop and restaurant too, and **fishing** on the lake and Kylemore River can be arranged. Also on the lakeshore is a beautiful neo-Gothic **church**, which incorporates elements copied from the great English cathedrals of the late twelfth and early thirteenth centuries.

From the abbey, you can walk (20min) or catch a shuttle bus to the restored Victorian **walled garden**. Laid out in the 1860s with no fewer than 21 glasshouses, the huge garden deteriorated after the estate was sold in 1903, but an ambitious project has returned it more or less to its former state, using only original Victorian plant specimens. Beyond the beautifully tended ornamental flower garden lie stream and fern walks and beds of herbs and vegetables, with everything from dill to parsnips (all labelled), divided by a long herbaceous border. The head gardener's house and his workers' far more basic bothy have been refurbished, but the most striking remnants are the very fine, original cabbage trees.

Renvyle Peninsula

North of Letterfrack, it's well worth exploring the minor roads that crisscross the **Renvyle Peninsula**, eventually looping around by the gentle waters of Lough Fee to meet the N59 near Killary Harbour. On the south side of the peninsula, 3km from Letterfrack overlooking Ballynakill Harbour, you'll come to the **Ocean's Alive Visitor Centre** (March–Nov daily 10am–6pm; charge; http://oceanandalivevisitorcentre.ie), which features exhibits of sea life and local maritime history, lots of children's activities and hour-long wildlife cruises (charge) in a glass-bottomed boat four times a day until the end of October (if there are enough takers), to view deserted islands and, hopefully, seals and dolphins. From the museum quay, a walk up **Tully Hill** is highly recommended (about 3hr return), whose 355m summit affords a matchless panorama, with the towering mountains of Connemara arrayed to the east.

In summer, the **Renvyle Teach Ceoil** centre (095 41047), whose name means "music cottage", hosts a weekly show of Irish music, song, dance and storytelling (Tues

8.30–11pm). The peninsula's main settlements are the adjacent hamlets of **Tully Cross** and **Tully**, 4km north of Letterfrack.

ACCOMMODATION AND EATING   RENVYLE PENINSULA

Connemara Campsite 5km east of Tullycross, http://connemaracamping.com. This popular campsite is superbly situated right next to Lettergesh Beach, a concave stretch of fine sand with views of the offshore islands. Excellent facilities include camper's kitchen, laundry and indoor games room, and in summer, a café. €̄

Paddy Coyne's Tullycross, http://paddycoynespub.com. A 200-year-old pub noted for its food and traditional music; the menus showcase fresh mussels, wild salmon and grilled hake, but the signature dish is Renvyle scallops with black pudding. A good time guaranteed. €̄€̄

Renvyle Beach Caravan and Camping 2km west of Tully Cross towards end of peninsula, http://renvylebeach caravanpark.com. Hugely popular campsite, thanks in part to its location next to a fine beach, although it's modern facilities are also a welcome attraction. Closed Oct–March. €̄

Renvyle House Renvyle, http://renvyle.com. In a dreamy location, seemingly on the edge of the world, this relaxing luxury hotel occupies the former home of the surgeon, writer and wit Oliver St John Gogarty (see page 92). It is set amid pretty gardens, woodland and a lake, and comes with a long menu of facilities and activities such as croquet, tennis, lawn bowls, boating, and a heated outdoor swimming pool. The perfect place to de-stress, and it's not as extortionate as you'd think. €̄€̄€̄

ACTIVITIES

Diving Scuba Dive West in Glassillaun (http://scubadivewest.com) is a PADI 5-star resort offering courses and diving off the coast and nearby islands.

Killary Harbour

Killary Harbour is one of Ireland's very few fjords, a truly dramatic oddity with Connacht's highest mountain, Mweelrea (817m), plunging sheer into the dark water on its north bank. This glacial gouge runs for 16km between the uplands of Galway and Mayo, and with a typical depth of 15m is perfect for salmon and mussel farms, and for enjoying a relaxing boat cruise or indulging in some adventure sports. The only waterside settlement, **Leenane** (http://leenanevillage.com), enjoys a snug, scenic location near the head of the fjord.

Sheep and Wool Centre

Leenane • charge • http://sheepandwoolcentre.com

The **Sheep and Wool Centre** may not sound too promising, but makes for a fascinating visit. Accompanied by an enthusiastic guide, you'll get to see demonstrations of spinning and weaving; the centre also has a good, inexpensive café-restaurant.

ARRIVAL AND DEPARTURE   KILLARY HARBOUR

By bus A Bus Éireann service (Mon–Sat 1–2 daily) runs from Clifden.

TOURS AND ACTIVITIES

Boat tours Killary Fjord Boat Tours (http://killaryfjord.ie), based at Nancy's Point, 2km west of Leenane, offers 1hr 30min fjord cruises (March–Oct daily 10.30am, 12.30pm & 2.30pm & 4pm June–Aug; €26).

Activities Killary Adventure Centre (http://killaryadventure.com) about 5km west of Leenane on the N59, offers all manner of land and sea-based activities, from gorge walking and kayaking to high ropes and archery.

ACCOMMODATION AND EATING

Connemara Hostel Leenane (IHO), http://sleepzone.ie. A superb variety of en-suite hostel accommodation, including four- to six-bed rooms, twins and doubles, plus camping space for a small number of tents (walk-ins only). Daily bus service in summer from Westport to Galway. It's quite isolated and there's only a vending machine here so bring food supplies. €̄

Leenane Hotel Leenane, http://leenanehotel.com. A traditional coaching inn with a delightful garden and fountain right on the water's edge – an ideal location from which to launch yourself into a hike over the Maumturk Mountains. The majority of the sixty-odd rooms have watery views, with the remainder facing towards the mountains. €€

Portfinn Lodge Leenane, http://portfinn.com. In a magical location offering stunning views of the fjord and the mountains, this large modern bungalow offers bright, attractive en-suite rooms and an evening restaurant. €€

County Mayo

The wonderful mountain scenery found in Connemara marches on into the south of **County Mayo** (Maigh Eo), in the substantial shape of Mweelrea, the Sheefry Hills and the Partry Mountains. These ranges culminate in the conical peak of Ireland's holy mountain, **Croagh Patrick**, beyond which change is announced by the trough of **Clew Bay**, the extension of a geological fault that runs all the way to the Scottish Highlands. Unless you're beetling direct to Westport on the N59, two possible routes out of Connemara into south Mayo present themselves. You can detour east to the abbey town of **Cong**, right on the county border and sharing many similarities with Oughterard, to which it is linked by boat trips across Lough Corrib. Or you can forge through the heart of the mountains from Leenane to **Louisburgh**, which gives access to the islands of **Inishturk** and **Clare** at the mouth of Clew Bay. Either way, you're almost certain to end up in **Westport**, a refined, lively Georgian base, terminus of the railway line from Dublin and hub for local buses. The county's other main tourist centre is **Achill** at the northwest corner of Clew Bay, Ireland's largest island and a popular resort. Beyond this, there's kilometre after kilometre of wild, dramatic landscape, all now part of the **Wild Atlantic Way** driving route. Attractions include the remains of a Neolithic farm system at **Céide Fields**, which alone justify a journey to the north coast; the impressive **National Museum of Country Life** at Castlebar, and the **Great Western Greenway**, a gorgeous off-road walking and cycle track along a former railway line that stretches from Achill Island to Westport. Inland, a thirty-minute drive from here is the Wild Nephin National Park with many scenic walking trails. From the Brogan Caroll Bothy at the far edge of the park, you can do some of the best stargazing in the **Mayo Dark Sky Park** (www.mayodarkskypark.ie), alongside two other locations at Claggan Mountain near Mulranny, and Ballycroy Visitor Centre in Ballycroy.

ARRIVAL AND GETTING AROUND
COUNTY MAYO

By plane Some 40km east of Castlebar and 8km south of Charlestown, Ireland West Airport (http://irelandwestairport.com) provides a useful, often cheap, way into the county. Commonly known as Knock Airport, it's is served by the Bus Éireann Galway–Derry express service (#64) and a local service to Westport (see page 371). Car rental is available from several companies, and the useful Visitor Discovery Centre can furnish you with maps and info.

Cong

The pretty village of **CONG** sits right on the county border, between the green plains of south Mayo and Galway's Connemara Mountains, on the neck of land separating loughs Corrib and Mask. Its main claim to fame these days is that the film *The Quiet Man*, a famed if sentimental emigrants' portrayal of Ireland that starred John Wayne and Maureen O'Hara (who was herself born in Dublin), was filmed here in 1951.

Quiet Man Museum
April–Sept daily 10am–4pm • charge • http://quietmanmanmuseum.com

If you're happy to get into the kitschiness of it all, head for the **Quiet Man Museum** just around the corner from the tourist office, a painstaking replica of the cottage built for the making of the film; the only "real" thing in it is a horse's harness used in the film. Die-hards can follow in the footsteps of the protagonists on hour-long walking tours (noon) through the village, which take in some of the film's locations, including Pat Cohan's Bar and the Reverend Playfair's House.

Cong Abbey and the Cross of Cong

The village does boast a site of genuine historical interest, **Cong Abbey**, which was originally founded in the seventh century and rebuilt in the twelfth and thirteenth centuries by Turlough, Rory and Cathal O'Connor, kings of Connacht and the last high kings of Ireland. The ruined Augustinian abbey's sculpture-work suggests links with western France, particularly the very fine geometrical and foliate carvings on the doorways to the chapterhouse from the cloister. Inside, the elaborate **Cross of Cong**, which was created for Turlough O'Connor in 1123, reflects the place's former wealth.

At one time the abbey housed a population of three thousand, and the logistics of feeding such a crowd are hinted at in the **fishing house** over the River Cong, whence a line ran to a bell in the refectory to let cook know when fish had been caught. From the **bridge** over the river by the abbey, you can stroll through the woods to Lough Corrib, passing through *Ashford Castle Hotel's* grounds (see page 367), though in summer be aware that it charges €5 for the privilege.

10

ARRIVAL AND INFORMATION   CONG

By bus Bus Éireann run a Galway–Ballina service (Mon–Fri 2 daily) that stops at Cong each weekday, and a summer service via Lennana to Clifden.

Tourist information In the Old Courthouse on Abbey St (March–Oct Mon–Thurs & Sun daily 9.15am–5.15pm, closes 1–1.45pm for lunch; http://mayo.ie/visit), this friendly outlet has plenty of detailed literature about the area's sights.

Boat tours Corrib Cruises (http://corribcruises.com) operates a number of boat trips around and across Lough Corrib. From Lisloughrey pier (near the hostel) there's a one-hour history cruise (daily 11.15am; €20), and a two-hour island cruise (daily 3pm; €30).

ACCOMMODATION

Ashford Castle Hotel http://ashfordcastle.com. Standing at the point where the River Cong runs into Lough Corrib, this lavish – and eye-wateringly expensive – hotel was built by Sir Arthur Guinness in the nineteenth century. No stone has been left unturned in the pursuit of ultimate luxury, manifest in opulently furnished bedrooms and suites with custom-made carpets and chandeliers, and dining of the highest order. Its grounds are far larger than the adjoining village – expect fine views and a long list of amenities that includes a health spa, horseriding and falconry. €€€€

Lakeland House 2km from the centre of the village off the Headford road in Lisloughry (Án Oige, IHH & IHO), http:// lakelandhouse.net. This well-run, comfortable hostel offers a good choice of small dorms and private rooms, some ensuite, alongside a self-catering kitchen, sitting room and laundry. dorms €, doubles €€

★ **Michaeleen's Manor** http://michaeleensmanor.com. A smart, en-suite, *Quiet Man*-themed B&B (named after the film's drunken matchmaker), with each room (which includes a family one) bearing the name of a character in the film plus loads of memorabilia everywhere else. The owner, a *Quiet Man* tour guide, will happily regale you with stories over breakfast too. €€

EATING

★ **Cullen's at the Cottage** http://ashfordcastle.com. Housed in a traditional thatched cottage with outdoor seating in the grounds of *Ashford Castle Hotel*, this seasonal bistro (April–Oct) serves stunning plates, like *dukkah* crusted Irish trout with clams and asparagus, and saffron *pappardelle* with clams and lemon and chilli cream; there are also dedicated vegetarian and vegan menus. €€€€

Danagher's Abbey St, http://danaghershotel.com. In the smart hotel of the same name, reasonably priced bar meals, such as the ever-popular bacon and cabbage or Irish stew, plus salads and sandwiches. Expect plenty of music too. €€

Hungry Monk Café Abbey St, 094 954 5842. A smart little café near the tourist office, which rustles up wholesome meals, snacks, salads and sandwiches, as well as great coffee. €

Delphi

The obvious road north from Connemara into Mayo is the N59 from Leenane to Westport, but the seemingly impenetrable mountains on the north side of Killary Harbour conceal a far more scenic route. Winding between the Mweelrea massif and the Sheefry Hills, the R335 brings you first to the noted fishing lake at **DELPHI**, so named by the second Marquis of Sligo in the early nineteenth century: after swimming the Hellespont with Byron, the Marquis arrived at Delphi in the mountains of central Greece, where he was overcome with homesickness as it reminded him so much of his fishery back here in Mayo.

The Famine Memorial

Beyond Delphi, the road skirts the black water of Doo Lough, past an interesting **memorial**. In March 1849, hundreds of men, women and children marched the 16km from the small crossroads town of Louisburgh through this bleak, exposed valley to Delphi Lodge, where the Famine Commissioners were staying. When they arrived, the commissioners were eating a hearty lunch and would not be disturbed, then refused any help, leaving the starving people to struggle back through the snow to Louisburgh, a journey on which many of them died. Every year towards the end of May, a Famine Walk commemorates the event, as well as more recent famines.

ACCOMMODATION	DELPHI
Delphi Resort http://delphiadventureresort.com. A spa and adventure resort running activities and courses in surfing, canoeing, mountaineering, combat archery and much more, for both adults and children. You can	choose from a variety of rooms and suites (many catering to families) – all with stunning views – and an equally enticing number of dining options. €€

Louisburgh and around

With a range of cafés and accommodation choices, little **LOUISBURGH** makes an excellent base for exploring the area. The **Granuaile Centre** in the library (June–Sept Mon–Fri 10am–5pm; rest of the year Mon–Fri 11am–4pm; 098 66341; charge) focuses on seafaring in Ireland in the sixteenth century, in particular **Grace O'Malley** (Gráinne Ní Mháille, often corrupted to Granuaile; c. 1530–1603), the formidable sea captain and pirate queen of Clare Island, who ruled the sea from Galway Bay to Donegal Bay. Over the bank holiday weekend at the start of May, Louisburgh hosts a lively **festival** of traditional music, Féile Chois Cuain (http://feilechoiscuain.com), featuring concerts, classes and plenty of impromptu sessions.

The sparsely inhabited coastline southwest of Louisburgh is lined with sandy **beaches**, notably **White Strand**, a long, west-facing stretch around the mouth of a stream about 15km away, and **Silver Strand**, a great desert of a beach at the mouth of Clew Bay, a couple of kilometres on from the end of the road to the north of the town, that is flanked by rocks and low dunes in the shadow of bulky Mweelrea. About 4km west of town at Carrownisky Strand, Surf Mayo (http://surfmayo.com) offers **surfing** instruction and equipment hire all year round.

ARRIVAL AND DEPARTURE	LOUISBURGH AND AROUND
By bus Bus Éireann runs services to Louisburgh from	Westport (Mon–Sat 6 daily, Sun 3; 30 min).

Clare Island

Measuring just 8km by 5km, **Clare Island** features two hills – Knockmore (462m) and its little brother Knocknaveen (223m) to the east – behind which the mighty sea cliffs along the northwest shore are home to important breeding colonies of **seabirds**, notably fulmars. Other rare birds include peregrines, choughs and barnacle geese, while petalwort, a species of liverwort, figures among the notable plants. The harbour, which shelters a Blue Flag **beach** with fine views of the mainland mountains, is guarded by a well-preserved sixteenth-century **tower house** ruin, which was the stronghold of Grace O'Malley (see page 368). The main island **festivity** is a currach and yawl regatta in July.

> ## CLARE ISLAND ACTIVITIES
>
> A leaflet available on the boats details five **walks** on the island, including a complete circuit which takes about six hours, while **scuba diving** is available May to October with Islands West (http://islandswest.ie), and a variety of activities, including snorkelling, orienteering, rock-climbing and abseiling, is offered by **Clare Island Adventures** (http://clareislandadventures.ie). Ballytoughey Loom & Craft Shop (Mon–Sat 11am–5pm, Sun noon–4pm; http://clareislandhandweaver.com) offers courses in **weaving** and **spinning** (May–Sept) and has wool, linen and silk for sale.

The abbey

In the middle of the island's south shore, a mid-thirteenth-century Cistercian **abbey** (ask for the key at the nearby O'Malley's foodstore and post office) bears an ornate Gothic tomb in which Grace O'Malley – or more likely a relative of hers – is said to be buried. More notable from an artistic point of view are the **frescoes** in the chancel, among the finest extant medieval paintings in Ireland.

ARRIVAL AND DEPARTURE   CLARE ISLAND

By boat Ferries run from Roonagh Quay at Clew Bay, 6km west of Louisburgh (May–Sept 5 boats a day, July & Aug 6, rest of year 3–4; €17 return). Contact O'Malley's (http://omalleyferries.com) or Clare Island Ferry (http://clareislandferry.com), which operates up to six a day in summer, three or four in the shoulder seasons, and two in the winter.

GETTING AROUND AND INFORMATION

By bike and taxi You can rent bikes or hire a minibus taxi from the pier (098 25640).

Tourist information In the absence of a tourist office, try http://clareisland.info.

ACCOMMODATION

Macalla Farm & Yoga Retreat Centre Ballytoughey, in the north of the island, http://macallafarm.ie. This centre offers courses in yoga, meditation, mindfulness, natural horsemanship and vegetarian cooking. Residential courses and occasional self-catering are also available. Accommodation is in refurbished traditional cottages which use natural materials such as wood, hemp and terracotta. €€
Seabreeze Capnagower, above the harbour, 098 26746. This pleasant guesthouse, with both en-suite and standard accommodation, is an ideal base from which to roam around the island. Evening meals are available if requested in advance. €€

Inishturk

To the south of Clare Island lies the even smaller and less developed island of **Inishturk**, a tranquil, 200m-high lump of rock and grass that survives on farming and lobster fishing. From the tiny harbour, the island's paved road branches north and south: to the north, there's a particularly fine **walk**, veering west off the road around a small lake, before climbing to a ruined watchtower in around 45 minutes. The south road rises to the **community centre** after about fifteen minutes, opposite which a narrow gate points down through the fields to the island's finest sandy **beach**, a sheltered strand with clear blue water and views of the mainland.

ARRIVAL AND INFORMATION   INISHTURK

By boat The Inishturk passenger ferry (http://inishturkpassengerferry.ie) runs boats over from Roonagh Quay (2 daily, July & Aug 3; 50min; €10 return) though may be affected by weather.
Tourist information http://inishturkisland.com.

ACCOMMODATION

Tránaun Beach House 098 45641. A 5min walk up the south road at the post office, with en-suite rooms, pick-ups from the harbour and day-trips to other islands organized by the owners. You get complimentary tea and fresh scones on arrival, and lovely grilled mackerel at breakfast. The community centre next door doubles as the island pub in the evenings, with regular music sessions and ceilis, and serves evening meals such as fresh pollock and crab claws. €€

Croagh Patrick

Rising to 764m to the east of Louisburgh, the cone of **Croagh** (pronounced "croak") **Patrick** dominates Clew Bay and the Westport area. It was the pagan home of the mother goddess, now converted into the holiest mountain in Christian Ireland, and on a fine day offers an awesome panorama, stretching from the Twelve Bens in the south to Slieve League in the north. During his long missionary tour of the island, **St Patrick** is supposed to have passed the forty days of Lent in 441 alone on the mountain, finding time to hurl all of Ireland's snakes to their deaths over the precipice of Lugnanarrib just to the south of the summit. This association with the saint has made Croagh Patrick the focus of major **pilgrimages**, which take place three times a year, on March 17 (St Patrick's Day), August 15 (Assumption Day) and – the main event – on the last Sunday in July, Reek Day (which coincides with the pagan harvest festival of Lughnasa). On this day, tens of thousands of pilgrims still make the climb to attend Mass on the summit, some fasting and barefoot.

The starting point for the ascent of Croagh Patrick is the currently defunct **visitor centre** on the R335 on the north side of the peak, about halfway between Westport and Louisburgh. The **climb** itself, taking on average three and a half hours return, is easy to follow, though steep in places – you'll need good walking shoes and a stick, available from the visitor centre. At the summit you'll find a small **chapel** that took twelve men six months to construct in 1905.

The Famine Monument

In a small park opposite the visitor centre stands the national **monument** to *an nGórta Mór* (the Great Famine), commissioned in 1997 for the 150th anniversary. The bronze sculpture of a coffin ship, with skeletons floating around its masts and prow, looks more eerie and shocking now that it's been weathered green by the rain.

Murrisk Abbey

On the shoreline behind the Famine Monument, well-preserved **Murrisk Abbey**, which features some unusual battlements on the south wall of the church, was established by the O'Malley family in 1457. An Augustinian foundation dedicated to St Patrick, in former times it housed famous relics such as the Shrine of St Patrick's Tooth and his Black Bell, both now in Dublin's National Museum. From the abbey there are fine views of the islands of **Clew Bay**, which are actually half-submerged drumlins (see page 606); there are said to be enough of them for a year and a day – 366.

ARRIVAL AND DEPARTURE
CROAGH PATRICK

By bus If you're relying on public transport for a day-trip to Croagh Patrick, the best day to attempt the climb is Thurs (the main shopping day in Westport), with three or four buses in each direction between the town and Louisburgh; Tues and Sat are also possible.

ACCOMMODATION AND EATING

Croagh Patrick Hostel Murrisk, 098 64756. In a stunning location right beside Croagh Patrick, this sparklingly bright hostel is an ideal base, not only for climbing the mountain, but also exploring the Wild Atlantic Way or cycling the Greenway. As well as a double room, it has a selection of dorms (4–12 beds), all en-suite. Fully equipped with bike rack, drying room and a laundry service (wash, dry and fold). They also offer self-catering accommodation in stylish cottages. Continental breakfasts included. €

The Tavern Bar & Restaurant Murrisk, http://tavernmurrisk.com. With Clew Bay on its doorstep it's no surprise local lobster (served with sea lettuce) and Achill sea trout are menu staples. You can choose from pub grub or dine in the evening restaurant where prices are moderately higher. There's also a beer garden and outdoor tables. Closed Mon & Tues.

Westport

Set on the shores of Clew Bay, **WESTPORT** is an agreeable, easy-going town that matches its location with some fine architecture. Its main visitor attraction is **Westport House**, a graceful Georgian mansion now surrounded by a country park of rides and amusements, which separates the town centre from Westport Harbour. The centre itself was laid out in classical style in 1780 for the Browne family of Westport House by James Wyatt, who built a striking octagonal square and canalized the Carrowbeg River,

10

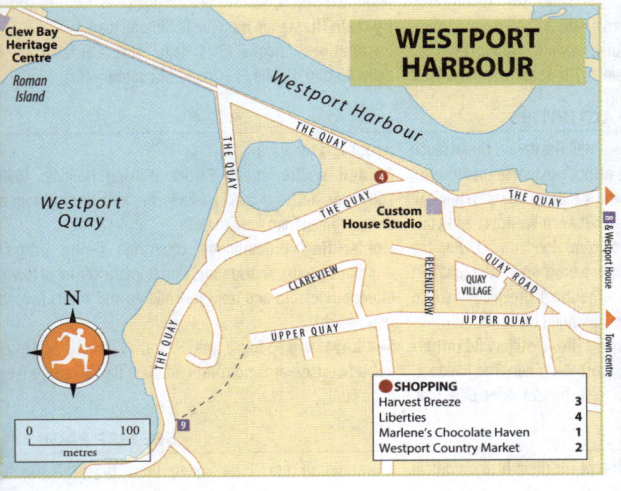

■ ACCOMMODATION	
Ardmore Country House Hotel	9
Carrabaun House B&B	6
Castlecourt Hotel	2
Mariner Hotel	7
Mulranny Park Hotel	1
Old Mill Hostel	4
Westport Town Campsite	8
Westport Plaza Hotel	3
Wyatt Hotel	5

● EATING	
An Port Mór	4
Il Vulcano	7
McCormack's	3
Sage	6
Sol Rio	2
The West Bar	1
Willow Café	5

● SHOPPING	
Harvest Breeze	3
Liberties	4
Marlene's Chocolate Haven	1
Westport Country Market	2

■ DRINKING & NIGHTLIFE	
Matt Molloy's	1
McGing's	3
Walsh's	2

flanking it with the tree-lined Mall. More recently, the town has developed an artsy, cosmopolitan feel, attracting many visitors and residents from other parts of Ireland and Europe. During the summer, the place is abuzz, especially for the prestigious six-day **Arts Festival** in late October (http://westival.ie). Another big attraction is the **Great Western Greenway** (http://greenway.ie), a lovely 42km cycling and walking route on traffic-free roads along a former railway track running from Westport to Achill Island.

Westport House

Entered from Westport Harbour • **House** tours hourly • charge • **Gardens** charge; Heritage Island • http://westporthouse.ie

Not one for the historical purists, **Westport House** has wholeheartedly embraced the concept of a former stately home as a modern pleasure ground. On the estate is a host of **attractions and rides**, such as a miniature railway, a log flume ride and swan pedaloes – and its new owners plan to develop these further. Meanwhile, the **gardens** are still well worth a stroll, and the creeper-clad Georgian **house** overlooking the lake is beautiful. It was built in 1730 by Richard Castle, with alterations later in the century by James Wyatt, and was owned until 2017 by the Browne family, descendants of the pirate queen, Grace O'Malley. Inside, highlights include the hall, with its fine barrel ceiling and ornate marble mantelpiece designed by Castle, the cantilevered marble staircase, executed by Italian craftsmen brought over specially for the purpose, and a delicate portrait by Sir Joshua Reynolds of Denis Browne, a member of Grattan's Parliament, in the Long Gallery. The large dining room is one of the finest examples of Wyatt's work, sporting boldly carved mahogany doors and relief medallions in Wedgwood style on playful classical themes. Upstairs look out for the playwright J.M. Synge's violin in one of the corridors.

Clew Bay Heritage Centre

Charge • http://westportheritage.com • Walking tours July–Sept Wed 11am (free)

Ten minutes' walk west around the harbour, **Clew Bay Heritage Centre** traces the history of Westport and the Clew Bay area through photographs, documents and other artefacts; it has a genealogical service and runs guided **walking tours** of the town, starting from the clock tower at the top of Bridge Street.

ARRIVAL AND DEPARTURE   WESTPORT

By bus Buses stop on Mill St.
Destinations Achill Island (1 daily; 1hr 10min–2hr); Athlone (3–4 daily; 2hr 50min); Ballina (2–5 daily; 55min–1hr 25min); Castlebar (hourly; 20min); Dublin (3 daily; 4–5hr 40min); Galway (5 daily; 1hr 35min); Ireland West

Airport (Mon–Sat 6 daily, Sun 4; 1hr 15min); Louisburgh (Mon–Sat 6 daily, Sun 3; 35min); Sligo (2–3 daily; 2–3hr).
By train The station is on the Ballinrobe road.
Destinations Athlone (3–4 daily; 2hr); Castlebar (3–4 daily; 15min); Dublin (3–4 daily; 3hr 35min–4hr).

INFORMATION AND ACTIVITIES

Tourist office Inside the Town Hall Theatre on The Octagon (Mon–Sat 9.30am–5pm; http://westporttourism.com). Dispenses maps of the town and leaflets on the Clew Bay Trail linking 21 archaeological sites between Westport and Clare Island (http://clewbaytrailride.com), looped walks and the Great Western Greenway. Ask for a brochure on the Gourmet Greenway (http://greenway.ie/gourmet-greenway), which details local artisan food suppliers along the route.
Bike rental Both Clew Bay Bike Hire, Distillery Rd (http://clewbaybikehire.ie) and Westport Bike Shop, The Paddock, Newport Rd (http://westportbikeshop.ie) offer bike hire,

repairs and servicing.
Guided walks Croagh Patrick Walking Holidays (098 26090) organizes guided walks in the area lasting from a day to a week from April to Oct.
Horseriding Drummindoo Equestrian Centre (http://drumindoo.com), Knockranny, 1km from the centre of town, offer both lessons and treks for children and adults (closed Oct–March).
Sea-kayaking Saoirse na Mara, Caraholly (http://irelandwestseakayaking.com) and Clew Bay Bike Hire (see page 606)

ACCOMMODATION   SEE MAP PAGE 371

Ardmore Country House Hotel The Quay, http://ardmore

countryhouse.com. Overlooking Clew Bay, this small,

fashionable hotel has thirteen rooms decorated and equipped in stunning style (including beautifully crafted wooden sleigh beds), and a superb breakfast menu that includes eggs Benedict and Achill kippers. Closed Nov to mid-March. €€€

Carrabaun House B&B On the road to Leenane, http://carrabaunhouse.ie. Highly recommended B&B, with a wide range of breakfast options and fine views, in a spacious, en-suite, period-style modern house with tastefully decorated rooms, either with a sea or garden aspect. €€

Castlecourt Hotel Castlebar St, http://castlecourthotel.ie. Together with the adjacent, co-owned *Westport Plaza*, this family-orientated hotel offers a swimming pool, gym, a wide choice of restaurants, a kids' club in school holidays, and all manner of themed breaks, half-board offers and other packages. €€€

★ **Mariner Hotel** Mill St, http://themariner.ie. A conveniently located hotel with an informal and friendly atmosphere just a few minutes' walk to the town centre. Slicked up rooms range from classic and premium king doubles to family rooms. Traditional rooms range from superior suites to doubles with queen-size beds. There's no restaurant here, but light bites are available in the *Front Room Café*. €€

Mulranny Park Hotel Mulranny, http://mulrannyparkhotel.ie. In a stunning location looking out over Clew Bay, this contemporary hotel, with a hot tub and pool, is ideally sited to explore the area, particularly as the Greenway trail runs behind it. Rooms are stylish and comfy; if you want extra space, opt for the seaview apartments but for a genuine touch of nostalgia you can stay in the John Lennon suite where the singer stayed with Yoko Ono in 1968 – albeit heavily refurbished since. €€€

Old Mill Hostel Barrack Yard, James St (IHH & IHO), http://oldmillhostel.com. Accessed through an archway, this former mill and brewery is now a comfortable hostel, with nine rooms ranging from four- to twelve beds (no singles or doubles), many still exhibiting the building's original wooden beams. There's a kitchen for use and a light breakfast is included in the price. Closed Nov–Jan. €

Westport Town Campsite http://westporthouse.ie. Campers should head for this park in the delightful grounds of Westport House estate – a perfect location from which to explore the town and countryside. Facilities include a large football field, recreation room and laundry, and of course you're right next to all the amenities of the house itself. Closed mid-Sept to late March. €

Westport Plaza Hotel Castlebar St, http://westportplazahotel.ie. Welcoming, elegant, chic and contemporary hotel, offering spacious and well-equipped rooms with kingsize beds, Italian marble bathrooms and hot tubs. Shares facilities with *Castlecourt Hotel*. €€€

Wyatt Hotel The Octagon, http://wyatthotel.com. Congenial hotel decorated in bare wood and bold colours, in an unbeatable central location. Plenty of dining options too, including *JW's Brasserie* and *Cobbler's Bar*. €€€

EATING

SEE MAP PAGE 371

An Port Mór Brewery Place, Bridge St, http://anportmor.com. Broad mix of modern Irish cuisine, especially fish and shellfish, artfully cooked and tastefully presented; creative set menu rate the likes of striploin steak with apple treacle and Armagh butter. €€€€

Il Vulcano High St, http://ilvulcano.ie. Bustling Italian restaurant with an open kitchen, just up from the clock tower, which provides pasta, risotto, pizza, and a fair number of meat and seafood main courses like oven baked fillet of lemon sole with calamari and courgettes. €€€

McCormack's Bridge St, 098 25619. Brightly painted, inviting café and art gallery above a butcher's, which serves coffee, salads, home-made soup and fine sandwiches. €

Sage High St, http://sagewestport.ie. Italian-influenced restaurant, serving delicious pasta dishes and a wide range of smartly-prepared meat and fish specials (seared scallops with cauliflower miso, Mayo lamb rump with smoked aubergine caviar) plus plenty of vegetarian options. Expect to pay around €32 for the early bird (5.30–6.15pm) two-course option. €€€

Sol Rio Bridge St, http://solrio.ie. Colourful and informal, if somewhat pricey, upstairs restaurant, with a Portuguese influence, that efficiently covers all the bases: salads, pasta, pizza and more expensive fish and meat dishes – with particularly good local mussels and oysters – augmented by posh sandwiches and wraps at lunchtime. €€€

The West Bar Bridge St, 098 56730. A gastropub that is noted for its chowder, platters of fish, cold meat and cheese, as well as surf 'n' turf, pasta, pork belly, burgers and steaks. Good range of cocktails too. €€€

★ **Willow Café** High St, http://thewillowcafe.weebly.com. An elegant tea room with outdoor tables beside the clock tower, strategically sited to view the bustling town centre. They offer an exquisite selection of organic and herbal leaf teas as well as Chinese flowering teas, home-made cupcakes, scones and gluten-free food at lunch time. €

DRINKING AND NIGHTLIFE

SEE MAP PAGE 371

★ **Matt Molloy's** Bridge St, http://mattmolloy.com. The town's most famous pub, owned by the eponymous Chieftains' flute player, is an affable place that fills up for its nightly traditional music sessions. A wide selection of craft beers is available.

McGing's High St, 098 29742. Congenial bar that boasts the cheapest (and many claim best) craft beer in Ireland: Paddy's Pilgrims Porter (3P for short), a traditional porter with deep roasted malty flavours made by the West Mayo microbrewery at Islandeady. The bright blue-and-yellow

10

exterior means you'll have no trouble spotting it.

Walsh's James St, 098 28760. Also known as *Blouser's*, this is a popular spot with a 30-something crowd, who come for the weekend DJ nights, and the live music gigs during the week.

SHOPPING

SEE MAP PAGE 371

Harvest Breeze Bridge St, http://harvestbreezewestport. ie. A celebration of lavender products and a sensory experience as you browse the shelves and tables. Closed Sun.

Liberties The Quay, http://liberties.ie. Large selection of fashion brands, accessories, gifts, art, jewellery, furnishings and homeware.

Marlene's Chocolate Haven Limecourt James St, http:// marleneschochaven.com. A mouthwatering selection of home-made chocolates (including some sugarless ones), ranging from truffles and nut pralines to luscious ganaches.

Westport Country Market James St car park, http:// mayofood.ie/markets/westport-market. Thursday market selling an appetizing array of local farm produce and home baking sold from stalls that draw crowds of both locals and visitors.

Castlebar and around

CASTLEBAR, the county town of Mayo, has a lot less going for it than Westport, just 18km away to the west. It's a busy workaday town with many long-established, family-run businesses. The oldest building, **Christ Church**, on the corner of the Mall, dates from 1769 and has survived rebellions, risings and the threat of demolition, but the main attraction hereabouts is the **National Museum of Country Life** at nearby **Turlough**.

National Museum of Ireland – Country Life

Turlough Park, 8km east of Castlebar off the N5 • Free • http://museum.ie/countrylife • A bus serves Turlough from Westport (Mon–Sat 9.55am, returning at 12.05pm); taxis are available in Castlebar on 094 903 4700

The sleek, modern **National Museum of Country Life** digs beneath the dewy-eyed nostalgia that besets popular images of rural Ireland to reveal the harsh realities of country life from 1850 to 1950. The museum is spread over three levels, with **Level C** housing the main exhibition area, chronicling the unremitting work of farming and fishing, of housewives, craftsmen and tradesmen – exhibits include a recording of a poignant letter home from an emigrant to America, and footage of men making a coracle on the River Boyne. The most interesting section here deals with the seasons and festivals and the traditions behind them: churning butter on May Day to ward off evil, leaving food and drink out for dead relatives on Halloween, and grainy footage of **Wren Boys**, who would do the rounds knocking on doors on St Stephen's Day (December 26) with the corpse of a wren, asking for money to bury it while singing songs and telling jokes – the money, of course, would be spent on a party.

While here, you can also look inside the adjacent "Big House" of the landowners, the nineteenth-century Gothic Revival **Turlough Park House**, designed by Thomas Newenham Deane, architect of the National Museum in Dublin (www.museum.ie) and set over 30 acres.

ARRIVAL AND DEPARTURE

CASTLEBAR

By bus Castlebar is served by buses from/to Ballina (5 daily; 35min), Dublin (3–5 daily; 4hr 50min), Galway (5 daily; 1hr 30min) and Westport (hourly; 20min).

Achill Island

The grandeur of **ACHILL ISLAND**'s scenery, with its towering sea-cliffs and bare mountains that rise above 650m, can seem forbidding in poor weather, but on a sunny day the Atlantic glitters as though stolen from the Aegean Sea. It's the largest of the Irish islands and, connected to the mainland by a road bridge, among the most developed, with plenty of accommodation and a ribbon of white-painted holiday homes on the south coast. Drawn by sweeping **sandy beaches** (five of which have earned a Blue Flag) and fairground rides, fun-seekers descend in droves on August

ACHILL ISLAND

weekends, when the place can get a bit rowdy. Germans are also attracted to Achill by associations with novelist and Nobel Laureate **Heinrich Böll**, who lived at Dugort in the 1950s. One of the best times to come is during **Scoil Acla** (http://scoilacla.com), a week of cultural programmes with plenty of traditional music at the end of July. There's also a walking festival over the St Patrick's bank holiday weekend in March, the Heinrich Böll literary festival across the May Bank Holiday weekend and a seafood festival in mid-July, Féile Na Mara, which includes seaweed tasting, yawl racing and boat trips.

The road bridge crosses the narrow, winding strait to the island at **ACHILL SOUND** (Gob an Choire), is not the best base for exploration though it has some useful facilities. On the island side of the bridge, there's an ATM at the side of *Sweeney's* restaurant and supermarket. The lively village of **KEEL** is the nerve centre for much of the island, boasting a lovely 3km Blue Flag sandy **beach**, backed by a large lake.

The south end of the island

The "Atlantic Drive", now part of the Wild Atlantic Way (see page 26), around the south end of the island from Achill Sound brings you after 6km to the ruined eighteenth-century **church** and holy well of Damhnait (Davnet or Dympna), a seventh-century saint who sought refuge and built a church (*cill*) here. Just beyond, its pink stone set attractively on the shoreline, rises the redoubtable outline of **Carrick Kildavnet**, an almost perfectly preserved, fifteenth-century, O'Malley tower house. Fantastic views of the Atlantic open up as you round the nearby headland, continuing as far as the village and Blue Flag beach of **Dooega**. Above the settlement looms **Minaun**, Achill's third-highest mountain; a left turn will bring you up to the TV mast near its summit for one of the island's most spectacular panoramas.

Dooagh and the west of the island

West along the road from Keel is the small village of **DOOAGH**, overlooking its own sandy beach as well as a newly returned beach. At its base here, the enterprising

10

AN AMATEURISH SET FOR A GHOST FILM

A couple of kilometres north of Keel, at **Slievemore**, lies a settlement of almost a hundred crumbling stone dwellings – but what led to its **abandonment** is still unknown. Its most recent period of habitation ended in the early twentieth century, when locals used it as a **booley**: during the summer, they would occupy the cottages while grazing their cattle on the mountainside, returning to their homes in Dooagh for the winter months. This is one of the last places in Europe to have practised *booley*-ing, or transhumance, and the village is being excavated by the Achill Field School (see page 376) every summer, in the hope that it will give up its secrets. German novelist Heinrich Böll (see page 375) described the deserted village as looking like "an amateurish set for a ghost film."

Achill Field School (098 43564, http://achill-fieldschool.com) lays on a raft of activities, including weekly lectures from June to August. The field school also runs one- to eight-week archaeology courses, featuring the dig and summer open days at the **Deserted Village** (see page 376).

Beyond Dooagh, the main road rises and descends very steeply to Blue Flag **Keem Bay**, a gorgeous strip of white sand hemmed in by steep, green slopes – on a sunny day, you'll feel as if you're looking down on a Mediterranean cove, with basking sharks often visible in the limpid waters. A turning off the up-slope towards Keem Bay will bring you to **Acorrymore Lough**, a black corrie lake, now reservoir, cradled by grassy scree slopes. From here you can set out on the steep ascent of **Croghaun**, the island's second-highest mountain (665m), which boasts spectacularly high cliffs on its seaward side.

The north end

Heading north from Keel, a side road runs along the west side of Lough Keel, then skirts east around **Slievemore**, Achill's highest mountain at 671m, before looping around the north end of the island. About 2km from Keel, you'll come to the strange sight of the **Deserted Village** (see page 376) over to the left, before a further 2km east on Slievemore's southern flank brings you to the start of a signposted ten-minute walk up from the road to a keyhole-shaped **dolmen** with fine views of Keel Bay. Less than a kilometre beyond **The Settlement** (see page 376) lies **Dugort Beach**, a gently curving, Blue Flag stretch of sand in the shadow of Slievemore, overlooked to the east by Dugort.

The Settlement

A kilometre or so to the north of the start of the dolmen walk is the site of **the Settlement**, the first Protestant mission in Ireland to minister in the Irish language. It was founded in 1834 by a Church of Ireland vicar, Edward Nangle, and at first proved successful, with stone cottages, schools, a small hospital and a printing press churning out regular publications. During the 1840s Famine, the Settlement came

THE BEACH THAT REAPPEARED

Did you hear the one about the beach that reappeared? It's not an old Irish joke but a fact. One of Achill's best-known strands, near Dooagh, was washed away by storms in 1984, leaving only rocks. But 33 years later, in 2017, after a freak tide it astonishingly **reappeared** to local, national and international excitement. The 300m stretch of golden sand restored to its rightful topographic place has captured the attention of many and brought an influx of new tourists to enjoy the island's delights. Meanwhile it has become a firm favourite again with dog-walkers, strollers, joggers and courting couples.

under fire for encouraging converts, known as "soupers" or "jumpers", with offers of soup and grain. The Catholic Church, which had previously been indifferent to the islanders' education, fought back by opening a National School in 1852, and the Settlement, further rocked by emigration and financial difficulties, eventually closed in 1886. Approached by an avenue of trees on the east side of the road, the mission's church of 1855 is still standing, containing a prominent memorial to Nangle.

ARRIVAL AND INFORMATION

ACHILL ISLAND

By bus Bus Éireann runs services from Westport to Achill Sound (Mon–Sat 6 daily, Sun 3; 1hr) and Dooagh (1hr 20min).

Tourist office Achill Sound (Mon–Fri 9am–6pm, plus Sat 10am–5pm in summer; http://achilltourism.com) sells detailed maps of the island and a guide to circular walks.

Achill Heritage Centre Bunacurry (Mon–Fri noon–5pm; http://achillheritagecentre.com). Traces two hundred years of Achill's history; also offers genealogy service and free walking tours.

ACCOMMODATION

ACHILL SOUND

Óstán Oileán Acla http://achillislandhotel.com. Immediately before you cross the bridge at Achill Sound stands this comfortable hotel with fine views of the island. It's a local social hub too, with a simple food menu (burgers, fish 'n' chips, chicken and steak) served all day. €€

DOOAGH

Teach Cruachan http://teachcruachan.com. On the west side of Dooagh, this comfy guesthouse has four en-suite rooms and good breakfasts, as well as laying on guided tours of the island. €€

West Coast House School Rd, http://achillwestcoast housebandb.com. Set on an elevated site in the shadow of the majestic Croaghaun mountain, this well-run bungalow offers superb sea views. Breakfast, too, is a fine affair, not least the Keel Bay smoked salmon and scrambled eggs. €€

DUGORT

Valley House Hostel http://valley-house.com. A fine, mid-nineteenth-century house, formerly the Earl of Cavan's hunting lodge, with a sociable courtyard bar and camping. Dorms (four to twelve beds) are basic but functional – it's the house that steals the show. €

KEEL

★ **Achill Cliff House** http://achillcliff.com. One of the island's best places to stay, this hotel in the centre of the village offers bright and spacious rooms, sea views, a sauna and a seafood restaurant for residents. €€

★ **Bervie Guest House** http://bervieachill.com. In a former coastguard station right by the beach, this place enjoys a dream location and is unquestionably Achill's best accommodation. Summery ground-floor rooms lead out to a pretty garden which brings you, via a small gate, right out on to the beach. Dinner is served each evening 7–8.30pm. Closed Dec–March. €€€

Ferndale Crumpaun, 098 43908. Hidden away 200m up the lane by the *Annexe* pub, this place has six lavishly furnished rooms. Its fabulous range of breakfasts includes eggs benedict, Barbary duck breast, Mexican omelette or a Mediterranean breakfast full of surprises. €€

Joyce's Marian Villa http://joycesachilll.com. First-class accommodation in a large seaside villa with fifteen bedrooms and a sunroom that looks out to the beach and the cliffs of Minaun. Breakfasts include local jams and preserves, as well as Achill smoked salmon and seasonal fruit. €€

Keel Camping http://keelcamping.ie. A swanky caravan park beside the beach, handy for the shops and cafés. Closed early Sept to March. €

EATING AND DRINKING

Amethyst Bar http://theamethystbar.com. Reviving the name of one of Achill's oldest hotels, which had long been closed, the *Amethyst* is a newly built two-storey property on the same site. The large, modern bar and grill room, featuring exposed brickwork and wooden beams, serves the likes of turkey and ham, seafood chowder or pasta with spinach and mushroom all day, while a more formal dinner is served upstairs in the spacious dining room.

★ **The Beehive** Keel, 098 43134. An informal daytime self-service café-restaurant and craft shop with outdoor tables on a terrace overlooking Keel beach. The menu promotes wholesome local produce, such as organic Clare Island salmon and Clew Bay mussels or smoked mackerel. €€

★ **Gielty's** Dooagh, http://gieltys.com. Large pub, restaurant and café at the west end of Dooagh village that claims to be Ireland's most westerly pub. Lunches and dinners served, with outdoor tables and live music, including regular weekend traditional sessions. €€

Céide Fields and around

8km west of Ballycastle · charge; Heritage Card · http://ceidefields.com

Isolated on Mayo's dramatic, cliff-girt north coast, the prehistoric site of **Céide** (pronounced "cage-a") **Fields** is difficult to get to but repays the effort. Here, archaeologists have discovered a unique, 5000-year-old agricultural landscape, miraculously preserved under a thick layer of peat and undisturbed by later farming. A highly organized system of **dry-stone field** dotted with individual houses and gardens in what were apparently peaceful times, covers an area of thirteen square kilometres, making Céide Fields the largest Stone Age monument in the world. Rough contemporaries of the tomb-builders of Newgrange (see page 141), these farmers cleared the area's forest to make field **walls** – said to be world's oldest – for their cattle, sheep, wheat and barley, and built **wooden houses**, of which trenches and postholes are now the only traces. However, after only five hundred years, the climate deteriorated, causing the bog gradually to rise up over their farms. What's remarkable about the site is its very ordinariness and similarity to much of the Irish countryside today, as Seamus Heaney noted in *Belderg*:

A landscape fossilized, its stone wall patternings
Repeated before our eyes in the stone walls of Mayo.

There impressive, well-designed **visitor centre** features exhibitions and audiovisuals on the history and geology of the area and the formation of the bog, as well as a viewing platform and a fine café. Regular fifty-minute guided tours take visitors outside to see excavated walls, animal and house enclosures and to learn about the ecology of the bog that swallowed them up. From the adjacent cliff-top viewpoint, you can see Donegal's Slieve League on a clear day, and in the near distance the sea stack of Downpatrick Head, neatly layered and tufted with grass: according to legend, this is the severed head of the last snake that St Patrick chased from Ireland.

Ballycastle

The nearest town to Céide Fields is **BALLYCASTLE**, which comes as a pleasant surprise among the barren, grossly proportioned mountains of North Mayo. Set in the broad Ballinglen valley, it's surrounded by green fields, trees and cattle, with a fine sandy beach at the river mouth. Changing exhibitions of works by internationally known artists attached to the local **Ballinglen Arts Foundation** are held at the gallery opposite *Polke's* pub. For further exploration of the coast, the **North Mayo Sculpture Trail** (http://northmayoarttrail.com), marked by brown *Tír Sáile* ("Land of the Salty Wind") signposts, is a striking series of modern outdoor sculptures, celebrating the wild beauty and cultural heritage of the area. It starts just west of the town.

ARRIVAL AND INFORMATION

BALLYCASTLE

By bus There's no public transport to Céide Fields but Ballycastle is linked by bus to Ballina, 28km to the southeast, which in turn has regular services to and from Galway (see page 330), Westport (see page 371) and Castlebar (see page 374).

Tourist information Information on the local attractions and the Wild Atlantic Way is available at the Ballycastle Resource Centre (Mon–Fri 10am–5pm; 096 43407) on Main St, which also houses a craft shop and displays the work of local artists. The town's website is http://ballycastle.ie.

ACCOMMODATION AND EATING

Keadyville B&B Carrowcubic, http://keadyvillehouse. com. A modern and friendly four-room guesthouse, convenient for a tour of North Mayo with views of Bunatrahir Bay. If you don't have transport the owners will take you out to the Céide Fields or Downpatrick Head. €€

Mary's Cottage Kitchen Main St, 096 43361. Breakfasts

and simple lunches (sandwiches, soups and wraps) are served at this welcoming café and bakery; be sure to sample their moist soda loaf, made with buttermilk. A sloping ceiling divides two rooms with flagstone floors while a turf fire burns all year round, giving it a homely feel.

Stella Maris Hotel http://stellamarisireland.com

Positioned on the Wild Atlantic Way, this elegantly refurbished former coastguard station and convent offers fine ocean views. The 11 luxurious rooms are individually furnished with their own antiques, and you can immerse yourself in the beauty of the Mayo landscape from the large conservatory. Dinner is served 7–8.30pm, with lamb's kidneys the most popular choice. Closed Nov–Easter. €€€

DRINKING AND NIGHTLIFE

Healy's Bar Main St, 096 43019. A family-run bar where occasional music sessions are held on Fridays. The beer garden and decking area is popular with party-goers and, during the August bank holiday (first weekend in Aug) they hold the Healy Fest, which attracts musicians from all over Ireland and further afield.

10

Sligo, Leitrim and Roscommon

STATUE OF W.B. YEATS IN SLIGO TOWN

Sligo, Leitrim and Roscommon

Sligo, Leitrim and Roscommon are blessed with majestic scenery, mighty castles and a countryside littered with antiquities. The area is also renowned for the flamboyance of its traditional music: known as the North Connacht style, it is characterized by flutes and fiddles. The principal hub, lively Sligo town, has the best facilities for visitors, and makes a good base for day-trips along the Wild Atlantic Way. This new driving route has been a boon to seaside resorts such as Mullaghmore and Rosses Point, while Strandhill has reinvented itself as a busy playground for watersports. Inland from here, you can visit the remarkable prehistoric graveyard of Carrowmore Megalithic Cemetery, at the foot of Knocknarea Mountain, whose summit is marked by Medb's Cairn, said to be the burial site of the ancient Queen Medb.

Lough Gill, its celebrated island **Innisfree** and a number of other sites in the north of Sligo are inextricably linked with W. B. Yeats, an appreciation of whose writing is enhanced by a visit to **Drumcliffe**, the place of his burial, set below Benbulben Mountain. The cultural highlight of Sligo, however, is the stunning **Lissadell House**, which has been extensively renovated and showcases some of Ireland's most precious treasures. Yeats's brother, the painter Jack B., was also inspired by the county's dramatic land- and seascapes, which continue to its northern tip with fine beaches such as at **Mullaghmore**.

Ireland's least populated county by some stretch, **Leitrim** crams a dizzying diversity into its landscape, though lacks any really notable sights. Bordering no fewer than six counties, Leitrim extends some 80km from its southeastern border with Longford to a narrow strip of Atlantic shoreline in the northwest, with the expansive **Lough Allen** at its core. Two of its most attractive assets – **loughs Gill and Glencar** – lie to the west, spanning the border with Sligo. In the south, the River Shannon is the principal feature, not least in the attractive boating town, **Carrick-on-Shannon**, while rolling countryside to the river's east, especially between **Keshcarrigan** and **Ballinamore**, is sprinkled with tiny lakes and drumlins.

County Roscommon may not feature prominently on tourists' itineraries but, in its far north, the **Arigna Mountains** provide a wild and vivid contrast to the flat landscape that defines most of Roscommon, and can be explored from the historic town of **Boyle**. Further south, sites around **Tulsk**, including the rebranded **Rathcroghan Centre**, are intrinsically associated with major events in Celtic mythology. The planned town of **Strokestown** features a memorable Georgian mansion with an impressive museum devoted to the Great Famine.

Sligo town

Bustling **SLIGO** town rose to prominence following the Anglo-Norman invasion of Connacht in 1235, its strategic importance linked to its location at the point where the River Garavogue enters the sea. A Dominican friary was founded here in 1252, but the town's shape was largely developed following the building of a castle by Richard de Burgo in 1310. This edifice lasted but five years, however, before it was destroyed by the O'Donnell clan which retained control of the burgeoning settlement over the next few centuries. After the terrible times of the Great Famine of the 1840s, Sligo re-emerged as a busy port and mercantile centre in the late nineteenth century.

The town has long been renowned for its **traditional music**, but is also firmly on the tourist trail thanks to its numerous associations with the poet **W. B. Yeats**, along with

LISSADELL HOUSE AND GARDENS

Highlights

The Model Sligo town's excellent art gallery is renowned for its exhibitions of experimental art and its Jack B. Yeats collection. See page 386

Lough Gill This utterly tranquil and unspoilt lake was the inspiration, along with its island, Innisfree, for much of the poetry of Yeats. See page 391

Lissadell House The ancestral home of the Gore-Booth family was the holiday retreat of W. B. Yeats and is a treasure trove of eclectic delights. See page 393

❹ Carrowkeel Cemetery The remains of a Bronze Age village, offering a stunning panorama of County Sligo from its hilltop position. See page 395

❺ Arigna Mining Experience Devoted to the vicissitudes of life for the miners who once literally scraped a living in the mountains here – completely gripping. See page 403

❻ Strokestown Park House Arguably the most eye-catching Plantation mansion in all of Ireland, whose former stables house the enthralling National Irish Famine Museum. See page 404

HIGHLIGHTS ARE MARKED ON THE MAP ON PAGE 384

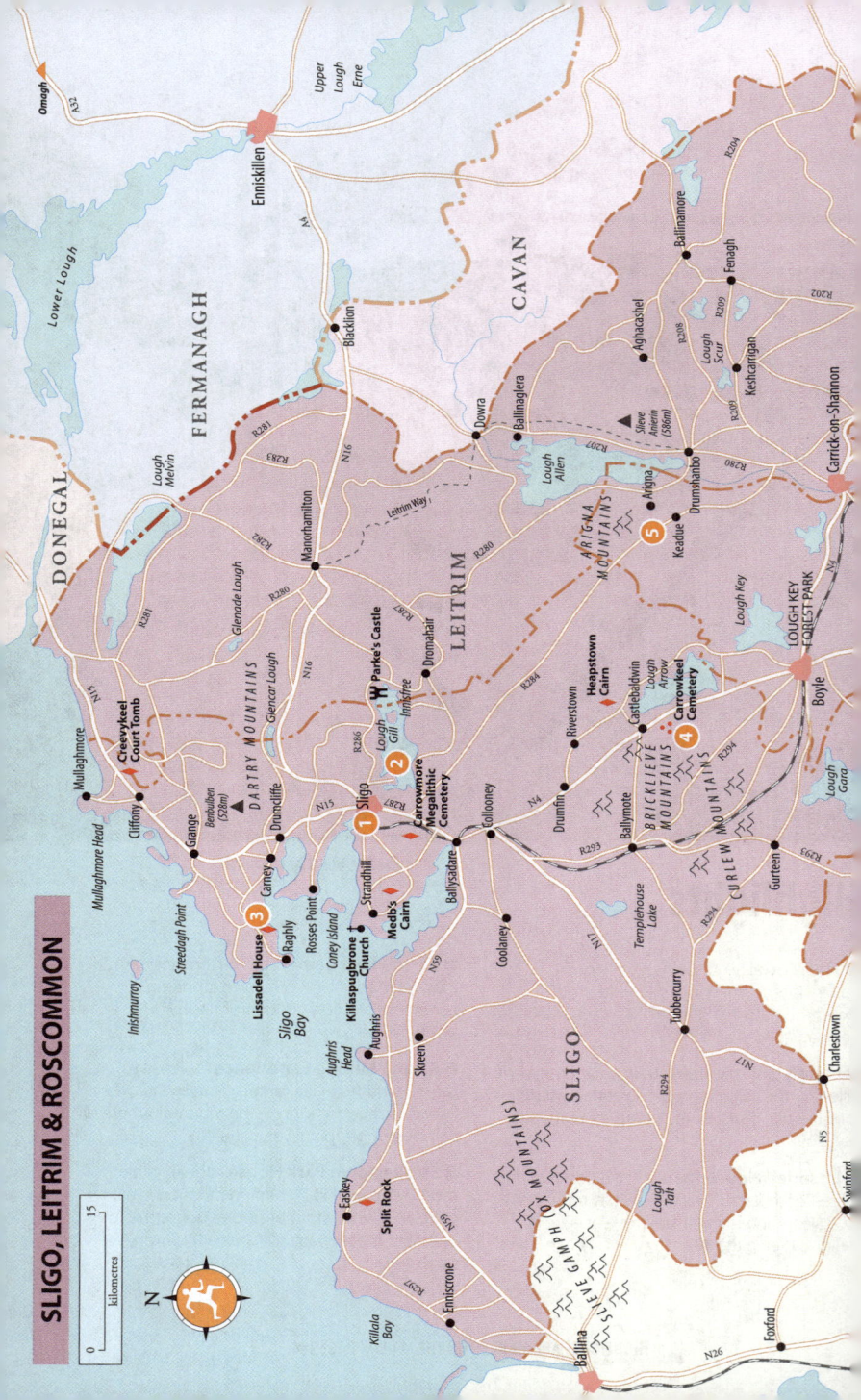

SLIGO, LEITRIM & ROSCOMMON

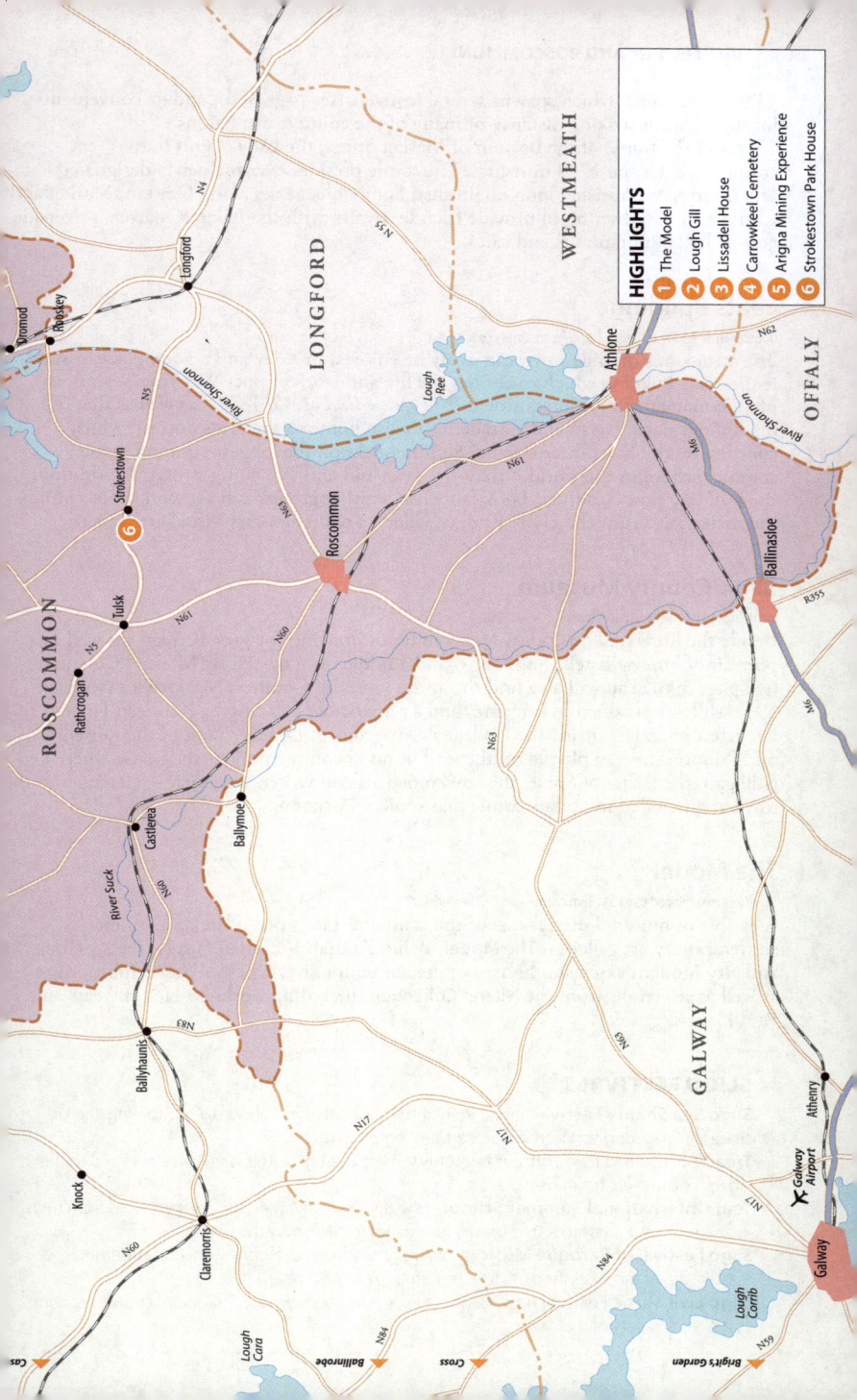

WESTMEATH

LONGFORD

OFFALY

ROSCOMMON

GALWAY

Dromod
Rooskey
Longford
N4
N55
Athlone
N62
River Shannon
Lough Ree
River Shannon
Strokestown
6
Roscommon
N61
M6
Ballinasloe
R355
Tulsk
N61
N63
N60
N5
Rathcrogan
N63
M6
Castlerea
Ballymoe
River Suck
N60
N83
Ballyhaunis
N63
N60
N17
N17
Galway Airport
Athenry
Knock
Claremorris
N17
N84
Galway
Lough Corrib
N59

Lough Cara
Cas
Ballinrobe
N84
Cross
Brigit's Garden

a lively arts scene, which spawns several **festivals** (see page 386), and its convenient location within striking distance of many of the county's attractions.

West of the **friary**, at the bottom of Market Street, the **Lady of Erin** statue commemorates the 1798 uprisings. The statue presides over the newly designated **Erin Quarter**, comprising long-established family businesses along Grattan, Market and Castle streets and set up to provide friendly rivalry with the Italian Quarter, a riverside area of Italian restaurants and cafés.

Yeats Building
Douglas Hyde Bridge • charge • http://yeatssociety.com

The attractions of Sligo town can easily be enjoyed in a day and a good place to start is the **Yeats Building** which celebrates the life and work of poet WB Yeats – courtesy of a permanent exhibition entitled *The Poetic Mind of WB Yeats* – as well as that of his siblings, Jack, Susan and Elizabeth. It's also home to the Yeats Society, which coordinates the Yeats International Summer School, the longest-running literary summer school in the world – sixty-five years old and still going strong. In addition, the building hosts readings, book launches, writing groups and art workshops, while the society also runs the Hyde Bridge Gallery, a contemporary visual arts gallery.

11

Sligo County Museum
Stephen St • Free • http://sligoarts.ie

Beside the library, **Sligo County Museum** holds drawings by Jack B. Yeats (as well as a portrait of him by Estella Solomons) and a fiddle once owned by Michael Coleman (see page 396). You will also find the apron worn by Countess Markiewicz (see page 393) while imprisoned in England, and a remarkable painting by Kathleen Fox of her arrest in 1916 outside the College of Surgeons in Dublin. West of the museum on Holborn Street, a **plaque** on the wall of no. 5 commemorates the house where Leo Milligan, the father of Spike, the late comedian and writer, was born – references to the town are included in Spike's comic masterpiece **Puckoon**.

The Model
The Mall • Free; guided tours Sat 3pm charge • http://themodel.ie

A couple of hundred metres east of the museum stands one of Ireland's finest contemporary art galleries, **The Model**. Behind a drab Victorian facade, the spacious and airy modern extension houses a range of temporary, experimental exhibitions, as well as selections from the **Niland Collection**, including works by Jack B. Yeats and Paul Henry.

SLIGO FESTIVALS

Sligo Sea Shanty Festival Rosses Point, http://wildatlanticshanty.eu. A rip-roaring line-up share their sea-dog songs in village bars and hotels in mid-June.

Tread Softly Sligo town, http://treadsoftly.ie. Held in August, this festival is dedicated to the legacy of the Yeats brothers.

Yeats International Summer School Hyde Bridge, http://yeatssociety.com. Runs from mid-June to early August, attracting literary luminaries from all over the world.

Sligo Festival of Baroque Music http://sligobaroquefestival.com. Concerts, ensembles, masterclasses and workshops, in late September/early October.

Sligo Live Music Festival http://sligolive.ie. An October festival of traditional music sessions, as well as a variety of major acts.

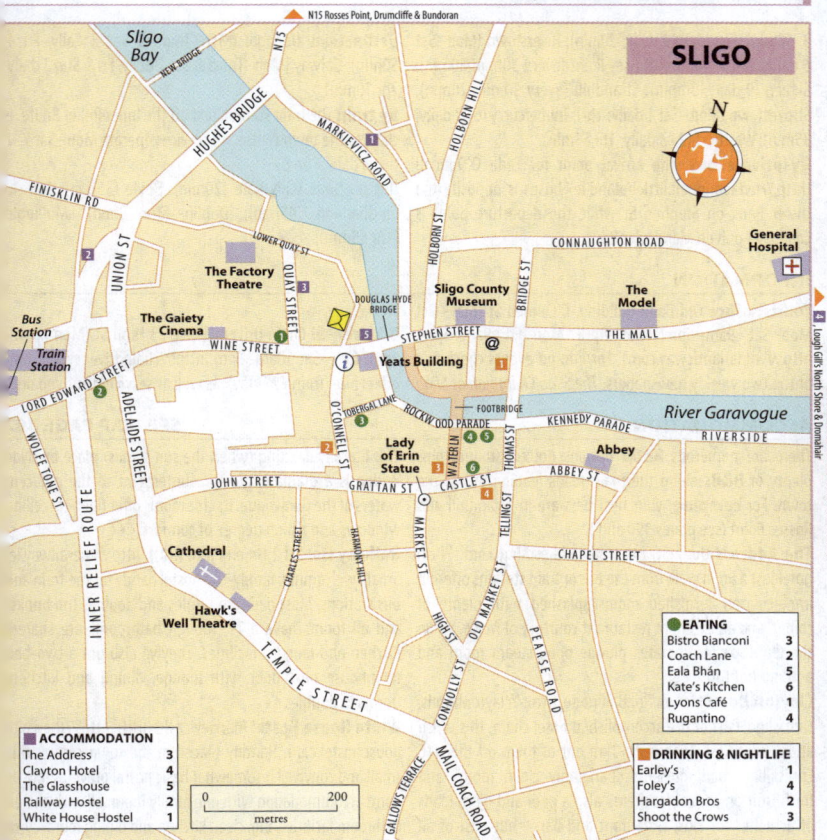

The Abbey

Abbey St • charge; Heritage Card • 071 914 6406

The Dominican friary, more commonly known as **the Abbey**, was founded around 1252 by Maurice Fitzgerald. Accidentally burnt down in 1412, it was rebuilt shortly afterwards and, unusually, continued to be occupied after the Reformation on condition that the friars became secular clergy. Damaged during a siege of the nearby castle (of which no trace remains) in 1595, the friary, along with most of the town, was sacked in 1641 by Sir Frederick Hamilton and his Puritan army, and its friars massacred. However, the friary's remains are in remarkably good condition and include a delicately decorated **high altar**, gracefully carved tombs and sculptures, and well-preserved **cloisters**. Seek out the love knot found in the Cloister East Ambulatory, said to represent the bond between earthly and spiritual love and, according to local custom, a wishing stone.

ARRIVAL AND DEPARTURE

SLIGO TOWN

By bus The bus station is on Lord Edward St.
Destinations Ballymote (Mon–Sat 7 daily, Sun 3; 35–45min); Ballyshannon (8–9 daily; 40min–1hr); Boyle (5–6 daily; 40min); Bundoran (8–11 daily; 35–55min); Carrick-on-Shannon (5–7 daily; 1hr); Derry (6–8 daily; 2hr 30min);

Donegal town (6–8 daily; 1hr 5min); Drumcliffe (9 daily; 15min); Dublin (5–7 daily; 3hr 15min–3hr 50min); Easkey (9 daily; 55min); Enniscrone (9 daily; 1hr 15min); Enniskillen (9 daily; 1hr 25min); Galway (5–7 daily; 2hr 45min); Gurteen (Mon–Sat 7 daily, Sun 3; 1hr); Keadue (Mon–Sat 6 daily, Sun

3; 50min); Lissadell (9 daily; 20min); Riverstown (Mon–Sat 6 daily, Sun 3; 40min); Rosses Point (every 30min; 20min); Skreen (9 daily; 30min); Strandhill (every 30min; 20min); Strokestown (Mon–Sat 1 daily; 1hr); Tubbercurry (6–7 daily; 35min); Westport (2–3 daily; 1hr 55min).

By private bus. The arrival point for Feda O'Donnell (http://fedaodonnell.littleireland.ie) buses is opposite the Ulster Bank on Stephen St while the departure point is *Connolly's* pub on Markievicz Rd.

Destinations Donegal (Mon–Thurs & Sat 2 daily, Fri 4, 50min); Galway (Mon–Thurs & Sat 2 daily, Fri & Sun 3 daily, 2hr 10min).

By train The train station, just off the Inner Relief Route, is close to the town centre. All services operate Mon–Sat 7–8 times daily, Sun 6.

Destinations Ballymote (20min); Boyle (35min); Carrick-on-Shannon (45min); Dublin (3hr 5min); Mullingar (1hr 55min).

INFORMATION

Tourist office Old Bank Building, O'Connell St (May–Oct Mon–Sat 9am–5pm; Nov–April Mon–Fri 9am–5pm; http://wildatlanticway.com). For info on events check one of the two weekly newspapers, *The Sligo Champion* or *Sligo*

Weekender.

Bike rental Chain Driven Cycles, 23 High St (Mon noon–6pm, Tues–Sat 10am–6pm; http://chaindrivencycles.com) offers hire (from €25/day), as well as servicing and repairs.

11

ACCOMMODATION

SEE MAP PAGE 387

There are numerous **hotel** options dotted around, plus plenty of **B&B**s along the main roads leading out of the town. For **camping**, your best bets are in Strandhill and Rosses Point (see pages 390 and).

The Address Quay St, http://theaddresssligo.com. Plush hotel just a 5min walk from the bus or train stations offering immaculately furnished rooms splashed with plenty of colour, and an excellent restaurant courtesy of *North*, while the Club Spa incorporates plunge pool, steam room and outdoor hot tub. **€€€**

Clayton Hotel Clarion Rd, Ballinode, http://claytonhotels. com/sligo. Part of the accomplished hotel chain, this swish and modern establishment, 1km out of town off the N16 Enniskillen road, presents sparklingly clean rooms and fresh fruit on the table; there's also a pool and gym, loads of activities for kids, restaurant and bar – but best of all perhaps is Auntie Sheila's sweet shop. **€€€**

★ **The Glasshouse** Swan Point, http://theglasshouse.ie.

This literally dazzling (when the sun shines) place by Hyde Bridge is a dramatic glassy counterpoint to the adjacent waters of the Garavogue. Its chic rooms offer floor-to-ceiling windows and a high degree of comfort. **€€€**

Railway Hostel 1 Union Place (IHO), http://therailway.ie. Small, welcoming, family-run hostel handy for the train and bus stations. Most beds are singles and doubles (no bunks and all rooms have a TV, though bathrooms are shared). Kitchen and laundry facilities. They've also got a two-bed townhouse next door with lounge, dining and kitchen. Dorms **€**, doubles **€€**

White House Hostel Markievicz Rd (IHH), http://thewhitehousehostel.com. Handily placed in the town centre, this small and convivial if somewhat basic hostel provides mostly dorm accommodation with one family room, all with shared bathroom facilities. Big, clean kitchen and dining room-cum lounge for guest use. Good location also for bus connections to Galway and Donegal. Closed Nov–March. **€**

EATING

SEE MAP PAGE 387

★ **Bistro Bianconi** Tobergal Lane, http://bistrobianconi. ie. Lively Italian restaurant in the flourishing Italian Quarter serving excellent pasta and pizza; they offer some good pizza with dips and drinks deals. **€€**

Coach Lane 1–2 Lord Edward St, http://coachlanesligo. com. The upstairs restaurant offers a diverse menu, with highlights including gnocchi Sorrentino (potato dumplings), Connemara lamb's liver or wild Atlantic cod. Eat downstairs at the bar and grill for cheaper meals such as fish pie and Italian meatballs served at red-check tablecloths. **€€–€€€**

Eala Bhán 5 Rockwood Parade, http://ealabhan.ie. Gaelic for "White Swan" (and you may occasionally see aforementioned bird on the neighbouring river) this fine dining establishment deals in modern Irish food with a French twist, hence dishes like smoked duck and plum bon bon. The three-course pre-theatre menu (daily 5–6.15pm) is decent value at €44. **€€€€**

★ **Kate's Kitchen** 3 Castle St, http://kateskitchen.ie. Call in for a coffee and sample some of the gourmet artisan products on the heaving shelves: handcrafted farmhouse cheese, elderflower cordial, Aine's handmade chocolate and home-made tea brack are a selection of the offerings. Closed Sun & Mon. **€**

Lyons Café Quay St, http://lyonscafe.com. Upstairs in one of Sligo's old family-run clothing stores, this time-burnished café (breakfasts, soups, cakes) has been a popular meeting place since it opened in 1923 – some of the original lights, tables and chairs are still in place. Closed Sun. **€**

Rugantino Rockwood Parade, http://rugantino.ie. This Italian brasserie serves up lunchtime standards of sandwiches, BLTs and salads and then reimagines its menu for a dinner of Toulouse sausage, glazed pork ribs, or parmigiana di melanzane. There's also an extensive cocktail list. Closed Mon & Tues. **€€€**

DRINKING AND NIGHTLIFE

SEE MAP PAGE 387

Earley's Bridge St, 071 914 2171. This cosy old bar features a great Thurs night session and other music on Sat and Sun. Beamish is one of the top-selling beers and much cheaper than some of their dark rivals.

Foley's 18 Castle St, 071 916 8900. Traditional bar with a superb range of whiskeys, and sessions year-round on Thurs & Sat, plus Wed from June to Sept.

★ **Hargadon Bros** 7 O'Connell St, http://hargadons.com. No visit to Sligo is complete without enjoying a drink or light meal in this early nineteenth-century pub with snugs, snob screens and marble-top counter to boot. For lunch (noon–3.30pm) small plates of oysters, mackerel timbale, or whiskey and oak cold smoked salmon are on the menu; dinner (4–9pm) features moules frites, broiled seabass, burgers or steak. Jazz on Thurs from 9.30pm, live music on Fri from 10.30pm. Closed Sun & Mon.

Shoot the Crows Grattan St. A long, narrow, slightly dishevelled bar across from the Lady of Erin statue, and a lively place to meet the locals. It has retained its original features including the timber wainscoting. Musicians frequently occupy a corner in the small bar at the front.

ENTERTAINMENT

The Factory Theatre Lower Quay St, http://blueraincoat. com. Hosts the innovative Blue Raincoat Theatre Company.

Hawk's Well Theatre Temple St, http://hawkswell.com.

Presents a range of dramatic productions and musical events.

Omniplex Cinema Wine St, http://omniplex.ie. A modern ten-screen cinema with a Kids' Club at 2pm at weekends.

SPORT

Football Sligo Rovers FC play in the League of Ireland Premier League at The Showgrounds on Knappagh Rd (http://sligorovers.com).

Horse racing If you fancy a flutter, head for the Sligo Races at Cleveragh Rd (http://countysligoraces.com) from May to Oct.

Around Sligo town

West of Sligo town lies the famous surfing beach at **Strandhill**, a grand base for exhilarating coastal walks, while inland is one of Europe's most significant collections of passage graves at **Carrowmore Megalithic Cemetery**. Both the resort and the graveyard are overlooked by the numinous Knocknarea Mountain, on whose summit sits the mystical **Medb's Cairn**.

Strandhill

Eight kilometres west of Sligo town and set against the backdrop of Knocknarea Mountain, seaside **STRANDHILL** boasts a gorgeous situation. It's just the way a seaside resort should be, too: traditional cafés and tea rooms, amusements, ice-cream parlours, beach stores and stunning sunsets. With the tagline "The Thrill of Strandhill", it has upped its game with a selection of trendy restaurants and bars, while the creative community has come together to hold a funky **Peoples' Market** on Sundays (11am–4pm; http://strandhillpeoplesmarket.ie) at Hangar 1 of Sligo Airport, selling local crafts, artisan foods, fresh fruit and vegetables.

Dolly's Cottage

49 Dorrin's Strand (beside the rugby club) • Free

On the way into the village look out for **Dolly's Cottage**, a tiny two-roomed thatched dwelling named after its last occupant, Dolly Higgins, who died in 1970. Maintained as it was, with a turf fire and a pouch bed, the cottage sells handicrafts as well as homemade jams and preserves.

The beach

Strandhill's renowned **beach** is a wild stretch pounded by huge Atlantic breakers. Because of rip currents it is absolutely unsafe for swimming but is massively popular with **surfers** and regularly witnesses the Sligo Open Championship over the first weekend in August. Right by the beach, the Perfect Day Surf School (087 2029 399) offers a range of classes. Adjacent on the front you can luxuriate in the curative and pleasantly soporific waters of the **Voya Spa Seaweed Baths** (daily 10am–8pm; charge; http://voyaseaweedbaths.com).

Killaspugbrone Church

The beach offers bracing walks, especially a few kilometres north towards **Killaspugbrone Church**, whose ruins largely date from the twelfth and thirteenth centuries, though its tower is a later addition. Visiting the church some centuries earlier, St Patrick somehow contrived to stumble and dislodge a tooth in the process, which he promptly donated to the sacristan, Bishop Bronus. This relic was kept and passed down, and, in the fourteenth century, an exquisite **casket**, the Fiacal Pádraig, was created to house it – the tooth subsequently disappeared, but its container is on view in the National Museum in Dublin (see page 67).

ARRIVAL AND TOURS
STRANDHILL

By bus There are regular buses from/to Sligo (4–7 daily; 20min).

Tours Seatrails (http://seatrails.ie) offers first-rate guided

mountain and coastal tours, run by maritime archaeologist Auriel Robinson. The Streedagh beach tour gives intriguing insights into the Spanish Armada landings of 1588.

ACCOMMODATION

Ocean Wave Lodge Top Rd, http://oceanwavelodge.com. An attractive guesthouse located on what is known locally as the "top road" in Strandhill, a 10min stroll from the seafront. The twelve rooms range from twins or doubles to family rooms, and there's also a reading room and well-equipped kitchen. Continental self-service breakfast included. **€€**

Strandhill Caravan and Camping Park Strandhill beach, http://sligocaravanandcamping.ie. Campers can choose from a large area of grass with a sandy base, which is mud-free even on wet days. Facilities include TV/games room, camper's kitchen, laundry and large outdoor play area. Ideally placed for exploration, and for activities ranging from swimming and surfing to horseriding and

golf. Closed Oct–March. **€**

★ **Strandhill Lodge and Suites** Top Rd, http://strandhilllodgeandsuites.ie. A sleekly designed boutique hotel overlooking Strandhill Bay. The modern bedrooms and suites, in calming cream and beige decor, are finished to a high standard; some come with a patio opening on to a courtyard. **€€€**

Surf n Stay Lodge Hostel and Surf School Shore Rd, http://surfnstay.ie. A good-value, well-equipped hostel near the beach, with small but well-presented dorms (two and four-bed) and tastefully furnished private rooms in the adjoining lodge. Handy for the bus connection to Sligo – the stop is just 100m away. **€**

EATING AND DRINKING

Mammy Johnston's Ice Cream Parlour Shore Rd, http://mammyjohnstons.net. Catch the right evening and MJ's is the best place from which to view the western sunset and Atlantic breakers while you agonize over a delectable choice of ice creams and sweet and savoury crêpes. They've been making ice cream since 1938, and the walls, adorned with pictures of old Strandhill, reflect the historic link. **€**

★ **Shells Café** Shore Rd, http://shellscafe.com. This delightful combination of fish restaurant and bakery is

a west of Ireland gem, with mismatched wooden chairs and an innovative menu that includes everything from buttermilk pancakes with bacon, vegan tacos, battered haddock and sardines on toast, to berries and wild garlic foraged from the beach. **€€**

Strand Bar Shore Rd, http://thestrandbar.ie. At the bottom of Shore Rd with a turf fire, cosy snugs and wholesome pub meals – there are lunch, pizza and evening menus –, this is a place where surfers meet the locals. **€€**

Carrowmore Megalithic Cemetery

4km west of Sligo town • charge; Heritage Card • http://heritageireland.ie

Carrowmore Megalithic Cemetery presents a remarkable array of some thirty megalithic passage tombs – easily the biggest prehistoric graveyard in Europe. The oval-shaped cluster of monuments spreads out within a 1km-by-600m field and ranges from the most basic, a small circle of stones surrounding a central roofed chamber, through to the largest, known as **Listoghill**, covered by an impressive rounded cairn. Excavations have uncovered cremated human remains as well as jewellery carved from bones and antlers.

Medb's Cairn

To get here from Carrowmore head west for 1km, take a right turn at the junction with the R292, then left at the first crossroads – after another 1km a lane leads right towards the car park at the base of the mountain, from where it's a steep 4km hike to the summit

Carrowmore is made all the more atmospheric for being set below one of Ireland's most significant burial places, the massive **Medb's Cairn** on the summit of **Knocknarea Mountain** – 55m wide and 10m high, and surrounded by a 3m-high earthen bank. Whether Medb, the legendary queen of Connacht and one of the protagonists of the **Táin Bó Cúailnge**, is actually buried here is unknown, since the site has not been excavated, but it's well worth making the trek, not only for views of the cairn itself, but for spectacular outlooks north to Donegal and west to Mayo. It takes around an hour to get to the top, following the 2.4km **Queen Medb Trail**; on your way up, pick up a stone and leave it on the cairn, making a wish as you do so and, as local legend has it, the force of Queen Medb may be with you.

11

Lough Gill

To the east of Sligo town lies one of Ireland's most entrancing lakes, **Lough Gill**, set beneath wooded slopes which provide the backdrop to almost all its 40km shoreline. The best route around the lough, and one easily navigable in less than a day's cycling, is to follow the shore clockwise by following the R286 from Sligo town, and taking in the plantation **Parke's Castle**, just inside County Leitrim, from where you can board a cruise boat and catch a sight of idyllic **Innisfree**.

Parke's Castle

Eastern end of Lough Gill • charge; Heritage Card • http://heritageireland.ie

Some 11km northeast of Sligo, towards the lake's eastern extremity, **Parke's Castle** is a plantation fort erected by Captain Robert Parke in the 1620s and elegantly restored in the late twentieth century by the Office of Public Works. A moated tower house once stood here, home of the Irish chieftain Brian O'Rourke, who in 1588 was charged with high treason after sheltering Francesco de Cuellar, one of the few survivors of the Armada ships wrecked off the Sligo coast. Wander around the battlements, admire expansive views of the lough and take in an **exhibition** on the remodelling of the castle with displays on other notable vernacular buildings.

Innisfree

Waterbus Easter–Sept daily 12.30pm; charge; http://roseofinnisfree.com

From the pier beside Parke's Castle, the "Rose of Innisfree" **waterbus** operates hour-long tours of Lough Gill, taking in views of Yeats's beloved isle of **Innisfree**, and featuring recitals of the poet's works by the skipper, almost certainly including the poet's **Lake Isle of Innisfree**:

*I will arise and go now, and go to Innisfree,
And a small cabin build there, of clay and wattles made:
Nine bean-rows will I have there, a hive for the honey-bee,
And live alone in the bee-loud glade.*

Alternatively, head a few kilometres southwards through Dromahair and pick up the R287. About 4km along this road a signposted lane leads down to the water where there's a fabulous view of the lough and Innisfree in all its serene beauty. If you fancy exploring the area on two wheels then the **Lough Gill cycle loop** is a 40km flat route that takes you through peaceful scenery and along quiet roads – bike rental is available in Sligo town (see page 388). Note that there's no access to the island itself.

North Sligo

The majority of **North Sligo**'s attractions are easily accessible from the county town. Much of the landscape is irrevocably associated with W. B. Yeats, particularly **Benbulben Mountain**, under whose green-tinged slopes and surmounting tableland the poet is buried at **Drumcliffe**. To the mountain's south lie the magical waters of **Glencar Lake** with its exhilarating waterfall, while to its west is **Lissadell House**, home to Yeats's friends Eva Gore-Booth and Constance Markiewicz, and a place filled with paintings, books and the lore of Irish cultural history. The coastline is less stimulating, though it includes a fine beach at **Mullaghmore**, a harbour village not far from one of Ireland's major funerary monuments, **Creevykeel Court Tomb**.

Rosses Point

Eight kilometres northwest of Sligo town, off the N15, **ROSSES POINT** is a seaside resort which has not moved with the times and is all the better for its lapse. There's a grand **beach**, ideal for swimming, and splendid views across the bay, both of which provided inspiration for Jack B. Yeats, the poet's artist brother. From here, fine, often blustery, walks lead around the headland.

ARRIVAL AND DEPARTURE ROSSES POINT

By bus Buses run from/to Sligo town roughly every 30mins (20min).

ACCOMMODATION AND EATING

Austie's Bar & Restaurant http://austies.ie. A convivial bar where retired sea captains hold court alongside local musicians. The wooden snugs and table which the musicians gather round on weekend nights are made from shipwrecked timber, and maritime memorabilia lines the walls. House burgers and pizzas comprise the bulk of the menu, alongside the odd wet offering like chowder and fisherman's pie. Closed Mon–Wed. €€

Rosses Point Caravan and Camping Park http://sligocaravanandcamping.ie. An efficiently run site close to two sandy beaches with TV/games room, camper's kitchen laundry and large outdoor play area. Good swimming and sailing facilities nearby. Closed mid-Sept to March. €

Yeats Country Hotel & Spa Leisure Club http://yeatscountryhotel.com. A sleekly designed boutique hotel looking out over Strandhill Bay, with bedrooms (almost one hundred) spread over three floors. The rooms (including enormous family rooms) come in beige and terracotta colour schemes, in keeping with the restful atmosphere of the hotel. Murder mystery weekends are a big hit. €€€

Drumcliffe

Eight kilometres north of Sligo along the N15, the tiny seaside village of **DRUMCLIFFE** is the site of a **monastery** established in 574 by St Colmcille, though only a round tower and an eleventh-century high cross, set on opposite sides of the main road, remain today. The graveyard of the adjacent and somewhat stark nineteenth-century **church** (which has a good café and craft shop next to it) is where the poet **W. B. Yeats** is buried and, as a consequence, is very much on the tourist trail. Yeats died in 1939 in Roquebrune, France, but before doing so requested that his body be interred locally for "a year or so" before being returned to Sligo. His wishes were granted in 1948 when his remains were transferred from France to Drumcliffe, where his great-grandfather had been rector, and buried, as one of his last poems stated, "Under bare Ben Bulben's head". His headstone, which also marks the resting place of his wife George, bears the last three lines of that poem, *Under Ben Bulben*:

Cast a cold Eye
On Life, on Death.
Horseman, pass by!

11

By bus Buses drop off/pick up on the main street in   and Sligo town (9 daily; 15min)
Drumcliffe, serving Ballyshannon (8–10 daily; 35–50min)

Glencar Lake

Heading east from Drumcliffe along minor roads, you'll come to **Glencar Lake** after
some 8km, gorgeously set amid tree-lined slopes. Near the eastern extremity of its
northern shore a signposted footpath leads up to an impressive 15m-high **waterfall**,
cascading down into a deep pool from the rocky mountainside above, which provided
the inspiration for part of Yeats's poem *The Stolen Child*:

Where the wandering water gushes
From the hills above Glencar,
In pools above the rushes that
Scarce could bathe a star.

11

Lissadell House

15km north of Sligo town • charge • http://lissadellhouse.com • Coming by car, turn off the main N15 Sligo–Donegal road, take a left turn
at Drumcliffe and follow the road northwest for 6km

Lissadell House, the lavishly restored ancestral home of the Gore-Booth family, whose
members Eva and Constance were close friends of W. B. Yeats, is a must-see attraction.
The house – an austere but classical residence built in 1833 – was an occasional retreat
of **W. B. Yeats** and the childhood home of Constance Gore-Booth, who later became
Countess Markievicz and fought in the 1916 Easter Rising in Dublin. She was the first
woman to be elected to the House of Commons (in 1918, although she did not take
her seat) and in the following year became the first female member of the Dáil, the
Irish Parliament, as Minister for Labour. The building is a storehouse of **family archives**
and other cultural treasures: the Billiard Room is dedicated to Henry Gore-Booth's
expedition to the Arctic in search of the explorer Benjamin Leigh Smith. The admission
price includes a tour of the house, entry to the exhibitions, and access to the **Alpine and
Victorian gardens**, which make for a pleasant stroll, as do the extensive woodland walks.

Creevykeel Court Tomb

Cliffony, 22km north of Sligo town • Open access

Just north of the village of Cliffony, **Creevykeel Court Tomb** is probably the best
example of its kind in Ireland. A cairn-covered, trapeze-shaped barrow constructed
between 3500 and 3000 BC, though now lacking many of its stones, the tomb features
two central burial chambers, faced by an oval-shaped court in which rituals were
conducted. Excavations in 1935 uncovered cremated remains, alongside Neolithic
pottery, axes and artefacts, all now held by Dublin's National Museum (see page 67).

Mullaghmore

Just before Creevykeel a lane leads northwards for 4km to **MULLAGHMORE**, an
enticing village set around a secluded, walled harbour with a glorious expanse of
sandy beach, offering fabulous views north to the mountains of Donegal and back
towards Benbulben.

Beach Hotel The Harbour, http://beachhotelmullaghmore.   and activity breaks. The 28 rooms are decorated in tranquil
com. Ideally situated at the waterfront with leisure facilities   pastels, and many have sea views and window boxes, while

the *Boatman's Bar* is a fine spot to chow down as you ponder the comings and goings in the harbour. €€€
Seacrest B&B The Harbour, 071 916 6468. A beautifully appointed guesthouse set in a stunning location beside the beach. The rooms look out over Benbulben Mountain and across Donegal Bay. €€

West Sligo

The shoreline of **West Sligo**, stretching from near Sligo town almost as far as Mayo's Ballina, is probably the least visited in the county. Yet set against the looming southern backdrop of the Ox Mountains, it offers plenty of diversions including bracing seascapes at **Aughris**, exhilarating surfing at **Easkey** and a dazzling beach at **Enniscrone**. A little way inland, the memorable funerary sepulchres at **Skreen** are well worth a detour en route.

Skreen and Aughris

Twenty-five kilometres west of Sligo town along the N59, the tiny village of **SKREEN** is worth visiting for the astonishing collection of 23 **box tombs** situated in its Church of Ireland's graveyard and created by a local family of stonemasons, the Diamonds, between 1774 and 1886. Named after one Andrew Black, who had the tomb erected in memory of his father in 1825, the most remarkable of these is the Black Monument, which carries an ornate carving of a ploughman, atypically dressed Fred Astaire-style in top hat and tails.

Back on the N59 and just west of the village, a signpost points towards the secluded hamlet of **AUGHRIS**. From the pier here you can follow a 5km cliff walk, which takes in splendid views, sights of numerous seabirds and, from June to August, basking dolphins.

Easkey

The village of **EASKEY**, 15km west of Aughris, began life as a monastic community, much later becoming the base for the MacDonnells, originally gallowglasses who served the ruling O'Dowd clan and built seaside **Roslee Castle** (now ruined) in the fifteenth century. Thanks to the constancy of its waves, Easkey is a popular **surfing** centre and houses the headquarters of the Irish Surfing Association (http://irishsurfing.ie).

Enniscrone

Some 14km southwest along the coast from Easkey, **ENNISCRONE** is blessed with a gorgeous 5km arc of golden **strand**. Its other main draw is **Kilcullen's Bath House** (June–Sept daily 10am–9pm; Oct–May Thurs–Sun noon–8pm; charge; http://kilcullenseaweedbaths.net) where you can wallow in a bath full of seaweed – the iodine-rich water is not only sheer relaxation but is also reckoned to offer relief for rheumatism and arthritis – before enjoying a hot steam in a cedarwood cabinet.

ARRIVAL AND DEPARTURE WEST SLIGO

By bus Buses (9 daily) run from Sligo town to Easkey (50min) and on to Enniscrone (1hr 15min).

ACCOMMODATION AND EATING

Atlantic and Riverside On the R297, Easkey, http://easkeybandb.com. Beside the River Easkey with comfortable en-suite rooms, convenient to shops and pubs, and an ideal stopover while touring the coastline. Excellent cooked-to-order breakfasts too. €€

★ **The Beach Bar** Aughris, http://thebeachbarsligo.com. A thatched pub serving such delights as creamy seafood chowder, freshly steamed mussels or Irish stew; it's also the best place around these parts to catch some live music. It also provides amenable en-suite B&B in the adjacent bungalow, including a room for a family of six. €€

South Sligo

South Sligo's attractions are spread over a wide area, ranging from the glorious **Lough Arrow** in the east, via megalithic sites, such as **Heapstown Cairn** and the atmospheric **Carrowkeel Cemetery**, set in the Bricklieve Mountains, to creeper-clad castles and **Lough Talt** in the west. Above all, however, the area is renowned for its **traditional music**, especially within the triangle of **Ballymote**, **Gurteen** and **Tubbercurry**.

Riverstown and Sligo Folk Park

Charge • http://sligofolkpark.com • Buses (Thurs & Fri 1 daily) run from Riverstown to Boyle (35min) and Sligo (40min)

The tranquil village of **RIVERSTOWN**, some 20km southeast of Sligo, is home to the **Sligo Folk Park**, a well-designed collection of buildings that includes a village street, cottage and farmhouse. The museum displays various aspects of rural life spanning more than 150 years, from the 1850's to the late 1900's and includes original artefacts belonging to Countess Markevich and her father Sir Henry Gore Booth – there's also a dedicated military display recalling the men of Sligo who lost their lives in the Great War. Strolling the six-acre site will bring you to the banks of the Unshin River, a special area of conservation where there's plenty of wildlife to look out for.

During the August bank holiday weekend Riverstown is taken over by the **James Morrison Traditional Music Festival** (http://riverstowncce.com), celebrating the music of the famous fiddler born in nearby Drumfin in 1893. He emigrated to the US in 1915 and became famous playing with his bands in the dancehalls of New York.

Heapstown Cairn and Lough Arrow

Five kilometres south of Riverstown, by the road to Ballindoon, stands the impressive **Heapstown Cairn**, which, at 60m in diameter, is Ireland's largest megalithic passage tomb outside the Boyne Valley. From the cairn it's a short jaunt to the eastern shore of **Lough Arrow**, whose limpid waters are peppered with tiny islands.

Castlebaldwin and Carrowkeel Cemetery

At **CASTLEBALDWIN**, 6km south of Riverstown on the N4, minor roads of diminishing width and reliability lead towards the Bronze Age **Carrowkeel Cemetery**. The last kilometre or so has to be negotiated on foot, but your efforts will be rewarded by a spellbinding panoramic view of the surrounding countryside. Here on the uplands of the Bricklieve Mountains is a remarkable collection of fourteen cairns, plus an assortment of other stonework. Excavation in 1911 produced a wealth of jewellery and relics, and several of the cairns, consisting of roofed, cruciform **passage graves**, can be entered. The most striking is **cairn K**, which, in complete contrast to County Meath's Newgrange (see page 141), is illuminated by the sun's rays during the summer solstice (June 21).

Ballymote and around

The largest place in southern Sligo is **BALLYMOTE**, 20km from the county town. Richard de Burgo built a **castle** here in 1300 which, switching ownership numerous times during its history, proved to be a veritable straw in the wind of Irish politics. In 1317 it fell to the O'Connors and remained in Irish hands until captured by Bingham, the governor of Connacht, in 1584. It was soon afterwards reclaimed by the McDonaghs who then sold it to Red Hugh O'Donnell (see page 433) for £400 and three hundred cows – he marched from here to catastrophic defeat at Kinsale in 1601. Later taken by Cromwell's army, it fell yet again to the O'Connors in 1690, before they in turn surrendered the castle to Williamite troops who determined to put an end to the whole farrago by tearing down much of the building and filling in the moat. The **ruins** lie just west of the town centre, and the stripped **interior** can be visited by acquiring a key from the Enterprise Centre (Mon–Fri 9am–5pm) on Emmet Street. Towards the end of the fourteenth century, the **Book of Ballymote** was assembled here, significant not just for the vast deal of information on Irish lore and history it contains, but also because it unlocks the secrets of the carved ogham letters that appear on numerous Neolithic standing stones. The book is held by the Royal Irish Academy in Dublin.

The **Paddy Killoran Traditional Music Festival** is held in Ballymote on the third weekend in June.

ARRIVAL AND DEPARTURE
BALLYMOTE AND AROUND

By bus Buses stop outside the Church of Ireland parish church on Main St.
Destinations Boyle (Mon–Wed & Sat 1 daily; 30min); Gurteen (Mon–Sat 7 daily, Sun 3; 20min); Sligo (Mon–Sat 7 daily, Sun 3; 40min); Tubbercurry (Wed 2; 30min).

By train Ballymote is on the Sligo–Dublin route (Mon–Sat 8 daily, Sun 5); the train station is opposite the castle ruins off the Tubbercurry road.
Destinations Boyle (15min); Dublin (2hr 40min); Sligo (18min).

ACCOMMODATION AND EATING

Hayden's Lord Edward St, 071 918 3188. An old-style welcoming bar that boasts 350 years of history and was the former home of the Sheriff of Sligo. Irish traditional music is played on Sun nights in the summer months.
Millhouse Keenaghan, on the southern outskirts of Ballymote, 071 918 3449. An agreeable, modern guesthouse with comfortable if slightly small bedrooms (singles, doubles, twins and triples) and delicious breakfasts. €€
Stonepark Teeling St. A central restaurant and café offering reasonably priced meals with main courses running

€9–14. The menu features burgers, chicken, pork, steak and fish. Daily 9am–9pm.
★ **Temple House** 5km northwest of town, http://templehouse.ie. The area's most exclusive accommodation offered in a lakeside setting. Dating originally from the late seventeenth century, this majestic country house offers ten of its hundred rooms as en-suite guest accommodation with breakfast taken communally at the huge mahogany dining table. Closed Dec–March. €€€

Gurteen

South of Ballymote the R293 runs parallel to the Dublin railway line before drifting away through fertile farmland and reaching the crossroads village of **GURTEEN** after 11km. Gurteen sits at the heart of South Sligo's **traditional music** scene, and its greatest son was the fiddler Michael Coleman (see box). Gurteen hosts the **Coleman Traditional Festival** over the last weekend in August.

MICHAEL COLEMAN

Arguably the greatest of Irish fiddlers, **Michael Coleman** was born in 1891 in Killavil, north of Gurteen, and grew up in a household noted for its strong musical tradition. Taking up the fiddle in childhood, he developed rapidly under the tuition of his elder brother James and acquired a phenomenally extensive repertoire. Coleman moved to **New York** in 1914, making a living playing first on the vaudeville circuit and in the city's Irish dancehalls and bars. With a ready-made Irish market for the nascent US recording industry, Coleman made his first 78s in 1921 and over the next fifteen years released numerous others on a variety of labels, while frequently broadcasting on the radio. He made his last commercial recording in 1936.

The impact of these recordings, the embodiment of the fluid **Sligo style** of music – characterized by its sweet tone and sometimes flamboyant ornamentation – was enormous, not just in the US but also back home, and the approach taken by Coleman and his fellow Sligo émigrés, Paddy Killoran and James Morrison (see page 395), came to dominate Ireland's traditional music. Coleman died in 1945, but you'll still encounter many a traditional session throughout Ireland where the sequence of tunes exactly replicates one of his 78rpm recordings.

Coleman Irish Music Centre

By the crossroads • shows (charge); exhibition charge • http://colemanirishmusic.com

Named after the renowned eponymous fiddler, the **Coleman Irish Music Centre** is Ireland's foremost centre dedicated to traditional music. As well as a 130-seat tiered theatre that regularly hosts concerts and events, there's an exhibition with audio-visual and touch screen facilities demonstrating the best of traditional Irish music, as presented by both older practitioners and more contemporary musicians. The shop, meanwhile, sells an excellent selection of books and CDs, including several collections of recordings from its own archives, plus instruments.

ARRIVAL AND ACCOMMODATION

GURTEEN

By bus Gurteen is served by buses from/to Ballymote (Mon–Sat 7 daily, Sun 3; 20min); Boyle (Thurs 2; 25min); Sligo (Mon–Sat 7 daily, Sun 3; 1hr); and Tubbercurry (Sat 1; 25min).

Church View B&B Main St, http://thechurchview.com.

A modern town house, centrally placed, with attractive en-suite rooms. Each room (a twin, double and triple) is decorated in a different colour scheme and comes with tea- and coffee-making facilities. Guests can avail themselves of a warming lounge and breakfast is optional. €€

11

Tubbercurry and around

Some 30km southwest of Sligo, **TUBBERCURRY** is a rather docile small town but traditional music thrives here, focused on the week-long **South Sligo Summer School** (http://southsligosummerschool.com) in mid-July, with classes, pub sessions and concerts. Tubbercurry's origins date back to the late fourteenth century, but it remained a sleepy little settlement until becoming a stop on one of Bianconi's coaching routes in 1853. The burgeoning town was all but destroyed by fire during a zealous Black and Tan reprisal in 1920, and little remains from earlier times.

Some 15km to Tubbercurry's west, along a lonely road that passes through flat land before rising into the Ox Mountains, lies **Lough Talt**. Trout-rich, the lake attracts plenty of anglers as well as walkers keen to enjoy the 6.5km path circumnavigating its waters.

ARRIVAL AND DEPARTURE

TUBBERCURRY AND AROUND

By bus There are bus connections with Ballymote (Wed 2; 30min); Galway (6–8 daily; 1hr 55min); Gurteen (Sat 1;

25min); Sligo (6–8 daily; 35min); and Westport (1–2 daily; 1hr 20min).

ACCOMMODATION AND EATING

Cawley's Emmet St, http://cawleysguesthouse.ie. A comfortable guesthouse with fourteen rooms and a restaurant is open to non-residents serving a mix of French-inspired and Irish cuisine. €€

Murphy's Hotel Teeling St, http://murphyshotel.ie. Well-equipped en-suite rooms and a range of meals in both its restaurant and bar, plus music sessions most weekends. €€

Carrick-on-Shannon and around

CARRICK-ON-SHANNON, Leitrim's county town, grew up around a strategic crossing point on the River Shannon, the importance of which was recognized by the English who began building a planned settlement that was incorporated as a borough in 1613. Modern Carrick developed after the 1840s when the Shannon navigation scheme reached the town; its stone bridge and quays date from this period.

At the tourist office you can pick up a booklet, *A Walk through Carrick-on-Shannon* (€2), detailing a signposted **trail** of the historic buildings. But Carrick's main draw is its proximity to the river, its busy **marina** often jam-packed with barges and cruisers – and a top-class selection of restaurants.

The Dock Arts Centre and Leitrim Design House

St George's Terrace • http://thedock.ie

Just above the river, off the top of Bridge Street, stands the former courthouse, built in 1821 and known as **The Dock**. The arts centre within includes a performance space staging theatre, comedy and music events, as well as a café. The building also houses the **Leitrim Design House**, showcasing contemporary works by local artists and craft workers, and hosts regular exhibitions.

St George's Heritage Centre

St Mary's Close • charge (includes admission to Workhouse) • http://stgeorgesheritagevisitorcentre.ie

The **Heritage Centre**, adjacent to St George's Church (1827), tells the story of Leitrim, its landscape and people through an engaging audiovisual presentation. The church is also worth visiting to see the magnificent altarpiece, *The Adoration of the Shepherds*, restored and hanging in a gilt frame.

11

Carrick Workhouse

Gallows Hill • charge (includes admission to St George's Heritage Centre) • http://carrickmacrossworkhouse.com

Carrick Workhouse opened in 1842 to accommodate eight hundred people but it was besieged during the Great Famine of 1845–47. With its long rectangular rooms, bare floorboards and whitewashed walls, it looks much as it did in the 1840s and is an atmospheric place to linger. The significance of the Workhouse has been interpreted by the Wexford artist Alanna O'Kelly through a permanent multimedia installation, *No Colouring Can Deepen the Darkness of Truth*.

Costello Memorial Chapel

Bridge St • Daily 11am– 4pm, or contact the tourist office for a key • Free • http://costellomemorialchapel.com

The restored **Costello Memorial Chapel** – supposedly the smallest chapel in Europe and second smallest in the world – was erected in 1879 by Carrick businessman Edward Costello in memory of his wife, Mary Josephine. The interior is lined with yellow Bath stone and its tiny dimensions measure a mere 5m long, 4m wide and 6m high.

James Gralton wall plaque

As you walk along Carrick's main street admiring the handsome shop fronts, you come to the site of the **Allied Irish Bank**, formerly a shop where **James Gralton** (1888–1945) worked in the early 1900s. Gralton was a left-wing political activist who joined the Revolutionary Workers Group, but following a political witch-hunt he became the only Irishman ever to be deported from his native land. His fascinating story is told in a 2014 Ken Loach film *Jimmy's Hall*. In 2013 a bilingual **memorial plaque**, in Irish and English, was erected in his honour on the outside wall of the bank as part of the Carrick-on-Shannon historic town trail.

GETTING OUT ON THE WATER IN CARRICK-ON-SHANNON

Moon River (http://moonriver.ie) runs €20 **river trips** with commentary, departing from the bridge. If you want to go it alone, Emerald Star (http://emeraldstar.ie) offers Shannon **cruisers** for weekly rental; expect to pay around €750–3000, depending on the size of the boat and season. Carrick Craft (http://carrickcraft.com) rents two to twelve-berth cruisers. Inland Waterways Association of Ireland (http://iwai.ie) supplies more **information** on the Shannon–Erne waterway and sells guides and navigation charts.

CARRICK-ON-SHANNON FESTIVALS AND EVENTS

Water Music Festival Held over the second weekend in July, featuring concerts ranging from traditional to classical music.

Carrick Rowing Club Regatta http://carrickrowingclub.com. At the beginning of August a lively regatta, run by the oldest rowing club in Ireland, is the high point of the boating season and attracts large crowds.

Coarse Fishing Festival 071 962 0313. In mid-September anglers come from many countries for a week-long festival devoted to coarse fishing.

ARRIVAL AND INFORMATION

CARRICK-ON-SHANNON

By bus Buses drop and collect near *Coffey's Pastry Case*, by the Shannon bridge.

Destinations Boyle (5–7 daily; 15min); Drumshanbo (Sat 1; 25min); Dublin (5–7 daily; 2hr 30min–3hr); Sligo (5–7 daily; 1hr).

By train The train station is a short distance off the Elphin road on the southern side of the river. All services operate

Mon–Sat 8 times daily, 5 on Sun.

Destinations Boyle (10min); Dublin (2hr 20min); Mullingar (1hr 10min); Sligo (45min).

Tourist office In the Old Barrel Store, under the bridge (mid-May to mid-Sept Mon–Sat 9.30am–5pm; http://leitrimtourism.com).

11

ACCOMMODATION

Bush Hotel Main St, http://bushhotel.com. The rooms at this traditional-style hotel range in size, though they are all well equipped and comfortable. A fascinating mini-museum of local photographic history lines the walls of the main corridor. €€€

★ **The Landmark Hotel** Dublin Rd, http://thelandmark hotel.com. A modern hotel with sprucely furnished rooms and views of the Shannon. Great cocktail bar, *Aroma's* café and *Boardwalk* restaurant too, for views of the riverfront with free newspapers. €€€

EATING

Café Lounge Mercantile Plaza, http://cafelounge.ie. Connoisseurs love this relaxing place where you can order your coffee black, milk-based, with syrup, or as a cocktail. Peruse papers and books while enjoying the barista's choice or the lounge blend along with a slice of decadent cake. Closed Sun. €

Coffey's Pastry Case Bridge St, 071 962 0929. A buzzy daytime café in a central location for coffee, muffins, scones, vegetarian pizza, salads and light bites; the seating upstairs is ideal for river gazing. €

The Cottage Restaurant Jamestown, 4km southeast of Carrick, http://cottagerestaurant.ie. Nicely located beside

the river, this is one of the classiest restaurants in the area presenting a dazzling, Asian-influenced menu; slow cooked duck leg with *kim chi* and miso cream sauce, and pan seared scallops with cumin potato and cinnamon curry dressing. Closed Mon–Wed. €€€

★ **The Oarsman** Bridge St, http://theoarsman.com. Almost as good as the *Cottage*, the imaginative, modern Irish cuisine here rates some thoughtfully prepared dishes such as Coolatin cheddar polenta with chargrilled watermelon and romesco sauce. Try some of their local craft beers including Sunburnt Red, Howling Gale Ale or Knock me down Porter. Closed Mon & Tues. €€€

DRINKING

Anderson's Thatched Pub 5km south of Carrick on the R368 Elphin road, 087 228 3288. An inviting bar with a pedigree stretching back to 1734. Sessions are held most nights from June to Aug (rest of the year Wed & Sat).

The Barrel Store Bridge St, http://thebarrelstore.ie. Styling itself as a craft beer haven, cocktail den and wine

haunt, this spacious bar stocks Carraig pale ales such as Grand Soft Day and Shepherd's Delight, as well as the famed Gunpowder gin from Drumshanbo. A light bar menu comprises half a dozen pizzas and burgers plus a few other nibbles and there's live music at the weekend, typically bands and DJs.

Drumshanbo and Lough Allen

Some 12km north of Carrick, **DRUMSHANBO** is a lively village with a strong musical tradition at the tip of **Lough Allen**'s southern shore. In the third week of July, the seven-day Joe Mooney Summer School (http://joemooneysummerschool.com) is held here, offering **traditional music** classes and concerts. At the end of June the village also hosts the **An Tostal Festival** (http://antostalfestival.ie) with a variety of music.

From Drumshanbo roads lead north along both eastern and western shores of **Lough Allen**. The western route crosses into Roscommon and skirts the Arigna Mountains (see page 402) while its alternative to the east heads up through bleak flatlands below Slieve Anierin. The waymarked 48km **Leitrim Way** (map available from local tourist offices) follows Lough Allen's shoreline before taking in higher ground on its way to the remote village of **Dowra**, the starting point for the **Cavan Way** (see page 161).

Sliabh an Iarainn Visitor Centre

Acres Lake on the Carrick-on-Shannon road, on the outskirts of Drumshanbo but within the limits of the town • http://sliabhaniarainnvisitorcentre.com

The **Sliabh an Iarainn Visitors Centre** is an excellent introduction to the area. Exhibitions feature topography and geology as well as musical heritage and scenic attractions. Audiovisuals take you on a local history journey, focusing on transport and industry. A **Musicians' Corner** showcases the flautist John McKenna and other renowned Leitrim musicians; you can listen to tracks featuring the different styles of the area's music.

ARRIVAL AND DEPARTURE   DRUMSHANBO

By bus Buses pick up and drop off opposite the library in the main street.
Destinations Ballinamore (Fri & Sat 1 daily; 25min); Carrick-on-Shannon (Sat 1; 25min); Dowra (Sat 1; 25min); Keadue (Fri 1; 15min); Sligo (Fri 1, Sat 2; 1hr 15min–1hr 40min).

ACTIVITIES

Lough Allen Adventure Centre Ballinaglera, 13km north of Drumshanbo, http://loughallenadventure.ie. Offers a variety of activities, such as windsurfing, kayaking, stand-up paddleboarding and hill-walking.

ACCOMMODATION AND EATING

Fraoch Ban 1km up the Dowra road, 071 964 1260. This comfortable modern bungalow surveying the lake makes an ideal location for walking, cycling or driving around the serene north Leitrim countryside Closed Nov–March. €€
Henry's Haven Convent Ave, 071 964 1805. The best place for good-value bar meals with all your standard staples like sausages and mash, and fish and chips. Beer's good too.
Lough Allen Hotel & Spa, http://loughallenhotel.com. Don't be put off by the approach road; the setting is a stunning location beside Lough Allen. Elegantly furnished bedrooms and spacious suites await you, as well as a spa, fitness centre and pool. €€€

East from Drumshanbo

KESHCARRIGAN, about 8km east of Drumshanbo on the Shannon–Erne Waterway, is worth a brief stop for its amiable bars. **FENAGH**, 6km east, was once an important ecclesiastical centre, founded by St Caillin in the sixth century. The area's history is recounted in the **Heritage Centre** (Wed–Sat 10am–5pm, Sun noon–5pm; free; http://fenagh.com), which also has a café. **BALLINAMORE**, 5km northeast of Fenagh, is a focus for **cruising** on the Shannon–Erne Waterway, with barges available from Riversdale Holidays (http://riversdaleholidays.com).

ACCOMMODATION AND EATING   EAST FROM DRUMSHANBO

The Commercial and Tourist Hotel High St, Ballinamore, http://hotelcommerical.com. A good base to explore the Erne–Shannon Waterway and surrounding countryside, with spacious, if slightly old fashioned rooms plus meals available. €€
Gerties Canal Stop Main St, Keshcarrigan, 071 964 2252. Beside Ballyconnell canal, this is an ideal place to tuck into cheap and hearty meals with a menu that includes steak, chicken and lasagne; equally good for a beer and watching sports on the big screens. €€
★ **The Old Rectory** Fenagh Glebe, Ballinamore, http://theoldrectoryireland.com. A child-friendly Georgian house (dating from 1827) on a working farm with well-kept en-suite period rooms (and some self-catering apartments) and with lovely views of Fenagh Lough from the grounds. It is popular with wedding parties, mind. €€

Boyle and around

Rising gently above its own namesake river, engaging **BOYLE** is a relaxed town with congenial bars, a couple of sites of noteworthy historical interest and a lively arts festival. It also makes an ideal base for exploring not only Roscommon's northern attractions, such as **Lough Key Forest Park**, but neighbouring Leitrim and South Sligo too. The town hosts several summer **festivals**, of which the biggest is the Boyle Arts Festival (http://boylearts.com) at the end of July with a broad-ranging programme of drama, concerts, exhibitions and lectures. Some 3km north of Boyle, overlooking the N4 Sligo–Dublin road where it skirts the Curlew Mountains, stands an intriguing metal **sculpture** representing Gaelic chieftain Red Hugh O'Donnell. Known locally as "the ass in the pass", artist Maurice Harron's work marks the site of the Battle of the Curleius between Irish and English forces in 1599.

Brief history

Boyle's origins lie in the establishment of a **Cistercian monastery** in 1161, but as it was situated on an important trading route, the abbey became embroiled in numerous internecine and Irish–English skirmishes and was sacked on a number of occasions. It lingered on for several decades after the Dissolution – its last abbot was executed in 1584 for refusing to disavow allegiance to Rome – and from 1599 until the end of the eighteenth century it was used as a barracks by the English and known as Boyle Castle. In 1603 the building passed into the hands of Sir John King and remained in the family's possession until 1892. It was Staffordshire-born King who transformed Boyle, constructing a grand **mansion** to the west of the abbey and an avenue (now the town's main street) leading up to it. At the same time he began to amass thousands of acres of land, which would eventually become the largest estate in County Roscommon, **Rockingham**.

11

Boyle Abbey

Less than 1km off the N4 Dublin–Sligo Rd • charge; Heritage Card • http://heritageireland.ie

It's easy to find your way around Boyle, and the town's two major attractions are well signposted from the centre. The first of these is **Boyle Abbey**, consecrated in 1218, whose alluring remains abut the river on the eastern side of town. Despite various onslaughts during the course of its history, it remains perhaps the finest surviving Cistercian church in Ireland and its sixty-year building process bears traces of both the Romanesque and the then newly arrived Gothic styles of architecture. The abbey's ruins are entered via its gatehouse, which contains an **exhibition** on the foundation's history and a model of how it once might have looked. Inside the nave the transition from Romanesque to Gothic is neatly contrasted by windows and arches, circular facing pointed. Some of the capitals bear intriguing secular decorations – one features little figures standing between trees and clutching the branches somewhat stiffly – while high on the western wall is a carving of a **Sheila-na-Gig** (see page 608).

King House

Military Rd • charge; Heritage Island • http://visitkinghouse.ie • 1hr weekday selfguided tours available

The original seat of the King family was destroyed by fire, but its replacement, **King House**, is well worth visiting. This impressive stone mansion was built around 1730 and sold to the War Office when the Kings moved to Rockingham, becoming the barracks for the Connaught Rangers from 1788 until 1922. The Irish Army then occupied the building until the 1940s, after which it passed into private hands, before falling into dereliction. Thoroughly restored, its ground floor now houses Boyle's **Civic Art Gallery**, largely displaying works by local painters, while upper storeys employ interactive high-tech gadgetry to retell the story of the house and the family who built it, with child-oriented exhibits. The story of Henry's son Edward, who built Rockingham, is wittily recounted in one exhibit, "How to become an earl in six easy stages", describing how he rose to become Earl of Kingston in 1768. One section of the house is devoted to the Connaught Rangers and recalls their role in various military campaigns.

Lough Key Forest and Activity Park

Just off the N4, 3km east of Boyle • **Rockingham Remembered Tour** charge; Heritage Island • http://loughkey.ie • **Boat trips** charge • http://loughkeyboats.com

Occupying what was once the focal area of the Kings' Rockingham estate (the demesne was abandoned by the family in 1957 after their mansion was destroyed by fire), **Lough Key Forest and Activity Park** offers a number of signposted **walking trails** – ranging from easy to strenuous – around the estate, and you can take a **boat trip** out on the lake, or rent a rowing boat during the summer months. Though almost all the park's woodland and trails remain unsullied, a massive commercial revamp has restricted access to certain areas, focal to which is the **Visitor Centre** at the end of a driveway 2km from the park's Gothic gateway on the N4. It's here that you can buy tickets to the **Rockingham Remembered Tour**, where information boards guide you along a walking trail through a segment of the park. The route takes you through two subterranean **servants' tunnels** that survived the mansion's fire, as well as to the top of the five-storey **Moylurg viewing tower**. From here, there are splendid vistas of the lake and its numerous islands, including **Trinity Island**, which was once the site of a Cistercian foundation and a medieval castle. The trail concludes with the 300m-long **Tree Canopy Walk** whose timber-and-steel construction rises steadily to a 9m-high view of the park from the treetops.

Near the visitor centre there's the children's outdoor **Adventure Play Kingdom** and **Boda Borg**, a Swedish-designed two-storey puzzle-house which relies upon teamwork to solve various, instruction-less problems. Other attractions include a zipwire, electric bike trails and woodland segways.

ARRIVAL AND INFORMATION

BOYLE

By train Boyle's train station is 200m south of the centre, just off Elphin St. All services operate Mon–Sat 8 times daily, Sun 5.

Destinations Ballymote (15min); Carrick-on-Shannon (10min); Dublin (2hr 35min); Mullingar (1hr 20min); Sligo (35min).

By bus Buses set down on Carrick Rd.

Destinations Ballymote (Mon, Wed & Sat 1 daily; 30min);

Carrick-on-Shannon (5–6 daily; 15min); Dublin (5–6 daily; 3hr); Gurteen (Thurs 2; 25min); Riverstown (Thurs & Fri 1 daily; 35min); Sligo (5–6 daily; 40min); Strokestown (Mon–Sat 1 daily; 40min).

Tourist office The Una Bhán tourist office (daily 9am–6pm; http://discoverboyle.ie) is just by the entrance to King House and stocks maps and other information on the area.

ACCOMMODATION AND EATING

Kate Lavin's Patrick St. All dark oak panelling and wooden benches, this old-style bar is a great place to meet the locals. Its strength is its simplicity: no television or pool table, but a glow from the turf fire and friendly welcome from the owners. The Guinness has a "short run" because it comes from underneath the stairs. Closed Mon–Thurs.

King House Tea Rooms 087 643 0326. Set within the grounds of King House, this café serves wholesome lunches;

poached eggs and bacon is the signature dish, but you'll also find salads and vegetarian options such as spinach and goat's cheese tart. €

★ **Lough Key Camping** Lough Key Forest Park, http://loughkey.ie. Lovely woodland camping in the grounds of Lough Key Forest Park (see page 402), with camper's kitchen, games room and plenty of recreation areas. €

The Arigna Mountains

The far north of County Roscommon stretches up to Lough Allen where gentle farmland ascends to the moors and lakes of the **Arigna Mountains**. Albeit small-scale, this was once one of the few areas of Ireland to play a role in the Industrial Revolution, based first on **iron** extraction for a fifty-year period after 1788 – the local ironworks forged pikes in preparation for the 1798 Rebellion – and, subsequently, **coal**, which was worked here until 1990. The **Arigna Miners Way** is a waymarked 120km walking trail through the area, linking up with both the Leitrim Way and a historical trail taking in Boyle and parts of Sligo.

Keadue

KEADUE, 12km northeast of Boyle, is an attractive village of traditional cottages, stone walls and well-kept gardens. It is associated with the blind harper Turlough O'Carolan (see page 579), whose grave lies by the ruins of Kilronan Abbey, just out on the Sligo road. The musician is commemorated at the **O'Carolan Heritage Park**, a well-kept public park in the heart of the village with, as its centrepiece, a bronze replica of one of his harps. Keadue also hosts a harp and traditional music festival (http://ocarolanharpfestival.ie) at the end of July/beginning of August.

ARRIVAL AND ACCOMMODATION · KEADUE

By bus Keadue is served by a weekly bus service on Friday from/to Drumshanbo (20min) and Sligo (50min).

Harp & Shamrock B&B Main St, http://harpandshamrock. net. A delightful combination of bar, beer garden, grocery shop and accommodation all rolled into one friendly service. None of the seven rooms is en-suite but there are three separate bathrooms along the corridor. €€

Kilronan Castle Hotel 2km down the Ballyfarnon road, http://kilronancastle.ie. This luxury hotel set in a tranquil parkland estate features a tidy ensemble of castle rooms and suites (none finer than the Castle Tower suite), most with antique furnishings and underfloor heating, plus a gorgeous spa – featuring an atmospherically-lit, 15-metre heated pool – and the *Douglas Hyde* restaurant, where mains might include fillet of dry-aged beef, rack of Irish lamb or roast monkfish. €€€

Arigna Mining Experience

Arigna Hall, 2km north of Arigna village • charge; Heritage Island • http://arignaminingexperience.ie

From the dusty village of **Arigna** itself, a little further north, a winding road leads a couple of kilometres upwards, past a smokeless fuel plant, to the **Arigna Mining Experience**. Perched high on a hilltop and commanding stunning views of Lough Allen, this brilliantly designed and enthralling museum is located around one of the last working pits in the area. The history of local coal mining is documented in the exhibition area, but, once equipped with a hard hat, it's the forty-minute **tours** of the mine (which are accessible to all) that are most informative and thought-provoking. Led by ex-miners, these are rich in anecdote and thoroughly explore both the nature of the industry and the atrocious and exploitative working conditions the miners endured – the tunnels are dark and foreboding, and the sound of dripping water and footsteps is amplified by the acoustics.

Strokestown and around

The impressively planned settlement of **STROKESTOWN**, with its wide, tree-lined mall, embodies Ireland's troubled history in microcosm. It is the ideal base from which to delve into the historic riches of this part of south Roscommon, an area of rolling agricultural land. At the western end of Strokestown's mall sits an octagonal church, now housing the **County Roscommon Heritage and Genealogy Company** (Mon–Fri 2.30–4.30pm; http://roscommonroots.com), which conducts research for anyone seeking to trace their Roscommon roots; the eastern end of the mall terminates in a three-arched gateway, marking the entrance to Mahon's massive estate.

Brief history

The land on which Strokestown lies, and the surrounding area, known as **Corca Achlann**, belonged for more than a thousand years to the MacBranan clan, underlords of the powerful O'Connor kings who ruled Connacht, until dispossessed by Cromwell in the 1650s. Subsequently, part of their territory was granted by Charles II to Nicholas Mahon, whose kin later amassed more than thirty thousand acres for their huge estate, second only in size to Rockingham (see page 401) in Roscommon, becoming one of the great landed families of Ireland in the process. In the early nineteenth century, his descendant Lieutenant-General Thomas Mahon, Second Lord Hartland, requiring a grandiose symbol reflecting the extent of his property, determined to have constructed a **central avenue** wider than Vienna's Ringstrasse.

Strokestown Park House

Bottom of Bawn St, 150m east of the crossroads in Strokestown • Charge; Heritage Island • http://strokestownpark.ie

The magnificent Georgian **Strokestown Park House** was the seat of the Mahon family from its completion in 1696 for almost three hundred years. This huge Palladian mansion originally consisted of a two-storey central block and basement until the 1740s when Thomas Mahon, MP for Roscommon, hired the architect Richard Castle to construct a third storey and two extra wings. Mahon's son, Maurice (who became the First Lord Hartland in 1800), made subsequent additions including the library and many decorative features, such as cornices and chimneypieces, while the Second Lord Hartland added the porch and its huge pilasters. The house remained in Mahon ownership until 1979 when it was sold, along with its contents, to a local garage owner who undertook restoration work and opened it to the public in 1987.

Few Irish "big houses" retain their original owners' property (in this case ranging from furniture to children's toys), which is a vital factor in making the **guided tours** so entertaining. The main hall features early eighteenth-century wood panelling, while the spacious dining room, decorated in rich rose-pink damask wallpaper, is equipped with furniture from the early 1800s and a mammoth turf-bucket. The library was originally a ballroom – hence the bowed space at one end, which housed musicians – and has glorious Chippendale bookcases, while the smoking room was converted into a laboratory and photographic darkroom by Henry Pakenham-Mahon in the 1890s. The north wing includes a superb kitchen, replete with spits and ovens, and a balustraded gallery, the only surviving example in Ireland of a kind favoured by Castle, from which the housekeeper could keep an eagle eye on business down below and, according to Strokestown legend, drop menus for the week's meals down to the cook.

National Irish Famine Museum

Among the property passed on by the Mahons were numerous documents and letters relating to the family's role in relation to the Great Famine of 1845–51. The house's former stables – marvellously vaulted buildings in their own right – house an often chilling and stimulating **museum** detailing the Famine's effects upon the Mahons' tenants and its wider impact across Ireland. The intricate, informative displays and films focus on the concatenation of factors in Ireland – the growth of the rural population, the conacre system of agricultural tenancy, the reliance on the potato crop and the spread of the potato blight – that combined with Britain's economic policy of non-interference to have such a devastating effect on human life. Exhibits also highlight the role in local events of **Major Denis Mahon**, who had inherited the Strokestown estate after the death of the third and last Lord Hartland in 1845. The malevolent major not only evicted the majority of his tenants, but contracted dangerously unseaworthy vessels (the infamous coffin ships) to transport some of them in atrocious conditions to North America. The displays document contemporary newspaper reports condemning his actions and, in 1847, his assassination by vengeful ex-tenants.

DOUGLAS HYDE

Born in Castlerea, 13km south of Frenchpark, to Anglo-Irish Ascendancy stock, **Douglas Hyde** (1860–1949) learnt Irish at an early age and developed a lifelong interest in the nation's rich vernacular tradition and folklore. After attending Trinity College, he became professor of **Modern Irish Language and Literature** at the National University of Ireland and produced numerous articles, essays and reviews in Irish, as well as collaborating on a number of Irish-language plays with Lady Gregory (see page343). Hyde travelled the country widely, gathering material, much of which was transcribed in collections such as the highly influential *Love Songs of Connaught*. In 1893, he was a co-founder of the **Gaelic League**, which aimed to enhance Irish culture via a revival of musical and linguistic traditions, though Hyde later became concerned by the League's increasing links with the Independence movement and resigned as its president in 1915. Elected to the Irish Senate in 1925, he retired from public life in 1932 until he was appointed the country's first **president** in 1938.

ARRIVAL AND DEPARTURE · STROKESTOWN

11

By bus The bus stop is 10m from the *Percy French Hotel* in Bridge St.
Destinations Boyle (1 daily; 40min); Dublin (6 daily; 2hr 25min); Frenchpark (7–8 daily; 25min); Sligo (Mon–Sat 1 daily; 1hr); Tulsk (6–7 daily; 15min).

ACCOMMODATION AND EATING

Hanly's Bridge St, 071 171 9584. This venerable institution is a great place to soak up some stories from the locals. It hosts traditional music sessions on the first Thursday of each month. Daily 6–11.30pm.

Percy French Hotel Bridge St, 071 963 3300. Lively social hub with eighteen pleasant en-suite rooms and a decent bar. Meals are available in the bar – carvery roasts are popular – throughout the day up to 9pm. €€

Douglas Hyde Interpretive Centre

Frenchpark, 26km northwest of Strokestown • Open by appointment May–Sept • Free • 087 782 3751

A forty-minute drive from Strokestown lies the village of **Frenchpark**, where the former Church of Ireland parish church is home to the **Douglas Hyde Interpretive Centre**. The centre recounts the life of **Douglas Hyde** (see box), one of the key figures in the Irish cultural revival, with informative displays and an entertaining video. Note that it is essential to phone in advance to gain admission to the centre.

Tulsk

Located around the village of **TULSK**, 15km southeast of Frenchpark, is **Rathcroghan**, a rich array of earthworks, ring forts, standing stones and caves betokening one of Ireland's major mythological areas. According to *The Annals of the Four Masters* (see page 414) it was here that Medb, the warrior queen and earth goddess who features heavily in the *Táin Bó Cúailnge* (see page 154), sited her palace Cruachan, the location of the epic's opening and gory conclusion.

Rathcroghan Visitor Centre

Just west of the crossroads in Tulsk • charge combined tour price • http://rathcroghan.ie

Before visiting the monuments, it's wise to head for the **Rathcroghan Visitor Centre**, where audiovisuals bring the history of the site to life: you'll see a reconstruction of the **Oweynagat** ("the cave of the cats"), which supposedly provided the entrance to the Irish Otherworld, the origin place for the global festival of Halloween, which originated in Ireland – ancient Samhain. Highlights include Iron Age and medieval Gaelic figures, and the collection of ten black-and-white facsimile illustrations of the *Táin*, drawn by the late Irish artist Louis le Brocquy.

Donegal

HIKING THE SLIEVE LEAGUE

Donegal

Second in size only to County Cork, County Donegal has unquestionably the richest scenery in the whole of Ireland, featuring a spectacular 300km coastline – an intoxicating run of headlands, promontories and peninsulas rising to the highest sea-cliffs in Europe. Perhaps the most satisfying landscape is that of northern Donegal, not least the Rosguill and Inishowen peninsulas, while the interior region around Errigal Mountain, Lough Beagh and Lough Gartan merits an extended visit. Elsewhere, Donegal manifests a wonderful, and often wonderfully bleak, terrain of glens, rivers and bogland hills.

Donegal's original name was *Tír Chonaill*, which translates as "the land of Conal"; Chonaill was one of the twelve sons of Niall of the Nine Hostages, reputed to have ruled Ireland in the fifth century. After the Flight of the Earls in 1607 (see page 562), the English changed the name to that of their main garrison *Dún na nGall* ("fort of the foreigners"), which has a certain irony, because Donegal always eluded the grip of English power thanks to its wild and infertile terrain. Donegal is the most northerly part of Ireland, which confuses some into believing that it is part of Northern Ireland. It never actually has been, since in 1922, at the time of Partition, the Unionists believed that Donegal's Catholic population would threaten the stability of the new statelet by voting the county and the whole of the North back into the Republic.

Aside from the aforementioned places, Donegal's best-known destinations are the **Glencolmcille Peninsula** and around **Ardara** and **Glenties** in the southern part of the county, while other noteworthy areas are **the Rosses** and **Gweedore**, which are reminiscent of the more barren stretches of Connemara and make up the strongest Irish-speaking districts (*gaeltacht*) in the county.

GETTING AROUND   **DONEGAL**

By bus The county has an extensive network of public and private bus services, with the sporadically interesting towns of Letterkenny and Donegal serving as its major transport hubs. However, there are limited services to some areas, especially outside high season.

By car You'll need your own transport to reach some outlying attractions, such as Glenveagh and parts of the Rosguill, Fanad and Inishowen peninsulas.

South Donegal

Entered via the N15 from Sligo (which now largely bypasses the most scenic spots), **south Donegal** might lack the wildness characteristic of much of Donegal's coastline, but the area still has some marvellous beaches, especially at **Bundoran** and **Rossnowlagh**, both popular surfing spots, while **Ballyshannon** is an attractive hillside town situated at the mouth of the River Erne. Further north, **Donegal town** has a pleasant bayside setting and remains of a notable castle, while to its north and southeast respectively lie graceful **Lough Eske** and **Lough Derg**, a major site for Catholic pilgrimage.

Bundoran

Once described by an Irish newspaper as like "the back streets of Las Vegas only with cheaper hookers", **BUNDORAN** isn't quite that bad, but it's hard to avoid

PRETTY BUNBEG

Highlights

❶ Slieve League No visit to Donegal would be complete without a walk along the top of this mountain's awesome sea-cliffs. See page 419

❷ Teach Húdaí Beag's pub Unquestionably one of the best traditional music sessions in Ireland takes place here in the small village of Bunbeg on Monday nights. See page 426

❸ Tory Island Bleak, barren, wet and windy – why would anyone choose to live here? Take a trip and discover a thriving local culture and a world quite different from the mainland. See page 426

❹ Glebe House Home of the late artist Derek Hill, Glebe House contains some of the most remarkable modern art in Ireland. See page 430

❺ The Grianán Ailigh This restored, circular stone fort commands unbeatable panoramic views of Donegal from its hilltop setting. See page 438

❻ Malin Head Ireland's most northerly point offers dramatic seascapes and, thanks to a lack of visitors, wonderfully unspoilt landscapes too. See page 442

HIGHLIGHTS ARE MARKED ON THE MAP ON PAGE 410

DONEGAL

HIGHLIGHTS

1. Slieve League
2. Teach Húdaí Beag's pub
3. Tory Island
4. Glebe House
5. The Grianán Ailigh
6. Malin Head

THE DONEGAL CYCLE ROUTE

A 200km scenic cycle route which snakes around the Donegal coastline, the **DCR** is the best way to explore the area by bike. Taking in some of the county's most spectacular landscapes, it has been broken down into fourteen manageable stages. Although it officially starts in Newtowncunningham, it's more straightforward to start in **Letterkenny** and finish in **Donegal town**. The route is well signposted throughout, but as this is Donegal, expect some steep climbs and narrow roads where extra care should be taken. For downloadable **maps** and route-planning, visit http://donegalcycleroute.ie.

BIKE RENTALS AND REPAIRS

The Bike Stop Bundoran, http://thebikestop.ie.   **Ireland by Bike** Carrick, http://irelandbybike.com.
Don Byrne Bikes Ardara, http://donbyrnebikes.com.   **LK Bikes** Letterkenny, http://lkbikes.com.

---

disappointment if the town is your first sight of Donegal. Lying at the county's southern extreme, this popular, though intermittently tacky, seaside resort offers little indication of the pleasures that lie beyond. Its 5km of Blue Flag **beaches, however,** are among the finest in the country, and are a real pull for surfers of all abilities.

The tiny River Doran separates the more genteel **West End** from the **East End**, with its down-at-heel Main Street and a headland dominated by a **golf course**. Bundoran's chief attraction is the lovely golden-sanded **Tullan Strand**, a bracing stroll along the coastal promenade from the northern end of the town beach. The walk takes in rock formations known as the **Fairy Bridge** and the **Puffing Hole**, with the Atlantic thundering below and appetizing views across to the much more rewarding Glencolmcille Peninsula.

ARRIVAL AND DEPARTURE

BUNDORAN

By bus Buses stop at various points along Main St. Destinations Ballyshannon (Mon–Sat 8–11 daily, Sun 4; 10min); Donegal town (Mon–Sat 7 daily, Sun 5; 30min); Sligo (Mon–Sat 7 daily, Sun 5; 35–50min).

INFORMATION AND ACTIVITIES

Tourist office By the bridge on Main St (Mon–Fri 9.30am–5pm, Sat & Sun 11am–5pm; http://discoverbundoran.com).
Surfing Tullan Strand and Rossnowlagh beach (see above) are exciting surfing spots, and tuition is available from Bundoran Surf Co., Main St (http://bundoransurfco.com), who also rent stand-up paddleboards, and Surfworld, Main St (http://surfworld.ie).

ACCOMMODATION AND EATING

Great Northern Hotel On the headland east of town, http://greatnorthernhotel.com. Prominently sited, this huge hotel adjoining the fabulous Bundoran golf course has glorious views from just about every room; facilities include a spa and gym. €€€
Maddens Bridge Bar West End, near the Protestant Church, http://maddensbridgebar.com. Wonderful, woody bar cluttered with hanging pots, jars, boots and suchlike. Heading upstairs to the restaurant, grab a window seat and soak up the sparkling ocean views while tucking into meaty dishes like Lough Erne lamb shank and beef and Guinness casserole. €€€

Ballyshannon

The lively town of **BALLYSHANNON**, 6km north of Bundoran, was the site of a major battle in 1591 when Hugh Roe O'Donnell saw off the besieging English army, but nowadays its hilly streets become most animated during several upbeat festivals (see box).

St Anne's Church

Upper Main St · 074 9734025

Ballyshannon's main arteries form a wishbone leading up the town's steep northern slope, and signposted near the top of the left-hand branch is **St Anne's Church** and graveyard, built on the site of the ancient palace of Mullaghanshee. A simple marble slab, inscribed with the word "poet", lies left of the church, marking the burial place of locally born **William Allingham** (1824–89). His first volume, *Poems* (1850), includes his best-known work, *The Fairies* ("Up the airy mountain/Down the rushy glen/We daren't go a-hunting/For fear of little men…"). Such verse attracted him to the Pre-Raphaelites – another work, *Day and Night Songs*, was illustrated by Rossetti and Millais – before Allingham moved on to the more serious poetic subject of his homeland. His posthumously published *Diary* recounts his friendships with literary contemporaries, most notably Tennyson.

Ballyshannon Museum

Slevins Department Store, Market Yard • Free • 087 193 7166

To gain further insight into the history of the town – it lays claim to being Ireland's oldest – pop your head into the **Ballyshannon Museum**, peculiarly located on the top floor of the local department store (past the beds). In truth, it's a curiously mixed bag, with exhibits ranging from a cannonball from the Battle of Ballyshannon and wreckage retrieved from one of the three ships from the Spanish Armada sunk in the waters hereabouts, to some personal effects belonging to local notables William Allingham (first editions, writing box and ink well) and the legendary, and much loved, rock star Rory Gallagher (see box).

ARRIVAL AND DEPARTURE

BALLYSHANNON

By bus Buses drop off on, and depart from, the bottom of Main St, near the bridge.

Destinations Belleek (9 daily; 10min); Bundoran (Mon–Sat

8–11 daily, Sun 4; 10min); Donegal town (Mon–Sat 7 daily, Sun 5; 25min); Sligo (Mon–Sat 7 daily, Sun 5; 45min–1hr).

ACCOMMODATION AND EATING

Dorrian's Imperial Hotel Main St, http://dorrians imperialhotel.com. Handsome eighteenth-century building with warm and comfortable, if agreeably old-fashioned, and slightly overpriced, rooms and public spaces, plus a decent bar and restaurant. €€€

Lakeside Caravan and Camping Off the R230 Belleek Rd, http://lakesidecaravanandcamping.com. Superb lakeside campsite with a full complement of facilities including modern shower blocks, laundry, games room plus a kids' playground. Canoe rental available too. Closed Nov to early March. €

Nirvana The Mall, http://nirvanarestaurant.ie. Sharp-

looking restaurant-cum-wine-bar, serving some beautifully conceived dishes, such as pan-fried duck breast with figs and a Cointreau reduction – veggie and vegan options are unusually strong too, such as stuffed courgette flowers, and bamboo steamed sesame and tofu dumplings. Shame about the short opening hours though (closed Mon–Thurs). €€€

★ **The Thatch** Bishop St, 071 985 1147. An old fisherman's haunt, this diminutive pub manifests a sweet cottage-kitchen interior with white-painted walls and red-painted doors – it's known for its legendary traditional music sessions, which could be any night the pub happens to be open.

ENTERTAINMENT

The Abbey Centre Market St, http://abbeycentre.ie. Dynamic arts centre hosting a range of musical, cinematic and theatrical events, plus a regular, rotating programme of

exhibitions. It's also one of the main venues for the town's several festivals.

BALLYSHANNON FESTIVALS

The town's main event is the **Folk Festival** (http://ballyshannonfolkfestival.com) over the first weekend in August, featuring major Irish and international musicians. Sticking with the musical theme, the **Rory Gallagher International Festival** (http://rorygallagherfestival.com) at the beginning of June pays homage to the local guitar legend, with concerts on several stages throughout town. Lastly, in November, the **Allingham Arts Festival** (http://allinghamfestival.com) brings to life the works of the native poet, through storytelling, screenings and workshops.

12

Donegal town and around

DONEGAL town is not the most exciting of places, but it's a pleasant enough spot to pass a few hours, rating one or two attractions and a fair sprinkling of hotels and restaurants clustered around its triangular and central **Diamond**, the old marketplace.

Many tourists head for the town in the mistaken belief that they'll find themselves in the midst of the county's famously wild terrain, and then discover its rather more sedate setting. However, southeast of the town, the landscape is replete with little lakes well stocked for fishing; the largest of these, and a place of pilgrimage, is **Lough Derg**. Less than 8km upriver from Donegal town is another spot of gentle natural beauty, **Lough Eske**, from where you can walk into the wilds of the **Blue Stack Mountains**, which rise to the north.

Donegal Castle

Tirconnell St • charge; Heritage Card • 074 972 2405

Donegal's original "fort of the foreigners" was thought to have been built on the banks of the River Eske by invading Vikings. Later, the first Red Hugh O'Donnell, king of Tír Chonaill, had a Norman-style tower house, known as **O'Donnell's Castle**, constructed on its site in the fifteenth century. When the English defeated the second Red Hugh in 1603, Sir Basil Brooke was given command of the town and it was he who rebuilt and extended the old castle, retaining the lower parts of the original tower, which had been razed to the ground by Red Hugh to prevent its capture. This well-restored example of Jacobean architecture is a fine marriage of strong defence and domestic grace, featuring mullioned windows, arches, ten gables and no fewer than fourteen fireplaces, over the grandest of which are carved the escutcheons of Brooke and his wife's family, the Leicesters. Brooke topped the tower with a Barbizon turret and added the mansion on the left, with the kitchens and bakery on the ground floor and living quarters on the floor above. Brooke was highly prolific in Donegal and was responsible for the overall design of the town.

Donegal Railway Heritage Centre

Tirconnell St • charge • http://donegalrailway.com

Railway fans will enjoy a visit to the **Donegal Railway Heritage Centre**, which occupies the Old Station House, standing just as it did when the County Donegal Railway, which ran from Derry to Ballyshannon, closed in 1959. Inside you'll find a model of the old railway alongside nostalgic memorabilia and some of the original station signs. Outside, you can enter a restored nineteenth-century coach and railcar, and while there's nothing inside, save for a DVD on the history of the railway, you may be lucky enough to catch one of the model railway exhibitions that are often held here.

THE ANNALS OF THE FOUR MASTERS

In Donegal town's Diamond stands an obelisk commemorating the compilers of the famed **Annals of the Four Masters**. The Annals were begun in the town's **Franciscan friary**, whose ruined remains stand on the left bank of the River Eske, and were a systematic attempt to collect all known Irish documents into a history of the land beginning in 2958 BC, including mythical invasions by Firbolgs and Milesians, and ending in 1616 AD. The friary itself was built in 1474 by the first Red Hugh and his wife Nuala O'Brien of Munster. It was occupied by the English in 1601 and seriously damaged by the besieging O'Donnell army, being finally abandoned after the Flight of the Earls (see page 562). The Annals were completed by friars who had moved to a site by the River Drowse, near Kinlough, Country Leitrim. Manuscript copies of the Annals are occasionally on display at **Trinity College library** in Dublin.

Donegal Craft Village

Just outside town, down the Sligo road • http://donegalcraftvillage.com

The **Donegal Craft Village** comprises half a dozen or so workshops showcasing a range of local crafts, including glassware, textiles, painting and ceramics, jewellery and wood sculpture. Many of the items are available to buy, and there's a fabulous little café here too (see page 416).

Lough Eske and the Blue Stacks

The soft beauty of **Lough Eske** is easily accessible from Donegal town. To get here take the minor road that runs north of the river, signposted "Lough Eske Drive", 500m out on the Killybegs road. This leads to a forgotten forested estate, once belonging to the Brooke family but now owned by the Forestry Commission. The lough is no longer a particularly great fishing spot, though it is known as a place to catch char, a tasty 20cm-long species of the salmon family, which lurk in the depths at the centre of the lake, moving out to the shallower edges around late October, where they can easily be fished using worms. The sandy banks of the River Eske are also known for freshwater oysters – some of which are reputed to contain pearls – but they're a protected species so it's illegal to take them. The ruins of an **O'Donnell tower**, once a prison, stand on one of the small islands on the lake.

Carrying on along the western shore of Lough Eske, you'll reach the spot where the river flows in at the lough's northern tip. A dirt road here runs off to the left into the **Blue Stack Mountains**.

At the top of the pathway that leads on from the track there are superb views over the lough. From here you can join the waymarked **Bluestack Way**, which passes Lough Belshade, guarded in legend by a huge black cat. If you're intending to tramp around the mountain range, it's best to keep to the skirts of the hills as there are many marshy patches on lower ground – and be prepared for misty pockets during bad weather.

Lough Derg and Station Island

5km east of Donegal town • Retreats May to end Sept • http://loughderg.org • Buses from Ballyshannon or Enniskillen drop you in Pettigo village (9km south), though some continue to Lough Derg in the summer

In the middle of **Lough Derg** is a rocky islet known as **Station Island** or, more popularly, St Patrick's Purgatory, a retreat for Catholics needing rigour and solitude to recharge their faith. A national shrine of pilgrimage since the fifth century, it was described by Giraldus Cambrensis in *Topography of Ireland* (1186) as "an island, one part of which is frequented by good spirits, the other by evil spirits". Contemporary scholars have argued

DONEGAL TOWN

Donegal Railway Heritage Centre

MEETING HOUSE STREET

TIRCONNELL STREET

NEW ROW

NEW ROW

CASTLE STREET

WATER STREET

KILLYBEGS ROAD

BRIDGE STREET

Donegal Castle

MAIN STREET

UPPER MAIN STREET

Obelisk

THE BANK WALK

QUAY STREET

QUAY BRAE

River Eske

Lough Eske / Blue Stack

Harvey's Point (7.5km) & Letterkenny

Donegal Waterbus

Friary

BALLYSHANNON ROAD

Donegal Bay

, Ballyshannon, Sligo & Donegal Craft Village

12

DRINKING & NIGHTLIFE	
The Reel Inn	1

ACCOMMODATION	
Atlantic Guest House	3
The Central Hotel	4
Harvey's Point Country Hotel	2
Lough Eske Castle	1

EATING	
Aroma	5
The Blueberry Tearooms	2
Chandpur	3
The Harbour	4
La Bella Donna	1

that, as St Patrick never referred to Lough Derg in his writings, he probably never visited the island, but nevertheless it still thrives today as a strong centre for **pilgrimage**.

Some retreat programmes are more challenging than others, with the one-day activities offering a shorter retreat experience where shoes remain on and lunch is served. The **Three Day Pilgrimage**, as written about down the centuries, is a powerful experience that requires endurance (24hr Vigil, walking barefoot in prayer and fasting with one simple meal of dry toast or bread, oatcakes and black tea or coffee) and an openness to enter deeply into the spirit of the pilgrimage. *Station Island*, a collection by Seamus Heaney, contains a number of poems dealing with the mystique surrounding this ritual, while the late Pete McCarthy graphically recounted his experience of a retreat in *McCarthy's Bar* (see page 601). The island is approached via the R233 from the village of **Pettigo**, 9km south.

ARRIVAL AND DEPARTURE

DONEGAL TOWN AND AROUND

By bus Buses stop outside the *Abbey Hotel* on The Diamond. Destinations Ardara (Mon–Sat 3 daily, Sun 1 daily; 50min); Ballyshannon (Mon–Sat 7 daily, Sun 5; 20–30min); Bundoran (Mon–Sat 7 daily, Sun 5; 30min); Derry (6–7 daily; 1hr 25min); Dungloe (Mon–Sat 3 daily, Sun 1; 1hr 30min); Enniskillen (8 daily; 1hr 10min); Glencolmcille (2–4 daily; 1hr 15min–1hr 30min); Glenties (Mon–Sat 3 daily, Sun 1; 35min–1hr); Killybegs (Mon–Sat 3 daily, Sun 1; 30min); Letterkenny (6–7 daily; 50min); Sligo (6–7 daily; 1hr 5min).

INFORMATION AND ACTIVITIES

Tourist office The tourist office is located in a waterside building in The Quay car park (Tues–Sat 9am–5pm, plus June–Sep Sun 10am–4pm; http://govisitdonegal.com).

Boat tours Down at the quay, a Waterbus offers trips around Donegal Bay (€25; http://donegalbaywaterbus. com; 1hr 15min).

ACCOMMODATION

SEE MAP PAGE 415

Atlantic Guest House Main St, http://atlanticguesthouse. ie. The best-value, and certainly the most hospitable, place in town, offering brightly coloured, if modestly sized, rooms, most with bathrooms but some just with sinks. €€

The Central Hotel The Diamond, http://central hoteldonegal.com. Prominently positioned on the main town square, this refined hotel has bright and airy rooms (some overlooking the bay), and its own leisure centre with pool; although it's not cheap, they do offer some good deals. €€

★ **Harvey's Point Country Hotel** Towards the southern end of Lough Eske, http://harveyspoint.com. The rooms – essentially mini-suites – here offer nothing less than unbridled luxury, from the magnificently upholstered furnishings to the sumptuous, marble-tiled bathrooms and imperious lake views. The restaurant, with its theatrical open kitchen, is no less impressive. €€€

Lough Eske Castle South of the Lough (and best approached from Donegal town via the N15 Lifford road), http://lougheskecastlehotel.com. This glorious five-star hotel and spa is set within a renovated Victorian castle in perfectly maintained grounds. Accommodation here ranges from swish doubles to lavish suites. Here too are all manner of dining possibilities and a fancy spa. €€€€

EATING

SEE MAP PAGE 415

Aroma Donegal Craft Village, just outside town, down the Sligo road, http://donegalcraftvillage.com. Exceptionally good coffee shop and home bakery serving a range of salads and savouries, including some spicy Mexican specials, plus lush cakes fresh from the oven. Closed Sun. €

The Blueberry Tearooms Castle St, http://theblueberry tearooms.ie.. A friendly place with a pretty, fairy-lit interior, serving excellent soups, sandwiches, hot wraps and quiches, the latter baked fresh on the premises each day. For a real treat, try one of the desserts (also made here), perhaps the steamed chocolate pudding or a slice of home-made blueberry pie. €€

Chandpur Main St, http://chandpurdonegal.com. Serving some of the best Indian food in the country, this multi-award-winning restaurant always lives up to the hype. With plush decor, friendly staff and a cracking atmosphere, it's the food that steals the show; try the Shami Kebab, followed by the Monkfish Curry. €€€

The Harbour Quay St, http://harbourdonegal.ie. Long standing, local institution offering a wide-ranging mix of menus comprising seafood (oven baked hake with creamy mash), chicken and steaks alongside stone-baked pizzas. €€€

La Bella Donna Bridge St, http://labelladonnarestaurant. com. This sleek Italian establishment just about shades it as the pick of the town's restaurants, offering up some interesting variations on traditional dishes, such as Italian sausage and wild mushroom tagliatelle. €€€

12

DRINKING

SEE MAP PAGE 415

The Reel Inn Bridge St, 087 11 9994. The place to come in town for traditional music – it's no exaggeration to say that there's something on here every night of the week, every day of the year. Music aside, this is a real boozer's pub with oodles of character, and characters.

Southwest Donegal

The most appealing route out of Donegal town heads west along the shore of Donegal Bay all the way to Glencolmcille, some 50km away. Highlights along this coast include the tapering peninsula leading to **St John's Point** and extraordinarily dramatic coastal scenery, which reaches an apogee in the mammoth sea-cliffs of **Slieve League**. The **Glencolmcille Peninsula** is a Gaeltacht (Irish-speaking area) and its attractive villages are rich in traditional folklore and music.

St John's Point

Just west of the single-street village of **Dunkineely**, 17km west of Donegal town, a deviation left from the main road brings you down to *Castle Murray House Hotel* (see below). In the small car park opposite stands a sandstone rock **memorial** to some forty fishermen (it may have been more) who lost their lives in Bruckless Bay during a great storm on February 11, 1813; what is undisputed is that more than two hundred curraghs (wooden-framed boats covered in animal hides) were lost at sea that night. Though little documented, it constitutes one of Ireland's worst ever fishing tragedies.

From here, continue down a long, narrow promontory to **St John's Point**, where a crumbling castle stands at the tip and there are great **views** over Donegal Bay, especially back towards the narrow entry of Killybegs Bay, with **Rotten Island** at its mouth. This is one of the finest spots in all of Europe for scuba diving.

12

ACCOMMODATION AND EATING

ST JOHN'S POINT

Castle Murray House Hotel St John's Point, 087 649 4659. A high-end B&B with ten individually decorated boutique bedrooms, some with incredible views of the bay. Breakfast is very impressive, with in-house smoked fish, home-made preserves and granola, and local farm-to-fork full Irish. **€€€**

Killybegs

Sticking to the coast road west of Bruckless, you'll round Killybegs Bay and arrive in what was once the most successful fishing port in Ireland: **KILLYBEGS**, the halfway point between Donegal town and Glencolmcille.

After years of decline this atmospheric little town is on the up again, partly due to the ongoing development of the marina, though no less important has been the introduction of Killybegs as a destination for major cruise liners, this being one of very few deep sea ports in the country. Moreover, – and while there are no conventional sites following the recent sad closure of the Carpet Making and Fishing Centre – there are some excellent places to stay and eat at in and around town.

Around 8km west of town, en route to Kilcar, the road divides: for the scenic route, take the left-hand fork, a narrow switchback ride along the coastline with stupendous views over the ocean, especially from **Muckross Head**, and the looming presence of the hills and mountains to your right.

ARRIVAL AND INFORMATION

KILLYBEGS

By bus Buses generally stop off and pick up in front of the *Tara Hotel*.

Destinations Ardara (Mon–Sat 3 daily, Sun 1; 20min); Carrick (2–4 daily; 30min); Donegal town (Mon–Sat 3 daily, Sun 1; 30min); Glencolmcille (Mon–Sat 3 daily, Sun 1; 45min); Glenties (Mon–Sat 3 daily, Sun 1; 45min); Kilcar

(Mon–Sat 3 daily, Sun 1; 20min).
Tourist office The tourist office is located in a cabin on Shore Rd (Mon–Fri 10am–4.30pm; http://killybegs.ie);

they can book accommodation here. Note that there are no ATMs beyond Killybegs in the direction of Slieve.

ACCOMMODATION AND EATING

★ **Bay View Hotel** Main St, http://bayviewhotel.ie. Handsome harbour-facing building which mixes classic and contemporary styles to dazzling effect, from the cool, crisp all-white rooms to the glittering elegance of the restaurant, which is where breakfast is taken. Pool and sauna too. €€
Mrs B's Main St, http://mrsbscoffeehouse.com. Perky, cheerily staffed coffee shop knocking up freshly prepared

seafood chowder, sandwiches and quiches – including gluten-free options – but best of all, an enticing selection of home-made treats; takeaway coffee too. Closed Sun. €
Tara Hotel Main St, http://tarahotel.ie. A few paces from the *Bay View Hotel*, the *Tara* is a little more discreet, with sunny, if unspectacular, rooms facing either the harbour or, less attractively, the street behind. €€€

Kilcar

The roads meet again at **KILCAR**, a pleasant village and a centre for the Donegal **tweed industry**: there are a couple of small factories open to visitors; try Studio Donegal (Mon–Fri 9am–5.30pm, Sat 9.30am–5pm; http://studiodonegal.ie) at the Glebe Mill in the centre of the village, where you can watch the spinners and weavers at work (not on Saturdays). The village hosts a three-day folk, blues and bluegrass **festival** on the May bank holiday weekend, plus a raucous street festival over the first weekend in August and a week-long traditional music festival during the same month. There are traditional music **concerts** in the Community Hall on Saturday evenings in summer.

12

ARRIVAL AND ACCOMMODATION
KILCAR

By bus Buses drop off and depart from the main street. Destinations Carrick (Mon–Sat 3 daily, Sun 1; 15min); Donegal town (1 daily; 1hr); Glencolmcille (Mon–Sat 3 daily, Sun 1; 25min); Killybegs (Mon–Sat 3 daily, Sun 1; 20min).
Derrylahan Hostel 3km west on the coast road towards Carrick, http://derrylahanhostel.ie. This place, set on a

working farm, must be one of the friendliest hostels in the country, with a mix of small dorms, a kitchen, common room with turf fire, and laundry. Camping is also available, with its own washing and kitchen facilities. €
Ocean Spray On the road towards Muckross Head, 074 973 8438. A welcoming seaside B&B with three pine-heavy en-suite rooms, though only one has ocean views. €

Carrick and Teelin

Derrylahan Hostel (see above) is an ideal base for exploring the beautiful countryside around **CARRICK**, especially Teelin Bay and the awesome **Slieve League** cliffs to the west (see box). The southern road from Carrick to **TEELIN** follows the west bank of the River Owenee, whose rapids and pools are good for **fishing**. The village is Irish-speaking and rich in storytelling, with many stories having been recorded by the late Seán Ó'hEochaidh, Donegal's great folklorist.

ARRIVAL AND INFORMATION
CARRICK AND TEELIN

By bus Buses drop off on, and depart from, Main St. Destinations Donegal town (1–3 daily; 1hr–1hr 15min); Glencolmcille (Mon–Sat 3 daily, Sun 1; 15min); Kilcar (Mon–Sat 3 daily, Sun 1; 10min); Killybegs (Mon–Sat 3 daily, Sun 1; 30min).

Boat trips One hour 45 minute boat trips to the Slieve League cliffs are provided by Sliabh Liag Boat Trips, based down at the pier in Teelin (€25; http://sliabhleagueboattrips com). They also run bird, whale and dolphin watching tours as well as trips to some idyllic swimming spots.

ACCOMMODATION AND EATING

The Rusty Mackerel Teelin, 2.5km south of Carrick, http://therustymackerel.com. Teelin has a long musical tradition, and the best place to hear some local sounds is this cosy village pub, which has a dynamic Saturday session,

plus occasional music on other evenings too. They've also got some simple, spartanly furnished rooms. €€
Slieve League Lodge Carrick, in the centre of the village http://slieveleaguelodge.com. This jolly pub keeps twelve

WALKS AROUND SLIEVE LEAGUE

There are two routes up to the ridge of **Slieve League**. The less-used back one, known as Old Man's Track, follows the signpost pointing to the mountain just before **Teelin** and looks up continually to the ridge, while the frontal approach follows the signs out of Teelin to **Bunglass**, swinging you spectacularly round sharp bends and up incredibly steep inclines to one of the most thrilling cliff scenes in the world, the **Amharc Mór**. The sea moves so far below their peak that the waves appear silent, and the 600m face glows with mineral deposits in tones of amber, white and red. They say that on a clear day it is possible to see one-third of the whole of Ireland from the summit. **Sightseeing tours** of the cliffs from the waters below are organized from Teelin, weather permitting (see page 418).

If you want to make a full day of it, you can climb up to the cliffs from the Bunglass car park and follow the path along the top of the ridge, which eventually meets Old Man's Track. From here One Man's Pass, a narrow path with steep slopes on each side, leads up to the **summit** of Slieve League. Bear in mind that the route can often be muddy and very windy – it is certainly not advisable in misty weather or if you suffer from vertigo. From the top of Slieve League, you can either retrace your steps to Teelin or continue west over the crest of the mountain and down the heather-tufted western slope towards the headland village of **Malinbeg**, where there's a sublime, crescent-shaped golden strand enclosed by a tight rocky inlet. Malinbeg itself is a village of white bungalows, with the land around ordered into long narrow strips. On the cliff edge a ruined Martello tower faces **Rathlin O'Beirne Island**, 5km offshore, a place with many folklore associations. There are occasional boats across (enquire in Teelin), but nothing to see aside from some early Christian stone relics and a ruined coastguard station.

Beyond Malinbeg, it's relatively easy to extend your walk through **Malinmore** and on to Glencolmcille. The whole distance from Teelin to Malinmore can be comfortably completed in six hours.

ACCOMMODATION

The Malinbeg Hostel Malinbeg, http:// malinbeghostel.com. Just a 5min walk from the beach, this well-equipped hostel offers exhilarating views from most of its rooms, which comprise both dorms and private rooms, some ensuite. Kitchen, dining rooms and sitting room. €

ostel-type rooms, all en suite and sleeping between two nd four, plus a self-catering kitchen. The pub itself is arrick's social hub, and has traditional music sessions most weekends. Set to one side of the pub is *Kelly's Kitchen*, where you can pick up light lunches, cakes and coffee. €

Glencolmcille and around

As the road from Carrick approaches **GLENCOLMCILLE**, it traverses desolate moorland that's dominated by oily-black turf banks amid patches of heather and grass. After this, the rich beauty of the Glen, as it's known, comes as a welcome surprise. Settlement in the area dates back to the Stone Age, as testified by the enormous number of **megalithic remains** scattered around the countryside, especially court cairns and standing stones. There's evidence, too, of the Celtic era, in the form of earthworks and stone works. According to tradition, **St Columba** founded a monastery here in the sixth century, and some of the **standing stones**, known as the Turas Cholmcille, were adapted for Christian usage by the inscription of a cross. Every Columba's Day (June 9) at midnight, the locals commence a barefoot circuit of the fifteen Turas, including Columba's Chapel, chair, bed, wishing stone and Holy Well, finishing up with Mass at 3am in the village church. (Columba and Columbcille/Colmcille are the same person – the latter is the name by which he was known after his conversion, and means "the dove of the church".) Widespread emigration post-Famine and in the early twentieth century left the Glencolmcille area a typical example of rural decay. In 1951, however, a new and energetic curate, Father James McDyer, instigated efforts to revitalize the community, while retaining and strengthening its culture. Electricity arrived and road improvements reduced its isolation and allowed new collective enterprises in knitting and agriculture to thrive, and encouraged the development of local tourism.

Folk Village Museum and Heritage Centre

Doonalt, less than 1km west of Glencolmcille on the R263 • charge • http://glenfolkvillage.com

Just a stone throw's from the beach stands the wonderful **Folk Village Museum and Heritage Centre**, a cluster of replica thatched cottages, each equipped with the furniture and artefacts of the era it represents. Founded in 1967, the museum was the initiative of Father James McDyer (see above), whose life is celebrated in the first of the six buildings as you enter. The older cottages are notable for their bog oak and straw roofs and uneven flooring, in marked contrast with those from the mid-nineteenth century, which manifest smoother, neater lines.

One building introduces you to the area's history and cultural heritage, including a door from a cupboard reputedly used by Charles Stuart (Bonnie Prince Charlie), who sought refuge here following the Battle of Culloden in 1746. The **Dooey School House** replica has a display of informative photographs and research projects, and a section on the American painter Rockwell Kent, who painted marvellous treatments of the area's landscapes during his time here in 1926. Close by is a wonderful example of an old-style **Pub-Grocers**, few of which exist today, but sweetest of all is the tiny **Fisherman's cottage**, which relays the history of the local fishing industry.

Glen Head, Port and Glenlough

From behind *Dooey Hostel* (see below), **cliff walks** steer off around the south side of the bay above a series of jagged drops. Rising from the opposite side of the valley mouth, the promontory of **Glen Head** is surmounted by a Martello tower. On the way out you pass the ruins of **St Colmcille's Church**, with its "resting slab" where St Columba would have lain down exhausted from prayer. North across this headland you can climb and then descend to the forgotten little cove of **Port** a few kilometres away, a village deserted since the 1940s. Absolutely nothing happens here – although Dylan Thomas once stayed in the next valley at **Glenlough**, renting a cottage for several weeks in a doomed attempt to "dry out" in an area replete with poteen stills.

The Glengesh Pass and Maghera

Heading northeast from Glencolmcille, the minor road to Ardara runs through the heart of the peninsula, travelling via the dramatic **Glengesh Pass** before spiralling down into wild but fertile valley land. Just before reaching Ardara, a road to the left runs along the southern edge of **Loughros Beg Bay** for 9km to **MAGHERA**, passing the transfixing **Assarancagh Waterfall**, from where you can embark on a hardy 10km waymarked walk uphill to the Glengesh Pass.

Maghera itself is an enchantingly remote place, dwarfed by the backdrop of hills and glens and fronted by an expansive and deserted strand that extends westwards to a rocky promontory riddled with **caves**. One of the largest is said to have concealed a hundred people fleeing Cromwell's troops; their light was spotted from across the strand and all were massacred except a lucky individual who hid on a high shelf. Most of the caves are accessible only at low tide and a torch is essential. Beware of the **tides**, however, as even experienced divers have been swept away by the powerful currents. Behind the village, a tiny road, unsuitable for large vehicles, runs up to the **Granny Pass**, an alternative and very scenic route to Glencolmcille.

ARRIVAL AND DEPARTURE   **GLENCOLMCILLE AND AROUN**

By bus Buses stop in the centre of the village. Services to the Glencolmcille peninsula are much reduced outside

July and Aug.
Destinations Carrick (Mon–Sat 3 daily, Sun 1; 15min

Donegal town (1–3 daily; 1hr 15min–1hr 30min); Kilcar (Mon–Sat 3 daily, Sun 1; 25min); Killybegs (Mon–Sat 3 daily, Sun 1; 45min).

EATING

Folk Village Tearoom Folk Village Museum, Glencolmcille, http://glenfolkvillage.com. After visiting the Folk Village Museum (and even if you don't), the teahouse at the Folk Village makes for a welcome pit stop with its warming comfort food like minestrone soup and fresh brown bread, and apple pie with cream, all of which is freshly made/baked on the premises. €

Central Donegal

The area around the bustling town of **Ardara** contains some of the most contrasting landscapes in Donegal. Rugged mountains lie to the southwest, traversed by the steeply sinuous **Glengesh Pass** and fringed by the unspoiled expanse of **Maghera** strand. Inland to the northeast sits the stately village of **Glenties**, while to the north the coastline forms peninsulas punctuated by the **Gweebarra** River, which, in turn, leads inland to the tranquil villages of Doocharry and Fintown, virtually surrounded by mountain scenery of an almost lunar quality.

Ardara

Sixteen kilometres north of Killybegs on the N56 lies lively **ARDARA**. Traditionally a weaving and knitwear centre, this is an excellent place to buy cheap **Aran sweaters**. Molloy's, 1km south of town, is the biggest outlet, but Kennedy's, uphill from The Diamond, the main square, is handier (its owner is also a mine of local tourist information); both stores are well stocked with hand-loomed knitwear and tweeds.

The Catholic **church** west of Ardara's Diamond has a striking stained-glass window, *Christ among the Doctors*, by the Modernist-inspired **Evie Hone**, one of the most influential Irish artists of the twentieth century. The authors of the Gospels are depicted symbolically with the infant Christ at the centre and David and Moses above and below. Traditional music is big business in this part of Donegal, and Ardara stages a plethora of festivals, the best of which are the **Cup of Tae** traditional music festival over the first weekend of May and the **Johnny Doherty** Music and Dancing Festival (http://johnnydohertyfestival.com) at the end of September.

ARRIVAL AND INFORMATION ARDARA

By bus Buses drop off on, and depart from, The Diamond. Destinations Donegal town (Mon–Sat 3 daily, Sun 1; 50min); Dungloe (Mon–Sat 3 daily, Sun 1; 40min); Glenties (Mon–Sat 3 daily, Sun 1 daily; 10min); Killybegs (Mon–Sat 3 daily, Sun 1; 20min).

Tourist office Inside the Heritage Centre on The Diamond (Mon–Fri 10am–6pm, Sat 10am–4pm; http://ardara.ie).

ACCOMMODATION AND EATING

Brae House Front St, 074 954 1296. Spruce, mint-coloured townhouse with five pleasing rooms spread over two floors, generally painted in gentle mauve and magenta tones – and a super-friendly welcome is guaranteed too. €€

★ **Nancy's** Front St, 074 954 1187. Run by the same family throughout its 200 -year-old history, the warren of small, cosy rooms spreading out from a central front bar are utterly delightful. The food is first-rate too, with mussels in white wine and garlic typical of a largely seafood-oriented menu. They also serve some great craft beers on tap. €€

Nesbitt Arms Hotel The Diamond, http://nesbittarms.

com. Named after George Nesbitt, a prominent eighteenth-century landowner in these parts, this smart hotel harbours a variety of well-appointed rooms including triples and quads. Good dining, too, courtesy of the convivial *Rambler's Bar*, which also does takeouts. €€

Woodhill House 1km east of town, http://woodhillhouse.com. This stylish seventeenth-century manor house is set in its own extensive grounds with rooms in both the main house and converted outbuildings. Its restaurant offers classic Irish cuisine, such as slow-cooked Irish lamb with parsnip crisps. €€€

Glenties

Set at the foot of two glens 10km east of Ardara, **GLENTIES** is a tidy village, with a beautiful modern **church**, at the Ardara end of town, designed by the Derry architect Liam McCormack; its vast sloping roof reaches down to 2m from the ground, and rainwater drips off the thousand or so tiles into picturesque pools of water. In October, the town is overrun, thanks to the enormously popular **Fiddlers Festival**, when the town's pubs heave with fiddlers from across the world.

St Conall's Museum and Tea Room

Opposite the church • charge • 087 292 1016

The **St Conall's Museum and Tea Room** is charming little museum with an extensive collection of Patrick MacGill and Brian Friel literature, as well as items relating to the famine, the Donegal Railway and local history curios. The town's most famous son is author **Patrick MacGill**, whose semi-autobiographical *Children of the Dead End* brilliantly recounts the wayward lives of migrant navvies. A summer school is held in his honour in late July, attracting hundreds of people to its exhibitions, seminars and literary debates (http://macgillsummerschool.com).

ARRIVAL AND DEPARTURE GLENTIES

By bus Buses drop off on, and depart from, Main St. Destinations Ardara (Mon–Sat 3 daily, Sun 1; 10min); Donegal town (Mon–Sat 3 daily, Sun; 1hr); Dungloe (Mon–Sat 3 daily, Sun; 25min).

ACCOMMODATION AND EATING

Highlands Hotel Main St, http://highlandshotel.ie. Longstanding village hotel with comfortable, if occasionally dated, rooms. A plaque commemorates the room where actress Meryl Streep stayed for the local premiere of *Dancing at Lughnasa*. The Sunday night music sessions here are worth looking in for. €€

Kennedy's Main St, http://kennedysbarandrestaurant.com. Modern gastro-pub set over two floors serving big portions of steaming comfort food like beer-battered fish and chips, though it's just as much fun to take a stool at the long bar and kick back with a pint.

Lisnadar B&B Mill Rd, 074 955 1800. Just a 5min walk from the centre of the village, this is by far the most appealing of Glenties' several guesthouses. Set within extensive gardens, the house has four big rooms, with a guest lounge and breakfast conservatory attached – the hospitality is second to none. €€

The Dawros Head Peninsula and around

To the immediate north of Ardara, the **Dawros Head Peninsula** is much tamer than Glencolmcille, with many tiny lakes dotting a quilt of low hills. The terrain of purple heather, fields, streams and short glens makes a varied package for the enthusiastic walker. The first turning off the R261 Narin road leads to **ROSBEG**, an isolated village, straggling beside a series of rock-strewn coves, which nevertheless has a campsite (see page 423).

If you're heading directly from Ardara towards Narin and Portnoo, in **Kilclooney** look out for the **Kilclooney dolmen**, just before the pastel-shaded church on the right. These are probably the best-preserved portal stones in the country, with the capstone measuring over 4m long and the structure reckoned to date from around 3500 BC.

Doon Fort

Turn left at the "Rosbeg/Tramore Beach" signpost 1km or so before Narin, then head right up the lane just after a school; a few hundred metres later you'll see a sign for boat rental leading down to a farmhouse, where you can rent a rowing boat inexpensively to take you across to the island

Continuing onwards towards Narin, the most worthwhile sight on the peninsula is **Doon Fort**, which occupies an entire oval-shaped islet in the middle of **Lough Doon**. The idyllic setting, rarely disturbed by visitors, makes the hassle of getting there worth

> **JOHN DOHERTY**
>
> Fintown's cemetery is the resting place of Donegal's **greatest traditional fiddler**, **John Doherty** (1900–1980), whose dynamic yet intricate style remains a major influence on the region's fiddle players, over forty years after his death. Many of the tunes you'll hear played in Donegal today owe their origins to his repertoire and that of his brothers, Mickey and Simon, and several excellent CDs of his work are still available.

it: although its walls are crumbling, the fort has been untouched for over two thousand years. The walls stand 5m high and 4m thick; their inner passages were used in the 1950s for storing poteen.

Narin and Iniskeel Island

In **NARIN** the spearheaded, 4km-long **strand** is a wonderful beach, safe for bathing. At low tide you can walk out to **Iniskeel Island**, where St Conal founded a monastery in the sixth century. This has long since disappeared, but there are the ruins of two twelfth-century churches with some cross-inscribed slabs.

Doocharry

East of Narin the N56 hugs the shoreline, twisting and turning until it crosses the Gweebarra and enters Lettermacaward. From here a minor road follows the river 8km inland to tiny **DOOCHARRY**, with just a pub and a grocery, which acts as the gateway to some of the most dramatic scenery in the county. From here, you can head further upstream northeast along a narrow and tortuous lane past **Slieve Snaght**, through the **Glendowan Mountains** and skirting the southern edge of the **Glenveagh National Park** to **Lough Gartan** (see page 429). The desolate though beautiful countryside bears little sign of human impact and you'll be lucky to see any life beyond the odd sheep or fluttering bird.

12

Fintown

A more major road heads 9km southeast from Doocharry through rugged, rock-strewn moorland to **FINTOWN**, a simple roadside village set at the foot of towering mountains in the Finn Valley where the river broadens to form an elongated strip of lake.

Narrow-gauge railway

Village centre, just south of the main road • 40min journeys on the hour: June–Sept Mon–Sat 11am–4pm, Sun 1–5pm • charge • 074 954 6280

You can take a waterside trip along a restored section of the old County Donegal **narrow-gauge railway**. In its late nineteenth- and early twentieth-century heyday, the railway extended for some 200km, before the gradual increase in the use of road traffic to shift freight forced the line's closure in 1959.

ACCOMMODATION	DAWROS HEAD PENINSULA AND AROUND
Tramore Beach Rosebeg, 074 955 1491. Wonderful little camping spot among the dunes, with some two dozen	pitches and decent facilities including camper's kitchen, laundry, play area and tennis court. Closed Oct–April. €

The Rosses

The **Rosses**, a vast expanse of rock-strewn land and stony soil, is a strong Gaeltacht area. Dotted with over 120 tiny lakes, the crumpled terrain stretches from **Dungloe** in

> ### PADDY "THE COPE" GALLAGHER
>
> Dungloe is synonymous with the rejuvenating work of **Paddy "the Cope" Gallagher** (1871–1966), who envisaged the salvation of the Rosses' then poor communities through cooperative ventures, in particular by reducing their dependency on moneylenders. Oddly enough, the enterprise's practical origins lay in Paddy's discovery that the price of manure was reduced when purchased by societies. As a result, he founded the Templecrone Co-operative Agricultural Society (the "Cope") in 1906, and its central branch still stands proudly on Dungloe's main street, with others elsewhere in the Rosses.

the south to **Crolly** in the north, but the forbidding nature of much of the landscape meant most settlements could only survive near the sea, so following the shoreline route around the Rosses is far more rewarding than the more direct road north.

Dungloe

An Clochán Liath is the name you'll see on signposts approaching **DUNGLOE**, referring to the grey-coloured stepping stones that were once used to cross the river here. The modern Anglicized version comes from Dún gCloiche, the name of a stone fort situated on a rock a few kilometres offshore. When the fair that was held at the fort moved in the eighteenth century to the village of An Clochán Liath, which had grown up around the stepping stones, the fort's name stuck, though Irish-speakers still refer to the town by its original name. For fans of Daniel O'Donnell aside, there's little to detain you here, but at the end of July, the **Mary From Dungloe festival** (http://maryfromdungloe.ie), centred around a rather wholesome beauty pageant, provides a good pretext for general festivities, plenty of music and street entertainment. There's no antiquity behind the festival's origins or name – it dates from 1968 and the title comes from an Irish hit single by the Emmet Spiceland band.

ARRIVAL AND INFORMATION
DUNGLOE

By bus Buses drop off on, and depart from, Main St. Destinations Ardara (Mon–Sat 3 daily, Sun 1; 35min); Donegal town (Mon–Sat 3 daily, Sun 1; 1hr 25min); Glenties (Mon–Sat 3 daily, Sun 1; 25min).

Tourist office The tourist office is on Chapel Rd, in the old church just off the top of Main St (Mon–Fri 10am–5pm, plus July & Aug Sat 11am–4pm; 074 952 1297).

ACCOMMODATION AND EATING

Doherty's 16 Main St, 074 952 1654. A no-fuss all-rounder serving breakfasts, lunches and dinners, plus takeaways. Coffees and pastries too.
Patrick Johnny Sally's Bar Main St, 074 952 1479. At the top of the street, this chunky grey-stone building is a genuine old-timers' pub, with a terrace offering fabulous views of the ocean. No TVs or music, just a good old-fashioned drinking den.
Radharc an Oileain Quay Rd, http://dungloebedand breakfast.com. Located a few mins' walk from Main St, this modern, family-run bungalow has three terrific en-suite rooms, with wet rooms, all of which overlook the bay. €€

Burtonport

Seven kilometres northeast of Dungloe, **BURTONPORT** is the embarkation point for **Arranmore Island** and, if you can find a boatman at the harbour to take you out, for other smaller islands. In the late eighteenth century, the village's founder, William Burton, attempted to establish **Rutland Island**, just offshore, as a major trading centre, and consequently this area became the first English-speaking district in the whole of Donegal. During the 1798 Rebellion **James Napper Tandy** landed on the island with French troops, but became somewhat inebriated on hearing of Wolfe Tone's capture and was carried back on board (see page 564). Apart from busy activity at the harbour, Burtonport has little to say for itself.

Arranmore Island

Arranmore's permanent population of around eight hundred people is almost entirely concentrated along the eastern and southern coastlines – the island's main village, **LEABGARROW**, is on the eastern side. The high centre-ground of bogland and lakes reaches a greater altitude than anywhere else in the Rosses, and it's well worth hiking a few hundred metres upland for great views back across the water to Burtonport.

A circuit of the whole island, with cliff-top views of the Atlantic, takes around six hours, and the terrain isn't especially taxing, though it can be blustery. Many ships have foundered in the choppy seas hereabouts, but in 1983 the lone American yachtsman Wayne Dickenson landed on the island's west coast after 142 days at sea in the smallest boat ever to cross the Atlantic. In the cliffs below St Crone's Church on the southern shore is **Uaimh an Áir** (the "cave of slaughter"), where seventy hiding islanders were massacred in the seventeenth century by a certain Captain Conyngham, in an action that lay somewhat outside his remit from Charles I to rid the Rosses of "rogues and rapparees". Two islanders later took revenge by killing the captain in Dunfanaghy. Uninhabited **Green Island**, at the southwestern tip, is now a **bird sanctuary** and rare species have been spotted hereabouts, including the snowy owl in 1993. The most dramatic of the several **beaches** is at the northwestern end of the island, on the way to the lighthouse and approached by a set of steps down the side of a perpetually crumbling cliff.

Note that **facilities** on the island are limited, but there are a number of places to sleep, and several pubs – none particularly stands out, but they suffice for a pint and some local banter.

12

ARRIVAL AND ACCOMMODATION | ARRANMORE ISLAND

By boat Arranmore Ferry runs a car ferry (6–9 sailings daily; 15min; €15 return, €30 with car; http://arranmoreferry. com), as does the almost identically titled The Arranmore Ferry (5–7 sailings daily; 15min; same prices; http:// thearranmoreferry.com).

Glen Hotel Leabgarrow, http://theglenhotel.weebly.com. Nineteenth-century hotel in pleasant grounds just a 5min walk from the ferry pier; the rooms won't set the pulse racing, but they're clean and decently priced. The restaurant here is the best place to eat on the island. €

Gweedore and Tory Island

Like its southern neighbour, the Rosses, the interior of the **Gweedore** district is largely desolate and forbidding country, and settlements again cling to the shoreline. To the southwest lie the villages of **Bunbeg** and **Derrybeg**, their cottages sprinkled across a blanket of gorse and mountain grasses. The ruggedness intensifies as it continues up the coast and round the Bloody Foreland to Gortahork in the Cloghaneely district, yet surprisingly, there has been significant house building here and the area is quite densely populated. Some distance offshore lies Ireland's most literally isolated community, Irish-speaking **Tory Island**, a place rich in folkloric and musical traditions.

Bunbeg

The main appeal of the roadside village of **BUNBEG** is its gorgeous little harbour, 1.5km from the village along an enchanting rollicking road. Packed with smallish trawlers, it's also the departure point for year-round **ferries** to Tory Island (see page 426), as well as boat trips to uninhabited **Gola Island** in summer (€10; 087 660 7003). The village pubs also host excellent traditional music nights.

Bunbeg House By the harbour, http://bunbeghouse.com. Pleasant B&B in a fantastic spot, with sparky little rooms offering waterside views. It's almost worth staying here just to enjoy breakfast on the outdoor terrace. Closed Nov–Feb. €€

★ **Leo's Tavern** Meenaleck, 5km south of Bunbeg, http://leostavern.com. This famous pub is run by a member of the Brennan family. Parents, Leo and Baba, were both well-known on the dance band circuit in the 1950s and 1960s, though other family members have achieved greater fame. Three of their children (Máire, Pól and Ciarán) were members of the group Clannad, and another is the celebrated singer/

musician Enya – the pub's walls are decorated with a variety of awards and mementos. As you might expect, the music sessions, including open-mic nights, are superb.

★ **Teach Húdaí Beag** By the harbour crossroads, http://teachhudaibeag.ie. Fantastic pub, which hosts a famous Mon night traditional session, sometimes involving as many as twenty musicians, as well as a smaller Fri night one too. Best of all, though, is the riotous Cabaret Craiceáilte on the last Sat of the month, where all manner of genres (roots, reggae, contemporary) are performed in Gaelic. Like *Leo's*, it pulls in some stellar names.

Glassagh

At **GLASSAGH**, about 7km north of Derrybeg, the road climbs abruptly to Knockfola, loosely translated as the **Bloody Foreland**, a grim, stony, almost barren zone, crisscrossed by stone walls, and so-called because of the red hue acquired by its heather from the light of the setting sun. From Knockfola, the road turns eastwards hugging the side of the mountain, with the bogland and its hard-worked turf banks stretching below towards the Atlantic. You should be able to spot the distinctive shape of **Tory Island** far out to sea and, at **Magheroarty**, 8km east of Derrybeg, a road runs down to the pier, where you can pick up a ferry to the island (see page 427) and possibly arrange a trip to largely deserted **Inishbofin**, just offshore.

Teac Jack Glasslagh, http://teacjack.com. If you fancy lingering a while, the best place to stay is this prominent roadside hotel, with 26 en-suite rooms. The hotel's

enormous horseshoe-shaped bar, meanwhile, is a great venue for the regular programme of music and dancing, typically Tues, Thurs and Sat nights. €

Tory Island

With its ruggedly indented shores pounded by the ocean, **TORY ISLAND**, though only 12km north of the mainland, is notoriously inaccessible. Only 4km long and less than 1.5km wide, its vulnerability to the elements means little can grow here. Yet despite the island's barren landscape and the ferocity of the elements, the Tory islanders are thriving, a situation no one could have predicted thirty years ago. Back then, conditions on the island were very poor, lacking essential amenities such as a water supply, proper sanitation, reliable electricity and a ferry service. The arrival of a new priest, **Father Diarmuid Ó Péicín**, in the early 1980s stimulated a transformation. Rallying the islanders, the pastor began to lobby every possible target, securing backing from such disparate characters as the US senator Tip O'Neill (who had Donegal ancestry) and the late Ian Paisley. The campaign attracted media attention and conditions gradually began to improve. Nowadays, around 150 people live permanently on the island.

Brief history

According to local mythology, Tory was the stronghold of the **Fomorians**, who raided the mainland from their island base and whose most notable figure was the cyclops **Balor of the Evil Eye**, the Celtic god of darkness. Intriguingly, the local legend places his eye at the back of his head. There's also said to be a crater in the very heart of the island that none of the locals will approach after dark, for fear of incurring the god's wrath. In the sixth century, **St Colmcille** landed on Tory with the help of a member of the Duggan family. In return, the saint made him king of the island; the line has been

---

THE TORY ISLAND ARTISTS

Tory islanders are famed for their **painting**, a development that originated in a chance encounter between the English painter Derek Hill and one of the island's fishermen, **James Dixon**, in 1968, both now deceased. Dixon had never lifted a brush before the day he told Hill that he could do a better job of painting the Tory scenery, but he went on to become the most renowned of the island's school of **primitive painters** – Glebe House has a remarkable painting by him (see page 430). You can view the islanders' work and, more than likely, meet the artists, at the **James Dixon Gallery**, the originator's former home, a little way to the east of the harbour.

---

unbroken ever since, and you're more than likely to meet the present king, **Patsy Dan Rodgers**, who regularly greets arrivals at the harbour.

Around the island

Some monastic relics from St Columba's time remain on Tory, the most unusual of which – now the island's emblem – is the **Tau Cross**. Its T-shape is of Egyptian origin, and is one of only two such monuments in the whole of Ireland. It has now been relocated and set in concrete on Camusmore Pier in West Town, one of the island's two villages. There are other mutilated stone crosses and some carved stones lying around, several by the remains of the **round tower** in West Town, which is thought to date from the tenth century and is uniquely constructed from round beach stones. A local superstition focuses on the **wishing stone** in the centre of the island, three circuits of which will supposedly lead to your desires being granted.

12

ARRIVAL AND ACCOMMODATION TORY ISLAND

By boat Turasmara (http://toryferry.com) operates a year-round, passenger-only service from Magheroarty, with 2–3 sailings daily (times vary depending on the season; services are often affected by the tides and the weather, so always call ahead to check; €28 return).

Tory Island Harbour View By the landing stage, http://hoteltory.com. Translating as the "Harbour View", this place provides comfortable accommodation in twelve rooms, plus one of only two bars on the island, and a fine seafood restaurant. The owners also organize a range of summer events, including traditional music and song, painting and birdwatching weekends, as well as running the Dive Tory centre for aquatic fans. €€

The Derryveagh Mountains and Glenveagh

Inland from Gweedore lies some of the most dramatic scenery in Donegal, an area dominated by mountains such as **Errigal** and **Slieve Snaght**, and loughs of startling beauty. This is popular hill-walking country, especially along the **Poisoned Glen,** part of the much-visited **Glenveagh National Park**. Further on, towards Letterkenny, the countryside becomes gentler and increasingly verdant, especially in the environs of **Lough Gartan**, an area rich in associations with St Columba.

The loughs and Mount Errigal

Heading east on the N56 from Gweedore, the imposing and starkly beautiful mass of **Mount Errigal** becomes increasingly prominent. From a distance the mountain appears to be snow-covered, but skirting the northern shore of **Lough Nacung**, it becomes apparent that the white coloration has geological, rather than meteorological, causes.

Quite often the area around Errigal is shrouded in mist, but on a clear day the beauty of the mountain is unsurpassable, its silvery slopes resembling the Japanese artist Hokusai's images of Mount Fuji. The hour-long hike up to the **summit** is a must, and there's a waymarked trail from the road, 2km past the Poisoned Glen turn-off, up the southeast ridge. You'll be rewarded with stupendous **views**: virtually all of Donegal, and most of Northern Ireland, is visible, and you could easily spend several hours just sitting and absorbing the contrasts provided by coastline, loughs and mountains.

Dunlewey Lakeside Centre

Lakeshire, Dunlewey Lough • Daily 10.30am–5pm • Tour of cottage, farm and outbuildings charge; boat trip and other activities charge • http://dunleweycentre.com

Back down in Money Beg, a lane runs south to the narrow strip of land which divides Lough Nacung from Dunlewey Lough. On the way there's the **Dunlewey Lakeside Centre**, an impressive visitor centre by the shore. The key attractions here are a tour around the cottage of the notable local weaver, Manus Ferry, where you'll get to see demonstrations of spinning and weaving, and a **boat trip** around Dunlewey Lough, which is a lovely thirty-minute excursion. This extremely child-friendly centre extends to a small farmyard "zoo", adventure playground (included in tour price) and pony rides; the trekking centre here also offers a range of cross-country treks. And once you're done with that little lot, there's an excellent **restaurant** and a crafts shop.

Dunlewey is also an important centre for traditional music and there are concerts (charge) in the centre every Sunday from 1.30–3.30pm.

An Chúirt Hotel On the N56, 5km east of Bunbeg, http:// gweedorecourthotel.com. You can stay very comfortably at the rather grand *"Gweedore Court" Hotel*, which, although largely catering to wedding parties, makes for a good base if spending some time in the loughs. Dining options include *table d'hote* in the restaurant, a Sunday carvery and more informal food in the *PJD Bar*. €€€

Errigal Hostel Dunlewey, 074 953 1180. Situated in the shadow of Mount Errigal, this is a stunning purpose-built place, entirely in keeping with the area. It features private en-suite doubles, plus four-bed rooms and innovative split-level six-bed dorms, internet room, laundry and self-catering kitchen, plus bike rental. Closed Nov–Feb. €

Glenveagh National Park

According to legend, the **Poisoned Glen** – east of Dunlewey Lough, and one of the most popular spots of the **Glenveagh National Park** – is where the cyclops Balor of the Evil Eye (see page 426) was slain by Lugh, poisoning the ground on which his single eyeball fell. There are many other explanations for the origins of its name, from the darkly conspiratorial (the glen's waters were polluted to kill English soldiers) to the purely botanical (poisonous Irish spurge used to grow here).

National Park Visitor Centre

Northernmost end of Lough Veagh • Free • http://nationalparks.ie/glenveagh

The **Glenveagh National Park Visitor Centre** has detailed and interactive displays on the area's ecology and geology. More interesting is the exhibition on the park's wildlife, and in particular its eagles, whose population died out here in the early 1900s; in 2000, a programme to reintroduce golden eagles was established, and it is estimated that there are currently around two dozen in this corner of County Donegal. There's also a reasonably priced restaurant here, though it's not as enjoyable as the Castle tearooms.

Glenveagh Castle

Charge • Minibuses (charge) from visitor centre (no cars beyond here), otherwise a 40min walk

From the visitor centre, minibuses shuttle back and forth to **Glenveagh Castle**, built on a small promontory for wealthy landowner George Adair between 1870 and 1873. Adair was the creator of the estate that now forms much of the park, but while you might admire the end product, it's impossible to condone the means by which it was achieved. Though some land was obtained through purchase, during what is now

WALKING IN GLENVEAGH

To reach the **Poisoned Glen**, head a little way further east of Money Beg on the R251 and take the signposted lane leading downhill to the right. Just below the ruined church at the eastern end of Lough Nacung turn off to the left and follow the track over the old bridge. The path dwindles and you should follow the left bank of the river deep into the gorge until it turns sharply left. Walk through the water here, usually just a trickle in summer, to the opposite bank and climb up towards a granite crest. From here, walk beside the small stream through a gully and finally you'll emerge on a ridge. It's not an easy tramp, for a lot of the ground is marshy, but the views are fantastic, with the River Glenveagh flowing into Lough Beagh down below.

You're now in the **Glenveagh National Park** and may well see deer hereabouts. If you don't want to retrace your tracks and are prepared for a longer hike, you have a number of options. However, it's vital to follow all the basic rules of hill-walking and essential to keep to the designated roads and paths during the winter deer-culling season (Sept–Feb), or you run the risk of being **shot**. Experienced hill-walkers will probably be tempted by the sight of **Slieve Snaght**, the highest point in the park, off to the southwest. Alternatively, if you head downhill to the southeast, the Glendowan road at the bottom leads eastwards to **Lough Gartan** (see page 429) and westwards to **Doocharry** (see page 423). If you take the road east towards Gartan for a short distance, an old disused vehicle track to the left will lead you down the barrel of the glen alongside the river to Lough Glenveagh.

known as the **Derryveagh Evictions**, Adair evicted 244 tenants during the bitterly cold April of 1861, forcing many into the workhouse and others to emigrate to Australia. The rhododendron-filled gardens surrounding the castle were very much the work of Adair's wife, Cornelia, who also introduced herds of red deer to the estate. The steep ascent to the viewpoint behind the gardens is more than worthwhile for the wonderful views down to the castle and along the lough deep into the glen. From here it's easy to imagine why the castle was so popular during the Golden Age of Hollywood, with Greta Garbo, Marilyn Monroe and Clark Gable all spending time here. Guided tours of the castle focus on the furniture and artwork collected by the millionaire Irish–American, Henry McIlhenny, the last owner of Glenveagh, who in 1983 bequeathed the castle and its contents to the nation.

12

Lough Gartan and around

The environs of **Lough Gartan** are one of the supreme beauties of Ireland. **St Colmcille** was born into a royal family here in 521; his father was from the house of Niall of the Nine Hostages and his mother belonged to the House of Leinster. If you walk over from Glenveagh you'll pass Colmcille's **birthplace** – take the first road right at the first house you see at the end of the mountain track, and you'll come to a colossal **cross** marking the spot; the site is also signposted from the road running along the lough's southern shore. Close by is a slab known as the **Flagstone of Loneliness**, on which Colmcille used to sleep, thereby endowing the stone with the miraculous power to cure the sorrows of those who also lie upon it, though nowadays it's bestrewn with coins. During times of mass emigration, people used to come here on the eve of departure in the hope of ridding themselves of homesickness. Archaeologically, it's actually part of a Bronze Age gallery tomb and has over fifty cup marks cut into its surface.

Going back to the track leading downhill will bring you to the lakeside road, where a left turn leads to the remains of a church known as the **Little Oratory of St Colmcille**. It's an enchanting ruin, no larger than a modern living room, with a floor of old stone slabs with grass growing up through the cracks. A holy well is here too and nearby the Natal Stone, where the baby Colmcille first opened his eyes; to this day pregnant women visit the slab to pray for a safe delivery.

Glebe House

Northwest shore of Lough Gartan · Visits by guided tour late May to Sept daily 11.30am–5.30pm · charge · http://glebegallery.ie

Glebe House is a gorgeous Regency building set in beautiful gardens on the northwest shore of Lough Gartan. Richly decorated both inside and out, it owes its fame to the time of its tenure by the English artist Derek Hill (1916–2000), though it's now run as a **gallery** by the Heritage Service. The converted stables are used for visiting exhibitions, while the rooms of the house itself display a rich collection of paintings, sketches and numerous other items once owned by Hill, including works by Kokoschka, Yeats, Renoir and Picasso. The study is decked out in original William Morris wallpaper and there are Chinese tapestries in the morning room. The kitchen has various paintings by the Tory Island group of primitive painters (see page 427), most remarkably James Dixon's impression of Tory from the sea.

Colmcille Heritage Centre

Northeast shore of Lough Gartan, opposite Glebe House · charge · http://colmcilleheritagecentre.ie

Moving on round the northeast of the lake, in the direction of Church Hill, a right turn immediately after crossing the bridge will take you down to the modern **Colmcille Heritage Centre**, on the opposite shore from Glebe House. The exhibition space is devoted to St Colmcille's life and the spread of the Celtic Church throughout Europe. If you have no interest in ecclesiastical history, there are other intriguing items, including very beautiful stained-glass windows of biblical scenes by Ciarán O'Conner and Ditty Kummer, and a step-by-step illustration of vellum illumination and calligraphy.

Doon

Lying a few kilometres northeast of Lough Gartan, **the Rock of Doon** and **Doon Well** are signposted off the R255 shortly after the village of **Termon** on the way to Kilmacrennan. Following the directions leads to a rural cul-de-sac right next to the well. A path from here ascends to a large bushy outcrop that is the Rock of Doon. From 1200 to 1603 this was the spot where the O'Donnell kings were crowned, standing above a huge gathering of their followers. The inauguration stone on the summit is said to bear the imprint of the first Tír Chonaill king, a mark into which every successor had to place his foot as his final confirmation. Doon, an ancient pagan healing **well**, is still a place of pilgrimage, marked out by a bush weighed down with personal effects left behind by the sick, hoping for a cure.

Kilmacrennan

KILMACRENNAN is a crossroads village 10km north of Letterkenny on the N56. Four hundred metres towards Ramelton is yet another site with Colmcille connections, **Cill Mhic n-Eanain**, where Columba was fostered and educated by Cruithnechan in around 528. A monastery stood here from the sixth century to 1129, and it was also the site of the O'Donnells' religious inauguration following the rites at Doon. The ruins on the left are of a sixteenth-century Franciscan **friary**, while the Church of Ireland building to the right dates from 1622 and fell into disuse around 1845.

The north Donegal coast

Running from the Cloghaneely district, which adjoins Gweedore, the **north Donegal coast** holds some of the most spectacular scenery in the whole country, where the battle between the elements is often startlingly apparent. Overshadowed at first by the bleak beauty of **Muckish Mountain** to the south, the main road from **Gortahork** to Milford passes through verdant countryside as it meanders around the deep bays and inlets and alongside the glorious and often deserted beaches which punctuate the shoreline. On the way, the Plantation town of **Dunfanaghy** provides a good base for exploring one of the coastline's two breathtaking peninsulas: **Horn Head**, with its rugged, sea-battered cliffs; and, further to the east, **Rosguill**, almost circumscribed by the marvellous Atlantic Drive.

Gortahork to Falcarragh

The first place you'll encounter in **Cloghaneely**, east of the Bloody Foreland, is **GORTAHORK**, an Irish-speaking village with a strong cultural history, albeit with little in the way of sights.

Three kilometres east of Gortahork, **FALCARRAGH** is livelier and better supplied with shops. A short distance east of the central crossroads is **An tSean Bhearic** (Falcarragh Visitor Centre; Mon–Fri 10am–5pm, Sat 11am–5pm; free; 074 918 0655), housed in the old police barracks. This has a craft shop and café, as well as displays on the town and its policing history, and regularly hosts temporary exhibitions and cultural events. Falcarragh **beach** is reached by heading north at the village crossroads and turning right about 1.5km further on, then continuing east for 3km. This is one of the more beautiful strands on this northwest coast, but a strong undercurrent makes it **unsafe for swimming**.

Muckish Mountain

The road south from Falcarragh to Glenveagh passes through **Muckish Gap**. The slate-grey mass of **Muckish Mountain** dominates the view, its sides pitted with old workings where quartzite sand was extracted for the manufacture of optical glass. It's a relatively easy climb from the roadside shrine at the Gap up a grassy ridge to the **summit** and, on a clear day, the entire coastline from the Bloody Foreland to Malin Head is splendidly visible from here.

12

Dunfanaghy

The small Plantation town of **DUNFANAGHY**, 10km east of Falcarragh, is the gateway to the **Horn Head Peninsula**, and while there's little to get excited about in the town itself, it is a good little base, and there are a couple of fabulous places to eat.

Workhouse Heritage Centre

Figart, Dunfanaghy, just off the N56 · charge · http://dunfanaghy.info

On Dunfanaghy's western outskirts you'll find the **Workhouse Heritage Centre**, sympathetically restored as a local history and community resource. Built in 1845 on the eve of the Great Famine, at first it had only five inmates, but by 1847, as the Famine intensified, over six hundred people were crowded inside. The Famine story is recounted upstairs through the tale of one local inmate, Hannah Herrity, who lived until 1926 – though the narrative method (a distinctly dull and disappointing series of tableaux) undermines the power of her story. The centre also displays work by local artists, and it has a coffee shop, and, somewhat surprisingly, a screen for film viewings, which usually take place on the last weekend of each month.

ACCOMMODATION AND EATING   **DUNFANAGHY**

Arnold's Main St, http://arnoldshotel.com. The rooms here are nothing beyond the ordinary, but as it's the town's sole hotel, the prices are rather inflated; much better is the food, served in both its bar and restaurant. They also organize a variety of activities (including writing, photography and cycling). €€€

The Mill By the lake on the western edge of town, http://themilldunfanaghy.com. This family-run restaurant serves scrumptious evening meals, its seafood being especially well regarded, for example spiced Greencastle Monkfish and grilled Killybegs turbot. It also has superbly furnished en-suite rooms (available March–Nov), four of which have lake views. €€

Muck'n'Muffins The Square, http://mucknmuffins.ie. This once derelict grey-stone building is now a super little pottery studio and café; watch the ceramicists at work downstairs before heading upstairs to the warm café for coffee and a pastry. €

Horn Head

Horn Head is magnificent, an almost 200m rock face scored by ledges on which perch countless guillemots and gulls, and small numbers of puffins. The best view of the cliffs, sea stacks and caves is from the water, but the cliff road is vertiginous enough in places to give you a good look down the sheer sides.

To get here, take the slip road at the western end of Dunfanaghy village; it descends to skirt the side of a beautiful inlet before rising steeply to go round the east side of the head. A spectacular vista of headlands opens up to the east – Rosguill, Fanad and Inishowen – but none can match the drama of Horn Head's **cliffs**, their tops clad in a thin cover of purplish heather. Alternatively, you can walk from Horn Head Bridge, 800m from Dunfanaghy on the Horn Head road, and head west across the dunes to **Tramore Beach**. Then follow the sheep track north, passing two small blowholes called the **Two Pistols** and then a much larger one, **McSwyney's Gun**, so-called because of the power of the sonic boom produced by the explosion of compressed air from the cavern. Erosion has occurred over the years, however, and you'll be lucky to hear anything these days. Continuing onwards, you'll come to **Pollaguill Bay** and beach. The next wondrous site is the more than 20m-high **Marble Arch**, cut by the sea through the base of Trawbreaga Head. Horn Head itself soon becomes visible as you ascend the next headland.

The **walk** as far as here takes around two hours from Dunfanaghy, and you can either complete the whole circuit of the peninsula (allow for a further 1–2hr) or head back by road.

Marble Hill and Ards Forest Park

East of Dunfanaghy, the road follows the edge of **Sheephaven Bay**, and, shortly after passing through Portnablagh, a signposted turn-off leads to **Marble Hill Strand**, a vast, glorious sweep of sand. Overlooking the strand, Marble Hill House was once owned by **Hugh Law**, MP for Donegal from 1902 to 1918 and TD for the county from 1927 to 1932, who entertained all manner of celebrities here, including W.B. and Jack Yeats. Nearby, **Ards Forest Park** (free, cars charge) occupies the former demesne of the Capuchin friary of Ard Mhuire; a 1.5km-long avenue alongside Lough Lilly takes you into its centre, where there are fine walks through the woodland as well as along the shore of Sheephaven Bay.

Creeslough and around

The sleepy village of **CREESLOUGH** occupies a slope commanding gorgeous views across the head of Sheephaven Bay. Partway down its main street is a **church** designed by Liam McCormack, its whitewashed whorl and back-sloping table roof reflecting the thickly set Muckish Mountain nearby. **Lackagh Bridge**, about 6km east of Creeslough, offers a tremendous viewpoint of Sheephaven Bay, the curving silted shoreline lying downstream and a ginger-brown picture of rushes and heather reaching deep into the hills. Immediately after the bridge there's a turn-off running for 3km to **Glen**, well worth taking for the opportunity to drop in at the *Olde Glen* bar (see below). A minor road south from Glen leads up through gorgeously lonely landscapes and past a tremendous viewpoint overlooking Lough Salt before descending to Termon (see page 430).

Olde Glen Glen, http://oldeglen.ie. Great-looking red-and-white-painted pub with an atmospheric, low-ceilinged interior and wonky stone flooring. People come from miles around to try the crab linguine or roasted duckling in the modern restaurant, but it's equally fab just for a pint of ale (or a whiskey) and some chatter in the front bar. Closed Mon. €€

The Rosguill Peninsula

The route onto the extremely beautiful and very manageable **Rosguill Peninsula** starts by the side of the church in **Carrigart**, 13km northeast of Creeslough, and passes rabbit-infested dunes at the back of a tremendous and usually deserted **beach**. At the top of the strand is **DOWNINGS**, a sprightly holiday centre patronized mainly by Northern Irish tourists, with caravan sites hogging the rear end of the beach and holiday chalets creeping up the hillside behind the village.

Downings' main street heads northwards to become the panoramic **Atlantic Drive**, which runs around the headland and also makes for a stupendous 13km walk. The range of views encompasses the essence of Donegal – rugged landscapes in constant tussle with the Atlantic Ocean – though, sadly, this is becoming increasingly blighted by large numbers of newbuild houses and caravan sites. About halfway along, a turning leads to **Melmore Head**, where you'll find the rather fine **Trá na Rosann** beach. A quicker way to get here is to take the right-hand fork on the way into Downings from Carrigart.

Harbour Bar Uphill at the far end of Downings, 074 915 5920. This is one of the most enjoyable pubs along this stretch of coast; along with glorious views of the bay, there's a toasty fire, lots of *craic* and music at weekends.

Rosapenna Hotel Downings, http://rosapenna.ie. Three of the north coast's finest golf courses straddle this upmarket hotel whose rooms are as plush as you might expect and, naturally, have stunning ocean views. Closed Nov–March. €€€

The Singing Pub 5min drive from Downings, 087 917 1950. The perfect pitstop on the Wild Atlantic Way, this welcoming pub has a traditional thatched roof, warm open fires and plenty of character. The menu changes weekly, with freshly caught seafood a regular feature.

Trá na Rosann Hostel Downings, 074 915 5374. Designed by Edwin Lutyens, this erstwhile hunting lodge – a listed building – is now a superb alpine-style hostel with a mix of dorms and a self-catering kitchen. Closed early Sept to May. €

McNutt of Donegal The Pier, Downings, http://mcnuttofdonegal.com. For over seventy years the McNutt family have been making some of the world's finest weaves, from Donegal tweed to Irish linen, at their mill in Downings. The shop contains a wealth of crafts and gifts, with a tour of the factory also available.

The Fanad Peninsula

The least tempting of Donegal's peninsulas is **Fanad**, circumnavigated by the well-signposted **Fanad Drive**. The western shoreline has little to offer scenically, and the whole peninsula is best approached from Kilmacrennan through the pleasant towns of **Ramelton** and **Rathmullan**, the latter with some very swish accommodation, before heading on to **Fanad Head** itself.

Rathmullan and around

Heading east out of Kilmacrennan, it's worth a quick stroll through **Ramelton**, a quaint and sedate little town sitting attractively on the eastern bank of the broad black flow of the salmon-rich River Leannan. Beyond here, **RATHMULLAN** is no less pretty, with its long row of multicoloured houses facing **Lough Swilly**; like Ramelton, though, the town has suffered badly in recent years, and many places have closed down. In 1587 the rebellious **Red Hugh O'Donnell** was lured onto a British merchant ship here on the pretext of a merry drink, and ended up in Dublin gaol for six years; and in 1607

Rathmullan was a departure point for the **Flight of the Earls**, the event that marked the end of the Gaelic nation. In October 1798 the French frigate *Hoche*, with Wolfe Tone on board, was intercepted in the lough nearby and Tone was captured and taken to Dublin for trial.

ARRIVAL AND DEPARTURE   RATHMULLAN

By boat The Lough Swilly ferry (http://swillyferry.com) operates a summer (June–Sept) service between Rathmullan and Buncrana, with 5–7 sailings daily (passenger €9 return, car €30 return).

ACCOMMODATION AND EATING

Pavilion Pizzas on the Lawn Rathmullan House, by Lough Swilly, http://rathmullanhouse.com. This terrific summer only venture at Rathmullan House sees a huge marquee erected on the lawn, within which delicious stone baked pizzas, alongside homemade ice cream, are served; craft beers from the neighbouring Kinnegar Brewery are also served, as is coffee. €€

★ **Rathmullan House** By Lough Swilly, http://rathmullanhouse.com. Gracious country house set amid lush, landscaped gardens. Most of the magnificent, classically furnished rooms have water views, while some have their own patio. Meanwhile, log fires burn away in sumptuously furnished lounges, but if you fancy more vigorous activity, you can avail yourself of the stunning indoor pool. €€€

Portsalon

North of Rathmullan the R247 climbs to give great views across to **Dunree Head** and the **Urris** range of mountains on the Inishowen Peninsula to the east. Taking the first right turn will lead you along a minor road hugging the coastline, as it twists and turns up to the cliff-top approach to **Saldanha Head**. Here you'll witness the most spectacular views on the entire peninsula, looking across to Inishowen and down onto the 5km stretch of golden sand at Ballymastocker Bay.

ACCOMMODATION AND EATING   PORTSALON

★ **Portsalon Luxury Camping** Cashelpreaghan, Portsalonough, http://donegalglamping.com. With stunning views of Lough Swilly, the five luxury yurts in the grounds of this beautifully restored traditional farmhouse have kingsize beds, sofas and wood-burning stoves – about as romantic as it gets. Self-service, so no breakfast included. Minimum two-night stay in July and Aug. Adults only. Closed Oct–May. €€€

Fanad Head

Most of the 8km route north from Portsalon to **Fanad Head** is through humpy and barren land, with clusters of granite pushing through marshy ground. Before reaching the Head, there is one curiosity worth taking in, just 2km north of Portsalon: the rock formation known as the **Seven Arches**, created by the constant erosive battering of the waters. To get here, follow the signpost on the right of the road, then take the path down to the new house, and finally cross the fields to the rocky strand. From here the main road leads straight on to **Fanad Head**, where it reaches a dramatically placed cliff-edge **lighthouse**.

Letterkenny

Whatever your means of transport, if you're travelling through northern Donegal, you're almost certain to pass through **LETTERKENNY**, the county's largest town. There's very little by way of actual sights in the town itself, which has undergone massive redevelopment in recent years, though it does retain a lively arts scene and some thriving nightlife. Its most notable visual element is the huge nineteenth-century **Cathedral of Saints Eunan and Columba** at the top of Church lane, with intricate stone-roped ceiling, flying buttresses and Gaelicized Stations of the Cross.

Donegal County Museum

High Rd • Free • 074 912 4613

The main point of interest in town is the **Donegal County Museum**, housed in part of the old Letterkenny workhouse. Temporary exhibitions occupy the downstairs area while the display in the first-floor gallery highlights the history of Donegal from the prehistoric period to the twentieth century using artefacts, archives and images. Visitors can also view both the Northwest Film Archive and Islands Archive which contain over a hundred hours of documentaries, news and drama.

Tropical World

Alcorns Garden Centre, Loughnagin, 3km north of town on the R245 to Ramelton • charge • http://tropicalworld.ie

The Alcorns garden centre north of town is the unlikely setting for the sweet little **Tropical World**, which comprises a **mini-zoo**, housing sections on mammals (including lemurs, raccoons and otters), reptiles (snakes, geckos and lizards), creepy crawlies

LETTERKENNY

12

● **EATING**
The Lemon Tree	3
Mulberry	4
The Quiet Moment	1
The Yellow Pepper	2

■ **DRINKING & NIGHTLIFE**
The Brewery	1
McGinley's	3
Voodoo Lounge	2

■ **ACCOMMODATION**
Castle Grove Country House	1
Dillons Hotel	3
Oaklands	2
Radisson Blu Hotel	4
Station House Hotel	5

0 — 200
metres

and birds. Here, too, is a wonderful **Butterfly House**, with a fabulous array of colourful specimens from around the world. Afterwards, parents can partake in some refreshment in the tea room while the little ones fool around in the excellent monkey swing indoor play area.

ARRIVAL AND INFORMATION — LETTERKENNY

By bus The bus station is at the bottom of Port Rd. Destinations Ballyliffin (Mon–Fri 4 daily, Sat 1; 1hr 10min); Ballyshannon (6 daily; 1hr 5min); Buncrana (Mon–Fri 4 daily, Sat 1; 45min); Bundoran (6 daily; 1hr 15min); Derry (9 daily; 45min); Donegal town (8 daily; 50min); Lifford (hourly; 40min); Moville (Mon–Sat 4 daily, Sat 3; 50min); Raphoe (Mon–Sat 6 daily; 30min); Sligo (6 daily; 2hr). **Tourist office** The tourist office is on Neil T. Blaney Road, by the roundabout 800m out of town towards Derry (Tues–Sat 9am–5pm; http://letterkennytourism.ie).

ACCOMMODATION — SEE MAP PAGE 435

Castle Grove Country House Ballymaleel, 3km out on the Ramelton road, http://castlegrove.com. This elegant seventeenth-century house, pitched among stately grounds overlooking Lough Swilly, offers splendidly furnished, Georgian-era rooms. €€€
Dillons Hotel 29–45 Main St, http://dillons-hotel.ie. This most central of hotels offers impeccably turned out rooms, alongside a classy bistro and bar. €€
Oaklands 8 Oaklands Park, Gortlee Rd, http://letter kennybandb.com. A 10min walk from the centre, this tidy B&B is a little tricky to find – it's at the end of a residential cul-de-sac – but the six rooms are immaculately kept and the hospitality is genuinely warm. €

Radisson Blu Hotel The Loop Road, http://radissonhotels. com. The location, on a main road opposite a retail park, is rather dull, but this discreet high-rise is as plush as you'd expect from this hotel chain; the rooms are supremely comfortable, the service is impeccable, and there are a couple of superb eating areas (see below). €€
Station House Hotel Lower Main St, http://station houseletterkenny.com. You wouldn't think so to look at it, but this is the old station house building, hence the name and the occasional nod to the old railway that used to run through these parts; bright, light-filled corridors lead to perky rooms with gleaming glass-panelled bathrooms. €€

EATING — SEE MAP PAGE 435

The Lemon Tree Lower Main St, http://thelemontree restaurant.com. Delicious modern Irish cuisine with a discernible French influence, manifest in dishes like roast duck breast with celeriac terrine and roast shallot blackberries; the restaurant, with its subtle pastel colours and candle-topped tables, looks fantastic. Closed Mon & Tues. €€€
Mulberry Radisson Blu Hotel, http://radissonhotels. com. Tip-top dining in the *Radisson*'s dazzling restaurant, featuring a great (if meat-heavy) menu, with exceptional steaks, as well as seafood and gourmet burgers. A terrific selection of craft beers and cocktails too. €€€
The Quiet Moment Upper Main St, http://quietmoment.

ie. Letterkenny's most enticing café captures the ambience of Dublin's *Bewley's* (see page 101) with some success, thanks to its thick, oak-panelled walls and deep green leather armchairs; great coffee, snacks, lunches and breakfasts. Closed Sun. €
★ **The Yellow Pepper** 36 Lower Main St, http:// yellowpepperrestaurant.com. The cast-iron pillars and thick stone walls are reminders of what was once an old shirt factory; these days, however, this is a cheery, family-run restaurant where you can tuck into dry-aged sirloin and seafood platters along with one of the many bottles of wine stacked up high behind the bar. Exemplary service too. €€€

DRINKING AND NIGHTLIFE — SEE MAP PAGE 435

The Brewery Market Square, http://thebrewerybar.com. Popular bar-restaurant with a striking all wood and brass interior. An exciting line-up of more than twenty craft beers complements fine menus in both the bar and restaurant. Live music several nights a week.
McGinley's Lower Main St, 086 784 0783. Of all this street's many hostelries, *McGinley's* is by far the most agreeable –

and most frequented – thanks to its dark yet cosy bar, and pretty much nightly music sessions, the most popular of which takes place on Wed.
Voodoo Lounge 36 Lower Main St, 074 910 9815. Good-time, state-of-the-art multi-roomed club with top-name DJs at weekends and occasional live bands; they also offer food.

ENTERTAINMENT

An Grianán Port Rd, http://angrianan.com. Top-notch local theatre offering an impressive drama programme, that's also one of Ireland's best music venues, from

traditional to classical. There's a super little café here too.
Regional Cultural Centre 46 Port Rd, http:// regionalculturalcentre.com. Just behind An Grianán, the

12

regional cultural centre mounts a variety of exhibitions and a regular programme of concerts, covering jazz to traditional music. It's also the principal venue for the two-week Earagail Arts Festival in mid-July (http://eaf.ie).

Raphoe

Thirteen kilometres southeast of Letterkenny, **RAPHOE** is set trimly around one of the largest Diamonds in the county. Once a see in its own right, its ecclesiastical importance is still indicated today by its inclusion in the Church of Ireland bishopric of Derry and Raphoe. The town's **cathedral**, dedicated to St Eunan (the biographer of St Columba), was founded in the ninth century, but the present plain Gothic-cathedral version dates merely from 1702. Transfixed in the inner wall is a stone block with some peculiar, indecipherable carvings, and there's a very impressive and resonant wooden baptismal chapel.

Beltany Stone Circle

Three kilometres south of Raphoe is the **Beltany Stone Circle**, one of the best-preserved circles in the country. Consisting of approximately sixty stones, varying in height between 30cm and over 1m, it provides an atmospheric vantage point for a marvellous panoramic view of the local valleys and distant mountains. To get here, follow the signs from the south of The Diamond in Raphoe and you'll arrive at the entrance to a farm. The circle is 400m up the bridle path to the right, over a stile and across a field full of sheep.

ARRIVAL AND DEPARTURE   **RAPHOE**

By bus Buses serving Letterkenny (Mon–Sat 6 daily; 30min) and Lifford (Mon–Sat 5 daily; 15min) stop in the centre of the village.

Lifford and around

Six kilometres southeast of Raphoe, **LIFFORD** was formerly Donegal's legal centre and the County Council is still based here. The graceful **Old Courthouse**, dating from 1746, houses a **visitor centre** on The Diamond (Mon–Fri 10am–4.30pm; charge; http://liffordoldcourthouse.com) which tells the story of the O'Donnell clan and Napper Tandy (see page 424), as well as notable events in Donegal's history. You can visit the cells, either on a self-guided or guided tour, the latter lasting around forty-five minutes; and you can even have your mugshot taken behind the bars.

Standing 3km northwest of Lifford, off the N14, **Cavanacor House** (Tues–Sat 2–6pm; free; 085 164 2525) is a fine seventeenth-century mansion where **James II** dined in 1689, and which was also the ancestral home of **James Knox Polk**, US president from 1845 to 1849. The real treat is its **art gallery**, displaying a changing array of work by contemporary Irish and international painters and sculptors.

ARRIVAL AND DEPARTURE   **LIFFORD AND AROUND**

By bus Lifford is served by buses from/to Letterkenny (hourly; 40min) and Raphoe (Mon–Sat 5 daily; 15min).

The Inishowen Peninsula

The **Inishowen Peninsula** in the northeast of County Donegal is perhaps the great overlooked treasure of the Irish landscape (and certainly has the longest signposted scenic drive – the "Inishowen 100"), offering a diverse and visually exciting terrain, where the views usually encompass the waters of the loughs or the Atlantic waves. Virtually every aspect of the landscape is superb – the **beaches** (especially Kinnego Bay, Culdaff, Tullagh and Pollan), the towering headland bluffs (Malin, Inishowen,

Dunaff and Dunree) and the central mountain range, with towering **Slieve Snaght** at the middle of it all.

The peninsula derives its name from **Eoghán**, who was made First Lord of the island by his father Niall, High King of Ireland. Phases of the peninsula's history before and after Eoghán have left a legacy of fine antiquities, from the **Grianán Ailigh** fort to a host of beautiful early **Christian crosses** (Cloncha, Mura, Carrowmore and Cooley).

GETTING AROUND THE INISHOWEN PENINSULA

By bus Services on the peninsula are extremely limited and, though you can reach places such as Buncrana and Ballyliffin fairly easily, you'll certainly need your own transport to explore Malin Head.

Burt Church

Near Bridgend on the N13 Letterkenny–Derry road • 074 936 0151

The approach to the most stimulating of all Inishowen's sights, the ancient fort known as the Grianán Ailigh, passes the Liam McCormack-designed **Burt Church**, the most beautiful twentieth-century church in all Ireland – like other McCormack designs in Donegal (see pages 422 and 432), its structure is evocative of the mystical landmark nearby. The seating is set concentrically, under a whitewashed ceiling that sweeps up into a vortex to allow sunlight to beam down directly upon the altar; the allusions in every detail to Neolithic sepulchral architecture, especially Newgrange (see page 141), are fascinating and very atmospheric. In a survey of Irish architects the church was voted Ireland's building of the twentieth century.

To learn more about the church and its legends, head to the *An Grianan Hotel*, just down the road in the village of **Burt**, which incorporates the somewhat confusingly named **Old Church Visitor Centre** (daily 11am–5.30pm; charge; http://oldchurchvisitorcentre.com), which concentrates on both Burt Church and the area's myths and legends.

Grianán Ailigh

3km up the hill from Burt Church • Open access

The origins of the **Grianán Ailigh** date from 1700 BC, and it's thought to be linked to the Tuátha Dé Danann, pre-Celtic invaders. It was sufficiently significant to be included by Ptolemy, the Alexandrian geographer, in his second-century AD map of the world, and was the base of various northern Irish chieftains. Here, in 450, St

---

DRIVING DONEGAL'S WILD ATLANTIC WAY

Arguably the most spectacular portion of the **Wild Atlantic Way**, the Donegal route hugs the coastline right up to Ireland's most northerly point. Taking in major sites such as Glenveagh National Park, Malin Head, Tory Island and Slieve League, it's the constant and breathtaking scenery that makes it so special. Although it's best to explore the area at a leisurely pace, if your time is limited you could follow the handy one- or two-day itinerary suggested below.

Day 1 consists of a looping 154km trip which begins and ends in Buncrana. Traveling along the R238 there are stops in Grianán Áileach, Greencastle and Malin Head, with plenty to see in between. The total drive time should be about three hours. **Day 2** again begins in Buncrana, this time taking the N13 to Rathmullan. From there it's a forty-minute drive along the R268 to **Fanad Head**, home of the Wild Atlantic Way's iconic lighthouses. From there it's on to **Glenveagh National Park** with a stop in The Singing Pub on the way. The time spent driving should be around two hours forty-five minutes.

Patrick is said to have baptized Eoghán, the founder of the O'Neill clan that ruled the kingdom of Ailigh for more than five hundred years. In the twelfth century, the fort was sacked by Murtagh O'Brian, King of Thomond, in retribution for a raid on Clare, and a large amount of its stone was carried away. Today's impressive building was largely reconstructed in the 1870s by Walter Bernard from Derry and is the only remaining terraced fort in Ireland.

Fahan and Buncrana

FAHAN, 6km north of **Burnfoot**, a main entry-point to Inishowen, boasts impressive monastic ruins. The first abbot here was St Mura, and surviving from his time is a seventh-century **cross slab**, a spellbinding example of early Christian stone decoration. Long-stemmed Latin crosses are carved on both faces with typical Celtic interlacing.

Five kilometres north of Fahan, **BUNCRANA** is the largest town on Inishowen and bills itself as a resort, though, frankly, the town's only attractions are its Lough Swilly setting some distance west of the centre. That said, Inishowen's sole tourist office is located here, and there are some enticing possibilities for sleeping and eating.

ARRIVAL AND INFORMATION
FAHAN AND BUNCRANA

By bus In Buncrana buses set down on Market Square in the centre of town, and on Corkhill Rd, the main road heading north. In Fahan they stop on the main road by the old rectory, at the south end of the village. Destinations Ballyliffin (Mon–Fri 4 daily, Sat 1; 25min); Derry (Mon–Sat hourly, Sun 2; 35min); Letterkenny (Mon–

Fri 4 daily, Sat 1; 45min); Malin (Mon–Sat 1 daily; 40min); Moville (Mon–Fri 3 daily, Sat 1; 1hr).
Tourist office The Inishowen tourist office is on Railway Rd, the main road leading into Buncrana (Mon–Fri 9.30am–5.30pm; http://govisitinishowen.com). Its friendly staff can supply you with information on the whole peninsula.

ACCOMMODATION AND EATING

★ **Beach House** The Pier, Swill Rd, Buncrana, 074 936 1050. Not only the best restaurant in Buncrana, but one of the finest on the peninsula; the glorious views aside, the food here is exceptional, with a main dinner menu featuring the likes of Silverhill duck breast with salt baked celariac (€21.95), and a lighter lunch-time café menu, which might include a Lough Swilly seafood chowder.
Inishowen Gateway Hotel Railway Rd, Buncrana, http://inishowengateway.com. The most prominent

accommodation in town is this large roadside hotel, with spruce rooms, its own leisure centre and pool, spa and wellness centre. €€
Tullyvaran Mill Off Drumree Rd, 2km north of Buncrana, http://tullyarvanmill.com. This renovated corn mill, picturesquely set on the banks of the Crana River, has spotless en-suite dormitory, family and private accommodation, and a self-catering kitchen. It is, though, heavily group oriented. €

12

Fort Dunree

Dunree Head, 10km north of Buncrana • charge • http://fortdunree.com

Perched on a headland overlooking the mouth of Lough Swilly, just past the village from which it takes its name, **Fort Dunree** began life as a Martello tower and stands near the spot where Wolfe Tone was brought ashore in 1798. The tower was subsequently enlarged into a fortress to guard against the possible return of the French and was further developed in the late nineteenth century. It now has a **museum** of predictable military memorabilia, with interactive displays providing an insight into the fort's former use; more interesting is a Siemens searchlight dating from 1899, which is still put to use on special occasions. The fort's upper reaches, meanwhile, keep two impressive breach-loading guns dating from 1911. It also houses a Wildlife Discovery room, and a coffee shop with wonderful views.

Mamore Gap

North out of Dunree village the road climbs steeply past a scattering of weather-beaten thatched cottages before crossing a small bridge close to the **MAMORE GAP**, which seems like a chunk bitten out of the Urris Hills. From the top of the Gap the road spirals steeply downwards, each bend providing an ever wider and more spectacular view of the flat foreground to **Dunaff Head**. The gorgeous, 1.5km-long **Tullagh Strand** to the east of Dunaff Head is a safe bathing beach.

Ballyliffin

From Tullagh Strand, the route insinuates itself inland between the mountains to **Clonmany**, a neat village of predominantly cream-coloured houses, quiet for most of the year but hyperactive during its week-long **festival** in early August (http://clonmanyfestival.com). Two kilometres beyond is the more upmarket **BALLYLIFFIN**, home to the Ballyliffin **golf** club – comprising two championship links courses. Golfing aside, there is some excellent accommodation here, plus one or two enjoyable places to eat and drink.

ARRIVAL AND DEPARTURE BALLYLIFFIN

By bus Buses stop in the centre of the village. Destinations Buncrana (Mon–Fri 4 daily, Sat 1; 25min);

Letterkenny (Mon–Fri 4 daily, Sat 1; 1hr 15min); Moville (Mon–Fri 3 daily, Sat 1; 35min).

ACCOMMODATION AND EATING

Ballyliffin Hotel Main St, http://ballyliffinhotel.com. It's a toss-up between the four hotels in the village, but the Ballyliffin is as accomplished as any of them; warm, maroon-coloured rooms and a very creditable restaurant. €€

Nancy's Barn Main St, http://nancysbarn.ie. Handsome stone barn with a warming cottagey interior, serving great coffee, delicious home-baked treats and desserts,

and more substantial fare like warming soups and toasted sandwiches. In summer there are music sessions on Wed evenings. €€

The Rusty Nail Crossconnell, Clonmany, 074 937 6116. Cheery roadside pub offering good-value bar food, but better known for its gut-busting Sunday lunches, plus there's live music at weekends.

Carrickabraghy Castle and Doagh Isle

North of Ballyliffin is the entrancing **Pollan Strand**, at whose furthest tip stands the ruin of **Carrickabraghy Castle**, a sixteenth-century O'Doherty fortification. Much weathered by spray and sea salt, the castle's stones are streaked with colours ranging from the darkest hues to golden yellows. The strand itself has wonderfully wild breakers, which unfortunately make swimming dangerous. The castle sits on the western side of **DOAGH ISLE**, now linked to the mainland through centuries of silt accumulation, on whose eastern edge lies **Trawbreaga Bay**, an exquisite piece of coastline. The mouth of the bay is bewitching: strolling onto the beach here you'll discover rocks fashioned into extraordinary shapes and colours by the sea.

Doagh Famine Village

Lagacurry, 6km north of Ballyliffin • charge • http://doaghfaminevillage.com

One sight not to be missed in this part of the peninsula is the outdoor **Doagh Famine Village**, which, for the most part, recalls the struggles of those who lived through the Famine of the 1840s. That aside, the museum manifests an enlightening, if slightly peculiar, coterie of attractions, including a Wake House, a Republican Safe House and an eviction scene. Visitors are free to nosey around by themselves, but you'll get much more out of the visit if you partake in one of the hugely entertaining **guided tours** (included in the price) – and once you're done, you'll be invited inside the teahouse for a cup of tea and some wheaten bread with jam, which is also included.

Culdaff

CULDAFF is a cosy village whose nearby **beach** forms a stunning natural crescent. There's a major **sea-angling festival** here at the end of July and, in early October, a cultural weekend commemorates the eighteenth-century actor, **Charles Macklin**. Otherwise, its main point of interest is the superb village hotel/pub.

ARRIVAL AND DEPARTURE CULDAFF

By bus Buses drop off on, and depart from, Main St. Destinations Ballyliffin (Mon–Fri 2 daily, Sat 1; 25min); Buncrana (Mon–Fri 2 daily, Sat 1; 55min); Letterkenny

(Mon–Fri 2 daily, Sat 1; 1hr 40min); Malin town (Mon–Fri 2 daily, Sat 1; 5min).

ACCOMMODATION AND EATING

McGrory's Main St, http://mcgrorys.ie. This fabulous all-rounder offers classy rooms, many having retained

their original exposed brickwork, and an equally fine bar, offering cracking meals including locally caught shellfish.

12

Entertainment-wise, its *Backroom* is one of the best venues in Ireland for live music, regularly pulling in some big names, while the Front Bar hosts traditional sessions, typically on Tues and Fri. €€

Malin and Malin Head

Seven kilometres west of Culdaff is the planter settlement of **MALIN**, tucked picturesquely into the side of Trawbreaga Bay, with a charming grassy Diamond at its centre. A little way north of Malin, a signpost points to **Five Fingers Strand**, across the bay from Doagh Isle – it's worth the diversion to experience the ferocity of the breakers on the beach and the long walks on its sands, though the strand has undergone recent severe coastal erosion.

Sixteen kilometres north of Malin village, **Malin Head**, the northernmost extremity of Ireland, might not be as stupendous as other Donegal headlands but is nevertheless excellent for blustery, winding coastal walks – and for ornithologists: choughs, with their glossy black plumage, red legs and bill, inhabit the cliffs, and the rasping cry of the rare corncrake can be heard in the fields. The tip of the headland is marked by **Bamba's Crown**, a ruined Napoleonic signal tower, and the western path from here heads out to **Hell's Hole**, a 75m chasm in the cliffs, which roars with the onrushing tide.

ARRIVAL AND DEPARTURE
MALIN AND MALIN HEAD

By bus Buses drop off on and depart from the Diamond. Destinations Buncrana (Mon–Fri 2 daily, Sat 1; 40min); Culdaff (Mon–Sat 1 daily; 5min); Derry (Mon–Sat 2 daily; 1hr).

ACCOMMODATION AND EATING

Sandrock Holiday Hostel Port Ronan Pier, http://sandrockhostel.com. In a fantastic location just above the beach, this bungalow-like building has two simple dorms, each sleeping ten, and both with wonderful sea views. Self-catering kitchen, lounge with library, and bikes for rent. It stays open for most of the year, but does close occasionally so it's worth checking online ahead of time. €

Seaview Tavern Malin Head, http://seaviewtavern. ie. Attached to a tiny bar, this rather ordinary-looking restaurant is actually very good, though you'll not want to venture far from the ocean-facing terrace in warmer weather. Its speciality is fish straight off the boat, including unbeatable Atlantic wild lobster. The guesthouse has some very comfortable rooms at decent prices. €€

★ **Whitestrand B&B** Malin Head, http://whitestrand. net. Delightful three-room guesthouse just a short stroll from the beach, whose proprietor couldn't be more welcoming – you'll get home-baked goodies upon arrival and a sumptuous breakfast to see you on your way. €€

Greencastle

The harbour village of **GREENCASTLE** on the eastern side of Inishowen has a pleasant view across to Magilligan Strand on the opposite side of Lough Foyle, and there's a **ferry** from here to Magilligan Point in Derry. By the road to Stroove are the ruins of the fourteenth-century Anglo-Norman **castle** from which the village gets its name, built on a rocky knoll to guard the narrowest part of the lough.

Maritime Museum and Planetarium

Greencastle harbour • charge • http://inishowenmaritime.com

By the harbour, in the old coastguard station, is the **Maritime Museum and Planetarium**, which recalls maritime travel from bygone times through a range of Irish boats from 2m to 20m in length. Among the maritime memorabilia, pride of place goes to a nineteenth-century rocket cart used to fire flares to aid survivors of wrecked ships. The state-of-the-art planetarium takes you on exhilarating trips through the universe, while regular laser light shows feature a traditional-music soundtrack; there are also custom shows (minimum ten people) where you can choose your own musical backing.

ARRIVAL AND DEPARTURE

GREENCASTLE

By bus Buses from/to Derry (Mon–Sat 4 daily; 1hr 10min) and Moville (Mon–Sat 4 daily; 25min) stop on Main St.

By boat Magilligan Point (daily on the hour: March–June, Sept & Oct 9am–7pm; July & Aug 9am–8.15pm; Nov–Feb 9am–5pm; pedestrians €4 single, €7 return; cars €22 single, €32 return; http://loughfoyleferry.com).

EATING AND DRINKING

★ **Kealy's** The Harbour, http://kealysseafoodbar.ie. Unsurprisingly, Greencastle is a great spot for seafood, but the one place to aim for is *Kealy's* seafood bar, reckoned to be one of the best in Donegal, and here's why: lobster thermidor, pan-fried medallions of monkfish, whole Dover sole on the bone with capers, plus loads more. Closed Mon–Wed. €€€

12

Belfast

TITANIC BELFAST

13 Belfast

Bustling and vibrant Belfast is a city reborn. Not only has Northern Ireland's capital successfully shaken off the "war-torn" label it earned during the Troubles – it's fair to say the city has undergone a full-blown renaissance. In the aftermath of the peace process, instigated by the 1998 Good Friday Agreement, investment has poured in, resulting in a thriving restaurant scene and a buzzing café culture, while new hotels – running the gamut from five-star glitz to funky and boutique – have sprung up in response to dramatically increasing tourist numbers. In keeping with its long tradition of supplying a stream of musicians, poets, artists and writers to the world stage, Belfast welcomes several first-rate arts and music festivals: the Belfast International Arts Festival takes place every autumn, while the Belfast Vital, and Belsonic Music Festivals, the Festival of Fools, Cinemagic Film Festival and the Cathedral Quarter Arts Festival (CQAF) are also established fixtures in the city's calendar.

At first glance, Belfast has much in common with the large industrial ports found elsewhere in the UK, with its docklands and business districts. But then you encounter the people, a set of inhabitants whose pride and sense of humour remained undimmed even as the world's media camped on their doorstep, broadcasting their woes and turmoil around the globe. It is they, together with the near-miraculous revival in their city's fortunes over the past decade, that really set the place apart. You can easily – and richly – fill at least a few days here, although the geography of the North makes Belfast a good base for exploring virtually anywhere else in the province.

Though the **city centre** is still characterized by numerous elegant Victorian buildings, there's been an enormous transformation, not least in the greater prosperity of the shopping streets. Big brands that once shunned Belfast because of its escalating insurance costs now occupy large units in the main commercial drags leading off from **Donegall Square North** (home to the iconic City Hall with its distinctive copper dome) and in the upmarket shopping complex, Victoria Square.

The rejuvenated area of refurbished warehouses and shop fronts from Ann Street to Donegall Street is now known as the **Cathedral Quarter** and plays host to a lively arts scene and a fantastic choice of bars and restaurants. A short walk northeast across the River Lagan brings you to the newly developed **Titanic Quarter**, where the multi-million pound **Titanic Belfast** visitor attraction charts the design, build, launch and sinking of the world's most famous ocean liner, RMS *Titanic*. This area is fast becoming the city's media hub with the enormous Paint Hall Studios one of the main filming locations for the globally successful HBO fantasy series, *Games of Thrones*. To the south of the city centre proper lie **Queen's University** and the extensive collections of the superb **Ulster Museum**, set in the grounds of the **Botanic Gardens**.

Further out, around 3km to the north, a climb up **Cave Hill** rewards with marvellous views of the city, spread out around the curve of its natural harbour, **Belfast Lough**. The city's once-formidable security presence and fortifications are now virtually invisible, but the iron blockade known as the **Peace Line** still bisects the Catholic and Protestant communities of **West Belfast**, a grim physical reminder of sectarian divisions – but that's not to say the area isn't worth a visit. A short bus ride to the east of the city delivers visitors to the **Stormont Estate**, home to the Northern Ireland Assembly. On a sunny day, the grounds surrounding the instantly recognizable "white house on the hill", as locals refer to it, provide the ideal picnic spot with woodland walks.

Highlights

The Cathedral Quarter Belfast's cultural hub, with a plethora of great restaurants, cafés, pubs, arts centres, music venues and its very own Cathedral Quarter Arts Festival (CQAF). See page 451

The Titanic Quarter The city's redeveloped docklands are home to the multimillion-pound interactive visitor centre, Titanic Belfast, which tells the story of the ill-fated RMS *Titanic*. See page 453

Ulster Museum A multitude of fascinating exhibits dating back to prehistoric times, as well as one of Ireland's major art collections and a superb children's zone. See page 456

❹ Stormont The seat of government in Northern Ireland is set in glorious parkland to the east of the city. See page 460

❺ Cave Hill The best spot for a panoramic view of the city, with Belfast Lough spread out below. See page 460

❻ West Belfast An essential part of any visit to the city: the murals, Peace Line, cemeteries and fortified bars put everyday life into stark political context. See page 461

HIGHLIGHTS ARE MARKED ON THE MAPS ON PAGES 449 AND 456

13

Brief history

Belfast began life as a cluster of forts built to guard a ford across the **River Farset**, which nowadays runs underground beneath the High Street. An **Anglo-Norman castle** was built here in 1177, but its influence was limited, and within a hundred years or so control over the Lagan Valley had reverted firmly to the Irish, under the O'Neills of Clandeboye. In 1604, **Sir Arthur Chichester**, whose son was to be the First Earl of Donegall, was "planted" in the area by James I, and shortly afterwards the tiny settlement was granted a charter creating a corporate borough. It was not until the end of the seventeenth century, though, that Belfast began to grow significantly, when French Huguenots fleeing persecution brought skills which rapidly improved the fortunes of the local **linen industry** – which, in turn, attracted new workers and wealth.

The eighteenth and nineteenth centuries

Through the eighteenth century, the cloth trade and **shipbuilding** expanded tremendously, and the population increased tenfold in a hundred years. With economic prosperity, Belfast became a city noted for its **liberalism**: in 1791, three Presbyterian Ulstermen formed the **Society of United Irishmen**, a gathering embracing Catholics and Protestants on the basis of common Irish nationality, from which sprang the **1798 Rebellion**. However, the rebellion in the North was quickly and ruthlessly stamped out by the English, and within two generations most Protestants had abandoned the Nationalist cause. Presbyterian ministers began openly to attack the Catholic Church, resulting in a **sectarian divide** that as time drew on became wider and increasingly violent. At the same time, the nineteenth century saw vigorous commercial and industrial expansion, and by the time Queen Victoria granted Belfast **city status** in 1888, its population had risen to 208,000, soon exceeding that of Dublin.

The twentieth century to the present day

With **Partition** came the creation of Northern Ireland with Belfast as its capital and Stormont as its seat of government. Inevitably, this boosted the city's status but also ensured that it would ultimately become the focus for much of the Troubles. The economic status of the Catholic population was deliberately maintained at a low level by a **Stormont government** that largely consisted of Protestant landowners and businessmen and saw no reason to challenge existing sectarian employment, housing and policing policies – all fuel to the fire which was to follow.

For 25 years from 1969, Belfast witnessed the worst of the **Troubles** (see pages 462 and 571), and by the time the IRA declared a **ceasefire** in 1994, much of the city resembled a battle site. There then followed a sea change in the city's fortunes as Britain and the EU funded a **revitalization** programme costing billions of pounds. Major shopping centres were built, swish hotels, bars and restaurants seemed to spring up almost overnight, and buildings such as the Waterfront Hall and Odyssey complex fundamentally altered the city's skyline. In the past decade, a crop of new entrepreneurs returned home, many having cut their teeth in businesses, restaurants and bars overseas, and set about effecting a new round of changes. Derelict buildings have been successfully restored and reopened in various guises, serving as everything from restaurants to accommodation options for all budgets. At times, sectarianism still raises its ugly head – but on the whole, vibrant new areas such as the Cathedral and Titanic Quarters keep Belfast looking to the future.

The city centre

The core of Belfast is stately **Donegall Square**, home to the copper-domed City Hall and its pristine gardens, where locals and visitors congregate for lunchtime picnics

13

in fine weather. Buses and taxis depart for every part of the city from the sides of the square, ensuring that it's always busy with both pedestrians and traffic. The city's main shopping area once lay a stone's throw to the north until upstaged by the Victoria Square complex, with its raft of upmarket retailers, just to the east. Entertainment and accommodation options proliferate immediately south and north of the square, although the rejuvenation of St Anne's Square has helped to establish the **Cathedral Quarter** as Belfast's coolest night-time hub. Most of the grand old Victorian buildings that characterize the city are to the north and east, towards the river, including St Malachy's church.

The **River Lagan** flows towards Belfast Lough along the eastern side of the city centre, offering excellent riverside walks. It is also home to the first of the city's radical new developments in peace times, the **Laganside**, focused on the Waterfront Hall and the Odyssey Complex across the water. Beyond the Odyssey, in the heart of the **Titanic Quarter**, stands the city's biggest success story, **Titanic Belfast**, a fully interactive museum built to commemorate the centenary of the ill-fated RMS *Titanic*.

City Hall

Donegall Square North •Mon–Fri 9.30am–5pm, Sat 10am–5pm; tours (45min) Mon–Fri 11am, 2pm & 3pm, Sat & Sun noon, 2pm & 3pm • Free • http://belfastcity.gov.uk/cityhall

The vast Neoclassical bulk of **City Hall** dominates Donegall Square and the entire centre of Belfast. Completed in 1906 and made of bright white Portland stone, its turrets, saucer domes, scrolls and pinnacle pots are all representative of styles absorbed by the British Empire. In front stands an imposing statue of Queen Victoria, the apotheosis of imperialism, while at her feet, sculpted in bronze, proud figures show the city fathers' world-view: a young scholar; his mother with spinning spool; and his father with mallet and boat, the three representing "learning, linen and liners", the alliterative bedrock of Belfast's heritage.

Inside, arching almost 50m above you, is the **main dome** with its (inaccessible) whispering gallery; modelled on St Paul's Cathedral in London, it is adorned around its rim with zodiac signs, both painted and in stained glass. The palatial marbled **entrance hall** features staircase pillars, colonnades and bronze and marble statues, while the principal landing is graced by a **mural** executed in 1951 by John Luke, celebrating Belfast's now mostly defunct traditional industries – rope-making, shipbuilding, weaving and spinning. The building's highlight is the oak-decorated **council chamber**, with its hand-carved wainscoting and councillors' pews as well as a visitors' gallery.

Free guided **tours** show visitors around the building, but more illuminating is the ground floor **exhibition**, which charts the city's history courtesy of sixteen differently themed rooms. Starting with the construction of City Hall itself – exhibits include the ceremonial trowel and the bill of sale for the plaster and marblework – further themes include work, focusing on the city's big three industries, namely shipping (look out for a beautifully crafted sideboard made for the *Titanic* but which never made it onto the ship), linen and ropework; play, which dwells on the city's sporting passions, among them football, boxing, and, yes, pigeon racing; culture, which considers the city's influential temperance movement; and perhaps most enjoyably, language, where you can try and get to grips with the nuances of the irrepressible Ulster dialect. Ending on a celebratory note, the exhibition pays homage to the good and great of the city, and there have certainly been some characters, among them Van Morrison, the snooker legend Alex "Hurricane" Higgins, and of course, George Best. It's worth pausing part way through for some light refreshment in the excellent *Bobbin Coffee Shop*.

Linen Hall Library

17 Donegall Square North (entrance at 52 Fountain St) • Mon–Fri 9.30am–5.30pm • http://linenhall.com

At the northwest corner of Donegall Square stands Belfast's oldest library – and Northern Ireland's last subscription library – the substantially revamped **Linen Hall Library**, established in 1788. The library's **Political Collection** – a unique accumulation of over 100,000 publications reflecting every aspect of Northern Irish political life since 1966, including prison letters smuggled out of the Long Kesh detention centre (aka Maze Prison) – is no longer viewable to the public, unless you make a prior appointment, But what you will see is the impressive Vertical Gallery – four floors of wall-bound political posters from The Troubles: *Terrorism Stop the Beatings*, *Remember Derry*, *Smash Stormont*, and so on. The library also boasts excellent facilities for tracing family trees, a café, and stocks all the daily newspapers. Regular literary events take place throughout the year, including specialist workshops.

The Entries and around

A little way northeast of Donegall Square, a handful of narrow alleyways known as the **Entries** links Ann Street and the High Street. You'll stumble across some great old saloon bars down here, such as *The Morning Star* in Pottinger's Entry, with its large frosted windows and Parisian-café-like counter (see page 469), and *White's Tavern* in Winecellar Entry, which dates from the seventeenth century (see page 469). Crown Entry was where the Society of United Irishmen (see page 564) was born, led by the Protestant triumvirate of Wolfe Tone, Henry Joy McCracken and Samuel Nielson. Nielson also printed his own newspaper in this area, the *Northern Star*; heavily influenced by the French revolutionary ideals of liberty, equality and fraternity, the newspaper's inflammatory material led to his being hounded out of town.

Just to the north, no. 2 Waring Street was originally built as a market house in 1769, but is more renowned as the venue for the **1792 Belfast Harp Festival**: by the end of the eighteenth century, the old Gaelic harping tradition had reached almost terminal decline and the convention was a deliberate attempt by its organizers, the United Irish Society, to record some of the harpers' airs for posterity. The transcriber, Edmund Bunting, was stimulated to tour Ireland collecting further airs, 77 of which were published in his illustrious collection of 1809.

The Cathedral Quarter

The area north of Waring Street has experienced more than two decades of regeneration, a process kick-started when chef Nick Price gambled on the then mainly derelict area by opening his *Nick's Warehouse* restaurant in 1989. With Price's retirement, that Hill Street venue, which proved a huge success, is now *The Harp Bar* (see page 469). His punt, meanwhile, is looking a sure thing, with an ever-increasing number of restaurants and bars and a fresh title, the **Cathedral Quarter** (http://cathedralquarterbelfast.com), for this once-scruffy patch. Testament to the changes is that the city's venerable five-star hotel, *The Merchant* (see page 466) – whose owner, Bill Wolsey, has converted building after building in the Quarter – is located here.

The University of Ulster's Belfast Campus sits across from the Metropolitan Arts Centre – better known as the **MAC** (see page 471) – on the edge of **St Anne's Square**, a foodie honeypot with some of Belfast's finest restaurants in residence around its fringes, *Coppi* (see page 468) and *House of Zen* (see page 468) among them. Arts and music venues such as the *Black Box* (see page 471) and *Oh Yeah Music Centre* (see page 471) and live music pubs throng the cobbled streets, while the Quarter's cultural hub status is cemented by its hosting of a number of Belfast's more bohemian **events**, including the Cathedral Quarter Arts Festival (see page 470) and the quirky Out to Lunch Festival.

13

Belfast Cathedral

Donegall St • Mon–Sat 10.30am–4pm • charge • http://belfastcathedral.org

A couple of hundred metres up Donegall Street from where it meets Waring Street you'll find the most monolithic of all the city's grand buildings: the Protestant **Belfast Cathedral** (still known locally as St Anne's), a neo-Romanesque basilica started in 1899, but not fully completed until 1981. Entrance is via the huge west door, immediately to the right of which is the baptistery, with an intricately designed representation of the Creation on its ceiling consisting of 150,000 tiny pieces of glass. Most significant, however, is the cathedral's only tomb, marked by a simple slab on the floor of the south aisle, which contains the body of **Lord Edward Henry Carson** (see box). The symbol of Partition, he's seen either as the province's saviour or as the villain who sabotaged Ireland's independence as a 32-county state. The cathedral attracts a lot of media attention in the run-up to Christmas each year as the incumbent Dean undertakes a "sit-out" on Donegall Street to collect donations for the poor and charitable causes, a tradition started by Dean Sammy Crooks in 1976. Dressed in the black Anglican clerical cloak, he is referred to as "Black Santa".

Great Victoria Street

The strip of Belfast running south along **Great Victoria Street** to Shaftesbury Square and thence to the university area and beyond was once known as the "Golden Mile". It's rarely called that these days, but Great Victoria Street itself is worth checking out, not least for the grandiose Victorian **Grand Opera House** (see page 471), which sits at its northern end. Although locals complained about the modern extension added to the theatre in 2006, it is now accepted as part and parcel of the city skyline. A few paces south lies the **Europa Hotel**; once renowned for being Europe's most bombed, it now stands as one of Belfast's finest. Almost opposite the *Europa* stands one of the greatest of Victorian gin palaces, the **Crown Liquor Saloon** (see page 468), now owned by the National Trust. The saloon has a glittering tiled exterior resembling a spa baths more than a serious drinking institution, while inside, the scrolled ceiling, patterned floor and the golden-yellow and rosy-red hues led John Betjeman to describe it as his "many-coloured cavern".

The Laganside

The beginning of the **Laganside** area is marked at the High Street's eastern end by the **Prince Albert Memorial Clock Tower**. Built in 1867–69 and tilting slightly off the perpendicular as a result of its construction upon gradually sinking wooden piles, it's a strange memorial – especially as Prince Albert never had anything to do with Belfast – but it's a handy landmark.

LORD EDWARD CARSON

Lord Edward Carson is a name that Northern Ireland has never forgotten. A Dubliner of Scots-Presbyterian background, he took the decision in 1910 to accept the leadership of the opposition to Home Rule, which in effect inextricably allied him to the **Ulster Unionist** resistance movement. Yet, though this association is about the only thing for which he is remembered, his personality and integrity went far deeper than this. He abhorred religious intolerance, and behind the exterior of a zealous crusader was a man who sincerely believed that Ireland couldn't prosper without Britain and only wished that a federalist answer could have involved a united Ireland. Nonetheless, this was the same man who, as a brilliant orator at the bar, and in the role he loved the most, brought about the humiliating destruction of Oscar Wilde at the writer's trial in 1895.

North of the Albert Clock, along Dunbar Link, you'll come across a series of grand buildings, chief among which is the restored **Custom House** on Donegall Quay – a Corinthian-style, E-shaped edifice designed between 1854 and 1857. Unfortunately, it's not open to the public, leaving you unable to verify rumours of fantastic art masterpieces stored in its basements – though it's known that Anthony Trollope, the nineteenth-century novelist (and inventor of the pillar box), once worked here as a surveyor's clerk.

Just beyond the Custom House on Donegall Quay is the ambitious **Laganside** development project, the first component of which to be completed was the **Lagan Weir**, designed to protect the city against flooding. Millions of pounds have been pumped into dredging the river to maintain water levels and revive the much depleted fish population – successfully it seems: there was salmon fishing on the weir's inauguration day in 1994. Look across the river to the **Harland & Wolff shipyard** (see page 454) and you'll spot its landmark yellow cranes ("Samson" and "Goliath").

Further south along Oxford Street, on Lanyon Place, stands a 20m-high metal **statue** depicting a girl holding aloft a ring of thanksgiving (for the peace process). Erected in 2007, *Beacon of Hope* (or "Nuala with the Hula", as locals affectionately call her) has fast become a city icon. Nearby sits the glittering 2000-seater **Belfast Waterfront** concert hall and conference centre.

The Titanic Quarter

Located across the river from the city centre on Queen's Quay, a 10min walk from Donegall Square (alternatively take Metro bus #26 from Donegall Square West or the train from Belfast Central or Great Victoria St, disembarking at the Titanic Quarter stop)

Across the river on Queen's Quay, the massive **Odyssey Place** leisure complex marks the beginning of the **Titanic Quarter** (http://titanicquarter.com), an area of the city that has seen huge financial investment in recent years. Luxury apartments now line the water's edge, overlooking the area's eye-catching figurehead, **Titanic Belfast**, an immersive visitor attraction dedicated to the world's most famous ocean liner. Alongside it, the **SS Nomadic Belfast** was the *Titanic*'s tender ship and is the last remaining White Star Line ship in the world – it's now permanently moored in Hamilton Dock, and visitors can step on board to explore a century of maritime history. The Quarter is gaining a reputation as a media hub, with Paint Hall studios the setting for several big-budget Hollywood movies and the HBO series, *Game of Thrones*, and the sprawling Belfast Harbour Studio. To the rear of the Odyssey building is the **W5** scientific discovery centre (http://w5online.co.uk), with more than 150 interactive exhibits, aimed primarily at children. For more grown-up insights, it's worth taking a tour of the area (see page 466). Further along what has been rebranded the Maritime Mile is the marvellous HMS **Caroline** and the new **Titanic Distillery**.

Titanic Belfast

1 Olympic Way, Queens Rd • Daily: April, May, Sept & Oct 9am–6pm; June 9am–7pm; July & Aug daily 9am–7.30pm; Sept daily 9am–6pm; Nov–March 10am–5pm • charge • http://titanicbelfast.com

Titanic Belfast opened its doors on the ship's centenary in April 2012 to great aplomb, with a concert staged on the slipway where the ill-fated liner was first launched. The prow-like structure is the same height as the ship's hull (38m) and glistens in the sunlight courtesy of some three thousand silver-anodized aluminium shards. Such is the attraction's popularity that it's worth considering very carefully when to visit, which generally means avoiding the middle of the day, weekends and holidays, if at all possible.

Once inside, you are funnelled through a series of galleries variously pertaining to the city's industrial past, the history of Harland and Wolff and the construction of *Titanic*, and, ultimately, its fateful journey. There's also fascinating coverage of *Titanic*'s recovery in 1998, as well as a cleverly conceived shipyard ride (on a gondola-type contraption),

13

THE DOCKS AND THE RMS TITANIC

Much of Belfast's waterside heritage is associated with English engineer Edward James Harland (1831–95) who, together with his German-born assistant Gustav Wilhelm Wolff (1834–1913), founded the **Harland & Wolff** shipbuilding company here in 1861. Starting from a small shipyard on Queen's Island, the company grew rapidly and over the following decades had gained a reputation for innovations such as iron (rather than wooden) decks and flatter, squarer hulls designed to maximize capacity. The firm continued to flourish after Harland's death and Wolff's retirement, most notably when it constructed three steamships for the **White Star Line** – the *Olympic*, the *Britannic* and, most famously, the **Titanic**. Completed in 1912, the RMS *Titanic*, then the world's largest passenger-carrying steamship, sank on April 14 of the same year, just four days into her maiden voyage from Southampton to New York, having collided with an iceberg in the North Atlantic. More than 1500 of the 2200-plus passengers and crew drowned, a tragedy that continues to hold a macabre fascination today. Belfast is still proud of its role in creating the world's most famous ship ("She was fine when she left here" goes the saying, along with "Built by Irishmen, driven by an Englishman"), and the centenary of her launch was marked by numerous events focused upon the Laganside and the new Titanic Quarter.

which takes you on a journey through the sights, smells and sounds of the dockyard during the ship's construction. It's probably fair to say that, for the most part, the layout is too haphazard (and it's often just too busy) to make this the genuinely moving attraction it should be, but that all changes at the conclusion of the exhibition. Here, in the basement – and to the soundtrack of sombre music – several glass cases hold some extraordinary artefacts retrieved from the ocean floor, including a deckchair, hip flask, walking cane, and – most famously – the violin belonging to Wallace Hartley, the ship's bandmaster, while a "glass floor" floats above the decaying remains of the doomed vessel.

HMS Caroline

Alexandra Dock, Queens Rd · Fri–Sun, tours at 10am, 11.30am, 1.30pm & 3pm, but do check times beforehand · charge · http://nmrn.org.uk

After an extensive restoration project to halt the deterioration of the World War One light cruiser, **HMS Caroline** is now welcoming back visitors on board. One of the most enjoyable of all Belfast's visitor attractions, the bare facts are impressive: built over a nine-month period in 1911, she's not only one of just three surviving World War I warships, but the sole survivor from the Battle of Jutland, the largest sea battle of the war, which took place over just two days at the end of May in 1916, resulting in over 6,000 British and 2500 German casualties. Decommissioned as recently as 2011 (which made her the second-oldest serving ship after HMS *Victory*), *Caroline* was a scouting ship and is also now the only one with her original engines still *in situ*. The visit begins with a dramatic recreation of the battle in the old drill hall (which was actually added in 1924), before you are led on an enlightening tour of various parts of the ship, including the mocked-up captain's quarters – among Captain Henry Cooke's many privileges was a three-course silver service each day and his own bath, while ratings slept in hammocks. And if you fancy some refreshments, you can buy a drink and a snack from the café located in the original mess kitchen.

Titanic Distillery

Alexandra Dock, Queens Rd · Daily: 10am–7pm · charge · http://titanicdistillers.com

Belfast's whiskey heritage is often given short shrift, but alongside shipbuilding and linen, whiskey was at the heart of the city's industrial revival. Occupying the hitherto derelict Old Pumphouse (part of the Thompson Dock) is the **Titanic Distillery**, which, when it opened in 2023, became the city's first working distillery since Dunville & Co shut up shop in 1935 – that largely being the result of the growing temperance movement (in the North). The hour-long signature tour is as much about this magnificent building itself as it is about the whiskey, and to this end you'll get to see some of the original early 20th century machinery, as well as the three 1950s pumps which were used to drain the water from the dock. The distillery's first single malt won't be on stream until 2026, but available at present is a triple-distilled blended (and slightly peaty) whiskey, as well as a vodka made with sugar beet, both of which you'll get to sample at the end of the tour. You'll also receive a voucher for a hot drink and traybake.

South Belfast

Towards the old Golden Mile's southern extremity lies the **university area**, the focal point for South Belfast's attractions (http://forwardsouth.org), with plenty of eating places, pubs and a range of budget accommodation options. Near Queen's University are the lush **Botanic Gardens**, within which sits the vast **Ulster Museum**, displaying everything from dinosaur bones and an Egyptian mummy to contemporary art and a 77m hand-embroidered *Game of Thrones* tapestry. Heading south from here along Stranmillis Road it's a relatively short step east to the river-skirting **Lagan Towpath**, which runs several kilometres southwest to Lisburn, while a detour along the way leads to the Neolithic earthwork known as the **Giant's Ring**.

The University Quarter

Just south of Shaftesbury Square stand three churches – Moravian, Crescent and Methodist – whose distinctive steeples frame the entrance to the **University Quarter**. From here, leading up to the university buildings, the roads are lined with early Victorian terraces that represent the final flowering of Georgian architecture in Belfast. The **Upper Crescent** is a magnificent curved Neoclassical terrace, built around 1845 but sadly neglected since; it is now used mainly for office space. The **Lower Crescent**, perversely, is straight.

Queen's University
University Rd • Visitor centre Mon–Fri 8.30am–5pm • Free • http://qub.ac.uk/home/welcome-centre

Queen's University is the architectural centrepiece of the area, flanked by the most satisfying example of a Georgian terrace in Belfast, **University Square**, where the red brickwork mostly remains intact, with the exception of a few bay windows added in the Victorian era. The university building itself was constructed in 1849 as a mock-Tudor remodelling of Magdalen College, Oxford, to a design by Charles Lanyon, and houses a **visitor centre** which provides information about the university and runs guided tours.

The Italianate **Union Theological College**, nearby on College Park, also by Lanyon, was temporarily the site of the Northern Ireland Parliament until 1932 when Stormont was built.

The Botanic Gardens
College Park, Botanic Ave • Daily 7.30am–sunset; Palm House April–Sept 10am–5pm, Oct–March 10am–4pm; Tropical Ravine Tues–Sun 10am–5pm • Free • Buses #8A, #8B and #8C from Donegall Square East

Just below the university are the popular **Botanic Gardens**, first opened in 1827 and well protected by trees from the noise of the surrounding traffic. Within the gardens

13

is the **Palm House**, a hothouse predating the famous one at Kew Gardens in London, but very similar in style, with a white-painted framework of curvilinear ironwork and glass. It was the first of its kind in the world, another success for Lanyon, who worked in tandem on this project with the Dublin iron-founder Richard Turner. The nearby **Tropical Ravine** is a classic example of Victorian light entertainment – a hundred-year-old sunken glen chock-full of "vegetable wonders" extracted from far-flung jungles and replanted for the delight of the visiting Belfast public.

Ulster Museum

Tues–Sun and bank holiday Mondays 10am–5pm • Free • http://ulstermuseum.org

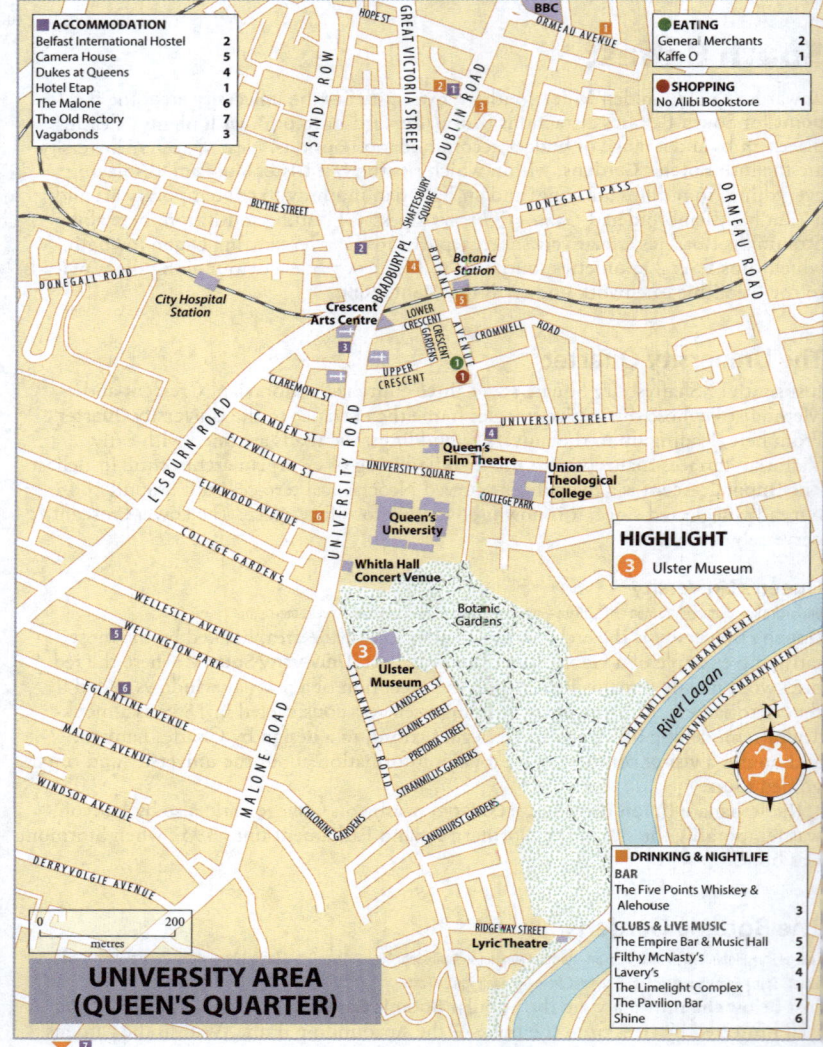

ACCOMMODATION

Belfast International Hostel	2
Camera House	5
Dukes at Queens	4
Hotel Etap	1
The Malone	6
The Old Rectory	7
Vagabonds	3

EATING

General Merchants	2
Kaffe O	1

SHOPPING

No Alibi Bookstore	1

HIGHLIGHT

3 Ulster Museum

DRINKING & NIGHTLIFE

BAR

The Five Points Whiskey & Alehouse	3

CLUBS & LIVE MUSIC

The Empire Bar & Music Hall	5
Filthy McNasty's	2
Lavery's	4
The Limelight Complex	1
The Pavilion Bar	7
Shine	6

UNIVERSITY AREA (QUEEN'S QUARTER)

13

The Botanic Gardens also house the **Ulster Museum**, whose clever design sheds light both literally and figuratively on subjects ranging from the North's troubled history to Ireland's geological past. The grand, open-plan **ground floor** includes everything from an impressive dinosaur skeleton to contemporary haute couture. From here, the curators recommend heading up to the **third floor** to explore the art exhibits, where the **modern art collection** is home to Francis Bacon's macabre *Head II*, Bridget Riley's unnerving *Cataract IV* and Stanley Spencer's thought-provoking *The Betrayal*. You'll also find some stunning landscapes and rural scenes up here, by painters such as Belfast's Sir John Lavery, plus Turner's highly symbolic *Dawn of Christianity*.

The **second floor** features the "**Nature Zone**", depicting the Earth's origins and Ireland's development up to the Ice Age. Far more engrossing are the **first floor**'s **history** galleries, which begin with Neolithic remains and Bronze Age finds (including a remarkable decorated shield), before taking a detailed look at the **medieval** period – two exhibits to look out for here are the somewhat skewwhiff stone inauguration chair of the O'Neills of Clandeboye and the silver gilt arm-reliquary supposedly created to house St Patrick's hand. The **Armada gallery** includes plenty of relics from the ill-fated *Girona*, which sank off the Antrim coast in 1588, while the Ascendancy section

---

GEORGE BEST

Maradona good, Pele better, George Best

popular Belfast sporting adage

Born in East Belfast in 1946, **George Best** became (and remains to this day) Northern Ireland's most celebrated footballer, signed by Manchester United after being rejected by local clubs. Making his debut aged 17, Best starred in the 1964–65 and 1966–67 league-winning teams, cementing his reputation as a dazzling, jinking and goal-scoring winger. His good looks, long hair, gift of the gab and love of the high life also led to his acquisition of the sobriquet "the fifth Beatle". Further fame was assured when United beat Benfica 4–1 in the 1968 European Cup Final, Best scoring one of the goals and running the Portuguese team's defence so ragged before a vast televised audience that his award of **European Footballer of the Year** was a foregone conclusion.

The latter half of the 1960s saw Best's celebrity lifestyle (by then he owned nightclubs and boutiques and had dated at least one Miss World) consumed by gambling, **alcoholism** and chasing women. He walked out of United in 1974, and after that his footballing career declined rapidly, taking in spells in the US and Australia. Alcohol addiction led to a stint in prison in 1984, after which Best was found guilty of drunk driving and assaulting a police officer. By 2002 his health was so poor that he underwent a liver transplant, but continued to drink after its success and eventually succumbed to multiple organ failure in November 2005.

Some 100,000 mourners lined the streets of Belfast as Best's coffin travelled to his **funeral** service at Stormont. Belfast City Airport was subsequently renamed in his honour and, in 2006, the Ulster Bank issued one million £5 notes bearing his picture – the entire issue was rapidly snapped up for keepsakes. The great sadness of Best's football career was that, despite 37 caps for Northern Ireland, he never appeared in a major international competition such as the World Cup, but he inspired a host of young footballers and, indeed, numerous jokes, not least his own oft-quoted remark: "I spent a lot of my money on booze, birds and fast cars. The rest I just squandered." Avid fans can book onto a guided tour of the Best family home at 16 Burren Way on the Cregagh Estate (April–Sept Fri; charge; http://georgebesthouse.com); Eastsider Pete McCabe provides fascinating tours of the house, which has been retro-fitted to 1961, the year George left for Manchester United, though his father remained here until his death in 2008 – indeed, the Best's were the only family to have lived here. Better still, it's now even possible to stay here (see page 467).

13

includes a remarkable rag-bound tally-stick, used to record the number of prayers said during the then illegal outdoor Catholic service, as well as highlighting the effects of the Great Famine. From here the exhibits quicken up a pace, especially when focusing upon the **War of Independence** and the North's resistance to Dublin rule, before looking at Belfast during World War II and concluding with a space devoted to the **Troubles**. A very popular addition to the museum is a 77m-long hand-embroidered tapestry depicting the story of the **Game of Thrones** (the HBO series filmed on location in Northern Ireland) in its entirety.

The Lagan Towpath and Giant's Ring

Beyond the university area lie the glades of middle-class suburbia. A gate at the southern tip of the Botanic Gardens leads to the river and the **Lagan Towpath**. This tarmacked trail can be tramped for about 13km south to Lisburn, passing old locks and lock houses, woodland and marshes on the way. The waterway became fully navigable in the late 1790s, ready to carry the newly discovered coal from Lough Neagh, but its utility declined with the advent of the railway in 1839. Today, it's been harnessed as part of the Ulster Way, for rambling and canoeing enthusiasts.

Giant's Ring

Off Ballynahatty Rd, Lisburn, 1.5km south of Shaw's Bridge • Free access dawn to dusk

If you leave the towpath at Shaw's Bridge (the ring-road crossing), it's a 1.5km signposted walk along country lanes to the **Giant's Ring**, a colossal, 183m-wide earthwork thought to have served as a burial ground or meeting place. You wouldn't be far wrong in thinking that its inwardly sloping wall would make an excellent speed-track circuit, for in the eighteenth century it was used for horse racing: six circuits made a two-mile race, with the punters jostling for position on the top of the rampart. Most captivating of all is the huge **dolmen** at the central hub of this cartwheel structure. As a single megalithic remain, it's immediately more impressive than even the great structures of the Irish High Kings at Tara, though here there's little information concerning its origins and usage. The setting chosen for the site, high above the surrounding lowlands (probably once marshy lake), is impressive – there's a powerful feeling that the great dramas and decision-making of the ancient northeast must have been played out here.

East Belfast

From Donegall Square West, the Metro bus #4A runs every 8min to East Belfast; alternatively, from Belfast Central train station, it's a 25min walk straight down the Alberbridge Rd to the Holywood Arches • http://ulstermuseum.org

East Belfast's skyline is dominated by the cranes – named "Samson" and "Goliath" – which tower above the **Harland & Wolff shipyard** (see page 454). The shipyard is the city's proudest international asset – though the company's work is nowadays centred on offshore wind farm installations – and is said to possess the largest dry dock in the world: over 600m long and 90m wide. The surrounding area is now home to one of Europe's biggest redevelopment projects, the Titanic Quarter (see page 453), and increased financial investment is being channelled towards housing developments and retail outlets as well as community and cultural projects.

The area's pride in the famous figures it has given to the literary, sporting and music worlds remains undimmed; the theologian and author of the Chronicles of Narnia, **C.S. Lewis**, was born in Dundela Villas, and there's a plaque commemorating him at Dundela Flats. Fans of the Chronicles should also pay a visit to the Holywood Arches railway bridge, where a magnificent **bronze statue** depicts one of the Narnia characters, Digory Kirke, peering into the famous

13

wardrobe. Next door is **C.S. Lewis Square**, a spruce public place with seven sculptures celebrating the acclaimed writer's most famous characters. Here too is the **EastSide Visitor Centre** (daily 10am–4pm; http://visiteastside.com), which is part of the EastSide Partnership (http://eastsidepartnership.com), a local charity who are pushing hard to regenerate the area.

Another plaque on Burren Way in the Cregagh Estate marks the childhood home of the late footballer **George Best** (see box), while fans of **Van Morrison** (see box) might want to seek out his birthplace, a private house (with no public access) at 125 Hyndford Street, off Beersbridge Road, and the many streets that feature in his songs (Cyprus Avenue, Castlereagh Road and others). The Connswater Community Greenway group has developed a series of **trails** (available to download on http://eastsidegreenways.com) for all three East Belfast sons, each leading you through the streets where the men grew up and the places that influenced and inspired them, as well as several others pertaining to the area's industrial heritage.

Templemore Baths
96 Templemore Av • Mon–Fri 9am–4pm • Free • http://better.gov.uk

Further proof of the area's renaissance can be seen in the redevelopment of the old **Templemore Baths**. Dating from 1893 and the sole surviving Victorian baths on the island of Ireland, Templemore was a popular venue among families (mostly men working at Harland & Wolff) living in East Belfast who at that time had no access to sanitary facilities, while it also served as a makeshift morgue during World War II. The original building has been repurposed as an interactive heritage centre, with many of the original features – such as the administrative office, waiting rooms, and first and second-class admission entrances – having been sympathetically restored; note the cigarette-stubbed tiles. The former minor pool, which has been glassed over, holds a superb exhibition, where you can listen to testimonies from many of the bath's former users, who have also donated various bits of memorabilia: swimwear, medals and certificates, logbooks, photos and so on. The superbly renovated main pool itself has been joined by a spanking new modern extension with a six-lane pool and spa facilities.

VAN MORRISON

Belfast boasts an impressive roster of musical talent, from singer Ruby Murray (the Madonna of the 1950s, in terms of chart success), flautist James Galway and pianist Barry Douglas, to rock guitarists Eric Bell and Gary Moore, both of whom played with Thin Lizzy. Without doubt, however, Belfast's most renowned musical son – and the one who most vocally celebrates his Belfast beginnings – is **Van Morrison**. Emerging from the city's early 1960s' blues scene with the group Them, it was Morrison's first solo single **Brown Eyed Girl** that brought him international success. He followed this up with **Astral Weeks** in 1968, an impressionistic song cycle drawing on his experiences growing up in Belfast, which remains his masterpiece. Throughout his subsequent career he has embraced jazz, folk and blues, producing a body of work that, for sheer quality and diversity, is rivalled only by Dylan.

Whatever the style of music, Morrison frequently harks back to his East Belfast childhood: he often name-checks specific streets and places, including Hyndford Street where he was born, and the nearby Cypress Avenue; and his collaboration with traditional Irish musicians The Chieftains in 1988 on their Irish Heartbeat album included *I'll tell Me Ma*, a traditional Belfast children's rhyme. In 2013 he was granted the freedom of the city, and in 2015 he played two ecstatically received concerts on the occasion of his seventieth birthday on Cypress Avenue, attracting local politicians and Hollywood stars. The **Van Morrison Trail** is a roughly 3km self-guided walk taking in eight places that were important to Morrison and inspirational to his music.

13

Stormont

6.5km east of the centre, off the Newtownards Rd • Mon–Fri 9am–4pm; guided tours Wed–Fri noon & 2pm • Free • http://niassembly.gov. uk • Buses #20A and #23 from Donegall Square West

The home of the Northern Ireland Parliament until the introduction of direct rule in 1972, **Stormont** now houses the Assembly created by the 1998 Good Friday Agreement. It's a magnificent sight, a great, white Neoclassical mansion crowning a rise in the middle of a park at the end of a long, straight drive. You can wander freely in the grounds, and free public tours have recently been introduced. There's also a wonderful children's playground, named in honour of the late Mo Mowlam, previous Northern Ireland Secretary of State. Also here, though not open to the public, is **Stormont Castle**, the office of the British Secretary of State for Northern Ireland.

North Belfast

North Belfast boasts baronial **Belfast Castle**, the impressive wildlife collection of **Belfast Zoo** and superb panoramic city views from **Cave Hill**. The castle and the city's zoo, both out on the Antrim Road, sit conveniently alongside one another on the slopes of Cave Hill, served by bus #1 from Donegall Square West.

Belfast Castle

Antrim Rd • Daily 9am–9pm,• Free • http://belfastcity.gov.uk

Built in 1870 to the designs of Lanyon and surrounded by a wooded estate, the sandstone **Belfast Castle**'s exterior is in Scottish Baronial style, inspired in part by the reconstruction of Balmoral Castle in Aberdeenshire in 1853. It features a six-storey tower, a series of crow-stepped gables and conically peak-capped turrets, but the most striking feature of all is the serpentine Italianate stairway that leads down from the principal reception room to the garden terrace below. Restored and refurbished in 1990, the interior is, however, virtually empty of Victorian period accoutrements. Upstairs, the **visitor centre** traces the locality's history from prehistoric cave-dwellers to the castle's construction. It also houses a restaurant and pub, and there's a children's adventure playground in the grounds of the estate.

Belfast Zoo

Antrim Rd • Daily: April–Sept 10am–6pm; Oct–March 10am–4pm • charge • http://belfastcity.gov.uk

Adjoining the castle is the well-landscaped parkland of **Belfast Zoo**, which stretches up towards Cave Hill. Within its impressive layout, you'll find primates and big cats, elephants, penguins and sea lions, and a free-flight aviary, where rare species have room to breed. There's also an impressive annual programme of family-friendly events.

Cave Hill

Castle and zoo aside, it's **Cave Hill** itself that should be your main port of call in North Belfast. Several paths lead up from the castle estate to the hill's summit – a rocky outcrop known as "Napoleon's Nose" (believed to have been an inspiration for Jonathan Swift's novel, *Gulliver's Travels*) – which affords an unsurpassable overview of the whole city and lough. From here you can't help but appreciate the accuracy of the poet Craig Raine's aerial description of the city in his *Flying to Belfast* as "a radio set with its back ripped off". Cave Hill was once awash with Iron Age forts, for there was flint (for weapon making) in the chalk under the basalt hill-coverings. In 1795, Wolfe Tone, Henry Joy McCracken and other leaders of the United Irishmen stood on the top of Cave Hill and pledged "never to desist in our efforts until we have subverted the authority of England over our country and asserted our Independence".

13

West Belfast

Metro bus #11A/B/C/D runs down the Fall from Chichester St; for the Shankill, take Metro bus #10A/B/C/D/E/F/G/H from Queen St

Though the nexus of the Troubles for 25 years, today **West Belfast** (http:// visitwestbelfast.com) is as safe as anywhere else in the city to visit, as well as being one of the most interesting. There is, however, little of architectural note among the mainly residential streets, and most of the "sights" are associated with the area's troubled past. Much of the old terraced housing has been replaced in recent years by rows of modern estates, but it's impossible to miss examples of the partisan **mural paintings** that decorate walls and gable ends in both Catholic and Protestant areas (see page 463). As in East Belfast (which, helpfully, is connected to West Belfast by the Glider bus service), members of the local community are making a concerted effort to draw more people into the area, and to this end, it's well worth popping into the Culturlann Arts & Culture Centre (see page 471). You might also consider taking a Black Taxi Tour (http://niblacktaxitours.com) covering both sides of the Peace Line – a divide longer than the Berlin Wall.

The Falls Road

From the city centre, Divis Street, a westward continuation of Castle Street, leads to the **Falls Road**, which heads on for a further 3km west past Milltown Cemetery and into Andersonstown. The first part of the Falls Road is known as the **Lower Falls** where, these days, most of the land to the left (south) consists of modern red-brick terraced housing. The right-hand side of the road features some of the main local landmarks, including the bright blue and pink leisure centre and the last remaining of the three Carnegie Libraries built in Belfast, this one dating from 1908. Turn right off the Falls Road at the leisure centre on to North Howard Street and Cupar Way and you'll encounter the infamous **Peace Line** – a wall of concrete and iron separating the area from the Protestant working-class district of Shankill; there are, in fact, more than twenty miles of peace lines across Northern Ireland, the majority in Belfast. Located at various points along the wall, peace gates, or "interfaces", are open during the day but do close at night, usually between 7 and 8pm.

Conway Mill

5–7 Conway St • Tues–Sat 10am–2pm • http://conwaymill.org

Down Conway Street stands the old **Conway Mill**, much revitalized by the local community. Inside you can investigate the wares of the numerous small businesses and local artists who operate from here, as well as an art gallery and a small exhibition depicting the mill's linen history. The Eileen Hickey Irish Republican History Museum (http://eileenhickeymuseum.com) is also housed in the former mill, boasting a vast collection of prison artefacts, such as a wooden harp crafted by inmate Johnny Haddock during his incarceration at Long Kesh in the 1970s. Note, though, that the museum's opening times are erratic.

Cultúrlann MacAdam Ó Fiaich

216 Falls Rd • Mon–Thurs 9am–6pm, Fri & Sat 9am–9pm, Sun 11am–4pm • http://culturlann.ie

Housed in a disused Presbyterian church, the **Cultúrlann MacAdam Ó Fiaich** is a cultural centre for Irish-speakers, housing an extensive bookshop (that also sells traditional music CDs), an excellent café and a thriving theatre, often host to musical events.

13

Although you're unlikely to hear it spoken on the streets or in most pubs, the Irish language is flourishing in Catholic areas of Belfast and throughout the North.

James Connolly Visitor Centre

376 Falls Rd • Mon–Fri 9am–4pm, Sat 10am–2pm • http://arasuichonghaile.com

Located some half a mile further on from **Cultúrlann,** a statue of the Irish trade unionist and revolutionary James Connolly, marks this out as the **James Connolly Visitor Centre**. At the heart of the centre is the Connolly Experience (charge), which celebrates his life, primarily through his trade union activities and his prominent role in the Easter Rising; to this end there is his tunic and belt, a door knocker from the General Post Office, and one of the few remaining original proclamations together with some of the printing blocks used to publish it. Connolly actually lived in a house just a few paces away between 1911 and his execution in Dublin in 1916. There's also a super café here serving breakfast baps, snacks and light lunches.

The Shankill Road and around

The Protestant population of West Belfast lives in the area abutting the Falls to the north, between the **Shankill Road** and the Crumlin Road, with a Peace Line running along Alliance Avenue. As an interface between the Protestant and Catholic communities, the Crumlin Road area was the scene of many violent sectarian incidents during the Troubles – and despite regeneration and new housing developments it remains a potential flashpoint, particularly during the July marching season. As with the Falls, the main draw for visitors to the area is the **murals**.

Crumlin Road Gaol

53–55 Crumlin Rd • Daily: first tour 11am, last tour 3pm (1hr 15min) • charge • http://crumlinroadgaol.com

---

THE TROUBLES IN WEST BELFAST

The **Troubles in West Belfast** have their origins in the nineteenth century, when the city's population expanded dramatically as people flocked from the countryside to work in the booming new flax and linen industries. Many of these migrants were crammed into jerry-built housing in the grids of streets which still today define this part of the city. Conditions were deplorable and did nothing to ease tensions between Catholic and Protestant residents. There were numerous **sectarian riots** – the worst was in 1886, during the reading of the Home Rule Bill, when 32 people died and over 370 were injured – leading to the almost inevitable definition of two separate neighbourhoods, as Protestant and Catholic families alike began to migrate to more secure surroundings.

In 1968 and 1969, this division was pushed to its limit when, across the city, sectarian mobs and gunmen evicted over eight thousand families from their homes, mainly in Catholic West Belfast. The Royal Ulster Constabulary, or **RUC**, called for government assistance, and **British troops** arrived on the streets on August 15, 1969. A month later the makeshift barrier dividing the **Catholic Falls** from the **Protestant Shankill** had become a full-scale reinforced "peace line". British intervention may have averted a civil war, but it failed to prevent an escalation in sectarian conflict. Indeed, the army soon came to be viewed as an occupying force and a legitimate target for a reviving IRA, though local sympathies for its aims were much diminished by the 1972 Bloody Friday bombings (see page 572). In return, Loyalist paramilitaries sought to avenge Republican violence, often through indiscriminate killings. A cycle of tit-for-tat attacks ensued, finally reaching its nadir with the **Shankill Road bombing**, a botched attempt to blow up Loyalist paramilitary leaders supposedly meeting above a fish shop on the Shankill Road in 1993, which instead killed customers and the shop's owner.

BELFAST'S MURALS

The politically inspired **murals** of Northern Ireland are among the most startling sights not just in Belfast, but in the whole country. This ephemeral art form, which recycles the images and slogans of the **Troubles**, characterizes the violent struggles of the last few decades. Though many have been in place now for over a decade, some of the slogans and murals mentioned here may have vanished by the time you visit: new murals are painted over old ones or the houses they adorn are demolished. One of the consequences in the immediate aftermath of the Good Friday Agreement (see page 573) was that many of the sectarian Loyalist murals were replaced by murals celebrating sporting heroes and local history, including the *Titanic* – yet when trouble flares or discontent rises, the old-style murals frequently reappear. A detailed **archive** of Northern Ireland's murals is maintained by the University of Ulster at http://cain.ulst.ac.uk/mccormick.

LOYALIST MURALS

For most of the twentieth century, mural painting in Northern Ireland was a predominantly **Loyalist** activity. The first mural appeared in East Belfast in 1908 and, like many of its successors, celebrated William of Orange's (King Billy) victory at the **Battle of the Boyne**. Loyalist murals have tended to use imagery symbolic of power, such as the clenched scarlet fist, known as the **Red Hand of Ulster**, or flags, shields and other heraldic icons. However, the Loyalist response to the Troubles translated into what is now the most common form of painting, the militaristic mural. The greatest concentration of Loyalist murals is to be found on and around the **Shankill Road**, especially the Shankill Estate, to the north, and Dover Place, off Dover Street, to the south. Other areas are Sandy Row and Donegall Pass in South Belfast, and Newtownards Road, Martin Street and Severn Street in East Belfast.

REPUBLICAN MURALS

Republican murals were at first limited to simple sloganeering or demarcation of territory, the best-known example being the long-standing "You are now entering Free Derry" in that city's Bogside district (see page 499). As with much else in Republican politics, however, the 1981 hunger strikes had a significant influence. Murals in support of the ten hunger strikers abounded and the (usually smiling) face of **Bobby Sands** – the IRA commander in the Maze prison who led the strike – remains an enduring image. Murals soon became a fundamental part of the Republican propaganda campaign: prominent **themes** have been resistance to British rule, the call for the withdrawal of troops and questioning the validity of the police. More recently, however, Republican muralists have turned increasingly to Irish legends and history as their sources of inspiration, and the only militaristic murals tend to be found in flashpoints such as the Ardoyne area of North Belfast. Equally, artists have paid tribute to other international liberation movements, as in a striking series of murals on Divis Street just before the beginning of the Falls Road; the murals here change regularly, with recent ones focused on the war in Gaza. Further Republican murals can be found nearby on Beechmount Avenue, further west on Lenadoon Avenue in Andersonstown, and on New Lodge Road in North Belfast.

From the Westlink, it's a short walk to the notorious **Crumlin Road Gaol**, a foreboding, basalt rock building opened in 1846 and which closed in 1996. Its list of former inmates includes Éamon de Valera, Gerry Adams, Martin McGuiness and Ian Paisley, while the last of seventeen executions here was that of Robert McGladdery in 1961. Women and children were also detained here, including members of the Ulster Suffragettes in 1914, who were in fact the first group to go on hunger strike in an Irish prison. One of the four wings has been refurbished with a number of cells holding hologram characters that crackle into life as they recall what life was like at the Crum (as it was colloquially known) alongside former loyalist and republican inmates. Linked

13

to the gaol via an underground tunnel – a short section of which you can venture into on the tour – is the old **Courthouse**, dating from 1849 and whose derelict remains scar the landscape opposite the gaol; subject to two huge fires, in 2009 and 2020, the building seems ripe for a luxury hotel investment. The gaol also has an excellent on-site restaurant (see page 499)

ARRIVAL AND DEPARTURE   BELFAST

Belfast's two **airports** are well connected to the city centre by public transport, while a limited Metro bus service operates between the city centre and the **ferry terminals** Mon–Fri. The city also has an efficient bus network. Visit the excellent journey planner at http://translink.co.uk (or get the associated app) to fine-tune your rail and bus journey to and from Belfast.

BY PLANE

Belfast International Airport http://belfastairport. com. The larger of the city's two airports is located 30km west of the city in Aldergrove; from here, the 24hr Airport Express 300 bus drops passengers at the city's Europa Buscentre (30–40min; £8.50 single, £12.50 return). A metered taxi to the city centre costs around £35 (for a meet-and-greet service try http://belfastairporttaxis.com).

George Best Belfast City Airport http://belfastcity airport.com. Many domestic flights from Britain use this airport, just 5km northeast of the centre, from which the Airport Express 600 bus runs to the Europa Buscentre (Mon–Fri every 20–35min 6am–10.05pm, Sat every 20–40min 6am–9.50pm, Sun every 40–50min 7.30am–9.45pm; £2.60 single, £4 return). Alternatively, take the free shuttle bus to Sydenham train station and hop on a train to Lanyon Place station (Mon–Fri every 20–30min 6.20am–10.50pm, Sat every 30min 6.35am–10.50pm, Sun hourly 9.20am–10.20pm; £2.20). A taxi from City Airport to the city centre costs around £10 (http://valuecabs.co.uk).

BY BOAT

Larne P&O ferries (http://poferries.com) from Cairnryan in Scotland dock at the town of Larne, 32km to the north, which is connected by Ulsterbus to the Europa Buscentre and by train to Lanyon Place station.

West Bank Road terminals Stena ferries (http:// stenaline.co.uk) from Cairnryan and Liverpool dock here, a 30min walk from Donegall Square. A metered taxi costs around £9 (http://fonacab.com). Metro Bus 96 runs daily to Belfast High St (limited weekend service).

BY TRAIN

The closure in 2024 of Great Victoria Street Station means that all trains now arrive and depart from Lanyon Place Station (formerly Belfast Central) near the Waterfront Hall on East Bridge Street, a little way east of the centre.

Getting into town Various Metro buses stop outside Lanyon Place Station en route to Donegall Square – travel is free to holders of railway tickets. From Lanyon Place Station you can also hop on a connecting train for the short journey to Botanic and City Hospital stations, both of which are useful if you're staying in the University Quarter. Alternatively, a 5min journey in the opposite direction will take passengers to the Titanic Quarter.

Destinations from Belfast (Lanyon Place) Bangor (Mon–Sat every 15–30min, Sun hourly; 20–30min); Carrickfergus (Mon–Sat every 30min, Sun 9; 25min); Cultra for the Ulster Folk and Transport Museums (Mon–Sat every 20–30min, Sun hourly; 15min); Derry (Mon–Sat hourly, Sun 6; 2hr); Drogheda (8 Mon–Sat, 6 Sun; 1hr 35min); Dublin (8 Mon–Sat, 6 Sun; 2hr–2hr 15min); Larne harbour (Mon–Sat hourly, Sun 10; 55min); Larne town (Mon–Sat hourly, Sun 10; 50min); Newry (8 Mon–Sat, 6 Sun; 55min).

BY BUS

Express buses arrive at one of Belfast's two stations. The Europa Buscentre, accessed via the Great Northern shopping mall on Great Victoria St, handles services to the Republic and the airports. It also serves all parts of Northern Ireland except North Down and the Ards Peninsula, which utilize the Laganside Buscentre in Queen's Square (near the Albert Clock), though on weekday evenings and Sundays even these use the Europa. Aircoach (http://aircoach.ie) services from Dublin Airport arrive at Glengall St.

Destinations from Belfast (Europa) Armagh (Mon–Fri hourly, Sat 7, Sun 6; 1hr 5min–1hr 25min); Derry (Mon–Sat every 30min, Sun hourly; 1hr 45min–2hr); Downpatrick (Mon–Sat every 30min, Sun 9; 50min–1hr); Drogheda (14 daily; 1hr 40min–1hr 55min); Dublin (every 30min–1hr; 2hr 40min–2hr 55min); Dublin Airport (every 30min–1hr; 2hr 10min–2hr 35min); Dungiven (Mon–Fri every 30min, Sat 20, Sun 11; 1hr 5min); Enniskillen (Mon–Fri hourly, Sat 6, Sun 5; 1hr 50min–2hr 20min); Hillsborough (Mon–Sat every 30min, Sun hourly; 25min); Larne (Mon–Sat hourly, Sun 6; 55min); Newcastle (Mon–Sat every 30min, Sun hourly; 1hr 10min); Newry (Mon–Fri every 30min, Sat hourly, Sun 8; 1hr 10min); Omagh (Mon–Sat hourly, Sun 6; 1hr 30min–1hr 50min).

Destinations from Belfast (Laganside) Bangor (Mon–Sat every 30min, Sun 8 daily; 45min); Cultra for the Ulster Folk and Transport Museum (Mon–Sat every 30min, Sun 8 daily; 30min); Newtownards (Mon–Sat very frequent, Sun 10 daily; 35min); Portaferry (Mon–Fri 10 daily, Sat 9, Sun 2; 1hr 15min–1hr 45min).

13

GETTING AROUND

Although you can easily **walk** around the city centre, distances to some of the outlying attractions are considerable, and a number of **places to stay** are also a little way out.

BY BUS

Network and times The excellent Metro service (http://translink.co.uk) provides frequent buses to almost every conceivable destination within the city, while the blue-and-white, long-distance services of Ulsterbus (which principally covers the rest of the North beyond Belfast's boundaries) connect to some of the sights on the city's fringes, such as the Giant's Ring. Almost all Metro buses set off from Donegall Square or the streets immediately around it, while Ulsterbus uses the Europa Buscentre on Great Victoria St. You can pick up a network map from the Visit Belfast Welcome Centre. In general buses operate 6am–11pm from Monday to Saturday, and 9am–11pm on Sunday.

Tickets and fares Metro fares are determined by a zonal system within twelve geographical corridors. An unlimited Metro Day Travel ticket that is valid network-wide costs £5 (5 days £19.50, 10 days £38). Alternatively, there's a Belfast Visitor Pass available for unlimited bus and rail travel over one (£7), two (£13) or three (£17) consecutive days (it also provides discounts to many visitor attractions, tours, shops and restaurants). Cards can be purchased from the Visit Belfast Centre, the two central bus stations and any Smartlink agent (including many newsagents).

BY TAXI

Metered black taxis, based at the main rank in Donegall Square East and other points throughout the city, charge a minimum of £3, which rapidly starts to increase if you're going any distance. Alternatively, you can phone a minicab (try fonaCAB or 2890 333333 or Value Cabs 02890 809080); these too are metered, charge similar rates to the black cabs and are a good idea late at night as passing taxis are hard to grab.

BY BIKE

The Belfast Bikes public rental scheme (http://belfastbikes.co.uk) has around four hundred unisex bicycles and nearly fifty docking stations located throughout the city. Users can choose to register online for either a 3-Day Account or an Annual Fee (£6 or £25). Usage is free for the first 30min and thereafter 50p for up to an hour, then £1 per hour up to 4hr, and then £2 for every extra 30min up to 24hr.

INFORMATION

Tourist information The Visit Belfast Welcome Centre at 9 Donegall Square North, opposite the City Hall (Mon–Sat 9am–5pm, Sun 11am–4pm; http://visitbelfast.com) is superb, stocking a vast range of information on the city and the rest of the North, courtesy of dozens of touch-screen terminals and tonnes of printed matter. It also provides an accommodation booking service (Northern Ireland) and has the only left-luggage facilities in the city (£4 per item for up to 4hr, £6 for the day, no overnight facility). It also sells tickets for tours and events. The West Belfast Tourist Information Point is in the Culturlaan arts centre (see page 471).

Listings Consult the monthly listings freesheet *The Big List* (http://thebiglist.co.uk), the free official guide, Visit Belfast's Belfast City Guide (http://visitbelfast.com/whats-on) or *Belfast in Your Pocket* (http://inyourpocket.com/belfast), all available at the Welcome Centre and from pubs, clubs and record shops. There's also *Love Belfast* (http://lovebelfast.co.uk), providing listings and blogs on local events for visitors to the city. Families should check out *ni4kids*, a free monthly paper and online resource that focuses on family-friendly activities and events in Belfast and beyond (http://ni4kids.com). The *Belfast Telegraph* newspaper (http://belfasttelegraph.co.uk) also has daily listings.

TOURS

Many of the tours listed below can be booked at the **Visit Belfast Welcome Centre** (see above), which also publishes a visitor map with information on Belfast tours.

WALKING TOURS

Political tours The "A History of Terror in Belfast" tour (http://deadcentretours.com; £22), led by a conflict resolution specialist, lasts 2hr 30mins and covers over 3km of the city, visiting places significant to the Troubles. There are also various political walking tours of West Belfast, delivered by former political prisoners (£15; http://coiste.ie), which depart from the Divis Tower at the city end of the Falls Road; advance booking is essential.

Other tours The "Hidden Belfast Walking Tour" (£12; http://belfasthiddentours.com) lasts 1hr 30min and aims to uncover the city's less well-known gems, both historical and recent. There are also walking tours (http://titanictourbelfast.com; £12.50) around the docks, taking in the Titanic's Docks and Pump House (meeting at the Titanic Belfast Plaza), and a pub crawl that hits the city's finest watering holes (Fri & Sat 8pm, meeting at the Albert Clock; £15; bhttp://belfastcrawl.com). There's also the "Belfast Food Tour", providing a 4hr guided tour sampling some of the city's most memorable food and drink spots – options include the Belfast Gin Jaunt and the Belfast Whiskey Walk (online booking essential; from £65; http://tasteandtour.co.uk).

13

BUS TOURS

Several companies operate hop-on, hop-off open-top bus tours, with most taking in the Laganside, city centre, Titanic, Cathedral and University quarters and West Belfast, including City Sightseeing (daily 10am–4pm, every 20–30min; http://belfastcitysightseeing.com; £20/one day, £25/two days), and City Tours Belfast (daily 10am–4pm; http://citytoursbelfast.com; £19/one day, £24/two days), both of which start at Donegall Square West.

TAXI TOURS

West Belfast is one of the features of several guided taxi tours, including the recommended Paddy Campbell's "Famous Black Cab Tours" (http://belfastblackcabtours.co.uk), World Famous Belfast Black Taxi Tours (http:// belfasttours.com) and Belfast Taxi Tours (http://taxitrax.com). Each tour lasts around 1hr 30min, exploring the Falls and Shankill roads (including the murals and the Peace Line), plus Milltown Cemetery, the docks and the university. Tours operate daily, must be pre-booked and usually cost between £50–60 for two or three people.

BOAT AND BIKE TOURS

The Titanic Quarter and docklands can be enjoyed via ninety-minute boat tours (http://ladyofthelagan.com; £25) departing from Donegall Quay, which relates Belfast's rich maritime history. Belfast City Bike Tours (http://belfast citybiketours.com) run three-hour guided cycling trips around the city departing from Norm's Bikes, 18 Winetavern St (Thurs–Sat 10am–1pm; £35).

ACCOMMODATION

Belfast has a broad range of **accommodation**, especially at the top end of the market, while the recent tourist boom has seen a number of well-known **budget hotels** open up across the city. The main concentration of hotels can be found on Great Victoria Street, around the University area and in the Cathedral Quarter.

CITY CENTRE, SEE MAP PAGE 449

Bullitt 40a Church Lane, http://bullitthotel.com. One of the city's coolest hotels, *Bullitt* offers uber-stylish "Dinky", "Comfy", "Roomy" and "Biggy" rooms, plus free "Grub to Go" bags with granola, fruit and orange juice when setting off to explore. Arrive back to a top-notch meal at the *Taylor & Clay* restaurant and a nightcap in one of the hotel's three bars. £££

Europa Hotel Great Victoria St, http://europahotelbelfast.com. Belfast's Grand Old Dame, looking resplendent after a multimillion-pound refurbishment, offers views across the city with modern, spacious and luxurious bedrooms and suites all with a/c and automated window blinds. £££

The Fitzwilliam Hotel 1–3 Great Victoria St, http://fitzwilliamhotelbelfast.com. One of the latest additions at the city's luxury end of the market features astonishingly well-equipped and thoughtfully accoutred rooms, with kingsize beds sheeted in Egyptian cotton, mini hi-fi systems and flatscreen TVs. £££

★ **room2** 32–36 Queen St, http://room2.com. With its net zero commitment and low carbon renewable energy schemes, *room2* is a most worthy addition to the city's accommodation stock. Rooms range from your standard double to studios with kitchenettes and large lofts equipped with a double and a bunk bed. The evening buzz is provided by nightly musicians in the lounge bar, while breakfast is taken in the colourful, convivial *Winnie's Café*. Gym and laundry facilities too. ££–£££

Ten Square 10 Donegall Square South, http://tensquare.co.uk. A gem of a hotel in a much-refurbished former linen house bang opposite City Hall, featuring bespoke rooms, with an utterly opulent feel that draws its influences from colonial Shanghai. The hotel also houses the excellent *Josper's Steakhouse* and the classy *Loft* cocktail bar, for which guests receive a complimentary drink. £££

CATHEDRAL QUARTER, SEE MAP PAGE 449

Malmaison 34–38 Victoria St, http://malmaison.com. Installed in an elegantly converted warehouse on the periphery of the city's cultural hub, *Malmaison* features chic doubles, sumptuous suites named after the Samson and Goliath cranes (see page 453), and an attractive bar and restaurant. £££

★ **The Merchant** 16 Skipper St, http://themerchanthotel.com. Once the HQ of the Ulster Bank, this Victorian sandstone edifice has been converted into a wonderful hotel, complete with many of the original Italianate fittings and its own art gallery and spa. Rooms are spacious and luxuriously furnished in either Victorian or Art Deco style – the latter slightly larger and with floor-to-ceiling windows – and its suites are impeccably elegant. Breakfast, meanwhile, is a sumptuous affair. ££££

Ramada by Wyndham 20 Talbot St, http://wyndham hotels.com. Sitting on the edge of St Anne's Square and surrounded by some of the area's finest restaurants, the reasonable room rates here mean more money for eating out. The 165 rooms are bright and contemporary, all with en-suite wet rooms. ££

UNIVERSITY AREA (QUEEN'S QUARTER) AND AROUND, SEE MAP PAGE 456

Belfast International Hostel 22–32 Donegall Rd, http://hini.org.uk. Large HINI hostel with twins and a couple of en-suite doubles, but mainly four- and six-bed dorms. There's also a café, self-catering kitchen and laundry, and tours of Belfast and to the Giant's Causeway are offered. £

Camera House 44 Wellington Park, http://camera-guest

house.co.uk. So-named after the many photographers who used to stay here, this elegant, family-run guesthouse offers double and triple en-suite rooms and a living room with an open fire. There's a top notch cooked Irish breakfast to see you on your way. ££

Dukes at Queens 65–67 University St, http://dukesat queens.com. Smart, modern, four-star redevelopment of a fine Victorian building, a few minutes' walk from the university, featuring luxurious bedrooms and a fashionable bar. £££

Hotel Etap 35 Dublin Rd, http://all.accor.com. Modern, minimalist, clean and budget pretty much sums this place up. Ideal if you're not bothered about the absence of frills. Continental breakfast costs extra. ££

The Malone 60 Eglantine Ave, http://themalonehotel. com. Welcoming and well-equipped hotel near Queen's, with off-street parking, pleasantly decorated rooms and a notable restaurant, *The Gallery*, where you can have a three-course meal for £28. £££

The Old Rectory 148 Malone Rd, http://anoldrectory. co.uk. This beautifully converted former clergyman's house (Church of Ireland), around 1.5km south of the university, offers seven delightfully appointed rooms variously furnished with sofas, armchairs and writing desks. Plus books and magazines – a real home from home. ££

★ **Vagabonds** 9 University Rd, http://vagabondsbelfast. com. This modern and funky hostel in the Queen's Quarter (close to bars, restaurants, the Botanic Gardens and Ulster Museum) is designed and run by seasoned travellers, Tara and Curt, meaning that nothing is too much trouble. £

EAST BELFAST, SEE MAP PAGE 449

★ **George Best House** 16 Burren Way, Cregagh Estate, http://georgebesthouse.com. An extraordinary opportunity to spend the night in George Best's old bedroom in his family home. Landmark East purchased the house in 2011 and have lovingly restored it to the way it would have looked before George left to join Man Utd in 1961. There are two double bedrooms and one single bedroom (George's old bedroom), while there's a fully fitted kitchen featuring Dick Best's old hob. To get here, take bus #6A to the Greenway stop, from where it's a two-minute walk beyond the shops. ££

EATING

There are plenty of options for food during the day in the city centre and around the university area, ranging from **cafés**, many of which in the city centre stay open until 8.30pm on Thursday nights, to award-winning **restaurants** and **traditional pubs**. Most of the city's well-established **restaurants** are around Donegall Square, although the Cathedral Quarter has fast become a dining-out hub. Restaurants are often fully booked on Friday and Saturday evenings, so **reserving** is essential unless you're prepared to eat early. There's a great range of cuisine, from modern Irish and European, with French and Italian especially popular, to a smattering of Indian and East Asian restaurants and some new chicken and barbecue joints.

CAFÉS

★ **Dock Café** 2K Queens Rd, http://thedockchurch.org. The perfect place in which to kick-back after exhausting the Titanic Quarter, there's a little bit of something for everyone here, with squashy sofas to sink into while admiring the comings and goings of the marina through the big floor-to-ceiling windows, wall-bound artwork and photographs to peruse, different play areas for kids and even a prayer garden. The choice is mercifully simple: filter coffee, scones and cakes, for which you pay you want/can afford. Closed Sun & Mon. £

★ **Established Coffee** 54 Hill St, http://established. coffee. Award-winning barista Mark and his partner Bridget offer arguably the city's finest coffee (though *Kaffe O* fans might disagree) here in the Cathedral Quarter, using filter, Chemex and Aeropress. Expect simple industrial decor (and beards) and a warm and welcoming atmosphere.

SEE MAP PAGES 449 AND 456

General Merchants 361 Ormeau Rd and 481 Upper Newtownards Rd, http://generalmerchants.co.uk. Australian inspired all-day breakfasts that are hearty and tasty yet packed with superfoods for a healthy, nutritious kick. The Brisbane Breakfast comes Aussie style, complete with guacamole and Vegemite.

★ **Grapevine** 5 Pottingers Entry, 07794 653259. Tucked away but worth seeking out for soul-warming soups, stews and gumbo plus homemade sandwiches that cost under £5 (gluten-free options too).

Kaffe O 411 Ormeau Rd and 73 Botanic Ave, http://kaffeo. coffee. For coffee aficionados, either branch of this Nordic-inspired café is well worth visiting. Simple vegetarian, often vegan, soup, stews and salads occupy the menu alongside locally smoked salmon and smoked meats. Lunch and a sublime coffee experience for around £10.

Lampost Café 19 Upper Newtownards Rd, http:// thelampostcafe.com. Probably the best of the many terrific Eastside cafes, the *Lampost* is all mirrored walls, vintage crockery and potted plants, plus lots of Narnia quotes – and the food is spot on too, from a Lampost Fry to an Irish stew. Very enjoyable indeed.

RESTAURANTS

Boojum 67–69 Botanic Ave, http://boojummex.com. Minimalist interior with a canteen feel but serving the best burritos in Belfast for less than £10, which the long lunch queues attest to. There are also branches on Great Victoria St, Lisburn Rd and in Victoria Square. £

Bubbacue 12 Callender St, http://bubbacue.com. Deep South barbecue cooked to perfection for twelve hours in

13

a traditional smoker. Pulled pork and beef brisket are the house specialities with a choice of home-made barbecue sauces, but there are loads of other goodies. $\overline{\underline{£}}$

Coppi St Anne's Square, http://coppi.co.uk. Contemporary Italian cooking, serving up a range of *cicchetti* (small plates of the kind traditionally served in Venetian bacari bars) plus exciting mains like slow braised beef shin lasagne and duck ragu and tempting desserts. £££

Cuffs 53–55 Crumlin Rd, http://cuffsgrillbar.com. The clue's in the name. Occupying the old kitchen area of the Crumlin Road gaol, the very creditable restaurant serves an accomplished menu (Daube of beef, pan-fried Teriyaki salmon) but it's the gargantuan Sunday roast (three-courses £25) that really pulls in the punters. £££

Cyprus Avenue 228 Upper Newtownards Rd, http://cyprusavenue.co.uk. Named after the nearby leafy street that Van Morrison made famous nearly sixty ago, this terrific restaurant hits the mark with cooked breakfasts, delicious fish dishes and mouthwatering steaks, and a dedicated plant-based menu. £££

★ **Deanes Meat Locker** 28–40 Howard St, http://michaeldeane.co.uk. No prizes for guessing what comprises the bulk of the menu here at Michael Deane's classy outfit, and while steak is the main offering, there's much else besides, including seafood chowder, and Korean fried tofu and Asian salad. Closed Sun & Mon. ££££

★ **Fish City** 33 Ann St, http://fish-city.com. Far more than just a fish and chip restaurant, this sparkling little restaurant has all manner of wet treats, from tuna spring rolls to pan roast cod with clam *beurre blanc* plus some appetizing desserts like red wine poached pear with bergamot curd. Impeccable service too. ££££

Home Restaurant 22 Wellington Place, http://homebelfast.co.uk. Originally a pop-up restaurant, *Home's* simple, hearty offerings proved to be such a success that it's now moved to permanent premises and continues to be a huge hit with local foodies and critics. Spectacular dishes include the likes of sesame duck croquettes and hot miso dressing, and roast lamb rump, harissa vegetables and saffron yoghurt. Excellent three-course prix-fixe menu for £26 (noon–3.30pm & 5–6.15pm). £££

House of Zen 3 St Anne's Square, http://houseofzenbelfast.co.uk. Fine Asian cuisine served in the beautiful setting of St Anne's Square. In addition to the a la carte menu (crab meat soup, roast duck with Fu Rong egg white sauce), there are various set menus including a super value three-course pre-theatre meal (5–6.45pm) for £23.95. £££

Howard Street 56 Howard St, http://howardstbelfast.com. This has fast become one of the city's finest restaurants, offering wholesome dishes ranging from beer-battered fish to dry-aged steaks and an excellent range of vegetarian options. Located near to the Grand Opera House, its three-course pre-theatre menu (Tues–Sat 5–6pm) at £36 is a firm favourite with theatre-goers. £££

James St 21 James St South, http://jamesst.co.uk. Chargrilled steaks, fresh fish dishes and heavenly Sunday roasts are the big appeal here but for special occasions, push the boat out with the Co. Antrim dry-aged fillet. £££

Mourne Seafood Bar 34–36 Bank St, http://mourneseafood.com. Cracking place for all piscivores, serving everything from shellfish and oysters to exotic dishes incorporating hake or monkfish. Reasonably priced too, and there's even an on-site fishmonger's if you fancy cooking your own. £10 will buy you a plate of baked oysters topped with bacon crumb and garlic cream spinach. £££

★ **OX** 1 Oxford St, http://oxbelfast.com. Attracting culinary praise from foodies far and wide for its creative use of local produce, the one-Michelin starred *OX* is worth a visit if you're keen to sample the city's finest dining, with seasonal dishes that showcase Northern Ireland's local produce: smoked veal, pea, elderflower and black garlic, and Mourne lamb with lavender and white asparagus are two such dazzlingly inventive plates. To sample the restaurant's very best, opt for the six-course tasting menu at £60/person. ££££

DRINKING

SEE MAP PAGES 449 AND 456

Whether you're after raucous dancing, **traditional music** or simply a quiet pint of the black stuff, you're going to be spoilt for choice. First-time visitors tend to be drawn to the older pubs on **Great Victoria Street**, while the city's trendier residents and students frequent the **University Quarter** and the **Lisburn Road**. For a more eclectic mix of pubs in a smaller area (making for a great pub crawl), head to the **Cathedral Quarter**. A good resource for pub reviews is http://belfastbar.co.uk.

★ **The Crown Liquor Saloon** 46 Great Victoria St, http://nicholsonspubs.co.uk/thecrownliquorsaloonbelfast. Owned by the National Trust, Belfast's most famous and spectacular pub is an old Victorian gin palace with an ornate ceiling, painted mirrors and frieze-decorated oak panelling. Once armed with drinks, try to grab one of the snugs, where you press a button to receive service. If the snugs are busy, it's still a great experience to linger at the bar, with its carved-timber dividing screens. There's a good repertoire of Northern Ireland food on offer too, along with pints of Strangford oysters, when Oyster season descends in Sept.

★ **The Duke of York** 11 Commercial Court, off Donegall St, http://dukeofyorkbelfast.com. Nestled on a cobbled alleyway in the Half Bap area in the heart of the Cathedral Quarter. The decor takes you back to bygone times, its walls strewn with memorabilia and antiquities. Regular traditional music sessions and outdoor benches for balmy summer evenings.

The Five Points Whiskey & Alehouse 44 Dublin Rd, http://pointsbelfast.com. Named after a notorious area in New York City where Irish Immigrants ruled the streets, this terrific Belfast pub serves up an impressive range of whiskies and craft beers to a live soundtrack of traditional Irish music.

The Harp Bar 35 Hill St, http://dukeofyorkbelfast.com. The more refined big brother of the *Duke of York*, housed in the former head office of the Old Bushmills whiskey distillery. Plush, red-velvet fabrics and antique furnishings recall Victorian Belfast, and there's an impressive range of whiskies and independent draught beers. Regular music nights upstairs.

The John Hewitt 53 Donegall St, http://boundarybrewing.coop. Despite the well-worn exterior, this fine pub run by the Belfast Unemployed Resource Centre and the city's first social enterprise bar, is a great place to while away a few hours sampling local craft beers and ciders. There are also traditional and jazz sessions (Thurs–Sat), as well as singer-songwriters on Mon (9pm) and various other events during the week. Also serves reasonably priced meals Fri & Sat.

Kelly's Cellars 30 Bank St, 02890 246058, http://kellyscellars.co.uk. Belfast's oldest-surviving continuously run pub was opened in the sixteenth century. According to legend, it was a frequent meeting place for the United Irishmen behind the doomed 1798 Rebellion (Henry Joy McCracken is said to have hidden under the bar counter from British soldiers). Good lunches, including thumping portions of home-made Irish stew and steak pie, a turf fire, traditional music midweek, and live bands Fri–Sun in summer.

The Morning Star 17 Pottingers Entry, http://themorning starbar.co.uk. This fine old-fashioned bar is something of a living museum, retaining many of its original fittings and fixtures including the original mahogany counter. It tends to be busy by day and quiet at night, and its *Lounge* restaurant is up there with the best in the city..

Muriel's Café Bar 12–14 Church Lane, 02890 332445. Named after a Belfast Madam who, rumour has it, sold hats by day and ran a brothel by night, the ground floor here is themed on a 1920s millinery shop while the upstairs lounge area is all "Parisian boudoir", with its opulent furnishings and candlelight. The food is top-notch, with a full bistro menu and deli-style platters on offer.

★ **Sunflower** 65 Union St, http://sunflowerbelfast.com. This former working man's drinking den has had a revamp, turning it into quite a cool pub, with an interior that offers more than a passing nod to the Seventies and Eighties. Regular live music upstairs and impromptu traditional sessions downstairs make it a popular haunt for the city's music lovers. Also holds comedy nights.

White's Tavern 2–4 Winecellar Entry, High St, http://whitestavernbelfast.com. Founded in 1630, *White's* is an atmospheric old Entries bar, with stone floors and an open fire, serving excellent lunches and hosting traditional sessions downstairs. Upstairs is *Vandal*, a dedicated "geek and movie bar" serving pizzas with a licensed cinema. They also offer seasonal outdoor retro screenings in the courtyard.

NIGHTLIFE

SEE MAP PAGES 449 AND 456

As in most UK cities, Belfast's "superclubs" have long gone, replaced with numerous smaller **clubs**, usually housed in an upstairs room above a popular city bar and catering for all tastes. **Admission** may be free early in the week (and at some places all week) and as low as £2 or £3 up to Thurs, while weekend prices are usually around £5 to £15. For the latest **listings**, the monthly listings freesheet *The Big List* is essential (online version at http://thebiglist.co.uk). As well as the traditional **music** on offer in pubs, Belfast also benefits from a thriving, grass-roots indie and rock scene, while the number of visiting international performers has increased dramatically since the arrival of the Waterfront Hall and Odyssey Complex with its SSE Arena (see page 471).

CLUBS AND VENUES

Lavery's 12–18 Bradbury Place, http://laverysbelfast.com. A Belfast institution, particularly popular with students, with "Retro Disco" and "Rip It Up" (soul, funk and indie) nights currently alternating on Sat in the Back Bar, and "Beat Connection" (funk, soul, hip-hop and house) in the Ballroom. On Sun night in the Ballroom it's DJ request night, with punters racking up their next game of pool to a soundtrack of favourites.

Ollie's 16 Skipper St, http://olliesbelfast.com. Part of the five-star *Merchant* hotel, *Ollie's* delivers all that you might expect to entail, with a decadent, velvet-and-mahogany bedecked club area alongside a private members' bar. Club nights Fri & Sat.

Shine Queen's University Student Union, http://shine.net. *Shine* has a UK-wide reputation, spanning almost twenty years, for attracting the biggest DJs to Northern Irish shores, from Felix Da Housecat and David Guetta to Deadmau5 and Dave Clarke. Attracts major bands too including the likes of War on Drugs and PJ Harvey.

LIVE MUSIC

The Dirty Onion 3 Hill St, http://thedirtyonion.com. This live music pub, a clever conversion of one of the city's oldest buildings, offers something different every night – from *bodhrán* lessons to bluegrass sessions. Excellent on-site chicken rotisserie restaurant, *The Yardbird*, too.

The Empire Bar & Music Hall 42 Botanic Ave, http://thebelfastempire.com. Cellar bar in a former church just up from the station, with a boisterous beer-hall atmosphere. Good-value food and bands most nights of the week with DJs and bigger name bands upstairs.

Filthy McNasty's 45 Dublin Rd, http://filthysbelfast.co.uk. With a secret garden, a club room (the "gypsy lounge") and a backdrop of quirky furnishings, local Belfast musicians can be heard doing their thing from 10pm most nights, with an

13

open mic session on Sun.

★**The Limelight Complex** 17 Ormeau Ave, http://limelightbelfast.com. This Belfast institution – one of the North's leading live music venues – is home to two music venues, a bar and the open-air, roof terrace "Rock Garden".

Expect an eclectic mix of singers and bands, plus DJs and club nights.

The Pavilion Bar 296 Ormeau Rd, http://pavilionbelfast.com. Possibly *the* place to catch up-and-coming young indie bands as they take to the stage to pedal their tunes.

FESTIVALS IN BELFAST

Belfast has some cracking festivals, a list of which can be found at http://visitbelfast.com/whats-on/festivals-in-belfast for a full calendar. Note that although **Open House Festival** (http://openhousefestival.com) has officially relocated to nearby Bangor, there are still Open House events held around the Cathedral Quarter at various dates throughout the year.

FEBRUARY, MARCH & APRIL

St Patrick's Day http://belfastcity.gov.uk/stpatricks. Carnival parade on March 17, followed by a major open-air concert in Custom House Square.

Belfast Film Festival http://belfastfilmfestival.org. The second half of April sees a host of left-field films and related events with screenings in cinemas, pubs, clubs and other venues. Note, though, that the month can change.

MAY & JUNE

Festival of Fools http://foolsfestival.com. Five-day international street-theatre festival, held over the first weekend in May, with events around the city centre.

Belsonic http://belsonic.com. The month of June sees A-list music acts giving open-air performances in Ormeau Park. Previous headliners have included Becky Hill, Biffy Clyro, Chemical Brothers and Rag'n'Bone Man.

Belfast City Blues Festival http://belfastcityblues.com. Three days of 12-bar honky-tonk and foot-stomping riffs at the end of June.

JULY & AUGUST

Orangefest Orange Order Lodges throughout Belfast commemorate the Battle of the Boyne with parades on July 12.

Belfast Pride http://belfastpride.com. At the end of July, over a hundred LGBTQ events take place across the city over a ten-day period, culminating in the Belfast Pride Parade.

Féile An Phobail http://feilebelfast.com. Week-long music and dance festival at the beginning of August, based in West Belfast.

Woodstock Rhythm & Blues Festival. East Belfast's grassroots music festival continues to grow year on year, now providing a long weekend of live music events in mid-August, showcasing new local talent alongside perennial favourites.

Belfast Mela http://belfastmela.org.uk. The region's largest multicultural festival, celebrating South Asian culture through live music, dance, food, arts and crafts in the city's Botanic Gardens (see page 455) at the end of August.

SEPTEMBER & OCTOBER

Cathedral Quarter Arts Festival (http://cqaf.com) Lively arts festival, featuring Irish and international acts (music, comedy, film and theatre) spread over ten days in early September.

Cinemagic Festival http://cinemagic.org.uk. The month of October sees an impressive programme of film screenings and workshops take place across Belfast, aimed at a youth audience with bespoke family events. Expect some Hollywood A-listers to be in town to lend their support.

Belfast International Arts Festival http://belfastinternationalartsfestival.com. Fortnight-long event held in late October which claims to be Britain's second-biggest arts festival after Edinburgh.

ENTERTAINMENT

CONCERT VENUES AND THEATRES
Belfast Waterfront Lanyon Place, Laganside, http://waterfront.co.uk. Hosts classical music and ballet, comedy, mainstream jazz and occasional big names from the world of middle-of-the-road pop and rock.

Grand Opera House Great Victoria St, http://goh.co.uk. Belfast's most prestigious venue, featuring regular operatic performances as well as many of London's West End productions.

Lyric Theatre 55 Ridgeway St, off Stranmillis Rd, http://lyrictheatre.co.uk. The Lyric's stages serious contemporary drama along with family performances.

Oh Yeah Music Centre 15–21 Gordon St, http://ohyeahbelfast.com. A music venue in the heart of the Cathedral Quarter that aims to showcase local music and educate the ears of the good people of Belfast. A hidden gem worth seeking out for live gigs and DJ sets.

SSE Arena 2 Queen's Quay, http://ssearenabelfast.com. Where the biggest rock and pop singers and bands perform when they come to town.

Ulster Hall Bedford St, http://ulsterhall.co.uk. Most of the city's classical music performances are given by the Ulster Orchestra (http://ulsterorchestra.org.uk); the hall is also used for big rock and pop concerts.

Whitla Hall Queen's University, 02890 245133. Stages some professional and amateur classical concerts.

ARTS CENTRES AND CINEMA
Black Box 18–22 Hill St, http://blackboxbelfast.com. An arts and performance space in the Cathedral Quarter with an eclectic programme of live events and exhibitions including art, dance and music.

Crescent Arts Centre 2–4 University Rd, http://crescentarts.org. A focus for much of Belfast's left-field arts and performance activities.

Culturlaan 216 Falls Rd, http://culturlann.ie. Arts centre with an exciting and vibrant programme that promotes the Irish language and culture. Also houses the West Belfast Tourist Information Point.

The MAC Saint Anne's Square, http://themaclive.com. The Metropolitan Arts Centre (MAC) occupies a modern six-storey building in the Cathedral Quarter with a programme that focuses on experimental and fringe productions, while also hosting major art exhibitions. Superb cafe too.

Queen's Film Theatre (QFT) 20 University Square, http://queensfilmtheatre.com. Two-screen independent cinema, showing art-house movies at exceptionally good prices.

LGBTQ+ BELFAST

The number of LGBTQ **bars** and **venues** in Belfast has increased substantially over the last few years and the majority are geared towards men. The area around **Union St** is affectionately known as "Queer Quarter" or the "Gay Village" by the city's LGBTQ community. **Pride** (http://belfastpride.com) week begins on the last Sat in July.

RESOURCES
The main resource for Belfast's LGBTQ scene is Queerspace at 23–31 Waring St. It's part of Cara-Friend, a collective that aims to serve the needs and raise the profile of the LGBTQ community of Belfast and Northern Ireland. It holds collective meetings on the afternoons of the first and third Sat of the month (2.30pm), followed by drop-in sessions at their *InSpace Coffee Lounge* (3.30pm). Helpline service provided by Cara-Friend (0808 8000390; Mon–Fri 1–4pm, Wed 6–9pm http://cara-friend.org.uk).

BARS AND CLUBS, SEE MAP PAGE 449
Kremlin 96 Donegall St, http://kremlin-belfast.com. Fronted by a statue of the eponymous Soviet leader, this is Ireland's biggest LGBTQ venue, featuring three bars and various themed nights of music, fun and games, including the hugely popular "Revolution" on Sat.

Maverick 1 Union St, http://themaverickbelfast.com. Billing itself as a "Den, Lounge & Disco", this,colourful joint offers plenty of kitsch decor and an eclectic mix of theme nights.

Union Street Bar 8-14 Union St, http://unionstreetbar.com. This trendy daytime gastropub has been a firm favourite in Belfast's LGBTQ scene since first opening its doors back in the early 2000s, offering a variety of themed nights for men seven days a week, ranging from karaoke to bingo, via deck-thumping DJs.

SPORT

The Northern Irish are very passionate about their sport, with a reputation for producing excellent **individual players**, such as George Best (football), Mary Peters (athletics), Dennis Taylor and Alex Higgins (snooker), Joey Dunlop (motorcycling), Carl Frampton (boxing) and Rory McIlroy (golf).

Football (soccer) Northern Ireland's team has enjoyed little success on the international stage over the last thirty years but did qualify for the 2016 European Championships in France, qualifying from their group and losing narrowly to Wales in the second round. Back home, international games attract a loyal following at Windsor Park (the home ground of the Linfield club) near the Lisburn Rd. On the domestic front, four Belfast teams – Cliftonville, Glentoran, Linfield

ST GEORGE'S MARKET

Belfast is immensely proud of **St George's Market** (East Bridge St; Fri 8am–2pm, Sat 9am–3pm, Sun 10am–4pm), which first opened as a covered market in the 1890s and retains its Victorian charm. The Friday food and variety market is by far the most popular, with about two hundred traders taking part, while Saturday focuses on organic produce and gardens. The Sunday market operates at a more leisurely pace, with arts and crafts stalls thrown into the mix.

and Crusaders – play in the Irish League Premiership for which tickets are easy to come by.

Gaelic football (GAA) and hurling Although both are immensely popular nationwide, neither sport has a huge following in Belfast city. However, you can still see both sports being played most weekends at Roger Casement Park, on Andersonstown Rd.

Rugby Union The provincial team, Ulster Rugby, has an ever-growing fan base that has resulted in a significant extension at the club's Kingspan Stadium (85 Ravenhill Park) in East Belfast. It can now hold over 18,000 spectators, yet many home games are sold out. Cup and league successes have seen the team go from strength to strength in recent years, regularly supplying the national squad (Ireland) with players, along with the British & Irish Lions.

Ice hockey The Belfast Giants are one of the powerhouses of the UK's Elite Ice Hockey League, winning the title three times between 2018/19 and 2022/23 (with two seasons cancelled owing to the Covid pandemic)– and regularly play at the SSE Arena in front of over four thousand fans. The SSE Arena also plays host to the annual Friendship Four Ice Hockey Tournament every Thanksgiving, showcasing talent from four of America's top universities.

SHOPPING

SEE MAP PAGES 449 AND 456

Shopping in Belfast has vastly improved in recent years with the arrival of many high street names. The **Victoria Square** shopping centre (http://victoriasquare.com) is home to over fifty different stores, including a multi-floored House of Fraser, while the top two floors feature a multiscreen Odeon cinema and a number of well-known restaurants that had previously ignored Belfast. The mall is open daily, with late-night shopping until 9pm Thursday and Friday. Take the lift to the **Viewing Dome** for spectacular vistas across the city and beyond.

Fresh Garbage 24 Rosemary St, http://freshgarbage. co.uk. This Belfast institution first opened in 1969 and is awash with band memorabilia, tour T-shirts, jewellery and funky accessories. Locals often refer to it simply as "Fresh".

No Alibi Bookstore 83 Botanic Ave, http://noalibis.com. A specialist crime fiction store immortalized in local author Colin Bateman's *Mystery Man* series. The staff are friendly and passionate about the genre, and there's a coffee and reading area. Regularly readings and literary events too.

Sawers Fountain Centre, College St, http://sawersbelfast. com. This Aladdin's cave of tasty local delicacies and exotic delights from far-flung shores was first established in 1897 and once had outlets in Glasgow, Birmingham and Dublin; the Belfast store is the only one that remains.

DIRECTORY

Hospital Royal Victoria Hospital, Grosvenor Rd, 02890 240503.

Laundry Globe, 39 Botanic Ave (Mon–Fri 9am–5pm, Sat 9am–6pm, Sun noon–4pm; 02890 243956).

Left luggage Visit Belfast Welcome Centre (see page 465), 9 Donegall Square North.

Lost property Musgrave St police station, off Ann St, 02890 650222.

Police In an emergency, call 999 or 112. The main city centre police station is in North Queen St.

Post offices 16 Howard St; 1–5 Botanic Ave; and 12–16 Bridge St (Mon–Sat 9am–5.30pm).

Antrim and Derry

DARK HEDGES

Antrim and Derry

Much of the coastline of County Antrim is as spectacular as anything you'll find across the whole of Ireland – consequently, unlike other parts of the North, it has always attracted an abundance of tourists. Beyond the fabulous Gobbins cliff path, the A2 coast road takes in attractive villages and small towns, such as Carnlough, Cushendall and the port of Ballycastle, all set against or within the verdant Antrim Glens. A short boat trip from Ballycastle, meanwhile, is rugged Rathlin Island, while further along the coast to the west, blustery cliff-top walks lead to the strange basalt formations of the Giant's Causeway. With an attractive backdrop, Portrush and, just over the county border in Derry, Portstewart are popular seaside holiday resorts.

14

County Derry's coastline is also blessed with wonderful strands, though most visitors make an immediate beeline for **Derry city** itself; set on the banks of the Foyle, with its hilltop core enclosed by some of the best-preserved city walls in Europe, Derry was at the forefront of the Troubles, and the city's past struggles are documented in a couple of superb museums. The county's hinterland is more dramatic than Antrim's, especially where it skirts the Sperrin Mountains. The flatter territory towards Lough Neagh features some noteworthy Plantation settlements at **Magherafelt** and **Moneymore**, though the most noteworthy destination hereabouts is **Bellaghy**, home to the superb Seamus Heaney HomePlace.

GETTING AROUND

ANTRIM AND DERRY

By train From Belfast, trains run to Larne via Carrickfergus but go no further up the Antrim coast; otherwise, the other main line through Antrim heads south to Lisburn before looping up towards Ballymena and Coleraine, where it branches off, with one line going to Portrush and another to Derry.

By bus Both Antrim and Derry are well served by buses, with most services operated by Translink (http://translink.co.uk). The hop-on, hop-off Causeway Rambler (#172/#402) runs daily (June–Sept every 30min–1hr) from Coleraine to Ballycastle via Bushmills, the Giant's Causeway, Dunseverick

Castle, Ballintoy and Carrick-a-rede; weather permitting, some of these are open-top buses. Between May and September the Antrim Coaster (#252) runs Mon–Fri from Larne via the Glens to Ballycastle, with a further connecting service from Ballycastle to the Giant's Causeway, Bushmills and Coleraine. Departures from Larne are at 10.20am and 3.20pm, with the returns from Ballycastle at 12.05pm and 5.05pm. Buses from Belfast's Europa Buscentre will take you to Larne.

By ferry P&O ferries (http://poferries.com) operate between four and six crossings daily (2hr) from Larne, 35km north of Belfast, to Cairnryan in Dumfries, Scotland.

North from Belfast

The coastal strip heading **north from Belfast** to Larne is largely uninspiring farmland, although there are a few spots to detain you as you head towards the more enticing Antrim Glens further north, notably the spectacular Gobbins cliff path.

Carrickfergus Castle

Marine Highway • Tues–Sun: April–Sept 9.30am–5pm; Oct–March 9am–4pm • charge • http://discovernorthernireland.com • Can be reached from Belfast by train (every 30min–1hr; 25min) or bus (every 20–30min; 40min)

Heading out of Belfast's northern suburbs, the A2 skirts the edge of Belfast Lough before reaching the unremarkable town of **CARRICKFERGUS**, whose seafront is dominated by the well-preserved **Carrickfergus Castle**. One of the earliest and largest

THE GIANT'S CAUSEWAY

Highlights

The Gobbins Dramatic and ingenious in equal measure, this 3km-long cliff-face path is utterly enthralling. See page 480

Causeway Coast Road The route from Larne to Portrush, skirting the Glens of Antrim, is one of Ireland's most scenic, with magical seascapes, staggering cliff-top walks and some of the North's prettiest villages. See page 480

Rathlin Island Northern Ireland's only inhabited offshore island, Rathlin offers exhilarating walks and views, top-class birdwatching opportunities and insights into a thriving local culture. See page 485

The Giant's Causeway Get there early to beat the crowds and marvel at one of the strangest geological formations in Europe. See page 487

Portstewart Strand The north coast's top beach where you can swim, surf, sunbathe or walk the dunes before ending your visit with dinner at the rustic *Harry's Shack*. See page 491

Walls of Derry A circuit of these seventeenth-century defences is an essential part of any visit to the "Maiden City". See page 496

Seamus Heaney HomePlace Immerse yourself in the life and works of one of Ireland's foremost poets, and Nobel Laureate. See page 504

HIGHLIGHTS ARE MARKED ON THE MAP ON PAGE 478

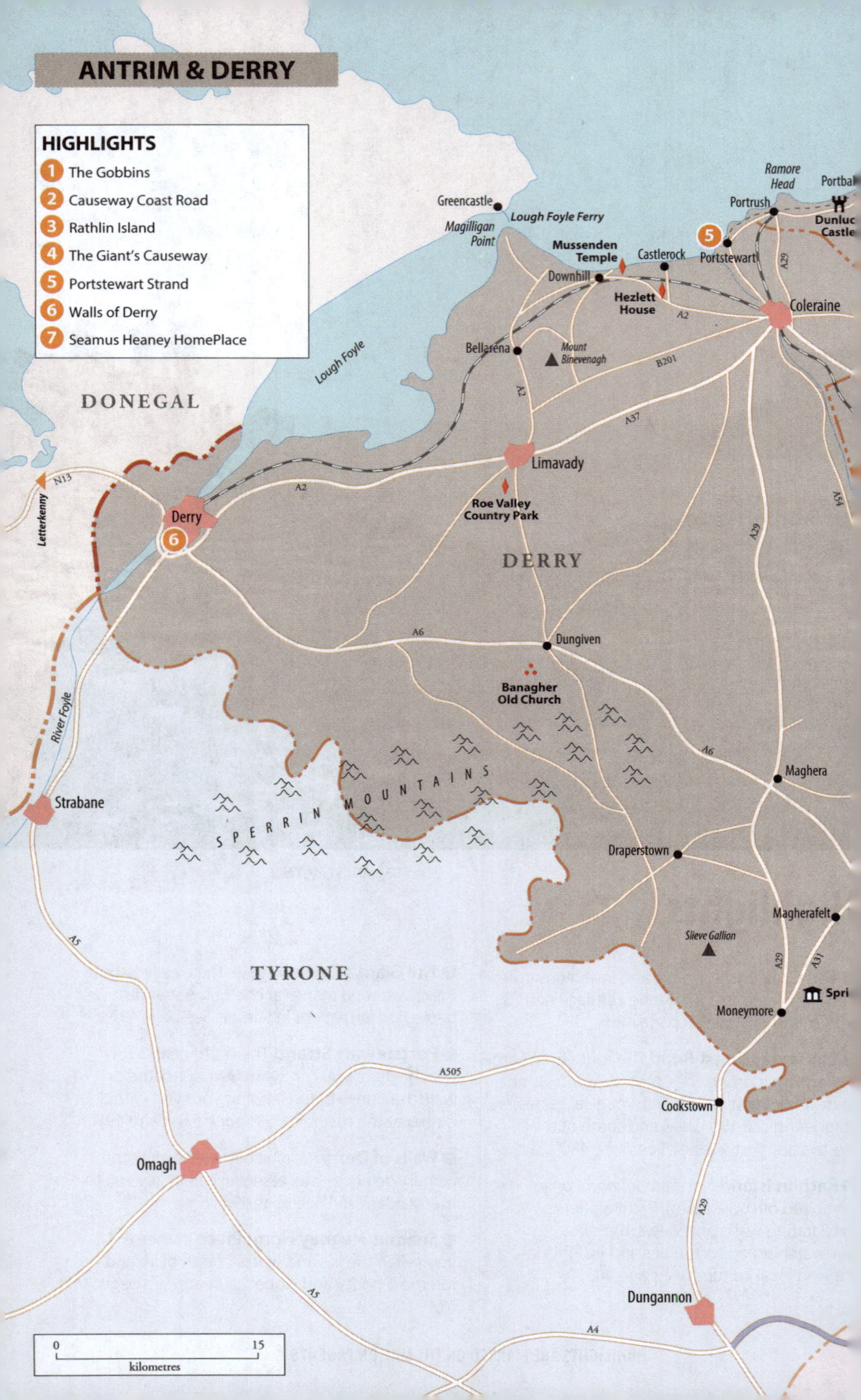

ANTRIM & DERRY
HIGHLIGHTS
1 The Gobbins
2 Causeway Coast Road
3 Rathlin Island
4 The Giant's Causeway
5 Portstewart Strand
6 Walls of Derry
7 Seamus Heaney HomePlace
DONEGAL
DERRY
TYRONE
Lough Foyle
Greencastle
Magilligan Point
Lough Foyle Ferry
Mussenden Temple
Castlerock
Downhill
Hezlett House
Ramore Head
Portrush
Portstewart
Dunluc
Castle
Portbal
Coleraine
Bellarena
Mount Binevenagh
Limavady
Roe Valley Country Park
Derry
Letterkenny
N13
A2
A37
B201
A29
A54
A6
Dungiven
Banagher Old Church
River Foyle
Strabane
SPERRIN MOUNTAINS
Maghera
Draperstown
Magherafelt
Slieve Gallion
A31
Spri
Moneymore
A5
A505
Cookstown
Omagh
Dungannon
A4
0
15
kilometres

Irish castles, built on a rocky promontory above the harbour around 1180 by the Anglo-Norman invader John de Courcy (and garrisoned until 1928), the castle reflects the defensive history of this entire region. In 1315, the castle endured a year's siege before falling to the combined forces of Robert and Edward Bruce, after which the English retook it. It's great fun exploring the castle's warren of dank passages and staircases, and there's also an informative exhibition on its history.

14 The Gobbins

68 Middle Rd, Islandmagee • Visitor Centre daily 8.30am–5pm; tours (must be pre-booked) • charge • http://thegobbinscliffpath.com

Dramatically cut into the rock face on the eastern flank of the long, crooked-finger-like peninsula of Islandmagee is the **Gobbins cliff path**. The path was originally constructed in 1902 by railway engineer Berkley Dean Wise as part of his grander vision to expand tourism in the area – indeed it was quite the tourist attraction back in the day. Numerous factors contributed to its eventual decline and the path closed in the early 1960s, thereafter falling into a state of disrepair.

Following a safety briefing, and kitted out with hardhat and appropriate footwear (boots can be supplied if yours aren't sturdy enough), visitors are bussed down to the start of the path. First off, you head up to a **viewing point** affording tremendous views of the sea-bitten coastline and, in the distance, the distinctive hump of Ailsa Craig just off the Ayrshire coast. Passing through **Wise's Eye** – the original, and surprisingly small, hole in the rock face – the new path roughly tracks Wise's original, albeit now almost totally eroded, version; the 3km path runs through a series of dramatic **tunnels**, **staircases** and **suspension bridges**, including a replica of Wise's iconic tubular bridge. Aside from birdlife, you may also get to see dolphins, porpoises and seals along the way. Note, though, that the path is not always open in its entirety (variously due to inclement weather, path maintenance or breeding birds), and while the walk – which takes around two and a half hours – is not especially demanding, a reasonable degree of fitness is required.

Before heading out, allow yourself a little time to peruse the illuminating **exhibition** inside the visitor centre, which relays the history of the path courtesy of some captivating black and white photos and informative wall panels; there's also one of the pillars from a section of the original railing. You can also enjoy some refreshments in the café.

The Glens of Antrim

The Causeway coast road surges north in quite spectacular fashion along the nine **Glens of Antrim**, a curious landscape in which pretty seaside villages – notably **Glenarm**, **Cushendall** and **Cushendun** – contrast vividly with the rough moorland above, which itself affords some memorable walking. The Glens' largest town is **Ballycastle**, a sprightly little spot on the northern tip, which is also the departure point for the ferry to rugged **Rathlin**.

Glenarm

The southernmost of the Glens, **Glenarm**, is headed by a village of the same name, which grew up around a hunting lodge built by Randal MacDonnell after Dunluce Castle, further up the coast, was abandoned (see page 489). Set around a graceful sandy bay and run through with handsome Georgian buildings, Glenarm is a delightful spot to linger in, and makes a great base for local walks. The village is also the location for the prestigious **Festival of Voice** (http://niopera.com), a three-day series of recitals and events in mid-August.

Glenarm Castle and the Walled Garden

2 Castle Lane • Walled Garden Easter–Sept Daily 9am–5pm • charge • http://glenarmcastle.com

Dominating the village, **Glenarm Castle** was built in 1636, becoming the major seat of the Earls of Antrim, though it was razed just a few years later – its current incarnation dates from 1756. Today the castle is a private residence, hence is off-limits (save for a handful of days when special events are on – check the website), but the stunning **walled garden** is open to the public and certainly worth an hour or so of your time. Highlights here include the circular yew hedge, a zesty-smelling herb garden (unusual for its four capitols), kitchen garden and glasshouse, which backs onto a row of whitewashed bothies – formerly gardeners' residences but which now accommodate various craft shops. Bring a picnic and make the most of the setting, or failing that, retire to the posh little tearoom for a cuppa and a slice of cake.

14

ARRIVAL AND INFORMATION   GLENARM

By bus Glenarm is served by buses from/to Carnlough (Mon–Fri 10 daily, Sat 6; 10min) and Larne (Mon–Sat 6–7 daily; 25min).

Tourist information Glenarm Visitor Centre is in the Harbourmaster's building at 16 New Rd (March–Sept Mon–Fri 10am–12.30pm & 1.30–4pm, Sun 1–4pm; http://glenarmtourism.org); the super-helpful staff here can assist on any aspect of visiting the Glens and the Causeway coast, including organising local walks.

ACCOMMODATION

★ **Water's Edge** 11–13 The Cloney, http://watersedgeglenarm.com. Occupying Glenarm's erstwhile police station, on the coastal road heading towards Carnlough, this fabulous self-catering apartment has two ground floor double bedrooms (both ensuite), plus a pull-out in the lounge – every room has unencumbered sea views, Two-night minimum stay. £££

Carnlough

Rounding the next bay from Glenarm, you'll arrive at **CARNLOUGH**, standing at the head of **Glencloy**. Until the 1960s, Carnlough's way of life was linked to its limestone quarries, and the village's most striking feature today remains its sturdy limestone buildings, dating mainly from the mid-nineteenth century. Right in the village centre, running over the main road, there's a solid **stone bridge** that once carried a railway bringing material down to the **harbour**, which itself has an impressive breakwater, clock tower and limestone courthouse. The harbour has also served as the setting for several *Game of Thrones* scenes (see page 481), and is the departure point for half-hour boat trips out to Black Rock.

> ## GAME OF THRONES
>
> Winterfell, House Stark, Vaes Dothrak, Renly's Camp, and the Wildling Pit – all of these names will be familiar to fans of the fantasy drama, **Game of Thrones**, which has principally been filmed in Northern Ireland, since series one aired in 2011; the eighth (and last) series hit the screen in 2019. Legions of fans make the trip here to seek out **filming locations** like Ballintoy and Carnlough harbours, Castle Ward, Cushendun Caves, Inch Abbey and Tollymore Forest. The most iconic, however, is the **Dark Hedges**, near Armoy some 13km southwest of Ballycastle; a remarkable, haunting avenue of enormous beech trees planted by the Stuart family in the eighteenth century, they have become one of the most visited sites in the country. In 2016 storms brought down a number of these trees, the result being that the wood was salvaged and transformed into a set of ten **doors**, each one intricately carved with a scene from series six; these are now *in situ* at ten pubs, or inns, across the country, for example *Fiddler's Green* in Portaferry (see page 517), *Mary McBride's* in Cushendun (see page 483), and *Blakes of the Hollow* in Enniskillen (see page 551).

ARRIVAL AND TOURS
CARNLOUGH

By bus Carnlough has bus services from/to Cushendall (Mon–Fri 3 daily; 25min); Glenarm (Mon–Fri 10 daily, Sat 6; 10min); and Larne (Mon–Sat 6–7 daily; 35min).

Boat trips Carnlough Bay Boat Tours (http://carnloughboattours.weebly.com) offers 45min tours out to Black Rock (£6), as well as longer tours.

ACCOMMODATION AND EATING

★ **Londonderry Arms Hotel** 20 Harbour Rd, http://londonderryarmshotel.com. A former coaching inn once briefly owned by Winston Churchill, the *Londonderry* oozes character. The building comprises a warren of agreeably old-fashioned rooms variously conferred with carved oak and antique furnishings, while the *Coach House* is a convivial spot to chow down on the likes of pan roast chicken with champ and bacon and leek cream. Once done there, sidle next door to the *Arkle* bar, whose collection of mementos celebrates the legendary 1960s champion steeplechaser. **££**

Cushendall and around

CUSHENDALL, which lies at the head of three of the nine Glens, is a delightfully understated village, its charming colour-washed buildings grouped together on a spectacular shore. The red-sandstone **tower** at the central crossroads was built in 1817 by Francis Turnley, an official of the East India Company, as "a place of confinement for idlers and rioters", and the village makes a fine base for exploring the countryside and catching a traditional music session. If possible, time your visit to coincide with the **Heart of the Glens** festival in early August, one of the area's oldest events, replete with music, sporting events and much merriment, culminating in a huge street ceili on the Sunday.

ARRIVAL AND INFORMATION
CUSHENDALL AND AROUND

By bus There are buses from/to Carnlough (Mon–Fri 3 daily; 25min) and Cushendun (Mon–Fri 8 daily, Sat 3; 15min).

Tourist information The tourist office is a few paces west of the central crossroads at 25 Mill St (June–Sept Mon–Sat 10am–5pm, Sun noon–4pm; Oct–March Mon–Sat 10am–2pm; http://visitcausewaycoastandglens.com).

ACCOMMODATION

Cushendall Caravan Park 62 Coast Rd, http://glenscoast caravanparks.com. Hovering right over the water's edge at the entrance to the village (from Carnlough), this small but well equipped campsite also has four wooden camping pods, with artificial turfed roofs and bench-like beds. Closed Nov–March. **£**

The Meadows 81 Coast Rd, http://themeadowscushendall. com. A quiet but friendly B&B located at the entrance to the village (just beyond the caravan park) with six spacious rooms, each with a double and single bed. Also offers disabled access. **££**

Sundial House 11 High St, http://sundialhouse.weebly. com. Super-friendly hostel-cum-guesthouse located on the steep hill just north of the tower offering a double (en suite), and three triple-bedrooms; self-catering kitchen plus lounge with log fire too. **£**

The Village B&B Mill St, http://thevillagebandb.com. Welcoming, central option with nine generously sized en-suite rooms, including singles doubles and family rooms. Walkers and bikers are particularly welcome, and the owner dispenses maps, logistical and practical information, and will enrich your stay with local cultural history. Closed Nov–Feb. **££**

EATING AND DRINKING

Harry's 10 Mill St, http://harryscushendall.co.uk. This hugely popular two-floored bistro won't win any prizes for culinary flair, but it serves good-value, big portion meals, such as freshly battered scampi with chunky chips and tobacco onions. **££**

★ **Johnny Joe's** 23 Mill St, 028 2177 1992. A convivial, cottage-style pub which hosts traditional music sessions on Fridays, in addition to music on Tues, Sat and Sun in high season.

Cushendun and around

The once-fashionable resort of **CUSHENDUN**, some 8km northwest of Cushendall, is an architectural oddity almost entirely designed by Clough Williams-Ellis, the innovative architect of Portmeirion in Wales, and constructed between 1912 and 1925. Built to a commission from Ronald McNeill, the first (and last) Baron Cushendun, and his Cornish wife, Maud, Cushendun's houses are of rugged, rough-cast whitewash with slate roofs – a Cornish style that clearly weathers the sea storms as efficiently here as in Cornwall. Much of Cushendun is National Trust property, and it shows: it's a tiny and well-tended place.

The main road from Cushendun northwest to Ballycastle runs inland, traversing some impressively rough moorland, and passes **Loughareema**, the "vanishing lake", so termed because of its tendency to drain away completely in hot weather. The narrow, winding coastal road is a better bet, however; edged with fuchsia and honeysuckle, it switches back violently above the sea to **Torr Head**, the closest point on the Irish mainland to the Mull of Kintyre in Scotland.

14

ARRIVAL AND DEPARTURE

CUSHENDUN AND AROUND

By bus Cushendun is served by buses from/to Cushendall   (Mon–Fri 8 daily, Sat 3; 15min).

ACCOMMODATION AND EATING

Mary McBride's 2 Main St, 028 2176 1511. Wonderful, warming pub that's as popular these days for its *Game of Thrones* door (see page 481) as its fabulous Saturday evening and Sunday afternoon music sessions; good pub grub too (beef and guinness pie). Upstairs you'll find the *Little Black Door*, the pub's superbly accomplished seafood bistro (spiced cod with babagnash and prawn croquettes). **££**

Sleepy Hollow 107 Knocknacarry Rd, 028 2176 1513. 1.5km or so back down the road from Cushendun, this small but perfectly formed B&B comes with kingsize beds and sweeping views of the countryside; an ideal location for exploration of the coast and glens. **££**

Murlough Bay and Fair Head

Murlough Bay is the most spectacular of all the bays along the northern coast. From the rugged cliff-tops, the hillside curves down to the sea in a series of wildflower meadows that soften an otherwise harsh landscape. The last headland before Ballycastle is **Fair Head**, whose massive 200m cliffs offer stunning views across the North Channel to Scotland – the Mull of Kintyre and further to Islay and the Paps of Jura – a proximity that sheds light on the confusion of land ownership between Ireland and Scotland. A prime example is Rathlin Island (see page 485), which was hotly contested up until the seventeenth century. **Lough na Cranagh**, one of three lakes in the hinterland behind the cliffs, houses a *crannóg*, encircled by a parapet wall. A walk from the Fair Head car park to Murlough Bay takes 45 minutes, but muddy paths and changeable weather make walking boots and waterproofs essential.

Ballycastle

The lively market town and port of **BALLYCASTLE** sits at the mouth of the two northernmost Antrim Glens, **Glenshesk** and **Glentaisie**, and makes a pleasant base for exploring the Causeway Coast or the Glens themselves. The best time to visit Ballycastle is for the **Ould Lammas Fair**, Ireland's oldest fair, dating from 1606. Held on the last Monday and Tuesday in August, it features sheep and pony sales, while stallholders do a roaring trade in dulse, an edible seaweed, and yellowman, a tooth-breaking yellow toffee that's so hard it needs a hammer to break it up. These delicacies feature in a sentimental song that originates locally:

Did you treat your Mary Ann
To dulse and yellowman
At the Ould Lammas Fair in Ballycastle–O?

Ballycastle has a prosperous feel about it that derived originally from the efforts of an enlightened mid-eighteenth-century landowner, Colonel Hugh Boyd, who developed the town as an industrial centre, providing coal and iron ore mines, a tannery, a

14

brewery and soap, bleach, salt and glass works, all now defunct. It was from its **coal mines** particularly that the town garnered most of its wealth; lignite was mined at Ballintoy on the coast a few kilometres further west, an enterprise which came to an abrupt end when the entire deposit caught fire and burned for several years.

At the seafront there's a memorial to **Guglielmo Marconi**, the inventor of wireless telegraphy, who in 1898 made his first successful radio transmission between Ballycastle and Rathlin. From here, Quay Road leads gradually uphill past houses and shops to **The Diamond**, the town's focus, and thence up the steeper Castle Street.

Ballycastle museum

59 Castle St • Free • 028 2076 2225

The tiny but highly engaging **Ballycastle museum** occupies the old eighteenth-century courthouse, whose former cells now hold a collection of artefacts produced by the pre-World War I Irish Home Industries Shop – mostly exquisite wood-carved furnishings. Elsewhere, there are Stone Age tools from Rathlin Island and a replica of Marconi's oscillator (one of just ten in existence), though pride of place goes to the Glentaisie banner for the first *Feis na nGleann* ("festival of the Glens") in 1904.

Bonamargy Friary

1.5km south of town on the Cushendall Rd • Open access

Just out of town lie the ruins of **Bonamargy Friary**, founded by the dominant MacQuillan family around 1500. One family member, Julia, insisted on being buried in the main walkway, so that she might be humbled for eternity by the stepping feet of others. A number of the rival MacDonnell family are also buried here, including the hero of Dunluce Castle, Sorley Boy MacDonnell, and his son Randal, first Earl of Antrim (see page 489). An indication of the erstwhile strength of the Irish language in these parts is that the tomb of the second earl, who died in 1682, is inscribed in Irish as well as the usual English and Latin; the Irish translation reads, "Every seventh year a calamity befalls the Irish" and "Now that the Marquis has departed, it will occur every year". The **River Margy**, on which the Friary stands, is associated with one of the tragic stories of Irish legend, that of the Children of Lir, whose jealous stepmother turned them into swans and forced them to spend three hundred years on the Sea of Moyle (the narrow channel between Ireland and the Scottish coast).

ARRIVAL AND INFORMATION

BALLYCASTLE

By bus Ballycastle is well served by local buses.

Destinations Ballintoy (every 30min; 15min); Bushmills (every 30min; 35min); Cushendall (Mon–Fri 3 daily; 35min); Cushendun (Mon–Fri 3 daily; 30min); Giant's Causeway (every 30min; 25min); Glenarm (July & Aug Mon–Fri 2 daily; 1hr 15min).

Tourist information Opposite the marina in Portnagree House, 14 Bayview Rd (July & Aug Mon–Sat 9am–6pm, Sun noon–4pm; Sept–June Mon–Sat 9am–5pm; http://visitcausewaycoastandglens.com), the welcoming visitor centre has stacks of info on the region as well as an accommodation booking service.

ACCOMMODATION, EATING AND DRINKING

Cellar 11b The Diamond, http://cellarballycastle.com. A distinctive tangerine-and-green-painted frontage conceals an atmospheric little cellar restaurant with layered slate walls and cosy, compartmentalized seating areas with low-hanging lights; the menu is locally-oriented such as Carrick-a-Rede salmon and rump steak from Antrim; there's a terrific-value early bird menu. **£££**

Central Wine Bar 12 Ann St, 028 2076 3877. A hostelry of sorts since 1861, and distinguished by its three thatched "eyes" above the entrance, this lively barn of a bar/restaurant is the most spirited place in town. The food is

terrific, for example seafood cassoulet or the three-course Sunday lunch, while the nightly music sessions pull in the punters by the shedload.

The House of McDonnell 71 Castle St, http://houseofmcdonnell.blogspot.com. Also known as Tom's, this bar has been in the same family for an astonishing fourteen generations, stretching back to 1766, and is just the place to channel the "spirit" of an older age via Irish, American or Scotch whiskies galore. Friday is music night, attracting visitors and youngish locals.

Marine Hotel 1–3 North St, http://marinehotelballycastle

com. This prominent and well-run hotel with 51 comfortable bedrooms is handy for the ferries to Rathlin Island (or simply gazing across to it), though it's slightly overpriced for what it is; the corner coffee bar is worth venturing to if waiting for a ferry. £££

★ **Ursa Minor** 45 Ann St, http://ursaminorbakehouse. com. A gorgeous waft of freshly baked bread hits you smack in the face as soon as you enter the "Little Bear" bakehouse,

part of a local Économusée project designed to showcase local crafts and artisan producers; you can even venture downstairs to see the breads being prepared. Back upstairs in the lovely, sparingly furnished café, scrumptious offerings include fried eggs on sourdough with cherry tomatoes and salsa verde, while the coffee, which comes with notes of origin, isn't half bad either. Closed Sun & Mon. £

Rathlin Island

Shaped like a truncated figure seven, **Rathlin Island**, 8km north of Ballycastle and just 21km west of the Mull of Kintyre in Scotland, is an impressive, craggy place, with a coastline consisting almost entirely of cliffs, and a lighthouse at each tip. The sea dominates the landscape and its salty winds discourage the growth of vegetation – wind turbines harness this energy source for electricity generation. A great time to be here is the end of May for the **Rathlin Sound Maritime Festival** (http://rathlinsoundmaritimefestival.com), a ten-day programme of events, the highlight of which is the opening, and quite spectacular, Blessing of the Boats ceremony.

Brief history

In 795 AD Rathlin was the first place in Ireland to be raided by the **Vikings**. Later raids saw two bloody massacres, first by the English and then by the Scots. In 1575, the mainland MacDonnells sent their women, children and old people to Rathlin for safety from the English, but that didn't stop the invading fleet, under the Earl of Essex (whose soldiers included Sir Francis Drake), from slaughtering the entire population. In 1642, a later generation of MacDonnells was then butchered by their Scottish enemies, the Campbells, causing Rathlin to be deserted for many years afterwards.

Church Bay and around

The presence of dry-stone walls and numerous ruined cottages points to a time when the population was far larger than the 150 or so current inhabitants concentrated around the shallow arc of **Church Bay**. Halfway towards the western lighthouse is the site of a **Stone Age** axe-making site, and, to its north, earthworks known as **Doonmore**. In the early Christian period, the island was a haven for monks, who left evidence of their presence in the form of a sweathouse (a kind of primitive sauna) at **Knockans**, back towards Church Bay. You can discover more about the island's history and culture in the **Boathouse Visitor Centre** (see page 485); at the southern end of the harbour; here, too, are photos of Richard Branson after his hot-air balloon infamously crash-landed just off the island's west coast in 1987. From the Boathouse, there's a fine 5km walk down to **Roonivoolin** ("Point of the Gulls") on the island's southern tip; along the way, you've got a good chance of spotting seals as well as oystercatchers and ringed plovers.

BIRDS AND WILDFLOWERS ON RATHLIN ISLAND

The island's cliffs are superb for **birdwatching**, particularly Bull Point, on the western tip, part of a large RSPB nature reserve. The **West Light Seabird Centre** (April to mid-Sept daily 9am–5pm; charge; free to RSPB members), inside the western lighthouse, provides wonderful views of Northern Ireland's largest colony of seabirds that includes puffins, guillemots and razorbills. If you are here in the spring you may also see a rare **wildflower**, the sky-blue pyramidal bugle, which is widespread from near the West Lighthouse to the north of Church Bay – the only recorded sighting of it in Northern Ireland. During summer, a minibus (£5) plies between the seabird centre and Church Bay in summer.

14

Bruce's Cave

On the northeast point of the island, below the lighthouse, is **Bruce's Cave**, a cavern carved in the black basalt where, in 1306, so the story goes, the despondent Robert the Bruce retreated after being defeated by the English at Perth. Seeing a spider determinedly trying to spin a web gave him the resolve to "try, try and try again", so he returned to Scotland and defeated the English at Bannockburn.

ARRIVAL AND INFORMATION   RATHLIN ISLAND

By ferry Two ferries (http://rathlin-ferry.com) make the trip from Ballycastle harbour to Rathlin: the *Spirit of Rathlin* vehicle ferry (April–Sept 4 daily; 40min) – though note that vehicles can only be taken across if you're staying on the island for six nights or more – and the *Kintra II* passenger-only ferry (April–Sept 4–5 daily; 30min); services are much reduced during the winter. A return ticket costs £16, bikes £4.40.

Bike Hire Bikes can be hired from Sorneog View, a 10min walk to the south from Church Bay (May–Aug daily 10am–5pm; 028 2076 3954).

Tourist information Housed inside the old boathouse, the visitor centre is a 5min walk south of the ferry slip (mid-March to Sept Mon–Sat 9am–1pm & 1.30–5pm; 028 2076 2024). A useful website is http://rathlincommunity.org.

ACCOMMODATION AND EATING

Manor House Church Bay, http://manorhouserathlin.com. A few paces from the ferry port, this beautifully restored late Georgian home dates from around 1760 on the site of weavers' cottages and is now run by the National Trust. The eleven stylish rooms are painted in a fetching green-blue colour and fitted with low sash windows through which you can savour the splendid sea views. Closed Nov–Easter. <u>££</u>

McCuaig's Bar Church Bay, 028 2076 0011. The island's social hub combines a plain but convivial bar/restaurant offering lunches and early evening meals such as apple and pork burger with fries, sandwiches and paninis; there's occasional music and other events too. <u>£</u>

The north Antrim coast

The north coast of County Antrim, west of Ballycastle, is dominated, from a tourist perspective, by Northern Ireland's most famous tourist attraction, the bizarre formation of basalt columns at the **Giant's Causeway**, a UNESCO World Heritage site. On the way, near the town of **Ballintoy**, there are several pleasant diversions, not least the precarious rope bridge to **Carrick-a-rede Island**. West of the Causeway, you can sample some whiskey at **Bushmills** and visit the imposing and well-preserved remains of **Dunluce Castle**, the stronghold of the local MacDonnell clan. The coastline west of Dunluce is another major holiday spot, with **Portrush** filled with tourists in summer and students the rest of the year.

Carrick-a-rede Island

Rope bridge Daily, weather permitting: Feb 9.30am–5pm; March–June, Sept & Oct 9am–4.30pm; July & Aug 9am–5pm; Nov–Jan 10am–2.30pm • charge • http://nationaltrust.org.uk/carrick-a-rede

As you draw level with **Carrick-a-rede Island**, not far before Ballintoy on the coast road west from Ballycastle, you'll see the island's **rope bridge**, first erected some 350 years ago. Strung almost 30m above the sea, the rope-connected planks lead to a commercial salmon fishery on the southeast side of Carrick-a-rede (the name means "rock in the road": the island stands in the path of migrating salmon) – but its main function seems to be to scare tourists, something it does very successfully. Like the Giant's Causeway, it gets murderously busy, so you'd do well to visit as early in the day as you can.

Ballintoy and around

Around 1.5km beyond the village of **BALLINTOY**, a road snakes down to a dramatic **harbour**, without doubt one of the most picturesque spots anywhere along the Causeway coast. Lively with boats in the summer, but bleak and exposed in winter, it's much loved by artists, with a dark, rock-strewn strand contrasting oddly with the neat, pale-stone breakwater. At the top of the harbour road stands a little white **church**, which replaced an earlier one in which local Protestants took refuge from Catholics in 1641 before being rescued by the Earl of Antrim.

Portbraddan and Dunseverick Castle

The coastal path from Ballintoy leads west to **PORTBRADDAN**, a tiny hamlet of multicoloured houses, where St Gobban's, a slate-roofed little church, just 3.5m by a little under 2m, is supposedly the smallest church in Ireland. Needless to say, there are other contenders: the ruins of an even smaller one, St Lasseragh's, stand on the cliff above.

From Portbraddan the coast path leads round a headland, through a spectacular hole in the rock and then, by degrees, up to the cliffs of **Benbane Head**. The road and path almost converge at the ruins of a sixteenth-century gatehouse, all that's left of **Dunseverick Castle**. This was once the capital of the old kingdom of Dalriada, which spread over north Antrim and Scotland, and the terminus of one of the five great roads that led from Tara, the ancient capital of Ireland.

ARRIVAL AND DEPARTURE
BALLINTOY AND AROUND

By bus Ballintoy is served by buses from/to Ballycastle (every 30min; 15min); Bushmills (every 30min; 20min); and Giant's Causeway (every 30min; 15min).

ACCOMMODATION AND EATING

Fullerton Arms 22 Main St, http://fullerton-arms.com. A comfortable, family-run guesthouse with twelve elegantly furnished rooms, some of which are dog-friendly. Just as good is the restaurant, entered via another *Game of Thrones* door (see page 481), offering tasty, traditional staples like steak and guinness pie, and fish and chips. **££**

Whitepark Bay Hostel 157 Whitepark Rd, 3km west of Ballintoy, http://hini.org.uk. With glorious views over Whitepark Bay, this seasonal hostel offers four- and six-bed dorms, as well as twins; all rooms are en suite while the twin rooms have TVs and tea/coffee making facilities. Closed mid-Oct to mid-March. **£**

The Giant's Causeway

Ever since 1693, when the Royal Society first publicized it as one of the great wonders of the natural world, the **Giant's Causeway** has been a major tourist attraction. The highly romanticized pictures of the polygonal basalt rock formations by the Dubliner Susanna Drury, which circulated throughout Europe in the eighteenth century, did much to popularize the Causeway; two of them are on show in the Ulster Museum in Belfast (see page 456). Not everyone was impressed, though. A disappointed William Thackeray commented, "I've travelled a hundred and fifty miles to see *that*?", and especially disliked the tourist promotion of the Causeway, claiming in 1842 that "The traveller no sooner issues from the inn by a back door which he is informed will lead him straight to the causeway, than the guides pounce upon him." Although the tourist hype is today less overtly mercenary, the Causeway (now managed by the National Trust) still attracts hundreds of thousands of visitors annually; indeed, the site can get crushingly busy, which can really put a dampener on the visit, so you'd do well to visit as early (or as late) in the day as you can. It's worth pointing out that you only have to **pay** if you're parking at the site or accessing the stones via the Visitor Experience (see below) – otherwise follow the signposted path to the stones that starts near (but bypasses) the Visitor Experience.

For sheer otherworldliness, the Causeway can't be beaten. Made up of an estimated 37,000 **black basalt columns**, each a polygon (hexagons are by far the most common, with pentagons second, though sometimes the columns have as many as ten sides), the sight is the result of a subterranean explosion, some sixty million years ago, that stretched from the Causeway to Rathlin and beyond to Islay, Staffa (where it was responsible for the formation of Fingal's Cave) and Mull in Scotland. A huge mass of molten basalt was spewed out on to the surface, which, on cooling, solidified into what are, essentially, crystals.

14

FIONN MAC CUMHAILL: THE GIANT OF THE CAUSEWAY

According to mythology, the Giant of the Causeway was Ulster warrior **Fionn Mac Cumhaill** (also known as Finn McCool), and two legends of Fionn's exploits provide an entertaining alternative to geologists' explanations of the Causeway's origins. In one, Fionn became besotted with a woman giant who resided on the Scottish island of Staffa (where the Causeway's fault-line resurfaces) and constructed a **highway across the sea** by which he could travel to woo her. An alternative version of the story suggests that Fionn built the Causeway in order to head over to Scotland to give another giant a good kicking, but, when confronted by his enemy's superior size, fled back to Ireland and hid in an extra-large cot which he'd persuaded his wife to construct. When the pursuing Scots giant arrived, he took just a glance at the sheer size of Fionn's supposed "baby" and fled back to Scotland.

Giant's Causeway Visitor Experience

60 Causeway Rd • March–June, Sept & Oct 9am–5pm; July & Aug 9am–6pm; Nov–Feb 10am–4pm; last admission to centre 1hr before closing • charge; price includes parking, a guided tour, and an audio-guide for visiting the stones • http://nationaltrust.org.uk and http://giantscausewaytickets.com

Sunken into the ground and made from locally quarried basalt, the **Giant's Causeway Visitor Experience** blends into the landscape with indigenous grasses on the roof providing a habitat for wildlife. Inside, a rather haphazard set-up features exhibition panels and 3-D displays providing detail on the geological and scientific nature of the area, while you get to meet the various characters that have shaped the landscape hereabouts – most of it, though, just seems to be taken up by the enormous National Trust shop.

The stones

From the visitor centre, it's a fifteen-minute walk down to the stones, though there is also a minibus that shuttles back and forth (£1 one way; free to NT members). The first of the distinctive stone columns once you reach the pavement are the 12m-high **Organ Pipes**. Many of the other formations have names ("the Camel", "the Wishing Chair" and "the Granny") invented for them by the guides who so plagued Thackeray and his contemporaries. At least one, **Chimney Point**, further north, has an appearance so bizarre that in September 1588 it persuaded the crew of the *Girona*, a ship of the Spanish Armada, to think it was Dunluce Castle (see page 489), where they thought they might get help from the MacDonnells. Instead, their vessel was wrecked on the rocky shore at Port-na-Spánaigh, just before Chimney Point. Its treasure was recovered by divers in 1968, and some of the items are on show in the Ulster Museum in Belfast (see page 456) and in Derry's Tower Museum (see page 496). Guided tours (hourly from 10am, every 30min in July & Aug) of the stones depart from the visitor centre and are included in the admission charge.

ARRIVAL AND INFORMATION   **THE GIANT'S CAUSEWAY**

By bus The Causeway is served by a number of buses, including the Causeway Rambler and the Antrim Coaster (see page 476).

By car The roads around the Causeway are congested, particularly on weekends, so it's best to use the park-and-ride bus from the Dundarave car park in Bushmills (March–Oct), which also entitles you to buy a Green Ticket, thereby saving £4.50 on the normal admission price to the Visitor Experience.

Visitors arriving by bike or on foot also receive a £1.50 discount. **By train** A restored narrow-gauge railway runs between the Causeway and Bushmills (June, Sept & Oct Sat & Sun; July & Aug daily; 6 trains daily on the hour 11am–5pm (except 1pm), returning 30min later from Bushmills; 028 2073 2844, http://giantscausewayrailway.webs.com; £6 one-way).

Tourist information The tourist office is located inside the Giant's Causeway Visitor Experience (same opening times).

Bushmills

Distillery 2 Distillery Rd • Tours Mon–Sat 10am–5pm, Sun 11am–5pm • charge • http://bushmills.eu

The foremost attraction in **BUSHMILLS** is the **Old Bushmills Distillery** on the outskirts of town, where whiskey has been distilled here legally since 1608, making it the oldest licit distillery in the world. Bushmills whiskey – of which there are five core products – is distilled three times, once more than Scotch, but perhaps the biggest surprise is just how little subtlety is involved in the industrial manufacture of alcohol, despite all the lore that surrounds it. You can enjoy learning about the process on a guided **tour,** which takes in the mash house, the malt barn (though malting is not done on site), the vast warehouse, and the equally impressive bottling plant; the tour ends with a complimentary tasting.

ARRIVAL AND INFORMATION   BUSHMILLS

By bus Buses drop off and pick up at the War Memorial on Main St, from where it's a 10min walk to the distillery. Destinations Ballintoy (every 30min; 20min); Ballycastle (every 30min; 35min); Coleraine (every 30min; 40min); Portrush (every 30min; 25min).

Tourist office 44 Main St (March–May & Oct Mon–Sat 9am–5pm; June & Sept Mon–Sat 9am–5pm, Sun noon–4pm; July & Aug Mon–Sat 9am–6pm, Sun noon–4pm; http://visitcausewaycoastandglens.com).

ACCOMMODATION AND EATING

★ **Bushmills Inn** 9 Dunluce Rd, http://bushmillsinn.com. This former coaching inn has a pleasantly rambling, cottage-style interior replete with inglenook turf fires, hayloft snugs and the like. Rooms come in several categories, though all are impeccably turned out, while the smart restaurant, located in the old stables building, features traditional dishes such as the Botchan (local soup) or Dalriada cullen skink (smoked haddock fillet). Better still is the atmospheric, gas-lit *Gas Bar* where, at weekends, there are live acoustic sessions. £££

Bushmills Youth Hostel 49 Main St, http://hini.org.uk. Rather clinical, but modern, clean and very convenient hostel with three-, four- and six-bed dorms, plus, twins, all of which are en suite; facilities include a large self-catering kitchen. £

Dunluce Castle

8km southwest of Giant's Causeway • Daily: Feb–Nov 9.30am–5pm; Jan & Feb 9.30am–4pm • charge • http://discovernorthernireland.com

The most impressive ruin of this entire coastline is the dramatically sited sixteenth-century **Dunluce Castle**. Perched on a fine headland, high above a cave, it looks as if it only needs a roof to be perfectly habitable once again. Its history is inextricably linked to that of its original owner, **Sorley Boy MacDonnell**, whose clan, the so-called "Lords of the Isles", ruled northeastern Ulster from this base. English incursions into the area culminated in 1584 with Sir John Perrott laying siege to Dunluce, forcing Sorley Boy ("Yellow Charles" in Irish) to leave the castle. But as soon as Perrott departed, leaving a garrison in charge, Sorley Boy hauled his men up the cliff in baskets and recaptured the castle, later repairing the damage with the proceeds of the salvaged wreckage of the *Girona* (see page 488) and arming the fort with three of its cannons. Having made his point, Sorley Boy agreed a peace with the English, and his son, Randal, was created Viscount Dunluce and Earl of Antrim by James I. In 1639, Dunluce Castle paid the penalty for its precarious, if impregnable, position when the kitchen fell off the cliff during a storm, complete with cooks and dinner. Shortly afterwards, the MacDonnells moved to more comfortable lodgings at Glenarm, and Dunluce was left empty.

The castle remains an extraordinary place. The MacDonnells' Scottish connections – Randal continued to own land in Kintyre – are evident in the **gatehouse**'s turrets and crow-step gables, and in the tapering chimneys of the seventeenth-century **Great Hall**. There's a strange touch of luxury in the **loggia**, though it oddly faces away from the sun. A steep path takes you down to the **cave** below the castle that pierces right through the promontory, with an opening directly under the gatehouse.

Portrush

The town of **PORTRUSH** has everything you'd expect from a seaside resort: sandy **beaches** backed by dunes, which run both east and west, a raft of waterborne activities,

14

along with amusement arcades and funfairs galore. Moreover, the huge popularity of the local dance scene draws clubbers from all over the North, meaning the town can have a distinctly raucous feel at weekends. The long, sandy **beach** towards Dunluce ends at the **White Rocks**, where the weather has carved the soft limestone cliffs into strange shapes, most famously the so-called **"Cathedral Cave"**, nearly 60m from end to end. This is **surfing** country par excellence and there is rewarding surfing off the West Strand and White Rocks, as well as good **paddleboarding**.

Much of the townscape changed dramatically for the 2019 Open Golf championship (one of golf's four majors), which was quite some coup for Portrush given that Northern Ireland hadn't staged the tournament since 1951; following on from this, the championship will be held here again in 2025. Otherwise, Portrush is certainly not short on annual events, with the perennially popular **North West 200 motorbike race** (http://northwest200.org), a manic six days in mid-May; the **Portrush Raft Race** (http://portrushraftrace.co.uk) at the end of May, which sees participants race each other across the harbour on all manner of wacky home-made rafts; and the spectacular two-day **Northern Ireland International Air Show** (http://airshowni.com) at the beginning of September, based around the East Strand – though this has only been held intermittently in the last few years.

ARRIVAL AND DEPARTURE

PORTRUSH

By train The train station is a short hop south of the town centre on Eglinton St.
Destinations Coleraine (hourly; 15min) for connections to Belfast (hourly; 1hr 20min) and Derry (Mon–Sat hourly, Sun 6; 40min).

By bus The bus station is near the train station on Dunluce Ave.
Destinations Bushmills (every 30min; 25min); Coleraine (every 15–30min; 15–25min).

INFORMATION AND ACTIVITIES

Tourist office Town Hall, 2 Kerr St (April–Oct Mon–Sat 9am–5pm, plus June–Sept Sun noon–4pm; http://visitcausewaycoastandglens.com).
Surfing and paddleboarding Surfing (£42/2hr),) and SUP lessons (£55/2hr), as well as board hire (£10/hr) and gear, are offered at the Portrush Surf School (http://portrushsurfschool.com), located at the Yacht Club in the harbour, and Alive Adventures on the West Strand beach (http://aliveadventures.co.uk) who also offer guided

kayaking tours.
Golf Royal Venue for the 2025 Open Championship, Portrush Golf Club (http://royalportrushgolfclub.com) is the North's premier club, boasting two eighteen-hole courses; the championship Dunluce course (£340/18 holes) and the Valley course (£140/18 holes). Demand is high in the summer but in any case you'll need to book ahead; note that green fees are much reduced in winter.

ACCOMMODATION

Adelphi Portrush 67–71 Main St, http://adelphiportrush.com. The wide selection of rooms, including triples and quads, in this centrally located hotel feature contemporary elegant design, some with sea views. Good off-season special deals are available Oct–March; the rate includes access to the hotel's spa facilities and there's a very creditable restaurant here too. <u>££</u>

Beulah Guesthouse 16 Causeway St, http://beulahguesthouse.com. A super-friendly welcome and nine well-presented rooms await guests at this adult only B&B near the East Strand beach. There's a lovely guest lounge with antique piano, and splendid breakfasts covering everything from the full fry-up to gluten-free and vegetarian dishes. Closed Nov–Feb. <u>££</u>

EATING AND DRINKING

★ **Arcadia Beach Café** West Strand Ave, http://arcadiaportrush.com. Once known as the Ladies' Bathing Place, this landmark building perched on the water's edge was a popular ballroom venue in the 1950s and 1960s. Today, it's a popular spot for breakfasts (such as French toast with cinnamon and maple syrup) and lunches (wraps, melts), with coffee, cake and ice cream adding to the seaside vibe. Dine outside, where

there's a little splash pool for kids, and gaze across to the Skerries or watch the waves break on the beach. The upstairs art gallery rounds things off beautifully. <u>£</u>
Kiwi's Brew Bar 47 Main St, http://kiwisbrewbar.com. This banging little bar is one of the best places on the coast to sample Ireland's terrific craft beers – including those from breweries in Cork, Armagh and Donegal as well as the

local Lacada brewery. On Wednesdays there's an acoustic session at 9pm, on Fridays live music and guest beers, and at 4.30pm on Sundays, it's the superb "Brews and Blues" session.

Neptune & Prawn 54 Kerr St, http://ramorerestaurant. com/restaurant/neptuneandprawn. The best of the bunch of restaurants clustered around the harbour, this is arguably more style than substance (and children are not allowed) – lots of white wood panelling and bare brick walls, and

picture windows showing off the harbour – but the largely Asian-tinged food is worth a punt – try the Portrush lobster with special fried rice and coconut sauce. The upstairs cocktail bar, meanwhile, is frequented by an altogether glitzier crowd. Closed Mon & Tues. **£££**

Springhill Bar 17 Causeway St, 028 7082 3361. Lively locals' bar located just off the main strip, with a traditional session every Thursday from 9.30pm, plus open mike sessions on Wednesdays.

14

Northern County Derry

West of Portrush the A2 continues to hug the coastline as it traverses the northern part of County Derry, taking in marvellous beaches all the way from **Portstewart**, near which it crosses the River Bann, to **Magilligan Point**. On the way there are impressive seascapes visible from the cliff-top **Mussenden Temple** and stunning views from the land around **Mount Binevenagh**.

Portstewart

Derry's largest coastal resort, **PORTSTEWART**, like its near neighbour Portrush, is full of Victorian boarding houses. Of the two, Portstewart is decidedly more sedate and has always had more airs and graces: the train station is said to have been built away from the town centre to stop hoi polloi from coming. In terms of sheer location, though, Portstewart wins hands down.

Portstewart Strand

Cars March–June & Sept £4.50, July & Aug charge, free to NT members

Just west of the town is the National Trust-owned **Portstewart Strand**, a glorious, 3km stretch of sand firm enough to drive on – which the locals delight in doing – with some of the best **surfing** in the country. It's a grand place, too, if you hit fine weather and feel like getting out your bucket and spade. The best way to take the sea air is the bracing **cliff-side walk**, which runs between the beach and the town, passing battlements and an imposing Gothic mansion, now a Dominican college.

ARRIVAL AND DEPARTURE

PORTSTEWART

By bus There are regular buses between Portstewart and Portrush (Mon–Sat every 30min, Sun 5; 15min).

ACCOMMODATION

Cul-Erg House 9 Hillside, http://culerg.co.uk. Just a couple of minutes from the strand, this large Victorian guesthouse offers fourteen rooms – mostly ensuite and some with sea views – a daytime eatery for snacks and lunches, and a private kitchen for guests. **££**

Juniper Hill Caravan Park 70 Ballyreagh Rd, 028 7083 2023. Space for caravans and camping about 1.5km down

the A2 towards Portrush. Closed Nov–March. **£**

Rick's Causeway Coast 4 Victoria Terrace (IHH), 028 7083 3789. Well-run hostel with rooms sleeping between two and six (some en suite) that's also handy for the many cafés, bars and restaurants on the nearby seafront. Price includes breakfast. **£**

EATING AND DRINKING

Amici Ristorante Portmore Rd, http://amiciportstewart. co.uk. Transformed from an old golf clubhouse, this is one of the most scenically sited of all the north-coast restaurants. You can keep it simple, with the likes of pulled pork burger and loaded fries, or plump for more sophisticated dishes

such as fresh goat's cheese, honey and walnut ravioli. **£££**

★ **Harry's Shack** The Strand, 028 7083 1783. Boasting an unbeatable beachside location, a beautifully styled interior – raw wood tables and big bay windows – and exquisite food, *Harry's* ticks all the boxes. Starters might be smoked mackerel fish cakes or shoreline mussels in cider with sourdough, while main course favourites include hake or plaice fresh from Greencastle in Donegal; alternatively, make for the canopied terrace where cheery staff dispense coffees and ice creams from a little wooden cabin. **£££**

Warke's Deli 1 Carrig na cule, 028 7083 3388. Tucked away at the northern end of the promenade away from the general hubbub, this super little deli quietly goes about its business offering the likes of pancakes with bacon and maple syrup for breakfast and warm goat's cheese salad for lunch.

Hezlett House

Mussenden Rd • April to mid-Sept daily 10am–5pm; mid-Sept to March Sat & Sun 11am–5pm • charge, includes Mussenden Temple (see page 492) • http://nationaltrust.org.uk

Lying 11km west of Coleraine along the A2, at the Castlerock crossroads, is **Hezlett House**, built in 1690. The house is a fine example of cruck-truss construction, an early method of prefabricated building using wooden frames filled with clay and rubble that was common in England but is enough of a rarity here to warrant preservation by the National Trust. The last owner of the house is buried in the graveyard at Downhill (see below), where his gravestone quaintly bears both his own version of the spelling of his name and that of his father, a Mr Hazlett.

Downhill Palace

Mussenden Rd, Castlerock • Daily dawn–dusk • Free

Ornate gates alongside the A2 mark the main entrance to the ruins of **Downhill Palace**, built in the 1780s by **Frederick Augustus Hervey**, Anglican Bishop of Derry and fourth Earl of Bristol. Hervey was an enthusiastic grand traveller (all the many Hotel Bristols throughout Europe are named after him), and was also an art collector and sportsman, once organizing a preprandial race between Anglican and Presbyterian clergy along the local strand. His palace, accessed through pleasant **gardens**, was last occupied by US troops, billeted here during World War II, and was dismantled on their departure.

Mussenden Temple

Mussenden Rd, Castlerock • Call 028 7084 8728 for opening times • charge, includes admission to Hezlett House • http://nationaltrust.org.uk

Across fields at the back of Downhill Palace is the diminutive **Mussenden Temple**, which clings precariously to the eroding cliff-edge and offers stunning sea views. Its classic domed **rotunda** was apparently modelled on the Temple of Vesta in Rome and was built by Hervey in honour of his cousin Mrs Frideswide Mussenden, who died aged 22 before it was completed, after which it was used as a summer library. Later, with characteristic generosity and a fairly startling lack of prejudice, Hervey allowed a weekly Mass to be celebrated in the temple, as there was no local Catholic church. The inscription on the temple **frieze** translates rather smugly as: "It is agreeable to watch, from land, someone else involved in a great struggle while winds whip up the waves out at sea." Overlooked by Mussenden Temple on the cliff-edge above is the enormously long **Downhill beach**, which is accessible by car. From Downhill Palace it's possible to take the Bishop's Road (constructed at Hervey's bidding) southwards to reach **Mount Binevenagh** and its fabulous viewpoints.

Limavady and around

LIMAVADY was once a major settlement, its old site lying 3km further south down the valley of the River Roe. The town was refounded as Newtown Limavady in the early seventeenth century by Thomas Phillips, speaker of the Irish House of Commons. It still possesses a few features of its illustrious past: the six-arch **bridge** spanning the river was built in 1700, and Main Street, which runs down from it, is still recognizably Georgian. In early July, Limavady hosts the three-day **Stendhal Festival** (http://

DANNY BOY

The lyrics for the quintessential "Oirish" ballad **Danny Boy** were actually composed by an English lawyer, Fred E. Weatherley, in 1912 and, a year later, fitted to *The Londonderry Air*, a tune collected by Jane Ross, a resident of 51 Main St, Limavady, from a travelling fiddler in 1851. The song achieved renown in Ireland when recorded in the 1930s by Margaret Burke-Sheridan and has since seen many other tear-jerking renditions (Sinéad O'Connor recorded an idiosyncratically spine-tingling version); it still remains endearingly popular with dewy-eyed expats and Irish-Americans. Limavady holds the annual **Danny Boy Jazz and Blues festival** in June, featuring a variety of music.

14

stendhalfestival.com), one of Ireland's finest small music festivals, while in late October, there's the lively **Roe Valley Folk Festival** (http://roevalleyarts.com). June, meanwhile, sees the town host the annual **Danny Boy Jazz and Blues Festival** (see box).

Roe Valley Country Park

41 Dogleap Rd, 3km south of Limavady • **Visitor centre** April–Sept daily 9am–6pm; Oct–March Sun noon–4pm • Free • **Museum** April, May & Sept Sat & Sun 1–4.45pm; June–Aug daily 1–4.45pm • Free • 028 7772 2074

The **Roe Valley Country Park** preserves Northern Ireland's first hydroelectric power station, opened in 1896, with much of the original equipment intact and viewable, as well as a **visitor centre** and the **Green Lane Museum**. This focuses on the area's history, including its erstwhile importance in linen production, and features craft displays on Saturdays (2–4pm).

ARRIVAL AND INFORMATION

LIMAVADY AND AROUND

By bus Limavady Buscentre is northeast of town, just off Main St.

Destinations Castlerock (Mon–Sat 6–10 daily; 45min); Derry (Mon–Sat every 30min, Sun 4; 40–55min); Dungiven (Mon–Fri 5 daily; 35min).

Tourist information Roe Valley Arts Centre, 24 Main St (Mon–Fri 9.30am–5pm, Sat 10am–1pm; http://roevalleyarts.com).

Derry

DERRY, which lies at the foot of Lough Foyle, is a crossroads city in more ways than one: roads from all cardinal points arrive here, but it was also a major point of emigration from the eighteenth century onwards, an exodus that reached tumultuous proportions during the Great Famine. Derry is the fourth-largest city in Ireland and the second biggest in the North, but it has a markedly different atmosphere from Belfast, being two-thirds **Catholic**. While roads into the city are signposted in Irish welcoming visitors to Derry, the city still appears as "**Londonderry**" on many road maps and signs, a preference adhered to by the British government, Unionists and television news bulletins. It is referred to by the press and broadcast media as "Derry-Londonderry", a tactful placating of both Nationalist and Unionist.

Approached from the east in winter twilight or under a strong summer sun, the city presents a beguiling picture, with the vista of the **River Foyle** and the rise of the city's two hillsides, terraced with pastel-shaded houses and topped by the hueless stone spires of the ever-present religious denominations. With its rich history, Derry has a clutch of worthwhile attractions, mostly enclosed within the seventeenth-century **walls**, themselves the most significant reminder of the city's past.

Brief history

Though **St Columba** established a monastery here in 546 AD, the development of Derry (originally called Doire Calgaigh, "oakwood of Calgach", after a legendary warrior) only really began in medieval times, when in the fourteenth century it was granted to the Anglo-Norman de Burgos. By 1500, the power of the O'Dohertys had spread from Inishowen and they constructed a tower house, which was later absorbed into the seventeenth-century walls.

Towards the end of the sixteenth century the uprising of Hugh O'Neill, Earl of Tyrone, provoked an English invasion. Doire's strategic position on the River Foyle was quickly appreciated, though it took some years for it finally to be captured. In 1600, the English commander **Sir Henry Docwra** began fortifying the remains of the medieval town as a base for incursions against the Irish, but in 1608 Sir Cahir O'Doherty rebelled against Docwra's successor, Pawlett, and burnt Doire, by now anglicized as Derry, to the ground. This destruction made the city ripe for the plantation of English and Scottish settlers, and the financial assistance of the wealthy businessmen of the City of London was obtained to achieve this. A new walled city was constructed and

14

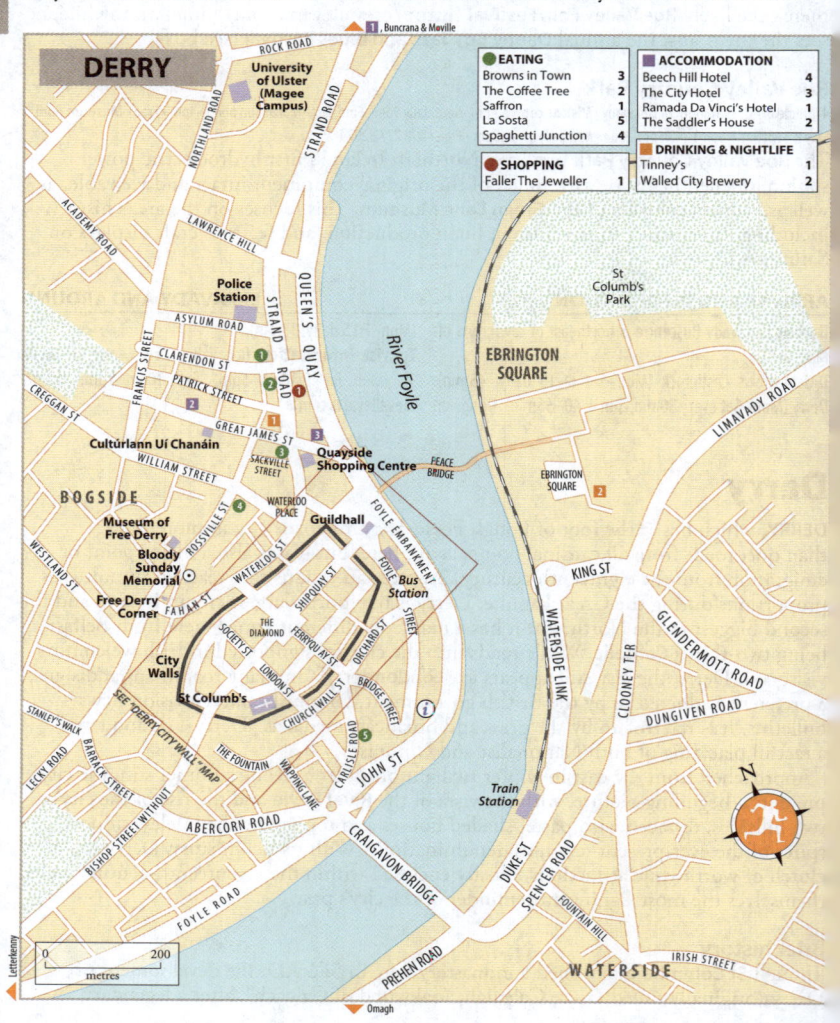

renamed **Londonderry** in 1613 in honour of its backers, the Twelve Companies of the Corporation of London.

The seventeenth century was the most dramatic phase of Derry's evolution, culminating in the **siege** of 1688–89 (see page 498). Following this, many Derry people emigrated to America to avoid harsh English laws, and some of their descendants, such as the pioneer frontiersman Daniel Boone, achieved fame there. Derry's heyday as a **seaport** came in the nineteenth century, a period when industries such as shirt-making began to flourish – by the beginning of the twentieth century the city was the largest shirt-manufacturer in the UK. However, after **Partition**, the North–South dividing line lay just over 3km from Derry's back door, and the consequent tariffs reduced much of its traditional trade. The shirt industry began its long decline, finally being phased out in the face of much cheaper imports from Asia.

Though Derry remained relatively peaceful after Partition, its politics were among the North's most blatantly discriminatory, with the substantial Catholic majority denied its civil rights by gerrymandering geared towards ensuring the Protestant minority's control of local institutions. In October 1968 Derry witnessed a two-thousand-strong **civil rights march**. Confronted by the batons of the Protestant police force and the notorious B Specials, rioting spilled over into the Catholic Bogside district and over eighty people were injured. The clash is seen by many as the catalyst for the modern phase of the Troubles: faith in the impartiality of the Royal Ulster Constabulary was destroyed once and for all, and the IRA was reborn a year or so later. The following year's Protestant **Apprentice Boys' march** (see page 498) was another significant step, and, on January 30, 1972, came **Bloody Sunday** (see page 500).

These days Derry is a quite different place. Its stint as the UK's City of Culture in 2013 was the catalyst for a major facelift, which included the renovation and repackaging of much of the city's built heritage. Meanwhile, one of the legacies of the peace process has led to the opening of the spectacular **Peace Bridge**. More recently, Channel 4's hugely successful, and very funny, programme, *Derry Girls*, has introduced the city to a whole new audience.

Peace Bridge and Ebrington Square

Forming a graceful arc across the River Foyle, the **Peace Bridge**, which opened in 2011, represents a symbolic, curvilinear-shaped handshake between the city's largely Protestant east bank and the overwhelmingly Catholic west bank – a new landmark that has helped rebalance the communities, meaning that the Foyle is no longer seen as a religious divide. Popular with walkers, joggers and cyclists, the bridge links the city centre with **Ebrington Square**, a redeveloped military parade ground that is now a thriving cultural hub, home to all kinds of restaurants and bars, and a venue for open-air concerts. It will also be home to a new Maritime Museum, possibly as early as 2026.

The Guildhall

Guildhall Square • Mon–Fri 9am–8pm, Sat & Sun til 6pm • Free • http://guildhallderry.com

Just outside the city walls stands the neo-Gothic **Guildhall**, whose largely ecclesiastical appearance belies its function as the place where the political parties hold their monthly meetings. Inside, you can nose around the main hall, with its elaborate ceilings, baronial wood panelling and magnificent organ (there are free, weekly recitals throughout August), while the city's history is depicted in a series of beautifully restored stained-glass windows. On the ground floor, a permanent **exhibition** tells with flair and imagination the story of the Plantation of Ulster and the building of the walls; here, too, on the ground floor is a Carrara marble statue of Queen Victoria, minus her hands, which were blown off when the Guildhall was bombed by the IRA in 1972. The terrace at the very agreeable *Guild Café* offers fine views of the Peace Bridge, while the main hall makes for an atmospheric venue for the many gigs take place here.

The medieval walls and within

Derry's centre, focused on its **medieval walls**, is remarkably compact, and it's easy to combine all the main attractions in one circuit. The walls are one of the best-preserved defences in Europe. Spanning 1.6km in length and as high as a two-storey house in places, they are reinforced by bulwarks and bastions and a parapeted earth rampart as wide as any thoroughfare. Within their circuit, the original medieval street-pattern has remained, with four **gateways** surviving from the original construction, albeit in slightly revised form.

The Tower Museum

Union Hall Place • Daily 9am–5.30pm • charge • http://towermuseumcollections.com

A reconstruction of the medieval O'Doherty Tower houses the **Tower Museum**, whose two permanent exhibitions are very worthwhile. The first of these recounts the **history of Derry** in easy to follow chronological fashion, from the Plantation period and the Siege (including the original effigy template of Robert Lundy), through to the Troubles, which is, inevitably, the section in which most visitors linger longest – on display are uniforms of the British army and the Royal Ulster Constabulary, as well as IRA combat jackets and balaclavas, canisters and bullet casings, and a piece of stained glass window from the Guildhall, when it was bombed in 1972.

The second exhibition focuses on the *La Trinidad Valencera*, from the **Spanish Armada**, which sank in Kinnegoe Bay (off Inishowen) in 1588, but was only discovered in 1971. Among the extraordinary, and extraordinarily well preserved, treasures brought to the surface were fragments of clothing, pewter dishes, a pair of exquisite salt cellars, and some finely worked jewellery; most impressive of all, however, is the ship's cannon.

St Columb's Cathedral

17 London St • April–June & Sept Wed–Sat 10am–3pm; July & Aug Mon–Sat 10am–4pm • suggested donation • http://stcolumbscathedral.org

Occupying the southwestern corner of the walled city, the Church of Ireland **St Columb's Cathedral** was built in 1633 in a style later called Planters' Gothic and was the first post-Reformation cathedral in the British Isles. Displayed in the entrance porch is a cannon shell catapulted into the church during the 1688–89 blockade by the besieging army – their terms of surrender were attached. The cathedral was used as a battery during the siege, its **tower** serving as a lookout post; today it provides the best view of the old city. The present **spire** dates from the late Georgian period, its lead-covered wooden predecessor having been stripped to fashion bullets and cannon shot during the siege.

Inside, an open-timbered **roof** rests on sixteen stone corbels carved with figures of past bishops. Other things to look out for are the finely sculpted stone reredos behind the altar, the eighteenth-century bishop's throne and the window panels showing scenes as diverse as the relief of the city on August 12, 1689, and St Columba's mission to Britain. In the **chapterhouse museum** are more relics of the siege, including the padlocks and keys used to lock the city gates, plus the grand kidney-shaped desk of the eighteenth-century philosopher George Berkeley, erstwhile dean of the cathedral (who only visited Derry once), and mementos of Cecil Frances (1818–95), wife of Bishop Alexander and composer of the famous hymns *Once in Royal David's City* and *There is a Green Hill Far Away*.

The Courthouse and The Fountain

Close to Bishop's Gate stands the **courthouse**, built of white sandstone from Dungiven in crude Greek-Revival style. The gate itself was remodelled for the first centenary of the siege and reopened in 1789. Immediately outside the walls here is **The Fountain** area, named after the freshwater source that once supplied the city, though few

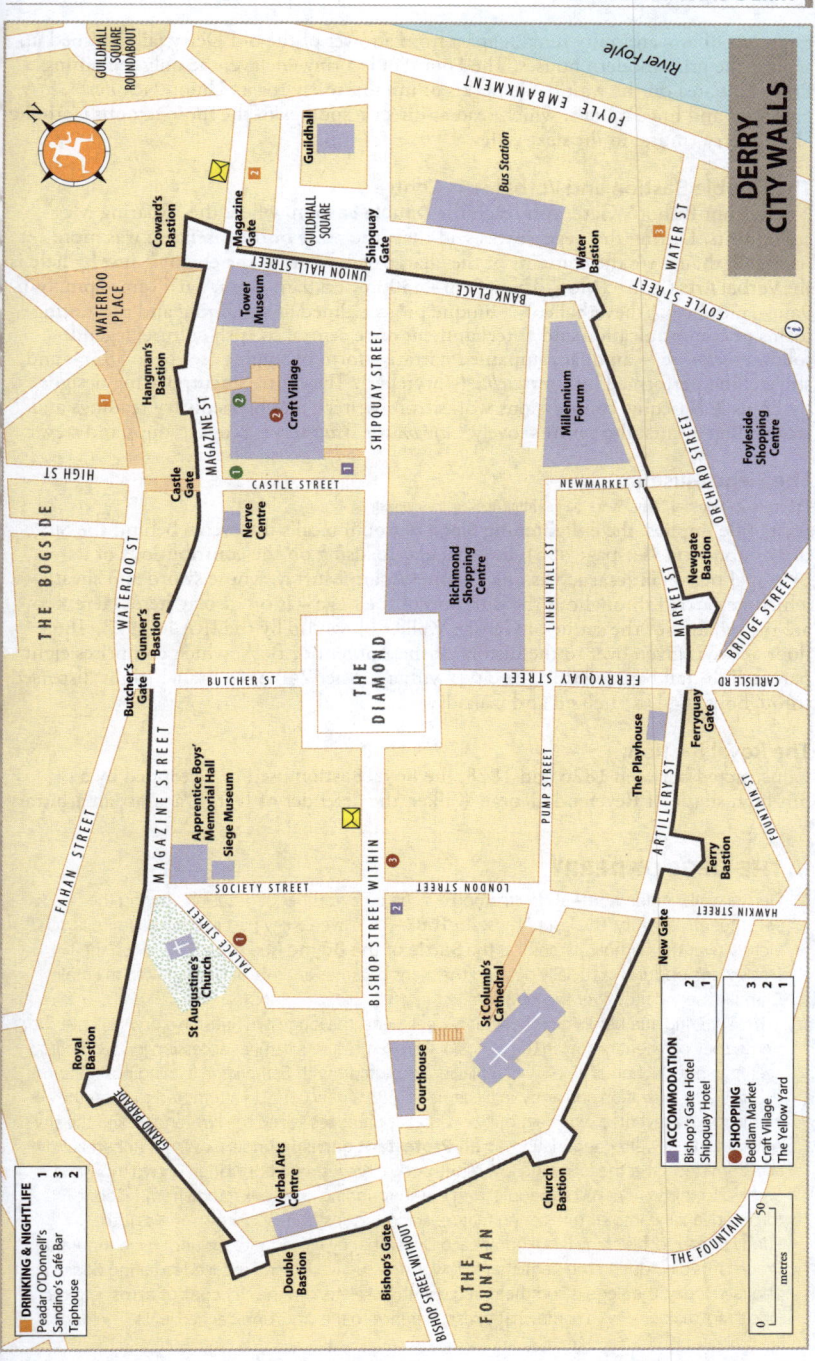

14

DERRY CITY WALLS

River Foyle

FOYLE EMBANKMENT

GUILDHALL SQUARE ROUNDABOUT

Guildhall

GUILDHALL SQUARE

Magazine Gate

Coward's Bastion

WATERLOO PLACE

Tower Museum

Hangman's Bastion

MAGAZINE ST

Castle Gate

CASTLE STREET

Nerve Centre

Craft Village

Shipquay Gate

UNION HALL STREET

SHIPQUAY STREET

Water Bastion

BANK PLACE

WATER ST

FOYLE STREET

Bus Station

Foyleside Shopping Centre

ORCHARD STREET

Millennium Forum

NEWMARKET ST

Richmond Shopping Centre

LINEN HALL ST

Newgate Bastion

MARKET ST

BRIDGE STREET

HIGH ST

THE BOGSIDE

WATERLOO ST

Gunner's Bastion

Butcher's Gate

BUTCHER ST

THE DIAMOND

FERRYQUAY STREET

Ferryquay Gate

CARLISLE RD

FAHAN STREET

MAGAZINE STREET

Apprentice Boys' Memorial Hall

Siege Museum

SOCIETY STREET

BISHOP STREET WITHIN

PUMP STREET

The Playhouse

ARTILLERY ST

Ferry Bastion

FOUNTAIN ST

St Augustine's Church

PALACE STREET

LONDON STREET

HAWKIN STREET

New Gate

Royal Bastion

GRAND PARADE

Courthouse

St Columb's Cathedral

Verbal Arts Centre

Double Bastion

Bishop's Gate

BISHOP STREET WITHOUT

THE FOUNTAIN

Church Bastion

THE FOUNTAIN

0   50
metres

DRINKING & NIGHTLIFE
Peadar O'Donnell's	1
Sandino's Café Bar	3
Taphouse	2

ACCOMMODATION
Bishop's Gate Hotel	2
Shipquay Hotel	1

SHOPPING
Bedlam Market	3
Craft Village	2
The Yellow Yard	1

remnants of any antiquity remain apart from a tower of the old Derry jail, jammed up against the grim modern houses. The Fountain is a tiny enclave, the only remaining Protestant area on the west bank, and is of interest solely for its Union Jack kerb paintings and huge **murals**, which read as direct responses to the more famous Catholic "Free Derry" mural in the next valley.

The Double Bastion and Verbal Arts Centre

North from Bishop's Gate, you reach the **Double Bastion**, where the "Roaring Meg" cannon sits. During the siege, it was said that "the noise of the discharge was more terrifying than were the contents of the charge dangerous to the enemy". Just by here is the **Verbal Arts Centre** (Mon–Thurs 9am–5.30pm, Fri 9am–4pm, Sat 11am–2pm, Sun 9am–1pm; http://theverbal.co), a unique project aimed at sustaining and promoting forms of communication and entertainment once central to Irish culture: legend, folklore, *sean-nós* – an unaccompanied narrative form of singing (see page 583) – and storytelling performed by a *seanachie* (storyteller). The centre, incorporating designs by Louis le Brocquy, commissions works from writers, and hosts poetry readings and storytelling events; the centre's lovely *Café on the Walls* serves scones, soups and stews.

The Siege Museum

13 Society St • Mon–Sat 10am–5pm • charge • http://thesiegemuseum.org

As its title implies, the enlightening **Siege Museum** recalls the events behind the Siege of Londonderry (see page 498), in particular focusing on the contributions of its principal personalities, such as one Colonel Adam Murray, whose sword and sheath – which he carried throughout the duration of the siege – is on display here. Here, too, are the remains of the statue of George Walker blown up by the IRA in 1973. The floor above is given over to the history of the Apprentice Boys, which comprises eight parent clubs (all based within the city), with a further 240 or so branch clubs dispersed throughout the UK, Ireland and Canada.

The Royal Bastion

Constructed between 1826 and 1828, the **Royal Bastion** used to be topped by a 3m-high statue of Reverend George Walker, the defender of Derry "against an arbitrary

---

THE SIEGE OF DERRY

Derry's walls underwent – and withstood – siege on a number of occasions during the seventeenth century. The last of these, in **1688–89**, played a key part in the Williamite army's victory over the Catholic James II at the **Battle of the Boyne** (see page 563), when the Derrymen's obduracy crucially delayed the plans of James and his ally Louis XIV to maintain Catholic ascendancy over the kingdom.

The suffering and heroism of the fifteen-week siege, the longest in British history, still have the immediacy of recent history in the minds of Derry Protestants. James's accession in 1685 had seen the introduction of a policy of replacing Protestants with Catholics in leading positions in the Irish administration and army. In December 1688, a new garrison attempted to enter the city, but was prevented when a group of young apprentices seized the keys and locked the city's gates. Eventually, after negotiation, an **all-Protestant garrison** under Governor Robert Lundy was admitted. Over the following few months the city's resident population of two thousand swelled to thirty thousand as people from the surrounding area took refuge from Jacobite forces advancing into Ulster. Fearing that resistance against the Jacobite army was futile, Lundy departed; his effigy is still burnt each December by Protestants. Around seven thousand Protestants died during the siege that followed, the survivors being reduced to eating dogs, cats and rats. Today, the siege is commemorated with a skeleton on the city **coat of arms**, and the lyrical tag "maiden city", a somewhat sexist reference to the city's unbreached walls.

BOGSIDE MURALS

Spanning much of the length of Rossville Street is an eye-catching panorama of twelve **murals** – collectively entitled the **People's Gallery** – painted between 1994 and 2006 by Bogside artists Kevin Hasson, Tom Kelly and William Kelly. One, a gable-end mural, shows the former Independent Republican MP and one of the organizers of the People's Democracy movement, Bernadette Devlin, megaphone in hand, in front of the old "You are now entering Free Derry" mural. Nearby, and perhaps the most affecting mural, is the "**Death of Innocence**", which commemorates a 14-year-old girl, Annette McGavigan, who died in 1971, caught in crossfire between the British Army and IRA. Just around the corner, on Westland Street, another mural depicts those killed on Bloody Sunday. There are also striking murals featuring a gas-mask-clad petrol bomber and a British soldier smashing down a door with a sledgehammer during Operation Motorman (see page 500).

14

and bigoted monarch" (to quote the still-legible inscription); the statue was blown up by the IRA in 1973. The Bastion and surrounding area remains the focal point for the annual Relief of Londonderry parade every August 12 when the Apprentice Boys march in their predecessors', and Walker's, memory. The view from here across the Bogside district is expansive.

The Bogside

In the valley below the northern city walls is the Catholic **Bogside** district where, at the start of the Troubles, ferocious rioting took place following the Apprentice Boys' march, with the army and police responding to bricks and petrol bombs with tear gas, rubber bullets and careering Saracen armoured cars. The area at the foot of the escarpment used to be full of streets of compact terraced housing, but was redeveloped in the 1960s in the form of a dual carriageway, an estate of tenement flats and empty concrete precincts. Clinging to the opposite hillside, and in stark contrast, are early twentieth-century terraces of stucco façades, blue tile roofs and red chimney stacks.

The Museum of Free Derry

55 Glenfada Park, off Rossville St • Mon–Sat 10am–4pm, plus May–Sept Thurs til 6pm, Sun 10am–4pm • charge • http://museumoffreederry.org

Brilliantly conceived from an old block of flats that had long gone to rack and ruin is the superb **Museum of Free Derry**. Inside, bare concrete walls provide a suitably chilly backdrop to the history of the Bogside. Following coverage of Ireland's civil rights heritage, the focus turns to the Battle of the Bogside of August 1969, with a selection of items, including flags, rubber bullets and canisters, and (now colourfully decorated) metal bin lids that were used to signal an impending army raid.

The greater part of the museum is given over to events surrounding Bloody Sunday (see page 500). With live British Army radio commentary playing in the background, the exhibits on show are truly sobering, and include the banner carried on the anti-internment march that day, blood-soaked and bullet-pierced items of clothing of some of the victims (for example the jacket belonging to Michael McDaid, bullet hole clearly visible in the back – above this is a photo of him just moments before being shot), and the blood-soaked handkerchief waved by priest Edward Daly, as recalled in the iconic piece of television footage (and photograph) of him escorting a group carrying the mortally-wounded Jackie Duddy. Back outside, and to the rear of the museum, is a glass-encased section of bullet-riddled wall.

ARRIVAL AND DEPARTURE   **DERRY CITY**

By plane The tiny City of Derry Airport (http://cityofderry   airport.com) is 11km northeast of town on the A2 road. It's

14

connected by Ulsterbus services #44, #143 and #234 to the train station and Foyle St bus station. A taxi from the airport to the city centre costs around £15.

By train Derry's train station is in the Waterside district on the east bank, from where it's a 15min walk to the town centre across the Craigavon Bridge, or there's a free shuttle bus service (Mon–Sat), which drops you in Foyle St.

Destinations Belfast (Mon–Sat hourly, Sun 6; 2hr); Coleraine (Mon–Sat hourly, Sun 6; 35min).

By bus The central bus station on Foyle St is served by Ulsterbus for all the main Northern Ireland destinations and Bus Éireann (information from Ulsterbus), which operates buses to Dublin, Donegal town, Galway and Sligo. In addition, Foyle Coaches (http://northwestbusways.ie) run services across the border into Donegal, with buses

departing from Patrick St, while McGonagle Bus and Coach Hire (http://mcgonaglebushire.com) operates a service between Derry (Guildhall) and Buncrana (Main St).

Destinations Belfast (every 30min; 1hr 50min); Buncrana (McGonagle: Mon–Fri 7 daily, Sat 5, Sun 2; 35min); Carndonagh (Foyle Coaches: Mon–Sat 3–4 daily; 45min); Culdaff (Foyle Coaches: Mon–Fri 2 daily, Sat 1; 55min); Donegal town (Bus Éireann: 6–8 daily; 1hr 25min); Dublin (Bus Éireann: 11 daily; 4hr); Greencastle (Foyle Coaches: Mon–Sat 4 daily; 1hr); Letterkenny (Bus Éireann: every 1–2hr; 40min); Monaghan (Bus Éireann: 11 daily; 1hr 50min); Moville (Foyle Coaches: Mon–Sat 5 daily; 40min); Omagh (Mon–Sat hourly, Sun 7; 1hr 5min); Sligo (Bus Éireann: 5–7 daily; 2hr 40min).

GETTING AROUND AND INFORMATION

By taxi Taxis wait on Foyle St and William St, or call Delta Cabs (028 7127 9999) or the Derry Taxi Association (028 7126 0247).

Tourist office 1–3 Waterloo Place (Mon–Fri 9am–

6pm, Sat & Sun 10am–5pm; http://visitderry.com). As well as furnishing you with stacks of info, they offer an accommodation booking service, left luggage facility (£6/day) and phone charging.

TOURS

Walking tours The well-established and hugely popular Martin McCrossan city walking tours take in a full circuit of the city walls, leaving from the tourist office (10am, noon, 2pm & 4pm; £6; http://derrycitytours.com), plus

other tours like a Derry Girls Tour and a Food Tour. Departing from the Guildhall, Bogside History Tours (daily 11am & 1pm; £10; http://bogsidehistorytours.com) take in the politics and murals of the area.

ACCOMMODATION
SEE MAPS PAGES 494 AND 497

Although Derry has plenty of upper-end **accommodation**, finding a more economically priced room in the centre can

be difficult, especially in high season and at weekends.

★ **Beech Hill Hotel** 32 Ardmore Rd, 4km southeast of

BLOODY SUNDAY

For the first two years of the Troubles, the part of the Catholic Bogside area beyond the original "Free Derry" mural was a notorious no-go area, the undisputed preserve of the IRA, its boundary marked by a gravestone-like monument declaring: "You are now entering free Derry". This autonomy lasted until 1972, when the British army launched **Operation Motorman**; the IRA men who had been in the area were tipped off, though, and got across the border before the invasion took place.

To the right of the "Bernadette Devlin" mural in the Bogside stands a **memorial pillar** to the thirteen Catholic civilians killed by British paratroopers (a fourteenth died later of his wounds) on "**Bloody Sunday**", January 30, 1972, in the aftermath of a civil-rights demonstration. The soldiers immediately claimed they had been fired upon, an assertion later disproved, though some witnesses came forward to report seeing IRA men there with their guns. The bitter memory of the subsequent Widgery Commission's failure to declare anyone responsible for the deaths festered in Catholic Derry, and pressure was maintained on successive governments to reopen investigations. In 1999, after years of mounting demands for a full examination, the British government established the **Saville Inquiry**, which conducted its proceedings in Derry's Guildhall until moving to Westminster in 2002. It finally reported in June 2010, concluding that the British Army's actions were "unjustified and unjustifiable", that all those killed or wounded were innocent victims and that some soldiers had committed perjury in giving their evidence. However, no single member of the British Army has ever been prosecuted.

the city centre, http://beech-hill.com. In a wonderfully tranquil setting away from the centre, *Beech Hill* is a graceful eighteenth-century country house that has hosted many of the world's top politicians, actors and musicians in its time. Rooms are impeccable, as is the service, while the hotel's fascinating museum room documents the exploits of the United States Marine corps who were stationed here during World War II. **£££**

★ **Bishop's Gate Hotel** 24 Bishop St, http://bishopsgate hoteldery.com. From the original revolving wooden doors and the magnificent sweeping staircase above reception, it's pretty obvious that this Edwardian hotel – an erstwhile gentleman's club – is something special. The thirty-one rooms don't disappoint either, coloured dove grey and orange, sage green, and plum, with oak writing desks and antique phones, and beautifully tiled-bathrooms with enormous rain showers; once settled in, pop down to the gorgeous *Wig & Gown* champagne bar for a drink or two. The cooked-to-order breakfast is nigh on perfect. **£££**

The City Hotel 14–18 Queens Quay, http://cityhoteldery. com. A prominent building overlooking the Foyle, this

fashionable hotel offers spacious rooms furnished in a warm, contemporary style, and all the leisure facilities imaginable. **££**

Ramada Da Vinci's Hotel 15 Culmore Rd, http://davincis hotel.com. This impressively modish hotel offers a wide range of crisply furnished rooms, while its small coterie of lively bars means that you can forego the rather dull traipse into town. **££**

The Saddler's House 36 Great James St, http:// thesaddlershouse.com. Stylish, period-furnished Victorian town house B&B with seven tidy rooms, either double or twins, in a fairly peaceful spot very near the city centre. Guests are encouraged to avail themselves of the lounge, while breakfast is taken around a large, communal table. Closed Jan & Feb. **££**

Shipquay Hotel 15–17 Shipquay St, http://shipquayhotel. com. After the *Bishop's Gate*, this is the city's classiest outfit, a superbly renovated former bank building with 21 modestly sized but exquisitely appointed rooms, some adorned with prints by Irish artist Terry Bradley. Superior rooms, which cost around £40 more, have river views. **£££**

EATING
SEE MAP PAGE 494

Derry's eating options are vastly improved these days, with a core selection of accomplished establishments to choose from; for more high-end stuff, head for the smarter hotel restaurants. And if you're here on the first Saturday of each month, make for the **Walled City Market** in Guildhall Square, where you can partake in some fabulous local produce and delicious street food.

Browns in Town 23 Strand Rd, http://brownsintown.com. A sleek candlelit city-centre restaurant that showcases the likes of Greencastle seabass and squid, as well as Donegal crab, turf smoked beef, lamb and duck, while for veggies and vegans there is, commendably, a dedicated menu. The three-course early bird (5–6.30pm) is excellent value at £30. **£**

★ **The Coffee Tree** 49 Strand Rd, 07472 466414. Despite its rather anonymous location, this good-looking, cheerfully staffed café is one heck of a popular place, and rightly so. Plonk yourself down on one of the deep leather sofas and enjoy a steaming bowl of yellow split pea soup with sweet potato and a hunk of doughy bread, or a gooey chocolate

brownie with a cup of coffee. Closed Sat & Sun. **£**

Saffron 2 Clarendon St, http://saffronderry.co.uk. The city's longest-established Indian restaurant is still the best, offering a well-priced menu with tandoori dishes and Punjabi cuisine a speciality. Takeaways too.

La Sosta 45a Carlisle Rd, http://lasostaderry.com. Secreted away in a rather unprepossessing location, this longstanding, family-run establishment is deservedly a locals' favourite. The Italian-inspired food is as authentic as you could wish for, with the likes of fillet of rigatoni with pancetta, vodka, tomato sauce and cream, and pea and lemon zest risotto with mint and mascarpone; the wine card is of a similarly high order. Closed Sun & Mon. **£££**

Spaghetti Junction 46 William St, http://spaghetti junctionderry.com. The clue's in the name, though there's far more to this fun, wildly colourful *trattoria* than mere spaghetti: how about monkfish risotto or black penne with squid and pistachio cream sauce, washed down, naturally, with a bottle of Peroni? There's live music at weekends too. Closed Sun. **£££**

DRINKING AND NIGHTLIFE
SEE MAPS PAGES 494 AND 497

Peadar O'Donnell's 59 Waterloo St, 028 7126 7295. In the same family since 1847, *Peadar's* and the attached *Gweedore Bar* are at the social and musical centre of the city – there's traditional music every night in the former while its neighbour is more DJ-centric with music on Fridays and Saturdays.

Sandino's Café Bar Water St, http://sandinoscafebar. com. Despite its somewhat dishevelled exterior, this is Derry's hippest hangout, featuring a variety of live music in its back bar and club room; the place, incidentally, is named

after a Nicaraguan revolutionary

Taphouse 5 Guildhall St, 028 7136 4888. Cool, contemporary bar with a darkened interior sprinkled with fairy lights and a long bar stocking some of the best ales in town, including Brewdog from Scotland and a selection from the Derry-based Dopey Dick brewery; soak it all up with a house steak sandwich, or, on Thursdays, a curry. Tuesday is games night while Wednesdays are reserved for trad music.

Tinney's 3–4 Patrick St, 028 7136 2091. One of the best

14

places for traditional music with a regular Tues night session. You can also get the lowdown here on "the bars", which is how local news and gossip is referred to in Derry.

★ **Walled City Brewery** 70 Ebrington Square, http://walledcitybrewery.com. Adding a welcome dollop of colour to the city's east side, this erstwhile medical centre in the centre of the old barracks quarter has been superbly repurposed as a craft brewery, the first in Derry for more than a century. Beers are brewed on site and there are typically ten or so on the go at any one time, which you can enjoy with *pinxtos* (Basque-style tapas), such as gazpacho or smoked mackerel, or more substantial fillers like house smoked braised beer pork. It also hosts its own Gin & Tonic festival at the beginning of June.

ENTERTAINMENT

Cultúrlann Uí Chanáin 37 Great James St, http://culturlann.org. Dedicated to the promotion of the Irish language, arts and culture and hosts occasional events, such as traditional music concerts.

Millennium Forum Newmarket St, http://millennium forum.co.uk. This huge theatre offers a broad if somewhat middle-of-the-road programme, including well-known ballets and opera.

Nerve Centre 7–8 Magazine St, http://nervecentre.org. The main focus of Derry's dynamic cultural world, the Nerve Centre contains sound, film and video studios and editing suites, an art-house cinema, two music venues, a bar and café; it stages regular screenings of left-field films.

The Playhouse Artillery St, http://derryplayhouse.co.uk. A more innovative range of theatre, dance and comedy is on the bill at The Playhouse.

Waterside Theatre Glendermott Rd, http://waterside theatreni.com. Across the river and dishing up a mixed bag of a programme, ranging from classic drama to local versions of TV game shows.

SHOPPING
SEE MAPS PAGES 494 AND 497

Bedlam Market 20 Bishop St, 028 7136 4613. Up to fifteen traders operate in an eclectic maze of rooms brimful of vintage clothes, holistic treatments, antiques and everything retro imaginable. Mon–Sat 10am–5.30pm.

Craft Village Shipquay St, http://derrycraftvillage.com. A wonderful array of craft and artisan producers come together in this collective that has re-created life between the sixteenth and nineteenth centuries. You'll find tweeds and knitwear, exquisite jewellery and glass, soaps and candles and secondhand books. Closed Sun.

Faller The Jeweller 12 Strand Rd, http://faller.com. Look out for the golden teapot that hangs outside the shop and discharges a plume of environmentally friendly smoke from its spout. Inside you can buy a selection of brooches and charms from their "Drop of Derry" range, which reflects the city's culture. Closed Sun.

★ **The Yellow Yard** 2 Palace St. Housed within an old shirt factory, Yellow Yard is a quartet of local enterprises namely a bookstore, record shop, gift shop and café, the latter making for a relaxing pit stop after a lengthy browse around the shops. Look out for the occasional Sunday flea market held in the yard outside.

DIRECTORY

Hospital Accident and emergency department, Altnagelvin Hospital, Glenshane Rd (028 7134 5171); call this number also for dental emergencies after working hours or at weekends.

Police The main police station is located on Strand Rd (028 7136 7337).

Post Office 3 Custom House St (Mon & Wed–Fri 9am–5.30pm, Tues 9.30am–5.30pm, Sat 9am–12.30pm).

DERRY'S FESTIVALS

Derry is awash with great festivals. In early March, a week-long **drama festival** is held at the Waterside Theatre (see below) while early May sees the five-day **Jazz and Big Band Festival** (http://cityofderryjazzfestival.com) come to town, the biggest and most prestigious jazz festival outside of Cork. In late June, the **Celtronic Dance Music Festival** (http://celtronicfestival.com) takes over various venues across the city, while the second week of August witnesses the **Maiden City Festival** – a four-day programme of dance, theatre and music organized by the Apprentice Boys of Derry, culminating in the Relief of Londonderry parade (see page 499). The **Big Tickle Comedy Festival** occupies eleven days in early September, followed by the long-running **Foyle Film Festival** in November (http://foylefilmfestival.org). Finally, there's the mammoth **Halloween Carnival**, - reputedly Europe's largest – five days of mayhem culminating in a massive costume parade and spectacular fireworks display on October 31.

Southern County Derry

The Derry–Antrim A6 road follows a river valley through fertile farmland then ascends to the Glenshane Pass on the northeastern fringe of the **Sperrin Mountains**. Southeast from here are Magherafelt and Moneymore, two attractive and entirely **planned towns**, the latter adjacent to the grand Plantation manor house of **Springhill**. The huge expanse of Ireland's biggest lake, **Lough Neagh**, laps against the county's southeastern corner, which is where you'll also find the village of **Bellaghy**, a place of pilgrimage for fans of Seamus Heaney.

14

The plantation towns and around

Southeast of Dungiven and over the Glenshane Pass on the way to the northern tip of Lough Neagh, it is worth making a detour to see some examples of town planning – the **plantation towns** of the London companies, most of them characteristically focused around a central Diamond. One example is **Magherafelt**, granted to the Salters' Company by James I, which has a wide, sloping main street and makes a reasonable base for exploring the lough and the Bellaghy area. **Moneymore**, about 8km further south, was originally constructed by the Drapers in the early seventeenth century (and restored by them in 1817), and was the first town in the North to have piped water – amazingly enough, as early as 1615.

Springhill

20 Springhill Rd, around 1.5km outside Moneymore off the B18 • **House** April, May, Sept & Oct Sat & Sun noon–4pm; June Sat & Sun 11am–5pm; July & Aug daily noon–4pm, • **Grounds** Daily 10am–5pm • charge • http://nationaltrust.org.uk/springhill

Springhill is a grand Plantation manor house built between 1680 and 1700 by William "Good Will" Conyngham in order to fulfil a marriage contract with the father of his bride-to-be, Anne Upton. Elegant both without and within, its sober whitewashed architecture houses fine rooms, equipped with original period furniture and paintings belonging to William and his descendants, who occupied the house until 1959. Upstairs, the **Blue Room** is said to be haunted by the ghost of Olivia Lenox-Conyngham, whose husband George was found shot here in 1816. Outside, the stables house a **costume collection**, which adopts a specific theme each year, drawing upon three thousand items collected from the mid-seventeenth century to the 1970s. There are delightful **gardens**, a tower dating from the 1730s, which was probably originally part of a windmill, and a pleasant walk through beech and yew trees.

ARRIVAL AND INFORMATION

By bus Buses run from Magherafelt to Bellaghy (Mon–Sat 5–8 daily; 15min) and Moneymore (Mon–Fri 10 daily, Sat 3; 15min). From Moneymore, buses run to Magherafelt (Mon–

THE PLANTATION TOWNS AND AROUND

Sat 6 daily; 15min).
Tourist information The Bridewell, 6 Church St (Mon–Fri 9.30am–5.30pm, Sat till 5pm; http://visitmidulster.com).

ACCOMMODATION AND EATING

Church Street Brasserie 23 Church St, Magherafelt, http://churchstreetbrasserie.co.uk. Church-style furnishings (pointy, high-backed chairs) and crisply laid tables await at this classy establishment just across the road from *Laurel Villa*. The menu runs the gamut from smoked trout and crab with apple and cucumber (£7.50) to fennel seed and maple glazed barbary duck breast, all of it beautifully executed, and there's a very creditable wine menu too. Closed Mon, ££

Laurel Villa 60 Church St, Magherafelt, http://laurel-villa.com. A graceful Victorian town house with four elegantly furnished, personality-packed rooms, each named after a poet, namely Kavanagh, Longley, MacNeice and, of course, Heaney, whose gorgeous little attic room features framed versions of his best-known work. Indeed, as an expert in all things Heaney, the owner organizes tours of Heaney country as well as an annual festival in Sept. ££

Lough Neagh

East of Magherafelt and Moneymore are the fish-filled waters of the biggest lake in Ireland, **Lough Neagh**. Tributaries flow from every point of the compass: the Lower Bann, which drains the lake and runs north to **Lough Beg** (finally reaching the sea north of Coleraine), contains some huge trout, including the dollaghan, unique to these waters. Similar to salmon (which are also common), dollaghan grow by three pounds every year and can be caught by spinning, worming and fly-fishing: the Ballinderry Black and the Bann Olive are famous flies derived from this region. The best fishing is from mid-July to October, but you will need a Fisheries Conservation Board Rod **licence**, available from tourist offices; they can also prove information on day-tickets for fishing and specialist boat-trips, which are issued and run by the Lough Neagh Angling Association.

14

Bellaghy

Like many of the plantation settlements in the area, **BELLAGHY**, just west of Lough Beg, has a history that reflects the divisions between communities. Indeed, two of the ten 1981 hunger strikers (see page 572) – cousins Francis Hughes and Thomas McElwee – came from the village, and Orange parades have been a regular flashpoint.

Bellaghy Bawn
20 Castle St · Easter–Sept Sun noon–4pm · Free · 028 9082 3207

Bellaghy is neatly laid out around a T-junction, and wandering south past the whitewashed terraces on Castle Street leads to one of the best surviving examples of a Plantation castle, **Bellaghy Bawn**, built in 1618 by the Vintners' Company. Most of its fortifications were lost in 1641, but it still retains a striking circular flanker tower which has been well restored. Inside you'll find fascinating interpretive **displays** explaining the 7000-year-old history of the settlements in this area, the construction of the village – today's houses still occupy the same original allocated plots of land – and the diverse ecology of the Lough Beg wetland area. It was here that Seamus Heaney's father rented grazing rights on the strand at Lough Beg; in his poem *Ancestral Photograph*, Heaney recalls helping to herd the cattle that grazed there down Castle Street on their way to market.

Lough Beg and Church Island

You can see the shimmering Lough Beg from the windows of the Bawn's flanker tower, and a stroll down to the lake is well worthwhile. In summer, its waters recede and **Church Island** becomes accessible from the shore. Besides a walled graveyard, you'll find the ruins of a medieval church here, said to have been founded centuries before by the ubiquitous St Patrick, with a tower and spire added in 1788 by the eccentric Frederick Augustus Hervey (see page 492) to improve his view from Ballyscullion House on the mainland nearby. He commissioned Charles Lanyon to build a huge replacement for the original house which stood here with, apparently, 365 windows, but died abroad before ever moving in, and the building subsequently fell into ruin.

Seamus Heaney HomePlace
45 Main St · Mon–Sat 10am–5pm, Sun 1–5pm · charge · http://seamusheaneyhome.com

Whether you're a fan of Seamus Heaney or not, the **Seamus Heaney HomePlace** is well worth an hour of your time, reflecting as it does on the extraordinary life and works of one of the world's greatest contemporary poets. Housed within the village's old police station, now sporting a handsome stone and wood clad exterior, the exhibition is split into two parts: on the ground floor, "People and Place" documents the poet's prodigious output, with Heaney himself reciting many of his poems; this section is augmented by handful of personal belongings, like his school bag and a duffel coat, as well as some beautiful, mostly family-oriented, photographs. Upstairs, "Imagination and Inspiration" dwells on some of the many objects that fired Heaney's imagination, for example a fireman's helmet from Boston (*Helmet*), an anvil (*The Forge*), and a turf spade (*Digging: Death of a Naturalist*). Here, too, is a mock up of his Dublin attic study, with a collection of his books and manuscripts, and footage of him receiving the

SEAMUS HEANEY (1939–2013)

It's impossible to conceive of a contemporary poet, Irish or otherwise, whose works are more evocative of time and place than **Seamus Heaney** who, at the time of his death aged 74 on August 30, 2013, was arguably the best-known poet in the world. Heaney was born, the eldest of nine children, on the family farm of Mossbawn (itself the title of two poems in his fourth collection, *North*), in the townland of Tamniarn, near Castledawson, on April 13, 1939. Heaney's family background, his Catholic upbringing and his study of Irish at school imbued him with a strong sense of being Irish in a state that considered itself British, a paradox that would form a major motif in his work during the 1970s. While at Queen's University, Belfast, he was further influenced by the literature he discovered in Belfast's **Linen Hall library** (see page 450), especially the works of John Hewitt, the Antrim-born "Poet of the Glens", and the English "naturalist" poet Ted Hughes, in whose work he found an "association of sounds in print that connected with the world below".

Heaney's first poem, *Tractors*, was published in the *Belfast Evening Telegraph* in 1962. His first significant collection, *Death of a Naturalist*, followed in 1966 and was immediately recognized for its earthiness and command of diverse metrical forms. In the 1960s, while lecturing at Queen's, Heaney's career expanded into journalism and television and he became increasingly involved in the **civil rights movement**. His response to the Troubles saw him seeking for "images and symbols adequate to our predicament" and he began to see poetry as a mode of resistance. Eventually, though, the violence so disturbed him that he moved with his family to County Wicklow, prompting Ian Paisley's *Protestant Telegraph* to bid farewell to "the well-known papist propagandist" on his departure to his "spiritual home in the popish republic". While his 1970s collections *North* and *Field Work* had mixed receptions – some saw the strong influence of Robert Lowell on the former – Heaney found himself turning increasingly to his **Irish heritage** as a source of inspiration, particularly the long medieval poem *Buile Suibhne* (*The Madness of Sweeney*), and published his own *Sweeney Astray* collection in 1983. The following year's *Station Island* drew on his experiences as a participant in St Patrick's Purgatory (see page 415).

The hunger strikes of the early 1980s brought a new urgency to Northern politics and a revival of Heaney's polemicism. Prompted by the staging in Derry in 1980 of Brian Friel's play *Translations*, which showed English surveyors travelling through eighteenth-century Ireland anglicizing all the place names, Heaney co-founded the **Field Day Theatre Company** with Friel, his old friend and fellow academic Séamus Deane, the actor Stephen Rea and others. While the group's theatrical activities were themselves controversial, it was their publications that engendered the most antipathy. Their pamphlets were criticized as attempts to over-intellectualize the Troubles, and the 1991 *Field Day Anthology of Irish Writing* was decried for its under-representation of work by women writers, though a subsequent volume entirely devoted to them has since been published.

In 1995, Heaney's body of work was more widely recognized by the award of the **Nobel Prize for Literature**. His later works included a translation of the Anglo-Saxon epic poem *Beowulf*, his dramatic retelling of this tale of monster- and dragon-slaying managing to breathe new life into a work that was long considered too dense and metaphorical for a modern readership; his collection, *District and Circle*, which won the prestigious T.S. Eliot Prize for Poetry in 2006; and his twelfth and final collection, *Human Chain* (2010), which is overshadowed by ageing and mortality.

Nobel Peace Prize in 1995. Throughout the year there are special exhibitions, events, workshops and tours.

From the HomePlace, it's a ten-minute walk through the village to St Mary's church and Heaney's **grave**, tucked away in one corner of the graveyard and whose plain, grey headstone simply reads "Walk on air against your better judgement", a line from his poem *The Gravel Walks*.

ARRIVAL AND DEPARTURE   BELLAGHY

y bus Magherafelt (Mon–Sat 5–9 daily; 15min).

Down and Armagh

THE MOURNE MOUNTAINS

Down and Armagh

Counties Down and Armagh occupy the southeastern corner of Northern Ireland, between Belfast and the border, and contain some of the region's most attractive countryside, especially around the coast. You're also never far away from places associated with St Patrick, who sailed into Strangford Lough to make his final Irish landfall in County Down, founded his first bishopric at Armagh and is buried at either Downpatrick or Armagh, depending on whose claim you prefer.

Heading south from Belfast, the glowering **Mourne Mountains** increasingly dominate the panorama, and it's in this direction that most of the attractions lie. If you simply take the main roads in and out of Belfast – the A1 for Newry and the border, or the M1 motorway west – you'll come across very little to stop for: it's in the rural areas, the mountains and coast, that the charm of this region lies. One of the best options is to head east from Belfast around the Down shore – past the **Ulster Folk and Transport Museum**, one of the best in the North, and the blowsy suburban resort of **Bangor** into the **Ards Peninsula** or along the banks of **Strangford Lough**. Near the Lough's southern tip, **Downpatrick** is closely associated with the arrival of St Patrick. There are plenty of little beaches, early Christian sites, defensive tower houses and fine mansions to visit on the way towards **Newcastle**, the best base for excursions on foot into the Mourne Mountains. Beyond the Mournes a fine coast road curves around to **Carlingford Lough** and the border. Inland, **Hillsborough** resembling an English Cotswolds-style village, is closely linked to the political development of the North.

Below **Lough Neagh**, **Armagh city** is well worth visiting for its ancient associations, cathedrals and fine Georgian streets, while the nearby village of **Loughgall** is a popular stop off for those wishing to explore the region's strong Protestant links; moreover, **The Argory**, a fine stately home, lies close by. The villages of **South Armagh** – a predominantly Catholic area – were the heartland of violent Republicanism, and are still often referred to as "Bandit Country" or "The Killing Fields", even by locals. However, don't let that be a deterrant, the region possesses some startlingly attractive countryside, especially around the peak of **Slieve Gullion**, a short way south of **Newry**.

Hillsborough

Around 20km southwest of Belfast, the historic village of **HILLSBOROUGH** merits a quick detour, courtesy of its stately castle and chintzy ambience, which is reinforced by a sprinkling of tea rooms and antique shops lining the main street and its pleasing Georgian architecture. Indeed, it's one of the most sought-after places to live in Northern Ireland.

You get the best of Hillsborough by following a route that starts from the **war memorial** and heads up the magnificent approach to the eighteenth-century Gothic **parish church**. Bear right here for the main entrance to Hillsborough's elegant but ruined **fort**, constructed by Colonel Arthur Hill (after whom the village is named) in 1650 and remodelled in the eighteenth century as a venue for family feasts, weddings and entertainment. Beyond this, a deciduous **forest** opens up, curving around a **lake** stocked with brown and rainbow trout. Footpaths meander through the trees in all directions – a simple circuit of the lake takes around thirty minutes.

Highlights

The Ulster Folk and Transport Museum Possibly the best museum in Northern Ireland – it consummately encapsulates much of the North's cultural and industrial history. See page 513

Portaferry A superb waterside location, tremendous sunsets and the best base for exploring Strangford Lough and the Ards Peninsula. See page 517

The Mourne Mountains Brooding and dominating South Down, the Mournes offer magnificent walking, intoxicating views and total escape from the contemporary world. See page 525

Slieve Gullion Drive or hike to the top of this mountain and enjoy the panorama of the unmissable South Armagh countryside laid out below. See page 530

Armagh city Probably the most graceful city in the North, with two cathedrals and a captivating Mall. See page 532

The Argory A magnificent nineteenth-century mansion, set in gorgeous grounds and featuring one of the most illuminating guided tours in Ireland. See page 537

HIGHLIGHTS ARE MARKED ON THE MAP ON PAGE 510

Hillsborough Castle

The Square • castle tours charge; gardens free • http://hrp.org.uk/hillsborough-castle

Dominating the town is **Hillsborough Castle**, built in 1770 by Wills Hill, the first
Marquis of Downshire; indeed, the Hills were, at one stage, the largest landowners
in Ireland. From 1925, it was the residence of the governor of Northern Ireland, but
since 1973 – following the imposition of direct rule from London – it has been the
official residence of the British secretary of state for Northern Ireland. Hillsborough has

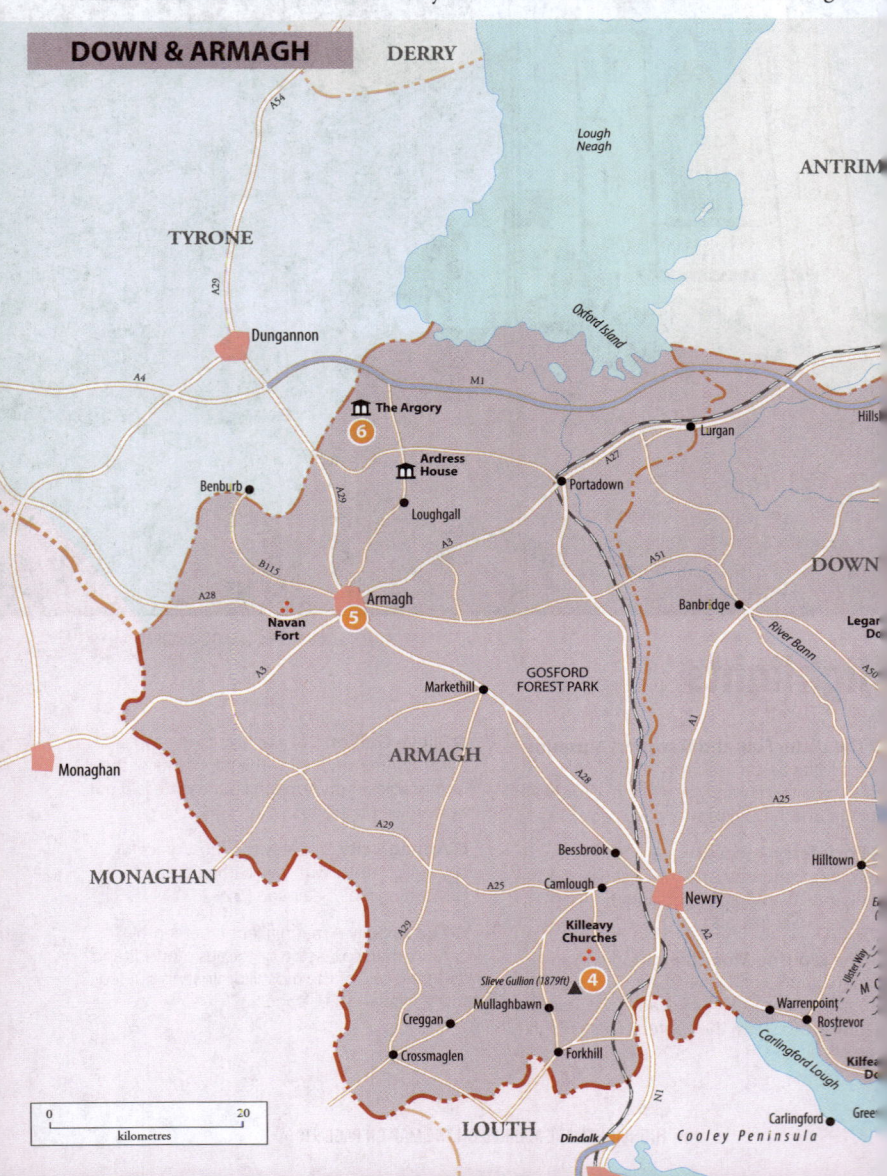

also played an important role in the peace process, for it was here that the **Anglo-Irish Agreement** was signed in 1985, while informal negotiations leading up to the Good Friday Agreement were also held here.

Guided **tours** of the interior take you through half a dozen or so rooms, including the State Drawing and Dining Rooms, replete with Georgian furniture and silver from HMS *Nelson*. Most rooms, too, have a smattering of important paintings from the Royal Galleries collection, including ones of Charles II, William of Orange and

James II, while there are photos galore of notable politicians, alongside snaps of visiting royalty. The **gardens**, meanwhile, are lovely, particularly in May and June when the many roses and Europe's largest rhododendron bush are in bloom. As part of a recent overhaul of Hillsborough, the walled garden has been sensitively reimagined, as it might have looked in the eighteenth-century, today stocked with blue nepeta, irises, and Espalier fruit trees (apple and pears) which crawl along the walls and are likely to have been planted up to a hundred years ago. There are several marked-out walks around the gardens, which take in numerous monuments, including the restored Lady Alice's Temple – given as a wedding gift to the daughter of the fourth Marquess of Downshire – the Quaker Burial Ground, Ice House and Cromlyn Ruin, a late eighteenth-century sham ruin of standing stone and lintel. Note that visits to the interior of the castle were not running at the time of writing.

ARRIVAL AND INFORMATION HILLSBOROUGH

By bus Buses from/to Belfast (Mon–Sat every 30min, Sun hourly; 25min) pull in at the War Memorial towards the bottom of Main St.

Tourist office The tourist office is housed in the elegant Georgian courthouse on The Square at the top of Main Street (Mon–Sat 9.30am–5.30pm, plus April–Sept Su 11am–4pm; http://visitlisburncastlereagh.com).

ACCOMMODATION AND EATING

Dunhill Cottage 47b Carnreagh, http://dunhillcottage. co.uk. A 10min walk from Hillsborough on the A1 Lisburn road, this ecofriendly guesthouse has six modern rooms in two buildings, all tidily furnished with marble tiling and walk-in showers. ££

Out of Habit 21 Lisburn St, 07803 795587/028 9268 8191. Easily recognizable by its sunflower-yellow stable door, this sweet little two-floored café-cum-art gallery serves up good, strong coffee, sandwiches, and a delectable array of tray bakes. Mon–Sat 8.30am–4pm.

The Plough Inn 3 The Square, http://ploughgroup.com Centuries-old coaching inn comprising a great-looking bistro and the retro-vibed *Vintage Rooms*, the former serving dishes such as pork belly with blue cheese sauce and truffle polenta chips, alongside posh burgers and gri dishes, the latter offering everything from breakfasts an tapas to tea trays for two.

East of Belfast

Heading east into County Down from Belfast, you've a choice of two routes: the A20, which heads due east past Stormont (see page 460) to **Newtownards**, at the head of Strangford Lough; or the A2, which heads northeast past the excellent **Ulster Folk and Transport Museum** to **Bangor**.

Scrabo Tower

16km east of Belfast on the A20 · Easter week, April–June & Sept daily 1–5pm; July & Aug daily 10am–5pm; Oct Sun noon–4pm · Free

Following the A20, the single interesting sight as you near Newtownards is **Scrabo Tower**, whose looming presence dominates the surrounding area. The tower protrude from the top of a rocky, gorse-strewn hump of a hill (a long-extinct volcano) – follow the signs to **Scrabo Country Park** and you'll arrive in the car park just below. The hill itself is pitted with quarries used to extract Scrabo stone, employed for all manner of local buildings. Built in 1857 as a memorial to the third Marquess of Londonderry, in recognition of his efforts for his tenants during the Great Famine, the tower looks like a monstrous rocket in its launcher, hewn out of rough black volcanic rock. The spot was originally a Bronze Age burial cairn, probably the resting place of one of the grand chieftains of the area, and there's evidence of a huge hill fort here, too. It's well worth ascending the 122 steps to the tower's top for the wonderful **views** across Strangford Lough and the healthy, blustery weather that often curls around the side of the hill.

Ulster Folk Museum and Ulster Transport Museum

11km east of Belfast on the A2 • Tues–Sun 10am–5pm March–Sept Thurs–Sun 10am–5pm; Oct–Feb Thurs & Fri 10am–4pm, Sat & Sun 11am–4pm • charge • http://ulsterfolkmuseum.org and http://ulstertransportmuseum.org • Train from Belfast Central to Cultra or bus #1 or #2 from Belfast's Laganside Buscentre (every 30min–1hr; 30min)

Two of the most fascinating museums in all of Ireland, the **Ulster Folk Museum and Ulster Transport Museum** comprises two distinct, and very large, sites straddling the A2: on one side of the road is the Folk Museum, and on the other, the Transport Museum – indeed, you'd do well to take a lengthy pause in between visiting each one.

Ulster Folk Museum

The **folk museum** is an open-air **village** where about thirty typical buildings from all over the North, some dating from the eighteenth century, have been taken from their original sites and rebuilt here, complete with authentic furnishings. Furthermore, many of them are "inhabited" by a member of staff, garbed in period costume and keen to offer information about the buildings and their origins.

Just beyond the entrance you enter **Ballycultra Town**, whose focal point is the Diamond, framed by an assortment of community buildings, such as the late eighteenth-century **Kilmore church** (moved here in 1976), a mid-nineteenth century courthouse from Cushendall, and the delightful **Gilford Picturehouse** from County Down, a silent cinema dating from the 1850s that functioned until 1929. Just beyond here is the old **rectory**, a thatched, two-storey dwelling where you can sample some soda bread baked on the open fire. More widely dispersed is **Discovery Farm,** a vast rural area of a dozen or so traditional farm dwellings, and other buildings used in light manufacture, with assorted livestock roaming between them. Farms range from the fairly luxurious – for example the handsomely furnished **Drumnahunshin Farm** from County Armagh – to the basic (but cosy), like the **Duncrun Cottier's House**. Don't miss the **Coalisland Spade Mill,** complete with a fine cast-iron wheel; inside, an illuminating exhibition reveals that during the nineteenth century there were more than sixty spade mills in Ulster, with more types of spade produced here than in any other European country – a fact possibly explained by the fact that a sixth of Ireland's land surface is bog, from where turf (peat) is dug.

15

Ulster Transport Museum

The superb **transport museum** packs in every conceivable form of transport, from horse-drawn carts to lifeboats and even a vertical take-off plane. First up is the **rail gallery**, featuring a stellar cast of locomotives arranged around an original turntable, the pick of which is **Old Maeve**, the largest loco ever built in Ireland. Highlights from the remarkable **road transport gallery** include a Belfast Telegraph van from 1952 and, from the late nineteenth century, a wonderfully old-fashioned ice-cream van and a Giant's Causeway tram, the first tram system in the world to be operated by hydro-electricity. Below here, in the voluminous **car gallery**, is a Model T Ford, a Sunbeam that won the 1924 Spanish Grand Prix, and a DeLorean sports car (of *Back to the Future* fame) from the infamously defunct factory.

As a fascinating aside, the **Titanica** exhibition documents the origin and fate of the *Titanic* as well as of her sister ships, *Olympic* and *Britannic*, built by the Harland and Wolff shipyard and collectively known as *Olympic*-class (see page 454). Inevitably the focus is on the *Titanic* itself, with a stack of artefacts salvaged from the wreck, including part of a porthole, a soup tureen and a launch ticket among other poignant items. Also on this site is a miniature railway that runs on summer Saturdays. You'd be wise to bring a picnic, but if you haven't, there are **tea rooms** on both sites.

Crawfordsburn Country Park

Bridge Road South, Helen's Bay • Daily: March, April & Oct 9am–7pm; May–Sept–Oct 9am–9pm; Nov–Feb 9am–4.30pm; Visitor Centre daily 10am–4pm • Free • http://discovernorthernireland.com

The short stretch of coast east from Helen's Bay is part of the **Crawfordsburn Country Park**, an estate handed down from the Scottish Presbyterian Crawford family, then acquired by Lord Dufferin (whose mother Helen gave her name to the bay) and which is now in public hands. Its glens and dells are replete with beeches, cypresses, exotic conifers, cedars, the usual burst of rhododendrons and also a Californian giant redwood, but the park's best features are the wild-flower meadow and the woodland planted with native species. From the visitor centre, there are three delightful **trails**: the Glen trail (45min), the Meadow trail (1hr 15min) – part of which skirts **Crawfordsburn beach** – and the Coastal trail (2hr), which heads down to **Helen's Bay beach** and then onto Grey Point Fort.

Grey Point Fort

The Fort, Bangor • April to mid-Sept daily 10am–5pm; mid-Sept to March Sat & Sun 10am–4pm • Free • 023 9082 3207

From Crawfordsburn Country Park, the path to **Grey Point Fort** leads through the best of the woodland, under a fine nineteenth-century railway viaduct and up to a waterfall at the head of the glen and thence to the bay. Positioned to command the mouth of Belfast Lough, along with its sister fort at Kilroot on the other side, Grey Point has an impressive battery of gun emplacements, ready to challenge the shipping that entered the lough during the two world wars. In the event, the two six-inch breech-loading guns were never fired except in practice (local residents had to be warned to open their windows and doors to prevent blast damage), apart from one occasion in World War II, when a merchant ship failed to respond to the signal "heave to or be sunk" and received a warning shot across its bows. The guns were sold for scrap in 1957 when the Coast Artillery was disbanded. After the fort was opened to the public in 1987, an identical six-inch gun was relocated here from the prison on Spike Island in Cork harbour. There's also a selection of photos showing the original guns and their positions; but it's really as a **viewpoint** that the fort is worth a visit for nowadays.

Bangor and around

With a curving bay set between a pair of symmetrical headlands, **BANGOR**'s sheltered position made it ideal for exploitation as a holiday resort. The town has been hugely popular with Belfast people since the railway came in the 1860s, but today it's as much a suburb of Belfast as a holiday spot. Still, it's well worth a visit for its renovated waterfront, while inland, the superb little museum and walled garden – inside the old castle grounds – make for a most enjoyable hour or two. If you're here in August it's well worth seeking out what's on as part of the **Open House Festival** (http://openhousefestival.com), an inspired, month-long programme of music, art and culinary happenings taking place in locations all over town, and the suburbs.

North Down Museum

Town Hall, Castle Park Ave • Tues–Sat 10am–4pm, Sun noon–4pm • Free • http://andculture.org.uk

Bangor's period of greatest historical significance was almost entirely associated with its **abbey**, which was founded by St Comgall in 586 AD, and from which missionaries set forth to convert pagan Europe. Though the abbey remained powerful for eight hundred years, there's not a trace of the building left. The only vestige of its fame is the *Antiphonarium Benchorense*, one of the oldest-known ecclesiastical manuscripts, consisting of collects, anthems and some religious poems; the original now lies in the Ambrosian Library in Milan, but you can view a facsimile of it in the **North Down Museum**, tucked away in the old stables of Bangor Castle. Other displays trace the rise of the Ward family (see page 522), who were largely responsible for the town's development and who built the castle.

Best of all are the archaeological discoveries, notably the Ballycroghan swords, three superb bronze weapons dating from 500 AD, and the ninth-century Bangor Bell, a splendid one-piece casting which was retrieved from a local graveyard in 1780. On a more recent note, there's a lovely little exhibition on the history of local cinematography and, more specifically, the once beautiful Art Deco Toni cinema, which stood on Hamilton Road; once the hub of Bangor's social scene – it also functioned as a ballroom – the cinema's last screening was in 1983 before it burnt down in 1992.

Bangor Castle Walled Garden

Castle Park • April, May, Sept & Oct daily 10am–6pm; June–Aug Mon–Thurs 10am–8pm, Fri–Sun 10am–6pm; Nov–March daily 10am–3pm • Free • 028 9127 1200

A short walk from the North Down Museum, through the tree-laden Ward Park, you'll come to the delightful **Bangor Castle Walled Garden**. Originally the site of a Victorian walled garden, which supplied the castle kitchen with vegetable, fruits and herbs, the garden fell into disrepair after World War I, before it quite spectacular renovation around fifteen years ago. Hidden beyond a 4m-high redbrick wall, the garden is divided into quadrants, namely, the flower garden, the herb and topiary garden, kitchen garden and damp garden; separating these are neatly gravelled avenues with fragrant, rose-covered arches, while a beautifully sculpted fountain stands as the garden's central feature. On a warm summer's day, it's a wonderful spot to rest up, and there's a café on-site too.

Somme Museum

233 Bangor Rd, 8km south of Bangor on the A21 • Visits by guided tour, see website for specific days and times • charge • http://sommeasscoiation.com

The **Somme Museum** features re-created front-line trenches staffed by guides in battledress who provide a sobering and moving account of the role of the Irish and Ulster divisions in the futile World War I battle that took place in July 1916 – 5500 men of the 36th (Ulster) Division alone were reported dead, wounded or missing in only the first two days. The Battle of the Somme itself is brought to life courtesy of an unusually informative audiovisual presentation.

ARRIVAL AND DEPARTURE · BANGOR AND AROUND

By train The train station is at the top of Main St, which itself leads down to the waterfront.
Destinations Belfast (Mon–Sat every 15–30min, Sun hourly; 30–40min).

By bus The bus station is adjacent to the train station.
Destinations Belfast (Mon–Sat every 20–30min, Sun 5; 50min); Newtownards (Mon–Sat every 30min, Sun 7; 20min).

INFORMATION AND ACTIVITIES

Tourist office Down by the marina in the Tower House at 34 Quay St (Mon–Fri 9.15am–5pm, Sat 10am–4pm Jun–Aug til 5pm); http://visitardsandnorthdown.com).
Fishing and boat trips Bangor Boats (07510 006 000) runs family-friendly, deep-sea fishing trips from the harbour (July & Aug daily 9.15am & 6.30pm; June, Sept & Oct call for times; £20), and short boat trips (July & Aug 2pm; £5) around the bay from the Pickie Fun Park.

ACCOMMODATION

★ **Cairn Bay Lodge** 278 Seacliff Rd, http://cairnbaylodge.com. Charming, family-run guesthouse with eight beautifully finished rooms, all quite distinct from one another, and some of which have stunning bay views. The gourmet breakfast is reason alone to pitch up here: smoked salmon omelette with rocket and lemon crème fraiche, or crab with scrambled eggs and chilli jam are just two of the possibilities. **££**

The Nines 10–12 Seacliff Rd, http://theninesbangor.com. By far the most attractive of an otherwise unappealing cluster of hotels down by the marina, this new kid on the block has a fabulous suite of beautifully appointed rooms, some with sea views. The restaurant serves up excellent bar standards alongside more quality offerings like slow cooked lamb shank, pea, shallot and wild garlic fricassee, while a drink in the cool cocktail bar should round things off quite nicely. **£££**

Old Inn Main St, Crawfordsburn, 4km west of Bangor, http://theoldinn.com. This rambling, centuries-old inn is where CS Lewis honeymooned with his wife, Joy Gresham, in 1958. Little has changed since that time, it would seem, though that's no bad thing; the individually designed rooms, variously sporting oak beamed ceilings, wood-panelled walls and sumptuous fabrics, are run through with character. **££**

15

EATING AND DRINKING

Blu BBQ 52 High St, http://blubbq.co.uk. Authentic wood-smoked barbecued meats from the grill, including beef ribs and peppered burger with sautéed mushrooms, make this a tempting possibility for dinner; the decor is muted and the atmosphere pleasingly informal, though better still is the roof terrace. BYO too. Closed Sun & Mon. £££

Jamaica Inn 188 Seacliff Rd, http://thejamaicainn.co.uk. In a fantastic location overlooking the bay, this warm and lively inn is by far the best spot in Bangor for a good night out, with live music (folk, rock, bluegrass) several nights a week and a rollickingly good pub quiz on Tues.

The Starfish 278 Seacliff Rd, http://cairnbaylodge.com. As warm and welcoming as the guesthouse it's housed in, the super daytime café – park yourself outside on the summery terrace – offers up a wicked section of breakfast and brunches (chilli eggs, steak burger), though most punters make a trip here to inspect the awesome crabs benedict.

Strangford Lough

15

Ancient annals record that **Strangford Lough** was formed around 1650 BC by the sea sweeping in over the lands of Brena. This created a beautiful, calm inlet, the archipelago-like pieces of land along its inner arm fringed with brown and yellow bladderwrack and tangleweed, and tenanted by a rich gathering of bird life during the warmer months and vast flocks of geese and waders in the winter.

Travelling the scenic **western shore** is enjoyable in itself, but there are a couple of spots worth making for, the first of which is **Castle Espie Wildfowl and Wetland Centre**, from where narrow roads wind down to **Mahee Island**. From here, back on the road along the lough, follow the signs to Ardmillan, Killinchy and then Whiterock to reach **Sketrick Island**. The tiny coves and inlets at the feet of little drumlins continue as far as Killyleagh, almost any of them worth exploring. The **eastern edge** of Strangford Lough is not as indented as its opposite shore but betters it in having a major road (the continuation of the A20) that runs close to the water virtually all the way down. Also, the scenery is delightful, and there's the engrossing **Mount Stewart** house and gardens to stop off en route to **Portaferry**.

Mount Stewart House and Garden

8km southeast of Newtownards • Gardens daily: March–Oct 10am–5pm; Nov–Feb 10am–4pm; house daily April–Oct 11am–5pm; Nov–March 11am–4pm • charge • http://nationaltrust.org.uk/mount-stewart • Bus #9 and #10 (Mon–Sat 9 daily, Sun 2) from Belfast's Laganside Buscentre

Pressed up hard against the shore road is **Mount Stewart House and Gardens**, the ancestral home of the Londonderry family. Leading protagonists of the Protestant Ascendancy, its members included Lord Castlereagh, who was Foreign Secretary under Pitt the Younger and is best remembered for guiding the Act of Union into operation.

The gardens

The undoubted highlight of the estate is the 98 acres of **gardens**, laid out by Edith, Lady Londonderry, wife of the seventh marquess, in the 1920s – and a thorough job she made of it: among others, there are **Spanish** and **Italian** gardens, a **Sunk Garden**, and the **Shamrock Garden** (with a topiary harp and an appropriately leaved Red Hand of Ulster). The trees and shrubs here are no more than seventy to eighty years old, but they've grown at such a remarkable rate that they look twice that. The principal reason for this is the unusually warm and humid microclimate: the gardens catch the east-coast sun, causing a heavy overnight dew, and the Gulf Stream washes the shores only a stone's throw away. Despite the northerly latitude, conditions here rival those of Cornwall and Devon. Amid all this lush greenery, look out for the **Dodo terrace** which flaunts various bits of giant statuary, including the eponymous bird alongside lizards, griffins and the like. There are numerous marked **trails**, too, ranging from just under 1km to 3km.

The house

The **house** itself is certainly worth viewing, with guided tours (every 15min) in the morning, and a free-flow system in place from 1pm. Among the splendid (and occasionally eccentric) furniture inside is a set of 22 Empire chairs used by the delegates to the Congress of Vienna in 1815, who included the Duke of Wellington and Talleyrand; the chairs were a gift to Castlereagh's brother Lord Stewart, another high-ranking diplomat of the time. The Continental connection is flaunted further in bedrooms named after various historically important cities: Rome, St Petersburg, Madrid, Moscow and Sebastopol (from the time of the Crimean War). The house contains a number of **paintings**, particularly portraits of Castlereagh's political contemporaries, but the most notable and largest is **Rubbing Down** (1799) by George Stubbs, showing the celebrated thoroughbred, *Hambletonian*, being rubbed down after a victory at Newmarket. Continuing the horsey theme, in the dazzling silver collection, look out for a pair of hooves (which have been fashioned into inkwells) that belonged to Fighting Charlie, winner of the 1965 Ascot Gold Cup and ridden by the great Lester Piggott.

15

Portaferry

Portaferry, at the mouth of the lough, is a pretty spot from which to admire the marvellous **sunset** looking across the "Narrows" to Strangford, a view enhanced by a ten-minute climb to the stump of the old windmill just behind the town. It's quite likely that you'll wind up here, as it's the departure point for ferries across to Strangford and the Lescale Peninsula.

Exploris Aquarium

Castle St • Daily 10am–5pm (last admission 4pm) • charge • http://explorisni.com

Portaferry's principal attraction is the **Exploris** aquarium, featuring the North's only **seal sanctuary**, where they've been rescuing and rehabilitating common and grey seal pups for nearly thirty years. Much better than your average aquarium, it has bright, well-kept tanks containing native and tropical fish, alongside menacing black-tip and white-tip reef sharks, an otter enclosure and a reptile room. The aquarium also has a "touch tank" for lots of hands-on fun, plus daily feeding sessions for otters and seals, and various talks.

ARRIVAL AND INFORMATION

PORTAFERRY

By bus Buses depart from the main square. **Destinations** Belfast (Mon–Sat 3 daily; 1hr 25min); Newtownards (Mon–Sat every 30min–1hr, Sun 4; 50min–1hr 10min).
By ferry Regular ferries make the 5min ride across the

lips of the lough to Strangford (every 30min, Mon–Fri 7.45am–10.45pm, Sat 8.15am–11.15pm, Sun 9.45am–10.45pm; http://nidirect.gov.uk; £1.30 single, £2.60 return; car £7.70 single, £13.30 return).

ACCOMMODATION AND EATING

Fiddlers Green 10 Church St, http://fiddlersgreen portaferry.com. You can't miss the turquoise-green painted exterior of this erstwhile grocery store – or one of the 'Game of Thrones' doors (see page 481) – now a convivial hostelry, with sing-along folk sessions and traditional music on Fri and Sat, plus quiz night on Thurs.
Portaferry Hotel 10 The Strand, http://theportnicom.

This distinctive all-white building right by the ferry harbours fourteen decent, high-ceilinged rooms with antique furnishings and smart sash windows; there's a £20 supplement for lough-facing rooms. At the hotel's restaurant or bar (they serve the same menu), you can feast on the likes of Strangford Lough mussels in garlic, or smoked haddock chowder. **££**

Ballyquintin Point and Kearney

The coast road south of Portaferry leads to **Ballyquintin Point** and, on the way, passes the entrance lane to **St Cowey's Wells**, where the faithful optimist is spoilt for choice:

there's a drinking well, a wishing well and a well for bathing sore eyes. Look out for the rock nearby – the indentations are supposed to mark the places where the saint's hands and feet rested as he prayed. Northeast from here **KEARNEY** is a charming seaside village, consisting almost entirely of whitewashed cottages and now mostly owned by the National Trust. You can walk from here to **Kearney Point**, an often blustery ten-minute stroll with panoramic views across the Irish Sea.

Castle Espie Wildfowl and Wetland Centre

78 Ballydrain Rd • Daily 10am–5pm • charge • http://wwt.org.uk/wetland-centres/castle-espie

At the **Castle Espie Wildfowl and Wetland Centre**, admission earnings are ploughed back into conserving the wetlands area for the seven thousand birds that visit it as well as the resident population of waterfowl, including the largest gathering of ducks, geese and swans in Ireland; the outdoor duckery is not to be missed, particularly in summer when the new hatchlings arrive. Part of the wetlands site was formerly a brick and lime works, and the old kiln here has been superbly converted into the **Limekiln Observatory**, now the centre's principal birdwatching spot. The centre also has a coffee shop and art gallery and hosts numerous events throughout the year, related both to ornithology and arts and crafts, as well as plenty of activities for children, including a climbing wall in the Limestone Pavilion nearby.

Mahee Island

Visitor Centre Easter–Sept daily 10am–6pm; Oct–Easter Sun noon–4pm • Free • 028 9182 6846

Mahee Island, named after St Mochaoi, supposedly the first abbot of the island, is reached via a twisting lane and several causeways. Heading past the crumbling remains of sixteenth-century Mahee Castle at the entrance to the island, and over the final causeway, you come to the Celtic **Nendrum Monastic Site**, a few hundred yards further on. It's a marvellously isolated spot, surrounded on three sides by water. Annals and excavations indicate that a sizeable community lived here from the seventh century onwards, but the remaining ruins probably date from the twelfth century at the very earliest. It was clearly a substantial establishment, with church, round tower, school and living quarters all housed in a cashel of three concentric wards. Today, the inner wall shelters the ruined church, and a reconstructed sundial uses some of the original remnants. There's an illuminating reconstruction map at the site and a helpful visitor centre.

The Lecale region

Jutting into the southern reach of Strangford Lough, the **Lecale Peninsula** is above all **St Patrick** country. Ireland's patron saint was a Roman Briton, first carried off as a youth from somewhere near Carlisle in northern England by Irish raiders. He spent six years in slavery in Ireland before escaping home again and, at the age of 30, decided to return to Ireland as a bishop, to spread Christianity. Christianity had already reached Ireland a while earlier, probably through traders and other slaves, and, indeed, St Patrick was not in fact the first bishop of Ireland, but he remains easily the most famous. He arrived in Ireland this second time, according to his biographer Muirchú (also his erstwhile captor, converted), on the shores of the Lecale region, and his first Irish sermon was preached at **Saul** in 432. Today the region commemorates the association with sites at Struell Wells and Saul, as well as at **Downpatrick**.

A great way to see the region is to tackle the **Lecale Way**, a 75km waymarked walking tour of the peninsula starting in Downpatrick and running to Strangford and thence around the coast to Killough and onwards to Newcastle – maps are available from the Downpatrick tourist office (see page 521).

Downpatrick

DOWNPATRICK, 37km south of Belfast, is a pleasant enough place of little more than ten thousand people, and its compact size and the proximity of some rich and well-preserved historical sites make for an easy and worthwhile day's visit.

The **Hill of Down**, at the north of the town, was once a rise of great strategic worth, fought over long before the arrival of St Patrick made it famous. A **Celtic fort** of mammoth proportions was built here and was called first Arús Cealtchair, then later Dún Cealtchair. Celtchar was one of the Red Branch Knights, a friend of the then King of Ulster, Conor MacNessa, and, according to the *Book of the Dun Cow*, "an angry terrific hideous man with a long nose, huge ears, apple eyes, and coarse dark-grey hair". The Dún part of the fort's name went on to become the name of the county, as well as the town.

By the time the Norman knight **John de Courcy** made his mark here in the late twelfth century, a settlement was well established. Pushing north out of Leinster, and defeating Rory MacDonlevy, King of Ulster, de Courcy dispossessed the Augustinian canons who occupied the Hill of Down to establish his own **Benedictine abbey**. He flaunted as much pomp as he could to mark the occasion, and one of his festive tricks was to import what were supposedly the disinterred bodies of St Brigid and St Columba to join St Patrick, who was (allegedly) buried here. One of the earliest accounts of Patrick's life asserts that he's buried in a church near the sea; and since a later account admits that "where his bones are, no man knows", Downpatrick's claim seems as good as any.

St Patrick Centre

St Patrick's Square • Mon–Sat 9am–5pm, plus July & Aug Sun 9am–5pm • charge • http://saintpatrickcentre.com

Just off the main drag, Market Street, the large glass-and-brick-built **St Patrick Centre** aims to recount the life of the saint and his influence in extensive detail. Its hagiographic, multimedia approach is pretty arid, however, and by the time you've been round its maze of interactive displays and sat through the five-screen 180-degree virtual helicopter ride through Christian history, you might even wish you'd never heard of him.

Down Cathedral

36 English St • Mon–Sat 10am–4pm • Free • http://downcathedral.org

Uphill from the St Patrick Centre, you'll reach the elegant, spacious Mall, at the end of which stands **Down Cathedral**. Built by John de Courcy, the cathedral was destroyed in 1316 during Edward Bruce's invasion, and a new abbey erected in the early sixteenth century was even more short-lived. Today's cathedral dates basically from the early 1800s, though it incorporates many aspects of earlier incarnations. Its unique feature is the private box-pews, characteristic of the Regency period and the only ones remaining in use in Ireland.

In the adjacent graveyard, you'll find the site of Patrick's supposed **grave**, marked today by a rough granite boulder put there around 1900 by Francis Joseph Biggar to cover a huge hole created by earlier pilgrims searching for the saints' bones.

Down County Museum

The Mall • Tues–Sat 10am–4.30pm • Free • http://downcountymuseum.com

Where the Mall segues into English Street, both streets crowded with handsome Georgian buildings, you come to the eighteenth-century jail, now home to the **Down County Museum**. The three-storey Georgian **Governor's House** in the centre of the walled courtyard houses a local history gallery entitled "Down through Time"; the displays are both varied and enlightening, ranging from some superb artefacts – notably Bronze Age tools and Norman grave covers – to photos of local worthies, including the town's most famous musical export, the indie band, Ash. Not to be missed, either, are a couple of beautifully embroidered **quilts**: the Ballybranagh Quilt, dating from 1849, depicts biblical scenes, as well as important events that have taken place in Down, while the Killyleagh Quilt is a dazzling velvet and silk patchwork made by local girl Martha Geddis in 1894.

15

ON THE TRAIL OF ST PATRICK

About 6.5km west of Inch Abbey (take the B2 to Annacloy and then the first turning on the left), **Loughinisland** is probably the most worthwhile of all the sites in the area associated with St Patrick, and indeed one of the most idyllic spots in County Down. It comprises a reed-fringed lake contained by ten or so little drumlin hills, one of which forms an island in the lake. Here, across a short causeway, are the ruins of three small churches, set next door to each other. The smallest one, **MacCartan's Chapel** (1636), has an entrance door little taller than a metre high. The larger northern church was used by both Catholics and Protestants until they quarrelled on a wet Sunday around 1720 over which camp should remain outside during the service. The Protestants left and built their church at Seaforde instead.

The next St Patrick landmark is at **Saul**, around 3km northeast of Downpatrick off the Strangford road. St Patrick is said to have landed nearby, sailing up the tiny River Slaney, and it was here that he first preached, immediately converting Dichu, the lord of this territory. Dichu gave Patrick a barn as his first base and the saint frequently returned here to rest from his travelling missions – legend has it that he died here in 461. Today a **memorial chapel** and round tower in the Celtic Revival style, built of pristine silver-grey granite in 1932 to commemorate the 1500th anniversary of the saint's arrival, is open to visitors (daily 9am–5pm; free). Two cross-carved stones from between the eighth and twelfth centuries still stand in the graveyard, though there's not a trace of the medieval monastery built here by St Malachy in the twelfth century.

A short distance further south, between Saul and Raholp, **St Patrick's Shrine** sits atop Slieve Patrick, a tract of hillside much like a slalom ski-slope, with the Stations of the Cross marking a pathway up. This huge Mourne-granite statue, clad at the base with bronze panels depicting Patrick's life, was erected in the same year as Saul church. The summit is no more than a twenty-minute climb and offers a commanding view of the county, a vista of the endless little bumps of this drumlin-filled territory.

At **Raholp** is the ruined church of **St Tassach**, named after the bishop from whom the dying Patrick received the sacrament. Patrick gave Raholp to Tassach as a reward for crafting a case for Christ's crozier, the Bachall Isú, one of Ireland's chief relics until its destruction in 1538. The ruins here were mainly restored in 1915 from the rubble that lay around, but their material is thought to date from the eleventh century. If you're eager for the complete St Patrick experience, it's 1.5km from the car park of the *Slaney Inn* in Raholp to the spot on the lough shore where he is believed to have first landed: head towards Strangford, then left down Myra Road; cross the main Strangford road and turn left at the first fork; at the bottom of the hill, take the track on the right to the shore.

The easiest way to find the last St Patrick site, **Struell Wells**, is to return to Downpatrick. Take the Ardglass road southeast, turn left just past the hospital, then right down a narrow track into a secluded rock-faced valley and you'll come to the wells. The waters here, believed to be the wells referred to in early accounts of Patrick's mission, have been attributed with healing powers for centuries. In 1744 Walter Harris described the scene: "Vast throngs of rich and poor resort on Midsummer Eve and the Friday before Lammas, some in the hopes of obtaining health, and others to perform penance." The site contains a couple of wells, one for drinking and another known as the eye well whose waters are supposed to have curative powers, and men's and women's bathhouses. Mass is still said here on midsummer night, and people bring containers to carry the water home with them.

The **cell block** at the back of the enclosure once held the United Irishman Thomas Russell, who had already survived the 1798 Rebellion but was found guilty of complicity in Robert Emmet's uprising and was duly hanged in 1803 from a sill outside the main gate of the jail; the restored cells remain, while an exhibition in the neighbouring room displays one of the original, graffiti-strewn doors. Here, too, you can view the last speech of William Gaddis before his execution for the murder of one Adam Heslip during a robbery in 1818, and a selection of hideous contraptions, notably a "Scold's Bridal", an iron muzzle designed to stop women gossiping.

To the rear, a specially constructed extension houses the 1100-year old **Downpatrick High Cross**. Ornamented with biblical scenes, this Mourne granite cross had, from 1897 to 2014, stood outside the east end of the cathedral, before it was dismantled, cleaned up and reassembled; a replica now stands in its place outside the cathedral. Film footage recalls the various stages of the project, but otherwise this illuminating little exhibition includes stone architectural fragments and some exquisite metalwork.

Mound of Down

Between the jail and the barricaded courthouse and inauspiciously tucked behind a secondary school, you'll find the **Mound of Down**, a smaller prominence than the Hill of Down and half-submerged in undergrowth. It's in fact 18m high and inside its outer ditch is a horseshoe-shaped central mound of rich grass. Once a rath, or round hill fort, it was considerably altered and enlarged to create a Norman motte-and-bailey fortification, with a **bretasche** (a wooden archery tower) at the centre. Its view of the Hill of Down clearly displays the attractions the hill had for its earliest settlers; it's believed by some to be the site of the palace of the kings of Ulster.

15

Downpatrick and County Down Railway

Market St • Mid-June to mid-Sept Sat & Sun 12.30–5pm, plus bank holidays and special event days • charge • http://downrail.co.uk

At the rear of the market car park is the enthusiast-run **Downpatrick and County Down Railway**, which operates short steam-train trips along a restored section of the Belfast–Newcastle main line to Inch Abbey. The station has a small photographic exhibition (free) on railways in County Down, as well as several steam and diesel locomotives on show.

ARRIVAL AND INFORMATION
DOWNPATRICK

By bus The bus station is on Market St, 100m or so south of the St Patrick Centre.
Destinations Ardglass (Mon–Fri hourly, Sat 7; 25min); Belfast (Mon–Fri every 30min, Sat hourly, Sun 8; 1hr); Castlewellan (Mon–Fri 11 daily, Sat 8, Sun 5; 30min); Killough (Mon–Fri hourly, Sat 7; 20min); Newcastle (Mon–

Fri hourly, Sat 7, Sun 5; 20–35min); Newry (4–6 daily; 1hr 15min); Strangford (Mon–Fri hourly, Sat 4; 30min).
Tourist office Inside the St Patrick Centre (Mon–Sat 9am–5pm; plus Sun 9am–5pm July & Aug; 028 4461 2233); offers an accommodation booking service.

ACCOMMODATION

Denvir's 16 English St, http://denvirs.com. One of Ireland's oldest coaching inns, with six en-suite rooms that are surprisingly simple, furnished throughout in dark, heavy wood, but cosy all the same. **££**
Dunleath House 33 St Patrick's Drive, http://dunleathhouse.com. Tucked away in a residential area very close to the centre of town, this welcoming family home has three good-sized, ground-floor rooms with French doors leading

off to a patio area; cracking breakfast as well. **££**
The Mill Drumcullen Rd, Ballydugan, http://ballyduganmill.com. This converted flour mill, dating from 1792, retains twenty-two rustically styled rooms on the building's upper two floors, each with exposed beams and rough-hewn stone walls and variously sleeping one- to four people. The Mill also has its own café and restaurant. **££**

EATING AND DRINKING

The Daily Grind 20a St Patrick's Ave, 028 4461 7173. The packed tables will tell you how popular this place is; pop in for late morning coffee or one of the scrumptious fruit salads. Closed Sun. **£**
Denvir's 16 English St, http://denvirs.com. Chunky oak

beams, flagstoned floors and a fine inglenook fireplace comprise the restaurant, lounge and snug bars of this hotel, and provide the setting for a creditable menu, for example seafood chowder, and beef and Guinness pie with colcannon, in addition to some lovely Sunday roasts. **£££**

ENTERTAINMENT

Down Arts Centre 2–6 Irish St, 028 4461 0747. The excellent Down Arts Centre has an extensive programme

of events, and you'll find all genres of art and performance here, from poetry and painting to music and comedy.

Inch Abbey

Around 1.5km northwest of Downpatrick • Open access

Lying on the other side of the Quoile Marsh from Downpatrick are the remains of the Cistercian **Inch Abbey**. The exquisite setting is visible from the town, but the river's intervention means that the only access is 1.5km out along the Belfast road, taking the left turn down Inch Abbey Road just before the defunct *Abbey Lodge Hotel*, followed by another signposted left turn shortly afterwards – alternatively, you can take a train ride from Downpatrick (see page 521). The site was once an island, and an earlier nearby foundation was destroyed by John de Courcy in 1177 because it was fortified against him. In atonement he built a replacement here and, in 1180, invited Cistercian monks from Furness Abbey in Lancashire over to populate the building, with the intention of establishing a strong centre of English influence. Little of it is now left standing – it was burnt in 1404 and monastic life was completely over by the mid-sixteenth century. Still, its setting, among small glacial drumlins and woodland, is picturesque, and strolling up the valley sides is a pleasant way to pass half an hour or so.

15

Strangford

If you're following the A2 round the coast of the Ards Peninsula, your arrival on Lecale will be at tiny **STRANGFORD** village, directly opposite Portaferry and linked by a regular ferry service (see page 522). The earlier name of this inlet was Lough Cuan (*cuan* being Irish for "harbour" or "haven"), but it was renamed Strangfiord by the Vikings over a thousand years ago because of the strong eight-knot current in the narrows. The centre of the village is a neatly manicured green framed by pastel-coloured stone tenements, while its small harbour makes a pleasant setting for watching the to and fro of the ferry boats. Good (if busy) times to be here are at the beginning of July for the **Strangford Sailing Regatta**, and the end of August for the **Strangford Festival**, when the quayside and village green burst into life with all manner of activities, including traditional music, food and craft fairs, and raft races.

ARRIVAL AND DEPARTURE STRANGFORD

By bus Buses from/to Downpatrick (Mon–Fri 10 daily, Sat 5; 30min) stop by the main square just up from the ferry landing stage.

By ferry Regular ferries make the 5min trip across to Portaferry (every 30min, Mon–Fri 7.30am–10.30pm, Sat 8am–11pm, Sun 9.30am–10.30pm; http://nidirect.gov.uk; £1.30 single, £2.60 return; car £7.70 single, £13.30 return).

ACCOMMODATION AND EATING

★ **The Artisan Cookhouse** 4 Kildare St, http://artisan cookhouse.com. A short distance up from the village green on the Downpatrick road, this sparkling little bistro is highly rated in these parts with a stylish menu covering all bases: Tempura cod with pea and spring onion *concasse*, and vegetable madras, shallot bhaji and mnt and cucumber yoghurt. Closed Mon–Wed. £££

The Cuan Village green, http://thecuan.com. This long-established inn offers nine elegantly furnished, fragrant-smelling rooms with splashes of artwork. In addition, there's a splendid restaurant with plenty of fish dishes on offer; and if you fancy a quiet pint, make for the sociable bar, which had the honour of receiving the first *Game of Thrones* door (see page 481). ££

Lobster Pot 9–11 The Square, 028 4488 1288. If fresh lobster straight off the boat takes your fancy, then look no further than this smart but easy-going, restaurant; lobster, prawn and mussel tagliatelle, and hot smoked mackerel with Jersey Royals, are typically mouthwatering dishes. £££

Castle Ward

1.5km west of Strangford on the A25 • House Mon & Wed–Sun mid-March to Oct 11am–4pm; grounds daily: April–Sept 10am–6pm; Oct–March 10am–4pm • charge • http://nationaltrust.org.uk/castle-ward

The most worthwhile place in the immediate surrounds of Strangford is **Castle Ward**, the eighteenth-century residence of Bernard and Anne Ward, later Lord and Lady Bangor, but now owned by the National Trust. It's a thoroughly eccentric building, thanks to the opposing tastes of its creators (they later split up): Bernard's half is in the Classical Palladian style, Anne's neo-Gothic, a split carried through into the design and decor of the rooms inside. This is manifest in Anne's Arabesque boudoir, all flowing, fancy curves and pointy bits, a stark counterpoint to the neat straight lines of Bernard's drawing room. There are some entertainingly oddball exhibits too, not least a display of stuffed squirrels posing as boxers, believe it or not.

Having absorbed all that the house has to offer, there's plenty to explore within the extensive **grounds**, including a sixteenth-century tower house (Old Castle Ward) and the fifteenth-century **Audley's Castle** just outside on the lough shore, with a superb view across the lake. Castle Ward has also featured prominently in *Game of Thrones*, so fans might like to pick up a filming locations map at reception.

Cloghy Rocks

A signposted turning 1.5km south of Strangford directs you to the **Cloghy Rocks** observation point. The rocks themselves are 20m or so out in the lough and for most of the day look decidedly inconsequential, but this is the best place to spot basking **seals**, both common and grey seals. They're well camouflaged against the seaweed, so a pair of binoculars would be handy. Here, too, you can see herons, redshank and oystercatchers, and you may even be lucky enough to spot an otter or two.

St Patrick's Well

1.5km south of Ballyhornan

St Patrick's Well is set on a wonderful rocky shore between Ballyhornan and Chapeltown. You can get to within a few hundred metres of the well by road, but the best approach is to start from Ballyhornan – where you'll see a narrow strip of water separating the village from Guns Island, accessible at low tide and still used for grazing – and follow the foreshore path for about a 1.5km. The well is easily spotted: it looks rather like a sheep dip with concrete walls, but with a crucifix at its head. Its holy water has turned into something closer to stagnant consommé than an ever-youthful source of new life.

Ardglass

ARDGLASS is set on the side of a lovely natural inlet. Its domestic buildings, rising steeply from the harbour, are interspersed with seven fortified mansions, towers and turrets, dating from a vigorous English revival in the sixteenth century, when a trading company first arrived to found a colony here. In the nineteenth century, Ardglass was the most thriving **fishing** port in the North; and even today, aside from the prawns, herrings and whitefish brought in by the fishing fleet, there's very good rod-fishing to be had off the end of the pier for codling, pollack and coalfish. It's often sometimes possible to buy direct from fishing boats or from the cannery on the quay.

The castles

The best preserved of the fortifications, though it's no longer open to the public, is **Jordan's Castle**, next door to the *Anchor* pub on the Low Road, the most elegant and highly developed of all the Down tower houses. The tall, crenellated building with white-plaster trimming up on the hill was once **King's Castle**; its nineteenth-century renovation is obvious, as is modern work to turn it into a nursing home. The lone ornamental-looking turret on the hilltop is **Isabella's Tower**, a nineteenth-century folly created by Aubrey de Vere Beauclerc as a gazebo for his disabled daughter.

ARRIVAL AND DEPARTURE   **ARDGLASS**

By bus Buses stop on the main road just above the harbour.   30min); Killough (Mon–Fri hourly, Sat 7, Sun 2; 5min).
Destinations Downpatrick (Mon–Fri hourly, Sat 7; 20–

ACCOMMODATION AND EATING

Aldo's 7 Castle Place, 028 4484 1315. Well-regarded restaurant that's been in the hands of the same Italian family for more than forty years, though (the house lasagne aside), there's little actually Italian on the menu; instead, you've got the likes of wok-fried monkfish with pea risotto, and Irish lamb rump with carrot jam and goats cheese mousse. **£££**

★ **Margaret's Cottage** 9 Castle Place, http://margarets-cottage.com. Named after the adjoining fifteenth-century tower house, this home-from-home guesthouse, directly opposite the golf course, offers three pretty rooms, two of which offer fantastic sea views. Guests are positively encouraged to avail themselves of the warming lounge – with papers galore, a roaring log fire and selection of lush, home-baked goodies rustled up by Ciara, *Margaret's* charming host. She also does a tremendous afternoon tea for £19.50. **££**

Killough

KILLOUGH, a few kilometres west of Ardglass, is a tranquil village stretching around a harbour that is much larger than its neighbour's but is now silted up. Killough's main street is a fine French-style avenue of sycamores with a string of picturesque cottage terraces at its southern end, making an unlikely major thoroughfare. The Wards, of Castle Ward, built the harbour in the eighteenth century, and there's still a road running inland, virtually in a straight line, from Killough to their castle. Untouched by tourism, there is no accommodation in the village and only bar meals in a couple of pubs.

St John's Point

From the southern end of Killough you can head out to **St John's Point** – much favoured by birdwatchers – on which lie the ruins of one of the North's best examples of a **pre-Romanesque church**; it's an enjoyable 4km walk. The tiny west door of the tenth-century church has the distinctive sloping sides, narrowing as the doorway rises, that were a common feature of these early churches. Also still apparent are the **antae**, enclosures created by the extension of the west and east walls to give extra support to the roof. Excavations in 1977 showed up graves that extended under these walls, indicating that an even earlier church existed in the early Christian period, probably made of wood.

ARRIVAL AND DEPARTURE

KILLOUGH

By bus Buses stop in the centre of the village.
Destinations Ardglass (Mon–Fri hourly, Sat 7, Sun 2; 5min); Downpatrick (Mon–Fri hourly, Sat 7; 15min).

Newcastle

NEWCASTLE, with its lovely stretch of sandy beach, is the biggest seaside resort in County Down – packed with trippers from Belfast on bank holidays and summer weekends. Although the resort isn't exactly exciting – there's next to nothing by way of sights, and the main strip is interspersed with tacky amusement arcades and souvenir shops – it does have some superb dining possibilities, and, with Slieve Donard rising behind the town, it's by far the best base if you want to do any serious walking or climbing in the nearby **Mourne Mountains**.

The town has a few literary connections too: **Seamus Heaney** was a waiter in the 1950s at the long-gone *Savoy Café*; Brook Cottage, on Bryansford Road, was home to the dramatist and dialect-poet Richard Valentine Williams, better known as Richard Rowley; and a fountain on The Promenade commemorates the popular Irish songwriter Percy French, composer of *The Mountains of Mourne* and numerous comic songs.

ARRIVAL AND INFORMATION

NEWCASTLE

By bus The bus station is on Railway St at the eastern end of Main St. The year-round Mourne Rambler (service #405; 9am, noon & 3pm; all-day ticket £6.50) is a circular service starting in Newcastle with numerous stops including

Tollymore and the Silent Valley.

Destinations Belfast (Mon–Sat every 30min–1hr, Sun hourly; 1hr 10min–1hr 30min); Castlewellan (Mon–Sat every 30min–1hr, Sun 5; 10min); Downpatrick (Mon–Fri hourly, Sat 7, Sun 5; 25–35min); Newry (4–6 daily; 55min).

Tourist office The tourist office is at 10–14 Central Promenade (Mon–Sat 9.30am–5pm; http://visitmourne mountains.co.uk) and has stacks of info on walking in the Mournes.

ACCOMMODATION

Beach House 22 Downs Rd, 028 4372 2345. The chief appeal of this refurbished Victorian dwelling is the sea view from each of the three, mostly all-white, rooms (two twins and a double). Closed Nov–Jan. **££**

Hutt Hostel 30 Downs Rd, http://hutthostel.com. Occupying a fine seafront town house, this buzzy, well-appointed hostel has a variety of three- to eight-bed dorms, plus "The Padd", an apartment-like annexe sleeping six. There's also a cool lounge with woodburner, a games room,

and a large self-catering kitchen for use, though breakfast is included. **£**

Slieve Donard Downs Rd, http://marineandlawn.com. This ostentatious redbrick pile, positioned on the beachfront and next to the Royal County Down golf course, is Newcastle's premier hotel, a mega-luxurious establishment with grand rooms in all manner of category – most with a sea view – and its own spa. **£££**

EATING AND DRINKING

Great Jones Craft & Kitchen 51 Central Promenade, http://greatjones.uk. Named after the street in New York on which the founders worked, this modern-looking restaurant serves up US-inspired plates of food like jerk chicken burger, and pulled pork or Cajun fish tacos, but with a nod to local (fish and chips, lamb rump). The quarter of veggie/vegan dishes are more than token affairs, for example spiced red lentil falafel tacos. And as the name suggests, there's a

decent line up of craft beers to sup on. **£££**

Railway St 2 Railway St, 028 4372 5620. There are dozens of cafés around town, but this great-looking coffee house opposite the *Slieve Donard* resort is the best by a country mile, serving up Aussie-inspired brekkies and lunches (fried chicken and smoked tomato aioli on toasted sourdough) and the freshest, tastiest coffee in town. Closed Tues. **£**

The Mourne Mountains

The **Mourne Mountains** are a relatively youthful set of granite mountains, which explains why their comparatively unweathered peaks and flanks are so rugged, forming steep sides, moraines and occasional sheer cliffs. Closer up, these give sharp, jagged outlines; but from a distance they appear much gentler, like a sleeping herd of buffalo. The wilder topography lies mostly in the east, below Newcastle, although the fine cliff of **Eagle Mountain** (636m), to the southwest, is wonderful if you can afford the time and effort to get there, and the tamer land above Rostrevor has views down into **Carlingford Lough** that rival any in Ireland.

In summer at least (winters can be surprisingly harsh), there are plenty of straightforward hikes in the Mournes that require no special equipment, with obvious tracks to many of the more scenic parts. There are also more serious climbs and **climbing courses** in the Mournes run by the Tollymore National Outdoor Centre in Bryansford (http://tollymore.com), but they must be booked well in advance.

The Legananny dolmen

The **Legananny dolmen** is worth a considerable detour, which it will be, wherever you are, due to its remoteness; it's signposted at the village of Leitrim, 5km north of Castlewellan. Approaching the site, you'll find yourself on narrow humped lanes, gradually ascending the southern edge of the Slieve Croob range, and feeling increasingly distant from modern realities. You may also experience a sense of *déjà vu* when you arrive at the site, for the dolmen is a popular choice of guidebook and tourist-board photographers. There's no doubting the impressiveness of the structure, looking for all the world like a giant stone tripod.

15

WALKS IN THE MOURNES

While there's little to see in Newcastle itself, the **Mourne Mountains** offer some beautiful walks close to town, as well as plenty of more serious hiking routes, including the **Newcastle Way**, a two-day, 45km-long waymarked hike, split into six sections, starting and finishing in the town; see http://walkni.com for more details. There's also an annual **walking festival** over three days at the end of June, featuring a variety of lowland and mountain walks, rambles and hikes.

SLIEVE DONARD

The climb up **Slieve Donard** (850m), just south of Newcastle, is the obvious first choice. Although it's the highest peak in Northern Ireland, there are two relatively easy **ascents** from town: one on a well-marked trail that starts around 5km south of town on the Annalong road at Bloody Bridge (see page 526), and another (slightly shorter) trail from the Donard Park car park – both end at the massive hermit cell on the summit, from where there are stupendous views.

For gentler local walking, there are several pleasant parks created from the estates of old houses in the vicinity. The nearest is **Donard Park** (free access) on the slopes of Slieve Donard. There's a good meander along the River Glen from Newcastle town centre to the park, and if you keep following this path uphill you'll emerge on the other side and eventually come to the Saddle, a col between the two mountains of Slieve Donard and Slieve Commedagh. If you want to carry on further into the mountains from here, a good route is via **Trassey Burn** towards the **Hare's Gap**, where minerals have seeped through the rock to form precious and semiprecious stones – topaz, beryl, smoky quartz and emerald – in the cavities of the **Diamond rocks** (hidden behind an obvious boulder stone on the mountainside).

TOLLYMORE FOREST PARK

Around 3km inland from Newcastle, along the Bryansford road, **Tollymore Forest Park** (daily 10am–dusk; cars £5; http://nidirect.gov.uk) is considerably bigger and better equipped than Donard, and has a **campsite**. The park creeps up the northern side of the Mournes, and its four picturesque **trails** (ranging from less than 1km to 8km in length) wind through woodland and beside the river. You enter the park by one of two ornate Gothic folly gates, and there's an information kiosk in the car park.

CASTLEWELLAN FOREST PARK

Castlewellan Forest Park (daily: March & Oct 9am–6pm; April–Sept 9am–9pm; Nov–Feb 9am–5pm) is also inland, about 8km further north, outside the elegant market town

Silent Valley

Daily: April, Sept & Oct 10am–6.30pm; May–Aug 10am–9pm; Nov–March 10am–4pm; café daily: April–Sept 10am–5pm; Oct–March 10am–4pm • charge, parking charge • Sandy Lough shuttle bus May, June & Sept Sat & Sun; July & Aug daily (charge) • http://niwater.com/silent-valley

The A2 south along the coast from Newcastle is a beautiful road, trailing the shore around the edge of the mountains. It takes you past the chasm known as **Maggie's Leap**, after a local woman who jumped to avoid the attentions of an unwanted suitor, and over the **Bloody Bridge**, reputedly so-called because of a nearby massacre during the 1641 Rebellion. Inland, 1.5km or so from the fishing village of Annalong (11km south of Newcastle) and serviced by the summer-only Mourne Rambler bus (see page 524), signposts point to the aptly named **Silent Valley**, where you'll find Belfast and County Down's **reservoir**, a huge thirty-year engineering project that was completed in 1933. There's a car park by the lower reservoir, bounded by the Mourne Wall, a sturdy 35km-long granite boundary to the catchment area that links the summits of fifteen mountains along its route. The views out to Slieve Binnian and Ben Crom, behind it to the west, of Castlewellan. The estate lies in the foothills of the Mournes, and a 4km trail from the entrance leads to the highest point in the forest, **Slievenaslat**, providing panoramic views. A wonderful **arboretum** is the forest park's outstanding feature: the sheltered south-facing slopes of its hills, between the Mournes and the Slieve Croob range, allow exotic species to flourish. There's trout **fishing** in its main lake and coarse fishing in the smaller lakes (enquire at the Newcastle tourist office for details).

There's a pleasant **campsite** in the park here, too, as well as the Life One Great Adventure centre (http://onegreatadventure.com), which offers a large number of land and water based activities, including guided and self-guided **canoeing**, stand up paddleboarding and **kayaking**, as well as trail **biking**. Nearby **riding schools** offering trekking through the forest parks include Mount Pleasant Riding and Trekking Centre, 15 Bannanstown Rd, Castlewellan (http://mountpleasantequestrian.co.uk) and Mourne Trail Riding Centre, 96 Castlewellan Rd, around 3km out of Newcastle on the A50 (028 4372 4351); expect to pay around £25 for an hour's ride.

15

LONGER HIKES

If you're planning on more serious hiking in the Mournes, heights worth chasing include **Slieve Binnian** (747m), beyond the Hare's Gap, reached through the Brandy Pad passes by the Blue Lough and Lough Binnian; **Slieve Commedagh** (767m), with its Inca-like pillars of granite; and **Slieve Bearnagh** (739m), up to the right of the Hare's Gap. Also, try and cross the ridge from **Slieve Meelmore** (681m) to **Slieve Muck**, the "pig mountain", descending to the shores of Lough Shannagh, where there's a **beach** at either end – useful for a dip, though the water's freezing. In the panorama beyond the Hare's Gap, the places not to miss are the eastern slopes of the **Cove Mountain** and **Slieve Lamagan** (704m). If you're sticking to the roads, all you can really do is circle the outside of the range, though there is one road through the middle, from Hilltown to Kilkeel.

ACCOMMODATION IN THE MOURNE MOUNTAINS

Castlewellan Camping Castlewellan Forest Park (signposted), 028 4377 8664. This basic but pleasant campsite offers showers, fresh water, and dishwashing station and electric hook-ups. Closed Nov–March. £̄

Meelmore Lodge 52 Trassey Rd, Bryansford, http://meelmorelodge.co.uk. Superbly positioned complex some 10km west of Newcastle, just beyond Tollymore Forest Park, offering hostel accommodation (dorms and private en-suites), a field for camping and two basic pods (sleeping up to four). Also has a smashing little café (Sat & Sun 8.30am–6pm; daily during school hols). £̄–££

Tollymore Caravan and Camping Tollymore Forest Park (signposted), 028 4372 2428. Like Castlwellanm this is a basic site with decent facilities including showers, compost loos and electric hook-ups but is also open year-round. £̄

are worth the effort of the 5km circular **Viewpoint Walk** (starts at the car park). Less energetic, but still superb, is the less than 1km Sally Lough stroll up to the dam at Ben Crom; again the views are spectacular. Halfway between the car park and the dam there's a small café and a **visitor centre** exhibiting displays on the reservoir's development.

Rostrevor

On the western edge of the Mournes, 24km further on from Annalong along the A2, a signpost points to the **Kilfeaghan dolmen**, 500m inland then a short walk through a couple of fields and kissing gates. Its capstone is enormous and could only have arrived here during the retreat of the glacial drift.

Further up the lough, the village of **ROSTREVOR** lies at the point where the bay waters dramatically begin to narrow towards Newry – and where the population and political climate turn more in favour of the Nationalist communities of County Armagh and those across the ever-nearing border. Rostrevor is a charming and sleepy village of Victorian terraces and friendly pubs, meandering up the lower slopes of **Slieve Martin**. A good time to be here is the last week of July for the Fiddler's Green Festival (http://fiddlersgreen festival.com), a major event attracting folk and traditional musicians from across Europe.

ARRIVAL AND DEPARTURE ROSTREVOR

By bus Buses drop off on, and depart from, Warrenpoint Rd, the main through road.
Destinations Newry (Mon–Sat hourly, Sun 5; 25min); Warrenpoint (Mon–Sat hourly, Sun 5; 10min).
By ferry The Carlingford car ferry (http://carlingfordferry. com) makes the 15min journey across Carlingford Lough

from Greencastle, 14km south of Rostrevor, to Greenore, near Carlingford in County Louth; from Greencastle ferries depart on the hour (April–Sept daily 10am–6pm) and from Greenore on the half hour (daily 10.30am–6.30pm; passengers €2.25, cars €11).

ACCOMMODATION AND EATING

Kilbroney Caravan Park Shore Rd, 028 4173 8134. Camping is available at this park where you can hike up the hill to the thirty-ton Cloughmore ("big stone") for views across the lough to the Cooley Mountains over the border. Facilities include laundry, tennis courts, play areas and café. Closed Oct–March. **£**
The Old School House 39 Church St, http://oldschool houserostrevor.com. The erstwhile school house might look quite ordinary, but the food here is anything but; beyond

light lunches, you can sit down to more substantial, and sophisticated, evening fare later in the week with the likes of tandoori monkfish with roast peppers and garlic potatoes. **£££**
The Sands 4 Victoria Square, http://thesandsbnb.com. Fabulously located B&B on a spruce Victorian square out on the road towards Newcastle, offering one double and one twin room, each with a clear sea view. **££**

Warrenpoint

Warrenpoint is as picturesque as Rostrevor, with a colourful esplanade of seafront housing and a spacious central square. It's a much more traditional seaside resort than its neighbour and has been attracting visitors since the early nineteenth century, when an enterprising local man advertised warm baths for the "gentry, nobility and public". The town really only comes alive, however, during the week-long **Blues on the Bay music festival** in late May (http://bluesonthebay.co.uk), and for the **Warrenpoint Loughside festival** (http://maidenofthemournes.com), which takes place in mid-August, a local version of the Rose of Tralee (see page 296).

ARRIVAL AND INFORMATION WARRENPOINT

By bus Buses drop-off on, and depart from, Church St. Destinations Newry (Mon–Sat hourly, Sun 5; 15min); Rostrevor (Mon–Sat Mon–Sat hourly, Sun 5; 10min).

Tourist office Easy to miss, the tourist office is in the town hall on Church St (Mon–Fri 9am–1pm & 2–5pm; 028 4175 2256).

ACCOMMODATION AND EATING

Whistledown Hotel 6 Seaview, http://thewhistledown hotel.com. Tidy boutique hotel with coloured furnishings, stripey carpets and regulation mod cons. Grab a posh pizza from the garishly decorated *Finn's Bar*, or treat yourself to more refined fare in the bistro. **££**

Ye Old Ship Inn 14 The Square, 028 4175 3125. A venerable old pub with a distinct nautical theme, from the wood-panelled bar to the sweet little table lamps; top-notch beer – try the local Mourne Mist – and live music Thurs–Sat.

Newry

Although **NEWRY**, astride the border of Down and Armagh, is this region's most important commercial centre and bustles with an urban vibrancy, it's worth little more than a short visit. However, its key position means that you're highly likely to pass through here, and it does make a possible base for exploring Slieve Gullion and the south Armagh district.

Newry was founded by Cistercian monks in 1144, but for most of its history has been a **garrison**, guarding the borders of Northern Ireland at the narrow point between hills on either side known as the Gap of the North. There's no trace at all of the bitterly contested early fortresses; what you see dates mostly from the eighteenth and nineteenth centuries, when a canal to Lough Neagh (cut in 1742, the first in the British Isles) brought the produce of the inland towns to the markets here; indeed, **market days** (Thurs & Sat) remain integral to the town.

Catholic Cathedral

Hill St • Daily 8.30am–5pm • Free • 028 3026 2586

One of the most interesting buildings in town is the **Catholic Cathedral**, constructed in 1829 and the first such building to be opened following Catholic Emancipation. Despite an unpromising granite exterior, the rich mosaic pattern along its interior walls gives a Byzantine feel, and there's also a striking vaulted ceiling of decorative sweeping plaster arcs and vivid stained-glass windows. Nearby, there's a strange bronze totem pole by sculptor Paddy McElroy, which depicts, in tortured relief, scenes from Newry's past.

15

Bagenal's Castle

Castle St • Museum Tues–Sat 10am–4.30pm • Free • http://visitmournemountains.co.uk/museums

A short walk from the centre of town, **Bagenal's Castle** is a superb example of a fortified house. Located within the environs of a Cistercian abbey, the castle was confiscated during the Reformation of 1548, and the premises were leased to a certain Nicholas Bagenal, who had apparently earlier fled his native Staffordshire to escape indictment for murder. After acting as a secret agent infiltrating the O'Neill clan, he was granted a pardon and subsequently became marshal of the English army in Ireland and established a garrison in Newry. While Bagenal was largely successful in defending the area against the O'Neills, his daughter Mary eloped and married Hugh O'Neill, a story that became the subject of Brian Friel's play *Making History*. The castle functioned as McGann's bakery for more than a century, until its closure in 1996.

Newry and Mourne Museum

The castle is now home to the nicely presented **Newry and Mourne Museum**, where you can inspect some of the building's original elements, most notably a cross section of its sixteenth-century cellar, which contains the original bread oven. Upstairs, in the impressively authentic Great Chamber, you can't miss the crater-like holes along the walls where the joists were removed years ago. There's a fascinating local history exhibition too, with an emphasis on the area's strong folk traditions. There's coverage, too, of life here during the Troubles, when Newry – the so-called capital of "Bandit Country" – was at the bloody forefront of the struggles; exhibits include British coins overstamped with IRA insignia, and an order of service for the ten men gunned down in the infamous Kingsmill massacre of January 1976.

ARRIVAL AND INFORMATION   NEWRY

By train The train station is 500m west of town on Millvale Rd and connected to the centre by local bus #41H (free with valid rail ticket).
Destinations Belfast (Mon–Sat 8 daily, Sun 5; 55min–1hr 5min); Drogheda (Mon–Sat 8 daily, Sun 5; 40min); Dublin (Mon–Sat 8 daily, Sun 5; 1hr 10min–1hr 30min).
By bus Newry's bus station is on The Mall alongside the canal.
Destinations Armagh (Mon–Fri 8 daily, Sat 7; 50min);

Belfast (Mon–Fri every 30min, Sat hourly, Sun 9; 1hr 10min); Carlingford (Bus Éireann: Mon–Sat 3 daily; 20min); Crossmaglen (Mon–Sat 5–6 daily; 55min); Downpatrick (4–6 daily; 1hr 15min); Dublin (hourly; 1hr 30min); Newcastle (4–6 daily; 55min); Rostrevor (Mon–Sat hourly, Sun 5; 25min); Warrenpoint (Mon–Sat hourly, Sun 5; 15min).
Tourist office In Bagenal's Castle on Castle St (Tues–Sat 10am–4.30pm; http://visitmournemountains.co.uk).

ACCOMMODATION AND EATING

Canal Court Hotel Merchants Quay, http://canalcourt hotel.com. On the opposite side of the canal from the bus station, this vast hotel is run through with class, from the opulent reception area to the extravagantly decorated rooms; it's also equipped with a gym and sauna. **££**

Grounded 25 Merchants Quay, 028 3083 3868. There aren't many places in Newry where you can grab a hearty lunch or a decent cup of coffee, but you can do just that at *Grounded*, an easy-going café a few paces along from the *Canal Court Hotel*; moreover, the squishy leather sofas and floor-to-ceiling windows are perfect for people-watching. **£**

South Armagh

Overshadowed by Slieve Gullion, the **South Armagh** countryside is among the most attractive in the North. Proximity to the border and a predominantly Catholic population resulted in this once being a nucleus of resistance to British rule. There's much evidence of prehistoric settlement here, important ecclesiastical remains and plenty of traditional music.

The Ring of Gullion

Most of South Armagh's attractions are concentrated in and around the area known as the **Ring of Gullion**, a naturally formed ring-dyke of low-lying hills that encircles (and predates) the mountain at its core. People have lived here for more than six thousand years, and there's a rich heritage of remains and monuments. On the ring's western fringe is the **Dorsey Enclosure**, two huge earthen banks and ditch ramparts dating from the Iron Age, running for 500m either side of the old route to Navan Fort. Elsewhere are numerous dolmens and cairns, Christian relics and monuments from the Plantation era.

Slieve Gullion, which dominates the southeastern corner of County Armagh, is one of the most mysteriously beautiful mountains in the country. A store of romantic legends is attached to it, especially concerning **Cúchulainn**, the hero of the **Táin Bó Cúailnge** (see page 154), who took his name here after slaying the hound (Cú) of the blacksmith Culainn. Due south at Glendhu is where Cúchulainn single-handedly halted the army of Queen Medb of Connaught, who was intent on capturing the great bull of Cooley. **Fionn Mac Cumhaill**, who founded the **Fianna**, a mythical national militia whose adventures are told in the *Fenian Cycle*, also appears in stories here.

Bessbrook and Killeavy

A scenic way to **approach Slieve Gullion** is from the north, passing the turning to **BESSBROOK**, a nineteenth-century model village developed by a Quaker linen entrepreneur; the Cadbury family's Bourneville estate in Birmingham, England, followed a very similar layout. After **Camlough** turn off the main road to go down by the eastern slopes of Camlough Mountain and you'll see the beautiful **lake**, set like a jewel within its green banks. A little further on, between Camlough Mountain and Slieve Gullion, are the ruined **Killeavy churches**. Two churches of different periods share the same gable wall: the west church is pre-Romanesque and one of the most important survivors of its kind in the country; the other, larger, church dates from the thirteenth century. A granite slab marks the **grave of St Monenna**, the founder of a fifth-century nunnery sited here – there's a holy well dedicated to her a little further up the slopes of Slieve Gullion, which pilgrims visit on her feast day (the Sunday nearest to July 6).

The official, tarmacked, **entrance** up into Slieve Gullion is on the mountain's forested southern face, after you've passed through the village of **KILLEAVY**. You'll find a small **forest park** (daily 10am–dusk; free), fronted by the **Courtyard Centre**, where there's a small exhibition on the area, craft workshops and a café. From the centre it's a 13km winding drive up to the summit (or you can follow a walking trail), where there's a couple of megalithic **cairns**. Fionn Mac Cumhaill was legendarily bewitched here by Miluchra, and local superstition holds that bathing in the small summit **lake** will turn your hair white; another tale states that under certain conditions a visitor to the site will be given the power to foresee everything that will happen that day. Various vertiginous spots offer spectacular **views** over the Ring of Gullion and the surrounding countryside.

Crossmaglen and around

In the far southwestern corner of Armagh just inside the border, **CROSSMAGLEN** has reputedly the largest market square in Ireland, the scene of a fortnightly Friday **market**. During the Troubles the town's reputation for armed struggle against the British was fearsome, and, in truth, it has been a cauldron of activity ever since Partition. Indeed, had the 1924 Boundary Commission's proposals been fully implemented, the town and surrounding countryside would have been transferred to Dublin rule rather than staying inside the North. All this said, on arrival you'll find the pubs much friendlier than you might have expected.

Around 3km east of Crossmaglen on the B30 Newry road, **CREGGAN** has a **Poets' Graveyard**, so named because three eighteenth-century Gaelic poets are buried here: Art Mac Cooey, Patrick Mac Aliondain and Séamus Mór Mac Murphy (who was also an outlaw of some notoriety). The inscription on Mac Cooey's stone is taken from his most famous poem, *Úr-Chill an Chreagáin* – "That with the fragrant Gaels of Creggan I will be put in clay under the sod".

Crossmaglen is at the forefront of the local revival of interest in Gaelic games, and the town's **Gaelic football** team, Crossmaglen Rangers, is consistently strong, though the last of their six All-Ireland championship victories came in 2012. If you fancy watching a game, their ground is St Oliver Plunkett Park.

ARRIVAL AND INFORMATION

CROSSMAGLEN AND AROUND

By bus Buses from/to Newry (Mon–Fri 6 daily, Sat 4; 55min) drop off on, and depart from, Ó Fiaich Square.

Tourist office The tourist office is in Ó Fiaich House on The Square (July & Aug daily 9am–6pm, Sept–June Mon–Fri 9am–5pm; http://visitmournemountains.co.uk).

ACCOMMODATION AND EATING

Cross Square Hotel 4–5 Ó Fiaich Square, 028 3086 0505. Very amenable accommodation in the centre of town, and though the rooms are slightly on the old-fashioned side, they're immaculately kept, and the staff couldn't be friendlier. The hotel's restaurant, meanwhile, is noted for its superb steaks. **££**

Keenans Bar Ó Fiaich Square, 028 3025 2767. The most agreeable of the town's pubs, this place has been around for the best part of eighty years, and hosts a notable traditional music session on Thurs.

ARMAGH FESTIVALS

Armagh has a tremendous roster of annual events, and, as you'd expect, the local **St Patrick's Day Parade** (March 17) is one of the largest in the country. Armagh is particularly well known for its **choral music**, and this manifests itself in the annual week-long **Charles Wood Festival of Music and Summer School** in mid-August (http://charleswoodsummerschool.org), featuring a daily series of recitals in the city's cathedrals and churches. In September, the four-day **Armagh Food and Cider Festival** (http://visitarmagh.com/festivals/foodandcider) celebrates the region's cuisine, with tours, tastings and suppers at various venues around town; while November sees the staging of the prestigious **John O'Connor Literary Arts Festival**, and the four-day **William Kennedy Piping Festival** (http://armaghpipers.org/wkpf), one of Ireland's major *uilleann* piping events (see page 580).

(see page 580)

Armagh city and around

ARMAGH is one of the most attractive places in the North, and the rich history of the city and its surroundings has plenty to keep you occupied for a day or two. The city offers **cathedrals** and **museums** set in handsome Georgian streets, and 3km west is the ancient site of once-grand **Navan Fort**. Armagh has been the site of the **Catholic** primacy of All Ireland since St Patrick established his church here, and has rather ambitiously adopted the title of the "Irish Rome" for itself – like Rome, it's positioned among seven small hills. Paradoxically, the city is also the seat of the **Protestant** Church of Ireland's archbishop of Armagh.

St Patrick's Roman Catholic Cathedral

Cathedral Rd • Free • http://armaghparish.net

The best way to get your bearings is to walk up the steps of **St Patrick's Roman Catholic Cathedral**, built on a hillside just northwest of the Shambles Market. The view of the town from here is impressive, and you should be able to identify most of the key sites spread out below. The cathedral's foundation stone was laid in 1840, but completion was delayed by the Famine and a subsequent lack of funding. While the pope and local nobility chipped in, money was also raised by public collections and raffles – one prize of a grandfather clock has still not been claimed. On the outside, the cathedral first appears little different from many of its nineteenth-century Gothic-Revival contemporaries, but it is impressively large and airy. Inside, as befits the seat of the cardinal archbishop, every inch of wall glistens with **mosaics**, in colours ranging from marine- and sky-blue to terracotta pinks and oranges. Other striking pieces include the white-granite "pincer-claw" **tabernacle**

15

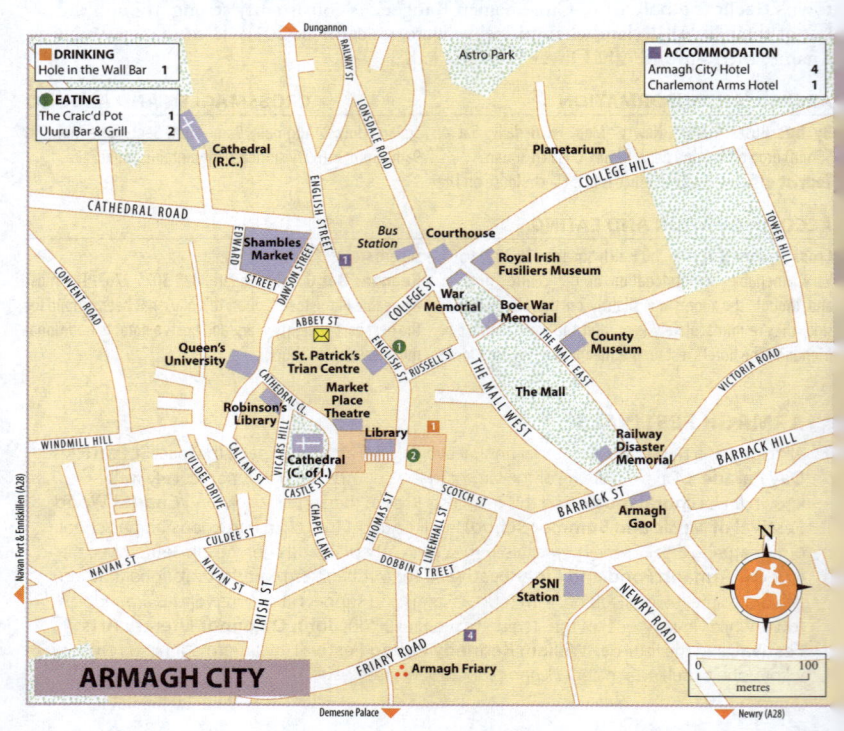

holder, reflected in a highly polished marble floor, and a **statue** of the Crucifixion, which suggests (deliberately or otherwise) the old city's division into **Trians**.

St Patrick's Church of Ireland Cathedral

Cathedral Close • April–Sept Mon–Sat 9am–5pm; Oct–March Mon & Wed–Sat 9am–1.30pm • charge • http://stpatricks-cathedral.org

St Patrick's Church of Ireland Cathedral lays claim to the summit of the principal hillock, Drum Saileach, where St Patrick founded his first church in 445 AD. It commands a distinctive Armagh view across to the other hills and down over the clutter of gable walls and pitched roofing on its own slopes. A series of churches occupied the site after 445, and, although the core of the present one is medieval, a nineteenth-century restoration has coated the thirteenth-century outer walls in a sandstone plaster of which Thackeray remarked, "It is as neat and trim as a lady's dressing room." Many of the ancient decorations were removed, leaving the spartan interior you see today. Just as you enter from the highly distinctive timber porch, you'll see a few remnants of an eleventh-century **Celtic cross** and a startling **statue** of Thomas Molyneux. Inside, high up, you should be able to sight the medieval carved heads of men, women and monsters. One other unusual feature is the tilt of the chancel, a medieval building practice meant to represent the slumping head of the dying Christ. The **chapterhouse** has a small collection of stone statues (mostly gathered from elsewhere), the most noticeable of which are the Stone Age **Tandragee Idol** and a Sheila-na-Gig (see page 608) with an ass's ears. Outside the north transept a plaque on the west wall commemorates the burial of **Brian Ború**. There's also a plaque dedicated to composer Charles Wood, who was born just across the way on Vicars' Hill and who was himself a chorister in the cathedral.

Armagh Robinson Library

43 Abbey St • guided tours on request • Free, donations welcomed; tours charge • http://armaghrobinsonlibrary.co.uk

The wonderful **Armagh Robinson Library** is Ireland's oldest, founded in 1771 by Archbishop Richard Robinson (1708–94), who was described as converting Armagh "from mud to stone" and who is responsible for almost all the older buildings in the city – the nearby infirmary was one of his, too, though it's now occupied by the university. The core of the collection is Robinson's own library, mostly seventeenth-and eighteenth-century books on theology, philosophy, politics and the sciences, though there is also a superb collection of medieval manuscripts and incunabula. Among the many rare tomes is a first edition of **Gulliver's Travels** annotated by Swift himself, and an early copy of Handel's **Messiah**, plus material belonging to Charles Wood (born just a few doors away).

The Mall

The Mall is an elegant tree-lined promenade fringed to the east by two terraces of handsome Georgian houses designed by the Armagh-born architect Francis Johnston at the behest of Archbishop Robinson. Johnston was responsible for many of Dublin's best Georgian buildings, including its GPO (see page 80), and you'll encounter more examples of his work around town, including the classical **courthouse** at The Mall's northern end; the former **jail** occupies the southern end. The Mall owes its largely oval shape to the fact that it was once a racecourse in the late eighteenth century; nowadays, there's nothing more athletic taking place than the occasional jogger and Saturday cricket matches.

Dotted throughout the park are three **memorials**; at the northern end, you'll find two monuments to those who fell during the Boer War and World War I, while at the southern end is the Railway Disaster Memorial, which remembers the 89 people who were killed in the crash in 1889 (see below); a simple yet affecting piece, it portrays a young girl holding a bucket and spade.

15

Armagh County Museum

The Mall East • Free • 028 3752 3070

A former schoolhouse on the east side of The Mall houses the **County Museum**, a charmingly old-fashioned space with all the usual local miscellany on display, including an alarmingly vivid collection of stuffed wildlife. One display devoted to railway history recounts the story of Ireland's worst **railway disaster**, when two passenger trains collided outside Armagh in 1889, killing 89 people, many of whom are buried in nearby St Mark's churchyard. Along with photos of the wreckage, there's a rather poignant letter, written in 1958, from one of the survivors, in which he recalls the events of that day.

Rotating art exhibitions complete the museum's ensemble, though one picture on permanent show is local artist J.B. Vallely's *The Red Fiddle*, a superb oil showing five musicians enjoying a session; the theme of traditional music figures in more than three thousand of Vallely's canvases (some of which are occasionally on display here), and, with his wife Eithne, he currently runs the town's Armagh Pipers' Club.

The Royal Irish Fusiliers Museum

The Mall • Free • http://royairishfusiliersmuseum.com

Occupying Sovereigns House, the leftovers of the courthouse, is the **Royal Irish Fusiliers Museum**. It's pretty much as you'd expect: tons of weaponry, uniforms, medallions and silverware from the regiment formed in 1793 in response to the Napoleonic crisis and subsequently known as the Faughs, from their battle cry *Faugh a Ballagh!* ("Clear the way!"). The Fusiliers subsequently fought in the Crimean and Boer wars (where they relieved the Siege of Ladysmith) and in both world wars before amalgamating with the Inniskilling Fusiliers (see page 550) and Ulster Rifles in 1968 to form the Royal Irish Rangers; in 1992, they joined with the Ulster Defence Regiment to form the present-day Royal Irish Regiment.

Armagh Planetarium

College Hill • shows 30–40min each • charge; Astropark free • http://armagh.space

The **Armagh Planetarium** boasts "the world's most advanced digital production projection system, Digistar 3", with full animation of the planetarium's dome (and reclining seats to enjoy the full effects), as well as an extraordinarily good sound setup. Various shows are on offer, including the child-oriented "Secret of the Cardboard Rocket" which explores the solar system; "Pole Position", touring the constellations; and "Violent Universe", a crash-and-burn account of comets and meteors. Inside there's also an exhibition hall featuring a range of high-tech interactive displays of the cosmos, as well as images of deep space and an assortment of meteorite chunks from the Moon and Mars. Outside there's the landscaped Astropark, a series of trails depicting the extent of the solar system in comparison to the known universe – a stroll up the Hill of Infinity leads to its very edge and also offers a glorious view of the city.

Armagh Friary and Demesne Palace

The ruins of **Armagh Friary** (open access), founded by the Franciscans in 1263, lie within easy walking distance south of the city centre on Friary Road, though they are marred somewhat by the continuous roar of traffic. Nearby is the entrance to the grounds of the Archbishop's Palace, otherwise known as the **Demesne Palace**; it now houses the District Council offices, hence is off-limits to the public, but you can wander around the adjacent **Palace Stables** – which is home to a superb restaurant (see below) – along with a well-preserved **ice house**, a curious **tunnel** by which servants accessed the basement kitchens, and a stimulating **sensory garden**.

ROAD BOWLS

The sport of **road bowls** is popular in Holland and Germany and was once played throughout Ireland, but is now limited mainly to Cork and Armagh, where it's also known as "road bullets".

The principle of the game is simple: a pair of rival contestants each propels an 800g (28oz) solid-iron ball along a course of country roads (usually about 4km long), the winner being the player who reaches the finishing line with the **fewest number of throws**. In practice, it's a complicated business. The Armagh roads twist and turn, up and down, and bowlers are assisted by a team of camp followers, including managers and road guides who advise on the most advantageous spots to aim for and the force of the throw.

Roads around Armagh where you're likely to catch sight of the game – usually on Sunday afternoons – include Cathedral Road, Knappagh Road, Blackwater Town, Rock, Tassagh, Newtownhamilton and Madden roads. The most reliable information on forthcoming games is probably to be had in local pubs. The **Ulster Finals** are held in the city over two weekends in late June or early July, with the **All-Ireland Road Bowls Final** in early August.

15

ARRIVAL AND DEPARTURE
ARMAGH CITY

By bus The Ulsterbus station is on Lonsdale Rd, just north of the centre.
Destinations Belfast (Mon–Fri hourly, Sat 8, Sun 5; 1hr 15–

25min); Loughgall (Mon–Fri 7 daily; 15min); Monaghan (Mon–Fri 10 daily, Sat 4, Sun 2; 40min); Newry (Mon–Fri hourly, Sat 8; 50min).

ACCOMMODATION
SEE MAP PAGE 532

Armagh City Hotel 2 Friary Rd, http://armaghcityhotel. com. Behind the facade of its somewhat bland exterior, there's a great buzz about this large, modern hotel, which offers plush accommodation in a range of room categories; note, though, that its main business is conferences and weddings, so you'll need to book well in advance. **££**

Charlemont Arms Hotel 57–65 English St, http:// charlemontarmshotel.com. It doesn't look particularly exciting from the outside, but this long-established, family-run establishment offers polished rooms, a congenial welcome and is in a terrific location just a few paces from the city centre. **££**

EATING
SEE MAP PAGE 532

The Craic'd Pot 25 Upper English St, 028 3778 9657. Justifiably a local favourite, this cracking espresso café offers a delicious array of caffeine fixes, brewed various ways, for example Aeropress, Chemex and French Press; if you fancy something truly heart-stopping, ask for a *hammerhead* (filter with double espresso); the pastries aren't half bad either. **£**

Uluru Bar & Grill 3–5 Market St, http://ulurubarandgrill. com. Ostensibly an Australian restaurant (to be fair, there is kangaroo loin on the menu), the real draw here is the josper charcoal grill, where you can tuck into any number of juicy burgers and steaks, served, perhaps, with tobacco onions and a green peppercorn sauce. There are also a handful of veggie/vegan dishes. Closed Mon. **£££**

DRINKING
SEE MAP PAGE 532

Hole in the Wall Bar 9 Market St, 028 3752 3515. Dating from the early seventeenth century, this dark, low-beamed inn was the former holding centre for the town's prison.

It's the most inviting hostelry around, with great beer, interesting characters and a resident parrot if you're stuck for conversation.

Navan Fort

81 Killylea Rd, 4km west of Armagh • **Fort** Open access • Free • **Navan Centre** • charge • http://visitarmagh.com • Bus #73 from Armagh

For nearly seven hundred years **Navan Fort** was the great seat of northern power, rivalling Tara in the south. It was here that the kings of Northern Ireland ruled and Queen Macha built her palace on the earthwork's summit. It's a site of deeply mystical significance, but also one of enormous archaeological interest. The court of the **Knights of the Red Branch**, Ireland's most prestigious order of chivalry, was based here too. The knights, like those of the Round Table, are historical figures entirely subsumed into legend, their greatest champion being the legendary defender of Northern Ireland, **Cúchulainn** (see pages 154 and 530). The stories of these warriors' deeds are recited and sung in what's now known as the **Ulster Cycle**. Their dynasty was finally vanquished in 332 AD, when three brothers (the Collas), in a conquest known as the Black Pig's Dyke, destroyed Navan Fort, razing it to the ground and leaving only the earthen mounds visible today. The defeated Red Branch Knights were driven eastwards into Down and Antrim, and were little heard of again.

Before visiting the site, you may wish to pop into the **Navan Centre**, which features an exhibition on the fort, courtesy of various archaeological bits and bobs excavated from the site, and a multimedia show on the Ulster Cycle – in itself though, it's not really worth the entrance fee. Skirting the centre, you'll discover that the site area is defined by a massive bank with a defensive **ditch**. When you reach the fort, you'll find an **earthen mound**, which gives a commanding view but no hint of its past. Excavation of the mound took place over a ten-year period (1961–71) and revealed a peculiar structure, apparently unique in the Celtic world. Archaeologists reckon that around 100 BC the buildings that had existed since the Neolithic period were cleared, and a huge structure 33m diameter was constructed. An outer wall of timber surrounded five concentric rings of large posts, 275 in all, with a massive post at the very centre. This was then filled with

15

THE ORANGE ORDER AND THE MARCHING TRADITION

Ireland's oldest political grouping, **The Grand Orange Lodge of Ireland**, was founded in September 1795 following the so-called **Battle of the Diamond**, which took place in or near **Dan Winter's farm** near Loughgall. The skirmish involved the Peep O'Day boys (Protestants) and the Defenders (Catholics) and was the culmination of a long-running dispute about control of the local linen trade. The Defenders attacked an inn, unaware that, inside, the Peep O'Day boys were armed and waiting. A dozen Defenders were killed, and in the glow of victory their opponents formed the **Orange Order**.

The first Orange Lodge march in celebration of the 1690 **Battle of the Boyne** (see page 563) took place in 1796, and they've been happening ever since. The Boyne is the Loyalist totem, even though the actual battle at Aughter that ended Jacobite rule did not take place until the following year. **William of Orange** is their icon, despite the fact that his campaign was supported by the pope and most of the Catholic rulers of Europe, and that William himself had a noted reputation for religious tolerance. For Protestant Northern Irish, the Boyne came to represent a victory that enshrined Protestant supremacy and liberties, and the Orange Order became the bedrock of Protestant hegemony. Between 1921 and 1969, for example, 51 of the 54 ministers appointed to the Stormont government were members of the Orange Order; at its peak, so were two-thirds of the Protestant male population of the North.

The **Loyalist** "marching season" begins in March and culminates in celebration of the Battle of the Boyne on July 12, followed by the **Apprentice Boys'** traditional march around the walls of Derry on August 12. Most Loyalist marches are uncontentious – small church parades, or commemorations of the Somme – but it can't be denied that some of them are something other than a vibrant expression of cultural identity. Marching can be a means by which one community asserts its dominance over the other – Loyalists selecting routes that deliberately pass through Nationalist areas, for instance, or their "Kick the Pope" fife-and-drum bands deliberately playing sectarian tunes and making provocative gestures such as the raising of five fingers on Belfast's **Lower Ormeau Road** (where five Catholics were shot dead in 1992). Though Loyalist marches have tended to be the flashpoints for major disturbances in recent years, not least in the late 1990s at **Drumcree** near Portadown, it shouldn't be forgotten that the marching tradition is common to both communities. Around three thousand marches take place throughout Northern Ireland each year and, although the vast majority are Loyalist parades, a significant number are **Nationalist**. The latter include the St Patrick's Day (March 17) marches of the Ancient Order of Hibernians and the Irish National Foresters, and commemorative parades and wreath-laying ceremonies by Sinn Féin and other Republican bodies on Easter Monday and various anniversaries.

limestone boulders and **set on fire**, creating a mountain of ash that was then covered with sods of clay to make a high mound. It is anybody's guess what the purpose of the structure was – possibly a temple, or maybe a monumental funeral pyre.

It's worth heading over to "Living History" (April–Sept only; included in Navan Centre ticket price), where, in a reconstructed Iron Age dwelling, costumed characters regale visitors with ancient stories, demonstrate various crafts and prepare food on an open fire. Adults will find it just as entertaining as kids. There's a very agreeable café in the centre too when in need of refreshments.

Loughgall and around

LOUGHGALL, a tranquil and pretty estate village about 8km north of Armagh, lies in the middle of apple-orchard country, beautiful in the spring, and is worth visiting mainly for its historical connections. Like many of its neighbours in Armagh's rural north, Loughgall is strongly **Protestant**; indeed it was at Diamond Hill, a few kilometres away, that the Battle of the Diamond took place in 1795, which led to the foundation of the first Protestant **Orange Order** (see page 536).

15

Museum of Orange Heritage

36 Main St • charge • http://orangeheritage.co.uk

The history of the Orange Order is comprehensively relayed in the **Museum of Orange Heritage**, which occupies Sloan's House – the house owned by James Sloan, one of the Order's three founders, the others being James Wilson and Daniel Winter (see page 537). The parlour in which the Order came into being still has the original table and gavel (ceremonial mallet) used by Sloan while chairing the meeting; it was here, too, that the first warrants were signed for the Order's various lodges. Elsewhere, there's stacks of memorabilia from Orders around the world: documents, sashes and other regalia accessories, plus a few pieces of weaponry used in the Battle of the Diamond, though you may have to ask to view these as they're usually locked away.

To the rear of the building, the **Garden of Remembrance** has 68 plaques listing the names of all those Orangemen killed in the county during the Troubles. Having perused the exhibition, pop into the very pleasant *Sloan's* coffee shop, on the ground floor of the building.

Dan Winter's Cottage

9 Derryloughan Rd, 5km northeast of Loughall • Voluntary donation • http://danwinterscottage.com

Positioned directly across from the site of the Battle of the Diamond, **Dan Winter's Cottage** is where the initial discussions regarding the formation of the Orange Order took place, though the order was officially formed at Sloan's House. The cottage itself – whose roof still contains original lead shot from the battle – dates from 1703, and has been the ancestral home ever since Dan Winter lived here. Inside, you can see maps and relics from the battle, family photos, and a hoard of banners and sashes. There's some notable seventeenth-century furniture here too.

The Argory

144 Derrycaw Rd, Dungannon • Visits by guided tour (hourly) • charge • http://nationaltrust.org.uk/the-argory

Set in 350 acres by the River Blackwater, 9km north of Loughgall, **The Argory** is a fine Neoclassical building dating from 1824. The **grounds** are splendid, but it's the **house** that's the real attraction. Built of Caledon stone, its entrance hall features a fine cantilevered staircase, and the rooms contain Victorian and Edwardian furniture among many other period items, including a fabulous cabinet barrel organ. The house is still lit by an original 1906 acetylene gas plant in the stable yard, and during the summer it stages musical events and garden walks. Tours provide entertaining anecdotes about the house's owners, the McGeough-Bonds.

Tyrone and Fermanagh

SUNSET OVER LOUGH NEAGH

Tyrone and Fermanagh

Much of inland Northern Ireland is formed by neighbouring Tyrone and Fermanagh, predominantly rural counties whose few sizeable towns, with the exception of Omagh, lie at the eastern and western fringes of the region. Stretching from the shores of the vast Lough Neagh in the east to the Donegal border in the west, Tyrone is primarily a farming country with little evidence of industrialization apart from the neat planters' villages that grew up with the linen industry and a smattering of heavier industries in the towns near Lough Neagh.

The county's chief scenic attractions can be found in the wild and desolate **Sperrin Mountains** in the north, where the village of **Gortin**, on the Ulster Way footpath, makes a good base. The region's towns hold little of interest, though the largest, **Omagh**, is near the **Ulster American Folk Park**, which explores the connections between the Northern Ireland province and the US.

In contrast to Tyrone, **Fermanagh** attracts plenty of visitors – chiefly for its watersports, boating and fishing. Justly famous for the intense beauty of its lakes, much of the landscape is dominated by their waters, which, along with numerous rivers, constitute more than a third of the county's area. At its core is **Lough Erne**, a huge lake complex dotted with islands and surrounded by richly beautiful countryside. Lower Lough Erne, in the northwest, draws the most visitors, but the Upper Lough in the southeast also has its attractions, its hills wooded with oak, ash and beech. There are plenty of opportunities for watersports, while the less energetic can get onto the lough by renting a boat or taking a cruise. Walkers will find mostly gentle hills and woods which rise to small mountains in the south and west of the county, made accessible by the **Ulster Way**. For cyclists, there are well-surfaced, empty roads, though routes around the Upper Lough are harder to negotiate, with little lanes often leading to the reed-filled shore – an atmospheric spot for a picnic.

At the point where the Upper and Lower loughs meet, the county town of **Enniskillen** has long been a strategic bridging point: today, with more amenities than the rest of Fermanagh put together, it makes an ideal base for touring the area and getting out on the water. With your own transport you can easily access Fermanagh's impressive series of **planters' castles**, along with two of the country's finest stately houses in **Florence Court** and **Castle Coole**.

16

GETTING AROUND

In both Tyrone and Fermanagh, the sights of interest are dispersed, and buses can be very infrequent away from the main routes – you're likely to see little of the most interesting parts of the region without a car or a bike. In the Sperrins, hiking is the best way to get around, although sporadic buses also serve the area.

Omagh and around

The name of Tyrone's largest town, **OMAGH**, is synonymous with the worst single atrocity in the history of the Troubles when, on the afternoon of Saturday August 15, 1998, a five-hundred-pound **car bomb**, planted by the dissident Republican group the Real IRA, exploded on Market Street. Twenty-nine people, and two unborn twins, died and more than two hundred were injured. Much of the eastern part of Omagh's main street was devastated by the bombing, though has since undergone major reconstruction. Two sites that recall that day form part of the

DEVENISH ISLAND

Highlights

❶ Ulster American Folk Park Plot your way around this wonderful assemblage of vernacular buildings, which recall the history of Irish emigration to America. See page 543

❷ The Sperrin Mountains Ruggedly picturesque, the Sperrins offer a splendid variety of hikes and trails. See page 544

❸ Beaghmore Stone Circles Seven Bronze Age stone circles and relics set in a lonely spot with tremendous views. See page 545

❹ Lough Neagh Ireland's largest lake – and indeed the biggest in the British Isles – is best viewed from the churchyard at Ardboe. See page 546

❺ Castle Coole Perhaps the most magnificent building of its kind in Northern Ireland, this gorgeous eighteenth-century mansion is richly decorated inside and set in wonderful grounds. See page 550

❻ Devenish Island Getting out on the water is an essential part of any trip to Fermanagh, and there's no better place to do it than at this former monastic settlement in Lower Lough Erne. See page 552

❼ Marble Arch Caves Take a boat trip along a subterranean river to view these caves filled with stalactites and other marvellous rock formations. See page 557

HIGHLIGHTS ARE MARKED ON THE MAP ON PAGE 542

Town Trail, which is well worth an hour or so of your time; a copy of the trail can be picked up at the tourist office.

The area uphill to the west contains two adjacent buildings that would grace any town – the fine classical **courthouse**, adorned with a splendid Tuscan columned portico; and the irregular twin spires of the Catholic **Sacred Heart Church** – inside, take a look at the Rose Window above the high altar. Though there's little else to see in the town itself, it's a useful place to base yourself for exploring the area and has all the ameneties you need.

The Glass Pillar and Memorial Garden

At the bottom of Market Street, a 4m-high cenotaph-like **Glass Pillar** – with a three-dimensional heart inside – stands at the point where the bomb exploded, next to a plaque on the wall. From here, head across the Strule Bridge to the **Memorial Garden**, a beautifully landscaped park with thirty-one pole-mounted mirrors strategically placed so that when the sun shines, they direct light on to the glass pillar, a rather ingenious feat of engineering. Engraved on a semicircular granite wall are the names of all those who died, which included six children – despite the traffic rushing by, it's a deeply affecting place.

TYRONE AND FERMANAGH

HIGHLIGHTS

1. Ulster American Folk Park
2. The Sperrin Mountains
3. Beaghmore Stone Circles
4. Lough Neagh
5. Castle Coole
6. Devenish Island
7. Marble Arch Caves

ARRIVAL AND INFORMATION

By bus The bus station is just across the river from the town centre in Mountjoy Rd.

Destinations Belfast (Mon–Sat hourly, Sun 6; 1hr 45min); Derry (Mon–Sat hourly, Sun 7; 1hr 10min); Dublin (Bus Éireann; 7 daily; 2hr); Enniskillen (Mon–Fri 6 daily, Sat 3, Sun 1; 1hr); Gortin (Mon–Fri 7 daily; 25min); Letterkenny (Bus Éireann; 7 daily; 1hr 5min); Monaghan (Bus Éireann; 10 daily; 45min); Ulster American Folk Park (Mon–Sat hourly, Sun 5; 15min).

Tourist office On the ground floor of the riverside Strule Arts Centre on Townhall Square, just west of the bus station (Mon–Sat 10am–5.30pm; http://exploreomaghsperrins.com).

ACCOMMODATION AND EATING

Number 19 19 High St, 028 8225 7772. In a town with limited dining possibilities, this popular place is as good a spot as any for a bite to eat (snacks and hot lunches) or a coffee. Its sunny floral interior comes with leather couches and big bay windows looking out onto the street. **£**

The Riverfront Café 38 Market St, 028 8225 0011. Directly opposite the glass pillar memorial, this is a cosy hideaway for a quiet mug of coffee and slice of cake, or perhaps a warming lunch; super home-made ice cream too. Mon–Sat 8.30am–5pm.

Silverbirch Hotel 5 Gortin Rd, http://silverbirchhotel.com. Although aimed largely at the business end of things, this rather ungainly low-rise, out on the Gortin road, is the only hotel in town and the rooms offer a high level of comfort. Some good deals available too. **££**

ENTERTAINMENT

Dún Uladh Cultural Heritage Centre Drumnakilly Rd, 8km east of town off the B4 http://dunuladh.ie. Fabulously vibrant regional centre that promotes traditional Irish music and culture, with some big names; there's also a traditional session on Saturday nights.

Strule Arts Centre Townhall Square, http://struleartscentre.co.uk. Stages a lively programme of music, drama and other events, and has a regular roster of excellent touring companies.

16

Ulster American Folk Park

Mellon Rd, Castletown • charge • http://ulsteramericanfolkpark.org • Bus #273 Belfast to Derry from Omagh

The most successful of Northern Ireland's American-heritage projects is the wonderful **Ulster American Folk Park**. The first significant emigration from Ireland to North America was that of Northern Irish folk in the early eighteenth century, many of whom were of Scottish Protestant origin. Of all the immigrant communities in the United States, it was the Irish who most quickly – and profoundly – made their mark; the three first-generation US presidents were of Irish origin were all of Ulster stock, and thirteen overall could trace their roots to here. Throughout the eighteenth and nineteenth centuries, thousands of people left to establish new lives in North America, a steady flow of emigrants that became a torrent during the Famine years.

Before heading out to the park itself, have a nose around the indoor **Emigrants Exhibition**, just beyond the reception desk, which documents the causes and patterns of migration, though, regrettably, little attention is paid to the Native Americans dispossessed by the Northern Ireland settlers.

The Park

You enter the park in the **Old World**, where original buildings have been transplanted or replicas constructed to provide a sense of Northern Irish life in the past. Throughout, costumed guides and craftworkers cheerfully answer questions and explain their activities, augmenting the folk park's attention to authenticity.

The disparity in living conditions in nineteenth-century Ireland is illustrated by the juxtaposition of a typical pre-Famine **single-room cabin,** from the Sperrins, with the **Mellon Homestead**, a significantly more substantial dwelling and the only structure in the park in its original location; it was in this house that Thomas Mellon – founder of the Mellon Bank in 1869 in Pennsylvania, which now trades as The Bank of New York Mellon – was born in 1813, before the family emigrated five years later. Fittingly, the park was opened by descendants of Mellon in 1976. Even more impressive is the thatched, double-storey **Campbell House**, the ancestral home of Hugh Campbell, who also emigrated and became a successful Philadelphia merchant.

Look out, too, for the **Hughes House**, the one-time home of John Hughes, another successful émigré who became the first Catholic Archbishop of New York in 1842, though if his nickname, "Dagger John", was anything to go by, not a particularly popular one; one peculiar feature of this house is the "jamb" wall, a single brick wall between front door and hearth which prevented draughts, as well as offering a degree of privacy. A few paces away is the Victorian **schoolhouse**, which functioned from 1845 to 1950; it's furnished with its original, graffiti-strewn desks and is overseen by a suitably stern mistress quick to admonish anyone that steps out of line. A re-created Ulster **street**, including the impressively authentic O'Doherty's Spirit Grocers, whose shelves are packed with appropriate period stock, leads to the *Union*, a full-sized **brig**, reconstructed to demonstrate the gruelling conditions endured during the voyage across the Atlantic; with a thirty percent mortality rate, it's little wonder that they were coined "coffin ships".

Upon disembarking, you enter the **Old World**, starting with an American street featuring, among other concerns, a reconstruction of the first Mellon Bank. From here, leafy lanes wind down to edifices constructed by the Pennsylvanian settlers, notably a massive six-roomed log **farmhouse** and a Tennessee plantation house. One event of note here is the annual **Bluegrass Festival** held over the May Day bank holiday weekend.

16

The Sperrin Mountains

The impressive, undulating **Sperrin Mountains** form the northeastern limits of County Tyrone. Wild, empty and beautiful, they reach 680m at their highest point, yet the smooth and gradually curving slopes give them a deceptively low appearance. The covering of bog and heather only adds to this effect, suggesting nothing more than high, open moorland. For all this, views from the summits are panoramic, and the evenness of texture can make the mountains sumptuous when bathed in evening light. It's impossible not to catch sight of **wildlife**, too. Sparrowhawks and kestrels fly above, and you might see buzzards or the rare hen harrier, attracted by a rich range

---

WALKING THE SPERRINS

The 64km-wide range of the Sperrin Mountains offers good long-distance **walking**, without necessarily involving steep inclines. You can ramble wherever you like, but remember that – despite appearances – these are high mountains, and changeable weather makes them potentially dangerous. A map and compass are essential for serious excursions.

The **Central Sperrins Way** (map available from most tourist offices) is a 40km waymarked trail, which begins and ends at Barnes Gap, halfway between Plumbridge and Cranagh. The two-day walk takes in a variety of countryside with spectacular views of the mountains, moorland and Glenelly Valley. The exposed moorland can often be very wet and boggy underfoot and, as there is no accommodation en route, taking a tent is essential.

For those not equipped for the high ground, the **Glenelly and Owenkillen** river valleys run through the heart of this fine countryside from Plumbridge and Gortin respectively and are particularly enjoyable for cyclists; you can pick up a copy of the Sperrins cycling guide from tourist offices. The **Sperrins and Killeter Walking Festival** (http://sperrinskilleterwalking.com) is held in mid-September and involves various guided walks, graded according to difficulty.

of prey in a landscape mostly undisturbed by development: the Sperrins teem with assorted mammals, including even the rare Irish hare. Over the years there's been many a tale about the discovery of "gold in them there hills", and you might encounter the occasional panner testing the story's veracity.

Much depopulated over the years, the local sheep-farming community is now sparsely scattered across the region; there are few **facilities** such as shops or pubs and little accommodation, except in Gortin, so planning ahead is essential if you're intending to walk in the mountains.

Gortin

The best base for exploring the Sperrins is the one-street village of **GORTIN**, 16km north of Omagh. Around 5km south of the village is the **Gortin Glen Forest Park** (daily 10am–dusk; cars charge), with a 8km **forest drive** and various **trails** leading to viewpoints of the area. For mountain bikers, there are three variously graded trails in the park's northern reaches, above the Glenpark Road. The park's most popular attraction, however, is its herd of **Sika deer**, which are particularly fun to watch in rutting season, typically from the end of September through to November. Gortin Glen is accessible on any bus between Omagh and Gortin (see page 545).

Beaghmore Stone Circles

Tyrone is peppered with **archeological remains**: there are more than a thousand standing stones in the Sperrins alone, and the county as a whole boasts numerous chambered graves. The most impressive relics are the Bronze Age **Beaghmore Stone Circles**, in the southeast of the Sperrins. From Gortin, take the B46 east onto the A505, from where they're well signposted up a track just over 5km north off the road. Although most of the stones on this lonely site are no more than a metre high, the complexity of the ritual they suggest is impressive: there are seven stone circles, ten stone rows and a dozen round cairns (burial mounds, some containing cremated human remains). All of the circles stand in pairs, except for one, which is filled with over eight hundred upright stones, known as the **Dragon's Teeth**. The alignments correlate to movements of the sun, moon and stars; two of the rows point to sunrise at the summer solstice.

An Creagán Visitor Centre

24km east of Omagh on the A505 • Free • Bike rental £10/day • http://ancreagan.com

Modelled on the many surrounding cairns, the **An Creagán Visitor Centre** explores the rare, raised bog terrain all around with interpretive **displays** and signposted **walking and cycling routes** over the countryside; the longest of the three trails is the circular, 5km-long Forest Walk. The farmers driven to these bogs in the eighteenth century made huge efforts to reclaim the soil: there are limekilns from which they treated the reclaimed land, and you can still see their **potato ridges** – these grassed-over Copney spade ridges point back to the devastating Famine of 1845–51 and illustrate the farmers' desperate attempts to survive.

An Creagán is, however, more of a **cultural centre** than a museum, with locals coming along to occasional traditional music concerts, dancing, storytelling and singing events; there's also a restaurant here.

ARRIVAL AND DEPARTURE | **THE SPERRIN MOUNTAINS**

By bus The Central Sperrins are tricky to reach without your own transport, but there is the useful Sperrin Rambler bus (£9), which runs from Omagh throughout the year (currently Mon–Fri 9.15am & 1.15pm) via Gortin through the Sperrins to Cranagh and on to Magherafelt in Co. Derry (the return service from Magherafelt operates Mon–Fri

9.10am & 1.10pm).
Destinations An Creagán Centre to Omagh (Mon–Fri

2 daily, Sat 1; 50min); Gortin to Omagh (Mon–Fri 7 daily; 25min).

ACCOMMODATION AND EATING

An Clachan Cottages An Creagán, http://ancreagan.com. Eight self-catering cottages (with one to three bedrooms) are available in the traditional *clochán* settlements; the open turf fires are supplemented, fortunately, by central heating. Two-night minimum stay. **£££**

Foothills 16 Main St, Gortin, 028 8164 8157. You can eat really well at this snug restaurant/bar, where there's contemporary Irish cooking of the highest order; try the steak with whiskey and blue cheese sauce. **££**

Gortin Accommodation Suite 62 Main St, Gortin, http://gortincentre.com. A friendly, multi-functional venue offering a range of self-catering units, six- and eight-bed dorms and family rooms sleeping up to four. A range of on- and off-site activities are available, including canoeing and cycling. Dorms **£**, self-catering **££**

Eastern Tyrone

The dominant feature in the east of County Tyrone is the western shore of **Lough Neagh**, while there are a number of relics of both the region's historical heritage, such as the high cross at **Ardboe**, and its more recent industrial past at the **Wellbrook Beetling Mill**, close to Cookstown. The village of **Benburb**, to the south, is one of the most attractively situated in the North.

16 Lough Neagh

According to legend, **Lough Neagh** (pronounced "nay") owes its origins to the mythical giant Fionn Mac Cumhaill, who was so unimpressed by east Tyrone's low-lying terrain that he took a massive lump of land from Ulster and hurled it across the Irish Sea. It landed midway and became the Isle of Man, and the hole it left behind became the lough. Its shores provide excellent fishing and plenty of bird life, though both the surrounding land and lake itself are almost featureless. Small settlements house eel fishermen, whose catches go to the Toome Eel Fishery at **Toome** at the northern tip of the lake.

Ardboe high cross

Slight relief from the featurelessness is to be found at lakeside **Ardboe**, halfway along the lough's western shore, where there's a tenth-century **high cross**. The elements have eroded the various biblical scenes carved onto the sandstone almost beyond recognition, but its exceptional size – almost 6m high – is impressive. The cross stands in the grounds of an early monastery associated with St Colman, but the ruined church nearby dates from the seventeenth century and is of little interest. On a humid day in early summer, you'll also not fail to be impressed by the swarms of black Lough Neagh mayflies.

Wellbrook Beetling Mill

20 Wellbrook Rd, 10km west of Cookstown • July & Aug Sat & Sun 1–5pm • charge • http://nationaltrust.org.uk/wellbrook-beetling-mill

Positioned on a pretty stretch of the Ballinderry River, the eighteenth-century **Wellbrook Beetling Mill** is the last functioning water-powered linen mill in the country. "Beetling" was the final stage of production whereby linen was given a sheen and smoothness by hammering with heavy wooden "beetles". Harnessing the waters from the river is the superb almost-5m waterwheel, and although the mill ceased operation in 1961, it is extremely well preserved, and all the engines still work. The guides here are extremely enthusiastic and knowledgeable, and will give you a demonstration; it's also possible to have a go yourself; it's just a shame about the extremely limited opening hours.

Benburb

Lying 11km northwest of Armagh (see page 532), the picturesque village of **BENBURB** merits a detour. Main Street's tiny cottages were once apple-peeling sheds, and the parish **church**, dating from 1618, is one of the oldest still in regular use in Ireland. It stands next to the gates of a **Servite priory** – the monastic order of Servants of the Virgin, which, though founded in Florence in 1233, did not establish itself in Ireland until 1948. The priory grounds offer a pleasant stroll, but far better are the walks along the Blackwater River in **Benburb Valley Park** (daily 9am–dusk; free), where, perched on a rock 30m or so above the water, are the substantial remains of a **castle** built by Viscount Powerscourt in 1615, which offer commanding views of the Blackwater valley.

Enniskillen and around

A pleasant, conservative little town, **ENNISKILLEN** sits on an island like an ornamental buckle, the two narrow ribbons of water that pass each side connecting the Lower and Upper lough complexes – hence it can lay claim to being Ireland's only island town. The strategic strength of this position has long been recognized – indeed, the town takes its name from Innis Ceithleann, "the island of Kathleen", wife of Balor, who sought refuge here after a defeat in battle. Later the island became a Maguire stronghold before William Cole, a planter from Cornwall, was appointed governor in 1607. The town played a major role in the 1641 Rebellion and the later Williamite Wars, the latter leading to the formation of its two famous regiments, the **Inniskilling Dragoons** and the **Royal Inniskilling Fusiliers**, which played a significant role in the victory at the Battle of the Boyne. Much of Enniskillen's character comes from wealth derived from the care of a colonial presence, and evidence of British influence is widespread, not least in the stately **Portora Royal School**, which serves as a reminder of the continued elitism in the social order. Founded by Charles I in 1626, old boys include **Oscar Wilde** – the pride of the school, until his trial for homosexuality – and **Samuel Beckett**, after whom the town's most prestigious festival is named (see page 549).

16

However, the name Enniskillen is still often associated with one of the most devastating atrocities of the Troubles: on Remembrance Day 1987, an IRA **bomb** killed twelve and injured 61 people as they gathered to commemorate the dead of the two world wars. The resulting widespread outrage was instrumental in directing parts of the Republican movement towards seeking a political solution to the Troubles. Today, Enniskillen is worthy of a day's visit in its own right, with its **castle** and proximity to the elegant **Castle Coole**, plus a town centre relatively unspoilt by shopping developments. It's also ideally situated as a base for exploring Lough Erne and touring the attractive local countryside.

The main street

The centre invites strolling: the main street undulates gently, lined with sturdy Victorian and Edwardian town houses, thriving shops and smart pub fronts, and, clustered together, three fine **church** buildings – Church of Ireland, Catholic and Methodist. This street changes its name six times between the bridges at either end, running from Ann Street to East Bridge Street; to either side, lanes drop down towards the water. On Down Street, just off the High Street, pop your head into the **Buttermarket** (Mon–Sat 10am–5.30pm; thebuttermarketenniskillen.com), a superbly renovated dairy-market dating from 1835 that's now a craft and design centre where a range of artisans – potters, jewellers, woodturners and the like – happily ply their trade.

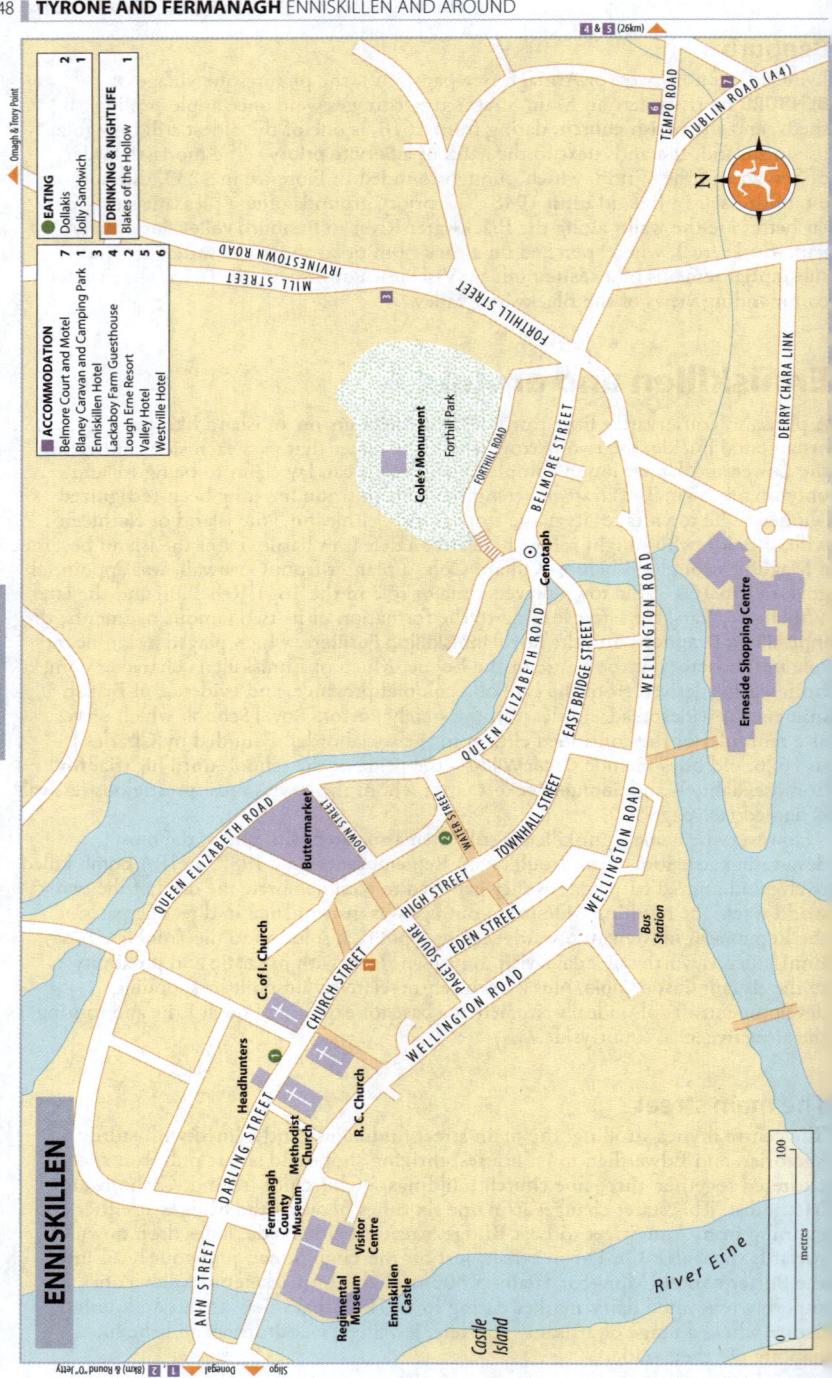

ENNISKILLEN FESTIVALS

Although no longer as big as it was, the town's chief annual event remains the Samuel Beckett-inspired **Happy Days Festival** (http://artsoverborders.com) at the end of August, which celebrates the eponymous novelist and playwright with a fantastic multi-arts programme of theatre, music, talks and readings in venues as diverse as the Buttermarket (see page 547) and the Marble Arch Caves (see page 557). **Fermanagh Live** (http://flive.org.uk), at the beginning of October, is a vibrant four-day festival of high-class music, drama and visual arts. Otherwise, there's the nine-day **Enniskillen Drama festival** (http://enniskillendramafestival.org) in March, hosted by the Ardhowen Theatre, while you should check with the tourist office for dates of the county **Fleadh**, the competitive traditional-music festival, in June (though it sometimes takes place in Derrygonnelly).

At the far end of East Bridge Street is the **cenotaph**, scene of the 1987 bombing; inscribed on a plaque are the names of those killed, along with twelve bronze doves, while a dedicated memorial was finally unveiled in 2022 on the wall of the rebuilt Clinton Centre, which was the site of the attack.

Headhunters

5 Darling St • Free • http://headhuntersmuseum.com

"The Barber Shop with a difference" is how **Headhunters** styles itself – and indeed, this barber shop-cum-railway museum is quite unique. Entering the shop up on the first floor, you'll immediately be struck by the rather surreal sight of customers having a haircut amid a wonderful clutter of **railway memorabilia**, including locomotive nameplates, station signs and photos. Beyond the shop itself, several rooms offer up a voluminous array of exhibits – signalling equipment, lamps, timetables, tickets and so on – that recall the heyday of the long-defunct Great Northern Railway, which closed in 1958; ask, too, to see the fabulous model railway up on the second floor. And if you fancy a trim afterwards…

Coles Monument

5 Forthill Park • April–Sept Sat & Sun, 2–4.30pm, tours every 30mins • Free • http://enniskillencastle.co.uk

Hidden away in a small park just beyond the cenotaph is one of Ennikillen's less visited sights. Completed in 1857, **Coles Monument** honours the distinguished general and parliamentarian Sir Galbraith Lowry Cole, a statue of whom tops the graceful, 30m-high doric-like column. Climbing the 108 stone steps brings you out onto a shallow, balconied platform affording a superlative panorama of the Fermanagh countryside – better still, you're likely to have the view all to yourself. Note, though, that to visit the inside you must pre-book onto one of the twenty-minute tours.

Enniskillen Castle

BT74 7HL • Charge • www.enniskillencastle.co.uk

Waterways loop their way around the core of Enniskillen, their glassy surfaces imbuing the town with a pervasive sense of calm and in places reflecting the mini-turrets of seventeenth-century **Enniskillen Castle**, which stands next to the island's westerly bridges. The castle was rebuilt by William Cole on the site of an old Maguire fort damaged by siege in 1594, and Cole's additions show obvious Scottish characteristics in the turrets corbelled out from the angles of the main wall. Today the castle grounds hold the town's two principal museums, which are accessed via a sparkling new visitor centre (see page 550).

Fermanagh County Museum

Charge • http://enniskillencastle.co.uk

The old barracks now house the intermittently stimulating **Fermanagh County Museum**, which covers in some depth the region's history, mainly through archaeological displays. The most interesting of these concerns the Drumclay crannog, which was excavated in 2012 and is believed to have been inhabited between the seventh and eighteenth centuries. Among the many superb finds on show here are bone combs, medieval dress pins and a pair of iron sheers; at one point there were nearly 140 crannogs (artificial island settlements) in Fermanagh alone. Other eye-catching exhibits include the River Erne Horn, ringed by nine bands of bronze, an immaculate bronze bell from Devenish Island, and a series of stone heads – look out for the suggestive male exhibitionist figure. The history of Enniskillen itself is covered downstairs, though disappointingly there's nothing on the town's recent past. The exhibition continues in a smaller building just beyond the visitor centre, though its displays pertaining to rural life in Fermanagh are eminently missable.

Regimental Museum of the Royal Inniskilling Fusiliers

Same hours and ticket as Fermanagh County Museum

Occupying the adjacent keep is the **Regimental Museum of the Royal Inniskilling Fusiliers**, a proud and polished display of the uniforms, flags and paraphernalia of the town's historic regiment; formed in 1881 as an Irish infantry regiment of the British Army, the Fusiliers amalgamated with the Royal Ulster Rifles and the Royal Irish Fusiliers to form the Royal Irish Rangers in 1968, before their latest reincarnation, in 1992, as part of the Royal Irish Regiment.

Castle Coole

1.5km southeast of Enniskillen · House guided tours hourly, last tour starts 1hr before closing · charge · http://nationaltrust.org.uk/castle-coole · The house can be approached either from the Dublin road (signposted just opposite the Ardhowen Theatre) or across the golf course from the Castlecoole road

Evidence of how the richest of the Enniskillen colonists lived can be found just outside town at **Castle Coole**, designed by James Wyatt and completed in 1797 as the lakeside home of the Earls of Belmore; the eighth earl and his family still live on site. A perfect Palladian-fronted building of silver Portland stone, the mansion is part of a huge seven-hundred-acre estate, whose beautiful landscaped **grounds** feature an impressive avenue of stately oak trees and a wealth of woodland walks.

Inside, the lavishly furnished **house** – indeed Wyatt indebted himself such was his extravagance – features scagliola (imitation marble) columns, exquisite plasterwork, Carrerra marble fireplaces, Cuban mahogany and an elegant library boasting Regency furnishings. A cantilevered staircase leads up to a dramatic and unusual lobby space and oval skylight, beyond which is a state bedroom decorated for George IV (who didn't actually come – in fact, the room was only ever used once, by the Bishop of Armagh in 1896). The tour ends in the labyrinthine basement, with its magnificent brick-vaulted cellar and capacious kitchen.

ARRIVAL AND INFORMATION

By bus Enniskillen's bus station is a 5min walk from the town centre on Wellington Rd.

Destinations Ballyshannon (Bus Éireann; 7 daily; 45min); Belcoo (Mon–Sat 3 daily; 25min); Belfast (Mon–Fri hourly, Sat 8, Sun 5; 2hr 15min); Belleek (Bus Éireann; 7 daily; 35min); Belturbet (Bus Éireann; 8 daily; 30min); Cavan (Bus Éireann; 8 daily; 50min); Clones (Mon–Sat 4 daily; 55min); Donegal town (Bus Éireann; 8 daily; 1hr 10min); Lisnarick (Mon–Sat 3–5 daily; 20–35min); Lisnaskea (Mon–Fri 8 daily, Sat 5; 30min); Omagh (Mon–Fri 5 daily, Sat 2, Sun 1; 1hr); Sligo (Bus Éireann; Mon–Sat 4 daily, Sun 2; 1hr 25min).

Tourist office The tourist office is inside the castle's visitor centre on Wellington Rd (Mon–Fri 9.30am–5pm, Sat 11am–5pm, plus June–Sept Sun 11am–5pm; http://fermanaghlakelands.com); this is also the place to come for information on all aspects of visiting Lough Erne, including fishing licences and permits.

ACCOMMODATION

SEE MAP PAGE 548

★ **Belmore Court and Motel** Tempo Rd, http://motel. co.uk. There's a decent choice of different accommodation here in this super-friendly hotel/motel; the motel, which is actually a large row of townhouse conversions, offers doubles, twins and family rooms, all with kitchenettes for self-catering, while the hotel itself has coolly furnished rooms with all mod cons. Breakfast is included but if staying in the motel costs extra. ££

Blaney Caravan and Camping Park 21km northwest of Enniskillen, off the A46 directly behind the Blaney service station, http://blaneycaravanpark.com. A beautifully situated and well-equipped campsite that's ideal for families. Modern shower block, laundry and play area. Closed Nov to mid-March. £

Enniskillen Hotel 72 Forthill St, http://enniskillenhotel. com. The building exterior is unremittingly dull, but the rooms looks fabulous in their various shades of grey, from the carpets and upholstery right down to the light switches; the only exception to the grey is the individually painted wall mural in each room. ££

Lackaboy Farm Guesthouse 51 Old Tempo Rd, http:// lackaboyhouse.com. Good-quality B&B in a rural setting 1.5km northeast of town, whose six florally patterned, en-suite rooms (including singles) promise a restful stay. There's

a guest lounge with large flatscreen TV and open fire, plus lovely little extras like home-made tray bakes upon arrival. ££

Lough Erne Resort Belleek Rd, 8km northwest of Enniskillen, http://lougherneresort.com. Spectacularly sited amid two lakeshore golf courses, *Lough Erne* offers large and supremely comfortable rooms – many with lake views – in its main building, alongside striking, turreted lodges sleeping up to six. Rooms, ££, lodges £££

Valley Hotel 60 Main St, Fivemiletown, 26km east of Enniskillen, http://thevalleyhotel.com. This smart, family-run hotel is a good choice if you're wanting to stay in the heart of the Tyrone countryside and also serves as a useful gateway to the Fermanagh countryside; good-sized, well turned out rooms are complemented by a very creditable restaurant/bar that functions as the lively hub of the local community. ££

Westville Hotel 14–20 Tempo Rd, http://westvillehotel. co.uk. The location is distinctly underwhelming and the grey, rough-hewn exterior is far from enticing, but this is actually a sparkling little boutique hotel offering tastefully designed rooms in warming chocolate brown and beige, or turquoise, colours. ££

16

EATING

SEE MAP PAGE 548

Dollakis 2b Cross St, 028 6634 2616. Three separate menus comprise this authentic Greek restaurant's offering: a lunch menu (noon–3pm) followed, between 5 and 7pm, by a meze menu, after which the à la carte menu is wheeled out; expect beautifully prepared dishes like feta cheese and honey filo pastry, or yoghurt-marinated chicken with chorizo souvlaki, then round it off with a glass of Metaxa or

frozen ouzo. Closed Sun. £££

Jolly Sandwich 3 Darling St, 028 6632 2277. Jolly by name, jolly by nature, this busy, buzzy daytime café/deli, laid out with dinky tables and bar stools, serves all-day breakfasts, hot wraps, salads and an eye-popping selection of cakes and scones. Closed Sun & Mon. £

DRINKING

SEE MAP PAGE 548

Blakes of the Hollow 6 Church St, http://blakesofthe hollow.com. With a *Game of Thrones* door in situ (see page 481), this agreeably careworn Victorian establishment should be your first port of call for a pint (the Guinness

is reckoned to be the best in town), its dark wooden snugs perfect for cosying up in. Live music on Fridays and Saturdays, which could be either rock and pop or traditional.

ENTERTAINMENT

Ardhowen Theatre Dublin Rd, http://ardhowen.com. The hub of Enniskillen's arts scene has a year-round programme of top-quality drama, film and ballet, and hosts a great

range of music events as well as productions by local community groups.

Lough Erne

Lough Erne has a profoundly important place in the history of Fermanagh. The earliest people to settle in the region lived on and around the two lakes, and many of the islands here are in fact *crannógs*. The lough's myriad connecting waterways were impenetrable to outsiders, protecting the settlers from invaders and creating an enduring cultural isolation. Evidence from stone carvings suggests that Christianity was accepted far more slowly here than elsewhere: several **pagan idols** have been found on Christian sites, and the early Christian remains to be found on the islands show the strong influence of pagan culture. Here, Christian carving has something of the stark symmetry, as well as a certain vacancy of facial expression, found in pagan statues. Particularly suggestive of earlier cults is the persistence of the human-head motif in stone carving – in pagan times a symbol of divinity and the most important of religious symbols.

Devenish Island and **White Island**, the most popular of the Erne's ancient sites, are on the Lower Lough, as is **Boa Island** in its far north, which is linked to the mainland by a bridge at each end. The **Upper Lough** is less rewarding, but has interesting spots that repay a leisurely dawdle. Aside from **cruising** the waterways (see page 553) and visiting the islands, there are a number of minor attractions around the loughs that are worth dropping into during your stay. Perhaps the most impressive are the early seventeenth-century planters' **castles** scattered around the shoreline.

Devenish Island

Heading around the eastern shores of Lower Lough Erne, **Devenish Island** is the easiest place to visit from Enniskillen without your own transport. A monastic settlement was founded on Devenish by St Molaise in the sixth century and became so important during the early Christian period that it had 1500 novices attached. Though plundered by Vikings in the ninth and twelfth centuries, it continued to be a major religious centre up until the early 1600s. It's a delightful setting, not far from the lough shore, and the **ruins** are considerable, spanning the entire medieval period. Most impressive are the sturdy oratory and perfect round tower, both from the twelfth century; St Molaise's church, a century older; and the ruined Augustinian priory, a fifteenth-century reconstruction of an earlier abbey with a fine Gothic sacristy door decorated with birds and vines. To the south is a superb **high cross**, with highly complex, delicate carving. Other treasures found here – such as an early eleventh-century book shrine, the Soiscel Molaise – are now kept in the National Museum in Dublin (see page 67).

16

ARRIVAL AND DEPARTURE | DEVENISH ISLAND

By ferry Erne Water Taxis (http://ernewatertaxi.com) operates ferries to the island from Trory Point, around 6.5km north of Enniskillen off the A32 Irvinestown road (July & Aug daily hourly 10am–5pm; June & Sept Mon, Thurs, Fri, Sat & Sun hourly 11am–3pm; Oct Sat & Sun hourly 11am– 3pm; £5 return), though it's wise to check times before setting out, as poor weather can sometimes delay or cancel departures. To get to Trory Point from Enniskillen, take the Omagh bus to the Kesh turn-off.

Castle Archdale Country Park

Near Lisnarick, about 6km north of Enniskillen, off the B82 Kesh road • Mid-March to Oct daily 9am–5pm; visitor centre Sun noon–4pm • Free • http://castlearchdale.com

THE KINGFISHER CYCLING TRAIL

Enniskillen is a good starting point for the 480-odd-km **Kingfisher Cycling Trail**, whose circular route skirts Lower Lough Erne to Belleck and then south to Blacklion before running through the Leitrim lakelands to Carrick-on-Shannon (see page 397), then east to Belturbet in County Cavan (see page 160), and back, via Clones in County Monaghan (see page 157), around the Upper Lough to Enniskillen. The route passes through a wonderful variety of countryside, and though some of the hills are pretty steep, they are rarely too arduous to deter cyclists; the website has a list of places to stay along the route.

LOUGH ERNE CRUISES, RENTALS AND ACTIVITIES

The MV *Kestrel*, run by Erne Tours (May & Sept Tues, Sat & Sun 2.15pm & 4.15pm; June daily 12.15pm, 2.15pm & 4.15pm; July & Aug daily 10am, 12.15pm, 2.15pm & 4.15pm; 1hr 45min; http://ernetours.com; £13), sails from the **Round "O" Jetty** in Enniskillen around the Lower Lough, calling at Devenish Island. They also run two-hour sunset cruises on Saturdays between late May and early September July and August (£22).

A number of companies offer possibilities to **rent your own boat**, with or without outboard motor. A good bet is Erne Boat Hire (http://erneboathireltd.com), based at the Regal Pass Jetty near the Erneside Shopping Centre in Enniskillen, whose boats take up to six people (£65/4hr). Unless you're going out on a small lake, you should always let the boat owner know where you're heading and ask to borrow navigation charts – Lough Erne can be dangerous, especially outside the summer months. Share Discovery Village also offers a host of water-based activities, including **windsurfing** (£15/2hr) and **stand-up paddleboarding** (£8/hr) taster sessions, as well as **canoe** and **kayak** hire (£10–12/hr).

To immerse yourself thoroughly in the beauty of the lough scenery, it's well worth making a trip to **Castle Archdale Country Park**. The eighteenth-century manor house, on which the estate is centred, houses tea rooms and a small **visitor centre**, whose exhibits focus on local wildlife and Castle Archdale's role during World War II when flying boats were based here. The park is also perfectly placed for getting out on the lough, with bike and boat rental available, as well as a campsite. You can also take a ferry from the nearby marina to White Island (see below).

16

ARRIVAL AND GETTING AROUND   CASTLE ARCHDALE COUNTRY PARK

By bus The only public transport here is the Pettigo bus to Lisnarick, 3km away.

Bike and boat rental Between Easter and September, you can rent bikes (£10/half-day), canoes (£40/2hr), kayaks (£20/2hr), hydrobikes (£20/1hr) and katakanu boats holding up to six people (half-day £70, full day £100) from Castle Archdale Boat Hire (http://castlearchdaleboathire. com).

ACCOMMODATION

Castle Archdale Caravan Park http://castlearchdale. com. In the grounds of Castle Archdale Country Park, by the shore of the lough, this fantastically well-equipped site also has camping and glamping pods all sleeping four, the latter with kitchenette; the campsite has a small supermarket and a café in high season. Closed Nov–March. £

White Island

Castle Archdale Boat Hire operates a ferry from Castle Archdale Country Park marina to White Island: July & Aug daily 10.30am, 11.30am, 2.30pm, 3.30pm, 4.30pm; call in advance for travel on the ferry outside these months • charge

Mounted on the wall of a **ruined abbey**, the seven early Christian carvings of **White Island** look eerily pagan. Discovered early in the nineteenth century, they are thought to be caryatids – columns in human form – from a monastic church of the ninth to eleventh centuries. The most disconcerting statue is the lewd female figure known as a **Sheila-na-Gig** (see page 608), one of the best preserved in Ireland. Less equivocal figures continue left to right: a seated Christ holding the Gospels on his knees; a hooded ecclesiast with bell and crozier; David carrying a shepherd's staff, his hand towards his mouth showing his role as author and singer; Christ the Warrior holding two griffins by the scruff of their necks; and another Christ figure with a fringe of curly hair wearing a brooch on his left shoulder and carrying a sword and shield – here he is the King of Glory at his Second Coming. There is an unfinished seventh stone and, on the far right, a carved head with a downturned mouth, which is probably of later origin than the other statues. The **church** of White Island also contains eleventh-century gravestones; the large earthworks round the outside date from an earlier monastery.

Boa Island

10km west of Kesh at the northern end of the Lower Lough

One of Lough Erne's most evocative carvings is on **Boa Island** (barely an island at all these days, as it's connected to the mainland by bridges), which takes its name from Badhbh, a Celtic war-goddess. The landmark to look out for is **Caldragh cemetery**, signposted off the A47 about 1.5km west of Lusty Beg Island. Follow the signs down a lane and the graveyard is through a gate to your left. Here in this ancient Christian burial ground of broken, moss-covered tombstones, encircled and shaded by low hazel trees, you'll find a double-faced **Janus figure**. An idol of yellow stone with very bold, symmetrical features, it has the phallus on one side and a belt and crossed limbs on the other. The figure was probably an invocation of fertility and a depiction of a god-hero, the belt being a reference to the bearing of weapons. Alongside it stands the smaller "**Lusty Man**", so called since it was moved here from nearby Lustymore Island. This idol has only one eye fully carved, maybe to indicate blindness – Cúchulainn (see page 530) had a number of encounters with war-goddesses, divine hags described as blind in the left eye.

ACCOMMODATION AND EATING
BOA ISLAND

Lusty Beg Island http://lustybegisland.com. Set amid beautiful woodland just off Boa Island, this popular weekend retreat (accessible via a free car ferry; 5min) offers a host of accommodation, including B&B in its *Courtyard* guesthouse, lakeside cabins (each with a double bed), and self-catering chalets and luxury lodges (sleeping 4–6). First-rate spa facilities, a cracking restaurant and bar, and all manner of land and water-based activities add to its appeal. **££–££££**

16

Forest of Castle Caldwell

Over towards the western extremity of Lower Lough Erne, the **forest of Castle Caldwell** is formed by two narrow promontories, which make it a natural breeding site for waterfowl and a habitat of rarities such as the hen harrier, peregrine falcon and pine marten. Its seventeenth-century **castle** has long been dilapidated, and the surrounding estate is now a commercial, state-owned forest of spruce, pine and larch. At the castle's entrance, look out for the giant stone fiddle in front of the gate lodge, the sobering memorial to Denis McCabe, a local musician who in 1770 tumbled from the Caldwells' barge while inebriated and drowned. Its inscription "DDD" supposedly stands for "Denis died drunk!".

Belleek Pottery

3 Main St • http://belleekpottery.ie

BELLEEK owes its fame to the local **Belleek Pottery**, Ireland's oldest, which was established in 1857. The enlightening 45-minute **tour** takes in the various stages of production, from mould-making and casting through to fettling – the process of sharpening or delineation of the pattern on the pottery – and dipping, where the glaze is added. As informative as the tour is, you'll be far more distracted by watching the craftsmen and women at work, especially the basket-makers – the level of skill required is quite something; indeed, a typical apprenticeship is anywhere between three and five years. The **museum** exhibits numerous pieces, from early hunting bowls and domestic sanitary ware to more recent decorative items, while the **shop** offers up the chance to buy its extraordinary array of products. There's a lovely tea room here too, where you can sit down to a substantial lunch or a cup of tea and one of their home-baked scones – all served, naturally, in the finest Belleek tableware.

ACCOMMODATION AND EATING
BELLEEK POTTERY

Fiddlestone Main St, Belleek, 028 6865 8008. Although it's unlikely you'll need to stop over, the village's main pub does have half a dozen solidly old-fashioned rooms, in addition to a little guest lounge. Otherwise, drop in for a

pint or a bit to eat. ££
Thatch Café Main St, Belleek, 028 6865 8181. Sweet little thatched cottage with an inviting, warm interior complete with a thick-set stone fireplace and wood-burning stove –

perfect for coffee, or something from the lunch menu like a baked potato with smoked salmon followed by a slice of home-baked blueberry pie. Closed Sun. £

Monea Castle to Lough Navar Forest

In a beautiful setting at the end of a beech-lined lane, **Monea Castle** (free access), 11km northwest of Enniskillen off the B81, is a particularly fine ruin of a planters' castle. Built around 1618, it bears the signs of Scottish influence in its design, with similar features to the reworked Maguire Castle in Enniskillen (see page 549). It was seriously damaged first by fire in the Great Rebellion of 1641 and later by Jacobite armies in 1689, and was eventually abandoned in 1750 after another fire. Lying 8km further north, beyond Derrygonnelly, are the fortified house and *bawn* of restored **Tully Castle** (June–Sept daily 10am–5pm; Oct–May Sun noon–4pm; free), itself burned by the Maguires in 1641, down by the lough shore. Further to the west, there are tremendous views of the lough and surrounds from **Lough Navar Forest** (daily 10am–dusk; parking charge).

Upper Lough Erne

Upper Lough Erne possesses neither the historic sites nor the scenic splendour of the Lower Lough, but it does have the best preserved of the planters' castles nearby in the **Crom Estate**. There's little to see in the region's main town, **Lisnaskea**, save for the ruins of **Castle Balfour** (free access), which was built for Sir James Balfour, a Scottish planter, in the early seventeenth century; it manifests strong Scottish characteristics in its turrets and parapets, high-pitched gables and tall chimneys.

Crom Estate

5km west of Newtownbutler • Charge • http://nationaltrust.org.uk/crom

On the eastern shore of the lough, the National Trust's **Crom Estate** has the largest surviving area of **oak woodland** in Northern Ireland, home to rare species such as the purple hairstreak and wood white butterflies. Unfortunately, the modern Crom Castle is privately occupied and not open to the public, though you can visit the ruins of the **old castle**. There is also a café and interpretive centre here, and you can rent **outboard engine boats** (£30/4hr), **rowing boats** (£7.50/hr) and **Canadian canoes** (£15/4hr). The estate has an interesting range of accommodation available too.

16

INFORMATION | UPPER LOUGH ERNE

Tourist office The Upper Lough Erne region's visitor centre is in Lisnaskea, 8km north of Crom Castle, at 113 Main St (Mon–Fri 9am–5pm, plus June–Aug Sat 10am–4pm; 028 6772 3590).

ACCOMMODATION AND EATING

The Kissin Crust 152 Main St, Lisnaskea, 028 6772 2678. Prettily-decorated café with chatty staff and a cracking little menu, including a steaming seafood chowder and a mouthwatering selection of home-baked treats like lemon cheesecake. The afternoon tea (3–4.30pm; £12) is great fun, but does need to be pre-booked. Closed Sun. £

Mullynascarthy Caravan Park Gola Rd, 3km north of Lisnaskea, http://mullynascarthyholidaypark.com. Picturesquely located on the banks of the Colebrook River, this clean and pleasant site has decent facilities include showers, laundry and a play area for kids. Closed Nov–March. £

Western Fermanagh

The stretch of countryside on the western edge of the county offers some good **walking** opportunities, particularly in the hills to the south. The **Ulster Way** (see page 556), which runs northwest from the Upper Lough and east towards Tyrone, makes the riches of the terrain easily accessible.

This region also has two attractions that are well worth seeking out. The magnificent eighteenth-century **Florence Court** is the most assured achievement of the colonists, built 150 years after the initial defensive planters' castles. If you have your own transport, a visit to the house can be combined with an hour or so at the **Marble Arch Caves**, the finest cave system in Northern Ireland. Walkers can reach both along the Ulster Way, accessible from the A4 near **Belcoo**; the path runs 6.5km south past **Lower Lough Macnean** to the Marble Arch Caves and then a further 8km east to Florence Court.

Florence Court

13km southwest of Enniskillen, just off the A32 • Charge • http://nationaltrust.org.uk/florence-court

The magnificent three-storey mansion of the National Trust-owned **Florence Court** was commissioned by John Cole and named after his wife. The house, completed around 1775, is notable for its restored rococo plasterwork and rare Irish furnishings, though overall the rooms are surprisingly modest in size. The **dining room** is especially lavish, its ceiling hosting a cloud of puffing cherubs with Jupiter disguised as an eagle in the centre, all flying out of a duck-egg-blue sky. There are some notable exhibits too, not least a chunky travel chest belonging to William of Orange. In 1955, a fire destroyed the top floor of the house, which has never been renovated internally.

Beyond the house lie the **pleasure gardens**, a lovely expanse of park and woodland, where you'll also find an ice-house, sawmill, and a pretty thatched summer house,

16

THE ULSTER WAY

From Marble Arch Caves the southwestern section of the **Ulster Way** (http://walkni.com/ulsterway) heads past Lower and Upper Lough Macnean before traversing the bog and granite heights of the Cuilcagh Mountains to **Ballintempo Forest** with its fabulous views over the loughs. The Way then continues north, through the **Lough Navar Forest**, a well-groomed conifer plantation with tarmacked roads and shorter trails. Although a great deal of fir-plantation walking is dark and frustrating, this forest does, at points, provide some of the most spectacular views in Fermanagh, looking over Lower Lough Erne and the mountains of surrounding counties. The Lough Navar Forest also sustains a small herd of red deer, as well as wild goat, fox, badger, hare and red squirrel.

ACCOMMODATION AND EATING

Finding somewhere to stay and eat along this section of the Ulster Way is fairly tricky, though there are several possibilities near **Belcoo**, 4km west from the trail's ascent to the Ballintempo Forest, plus one or two options in neighbouring Blacklion (see page 161), over the border in County Cavan.

Customs House Country Inn 25–27 Main St, Belcoo, http://customshouseinn.com. The nine rooms in this rambling country house are beautifully designed, with all mod cons and luxury features such as Italian marble and handmade pewter tiling. The inn's *Boutique* restaurant is not half bad either, with very reasonably priced dishes such as salmon with spring onion mash and sauvignon sauce. $\overline{\underline{\pounds\pounds}}$

Lough Melvin Holiday Centre 028 6865 8142. A bit further away from the route of the Way, west near the border at Garrison (take the minor road from Derrygonnelly), this place offers hostel-style accommodation and camping alongside numerous activities, including archery, caving, canoeing and wind-surfing. $\overline{\underline{\pounds}}$

Rushin House Caravan Park Holywell, http://rushinhouse.com. 1.5km up the road from Belcoo, this smart caravan park, attractively sited on the shores of Lough MacNean, has comprehensive facilities including barbecue, picnic and play areas, and a service block with kitchen and laundry. Closed Nov–Feb. $\overline{\underline{\pounds}}$

now restored after having burnt down in 2014 and offering marvellous views across to Benaughlin mountain. On the opposite side of the estate, a glorious walled **garden** comprises rows of neatly tended flowerbeds, vegetable plots and an apple orchard. If you want to go the whole hog, there are some 15km of **trails** to enjoy, after which you can repair to the fabulous Stables **tea room**.

Marble Arch Caves

8km west of Florence Court in Legnabrocky • tours roughly every 20min • Charge • http://marblearchcaves.co.uk

Fermanagh is renowned for its cave systems, the most spectacular of which is the **Marble Arch Caves**. The caves are one of seven geoparks in the UK (run under the umbrella of UNESCO), although the Marble Arch Caves Global Geopark – to give it its full title – also incorporates Cavan across the border (see page 161), thus making it the first cross-border geopark in the world. The caves were first discovered in 1895 by Frenchman Edouard Martel and Dublin zoologist, Lyster Jameson, with more extensive explorations undertaken in the 1930s by the Yorkshire Rambler's Club; they were finally opened to the public in 1985.

Following a pleasant little walk down through the reserve, the **tour** (which lasts around an hour and a quarter) begins with an atmospheric five-minute boat journey along the subterranean **Cladagh river**, before continuing through a succession of atmospherically lit chambers and passages. Throughout there are clusters of weirdly shaped stalactites and stalagmites, as well as other impressive formations, such as flowstones and scallops (sculpted indentations caused by water flow). Following a heavy Irish downpour, the caves are prone to flooding, so do check before you visit.

From whichever direction you approach the caves, you'll travel along the **Marlbank Scenic Loop**, with tremendous views of Lower Lough Macnean, and on either side you'll see limestone-flagged fields, much like those of the Burren in County Clare. It was fifty thousand years of gentle water seepage through the limestone that deposited the calcite for the amazing stalactite growths in the caves below.

Legnabrocky Trail and Cuilcagh Mountain

Almost opposite the entrance to the Marble Arch Caves is the start of the 7.5km-long **Legnabrocky Trail**, which runs through rugged limestone scenery and peatland to the shale-covered slopes of **Cuilcagh Mountain** (666m), Fermanagh's highest peak. This forms part of an environmental conservation area and offers a wonderful, if strenuous, six- or seven-hour walk to the mountain's summit and back (be prepared to turn back if the weather turns sour) – on a clear day it's possible to see the Mourne Mountains. A part of the Marble Arch Caves centre is now devoted to an exhibition describing the restoration of the mountain park's damaged peatland and bogland habitats.

16

MUIREDACH'S HIGH CROSS

Contexts

History

Ireland's history is as rich and colourful as that of any European nation, and comprehending its troubled past is vital to an understanding of its current situation. Though the following pages can merely summarize key events, our book list (see page 597) provides sources of further enlightenment.

Prehistory

Originally connected to mainland Europe, and at times completely glaciated, Ireland's geographical form has developed over the last two million years as a result of global climate change. The end of the last major **Ice Age** saw sea levels rise and the gradual separation of both Britain and Ireland from the European landmass, leaving just a few connections between the two regions. The first plant life is reckoned to have appeared around 12,000 BC, and the first mammals, such as reindeer, arrived a millennium or so later. A subsequent period of glaciation resulted in their extinction in Ireland, though warming again occurred around 9000 BC, at which point the country began its long process of forestation and various animals crossed the last remaining land-bridges.

The **first human settlements** are thought to date from around 8000–7000 BC. These Mesolithic hunter-gatherers, who made various implements and artefacts from flint, lived largely around coastal areas, such as Belfast Lough and the Shannon estuary. Developments

---

IRELAND'S PREHISTORIC TOMBS

Ireland is sprinkled with an extraordinary number of megalithic tombs, of which more than 1500 examples have been identified, and many are in remarkably fine condition. The oldest tomb-form, dating from around 4000 BC, is the **passage grave**, consisting of a rounded mound or cairn with a stone-lined passage leading from the perimeter to a central chamber. Of the three hundred-plus surviving examples, mostly found in Ireland's north and east, **Newgrange** (see page 141) is the most renowned, remarkable not just because of its intricate construction – and the site's sheer scale – but also for its implicit associations with magic and ritual.

Dating from before 3000 BC, **court tombs** feature an open area beside the entrance, probably used for religious ceremonies. The majority are found in the country's north, **Creevykeel** in County Sligo being the best known (see page 393).

Portal tombs (known as **dolmens**), from around 2500–2000 BC, are the most easily recognizable form, consisting of three or more sturdy upright boulders, dragged into position, on which an often bigger capstone was placed. This tripod-like structure would then have a gallery tomb excavated beneath. Found in the north, west and southeast, a particularly fine example is at **Kilclooney** in County Donegal (see page 422).

Lastly, **wedge tombs** date from the early Bronze Age (around 2000–1500 BC), and are so termed because their burial chamber narrows and decreases in height as one moves inwards. More than a quarter of the recorded four hundred examples are located in **the Burren** in County Clare (see page 323).

---

c. 11,000 BC	c. 8000–7000 BC	c. 4000 BC	c. 2000 BC
The first mammals arrive in Ireland	The first human settlements: Mesolithic hunter-gatherers	The first passage graves appear	The arrival of bronze casting

elsewhere were slow to reach Ireland and it was not until the **Neolithic** period, around 3500 BC, that people skilled in farming settled here – equipped with stone axes (numerous examples have been found across the country), they were capable of clearing forests for their crops and animals. Subscribing to ritual and magic, notably in their burial ceremonies, they left numerous megalithic monuments across Ireland, including graves and stone circles (see box) similar to those found throughout Western Europe's coastal areas, indicating their place in a much broader network. Archaeological discoveries reveal the increasing subtlety of the products of this culture, first in the form of pottery and later, after the arrival of bronze casting techniques around 2000 BC, jewellery.

The Iron Age

Ireland is usually considered a **Celtic** country, one colonized by the Indo-European people who spread rapidly across continental Europe from the East from around 1000 BC onwards. However, while they certainly reached the French coast, recent evidence suggests that far from being Celtic themselves, the peoples of Britain and Ireland gradually became Celticized through contact with traders. As a result, iron reached Ireland around 700 BC and, over the course of the next few centuries, the island's inhabitants adopted the Celtic ritual-based culture and language, though this would diversify significantly over the next millennium.

Other innovations followed, including the development of stone-built ring forts, a response to the need for protection brought about by Celtic systems of land ownership and fealty, which increasingly provoked intertribal warfare. A hierarchical system was gradually established, with individual **kingdoms** forming parts of larger fiefdoms based on the five provinces of Connacht, Leinster, Meath, Munster and Ulster. These fiefdoms in turn supposedly paid homage to a High King (*Ard Rí*) based at Tara, though in fact no such regal figure gained sway over the whole of Ireland until Brian Boru. However, like its Norse contemporary, this was also a myth-making culture, based on the cult of the hero. One of these, Cúchulainn, stars in the Irish epic nonpareil, the *Táin Bó Cúailnge*, a bloodthirsty tale of war and revenge whose characters are ever prey to the whims of their gods.

Early Christianity

If the myths are to be believed, Ireland subsequently embraced **Christianity** with remarkable rapidity thanks to the efforts of its patron saint, **St Patrick** (who also eradicated the snakes that had never inhabited the island). Truth be told, the process was far more gradual and never entirely included the abandonment of Celtic pagan beliefs, as proven by the presence of Sheila-na-Gigs (see page 608) in medieval church-building. Missionaries began to arrive from the fourth century AD onwards, though the establishment of monastic settlements did not really begin for another two hundred years. By the eighth and ninth centuries monasteries such as Clonmacnois in County Offaly and Lismore in County Waterford had risen to become major seats of learning in an increasingly church-focused Europe. Extant evidence of such prowess exists in the form of **illuminated manuscripts**, such as the *Book of Durrow* and the renowned *Book of Kells*, on show in the Library of Trinity College, Dublin.

c. 700 BC	**Fourth century AD**	**c. 800**
Iron reaches Ireland	Christian missionaries begin to arrive	Production of the magnificent illuminated manuscript, the *Book of Kells*

The Vikings and the Normans

The **Vikings** reached Ireland towards the end of the eighth century and conducted sporadic raids on coastal areas, usually on monasteries – the defensive round tower dates from this period – before embarking on a more coordinated assault in 914. The upshot was the formation of fortified settlements at places such as Dublin, Cork and Waterford, though one hundred years later the Norsemen were vanquished at the Battle of Clontarf by the *Ard Rí*, Brian Boru.

One branch of the Norsemen, in the shape of the **Normans**, did finally conquer England in 1066, but it was more than a century before a successful Anglo-Norman incursion was made into Ireland, when Irish infighting resulted in Dermot MacMurrough, the dethroned king of Leinster, seeking the support of Henry II to regain his throne. The English king agreed to allow one of his knights, Richard FitzGilbert de Clare ("Strongbow"), to take a contingent of troops across the Irish Sea, but soon became concerned by the extent of Strongbow's success and arrived shortly afterwards to claim sovereignty over Ireland and establish a court in Dublin.

Norman rule over Ireland was largely restricted to the former Viking townships, and attempts to introduce feudalism foundered against the resistance of the Irish chieftains. In reality, the process of assimilation, which saw many of the victors becoming "more Irish than the Irish", resulted in the conquest becoming limited to a small area surrounding Dublin. This became known as the "English Pale" (from the word for an enclosure), and those who lived beyond its bounds were demeaningly described as "**beyond the pale**", a term which subsequently became synonymous with barbarism.

Attempts to coerce the Irish into submission by force were abandoned, and those Norman settlers who had established themselves gradually became integrated into a society, now usually described as Gaelic, founded on the domains of Irish chieftains. The outcome was a flowering of **Gaelic culture**, with its emphasis on the place of the bard (a court musician-cum-poet) in storytelling and music-making. However, this did not prevent certain Anglo-Norman dynasties from broadening their own power bases, not least the de Burgo family in Ulster and Connacht, and the Fitzgeralds of Kildare.

Tudor and Stuart incursions

The succeeding centuries saw various English interlopers attempting to establish themselves in Ireland, but it was not until **Henry VIII** broke with Rome that a concerted effort to demolish the hegemony of the Irish overlords began, linked to the dissolution of the powerful Irish monasteries with their wealth up for the grabs of any supporter of the Tudor regime. An abortive insurrection in 1534 offered Henry the excuse to send troops to Ireland, quash the revolt and establish himself as both sovereign ruler and ecclesiastical head of his domain.

His daughter **Elizabeth I** continued the process, but adopted much more stringent and far-reaching tactics, geared towards undermining Gaelic authority and its allegiance to Catholicism while simultaneously reinforcing Ireland's position as an English colony. Taking up her elder sister Mary's policy of **plantation**, which had seen parts of Laois and Offaly sequestered from their Irish owners, Elizabeth unsuccessfully attempted to "plant" colonists from Scotland in the area around Belfast Lough during the 1570s.

795	**1169**	**1534**
The Vikings begin their century-long plunder of Irish monasteries, before building fortified settlements	Henry II of England's barons land at Wexford, kicking off the 750-year colonization of southern Ireland	Henry VIII sends the troops in to establish his hegemony

The threat of further infiltration provoked Irish offensive reaction, of which the most crucial was the revolt led by **Hugh O'Neill** of Northern Ireland. This chieftain had been deliberately targeted by the Tudors as a potential convert to the Protestant plantation process, but, realizing he had been duped, he took up arms against the Crown. At first successful, his armies were crucially defeated at Kinsale in 1601 and, finally forced into submission by a siege at Mellifont in County Louth in 1603, he signed a treaty granting all his land and that of his underlords to the English, which was leased back to them under an oath of fealty. This opened the door for a flood of "planters", mainly ex-soldiers from England and the Scottish Lowlands who were encouraged to establish themselves in the newly gained territories. Though the Irish chiefs were still ostensibly in control of their land, their power was fatally diminished and a significant number decided to leave their country en masse in 1607, embarking from Rathmullen, County Donegal, in what was later described as the **Flight of the Earls**, heading variously for Flanders and Italy. The power of the old Gaelic kingships was at an end, and the plantation broadened its scale as **James I** urged more Lowland Scots to cross over to Northern Ireland and take over the Earls' impounded lands. This established a significant division between the Protestant planters and the evicted Catholic Irish, the ramifications of which endure to this day.

The 1641 Rebellion and Oliver Cromwell

Concerns about the apparently pro-Catholic religious policies of James I's successor, **Charles I**, resulted in a Scottish rebellion in 1640. Having failed to persuade parliament to vote for taxes to raise new troops to quell the Scots, Charles negotiated a deal with Irish Catholics whereby their troops would be provided to suppress the rising in return for concessions regarding land ownership and religious tolerance. Alarmed that the king might be about to impose Catholicism across his dominion, a Scottish–Parliamentarian alliance proposed invading Ireland to subdue the population. A small group of Irish landowners planned their own rebellion in turn, conspiring to take Dublin Castle, Derry and other northern towns in October 1641. Their assault on Dublin was foiled by an informer, but their Northern Ireland campaign, led by Phelim O'Neill, was initially successful. Charles himself sent an army to put down the rising (and the Scots sent their own to protect Ulster Protestants, four thousand of whom had died in the fighting and a further eight thousand succumbed to the harsh winter conditions after being expelled from their homes by O'Neill's army), but the outbreak of the English Civil War delayed the resolution of the Irish question.

An Irish alliance called the **Catholic Confederation** was created to coordinate attacks on English and Scottish troops in Ireland, though **Oliver Cromwell**'s victory in the Civil War saw the overthrow of the monarchy and a determination to conquer all of Ireland. Cromwell arrived in Dublin with a large contingent of his New Model Army in August 1649 and embarked on a merciless and bitterly fought crusade to establish his authority. His prime targets were those towns occupied by Royalist garrisons, first taking Drogheda, where he massacred the troops and numerous citizens, before sweeping down through the southeast of Ireland and on to Cork and Kinsale. By 1652 all of Ireland was under Cromwell's control, his bloodthirsty troops slaughtering a quarter of the Catholic population in the process and dispatching many others into slavery in the Caribbean. The subsequent **Act of Settlement** saw widespread sequestration of

1601	1607	1649
The Irish chieftains are decisively defeated by Elizabeth I at the Battle of Kinsale	Many of them flee to Europe – the "Flight of the Earls" – opening the way for mass plantation of Ulster	Oliver Cromwell descends on Ireland with legendary cruelty

Catholic-held land and all the evictees were instructed to move west of the Shannon River by the beginning of May 1654 or face death – in Cromwell's cold terms, "to Hell or to Connacht". Many more died on the journey to places such as Connemara and the boglands of Mayo, while Cromwell's troops were rewarded with their confiscated land. Unsurprisingly, Cromwell's name remains reviled across much of Ireland.

The Williamite War and the penal laws

Though the monarchy was restored in 1660, Charles II remained in thrall to his Protestant Parliament and it was not until he was succeeded by his brother, the Catholic **James II** in 1685, that Irish hopes were revitalized. However, anti-Catholic concerns, particularly about James's close relationship with Louis XIV of France, led the English Parliament to offer the throne to the Dutch **Prince William of Orange**. James fled to Ireland and enlisted an army to try and overthrow what had become known as the "Glorious Revolution". Though initially successful, the city of **Derry** presented a major stumbling block (see page 498), allowing William's forces the time to arrive in Ireland. James was finally defeated at Limerick, though the most celebrated encounter in William's campaign took place earlier, on July 12, 1690, when he was victorious at the **Battle of the Boyne**, an event commemorated as the highpoint of the Loyalist marching season (see page 536).

Subsequently, under William, the English Parliament consolidated the legal process (begun under Charles II) of furthering control over Ireland by diminishing the rights of the native Catholic population in terms of land ownership, marriage, religion and enfranchisement. A series of Acts passed between 1695 and 1728, which later became known as the **penal laws**, aimed at safeguarding the Protestant planters while suppressing Irish Catholic identity and culture and dragging the population into penury. Catholics were barred from purchasing land and on a landowner's death his property was split equally between all of his sons, thus incrementally diminishing familial wealth by each generation (an essential factor in the Great Famine of the nineteenth century – see page 565), though any son who converted to Protestantism became entitled to his brothers' inheritance. Catholic priests were banned from practising unless they paid two £50 bonds for registration, and even then were not allowed to say Mass; alternatively, conversion to the Church of Ireland attracted a £20 stipend, levied on their former congregations. Targeting cultural transmission, Catholics were barred from teaching, though some operated surreptitious "hedge schools" in the countryside, using the Irish language as a medium. Despite these exigencies, native Irish culture somehow survived.

Revolution and rebellion

Towards the end of the eighteenth century, revolution was in the air throughout much of bourgeois Europe. Its initial catalyst was the **American War of Independence**, which saw British troops diverted across the Atlantic from Ireland. The series of laws establishing the primacy of the Anglican Church had not only affected Irish Catholics, but Presbyterian Northern Ireland planters, too, many of whom had emigrated to the Americas (see page 543), bringing about some sympathy among Ireland's burgeoning

1690	1695–1728	1795
Protestant William of Orange decisively defeats Catholic James II and the French at the Battle of the Boyne	Passage of the penal laws, suppressing Irish Catholics, their culture and identity	Northern Protestants found the Orange Society (later Orange Order) to oppose Catholic emancipation

Protestant mercantile class for Washington's campaign demand of "no taxation without representation". Though not directly taxed by the English Parliament, Ireland was the subject of numerous trade levies and the American war led **Henry Grattan**, leader of the Patriot Party, not only to make increasing demands for proper representation at Westminster and some form of constitutional independence, but to recruit troops to replace the departing English militia in order to defend Ireland against the threat of a French invasion.

More crucially, segments of the Irish middle class saw the **French Revolution** of 1789, with its underlying concepts of liberty, equality and fraternity, reinforced by the publication of Thomas Paine's *Rights of Man* (1792), and the consequent possibility of an invasion from France, as the potential means of securing independence. Formed by Belfast Protestants in 1791, the **Society of United Irishmen** promulgated Nationalist views regarding democratic reform and Catholic emancipation never likely to be taken up by the Grattan Parliament. After the English declaration of war against France in 1793, the Society was forced underground, and adopted agitational policies aimed at severing the link with Britain, linking with militant Catholic agrarian groups in the process. France became the means of breaking the connection with England, and one of the Society's leaders, Theobald **Wolfe Tone**, a Dublin Protestant barrister, was sent there to secure French support for an insurrection. Realizing the possibility of gaining a back-door victory over England, a French army set sail to invade Ireland, but was prevented from landing in Bantry Bay in 1796 by bad weather and indecision (see page 258).

Plans revised, the **Rebellion** took place in 1798 (see page 198), but met brutal English resistance, supported, especially in the North, by Protestant yeomanry, many of whom belonged to the Orange Society (later Orange Order), established in 1795 to oppose Catholic Emancipation (see page 536). The French, under General Humbert, finally landed at Killala, Mayo, in late August, by which time much of the uprising had been quelled. Drawing local support, they marched towards Dublin, until defeated at Ballinamuck in Longford. Subsequently, a larger Gallic force, with Tone on board, tried to land in County Donegal, but was intercepted by the British navy. Tone was taken to Dublin and sentenced to death, but slit his own throat before the execution.

As a result, the British enacted the 1801 **Act of Union**, dissolving Dublin's Parliament and ensuring total legislative control over Ireland, which now became part of the United Kingdom. The act did not deter one further Irish revolutionary, **Robert Emmet**, whose wholly ill-planned attempted coup failed ignominiously in 1803.

Catholic Emancipation

The cause of Catholic enfranchisement became the major focus for agitation. Its catalyst was the lawyer **Daniel O'Connell**, who founded the Catholic Association in 1823 to build on successful British popular campaigns to expand the franchise beyond its previously limited bounds, and was returned to the British Parliament as MP for Clare in 1828. Though legislation prevented him from taking up his seat, his victory played no small part in the subsequent passage of the Catholic Emancipation Act, which, though only enfranchising a tiny number of middle-class voters, had enormous repercussions by making Catholics eligible for a number of previously excluded public offices.

1798	**1801**	**1829**
The '98 Rebellion, led by the United Irishmen, is brutally defeated	The Act of Union dissolves the Parliament of Ireland, which becomes part of the United Kingdom	The Catholic Emancipation Act gives limited rights to Catholics

THE IRISH DIASPORA

Even when Ireland's Great Famine was finally quelled, a pattern had been set, with **emigration** becoming regarded as the only means of escaping poverty. Sixty years after the Famine, Ireland's population had sunk to just over half its 1841 level of 8.2 million, and further waves of emigration occurred during the twentieth century. This **diaspora** established large Irish communities in other countries, especially Britain (where ten percent of the population are now thought to have an Irish grandparent) and the USA, where **Irish-Americans** played a major role in supporting moves towards independence and still remain a powerful lobbying group. The list of US presidents with Irish roots now runs into the low twenties (including Ulysses S. Grant, John F. Kennedy, Ronald Reagan, Bill Clinton and perhaps more tenuously Barack Obama), and over forty million Americans, one fifth of the white population, claim Irish descent. Other countries with significant populations of Irish descent include Australia, Canada, South Africa and, perhaps more surprisingly, Mexico and Argentina, the latter explaining how the great Latin American revolutionary Che Guevara came to have an Irish grandmother.

O'Connell was elected as Dublin's first Catholic Lord Mayor in 1841 and subsequently embarked on a campaign to repeal the Union with Britain. Adopting populist techniques acquired from the Chartists, he called a series of "**monster meetings**" across all of Ireland except Ulster, attended on each occasion by as many as 100,000 people. Alarmed, the British government outlawed his October 1843 assembly at Clontarf and jailed him for sedition. More radical supporters of independence, the Young Ireland Movement, attempted their own uprising in 1848, but such was its lack of support that it became known as "The Battle of Widow McCormack's Cabbage Patch".

The Great Famine

The **Great Famine** of 1845 to 1851, during which Ireland's population declined by 1.5 million – almost twenty percent – was one of the most devastating tragedies in human history. In the early 1840s a potato blight spread across Western Europe, and, while resolved reasonably well elsewhere, struck at the core of an Irish peasantry excessively dependent on their potato yields. Britain's laissez-faire economic policy throughout the Famine years allowed continued export from Ireland of other agricultural products, which might have alleviated the situation. By the worst year of the Famine, Black '47, hundreds of thousands faced starvation, a situation exacerbated by mass evictions across Ireland as landlords removed tenants unable to pay their dues. Workhouses were crammed to overcapacity and, while some were fed by soup kitchens or received support from individual landlords, the majority faced death or emigration.

Though Dublin, Belfast and much of the Northern Ireland province remained relatively unscathed, at least a million people died during the Famine and hundreds of thousands migrated to Britain or risked death by travelling on one of the infamous "coffin ships" to North America or Australasia, which, often crammed beyond capacity, were not fit to sail and floundered en route.

1841	1845–51	1848
Daniel O'Connell is elected as the first Catholic Lord Mayor of Dublin	Around a million people die and hundreds of thousands emigrate in the Great Famine	Unsuccessful uprising in favour of independence by the Young Ireland Movement

Nationalist action had been fuelled by British policy during the Famine years. The **Irish Republican Brotherhood** (sometimes termed Fenians and funded in part from the US) carried out an abortive uprising in 1867 and incurred a massive backlash, though this failed to destroy the organization. Agrarian groups focused particularly on **absentee English landlords** and those who continued to evict tenants unable to pay their rent – one of the most notorious wide-scale evictions took place at Derryveagh in Donegal (see page 429).

The Home Rule Movement

Over the remaining decades of the nineteenth century the struggles over land and tenants' rights retained pivotal importance and were accelerated by **Michael Davitt**'s formation of the **Land League** in 1879. Its aims, however, became increasingly linked to a concerted campaign to secure independence via parliamentary democracy. The movement's guiding light was **Charles Stewart Parnell** (1846–91), who won County Meath for the **Home Rule Party** in the 1875 election and became its leader two years later. Parnell gained huge popularity in Ireland for his support of the ideal of an Irish Parliament, his use of obstructive tactics in the House of Commons and his full-blooded backing for agrarian action against recalcitrant landlords and their agents, using the tactic of social excommunication. One of the first victims, in 1880, of this device was a Mayo estate factor, Captain Charles Boycott – the action introduced his eponym into the English language.

William Gladstone's government put Parnell, Davitt and other leaders of the Land League on trial for seditious conspiracy in 1881 and, though the jury failed to agree a verdict, Davitt was shortly afterwards re-arrested for breaching his "ticket of leave". A new Land Act, based on the principles of fair rent, fixed tenure and freedom of sale, became law later that year, but was rejected by the Land League which embarked on a new campaign of violence against landowners and thus was declared illegal. On the very day of Davitt's release from prison the following year, the British viceroy Lord Frederick Cavendish and his Under Secretary T.H. Burke were assassinated in Phoenix Park by a Fenian group calling itself "The Invincibles". Parnell denounced the murder in the Commons, but attitudes hardened against the Irish.

Though Gladstone had been persuaded by Parnell's arguments, his first Home Rule Bill failed in 1886 (as did his second in 1893), while Parnell's political career was terminated when his long-term affair with Kitty O'Shea saw him named as co-respondent in a divorce trial launched by her husband.

Towards identity

From the late nineteenth century onwards Nationalist ideas became increasingly intertwined with the concept of cultural revival, especially via the establishment of two new opinion-forming organizations. Founded in 1884, the **Gaelic Athletic Association**'s fundamental aim was to preserve and nurture Irish sports such as Gaelic football and hurling. Avowedly Nationalist, its members were banned from playing foreign games and Crown forces were excluded from membership. The **Gaelic League** was formed in 1893. While aiming to preserve and maintain the Irish language and native

1867	**1877**	**1884**
Abortive uprising by the Irish Republican Brotherhood	Charles Stewart Parnell, the "uncrowned king of Ireland", becomes leader of the Home Rule Party	Foundation of the Gaelic Athletic Association to nurture Irish sports

culture, it too became increasingly nationalistic, viewing its goals as central to the "de-Anglicization" of Ireland. At the same time, a group of writers, centred on W.B. Yeats and Lady Gregory, set about establishing a **cultural revival**, based on the creation of distinctly Irish works written in English.

Almost simultaneously, and in response to Parnell's failure to achieve Home Rule via parliamentary means, a current of opinion was developed and promulgated by a Dublin printer, **Arthur Griffith**, in his newspaper *The United Irishman* (established 1898). Initially, this espoused self-determination, involving the withdrawal of Irish MPs from Westminster and the formation of an independent Irish Parliament in Dublin as the only means to achieve economic and political freedom. Supporters of this view coalesced to form the political party **Sinn Féin** in 1905, an organization increasingly influenced by the views expounded by Scotsman **James Connolly**'s Irish Socialist Republican Party, which sought to establish a workers' republic in Ireland. A significant further factor was the rise of the trade-union movement in Ireland, especially the role of the militant workers' leader **James Larkin**, who formed the Irish Transport and General Workers' Union in 1909. Its philosophy was encapsulated in Larkin's slogan, "The land of Ireland for the people of Ireland".

Resistance ...

The General Election of 1910 resulted in the slimmest of majorities for Asquith's Liberal Party, leaving it utterly reliant on the Irish Nationalist Party to enact legislation. Seizing the moment, the Nationalists pressed for a new Home Rule Bill, which the Commons passed in 1912. This aroused a bitterly intransigent response from Northern Protestants who united under the direction of **Sir Edward Carson**, a Dublin barrister, Tory MP and leader of the Irish Unionists. In September 1911 he and James Craig initiated a campaign to resist Home Rule and any threat of the imposition of Catholicism on Protestant Ulster. More than 200,000 signed up to a covenant pledging to defeat Home Rule by "all means necessary". In readiness for such action, Protestants formed their own militia, the **Ulster Volunteers**, which was armed by munitions from Germany. Indeed, Carson went so far as to lunch with the Kaiser in 1913 to discuss German aid for the resistance strategy.

Unsurprisingly, Nationalists and the British responded vigorously. The former founded its own armed force, the **Irish Volunteers**, the second Nationalist militia to form after James Connolly's Irish Citizen Army. The British responded by banning the use of armed weapons in Ireland and went so far as to plan a raid on the Ulster Volunteers, though this was abandoned when troops stationed in Northern Ireland refused to take action against the militia. Lloyd George devised a compromise whereby the province of Northern Ireland would be excluded from the introduction of Home Rule for six years, but the whole issue was deferred when war broke out between Britain and Germany late in the summer of 1914.

... and revolt

While Carson and the Irish Nationalist leader **John Redmond** pledged the support of both the Ulster and Irish Volunteers in guarding Ireland from German invasion

1893	1905	1912
Foundation of the Gaelic League to nurture Irish language and culture	Formation of the Sinn Féin ("We Ourselves") political party	Home Rule Bill passed by the House of Commons — but deferred with the outbreak of World War I in 1914

(and, indeed, more than 230,000 Irishmen enlisted in the British Army), others saw the war as a fruitful opportunity ripe for the picking. In particular, leaders of the **Irish Republican Brotherhood** (IRB) made preparations for a rising, using the strength of the Irish Volunteers, to be instigated if the Germans entered Ireland or if the British tried to implement conscription. When army and police embarked on a series of raids against Irish Nationalist and revolutionary newspapers in late 1914, plans were made for a rising in September 1915, but were deferred when the Irish Volunteers' leaders declared themselves unready. The IRB sent an envoy to Germany, the former British diplomat **Sir Roger Casement**, who successfully secured German support for the rising.

When it finally occurred on Monday April 24, 1916, the **Easter Rising**, as it became known (see page 82) was a drastically limited affair. The British had already captured the German ship bringing arms and had arrested Casement when he landed from a German submarine in Cork four days earlier. Tipped off by informers, the British had also made plans to arrest all the leaders of the various organizations involved on that Easter Monday (though such action was then largely deferred until the rebels' surrender), and the leader of the Irish Volunteers, Eoin MacNeill, ordered his men not to take part in the rebellion. In the regions, action was limited to the north of County Dublin, Enniscorthy in Wexford and parts of County Galway, while the focus for the rebels' action became the Dublin General Post Office with simultaneous assaults on key targets across the city. Patrick Pearse, a poet and political activist, delivered the **Proclamation of the Irish Republic** from the steps of the GPO, but the rebels were powerless to resist the heavy British bombardment that ensued. After five days of fighting, the leaders surrendered, though it was two more days before combat ended. Over the course of the week, more than 1350 people were killed or wounded and numerous buildings in central Dublin destroyed.

Dubliners were initially aghast at their city's devastation, but public anger turned to outcry when all of the Rising's leaders and numerous other insurgents, with the exception of **Éamon de Valera** who had US citizenship, were executed by the British at Kilmainham Gaol in Dublin after a secret court martial. Connolly himself was so ill from infected wounds that he wouldn't have survived long enough for the planned execution and was shot while tied to a chair. As a consequence of the resulting public revulsion, all other death sentences were commuted, with the exception of Casement, who was hanged in London in August.

The War for Independence

Far from losing support, as the British had hoped, the rebels' ideals were embraced by the next wave of leaders. Key figures were **Michael Collins**, working within the Irish Volunteers, and de Valera, who was elected MP for East Clare in 1916. The Volunteers grew in strength and Sinn Féin achieved a crushing success in the 1918 General Election, though none of its elected members took their seats, instead convening as the Dáil Éireann ("Ireland's Parliament") and issuing a declaration of independence. With de Valera as its leader and Collins as Minister of Finance, the Dáil reorganized the Volunteers and Citizen Army under the new name of the **Irish Republican Army (IRA)**. The British poured troops into Ireland and war effectively began in September 1919, when a soldier was killed in Fermoy, County Cork, and the British subsequently sacked the town.

1912	1913	1916
Formation of the Ulster Volunteers to oppose home rule	Formation of the Irish Volunteers to oppose the Ulster Volunteers	The Easter Rising wins widespread sympathy only after the brutal execution of its leaders

In consequence, a campaign of guerrilla warfare broke out across most of Ireland which the Royal Irish Constabulary proved powerless to restrain. Irish sentiment was much heightened by the arrival of the **Black and Tans**, British soldiers re-recruited after World War I (and so called because of the colour of their uniforms), whose reprisals were merciless. However, even they were unable to prevent the situation of virtual stalemate, which dragged on until a truce was called in July 1921.

Meanwhile, in 1920 Westminster passed the **Government of Ireland Act**, establishing separate new parliaments for the six counties of "Northern Ireland" and the residual 26 of "Southern Ireland". Elections the following year resulted in a simple reinforcement of the Nationalist majority in the latter, which promptly reconstituted itself as Dáil Éireann, led by de Valera, and demanded independence as a 32-county state. Since Ulster's Protestants clearly held sway in the North and the armed independent struggle had reached deadlock, de Valera sent a delegation to London to negotiate an agreement with Lloyd George (thus absolving himself of any role in the process). In the face of the British prime minister's intransigence regarding the Unionist stand-off, the representatives, who included Michael Collins, agreed to the partition of Ireland as defined by the 1920 legislation, with the South gaining independence as the Irish Free State but retaining allegiance to the Crown through membership of the Commonwealth.

The Irish Civil War

A provisional government was established in the South shortly after the signing of the **Anglo-Irish Treaty** in December 1921, which granted independence at the cost of partition. However, while Collins had signed the treaty on the basis that it was a major leap towards independence and a halfway step towards gaining control of all 32 counties, de Valera rejected the proposals as a diminution of Republicanism and refused to truck with their enactment. By July 1922, pro- and anti-Treaty forces had become embroiled in a bitter **civil war** which would have a lasting impact on Ireland's politics and economy. Though most of the population of the 26 counties supported the "Free Staters", opinion was seriously divided owing to the scale of the fighting and the reprisals taken by the provisional government, not least the execution of the prominent Republican Erskine Childers (who had run guns into the country in 1914) after his arrest for possessing a revolver given him by Collins, and the counter-reprisals that ensued. Eventually, the much weaker Republican forces were restricted to control parts of the southwest and west and were forced to surrender in May 1923. Collins himself died in 1922 in an ambush in County Cork.

The Free State

Since one of the main candidates, Arthur Griffith, had also died (of a brain haemorrhage) during the civil war, leadership of the new government passed on to **William T. Cosgrave**, whose regime set about establishing a new infrastructure for the country's development, including the formation of a civil service and police force. Republicans boycotted the Dáil until 1926 when de Valera formed a new political party, **Fianna Fáil**, drawing members largely from the anti-Treaty element within Sinn Féin. Cosgrave remained in power until 1932, overseeing the initiation of the

1918	1919–21	1921
The first Dail Éireann ("Ireland's parliament") issues a declaration of independence and forms the Irish Republican Army	The War of Independence	Anglo-Irish Treaty signed, setting up the Irish Free State in 26 of Ireland's 32 counties

Shannon hydroelectric scheme and the foundation of the Electricity Supply Board, but his Cumann na nGaedheal party lost the election that year to Fianna Fáil ushering in de Valera's subsequent sixteen-year reign as Taoiseach. Cumann na nGaedheal itself merged with the National Centre Party and the right-wing Army Comrades Association (known as the "Blueshirts") the following year to form **Fine Gael**.

Throughout this period, the economic situation remained austere, exacerbated first by the Depression after 1929 and then by high British trade-levies on imports from Ireland, a result of de Valera's refusal to repay land annuities to Britain, which forced his government into frugality and self-sufficiency. These stern policies were reflected in Ireland's social and cultural life, and ties with the Catholic Church were reinforced at the time. However, de Valera's government also saw the establishment of state boards for road, rail and air transport (Aer Lingus) and peat production.

De Valera's determination to sever links with Britain resulted in a new **constitution** in 1938 whose central premise was the renunciation of Crown sovereignty and a new system of government for the state henceforth known as **Éire**. The model adopted was bicameral with the Dáil retained, but with a new upper chamber, the Seanad (or Senate), added, and the role of president (Uachtarán) created – the first holder of the office was the Protestant Douglas Hyde (see page 405).

Northern Ireland's first decades

Following the enactment of the Anglo-Irish Treaty, Northern Ireland's new-found status as a largely self-governing entity had begun in June 1921 with the establishment of its parliament under James Craig, whose **Ulster Unionist Party (UUP)** would run the mini-state until 1972. Rather than including all nine counties of the Ulster province, leaders of the majority Protestant community had negotiated a settlement for their separation from the Free State on the basis of just six, thus ensuring the retention of a secure mandate which might have been threatened by the inclusion of the largely Catholic counties of Donegal and Cavan. Though a significant and gradually increasing Catholic minority remained, it was largely concentrated on agricultural areas west of the River Bann, plus the city of Derry, while the economically thriving linen and shipbuilding industries east of the river remained almost entirely in Protestant hands.

Britain needed Belfast's industrial strength as much as the UUP wanted Britain's economic and financial support and Unionists quickly set about reinforcing their domination. As well as establishing a largely Protestant police force, the **Royal Ulster Constabulary (RUC)**, and a military adjunct, the B Specials, the new parliament (originally based in Belfast, but moved to Stormont in 1932) strengthened its position by favouring the Protestant population with economic support, housing allocations and gerrymandering (for example, Derry's electoral boundaries were changed to ensure a Protestant council remained in power for decades despite the city's two-thirds Catholic majority).

World War II

As part of the United Kingdom, Northern Ireland was heavily involved in the war effort, particularly Belfast, whose shipyards proved a major target for German bombing

1922–23	1926	1932	1933
Civil War between pro- (led by Michael Collins) and anti-treaty (led by Éamon de Valera) forces	De Valera forms a new political party, Fianna Fáil ("Soldiers of Destiny")	De Valera wins the general election, at the start of a sixteen-year reign as prime minister	Formation of the Fine Gael ("Tribe of the Irish") political party out of pro-treaty elements in Sinn Féin

raids. In contrast, Éire adopted a position of neutrality throughout and negotiated its security with Germany, though it did make certain concessions to the UK regarding flights over its airspace. It also remained utterly dependent on imports from the UK and suffered drastically when British ships carrying goods such as coal and cattle feed were attacked by U-boats. In recent years the Irish Republic's neutral role in World War II has been re-examined to some extent. New estimates suggest that despite the position adopted by de Valera's government during "The Emergency", as it termed World War II, around fifty thousand Irishmen from south of the border volunteered to fight for the British army, roughly the same as those from the north.

The postwar Republic

De Valera lost the 1948 election to a wide-ranging coalition of opposition parties, led by John A. Costello's Fine Gael, which set about the removal of any surviving legislative links with Britain by establishing Éire as the **Republic of Ireland** in 1949. However, the new Republic's economic position remained dire and the early 1950s were characterized by fresh waves of rural depopulation and migration both to Dublin and abroad. De Valera was returned as Taoiseach twice during the decade (in 1951 and 1957), but it was not until his long-serving deputy Seán Lemass took office in 1959 that the policies needed to boost Ireland's stagnant economy began to be enacted. Lemass directed Ireland away from protectionism and firmly towards free trade, drawing foreign investment in the process, and sowed the seeds of membership of the **European Economic Community** in January 1973 – though by this time Jack Lynch's government was fully embroiled in developments in the North (see below).

While the Republic, not least its farmers, initially prospered from EEC membership, the country suffered badly during the recession of the early 1980s, leading to a new wave of emigration. Its remaining population seemed to become increasingly conservative, rejecting referenda to allow abortion and divorce in 1983 and 1986 respectively.

The Troubles and the peace process

Though Northern Ireland had benefited hugely from the social policies begun by the post-World War II Labour government, not least in terms of health and social care, its Catholic population continued to suffer levels of social deprivation far worse than anywhere else in the UK. In 1967 the **Civil Rights Movement**, a nonsectarian coalition demanding equal rights, was formed, promoting its campaign via protest marches. One of these, through Derry in 1968, saw demonstrators attacked by a police baton charge and television pictures of the West Belfast MP Gerry Fitt with blood streaming down his face from a wound – transmitted around the world, these provoked international condemnation of the RUC's tactics. Severe rioting the next year following the Apprentice Boys' August parade led to the barricading of the Bogside area of Derry and Irish Taoiseach Jack Lynch's movement of Irish troops to the border to await developments.

British troops arrived shortly afterwards, ostensibly to keep the peace in Derry and Belfast, where Protestant assaults on West Belfast's Catholics had taken place. Though initially welcomed by Catholics, the army soon shifted its approach in line with the

1938	1939–45	1949	1959
Promulgation of a new constitution for the State, henceforth to be known as Éire	Éire remains neutral in World War II, which is known as "The Emergency"	Éire becomes the Republic of Ireland and severs all remaining ties to Britain	Sean Lemass succeeds de Valera and begins to stimulate the economy

THE MAZE HUNGER STRIKES

In the late 1970s IRA inmates at Long Kesh prison (also known as **The Maze**) began a series of protests against the abolition of the Special Category Status they had been granted, which gave them the right to be treated as political prisoners. This began as a "**blanket protest**" in which prisoners refused to wear prison clothes, instead opting to remain naked under a blanket draped over their shoulders, and later moved on to the infamous "**dirty protest**" where the inmates smeared their cell walls with excrement rather than emptying their chamber pots. Despite a 1978 European Court of Human Rights verdict finding the British Government guilty of "inhuman and degrading treatment", the British position remained intransigent, both under the outgoing Labour Government and even more so when a new regime under Conservative leader Margaret Thatcher was elected in 1979. The H-blocks of The Maze had become a hotbed for Republican education and action and, in the early 1980s, a new tactic was employed – the **hunger strike**. The first of these ended ignominiously in 1980, but the second, led by **Bobby Sands**, commander of the Provisional IRA within the prison, who was elected MP for Fermanagh and South Tyrone in the course of the fast, had more effect. The hunger strike resulted in ten deaths, including Sands' own, but Thatcher remained obdurate despite worldwide condemnation of Britain's position.

laissez-faire and often repressive tactics of the RUC. After years in the wilderness, and bolstered by new recruits, the IRA took up the gauntlet as defenders of the Catholic turf, though its own internal disputes led to the formation of the **Provisional IRA**, which broke away from the Dublin-led Official IRA and began an armed campaign against the army, RUC and Loyalists. As a result, the British introduced **internment without trial**, indiscriminately rounding up any Catholic thought to be linked to the violence. On January 30, 1972, British paratroopers shot and killed thirteen unarmed civil-rights demonstrators in Derry in an incident known ever afterwards as **Bloody Sunday** (see page 500). Three days later, the British Embassy in Dublin was burnt down and shortly afterwards Westminster's direct rule was reinstated over Northern Ireland. On **Bloody Friday**, July 21, 1972, the IRA exploded twenty car bombs in Belfast's city centre, killing nine people and injuring 130.

Sunningdale and the mainland bombing campaign

The 1970s were marked by increasing violence and diplomatic attempts to produce a political solution. A first attempt at power-sharing, established by the 1973 **Sunningdale conference**, proved impossible to implement in the face of a massive campaign of disruption led by the **Reverend Ian Paisley** and the strike called by the Ulster Workers Council in May 1974, which paralyzed much of Northern Ireland. During the strike the Loyalist UDA (Ulster Defence Association) detonated three car bombs in central Dublin, killing 33 people. The power-sharing executive was disbanded and direct rule reinstated once again, which continued until 1999.

Meanwhile, the IRA had transferred its bombing campaign to mainland Britain in an attempt to force the reunification of Ireland, and in 1974 set off massive **explosions** in pubs in Birmingham, Woolwich and Guildford, killing 28 people. It declared a ceasefire later that year – subsequently discovered to be a consequence of clandestine

1967	1972	1973	1973
Formation of the Civil Rights Movement to demand equal rights in the north	Bloody Sunday: British paratroopers kill thirteen unarmed civil rights protestors in Derry	The Sunningdale Agreement, an unsuccessful attempt at power-sharing	The Republic joins the European Economic Community

negotiations with the British Government – but the failure to secure a lasting agreement led to the resumption of the campaign the following year. In retaliation, Harold Wilson introduced the **Prevention of Terrorism Act**, allowing extended detention without charge. In two major trials, those found guilty of the Guildford and Birmingham bombings were sentenced to life imprisonment, but increasing concerns about the reliability of the forensic evidence and their confessions led to the release of the Guildford Four in 1989 and the Birmingham Six in 1991.

Though refusing to respond to the Hunger Strikes (see box) by IRA inmates, Margaret Thatcher's government did attempt another power-sharing initiative with the formation of the **Northern Ireland Assembly** in 1982, but this was shunned by both Nationalists and Republicans. In 1984 the IRA notoriously bombed the Brighton hotel hosting the Tory party conference, in an unsuccessful attempt to kill Thatcher. However, parallel political developments saw a sea change in the form of the Republicans' tactical decision to employ the democratic process alongside the armed campaign. Instrumental in this strategy were two Republican leaders who would become pivotal figures in the peace process: former Maze internee **Gerry Adams**, from 1983 Sinn Féin's party leader and MP for West Belfast, and **Martin McGuinness**, a former member of the Provisional IRA and Sinn Féin's vice president from 1983.

Towards the Good Friday Agreement and the Assembly

The IRA kept up its bombing campaign during the 1990s, beginning with a brazen mortar attack on 10 Downing Street in February 1991 targeting a cabinet meeting chaired by the new British leader, John Major. Loyalist sectarian attacks on Catholics also continued relentlessly, matching the numbers killed by Republicans. Undeterred, Major concluded an agreement with the Irish Prime Minister Albert Reynolds in December 1993, the **Downing Street Declaration**, largely shaped by the diplomacy of the SDLP's leader, **John Hume**, which sought to bring peace to Northern Ireland by democratic means.

The IRA launched another audacious mortar attack, this time on Heathrow Airport, in March 1994, but after focused lobbying by Dublin and the US vice president Al Gore, announced a ceasefire at the end of August, followed two months later by a similar Loyalist move. The following year witnessed intense negotiations involving the London and Dublin governments and the Republicans, which floundered in the face of the IRA's refusal to decommission its weaponry. Its bombing of Canary Wharf in London's financial centre in February 1996 re-emphasized its determination to continue the armed struggle, but lobbying for all-party talks on a resolution of the settlement intensified further. The key players were John Hume, who repeatedly met Gerry Adams with the intention of restoring the IRA's ceasefire, and the US president **Bill Clinton**, whose involvement and support for change went way beyond any intention to bolster his Irish-American electoral support.

The most significant broker, however, became British Prime Minister **Tony Blair**, the Labour leader elected with a vast majority in 1997, alongside his Northern Ireland Secretary, **Mo Mowlam**. They targeted a solution by diplomatic discussions with Bertie Ahern's government and the securement of the commitment of the **David Trimble**-led Ulster Unionists and Gerry Adams to all-party talks on Northern Ireland's future. The IRA's resumption of a ceasefire in July 1997 eased the process, but continuing violence

1981	1983	1991	1993
Bobby Sands and nine other Republican prisoners die on hunger strike; Margaret Thatcher is unmoved	Gerry Adams and Martin McGuinness take control of Sinn Féin and Adams becomes MP for West Belfast	Mary Robinson becomes Ireland's first woman president	The Downing Street Declaration by the Irish and British prime ministers

throughout the following months, including the assassination of the LVF leader, Billy Wright, inside The Maze, provided further stumbling blocks.

Blair's commitment to a democratic solution culminated on April 9, 1998. After anxious negotiations late into the night, an accord was somehow agreed, and the **Good Friday Agreement** was signed the following morning. The Agreement committed its signatories "to exclusively democratic and peaceful means of resolving differences on political issues".

More vitally, the agreement laid down the principle that any subsequent changes in the government of Northern Ireland – whether it remained part of the UK or opted to amalgamate with the Republic – relied entirely on the consent of the majority of both the Catholic and Protestant communities. An **Assembly** would be elected, based on proportional representation, with an executive of ministers drawn equally from both camps operating departments previously run by the British. Political prisoners would be rapidly released and an independent commission appointed to determine the future of Northern Ireland's policing.

The agreement was ratified by the North's population in May, and elections in June 1998 saw the UUP's David Trimble returned as First Minister and the SDLP's **Séamus Mallon** as his deputy.

Impasse ...

Almost as soon as the agreement was signed, however, the new administration, opposed by **Ian Paisley**'s DUP and numerous other Loyalists, became embroiled in debate regarding the right of the Orange Order to march from a Church of Ireland in Drumcree, prior to celebrations of the Battle of the Boyne (see page 563), through Catholic areas of Portadown. Drumcree became a significant annual flashpoint over the next few years and the marching issue remains a significant element in the sectarian divide to this day.

It was not just Loyalist unrest that threatened to derail the peace process, though. A breakaway Republican grouping, the self-styled **Real IRA**, soon perpetrated the most murderous act of the whole history of the Troubles. As part of a campaign of town-centre assaults, it exploded a car bomb in the centre of **Omagh**, County Tyrone, on Saturday August 15, 1998, killing 29 people and injuring hundreds more. In the face of uniform condemnation, the group declared a ceasefire two weeks later.

David Trimble and John Hume were jointly awarded the **1998 Nobel Peace Prize**. However, while general optimism remained in place, the ramifications of parts of the Good Friday Agreement soon became apparent, as the UUP became concerned at the reduction of army numbers. Their worries were exacerbated by the report of the **Patten Commission** into the future of the **Royal Ulster Constabulary**, which proposed the force's abolition and replacement by a new body – with a new name – whose members were to be recruited equally from Catholic and Loyalist communities. The loss of the words "Royal" and "Ulster" from the new organization's title were impossible for Unionists to accept, and the new secretary of state, **Peter Mandelson** (who had replaced Mo Mowlam), bowed to pressure by rejecting many of the Commission's findings, despite strong Nationalist and Republican protest. The new **Police Service of Northern Ireland** (**PSNI**), however, came into existence in November 2001, but has not yet managed to recruit equally from the two communities.

1994	1998	1999	2000
Short-lived Republican and Loyalist ceasefires	The Good Friday Agreement commits all parties to democratic and peaceful solutions	The new Assembly convenes but is bedevilled by the issue of arms decommissioning	The IRA announces that it will initiate a process to put its arms beyond use

However, the two key issues, interrelated in the eyes of many Unionists, were the release of political prisoners and the **decommissioning of weaponry**. While the release of prisoners passed relatively smoothly, the operation of the Assembly was thoroughly bedevilled by the decommissioning issue from the day it opened for business on December 1, 1999, and over the next six years its powers were regularly suspended by a succession of different British Northern Ireland Secretaries.

On May 6, 2000, an unexpected and hugely significant **statement from the IRA's leadership** declared that, while they remained committed to a united Ireland, they would "initiate a process that will completely and verifiably put IRA arms beyond use". Neither the UUP nor the DUP, which despite its complete abhorrence of the Good Friday Agreement had taken its seats in the Assembly, would accept that the IRA really meant business, despite the reports of the independent arms inspectorate led by the Canadian General John de Chastelain. In response, Sinn Féin's leadership of Gerry Adams and Martin McGuinness argued that, as a political party, it had no powers over decommissioning. Many now worried for the future of devolution, fearing that this apparent stalemate would see many IRA members defecting to the reactivated Real IRA (which indeed subsequently began a bombing campaign in London), based on the belief that the Adams–McGuinness strategy for political progress had been a mistake. If Gerry Adams could not persuade the IRA to decommission, they reasoned, then nobody could.

As the impasse continued, conventional crime seemed to hoover up the activities of Loyalist and Republican paramilitaries. The former were involved in a violent feud over the illegal drugs trade, while in December 2004, a staggering £26.5 million **bank raid** of Belfast's Northern Bank had fingers immediately pointing towards the IRA (though only a financial adviser has been convicted of money laundering).

… and resolution

Local and national **elections** in May 2005 witnessed a sea change in public opinion. The SDLP suffered badly at the hands of Sinn Féin, while the UUP was virtually wiped off the political map by the DUP, leading to Trimble's resignation as minister. The centre ground had now completely disappeared, leaving hardline Republicans and Loyalists as the arbiters of the peace process's continuation. In September 2005, the IRA announced that it was putting all of its weaponry beyond use, thus effectively declaring the end of its armed struggle for unification and against British rule (the UVF would follow suit in 2007).

Assembly elections in early 2007 ratified the DUP's and Sinn Féin's positions as the North's two leading parties. Subsequently, following the ending of a suspension which had begun in late 2005, Ian Paisley and Martin McGuinness took up their positions as, respectively, leader and deputy leader of the Assembly. The DUP's **Peter Robinson** succeeded Paisley (who passed away in 2014) as both DUP leader and the Assembly's First Minister in 2008. Robinson and McGuinness continued their roles after the 2011 Assembly elections, which again returned the DUP and Sinn Féin as the largest parties.

… and a new stalemate

Early in 2016 Robinson resigned from politics to be replaced as DUP leader and First Minister by **Arlene Foster**. This led to yet another change in the political temperature, plunging the power-sharing Assembly at Stormont into its worst crisis in a decade. An

2001	2005	2007	2008
The Royal Ulster Constabulary becomes the Police Service of Northern Ireland	The more extreme DUP and Sinn Féin succeed the UUP and SDLP as the north's major parties	Ian Paisley (succeeded by Peter Robinson) and Martin McGuinness become leader and deputy leader of the Assembly	Fianna Fáil's Bertie Ahern resigns after eleven scandal-hit years as prime minister

added dimension was created with the **death of Martin McGuinness** in February 2017. Obituaries characterized McGuinness as a former IRA chief of staff who had his finger on the pulse – and the trigger – of terrorism, but who matured into an advocate of peace, becoming a lynchpin of the process that led to the Good Friday Agreement.

Michelle O'Neil, replaced McGuinness as deputy leader of the Assembly and leader of Sinn Féin, but relations between her and Foster became strained and the Assembly was **suspended**, pending negotiations. The disputed issues were over legal recognition for the Irish language, a new settlement for unsolved Troubles cases, legalizing same-sex marriage (the DUP was strongly opposed to it) and the underlying tensions of Brexit, the United Kingdom's exit from the European Union. The DUP also came in for criticism in June 2017 when they entered into an agreement with the minority Conservative government led by Theresa May after the party suffered a shock election loss. To retain her position as British Prime Minister, May struck a deal to secure the DUP's support, and in exchange the party received £1bn for investment in infrastructure projects in Northern Ireland. In 2019, Northern Ireland followed its neighbours in the south by decriminalising abortion, and the following year it legalized same-sex marriage.

Start, stop, start…

After a three-year suspension, the assembly resumed in January 2020 following a deal that resurrected a power sharing government in the region; key to this was the creation of two new language commissioners, part of a cultural policy to put Gaelic on the same legal standing as English at the same time as protecting Ulster British culture. In the meantime, both the DUP and Sinn Féin had suffered significant losses in the 2019 UK general election. Further trouble lay ahead for the DUP when, in 2021, Foster stepped down as DUP leader and First Minister following an internal revolt. She was succeeded by Paul Givan, although his tenure lasted just eight months, the First Minister resigning in protest at post-Brexit trade arrangements – which led to yet another suspension for the assembly. After two years of stasis, devolved government was restored to Northern Ireland in February 2024 following the DUP's decision to endorse a deal that ensued that there would no longer be physical or identity checks on goods entering the country from the rest of the UK; and with Sinn Féin as the largest party following the last assembly election, Michelle O'Neill became the country's first nationalist First Minister, with the DUP's Emma Little-Pengelly assuming the role of deputy first minister, the first Unionist to hold this position. Meanwhile, in the UK general election that same year Sinn Féin became, for the first time, the largest Northern Ireland party in Westminster, albeit without adding to their existing seven seats, the DUP losing three of its eight seats.

Nearly thirty years on from the IRA ceasefire of 1997 – and whatever the ongoing political bickering – a newly rich Northern Ireland is enjoying the greatest prosperity and longest period of peace in its history; it is a small country in transformation and an infinitely better place than the dark days of the Troubles.

Meanwhile in the Republic

While events in the North had been completely dominated by the peace process and the continuing wrangling at Stormont, the story of the Republic in the 1990s

2010	2011	2014	2015
Ireland accepts an €85 billion bailout to survive the international economic crisis	Enda Kenny of Fine Gael becomes prime minister	President Michael D. Higgins makes the first official visit by an Irish head of state to Britain	In a historic referendum, the Republic of Ireland votes overwhelmingly to legalize same-sex marriage

THE RISE AND FALL OF THE CELTIC TIGER

The 1990s witnessed a remarkable economic boom in the Republic, leading to the country's acquisition of the soubriquet **Celtic Tiger**. Ireland's emergence resulted from a combination of huge European Union subsidies (especially to farmers) and massive tax concessions to multinational companies, encouraging them to site operations in Dublin and elsewhere. For the first time in decades, Irish people actually returned home from abroad to seek work, reinvigorating an economy already bolstered by an increase in the number of graduates emerging from the country's universities. The most visible changes were apparent in the Dublin skyline, where new edifices seemed to emerge almost daily, and in the wave of "mansion" building reflecting the increasing affluence of Ireland's nouveaux riches. Additionally, sparked partly by the redevelopment of Dublin's Temple Bar, the vigorous local music scene (epitomized by the worldwide success of the band U2 and the singer Sinéad O'Connor) and the liberal tax concessions given to artists, writers and musicians, Ireland became for the first time a hip place to visit.

However, as it later emerged, the economy's growth was largely that of a boomtown built on silt, with vast wealth created for a relatively small number of investors in high-tech industries, bankers and property developers, but little legislation to tackle the social deprivation facing those way down the pecking order.

and 2000s was one of **rapid economic development** (see box) and a series of political scandals. The first major event of the new decade was the election of **Mary Robinson** as Ireland's first woman president in 1991. This heralded a more liberal outlook for the country, but her time as head of state was overshadowed by the resignation of two of Ireland's Taoiseachs. **Charles Haughey** was the first to go in 1992, his administration smeared by long-lasting and later substantiated allegations of corruption, and brought down by the revelation that journalists' private telephone calls had been tapped by the Republic's police. In 1994 his successor, **Albert Reynolds**, was also forced to resign after revelations that his government had covered up allegations of paedophilia made against a Catholic priest.

Following a brief interlude of a Fine Gael coalition under **John Bruton**, the Republic was run for fourteen years by a series of Fianna Fáil–headed alliances. The Taoiseach from 1997 until 2008 was **Bertie Ahern**, whose ministries were dogged by further revelations of financial corruption involving key members of his party, resulting in the establishment of the **Flood Commission**'s long-standing investigations into innumerable transactions, as well as major enquiries into the operation of Ireland's police force, centred on various nefarious goings-on in County Donegal.

Ahern's government somehow stumbled on until May 2008, when he resigned following the **Mahon Tribunal**'s investigation into corrupt payments to politicians. He was succeeded by **Brian Cowen**, whose 2007 budget while Minister of Finance was widely regarded as the biggest spending spree in Irish political history. However, the international monetary crisis of 2008–2009 saw all of Ireland's boom-and-bust economic chickens come home to roost in alarming numbers. Cowen's government (forced to enact three budgets within a calendar year) struggled to maintain control of a situation verging upon national insolvency, and enforced austerity measures

2016	2017	2018
The DUP's Arlene Foster becomes new first Minister of the Stormont Assembly, which is suspended over political bickering with Sinn Féin	Ireland elects Leo Varadkar, leader of Fine Gael, as its first openly gay prime minister	Ireland legalizes abortion; Northern Ireland follows suit a year later

which cut the salaries of public servants and lowered welfare benefits, while simultaneously attempting to safeguard the Irish banking system. Added to this was the 2009 **Murphy Report** which resulted from investigations into sexual abuse by priests and others within the Catholic archdiocese of Dublin which exposed widespread exploitation of children, numerous cover-ups and a widespread failure to prosecute the perpetrators.

In 2010, the government was forced to turn to the EU and the IMF for an €85 billion **bailout** to save the banks, which has put the country in hock for generations to come. Some optimism returned with the success of Fine Gael, led by Mayoman Enda Kenny and in coalition with Labour, in the 2011 election. By 2014, the unemployment rate had fallen to 11 percent and the country recorded a year-on-year economic growth rate of 7.7 percent, the highest in the Eurozone. Seasoned observers of Ireland's boom-and-bust economy, however, could only wince as newspapers coined the term "The Celtic Phoenix".

Since then the Republic has continued to prosper economically (albeit in a patchy manner outside the major cities): for four successive years, from 2014 to 2017 it was Europe's fastest-growing economy with GDP growth of 4.8 percent. At the same time, it has slowly been transformed into a more liberal and multicultural country. In a historic 2015 referendum, Ireland voted overwhelmingly in favour of legalizing **same-sex marriage**. The following year, the 2016 Census showed a population of 4.7m, and while it remains a predominantly Catholic country, the numbers identifying as such fell sharply from 84.2 per cent to 78.3 per cent, evidence that it is no longer in thrall to the Catholic Church. But the most astonishing political move came in the summer of 2017 with the election as Taoiseach of **Leo Varadkar**, the openly gay son of an Indian immigrant. He took over from Enda Kenny who led Fine Gael for fifteen years and was Taoiseach for six of them. Varadkar's appointment, which made headlines around the world, was seen by many commentators as a sign, not only of a generational shift in Irish politics, but also as a transition from conservative traditionalism to liberal modernity. As if to emphasize this fact, in 2018 the country voted by a landslide to **legalise abortion**, in what turned out to be the highest ever turnout for a ballot on social issues. In the 2020 general election, Sinn Féin made huge inroads into the long-standing Fine Gael-Fianna Fáil duopoly, taking 37 seats, just one behind Fianna Fáil. The centrist coalition government comprised Fianna Fáil and Fine Gael (the first time the two parties had governed together) alongside the Green Party, with Micheál Martin – leader of Fianna Fáil – as Taoiseach, a role Varadkar would take over again in 2022. In March 2024, Varadkar shocked the country by announcing that he was resigning as Fine Gael leader as well as standing down as Taoiseach, a decision that some attributed to the fact that his government had just suffered damaging defeats in two referendums on family and women in the constitution. He was replaced by **Simon Harris** who, at the age of 37, became the youngest Taoiseach in the country's history.

2020	**2022**	**2024**
Ireland forms a coalition government between Fine Gael, Fianna Fáil and the Green Party	Northern Ireland assembly suspended for a sixth time	Leo Varadkar quits as Taoiseach and as leader of Fine Gael, while Michelle O'Neill becomes Northern Ireland's first nationalist First Minister

Traditional music

Ireland and music are as inseparable as fish and chips. Though the country has developed a thriving rock music scene over the last forty years and artists such as U2, Sinéad O'Connor and Van Morrison have achieved massive international success, it's Ireland's traditional music that in many ways continues to hold centre stage.

The country's musical traditions remain essentially based on the age-old practice of passing down tunes and songs by oral transmission, from generation to generation and from friend to friend. Its core has become the **pub session**, where the richness of the musical tradition can be experienced at first hand, and the *craic* (or crack) – that idiosyncratically Irish, heady combination of drink-fuelled chat, banter and fun – simply takes over.

The best sessions are always the ones you never expected to find, spontaneous and uproarious affairs, and the areas where you'll most likely find them are in the counties along the western and southern seaboards, especially Donegal, Sligo, Galway, Clare, Kerry and Cork, though there are excellent session scenes in Belfast and Dublin. Otherwise, the places to visit are festivals, and we've listed the best of both these and the session pubs throughout the Guide. For more information on the music itself and its instruments, see page 580.

Irish music rediscovered

While the musical traditions of other Western European countries were dissipated by the process of industrialization and political change, Ireland's indigenous music remained at the centre of its people's social life until well into the twentieth century, when its survival became threatened by emigration and governmental controls aimed at curbing dance forms regarded as immoral. It needed two major shots in the arm in the 1960s – the **folk song boom**, which originated in the USA, and the pioneering work of **Seán Ó Riada** in establishing ensemble playing as the new norm – to reinvigorate its existence.

Ireland's greatest musical ambassadors, **The Chieftains**, emerged from Ó Riada's initiative in the 1960s, and the following decade saw the formation of the country's two most influential groups, **Planxty** and **The Bothy Band**. Their performances and recordings effectively laid out the ground for others to tread, not least **De Dannan**, the Donegal-based **Altan**, and, in more recent times, **Lúnasa**, **Danú** and the US-based **Solas**.

The tunes

Almost all of Ireland's traditional music tunes are based on imported **dance** forms. The only exceptions to this rule are slow airs which largely owe their origins to the song tradition (see page 582), a few special pieces belonging to the *uilleann* piping tradition (such as *The Fox Chase*, in which the instrument mimics the sound of fox, hunters and hounds), and a body of more than two hundred tunes composed by the blind itinerant harper **Turlough O'Carolan** (1680–1738), which carry some influence by Italian classical composers of that era.

There are several thousand reels, jigs (in various formats), hornpipes, barndances, strathspeys, waltzes and numerous other dance tunes, though many are only rarely played. At most sessions it is reels and jigs that predominate. Particular tune forms are favoured in different parts of the country – the polka for example is especially popular in Cork and Kerry. The authors of the vast majority of tunes are unknown, though some do bear their composer's name, such as *Martin Wynne's No. 1*, and many more are added to the canon

INSTRUMENTS AND PLAYERS

We've mentioned some of the best instrumentalists on the Irish music scene in this roundup of traditional instruments. If you get the chance to see any of them at the festivals, don't miss it.

UILLEANN PIPES

The English folk singer Martin Carthy once aptly described seeing the renowned **Séamus Ennis** playing the *uilleann* pipes as like "watching a man wrestling an octopus". The world's most complex set of bagpipes (variously pronounced "illun" or "illyun") is an extraordinarily temperamental creature and notoriously hard to master. The instrument has several components, consisting of a nine-holed chanter capable of producing a double-octave range, powered by air squeezed from a bag positioned under the left arm, itself driven by bellows pressed against the player's torso by his or her right elbow. The pipes also come equipped with three drones and a set of three regulators that can be flipped on and off to provide chordal accompaniment. No other instrument in the Irish canon is as capable of replicating the vocal ornamentations of *sean-nós* singers via the playing of slow airs.

Since the late nineteenth century two distinct styles of playing have evolved: one more gentle and ornamentally delicate, exemplified by Séamus Ennis and **Leo Rowsome**; and the other (often termed "open" or "legato") much more intricate, crisp, showy and rhythmically driven, and associated with members of the Traveller community who earned a living playing at country fairs – key protagonists of this style were the late brothers **Johnny and Felix Doran**, and, more recently, **Davy Spillane**.

Pipers have long held a special place in Ireland's musical heritage, one such virtuoso being **Liam O'Flynn**, who was famed for his solo recordings, work with the classical composer Shaun Davey and poet Seamus Heaney, and membership of Planxty. **Paddy Keenan**, memorably once described as "the Jimi Hendrix of the *uilleann* pipes", rose to fame via The Bothy Band and continues to produce performances of astonishing majesty. Other pipers of note include **Neillidh Mulligan**, one of the best exponents of slow airs, **Ronan Browne** (also adept on flute and whistles), the Belfast-born **John McSherry** and the phenomenally talented young Dubliner **Seán McKeon**.

FLUTES AND WHISTLES

The flute preferred by Irish musicians is the simple wooden version with fingers used to cover the holes rather than keys as in its classical cousin, though some players do employ semi-keyed instruments. The long-standing hotbed of Irish flute music is North Connacht, famed for its seeming production-line of players incorporating a mellifluous, sometimes flamboyant style, in their music. The best known of these is **Matt Molloy** of The Bothy Band and The Chieftains, although the late **Séamus Tansey** was also hugely influential. Belfast too has produced some fine flute players, often influenced by the North Connacht style or that of neighbouring Fermanagh (from which **Cathal McConnell** is a major figure), including **Desi Wilkinson** and **Harry Bradley**, while Dublin's **Paul McGrattan** has drawn much from the Donegal fiddle tradition.

The essential learning instrument of Irish music is the tin whistle, and one is still carried around by many players of other instruments keen to learn new tunes quickly – if you're tempted to buy one, make sure it's a D-whistle, as many tunes are played in this key. In the hands of a skilled operator – such as **Mary Bergin**, **Gavin Whelan** or **Bríd O'Donohue** – the whistle utterly surmounts its apparent technical limitations.

FIDDLES

The fiddle is Ireland's most popular traditional instrument and perhaps the best exemplar of regional musical styles (although these have been undermined as players learn their tunes and adaptations from the radio, CDs and MP3s rather than their neighbours). Donegal is famed for its captivating rhythmic style, often referred to as "driving" and best heard in the recordings of **John Doherty** (see page 423) and **Tommy Peoples**. The Sligo style, encapsulated in the recordings of **Michael Coleman** (see page 396) and **James Morrison**, is generally regarded as more ornamented and flashy, but continues to be a major influence. The eastern parts of Galway and Clare are noted for their more lonesome style, produced by a tendency to play in flattened key signatures and exemplified by the playing of **Martin Hayes**, who uses his native tradition as an extraordinary springboard for musical exploration. To the south, in Kerry and Cork, the polka remains the most popular dance tune and much of the most atmospheric playing dates back to the fiddle-master **Pádraig O'Keeffe**, though his enduring influence can be heard in the playing of **Matt Cranitch** and the late **Séamus Creagh**.

MELODEONS, ACCORDIONS AND CONCERTINAS

Squeeze-boxes come in a variety of shapes and sizes in traditional music. The simplest is the one-row button accordion, usually known as a melodeon in Ireland. One of its true masters was the Connemara box-player **Johnny Connolly**, generally regarded as the acme of accompanists for dancing. The far more popular two-row button accordion comes in a range of tunings, usually either B/C (favoured by the late **Joe Burke**), which produces a more rolling and frilly style of play, or the C sharp/D variety (whose well-known exponents include **Dermot Byrne** and the late **Séamus Begley**). Also well worth seeking out are **Jackie Daly** and **Máirtín O Connor**, both of whom play boxes in a variety of tunings, while the music of Clare's **Sharon Shannon** continues to attract a global audience. The piano accordion is less well favoured, though there are some cracking musicians using it, including **Alan Kelly**, **Mirella Murray** and **Martin Tourish**.

The smaller concertina was once thought of as primarily a women's instrument and was especially popular in County Clare (for too many reasons to list here). Again, it's ideal for accompanying dancers. Probably the best-known exponents are **Mary Mac Namara**, **Noel Hill**, **Micheál Ó Raghallaigh and the late Chris Droney**.

THE BOUZOUKI AND OTHER STRINGED INSTRUMENTS

The Greek *bouzouki* was first introduced to Ireland by **Johnny Moynihan** of the band Sweeney's Men in the late 1960s and made popular by **Dónal Lunny** of Planxty and The Bothy Band, and **Alec Finn** of De Dannan. Along with the guitar, it's the most common form of stringed accompaniment found at sessions, though, thanks to its open tuning and flat back, it's nowadays more akin to the mandolin than its Greek forebear. As a relatively quiet instrument, the mandolin itself, as played by **Paul Kelly**, is rarely seen at sessions, though you may see a larger version known as the mandola, whose well-known protagonists include **Andy Irvine**. Lastly, there's the banjo, an instrument reviled by many for its "plunker-plunker" sound, but which does have some exceptional exponents, including **Gerry O'Connor**.

THE BODHRÁN

This goatskin frame drum (pronounced "bore-run" or "bough-ron"), resembling a tambourine without jingles and played with the hand or a wooden beater, divides opinion among Irish sessioneers more than any other instrument. Some musicians appreciate the driving rhythm provided by a good percussionist (such as **John Joe Kelly**), but others regard it as the devil's detritus and sounding, in one fiddler's memorable words, "like a sack of spuds tipped down the stairs". Originally associated with the "wren boys" who went out revelling ("hunting the wren") and playing music on St Stephen's Day (Dec 26), it was adopted for ensemble playing by **Seán Ó Riada** in the 1960s. Many music or souvenir shops sell the drum and, if you're tempted to buy one, do listen to recordings of the best players (**Johnny McDonagh** and **Colm Murphy** with De Dannan or **Donnchadh Gough** with Danú) before even considering whether your own formative skills might be welcome at a session.

each year in the form of new compositions. Apart from such eponymous works, tune titles should not be taken as anything more than a labelling device (and some have particularly arcane titles – witness *Wallop the Spot* or *The Cat That Kittled in Jamie's Wig*).

This depth of the tradition owes much to fears at certain times in Ireland's history that it was on the wane, spurring collectors to amass as much information as possible from musicians. The most notable collector was **Captain Francis O'Neill**, erstwhile Chicago police chief, who in the early twentieth century gathered tunes together in publications such as *The Dance Music of Ireland*. Later collectors of note include **Séamus Ennis**, who assiduously accumulated material for Radio Éireann and the BBC, and **Breandán Breathnach**, who published several volumes of material under the title *Ceol Rince na hÉireann* ("Dance Music of Ireland"). Today Dublin's Irish Traditional Music Archive continues the process of storing and cataloguing newly found material.

While these tunes were originally played at house or "crossroads" dances (held in a suitable open space – frequently a road junction), and often at weddings or wakes, they form merely a staging post for skilled traditional musicians, who embellish their renditions with all manner of musical ornamentation, though rarely straying from the essential rhythms of the dance. Nowadays, most dance tunes are played as part of a set, usually consisting of two or three of the same form, each played through a couple of times (or sometimes more) before segueing into the next one.

Sessions

The pub session as we know it today is in fact another import, having emerged in pubs in London and elsewhere where there were plenty of Irish émigrés in the years following World War II. During the folk and ballad boom of the 1960s, led by **The Clancy Brothers and Tommy Makem** and their more raucous contemporaries **The Dubliners**, Ireland's pub landlords began to welcome traditional musicians and the practice continues to this day. The session has become the focal point for the tradition and usually consists of a regular and informal gathering of local musicians on a particular evening, one of whom is usually paid to ensure that it takes place.

The majority of sessions (except some in extremely popular tourist areas) are relatively informal affairs where the musicians play the tunes of their choice, breaking off whenever they feel like doing so for a chat or an outdoor fag-break. Sessions can be found throughout the year in cities such as Belfast, Cork, Dublin and Galway, but in smaller towns and rural areas the months between June and September are usually the best time. Most begin at around 9.30pm, though on the west coast in high summer you'll find plenty not starting until 10.30pm and sometimes later. The lure for the pub's punters is the chance to hear top-class musicianship for the price of a pint or two as well as participating in the associated *craic*.

Bear in mind that the musicians' seats are sacrosanct, so don't plonk yourself down next to a fiddler to enjoy the music from a closer aspect – the vacant seat you've just occupied was reserved for a musician who might or might not appear later.

You'll only rarely come across dancing at a session (and you'll probably be in Kerry or Clare if you do), thus the best bet, if you want to twirl the light fantastic, is to look out for a **ceili dance**. Plenty of these take place during local festivals, but there are also a number of renowned venues along the west coast that feature regular nights of set dancing to the accompaniment of a ceili band. These bands normally feature just the usual main traditional instruments, though some also include oddities such as the saxophone and accompaniment via piano and/or snare drum.

The song tradition

Sadly, unaccompanied songs play little part in today's sessions, despite Ireland's remarkable vocal tradition. Essentially, this falls into two categories: songs in the Irish language and songs in English. Many Irish-language songs are of great antiquity and together they form part of what has become known as **sean-nós**, which literally means "old style". The tradition is strongest in the Irish-speaking areas of the west coast, particularly in West Kerry (Dingle), Connemara and Donegal, and incorporates an unaccompanied singing style of great emotional intensity when applied to the "big songs" of the tradition – tales of love, loss and longing – or sprightly frivolity when handling more light-hearted matters. Singers essentially construct a soundscape in which their use of vocal ornamentation and changes in tempo and tone lead the listener through the lyrics' twists and turns. Though knowledge of the Irish language is essential to a full understanding of their abilities, even without this it's still possible to appreciate singing that can be very beautiful. Some of the best contemporary members of the tradition, not least **Iarla Ó Lionáird** (from West Cork), well known through his work with the Afro Celts fusion band, and **Lasairfhíona Ní Chonaola** (from the Aran Islands), have produced albums of extraordinary splendour.

Simultaneously, Ireland possesses a vast wealth of traditional songs in English, including many derived from the broadsheet ballad-sellers of the nineteenth and earlier twentieth centuries and others shared with the heritage of England and Scotland, and there are traditional singing clubs in several of Ireland's towns and cities. The country's foremost interpreter of these and many other contemporary songs is unquestionably **Christy Moore**.

DISCOGRAPHY

The following selection of albums provides a solid foundation for investigation of Ireland's musical traditions. They can be purchased at Custy's in Ennis (see page 315), other record stores and online.

Seamus Begley *The Bold Kerryman* (IRL Independent Records). Tender-voice west Kerry singer, accordionist and storyteller.

Mary Bergin *Feadóga Stáin* (Gael Linn). Marvellously adept whistle-playing.

The Bothy Band *The Bothy Band 1975* (Jasmine). Short-lived but still incredibly influential, this band set the template for so many others to follow.

Cran *Lover's Ghost* (Black Rose Records). A gripping melange of songs and flute/*uilleann* pipes interplay.

Séamus Creagh and Jackie Daly *Same* (Gael Linn). Polkas from the mountains of Sliabh Luachra on the Kerry–Cork–Limerick border and much more on this exhilarating fiddle/accordion album.

Martin Hayes and Dennis Cahill *Live in Seattle* (Green Linnet). Ireland's most soulful and imaginative fiddler, in cahoots with long-time guitarist buddy, produces one of the most invigorating live performances you'll ever hear.

Joe Heaney *The Road from Connemara* (Topic). A double-CD which encapsulates the singing of perhaps Ireland's finest exponent of the *sean-nós* style.

Noel Hill and Tony Linnane *Same* (Tara). Tremendous concertina/fiddle duets from the Clare duo, recorded when both were in their late teens.

Cathal Lynch *The Jolly Roving Tar* (Claddagh). The renowned traditional Tyrone singer has made a name touring extensively.

Seán Maguire *The Master's Touch* (Aínm Records). The multi-talented Belfast fiddle player died in 2005 but his music has been digitally remastered with classics such as The Blackbird, The Humours of Bandon and *Madame Bonaparte*.

Christy Moore *At the Point Live* (Columbia). Captures the singer in his heyday when he was justifiably regarded as a national treasure.

Maighread and Tríona Ní Dhomhnaill *Idir an Dá Sholas* (Gael Linn/Hummingbird). Glorious singing in both Irish and English.

Gerry O'Connor *Journeyman* (Lughnasa Music). One of the finest fiddle albums of recent years.

Máirtín O Connor *The Road West* (Sun Street Studios). Button accordionist O Connor teams up with some of Ireland's best musicians including Cathal Hayden, Nollaig Casey and Garry O Briain that will have you heading for the Wild Atlantic Way.

Planxty *Same* (Shanachie). AKA "*The Black Album*" and featuring a dazzling array of songs and tunes from Christy Moore, Andy Irvine, Liam Ó Flynn and Dónal Lunny, this magical release redefined Ireland's musical landscape.

Sharon Shannon, Frankie Gavin, Michael McGoldrick and Jim Murray *Tunes* (The Daisy Label). A splendid constellation of accordion, fiddle, flute and guitar.

Solas *Reunion* (Compass Records). A fabulous live recording (including film footage on DVD) of a concert reuniting the Irish-US band's former and present members.

Séamus Tansey *King of the Concert Flute* (Sound Records). Outstanding flute-playing from the Sligo master.

Various *The Rough Guide to Irish Folk* and *The Rough Guide to Irish Music* (both World Music Network). Two excellent compilations providing an overview, respectively, of the song and instrumental traditions.

Literature

For an island of fewer than six million people, Ireland has an astonishingly rich literary tradition, the oldest in Europe outside of Italy and Greece. While most of this literature up to the seventeenth century was written in Gaelic (usually called Irish in Ireland today), and to a lesser extent Latin, English would become pre-eminent from the eighteenth century onwards and is today the first language not just of most Irish writing but also of the vast majority of Irish people. Ireland's literary tradition has developed over two thousand years from the first markings on rocks around the time of Christ, to the acclaimed poetry, prose and theatre of writers such as W.B. Yeats, James Joyce and Samuel Beckett, producing startling works of originality and influence.

Beginnings

The oldest writing in Ireland was ogham script, a system of parallel notches that survives on standing stones from the fourth century AD, but was likely in existence for several hundred years previous. However, it was the arrival of Christianity in the fifth century that would have the most significant early influence on the emergence of literature in Ireland. With the growth of the monasteries between the seventh and tenth centuries, a rich culture of Latin manuscripts developed, the finest surviving example of which is the *Book of Kells* in Trinity College, Dublin (see page 65).

During the same period, a thriving literary culture in the vernacular of Irish life, Gaelic, began to emerge and develop, too. While the oldest surviving manuscripts in this language date from around the twelfth century, much of the material was copied and recopied for many hundreds of years before that. The oldest datable work of Gaelic literature is **Amra Choluim Chille** (Elegy of St Columba), a poem attributed to the poet Dallán Forgaill and written soon after the death in 597 of one of Ireland's most famous early saints, Colmcille, regarded as the patron saint of Irish poets. The Gaelic manuscripts also incorporated ancient, often fantastic and supernatural tales which had been preserved in a primarily oral culture. One such classic Irish story is the **Táin Bó Cúailnge** (The Cattle Raid of Cooley), which features the legendary figures of Cúchulainn, the larger-than-life Ulster warrior, and Queen Medb of Connaught.

While the manuscript tradition preserved tales concerning Cúchulainn, found in a larger narrative called the Ulster Cycle, a further popular hero in Gaelic oral culture was **Fionn Mac Cumhaill**, the leader of a band of warriors defending Ireland called the Fianna. The stories of Fionn and his men are commonly referred to as the *Fiannaíocht* tales and include the classic *Tóraíocht Dhiarmada agus Gráinne* (The Pursuit of Diarmuid and Gráinne), in which Fionn's intended, Gráinne, seduces one of his handsome warriors, Diarmuid, and elopes across Ireland, chased by Fionn and his men. Another famous early Gaelic tale is **Buile Shuibhne** (The Frenzy of Sweeney), the story of Suibhne Geilt, a king who, after being cursed by a local cleric, is transformed into a bird, banished and condemned to wander through Ireland's most desolate landscapes enduring great hardship and loneliness. These Gaelic legends have provided recurring inspiration for Irish writers, including W.B. Yeats, Synge, Joyce, Beckett, Flann O'Brien and Seamus Heaney.

The arrival of the Anglo-Normans in Ireland in the twelfth century brought another influence to bear on the Irish language and literature, and some of the finest poets of the Middle Ages would descend from Anglo-Norman stock, including in the fourteenth century Gearóid Iarla Fitzgerald, the Third Earl of Desmond. The thirteenth-century version of what is today known as Middle Irish was preserved as a literary language through the **bardic schools** that emerged in this period and continued in Ireland down to the mid-seventeenth century. These provided structured training for the *filí*, or poets, who were both feared and highly respected in a very hierarchical society. One significant aspect of poetry in this period was its close association with music, an association that would continue throughout the history of Irish literature. Surviving records suggest that bardic poetry was always performed with the accompaniment of the harp, the instrument that remains the national emblem of Ireland today. The esteem in which these poets were held is evident from the fact that many examples of this richly ornate and highly sophisticated bardic poetry survive, despite the tumultuous events that would lead to the decline of Gaelic Ireland.

Irish-language works of the seventeenth and eighteenth centuries

With the undermining of the Gaelic order following the Battle of Kinsale in 1601, the structures that had supported indigenous poetic and musical production went into decline. Furthermore, as the power of musicians and poets had been feared by the British establishment throughout the sixteenth century, efforts were made to persecute them and generally limit their influence. Previously exalted *filí* were now often reduced to **sráid-éigse** or "street poetry". The result was to bring the formerly independent professions of musician and poet together in the one performer whose compositions, particularly by the eighteenth century, gradually became more and more associated with the folk tradition of song. The passing on of Irish poetry through song ensured its survival and some songs from the eighteenth century, including *Dónal Óg* and *Úna Bhán*, continue to be sung today in the *sean-nós* or old-style tradition.

The eighteenth century would also witness, inspired by the Jacobite insurrections in Scotland of 1715 and 1745, the emergence of an indigenous, politically engaged poetry, as poets such as Piaras Mac Gearailt, Seán Ó Tuama, Seán Clárach Mac Domhnaill and Eoghan Rua Ó Súilleabháin produced work confident of the return of the Catholic Stuart kings to power and the revival of the Gaelic aristocracy. One of the most popular genres to evolve in this period was the **aisling**, its finest exponent **Aogán Ó Rathaille** in works such as *Mac an Cheannaí* (The Merchant's Son) and *Gile na Gile* (Brightness Most Bright). These "vision poems" feature the poet, on falling asleep, imagining he is visited by a beautiful woman who reveals herself as Ireland and laments her oppression. Such was the popularity of the *aisling* that one of the finest Gaelic poems of the eighteenth century is actually a parody of the genre, **Brian Merriman**'s *Cúirt An Mheán Oíche* (The Midnight Court). Here the poet encounters no beautiful maiden but rather an old hag, who summons him to a court where he witnesses an attack by Queen Aoibheal on the young men of Ireland for their refusal to marry and lack of virility. A ribald and satiric piece, regarded as the greatest comic poem in the language, it was banned in English when translated by Frank O'Connor in 1945, though the Irish-language version remained on the shelves.

Another highly accomplished Gaelic work of the eighteenth century is the *Caoineadh Airt Uí Laoghaire* (Lament for Art Ó Laoghaire), a long, traditional *caoineadh* or lament composed *ex tempore* by **Eibhlín Dhubh Ní Chonaill**, the aunt of Daniel O'Connell. It is a haunting piece lamenting the killing of Eibhlín's husband by the local sheriff, Abraham Morris, for refusing to sell his horse to him for £5, at a time when no Catholic was allowed under the hated penal laws to own a horse worth more than that figure.

The emergence of Irish literature in English

While Irish-language literature took a downturn from the seventeenth century onwards, Irish literature in English began to come to the fore, most importantly in the angry little shape of the poet, essayist and satirist **Jonathan Swift** (see page 79).

Other notable writers in English from the eighteenth century include **Laurence Sterne**, the Tipperary-born clergyman and author of the innovative and highly influential satire on the biographical novel, *The Life and Opinions of Tristram Shandy, Gentleman*; the Longford doctor, **Oliver Goldsmith**, best known for his elegy *The Deserted Village*, novel *The Vicar of Wakefield* and play *She Stoops to Conquer*; and **Richard Brinsley Sheridan**, author of *The Rivals* and *The School for Scandal*, one of the first in a long tradition of leading Irish playwrights in the English language.

Despite the decline of Irish language and culture, the late eighteenth and early nineteenth centuries were nonetheless important for the rejuvenation of Irish nationalism, Irish music and the emergence of a distinctive Irish poetry in English. The efforts of primarily Anglo-Irish antiquarians, concerned to promote the distinctiveness of the adopted country of their ancestors, would help to preserve some of the native literature and music. In 1789, the first translations of Gaelic poetry and songs, *Reliques of Irish Poetry*, were published by **Charlotte Brooke**, a pioneering mediator between the Anglo-Irish Ascendancy and the local tradition. Her work would inspire subsequent antiquarians such as **Sir Samuel Ferguson**, the most important collector and translator of Gaelic poetry and mythology in the nineteenth century and a crucial influence on the writers who emerged in the Literary Revival at the end of the century, including W.B. Yeats.

Thomas Moore and the Young Ireland Poets

In the early nineteenth century, "the darling of the London drawing rooms" was **Thomas Moore**, born of a Catholic family in Dublin, whose romantic and nostalgic nationalist compositions – such as the still-popular songs *The Minstrel Boy* and *The Last Rose of Summer* – were included in *Irish Melodies*, published in ten volumes between 1808 and 1834. These poems were set to traditional Irish tunes from Edward Bunting's *General Collection of Ancient Music of Ireland* (1796), a compilation of the airs of some of the few remaining Irish harpists who performed at the Belfast Harpers' Festival of July 1792. Moore's *Melodies* has been called "the secular hymn-book of Irish nationalism" in the nineteenth century and he was regarded by many during his lifetime as Ireland's national poet. He represents the beginnings of the articulation of Irish identity and culture, on a national scale, in the English language.

While Moore had found in Irish music a means of access to what he believed to be the national spirit, the **Young Ireland Poets** associated with the nationalist newspaper, *The Nation* (which began publication in 1842), would find similar sustenance in the ballad. Among the most influential contributors to *The Nation* were **Thomas Davis** and **James Clarence Mangan**, both of whom would be alluded to in the work of W.B. Yeats and Joyce. While Davis's *A Nation Once Again* is still sung and was given serious consideration as the national anthem of Ireland, his emphasis on the importance of literature for national identity would have a vital influence on the Literary Revival. Mangan's free translation of the Gaelic song *Róisín Dubh* (Dark Rosaleen) has been described as the "most widely known nationalist poem" of the nineteenth century, but his overall ambivalence towards the nationalist project would find resonance in the work of Joyce, who wrote an essay on the poet.

Irish playwrights of the nineteenth century

Born in Dublin of Huguenot stock, **Dion Boucicault** found inspiration in Irish history and legend for plays such as *The Colleen Bawn* (1860), *The Shaughran* (1875) and *Robert Emmet* (1884). His work was renowned for its humour and enjoyed considerable popular success in Ireland, Britain and the US during his life, but subsequent Irish writers and commentators would accuse him of perpetuating the figure of the drunken and pugnacious "stage Irishman", a popular stereotype that had gained currency in the early eighteenth century in the work of Irish playwright George Farquhar.

Better known to her readers by her pseudonym **Speranza**, Jane Francesca Wilde was an Anglo-Irish author and literary hostess who contributed nationalist poems and anti-British writings to *The Nation*. While her work was of limited artistic value, her son **Oscar Wilde** would become one of the most famous (and eventually infamous) dramatists of the British stage in the late nineteenth century. Oscar did not share his mother's engagement with Irish politics and left the country for England shortly after graduating from Trinity College, where he was an outstanding student of classics, in 1874. He was awarded a scholarship to Magdalen College, Oxford, where he joined the Aesthetic Movement, a society dedicated to making an art out of life. Although Wilde published prose – his novel *The Picture of Dorian Gray* provoked a storm of protests in Victorian society because of its implied homoerotic theme – and poetry, his dazzling plays, including *Lady Windermere's Fan* and *The Importance of Being Earnest*, enjoyed the most success during his lifetime and continue to be performed today. Wilde managed to satirize the pretensions of the English upper and middle classes with humour and insight in a way that only someone coming from outside this society could. He was respected on both sides of the Atlantic for his work and enthralling lectures, and admired in polite society for his ability as a raconteur – as he said himself, to W.B. Yeats, "we Irish have done nothing, but we are the greatest talkers since the Greeks". However, a homosexual relationship with Lord Alfred Douglas, son of the Marquis of Queensbury, would eventually lead to his demise following a conviction and imprisonment for gross indecency. He was sentenced to two years' hard labour, an experience, given chilling insight by one of his finest works *The Ballad of Reading Gaol*, that would break him both physically and psychologically. Wilde died in Paris on November 30, 1900, a broken man who could never ignite his fires of creativity after prison. He left not just great literature but also some of the most memorable aphorisms in the English language, some of which too sadly described his own fate: "The secret of life is to appreciate the pleasure of being terribly, terribly deceived."

The other major playwright to emerge in England in the late nineteenth century was also Irish, the Dublin-born, life-long socialist, **George Bernard Shaw** (see page 71), whose career and influence extended well into the twentieth century. Shaw's work for the theatre was ground-breaking in bringing his own economic, moral and political concerns to the fore, but like Wilde he was also a legendary wit, combining acerbic humour with potent insights into human nature: "Gambling promises the poor what property performs for the rich – something for nothing." Nothing short of prolific, Shaw wrote over sixty plays, including *Arms and the Man*, *John Bull's Other Island* and *Pygmalion*, as well as five less successful novels and an impressive array of literary criticism and political commentary, before his death at the age of 94 in November 1950.

The emergence of the Irish novel

A relatively new form that was to play an increasingly central part in cultural life in the nineteenth century, the novel in Ireland generally traces its beginnings to *Castle Rackrent* (1800), written by **Maria Edgeworth**. Although from an Anglo-Irish Ascendancy family, who gave their name to Edgeworthstown in County Longford, Edgeworth reveals the inequitable and sometimes abusive treatment estate tenants endured at the hands of their landlords. *Castle Rackrent* began one of the most popular genres in Irish literature, the "Big House" novel, concerning the experiences of the landholding class on an Anglo-Irish estate.

Though dominated by writers from the Ascendancy class in Ireland, the nineteenth century was also important for the emergence of female writers such as Edgeworth. Others include **Lady Morgan** (Sidney Owenson), whose *The Wild Irish Girl* (1806) is regarded as an important early feminist text, and the co-authors Edith Somerville and her cousin Violet Martin, known for works such as *The Irish R.M* written under their pseudonyms **Somerville and Ross**.

Other important writers of fiction to emerge in the nineteenth century include **William Carleton**, whose *Traits and Stories of the Irish Peasantry* would be a very influential text for writers such as Yeats; the brothers **John and Michael Banim**, whose major work is the 24 volumes of *The Tales of the O'Hara Family*; and Limerick-born novelist **Gerald Griffin**, whose *The Collegians* was based on events surrounding a trial in which Daniel O'Connell acted as attorney for the defence. The most popular novel in Ireland of the nineteenth century, however, was *Knocknagown; or The Homes of Tipperary* (1879), a convoluted and sentimental account of Tipperary rural life and critique of landlordism, written by the patriot and Young Irelander, **Charles Kickham**.

The Gothic genre was given much of its shape by Irish writers in this period, including **Charles Robert Maturin**, particularly in his dark tale of a man who sells his soul to the devil, *Melmoth the Wanderer* (1820); and **Joseph Sheridan Le Fanu**, the leading ghost story writer of the nineteenth century, best known for his novel *Uncle Silas* (1864) and collection of short stories *In a Glass Darkly* (1872). But they pale in comparison to **Bram Stoker**, whose *Dracula* (1897) is still one of the most popular and adapted works of fiction today. Born in Dublin and educated at Trinity College, Stoker spent most of his life in London as manager to the famous Shakespearean actor, Henry Irving.

The Literary Revival

While Oscar Wilde and George Bernard Shaw were dominating the stage in Britain at the end of the nineteenth century, Irish cultural nationalism was on the rise back home. This period is collectively referred to as the **Irish Literary Revival**, though there were at least two revivals apparent: the Anglo-Irish, concerned with the promotion of Hiberno-English, the English language as sculpted by the particularities of Irish accent and the structures of Gaelic; and the Gaelic Revival, focused on the Irish language, which by now had been devastated by famine, emigration, poverty, lack of support and, indeed, outright discouragement in education. During the Literary Revival, literature in both languages would become a central focus for the revitalization of Irish culture, though attempts were also made through organizations such as Conradh na Gaeilge (the Gaelic League), founded in 1893, to preserve and encourage indigenous musical practices. The League's first president, **Douglas Hyde**, who later became Ireland's first president, would do much to popularize the Gaelic poetic tradition through his translations in *Abhráin Grádh Chúige Connacht* (The Love Songs of Connacht; 1893) and *Abhráin Diadha Chúige Connacht* (The Religious Songs of Connacht; 1905). These collections were an important inspiration for both Irish- and English-language writers, contributing to the idealization of the rural peasantry of the west, particularly in Yeats's work, as the well-spring from which, it was thought, a new, invigorated Irish literature and identity would emerge.

W.B. Yeats

Though **William Butler Yeats** was born in Dublin in 1865 into an aristocratic Protestant family, it was Sligo in the west of Ireland, where he spent a considerable part of his formative years, that would fire his creative imagination. The most important writer of the Revival period, Yeats was in many ways the father of modern Irish literature. One of his major roles was in bringing material in Irish – including elements from the *Táin* and *Fiannaíocht* tales – into mainstream English-language literature through collections such as *The Wanderings of Oisin* (1889). But, more importantly, as a dramatist, essayist and, above all, poet, Yeats brought Irish culture onto a world stage, winning the Nobel Prize for Literature in 1923 and producing some of the finest poetry in any language of that era. While influenced by and commenting on the turbulent years in Ireland of the early twentieth century, his work resonated internationally in a time of calamity and change during and after World War I, with the lines of *The Second Coming*, published in 1921 as the Irish war of independence was coming to an end, still among the most quoted in modern literature:

Things fall apart; the centre cannot hold;
Mere anarchy is loosed upon the world,
The blood-dimmed tide is loosed, and everywhere
The ceremony of innocence is drowned;
The best lack all conviction, while the worst
Are full of passionate intensity.

From his Late Romantic beginnings, Yeats's work developed through the trauma of lost love – Maude Gonne, a recurring presence throughout his work – and the disappointment of the Ireland he saw emerging, more mercantile than artistic, to produce a harder, more realist and direct poetry. Among the best examples of this work are *September 1913*, *Easter 1916* – his elegy for the executed leaders of the Republican Rising of that year – and *The Fisherman*. But it was in Yeats's last decade that the challenges of ageing and declining health inspired some of the finest moments in modern poetry, including *Among School Children* and *Sailing to Byzantium*. Yeats died in January 1939 in France, with his body returning to Ireland after the war in 1948 to be reburied in Drumcliffe churchyard in County Sligo.

The Abbey and Synge

One of the major ambitions of Yeats, Lady Gregory and other leaders of the Literary Revival was the development of an Irish national theatre, realized with the opening of the **Abbey Theatre** in 1904. The Abbey would define a distinct form of Irish theatre, combining a concern with the English language as spoken in Ireland with an attempt to revive belief in the value of Irish culture. In its early years, its greatest playwright was **John Millington Synge**, whose work would provide some of the most memorable characters and narratives of this period, particularly in his masterpiece *The Playboy of the Western World*, first performed in 1907. This dark and yet at times very humorous play, featuring Christy Mahon who achieves fame in a rural Mayo community by claiming that he killed his father, was more than the nationalist audience of its day could accept and resulted in a riot during its first performance. Synge was not afraid to reveal the full gamut of the rural peasant's language, inflected with the Irish language, in both its vulgarity and wit, and an audience that had been conditioned to view the peasant as the very paragon of pure Irishness could not tolerate such a blasphemy. Synge died all too young at the age of 37 in 1909, but helped to inspire later dramatists to create realistic depictions of Irish life.

Joyce

James Joyce was born in Dublin in 1882 into a middle-class Catholic family, which by his early teens had declined into poverty, due largely to his father's carelessness with money. Joyce's challenging experiences, however, provided considerable material for characters and narratives, giving rise to one of the most innovative and imaginative voices in English literature. Although Joyce began writing when the Literary Revival was at its height, he would become one of its strongest critics: as Stephen Dedalus, the protagonist of his semi-autobiographical *A Portrait of the Artist as a Young Man* (1916), remarks to his nationalist school-friend Davin, "You talk to me of nationality, language, religion. I shall try to fly by those nets." For Joyce, each of these elements placed constraints on the writer that could only limit his creativity and expression, something he could not countenance. In the end, he found Ireland too oppressive socially and culturally for his art and headed for the continent, rarely returning to the country of his birth after 1904, and visiting for the last time in 1912. However, while much of his writing was done in Trieste, Paris and Zürich – the city in which he died in 1941 – Ireland, and particularly Dublin, remained the central locale of his work. Indeed, arguably no other writer in twentieth-century literature mapped a city so effectively, epitomized in his finest work, *Ulysses* (1922), which recounts the happenings of a single day in the life of Dublin. Joyce's partner, and eventual wife, during his years on the continent was Nora Barnacle, and the day on which they first met in Dublin, June 16, 1904, has become immortalized as "Bloomsday" (see page 84), the day on which all the events of the novel, concerning the life and ruminations of a Jewish advertising canvasser, Leopold Bloom, take place.

Irish fiction after Joyce

The short story, a form pioneered in Ireland by George Moore in *The Untilled Field* (1903) and developed by Joyce in *Dubliners* (1914), has been an important genre for Irish writers ever since. **Liam O'Flaherty**, born in 1896 on the Irish-speaking Aran Islands off Galway, wrote several acclaimed novels, including *The Informer* (1925), a salty tale of an ex-IRA man who betrays an associate to the police and is hunted down by his former colleagues. However, it is his short stories, in both English and his native Irish, including "Going into Exile", "The Shilling" and his Irish-language collection, *Dúil* (1953), that constitute his best work. Two other notable exponents of the short-story form were **Seán Ó Faoláin** and **Frank O'Connor**. Among Ó Faoláin's finest collections are *Midsummer Night Madness and Other Stories* (1932) and *The Man Who Invented Sin* (1948), while his story "Lovers of the Lake" remains a classic in modern Irish writing. Ó Faoláin was also an editor of the seminal literary journal of the 1940s and 1950s, *The Bell*, and an outspoken critic of the anti-intellectualism that characterized Irish society during his life, under the considerable influence of the Catholic Church. O'Connor is best remembered for the short stories "The First Confession" and "The Luceys", and the collection *Guests of the Nation* (1931).

One of the most experimental writers of the twentieth century was **Flann O'Brien**, born Brian Ó Núalláin in 1911. While O'Brien's finest work is arguably found in the novel *At Swim-Two-Birds* (1939), his wonderfully surreal and funny *The Third Policeman* (1967) enjoyed renewed popularity after its brief appearance in the TV serial *Lost*. O'Brien's first language growing up in Tyrone and later Dublin was Irish, and he also wrote some of the most satirically humorous work in this language, including *An Béal Bocht* (The Poor Mouth; 1941), published under the pseudonym Myles na gCopaleen ("Myles of the little horses"). A parody of the celebrated Blasket Island autobiographies of writers such as Tomás Ó Criomhthain and Peig Sayers, *An Béal Bocht* is an unrestrained attack on the pretensions of the Irish-Ireland movement.

Irish poetry after Yeats

The generation of poets that followed Yeats could not escape the long shadow cast by the Nobel Laureate, but were also concerned to critique the legacies of the Literary Revival, especially its reliance on the idealization of the peasant. While **Austin Clarke** charted the urban experience, Patrick Kavanagh's work provided one of the first authentic catalogues of rural life in twentieth-century poetry. Clarke began writing verse in the 1910s much influenced by early Yeats and concerned with similar goals of bringing Gaelic literature into the English language; for example in his free translations of stories about Fionn Mac Cumhaill in *The Vengeance of Fionn*. As his work matured, he became one of the most consistent and acerbic commentators on Irish life and particularly the suffocating influence of the Church, apparent in one of his finest poems *Martha Blake at 51*, and his short lyric *Penal Law*:

Burn Ovid with the rest. Lovers will find
A hedge-school for themselves and learn by heart
All that the clergy banish from the mind,
When hands are joined and head bows in the dark.

Clarke's legacy has been particularly influential in the work of **Thomas Kinsella**, who continues Clarke's mapping of the urban geography of Dublin. Kinsella has also turned to Gaelic literature and Irish mythology for themes and motifs in his work and, influenced by Jungian psychology, as part of his exploration of his own unconscious, in collections such as *Notes from the Land of the Dead* (1973) and *Fifteen Dead* (1979). Kinsella has also been one of the most important translators of Gaelic literature into English, in works such as *The Táin, An Duanaire 1600–1900: Poems of the Dispossessed* and *The New Oxford Book of Irish Verse*.

The poetry of **Patrick Kavanagh**, who was born in 1904 and raised on a small farm near Inniskeen, County Monaghan, revealed the challenges of rural life in a manner that included an implicit, and sometimes explicit, critique of the Revival's pretensions. Though his work also includes striking lyrics recognizing the power and beauty of the natural world – "the spirit-shocking wonder of a black slanting Ulster hill" – for Kavanagh rural life was often characterized by deprivation, both physical and psychological, as demonstrated in *The Great Hunger* and the pounding rhythms of *Stony Grey Soil*:

O stony grey soil of Monaghan
The laugh from my love you thieved;
You took the gay child of my passion
And gave me your clod-conceived.

Kavanagh, who died in 1967, was arguably the most influential Irish poet after Yeats for poets such as Seamus Heaney and **John Montague**. Raised in Tyrone, Montague inherited Kavanagh's rural concerns, but added to them a political consciousness focused on the Troubles in Northern Ireland, apparent in the volume *The Rough Field* (1972).

As Montague's work, and that of other Northern poets suggests, the setting-up of Northern Ireland in 1920 created distinct historical and political processes within that region. Issues such as culture, language, history and identity became all the more important to writers attempting to articulate distinctive voices in a contested space, coming to a head with the outbreak of the Troubles in the late 1960s. However, these themes were already apparent in the work of the major writers from Northern Ireland in the early and mid-twentieth century: **John Hewitt** and **Louis MacNeice**. In the work of MacNeice, who is often associated with the British poetry movement of the 1930s that included Cecil Day Lewis, Stephen Spender and W. H. Auden, one finds an ambiguous relationship with the country of his birth, though his focus on the west of Ireland in particular, in poems such as *Galway* and *Western Landscape*, anticipates the concern with this part of the island in the work of the next generation of Protestant poets, Michael Longley and Derek Mahon. Meanwhile Hewitt promoted his belief in cultural regionalism, in writing from and for the community in the North from which he emerged:

I write for my own kind
I do not pitch my voice
that every phrase be heard
by those that have no choice:
their quality of mind
must be withdrawn and still,
as moth that answers moth
across a roaring hill.

Irish-language literature in the twentieth century

The Revival was important for the emergence of prose writers in Irish in the twentieth century, most notably Galway-born **Pádraic Ó Conaire**, the author of over four hundred short stories, several plays, numerous essays and the ground-breaking novel *Deoraíocht* (Exile; 1910), still one of the most remarkable Irish works of fiction and regarded as the first modern novel in the Irish language. Set in London at the beginning of the twentieth century, the narrative concerns an Irish emigrant, who after losing an arm and a leg and being seriously disfigured in an accident shortly after arriving from Galway, ends up working in a travelling circus as a sideshow freak.

Autobiography emerged as an important form in Irish-language literature in the early twentieth century. This was most apparent in the work of writers from the now-uninhabited **Blasket Islands** (see page 292) off the coast of Kerry, including Peig Sayers, Muiris Ó Súilleabháin and Tomás Ó Criomhthain, whose *An tOileánach* (The Islandman; 1929) is probably the most accomplished of all these texts.

The dwindling audience for Irish-language literature would be a matter of concern for writers throughout the twentieth century. As **Máirtín Ó Cadhain**, author of the century's most innovative novel in Irish, *Cré na Cille* (Graveyard Clay; 1948, translated as *The Dirty Dust* and republished in 2015), remarked, "[i]t is hard for a man to give of his best in a language which seems likely to die before himself, if he lives a few years more". Despite the decline in the number of native speakers, however, writers such as Eoghan Ó Tuairisc, Breándán Ó hEithir, Pádraig Standún, Mícheál Ó Siadhail and Pádraig Ó Cíobháin have all produced substantial fiction in Irish, while Pádraic Breathnach, Alan Titley and Micheál Ó Conghaile continue to produce critically acclaimed collections of short stories.

In poetry, the major Irish-language writers to emerge in the mid-twentieth century were **Máirtín Ó Direáin**, **Máire Mhac an tSaoi** and **Seán Ó Ríordáin**. For Ó Direáin, from his first self-published collection, *Coinnle Geala* (1942), the speech of the Aran Islands where he grew up was an important source, but he would turn, particularly from the collection *Ó Mórna agus Dánta Eile*, to forms apparent in the work of earlier Gaelic poets. Mhac an tSaoi would bring a thorough knowledge of the Gaelic literary tradition to her work, reflected in her use of both bardic and *amhrán*, or Gaelic song, metres in poems such as *Caoineadh* and *Ceathrúintí Mháire Ní Ógáin*. For collections such as *Brosna* (1964), Ó Ríordáin is regarded as the great modernist of Gaelic poetry, whose conscious rearranging of language would produce an original and, for many, controversial, poetics in Irish.

Other accomplished Irish-language poets over the past forty years have included Michael Hartnett – who was also a major poet in English – Michael Davitt, Gabriel Rosenstock, Liam Ó Muirthile, Nuala Ní Dhomhnaill, Cathal Ó Searcaigh, Gréagóir Ó Dúill, Micheal Ó Siadhail, Áine Ní Ghlinn, Biddy Jenkinson, Colm Breathnach and Louis de Paor.

Irish theatre after Synge

Whereas Synge had focused on rural Ireland, the Abbey's next great dramatist, **Sean O'Casey**, would bring the lives and challenges of the urban poor onto the stage, in some of the theatre's most famous and controversial productions, including *The Shadow of a Gunman* (1923) and *Juno and the Paycock* (1924). As with Synge's *Playboy of the Western World*, O'Casey's next, and arguably finest play, *The Plough and the Stars*, resulted in a riot in the theatre when first staged in 1926. Depicting the events of the 1916 Rising from the perspective of ordinary tenement-dwellers in Dublin, O'Casey cast a critical eye over events considered sacred in Irish nationalist history, regarding the leaders as more concerned with their own egos than with the welfare of the populace. O'Casey, however, felt suffocated as many Irish writers before and after by the oppressive forces of religion and orthodoxy in Ireland. After his subsequent play, the experimental *The*

Silver Tassie, dealing with World War I, was rejected by the Abbey, he left Ireland in 1928, spending the remainder of his life in Devon, England.

Among those who assisted James Joyce in his work during his years in Paris was a young writer who had similarly left Ireland in his early twenties, and would himself go on to achieve worldwide fame as a modernist writer: **Samuel Beckett**. While creating some of the century's most memorable dramatic works – including *Waiting for Godot* (1952), *Endgame* (1958) and *Krapp's Last Tape* (1959) – Beckett developed a minimalist and sometimes severe theatre of the absurd, if one relieved by occasional moments of insight and humour. He brought to his writing the attention to detail characteristic of one writing in an acquired tongue (many of his greatest works were written in French) and was awarded the Nobel Prize for Literature in 1968.

Brendan Behan is today unfortunately remembered almost as much for his effusive personality and drunken interviews as for his important literary work, which included the autobiographical *Borstal Boy* (1958) and the plays *The Quare Fellow* (1954) and *The Hostage* (1958; originally produced in Irish as *An Giall*), a piece that in many respects anticipated the narrative of Neil Jordan's Oscar-winning 1992 film, *The Crying Game*. Behan's weakness for alcohol was a major factor in both his small, if accomplished, output as a writer and his early death at the age of 41.

Contemporary theatre

Among the recurring themes of Irish theatre since the middle of the twentieth century has been the legacy of colonialism, including the Troubles in Northern Ireland. Reflecting the nationalist standpoint, **Brian Friel**'s *Translations* (1980) and *Dancing at Lughnasa* (1992) remain modern classics of the Irish stage. One of the most important studies of Unionist identity is found in the Donegal-born **Frank McGuinness**'s *Observe the Sons of Ulster Marching Towards the Somme* (1985). Similar critical acclaim has attended **Thomas Kilroy** (*The Death and Resurrection of Mr Roche*, 1968; *The O'Neill*, 1969; *Sex and Shakespeare*, 1976) and **Tom Murphy** (*Famine*, 1968; *Conversations on a Homecoming*, 1985; *Bailegangaire*, 2001), while **Hugh Leonard** and **John B. Keane** have written some of the most popular dramatic works since the 1960s, several of which have been adapted for film, including Leonard's *Da* (originally produced in 1977) and Keane's *The Field* (1965).

A significant development over the past forty years has been the emergence of new theatre companies to challenge the dominance of the Abbey, including **Field Day**, founded in 1980 in Derry by Seamus Heaney, Brian Friel and Thomas Kilroy, among others. Galway's **Druid Theatre** has produced some of the most important contemporary works on the Irish stage, including the plays of **Martin McDonagh**, born in London of Irish descent. McDonagh, who won an Academy Award for best short film in 2006 and a BAFTA for 2008's *In Bruges*, has garnered widespread critical acclaim for his provocative and violent work, notably *The Beauty Queen of Leenane* (1996) and *The Cripple of Inishmaan*, a dark comedy which had successful runs in the West End and off-Broadway. A feature of younger playwrights such as **Conor McPherson**, **Enda Walsh** and **Mark O'Rowe** has been a willingness to bring the vernacular and popular culture onto the stage. Each of these writers has moved between theatre and film, with Walsh's *Disco Pigs* (1996) being adapted for the screen by Kirsten Sheridan in 2001, O'Rowe providing the script for one of the most successful independent Irish films in recent years, *Intermission* (2003), and McPherson going on to direct his own films, including *Saltwater* (2000) and *The Actors* (2003) starring Michael Caine. One of the most significant new voices to have emerged from the North is **Gary Mitchell**, whose plays such as *As the Beast Sleeps* (1998), *The Force of Change* (2000) and *State of Failure* (2006) draw strikingly on his own Belfast working-class Loyalist experience. However, following first threats then full-scale intimidation by the paramilitaries (angered by TV adaptations of his work), Mitchell and his family were forced to flee Belfast in 2005 and live in hiding for five years. Other playwrights of note to emerge in recent years include Paul Mercier, Marina Carr, Christian O'Reilly and **Sebastian Barry**, who has also achieved recognition for his fiction, including *A Long Long Way* (2005) and *The Secret Scripture* (2008), which were both shortlisted for the Man Booker Prize. In 2016 his novel, *Days Without End*, set partly during the American Civil War, won the Costa Book Award.

Contemporary Irish poetry

Undoubtedly the leading light of the contemporary poetry scene has been the late Nobel Prize-winner **Seamus Heaney** (see page 505), who built on the legacy of Patrick Kavanagh to produce lyrical verse relating the experiences of rural life. Heaney unearthed empowering metaphors in the Irish, and Danish, landscape, particularly bogs, for the Troubles, finding parallels for contemporary violence in ancient ritualistic killings, in poems such as *Bogland*, *Punishment* and *Tollund Man*:

Out here in Jutland
In the old man-killing parishes
I will feel lost,
Unhappy and at home.

Michael Longley, born in Belfast in 1939, the same year as Heaney, has written some of the most evocative poems of the Troubles, including *Wounds* and *Ceasefire*, which draws on Book XXIV of the *Iliad* and was printed on the front page of the *Irish Times* on the eve of the IRA ceasefire on August 31, 1994. Indeed, Northern Ireland has been a particularly fertile ground for poetry since the 1960s. Other poets of note from the region include **Padraic Fiacc**, **Derek Mahon**, **Paul Muldoon**, the Armagh-born but American-based poet whose collection *Moy Sand and Gravel* won the 2003 Pulitzer Prize for poetry, and the late **Ciaran Carson**, who had been one of the most distinctive and innovative voices to have emerged since the 1970s witnessed in novels such as *The Star Factory*, *Fishing for Amber* and *Shamrock Tea*.

Significant women's voices in Irish poetry have emerged, including **Eavan Boland**, **Eiléan Ní Chuilleanáin**, **Medbh McGuckian**, **Paula Meehan**, **Rita Ann Higgins**, **Mary O'Malley** and **Sinead Morrisey**, each of whom has brought the female experience to the fore, while critiquing previous representations of women in a primarily male-dominated canon. Another important development in recent years has been the growing number of literary festivals – including the Cúirt Festival in Galway, Listowel Writers' Week and the Dublin Writers' Festival – and the increasing engagement of contemporary poets in the performance of their work. Audiences have had many more opportunities to encounter new writers, and poets such as **Paul Durcan** and **Gearóid Mac Lochlainn**,– not to mention the late **Brendan Kennelly** – have established considerable reputations through performing.

Contemporary Irish prose

Much as in poetry, the North of Ireland has produced some of the most popular prose writers. One of the most admired since World War II is **Bernard MacLaverty**, whose most famous novels are *Lamb* and *Cal*, both of which he adapted for the screen, while his most recent books, *Midwinter Break* (2017) and *Blank Pages* (2021) have both been critically acclaimed. **Eoin McNamee**'s *Resurrection Man* (1994) is a disturbing fictionalized account of the notorious Loyalist paramilitaries, the Shankill Butchers, while **Glenn Patterson** has turned to moments before the Troubles to explore other possibilities that might have emerged, in *Burning Your Own* (1988), *The International* (1999), *The Mill for Grinding Old People Young* (2012) and *Where Are We Now?* (2020). One of the North's most innovative voices has been **Robert McLiam Wilson**, notably in his 1996 novel *Eureka Street*, focusing on the relationship between a Catholic and a Protestant before and after the IRA ceasefire in 1994. Meanwhile, Derry-born **Sean O'Reilly** has been compared to Isabel Allende, producing experimental and magical realist prose in works such as the short-story collection *Curfew and Other Stories* (2000) and novel *Watermark* (2005).

The death in 2006 of **John McGahern** robbed contemporary readers of one of the finest Irish writers since Joyce. McGahern had an almost uncanny insight into human nature and rural Irish society – he was born and lived for most of his life in County Leitrim – and rarely has a writer managed to realize as effectively the details of his life experience in literature. From his first novel *The Barracks* (1963) to his final autobiographical work *Memoir* (2005), McGahern's work evinced a deceptively accessible plain technique, which disguised a unique stylistic meticulousness and inner order.

While Wicklow-born **Claire Keegan**'s work – including her acclaimed 2007 short-story collection *Walk the Blue Fields* – has been indebted in style and theme to McGahern, **Colm Tóibín** has also been regarded as the heir to the Leitrim writer in his focus on aspects of the rural Irish experience. Tóibín's childhood town of Enniscorthy provides the setting for some of his most accomplished work, including *The Heather Blazing* (1992), *The Blackwater Lightship* (1999), a novel that explores the theme of homosexuality in contemporary Ireland, and 2014's *Nora Webster*. Fellow Wexford-born novelist **John Banville** has, like many of his contemporaries, moved outside the Irish context, with subjects ranging from eminent European scientists (*Dr Copernicus, Kepler* and *The Newton Letter: An Interlude*) to reflections on a European city (*Prague Pictures: Portrait of a City*). He remains the most critically acclaimed of modern Irish authors, winning the Man Booker Prize in 2005 for his novel, *The Sea*.

Colum McCann has also moved outside his Irish roots for inspiration and subject matter, in novels such as *The Dancer* (2003), concerning the Russian ballet legend Rudolf Nureyev, *Zoli* (2007), which focused on the gypsies of Eastern Europe, and *American Mother* (2024), which recalls the kidnapping and murder of a US journalist. A key influence on McCann's work was the novelist and short-story writer **Desmond Hogan**, who along with Neil Jordan founded the influential **Irish Writers' Cooperative** in 1974. Hogan focuses repeatedly on the marginalized, isolated and unconventional, in settings that include rural County Galway where he grew up (*The Ikon Maker*) and 1950s Dublin (*The Leaves on Grey*). While **Neil Jordan** is better known today for his Oscar-winning film work, he continues to produce well-crafted and, indeed, powerfully visual literature, including his 2004 gothic tale *Shade*, entirely narrated by a murder victim.

Other members of the Writers' Cooperative include **Ronan Sheehan**, author of *The Tennis Players* and *Foley's Asia*, and **Dermot Bolger**. A poet and dramatist as well as novelist, Bolger has charted Dublin life, especially the Northside, since his first novel *Night Shift* (1985), including reimagining in the context of contemporary working-class Dublin *Caoineadh Airt Uí Laoghaire* (see page 585) as the play *The Lament for Arthur Cleary* (1989). Bolger also founded Raven Arts Press in 1979, one of several Irish publishers, including Dolmen, Gallery, Brandon, Salmon and Arlen House, that have emerged since the 1960s to provide a vital outlet for the work of Irish writers.

Clones-born **Patrick McCabe** has written some of the most provocative and sometimes deeply unsettling fiction of the past twenty years, including *The Butcher Boy* and *Breakfast on Pluto*. Meanwhile, few have managed as successfully to chart the urban experience in contemporary Ireland as **Roddy Doyle**, notably in the Barrytown trilogy (*The Commitments, The Snapper* and *The Van*) and the 1993 Booker Prize-winning *Paddy Clarke Ha Ha Ha*, an absorbing portrayal of a child's experience growing up in Dublin in the 1960s. His 2007 collection of short stories, *The Deportees*, is just one of a growing number of texts focusing on multicultural Ireland.

Edna O'Brien, now well into her 90s, has remained in the vanguard of Irish novelists since her pioneering work charting the female experience in 1960s Ireland, including the Country Girls trilogy: *The Country Girls, Girl with Green Eyes* and *Girls in Their*

Married Bliss. Her 23rd book (and first for ten years) *The Little Red Chairs*, about a war criminal who reinvents himself in an Irish village, was published to acclaim in 2015 when she was 85 and described by critics as "a chilling masterpiece." Meanwhile, the award of the 2007 Man Booker Prize to **Anne Enright** for her fourth novel *The Gathering*, a powerful study of the trauma of suicide for those family members left behind, confirmed her position as one of the leading novelists of her generation. Described by John Banville as "one of the subtlest and most penetrating of the latest generation of Irish writers", **Mary Morrissy** has followed Banville in focusing on non-Irish themes, in particular in *The Pretender* (2000), the story of a Polish factory worker who claims to be the daughter of the last tsar of Russia. **Eilís Ní Dhuibhne**, who writes in both Irish and English, has also attracted increasing attention for her work internationally, including her 1999 novel *The Dancers Dancing*. One of the most innovative voices to emerge from Northern Ireland in the 1990s was **Antonia Logue**, notably in *Shadow Box*, while **Anne Haverty's** *The Free and Easy* (2006) marked a movement among contemporary novelists to finally explore twenty-first-century Ireland in their work.

In similar vein, Cork-born poet, short-story writer and novelist **William Wall** wrote in 2005 a pointed critique of the Celtic Tiger, *This is the Country*, featuring a man trying to leave a life of drug abuse behind in an increasingly corrupt and uncaring Ireland. **Mike McCormack** also cast a critical eye on the new Ireland, though in a futuristic context, in *Notes from a Coma* (2005), an account of a penal experiment in which five volunteers, including the former Romanian orphan J.J. O'Malley, are kept in a coma for three months aboard a prison ship in Killary Harbour. His novel *Solar Bones* was shortlisted for the Man Booker Prize in 2017. The late **Seamus Deane** emerged as one of the most accomplished contemporary writers with the 1996 publication of his semi-autobiographical *Reading in the Dark*. While Deane focused on his formative experiences in the North, one of the most popular recent works of autobiography was **Frank McCourt's** Pulitzer Prize-winning *Angela's Ashes* (1996), an evocative, and at times deeply moving, account of growing up in poverty in 1930s Limerick which in 2017 was turned into a smash hit musical. While **Joseph O'Connor** (brother of the late Sinead O'Connor) began his career as a journalist and writer of popular nonfiction – including the satirical and insightful *The Secret World of the Irish Male* (1994) – he has turned in recent years to fiction, often informed by a meticulous study of history. His 2002 bestselling novel *Star of the Sea* explored the experiences of travellers on a famine ship sailing to the United States in 1847.

The remarkable boom in Irish writing since 2012 has led to critics referring to a new **Irish Literary Renaissance**. The leaders of this youthful charge include Donal Ryan (*The Spinning Heart*, 2012, and *All We Shall Know*, 2016), Eimear McBride, author of the prize-winning *A Girl is a Half-formed Thing* (2013), and Kevin Barry whose novel *City of Bohane* won the 2013 International IMPAC Dublin Literary Award; Barry's other titles include *There are Little Kingdoms* (2007) and *Beatlebone* (2015), which won the Goldsmiths Prize. In her writing, Lisa McInerney, famous for her Arse End of Ireland blog, combines the tradition of Irish crime writing with a foul-mouthed wit. Her novel, *The Glorious Heresies*, featured a cast of low-life Cork city types for which she won the Baileys women's prize for fiction in 2016. Her sequel, *The Blood Miracles*, is a story of drugs and descent in the Cork criminal underworld.

Seán Crosson, with additional contributions by Paul Clements

Books

Most of the books listed below should be available around the English-speaking world, though you may need to visit one of Ireland's many good bookshops to track down one or two.

CLASSIC FICTION

★ **J.P. Donleavy** *The Ginger Man*. Riotous and roguish, this is a semi-autobiographical tale of a Trinity College student, full of energy and humour, which unsurprisingly fell foul of the Irish censor in the 1950s. Reprinted in 2015 for its sixtieth anniversary.

★ **Myles na gCopaleen** *The Best of Myles*. Funny, quirky collection of *Irish Times* columns, under Flann O'Brien's other pseudonym.

Oliver Goldsmith *The Vicar of Wakefield*. Goldsmith used his experiences as the son of a clergyman to write his most successful novel, a masterpiece of gentle irony.

★ **James Joyce** *Portrait of the Artist as a Young Man*; *Ulysses*. A largely autobiographical tale of a claustrophobic religious education and social oppression, *Portrait* is Joyce's most accessible novel, while *Ulysses* is one of the greatest modernist works, a stylistically brilliant parody of Homer's *Odyssey* that roams over Dublin in a single day.

Brian Moore *The Lonely Passion of Judith Hearne*. Set in Moore's native Belfast, a moving tale of a lonely Catholic woman's descent into alcoholism and mental breakdown.

★ **Flann O'Brien** *At Swim-Two-Birds*. Hilariously subversive reworking of *Buile Shuibhne*, the medieval saga of the mad King Sweeney, in which the characters try to take control of the story from their "author". *The Third Policeman* is a darkly absurdist vision of Purgatory. See also Myles na gCopaleen.

★ **Laurence Sterne** *The Life and Opinions of Tristram Shandy, Gentleman*. An eighteenth-century comic masterpiece, described as "the greatest shaggy-dog story in the English language".

Bram Stoker *Dracula*. Stoker penned his most famous novel as a psychological thriller, though it's taken on a life of its own since then.

★ **Jonathan Swift** *Gulliver's Travels*; *The Tale of a Tub and Other Stories*. Glorious satires by the Dean of St Patrick's Cathedral, Dublin (see page 79).

★ **Oscar Wilde** *The Picture of Dorian Gray*. Wilde developed similar Gothic themes to his acquaintance Bram Stoker's in this novel, an allusive exploration of "the enemy within".

MODERN FICTION

★ **John Banville** *The Sea*. One of Ireland's most innovative stylists, the former literary editor of the *Irish Times* won the 2005 Booker Prize for this tale of a widower returning to the seaside village where he spent a formative childhood summer. His recent, prolific output includes *Snow* (2021), and *The Lock-Up* (2023), two superlative crime thrillers. Look out also for his superior crime fiction, written under the pen name Benjamin Black.

Kevin Barry *City of Bohane*. High-energy, muscular gangland thriller, set somewhere between Cork and Limerick in the not-too-distant future.

Sebastian Barry *The Secret Scripture*. Perhaps Barry's finest work, this engrossing tale of a woman's mental breakdown and subsequent committal is firmly set within the last century's social and political changes. Beautifully written and observed, it packs a powerful finale.

Dermot Bolger *The Valparaiso Voyage*. A tale of a violent homecoming, dealing with themes of political corruption and alienation in contemporary Ireland. *The Family on Paradise Pier* is a vivid account of an eccentric Protestant Big House family as their world collapses after 1915.

Anna Burns *Milkman*. As Northern Ireland's first Booker Prize winner (in 2018), this novel is as important as they come. Set in an unnamed town during the Troubles, and seen from the perspective of an 18-year old girl in a relationship with an older man (a paramilitary), *Milkman* is both original and funny, albeit not an entirely easy read.

★ **Ciaran Carson** *Fishing for Amber*. A "long story" by one of Ireland's most original writers, who died in 2019, that pulls together Irish fairy tales, Ovid's *Metamorphoses* and the history of the Dutch Golden Age into the form of a magic alphabet. *Shamrock Tea* is a wildly imaginative fantasy based on a herbal remedy that can cleanse the windows of perception infiltrating a Belfast reservoir.

Emma Donoghue *The Wonder*. Dublin-born Emma Donoghue shot to international fame with her 2010 novel *Room*, shortlisted for the Man Booker and Orange prize, about a 5-year-old boy and his mother, held in captivity. Her most recent novel, *The Wonder*, tells a story of a "fasting girl" in an Irish midlands village in the 1850s.

Roddy Doyle *Barrytown Trilogy* (*The Commitments*, *The Snapper* and *The Van*). The former Dublin teacher made his name with these humorous tales of the ups and downs of working-class Dublin life, and later won the 1993 Booker Prize for *Paddy Clarke Ha Ha Ha*, which shifted the focus, still laced with comedy, to family breakdown. In 2014, he ghost-wrote a memoir of footballer and manager Roy Keane, *The Second Half*. Coming closer to the present, *Love* (2020) has two old friends (re)bonding – sometimes awkwardly – over several pints or more in the familiar setting of a Dublin locale.

Anne Enright *The Pleasure of Eliza Lynch*. Historical novel, based on the true story of the nineteenth-century Irish courtesan, who became the richest woman in the world, and her adventures in Paraguay. In 2007, Enright's *The Gathering*, a bleak, compelling tale of family dysfunction, won the Man Booker Prize. *The Green Road*, a moving family drama set in the west of Ireland, was published in 2015, while *The Wren, The Wren* (2023) continues in much the same vein, with each chapter told from the point of view of a different family member, at the head of which is the philandering father, Phil.

Karl Geary *Juno Loves Legs*. This compassionate coming of age story tells of the deepening friendship between its two main protagonists – Juno and Legs – as they contend with poverty and social isolation amid the turmoil of 1980s Dublin. A richly rewarding read.

Dermot Healy *Sudden Times*. A rich tale of paranoia, innocence and the tragedy of the working-class Irish in England. Healy has also published some fine poetry collections, including *A Fool's Errand*, which charts the annual migrations of barnacle geese between their breeding grounds in Greenland and their winter quarters in Sligo, where he lived until his death in 2014.

Claire Keegan *Small Things Like These*. In the author's latest, and best, short novel – one that was Booker-shortlisted – a father confronts the truth behind one of Ireland's infamous Magdalene Laundries. Tender, yet powerful, the book was adapted for the big screen in 2024, starring Cillian Murphy.

Paul Lynch *Prophet Song*. Winner of the 2023 Booker prize – remarkably yet another winner from Ireland – this is an enthralling, dystopian tale of a counterfactual Ireland in the grip of a totalitarian regime; a novel very much of our time.

Patrick McCabe *The Butcher Boy*. Darkly humorous – and at times disturbing – tale of rural Ireland that was nominated for the Booker Prize.

Colum McCann *Thirteen Ways of Looking*. This lyrical novella and three short stories includes the remarkable story of a mother and son adrift on the west coast of Ireland. McCann has also written *Let the Great World Spin* (2009), which won the National Book Award in the US, and *This Side of Brightness* (1998), regarded as his breakthrough novel. His most recent – and very human – books are *Apeirogon*, based on the true-life friendship of two men whose daughters were killed in the Middle East, and *American Mother*, a searing memoir written in conjunction with Diane Foley, mother of murdered US journalist James Foley.

John McGahern *The Leavetaking*. Semi-autobiographical tale, in which a teacher at a Clontarf national school

reviews his life on the day he expects to be sacked for marrying an American divorcee. One of McGahern's finest works is *Amongst Women*, which details the final years and recollections of a disillusioned former IRA soldier, who dominates the women of his family on a small farm in the west of Ireland. *That They May Face the Rising Sun*, McGahern's last novel, is a dark and elegiac narrative set in rural County Leitrim (published as *By the Lake* in the US).

Bernard MacLaverty *Cal*. The Belfast-born writer's best-known book, which tells of the tragic relationship between a young IRA man and his victim's wife. In 2017, *Midwinter Break*, his first novel for sixteen years, features a married couple who go off to Amsterdam to take stock of their lives, while *Blank Pages* (2021) is a marvellous compendium of twelve short stories.

Eoin McNamee *The Ultras*. Set in 1970s Northern Ireland, this dark, claustrophobic tale centres on the disappearance of a captain in the British Army Special Forces, employing the film noir and postmodern stylistics found in McNamee's earlier works, *Resurrection Man*, about the Shankill Butchers, and *The Blue Tango*, about a real-life murder.

Deirdre Madden *Authenticity*. Evocative and ambitious novel, both a love story and a reflection on being an artist in contemporary society.

★ **Christopher Nolan** *Under the Eye of the Clock*. Powerful, largely autobiographical story of a boy with severe disabilities and joys.

Joseph O'Connor *Star of the Sea*. Rich, tragic historical thriller set on a refugee ship bound for New York in 1847. *Ghost Light* is a work of historical fiction set in the Dublin of the 1950s, while his most recent title, *My Father's House*, is a World War II-based literary thriller of the highest order.

Seán O'Reilly *Love and Sleep*. A bleak, distinctive novel set in Derry, blending hard-edged realism with vivid, dream-like qualities.

Keith Ridgway *The Long Falling*. Ridgway's often harrowing debut novel is both a love story and murder story, set in a Dublin that is dangerous and alienating. He followed it up with *The Parts*, a compelling and stylistically inventive mystery, also set in Dublin.

★ **Colm Tóibín** *Brooklyn* Tóibín's best-known novel is a keenly observed, humane story of 1950s emigration and return, set partly in the author's home town of Enniscorthy – which is also the setting of his exquisitely written follow-up novel, *Nora Webster*. Tóibín has been on cracking form for his two latest novels: *The Magician* (2022) – a thrilling fictionalised biography about the exiled German Nobel prize winner Thomas Mann – and *Long Island* (2024), which, as the title implies, is a sequel to *Brooklyn*.

William Trevor *The Story of Lucy Gault*. Nominated for the Booker Prize, this powerful tale beginning in rural Cork – where Trevor was born – during the troubles of 1921 tells the story of the disasters that ensued for one family. Regarded as one of the greatest writers in contemporary fiction, Trevor died in November 2016 leaving a string of elegiac novels such as *Love and Summer*, *The Children of Dynmouth*, *The Silence in the Garden*, *Reading Turgenev*, and a two-volume *Collected Stories*. He once said that his work involved making Irish provincialism universal.

POETRY

Samuel Beckett *Poems 1930–1989*. The most complete collection of Beckett's poetry, in both English and French (with his own translations), and including translations of major twentieth-century French poets such as Rimbaud and Eluard.

Eavan Boland *Collected Poems*. Ireland's leading female poet, also a central voice in American poetic circles, explores the boundaries of women's experiences.

★ **Paul Durcan** *Greetings to Our Friends in Brazil*. A good starting point for this accessible Dublin-born poet. Many of the poems centre on a priest who, far from being repressive and hypocritical as in his earlier works, is honourable and truly spiritual.

Michael Hartnett *Collected Poems*. A richly lyrical and rhythmical collection covering Hartnett's forty-year career.

★ **Seamus Heaney** *Opened Ground: Poems 1966–96* is a huge selection of Heaney's work (see page 505), while *New Selected Poems 1988-2013* features his later work up to the time of his death. *Finders Keepers* is an anthology of his energetic prose, consisting of essays and lectures written between 1971and 2001.

★ **Patrick Kavanagh** *Collected Poems*. Ireland's best-loved poet is perhaps most famous for *The Great Hunger*, in which he attacked sexual repression in 1940s Ireland.

Thomas Kinsella *Collected Poems: 1956–2001*. The full variety of Kinsella's work is on display here, employing modernist and traditional elements, on subjects ranging from love to political satire, social commentary and metaphysical speculation.

Michael Longley *Gorse Fires*; *The Ghost Orchid*; *The Weather in Japan*. Three fine collections, which show Longley as a highly skilled poet with a strong moral voice.

Nuala Ní Dhomhnaill *The Astrakhan Cloak*; *The Water Horse*. Good introductions to her work, in Irish and English, with translations in the former by Paul Muldoon, in the latter by Medbh McGuckian and Eileán Ní Chuilleanáin.

Derek Mahon *New Collected Poems*. A comprehensive fifty-year retrospective of this prodigious poet's far-ranging oeuvre that includes the much-loved "Disused Shed in Co. Wexford."

John Montague *Collected Poems*; *The Rough Field*. The first holder of the Ireland Chair of Poetry in 1998, Montague was much-garlanded, highly influential, and author of numerous slim volumes. Although he died in December 2016, his work continues to resonate as a master of *dinnseanchas* or "place wisdom".

★ **William Butler Yeats** *Collected Poems*. Love, anger, meditation and disillusionment from W.B., one of the greatest figures of twentieth-century literature.

GAELIC LITERATURE AND FOLKLORE

Ciaran Carson *The Midnight Court*. Vibrant rendering of Brian Merrimar's bawdy, eighteenth-century Gaelic poem, *Cúirt an Mheán Oíche*.

Seamus Heaney *Sweeney Astray*. The late Nobel laureate's version of *Buile Shuibhne*, the twelfth- or thirteenth-century tale of Sweeney's mad wanderings and healing.

Thomas Kinsella *The Táin*. The best translation of the *Táin Bó Cúailnge* (The Cattle Raid of Cooley), the heroic centrepiece of the Ulster Cycle.

Tomás Ó Criomhthain (aka Thomas O'Crohan) *An tOileánach* (The Islandman). Vivid insights into the cruelties of life on the Blasket Islands.

★ **Maurice O'Sullivan** *Twenty Years A-Growing*. The story of O'Sullivan's youth and the traditional way of life on the Blasket Islands in the early twentieth century, in a style derived from folk tales.

HISTORY AND POLITICS

Jonathan Bardon *A History of Ulster*. A comprehensive account from early settlements to the Troubles.

Michael Barry *Courage Boys: We are Winning, Illustrated History of the 1916 Rising*. The 100th anniversary of the Easter Rising in 2016 prompted a surge of new books and this one, moving from the panoramic to the particular, is brought alive with over five hundred stunning images telling the story in a clear but nuanced manner.

Angela Bourke *The Burning of Bridget Cleary*. Impeccably researched account of nefarious goings-on in Tipperary in the 1890s, describing the sensational case of a young woman supposedly taken by the fairies, tortured and murdered, and the subsequent trial of her husband, father, aunt and four cousins.

John Bowman (ed.) *Ireland: The Autobiography*. Engaging anthology of a hundred years' worth of storytelling, essays and journalism ranging from Patrick Pearse's letter to his mother to Fintan O'Toole's account of the Irish referendum in 2015 which legalized same-sex marriage.

Turtle Bunbury *Ireland's Forgotten Past*. If you ever wanted to know the answer to questions like: Why did the Romans never try to conquer Ireland, then this fabulous, and irreverent, book, will fill you in. There are thirty-six annals here, each and every one a gem.

Garrett Carr *The Rule of The Land: Walking Ireland's Border*. Variously travelling by foot and by boat, this is a compelling account of the author's jaunt along the border between North and South, in which he reflects upon the people, places and events that have shaped this often troubled landscape – it's an account that's more pertinent than ever following Brexit.

Feargal Cochrane *Northern Ireland: The Fragile Peace*. As well as providing a comprehensive, and lucid, account of the long struggle to achieve peace in the province, the author – a child of the Troubles - considers the ramifications of Brexit and the recent suspensions of the Northern Ireland Assembly.

★ **Tim Pat Coogan** *Ireland in the Twentieth Century*. An engrossing account of political and social developments, both North and South, by the former editor of the *Irish Press*, who has written many readable histories, notably *The IRA*, *1916: The Easter Rising* and biographies of Michael Collins and Éamon de Valera.

Richard English *Irish Freedom: A History of Nationalism in Ireland*. Lucid and fascinating scholarly dissection of Irish nationalism over the last three centuries.

Diarmaid Ferriter *The Transformation of Ireland 1900–2000*. Extensive and insightful account of the making of modern Ireland, combining politics, economics and social history.

Garret FitzGerald *Reflections on the Irish State*. The former Taoiseach offers perceptive insights and challenging theories on the big issues of Irish public life.

★ **R.F. Foster** *Modern Ireland 1600–1972*. The best history of the period, authoritative and comprehensive, though heavy going at times for the lay reader. In contrast, *Luck and the Irish* gambols entertainingly through the period from 1970 to 2000, while *The Irish Story: Telling Tales and Making It Up in Ireland* is a provocative, witty deconstruction of myth-making and clichés in Ireland's telling of its own history.

Tom Garvin *Preventing the Future: Why Was Ireland So Poor for So Long?* Perhaps the most important socio-historical analysis of postwar Ireland, not least in terms of the "lost" decades of the 1950s and 1960s. Garvin offers not only an acute analysis of the rotten core of Irish social policy but a persuasive and often witty account of its impact upon future generations.

★ **Robert Kee** *The Green Flag*. Lucid and incisive account of nationalism from the Elizabethan Plantations to "ourselves alone" after Independence.

Conan Kennedy *Ancient Ireland: The User's Guide*. Extremely useful descriptions of Ireland's various types of megalithic field monuments, plus a fascinating account of the place of magic, ritual and mythology.

★ **Declan Kiberd** *Inventing Ireland*. Witty and thought-provoking re-reading of the literature of the modern nation.

Christine Kinealy *This Great Calamity: The Irish Famine*. Unravels fact from fiction through systematic analysis of primary source material related to the Great Famine.

Susan McKay *Northern Protestants: An Unsettled People*. Utterly grim but absolutely essential account of the North's Protestant community and its disparate views, based on numerous interviews, simultaneously offering hope for the future and showing sheer desperation.

David McKittrick and David McVea *Making Sense of the Troubles*. Clear, dispassionate and authoritative crash-course on the conflict.

Ed Moloney *A Secret History of the IRA*. Authoritative account, with Gerry Adams as its sinisterly intriguing central character, of the struggle within the Republican movement over the last forty years.

George Morrison *The Irish Civil War*. A powerful collection of photographic images of the Civil War, accompanied by commentary by Tim Pat Coogan.

Henry Patterson *Ireland Since 1939: The Persistence of Conflict*. At times iconoclastic, Patterson's account of an Ireland divided not only by boundaries, but by ideologies and class-related interests, breaks new ground and provides utterly stimulating reading.

Patrick Radden Keefe *Say Nothing: A True Story of Murder and Memory in Northern Ireland*. Winner of the 2019 Orwell Prize for political writing, this is a compelling book about the Troubles, at the heart of which is a forensic dissection of the murder of Jean McConville by the IRA in 1972.

★ **Colm Tóibín and Diarmaid Ferriter** *The Irish Famine: A Documentary*. Highly readable analysis of the Great Famine, which takes an incisive look at both the complex issues surrounding the failure of the potato crop, and the inadequacy of previous historical accounts of the crisis.

BIOGRAPHY AND MEMOIRS

Christy Brown *My Left Foot*. Born with cerebral palsy, Brown painstakingly typed out this unsentimental autobiography, published in 1954 when he was 22, focusing on his upbringing in a huge Dublin family, dominated by the remarkable character and endurance of his mother.

Ruth Dudley Edwards *James Connolly*. A short biography of the socialist leader, which gathers pace around the time of his relations with Larkin, the 1913 Lock-Out in Dublin and the 1916 Rising.

★ **Richard Ellmann** *James Joyce*; *Oscar Wilde*. Ellmann's wonderful biography of Joyce is a literary masterpiece in its own right. His work on Wilde was, unfortunately, unfinished when he died, but is still an excellent insight into the work of this often misunderstood writer.

Christopher Fitz-Simon *The Boys*. Frank and conscientious biography of the founders of Dublin's Gate Theatre, Micheál Mac Liammóir and his equally mysterious lifelong lover, Hilton Edwards.

★ **R.F. Foster** *W.B. Yeats: A Life – Volume I, The Apprentice Mage; Volume II, The Arch-poet*. A magisterial work, the first fully authorized biography, incisive, exhaustive and compellingly readable.

Michael Harding *Staring at Lakes*. An absorbing memoir of love and magical thinking by a playwright and author who chronicles his ordinary life in the Irish midlands in a popular weekly column in *The Irish Times*.

James Knowlson *Damned to Fame: The Life of Samuel Beckett*. Excellent biography by one of the world's pre-eminent Beckett experts.

Hugh Leonard *Home before Night; Out after Dark*. Beautifully written evocations by the noted playwright of, respectively, his childhood and his adolescence in south Dublin around the 1940s. At times moving, often hilarious.

Kevin Myers *Watching the Door; A Single Headstrong Heart*. Controversial journalist and author who has pioneered the study of WWI in Ireland. Funny and moving, his memoir *A Single Headstrong Heart* is a prequel to *Watching the Door* about his early career in journalism.

Antoinette Quinn *Patrick Kavanagh: A Biography*. Astute and often gently paced account of the life and poetry of County Monaghan's favourite son.

MUSIC

★ **Helen Brennan** *The Story of Irish Dance*. Not just a fascinating history of the development of traditional dancing in Ireland, but a (literally) step-by-step guide to some of the most popular set-dances.

Victoria Mary Clarke and Shane MacGowan *A Drink with Shane MacGowan*. MacGowan's wife takes the late singer and songwriter through his personal history and several large martinis on the way.

Gerard Hanberry *On Raglan Road*. The story of the women who inspired Irish love songs such as "Galway Girl", "Nancy Spain", and "Down by the Salley Gardens".

Colin Harper and Trevor Hodgett *Irish Folk, Trad & Blues: A Secret History*. Fascinating accounts of key figures in Ireland's recent musical history, from Van the Man to Altan.

Colin Irwin *In Search of the Craic*. Wittily written account of a quest to hear some of the best of Ireland's traditional music.

★ **Christy Moore** *One Voice*. Not just a scintillating account of Moore's own life through song, but a hard-hitting analysis of Ireland over the last thirty years.

Pádraigín Ní Uallacháin *A Hidden Ulster*. Mammoth and utterly engrossing account of the Irish song tradition, centred on the area known as Oriel (containing parts of Armagh, Monaghan and Louth).

Tommy Sands *The Songman*. Illuminating, droll and incisive autobiographical account by the singer and broadcaster of growing up in 1950s rural Down, being enticed by and rejecting the idea of the priesthood, and moving on to a musical career whose increasingly sharp-edged political tone saw him play a pivotal role in the peace process.

★ **Fintan Vallely** (ed) *The Companion to Irish Traditional Music*. Provides constant delight in its copious accounts of the music's form, style and qualities, and brief biographies of many key participants; required reading.

Fintan Vallely and Charlie Piggott *Blooming Meadows: The World of Irish Traditional Musicians*. The fascinating biographical snapshots of a broad range of singers and musicians are enhanced by evocative photographs of their subjects.

Geoff Wallis and Sue Wilson *The Rough Guide to Irish Music*. A quintessential account of the roots and current state of traditional music in Ireland, containing a comprehensive directory of more than four hundred singers, musicians and groups, and details of the best places to see them in action.

MISCELLANEOUS

★ **Aalen, Stout and Whelan** (eds) *Atlas of the Irish Rural Landscape*. Fascinating, lucid exploration of the geography of the Irish landscape, illustrated with photographs and maps. *Newgrange and the Bend of the Boyne*, by Geraldine Stout, is an offshoot of the atlas.

Paul Clements *Wandering Ireland's Wild Atlantic Way*. Detours and diversions on a lively meander along the 2500km route of the Wild Atlantic Way. The author has also written *The Height of Nonsense*, a humorous account of his journey to the highest point of every county in Ireland, described by the *Irish Independent* as "gloriously daft yet irresistible".

Gordon D'Arcy *The Breathing Burren*. A personal tour and fascinating exploration of the remarkable area of limestone pavement in the Burren, Co. Clare. The author has also written a book on the Burren walls.

Deirdre and Laurence Flanagan *Irish Place Names*. Exhaustive guide to the names of over three thousand towns, villages and physical features and their derivations.

Alannah Hopkin *Eating Scenery*. The serenely beautiful "Independent Republic of West Cork" as it is sometimes known, is brought alive through interviews and reflection, quirky detail and laugh-out-loud snapshots. The author's collection of stories, *The Dogs of Inishere* is also worth looking out for.

★ **Pete McCarthy** *McCarthy's Bar*. Runaway bestseller by the late, former travel-show presenter and stand-up comedian. An extended crawl around the *McCarthy's* bars of Ireland provides occasion for insight and humour.

★ **Tim Robinson** *Connemara: Listening to the Wind*. Fascinating story of the Roundstone area around the author's home, ranging over everything from geology to folklore, written in a deceptively plain, easy style. *Connemara: The Last Pool of Darkness* gives similar treatment to the coast from Killary Harbour to Ballyconneely.

GUIDES

★ **Mairead Carew** *Tara: The Guidebook*. Quick-reference guide to one of Ireland's mythical sites, the Hill of Tara in Co. Meath, presented succinctly and with clarity.

Zoe Devlin The Wildflowers of Ireland. Lavishly illustrated with more than five hundred wildflowers and the author's photographs, this is an essential vade mecum. For a more specific book on flora, Charles Nelson's The Wild Plants of the Burren and the Aran Islands is recommended.

Paddy Dillon The Mournes Walks and The Complete Ulster Way Walks. A series of detailed, easy-to-follow guides covering mostly circular day-walks, with information about the wildlife and landscape.

Felicity Hayes-McCoy Dingle and its Hinterland. Dingle is a mecca for tourists but the western part of the peninsula is not so well known. This book offers both practical information and cultural insights into the area.

Neil Jackman Ireland's Ancient East. Historic treasures and the built heritage are showcased as part of the newly established Ancient East driving route from Co. Cork to Co. Louth.

★ **Joss Lynam** (ed) *Best Irish Walks*. Authoritative guide to over 75 hill walks all around Ireland. Lynam's *Easy Walks near Dublin* and the more recent *Leisure Walks near Dublin* each cover around forty mostly circular walks of between half an hour and three hours on the city's doorstep, mainly the Wicklow Mountains.

Dan MacCarthy *Cycling Munster*. Explore on two wheels the byways of the counties of Munster, including the thigh-burning Ring of Kerry, with this first-class guide complete with maps and gradient graphs. It is published by the Collins Press, which has produced numerous other excellent cycling and walking guides to different parts of Ireland.

Frank McNally *111 Places in Dublin That You Shouldn't Miss*. Filled with the strange and the incongruous, McNally – who writes the Irishman's Diary in *The Irish Times* – knows Dublin intimately and includes less obvious places in his ramblings.

The Irish language

You're most likely to hear the distinctive sounds of spoken Irish if you travel in the Gaeltacht regions, designated areas of Irish-speakers (*Gaeilgeoirí*), the largest of which are in Kerry, Galway and Donegal. Here in summer, you'll come on crowds of teenagers from all over Ireland who are passing through the annual ritual of Irish college, learning the language by immersion. If you're interested in having a go yourself, courses are run by the well-respected Gael Linn, 35 Dame St, Dublin (http://gael-linn.ie), whether in Dublin usually over six weeks or in summer staying for a week in the Donegal Gaeltacht; by the excellent Oideas Gael in Glencolmcille, Donegal; and in Connemara, Galway (see page 356). Among language-learning materials, Gael Linn produces *Gaeilge agus Fáilte*, an easy-to-follow combination of book and two CDs aimed at adult beginners.

Some history

Irish is one of the Celtic languages, along with Welsh and Breton, and belongs in particular to the **Gaelic** branch, sometimes known as **Goidelic**, which also includes Scottish Gaelic. Celtic language and culture had become dominant in Ireland by around 300 BC, but **Primitive Irish**, the earliest form known to us, is found only in **ogham** inscriptions on stone monuments, dating from the fifth to seventh centuries AD. This highly unusual script consists of tally-like notches cut along the edge of standing stones, rather than conventional letters. In the next linguistic phase, **Old Irish** (seventh to ninth centuries), the language changed quickly, as Christian monks, now writing in Latin script, adopted a more colloquial form of Irish; from this period comes a fine body of lyric poetry and the earliest version of the *Táin Bó Cúailnge* ("The Cattle Raid of Cooley"), the central saga of the Ulster Cycle. **Middle Irish** (eleventh to thirteenth centuries) was a phase of linguistic confusion and new grammatical forms, with the language going into a decline after the twelfth-century Anglo-Norman conquest. By the fourteenth century it had recovered, entering the period known as **Early Modern** or **Classical Modern Irish**. The use of the language was now governed by the **filí**, a class of professional scholars and poets, among whom the most respected might have the status of a bishop or minor king. Meanwhile, the Anglo-Norman settlers had mostly integrated with the native population, adopting Irish language and customs.

In the seventeenth and eighteenth centuries, however, with the Flight of the Earls, Cromwell's Act of Settlement and the penal laws, the structures of traditional society were comprehensively destroyed. At the beginning of the nineteenth century, just under half the population was purely Irish-speaking, mostly in poor rural areas. These were the very areas, however, that were decimated by the Great Famine of the 1840s and the mass emigration that followed. As early as 1851, the proportion of Irish speakers had declined to a quarter of the population, and by the end of the century it was down to one percent.

Despite the decline of Irish in the nineteenth century, several organizations dedicated to reviving its use sprang up, most notably the **Gaelic League** (Conradh na Gaeilge), founded in 1893 by Douglas Hyde and others. The League ensured that, after Independence in 1921, Irish was constitutionally recognized as the first official language, and was compulsory in the school system and for entry to the Civil Service. Today, around fifteen percent of the Republic's population have a good competence in Irish, 92,000 of whom live in the **Gaeltacht** areas, in counties Donegal, Mayo, Galway, Kerry, Cork, Waterford and Meath. A recent decline in the actual use of Irish in the *Gaeltachtaí* can be detected, however: a 1980s survey of schoolchildren there, for example, showed that nearly half of them spoke only English at home, while just twenty percent of them spoke only Irish.

Outside of the *Gaeltachtaí*, however, there's been a remarkable recent growth throughout the island, both North and South, in the number of **Gaelscoileanna**, schools in which every subject is taught in Irish and which are known for their high general standards of education. From just sixteen such schools in 1974, the figure has now risen to over two hundred. In **the North**, where the British government is committed to supporting Irish-medium education, the use of Irish has naturally been more politicized. However, about ten percent of the North's population can now speak Irish, and since the Good Friday Agreement of 1998 there's been an all-Ireland body to promote the language, Foras na Gaeilge (http://gaeilge.ie).

Set up in 1972, the **Irish-language radio station**, Raidió na Gaeltachta, known especially for its support for traditional music, has been broadcasting all over the country from its base in Connemara; it's now 24-hour, with studios in Donegal, Kerry, Mayo and Dublin. In 1996, it was joined in Connemara by a **national television station**, TG4 (Teilifís na Gaeilge Cathair), which, through its often progressive and upbeat programming, has tried hard to reinvigorate the language.

But despite the renewed interest, and the fact that the language as a communicative subject appears to be thrivingthe harsh reality is that the number of everyday Irish speakers is **declining**, albeit marginally, Although the number of Irish speakers in the country has grown since the census in 2016, in most cases they were speaking it less frequently; moreover, the proportion of Irish speakers in Gaeltacht areas has decreased from 69% in 2011 to 66% in 2022. Many feel the political will is simply not strong enough to promote the language, as well as other aspects of the culture such as traditional singing and dancing.

Basic pronunciation of Irish

Irish **pronunciation** is notoriously difficult for outsiders, bearing little resemblance to English pronunciation. A few basic, simplified pointers are given below. To complicate things further, Ulster, Connacht and Munster have distinct dialects, with different pronunciations and, to a lesser extent, grammars.

Vowels

Note the acute accent, a *fada*, which is used to lengthen vowels.

a as in "bat", or like the "o" in "slot"	**í** as in "machine"
á as in "paw"	**o** as in "ton"
e as in "bet"	**ó** as in "bone"
é as in "prey"	**u** as in "book"
i as in "bit"	**ú** as in "rule"

Consonants

Irish distinguishes between slender consonants – when beside an "e" or "i" – and broad consonants – when beside an "a", "o" or "u". For many consonants the slender pronunciation is different from the broad one.

bh broad, **mh** broad – "w" or "v"	**dh** broad, **gh** broad – "gh", like a voiced version of "ch" in "Bach"
bh slender, **mh** slender – "v"	
c – always hard, as in "cot"	**dh** slender, **gh** slender – "y" as in yes
ch – like Scottish "loch"	**fh** is silent
d broad – "th" as in "**th**is"	**g** – always hard, as in "**g**ift"
d slender – sharp "d", almost a "j" as in "jelly"	**ph** – as in "**ph**one"
	s broad – "s" as in "**s**ome"

s slender – "sh" as in "**sugar**"

sh, th – "h" as in "**hat**"

t broad – aspirated, with the tongue against the upper teeth, somewhere between the "t" in "toad" and the "th" in "**thin**"

t slender – as the "t" in "**tin**"

A FEW SIMPLE PHRASES

Hello (lit. "God be with you") Dia duit

Hello (in reply, lit. "God and Mary be with you") Dia is Muire duit

Welcome (lit. "a hundred thousand welcomes") Ceád míle fáilte

What is your name? Cad is ainm duit?

My name is… … is ainm dom

How are you? Conas atá tú?

Well Go maith

Please Más é do thoil é

Thank you (very much) Go raibh (míle) maith agat

I don't understand Ní thuigim

Goodbye (to the person staying) Slán leat

Goodbye (to the person leaving) Slán agat

Bye (more informal) Slán

SIGNS AND PLACE NAMES: SOME COMMON IRISH TERMS

an lár city centre

árd height

áth ford

baile town – often anglicized as "bally"

beag small – "beg"

bóthar road

bun base

caiseal stone ring fort – "cashel"

caisleán castle

carn cairn

carraig rock – "carrick"

cathair fort – "caher"

ceann head, headland – "can" or "ken"

cill church – "kill" or "keel"

cnoc hill – "knock"

doire oak wood – "derry" or "derreen"

dún fort

eaglais church

fir men

geill slí give way

glean valley – "glen"

go mall slow down

gort field

inis island – "inish"

leithreas toilet

leitir hillside – "letter"

lios ring fort – "lis"

loch lake – "lough"

mná women

mór big – "more"

mullach summit – "mullagh"

oileán island – "illaun"

páirc field – "park"

ráth ring fort

rinn point – "reen"

ros headland – "ross"

sliabh mountain – "slieve"

sráid street

teach, tí house, cottage

teampall church

tír country – "tyr"

tobar well

trá beach

Glossary

Ascendancy The Protestant aristocracy, whether descended from Anglo-Normans granted land in Ireland or plutocrat planters subsequently installed in the country from the late sixteenth century onwards. Often prefixed by the term "Anglo-Irish".

banjaxed Anything that is broken or beyond repair, ranging from the Government to a bicycle.

bawn Fortification around a castle enclosure or cattlefold.

big house Mansion built by the Ascendancy.

bodhrán (pronounced "bore-run" or "bough-ron" depending on the region of Ireland). A shallow, hand-held goatskin-frame drum, played either with a wooden beater or the hand.

bohreen (pronounced "bor-een") Resonant Irish term for a laneway.

B Specials Auxiliary Northern Irish police force formed after Partition and disbanded in 1971.

cashel A stone ring fort.

ceilidh/ceili An evening of Irish traditional dancing usually accompanied by a band.

clochán An early Christian beehive-shaped hut constructed of stones fitted tightly together without the use of mortar.

craic/crack General term for a good time, usually accompanying drinking. "What's the crack?" means "What's going on?"

crannóg A Bronze Age artificial island in a lough, constructed to camouflage an otherwise vulnerable dwelling.

Continuity IRA Irish Republican paramilitary group which claims to be the legitimate continuation of the IRA. Opposed to the Northern Ireland peace process.

culchie Pejorative term used by city-dwellers to describe their country cousins. May have originated from the Co. Mayo town Kiltimagh, or "Coillte Mach", with "culchie" emerging from the Irish word "coillte", meaning woods.

cute hoor From "cute" as in sly, and "hoor", as in whore, aimed at those in politics, business or any other profession where deals are cut; normally interpreted as an insulting term but can also be flattering.

Dáil Literally means "meeting", but has come to stand for the lower house of the Republic's parliament.

Diamond A central area in a planned Irish town, sometimes actually diamond-shaped, but often triangular, with streets surrounding an open space where usually some form of memorial is erected.

dolmen Dating from around 2500–2000 BC, a burial chamber set below an often-triangular placement of standing stones, surmounted by an impressively weighty capstone. Also called a portal tomb.

drumlin A small oval hummock resulting from Ice Age glacial retreat, found especially in County Monaghan.

DUP The Democratic Unionist Party. A staunchly traditional right-wing and often controversial Loyalist party, co-founded by Ian Paisley in 1971, opposed to any attempts at loosening Northern Ireland's ties with the United Kingdom. The party shot to prominence in 2017 when they entered into an agreement with the Conservative government led by Theresa May after the party suffered a shock election loss. To retain her position as British Prime Minister, May struck a deal to secure the DUP's support and in exchange the party received £1bn pounds for investment in the infrastructure of Northern Ireland.

Éire The Irish name for the island of Ireland; often used to mean the Republic of Ireland.

esker/eskar A ridge of gravel and sand formed by a retreating glacier.

famine wall/famine road An enterprise of local landowners during the Great Famine of 1845–51 whereby starving tenants would be rewarded for work given them to build a wall or road rather than aid through hunger-relieving largesse.

Fenian A member of the nineteenth-century revolutionary organization that fought for an independent Ireland; often used as an anti-Catholic term of abuse by Northern Irish Loyalists.

Fianna Fáil Irish Republic political party that emerged from the Civil War, opposing the partitioning treaty, to become a major force under its long-time leader Éamon de Valera. Still largely conservative in aspect, it has retained governmental control for most of the last eighty years, despite being embroiled in a farrago of financial and political scandals in recent decades.

First Minister and Deputy First Minister. The Office of First Minister and Deputy First Minister (known as OFMDFM) of the Northern Ireland Assembly based at Stormont.

Fine Gael The Republic's long-term and long-suffering (usually) opposition party, whose origins go back to Michael Collins' support for the Independence Treaty (see page 568). Little distinguishes it from Fianna Fáil, though its social policies seem a little more liberal, and its membership is largely drawn from agricultural areas.

Fleadh Literally meaning a "festival", the term has become associated with the Irish traditional-music organization Comhaltas Ceoltóirí Éireann's music competitions in which musicians and singers compete at county and provincial levels before going on to the annual Fleadh Cheoil na Éireann ("Ireland's music festival"). This also includes the winners of the UK and US *fleadhanna* (the plural of "fleadh").

Gaeltacht Regions of Ireland where the Irish language is the predominant vernacular tongue, mainly in the country's west.

gallivanting Gadding about. A much-used phrase in Ireland although it comes from early nineteenth-century English as a term for flirting with women.

galloglass An armed mercenary in medieval times (from the Irish for "foreign soldier").

Garda Siochána The police force of the Republic of Ireland.

High cross A tall stone cross in which normally the cross itself is surrounded by a circle. The earliest known Irish examples date from the seventh century and are often richly ornamented with biblical scenes.

IRA Irish Republican Army. Longstanding upholders of the Republican drive to restore a united 32-county Ireland. Particularly from the late 1960s onwards, it embarked on an armed struggle to force the British to withdraw from Ireland, with major bombing campaigns in the UK and Northern Ireland. The IRA unreservedly renounced its military initiatives in late 2005.

lash Give it a lash means to attempt something, while to go on the lash is drinking to excess.

lough A commonly used term for lake; also a narrow coastal bay.

Loyalist Hardline Northern Irish Protestant loyal to the British Crown, sometimes linked to paramilitary activity, largely existing only as a criminal group.

LVF Loyalist Volunteer Force. Paramilitary group based around Portadown and founded by Billy Wright.

Martello tower Circular coastal tower built for defence during the Napoleonic Wars.

MLA Member of the (Northern Ireland) Local Assembly.

motte An early medieval fortification, much used by the Normans, consisting of a circular earthwork mound, flattened on top, on which would be sited a primitive form of castle.

Nationalists Those wishing to achieve a united Ireland, usually by peaceful means.

The North Politically neutral euphemism for Northern Ireland.

ogham Ancient twenty-letter alphabet used in both Celtic and Pictish inscriptions on standing stones, comprising parallel carved lines or notches.

Oireachtas The Republic's parliament.

Orange Hall A local building where members of the Orange Order meet.

Orange Order Loyalist Protestant organization founded in 1795. Subdivided into local lodges, it derives its name from William of Orange (see page 536) and annually celebrates his victory over Catholic James

II at the 1690 Battle of the Boyne on July 12 with parades across Northern Ireland. The majority of Unionist politicians and many Presbyterian clergymen belong to the Order.

Palladian A style of architecture derived from the designs of the Italian Andrea Palladio (1508–80), whose work incorporated a rigid adherence to mathematical proportions, first promulgated by the Roman architect Vitruvius. Among the most stunning examples of Palladian architecture in Ireland are Castletown (see page 132), Russborough House (see page 127) and Florence Court (see page 556).

partition The division of Ireland into the 26 counties of the Republic and six of the North created by the 1921 Government of Ireland Act.

passage grave The oldest form of megalithic tomb, dating from around 4000 BC, consisting of a rounded mound or cairn with a stone-lined passage leading from the perimeter to a central chamber.

pishogue A charm, spell, superstitious practice or tall tale.

plámás Flattery or empty praise.

plantation The process of colonization of Ireland by the English Crown by which land was confiscated from the indigenous people and given to English and Scottish Protestant settlers.

poitín (pronounced "pot-cheen") Illicit home-made spirits, once distilled from potatoes in a little pot – hence the name.

portal tomb see "dolmen".

PSNI The Police Service of Northern Ireland (see also "RUC").

rath or ring fort The most common form of ancient monument found in Ireland, dating from between the late Neolithic period and early medieval times. Consists of a circular (sometimes oval or D-shaped) enclosure surrounded by an earthen bank rising from a defensive ditch. A roofed dwelling, of stone or timber, would be constructed within the enclosure.

The Real IRA Breakaway political faction which rejects the Northern Ireland political process and maintains the armed struggle. Calls itself simply "the Irish Republican Army" or "IRA"; the media sometimes calls it the "New IRA" after its 2012 merger with Republican Action Against Drugs.

Republicans Supporters of the ideals incorporated in the 1916 Proclamation of the Republic, the overthrow of British rule in Ireland and the promotion of Irish language and culture.

ring fort see "rath".

round tower Usually part of a monastic settlement, these lofty and slenderly tapering, circular stone towers range in height from around 20–35m and were often capped with a conical roof. The earliest examples of this uniquely Irish construction date from around the ninth century. The building would have had a variety of purposes, serving as a belfry, a lookout post and a place for storage of goods and valuables. The entrance was often set some 3–5m above ground level, allowing the means of access, a ladder, to be withdrawn inside the building in case of a Viking raid, some claim.

RUC Royal Ulster Constabulary. The Northern Ireland police force from 1921 until 2001, when it was replaced by the Police Service of Northern Ireland.

SDLP Social Democratic and Labour Party. A left-of-centre Northern Irish Nationalist party that has lost considerable political clout to Sinn Féin and won no seats in the UK 2017 General Election.

session Normally refers to a traditional Irish music session, the "sesh", or used in relation to party-going and drinking.

shebeen An old term for an unlicensed house selling drink.

Sheila-na-gig A carved stone representation of a squatting woman, often displaying an over-large vulva; believed to avert death and prevent evil, they are similar to the carvings of Yoni found on Hindu temples. Many Irish churches once bore these carvings, particularly above doors or windows, but they were often removed during the Victorian era. Well-preserved examples are visible on White Island, Co. Fermanagh, in Boyle Abbey and on the ruined church at Kilnaboy, Co. Clare.

Sinn Féin ("We, Ourselves"). Republican political party opposed to the 1921 political treaty that played a major role in the subsequent civil war. From the late 1970s onwards, and, allegedly, closely linked to the IRA, it rose to electoral prominence among the North's Catholics and achieved significant success in the Republic. Since 1983 its leader has been Gerry Adams, one of the key figures in the gradual move towards peace in Northern Ireland. It is now the leading Nationalist political party in the North.

The Six Counties Nationalist/Republican euphemism for Northern Ireland.

snug Small area of bar where women used to drink discreetly, now open to all-comers.

soft day Misty rain with hazy cloud to the point of invisibility with drizzle lingering in suspended animation.

souterrain Prehistoric underground passage which offered sanctuary for those fleeing their enemies;

in some mythical locations, seen as an entry to the otherworld.

stone circle A ring of spaced standing stones with a ritualistic purpose.

sweathouse A small stone-constructed, low-roofed building in which a turf fire was lit. Once sufficient heat had been generated, those suffering from aches and pains or a fever would enter and would stay long enough to generate a sufficient sweat before emerging to take a dip in the nearest cold stream. In other words, an early Irish version of the sauna.

Taoiseach Prime minister of the Republic of Ireland.

TD Teachta Dála. Member of the lower house of the Republic's parliament (see "Dáil").

townland An area of land, similar to a parish, but not necessarily a village, which could have ten fields in it or more than a hundred.

thon An Ulster-Scots word meaning "that", mostly heard in the North.

Troubles Euphemism for the vicious cycle of violence in Northern Ireland from the late 1960s to the announcement of the Good Friday Agreement in 1998.

trumpadóir Literal meaning is a "trumpeter", but can also mean an obnoxious loudmouth.

turlough A lake with a limestone base that causes water to drain away during drier months of the year.

Twenty-six counties Somewhat begrudging Republican description of the Republic of Ireland.

UDA (Ulster Defence Association)/**UFF** (Ulster Freedom Fighters) and **UVF** (Ulster Volunteer Force). Northern Irish Loyalist paramilitary organizations, which now seem more concerned about controlling the Northern Ireland drugs trade.

Ulster One of Ireland's four provinces, comprising Northern Irish counties Antrim, Armagh, Derry, Down, Fermanagh and Tyrone, plus Cavan, Donegal and Monaghan in the Republic. Often erroneously used by Unionists and journalists as a synonym for Northern Ireland.

Unionists A term describing those (mainly Protestant) who wish to maintain Northern Ireland's union with the rest of the UK.

UUP Ulster Unionist Party. The dominant party in Northern Ireland from 1921 to 1972, retaining control of its government for the period's entirety. Though initially retaining ascendancy under David Trimble following the enactment of the Good Friday Agreement in 1998, its support subsequently dwindled and it won no seats in the UK 2017 General Election.

Small print and index

A ROUGH GUIDE TO ROUGH GUIDES

Published in 1982, the first Rough Guide – to Greece – was a student scheme that became a publishing phenomenon. Mark Ellingham, a recent graduate in English from Bristol University, had been travelling in Greece the previous summer and couldn't find the right guidebook. With a small group of friends he wrote his own guide, combining a contemporary, journalistic style with a thoroughly practical approach to travellers' needs.

The immediate success of the book spawned a series that rapidly covered dozens of destinations. And, in addition to impecunious backpackers, Rough Guides soon acquired a much broader readership that relished the guides' wit and inquisitiveness as much as their enthusiastic, critical approach and value-for-money ethos. These days, Rough Guides include recommendations from budget to luxury and cover more than 120 destinations around the globe, from Amsterdam to Zanzibar, all regularly updated by our team of roaming writers.

Browse all our latest guides, read inspirational features and book your trip at **roughguides.com**.

Rough Guide credits

Editor: Kate Drynan
Cartography: Carte
Picture Manager: Tom Smyth

Layout: Pradeep Thapliyal
Head of DTP and Pre-Press: Rebeka Davies
Head of Publishing: Sarah Clark

Publishing information

Fourteenth edition 2025

Distribution

UK, Ireland and Europe
Apa Publications (UK) Ltd; sales@roughguides.com
United States and Canada
Ingram Publisher Services; ips@ingramcontent.com
Australia and New Zealand
Booktopia; retailer@booktopia.com.au
Worldwide
Apa Publications (UK) Ltd; sales@roughguides.com

Special Sales, Content Licensing and CoPublishing
Rough Guides can be purchased in bulk quantities
at discounted prices. We can create special editions,
personalised jackets and corporate imprints tailored to
your needs. sales@roughguides.com.
roughguides.com

Printed in China

Help us update

We've gone to a lot of effort to ensure that this edition
of **The Rough Guide to Ireland** is accurate and up-to-
date. However, things change – places get "discovered",
transport routes are altered, restaurants and hotels raise
prices or lower standards, and businesses cease trading. If
you feel we've got it wrong or left something out, we'd like
to know, and if you can direct us to the web address, so
much the better.

Please send your comments with the subject line
"Rough Guide Ireland Update" to mail@uk.roughguides.
com. We'll acknowledge all contributions and send a copy
of the next edition (or any other Rough Guide if you prefer)
for the very best emails.

Acknowledgements

Norm would like to thank Kate for getting this project off the ground, and patience thereafter. Huge thanks to Nicola
McCullough and Chloe McCloskey at Visit Belfast for their fantastic support; Julie McLaughlin at the EastSide Partnership,
Peter McCabe of the George Best House, and Tony McDonagh at Visit West Belfast. Most importantly, thank you to
Christian and Anna for their love and support.

ABOUT THE AUTHORS

Norm Longley has spent most of his working life in central/eastern Europe – he is the author
of the Rough Guides to Slovenia, Romania and Budapest – but more recently has turned
his hand to home shores, contributing to the Scotland, Wales and Ireland guides. He lives in
Somerset and can occasionally be seen erecting marquees on The Rec in Bath.
Kate Drynan is a regular contributor to Rough Guides. She has lived, worked and studied all
over the world, including France, Spain, Belgium, England and Dubai. An Irish national, she
now resides in her home country and is always happiest when out exploring new places and
expanding her knowledge.

Photo credits

(Key: T-top; C-centre; B-bottom; L-left; R-right)

YOUR TAILOR-MADE TRIP
STARTS HERE

Tailor-made trips and unique adventures crafted by local experts

Rough Guides has been inspiring travellers with lively and thought-provoking guidebooks for more than 35 years. Now we're linking you up with selected local experts to craft your dream trip. They will put together your perfect itinerary and book it at local rates.

Don't follow the crowd – find your own path.

HOW ROUGHGUIDES.COM/TRIPS WORKS

STEP 1

Pick your dream destination, tell us what you want and submit an enquiry.

STEP 2

Fill in a short form to tell your local expert about your dream trip and preferences.

STEP 3

Our local expert will craft your tailor-made itinerary. You'll be able to tweak and refine it until you're completely satisfied.

STEP 4

Book online with ease, pack your bags and enjoy the trip! Our local expert will be on hand 24/7 while you're on the road.

BENEFITS OF PLANNING AND BOOKING AT ROUGHGUIDES.COM/TRIPS

PLAN YOUR ADVENTURE WITH LOCAL EXPERTS

Rough Guides' English-speaking local experts are hand-picked, based on their experience in the travel industry and their impeccable standards of customer service.

SAVE TIME AND GET ACCESS TO LOCAL KNOWLEDGE

When a local expert plans your trip, you save time and money when you book, even during high season. You won't be charged for using a credit card either.

MAKE TRAVEL A BREEZE: BOOK WITH PEACE OF MIND

Enjoy stress-free travel when you use Rough Guides' secure online booking platform. All bookings come with a money-back guarantee.

WHAT DO OTHER TRAVELLERS THINK ABOUT ROUGH GUIDES TRIPS?

Trip to Spain

This Spain tour company did a fantastic job to make our dream trip perfect. We gave them our travel budget, told them where we would like to go, and they did all of the planning. Our drivers and tour guides were always on time and very knowledgable. The hotel accommodations were better than we would have found on our own. Only one time did we end up in a location that we had not intended to be in. We called the 24 hour phone number, and they immediately fixed the situation.

Don A, USA

Trip to Morocco

Our trip was fantastic! Transportation, accommodations, guides – all were well chosen! The hotels were well situated, well appointed and had helpful, friendly staff. All of the guides we had were very knowledgeable, patient, and flexible with our varied interests in the different sites. We particularly enjoyed the side trip to Tangier! Well done! The itinerary you arranged for us allowed maximum coverage of the country with time in each city for seeing the important places.

Sharon, USA

PLAN AND BOOK YOUR TRIP AT ROUGHGUIDES.COM/TRIPS

Index

Map symbols

The symbols below are used on maps throughout the book

	International boundary		International airport		Mountain peak		Zoo
	County boundary		Airstrip		Cave		Gate
	Chapter boundary		Transport stop		Waterfall		Statue
	Motorway		Place of interest		Gardens		Lighthouse
	Dual carriageway		Post office		Ruin/archeological site		Church (regional map)
	Main road		Internet access		Windmill		Church (town map)
	Minor road		Hospital		Castle		Market
	Pedestrianized road		Information centre		Tower		Building
	Steps		Parking		Fort		Stadium
	Railway		Viewpoint		Stately home		Park
	Path		Wildfowl reserve		Abbey		Cemetery
	Wall		Mountain range		Museum		Beach
	Ferry						

Listings key

Accommodation

Eating

Drinking/nightlife

Shopping

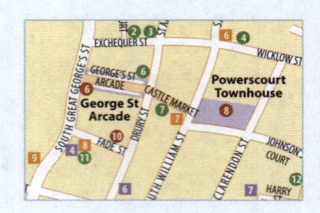